TRUCKBU

FROM DOGPATCH

THE *Combat Diary* OF THE 18ᵀᴴ FIGHTER-BOMBER WING IN THE KOREAN WAR 1950-1953

Library of Congress Cataloging-in-Publication Data

Connors, Tracy D.
Truckbusters From Dogpatch: The Combat Diary of the 18th Fighter-Bomber Wing in the Korean War, 1950-1953
Includes bibliographical references, index and glossary.
1. United States Air Force. Far East Air Forces. 2. Korean War, 1950-1953--Aerial Operations.

ISBN 0-9640138-2-7
LCCN 2004195557

Printed in the United States of America on acid-free papaer

Dedicated to

1ˢᵗ Lt. Archibald "Archie" Haddock Connors, Jr.

and the other 163 pilots and airmen
of the 18ᵗʰ Fighter-Bomber Wing who gave their
lives in defense of freedom during the Korean
War, 1950-1953

About the Author

Tracy D. Connors attended Jacksonville University, and earned Bachelor and Master of Arts degrees from the University of Florida and the University of Rhode Island, respectively. His management and military career includes over 40 years total experience in a variety of responsible positions in business, government and philanthropic organizations.

Since publication of his *Nonprofit Organization Handbook* (McGraw-Hill) in 1979, the first such management publication in that field, to the present *Nonprofit Handbook: Management Third Edition* (John Wiley & Son), the largest and most comprehensive management handbooks in print for nonprofit organizations have been those he prepared.

He enlisted in the Naval Reserve before graduating from high school and was a senior petty officer when he was commissioned after graduating from the University of Florida. After ten years Navy active duty, which included sea duty in USS F.D. ROOSEVELT (CVA-42) and on the Public Affairs Staff of Commander in Chief, U.S. Atlantic Fleet in Norfolk, he left the Navy entirely to pursue a business career in management of nonprofit organizations, management of advanced technology development programs, and, development of on-line publishing and communication programs.

In 1981, he was recommissioned in the Naval Reserve and earned Surface Warfare Officer qualification aboard USS SAIPAN (LHA-2). He was recalled to active duty frequently and for long periods of time from 1985 to 1999 to serve in a variety of highly responsible positions for the Secretary of the Navy, the Chief of Naval Operations, and other senior Navy commands in the National Capital Region prior to his Navy retirement in 1999.

Civilian positions included distance learning program management for the U.S. Chamber of Commerce, corporate communications management, and serving as chief of staff for a senior Member of Congress.

In addition to *Truckbusters From Dogpatch*, his other publications include:
- *Nonprofit Handbook: Management* (Third Edition + Annual Supplements), John Wiley & Sons, 1990-2001
- *Flavors of the Fjords*, Co-authored with Faith R. Connors, BelleAire Press, 1996
- *Volunteer Management Handbook*, John Wiley & Sons, 1995
- *Nonprofit Organization Handbook* (Second Edition), McGraw-Hill, 1979, 1985
- *Dictionary of Mass Media & Communication*, Longman, 1982
- *Financial Management for Nonprofit Organizations*, AMACOM, 1982

Periodical publications in national news media and trade press, include: *U.S. Naval Institute Proceedings* Magazine, *All Hands* Magazine, *Surface Warfare* Magazine, *Direction*, Navy News, Navy Wire Service, *International Defense Images*, *Public Affairs Communicator*, *National Productivity Review* and *Sea History* Magazine.

Captain Connors began *Truckbusters* as a memorial to his uncle, 1st Lt. Archie Connors, a Mustang pilot with the 67th Squadron. During a daring rescue mission on 25 June 1952, Lt. Connors was killed in action. The tribute to his uncle has grown into a much more comprehensive history of the 18th Wing in the Korean War.

Contents

Acknowledgements

The author gratefully acknowledges the following individuals or organizations for their invaluable assistance in the preparation of this manuscript:

18th Fighter Wing Association

Alachua County Public Library Staff, Gainesville, Florida

Ray Anwyl

Lt. Col. Timothy O. Austin, USAF (Ret.)

Frederick B. Ayer

Lt. Col. Kenneth H. Barber, USAF (Ret.)

Lt. Col. Vi Bielefeldt, USAF (Ret.)

Lt. Col. Duane "Bud" Biteman, USAF (Ret.)

Lt. Gen. Devol "Rock" Brett, USAF (Ret.)

Lt. Col. Walter H. Burke, USAF (Ret.)

Lt. Col. John Caldwell, USAF (Ret.)

Col. Stanley E. Chatfield, USAF (Ret.)

Dorothy Sharp Clements

William J. "Sandy" Colton

Faith R. Connors

W. Bruce Connors

Lt. Col. William Cothern, USAF (Ret.)

Robert Cranston

Lt. Col. Julian Crow, USAF (Ret.)

Joyce Eaton Dalton

Richard H. Deihl

Lt. Col. Donald Drage, USAF (Ret.)

Lt. Gen. Denis Earp, SAAF (Ret.)

Lt. Col. Howard "Ebe" Ebersole, USAF (Ret.)

Essex Public Library Staff, Tiverton, Rhode Island

William R. "Barney" Frampton

CAPT L. Tyke Furey, USN (Ret.)

Master Sergeant Bobby D. Holloway, USAR (Ret.)

Della Lear Holloway

CAPT Seth Hudak, USCG (Ret.)

Col. Howard "Scrappy" Johnson, USAF (Ret.)

Dr. Frances B. Kinne

Paul R. Kniss

Col. Edward J. Mason, USAF (Ret.)

Col. Charles E. McGee, USAF (Ret.)

David McLaren

Col. Harry Moreland, USAF (Ret.)

Col. Robert P. Pasqualicchio, USAF (Ret.)

Col. Joseph A. Peterburs, USAF (Ret.)

Col. James C. Peek, USAF (Ret.)

Maj. Gen. Walter D. Reed, USAF (Ret.)

Col. Ralph H. Saltsman, Jr., USAF (Ret.)

Col. Richard H. Schiebel, USAF (Ret.)

Col. Charles E. Schreffler, USAF (Ret.)

Col. Jack E. Shepard, USAF (Ret.)

Wilfred ("Budd") Stapley

CDR Richard Thompson, USN (Ret.)

Ernest Wakehouse

Col. Frederick L. Thomas, USAF (Ret.)

U.S. Air Force Historical Research Agency

U.S. National Archives and Records Administration

U.S. Navy Historical Center

Photographic Acknowledgements

Manual V. Andujar
Ray Anwyl
Fred Ayer
Lt. Col. Kenneth Barber, USAF (Ret.)
Lt. Col. Vi Bielefeldt, USAF (Ret.)
Stanley J. Bist
Lt. Col. Duane "Bud" Biteman, USAF (Ret.)
Elbert Duane Black
Frank and Erica Bolt
Lt. Col. Walter H. Burke, USAF (Ret.)
Allen A. Burns
Col. Stanley E. Chatfield, USAF (Ret.)
Everson O. Clark
William J. "Sandy" Colton
1st Lt. Archibald Haddock Connors, Jr., USAF
Lt. Col. John G. Corley, II, USAF (Ret.)
Lt. Col. Melvin J. Corley, USAF (Ret.)
Robert Cranston, Sr.
Lt. Col. Julian Crow, USAF (Ret.)
Lt. Col. John W. Dawson, USAF (Ret.)
Murritt Davis
Richard H. Deihl
Lt. Col. Donald Drage, USAF (Ret.)
Lt. Col. Howard "Ebe" Ebersole, USAF (Ret.)
Clarence E. Frownfelter
Dr. Morton A.A. Gross, DDM
Bobby D. Holloway
Della Lear Holloway
Dr. Vernon D. Holmes
Lt. Col. John A. Jansen, USAF (Ret.)
Col. Howard "Scrappy" Johnson, USAF (Ret.)
Master Sergeant Richard Joppru, USAF (Ret.)
Paul Kniss
Joseph Krakovsky
Col. Edward Mason, USAF (Ret.)

Master Sergeant Charles Maynard, USAF (Ret.)
Doris McElvey
Major Raymond McElvey, USAF (Ret.)
John "Jack" McLoughlin
Lt. Col. George C. McLees, USAF (Ret.)
Col. Bill E. Myers, USAF (Ret.)
Lois L. Moore
Charles R. Morehouse
Col. Harry "Mo" Moreland, USAF (Ret.)
Edward G. "Ted" Murphy
Richard E. Newell
Col. Robert P. "Pancho" Pasqualicchio, USAF (Ret.)
Charles W. Patterson
Col. James C. Peek, USAF (Ret.)
Col. Jame A. Peterburs, USAF (Ret.)
Major Mario Prevosti, USAF (Ret.)
Roy Pylant, Jr.
Earl W. Ramsdell
Major General Walter D. Reed, USAF (Ret.)
Lt. Col. Peter W. Richardson, USAF (Ret.)
Lt. Col. Richard H. Schiebel, USAF (Ret.)
Col. Charles E. Schreffler, USAF (Ret.)
Col. Jack E. Shepard, USAF (Ret.)
Donald Spry
Wilfred ("Budd") Stapley
Paul W. Stevens
Major General John Taylor, USAF (Ret.)
Col. Frederick L. Thomas, Jr., USAF (Ret.)
Brigadier General Robert F. Titus, USAF (Ret.)
William Timmons Urquhart
Ernest Wakehouse
Gill Wennes
National Archives and Records Administration
U.S. Air Force Historical Research Agency

Foreword

Lieutenant General Devol "Rock" Brett, USAF (Retired)

THE MISSION OF THE UNITED STATES AIR FORCE

IS TO FLY AND FIGHT

DO NOT EVER FORGET IT!

There can be no question the Truckbusters of Dogpatch understood completely the mission of the United States Air Force--with it being the bedrock of their lives. For those of us privileged and proud to be Truckbusters fighter pilots, we lived on a daily basis the dynamic application of the Air Force Mission made possible by the extraordinary efforts of all members of the Wing.

Time and time again our maintenance and armament personnel under the toughest climatic and environmental conditions prepared our war-weary Mustangs for combat. From a combat fighter pilot's viewpoint their efforts were never-ending miracles. The same held true for all members of the Wing with each in his own specialty contributing significantly to the Wing's effective achievement of the Air Force Mission.

I had the opportunity to verify over and over the awesome performance of the Truckbusters, first as a combat fighter pilot assigned to the 39th Fighter Squadron and later as its Operations Officer; and then as a Senior Operations Duty Officer in the Joint Operations Center (JOC) at Headquarters Fifth Air Force. In each of these positions I was always greatly impressed and pleased with the performance of the Truckbusters--dependability and effectiveness were always present in mission accomplishment.

Over the many years since those times I have been reminded of the awesome tactical fighter combat achievements of the Truckbusters when compared to other combat fighter units to which I have been assigned. The Truckbusters flew every possible type mission that could be done by a fighter aircraft and on almost a daily basis. During my observation time daily large formations north (Gaggles) to almost the Yalu River were done three times a day and into extremely well defended areas with aircraft shoot-downs and/or battle damage a constant hazard. These gaggles demanded the utmost from the maintenance and armament personnel in terms of rapid refueling, armament loading and battle damage repair to meet the need for a quick turnaround. At the same time there was always a squadron on Close Air Support (CAS) alert, again demanding quick turnarounds. And it never seemed to fail that a requirement for a special mission would be placed upon the Wing necessitating a unique configuration with an instant response.

I remember the day at K-46 [Hoengsong, SK] when the JOC needed immediately, as many as possible, of our aircraft configured with fuel tanks to search in the Yellow Sea for downed B-29 aircrews. The '29's had been on a daylight mission well north in North Korea. I had just returned from a gaggle and we did a quick turn around and headed out to sea. It was a very long mission--about seven hours--and we did spot some dingies (Yellow one-man inflatable life rafts) and directed the Dumbo's (SA-16 Amphibians) to them. Based on this mission and many other rescue escort missions I believe the Korean Mustangs were the founders of the A-1 Sandy roles in Vietnam and the current A-10 Sandy missions which were and are so critical to effective Combat Search and Rescue (CSAR) Escort Missions.

I honestly believe that no other Fighter Wing during the Korean War came even close to performing such diverse, challenging and tough missions, as did the Truckbusters. If one statistically measures the cost effectiveness of all types of ground targets destroyed the Truckbusters would come out clearly on top. Case in point, unlike the fighter bomber Jets, we Mustang drivers on almost every mission hit more than one target and frequently two, three or more with our bombs, rockets and .50-caliber ammo and rarely came home with any ordnance on board having expended it on either the assigned target or targets of opportunity. For us Mustang drivers North Korea was always a target rich environment, as we could take the time and get down low to find targets and then work them over with deliberate skill.

I would be in arrears if I did not dedicate some deserved space in this Introduction to Truckbuster personnel. When I was assigned to the 39th Fighter Squadron in August of 1951 I was a regular officer and

Four "Cobras." Lt. Ernest "Ernie" Wakehouse, Capt. John Taylor, Jr., Capt. Devol "Rock" Brett and Lt. Fred Rockmaker of the 39th Fighter-Interceptor Squadron after a 1951 mission with the 18th Fighter-Bomber Wing. (Cook)

a graduate of West Point. I had no combat experience, but had been assigned to two P-47 Fighter Units in Europe and had quite a bit of time in both the P-51D and P-51H. The personnel assigned to these outfits were all regular officers and enlisted. My first experience with Reserve and Air National Guard personnel was upon being assigned to the 39th. To me this was then and is now very important, as the Reserves, both officers and enlisted, made up the majority of Wing Personnel.

In every respect they were absolutely superior individuals, not only being incredibly dedicated and patriotic, but their experience and professional skills made the never-ending exceptional performance of the Truckbusters possible. In modern terms they made the outstanding performance of the Wing a "GIVEN"!

I still remember in detail many of these wonderful individuals and have treasured always my times with them. They taught me a great deal about combat fighter flying which served me well in my subsequent many years of flying fighters both in combat and peace; but most of all I learned from them the true meaning of the words dedication, loyalty and service; all of which equates to the motto of West Point, "Duty, Honor and Country."

It is a significant honor and privilege to be asked by Captain Tracy Connors to write the Introduction to the "*Truckbusters of Dogpatch*," as the story of this awesome and so unique a Wing is long over-due. It is a saga that clearly illustrates the gathering and performance of the best, brightest and bravest group of combat fighter pilots and their exceptional support personnel that I have ever known. For me my days as a Truckbuster are truly amongst the very finest days of my life and believe me, as I look back from my ninth decade there have been some great days.

With profound admiration and respect,

Devol "Rock" Brett
Mustang Pilot
Lt. General, USAF (Ret.)

Preface

William J. "Sandy" Colton

I'll never forget that early morning August flight from Ashiya, Japan to K-9 just east of Pusan Korea. It was dark when we took off. The center aisle of the C-46 was piled high with cases of supplies covered by a huge tarpaulin. The passengers sat slumped in hammock seats along each side. Most appeared deep in thought, some smoked nervously, one was asleep on the floor wrapped in the tarpaulin overhang.

Shortly after takeoff the sun rose, casting beams of light through the smoke filled cabin from the right side porthole like windows. I was a young, wet-behind-the-ears would-be writer about to enter my first combat situation and I was scared. Looking around me in the brighter light I could see many other apprehensive faces. I wasn't the only one afraid.

Peering out of the porthole window near me I soon saw an approaching coastline. Korea! Then came a terrible odor. The small figure under the tarpaulin woke up and shouted "Who shit!"

"You'd better get used to it," the crew chief shouted down to the small figure laying near his feet. "The Koreans fertilize their fields with the stuff and you can smell it at ten thousand feet!" It was later that I learned the small figure on the floor was Lt. Phil Conserva, an F-51 pilot with a great sense of humor.

We began to descend and soon made what sounded like a terrible landing on a runway made of perforated steel mats. I thought that the airplane was being torn apart! When the door was opened we had our first look at our new home, a former rice paddy turned into an air field! What a mess! But before I left this outfit, a much wiser young man, I was going to see many more messes, much worse than this one.

During my nine months with the 18th many things still stick in my mind. I don't remember which field it was but I remember a four-holer set out in the middle of a field all by itself for all to see that served officer and enlisted man alike. I remember the luxury of a makeshift cold shower--a 55-gallon drum hanging over your head!

I remember, sadly, the Army units pulling back through us at Pyongyang East [airfield] at Thanksgiving time after the Chinese entered the conflict. We fed them cold turkey in the drafty old hangar that served as our mess hall, one of the few good meals we had in those days. They looked terrible and had only the old horse hair sleeping bags. It was cold with those Siberian winds howling down out of the north. I remember too the exploding ammo and fuel dumps as we left that base.

At Wonsan we only used the base as a staging area but it gave me a chance to sneak away with the ROK Capitol division for awhile and see the 51's in action from the point of view of the infantryman on the ground in need of support. Later, when I was with the *Stars and Stripes*, I got to cheer them on many times while on patrols with the Army or Marines.

In June of 1950 when the North Korean Army invaded South Korea, it was five years since the end of World War II. Korea and Japan were staffed with garrison soldiers, spoiled and out of shape for combat. The brand new U.S. Air Force, competing with Russia's MIG fighters, had put all its money on jet fighters and air-to-air combat, ignoring ground support. The old and now obsolescent F-51's were shipped off to National Guard duty and military advisory groups around the world.

The jets at the time might have been great in a dog fight with another jet but lacked the fuel capacity to stay around very long and, because they were designed for speed, they could not get close enough to the ground to identify a small target. With the invasion of South Korea it was time to call in the obsolescent F-51s for much needed ground support. National Guard units throughout the United States lost their F-51s, which were loaded onto the aircraft carrier USS Boxer for rapid delivery to Korea. A few were rounded up around Asia and sent to Korea to join the few Col. Dean Hess and his KMAG [Korean Military Advisory Group] unit had. Pilots were also needed who knew how to fly the '51. For the most part that meant old WW II pilots [early in the war]. The 13th Air Force in the Philippines provided that first group, all volunteers and pulled out of their new jets to join Hess in Taegu and form a unit called "Bout One," later to become the 18th Fighter-Bomber Wing.

In those days, the pilots told me, they resorted to night flights. The North Koreans made easy targets then. They lit huge fires in their camps and convoys traveled with their headlights on. Imagine diving on a target at night at 400 miles per hour, aiming at your target, then covering your eyes, releasing your rockets and pulling up to avoid the bright glare from the rockets. That glare would temporarily blind a pilot used to the dark in his cockpit.

That's just one of many stories I was told by these brave men as I traveled with them from mud hole to mud hole. First K-9, then Suwon and Wonsan, Pyongyang East, back to Suwon and finally, for me, Chinhae. We were assigned to all the dusty, dirty, muddy fields, fields where the jets couldn't operate. The jet jockeys operated at first from Japan, later Pyongyang's main airport and then Kimpo near Seoul, where they had a cement runway and nice buildings left to live and work in.

The bulk of close support in Korea came from old propeller driven aircraft, the F-51s of the 18th, the South African and Australian squadrons, and the Navy and Marine F4Us, both carrier and land based.

For the most part it was tent living for us. The food was mostly terrible. At one point I remember being so sick of SPAM I never wanted to see it again. Officer and enlisted alike, we all ate the same food, lived in tents and suffered with the dust and mud and cold.

If you ever want to see devotion, watch a crew chief on a 51. He's usually up before daylight warming up the plane and checking out all of its systems. If there's any damage to the aircraft, and they frequently came back with holes, some large enough to stand up in, or a rough engine, the crew chief will be up all night, if necessary, trying to get his "bird" ready for flight again. Then, when the pilot shows up and climbs into his aircraft, the crew chief is right there to tuck him into his seat belt and shoulder harness.

When the pilot returns, the crew chief is the first one there on the wing to help the pilot out of the harness and ask if anything needs fixing. While the pilots are gone on a mission the crew chiefs gather together to play ball or just sit and wait, sweating out their return. Occasionally one or more does not return and those crew chiefs wait anxiously for one of the other pilots to tell him what happened. I've seen some of them cry! There is a wonderful closeness between the pilots and their crew chiefs.

It's a strange feeling of camaraderie that infected the whole unit, from the napalm mixers and armament crews at the end of the field to the pencil pushers at headquarters. In spite of the mud and dirt and lousy living conditions they're all proud as hell of their outfit and the exploits of its pilots.

They're proud of their heroes. Men like Major Lou Sebille, Commander of the 67th Squadron, the first to win the Congressional Medal of Honor! Possibly mortally wounded, a 250-pound frag bomb still hanging on his wing, he dove his plane into a line of North Korean trucks and tanks, radioing his wing man, "I'm going back and get those bastards!"

And other pilots like "Tamerlane Willie" Bryan, the 12th Squadron Commander, who helped the 18th earn the title

18th Group Commander Lt. Col. Ira Wintermute briefs Sgt. Sandy Colton before take-off from K-10 in Spring 1951. Colton was eager to write an eye-witness account of a Mustang strike against enemy targets in North Korea, and got more than he bargained for during the mission. Loaded down with equipment, Colton was barely able to squeeze into the samll space behind the cockpit of the "Pig," an F-51 with the rear gas tank removed. It is the only documented case in 18th Wing history of a non-commissioned officer flying a combat mission in a fighter-bomber. (Colton)

"Truckbusters." As the war grew older the North Koreans began to get smarter about hiding their trucks and tanks from the air. Some drove into hay stacks, a favorite target for the F-51 pilots who would ignite the stack with their .50-caliber wing guns and then buzz it to fan the flames!

Tanks frequently rammed into the mud houses to hide, but their tracks gave them away and the house and tank were blown to smithereens. Sometimes the North Koreans hid ammo in the mud houses and one of our pilots had the misfortune of strafing such a house only to have the whole house blow sky high. Unable to avoid it, the pilot flew right through the house and returned to base with a bent propeller, dents in the wings, and his air scoop loaded with mud and straw!

"Tamerlane Willie" became known among flying circles in Korea as the 18th's "secret weapon" for his ability to ferret out hidden trucks and tanks. How? He simply flew below tree height where he could spot the hidden vehicles—and taught his squadron to do the same!

Yes, flying very low, only a few feet off the ground; but, that was not unusual for this outfit. There were a couple of times that

I wrote about when North Korean troops actually surrendered to the low flying F-51s who then herded them down the road towards our troops by buzzing them from behind.

And then there was the time one of our pilots broke down during debriefing after a mission. It seems he went in so low to strafe some troops, the .50-caliber ammunition from his wing guns actually blew apart some of the troops he was strafing and his propeller may have cut into some too! He returned from that mission with blood all over his airplane and body parts in the air scoop! I felt very sad for that pilot.

I had, over time, become very close with many of the pilots. They even let me attend mission debriefings in search of stories, something not exactly legal. I knew I had it made when Captain Alma Flake shot down two Yaks on a mission, did a victory roll over the strip on his return and told the tower to tell Sandy to come to debriefing. I did get the story, and got into trouble. But more about that later.

My second biggest thrill came when I was actually taken on a mission. The 18th Group commander, Lt. Col. Ira Wintermute, was my pilot. The maintenance crews had somehow moved a spare gas tank and radio equipment back in a 51's fuselage so that they could squeeze in another seat behind the pilot. They called this aircraft the "Pig, but I don't know why. [Others recalled that "Pig" was shortened from "Piggy back" since it could carry a passenger in addition to the pilot.]

There were four aircraft in our flight. Our call sign was "Boxer." It was "Boxer one," "Boxer two," "Boxer three," and with me on board we were "Boxer four and a half!"

As I watched the other planes bounce up and down on our wing tip I fell deeply in love with that airplane. It was so personal. I felt I could reach out and touch the wing tips. The ground below went from brown to white snow as we crossed over into North Korea. I listened as the colonel called the air controller in the area seeking a target. I heard the reply, no targets, search and destroy targets of opportunity.

Then came the chatter between the colonel and the other pilots in our flight as we searched until one spotted a likely target—tire tracks and many footprints leading into some mud houses. The first two planes in our flight went down to strafe one of the buildings. Then we went in behind the number three plane. I got my camera up, ready to shoot, when the colonel set off our wing guns. Those six fifties startled me and shook the plane. Then, looking over the colonel's shoulder, I saw a fire ball ahead from the napalm dropped by the number three plane. We flew right through the flame and it felt like hitting a brick wall. The colonel then pulled up, my camera slammed down onto my lap and I felt like I was going to crash right out of the bottom of the plane. The G force was so heavy I couldn't lift my arms, much less my camera, until we were aloft again. The planes alternated going down on a target. Two go down first while the second two guard from above ["top cover"]. When napalm is dropped, the second plane machine guns the dropped napalm to ignite it in case its encased igniter doesn't work.

After more of this yo-yo-ing on our targets I was happy to return to base, watching this beautiful little airplane bob up and down on its wing tips and thinking how deadly it could be. I couldn't help but think too of the pilots, the shaking rattle of their fifties blazing away, the bump of flying through a napalm blast, and the terrible G forces they suffer when pulling out of a dive. I'd seen these men fly four and more missions every day!

That day helped explain the terribly tired look I'd seen many times on the pilots faces at mission debriefing when they had returned, especially at the end of the day. After just one mission my body ached!

But there were fun times too, times meant to take away the strain. Like the time one squadron began wearing long white silk scarves, until one of the pilots, whose name I won't reveal, got his sucked into his pee tube during a mission and it almost strangled him before he was able to get it off! Or when that same outfit brought back a bunch of motor scooters from Tokyo and staged races, white scarves flying in the wind as they madly and laughingly raced each other around a muddy field. As if there wasn't enough excitement in their lives already!

And then there was that Christmas dinner. Well, close to Christmas any way.

We were back at Suwon and some of our mail had finally caught up with us. We were all tired of eating Spam. My brother, a grocer at home, sent me a box of goodies, canned hams, chickens and such. With some other things that arrived a few of us had managed to go out and swap with the natives for fresh eggs and onions. We public information types were going to have our own feast in our small tent.

The Catholic chaplain, Father Westhoff, got wind of it and came through the tent flaps wearing a heavy jacket to keep out the cold. "Is the Protestant chaplain about," he asked. When we said no, he pulled out two bottles of wine from under his jacket and told us that this was his contribution! He'd swiped them from the protestant chaplain, he said! We all laughed and invited him to dinner.

There were a few tall tales too. I got bit at one debriefing when a then Captain Bud Biteman said he had a story for me and then described chasing a train into a tunnel.

"What did you do?" I asked excitedly.

"I went right in after it and blew it up!" he said.

"Oh, come on!" I said incredulously, "How did you get out?"

"I just reversed the pitch on my props and backed out." he replied.

Everybody got a laugh out of that one.

There were sad times too. Like the time Sgt. Boynton came into my office and sheepishly asked me if I could do anything with a poem he'd written. Boynton was crew chief for Captain Danny Leake who had not returned from a mission. The poem was beautiful and heartfelt. I made up a photo of a '51 on the ground with a photo of Captain Leake burned into the sky over it and sent it out with Boynton's poem. It was widely printed and, years later while visiting the Pentagon, I saw the framed photo hanging in one of the Pentagon hallways.

My saddest moment came after one evening sitting on the steps of our headquarters building with our executive officer, Lt. Col. "Milt" Gloesner. Understand, I was just a sergeant thoroughly indoctrinated with the military doctrine that officers and enlisted men don't mix.

It was different that night as the colonel tried to explain to me what being a fighter pilot was like. I felt a special closeness that night as we talked until dark.

The next day he did not return from a mission. His wing man said he'd crashed with no possibility of surviving. That's when I crashed too, literally. The air surgeon gave me a big yellow pill and I slept for two days.

These men, all of them, ground crews and pilots alike, were the bravest men I've ever known. I hated leaving them. That brings us back to the day Captain Alma Flake shot down those two Yaks. That day they held up mission debriefing while I got my story from Flake. I rushed into Pusan to file the story via the *Stars and Stripes* line into Tokyo. It was almost impossible to get a line into Tokyo from our base so I'd made this arrangement during a previous visit to Tokyo. The *Stars and Stripes* Tokyo office would clear my story with the Far East Air Forces PIO office in Tokyo before using it and the FEAF PIO could do with it what they willed.

When I returned to base and was sitting in our office the phone rang. "It's for you, Sandy," our PIO, Lieutenant Gallagher told me, handing me the phone. "It's General Nuckles!" I guess rank has its privileges. He was able to reach our base in Korea by phone from Tokyo while I could never get through to Tokyo. Nuckles was the man in charge of Far East Air Force public information.

When I answered the general said he'd just heard that one of our pilots downed two Yaks. "How about giving us the story?" he asked. Apparently my story had got into Tokyo before the intelligence report! I told the general that the story was already in Tokyo and that I'd filed it via the *Stars and Stripes*.

"God damn it Sergeant," he blew up, "you don't work for the *Stars and Stripes*! You work for me! I want you to get on an airplane right away, come to Tokyo, and report to me!"

The next day I caught a plane to Tokyo and reported to his office where I first saw Captain Sanky Trimble, his executive officer, with whom I'd made the deal to file via the Stripes line.

"Don't worry, Sandy," he said. "I've explained the whole thing to the general." With that I walked into the general's office, saluted, and waited for my reprimand. Boiled down it went something like this: "Sergeant, you have to understand that our taxpayers are paying for jets. You are getting too much publicity for a group of obsolescent airplanes! I want you to slow down."

I left his office fuming and walked directly to the *Nippon Times* where the *Stars and Stripes* offices were located. There I met with Lt. Col. Schuyler, the officer in charge of the Stripes. He had twice sent letters down the chain of command requesting that I be transferred to the Stripes and both times it was turned down. I asked him to send one more letter, went back to FEAF headquarters to see an old friend, the FEAF

sergeant major to explain the situation. Then I flew to Fifth Air Force headquarters in Seoul to see another old friend the sergeant major there.

Back at my own wing at Chinhae, I explained the situation to our sergeant major who happened to be a drinking buddy. Colonel Schuyler's letter went up and down the chain of command and I don't believe one officer saw it. My orders came through transferring me to the *Stars and Stripes* in Tokyo, thanks to the ingenuity of a few sergeants!

After that I returned to Korea as a Stripes correspondent, visiting various units from all the services for stories but frequently returning to the 18th to write about their exploits and enjoy the benefits of the best NCO club in Korea. But that's another story.

Sandy Colton

Following his service as an Air Force Journalist, Colton served in senior management positions with the Associated Press.

Introduction

Tracy D. Connors

Many of those whom you seek have mouldered away to nothing…

but their deeds live on…

Precious achievements, particularly those that changed history and protected freedom for subsequent generations, should survive all the erosions of time.

Despite the layering of other, more recent conflicts, the deaths of participants, and the shifting focus of media or historic attention, enough basic elements of the historical record remain to enable us to establish the combat record of the 18th Fighter-Bomber Wing during the Korean War as among the most illustrious of any U.S. military unit throughout our history. The 18th Wing's record is particularly noteworthy in light of its performance as a *U.S. Air Force unit*, since the Korean War was the first to be fought by the newly established, independent Air Force.

During three years of continuous combat in the Korean War, the component squadrons and support units of the 18th Fighter-Bomber Wing—

· Faced unrelenting sortie rates maintained in the face of weather;

· Overcame seasonal assaults of heat and cold;

· Maintained and flew aging aircraft, unsuited for the various missions it and its pilots were called on to fly; and,

· Sustained an operational level of flexibility and adaptability that is unparalleled in U.S. Air Force history.

For example, the 18th Wing is the only known Air Force flying unit to be asked to convert from one type of aircraft to another—while engaged in combat and without "standing down" from required combat mission completions—not once, but twice and while operating from crude "forward operating bases."

If anything, the intervening half cen-

> *Mustang pilots all are we.*
> *Fly any bird through eternity.*
> *So God have mercy on such as we,*
> *Who fly, fly, fly.*
> *…*
> *And our life and love shall last.*
> *We'll not pass nor be forgotten like the rest.*
>
> ***Excerpt from***
> ***Truckbuster's Song***

tury since the 18th fought so valiantly in Korea has improved our ability to evaluate its contributions by placing them in the context of fifty years of subsequent military history and evolution. We can more accurately assess the legacy it established for subsequent Air Force components, and indeed, the sons and daughters who today continue to serve in the 18th Wing.

American military progress and achievements have been significant over the intervening half century, and have enabled those that uphold freedom to generally prevail against oppressive governments and ideologies. We must not forget, however, that such progress was gained as a direct result of the richer heritage to which today's fighting men and women were born and inherited—a heritage established and advanced by pilots and airmen like those of the 18th Fighter-Bomber Wing during the Korean War.

Truckbusters From Dogpatch attempts to record and document the record

of achievement established by the 18th Wing during 37 months of arduous, costly combat—to chronicle the events, accomplishments and sacrifices by some of the bravest "characters" in American military history who bequeathed an important heritage to subsequent generations serving in the U.S. Air Force. It tries to convey a better understanding of the personalities behind the facts and data. It is not intended to be a comparative study of "props vs. jets" or to compare one unit's statistics to another and thereby declare a "winner."

Monthly, formerly classified, records and reports were used to establish a helpful context and matrix into which as much information as possible could be included that profiled and spotlighted the men who were actually flying the missions and keeping the planes in the air. As such, ***Truckbusters*** becomes for the reader a gritty, dusty, tent city full of the sounds, smells and character of those who served with the 18th in Korea—pilots, ammorers, mechanics, clerks, medics, and supply sergeants—who still live and speak and fret and worry about how to keep their "Spam Cans" flying. They also teach us important lessons about professionalism, dedication, commitment, bravery, fear, sacrifice and humanity—lessons we should never forget, lest democracy and freedom themselves become potential victims.

It is our pride, all of us who have worked on this book, contributed to this book, and breathed life into this book, that in doing so we have put new meaning into the lives of those who so honorably served in the 18th Wing during the Korean War—and that in doing so we have added a significance that will transcend death itself, which has already overtaken so many of these brave Americans.

One of those 18th Wing Veterans, Sandy Colton, sums up the overall story in *Truckbusters*.

"The 18th and its glorious men," wrote Colton, "is a story of how World War Two pilots who had flown the P-51 were asked to volunteer to give up their shiny new F-80 jets and leave the comfort of their homes and families in the Philippines to fly an obsolete F-51 in combat because the idiots in Washington all goofed! It was all jet bombers and jet air-to-air fighters after the big war. They never considered a ground support aircraft and got caught with their pants down when the Korea 'Police Action' came along. If it weren't for the F-51's and the Navy and Marine Corps F4U's, the South Koreans and our ill-trained garrison soldiers who were tossed into the mess would have had to swim back to Japan."

"It's a well known fact," Colton continued, "that MacArthur wanted to drop an atomic bomb on the North Korean troops massed in the Suwon plains but Harry S [Truman] said 'no.' If it had not been for the obsolescent aircraft and old men slowing things down until a major counter attack could be planned and put into effect, might Truman have been persuaded to change his mind, or would all of Korea be under the control of North Korea today?" Colton asked.

"The 18th got all the crappy jobs and bases—old aircraft constantly breaking down from wear and tear and lack of parts, assigned dusty, muddy airstrips all over Korea, sleeping in cold leaky tents or bombed out buildings, eating lousy food and frequently working on adrenaline for lack of sleep while the 'more glamorous' jet jockeys got all the credit and publicity. Newspaper men liked their comfort, too, so rarely visited the Dogpatch-like bases, but rather stuck around Fifth Air Force [Seoul] or Far East Air Forces [Tokyo] headquarters where the food and accommodations were better while they were fed all that jet propaganda. "Remember, Sergeant, the taxpayers are paying for jets!" one general officer reminded me. The job that the obso-

lescent F-51's and F4U's were doing was an embarrassment to the military brass. They made every effort to keep their exploits out of the lime light and to emphasize the exploits of jets. I'm still madder than hell," Colton recalled.

Those of us giving birth to *Truckbusters* know that we are fortunate in this quest, that before we die we have done our best to gather up as much as we could of this unsurpassed American military heritage and transmit it to our children—and your children—reaffirming in the honorable tradition of American fighting men, that they believed the price of freedom is worth the cost. Sometimes that price is simply the temporary inconvenience of an informed vote during an election. Sometimes, the price includes putting our military forces at risk in distant, dangerous territory. All too often the price of freedom involves pain, suffering or sacrifice. In Korea, that was certainly the case. However, without the sacrifices of U.N. soldiers, sailors and airmen, millions of Korean people would have been sentenced to slavery and repression—living lives devoid of hope or future.

Organization and Presentation

This book is written to honor the achievements and dedication of the men who served in and with the 18th Wing in Korea. It is their story, told as much as possible in their own words and photographs, taken from the monthly unit history reports, personal recollections, memoirs, scrap books and faded snap shots. *Truckbusters* attempts to convey for the reader a month-by-month sense of what was happening in the war overall, but especially at the Wing level, squadron level and in the tents and cockpits of the men who were trying to do their jobs, remain loyal to their fellow airmen, and to survive long enough to go home.

The 18th Wing and its component squadrons were called into action within hours of the North Korean invasion of South Korea. It stayed on the line, completing tens

of thousands of combat sorties from seven different air bases in both prop and jet aircraft, for the next three years—no matter what the weather or the state of its aging aircraft.

The passage of time for the men was measured in "how many days until I get rotated out of here." For the pilots, it was in the number of combat missions completed. Early in the war it was 100 missions—becoming a "Centurian." Later, as the Air Force "pilot pipeline" pumped too many pilots into the Wing, the number of required combat missions for pilots was lowered to 75 missions.

For individual units, time was measured by monthly unit historical reports—relatively candid assessments of combat tactics, results, materiel, personnel and morale. Each component filed these Secret classified reports regardless of what else was going on. They would not be declassified until nearly twenty years later.

Early in the compilation and distillation of information and materials, it was clear that a different framework was needed. There was not just one story, but many stories that ranged from sometimes dry reports up the chain of command to first person accounts that fairly crackled with emotion and adrenaline. Between these extremes were the day to day images and accounts that chronicled the lives and activities of the approximately 1,800 men that at any one time comprised the 18th Wing complement during the Korean War.

The eventual organization and presentation of materials in Truckbusters is unusual in that it more nearly compares to the layout of a magazine than of a typical book. A "monthly magazine" form of organization evolved that attempts to give the reader an overall understanding of what was happening in the Wing and in the war overall—month by month.

Most chapters in Truckbusters begin with a quote from a report or an account that captures some important development or action that took place that month. The first page has a summary of significant events for that month that provides a brief thumbnail for the reader of what else was happening in the Korean War.

[Note: each year begins with a summary of what happened that year to provide historical benchmarks for the reader on a larger scale. Every six months a time line or chronology is inserted to provide succinct, graphic cues for the reader regarding what happened during that period.]

The chapter narrative leads off with a summary of what the Wing reported to the Fifth Air Force regarding organization, manning and sorties flown. This is followed by more specific information detailing combat operations during that month, including excerpts from unit commanders regarding tactics, weapons, equipment, materiel and personnel. In so far as possible these insights are presented in the words of the commanders making the reports and providing the assessments.

As the monthly chapter content moves forward, the point of view shifts from Wing to Group to Squadron level.

[For most of the war, the 18th Group included at least three combat squadrons—12th, 67th, and 2 Squadron SAAF. For about a year in 1951-52, the 39th Fighter Interceptor Squadron also flew as a component organization of the 18th Fighter-Bomber Group.]

Each of these commanders had a different point of view depending on the month and what was happening in the squadron at that time. Each available unit history for each month for each squadron was reviewed and assessed for important developments or events that should be included because they helped explain or symbolize events at the squadron level.

Where information was available, combat statistical data were provided for each month—squadron sorties, aircraft lost in combat, pilots lost in combat and ordnance expended. Every month an average of 1.5 million rounds of .50-cal. Machine gun ammunition, thousands of aerial rockets, napalm bombs and fragmentation bombs were "expended." Each of these rounds, rockets or bombs had to be brought to the air base, stored safely, retrieved, loaded on the aircraft properly and safely, then carried to the target despite heavy ground fire and sometimes opposing fighter aircraft, to be delivered to the assigned target—a bunker, a depot, a convoy, a trench line, a rail road track, a supply line, a bridge, or a truck. The monthly numbers are staggering and they give us some idea of the enormous logistical effort that was required to keep 75-80 aging combat aircraft mission ready no matter what the weather, location or conditions.

Imagery in *Truckbusters* ranges from official photographs taken by usually unnamed Air Force personnel, to snap shots brought home by airmen and pilots, to copies of the actual documents that passed across their desks—frag orders, mess hall passes, letters, and other memorabilia. These images are presented to the reader, where ever possible, in the month during which they were recorded. The reader sees the images as they happen instead of having the images grouped elsewhere in the book, almost as an after thought. The sheer number of images is significant. Virtually every page has one or more images to help convey a sense of what was happening and who was involved. I wanted the reader to be able to "see" the war not only from the "front office" at Fifth Air Force or Far East Air Forces headquarters, but from the Orderly Rooms and berthing spaces at the squadron level.

Photographs were included, where available, of off duty entertainment activities and locations. The work days were awful and recreation was limited, but there was usually a movie in the evening. At some bases, there were clubs—primitive to be sure—but clubs where airmen and officers could try to relax with some beverage of choice, a game of cards, or a sing along. I tried to show a range of images that convey a sense of daily life at "Dogpatch."

Much of the information in *Truckbusters* is presented in "boxes." This enables the reader to obtain discrete information about a particular topic in a glance or very short read, then return to the main story of the chapter. Often *Truckbusters* looks more like a magazine than a typical book. Having a layout that presents information in easily identifiable blocks or units enables the reader to focus on the topic if it is of interest or move on by if their main interest lies further on. It also provides an effective way to present the first person accounts, many of them brief, using the exact words or even by-lines of those that lived through the experience.

Some of the chapters include first person accounts provided by pilots or airmen that were especially noteworthy for the understanding they provided about how individuals experienced the war and what they were thinking at the time. Although several are lengthy, these accounts are unsurpassed in their ability to convey thoughts, reactions, fears and motivations on the part of those who were actually fighting that war.

Chapters conclude with a summary of the significant events that took place that month. Enough information is provided about developments elsewhere in Korea to enable the reader to form a "big picture" of what else was going on in that theater of war. The major emphasis in this section, however, is on what had happened of interest or significance within the 18th Wing or its component squadrons that month. It is here that many of the aircraft accidents and crashes are reported—those that did not result in the death of the pilot. Not only were these "highlights" the subject of much animated discussion in the chow lines and clubs, but they graphically illustrate for *Truckbuster* readers the constant danger to which both pilots and ground crews were exposed.

Chapters conclude with a list of combat losses for that month. Some months, mercifully, ended with no killed in action or missing in action to report. Sadly, most months ended with several deaths—some months with as many as a dozen pilots. Ground crews could become victims as well to ordnance mishaps or accidents. To whatever extent is known, the circumstances surrounding the pilot's last flight or the fatal accident are noted. These were gleaned from sometimes very sketchy summaries in the unit histories or from reports submitted by surviving flight members.

The stories of these last missions are

18th Fighter-Bomber Wing Chronology
1950

January-June

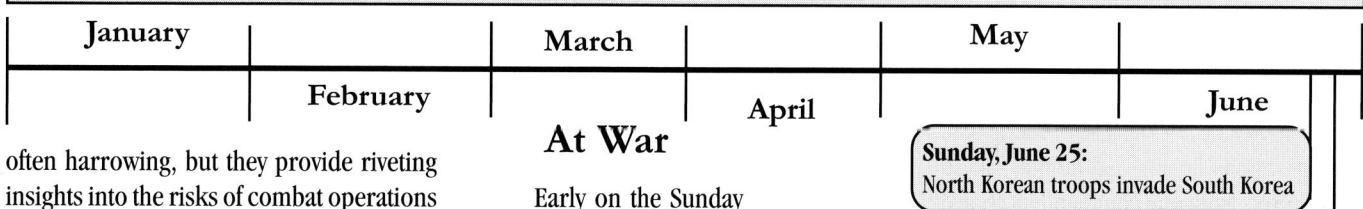

18th Fighter Bomber Group
Clark Field, Luzon, Philippines

January		March		May	
	February		April		June

often harrowing, but they provide riveting insights into the risks of combat operations and the incredible bravery shown by other members of the flight in trying to attempt a rescue or to ascertain exactly what had happened. In far too many instances, there is little or no information available about the last flight—the pilot simply failed to return from the mission. This listing appears at the end of the month in which the loss was sustained rather than as a list in the appendix of the book. If photographs are available, they appear nearby.

Biographical information on 2 Squadron SAAF losses was excerpted from materials and information provided by Lt. Col. Duane "Bud" Biteman.

When these elements are seen as a whole, *Truckbusters* emerges as a compilation of some 37 "books," each of them a month in the life of the 18th Fighter-Bomber Wing and its component commands. It is unlikely that *Truckbusters* will be read at one or even several sittings. Instead, most often, it will be reviewed by those interested in a specific time period, events or people. For unit members themselves or the families of 18th Wing veterans, the primary interest will be those months during which they or their family member served in Korea with the 18th. Designing each month as almost a "stand alone" facilitates the overall book's use in this way. It also facilitates its use as a reference or text book.

At War

Early on the Sunday morning of June 25, 1950, North Korean military forces poured across the 38th Parallel near Kaesong to invade the Republic of Korea (ROK). Almost immediately, North Korean fighter aircraft attacked both South Korean and United States Air Force aircraft and facilities at Seoul airfield and Kimpo Air Base, just south of Seoul. The brand new U.S. Air Force was involved in its first war as an independent United States military service.

In the first hours of the conflict, Air Force units helped evacuate Americans from the combat area, and also destroyed three North Korean fighters, the first aerial victories in the war, and the opening round of a constant struggle to gain and retain air superiority throughout the mountainous peninsula—the key that enabled United Nations forces to stay in the field.

By June 28th the Far East Air Force had been authorized to fly interdiction missions, photo-reconnaissance and weather missions, airlift missions, bombing and close air support missions for ROK troops.

On June 30th, President Harry S Truman committed U.S. ground forces to the battle, and shortly afterward, on July 7th, the United Nations established an allied command. U.S. Army General Douglas MacArthur was named UN Commander. The Fifth Air Force, commanded by USAF Major General Earle E. Partridge, established an advance headquarters in Taegu, SK, about

> **Sunday, June 25:**
> North Korean troops invade South Korea

> **Tuesday, June 27:**
> "Bout One," a composit unit of American and South Korean airmen organized by the 8th Fighter-Bomber Wing ordered to Taegu, SK (K-2)

140 miles southeast of Seoul.

During July, UN forces were forced by overwhelming numbers of North Korean troops to retreat down the peninsula until finally they were on the verge of being forced to consider evacuating the country entirely. During this period, the Air Force was desperately moving units from all over the world into place to provide the air support so badly needed. Later assessments would suggest that the "outbreak of this conventional limited conflict should have put the lie to the idea that the weapons designed to deter nuclear war were adequate to prevent conventional conflict. Instead, the Korean struggle was seen by most influential decision makers as merely a diversionary first phase of a European conflict that could well become nuclear." [1] As a result, much of the equipment that was beginning to flow towards Korea was anything but the best the Air Force had to offer.

The First Weeks of Combat

The 18th Wing newspaper later noted that when the Korean War began, the 18th Fighter-Bomber Wing was based in the Phil-

18th Fighter-Bomber Wing Chronology 1950

July–December

UN Defensive June 27–September 15, 1950		UN Offensive September 16– November 2, 1950	CCF Intervention November 3, 1950– January 24, 1951	
18th Group operates from K-2/Taegu, SK	18th FBG based in Ashiya, Japan	18th FBG operates from K-9/Pusan, SK	K-24 20 Nov- 16 Dec.	K-10/ Chinhae, SK

July   September   November

August   October   December

Sept. 8: 18th FBG moves to K-9/ Pusan
Sept. 15: Inchon invasion

Nov. 20: 6002nd TSW begins move from K-9 to Pyongyang East/K-24

Aug. 1: 51st Provisional Squadron redesignated 12th F-B Squadron
Aug. 5: Maj Sebille KIA
Aug. 6-7: 18th Group pulled back from Taegu, reunited in Ashiya, Japan.

Dec. 1: 18th FBW moves to K-13/Suwon

July 24: 18th Group Hqts, plus the 67th Squadron ordered to Johnson AB, Japan, then on to Taegu (K-2), Korea.
July 25: First KIA for 18th FBW, 2nd Lt. Billie Crabtree

Dec. 16: 18th FBW begins move to K-10/Chinhae.
2 Squadron SAAF joins 18th FBG

July 15: "Bout One" and "Dallas" Squadron cease to exist, merged into newly created 51st Fighter Squadron (Provisional) at Taegu. First combat mission flown from K-2.

July 3: FEAF directs 13th AF at Clark AFB to create new "Dallas Squadron" and deploy it to Japan to be equipped with F-51 Mustangs.

ippines "in a cadre state..." [2] Within a week of the North Korean assault, it was ordered to supply a single fighter squadron for duty in Korea. A contingent was identified and given the name "Dallas Project," which became the "Dallas Squadron," upon its arrival in Japan at Johnson Air Base on July 10, 1950. By July 27th, the squadron was based at Taegu Air Base, Korea. The first priority was to cross train the pilots from F-80s back into F-51s to satisfy Air Force mission requirements. After just four transition sorties, the "new" F-51 pilots were flying combat missions. The first Korean War combat mission by pilots of the 18th Wing was flown on July 12th.

The "51st Provisional," "Dallas," "Bout One," "Six-Double-O-Deuce" are all terms that marked the progress of the 18th Fighter-Bomber Wing "from a volunteer unit, hastily assembled in the Far East" in June-July 1950 until December 1, 1950 when it was moved "on paper" from the Philippines to Pyongyang, North Korea, absorbing the personnel, F-51 aircraft, and responsibilities of the 6002nd Tactical Support Wing.

"Two groups of volunteers, then known as "Bout One" and "Dallas," formed the 51st Provisional Squadron. They flew F-51s against the enemy forces during the early days in an effort to slow down the North Korean offensive and offer some protection to our withdrawing, greatly outnumbered, troops." [3]

Originally commanded by "calm, quiet-spoken Colonel Curtis R. Low from Needham Heights, Mass., the 18th was one of the first units to get into the Korean fray and has been part of the United Nations Team since that first hot July 12th when the first flight of F-51 Mustangs took off to strike an aerial blow for global peace and freedom." [4]

"Syngman Rhee, Republic of South Korea president, dubbed the unit 'The Flying Tigers of Korea.' The volunteer squadron grew rapidly. Col. Curtis R. Low assumed command and molded these squadrons, plus additional personnel into the 6002nd Tactical Support Wing. It was later redesignated the 18th Fighter-Bomber Wing, the name it carries today." [5]

From those "first humble beginnings" the 18th was destined "to play a prominent part in the Fifth Air Force's role on the peninsula. Despite the fact that the Wing moved five times in as many months, the all-important sortie rate did not drop and its fighting spirit never flagged for an instant."

The short range of the F-80 "Shooting Star" aircraft, coupled with the fact that they were based in Japan because of the lack of suitable air bases in Korea, left them with "only 10 or 15 minutes over the front lines, barely sufficient time to identify and attack targets when they were not controlled from the ground." [6] With the arrival of the "Boxer Boys" aboard the USS Boxer on July 23, 1950, along with 145 F-51 Mustangs, the Air Force quickly converted six F-80 squadrons to these aging World War II fighters—that could, however, operate from rough forward bases and remain over the target area for hours with rockets, bombs, napalm and machine gun ordnance. At the time the decision to provide close air support by returning the Mustangs to combat was "widely interpreted" as an admission that jets were unsuitable for the close air support role." In fact, Far East Air Forces (FEAF) had requested an additional 150 F-80s to provide that support. However, since the Air Force had only one-third of that number available versus over 1,500 of the WWII Mustangs, FEAF was forced to convert six formerly jet squadrons for the role instead. "The real reason for turning to Mustangs, namely the absence of jets in the inventory, could not be stated for national security reasons." [7]

Immediately upon the arrival of Air Force fighter-bomber units in mid-July, a tug of war began with Army planners. Behind the power struggles lay the Air Force conviction that as the front stabilized around Pusan, mission priorities should begin to shift away "from close air support and toward an interdiction program to isolate the battlefield. The Army, still being pushed back toward the southeastern corner of the peninsula, wanted to continue concentrat-

ing aerial firepower on the battlefield." [8] The differences between the Air Force and Army over air war doctrine and strategies would continue throughout the war and beyond. After the landings at Inchon, mission planning emphasis by the Air Force, with few exceptions from October 1950 until July 1953, was on shutting off enemy supply lines and reinforcements—"close air support sorties were overshadowed by interdiction and armed reconnaissance flights, sometimes by a ratio as high as twenty-five to one." [9]

Inchon Landings

The 18th played an important role in the first UN offensive against North Korean forces that began on September 15, 1950—the amphibious assault at Inchon. The 1st Marine Air Wing provided air support for the landing, while the Fifth Air Force supported the Eighth Army. In August and into September, all FEAF flying units had to fly from bases in Japan. Taegu/K-2 was used as a staging field to refuel and arm tactical aircraft. By September 9th, the 18th Fighter-Bomber Group was back in Korea flying from K-9, the first Air Force tactical unit to return to Korea—a week prior to the Inchon landings.

By October 1st UN units were crossing the 38th Parallel en route to Wonsan. By October 26th they reached the Yalu River at Chosan. Two days later, however, Chinese Communist forces counterattacked across a wide front, forcing UN forces into retreat and taking the war in an entirely new direction as the tide turned in favor of the Communist aggressors.

During the subsequent withdrawal down the Korean peninsula, the protection provided by the fighter-bombers of the 18th Wing and other units of the Fifth Air Force enabled UN forces, although hard pressed on all sides by overwhelming numbers of CCF, to withdraw in a generally orderly manner. Without highly effective close air support during those frigid weeks of withdrawal to the seaport of Hungnam, many thousands of UN troops would have faced almost certain death or cruel imprisonment. Truck-

busters includes a gripping account by 1st Lt. Ken Barber, an 18th pilot who had been sent on detached duty as a forward air controller to an infantry battalion slogging up close to the Yalu River, then back down to Hungnam for evacuation by the U.S. Navy from December 5-15. Barber kept a detailed diary and provided photography that tells this pivotal operation from a combat pilot's perspective.

After the Inchon landings, the 18th Fighter-Bomber Group had hop-scotched along behind the advancing troops by moving its advanced operating bases to newly captured North Korean air bases. It was the first UN squadron to fly combat missions from bases north of the 38th Parallel. It was newly augmented by the assignment to its operational control of 2 Squadron, South African Air Force (SAAF). It was the first unit to integrate another nation's air arm, thus creating a true United Nations fighter-bomber wing. Eventually, the 18th flying squadrons were moved to K-24, a base just east of Pyongyang, the North Korean Capital. Communist advances soon required that the 18th evacuate that base for others further south.

Constant hammering by UN air forces finally began to take its toll on the hordes of Chinese "volunteers" pouring down the peninsula. Due to the incessant and effective close air support and interdiction efforts by the 18th and other UN squadrons, by mid-December, Communist forces were moving mostly at night, although they were still advancing. It wasn't until January 15th that UN forces halted the Chinese and North Korean armies about 50 miles south of the 38th parallel.

When UN forces began taking the offensive on January 25, 1951, the military objective had changed from capturing territory to wearing down the enemy.

Combat Operations

"During the first six months operations in Korea, from July through December 1950, the wing moved five times and operated from three different areas," the *Air Force Times* noted on 30 May 1951. In less than six months of operations in Korea, the new Wing flew more than 6200 "effective combat sorties totaling 17,800 flying hours." It required that ground crews, maintenance, supply and "even administrative personnel" often worked up to 18 hours each day. "Enemy losses credited to pilots of the 18th through December 1950 included 16 enemy aircraft, almost 1,300 trucks, 190 tanks and 75 locomotives destroyed, and an estimated 10,150 enemy troop casualties. In one day alone 18th pilots destroyed an estimated 130 vehicles."

"The South African Air Force "2" Squadron joined the Wing in late 1950 as the third squadron. The 18th Wing claimed distinction of flying the first combat fighter planes on missions from an airstrip north of the 38th Parallel. On Oct. 14, shortly after it was captured, they flew out of the Wonsan airstrip."

Operations After the Chinese Communist Intervention

The 18th was operating from rough strips during "the big enemy breakthrough" in December 1950, the Wing's unit history recorded. "Throughout that period 18th pilots smashed enemy roadblocks, traps, and troop positions, supporting our withdrawing forces. When the pilots landed, their planes were refueled and rearmed while they were debriefed. They then climbed back into their readied Mustangs and returned to strike at the enemy again." [10]

Night flying was "not uncommon with the volunteer group. The pilots flew their Mustangs frequently through the inky darkness searching out enemy troops or equipment. When they spotted headlights, fires, or other tell-tale signs they dove in for the kill. These same pilots set a precedent early in the war by capturing and delivering enemy troops to UN forces while flying overhead at more than 250 mph, and without firing a shot. Two pilots lined up 12 enemy troops in a road and by buzzing low over

their heads marched them four miles down the road to UN troops. Later, more enemy troops—fearing the blazing guns, fire bombs, and low flying Mustangs—surrendered to the 18th pilots, who notified ground troops to 'walk in' and take over." [11]

"Along with Chinese Communist ground forces, the enemy threat now included jet fighter air craft—the MiG 15. A U.S. Air Force F-86 wing was immediately deployed from the United States to counter them. This gave the F-51s, F-80s, and the F-84s the protection needed to focus on the close air support needed to inflict heavy punishment on advancing Chinese forces. The combination of air interdiction strikes on North Korean road and railroad networks began to outnumber support strikes and became increasingly effective as Communist supply lines lengthened from the Yalu. Finally, the Communist drive was brought to a halt just south of Seoul.

"Last November fighter pilots of the 18th encountered the first MIG-15 enemy jets to be seen over Korea. In the first days of that month 18th pilots destroyed two conventional type YAK-3's, five YAK-9's, and probably destroyed two MIG-15's in aerial combat." Although Air Force reports and doctrine gave a Mustang virtually no chance against a jet aircraft, the pilots of the 18th proved them wrong on many occasions. In fact, specific tactics were developed by the 18th designed to use the Mustang's better maneuverability to advantage over the jet. It was never a "fair fight" between a MiG and a Mustang, but the 18th pilots often proved that it was anything but an assured victory for the jet.

"Pilots of the 18th Wing were the first to carry the new tank-demolishing 6.5 rockets into combat. One flight of F-51's equipped with the new rocket and led by Maj. Harry Moreland, was known as 'Moreland's Tank Busters' because of their feats."

"These pilots, in close support missions, knocked out enemy positions as close as 50 feet from our own troops, dropping napalm fire bombs, rocketing, and strafing."

Under pressure from Chinese Com-

munist Forces advances, the 18th moved on December 4, 1950 to Suwon AB, South Korea, and six days later to Chinhae, a former Japanese seaplane base, near Pusan.

1951 Major Offensive

The 18th Fighter-Bomber Wing completed its move from K-13 (Suwon) to K-10 (Chinhae) by January 4, 1951. "The landing strip at K-10 is dirt and problems were immediately encountered," the unit history recorded. "Large rocks on the runway were sucked into the propeller during run-ups, resulting in damage to numerous propellers and only extraordinary supply action kept such aircraft from becoming AOCP [Out of Commission for Parts]. [12]

Several "flying hazards" at K-10 greatly hampered night and early morning operations. The airstrip was bounded on three sides by mountains 2,000' high that are within 3 miles of the strip. The fourth side of the airstrip was formed by Chinhae Bay. Only 50 feet separates the entire length of the runway from the bay. A steel hangar was located at the south end of the runway and clears the runway by a mere 50 feet. Numerous pilots would be lost trying to take off or land from this dangerous air field.

Shortly after the 18th had moved its headquarters to K-10/Chinhae (near Pusan) in early January 1951, the UN launched its first major offensive since the Inchon landings. By February 10, 1951 UN troops had recaptured Kimpo AF near Seoul and were slowly advancing northward. The Communist air forces were beginning to establish such a strong air presence between the Chongchon and Yalu Rivers in northwestern Korean that the area was soon known as "MiG Alley." Although the U.S. began to move tactical fighter units equipped with F-86 Sabres from Japan to Korea to deal with the new threat, MiG fighters would continue to be a deadly threat to the Mustangs of the 18th Wing.

By mid-April 1951, UN forces had pushed north of the 38th Parallel, but were then halted by a North Korean and Chinese counterattack. The lines see-sawed back and forth for the next several months with

18th Wing Mustangs heavily engaged in close air support and bombing of North Korean airfields. On May 9th, Fifth Air Force (FAF) and Marine Corps fighters launched extended, heavy attacks on Sinuiju airfield in the northwest corner of Korea. The missions destroyed all North Korean aircraft on the field, most buildings, and several fuel, supply and ammunition dumps. No aircraft were lost during the raids. [13]

In May 1951, Far East Air Forces (FEAF) launched Operation Strangle, an interdiction campaign focused on destroying highways south of the 39th Parallel. A month later, the operation was extended to railroads—with great success.

By June 1951, the North Koreans, working through the Soviet Union, were proposing a cease-fire. Negotiations began at Kaesong, North Korea in July. They would continue, fitfully, for two more years. Hostilities continued throughout truce negotiations with each side launching operations or offensives designed to provide more leverage or bargaining power at the truce table.

Meanwhile, the 18th Fighter-Bomber Wing established itself at K-10 for most headquarters and heavy maintenance functions and used first K-16 (near Seoul) and later, K-46 (Hoengsong, east of Seoul) as advanced operations bases. Pilots and crew chiefs would leave K-10 for 3-5 days of heavy combat flying from the advanced base, and then return to K-10 for some measure of relaxation, better food and administrative duties. Eventually, a system was instituted that enabled most combat crews to come "off the line" every five weeks or so for a brief "R&R" in Japan.

As the ground war slowed from gaining territory to holding the line, the air war as 1951 advanced was hotter than ever. Missions for the Mustang pilots not only included ground support, but interdiction

18th Fighter-Bomber Wing Chronology

1951

January-June

CCF Attack 11/3/50-1/24/51	First United Nations Counteroffensive January 25-April 21, 1951	Chinese Communist Army Spring Offensive April 22-July 8, 1951

18th Fighter-Bomber Wing and Group based at K-10/Chinhae, SK	18th FBG flies most combat missions from K-16/Seoul, SK

January   February   March   April   May   June

Mar. 24-Apr. 23: During K-10 resurfacing, 18th FBG aircraft operated from K-1 and K-13. The majority of organizational and field maintenance was performed at K-1.

May 12: 39th FIS operational at K-10.

Feb. 24: 18th FB Wing 10,000th combat mission.
Mar. 4: MG Earle Partridge, CG, FAF honored Wing for 10,000 effective combat sorties.

May 9: 39th Fighter-Interceptor Squadron assigned to 18th FBG at K-10.

Feb. 1: Col. T. C. Rogers assumed command of 18th Wing from Col. Curtis R. Low.

May 8: 18th FBG begins staging combat operations from K-16.

Jan. 15: Red CCF Tide begins to turn. CCF begin a limited withdrawal.

Jan. 4: 18th FBW completes move from K-13/Suwon to K-10/Chinhae.

June 30: As of 30 June, the 18th FBG had flown 16,370 effective combat sorties during 36,758 combat flying hours.

18th Fighter-Bomber Wing Chronology 1951

July - December

United Nations Summer-Fall Offensive July 9-November 27, 1951	Second Korean Winter Nov. 28, 1951- April 30, 1952

18th Fighter Bomber Group based at K-10/Chinhae Flying combat missions from K-16 /Seoul	18th Fighter Bomber Group based at K-10/Chinhae. Flying combat missions from K-46/Hoengsong

July | August | September | October | November | December

Aug. 14: 18th FBG conducts major raid on P'yongyang.

Nov. 12: Peace negotiations moved to Panmunjom. UN Command ceases offensive ground operations.

July 5: A major firepower demonstration was held at "Dogpatch" by the 18th FBW commemorating its "First Anniversary" of combat in the Korean War. General Everest and Ambassador Muccio attended.

Oct. 25: Peace negotiations resume.

Oct. 1: 18th FBW personnel operating from K-16/Seoul AB ordered to establish a new advanced base of operations at K-46/Hoengsong, SK.

July 1: Communists first agree to truce negotiations.

July 9: 39th FIS completes first full year of combat with 8,911 combat sorties during 18,708 flying hours.

efforts that often took flights or "group gaggles" far into North Korean territory. Although UN F-86 Sabres were usually assigned as "cover" for the Mustangs, reports verify that often the rendezvous was not effected. The Mustangs often had to fend for themselves against the much faster MiGs.

By late 1951, the squadrons of the 18th—12th, 67th, 39th FIS, and 2 Squadron SAAF—were focused on railway interdiction throughout North Korea, in addition to Close Air Support and many other missions, including providing combat air patrols to help protect downed pilots and the helicopters that were often sent to rescue them.

As 1951 closed out, truce negotiations had resumed—at Panmunjom—and

Aug 29: 18th Wing completes 25,000 combat sorties, the first FEAF unit to reach this number.

UN ground forces had virtually ceased offensive actions. The UN allies were settling into a war of containment, but deadly air offensives continued—by both sides.

Static Ground War, Heavy Air Operations

In early 1952, as the front lines became static, the need for close air support declined significantly. The freed up fire

power of the fighter-bombers was then used to alternate aerial bombardment of enemy positions one day followed by artillery attacks of the same position the next day. The effectiveness of this tactic was undermined, literally, when the Chinese and North Korean troops soon dug even deeper positions and tunnels that were harder to find or to destroy by air or artillery attacks. The air strikes were soon discontinued.

The tactical focus then turned to means of applying military pressure against Communist forces by attacking targets previously exempted from lists of approved targets or returning to work over targets that had retained any potential value to the enemy. Interdiction mission planning began to shift from transportation networks to attacks on supply depots and industrial targets. In mid-1952, FAF [Fifth Air Force] fighter-bombers coordinated with U.S. Navy and Marine Corps units to attack electric power complexes at Sui-ho Dam, on the Yalu River near Sinuiju, followed by effective strikes against the Chosin, Fusen, and Kyosen power plants in northeastern Korea. Pyongyang also received heavy damage during this period.

Even though the battle lines were generally static, close air support remained an important mission for FAF fighter-bombers. Between 2,000-4,000 such missions were flown by Air Force, Navy and Marine Corps units each month.

During this period the Air Force continued to phase more F-86 Sabrejets into the mix of combat aircraft. The 18th Wing continued to fly its aging, obsolescent Mustangs throughout 1952.

In October 1952, UN negotiators broke off "peace talks" when the Chinese would not agree to non-forced repatriation of prisoners of war—only those POWs who wanted repatriation would be returned to Communist control. As the war entered its third winter, the conflict remained stalemated throughout the winter of 1952—at least in the ground war. The air war continued unabated.

Air Operations Hasten Armistice

Fifth Air Force and the hard-working 18th Wing pilots and ground crews, maintained a high tempo of combat missions to strike supplies, equipment, and troops up and down the entire length of North Korea. Even though destroyed supply lines, railroads and bridges were quickly put back into service, it was at great cost in men and material. By the end of March 1953, the Chinese government began to indicate a willingness to exchange injured and sick POWs and to discuss the terms of a ceasefire in Korea. On April 20, 1953, UN and Communist officials began an exchange of POWs—"Little Switch"—and six days later negotiations resumed at Panmunjom.

As Spring was turning into Summer 1953, Communist leaders decided to improve their military positions by launching a major offensive—even as they were negotiating an armistice. During the following UN drive to blunt, then halt, the offen-

18th Fighter-Bomber Wing Chronology 1952

January-June

Second Korean Winter November 28, 1951-April 30, 1952	Korean Summer-Fall 1952 May 1-November 30, 1952

18th Fighter-Bomber Group officially based at K-10/Chinhae, SK Flying combat missions from K-46/Hoengsong, SK	18th FBW based at K-46

January

February

March

April

May

June

18th FBG Mustangs penetrated deep into enemy territory. Communist rail lines, bridges, storage dumps, troop emplacements and vehicles suffered heavy losses. F-51's attacked 30 supply buildings near Sibyon-ni, rocketing and napalming until the entire area "was crackling in flames."

"We have been hitting, with the entire 5th Air Force, a small section of rails each day. The results have proven very satisfactory."

June 1: 18th FBG moves operations from K-10 to K-46.

June 24: FEAF flew 1,043 sorties, the highest daily total for the month FAF fighter-bombers flew over 250 sorties against North Korean targets.

In January, the rail interdiction program continued as a focus for combat operations. Most flights directed against railheads, communication lines and highways.

April 19: 39th FIS reassigned from 18th FBG to the 51st FIW.

Close support, interdiction, rail cutting, and rescue missions account for the largest number of sorties to be flown by the 18th FBG.

18th Fighter-Bomber Wing Chronology 1952

July - December

Korea Summer-Fall 1952 May 1-November 30, 1952	Third Korean Winter Dec. 1, 1952-Apr. 30, 1953

18th Fighter Bomber Group officially based at K-46/Hoengsong, SK

July   August   September   October   November   December

September: FEAF directed most air attacks against enemy industrial remnants and troop concentration areas. Many targets were in border areas, which had been virtually untouched by FEAF attacks.

Nov-Dec: 18th FBG's principal interdiction efforts "were directed against enemy troop concentrations and supplies. Close support again accounted for the largest portion of the effort. Armed reconnaissance and rescue combat air patrols were the other types of missons flown."

Aug. 29: FEAF conducted the largest air attack to date against Pyongyang as a dramatic military action during a visit by China's premier, Chou En-lai, to the Soviet Union.

October: Close support sorties increased during October to represent more than one-half of the effort for themonth. Armed reconnaissance, rescue air patrol, and road reconnaissance were the other types ofmissions flown by the 18th FBG.

July 11: Highlight for the pilots when "a maximum effort was directed at Ping Pong (Pyongyang East)."

July 9: Capt. Elliot Ayer, 67th FBS, completes 45,000th combat mission for 18th FBG.

Dec. 26: The 18th FBW transferred its headquarters from K-10/Chinhae "to the new base at Osan Airdrome (K-55)."

Close support, interdiction, road recces, and RESCAP missions were the main types of missons flown during July.

sive, its combined air forces broke previous records in flying close air support sorties.

Significantly, for the 18th Wing, in January 1953 it had finally begun the transition from the F-51D Mustang to F-86 Sabrejets. In doing so, it made Air Force history—again—by completing its second conversion from one type of aircraft to another—while engaged in combat and without "standing down" from required combat mission completions. Its pilots were now flying all of the typical "fighter" missions in high performance jets, but also using the sturdy, capable Sabrejets for "bomber" missions, as well.

When it finally converted to the F-86 Sabrejet, the 18th Fighter-Bomber Wing became the last American combat unit to fly the P/F-51 "Mustang" in combat. "The above aircraft were the last USAF single engine, propeller-driven aircraft to be flown in offensive combat. The excellent results of these two missions were a fitting tribute to the end of another phase of aviation development," the 18th Wing unit history recorded that month.

As the Chinese offense ground to a halt under the punishment inflicted by UN ground and air units, 18th Wing fighter-bombers were attacking power complexes, industrial and military targets throughout North Korea. Major irrigation dams were added to the list of approved targets. North Korean air fields were worked over thoroughly during this period.

An armistice ending the Korean War went into effect on July 27, 1953.

Air Force leaders often had to remind their Army counterparts that two air factors made possible the kind of ground action that took place in Korea. One vital factor was the defeat of the enemy's air force, both at the outset of the war and later after Russian and Chinese jets were introduced—air superiority. Ground forces had little need to fear enemy air attacks. The Air Force reminded the Army that it should not overlook the importance of air battles that took place far out of sight of ground units that provided the protection needed for them to operate confident of no aerial attacks. The second factor was the significant contribution made by Air Force units in preventing enormous quantities of enemy material and men from reaching the front lines. To the Air Force, these efforts were as important, if not more so, than direct close air support in determining the outcome of the battles." [14]

18th Wing Accomplishments in the Korean War

◪   Early in its combat role, the "*Truckbuster*" tag was applied to the 18th after its squadrons destroyed 126 trucks in one day. "This can be attributed to the 'Pioneer' volunteers who evolved low-level attack techniques that today are SOP when attacking enemy equipment." [15] Enemy losses credited to pilots of the 18th from July through December 1950 included 16 enemy aircraft, almost 1300 trucks, 190 tanks and 75 locomotives destroyed and an estimated 10,150 enemy troop casualties.

◪   Following the evacuation of all Air Force tactical units from Korea in August 1950 as the Pusan Perimeter was shrinking, the 18th F-B Wing was the first Air Force tactical unit ordered back into Korea and based at K-9, near Pusan.

◪   First unit to integrate another nation's air arm and forge a United Nations fighter-bomber wing when the 2nd Squadron South African Air Force joined the 18th in November 1950.

◪   First Air Force unit to have one its members receive the Congressional Medal of Honor for action in Korea (Major Louis J. Sebille), who, when mortally wounded, deliberately crashed his Mustang into an enemy armored vehicle, on August 5, 1950.

◪   First Air Force unit to fly combat missions from airstrips north of the 38th parallel. Four Fifth Air Force F-51 Mustangs, led by Major Arnold Mullins, CO of the 67th took off Sunday [October 15, 1950] from the newly occupied air field at Wonsan, above the 39th Parallel in North Korea, on the first mission to be flown from that strip," noted Captain Tom Baird in a *Stars and Stripes* article. "This was the first North Korean air field to be utilized by the UN forces since the beginning of Korea hostilities."

◪   First to encounter the MIG in combat

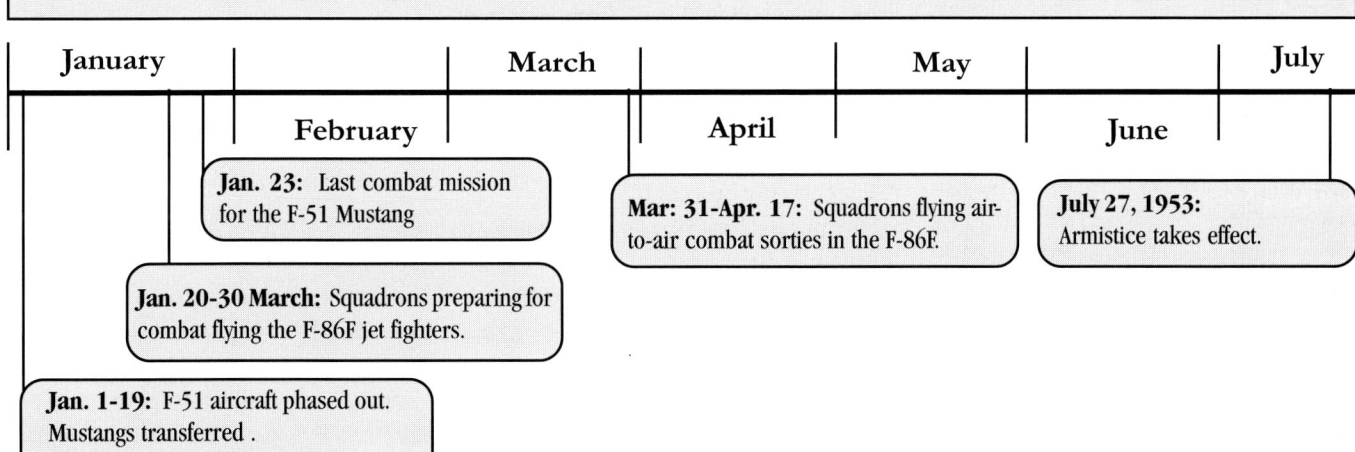

18th Fighter-Bomber Wing Chronology 1953

January-July

Third Korean Winter December 1, 1952-April 30, 1953	Korea Summer-Fall May 1-July 27, 1953

18th Fighter Bomber Group officially based at K-55/Osan-ni, SK

January		March		May		July
	February		April		June	

Jan. 23: Last combat mission for the F-51 Mustang

Mar: 31-Apr. 17: Squadrons flying air-to-air combat sorties in the F-86F.

July 27, 1953: Armistice takes effect.

Jan. 20-30 March: Squadrons preparing for combat flying the F-86F jet fighters.

Jan. 1-19: F-51 aircraft phased out. Mustangs transferred . Movement to K-55 completed.

over Korea. "Last November fighter pilots of the 18ᵗʰ encountered the first MIG-15 enemy jets to be seen over Korea. In the first days of that month 18ᵗʰ pilots destroyed two conventional type YAK-3's, five YAK-9's, and probably destroyed two MIG-15's in aerial combat."

⌕ First to employ 6.5 inch rockets in combat.

⌕ First in total number of effective combat sorties.

⌕ First Air Force unit to capture enemy troops while flying aircraft. Night flying was "not uncommon with the volunteer group. The pilots flew their Mustangs frequently through the inky darkness searching out enemy troops or equipment. When they spotted headlights, fires, or other tell-tale signs they dove in for the kill. These same pilots set a precedent early in the war by capturing and delivering enemy troops to UN forces while flying overhead at more than 250 mph, and without firing a shot. Two pilots lined up 12 enemy troops in a road and by buzzing low over their heads marched them four miles down the road to UN troops. Later, more enemy troops—fearing the blazing guns, fire bombs, and low flying Mustangs—surrendered to the 18ᵗʰ pilots, who notified ground troops to 'walk in' and take over." [16]

⌕ The 18ᵗʰ Wing is the only known Air Force flying unit to be asked to convert from one type of aircraft to another—while engaged in combat and without "standing down" from required combat mission completions—not once, but twice and while operating from "forward operating bases." In July 1950, 18ᵗʰ Wing squadrons were order to convert from F-80 "Shooting Star" jet aircraft to the aging F-51 "Mustang" fighter-bomber. In January 1953, 18ᵗʰ Wing Squadrons converted from the F-51 "Mustang" to the F-86 "Sabrejet"—again while in active combat and while meeting all operational commitments. In a 9 October 1997 letter to Lt. Col. Flamm D. Harper, USAF (Ret), the Air Force History Support Office noted "you stated your interest in gaining some recognition for the unique accomplishment of the 18ᵗʰ Fighter-Bomber Wing in converting from piston

engine F-51's to high performance jets (F-86F) at a new base, in winter, and in a combat zone." "We agree," wrote Col. Christine L. Jaremko, "in fact, we cannot find another example of a similar conversion in the history of the Air Force."

⌕ Also, the 18ᵗʰ Fighter-Bomber Wing was the last American combat unit to fly the P/F-51 "Mustang" in combat. Only in January 1953 was the 18ᵗʰ Wing converted to the F-86 fighter-bomber jet aircraft. "The above aircraft were the last USAF single engine, propeller-driven aircraft to be flown in offensive combat. The excellent results of these two missions were a fitting tribute to the end of another phase of aviation development."

This combat diary of the 18ᵗʰ Fighter-Bomber Wing during the Korean War was not prepared or based solely on a pains-taking accumulation of facts and dates and statistics. Rather, it is the goal of all who worked on **Truckbusters From Dogpatch** that it establishes the proud record of a venerable American fighting unit that has earned the right through grit, achievement and sacrifice to be remembered as among the very finest of military units, not just during the Korean War, but even when compared with American combat units of any period in our history.

Endnotes

[1] Schlight, John (2003). Help from Above: Air Force Close Air Support of the Army, 1946-1973. Washington, D.C.; Air Force History and Museums Program, p. 113.

[2] 18ᵗʰ Fighter Bomber Wing Album, October 1951, Foreword

[3] "Mustangs of the 18ᵗʰ F-B Wing Nearing Year of Fighting," Air Force Times, May 30, 1951, p. 10

[4] 18ᵗʰ Fighter Bomber Wing Album, October 1951, Wing Headquarters Squadron.

[5] Air Force Times, May 30, 1951, p. 10.

[6] Schlight, p. 122.

[7] Schlight, p. 154.

[8] Schlight, p. 123.

[9] Schlight, p. 135.

[10] Air Force Times, May 30, 1951, p. 10

[11] Air Force Times, May 30, 1951, p. 10.

[12] *USAFHRA. Monthly Historical Report, 18ᵗʰ Fighter-Bomber Wing, January 1951, p. 4.*

[13] Endicott, Judy (Editor), "U.S. Air Force in Korea, Campaigns, Units and Stations, 1950-1953, USAF Historical Research Agency, 2001, p. 23.

[14] Schlight, p. 141.

[15] 18ᵗʰ Fighter Bomber Wing Album, October 1951, Wing Headquarters Squadron.

[16] Air Force Times, May 30, 1951, p. 10.

TRUCKBUSTERS

FROM DOGPATCH

THE *Combat Diary* OF THE
18TH FIGHTER-BOMBER WING
IN THE KOREAN WAR
1950-1953

Talons and Beak

As the new decade of 1950 began, the 18th Fighter-Bomber Wing of the U.S. 13th Air Force was based at Clark Air Force Base, Philippines. Its component squadrons—including the three squadrons of the 18th Fighter-Bomber Group—67th FBS, 12th FBS and the 44th FBS—were still completing "the transition from combined forces to primarily an overall Air Force installation…" Nearly 80 percent of its personnel were Air Force and 22 percent were still SCARWAF (Special Category Army with Air Force).

[Acronyms will be spelled out the first time they are used in the text. An extensive Glossary can be found in the Appendices and includes all of the acronyms and technical terms used in this history.]

On 9 November 1949, Lt. Col. Henry H. Norman was the newly designated 18th Fighter Group Commander, replacing Col Marion Malcolm, who had completed his tour and returned to the Z.I. [Zone of the Interior, i.e. the continental United States]. Lt. Col. Ira F. "Ike" Wintermute was the Group Operations and Training Officer.

At about the same time, the 18th Group was given its first Lockheed F-80C "Shooting Star" aircraft. Actually, it was not the first F-80 the 18th squadrons had flown. Norman presented the F-80C to Major Louis J. Sebille, Commander of the 67th Squadron, since the 67th had been the first squadron in the 18th to receive the new jets in 1946, following the end of World War II. The Group had not kept the jets for long and there had been several different "primary aircraft" to fly in the nearly five years since World War II—from P-80s to P-51 Mustangs, to P-47s and back to F-51's again.

F-80 flight line at Roswell AFB, NM in 1948 for 33rd Fighter Group checkout. (Biteman)

On 16 January 1950, Lt. Kenneth Barber soloed in the F-80 Shooting Star. "What a wonderful feeling and such smooth flying. Lands like a dream, too!"

Lt. Alfred R. Braly, a pilot with the 67th Fighter Bomber Squadron, was killed on 3 February 1950. Braly was a recently commissioned bomber pilot assigned to fighters. Navy observers reported they "had seen a jet crash straight into Subic Bay. It was not on fire nor was there any indication that the pilot tried to bail out." Crash boats on the scene recovered his body.

"No one knows what caused this accident--but the general opinion is that he had anoxia while flying at altitude and didn't recover in time to pull out," Barber noted.

Braly's memorial service was held on 6 February at the Base Chapel. As taps was played and a squad fired a three volley salute, a flight of F-80's "buzzed low overhead making two passes in salute to the deceased member of their squadron."

"Life is a short and uncertain thing. We must always be ready for its termination, for it is not for us to know when the time or where the place. As I sat there in the service I kept thinking of how important it was for us to do our best in service to people while we can. My other thought was, when my time comes, what better way can there be to die, than in a Shooting Star? A good way to die!!"

On Saturday evening, 11 February, Lt. Barber attended a barbecue and beer bust that included singing and "ye ole guitar--much fun. Learned some good songs," he noted.

"Off we go into the wild, blue yonder—Crash

I hear those gentle voices calling—"Hey, Joe!"

Barber, Lt. Col. Kenneth. Korean War Diary Number One (unpublished), 5 August 1950.

The "new" Air Force redesignated many former Army Air Forces aircraft in 1947. The "Pursuit" Mustang was now the "Fighter" Mustang.

As 1949 turned into 1950, the 18th Fighter Group was re-designated the "18th Fighter-Bomber Group" and were once again heavily involved in converting to the Lockheed F-80C jet aircraft, a much improved version of the aircraft over its WWII predecessor.

Component squadrons of the 18th Fighter-Bomber Group, whose motto was "Unguibus et Rostro," meaning "with talons and beak," were completing the transition from prop aircraft into jet fighter aircraft.

[Note: "Unguibus et Rostro," was approved for the 18th Group on 21 Feb 1931 and for the 18th Wing on 17 Apr 1953 just prior to the Korean Armistice.]

"Our F-80's arrived, and after four years I finally got my chance to fly it," recalled Col. Howard "Scrappy" Johnson. "The group converted to brand new P-80C's in late 1949. They arrived by ship and were assembled at our depot. They painted big lightening stripes down the side and our names just below the canopy. They looked great sitting on the ramp. My first flight in one was a wonderful thrill. We flew our old P-51s down to Manila and gave them to the Philippine Air Force. I did not know it at the time, but the P-51 and I would cross paths again in the near future."

"The transition to F-80s did not go as smoothly as checking the kids out in the P-51," Johnson noted. "One day Lieutenant

New Year's Eve 1949. As the Forties faded into a memory, pilots and wives of the 18th Fighter-Bomber Group celebrated the conclusion of the first half of the 20th century. The photograph at right was probably taken on the patio of the "hospital club" at Clark Air Base. Flying squadrons from the 18th were often invited guests at the club. Former 44th Squadron flyer Ray Carter remembered New Year's Eve 1949 "because the 44th was thrown out of the Club for making too much noise?" Ray's wife, Erma did not arrive in the Philippines until March 1950, but remembers the hospital club was "pretty rowdy."

Flight line at Clark Air Base *in the Philippines in late 1949, prior to the 18th Group getting F-80's.* *(Burns)*

Lacy augured in on final approach. He'd obviously stalled it out turning on to final. I was the airdrome officer that day and was at the scene as the fire truck arrived. The plane was spread out over about one hundred yards. I found the firemen spraying foam on the tail section and angrily directed them to spray the cockpit. It wouldn't have

mattered though, the kid was already dead."

Captain Harry "Mo" Moreland was "in the mobile control to witness his landing. We used an overhead 360 degree landing pattern," Moreland explained. "His pattern was too tight and I instructed him to break it off, go around and try again. Instead he tried to pull it in tighter, stalled and crashed

New Year's Celebration

On December 16, 1949, Lt. Kenneth Barber reported to his new unit, the 44th Fighter Squadron, based at Clark AFB in the Philippines. That night he attended a "free beer bust" where he met many of his fellow pilots and their wives. "This sure is a partying base!" he wrote in his diary. "Loose as a goose too, I imagine." He made plans to enter the Wing boxing tournament, but first he had to get back into shape.

"What a party tonight," Lt. Barber noted on 31 December 1949. "It was held in the Officer's Club outdoor pavilion. The floorshow wasn't too bad—pretty fair sing-

ing, sorry hula dancers, and two fine acrobats. At midnight, amid much drunken uproar and loose kissing, the New Year came in. Strikes me as a poor but typical start of a New Year. Now that the world's chief pleasure is drinking and kissing, we have a fine New Year to look forward to."

Two weeks later, on 15 January, Lt. Barber noted that the "Little Theatre group is going strong." He was asked to play the part of Tony opposite Billie McManigal, one of the schoolteachers, in "You Can't Take It With You." It is a lot of fun and a good spare time hobby."

3

on the runway."

There were other young pilots in the air at the time taking their first test flights in the F-80. "As a result of that accident we almost had another one. A Lt. Lang was airborne at the same time on his first ride in the F-80. We had to close the runway due to Lt. Lacy's accident and were using the taxiway to land on. Lang was so shook up that it took several passes to get him on the ground and it was a rough landing," Moreland remembered.

There was an ironic but very sad aftermath to Lt. Lyle's death, Johnson recalled.

The following day, Lyle's wife arrived. "He had met her in a bar in San Francisco and had married her the day his ship sailed, after having known her for only two days. Lieutenants do strange things."

January 1950 was highlighted by a public demonstration of the F-80 "Shooting Star" that showed off its performance and flight characteristics for members of the Philippine press. During the demonstration that was held on the 19th, the 18th Fighter-Bomber Group put 12 F-80 Shooting Stars into the air simultaneously. The big problem they faced in doing this was not in the aerodynamics of the sleek new jets, so different from those of the F-51s, but the challenge of starting all of the aircraft simultaneously due to a shortage of auxiliary power units.

The Shooting Star fighters were brand new to the Far East Air Force (FEAF), but they were the oldest of the new Air Force's operational jets. "The F-80's that were sent to the 18th Fighter-Bomber Wing," Col. Stan Chatfield explained, "were new F-80C aircraft from the States. All three squadrons— the 12th, 44th and 67th—converted simultaneously to the new bird."

Chatfield, a native of Minot, North Dakota, was the eighth of nine children, six of whom were brothers that had served in uniform during World War II. After two years at the University of North Dakota in the late Thirty's, Chatfield had completed the Army's Aviation Cadet program by late 1942, and

Clark Field Administrative Building (Barber)

began flying P-39's in North Africa. After the Anzio landings, Chatfield's group was ordered to Karachi, India to pick up the new P-47, followed by a deployment to China.

Chatfield reported to the 18th in November 1949 as a Major, following his assignment after WWII at the USAF Fighter School, Williams AFB, Arizona, where he had been an Instructor Pilot in the F-51, T-33 and the F-80C. His original assignment for the 18th Group had been to replace one of the three squadron commanders who were about to be reassigned to the Zone of the Interior (ZI).

Originally, the F-80's had been designed as counter-air interceptors with their pri-

mary weapons being six .50-caliber machine guns mounted in the nose. The F-80's greatest weakness was its limited range. With an internal fuel tank, it had an action radius of approximately 100 miles. When equipped with two 165-gallon external fuel tanks, the operational radius was increased to approximately 225 miles. Not only was the operational radius extremely short, but it assumed that the jet would, for the most part, fly to and from the intended target at high altitudes (above 15,000 feet) where its jet engine was most economical. Time spent at low altitudes rapidly exhausted the F-80's radius of flight.

The severe limitations of the Shooting

Clark Field Base Operations Quonset Building in Spring 1950. (Biteman)

The 44th Fighter-Bomber Squadron was attached to the 18th Fighter-Bomber Group when it was based at Clark Field in the Philippines. When the 12th and 67th Squadrons were sent into combat in Korean, the 44th Squadron remained at Clark Field to provide sole air protection of the entire South Pacific, Philippine Islands and Formosa areas, with its single squadron of F-80Cs, while at the same time providing pilot rotation resources for the two 18th units fighting in Korea. The F-80 aircraft left behind at Clark by the 12th and 67th Squadrons furnished Far East Air Forces (FEAF) with a replacement pool for the many F-80s later to be lost in Korea.

Star in missions other than counter-air were well known to USAF planners. The Republic F-84E "Thunderjet," was considered to be better fitted for that role.

"Having flown the F-84 and having attended the Tech Rep School on the J-35 engine," Chatfield explained, "I can say that it was comparable to the F-80C as they were both limited to subsonic flight." The F-84 also took more runway to get airborne.

FEAF had been slated to receive some of the F-80 aircraft, but the Japanese airfields of the day were inadequate for the Thunderjets. An interim "jury rigged" solution was devised by two young Lieutenants who developed a modified 265-gallon fuel tank that increased the action radius to approximately 350 miles, depending on the nature of the mission. The Air Materiel Command would not approve the new tanks because they stressed the wing tips, but FEAF began installing them anyway in June 1950. [1]

In February 1950, Colonel C. W. "Skippy" Davies commanded the 18th Fighter Bomber Wing at Clark AFB on Luzon and Lt. Col. Henry H. Norman, com-

18th Group Pilots with Shooting Star. *18th Group Pilots from the 12th, 67th and 44th Squadrons at Clark Air Base were proud to pose on their new--to them--F-80 "Shooting Star." In a few short weeks, many of these pilots would be transferred to the sister squadrons of the 18th Fighter-Bomber Group and flying combat in Korea--in F-51 Mustangs. Seated (L-R): Lt. Bill Foster, Lt. Ray Carter, Lt. Patterson, Lt. Frank Buzze, Lt. Glessner, Capt. Bob Embery. Second Row Standing: (L-R) Capt. Howard "Scrappy" Johnson, Capt. Bill Slater, Lt. Jim Allen, Capt. Ross Cree, Lt. Herbie Brewer, Lt. Starck, Capt. Chuck Hauver, and Lt. Phil Conserva. Third Row On Plane (L-R): Lt. Campbell, Lt. Harlan Ball, Major Stan Chatfield, Lt. Ausman, Capt. Duane "Bud" Biteman, Lt. Paul Buttry, Capt. Jack Crawford, Capt. Pete Kane, Capt. Ed Hoagland and Capt. Nebinger. (Chatfield)*

5

manded the 18th Fighter Bomber Group that was equipped with F-80 type aircraft.

The 18th Wing at that time included such component commands, in addition to the 18th Fighter-Bomber Group, as the 18th Medical Group, the 6205th Air Police Group; the 6204th Photo Mapping Flight; 2nd Rescue Squadron; and the 21st Troop Carrier Squadron.

The Wing's primary mission was to maintain the 18th Fighter-Bomber Group "in the maximum state of combat readiness" according to the command history. It was also responsible for maintaining Clark Air Force Base, including base defense, and supporting two "tenant organizations," the 13th Air Force and the 6208th Depot Wing.

Operational missions for the Wing and its component Group "varied from routine training to simulated actual problems with friendly naval forces." Such a friendly force arrived late in February—U.S. Naval Task Force 73—included two aircraft carriers, the USS BOXER and HMS TRIUMPH of the Royal Navy. Joint exercises had been planned and would be carried out to "improve coordination between these different types of Services. The 18th Fighter-Bomber Group has been utilizing Navy facilities for dive bombing and strafing practice for several months; and the Navy has been using our pilots and aircraft for aiming and radar practice." [2]

Most Wing pilots were still heavily engaged in transitioning into the F-80 type aircraft. In March, a total of 1,534 hours were flown and in April, 1,548 hours were logged in the new (to them) jet fighters.

On the ground, the Air Police "maintained many patrols of the Base perimeter fence to prevent dissident Filipinos from entering the Base to steal supplies."

A practice alert on March 21st revealed that, "many deficiencies were found to exist in communications. These have been corrected by use of field phones and portable radios."

The unit reports for this period note that Saturday mornings were used for training in such subjects as "military discipline, cour-

*(Right) View from **Clark Air Force Base Control Tower** in Spring 1950. (Biteman)*

"During this period blacks were integrated into the services," Col. Howard "Scrappy" Johnson explained. "One day in Operations the pilots were talking about this tall black man, who was a new pilot in the squadron. He had scored 30 points for us in a basketball game the previous night. This turned out to be First Lieutenant Daniel "Chappie" James. Chappie was an extremely personable guy and was accepted in the squadron with open arms. However, I heard that his son "Spike" and daughter Denise did not fare as well. The kids were giving them a hard time at the school bus stop. Claude "Spud" Taylor, another one of our pilots, who had become a friend of Chappie's heard about this and for several mornings he escorted Spike and Denise to the bus stop, and convinced the other kids to cool it."

"Spud was a great saxophone player. He had played in a civilian band and had formed a band of his own that played at clubs on the base. Sometimes when his musicians were playing in two clubs on the same night, Chappie led one of them for him. Chappie could sing in a deep baritone voice and dearly loved to have a microphone in his hand," Johnson recalled.

Chappie was sent to the 18th fighter group when they broke up the all black outfit at Lockburn, Col. Harry H. Moreland explained. "There was a lot of skepticism around Clark when he arrived. It didn't last long. He was soon invited all around and became very popular. Beside singing

1st Lt. Daniel "Chappie" James

with Spud's band, he played football, tennis and golf. I know of a couple from lower Alabama who said they would never have a black in their house. It took all of a month before we went to their house for dinner. Chappie was everybody's friend."

"Back at Clark, Spud used to entertain us at the Officer's Club with his band and Chappie would join in and sing. Spud was shot down in North Korea and killed by his captors. This was a very difficult time for Chappie. When he would sing after that his rendition of "my buddy," it would bring tears to his eyes," Moreland remembered.

Chappie was a native of Pensacola, Florida and eventually retired as a four star general.

tesy, venereal disease and drill." Swimming lessons were held for those airmen who could not swim. "The required standard was that they be able to swim at least fifty yards." However, such training is not remembered by some of those who were assigned to the Group at the time. It would not be the first or last time that what was being reported "up the chain" by the squadrons and the Group differed from what was actually happening at the Squadron level.

A "special course in atomic and biological warfare" was attended by selected officers. While "it barely scratched the surface of the subject, it impressed those who were selected to attend of the possibilities of this type of warfare."

Even as it was pushing its pilots through the transition into jets, the Wing was reporting critical shortages of equipment, ranging from auxiliary power units to helmets, May Wests and life rafts. "It is felt that unless replacements for overage and worn-out May Wests and C-2 life rafts are forthcoming before 1 July 1950, a serious shortage will jeopardize the operational safety of the 18th Fighter Bomber Group." [3] The tight money policies in Washington for defense expenditures, in general, plus the costs to the Air Force of buying a new jet fleet were being felt all the way down to the squadron level.

During the first week of March, the pilots from the 18th Group conducted several missions against a task force that was "invading the Philippine islands." Units of the U.S. Navy and the Royal Navy played the role of aggressors while the 18th Fighter-Bomber Group, defended the islands. Missions included aerial cover, combat air patrols, simulated long-range dive bombing and strafing attacks and ground control interception, both scheduled and on scramble. These were the first simulated missions in the F-80 aircraft and the results were in line with the limitations of the aircraft, but very beneficial in terms of training. [5]

During the joint maneuvers Major Sebille, Captain Myers and Lt. Welch "had the opportunity to observe operations aboard the Aircraft Carrier BOXER. They all concurred that the U.S. Navy air arm is an effi-

Supreme Commander Allied Powers Headquarters building in Tokyo, Japan (squared off building at center background).

cient and important part of our national defense." [6]

The second week of March was used for routine training flights and to allow the engineering section to "recuperate" from the rigors of the previous week. The third week of March "flying began in earnest." Numerous aerial and ground gunnery missions were flown. "The hangar resounded to arguments involving colors and target sleeves and tired and happy pilots puffed hurriedly on a cigarette while zipping into a G-suit. The goal of 480 plus 10% flying hours in F-80's for the next month began to come into sight." [7]

Although the unit reported that G-suits were being used, neither Chatfield or Barber can remember "any G-suits being available."

Throughout March, the 18th Group pilots continued to gain experience in flying the F-80's, including many flight hours at night.

On Friday March 31st, the entire 67th Squadron went to a "cool mountain recess" for a well earned weekend of rest and relaxation. A most enjoyable Squadron barbecue and beer party at Baguio was held Friday night for Lieutenant Welch, as a final contribution before departing from the Squadron, where all the rage was for the food, beer and music. The rest of the weekend was spent by Officers, airmen and wives in taking advantage of the many facilities on

hand at Camp John Hay." [8]

A Final Peaceful Spring for the 18th FBW

In late April, the Intelligence Section of the 18th Wing "was beleaguered with reports of strange sightings, which, coincidentally, came simultaneously with the series of 'flying saucers' stories rampant in the United States. Thus far, it has been reasonably established that our local 'flying saucer' was a meteorological balloon."

In April the 18th Group participated in ferrying 75 F-51 aircraft to the Manila International Airport for transfer to the Philippine Air Force. "Ten pilots of this organization climbed into the old familiar "Spam-can" and the mission was completed successfully." These pilots had no idea that in just a few short weeks they would be flying "Spam-cans" again—and in combat.

The squadron postponed aerial gunnery due to an out of commission tow-reel in the B-26 tow plane. It did begin "standing four ships on five minutes alert from 0500 until 1815" from April 7-9. On the 8th, the alert flight was scrambled to intercept an unidentified aircraft. The interception was made north of the base, and the aircraft "was incorrectly identified as Chinese Nationalist. Clearer investigation revealed the C-47 to be British."

The additional flying resulted in a shortage of JP-1 fuel for the jets and flying was restricted for several days during the middle of the month to bring in more fuel.

Ground gunnery and dive bomb missions were emphasized during the third week of that month and "notable progress was evidenced in the scores of our trainee pilots."

On April 20th, Captain Robert W. Myers and Lt. Philip J. Conserva "buzzed the tower to terminate their ferry flight from Japan." The total distance covered was 1,980 miles, with an elapsed flying time of 4:45 hours, a new record for the trip.

The last week of this busy month "saw the 67th again standing alert. Major Sebille led two missions to provide target ships for the cruiser USS TOLEDO, simulated dive bomb, glide and torpedo runs were made on the ship at varying angles and speeds." The squadron also flew six ships and one spare, as a group formation "in commemoration of the officers and airmen lost aboard the C-54 which crashed in Japan." [10]

On May 16, the 18th Group participated in an Operational Test conducted by FEAF that examined the vulnerability of the USAF in the Philippine Islands. The Group was assigned the role of defending U.S. installations situated on Luzon. This "defensive role was accomplished by intercepting and engaging the invaders with the aid of GCI controllers. The mission was successful; the defense of the interceptor's home base was much better than expected." [11]

"In preparing all pilots of the 18th Fighter-Bomber Group for their respective roles in a tactical fighter-bomber unit, emphasis was placed upon intensive training in all phases of ground attack and ground support." All squadrons in the Group stressed dive-bombing, skip bombing, strafing, ground gunnery and aerial gunnery in an "accelerated program." Group leadership sensed that the potential for conflict in Korea was growing and it needed to have its pilots and crews prepared.

In May, Major Sebille "fired the high score of the 67th Squadron with 53 hits out of 400 rounds fired" during aerial gunnery drills. Captain Robert W. Myers departed for the Z.I. on May 5th. The squadron escorted his ship with a "farewell formation over the ship as it left Manila Harbor."

Tokyo, Japan, was the home of the Far East Air Forces (FEAF, pronounced like "leaf"). It had moved its headquarters from near Manila (Luzon), Philippines in September 1946, to the heart of the Japanese capital and into the Meiji building, all towering eight stories of the "skyscraper" located close by the wooded grounds of Emperor Hirohito's palace. (Bielefeldt)

The third week of May saw the 67th, the 44th and the 12th Squadrons "feverishly preparing for the impending FEAF Test." The Engineering Sections worked "night and day" to have as many aircraft as possible

Swan Dive for Pappy

by Col. Howard "Scrappy" Johnson

In the 12th Fighter Squadron I joined a flight led by Captain "Pappy" Hood. Pappy was a super guy from Georgia. He was only a couple of years our senior but the name fit him well. Pappy had a cotton top of hair, and a great sense of humor.

One Sunday, a group of our pilots were relaxing around the Officers' Club pool. Pappy and three others were playing bridge. The squadron adjutant's wife was sitting behind Pappy where she had a view of his hand. When Pappy and his partner contracted for a hand, she shook her head and said, "You'll never make that."

Pappy didn't like this lady to begin with and he responded with a little too much emotion by saying, "If I don't make this hand I'll do a swan dive off the high board.

Pappy didn't make it and did the swan dive off the high board. Since he didn't have a swimsuit with him, he dove off fully dressed. Clara, his wife, was pretty miffed at him because he had on a new pair of slacks and sport shirt that she had bought for him.

"really in commission." During the attack, the squadrons were disappointed to fly only a handful of sorties—"far short of our expectations." Three B-29s were intercepted and "notionally destroyed."

Most of the Group's aircraft "were on the ground during the test and a weary-vigil was kept by pilots strapped in the aircraft or in operations awaiting scramble."

On May 20th the squadrons participated in a "Group Formation in commemoration of Armed Forces Day." Bad weather intervened, however, breaking up the large formation. "After two unsuccessful attempts to penetrate the weather the Group proceeded south, around the build-ups, to return to base." A severe storm moved in on the field bringing cross winds of up to 35 mph. Colonel Norman led ten aircraft of the 12th Squadron to land safely at Clark. Six more jets landed at Florida Blanca. The remaining 23 aircraft were diverted to Manila. The Group could not reassemble until late the next day.

Not surprisingly, the squadrons soon "conducted a simulated let-down-through-overcast mission" that proved to be feasible.

During that period, Captain Arnold "Moon" Mullins, Operations Officer for the 67th, "towed with an F-80 for the first time."

The 18th Group was finally "Air Force." SCARWAF personnel "formerly assigned to this Wing have departed this station or have been assigned to Army Units within this Command." [12]

The Group used the first part of June to "continue its mission of training towards the goal of becoming 100% combat ready." Emphasis was placed on Skip and Dive Bombing, and simulated individual combat.

By June 2nd, the proficiency of the 67th squadron's "Peon" pilots was demonstrated with Major Sebille and Captain Mullins leading six trainees in a "review flight over the field. All pilots flew excellent formation and made a fine showing." The day was "climaxed by all pilots wearing red shirts, with the 'Fighting Cock' emblazoned on the front…to free beer."

The 18th Group was commanded by Lt. Col. H. H. Norman until 16 June, when he was succeeded by Lt. Col. Ira "Ike" L. Wintermute. Major Stan Chatfield replaced Lt. Col. Wintermute as Group Operations Officer.

A "Farewell" flight was flown for Colonel Norman, the departing Group Commander on June 17th. Eight planes from the 67th participated with four each from the 44th and 12th Squadrons. Following a general review, the 67th flew an "N" for Colonel Norman and a "C" for Colonel Carpenter. Lt. Col. Wintermute then assumed command of the 18th Fighter Group.

Endnotes

[1] Futrell, Robert F. **The United States Air Force In Korea: 1950-1953**. Washington, DC: Office of Air Force History, USAF, 1983. p. 58-60.

[2] USAFHRA K-SQ-FI-67-HI Jan-Oct 1950. History of the 18th Fighter-Bomber Wing, February-April, 1950.

[3] History of the 18th Fighter-Bomber Wing, February-April, 1950. USAFHRA.

[4] History of the 67th Fighter-Bomber Squadron, January 1950. USAFHRA K-SQ-FI-67-HI Jan-Oct 1950.

[5] History of the 67th Fighter-Bomber Squadron, January 1950. USAFHRA K-SQ-FI-67-HI Jan-Oct 1950.

Major Louis J. Sebille, *Commanding Officer of the 67th Fighter Bomber Squadron, (right) stands next to his F-80 "Shooting Star" fighter.*

(Below) *Major Sebille with his wife, Jane,* *inspects the "Fighting Cock" insignia of the squadron that was soon to be engaged in combat. Sadly, although Sebille led the 67th into combat, he was killed after only a few weeks in action. The Air Force released this photograph when it announced that Sebille was being awarded Posthumously the first Medal of Honor for Air Force action in Korea.* *(NARA)*

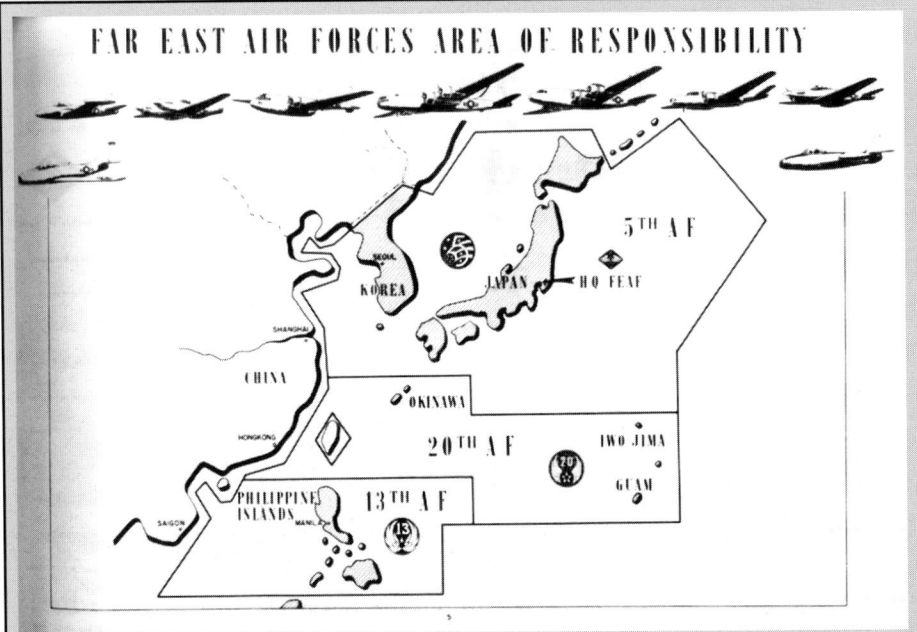

FAR EAST AIR FORCES AREA OF RESPONSIBILITY

As the air arm for General Douglas MacArthur's Southwest Pacific Area Theater, Far East Air Force's (FEAF) mission was to ensure an active air defense for the FEAF area, including Japan, the Ryukyus, the Marianas, and American bases in the Philippines. Its missions included that of maintaining a mobile air striking force and to provide air support of operations in cooperation with Army and Navy commanders. (NARA)

Days At Clark Field
by Col. Howard "Scrappy" Johnson

The Philippines was a super place for a fighter pilot. The weather was good, the scenery from the air was beautiful, and although the wheels had a lot of "Be No's," they were never in the air to find out whether we were complying with them or not. We had a lot of fun buzzing, rat racing, etc. And I had no additional duties outside the squadron! It was unbelievably great!

Clark Field was located in a plush, green valley dotted with bamboo-topped huts. The only interruption in the otherwise flat valley was the mountain called Arayat, which blossomed up in the center of it.

The day I landed at Clark Field there was a battle in progress between the Philippine Constabulary and the communist guerrillas called HUKs. These two factions were still fighting when I left the Philippines three years later. The battle was taking place on and around Mt. Arayat, which was within sight of Clark Field. Even before we landed we could see bursts of artillery shells on the side of the mountain. The Constabulary had the mountain surrounded, and were shelling it from the valley.

Two days later they closed the trap and drew a zero. The HUKs had filtered through their lines and dispersed. The HUKs mostly fought at night, and either hid in the jungles, or posed as ordinary citizens during the day. This fighting was not unusual. It occurred almost every night.

It seemed neither the HUKs nor the Constabulary were eager to come to close grips with each other. They would remain about a quarter of a mile apart and lob fifty-caliber machine gun rounds back and forth at each other. This was evidenced by the trajectory of tracers being lobbed through the night air.

Ominous Reports from South Korea

As winter turned into spring, the North Korean Army was growing rapidly. Originally formed around two divisions of Korean exiles and refugees that had served with the Soviet armed forces; this nucleus had been greatly augmented by experienced veterans from the Chinese Communist Army that had recently taken control of all of mainland China. At this point, the NKPA totaled over 100,000 troops organized into eight infantry divisions. The NKAF included an Air Division that flew some 132 combat aircraft, mostly IL-10 and Yak-3 fighter aircraft.

KMAG had reported that while no invasion of South Korea seemed imminent, the completion of Chinese Communist military campaigns in China would enable it to send additional troops into North Korea. In May 1950, the Korean Military Assistance Group (KMAG) relayed a report that the North Koreans would invade sometime in June 1950. KMAG operated as a unit of the U.S. State Department and reported to the U.S. Ambassador John J. Muccio. Far East Command Intelligence officers agreed with the quantitative assessments prepared by KMAG, but were not so sure of the exact date. FEAF intelligence recognized that North Korea now had enough military equipment and trained personnel to invade the South at any time it chose. FEAF predicted that once South Korea was invaded it would fall and that the invasion would begin whenever Soviet strategy dictated.

Futrell, Robert F. The United States Air Force In Korea: 1950-1953. Washington, DC: Office of Air Force History, USAF, 1983. p. 20.

---

[6] *History of the 67th Fighter-Bomber Squadron, January 1950. USAFHRA K-SQ-FI-67-HI Jan-Oct 1950.*

[7] *History of the 67th Fighter-Bomber Squadron, January 1950. USAFHRA K-SQ-FI-67-HI Jan-Oct 1950.*

[8] *Futrell, Robert F., p. 20.*

[9] *History of the 67th Fighter-Bomber Squadron, January 1950. USAFHRA K-SQ-FI-67-HI Jan-Oct 1950.*

[10] *USAFHRA. History of the 18th Fighter-Bomber Wing, May-June, 1950.*

[11] *USAFHRA. History of the 18th Fighter Bomber Wing, May-June, 1950. USAFHRA.*

When we flew at night it was standard procedure to make a steep climb out to avoid being fired at. We assumed that was by the HUKs.

Pitot Tube Cover

I had a great relationship with my crew chief. He was a staff sergeant and we both took a lot of pride in our P-51. When he'd pull an inspection on our plane, I would help him. About the only thing he asked for in return for his job well done was an occasional loan. Usually on about the 25th of the month I would loan him 20 bucks till payday.

When going to fly, I would ask him if the airplane was ready. If he said, "Yes, sir," which he always did, I wouldn't dare pull a detailed inspection on the ship for fear of hurting his feelings.

He slipped up one time, however. One night I took off on a pre-dawn flight with Don [Upshaw] leading. When we came in to land it was daylight. Just prior to landing, I asked Don if I could land on his wing. He suspected that I'd left the Pitot cover on and eased his ship down where he could see under my wing and I said, "Yeah, it's still there." Meaning I did not have any airspeed indication because my Pitot cover was left on. We landed OK and when I taxied up to the hardstand to park, Sergeant Shea saw that the Pitot cover was left on and tears appeared in his eyes.

Relief Tube Shower

Mo (Capt. Harry H. Moreland) was flying his P-51 one-day and decided it would be a good idea to clean out the cockpit. With this in mind he rolled the canopy back and proceeded to roll the airplane over on its back. His idea was to rid it of any debris that may have accumulated on the bottom of the cockpit. He did rid the P-51 of a lot of dust and other particles, but he also was drenched with a putrid smelling liquid.

Someone had used the relief tube without writing it up!

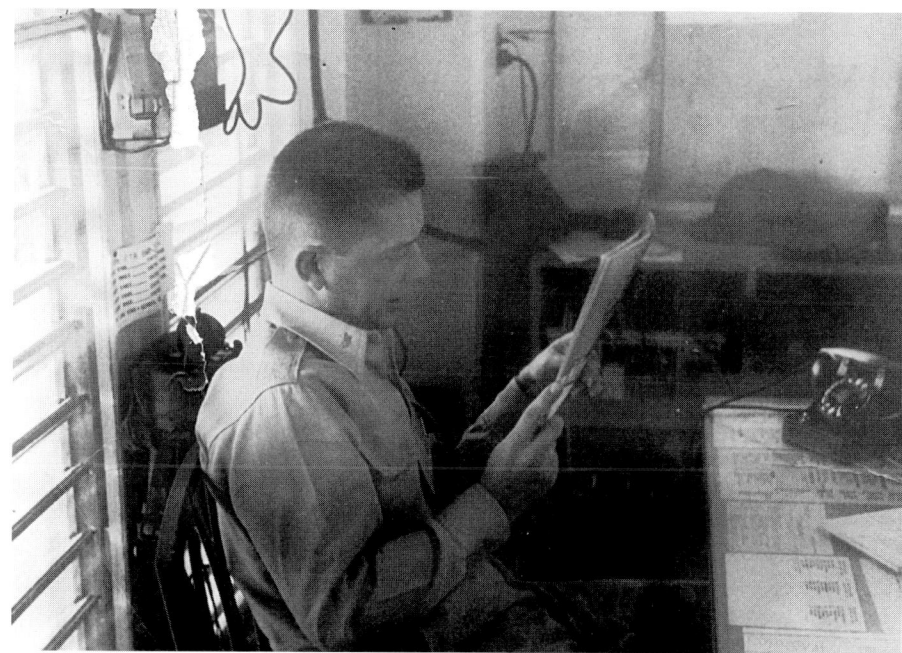

Group Operations Officer. Major Stan Chatfield at his desk as the 18th Group Operations Officer. Chatfield was posted to the 18th Fighter-Bomber Group in November 1949. Originally slated to replace one of the three Squadron Commanders— 12th, 67th or 44th Squadrons—who were being reassigned to the ZI. Instead, Chatfield replaced Lt. Col. Ira Wintermute as Group Operations Officer when Wintermute assumed command of the 18th Group on 16 June 1950. (Chatfield)

"Coach"

I made captain and became a flight commander. My first flight consisted of eight-second lieutenants, all fresh out of flying school. The problem was that they'd been sent to us because we were going to get F-80's. They had been trained to fly jets, and I had to check them out in the P-51. I was proud of the fact that I was able to do this without losing any of them or even having a bad incident.

I herded the flight around and taught them to fly in an operational fighter squad-

(Above) **67th Squadron Crew Chiefs** *at Clark Air Base in late 1949. (Burns)*

ron. We got along great. They called me "Coach" and spent half their off duty time at my house.

Yo-Yo Maneuver

In order to get in extra flying time I volunteered to slow fly F-51's when they'd had an engine overhaul. After this maintenance they needed to be flown at a low throttle setting for ten hours. An F-51 flying slow over Luzon, near Clark Field was a sitting duck for eager fighter pilots. It attracted them like honey would flies.

After having several passes made at me, I devised a way to prevent these over zealous pilots from having too much fun. When someone begins a pass at you, the proper reaction is to push the throttle to the stop and turn up into the aggressor. Since I was not supposed to use a lot of throttle, I was prevented from doing this.

So, when I observed someone diving at my plane from the rear, I'd do just the opposite. I'd wait until just the right moment, and retard the throttle and dive into their attack. Since they'd had already built up a lot of speed, this tactic often worked. They would overshoot me and go whistling by.

On another day, while in a mock dogfight with another pilot, I found myself turning the F-51 as tight as I could, and not improving my position. He was gaining slightly, or we were staying equal to each other in the turn. No matter how tight I turned, he was able to stay even. Without having any other ideas, I started diving the plane within the turn and pulling up towards my opponent's airplane and pulling up above the turning plane and diving at him. In this manner I was able to slowly gain and finally ended up on his tail.

Years later the fighter school at Nellis AFB started calling this maneuver the Yo-Yo. I'd been doing it for years and didn't know what it was!

12th Squadron. *Pilots and Airmen of the 12th Squadron pose for a unit photograph in late 1949. The Foxy Few was transitioning into the F-80 "Shooting Star" jet fighter. (Biteman)*

June 1950
North Korea Invades South Korea
Another Sunday Morning Surprise Attack That Should Not Have Been A Surprise

On Sunday, June 25th, FEAF duty officers at the Meiji GHQ building in Tokyo were shocked by reports early that morning coming from U.S. Korean Military Advisory Group (KMAG) field advisors that Communist North Korea troops had unexpectedly invaded the Republic of Korea (ROK). Thousands of North Koreans were pouring across the 38th parallel and forcing South Korean defenders to withdraw southward in the face of far superior numbers of troops and armor. By 0900 the South Korean town of Kaesong had fallen. This was no raiding party, this aggressive military force was organized, equipped and determined to conquer the Republic of Korea.

U.S. commands responded in those first hours by alerting its military personnel in the area to possible operations and preparing to carry out any directives and policy established by Washington. Military actions would depend on political decisions and orders.

"On Sunday, June 25th, the 18th Fighter-Bomber Wing was made aware of the invasion of South Korea," Col. Stan Chatfield recalled. "Sundays were not generally training days, although most of the personnel were on base at Clark AFB. I received a call from Lt. Col. Wintermute to meet with him and the Wing Commander, Colonel Davies, at Wing Headquarters, where we were briefed on the situation. We were told to make preparations for deployment to Korea of a cadre of pilots in the near future. This was to become the 'Dallas' Project."

The next morning, Monday, June 26, FEAF ordered Fifth Air Force (FAF) to provide fighter cover for freighters loading refugees in Inchon Harbor. It was the first U.S. military response. The Joint Chiefs also approved the use of armed force if it was necessary to ensure the safe evacuation of Americans from Korea.

[A time difference of 14 hours exists between Korea and Washington, D.C. Sunday, 0400 in Korea is the same as Saturday, 1400 in Washington, D.C.]

Fifth Air Force immediately set out to establish air superiority over South Korea, "partially to prevent the North Korean air force from attacking ROK forces and to protect evacuation forces." When North Korean aircraft appeared over Kimpo and Suwon Airfields, U.S. Air Force aircraft flying air cover engaged the enemy in the first air battle of the war.

By Monday evening, June 26th South Korean President Syngman Rhee was advising American Ambassador Muccio that the

Monthly Summary

Communist North Korea unexpectedly invaded the Republic of Korea (ROK), pouring across the line of demarcation, the 38th Parallel. South Korean defenders were forced southward by far superior numbers of troops and armor.

The United Nations (UN) Security Council condemned the North Korean invasion and authorized UN members to aid the ROK. The U.S. government was asked to establish a United Nations Command under a U.S. officer.

Despite hastily planned attacks by U.S. Air Force units, "the invaders quickly captured South Korea's capital, Seoul, overran the port of Inchon, seized the airfield at Kimpo, and threatened the city of Suwon."

Gen. Douglas MacArthur, USA, Commander, U.S. Far East Command, ordered weapons and ammunition shipped to South Korea and prepared to move U.S. ground troops from Japan to Korea. At the same time, U.S. naval units approached the peninsula to enforce a blockade of North Korea, as ordered by U.S. President Harry S Truman.

Maj. Gen. Earle E. Partridge, USAF, Commander, Fifth Air Force, ordered wing commanders "to prepare for air evacuation of U.S. citizens from South Korea. He also increased aerial surveillance of Tsushima Strait between Korea and Japan."

Fifth Air Force immediately set out to establish air superiority over South Korea,

"partially to prevent the North Korean air force from attacking ROK forces and to protect evacuation forces." When North Korean aircraft appeared over Kimpo and Suwon Airfields, U.S. Air Force aircraft flying air cover engaged the enemy in the first air battle of the war. [1]

[1] Adapted from U.S. Air Force Historical Research Agency. January 2002. The U.S. Air Force's First War: Korea 1950-1953 Significant Events. http://www.au.af.mil/au/afhra/wwwroot/korean_war/korean_war_chronology/kwc_1950.html

North Korean tanks then approaching Seoul could not be stopped and that the South Korean government was moving to Taejon immediately.

An emergency air evacuation from Seoul was ordered. Far East Air Forces used Kimpo Airfield near Seoul and Suwon Airfield some twenty miles south of the capital for emergency air evacuation of 748 persons to Japan on C-54s, C-47s, and C-46s. By midnight on June 27th, nearly 800 people had been flown to safety in Japan. All were removed safely, but only because Air Force fighter cover protected the transport aircraft from circling Yak fighters.

Fighter cover was all that U.S. air forces were providing at that early hour, FEAF planes were not released to go after North Korean ground forces. The U.S. was not about to enter a new war, less than five years after World War Two had ended, until it could be seen whether or not the South Korean military could win its own battles without outside assistance. That answer was not long in coming.

Within hours, the three ROK divisions protecting the South Korean Capital first attacked and then were driven back by the far better equipped North Korean forces. As the broken ROK units streamed toward the Han River, General MacArthur advised the JCS that the Republic of Korea would not survive without active American military assistance. [1]

Despite hastily planned attacks by U.S. Air Force units, "the invaders quickly captured South Korea's capital, Seoul, overran the port of Inchon, seized the airfield at Kimpo, and threatened the city of Suwon."

The United Nations (UN) Security Council on June 25th [2] condemned the North Korean invasion and authorized UN members to aid the ROK. The U.S. government was asked to establish a United Nations Command under a U.S. officer.

By Wednesday afternoon, Tokyo time, the JCS was advising Gen. MacArthur that all restrictions preventing FEAF from assisting in the defense of South Korean territory below the 38th Parallel had been lifted. The purpose now was to clear North Korean forces from the Republic of Korea.

General MacArthur ordered Far East Air Forces to attack North Korean units south of the 38th Parallel. He ordered Gen. Partridge, acting commander of FEAF to hit the North Koreans with everything the Air Force had at its disposal. MacArthur's hope and strategy was that early, devastating U.S. intervention from the air would drive the North Koreans back to their territory.

The JCS instructions and MacArthur's orders represented a major shift in U.S. policy towards Korea. It also represented a totally new mission for the FEAF, which until then had no combat mission for Korea— or planning for the brand new mission. FEAF planners labored far into the night issuing operational orders that dispatched sorties over Korea for reconnaissance and aerial attacks on the invading North Korean forces.

The U.S. Air Force was going to war for the first time as a separate and equal U.S. military service alongside the Army, Navy and Marine Corps.

On June 27th six U.S. pilots shot down seven North Korean propeller-driven fighters over Kimpo. It would be the highest number of USAF aerial victories scored in one day for all of 1950. Fifth Air Force established an advance headquarters at Itazuke, Japan and moved B-26s to Ashiya and RF-80s to Itazuke AB, Japan, they were now positioned for missions in Korea. The 8th Fighter-Bomber Wing (FBW) organized a composite unit of USAF and South Korean airmen at Taegu Airfield, South Korea, to fly F-51D Mustangs.

On Wednesday, just three days after crossing the border, North Korean Forces captured Seoul, forcing the ROK government to move to Taejon. Enemy forces also occupied nearby Kimpo Airfield (K-14) and, on the east coast, Mukho Naval Base below Kangnung. North Korean Yaks strafed Suwon Airfield (K-13), destroying two U.S. aircraft. And, in the first USAF air strikes of the Korean War, more than twenty B-26s of the 3rd Bombardment Group (BG) attacked Munsan railroad yards near the 38th Parallel and rail and road traffic between Seoul and the North Korean border.

On Thursday, June 29th, General MacArthur authorized General Stratemeyer to extend combat air operations into North Korea where he could attack air bases, depots, tank farms, troop columns and other military targets, as well as key bridges, highways and railway roadbeds. Based on a new directive from Washington, the orders broadened the scope of air operations, but said nothing about the introduction of ground combat troops into the fighting.

On Friday, June 30th during a 0930 meeting of key Secretaries and the JCS, President Truman ordered the use of U.S. ground troops in Korea and a naval blockade of North Korea. The United States was going to war to defend the sovereignty of the Republic of Korea.

Also on Friday, the 77th Royal Australian Air Force (RAAF) Squadron arrived in Korea to support the Fifth Air Force, to which it was subsequently attached. North Korean forces reached Samchock on the east coast and in the west crossed the Han River, threatening Suwon Airfield (K-13). Far East Air Forces began evacuating the airfield and authorized improvement of Kumhae Airfield, eleven miles northwest of Pusan, to compensate for the loss of Kimpo and Suwon. [3]

The 18th F-B Group "Is Ready"

In addition to its previous missions, late in June the 18th Fighter-Bomber Wing acquired a new mission "with the entry of the United States into the Korean incident"— the "support of the active units of the Far East Air Forces in any way that may arise." [4]

Following the "incident in Korea," the 18th Fighter-Bomber Group rapidly stepped up its preparations and readiness for whatever lay ahead. Emphasis was placed on tighter security measures, maintaining a current situation map, including publishing a study of Korea and surrounding areas with emphasis on "providing escape and evasion information. More time was devoted to aircraft recognition, security and indoctrination. The Flight Line, "previously guarded at night by Filipino guards, is now guarded by airmen from the 6205th Air Police Group."

Material readiness for potential combat operations was a constant issue in unit reports. "Maintenance problems continue to hinge on supply shortages." Fuel booster pumps, electrical hydraulic pumps, canopy assemblies, tires, tubes and brakes headed the long list of equipment needed. As of June 30th, 53 of the F-80 aircraft did not have the charges for the pilot ejection seats.

Officer personnel replacements were beginning to show up to fill shortages; however, "the replacements have not been adequately trained fighter pilots. Many are relatively inexperienced or have experience in other type aircraft."

One expedient temporary solution to stop personnel losses was the "freeze" of all military personnel following the "eruption in Korea." Those who were "scheduled to return to the ZI automatically extended for an indeterminable period. The freeze prevented the loss of certain key personnel in the Group. These personnel and replacements are making the situation much brighter." [5]

The invasion of South Korea by the Communists "electrified the entire Far East and the 18th Group stepped up its training flights to a maximum. Simulated Air Combat flights were flown throughout the week. Ground Control Intercept (GCI) flights took off from dawn to dusk and a four ship alert flight was kept in readiness."

As the situation "became considerably worse for the South Korean Forces and [with] the entrance of United States Air Forces into the fray, the entire [Clark AFB] base went on a seven day week." By working "night and day," the Engineering Section put 25 F-80s in commission.

"Intensive training in the past paid off" and the great majority of pilots in three squadrons of the 18th Group reported they were "combat ready." The "Fighting Cocks" of the 67th summed up the situation for the entire Group when it declared itself "prepared to mobilize." The 67th "is <u>ready to go</u>." [6]

June Significant Dates

June 16: Lt. Col. Ira L. "Ike" Wintermute succeeded Lt. Col. Henry H. Norman as Commander, 18th Fighter-Bomber Group.

June 25: North Korean troops invaded South Korea. Fifth Air Force began evacuating Americans from Seoul in 374th Troop Carrier Group aircraft with F-82's of the 339th Fighter AW Squadron and 68th Fighter AW Squadron. Operation under control of Commanding General, 8th Fighter-Bomber Wing, Itazuke. [8]

First North Korean aircraft shot down by 1st Lt. Charles B. Moran, 339th Squadron, in an F-82 when enemy aircraft "made pass at an evacuation C-54."

June 27: Fifth Air Force "ordered into shooting war."

"Bout-One," a composite unit of American and South Korean airmen organized by the 8th Fighter-Bomber Wing, ordered to Taegu (K-2).

Advance Headquarters of Fifth Air Force (FAF) established at Itazuke Air Base, Japan.

3rd Bomb Group moved to Ashiya, 8th Squadron of 49th Fighter-Bomber Group moved to Ashiya and 9th Squadron of 49th Fighter-Bomber Group moved to Itazuke.

June 29: General MacArthur authorized air attack north of the 38th Parallel. General MacArthur flew into Suwon. [9]

June 30: Detachment "1" of 36th Fighter Bomber Squadron (8th Grp) designated "Bout-One" organized at Itazuke. Mission assigned to train South Korean pilots in F-51s. "Bout One" arrives at Taegu in the evening. Its leader, Maj. Dean E. Hess, reports for duty to KMAG headquarters.

Han River line breached by North Koreans.

President Truman ordered use of U.S. ground troops in Korea.

Suwon abandoned.

RAAF Squadron 77 ordered into action in Korea.

Endnotes

[1] Futrell, Robert F. *The United States Air Force In Korea: 1950-1953.* Washington, DC: Office of Air Force History, USAF, 1983. p. 9.

[2] Futrell. p. 13.

[4] Adapted from U.S. Air Force Historical Research Agency. January 2002. The U.S. Air Force's First War: Korea 1950-1953 Significant Events. June, 1950.

[5] USAFHRA. History of the 18th Fighter-Bomber Wing, May-June, 1950.

[6] USAFHRA. History of the 18th Fighter-Bomber Wing, May-June, 1950.

[7] History of the 67th Fighter-Bomber Squadron, January 1950. USAFHRA K-SQ-FI-67-HI Jan-Oct 1950.

[8] NARA. Memorandum from Major James W. Ingram to MG E. J. Timberlake of 26 September 1950. Chronology of Fifth Air Force Activity in Korea.

[9] Ingram. Chronology of Fifth Air Force Activity in Korea.

Air Force Aviation Pipeline

The Aviation Cadet "Pipeline"

While the 18th Fighter-Bomber Wing was preparing to enter combat, back in the Zone of the Interior, the Air Force was beginning to cope with what was obviously going to be an urgent need for more pilots. New air cadets at several bases in Texas, were being roughly introduced to military life and learning the ropes as rooky pilots.

In 1950, the Air Force "pipeline" for would-be pilots started with applicants requesting appointment as an Aviation Cadet. Archibald "Archie" Connors of Jacksonville, Florida was typical of what would eventually be thousands of pilots the Air Force would train and send to Korea.

A Navy veteran of World War Two, Connors had used the new GI bill to attend Jacksonville Junior College (now Jacksonville University) where he was elected President of the student body. His goal was to become an Air Force pilot, even though he had to wait almost a full year after he applied before he was brought on active duty.

Like other young men of his age, Connors had decided to become a pilot. It seemed like a prudent thing to do. The country was at peace around the world. No wars or shooting conflicts were in sight and the commercial aviation industry was growing rapidly. The $50,000 cost of training a new pilot was paid by the taxpayers, and after serving their active duty military obligation for the training, military pilots could easily translate those skills into airline cockpits.

On December 7, 1949, 1st Lt. W. F. Knotts, the Assistant Adjutant General for the Air Training Command at Scott Air Force Base, Illinois signed out a letter that informed Connors he had been selected for assignment for aviation cadet training in Class 51-A. "To assure your availability for this class assignment, it will be necessary for this Headquarters to be in receipt, not later than twenty days from the date of this letter, of your agreement to accept an aviation cadet appointment."

The Agreement to Accept Aviation Cadet Appointment which Connors signed and returned, advised him that if he was married before or during the period of training that he would not be "extended privileges in addition to those afforded unmarried cadets." He would be required to live in barracks throughout the period of training and no travel allowance or quarters would be available for his dependents during the period. The Agreement listed an eclectic number of items that were prohibited at flying schools, including: pets, firearms, ammunition, motorcycles, personal airplanes, furniture, camera darkroom equipment, narcotics, personal bedding, alcholic [sic] beverages, cooking equipment, chemicals of explosive, poisonous, or harmful nature."

Items that were permitted at flying schools included: civilian clothing, athletic equipment, automobile ($5,000 and $10,000 property damage and public liability insurance, mandatory), small radios and record players, cameras, small electric fans, electric razors, typewriters, alarm clocks, books, musical instruments (not recommended), and model airplanes."

Connors was going to get his chance to become an Air Force pilot--but first he had to get through cadet training.

Aviation Cadets

On May 15, 1950, Connors heard from Air Training Command Headquarters at Scott Air Force Base, Illinois. "The Commanding General," wrote Captain John F. Taylor, "takes pleasure in informing you that you have been selected for aviation cadet appoint-

*Unidentified 2nd Classman "indoctrinating" 4th Classman **Aviation Cadet Archie Connors** (left). "That's sweat kid," Archie wrote on the back of this photograph he sent his fiance, Frankie Simpson. "But not anymore. I looked like h--- didn't I?"*

ment and assignment to pilot training." The letter was to serve as the authority for his enlistment in the Air Force and assignment to the 3565th Basic Pilot Training Wing at Connally Air Force Base, Waco, Texas. He was to report on May 29, 1950.

"In qualifying for this appointment, you have met the high standards necessarily required by the new United States Air Force. It is hoped that you will be successful in realizing an ambition to take your place in this organization as an officer and pilot," Taylor concluded his letter.

On May 26, 1950, Aviation Cadet A.H. Connors, Jr. enlisted in the USAF, and was assigned service number AF 14 353 100. On military active duty for the second time in his life, he had moved from Seaman First Class to Aviation Cadet, a rank he would hold for thirteen months.

On 1 June 1950, A/C A.H. Connors, Jr. was among those cadets assigned to the 3565th Training Squadron, Pilot Training Group (Basic) as a member of Aviation Cadet Training Class 51-D.

By June 2nd, A/C Connors had arrived at Connally AFB, Texas, and had prepared an Application for National Service Life Insurance. The principal beneficiary was his mother, Eva May Haddock Connors. Warrant Officer Hershell Winship, the Assistant Adjutant, certified "that applicant commenced regular and frequent aerial flights as an Aviation Cadet effective 1 June 1950 and is entitled to NSLI at Gov't expense under provisions of PL 658, 77 Congress."

Life As A Cadet

Like other Fourth Classmen, Aviation Cadet Connors lived in wooden barracks and wore a very basic uniform consisted of dungarees and a "fore and aft cap." When Reveille was sounded, they had to be ready to fall out in uniform literally within seconds of the "official" wake up alarm. Since shaving was impossible in the brief time allowed, they worked out a system of getting up before Reveille, then to quickly take turns shaving while classmates held a blanket over the window (to prevent any light from escaping from the officially still darkened barracks).

Meanwhile, Third Classmen, already up, shaved and dressed, were "patrolling" the areas outside the Fourth Classman barracks—looking for any lights. "If they spotted some light coming from your window, you had had it," Wilfred "Budd" Stapley remembered. [3]

[Budd Stapley was Connors' roommate during part of his pilot training and later they flew combat missions together as members of How Flight of the 67th Fighter-Bomber Squadron.]

They dared not get caught looking out of their room. Even a slight glance out of the window could earn the distracted Cadet another hour of military drill.

Just prior to Reveille, the shaved, uniformed Cadets would be poised by the door. At the sound of the wake up call, they would pour outside—"elbows over @#$$holes"—and into ranks, ready for inspection by Third Classmen ever ready to find flaws in uniforms or bearing. These meant Extra Military Instruction or EMI in the form of "tours" that were marched off—one hour of marching for each tour. Too many "tours" and a Cadet was washed out permanently.

"This is known as a 'Brace,' something that a person should never get into," Aviation Cadet Archie Connors wrote on the back of this snapshot sent to his fiance, Frankie. "The uniform that I am wearing is known as a 'raunchy' uniform." Then he added, "I love Frankie with all my heart!" and drew a heart. "Please note the wrinkles in my chin," he closed with a postscript.

Aviation Cadet Wilfred "Budd" Stapley put an arrow over his head to show his family where he was in this formation of Aviation Cadets marching to class. (Stapley)

1950
18th Fighter-Bomber Wing Chronology

UN Defensive June 27-September 15, 1950		UN Offensive September 16- November 2, 1950	CCF Intervention November 3, 1950- January 24, 1951	
18th FBG operates from Taegu, SK	18th FBG based in Ashiya, Japan	18th FBG operates from K-9/Pusan, SK	K-24 20 Nov- 16 Dec.	K-10/ Chinhae, SK

July   August   September   October   November   December

Sept. 8: 18th FBG moves to K-9/Pusan
Sept. 15: Inchon invasion

Nov. 20: 6002nd TSW begins move from K-9 to Pyongyang East/K-24

Aug. 5: Maj Sebille KIA
Aug. 6-7: 18th FBG pulled back from Taejon, reunited in Ashiya, Japan.

Dec. 1: 18th FBW moves from K-24/Pyongyang to K-13/Suwon

July 24: 18th FBG Hqts, plus the 67th FBS ordered to Johnson AB, Japan, then on to Taegu (K-2), Korea.
July 25: First KIA for 18th FBW, 2nd Lt. Billie Crabtree

Dec. 16: 18th FBW begins move to K-10/Chinhae. 2 Squadron SAAF joins 18th FBG

July 15: "Bout One" and "Dallas" Squadron cease to exist, merged into newly created 51st Fighter Squadron (Provisional) at Taegu.

July 3: FEAF directs 13th AF at Clark AFB to create new "Dallas Squadron" and deploy it to Japan to be equipped with F-51 Mustangs.

HQ FEAF

K-Bases in Korea

The spelling of Korean locations on maps varied greatly. Many villages had a Korean name as well as a Japanese name. A "K" number system was soon established that identified individual airbases in both northern and southern Korea by number to prevent confusion among locations.

K-1 Pusan West
K-2 Taegu No. 1
K-3 Pohangdong
K-4 Sachon
K-5 Taejon
K-6 Pyongtaek
K-7 Kwangju
K-8 Kunsan
K-9 Pusan East
K-10 Chinhae
K-11 Ulsan
K-12 Muan
K-13 Suwon
K-14 Kimpo
K-15 Mokpo
K-16 Seoul (Yongdungpo)
K-17 Ongin
K-18 Kangnung (Koryo)
K-19 Haeju (Kaishu)
K-20 Sinmak
K-21 Pyonggang
K-22 Onjong-ni
K-23 Pyongyang
K-24 Pyongyang East
K-25 Wonsan
K-26 Sondok
K-27 Yonpo
K-28 Hamhung West
K-29 Sinanju
K-30 Sinuiju
K-31 Kilchu (Kisshu)
K-32 Oesicho-dong
K-33 Hoemon (Kaibun)
K-34 Chongjin (Seishin)
K-35 Hoeryong (Kainsei)
K-36 Kanggye No. 1
K-37 Taegu No. 2
K-38 Wonju
K-39 Cheju-do Island No. 1
K-40 Cheju-do Island No. 2
K-41 Chungju
K-42 Andong No. 2
K-43 Kyongju
K-44 Changhowon-ni
K-45 Yoju
K-46 Hoengsong
K-47 Chunchon
K-48 Iri
K-49 Yangsu-ri
K-50 Sokcho-ri
K-51 Inje
K-52 Yanggu
K-53 not completed
K-54 not completed
K-55 Osan-ni
K-56 not completed
K-57 Kwangju

19

July 1950
Thrown Into Combat To Save A Shrinking Perimeter

Bout One Squadron

A week after the Korean War began, the Air Force was rapidly shifting from caught off guard defense to increasingly aggressive offense in its efforts to hurt the North Korean supply train and combat units enough to halt their advance and then cause them retreat behind their previous border. The limited use of jet aircraft, in particular the F-80 "Shooting Star," had given them enough data to make long range decisions that would affect many units and thousands of airmen for the next 2 ½ years of combat.

Meiji Building, Far East Air Forces Headquarters in Tokyo, Japan.

Not only could the fuel-sucking Shooting Stars not stay on station for very long, there were no runways in Korea that could handle their requirements for length and surfacing. The heavily loaded transport aircraft had already begun chewing up the

lightly surfaced runways in Korea. It was clear that all of the jets, for the time being, would have to be based in Japan. This, of course, reduced their combat effectiveness significantly. It was also clear to FEAF planners that they would need to use every possible conventional F-51 that could be secured. The jets were performing adequately but the Mustangs had far greater range, could loiter over targets for hours and could use shorter and rougher runways. [1]

Thirty Mustangs were rustled up from storage locations scattered around the FEAF area of operations. Plans were immediately

Monthly Summary

North Korean Army forces advanced steadily into South Korea despite U.S. air strikes north and south of the 38th Parallel. U.S. ground forces—ill equipped and inadequately trained—were introduced piecemeal and failed to stop the Communist advance. By the end of July, North Korean military forces had conquered the entire Korean peninsula except the area southeast of Hamch'ang and bordered by the Noktong River—the Pusan Perimeter.

The UN Security Council established the UN Command (UNC), designated the United States as executive agent for prosecuting the Korean War, and requested that the U.S. President appoint a UN Commander.

Gen. Hoyt S. Vandenberg, USAF, Chief of Staff, met in Tokyo with General Douglas MacArthur, now Commander of UN forces in the theater, and agreed on overall objectives for the air campaign. They agreed to allow George E. Stratemeyer, USAF, Commander, Far East Air Force to use some Su-

perfortresses against strategic and deep interdiction targets, such as chemical plants, oil refineries, marshalling yards, docks, and key bridges in North Korea. General MacArthur insisted that the bulk of U.S. air power be employed tactically against the advancing enemy troops.

The UN Command was formally established in Tokyo, Japan, commanded by General MacArthur, who assigned responsibility for ground action in Korea to Lt. Gen. Walton H. Walker, USA, Commander, Eighth U.S. Army; naval action to Vice Adm. C. Turner Joy, Commander, Naval Forces, Far East; and air action to General George Stratemeyer, Commander, Far East Air Forces.

Far East Air Forces (FEAF) tasked Fifth Air Force to establish and maintain air superiority, provide UN ground forces with close air support, and interdict NKA supplies and reinforcements, the goal being to isolate enemy forces on the front

lines. FEAF moved two fighter groups from the Philippines and Japan to South Korea and began replacing jet-powered F-80s with more fuel-efficient propeller-driven F-51 Mustangs. "Compared to the F-80s, the Mustangs could loiter far longer in a target area and better endure the primitive conditions of South Korean air bases." By the end of the month, the World-War II era fighters were flying from Taegu and Pohang Dong, while C-47 transports used the Pusan Airfield. B-26s of the 3d BG, based in Japan, often attacked bridges at night in enemy-occupied South Korea. Although the North Koreans shot down a few USAF airplanes, Far East Air Forces soon achieved air superiority over Korea.

Adapted from U.S. Air Force Historical Research Agency. January 2002. The U.S. Air Force's First War: Korea 1950-1953 Significant Events.

drawn up to use these weary war birds to equip a provisional fighter squadron that could operate from Japan until suitable facilities could be found and prepared in Korea.

Lt. Gen. Earle Partridge and Major Gen. Edward J. Timberlake agreed that they needed to operate as many conventional F-51 Mustangs—from Korean bases—as they could find and support. However, at the time, the only airfield that could be used without extensive repairs was located about five miles northeast of Taegu—a sod-and-gravel runway (full of pot holes), two dilapidated concrete buildings, and a wooden mess hall built by the Japanese during their Korean occupation. "K-2" as it was soon called, was soon identified as the destination of "Bout-One," a pick-up or composite squadron organized by the 8th Fighter-Bomber Wing on June 27 that included both U.S. and Korean pilots.

Korea Requests
Mustangs

At the outbreak of hostilities in Korea, South Korea's President Syngman Rhee had asked President Truman for an immediate show of airpower by the South Koreans to discourage the North Korean troops, Lt. Col. (then 1st Lt.) Duane "Bud" Biteman explained. On July 1st, 1950, President Truman authorized the transfer of ten airplanes. All of the fighter units in the Far East had already converted to the F-80 "Shooting Star" jets many months before. The only F-51s that were not mothballed and in storage were a few decrepit derelicts that were towing targets for aerial gunnery practice. All were stripped, dirty and "tired," but they were the only F-51's in the Far East available for immediate use. *[Biteman was an original member of the "Dallas Squadron," another composite unit from the 18th Group that was soon en route to Korea.]*

The "Bout One" Mustangs were ferried to Taegu by members of the 35th Fighter Group. On their way to Korea, they were asked to fly top cover for General MacArthur's C-54--"Bataan"--en route to

Major Dean "Preacher" Hess talks with two American pilots flying Korean marked F-51's from K-2 in August 1950. (Myers)

Suwon, where he was to confer with General Dean and look over the battle situation. "They chose the old derelict F-51s over the newer, faster F-80 jets," Biteman explained, "because the old Mustangs had enough fuel to circle the field the entire time MacArthur was on the ground conferring, then escort him all the way back to Pusan, and still had enough fuel to return for their original intended landing at Taegu!"

The U.S. air advisors were not at all convinced that the young Korean pilots could handle the ten Mustangs they had been provided. To provide more depth and on-scene

Bout One Briefing. Capt. James P. Beckett, briefs ten ROK pilots on the operation of the F-51 Mustang. Beckett was not a member of the Dallas Squadron. (NARA)

training, Major Dean E. Hess and nine U.S. Instructor pilots had been assigned to the unit, which moved to Taegu on the evening of June 30th and reported into the local KMAG Commander. At first, the Korean pilots were allowed to fly missions together with their American pilot colleagues. However, with the crash and death of the ROK commander, it was apparent that their long absence from the cockpits of the heavy, "tricky" F-51s required that the American pilots fly all the missions.

Upon arriving at Taegu, the "Bout One" commander, Major Dean Hess, and his crew, tried to teach the inexperienced South Korean pilots how to fly the high performance Mustangs from the rough, "cow pasture" runway at Taegu, Biteman explained.

Trying to upgrade the Korean pilots from a 650-hp T-6 trainer to a 1350-hp fighter while flying combat missions against the enemy was an impossible situation."

Soon enough, the "Bout One" pilots just left the Korean pilots on the ground at Taegu to refuel and re-arm the airplanes, and started flying the combat missions themselves," Biteman said.

At first Bout One pilots were assigned missions directly by KMAG. The "system" was very informal. On one occasion, "individuals came out from KMAG in the middle of the night, about three o'clock in the morning, and they requested an air strike verbally just by sticking their heads in the tent and asking for an air strike over a city at a certain time. Then they disappeared into the night," Hess remembered. The Bout One pilots gave a good account of themselves and could stay over enemy lines for hours, searching out targets when none were reported by the Army. [2]

Within a few days, as the "Dallas Project" pilots began arriving with no airplanes of their own, Headquarters FEAF decided to assign to them the nine remaining flyable F-51s—complete with South Korean insignia painted on the wings and fuselage. When more F-51s became available, Dean Hess moved to Masan, on the southern coast, and started a pilot training school for the South Korean pilots.

[Major Dean Hess later wrote a book

(L-R) Lt. Jack Crawford, Lt. Col. "Ike" Wintermute and Captain Harry "Mo" Moreland at K-2/ Taegu. Wintermute was commanding the 18th Group at the time, but had little fighter experience. (Moreland)

The Dallas Project

by Col. Harry "Mo" Moreland

The Dallas project was composed of volunteers from the three fighter squadrons at Clark and some others from various support units that had F-51's at the time. One pilot, Luke Warm, had no fighter time, at all."

We went from Clark to Johnson Field and Ashia to get our equipment. Most of it was shipped from Johnson to Ashia before we moved to Korea.

Once there, they merged us with the Bout One--nine American pilots and 9 aircraft--and designated us as the 51st Provisional Squadron.

Major Dean Hess did not join us.

The Bout One pilots were given a choice to stay with us or return to their parent units. All but one opted to return to their units and I was sort of glad because they did not want to do it our way.

Shortly thereafter the 51st Provisional Squadron was redesignated the 12th Fighter-Bomber Squadron and we were joined by the 67th Squadron from the Philippines.

Major Hess reorganized a Korean Training unit and moved to another base.

The USS BOXER soon brought more pilots and aircraft and we became a fully operational squadron.

The Bout One aircraft left much to be desired since they had been in mothballs for some time.

of his Korean experiences, which was made into the movie "Battle Hymn," starring Rock Hudson.]

Dallas Squadron

On Saturday, July 1, North Korean forces occupied Suwon, denying Far East Air Forces use of its airstrip. The 374th TCW began airlifting the U.S. Army (USA) 24th Infantry Division, the first U.S. troops to enter Korea since the war began, from Itazuke AB to Pusan. The 77th RAAF Fighter

Squadron was assigned to the FAF for operational control.

Far East Air Forces continued to airlift U.S. Army troops to Korea throughout the "weekend" of July 1-2, but substituted smaller C-46s and C-47s for the heavier C-54s, which had damaged the Pusan runways. Pilots of four F-80s on the first mission with external rockets reported excessive drag that shortened their range.

On that Monday, July 3rd, General Stratemeyer (FEAF) directed the 13th AF at Clark AFB in the Philippines to create another squadron of F-51s from the most qualified personnel of the 18th FBG. The new "Dallas Squadron" was soon headed to Johnson Air Base in Japan to be equipped with Mustangs.

At the beginning of July 1950, the 18th Fighter-Bomber Group was composed of a headquarters and three squadrons, including the 12th and 67th FBS, which had begun to participate "directly in the Korean Campaign," and the 44th FBS stationed at Clark AFB in the Philippines.

On July 5th, General Order 24 issued by the 18th FBW "directed the 18th Fighter-Bomber Group to organize a provisional squadron code named 'Dallas Squadron.' The officers and airmen of the former 12th Fighter Bomber Squadron were used as a nucleus to form this provisional squadron. On July 8th General Timberlake designated Taegu as the destination for the "Dallas" squadron, which departed Clark Air Force Base on 10 July 1950, via Troop Carrier aircraft for Johnson Air Base, Japan, where it was to receive TO&E [Table of Organization and Equipment, i.e. the mix of equipment and supplies that had been determined was required for it to perform its missions] property and aircraft." [3]

The newly created Dallas Squadron moved to Ashiya Air Base and then on to Taegu Airstrip (K-2, Korea. "The first combat mission was flown from that base on 15 July 1950," the 18th Group reported. "At K-2 the Dallas Squadron and the personnel from 'Bout One' were combined and redesignated as the 51st Provisional Squadron and were assigned to the 6002nd Fighter Wing. Major (then Captain) Harry H. Moreland was in command of the 51st."

Leaving Luzon

One of the first "axioms" any military recruit learned in the Forties and Fifties was "Never to volunteer for anything." Volunteers could get stuck with K-P or latrine cleanup or any number of other possible "choice assignments" that were often a part of military life, whether one was a "Soldier, Sailor or Marine."

Volunteers for new military assignments and missions could also find their decision

Dallas Squadron

On 5 July, the 18th Fighter-Bomber Wing issued Special Orders Number 124. Translated from the condensed message format language used as shorthand, the message read:

"The following officers and Airmen, USAF, organizations indicated, APO 74, are placed on Detached Service with the Dallas Squadron (Provisional), 18th Fighter Bomber Group, APO 74, for an indefinite period and will report to the Commanding Officer no later than 5 July 1950, for duty and administrative purposes...." The original members of the Dallas Squadron included:

12th Fighter-Bomber Squadron
Captain Harry H. Moreland
Captain Jerome R. Mau
Captain Howard C. Johnson
1st Lt. Harlan Ball*
1st Lt. Dewey Ballard*
1st Lt. Jim Glessner*
1st Lt. Charles D. Hauver
1st Lt. Daniel "Chappie" James*
1st Lt. Wendell J. Kistner
1st Lt. Alex Padilla*
1st Lt. William S. Slater, Jr.
2nd Lt. Billie R. Crabtree
44th Fighter-Bomber Squadron
1st Lt. James R. Allen
1st Lt Frank C. Buzze
1st Jack H. Crawford
1st Warren H. Kane
1st Edward M. Nebinger
1st Lt. Claude "Spud" Taylor*
67th Fighter-Bomber Squadron
1st Lt. Duane E. Biteman
1st Lt. William D. Bridges, Kr.
1st Lt. Philip J. Conserva
1st Lt. Mal Edens*
2nd Lt. Mike S. David

Headquarters and Headquarters Squadron, 18th FB Group
1st Jack Coghlin*
1st Lt. John P. McCann
1st Lt. Robert L. Naylor
1st Lt. Clair Potter*
1st Lt. Clarence H. Sonderman, Jr.
1st Lt. Melvin "Luke" Warm*
Airmen assigned to the Dallas Squadron, included:
M/Sgt. Solley
M/Sgt. Johnson*
Sgt. Edward B. Fraley, Jr.
Sgt. Jack N. Coffey
Cpl. Douglas L. Marshall
S/Sgt. James F. Curran
Cpl. Harol D. Jones
Pvt. Jesse S. Young
Sgt. William A. Wedell
Pfc Patrick J. Harrison
T/Sgt. Maynard O. Pierce
Sgt. Jack W. Sefton
Cpl. Corbert R. Contival
Cpl. Robert L. Hale
Pfc Robert C. Netherton
S/Sgt. Beachem Cockroft
Sgt. Dionicio Cudal
Cpl. Donald F. Haimes
Cpl. Ernest C. Busby

Note: Names marked by an asterisk were not included on Special Orders No. 124. Colonel Harry H. Moreland, original Commander of the Dallas Squadron, confirmed with the author that these individuals were also ordered to the Dallas Squadron.

might put their very life in danger. This was particularly true if "volunteers" were being sought for combat duty.

On Monday evening, July 3rd, 1st Lt. Duane "Bud" Biteman was attending a meet-

ing of the 18th Fighter-Group Headquarters Staff at Clark field on Luzon. The Korean invasion was moving into its second week and things were not going well at all, in fact, the ROK forces were being pushed down the rocky peninsula—they would soon run out of territory into which they could retreat. Volunteers were being sought from pilots and support personnel in the Group for duty as a member of a new composite unit that would be deployed almost immediately to Korea and into combat as the U.S. began to bring its military force to bear on the invading North Korean troops that had to be stopped before the Republic of Korea ceased to exist.

The choice for the 26-year old Lieutenant, married five years and with a young daughter—to leave a relatively secure assignment, with his wife and family nearby, to fly off to some dusty, dirty, almost unknown little oriental country to kill—or perhaps to be killed?"

For Bud Biteman, "it was a quick decision, but not necessarily an easy one." During those few minutes of the Headquarters Staff Meeting, he was torn between his "love and loyalty" for Helen and Carol (who were with him at Clark Field, P.I. and getting ready to return to the United States after two long years in the Philippines) and his "worrying families back in the States," and the "very strong obligation" he felt "to support what our country was doing to carry out a promise to protect a weaker nation." As Biteman saw it, he "had the required professional qualifications and was a qualified fighter pilot with "experience gathered over the years at the taxpayer's expense, so that I might someday repay them by fighting on their behalf." He wondered whether he "could live with myself, with my conscience, and the shame if I said "no" to a request for help?" [4]

The wrenching decision came down to "Helen, Carol and the families on one side, the duty obligations on the other." Biteman determined that "both causes could be served by sending my "gals" back to the safety of the United States, while I went north to Korea for a few months. In all likelihood, with the situation that existed at the time, I would probably get back to the U.S. sooner from Korea than I would from remaining as "home guard" at Clark Field."

Taking a very deep breath, Biteman added his name to the list of volunteers, even

When Lt. Kenneth Barber was notified about the invasion of South Korea by North Korea, he noted, "It is strange to think that the spotlight should shift to such a seemingly insignificant spot. I wonder what will come of this? I wonder what America will do now in the face of such Communist aggression?"

On 7 July, Lt. Barber volunteered but "was too late to make the Dallas Project. We will probably be called in a few weeks anyhow, so I guess it doesn't matter too much. Kind of strange feeling to see Jim, Nib and Mike leave."

"Big doings today," Lt. Barber noted on 15 July 1950. "It is a well founded rumor that the 67th Fighter Squadron is to follow the Dallas Project and I'm to be on it! Hot dawg! Major Dow is to command the Dallas Squadron, which will be renamed the 12th Fighter Bomber Squadron, and Major Louis B. Sebille will command the 67th."

When Barber told his wife, Carolyn ("Cassie"), she could not believe it. "After about two hours I managed to convince her," Barber noted. "She's not too happy over it. I feel eager to go, but at the same time hate to leave Carolyn. It's funny how one's viewpoint can change after being married awhile." Nevertheless, he told his diary, "I still have to have this adventure, however, such as it may be, and whatever it may lead to."

On 16 July, the "rumor" that Barber had heard turned out to be true. "I'm transferred to the 67th and we may leave Monday or Tuesday."

It would be more of an "adventure" than Barber could ever have imagined.

as he was "hoping that Helen would understand." They had not had a chance to discuss it at the time, but he "was sure that she approved—with considerable apprehension and reluctance."

Bud and Helen were both very sorrowful at the prospect of yet another lengthy separation, "the third in our young five years of marriage; but we had known what we were letting ourselves in for when I had come back on active Air Force duty in 1948. And I knew that, at the time, we just happened to be in the 'wrong place at the right time!'"

The volunteers for the new Dallas Provisional Squadron whose families were at Clark Field were offered the option of having them return to the 'States' immediately, or to remain in their present quarters on Clark Air Force Base. Several of the officers elected to have their families remain, but under the circumstances, Biteman remembered, "with our baggage all packed, and some of it already on its way, we decided that it would be best if Helen and Carol went on ahead, and waited for me in the safety of Los Angeles with her parents. We were still uncertain how widespread the Korean thing would develop and, since I would be a couple of thousand miles north, I would feel a lot more comfortable if I knew they were safe at home."

As soon as Biteman realized he was heading for the fight in Korea, he headed for the backrooms of the 13th Air Force Headquarters. He was on his first "mission"—searching for maps—of Korea. He managed "to drain 13th AFH stock of about a dozen sets (three charts covered the entire peninsula)." When he arrived at Ashiya, Japan prior to heading for Taegu, Korea, he hustled a set of those charts to the photo lab and "had them make monochrome photo copies in about 100 sets" which he then "took over to Korea with us, since all issue charts had already been removed from Base Operations at Ashiya. With the b/w photo copied charts, we could find the rivers and towns—but it's amazing how we had all come to depend upon the color gradations to help determine the mountains and valleys—of which the en-

Front Line Meeting. *Lt. General Walton H. Walker (left), Commanding General of the Eighth Army and Major General Earle E. Partridge, Commanding General of the Fifth Air Force, meet "somewhere in Korea" on July 16, 1950, to "discuss strategy prior to their take-off to inspect front line fighting. (NARA)*

tire country was filled!"

On July 7th, 1950, while the men of the 24th Infantry Division were being airlifted from Japan to Suwon and Kimpo airfields in South Korea, Biteman "was standing forlornly on the dock at Manila Bay, looking through misty eyes at an equally-forlorn pair standing at the rail on the deck of the naval transport USNS Gaffey." It was almost two years since the family separations had been reversed. In July 1948, he had left Helen standing on the dock at San Francisco. The band had been playing the same heart-tugging song, "Now Is The Hour, that we must say Goodbye." It was a song he'd not soon forget.

[To his final days, Biteman still got "a lump in his throat and a faraway look in my eyes whenever I hear it played." To him it would "always be a song of sadness, gathering up visions of a little girl, not yet quite three, holding onto her mother's skirt and wondering why her Daddy couldn't go along with her on the boat.]

Finally, as the ship pulled away from the dock, the band played "California Here I Come," the tune that had become the

Biteman's private theme song in the previous several months, as they had happily anticipated their going-home journey—together—back to the United States.

A very sad Lieutenant Biteman made the long drive from Manila back to their empty quarters on Clark Field. He couldn't help but wonder "how long it would be before we could be together again—three months—six months—or never?"

Reasoning that the "best cure for a lonely heart is intense activity," he got busy, very busy during his few remaining days at Clark Field.

Biteman was given a "double hat" assignment in Korea. He would serve as both the Dallas Squadron Intelligence Officer and its Assistant Flight Commander. It was "a very unusual combination of duties, that perhaps typified the screwy, topsy-turvy nature of our new little war," he explained. "Historically, Intelligence Officers were never allowed to go on combat missions because of the possibility that their knowledge of classified plans and codes could be "extracted" by their captors in the event they were shot down. Not so, in Korea. Qualified F-51 fighter pilots were in such short sup-

ply that they couldn't afford the luxury of having one around who couldn't fly combat missions."

The next few days were hectic—and productive to the farsighted Biteman who combed through offices and storerooms "collecting as many maps, charts and supplies as I could lay my hands." He managed to find ten complete sets of navigation charts, which he "guarded like valuable securities." Also high on his list of "collectibles" were Plexiglas sheets, map boards, grease pencils, paper clips, staplers, typewriters, lead pencils, pads and erasers—"all of the basic tools of the Intelligence Officer's trade, plus a small, two-inch glass ball—a "Crystal Ball"—went into my stock of supplies."

51st Fighter Squadron (Provisional)

Prior to the arrival of the "Dallas Squadron" at Taegu, FAF created on July 10th the 51st Fighter Squadron (Provisional) at Taegu, and authorized it to incorporate the American personnel from "Bout-One" and the "Dallas" pilots. At the same time, FAF created the 6002nd Air Base Squadron and sent it to Korea.

The "Dallas" pilots were quickly airlifted to Johnson AB on July 10th, checked out in Mustangs, drew their supplies and other equipment, then ferried their planes to Taegu, where they prepared to go into combat.

On the night of July 9th, 1950, fifteen F-51 pilots—"without a home, and without airplanes, went looking for a war," Biteman recalled. "We boarded a C-54 transport for the all-night flight to Johnson Field, Japan, the nostalgic site of my first assignment to Japan in 1948. While Captain Moreland, our designated CO, went on to Tokyo to arrange our airlift to Ashiya on the southern island of Kyushu, and to collect instructions and orders from FEAF Headquarters, the rest of us ranged across Johnson Field to beg, borrow or steal the supplies and equipment we would need in Korea. Lieutenant Chuck Hauver, our "chief thief" Supply Officer somehow managed a whole plane load of tents and a complete Field Kitchen; a notable accomplishment, inasmuch as the units at Johnson were reluctant to give up their equipment...they didn't know how soon they would need it themselves."

Biteman did his best to scrounge up needed supplies and equipment. "The best I could do was gather a couple of portable field tables, a packet of maps—and a bright young, able-bodied, red-headed Intelligence Clerk, Sergeant Dan Thornton who had worked for me at Clark, and had recently been transferred to Johnson." Biteman convinced Thornton to join us, telling him "we would arrange for his formal, written orders later. He probably never knew it, but he was subsequently declared AWOL (Absent Without Leave), and it took me weeks to get his records cleared, and convince the headquarters that he was, in fact, with us in Korea and doing one fine job."

That evening, July 10th, "we had three C-54 loads of equipment on their way to Ashiya," Biteman noted. "We rode "shotgun" to make sure no other Korea-bound outfit came along and hijacked the hard-won gear which we had so recently stolen. And, by that same day, the North Koreans had advanced rapidly southward in a three-pronged attack into the west, central and eastern parts of South Korea."

"While we were moving our gear from Johnson to Ashiya," Biteman recalled, "B-29s from Okinawa had bombed the rail and highway bridges at Pyongtaek, trying to slow the Reds western thrust. As the North Korean traffic piled up at the resulting roadblock, they were sighted by a lone F-51 pilot of the 35th Fighter Group, returning from an afternoon reconnaissance mission, who called for help. During the rest of the day, until it was too dark to see anything but the blazing wrecks, all available F-51s, F-80s, F-82s, plus the B-26 and B-29 bombers had a real "turkey shoot." When it was over, the Reds had lost 38 Russian-made tanks, 117 trucks and hundreds of troops. It was the first major air strike, and it slowed their advance toward Taejon enough for General Dean to pull some of his 24th Infantry troops together for a further delaying action.

Seven "Truman F-51's" being flown by members of the USAF 12th Squadron at Taegu, SK (K-2) in July 1950. (Biteman)

Arrival at Ashiya

"When the Dallas Squadron was formed, the advance party went to Johnson AFB to get support to equip the Dallas project," Col. Harry Moreland recalled. "I, with a few others, went to Ashiya to make arrangements to receive the Squadron. At that point I went to see General Timberlake to smooth out our move first to Ashiya and then on to Korea. I was a Captain at that time and when General Timberlake met me he immediately said he wanted to meet with the squadron commander not some Captain. At that point he called the CO of the 18th Group in the Philippines [Lt. Col. Ira "Ike" Wintermute], and was told that I was the squadron commander of the 12th, had flown two tours of combat in the ETO and that he considered me the man for the job. After that we had a good meeting to decide what to do with us--and that was to get ready for a move to K-2. Captain Jerry Mau, instead of remaining at Johnson, went on ahead to K-2 to size up the situation and to help facilitate our move a few days later. In less than three weeks, we went from an F-80 squadron based in the Philippine Islands, to an F-51 squadron flying combat missions in Korea. We had no time for training flights."

18th Group

Deploys to Korea

Advancing enemy troops forced the airborne control function to relocate southeastward from Taejon to Taegu. It was very early in the war and GHQ was reluctant to commit or authorize command movements that might be nullified by the unpredictable tactical situation. However, on July 13th, General Stratemeyer obtained permission to move the 18th Group to Japan. The Group Command was authorized to deploy to Korea via Japan, but only one squadron, the 67th Fighter-Bomber Squadron, would be moving out with the Group.

The unit history reflects the drastic expansion of the 18th Group's mission that is now "to seek out, engage and destroy the North Korean enemy; to neutralize his war making potential and to compromise his will and ability to fight." The combat components of the Group were to achieve the expanded new mission by "furnishing close air support to the United Nations ground forces, aerial reconnaissance of enemy-held territory, seeking military targets of opportunity and providing such other tactical operations as may be directed by higher headquarters to bring hostilities in Korea to a successful cessation." [5]

The 35th Fighter Interceptor Group (FIG), moved from Japan to a new airfield (K-3) at Pohang on July 14th, and became the first USAF fighter group to be based in South Korea during the war. The 6132nd Tactical Air Control Squadron, the first tactical air control unit in the war, went into operation at Taegu under Col. Joseph D. Lee, USAF. It provided forward, ground-based air control for aircraft providing close air support of UN forces. A Fifth Air Force-Eighth Army Joint Operations Center began to function at Taegu, and Fifth Air Force organized an advance headquarters at Itazuke AB, Japan.

The vital command and control capabilities were beginning to come together.

Within hours of their arrival at Taegu, the pilots of "Dallas" were part of a new command. "Bout-One" and "Dallas" had ceased to exist as independent units. Following their merger into the newly created 51st Fighter Squadron (Provisional) at Taegu (K-2), the eager pilots flew their first F-51 Mustang combat missions in Korea on July 15th. During their pre-briefing, a new Fifth Air Force operation order was brought to their attention. It assigned "Mosquito" call signs to airborne controllers in T-6 airplanes, and the name became the identifier for the aircraft—"Mosquito."

The new 51st Provisional Squadron was promptly assigned to the 6002nd Fighter Wing under the command of Captain Harry H. Moreland.

"At Taegu the 51st Fighter Squadron had wire communications with the air control center in Taejon, and its planes were available for scrambles when the ground situation demanded immediate air-support missions. In the early days at Taegu the Mustangs used light-case 500-pound bombs filled with thermite and napalm with great success against both tanks and troops." The treads of the Russian-built tanks were rubber covered and even a near miss with the flaming napalms would usually ignite the treads and eventually destroy the tank. "The enemy didn't seem to mind being blown up or shot," reported Major Hess. "However, as soon as we would start dropping thermite or napalm in their vicinity they would immediately scatter and break any forward movement." [6]

Carefully timing air strikes to coincide with the departure of USAF counter-air patrols for refueling, on July 10th four enemy Yaks bombed and strafed the US 19th Infantry Regiment at Chongju. The clever timing and success of the attack underscored the need to get as many F-51s into action as quickly as possible. The Close Air Support (CAS) mission desperately needed their loiter time over contested areas. That Monday also saw the Fifth Air Force begin using T-6 trainer aircraft for forward air control missions, because liaison airplanes previ-

Provisional Squadron Pilots. *(Far left) Capt. John Denman and Lt. Daniel "Chappie" James. (Sitting on wing): Captain Howard "Scrappy" Johnson (Flight Leader), 2st Lt. Ted "Mother" Baader, Capt. Ramon Roderick "Stoop" Davis. (Crouching in front) Capt. "Nickel's Worth" Micklewait and 1st Lt. Claude R. "Spud" Taylor (sitting on wheel). "Davis and Denman came over on the USS BOXER," recalled Col. James Peek. "Stoop was shot down, captured and never heard from again. He is still MIA," Peek said.*

ously used were not fast enough to elude enemy fire.

The Dallas Squadron Advance Party— Captains Moreland and Jerry Mau, and Lieutenants Frank Buzze and Chuck Hauver— "went over to scout the airfield situation at Taegu on July 12th, while the rest of us spent a couple of days at Ashiya, collecting more equipment and arranging for sea shipment across to Pusan. From there it would have to go by truck and rail to Taegu. Again, each load had to have one of our pilots go along to ride shotgun, to make sure it didn't go astray."

Biteman's intelligence gear was light enough to go by air. On July 14th, he finally received his bundle of black and white Korean air navigation charts (the only charts available in the area), which he had requested be printed on a "Priority Rush Job" by the Ashiya photo lab. Carrying the precious navigation prints by hand, he climbed aboard a heavily-loaded C-47 for the flight to their "new home-away-from-home at Taegu, Korea."

While at Ashiya, Biteman had managed to talk to pilots of the 35th Fighter Group, who were already flying F-51 missions against the Reds. "Things did not sound

good—the Reds had crossed the Han River at Seoul—our base at Kimpo had been captured, and they were approaching our airstrip at Suwon, which was 30 miles south of Seoul. Red air attacks had caught several of our C-54 and C-47 transports on the ground at Suwon, severely damaging them; the crews had then become foot soldiers and had joined the walking retreat toward Taejon, with the North Koreans hard on their heels."

On his last evening at Ashiya, as he finished his "last dinner on a tablecloth" at the Officer's club, Biteman had a chance meeting with "four great stars, resting heavily on the shoulders of Air Force Chief of Staff, General Hoyt S. Vandenberg, who had just arrived at Ashiya for a personal look at the war situation. We did a little "Alphonse & Garcon" dance routine, as each tried to step aside for the other to pass, then he smiled at me, and he, the General, stepped aside to let me, the Lieutenant, pass," Biteman recalled. "I was amazed at how tired he looked, not realizing that he was already ill with the cancer which would soon take his life. At that moment I was glad to be a lowly Lieutenant, with but one life to be concerned about, instead of a four-

F-51D taxies past flightline tents at Taegu in July 1950. (Biteman)

star General with a goodly portion of the weight of the world pressing on his shoulders."

Many years later, Biteman recalled his little "dance step" with the General, when he attended the dedication of the "great missile base in California—Vandenberg Air Force Base—in honor of the General I had 'danced' with at the Ashiya Officer's Club."

Combat Operations Taegu, South Korea

Pilots arriving at K-2, Taegu saw a few widely dispersed F-51s (with South Korean markings), one adobe building, and an awning-like affair over a low stack of packing boxes (that housed the "maintenance hangar"). In the distance to the north, up a steep hill, were a few one-man Pup tents.

The nerve center of the squadron—the Operations Office—was one small room of the adobe hut, "with a local area chart thumb-tacked to one wall, two or three wooden ammo boxes and a hand-crank field telephone," Biteman said.

Taegu airfield, in mid-July, 1950, was simply an open, dusty patch of pastureland approximately not quite a mile in length, about four miles north of Taegu City. The so-called "runway" ran east and west, and was little more than a dusty road with numerous pot holes and dips.

The "Front," was moving south so fast that it was impossible to identify any specific area as being in friendly or enemy hands.

Taejon Falls

The dangers of using B-29s for close air support were tragically emphasized on July 17th when three B-29s accidentally bombed

friendly civilians in Andong, South Korea.

On Thursday, July 20th, despite FEAF close air support, the North Korean Army took Taejon, forcing the remnants of the US 24th Infantry Division to withdraw to the southeast. U.S. ground forces defending Taejon had suffered almost thirty percent casualties in just one week of brutal fighting. Maj. Gen. Otto P. Weyland, USAF, arrived in the Far East to assume the position of FEAF Vice Commander for Operations. Fifth Air Force pilots in F-80s shot down two more enemy aircraft, the last aerial victories until November. Enemy air opposition had virtually disappeared, a sign that FAF was achieving its goal of air superiority.

The city of Taejon fell to the Communists the same day that Typhoon Gloria's low ceilings caused the few airplanes of the Dallas Squadron to stand down. Hundreds of UN troops were captured, including Major General Dean.

"I don't know how much difference our efforts would have made," Biteman noted, "had we been able to fly that one day. Although he acknowledged, "we couldn't stop the advance," perhaps if air cover had been available "we could have allowed our troops a little more of a fighting chance to regroup." For the Dallas Squadron, "it was a very sad, frustrating feeling. If only there were more of us, and if we had more planes ...or more hours in each day ...if, if, if....!"

Taejon's capture marked a major success for the North Korean's western forces. It made it possible, Biteman explained, for them to effect a risky end-around advance along the weakly-defended western and southern coasts of the peninsula and, at the same time, continue their steady advance down the east coast with their third force.

The Dallas Squadron became directly in-

volved with the end-around flanking movement on the west coast, but because of inadequate communications—as well as "too few airplanes to cover too much war, we failed to slow the Communist advance as we should have.

Telling Enemies From "Friendlies"

A Navy Lieutenant arrived at Lt. Bud Biteman's Intelligence tent the rainy day that Taejon fell, pleading with Biteman "to send some fighter support over to the west coast, beyond Taejon. He said he'd just come from there by road, and the Red troops were crossing the river estuary in small craft. If they weren't stopped then, while still vulnerable in their little boats, they would reach the south shore and be able to sweep through the city of Kwangju and the whole southwestern end of the country. I felt very badly, not being able to help him, but we couldn't possibly fly in the existing weather, and at that time didn't even know the status of our primary area of concern—Taejon."

Biteman told him that he would "try to get someone into that area to look over the situation as soon as the weather broke enough to get our ships into the air.

Early the following day, Biteman's flight attacked troops and tanks southeast of Taejon with his bombs and rockets, then "swung wide northwest of Kwangju, to look for signs of boats crossing the western estuary." They saw no boats, but as they flew low over the road leading south toward Chongjun, about thirty miles south of the estuary crossing, they "ran across ten olive-drab, open-backed trucks loaded with armed troops—they were southbound. Were they North or South Korean troops?"

Maintenance "Building" and tent for the 51st Provisional Squadron at K-2 in July 1950. "That was it," Lt. Col. Duane "Bud" Biteman explained. (Biteman)

Biteman had no way of knowing.

When Biteman made a second, "very low, slow pass to look them over, the men in the trucks displayed white cloth signal panels on the roof of the trucks' cab—even though panel codes had not yet been established that early in the war. The trucks were headed south, not north. Biteman was certain that they were enemy troops—why else would they be heading south, and the Navy officer had said they were crossing—ten truck loads, about 200 men. They were sitting ducks for his machine guns. It would have been a simple matter for him to halt them all in a matter of minutes. But, he dared not fire on them! There was no way to be absolutely sure that they weren't friendly troops, so he did not strafe.

After two more low, slow passes, all the while trying desperately to find a giveaway clue as to their true identities, he gave up and flew on southeastward toward Masan at low level. He saw no other troop move-

Lt. Pallor prepares to move into his "home" in Korea at K-2 in August 1950. (Myers)

ments of any kind, so he turned back north to his base at Taegu. When he filed his mission report with 5th Air Force after landing, he learned that "there were NO FRIENDLY TROOPS in the area where I'd found the convoy. The troops I had seen

were the spearhead of the advance that the Navy Lieutenant had told me about." He could have stopped it, or at least slowed if for awhile—if he had only known. "Troop identification was a continuing, and critical problem during those hectic, early days when the battle lines were changing from minute to minute," Biteman explained. "Our normal tactics, when operating in support of ground troops, would have included the use of bright-colored cloth panels displayed on the ground according to a "code of the day." But, because there was no communications yet established with the ground troops, they used the only colored panels available—white—and they were displayed by both the friendly and the enemy forces. It was a continuing, confusing mess."

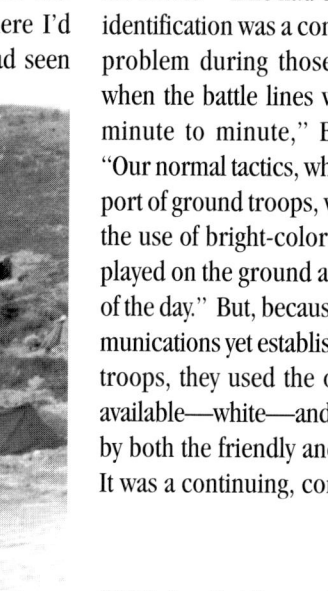

"BOQ Area" at Taegu air strip K-2 in August 1950. (Myers)

Kwangju Falls

Kwangju, the major city on the south-west interior, fell just a few days after Taejon. The pilots of the Dallas Squadron "were amazed at the speed and ease with which the Communists were able to take territory," Biteman explained. "Although we kept a daily reconnaissance over the areas, and found plenty of targets, we were able to slow down their advance hardly at all. How sorry I was that I hadn't been able to identify those first ten truck loads of troops—things might have been different in the south."

The main Communist thrust, down the west-central route to Taejon, had been redirected more to the east to follow the road and railroad corridor toward Waegwan. Clearly, they planned to cross the Naktong River to envelop Taegu. In just a matter of days, the war situation became desperate for the U. N. forces. "By the end of July our ground troops around Yongdong had managed to fight only enough of a delaying action to slow the thrust aimed at Taegu," Biteman explained. "Most of our close support bombing and strafing was concentrated in that area, close to our front (or 'rear') lines, and we were pleased with the reports from ground troops on how much damage our strikes were doing. Along those lines, however, some of those Army troops became pretty "itchy-fingered."

18th Fighter-Bomber Group Gets The Call

On July 24th, the 18th Fighter-Bomber Group, based at Clark AFB, plus the 67th Fighter-Bomber Squadron, received orders transferring the unit to Johnson Air Base, Japan, "for the purpose of staging and receiving aircraft and for further transfer to Taegu (K-2), Korea." The 67th was commanded by Major Louis J. Sebille until his death in combat on August 5th.

Until July 27th, the 18th Group, commanded by Lt. Col. Ira L. Wintermute, remained attached to the 18th Fighter-Bomber Wing at Clark AFB, Philippines. On that date "the Group was moved to Japan. The 44th

Fighter-Bomber Squadron remained at Clark AFB under the Command of Major Charles H. Gipson." [7]

On July 30th, the 18th Group and the 67th Squadron moved to Ashiya, and on August 3rd, the group headquarters moved to K-2.

Group Combat

Operations

Until it was called into the Korean War, the 18th Group had been flying the F-80 "Shooting Star" aircraft. However, "when the group was attached to the Fifth Air Force it was given F-51 aircraft to use in the Korean conflict. Ordinarily, when changing aircraft, checkouts[8] and transitional flying are in order. However, the exigencies of the situation precluded such action. For the most part, checkout and transition for pilots consisted of a three-hour ferry mission from Johnson AB to Ashiya AB. Several pilots checked-out and flew their first combat mission at the same time." [9]

The impact of the Mustang's relentless daylight fighter attacks became apparent rather suddenly during the last week in July. "Where the Reds had previously charged blindly ahead in full daylight, seemingly oblivious to the toll we were taking of their tanks, trucks and troops," Biteman recalled, "they all of a sudden began seeking concealment during the day, and making their advances only at night."

As the North Korean forces neared the Naktong River, the Mustang pilots "really had to search hard for them, looking under each tree and inside the buildings of each village. They would drive their tanks right through the walls of several buildings in the village, then drive their trucks and tanks inside and camouflage the openings with net or straw so they would not be detected from the air. Or, if there were no villages nearby, they would park under a clump of trees and spread netting and branches over the equipment."

The new concealment tactics "made it necessary for us to drastically change our tactics, because we had to search out the

targets at minimum altitude—literally lifting the branches of the trees to look underneath for their arms, or to find their tank tracks, where they'd failed to cover them."

There were just as many targets as there had been before, but it was much harder to find them. The Mustangs also "started picking up more holes in our ships from small arms fire while we were down on the deck searching for clues."

One new tactic became known to the pilots as "yo-yo" maneuvers. "Instead of two or more ships going in to search or attack a target simultaneously, we'd keep one ship high—above 2000 feet, just high enough to stay out of much small arms (rifle and machine gun) range—while the other went down onto the deck. Then, if the enemy fired on the attacking plane, the top-cover could usually spot the muzzle blasts and be able to dive in to attack, while the first attacker would pull up to fly "shotgun," continuing the one up, one down coverage for as long as there were targets in the area," Biteman explained.

When the Mustangs would locate "an especially lucrative or heavily-defended target, one that we had to hit repeatedly, we'd try to vary the patterns to be sure that we never made our attacks twice from the same direction. To do so was to invite disaster, because the gunners were able to take a sighting on one ship, then be all set to blast the next one down the 'chute.' Instead, we'd make sure that our attack headings were at least 60 to 90 degrees offset from the preceding ship." Biteman would "always let loose a short burst of machine gun fire just as I started in on the target, even at long,

Dusty Return to K-2. *A maintenance crew member rides on the wing of a Mustang returning to K-2 from a combat mission in July 1950. The plane stirs up a major dust cloud as it passes by the Maintenance, Intelligence and Operations "Offices" (tents). (Biteman)*

out of range distances—just to suggest the gunners put their heads down. They really didn't know whether I was shooting at them or not, so they'd often hold their fire for fear I'd see their muzzle blast and aim directly at them."

["We'd only fire a warning burst if we suspected 'friendlies,'" explained Lt. Col. Kenneth Barber. "'Moon' Mullins always taught us to 'shoot to kill.'"]

Once the attacking Mustangs had completed their run and passed the positions of the enemy on the ground "and they knew we couldn't turn on them—WOW!—all hell would break loose and everyone on the ground would swing their guns around and try to get us on the way out—unless my wingman was coming down the slot at the same time that I was pulling off." Biteman soon acquired the habit of "jinxing" the ship around as he approached the target, and especially as he pulled off.

"I'd push rudders, stick and ailerons all over the cockpit, to keep the ship flying as UNCOORDINATED as I could make it. If there was a hill nearby, I'd roll over on my back and scoot over the hill close to the ground, rolling right-side-up only after I was on the opposite side, where the targets' gunners couldn't take aim on me. Then, after a few miles or so on the other side, I'd pull up steeply to trade my excess full-throttle airspeed for a couple thousand feet of quick altitude, and start another attack from a far-different angle. My defensive techniques worked very effectively for me, and although most attacks were at low altitude, in heavily

Lt. Col. Ira L. "Ike" Wintermute, *Commanded the 18ᵗʰ Fighter-Bomber Group from 16 June 1950-20 February 1951, when he was relieved by Lt. Col. Homer M. Cox. Wintermute was then assigned to the Thirteenth Air Force. (Moreland)*

defended areas, few gunners were able to successfully take a bead on me. My Mustangs picked up very few holes," he remembered.

Han River Pontoon Bridge

Those tactics worked especially well on one "rough" mission, soon after the Mustangs were thrown into the war. They were assigned the task of "trying to knock out a pontoon bridge the Reds had set up across the Han River at Seoul," Biteman reported.

Heavy bombers had knocked out the road and railroad bridges across the river, but the Communists quickly brought in sections for a pontoon bridge, erected only at night, and dismantled and hidden during the day. "The bombers were unable to knock it out, because they seemed to always be just a few minutes too late, and couldn't catch the bridge in place. Since it was on their primary supply route and a choice target, the Reds had set up heavy anti-aircraft batteries on both ends of the bridge and in the towns on either side—one of the few such

(Continued on page 33)

USS BOXER Arrives With Pilots and Planes

The arrival on Sunday, July 23rd of the U.S. Navy aircraft carrier USS Boxer (CV 21), in Yokosuka, Japan was highly significant. It was crammed with 145 USAF F-51s, equipment and personnel on board following a record eight-day transit from Alameda, California.

The BOXER was completed in 1945, too late to take part in World War II, and joined the Pacific Fleet at San Diego in August 1945. From September 1945 to 23 August 1946 she operated out of Guam as flagship of TF 77 in the western Pacific. During this tour she visited Japan, Okinawa, the Philippines and China. She returned to San Francisco 10 September 1946 and operated off the west coast engaged in normal peacetime duty until departing for the Far East 11 January 1950.

Her service with the 7th Fleet in the Far East during the first half of 1950 included conducting joint operations with Air Force units in the Philippines. She returned to San Diego, arriving 25 June 1950. With the outbreak of the Korean conflict she was pressed into service to carry desperately needed Air Force planes to Korea. On 23 July 1950 she completed a record crossing of the Pacific from Alameda, Calif., to Yokosuka, Japan, in just 8½ days, carrying 145 P-51 *Mustang* and six L-5 aircraft for the Air Force, 19 Navy planes, 1,012 troops and 2,000 tons of supplies. On her return trip—27 July-4 August—she cut the record to 7 days, 10 hours, and 36 minutes. She departed for the Far East on August 24th to join TF 77 in providing air support to the troops. Her planes covered the landing at Inchon September 15th and other ground action until November, when she departed for the west coast and a much-needed overhaul.

On the same day the BOXER arrived in Japan, the 6132nd Tactical Air Control Group (Provisional) established a Tactical Air Control Center adjacent to the Joint Operations Center at Taegu, South Korea. The next day, FAF moved its advanced headquarters from Japan to Taegu, South Korea, locating it next to the Eighth U.S. Army Headquarters in Korea to improve overall communication and coordination between the two commands.

The USS Boxer (CV 21) arrived in Yokosuka, Japan on Sunday, July 23rd crammed with 145 USAF F-51s, equipment and personnel aboard following a record eight-day transit from Alameda, California.

"Boxer Boys." These pilots from the 27th Fighter Wing based at Bergstrom AFB, Texas departing Austin, Texas were en route to San Francisco, California, where they boarded the USS BOXER for a fast trip across the Pacific to Korea. The F-51's were off loaded in Yokohama, Japan, prepared for combat and flown to Taegu, Korea. (L-R) Jack A. Lightner, Ramon R. "Stoop" Davis, John A. Denman, Don E. Eberhardt, Norbourn A. Thomas, Robert D. Rohhlfs, William H. Alexander, Telbert B. Wormack, Neil R. Bartimus, Archibald Young, Edward F. Gossen, Raymond J. Frese, Kendal E. Carson, Robert B. Kelsey, Jan W. Barmore, James C. Peek, James S. Alford, Lee Gomes, Joseph V. LeRoy, John D. Duncan and Bernard L. Pearson. (Peek)

heavily defended sites in Korea at the time. Several of our fighter flights had been diverted by the heavy ground fire before they could take good aim on the bridge sections."

In late July 1950, 1st Lieutenants Bill Slater and Bud Biteman "were elected" to try again to knock out the pontoon bridge. Knowing the target was heavily defended, they planned the mission in more detail than most of their recent "armed recce" flights. "We knew we'd have to arrive over the river before dawn's first light to catch it in place or in use, but we'd need to have enough light to see and to aim at the bridge." They planned for two other ships to approach the area at higher altitude—above 10,000 feet and out of range of the flak—heading in a southwest to northeasterly direction.

At the exact time that the decoy planes would be over the bridge, holding the attention of all flak batteries, Biteman and Slater "would sweep wide around the low hills in the east, coming down the river flat on the water, to skip bomb the pontoons—we hoped—then continue down river, staying on the water, and on out to sea near Inchon before climbing to return toward the south."

Taking off at 0400 from the dark, unlighted, rough field at Taegu, blinded by dust from the two lead ships "was a memorable thrill in itself," he remembered, "but once airborne we could navigate through the dark by following the line of burning villages. In less than an hour we had reached our IP (identification point) south of Seoul, where the other pair of fighters continued their climb while Bill and I cautiously eased down into the dark hills, with just enough light growing in the east to tell when we were low enough for safety."

After reaching the Han River, about ten miles upstream from the bridge, Biteman signaled the others, who turned toward Seoul, while he and Slater "put on full throttle and dropped down into the river bed."

As expected, "all hell broke loose when the high flight approached the bridge, with four separate flak batteries lighting up the sky below them. We knew from their eva-

1st Lt. Bud Biteman (left) and *Capt. William S. "Wild Bill" Slater,* original members of the Dallas Squadron, "were elected" to take out the Han River Bridge in late July 1950. "All hell broke out!" (Moreland)

sive action that they'd never be able to get a halfway decent bombing run on the bridge, even if they were foolish enough to try it, but their decoy was working well, because all of the guns were shooting skyward—not one was aimed at us, yet."

Slater sighted on the south shore, when they got close enough to see the pontoons—with a tank and a truck still trying to make it across. Biteman, on his right wing, picked the north supports.

The pair raced down the river and toggled their bombs off simultaneously, broadside against the bridge, "and immediately rolled hard to the sides to miss our bomb blasts." Slater rolled up over the hill on the south, right over the flak batteries, and Biteman turned north over the town, momentarily, then rolled onto his back and angled back to the river just before coming abreast of Kimpo airfield. Rolling right-side-up again, he dropped as low into the river bed as he could "without hitting the water, and started making violent skidding turns from side to side, because when I looked behind me I could see a trail of large white puffs following each and every turn I made. The flak batteries at Kimpo had my altitude and range boxed in, but so far they hadn't tuned in to my airspeed—and I damned sure was not going to hang around and let them test their abilities."

As he jinxed away from the target as fast

as he could, Biteman huddled lower and lower into the cockpit, "to get as much protection as I could from the sheet of armor plate behind the seat." He almost did not see the set of high-tension power lines strung across the river west of Kimpo airfield. With a quick "pop" of the stick, he ducked under the lines, then pulled hard back, to climb for maximum altitude, still "towing" his trail of white flak puffs behind, "looking for all the world like a strange, surrealistic, giant popcorn string decorating a Christmas tree!"

He called Slater, who had stayed on the deck until he had passed the town of Suwon, before climbing to join the other pair of fighters, and told them he would meet them north of Taejon. As far as they knew, none of them had been hit by ground fire, and they had knocked out the prized pontoon bridge—"with a tank and a truck for good measure."

The successful flight "felt good" as they looked for more targets for their rockets and machine guns on the way back to Taegu. In fact, they "caught" several more trucks and "were back on the ground before breakfast—a very successful mission all the way around."

The North Koreans replaced the pontoon bridge less than a week later, but the risky sortie delayed supplies and caused them "to jam up on the roads and railroads north of the Han River, where a flight of B-29s caught a mass concentration a couple of days later," Biteman recalled.

By the end of July, North Korean military forces had conquered the entire Korean peninsula except the area southeast of Hamch'ang and bordered by the Naktong River—it was soon called "The Pusan Perimeter."

July Significant Dates

July 1: North Korean forces occupied Suwon, denying Far East Air Forces use of its airstrip.

"Bout One" is operational at K-2.

July 3: General Stratemeyer (FEAF) directed the 13th AF at Clark AFB in the Philippines to create new "Dallas Squadron" and deploy it to Johnson Air Base in Japan to be equipped with Mustangs.

First AOC organized at Itazuke.

July 5: General Order 24 issued by the 18th Fighter-Bomber Wing "directed the 18th Fighter-Bomber Group to organize a provisional squadron code named 'Dallas Squadron' with personnel of the former 12th Fighter Bomber Squadron to be used as a nucleus.

First three TACP teams began operating at Chonan.

July 6: 6002nd Air Base Squadron organized and moved to K-2.

July 7: Provisional Troop Carrier Unit 1 (C-47's and C-46's) organized at Ashiya.

July 8: General Timberlake designated K-2/Taegu as the destination for the "Dallas" squadron.

39th and 40th Squadrons of the 35th Fighter-Interceptor Group moved to Ashiya and 8th Squadron of 49th Fighter-Bomber Group moved from Ashiya to Itazuke.

July 10: "Dallas Squadron" departed Clark Air Force Base via Troop Carrier aircraft for Johnson Air Base, Japan, where it was to receive TO&E. "51st Prov. Ftr. Sq. (Dallas Project) organized at K-2." [10]

FAF created 51st Fighter Squadron (Provisional) at Taegu, and authorized it to incorporate the American personnel from "Bout-One" and the "Dallas" pilots. Simul-

Seoul's Kimpo Airfield on 27 July 1950, shows the damage inflicted on it after numerous attacks by Air Force bombers and fighter bombers in the early days of the Korean War. (NARA)

taneously, FAF created the 6002nd Air Base Squadron and sent it to Korea to provide logistical support for the provisional fighter squadron.

July 13: General Stratemeyer obtained permission to move the 18th FBG to Japan. The Group Command was authorized to deploy to Korea via Japan. Only one squadron, the 67th, would be moving with the Group.

General Walton Walker named ground force commander in Korea.

July 14: 35th Fighter Interceptor Group (FIG), moved from Japan to K-3 at Pohang, the first USAF fighter group to be based in South Korea during the war.

T-6 Mosquitoes began operating from K-2.

6132nd Tactical Air Control Group organized at Itazuke.

General Vandenberg visited Hq FAF at Itazuke and flew to Korea (including Taegu).

July 15: "Bout-One" and "Dallas" cease to exist as independent units following

merger into the newly created 51st Fighter Squadron (Provisional) at Taegu (K-2).

Eager pilots of the "51st" flew their first F-51 Mustang combat missions in Korea. "The 51st Fighter Squadron (Provisional) was dubbed 'The Flying Tigers of Korea' by Korean President Syngman Rhee, and was allowed to paint sharks teeth on the engine cowling of the aircraft, reminiscent of the Flying Tigers of World War II." [11]

Major Stanley Chatfield, was preparing to land his F-80 at Clark AB, circling over the field waiting until a T-33 jet trainer had taken off. The T-33 "had a flameout about the rotation time," and bellied in off the end of the landing runway. Chatfield "landed right away since the aircraft was a 12th Squadron aircraft and Chatfield was the new Commander of the 12th following the departure of Capt. Harry Moreland with the Dallas Project. Chatfield jumped into a jeep "and raced for the accident where the fire and crash crews were taking care of the situation." Also on the scene was Lt. Chappie James, who was in the process of lifting the

F-51 returns to K-2 in July 1950 to refuel and rearm for another mission. (Biteman)

canopy off the aircraft--with his back--and helping the pilot out. The pilot was not Spud Taylor, James' close friend, since "Spud had long ago checked out in the F-80 and was in no need for a check," Chatfield recalled. James did injure his back during the rescue and was taken off flying status by the Flight Surgeon to give the injury time to heal. This did not sit well with James, at all. "We were all getting ready to go to Korea, and Chappie is not going to be among the pilots." James went to Chatfield for help. "He pleaded with me to do something," Chatfield recalled, "so I went to the Command Surgeon and told him the story of the Group and the camaraderie of the pilots. I also told him--off the cuff,of course--that if Chappie did not go with the Group, that he said he would go AWOL and join them in Korea." The Surgeon relented and put James "back on flying status. I don't think that Chappie even knew that," Chatfield recalled.

July 19: JOC fully established at Taegu.

July 20: Taejon falls to NKA, forcing the remnants of the USA 24th Infantry Division to withdraw to the southeast.

July 23: USS BOXER (CV 21) arrived in Yokosuka, Japan loaded with 145 USAF F-51s, equipment and personnel aboard following a record eight-day transit from Alameda, California.

July 24: 18th Fighter-Bomber Group headquarters at Clark AFB, plus the 67th Fighter-Bomber Squadron, received orders transferring them to Johnson Air Base, Japan to receive aircraft and for further transfer to Taegu (K-2), Korea.

July 25: Second Lieutenant Billie R. Crabtree "was the first casualty of the unit [51st Provisional Squadron] … when he dove his F-51 too close to his target," S/Sgt. Sandy Colton recorded. [12]

July 27: 18th Fighter-Bomber Group, commanded by Lt. Col. Ira F. Wintermute, detached from the 18th Fighter-Bomber Wing at Clark AFB, Philippines and was ordered to Japan. The 44th Fighter-Bomber Squadron remained at Clark AFB under the Command of Major Charles H. Gipson."

July 28: In Special Orders #144, the 18th Fighter Bomber Wing directed Lt. Col. Ira F. Wintermute as Commander, 18th Fighter-Bomber Group, to move by airlift from Clark AFB to Japan for "subsequent movement to Taegu, Korea. Group staff officers going with Wintermute, included: Major Robert Dow, Major Stanley E. Chatfield, Capt. Edward C. Hoagland, Jr., and Capt. Charles E. "Slide" Trumbo, Jr.

The 18th Group was ordered deployed to Johnson Air Base in Japan "to pick up F-51 aircraft that had been brought over on the USS BOXER," Chatfield recalled. [The aircraft on board the Boxer were Air National Guard aircraft that had been hastily moved to the port in California for shipment. "They were in need of many things, not the least of which was ordinance," Chatfield explained.] "We wasted no time at Johnson. We were briefed that a C-54 would be our

1st Lt. Daniel "Chappie" James. (Moreland)

navigating escort. We formed up in a massive formation with the C-54 in the lead. Most of us had prior flight time in the F-51 so this was no big problem and the flight was without incident. Peeling off at Ashiya in southern Japan, all of the aircraft landing safely and were immediately serviced and inspected by the maintenance crews to see how many could be out in the air for combat."

July 30: 18th Group and the 67th Squadron moved to Ashiya, Japan from Clark AFB on Luzon. Command and Operations functions began to function immediately, Chatfield recalled. "As the Group Operations Officer, I made arrangements to go to Itazuke, where the 8th Fighter-Bomber Group was based, for a briefing on call signs, communications in the combat areas, operations that were under way, and for targets that our Group would be called on to strike. With appropriate maps and intelligence, I returned to Ashiya and briefed the Commander and the squadrons. We were available for operations."

A week later, the 51st Provisional, now redesignated the 12th Fighter-Bomber Squadron, and the Headquarters Squadron Section of the 18th Fighter-Bomber Group would be pulled back from Taejon to join the 67th and the other sections of the Group. The 18th Fighter-Bomber Group—the 67th FBS and the 12th FBS, plus supporting elements—was once again together as a fighting unit.

Combat Losses

2nd Lt. Billie R. Crabtree, 25 July 1950, "was the first casualty of the unit [51st Provisional Squadron] … when he dove his F-51 too close to his target," S/Sgt. Sandy Colton recorded.[12] The average experience level of the Dallas (12th) squadron pilots, "with a median age of 27, and 600 flying hours, paid dividends during those first couple of weeks of the Korean war," Biteman remembered. "Even though we lost a couple of airplanes, we didn't lose any pilots until the 25th of July. On that day, Billie Crabtree, a sharp young 2nd Lieutenant was our first casualty. He was working over a

railroad on the west coast near Kwangju, trying to skip-bomb a locomotive in a tunnel. He apparently started his pullout a fraction of a second too late for the heavy load he was carrying, for he mushed into the top of the hill at the same time that his bombs went off inside the tunnel. He wrapped his Mustang into a great ball of fire. Two days later the North Koreans had the tunnel open and usable again."

Endnotes

[1] *Futrell, Robert F.* **The United States Air Force In Korea: 1950-1953**. *Washington, DC: Office of Air Force History, USAF, 1983. p. 68.*

[2] *Futrell. p. 90.*

[3] *History of the 18th Fighter-Bomber Group, July-October, 1950. USAFHRA.*

[5] *History of the 18th Fighter-Bomber Group, July-October, 1950. USAFHRA.*

[6] *Futrell. p. 95.*

[7] *History of the 18th Fighter-Bomber Wing, July-August, 1950. USAFHRA.*

[8] *History of the 18th Fighter-Bomber Group, July-October, 1950. USAFHRA.*

[9] *History of the 18th Fighter-Bomber Group, July-October, 1950. USAFHRA.*

[10] *NARA. Memorandum from Major James W. Ingram to MG E. J. Timberlake of 26 September 1950. Chronology of Fifth Air Force Activity in Korea.*

[11] *USAFHRA. "The Story of the 18th Fighter-Bomber Group in the Korean United Nations Police Action." 6002 Tactical Support Wing, Public Information Office. S/Sgt Sandy Colton.*

[12] *USAFHRA. "The Story of the 18th Fighter-Bomber Group..." Colton.*

"Camouflage" and Protection

"In order to look more like Infantrymen, some of us traded our one-piece flight suits for two piece Army fatigues and had pencil pockets sewn on the sleeves," Lt. Col. Barber explained, "in case we got shot down and captured we didn't want to look like a 'pilot.'"

"In my case, I had a pile jacket sewn up by a Korean woman with gloves and headgear (warm) in the same shape as the backpad of the parachute. I then replaced the backpad with this expedient so if I crash landed or bailed out, I would always have these warm clothes with me."

Barber also had "a small holster made for my .25-caliber pistol and strapped it out of sight under my fatigues in case I was captured and the enemy removed my .45 from its shoulder holster."

As additional protections, Barber "strapped a switch blade knife in a small holster around my lower leg and connected under my fatigue pants." He was "loaded for bear" but hopeful that the "bear wouldn't come!"

Looking back, he found the psychological effects of flying combat missions "interesting." For the first 20-30 missions he "flew well prepared." Gradually, as the number of missions grew, he found himself gradually "slacking off in carrying additional protection."

When he reached 80-85 missions, and "had the feeling that I might make it through after all," he "started re-strapping the 'protection' on."

The First Few Weeks

by William J. "Sandy" Colton

On 25 June 1950 the North Korean Forces invaded South Korea. Armed and supplied by Communists there was no power to stop these hordes. The United Nations Security Council met and called upon the United States Army, Navy, Air Force and Marines.

The United States Air Force called upon the Fifth Air Force and the Far East Air Forces with bases in Japan, Okinawa and the Philippines. The FEAF had many types of aircraft and a limited number of personnel who were experienced in more than their own job. In Japan FEAF had F-51's, F-82's, and B-26's. In Okinawa there were F-80A's and F-80B's and in the Philippines there were the new F-80C's and the old reliable C-54, C-47 and C-46 aircraft of the 21st Troop Carrier Squadron, 347th Troop Carrier Wing.

On 15 July 1950 the 51st Fighter Squadron (Provisional) was formed from units of the 18th Fighter Bomber Group from Clark AFB, Philippines. This unit was airlifted to King Two (K-2) airstrip five miles north of Taegu, South Korea. They were armed with F-51 Mustangs and were composed of Officers and Airmen of the 12th Fighter-Bomber Squadron. This project was called "Dallas Squadron." 2nd Lt. Billie R. Crabtree was the first casualty of the unit on 27 July when he dove his F-51 too close to his target.

The 51st Fighter Squadron was dubbed "The Flying Tigers of Korea" by Korean president Syngman Rhee. They were allowed to paint shark teeth on the engine cowling of the planes after the AVG of World War II.

This unit went to K-2 located at Taegu. On 2 August they were greeted by advanced elements of the 18th Fighter-Bomber Group main body. This was short lived as on 4 August the whole Dallas Squadron and the Headquarters section of the Fighter Group were evacuated to Ashiya Air Force Base in southern Japan. The 67th Fighter Bomber Squadron had already started to operate from Ashiya when Dallas got there.

Lt. Billie Crabtree

The Headquarters section of the group and the 67th Fighter Bomber Squadron were moved from Clark Air Force Base, Philippines on 31 July 1950 and were set down at Ashiya.

The 18th Fighter-Bomber Group was attached to the 6002nd Tactical Support Wing which was newly organized from personnel in Japan and newly arriving personnel in the theater. Colonel Curtis R. Low was named wing commander and his staff included: Capt. Thomas Shockley, Adjutant, Lt. Col. Donald H. Lynch, Major Charles D. Yankhower as Operations and Intelligence Officer's respectfully, and Lt. Col. Kendall E. Carlson, as Base Maintenance Officer.

The group operated out of Ashiya AFB, 100 miles from Pusan, SK.

Their Frag Order read anything from North of the 38th Parallel to Taegu and the Naktong River. Once, pilots of the 67th were accused of bombing an airfield In Manchuria. Most of their missions were Armed Recce's of four to six hours duration. Frequently the aircraft would take off from Japan, hit the target, land at K-2 or K-13 (Pohang) and operate out of there until dark and return to Ashiya after their last strike. This put a strain on transports as mechanics, armorers and sometimes intelligence personnel had to be flown to K-2 or K-13 to handle the load as personnel there were inadequate.

During the brief thirty-four days the group stayed in Ashiya, it had four casualties of killed or missing in action. There were many ground loops either from battle damage or from existing weather conditions. A strong cross wind always seemed to prevail over Ashiya's one main runway which emptied out into the Japan Sea on the south end, and there was a town on the north end which made landing and taking off a cautious job. Conditions were crowded and everyone had to work out of packing cases—officers and line personnel alike.

The Ashiya Base Supply did its utmost to fulfill the needs of the group and its supporting elements.

The North American F-51 Mustangs received at Ashiya and at K-2 were aircraft which had belonged to National Guard units in the states and aircraft which were stored at Far East Air Materiel Command (FEAMCOM) in Japan. The National Guard aircraft

Base Operations and Tower at K-2/Taegu *not long after the 6002nd Provisional Fighter Squadron began combat operations in the Korean War. (Peek)*

Lt. Bill Slater's scruffy appearance scared even the Marine Corps. (Biteman)

Culture Shock for the Marine Corps

As 18th Group Operations Officer, Major Stan Chatfield "had the job of assigning and briefing missions on target areas." Remembering the "primitive" conditions, it is easy to imagine that the "whole group of pilots and crews were at best a motley lot. Unshaven, no showers for days, scruffy flight suits and appearance."

Soon after K-2 became operational, Chatfield was advised "that a flight of Marine aircraft would be coming into Taegu, from a carrier off shore, full armed and ready to do battle with the enemy," he rememebered with a smile.

Chatfield's responsibility was to brief them and to assign an F-51 pilot, with aircraft, "to usher them out to the target area where they would expend their ordnance and return to the carrier."

Lt. Bill Slater was assigned to the job, as well, and soon the Marine aircraft were on the ground and their pilots ready to be briefed.

The Marine Corps pilots "in their new shin-n-ny boots, clean flight suits, with helmets, took one look at us--especially Bill Slater--and I thought they would bolt and return to the ship," Chatfield remembered.

"This is the one who will show us to the target," they asked incredulously.

After the initial shock, however, "things went well and we did not see them again." Chatfield always wondered, "what they told the crews back on board the carrier?"

Marine Corps F4U Corsair taxies at Ashiya, Japan. (Burns)

went out as MONOLOGUE and the 67th Squadron had ELSEWHERE as its call sign.

The Flights—usually four Mustangs flying as a unit—were designated A, B, C, D and E, etc. or Able, Baker, Charlie, Dog and Easy. Able flight was usually the first flight off in the day. Later, the 12th Squadron started at Mike and went to Zebra and the 67th Squadron started at Able and went to Love.

Overall combat operations of the group did not change much from World War II. The ground controller, in a jeep (usually a USAF pilot), would call an L-5, with the radio call sign of "Mosquito" and tell him of a target for fighters. "Mosquito Wildwest" would call the flight leader, give him the coordinates and his flight would go in for the kill.

These F-51 flights were like an Aerial Guard duty—one flight would relieve the other. When operating from Japan "Elsewhere Easy" flight (a flight of four aircraft) would report to JOC with a call sign of "Mellow" at 1300 hrs. JOC would, in turn, tell the flight to report to "Mosquito Wildwest" in Area # ___, give the coordinates, and the flight would go to that area, relieve the preceding flight, be it USAF, Navy, Marines or Australian and report to "Mosquito Wildwest" and usually stay in that area for one to two hours, then the Air Controller would take over. Sometimes the F-51's worked with just the TACP or radio jeep. When the flights were going to and from Korea they would check in with "Mellow" so they would know if any aircraft were missing.

JOC—Joint Operations Center—was in 5th Air Force (Advanced) Headquarters at Taegu, then Pusan and on 15 September 1950, the center moved back to Taegu, then on to Seoul. After Seoul some of the Center personnel went to Anju. When the big winter Communists offensive started, JOC went back to Taegu.

JOC had complete control of every ground controller, Air Controller and every United Nations Aircraft in the Korean theater. This also was a cross-check for any missing aircraft.

were loaded on the "USS BOXER," aircraft carrier complete with pilots, twenty five in all. Those pilots were affectionately dubbed "The Boxer Boys" by the group pilots. The group's long-range recce's proved to be useful. Maj. Mullins, Capt. Price and Capt. Hoagland caught the first YAK fighter on the ground for the first aircraft destroyed on the ground for the group.

The operations of the group did not change much from World War II. They had two squadrons (one squadron under strength)—the 12th and the 67th Fighter-Bomber Squadrons. The 12th Squadron

North American
P-51 Mustang

The P-51 Mustang was designed in 1940 following a request by Great Britain to create an improved successor to the Spitfire. The prototype was designed and constructed in less than four months. Mustangs entered service in World War II in December 1943, as escorts for long range bombers. By war's end about a year and half later, Mustangs had destroyed nearly 5,000 enemy aircraft in the air--nearly half of the U.S. total--plus more than 4,000 on the ground.

In 1948, the new U.S. Air Force redesignated the nearly 5,000 surplus Mustangs as F-51s, most of them the "D" Model. During the Korean War, the F-51's were used primarily for close air support of ground forces until it was withdrawn from combat in January 1953. The 18th Fighter-Bomber Wing was the last U.S. Air Force unit to fly the Mustangs in combat.

General Characteristics of the F-51D

Primary function: long range fighter bomber

Power plant: one Packard V-1650-7 (license-built Rolls-Royce Merlin) liquid-cooled V-12 engine

Thrust: 1,590 horsepower

Wingspan: 37 feet

Length: 32.25 feet

Height: 13.65 feet

Weight, empty: 7,640 lb.

Weight, maximum: 12,110 lb.

Max. speed: 437 mph

Climb rate: 3,478 ft/min.

Ceiling: 42,000 ft.

Max. range: 2,068 miles

Armament: 6 .50-caliber machine guns, 2 500-pound bombs, or 2 external fuel tanks, 6 HVAR rockets

Crew: one pilot

Cost: $50,000

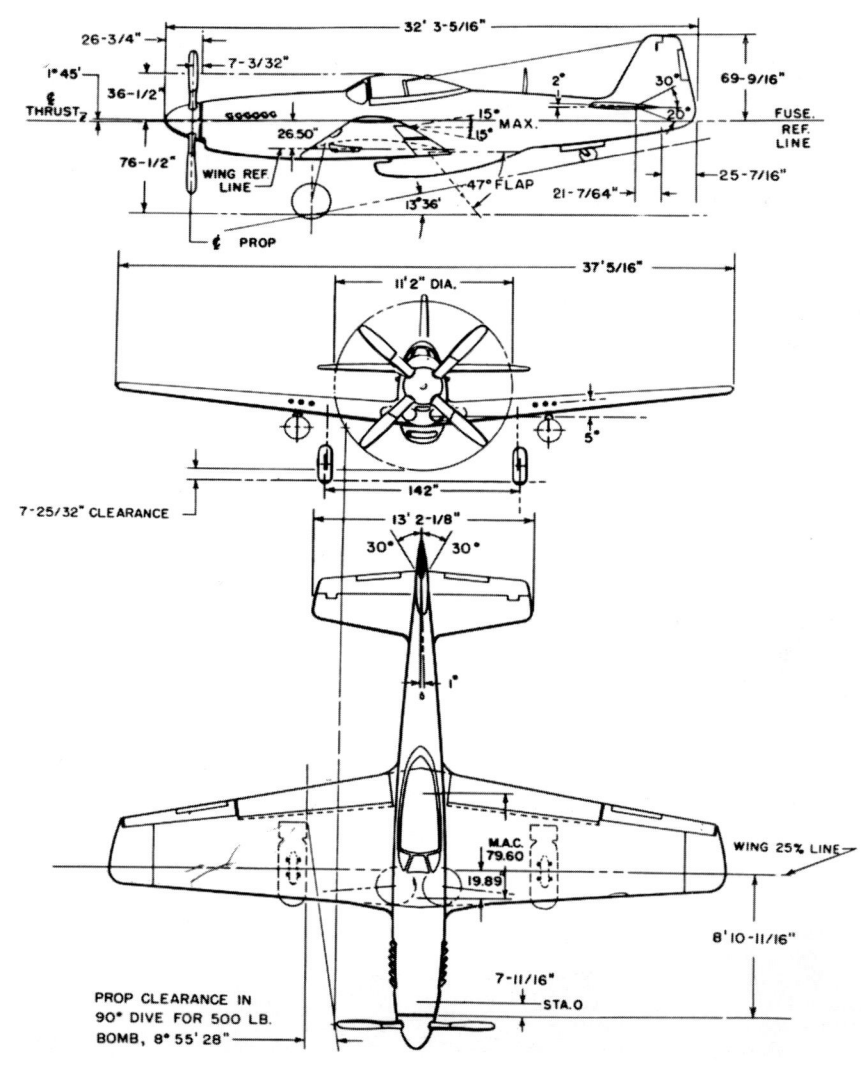

Pilot's F-51 Test

Among many other prerequisites to being certified ready to fly in combat, newly arrived pilots to the 18th Group were required to pass this test.

Q: The F-51 is powered with a Packard built Rolls Royce Merlin V-1650-3 or 7 engine. A: True

Q: The fuselage is a semi-monocoque, all metal structure and comparatively speaking, has a large amount of frontal area. A: False

Q: Sealed type ailerons are installed, giving lighter control stick pressues and at the same time more positive action. A: True

Q: Flaps range 50 degrees and may be controlled at 10 degree intervals. A: True

Q: Ordinarily Ram Air will be used for normal operation; however, during dusty operations the Filtered Air will be utilized. A: True.

Q: Due to the safety control lock on the landing gear handle of the F-51, accidental retraction of the landing gear is impossible. A: False

Q: You can release the landing gear in an emergency by means of a red handle just above the hydraulic gauge. Pulling this handle releases pressure in the hydraulic lines. The gear drops of its own weight providing the gear lever is in the down position. A: True

Q: Landing gear warning lights indicate when your gear is not locked. A: True

Q: The F-51 has two main tanks, one in each wing root (92 gallons each) and one auxiliary tank behind the pilots seat containing 85 gallons. A: True

Q: Coolant is distributed through two systems not connected in any way namely, engine coolant and after cooler. A: True

Q: The emergency cockpit canopy release is located directly above the pilot's head. A: False

Q: List the engine operating instruments. A: Tachometer, Manifold Pressure, Oil Temperature, Coolant Temperature, Oil Pressure, Fuel Pressure and Carburetor Temperature.

Q: IFF radio set is an identification device used in determining friend or foe. A: True.

Q: The oxygen system in the F-51 is the low-pressure demand type. A: True

Q: The F-51 has 6 .50-caliber machine guns, can carry six rockets and two 500-pound bombs. A: True

Q: How much ammunition does the F-51 carry when fully loaded? A: 1880 rounds.

Q: What type of gunsight is installed in the F-51 aircraft? A: K-14C

Q: Can rockets be fired in pairs? A: Yes

Q: Landing lights should not be operated on the ground for over 10 seconds because the heat will melt the plastic lens. A: True

Q: List the cockpit check to be made after entering the cockpit and prior to starting the engine. A: Flaps Up, Carburetor Air Filter, Forward, Trim Tabs set, Gear Handle DOWN, Throttle Quadrant SET; Fuel Boost ON, Altimeter SET, Gyros UNCAGE, Gas on L. MAIN, Hydraulic Valve IN, Radio OFF, Oxygen NORMAL.

Q: The starter may be used continuously for up to 30 seconds. A: False

Q: Landing gear may be lowered at any speed not in excess of 200 mph. A: False

Q: Do not attempt to turn after go-around until your flaps are up. A: True

Q: Lowering the flaps makes the F-51 nose heavy. A: True

Q: What is the desired operating range for the coolant temp. A: 100-110 Q: What is the maximum temp for operation. A: 121

Q: Mach number is the percentage of the speed of sound at which the particular airplane reaches compressibility. A: True

Q: The Mach number for the F-51 is approximately 67%, 75%, 85%. A: 75%

Q: Describe briefly the recommended spin recovery for the F-51D. A: 1) Controls with spin, 2) opposite rudder, 3) stick forward of neutral, 4) pull up gradually.

Q: List the following for bail out. A: 1) lower seat, 2) disconnect radio cords and oxygen, 3) roll canopy back, 4) duck head, jettison canopy, 5) dive out right side of aircraft.

Q: The greatest percentage of successful parachute jumps have been made to the (a. outside, b. inside) of the spin. A: inside.

Q: In case of complete engine failure, how may the gliding characteristics of the F-51 be increased? (Excluding dropping of external tanks and bombs.) A: prop pitch low, close coolant doors.

(18th Fighter-Bomber Group F-51 Questionnaire)

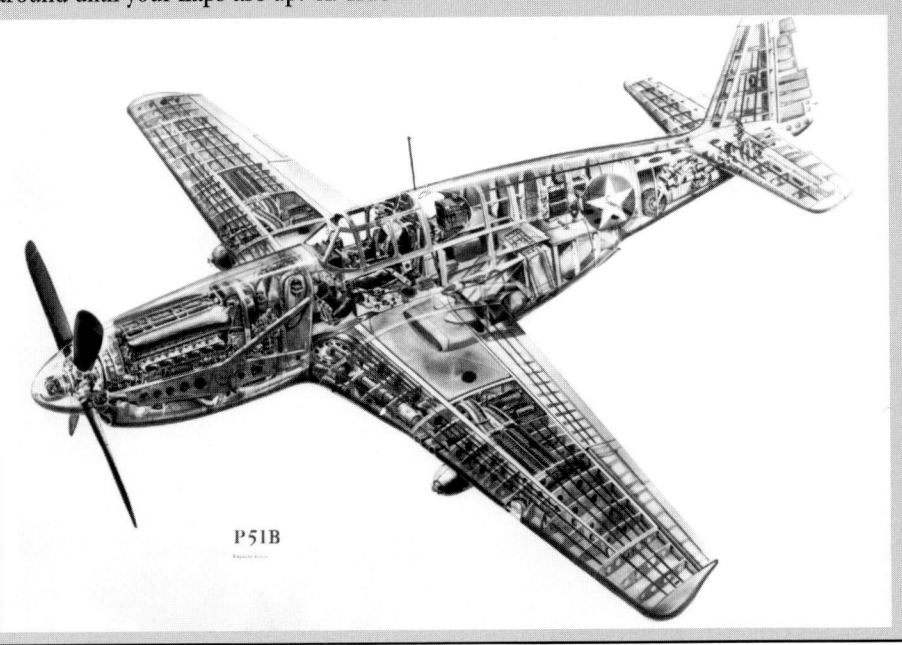

P 51B

The Police Action

by Col. Howard C. "Scrappy" Johnson

Even though "Mo" [Capt. Harry H. Moreland] was only a Captain, Colonel Henry H. Norman, 18th Group Commander, made him 12th Squadron Commander. They had become tired of squadron commanders who were reluctant flyers.

One day soon after, Mo called us together and told us we were going to Korea. We were supposed to be volunteers so there was some switching around between members of the 12th, 44th and 67th Squadrons. I suppose we were volunteers because we probably could have gotten out of it if we had wanted to.

There's an old saying in the military--"Never volunteer for anything." But, I was eager to go, because I had not served in combat in World War II and didn't want to miss this one. This was not so much because I was super patriotic or trying to be over dramatic, it was more about being around when your buddies are telling war stories and you're not being able to tell some too. I also felt that since I was being paid to be a fighter pilot, I ought to do some fightin'.

We called ourselves the "Foxy Few," and our logo was Renyard the Fox, portraying a baseball pitcher, throwing a whiskey bottle. We were all jubilant, and thought we could end the little skirmish in about two weeks. We did not realize how neglected our military had been since World War II.

The plan was for us to fly P-51's again. They were considered better than jets for the hilly terrain in Korea and had more range at low altitude, which gave us more time over the target. I could not have been more prepared. I had a lot of hours in the P-51 and was damn good at dive-bombing, rocket firing and strafing.

In high school my most ardent desire was to play football. I would have given anything to be the star halfback, but due to my size, it was not to be. Now I finally found something I could do well and size didn't matter. One evening we boarded a C-54 bound for Ashiya, Japan. Upon our arrival we found ourselves without airplanes. Ear-

Pilots Frank Buzze and Howard "Scrappy" Johnson.

lier we sent a forward party to K-2 (Taegu) to join Bout One. This project had turned out to be a loser. Several of the Korean pilots crashed, the American instructors had given up on them and were flying the missions themselves.

Our advanced detachment at K-2 was first called "Dallas," for reasons known only by the great ones in headquarters. Then it was almost immediately designated the 51st Provisional Squadron and Mo was still the squadron commander. The squadron flew 426 combat sorties from K-2 in July of 1950. Many times we were pulled off a target to orbit, waiting for a flight of F-80's to make a couple of fast strafing passes and head back to Itazuke, low on fuel.

At that time there were no navigational aids in Korea, no homers, no DFs (radio direction finders), no radar, no instrument procedures. Nothing, period. Standard procedure, when the weather turned bad, was to fly to Japan where the ground radar could give you a steer. The only other alternative was to fly out over the water, let down, and hope that you break out of the clouds before hitting something.

We were confident that we could end this skirmish quickly, but it wasn't long before we learned the facts of life. How the Commies only moved and fought at night, how they hid themselves and their equip-

ment in the day, and how difficult it was for us to find and destroy them.

As soon as I came to the conclusion that the war was not going to end quickly as I originally thought, I wanted Dorie and Ted, who had remained in the Philippines, to return to the States. The situation was very unstable and we did not know what was going to happen. I was afraid that the war would spread and that they'd be stuck there in enemy hands. I wrote Dorie and told her to head home as soon as possible. She left a few weeks after I departed for Korea. I did not know at the time, that I would even-

Captain Harry Moreland

41

tually return to the Philippines.

Around the dirt strip at K-2 there were remnants of WW II buildings, battle damaged and un-repaired. Twelve-man squad tents sheltered our operations, maintenance, billeting, and messing. We erected most of them ourselves. One night during a storm the tent next to ours blew down on top of its occupants, proving that good fighter pilots are not necessarily good tent erectors!

Mo had divided the Squadron pilots into two sections. Captain Jerome "Jerry" Mau headed one and I headed the other. One section flew mornings and the other flew afternoons. One morning when my section was on duty I went down to operations early. The FRAG (operations order spelling out the mission for the day) came in over a crank telephone from the command post, which was located nearby in Taegu. This morning the North Koreans, just south of Taejon, surrounded the 24th Army Division. The message said they had left thirteen carloads of arms and ammunition in the railway yard. The message ended with, "They have to be destroyed at any cost."

Major "Mo" Moreland's Airmanship

With Mo leading, we took off as a two-ship flight and headed for Taejon via the railroad. The weather was not too good and the clouds forced us lower and lower. We were right on the ground when Mo concluded this was not the answer. He decided the only way we were going to make it was to climb on top of the clouds.

He did this with me tucked in on his wing. We reached the tops at about 8,000 feet. He then flew time and distance and let down into the Kum-Gang valley where Taejon was located.

We did not know what to expect, but luckily broke out over Taejon at about 2,000 feet. We found the 13 railroad cars in the railroad yard, just as described on the frag. We thoroughly strafed and fire bombed all thirteen of the cars. I was wary of getting my butt blown out of the sky, but luckily all

"Mo's Machine." Cpl. Hoot Gibson, "Mo" Moreland's Crew Chief, oversees the process of "strapping in" before he takes "Mo's Machine" on a mission from Taegu. (Moreland)

we got was some fires started and a series of minor explosions. Now we had to get back to K-2. Mo worked the time-distance again and on arrival over Taegu we were lucky enough to find a small hole, which we dove through and landed. Even with a super leader like Mo, the idea of a time-distance letdown into the much smaller Kummo Valley at Taegu held no great appeal to me.

Another day we got a call to fly patrol over a bridge at Seoul that night. The bridge had been knocked out earlier but the Commies had rigged up a pontoon bridge and were moving supplies across the river every night. The 7th Air Force Headquarters wanted us to harass them when they turned on their lights and attempted to bring things across. It would mean keeping a P-51 over the area during the entire period of darkness.

Mo scheduled himself for one of the flights and asked for volunteers to fill the other five slots. I remember Captain William "Bill" Slater volunteered for one of the flights and squadron pilots filled the others. I did not volunteer for one. Later I regretted it. Mo and I were good friends and I should have backed him up on it.

When the North Korean Army finally got within seven miles of Taegu, you could hear the artillery from the airstrip. When we'd fly missions late in the evening we could see

refugees, mostly dressed in white clothing, crossing the Naktong River. I was flying one evening when the Forward Air Controller told me to strafe them. I replied, "They are civilians. They're in white clothes." The FAC replied, "Strafe them. There are North Korean troops mixed in and they will give our guys a hard time tonight if you don't." Knowing that our army troops were greatly outnumbered and trying to hold back the North Koreans, we strafed them.

Production Line

Armament

We were flying sorties so fast the maintenance and armament crews were having a problem turning the airplanes around. One day when my section was on duty, I devised a plan where the pilots would remain with the airplane, taxi it from the point where it was refueled to where it was armed, then move it up as various arms were attached to the ship. We called it production line armament. It worked so well that other flights from Itazuki and Ashya started to land at Taegu, refuel, re-arm and fly another mission on the way home. Moe told me later that they gave the armament officer a Bronze Star for implementing it. Some times that's the way the ball bounces.

Reinforcements Bring Changes

The rest of the Squadron joined us in the last week of July and we resumed our proper identity as the 12th Fighter-Bomber Squadron. Robert "Bob" Dow took over as squadron commander from Mo, effective the end of the month.

In my book this was a step backward.

Mo was a much better combat leader. Besides he got a spot promotion to Major shortly afterwards. With the rest of the squadron came the group and the Wing weenies like the wing commander who thought it was a wonderful idea to blow reveille on the anti aircraft guns! I kid you not. You will get out of bed in one hell of a hurry when two quad-forty millimeters start blasting away ten yards from your tent!

The 5th Air Force Commander, General Earle Partridge, had his executive B-17 parked near us on the airstrip. We joked about it by saying, "When that B-17 leaves, we're gettin in our P-51's and hauling ass for Itazuke."

Well, when the bomb line got within seven miles of K-2 we were ordered to go to Ashiya, Japan. We later found out the general had already departed several days earlier--leaving the B-17 at K-2 for "morale purposes."

Although the Commies never took K-2, they came very close.

Farr and Baader

At Ashiya I met two new friends--Daniel "Danny" Farr and Ted "Mother" Baader. They were occupying the BOQ room next to mine. One afternoon about four (almost bar time), I was in their room having a drink. Danny needed something out of his footlocker but he could not find the key. So he knocked on several doors nearby asking for a screwdriver or something to pry the lock off with. None of the occupants had come up with anything.

Back in his room he dragged the footlocker out on the porch, and with his .45-cal. pistol, he blasted off the lock. He was undoubtedly the most colorful character I knew during my Air Force Career. He'd graduated from West Point and all that discipline hadn't had a whit of effect on his way of doing things. He wore a Bancroft Flighter with his flying suit. (A Bancroft Flighter was an officer's hat with a flexible bill that was popular with pilots during WWII because it could be folded up.) Danny wore his with the flexible bill turned up like a baseball catcher.

[Farr also wore "obvious Argyle socks," recalled Col. Bill Myers.]

At K-9 I led Danny on his first combat mission, which was an uneventful two-ship flight. Afterwards he asked me, "How did I do"?

"You did fine," I answered, "except your formation flying was a little sloppy."

He retorted, "I don't think it was so bad considering the amount of time I have in the P-51."

Danny had sailed over on the aircraft carrier USS BOXER with a hundred pilots and a hundred forty-five P-51's. These planes were taken from the Air National Guard.

"Danny," I said, "I thought that all you pilots who came over on the BOXER had lots of P-51 time."

"I didn't," he smiled, "I just told them I did. Remember when you saw me ferry that airplane over here from Japan last week?"

"Yes," I replied."

"Well, that was the first time I ever flew a P-51. One of my buddies showed me how to start it."

Farr and Baader. *1st Lt. Danny Farr "was undoubtedly the most colorful character I knew during my Air Force Career," recalled Col. Howard "Scrappy" Johnson.*

2nd Lt. Ted "Mother" Baader, was the only 2nd Lt. in the unit at the time. "We called him 'Mother' because he did all the chores," Col. Harry "Mo" Moreland recalled. (Moreland)

43

Moreland's Moments

by Col. Harry H. Moreland

The North Koreans traveled at night and hid their vehicles before daybreak. It took a while to catch on to how and where they chose to hide them. Once we found out what they were doing and where they tried to hide their men and material the task of locating them became much easier. They would dig out an area in the side of a hill and drive the vehicle into the hole and then cover it up with branches. We learned to look for tire tracks off the road and follow them to a hidden target. They would drive a tank into the side of a small house, but the tracks would give the hiding place away. Another favorite spot was along a river bank. They would pick a location that had a high bank, then move up next to the river bank and cover the truck. Sometimes they were not so imaginative and would park in an open field under a hay stack. Again, the tracks leading to the vehicle were a dead giveaway.

Captain Harry H. "Mo" Moreland, Commander of the 51st Provisional Squadron and later the 12th Fighter-Bomber Squadron. (Moreland)

No Civilian Targets

On one occasion, I was leading a two-ship flight out of Taegu. Lt. Chappie James was my wingman. This was during that time when the North Koreans were almost at Taegu and we would soon have to evacuate that forward operating base. We were southeast of the base when we got a call from a mosquito pilot (airborne forward controller) that he wanted us to strafe a large number of troops who were going down the road. We proceeded to his location and he directed us to strafe people going down the main road. Before setting up for a strafing pass I decided to buzz the group to get a much closer look before attacking. Looking down during that high speed pass, I saw many women and children in the crowd. There may have been North Korean troops amongst them but I could not bring myself to strafe the crowd and so informed the FAC. We soon departed the area to look for clearly military targets.

Later, while flying up a valley I noticed tire tracks leading up the slope and stopping at a clump of bushes. So we took a close look and could make out a vehicle under each of about 20 large bushes. From that point on we had a heyday--strafing each target until we had most of them burning before we ran out of ammo. A much more rewarding mission than the alternative. Had we attacked the people on the road I would have had guilty feelings the rest of my life.

Panels for Identification

Spud Taylor(later KIA) and I had been on a two-ship napalm close air support mission. A FAC called us and said some of our ground troops were in need of help--then directed us to a location and showed us where our troops were located. [Our forces were well identified with panels made of colored cloth. Later on the North Koreans got wise and used panels to confuse us.]

The FAC then showed us where the enemy fire was coming from and we gave them a warm welcome with our napalm. The FAC said we were right on target and released us to recce the area while returning to K-2.

Fanning the Flames-- with Mustangs!

We were flying at about 1000 feet searching for targets of opportunity when I noticed some tracks in a large, open field leading up to a haystack. Upon a closer look at the haystack we could see that a tank was under it. We were down to .50-caliber ammo which doesn't offer much of a threat to a tank, but we decide to give it a try. So we each made a few strafing passes with no apparent damage.

Before departing I noticed smoke coming from the haystack. Apparently our ammo had started a small fire in the hay itself. So, we decided to help it. We each made low level passes placing our right wing over the tank to fan the flames. Much to our surprise it worked and we soon had a good fire going. We circled the tank and watched it blow up before departing for home plate.

Tank Gunnery Crew Souvenir

This flight occurred early August when the North Koreans had crossed the Naktong River. We received a new tank busting rocket that they wanted us to test. They only had a limited number of them so they asked that only the more experienced pilots use them and to use them on tanks only. Otherwise bring them back home.

I was on a two plane flight searching the valley on the other side of the mountain from K-2. We are only about 5 minutes from our base. There were several valleys to look at and in one of them we came across a T-34 tank that had parked along side of the road. An ideal target for our new weapon. We set up our firing passes to come in from different directions to make it more difficult on the gunners.

I have always found rockets hard to hit what you aimed at and this was no exception. We both made several passes and on my last pass I launched my last two rockets and at same time received several hits from the tank just as my rockets found their target. They were a success with the tank exploding.

The tank gunnery crew was not all that bad either. I had one bullet hole in the front part of the canopy and one just behind my head. I knew my plane had been hit so decided to return home and land. After the debriefing my crew chief said he would like to show me something. He showed me a bullet hole that had entered the underside or the airplane. En route it had clipped 5 strands from a 7 strand cable to my elevator. It also creased the coolant radiator, went thru the oxygen tank and exploded as it exited the fuselage. I kept that cable for years to remind me how lucky I was. A little closer it would have broken the cable, no elevator control, punctured the coolant tank, no power, exploded in the oxygen tank--no airplane.

How lucky can you get!

Capt. Frank Buzze

A Lucky Strike, Indeed

We had been at K-2 for a short period of time and were flying some old F-51s that had been in moth balls. This was a two ship mission to strike targets of opportunity around Taejon where our troops had recently left in a hurry. I was leading the mission with Frank Buzze on my wing. It was a routine flight to the target area. When we arrived over Taejon there was a mosquito pilot flying an AT-6 over the area. He asked us to attack some buildings at the edge of town. Buzze and I proceeded to strafe the buildings from different angles to reduce our vulnerability.

After a couple of passes one of the building blew up as I was firing at it. When I pulled up from the pass I noticed that I was losing coolant fluid from my engine. I immediately called Buzze and told him of my situation and was heading for home plate. There was a mountain range between us and K-2 so I climbed to about 8000 feet altitude to clear the mountains. I put the mixture control to full rich so the engine would run cooler. The engine began to overheat and I gradually started losing power and altitude. We did not know just how far the enemy had gotten, but I wanted to go as far as I could to get back near our field. The plane kept sinking as I was almost in a glide.

At about 1000 feet Buzze called and told me that I should bailout. I believed that it was too low to go over the side of the plane and felt my best chance was to go as far as I could and belly in. I spotted the Naktong river in front of us and noticed a large sand shoreline on the far side. So I decided to set it down there. The powers to be decided otherwise and I ran out of speed and altitude in the middle of the river .

Before touching down I remembered the pilots manual. In big bold print it said, do not ditch this airplane. Then it said if you have to, drop a wing into the water just before touchdown. It was contrary to everything I wanted to do, but I did it and placed my left arm over the gun sight to ease the possible blow and made sure the seat harness was tight. This caused the plane to veer sharply and hit the water almost sideways. A rough ride, but all in one piece.

I really don't remember how I got to the sand bar but it didn't take long.

Buzze was flying overhead and I waved to him to let him know that I was okay. A short time later men dressed in white frocks started coming from everywhere. There were several hundred of them. They surrounded me but kept about 15 yards away. As I walked toward them the circle would move. Apparently they didn't know if I was friend or foe and I wasn't exactly sure about them, either. I am not a smoker, but did carry a pack of cigarettes in my flying suit for just such a situation.

I removed the pack of Lucky Strikes and held it over my head. The circle immediately collapsed and I was mobbed.

Buzze thought they were attacking me and had taken the safety off his gun switch ready to let them have it. I waved to him and he saw that I was okay.

I passed the cigarettes around and waited for them to light up. They just stood there holding the cigarette in their hands and smiling. I couldn't figure why they didn't light up.

Then it dawned upon me. They were waiting for me, so I took one of the cigarettes from the nearest person, lit it and passed it back. At that point they all lit theirs took a couple of puffs and passed it around. After the smoke they all formed a long line and came by me gently touching me and saying aregotto--"thank you."

Into The Fray...

First Combat Mission

Taejon, South Korea

By Lt. Col. Duane E. 'Bud' Biteman

On 16 July, 1950, while our " Dallas Squadron " crews were flying combat missions out of Taegu airstrip with nine remaining "South Korean" Mustangs, the 40th Fighter Squadron from Johnson Field, Japan's 35th Fighter Group, was being re-equipped with other hurriedly refurbished F-51s, brought out of storage. They were promptly deployed to Korea at the old Japanese airstrip at Pohang, directly east of Taegu on the shores of the Sea of Japan. With the 40th's arrival, FEAF then had two under-strength USAF F-51 Mustang squadrons based on Korean soil.

Initially the 40th had its hands full trying to slow the advance of the North Koreans racing down the coastal highway on the eastern side of the Korean peninsula, while we at Taegu directed our primary efforts against the fast-moving enemy thrusts on the central and western side of the penninsula.

By the 19th of July my Squadron Intelligence operation was organized well enough that I could finally consider doing some flying. The telephone hook-up with 5th Air Force Advance headquarters in Taegu city was working, most of the time, enabling us to relay strike results and receive word on which areas were most in need of air support. Sergeant Thornton knew what to look for during pilot's post-mission interrogations, and how to plot heavy flak areas on our makeshift situation maps. It was time for me to "get my feet wet"--to start flying some combat missions.

I asked our CO, Capt. "Mo" Moreland to put me on the mission schedule whenever he had an opening; he wasted no time in setting me up for early the next morning—20 July, 1950. It had been over six months since I had last flown the F-51 Mustang, an airplane that requires a pilot's undivided attention even under the best of cir-

1st Lt. Duane "Bud" Biteman, at Clark Field, Philippines.

cumstances. With the change back to the "tail-dragger" (tail wheel) configuration, following the ease and good visibility of the F-80 Jet's nose wheel set-up, plus the challenge of Taegu's dusty, bumpy dirt strip and the Mustang's grossly changed handling characteristics with a full fuel and bomb load—I was somewhat apprehensive about my first "refresher" flight.

My thoughts and concerns with just getting the old bird up and down safely, were such that I didn't have time to think about the fact that I was going into a combat area where people on the ground would be trying their damndest to shoot me down!

The morning of the 20th dawned warm and clear, but 'way high we could see a layer of thin clouds forming, indicating the approach of the outer fringes of Typhoon "Gloria," which had passed the southern Philippine Islands on the previous day and was now headed for Japan. Our weather was forecast to remain reasonably clear for at least one more day.

On my first combat flight I was scheduled to fly as wingman for Captain Howard "Scrappy" Johnson, who had by then completed two or three missions into the Suwon-Taejon area during the past couple of days. We were limited to use of two-ships—flight leader and wingman—rather than the standard four-ship formation simply because we didn't have enough airplanes to

concentrate four at a time onto any one target area. On the other hand, two planes were minimum for mutual protection and area location, in case one should be knocked down.

With due respect for the heavy load I was carrying, and the numerous soft, sandy spots in our taxi trail, I proceeded with extra caution to the end of the dirt strip behind Scrappy's airplane. The great cloud of thick dust raised by his propeller made it necessary for me to fully close my canopy while taxiing, and to place my carburetor air filters in the "filter" position to keep at least part of the dust out of the vital internal parts of the engine. Unfortunately, this filtering reduces the volume of air to the coolant radiator and usually causes the engine temperature to rise above its normal range.

Upon arrival at the end of the runway the armament crews scurried under our wings to pull the safety pins from the rockets and bombs and, only when they had moved clear, did we make our engine run-up checks. My coolant temperature was still climbing toward the red-line on the coolant gage on the instrument panel, but I thought that it might be OK once I built up speed on take-off and had a lot of cooler air passing through the radiator.

I taxied to the upwind side of the strip as far as I could, hoping to stay out of Scrappy's dust and, as he accelerated to the point where I could see his tail rise, I added full power to start my take-off roll. Because of the billowing cloud of dust ahead, I had to leave my filters 'in', still reducing the amount of cooling air reaching the radiator.

With one eye on the coolant needle and the other looking ahead for chuckholes in the runway, I lumbered down the runway with my heavily loaded bird. After a seeming eternity of rough bouncing, fearful that the shaking would dislodge the 500-pound bombs under my wings, I was finally able to raise the tail and, with heavy back-pressure on the control stick, managed to force it, semi-stalled, into the air. I immediately retracted my landing gear and moved the air filter switch to the "unfiltered" position. But the unfiltered cooling air came too late;

Dust swirls at K-2, Taegu, South Korea in July 1950 as F-51's being flown by USAF pilots take off on yet another combat mission. (Biteman)

the steam was streaming out the right side of the nose, and I knew that I had "popped my coolant." The automatic pressure relief valve had opened from the excess heat of the over-heated engine coolant, and unknown quantities of the vital fluid had steamed out into the atmosphere. Even though I leveled off and reduced power immediately, the steam continued to pour out for several minutes.

My possible alternatives were quickly considered and discarded. But I could not dawdle too long, for my coolant temperature was still hovering on the redline, and I had no idea how long the engine would keep running with its minimum coolant level.

I could look for an uninhabited area somewhere in the vicinity, and jettison my bombs, hoping they wouldn't go off and hit someone. But I wasn't familiar with the locale, and didn't know where to find such a remote area—if there was one. I couldn't jettison my rockets, because the only way to get rid of them was to fire them off. With my luck, the prop would stop just about the time I decided to jettison my bombs—and I'd have to bail out. I decided to take my chances with a heavy-weight landing on Taegu's bumpy dirt strip rather than risk continuing to fly without sufficient coolant, where the hot-running liquid-cooled engine could (and probably would) heat up to the point of stopping the engine, and I'd hate to have that happen on my first mission over enemy territory.

Johnson was informed by radio of my predicament, and my decision to return to Base; he elected to circle the field, waiting,

while I went back in to have the tank topped off with additional coolant fluid. I made a wide, sweeping turn to the left, so as to set up for a very long, flat approach for landing.

Landing the F-51 Mustang with an almost-full fuselage fuel tank is, by itself, a tricky maneuver—even on a long, paved runway, because the rearward center of gravity often causes the need for forward stick pressure to keep the tail from dropping out faster than the nose—apprehensively referred as "the tail tucking under." But with full ammunition, plus armed rockets and bombs, as well, it would indeed have to be an extremely gentle landing or the live bombs could be shaken loose and it could become a really HARD touchdown!

Setting my final turn a good five miles out, I lowered landing gear and flaps, then coordinated my pitch angle and engine power to ease the nose down for a long, flat final approach. With airspeed stabilized at 125 mph, the controls felt extremely sensitive, but they continued to work in their proper directions: 'stick back, the nose came up, stick forward, the nose went down.' At 115-120 I was over the Mustang's normal approach speed, but I knew I'd need the extra speed to keep control of the heavy load through flare-out and touchdown. I'd worry about slowing down once I had it on the ground.

I skimmed the tops of trees a mile from the end of the dirt runway and held my gradual, controlled descent constant until just before touching down, when I eased the stick back and chopped the throttle for

a gentle, tail high, "wheel" landing. As I slowed on the ground, I had to push the stick forward to keep the heavy tail from banging down onto the ground too hard.

Then, with heavy braking, while holding the stick hard back, the Mustang slowed to a stop with no further problems. Our Line-Chief had been watching 'his' airplane like a mother hen from the time I had started the take-off roll, and knew exactly what I'd need when I came back in. He had picked up two five gallon cans of coolant and met me with the jeep as I turned off the runway. I shut off the engine and within five minutes he had me topped off and ready to go again.

Since the winds were calm, I restarted the engine and swung the tail around, making my second take-off in the opposite direction from which I had just landed. The coolant temperature remained slightly above normal for a few minutes, until after I had retracted my air filters; it then settled back into the "green" range and I felt better. After another five minutes I was sliding into position on Scrappy's left wing, heading west over the mountains toward the battle front near the city of Taejon.

Climbing leisurely on course toward the west, we crossed the Naktong River at two thousand feet. There was no need yet to climb very high, since we were still over friendly territory; we could have a better view from lower altitudes, of our primary navigation device: the railroad winding thru the low hills. Upon approaching Taejon, we made radio contact with a T-6 "Mosquito" spotter plane who was just returning to Taegu for fuel. When asked where we'd find the enemy, he just told us to take anything on the road north out of Taejon; it was all enemy. Swinging north to trace the road out of that city, we were over a heavy pall of smoke from the burning buildings. We could see flashes from the muzzle blast of tanks firing in both directions; the battle was raging in the streets of Taejon. Three miles north of the city we could see a trail of dust heading south on the road, then another and another; three Russian-made North Korean T-34 tanks were racing to join the battle. We climbed to 8000 feet and headed slightly east of the road to position ourselves into the bright morning sun for our bombing attack. Scrappy called to remind me to "arm" my bombs and rockets, and I reached down to the console panel by my knee, lifted the switch guards and moved both the bomb and rocket switches to the "armed" positions. That transferred control of the bomb release to the switches on the control stick; the red button at the top of the stick would release the bombs, and the button on the left of the stick would fire the rockets. The trigger on the front of the handgrip would fire the six machine guns simultaneously.

For "bombsights" our war-weary '51s had a very simple, but effective system—a series of one-inch red stripes painted on the leading edge of each wing, near the fuselage, radiating out at different angles from the pilot's line of sight. Another was painted on the top center of the nose cowling, extending from the windscreen to the prop spinner. In use, the pilot would simply fly off to one side far enough to keep his target in view along the side of the nose, then, as the target passed under the red wing stripe for the altitude he was flying, he would roll over into a steep 60 or 70 degree dive, and line the target up with the nose stripe. Finally, when approaching 4000 feet in the high-speed dive, it was necessary only to check that the needle and ball instrument was "centered", to be certain there was no skid or slipping of the aircraft, then press the bomb release button as the target passed

Captain Howard "Scrappy" Johnson

out of sight under the nose. As soon as the bombs were released, usually at about 2000 feet, a very sharp pull-up was necessary to keep from flying through the bomb's blast.

Johnson adjusted his heading slightly, then peeled off, rolling into a near vertical dive from 8000 feet, aiming for the first tank in the line and, after another couple of seconds, I rolled over into my dive bombing run. I fired a few short bursts of machine gun fire as I started down, checking to "clear" my guns, and also hoping to keep enemy gunners' heads down, to discourage them from shooting back as we made our attack. We both had close 'near misses' on the first and second tanks, hitting within 40 to 60 feet of each. But after the dust and debris had settled, the tanks were still moving. Russian T-34 tanks usually needed a direct hit with a 500-pound bomb to knock them out of action.

Dropping down onto the deck, we swung around to come at them from the side with our rockets. Again Scrappy aimed at the lead tank and I opened up on the second. We salvoed our six 5-inch HVAR rockets from about three hundred yards, and both got good hits against the tracks and wheels. Both tanks were badly damaged, but the crews quickly opened their hatches and started firing at us with their machine guns.

Discretion being the better part of valor, we then flew on north looking for other targets; we knew we couldn't finish off the tanks with just our machine guns, and the chances of knocking out the crews inside the tanks' steel armor plating were too slim for the risks involved; maybe we could catch them by surprise on our way back. We circled wide and came back down onto the road at about 200 feet, following it north, with Johnson on the west side of the road and me on the east.

Just south of Suwon we found a pair of south-bound trucks loaded with enemy troops. Scrappy blew the first one in the engine, on our initial pass, but we had come upon them so suddenly that I didn't have time to properly line up to take aim for a good shot. We swung around for another pass from the side, as the enemy troops were taking cover in the ditches and rice paddies alongside the road. I blasted the second truck with machine gun fire, while Scrappy spaced himself for a pass lengthwise with the road, strafing the ditches. The troops were all firing at us with their rifles, but their aim was off, and neither of our planes was hit. We made a third pass, strafing the ditches on both sides of the burning trucks, then continued north toward the airfield at Suwon. There was nothing moving there, and all we could see was the smoldering hulks of our two C-54s which had been damaged on the ground a few days before. Someone had finished the job with a good fire.

We retraced our route back toward Taejon, letting loose a short burst at a couple of soldiers standing near the burned trucks, then continued on to where we had attacked the tanks. We were starting to run low on ammunition and couldn't waste it on one or two stray soldiers. Two of the tanks were still where we'd left them, but the third was gone, hidden in the pall of heavy smoke which hung over the city of Taejon. We made one pass to look at a couple of troops standing by the side of the first tank, but pulled up sharply to get out of range of the rifle

On 31 July 1950, Lt. Ken Barber was told to fly an F-51 from Japan to Korea. He took off about 1500 enroute to Ashiya. "What a flight! I felt like a rookie on my first solo ride, and didn't know a thing about that F-51. The flight came as a surprise. Luckily, the flight went OK, and after a couple of hours I started to get the feel back." (Barber)

By Thursday, 20 July, Lt. Ken Barber's new unit, the 67th Squadron was "starting to draw equipment. Everything's in an uproar, and it seems that everybody wants in on the show." Sergeant Blough even gave up his chance to take the West Point exams. "Just about all the men are going," Barber noted.

A week later, on 27 July, Barber noted "everything's in shape to go—equipment all drawn." His friend, Jim Barnett, sold

Barber a "nice pair of boots right off his feet when he heard I was leaving and couldn't get a pair of paratroop boots to fit. Mighty nice of him."

"Major Dow should be an ideal combat leader. He is calm and unexcitable, plays no favorites, holds no grudges, doesn't constantly look over his subordinates' shoulders but lets them do their jobs. He goes to bat for his men at all times, and yet is detached enough so that losses wouldn't make him crack up. His only apparent faults are

lack of force and perhaps inability to express himself forcefully. He is a discerning person who sees and thinks more than he talks."

"Today we leave," Barber noted on 29 July 1950. "Sure do hate to leave Cassie, but there are things to be done and places to be seen." When the order came to board the cargo plane that would take them to Japan, "we piled on, after that last long kiss which will have to last for a long time."

and machine gun fire which we knew would be coming up at us from the town. As we rejoined the road on the east side, we could see our Army troops fighting a holding action, while a long line of our trucks and jeeps retreated toward the east.

We climbed back up to 8000 feet, where the air was cooler and more clear, and followed the railroad east to the Naktong River, our checkpoint for home base at Taegu. After crossing the river, we nosed down for a sweeping turn, in close formation, into a low, on-the-deck initial approach. Upon reaching the runway at about 350 mph, Scrappy pulled up into a steep chandelle as

he chopped his power for landing. Two seconds later I pulled up to take spacing behind him on downwind leg. With speed down, after the steep pull-up, we dropped our gear and turned onto a tight base leg, and were still turning slightly on final as we touched down onto the dusty runway.

Our mission on July 20th had been a good and successful one, despite my false start with the coolant problem. Neither Scrappy nor I had picked up a hole, and we could take credit for two seriously damaged tanks and two destroyed trucks. And, more importantly, for me, my nervousness about getting back into combat was under

control. I was tense with anxiety, but stimulated by the success of the mission, and ready for more.

That afternoon, as Harry Moreland was returning from a bombing and strafing mission in the same area, he was forced to belly-land in a dry river bed when his engine froze up as a result of a bullet hole in his coolant line. He wasn't hurt, but his plane was demolished. That brought us down to a total of eight flyable Mustangs in the squadron-- not much of a fleet to fight a war.

A Tale of Taegu

Anonymous parody included in early 18th Fighter-Bomber Group unit history. Provided by Col. Stanley Chatfield.

And in the year of the reign of the Emperor Harry, it came to pass that the chosen people found themselves in the Valley of Taegu. Came there people from a place called Taejon and spoke they thus to the newcomers...

Behold, the enemy cometh upon us even as they have in the North and felleth us with bullets, and smiteth us with divers munitions, and such of us he catcheth, he visiteth passing great atrocities upon. Therefore, heed ye, and listen for the sound of the panic button, and prepare ye to flee to the place which is called Pusan, for even though the waters open not, then shall ye hitchhike with the Navy. And so speaking, they broke such weapons as proved unserviceable and prepared themselves to quit the valley.

But the newcomers made as if they heard them not, and spake of great deeds of arms and of many of the enemy to be slain, though in secret their knees trembled and they were sore afraid. In the fullness of time, the radio spake of the approach of the enemy, and a voice spake of the approach of the glorious People's Army to liberate the Fatherland, and thus did it proclaim to all the land: The time cometh, Oh Imperialist Oppressors of the People."

So, the newcomers spake each unto the other, saying: "Wherefore this business of Imperialists, thou old oppressor, thou?"

And his neighbor spake, "Verily, I understand not this tale of Imperialism, for I desire only to return to Truman's Island, and to retire, wherefore I came into the Service."

Then the enemy drew yet closer, and the thunder of their wrath was heard in the hills, and many there were who climbed aboard chariots of the air and left the valley.

Then came unto the valley one who was called the "C.O." and he spake thusly.

"Verily I say unto ye, we shall stay here while yet the iron birds fly, and we shall heap napalm and leaden hail upon the heads of the enemy, and their arms shall not prevail against us. Wherefore, heed ye, and labor ye mightily upon the line, for know ye that I shall chew upon the posterior of each of the lowliest Lieutenant each day, else the enemy prevail upon us."

Then came he of the corncob pipe and iron bird named for a peninsula in the faraway southern islands [General MacArthur's plane was named "Bataan."], and strode out and thus did he speak to the multitude.

"Be ye of good cheer, for I shall stay." Then he returned forthwith to the nine and fortieth state, which is called "Nippon" whereof he is Governor.

Then, in due seriousness, the multitudes labored upon the line, loaded they aircraft, and shouted they over the radio and hauled they fuel, for the number of the enemy was as the leaves of the trees, and the hour of reckoning approached.

Wherefore, went he who was called C.O. unto the tent of him who was called Sergeant, and spoke thusly:

"Wherefore liest thou upon thy posterior in thy sack when even now the faithful labor upon the line? Laggards there are in thy section, players of cards, writers of letters to their wives, shooters of craps, yea, even drinkers of Budweiser there are. Wherefore laborest thou not upon the line and do likewise, and labor mightily, lest I chew again upon thy posterior until it becometh even as the sieve, which holdest not water."

So speaking, he who was called the C.O. departed in the fullness of his wrath, and he who was called Armament arose, and cursed, and broke wind, and scratched himself, and went forth to labor at the line. Then chewed he mightily upon the posteriors of the faithful, saying, "Wherefore labor ye not upon the line when thy brethren work their posteriors off. Wherefore shoot ye craps and drink ye even Budweiser, wherefore the Old Man cheweth again upon my posterior, which is passing tender lately?"

So sayeth he and they labored mightily.

And in the fullness of time the enemy came yet closer, and there was a pillar of fire by night and cloud of smoke by day, and each of the newcomers thought unto himself, "This time they snow us not, as they did when the smoke of locomotives was said to be the enemy, for we can see the flash of the rockets and the smoke of the bombs which even lately we have loaded."

"Verily, the enemy is upon us, and if we are taken we shall be castrated."

So, they thought, but they spake mightly of deeds of valor and of so many of the enemy are slain, spake each unto the other. Then each in his turn went into his tent and checked with loving care his carbine, and his ammunition therefore, and his pack with three days of C-rations, and his extra socks, and his map to Pusan.

And there were those among them who returned to their tents to change their drawers, for the thunder in the hills was passing close.

And in the fullness of their need for tools, the chosen ones went until him who was called XO, and called upon him, and he spake, saying, "Verily, brethren, do I know thy wants, but some son of a (gun) hath other xxxxated the Class 17 stock lists or brought them not, wherefore, when I call on FEAFCO without the stock number they send me divers strange implements, and he shewed the cowling wrenches for the V-12, and harmonization tools for the A-17, and offered them WAC shoes, and sent them on their way.

Even in greater numbers came the riders of great iron birds and left them to be reloaded while they strode to the tent of him who was called Intelligence, and spake to him of great deeds of arms and of weeping and wailing in the camp of the enemy. Wherefore, he who was called Intelligence caused it all to be written down, and caused it to be classified secret, and turned the crank and shouted unto the direct line to JOC, the telephone availed not.

Then he who was called Operations strode to the line and spake thusly, "Wherefore foul ye up? Wherefore load ye not more aircraft?"

In the fullness of his wrath, the Old Man shall descend upon me and I shall be cast into outer darkness. Even Generals are come to the line in chariots of blue and black to ask me questions. Wherefore can I answer these questions if ye load not aircraft? Therefore, labor ye well, else I turn ye in.

Wherefore the chosen ones went forth again and labored mightily upon the iron birds, saying each unto the other, "Verily, this man speaketh not with a forked tongue, for else we labor well, we shall be smitten by the enemy. And they called upon him who was called Ordnance, he of the foul cigar and purple cap, for more rockets of silver, and fat bombs, and shining ammunition. And he was called Ordnance, called upon FEAFCOM, saying, "Wherefore keepest thou me here if thou sendest not munitions?"

And on the days when there was no inventory, the chosen ones went forth to the PX, and saw there many of these who are called beetle crushers, and spake untu them saying, "Wherefore lengthenest thou our PX line, and what goeth with the war?"

And the warriors spake unto them, telling of the iron birds and of mighty feats of arms, and spake of seventy, yea even of one hundred and seventy groups, and of unification and divers other subjects. Wherefore the chosen ones spake each unto the other, saying, "Verily these people snow us not, for it is passing tough up on the line."

And each went in his turn unto his tent, and anointed his carbine with oil, and checked his escape kit.

And in the fullness of time it came to pass that three striken iron birds were made ready to fly again. And he who was called Base Operations spake unto him who was called Operations, saying, "Wherefore fly we not together with the A-3 these aircraft? Wherefore get we not in a few sorties ourselves?"

And ere they left the valley, there came unto the Operations Tent three newcomers whose loins were girden with parachutes and other personal equipment spake thusly, "Wherefore take these people our aircraft? Whosoever do they think themselves to be? Verily, I shall call upon Base Operations Officer was before him who answered the telephone, and he spake with a forked tongue, telling them that the radio availed him not."

So, the operation was carried forth, and great was the weeping and wailing in the camp of the enemy, for many of their war chariots ran not, and many were the war stories therefrom.

And many times there came unto the valley iron birds whose surfaces shown even as silver in the sunlight, and whose weapons were kept like watches. And among their riders, there were flight leaders who spake hopefully of promotions to bloody corporal, for these men used this word in their speech where ordinary men use commas. And, they spake to the chosen ones which were passing dirty bottles of Australian whisky they brought, and great was the rejoicing therefore. And great was the anguish in the camp of the enemy, for as pilots these men were passing hot, even as their whiskey.

Even yet on some days the face of the sun was hidden, and the hosts of the beetle crushers fought by themselves. And on those days, the chosen ones went unto the weather man, and spake, saying, "What of the weather, oh learned ones? If the face of the sun remaineth hiddeneth, then our aircraft shall fly not, and the enemy shall overcome us."

And the weather men answered not, but went unto their tents—and packed.

And fire and brimstone and napalm was heaped upon the enemy, and the hail of rockets and cal. 50s fell upon his head, and such of the enemy as remained, returned to the North. And the voice at the radio was stilled, and spake no more of Imperialists, and of liberation of the glorious People's Army. And they who were called beetle crushers lengthened not the PX, for they too had gone North.

And new aircraft came to the valley, and the chosen ones watched their ascensions and spake to the new ones of mighty deeds of arms and of the days when the thunder of the enemy was even greater than the thunder of the new aircraft.

Thus, in the fullness of time, peace came to the valley and he who was called C.O. sent his staff forth on their appointed rounds, and caused them to be shown the places in which great deeds had been done, and told them war stories, whereof they listened with interest and with expressions of astonishment, as was fitting.

And there were those among them who returned to Nippon and embraced their wives, and beat upon the posteriors of their children. And there were those among their wives who spake to them saying, "Wherefore comest thou not home as often as thy neighbor, who had seventeen R & R's during this Police Action. Verily, thou lovest me not."

And there came unto the valley squadron commanders, who checked their VD reports, beating their breasts and saying, "Woe is me, for the character guidance program availeth not. And they caused their men to place hats upon their heads, and to salute as it fitting and proper. And the chosen ones spake each unto the other, saying "Verily, this is Chicken. This place groweth more stateside each day."

And they placed hats upon their heads, and went forth to salute, as is fitting and proper. And there was building of organization charts and talk of ground safety and of I&E programs and much greasing of vehicles there was also. And inspectors also there came, each with the waxing and waning of the moon, for the thought of their tax exemptions was heavy upon them, and he who was called the C.O. rejoiced to see them, for then he knew that peace had at last come to the Valley.

August 1950
Facing Another "Dunkirk"

51ˢᵗ Provisional Becomes 12ᵗʰ Squadron

Due to the "untenable tactical situation and insufficient parking space it was decided to operate the 67ᵗʰ Squadron from Ashiya and the 51ˢᵗ Provisional Squadron from K-2. Immediate steps were taken to have the 51ˢᵗ redesignated the 12ᵗʰ Fighter-Bomber Squadron and this was effected on 1 August 1950 with Lt. Col. (then Major) Robert Dow commanding." By early August, ground forces were indicating that "possibly the Naktong River defense perimeter could not be held in the vicinity of Taegu."

Combat Squadron's "Typical" Day

August 5, 1950 was a very busy day for the 67ᵗʰ Squadron. It would also become for the U.S. Air Force an historic date. The day began well before the first flight lifted off at 0735. Before that rainy summer day

Monthly Summary

After nearly five weeks of fighting, at the beginning of August 1950, the North Koreans pressed their offensive ever-deeper into South Korea, now advancing on the UN's perimeter around Pusan from three directions: toward Masan from the west, toward Taegu from the northwest, and toward Pohang from the north. They established bridgeheads over the Naktong River, along which UN forces held a defensive line. However, UN ground forces launched their first ground offensive of the war, advancing from Masan westward toward Chinju to stabilize the southwestern end of the Pusan perimeter.

The tactical situation in Southeastern Korea was approaching desperate. The Communists were tightening their hold on South Korea and threatening a new "Dunkirk" for UN forces that were being increasingly forced into a salient in the lower southeast portion of the peninsula. The approach of enemy troops forced USAF units to evacuate Taegu and Pohang, where they had only recently arrived.

By early August 1950, "the momentum of the North Korean's three-pronged drive into the south had proved immensely successful," Lt. Col. Duane Biteman, USAF (Ret)

explained. "They had completed their end-around on the west and south coasts, their east coast drive had progressed far enough to force evacuation of USAF fighter squadrons from Pohang air base, and their central thrust was threatening to cross the Naktong River to knock on our last bastion of defense--our home base at Taegu. Their objective, to surround Taegu, then march on Pusan and have control of the entire peninsula, seemed just a few days short of accomplishment. We were in deep trouble!"

Even as the immediate tactical picture looked bleak, indeed, with UN forces barely hanging on, UN planners were hard at work on an entirely new and daring military operation that, if successful, would reverse the tide of the war to this point.

During August, General MacArthur and his staff drafted plans for the invasion of Inchon, near Seoul, which would take place in September. In support of the planned UN offensive, Far East Air Forces devoted most air resources to the interdiction campaign. By mid-August, each North Korean division was receiving less than a mere trickle of the food, fuel, and ammunition needed to maintain enemy positions against a UN attack. To coordinate the growing air-

lift between Japan and Korea and to prepare for the coming invasion, Far East Air Forces organized a provisional Combat Cargo Command. General Stratemeyer failed to persuade MacArthur to give Far East Air Forces sole responsibility for all air raids over North Korea.

The USAF moved two additional B-29 groups from the United States to the Far East, making a total of five in the theater. During August, the Superfortresses bombed marshalling yards, industrial targets, and port facilities in North Korea, plus marshalling yards in Seoul, and bridges in both North and South Korea, especially in the Seoul area. They also conducted one major carpet-bombing raid near the front.

The Fifth Air Force continued to raid enemy lines of communication, airfields, and close air support targets in South Korea. Fifth Air Force B-26s and F-82s conducted night raids south of the 38th parallel. The H-5 helicopters based at Taegu evacuated 124 casualties from the battlefields of South Korea.

Adapted from U.S. Air Force Historical Research Agency. January 2002. The U.S. Air Force's First War: Korea 1950-1953 Significant Events.

On 1 August, Colonel "Ike" Wintermute flew to K-2 (Taegu) "to see what the score is." The squadron sat around all day, and he returned with no information as to whether we'll move to K-2 or not. All of us are mighty eager to get into combat. Must be eagerness born of ignorance, but we're eager anyway."

The first combat mission of 24 planes from the 67th FBS "went out" on Wednesday, 2 August. All except for Lt. Kenneth Barber. His plane was out of commission. "Doggone it, I never have any luck! It sure would have been nice to make the first mission."

Barber got in his first mission on Thursday, 3 August. He escorted B-29s to Hamhung, "up near the 40th Parallel on the east coast of Korea. I was flying off Ed Hoagland's wing while Ray Carter was on the other side. Capt. Mullins led the first flight. I was flying on the land side most of

Lt. Col. Ira "Ike" Wintermute
Commander, 18th Fighter-Bomber Group

the time and really had my neck on a swivel, craning to all sides to try to spot any enemy aircraft first. We met the B-29's not far from our destination, and zigzagged over them until we were over the target area. Little black puffs of smoke from flak covered the sky under the B-29's but they were way above it. After they dropped their load, we

dove down and strafed a nearby Korean airfield. Ed and I strafed two ships in a field which I believe were just camouflage (dummy a/c), because they looked so messy. Capt. Mullins' flight passed over the field and ran into a lot of flak.

Ausman later asked "Were they really shooting flak?"

Mullins said "Damn right, didn't you see that solid line of white puffs behind you?"

"Oh, hell," replied Ausman, " I just thought that was a cloud bank."

The first mission "took quite some of the pleasure or anticipation of war away. Not only was my tail mighty sore from sitting on that dingy for 4 hours and 35 minutes, but also the idea of living to a ripe old age begins to appeal to one," Barber recorded.

Barber, Lt. Col. Kenneth. Korean War Diary Number One (unpublished), 5 August 1950.

concluded with the last mission touching down at the Taegu strip shortly after 10:00 p.m. that evening, the squadron had completed ten separate missions of 35 sorties. It had dropped 24 napalm bombs, 26 500-pound general-purpose bombs, and 72 rockets at the enemy. Four towns were reported destroyed, 20 buildings damaged, 12 vehicles destroyed and an equal number damaged, 3 field pieces destroyed, 10 railroad cuts inflicted, one bridge and two tanks knocked out, and 250 dead North Koreans.

The 67th did not come away unscathed. It lost two aircraft—and their pilots.

Elsewhere Able was wheels up at 0735 for a three-hour mission over and around Sachon. The weather was rainy with broken clouds at 2,500 – 3,500 feet. When the four F-51's arrived over the target at 0830, they checked in with the first of two different controllers—Mellow Mosquito Fox and Jig—that would direct and coordinate their attacks. Elsewhere Able bombed the Sachon airfield barracks with seven napalm canisters, and then strafed the airfield. When it finally departed an hour later, six buildings and the control tower

"were ablaze."

Elsewhere Bravo lifted off at 0746 and checked in with Mosquito Jig, which diverted the four F-51's to Poksong-dong, possibly because of the weather that included "rainstorms from Taegu to Pusan." Once over the target area, they "dumped eight napalm bombs on the town." All the bombs hit their targets and "started large fires." The Mustang quartet then "strafed the rest of the village area." Outside the town, they strafed five vehicles and tanks "in a ravine approximately one mile south and east of Poksong-dong." A two-story schoolhouse or warehouse was attacked with rockets. A nearby culvert in the road between Poksong-dong and the river was attacked with rockets because the pilots suspected that a "vehicle and possibly troops were hidden in the culvert." They reported seeing "moderate AA" concentrations in Poksong-dong and being fired on with light weapons but with heavy intensity. Fortunately, the fire was "inaccurate." They then returned to base by 0820, having been over the target for 75 minutes.

Elsewhere Charlie, a flight of two F-51's took off at 1100. It was not a successful

mission. Lt. Cree "aborted after take off." The single Mustang then continued the mission. The target area was supposed to include the "coastal area S.W. of Masan to Kogum-do." However, the pilot was unable to establish radio contact with a controller. The overcast conditions including a 2,000 foot ceiling complicated the search and the pilot reported, "no targets found." Returning to base about 1145, the pilot "dumped 2 napalms in bay west of Ashiya."

Elsewhere Dog took off at 1149, the three F-51's carrying bombs and rockets. Once it checked in with Mosquito Item, the three Mustangs were directed to a concentration of troops about one mile southeast of Hamchang. The area was protected by numerous 20-mm flak positions "on hill in village." The AA was both light and medium caliber and the fire was "heavy and accurate." The three aircraft first "attacked ground troops with bombs scoring four direct hits in troops." Then on a second pass they "used rockets on trucks, half tracks and hillside village," in the process destroying four armored vehicles. During this attack "Major Sebille in aircraft number 394, sustained flak damage and made a dive on

K-2 Operations

Napalm tanks are prepared for combat missions at K-2 in August 1950. One of the tanks offers "warm regards." (Myers)

halftrack, destroying target, aircraft and self." A handwritten addition in the National Archives record was penciled in after "self," adding "and numerous enemy troops." After strafing troops in the area, and a horse drawn artillery piece on the road from Naksong-dong, the remaining F-51's returned to base. Major Sebille had been the Commanding Officer of the 67th FBS. A year later he was awarded the Congressional Medal of Honor, one of only two awarded to Air Force personnel during the entire Korean War.

The flight record for **Elsewhere Easy** is missing from the National Archives records for this date.

Elsewhere Fox, four F-51's took off at 1225 and checked in with Mosquito Fox in the area of Chunju. The four first strafed Chungam, starting "numerous fires," then dropped six bombs into the village from about 7,000 feet using a 60 degree glide angle that "started fires." On the way back to base they observed "approximately 15 vehicles camouflaged as the flight approached Nomji-ri. Observed at 5,000 feet but not strafed due to shortage of fuel."

Elsewhere Golf took off at 1615 with four F-51s. There were "scattered storms and squalls" throughout the Taegu-Pusan area with the ceiling at 2,000-4,500 feet. Mellow control was "very difficult to contact" because the "channels were cluttered up with chatter." There were "troops and camouflaged equipment all over the general area" west of Waegwan. The AA from light guns was moderate, but "accurate." Finally, the Golf flight was "controlled by Mosquito Mike upon contact after failing to contact Mellow with any satisfaction." Golf

Flight then made "bomb runs" on four villages and a roadway, scoring seven direct hits on houses and a near miss on a secondary road near Poksongdong. During one of the bombing runs, Captain Bob Howell sustained damage to his aircraft "from light enemy ground fire on pull out from bomb run at approximately 1720." Howell's plane crashed into a hillside approximately eight miles west of Taegu. The flight continued its attacks and destroyed a truck and nine armored vehicles with .50-caliber machine gun fire. Lt. Patterson scored "a direct hit on a light gun emplacement with a rocket."

Elsewhere How took off at 1630 with four F-51's. After contacting Mellow, they were "passed to Mosquito Jig" who sent them to Wongyongdong, where they "bombed the town." Direct hits were scored with six 500-pound bombs, with two near misses with napalm on trucks and carts "camouflaged in a river bed near Wonyongdong."

Elsewhere Item lifted off at 1715 with three F-51's headed for the Inchon area "to attack reported 300-400 small vessels at sea. No vessels found after complete search

Preparing to evacuate Taegu. A scene of chaos. Supplies and equipment piled in disorder. Aircraft loading in the background. The squadron was "bugging out" to Ashiya, Japan on 6-7 August 1950. North Korean forces were about to overrun the advance operating base. (Biteman)

of shore line and sea area. Returned off west coast. Entered Korea at Taechon and proceeded to Taejon area." After the flight arrived over Taejon, it "dropped all bombs in RR marshalling yards." Direct hits were scored on tracks and surrounding houses. Four main lines of track were destroyed for approximately ¼ of a mile, including ten railroad cars. The round house was strafed

and direct hit on it scored with a rocket. After flying east to Waegwan, the flight strafed more railroad cars and a truck, before it "returned to base." During its debrief, the flight reported 300-400 personnel "in river bed between Kunchon and Kaeryong."

Elsewhere Juliett was the last flight of the day for the 67th on August 5th, taking off

at 1930 to fly cover for a search and rescue mission being undertaken by an SA-16. The pick up was not far away, the flight was circling overhead when the SA-16 made the pickup at 1930. The SA-16 was escorted to Wido Island and the flight returned at 2210.

August 5th was over. Ten missions, 35 sorties, four towns destroyed, 250 enemy killed, numerous enemy vehicles and railroad facilities destroyed, at a cost of 24 napalm bombs, 26 500-pound bombs, 72 aerial rockets—plus two aircraft destroyed and two American pilots killed.

Evacuation to Ashiya

On August 6-7 the 18th Fighter-Bomber Group headquarters and the 12th FBS were evacuated to Ashiya Air Base "where continuous and uninterrupted support of UN forces could be guaranteed. However, the 12th and 67th Squadrons continued staging from K-2 until the entire group moved to K-9 Airstrip on 7 September." [1]

Operations at Ashiya during August "left much to be desired. The mission was accomplished despite numerous handicaps. The shortage of TO&E authorized equipment plagued operations most. Personnel were required to work around-the-clock in many cases in order to accomplish their duties which would have been much easier had proper equipment been available." [2]

The 18th Fighter-Bomber Group at that time was composed of just the 67th Squadron and the 12th Squadron, Sergeant Sandy Colton explained, "and it was attached to the 6002nd Tactical Support Wing which had been newly-organized from personnel resident there and from personnel arriving from the Zone of Interior. Colonel Curtis H. Low was appointed Wing Commander, and members of his staff included: Lieutenant Colonel Donald H. Lynch, Operations Officer; Captain Thomas Shockley, Adjutant; Major Yankhower, Intelligence Officer, and Lieutenant Colonel Carlson, Base Maintenance Officer."

The 18th F-B Group operated from Ashiya Air Base, over 100 miles from Pusan, South Korea. "Fragmentation Orders called for operations from north of the 38th Paral-

Unsuccessful Camouflage. On August 11, 1950, FEAF fighter bombers noticed something unusal on the railroad track at Yongju west of Seoul. North Korean troops had covered the railroad engine (left) detached from its boxcars (right) with branches. The camouflage did not fool either the FEAF photo reconnaisance analysts nor the 18th Fighter-Bomber Wing pilots who quickly revisited the area. (NARA)

lel to Taegu and the Naktong River." Most missions lasted from four to six hours. "Frequently, aircraft would take off from Japan, hit the targets, land at K-2 or K-3 (Pohang), operate from there until darkness fell, and return to Ashiya after the last strike. This imposed a strain on transports, for mechanics, armorers, and at times, Intelligence personnel, had to be flown to K-2 or K-3 to handle the workload as personnel at the forward bases were present in inadequate quantities."[3]

"The North American F-51 Mustangs received at Ashiya and at K-2 were aircraft that had belonged to National Guard units in the Zone of Interior, as well as aircraft stored at the Far East Materiel Command (FEAM-COM) in Japan. The National Guard aircraft were loaded on the U.S. Navy aircraft carrier USS BOXER with their 25 pilots. These pilots were affectionately dubbed 'The Boxer Boys' by Group pilots," Colton explained.

Combat Operations With F-51's

Combat operations for Mustangs of the Group revolved around "the use of four-ship flights on close support missions." This tactic was "found to be the most effective and the most efficient." Two-ship flights were also used when needed "due to the requirements of the situation."

In general, the two-ship flights operated as a team, "often making simultaneous strafing runs from different directions in order to diffuse enemy fire. Passes were varied as much as weather and terrain permitted, taking advantage of the sun and natural cover to minimize the danger from anti-aircraft and small-arms fire."

Four-ship operations "were much the same" except that "while two of the ships were working over the target the other two ships would remain at a high altitude, affording top cover against air attack and spotting ground-fire sources, artillery and troop positions."

With time, as air operations became "more stabilized" the four-ship flight became the predominant type and "was very

Major "Moon" Mullins and Captain Bill Myers of the Dallas Squadron at Ashiya, Japan on 14 August 1950. (Myers)

"**Taegu is a very dusty place**—at least the airfield is," Lt. Ken Barber noted in his diary. "When I landed I thought I had blown my tail wheel tire the strip was so rough. They are completing a new steel landing strip now, which should improve conditions quite a bit. Harry Dugan is operations officer at Taegu for the next month. Mike David is a radio jeep controller in the front lines for three months [Forward Air Control Team leader]."

On Wednesday, 9 August, after asking the "girlsans" to do his laundry, breakfast and a trip to the library, Lt. Barber dropped in to visit Lt. Don Bolt, the "PIO" [Public Information Officer]. Bolt "wanted my story on the dead stick landing to send to the Stars and Stripes, Atlanta and San Antonio newspapers, plus a picture. Ha!"

On Saturday, 12 August, Barber reported "they abandoned K-3 yesterday. Looks like we need more troops mighty bad. Never seem to see much during the day. Our troops really catch it at night, however. During the recon today, I saw many burned out towns and trucks, but only a few people. War is a funny thing. You don't really see its horrors from the air." Barber could not know what was ahead for him, but he would soon be seeing war's horrors from the ground as well as from the air.

effective on ground support, reconnaissance and other type missions."

Some night intruder and reconnaissance missions—two-ship and four-ship efforts—were attempted by the Mustang pilots whose aircraft were ill equipped for such roles. The attempts "were not too successful." While it was not possible to accurately assess the "harassment value of these flights their destructive value was almost nil. Targets were located without too much difficulty, however the firing of either rockets or machine guns so blinded the pilot that accuracy was next to impossible. Dive-bombing at night in the F-51 did not prove very effective either, since targets were not easily discernible at dive-bombing height and faulty depth perception generally induced early releases resulting in inaccurate drops."[4]

Most armed reconnaissance flights ["recces"] were flown carrying napalm, rockets and .50-caliber rounds. "While adequate napalm targets were often located, nine times out of ten, rockets and/or .50 caliber would have proved as effective on the same target."

Just days into combat operations in the F-51 Mustang the 18th Group was reporting important lessons regarding combat operations in the now venerable aircraft. The "speed of the aircraft was not an essential factor in close support missions but rather an aircraft is ideal which is capable of short-field landings and take-offs, is capable of heavy striking power and is armored to the extent that the pilot and vital parts of the aircraft are protected against small-arms fire." [5]

Some of these "lessons" could be put into practice with changes to mission tactics, but others such as vulnerability to small arms fire would continue to cost the lives of Mustang pilots throughout the Korean War.

Refugees, Or Reds?

The "determining factor" to success in close support missions" is the quality both of the communications facilities and the communications operators. Even when using the best close support aircraft obtainable, no value will result unless coordinated communications, air-to-air and air-to-ground are of the best." [6]

"Close support missions are controlled in the most satisfactory manner by a person on the ground and at the spot where the action is taking place. In addition, this ground controller must be a pilot with sufficient combat experience to enable him to determine the best line of attack and to determine if air support is actually needed. Since it is impossible to have ground controllers at every frontline position, some improved method should be devised that could instantly advise the pilot of the identity of people on the ground."

On numerous close support missions it was found that the airborne controller lacked sufficient information regarding friendly troops. The practice by enemy troops of driving civilian refugees ahead of them created a large degree of confusion both for the controller and for the pilot, in that the pilots were often asked to strafe groups of people that obviously contained women and even children. The decision as to whether these groups of people were actually dangerous seemed to rest with the controller and some controllers would order an attack while others would dismiss them as refugees." [7]

The early system of target locating was not very efficient. A scarcity of maps and lack of a grid system made complete famil-

Colonel Curtis R. LOW
...from NEEDHAM HEIGHTS, MASS....38 YEAR OLD CHARTER 'C.O.' of the 18th.
...IN WWII, LOW COMMANDED the 12th BOMB GROUP in AFRICA.
NOW ASSIGNED to 5th AF HQ, as A-1, LOW will long be REMEMBERED by the MEN of the 18th as a GENTLEMAN, LEADER, and GREAT GUY!
CALM, QUIET-SPOKEN LOW was a FAMILIAR SIGHT AROUND the BASE in his TRADITIONAL JACKET AND FLYING SUIT...!
HOW'S it GOIN' SARGE?

iarity with the terrain an essential factor in locating controller or in pin-pointing targets. Although a grid system was worked out, it necessitated the carrying of a large number of maps which became unwieldy in the small fighter cockpit. Using the names of towns to locate targets was also ineffective since there is a great similarity between the names of Korean towns even within a small area. When the universal grid maps became available most of these problems were solved.

The decision to fire on "civilian refu-

Lt. Kenneth Barber flew his third mission on Sunday, 6 August—from Ashiya to Pusan and "on up to Taegu then over to Kunchon, N.W. of Taegu and across the Bomb Line. An L-5 tried to point out some trucks hidden in a draw, but we never saw them so we dropped our napalm bombs on Poksong-dong and strafed it well. This town is just north of Waegwon Ferry where the enemy is crossing the river. Looks like Taegu won't last much longer."

Group Headquarters was returning from Taegu. "Looks like there are going to evacuate it and move the 12th "Dallas Squadron" over here," Barber noted. "We may all go to some new base as the 18th Fighter Bomber Group."

"Looks like Mullins is our new C.O. Captain Trumbo said they'll probably promote him to Major. Good deal for him," Barber noted.

gees" or not was also made by the Mustang pilots of the 18th Group who were faced with emotionally wrenching "judgment calls"— stop the refugees, many of whom were North Korean infiltrators, or be overrun by the enemy.

"Despite our intensive firepower from dawn to dark every day, we just didn't seem to have enough airplanes or pilots to properly stem the Red tide," Biteman recalled. "As our defensive perimeter continued to shrink around Taegu, we became suddenly aware of the massed exodus of Korean refugees ahead of the battles."

The full impact of the refugee's presence did not strike home for Biteman and his fellow airmen, until the first few days of August, 1950, "when the stream of white-clothed humanity began to collect on the west bank of the Naktong River. Only then, as I sat in the narrow confines of my F-51's cockpit in relative 'comfort', patrolling the river to prevent their crossing, did I begin to feel the weight of the decisions which were suddenly forced upon me—decisions which my years of Air Force training had neglected to prepare me for—and which violently contradicted my Christian upbringing."

"Could I bring myself to fire my machine guns at those refugees in order to keep them from crossing the Naktong River?" Biteman asked himself. He knew that the Red army troops had dressed many of their soldiers as refugees, who then infiltrated behind UN lines to attack from the rear at opportune times. But Biteman also knew "that these thousands upon thousands of old people and young children had been forced from their homes in Seoul, or Suwon, then from Taejon, Kumsan, and all of the villages in between--carrying all that was left of their lifelong possessions. Many were Christians, for Korea had responded to missionary zeal for scores of years. I couldn't know how many could be praying to my Jesus for deliverance—at the exact instant that I was asking the very same Jesus for divine guidance, when the time came, that I might have to pull the trigger—on them!"

Operating From Japan

"During the brief 34 days the Group remained at Ashiya, it had four casualties, listed as killed or missing in action," S/Sgt. William J. "Sandy" Colton recorded. "Many ground loops occurred, either from battle damage or existing weather conditions. Strong crosswinds seemed to prevail over Ashiya's one main runway, which emptied into the Japan Sea at the south end. A town on the north end made landings and take-offs a cautious job. Conditions were crowded, and all personnel worked out of packing cases. Ashiya Base Supply did its utmost to fulfill the needs of the Group and its supporting elements." [8]

The 18th Fighter-Bomber Group then consisted of just two squadrons, one of which was under strength. There was little change in Group operations than in World War II. The 12th Squadron operated under the Call Sign MONOLOGUE, and the 67th Squadron as ELSEWHERE. "The Flights were A, B, C, D, and E. ABLE Flight was usually the first each day. Later, the 12th started at MIKE and went to ZEBRA and the 67th began at ABLE and ended with LOVE," Colton noted.

"The Ground Controller was normally in a jeep, and most often was a rated officer [a pilot], who would call an L-5, most likely with a radio Call Sign of 'Mosquito Wild West' and tell him of a target for fighters. 'Mosquito Wild West' would call the Flight Leader, give him his coordinates, and the flight would go in for the 'kill'."

These early F-51 missions "were reminiscent of an aerial guard duty, with one flight relieving another," Colton noted. When the Group operated from Japan, the procedure would be somewhat as follows: 'ELSEWHERE EASY' Flight (a flight of four aircraft) reported to JOC with a Call Sign of "Mellow" at 1300 hours. JOC would, in turn, tell the flight to report to 'Mosquito Wild west' in Area #xxx, give the coordinates, and the flight would proceed to that

---

"Two Men Killed Today..."

"The men [ground crews] have no tools or spare parts to use on the ships. They scrounge for everything they can, and are doing well to keep as many ships as they have in the air. A good many of them have nothing to do but sit around. I'm very definitely in favor of giving the men free afternoons every few days so they can go swimming, get laundry done, etc. No need in making them come down if there's no work to be done, but if they are on duty, they should work like everything. We'll be fortunate when our tools arrive by boat, but still no spare parts, no extra coolant, very few rockets. Tell me the AF is ready for any emergencies!"

"There were mighty long faces at the Club today after our two losses. Finally, I talked to Captain Flentke and Bob Embery, who were much more cheerful and philosophic about the whole thing. They said that this is much bigger than us as individuals and not to think bout being killed. That's quite true."

"Two men killed today—our Commanding Officer and one of the flight leaders. This war went sour for many today—it's not the romantic, lovely thing so many of us imagined it to be. I find myself praying for this war to end, and for God to give me some part in working for lasting peace.

I hope I am not making vain, war time promises to Him. War is so stupid. God gave us minds and brains to make us intelligent and superior to animals but here we are tearing each other apart in a way no animal would act, unless he were crazed. They usually kill only for food. This whole war is really messed up. The ground troops are getting beaten. We have no air opposition with which to contend, and I hope we're doing some good. I know we are! What will it accomplish in the long run? This is what we've trained for, I know, and why we're paid so well, but it is futile and stupid; still necessary to maintain our freedom. Why can't folks let others live in peace! There are enough different kinds of governments on this earth that a person can find some kind he wants to live in, instead of trying to change everyone else to suit himself. We must win in Korea, but here does not lie the root of the trouble. Dear Lord, bring peace and happiness to our world and our lives."

Barber, Lt. Col. Kenneth. Korean War Diary Number One (unpublished), 5 August 1950.

Mission Planning for Bridge Strike. *Mission planning photography for strikes on 2 August 1950 at 34 56 43 N Latitude, 127 29 42 East Longitude--near present day Sunch'on, South Korea, near the tip of the Korean peninsula. Several views of the bridge were taken and the target area marked with grease pencil. The "CP627672" refers to the location of the intended target on the knee map carried by the pilots in the cockpit for quick reference. These photographs were found in the National Archives and Records Administration materials for the 18th Wing. (NARA)*

Bridges were prime targets. Every effort was being made to slow the North Korean advance down the peninsula. (NARA)

area to relieve the preceding flight, be it USAF, Navy, Marine or Australian.

After reporting to 'Mosquito Wild West' a flight "usually remained in the area for two hours, at which time the Controller would take over. At times, the F-51's worked with the TACP or radio jeep. When the flights were going to and from Korea, they checked in with 'Mellow' to ascertain if any aircraft were missing."

"The Joint Operations Center was in the Fifth Air Force (Advance) Headquarters at Taegu, later at Pusan, and again on 15 September Taegu, followed by Seoul. After Seoul, a portion of the Center went to Anju, but when the big Winter Communist Offensive began, the Center returned to Taegu. JOC had complete control of every Ground Controller, Air Controller, and all United Nations aircraft in the Korean Theater. This system also provided a means of crosscheck for mission aircraft," Colton explained.

August Significant Dates

August 1: The 6147th Tactical Control Squadron, Airborne, was established at Taegu for forward air control operations with T-6 aircraft. The 51st Provisional Squadron was redesignated the 12th Fighter-Bomber Squadron with Lt. Col. (then Major) Robert Dow commanding. [Note: difference of date between unit history and FAF PIO chronology prepared for MG Timberlake that gives August 4th as date for redesignation of 51st.]

A group of 18th Wing pilots detailed to ferry the USS BOXER F-51's to Korea, departed Johnson AB flying the F-51s that "still bore the Guard markings," remembered Col. Stanley Chatfield. There were 64 Mustangs in the ferry group. Col. Ike Wintermute, Commander of the 18th Group, sent Major Chatfield "over to Itazuke to the 8th Fighter-Bomber Wing to get a situation briefing, maps of the front, call signs and a Frag Order. We were going into combat operations the next day," Chatfield recalled.

August 2: Major Stanley Chatfield led

the first four F-51s "off on the first mission of the 18th Fighter-Bomber Group from Ashiya to Korea." Chatfield contacted the Mosquito AT-6 "just west of Pusan for a target and was sent to the bridge at Chinju where enemy troops and tanks were crossing. I put the flight in spread formation and made my bomb run, north to south. No problem with that, except the only ordnance we could get at Ashiya at take off time was fragmentation bombs. We hit the bridge without doing much damage, but we did slow down the flow of troops. Just east of the bridge, I saw several tanks moving in an easterly direction and I called the flight to follow me in with the .50s. I had the first tank dead to right and when I pulled the trigger, only one of the six guns fired. The rest of the flight completed their runs and we returned to Ashiya, where I had a few choice words with the Armament people."

August 3: The 18th FBG headquarters moved from Japan to Taegu, South Korea, for expanded F-51 operations. SA-16 amphibious rescue aircraft began flying sorties along the Korean coast to retrieve U.S. pilots forced down during operations.

USMC aircraft in action for first time in Korean War.

August 4: 18th Fighter Group Headquarters and 67th and 12th Fighter-Bomber Squadrons arrived at K-2 from 13th Air Force. 51st Provisional Fighter Squadron discontinued and personnel and equipment absorbed by 12th Fighter Squadron. [9]

B-29 attacks against key bridges north of the 38th parallel initiated FEAF "Interdiction Campaign No. 1."

August 5: Maj. Louis J. Sebille, USAF, Commander, 67th FBS, dived his damaged F-51 into an enemy position. For this action he posthumously received the first Medal of Honor awarded to a USAF member, the first of but two awarded to Air Force personnel during the entire Korean War. Captain Bob Howell, 67th Operations Officer, was killed within the hour, just a short distance away. In the first SA-16 rescue operation of the war; Captain Charles E. Shroder led a crew in saving a Navy pilot who had crashed into the sea off the Korean coast.

Fighter Pilot

"It is impossible to fully describe the feelings of a Fighter Pilot—his pride in the title "Fighter Pilot," his incomparable thrill of feeling as his plane climbs into the limitless blue sky, the sensation of speed as he buzzes the earth, the eager tension as his wheels leave the ground in takeoff, the knowledge of power in his engine while it drives itself and him thru the sky, the shroud of gray mystery as he flies through rain or thunderstorms, the sudden tug of fear as his plane fails him in some respect, the rapture of beautiful mystery as he flies amid beautiful sunsets, towering cumulus clouds, or at night, under the bright stars. And occasionally he wonders, in his exultant life of loops, rolls, buzzing, gunner, war, if he may be the next man to go. He remembers his friends who are gone. And then this pilot leaves for war—but the beauty, power, and mystery of the sky ranges maintain their strong hold. He feels that "We live in fame or go down in flame" are more than mere words, and if he is to be a sacrifice to the inexorable Moloch of war, what better way is there to die!"

And I, a fighter pilot, can be glad of this life I lead, knowing that this short life is but a test of a wonderful life to come in which the head Pilot will tune all of our engines to perfection and a happiness of peace, and reunion."

Lt. Col. Kenneth. Barber. Korean War Diary Number One (unpublished), 1950.

A fuel truck explodes and burns furiously near Kumchong on 3 August 1960. (NARA)

August 6: Far East Air Forces began nightly visual reconnaissance of enemy supply routes.

8th Fighter Group Headquarters and 35th and 36th Fighter-Bombers Squadrons began move to Tsuiki, equipped with F-51s.

August 6-7: The enemy threat to Taegu forced the 18th Fighter-Bomber Group headquarters and the 12th FBS to evacuate to Ashiya Air Base. FAF PIO chronology gives movement date as August 9, 1950.

August 7: The 822nd Engineer Aviation Battalion completed the first phase of new runway construction, which allowed expanded USAF operations at Taegu.

39th Fighter Squadron (F-51s), moved to K-3.

August 12: USN Task Force 77 stopped close air support and interdiction strikes in South Korea and moved up Korea's west coast to attack interdiction targets in North Korea, leaving all air attacks in South Korea to Far East Air Forces.

August 13: Endangered by the NKA advance to Pohang, two squadrons of F-51s in the 35th FIG moved from nearby Yonil AB, South Korea, to Itazuki AB, Japan.

August 16: Because of the enemy threat to Taegu, the advanced Fifth Air Force headquarters moved to Pusan.

August 19-20: General Partridge moved the Joint Operations Center from Taegu to Pusan because of enemy advances.

August 23: General Douglas MacArthur

set September 15 as the date to invade Inchon.

August 25: Far East Air Forces directed Fifth Air Force to maintain constant armed surveillance of enemy airfields to prevent enemy build-up of air strength before the Inchon invasion.

August 27: Two USAF Mustang pilots accidentally strayed into China and strafed an airstrip near Antung, mistaking it for a North Korean airstrip at Sinuiju. The Chinese exploited the incident to the fullest for propaganda and diplomatic purposes. Far East Air Forces experimented with delayed action bombs to discourage enemy repairs on bridges.

August 31: After a ten-day lull in the ground fighting, North Korean forces launched a coordinated offensive against the entire Pusan perimeter. Fifth Air Force provided close air support for the defending UN troops.

Adapted in part from U.S. Air Force Historical Research Agency. January 2002. The U.S. Air Force's First War: Korea 1950-1953 Significant Events. June, 1950.

Combat Losses

Howell, Capt. Robert Operations Officer of 67th Squadron KIA on 5 August 1950. "Later, on the last mission of the day, Captain Howell had his rudder control shot away by ground fire. His wingman stayed with him as he made it back over the bomb line. He had jettisoned his canopy and was loosening his belts to bail out, when the plane suddenly nosed over and dove into the ground. His wingman saw it all. No one knows why he waited so long to get out. No one ever will know. No one ever does know what happens at these times, or what thoughts run through a man's mind." (Barber, Lt. Col. Kenneth. Korean War Diary Number One (unpublished), 5 August 1950.)

Jacobs, 1st Lt. Michael 12th Squadron pilot KIA in August 1950.

Lukakis, 1st Lt. George M. 39th FIS pilot KIA near Po'hang in August 1950.

Mathis, 1st Lt. James J. 39th FIS pilot KIA near Po'hang in August 1950.

Pitchford, 1st Lt. Donald L. 39th

Bridge Hits. *"Two probable" hits are made on August 6, 1950, on these railroad bridges that crossed the Kum River about 10 miles north of Taejon. On near bridge, left approach out; right line out; direct hit on bridge structure. On far bridge, direct hit. The type of aircraft making the attack are not identified. However, it was probably B-26 bombers. Fighter-bombers from the 18th Fighter-Bomber Group also attacked this bridge and finally knocked it out. (NARA)*

FIS pilot KIA near Po'hang in August 1950.

Sebille, Maj. Louis The 67th Fighter-Bomber Squadron lost both its Squadron Commanding Officer, Major Lou Sebille, and its Operations Officer, Captain Bob Howell, to enemy ground fire within hours of each other on August 5, 1950, near H'amchang. Maj. Sebille was later awarded the Medal of Honor for his final mission, the first of but two awarded to Air Force personnel during the entire Korean War.

Smith, Captain Robert 12th Squadron pilot KIA in August 1950.

Endnotes

[1] *History of the 18th Fighter Bomber Group, July-October, 1950. USAFHRA.*

[2] *History of the 18th Fighter Bomber Group, July-October, 1950. USAFHRA.*

[3] *USAFHRA. "The Story of the 18th Fighter-Bomber Group in the Korean United Nations Police Action." 6002nd Tactical Support Wing, Public Information Office. S/Sgt Sandy Colton.*

[4] *History of the 18th Fighter Bomber Group, July-October, 1950. USAFHRA.*

[5] *History of the 18th Fighter Bomber Group, July-October, 1950. USAFHRA.*

[6] *History of the 18th Fighter Bomber Group, July-October, 1950. USAFHRA.*

[7] *History of the 18th Fighter Bomber Group, July-October, 1950. USAFHRA.*

[8] *USAFHRA. "The Story of the 18th Fighter-Bomber Group in the Korean United Nations Police Action." 6002nd Tactical Support Wing, Public Information Office. S/Sgt Sandy Colton.*

[9] *NARA. Memorandum from Major James W. Ingram to MG E. J. Timberlake of 26 September 1950. Chronology of Fifth Air Force Activity in Korea.*

Close Air Support From K-2

By Lt. Col. Duane E. 'Bud' Biteman

Typhoon Gloria swept across Japan on July 22, 1950, and we in Korea caught the downpour on the fringes. We were missed by the highest winds, but the low clouds—right down onto the deck, and heavy rains prevented us from doing much flying. If we had sent anyone off, even for a weather check, he would never have been able to find his way back down to land at Taegu.

Flying weather improved enough on July 23rd to resume our mission pace, but the heavy rains had changed the red Korean dust to red Korean mud—sticky, clay-like mud. It stuck to our shoes, jeep tires, airplane landing gears—everything it touched. Our grimy flying suits, already filthy from sweat and dust, became caked with mud. At that time, our bathing facilities were limited to the water we could carry in a steel helmet. With little spare time, and less concern for personal appearances, we were dirty and unshaven most of the time during those first few weeks. We looked almost as bad as our airplanes.

Shortly after the rains, when we could finally stand it no longer, we had the Koreans build a framework to hold a couple of 55-gallon drums, and devised a shower head below. We had no clean water, except the little used for cooking, which was transported from the city, and we had to have water carried from a nearby creek to supply our "shower." It was cold water, even in late July, and it was far from being considered "sanitary," but we were finally able to rinse off part of the grime that had accumulated during the past weeks. The basic facilities were extremely primitive, but they were the least of our worries, and we soon became used to doing without the small amenities.

By July 30th, when the twenty-five "new" Mustangs arrived aboard the USS BOXER, with several new pilots as well, and the 67th Squadron arrived in Ashiya from the Philippines—things began to look up for the 12th Squadron's "Foxy Few," which we had chosen for our new logo. *[The Dallas Pro-*

Meeting President Syngman Rhee

Lt. Kenneth Barber's mission on 7 August "consisted of attacking artillery pieces in a tree row east of Chinju near Pansong with rocket and strafing attacks and bombing a couple of towns full of troops. I put my bombs in the center of the town and then worked over the entire area. It was a good mission. Marty got a tank in a haystack and a gun position."

The "Dallas Squadron" joined the Group at Ashiya on the 7th--"came back from K-2. The Commies are getting pretty close now. We'll probably be refueling and reloading at K-2 from now on. They sure are tired and dirty. Most of them have moved into De Gink, and think it's really luxurious compared to K-2. I'll bet."

Tuesday, 8 August 1950 was a three-mission day for Lt. Barber. "Leave here [Ashiya, Japan], bomb, land K-2 [Taegu], unload, land K-2, load, unload and return. As it turned out, we only flew two missions. We saw some box cars which look burned out, sitting on the Kijongbn Main Line near Kuksa-dong, halfway between Kumchon and Waegwan. I was under the impression that they were all bombed out, but pieces of cardboard flew off them…these N. Kore-ans sure know how to camouflage things. We bombed them, rocketed them, and strafed 'em so I think they're pretty well through. We then landed at Taegu. After a snack, we rested a bit."

Barber had to abort the final mission due to mechanical problems, and returned to Ashiya "with some Aussies." They were "standing around" near the Operations Center "when up drove a staff car with a General (1-star) who I later found out was Timberlake [Fifth AF Fighter CO], and a distinguished looking Asian man. They walked up to the four of us and the General said, "Mr. President, these are some of our Australian pilots." The President [Rhee], replied, "I want to meet all of you, personally," and shook our hands as we introduced ourselves. Then in fairly good English, he said, "I just want you all to know how much I appreciate what you're doing for my country."

Barber finally got the words out, "Thank you, Sir" or "something like that. Never thought I'd actually meet Syngman Rhee in person."

Lt. Col. Kenneth. Barber. Korean War Diary Number One (unpublished), 1950.

visional Squadron had been redesignated '12th Fighter-Bomber Squadron' the previous week.] I had just logged my twentieth combat mission—averaging two per day for ten straight days, three days of which I had to stay down to work my intelligence chores. My tail was beginning to drag from the intense pressure of the daily pace—flying combat during the days, and doing the vital paperwork far into the nights. On July 30th and 31st I flew four missions each day, hitting targets all along the battlefronts to the west, north and east of our tenuous little airstrip—all within 30 miles of our home base at Taegu.

We were getting our asses whipped, in no uncertain terms, and it was becoming just a matter of short hours before we would have to give up the base at Taegu—evacuate, or be over-run by the North Koreans.

The situation on the east coast, where the enemy in Hunghae were already shelling the airstrip at Pohang, was no more promising than ours at Taegu. We were fighting as if our heads were on the chopping block—because they were!

By early August, 1950, the momentum of the North Korean's three-pronged drive into the south had proved immensely successful. They had completed their end-around on the west and south coasts, their east coast drive had progressed far enough to force evacuation of the 35th Group fighter squadrons from Pohang air base after only a few days' active use of the strip, and their central thrust was in the process of crossing the Naktong River to knock on our last bastion of defense—our home base at Taegu.

The North Korean's objective, to surround Taegu, then march on Pusan and have control of the entire peninsula, seemed just a few days short of accomplishment. We were in deep, deep trouble!

Despite our intensive aerial firepower from dawn to dark every day, we just didn't seem to have enough airplanes or pilots to stem the North Korean's onrushing tide. In our favor, though, was the fact that we were forced to concentrate our air strikes over an ever-decreasing geographic area as the Reds tightened their noose around what ultimately became the "Pusan Perimeter." As the distances to the front lines shrunk, it meant that we would fly shorter missions—many as brief as 25 to 30 minutes from take-off to landing; and that, of course, had the same effect as multiplying our striking power.

On the darker side, it also increased the time we were actually in physical combat with the enemy. We were down close to the ground where they were shooting at us a much greater percentage of the time—with the result that we were taking a lot more battle damage, and losing many more airplanes to ground fire.

During the first ten days to two weeks of the war, the Reds had raced madly forward in broad daylight, with little opposition to hinder their movements. By the third week in July, when our meager Dallas Squadron opposition began to take effect, their losses mounted to an uncomfortable level, and the North Korean commanders were required to modify their tactics.

By the first week of August they were forced to travel only at night, and hole-up in the villages during the day, camouflaging their tanks and trucks inside buildings and under trees in an effort to keep them from our fighter pilot's sights. Their attempts at camouflage were rather futile at first, for we could usually pick out the tank tracks in the dirt leading thru the fields to a house or a grove of trees; and we would then conclude that there was a worthwhile target inside—as was usually the case. Their camouflage techniques improved with time and practice, but it was also a time-consuming precaution which helped to slow the momentum of their advance, because of the

Sergeant Arthur J. Repp of Phoenix, Arizona, installs the nose fuse in a rocket carried by an F-51 Mustang that is about ready to take-off on a night mission in August 1950 against a North Korean convoy. (NARA)

time it took prior to dawn each day to try to hide their equipment from us.

They found, too, that there was a maximum travel distance which they could move supplies within a single summer night's darkness, and as they tried harder to tighten our noose, needing more and more replacement arms, their supply lines became more and more exposed to our interdiction attacks. At some time during the long trip south from the Yalu River or from Pyongyang, every train, tank or truck would be exposed to our air attacks. But as the enemy lines closed in on Taegu from two directions--from the west and from the north, and our Army forces had to back steadily into an ever-shrinking defensive perimeter, we found it necessary to direct almost all of our mission effort to close tactical support of the frontlines, thereby reducing the number of sorties we could send north to interdict their replacement supplies.

It was a "Catch 22" situation: we couldn't afford to slack off on our interdiction attacks because the armor coming onto the line would jeopardize our fragile hold on the perimeter's front lines—but if we didn't help our troops on the front, there wouldn't be any perimeter left to defend!

It is not possible to adequately describe the intense feeling of gratification we fighter

pilots felt when we could hit the Reds attacking our front-line troops. By August there were enough radio jeeps operating on our frequencies, and airborne T-6 Mosquito spotter planes, that we could work with reasonable safety within just a few hundred yards of our own Army troops. When the verbal orders of the man on the ground were insufficient to tell us precisely where to strike, we'd ask the spotter to fire a smoke rocket, or the ground artillery to place a white phosphorus shell onto the target. With positive target identification like that, we could work over the Red's dug-in positions with a venegeance. It was doubly gratifying because we were not only taking the enemy pressure off of our troops, but they would often stand right up in plain sight to cheer us on.

We knew that our close-support efforts were deeply appreciated, so we would inevitably press our attacks a little harder—a little closer, or a little lower than was prudent for the safety of our own hides. But we knew, too, that when we finally ran out of ammunition and had to head back over the nearby hill to our base at Taegu, those poor characters below had to stay in their muddy foxholes all night to protect our position and our lives. Too often they didn't make it through the night, for that was when the Reds liked to attack--at night, when our

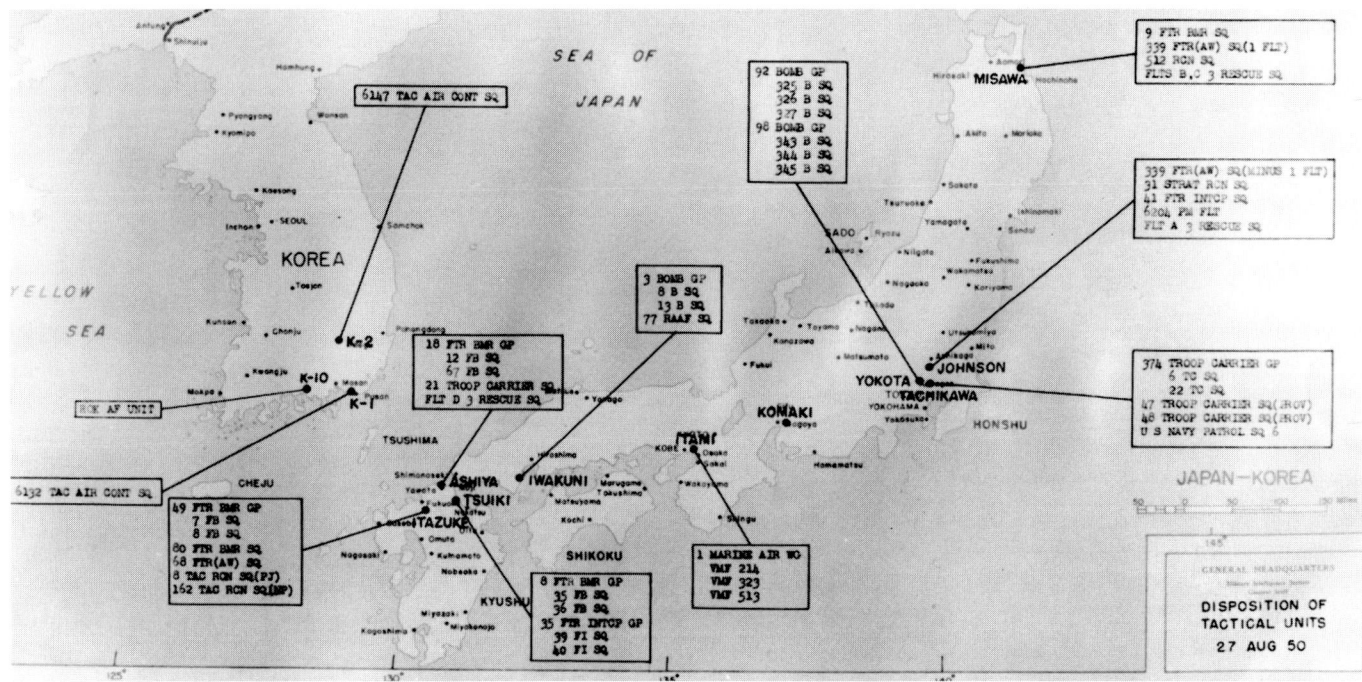

No Air Force Tactical Units in Korea. *By 27 August 1950 when this Disposition of Tactical Units Chart was prepared, UN forces were facing another "Dunkirk," on the Korean Peninsula. There were virtually no Air Force tactical units actually based in Korea, only two Air Tactical Control Squadrons flying out of K-2 and K-1. The 18th Group was then operating out of Ashiya, Japan with the 12th and 67th Squadrons. (NARA)*

planes weren't around to break up their thrusts. We picked up a lot of damage to our battered Mustangs on those close support missions, mostly small arms: rifles and machine gun fire which, if we could get the ships back to base, our mechanics could often quickly repair with a sheet of aluminum and a rivet gun--or, in an emergency, even a piece of cloth tape.

The F-51 was fondly nicknamed the "Spam Can" because, from the side, the shape of its fuselage looked as deep and flat-sided as the namesake tin-can used for packing the processed meat. In those days we, for a fact, used the tin from Spam cans to patch bullet holes in the skin of our airborne Spam Cans (it's true, I swear!)

Sadly, not all holes were minor; we started losing more and more pilots to enemy ground fire. Some were fortunate and were able to land unhurt, or with minor wounds--crash landing behind our lines to be picked up by the Army, as Danny Farr, Owen Brewer, Ed Hodges, Harry Moreland and several others of our group were able to do. Many were not so lucky, as our mounting casualty lists reflected.

But, unbeknownst to us or, reportedly, even to the 5th Air Force commander, General Partridge, the Army was planning to make last ditch stands north of Taegu and at the Naktong River.

So on the evening of August 5th we at Taegu air base were racing to complete our evacuation preparations before dark; 'planning to move out—to Bug Out, on the following day—on 6 August 1950.

Excerpted with permission from "Korean Tales, Unsung Heroes of the Korean Air War." Duane E. 'Bud' Biteman, Lt. Col. USAF (Ret.)

Rockets and Bombs. *Armorers load 500-lb General Purpose (GP) bombs and 5" HVAR rockets as they prepare a Mustang for its next combat mission. Note the crude bomb hoist that has been improvised by the crew. Not only in the early months of the Korean War were the squadrons short of supplies and materials, but for the entire period of combat. (Biteman)*

Major Lou Sebille's

Heroic Mission

Major Louis J. Sebille, was in command of the 67th Fighter Squadron when it arrived, without airplanes, at Ashiya, Japan on July 31, 1950, explained Lt. Col. Duane "Bud" Biteman. They were to receive twenty-five of the "new" F-51 Mustangs that had arrived the previous week aboard the Navy Carrier, USS BOXER. But because there was insufficient physical space--real estate, to park their planes and house their troops, to base them at Taegu with the rest of us--the 67th would, by necessity, have to remain at Ashiya, on the southern Japanese island of Kyushu, and receive logistic support from the 8th Fighter-Bomber Group at Itazuke, 40 miles south of Ashiya.

"It would be a crude, and probably unworkable wartime arrangement--with the 67th's parent organization, the 18th Group based at Taegu, but having to beg for vital support from a bunch of 'strangers' based forty air miles away. Lou Sebille was not a bit happy with that arrangement, and told Lt. Colonel Ira "Ike" Wintermute, our 18th Group C.O. what he thought the results would be. His angry response to the proposition was unlike the easygoing, friendly personality of Lou Sebille, and he was undoubtedly in a sour mood as he began re-indoctrinating his pilots--who, until that time had been flying the F-80C Lockheed jet fighters for the past year, as we had, training them once again to fly the propeller-driven F-51s, and rebuilding his combat outfit," Biteman recalled.

They started flying their first combat missions the following day.

By August 2nd Biteman could hear the "Elsewhere" flights ["Elsewhere" was the radio call sign for the 67th Squadron at that time] "operating alongside our elements all along the front lines. I could recognize many of the radio voices of pilots I'd flown with over the past couple of years, and it was hard not to exchange friendly greetings and small-talk over the busy tactical wavelengths. I talked with Bob Howell, 67th Operations Officer, (an old-time P-51 instruc-

"I'm hit bad..."

On Saturday morning, 5 August, Lt. Ken Barber was assigned to fly wingman for Major Louis Sebille. Over the channel, Barber's coolant started acting up and the temperature jumped to 150 degrees. His oil pressure was OK, but the radio was also "poor." He contacted Sebille to report his situation. Sebille sent Barber back to Ashiya and continued the mission. "Captain Johnson was his element leader, and they went on. Three hours later, Captain Johnson returned with his wingman. Major Sebille had gone in. Apparently, his coolant was hit by ground fire (which leaves the plane only from 3-10 minutes flying time before it overheats and freezes). Captain Johnson said, "Head SE and you'll make it to friendly territory."

Sebille answered, "I'm hit bad. I can't make it. I'm going to get that bastard."

Sebille "then turned and went back in the valley and crashed his plane into an enemy truck and the whole business went sky high. Damn!" Barber noted.

Barber, Lt. Col. Kenneth. Korean War Diary Number One (unpublished), 5 August 1950.

tor pilot who had given me my first P-51 check-out at Pinellas, Florida during World War II). Ross Cree, friend and fellow S-2 officer, Ed Hodges, Harry Moore, Joe Lane, Owen Brewer—the whole bunch was up in Korea to help extricate us from the damned bucket of worms we'd gotten ourselves into. We were extremely glad to have their help, for they were capable, experienced, hard-driving fighter pilots."

Three days later, on August 5th, while each was leading separate flights near H'amchang [36 degrees, 32'N,128 degrees,15'W] on the Naktong River, Lou Sebille and Bob Howells would both be killed within five miles and within minutes of each other--both within 15 miles of the base at Taegu!

H'amchang, the little village where Major Lou Sebille died, "was just one of many small groups of mud and straw huts that dotted the countryside along every road and trail in Korea. On the preceding night, August 4th, the North Koreans had managed to establish a minimal beachhead across the summer-shallow Naktong River and, although we were able to stop all daylight movement across the river, the tanks, troops and artillery that had crossed during darkness were moving steadily toward their objective—our nearby base at Taegu. Just a few more miles and they would be within artillery range of our primary airstrip."

Sebille, leading a flight of 67th Squadron Mustangs out of Ashiya, wound up with but three airplanes when his wingman [Lt. Ken Barber] was forced to return to Ashiya with a rough engine.

"Captain Martin Johnson, his element leader, with Lt. Charles Morehouse on his wing, were informed by the pilot of a T-6 Mosquito spotter, of enemy armor hidden inside several houses in the village of H'amchang. Enemy armor so close to Taegu made our military position "very precarious," to say the least," Biteman noted.

Sebille understood the critical tactical situation—perhaps the very success or failure of the US/UN stand in Korea depended on the effectiveness of his fighters.

After the T-6 spotter aircraft fired a target-marker smoke rocket identified the huts that were hiding the Red armor, Sebille began a medium angle dive bomb run. He planned to drop both of his 500-pound GP (general purpose) bombs on the first run. Only one of Sebille's bombs released on his first attack. The 500-pounds of extra, unbalanced weight under his left wing may have contributed to his near-miss on the target, Biteman noted. The enemy armor was still firing at Sebille's other element as

FIGHTER-BOMBER FINAL MISSION SUMMARY
(FEAF INTEL FORM #5)

UNIT: HEADQUARTERS, 67TH FIGHTER, BOMBER SQUADRON

MISSION NO. 26 _____ DATE 5 August 1950

1. NO. & TYPE A/C 3-FB 51
   (Indicate bomb carring fighter by "F/B")
   A. TAKEOFF TIME 1149 _____ LANDING TIME 1510
2. NO & TYPE A/C RETURN 2-FB 51
   (Indicate bomb carring fighters by "F/B")
3. MISSION (SPECIFIC) Controlled by Mosquito Item #2

4. NO, & TYPE OUR A/C LOST: (TOTAL) 1 - F/B 51
   A. TO A/C:
   B. TO AA: 1 - F/B 51 Number 394
   C. TO OTHER
   (Indicate if known)
5. OWN A/C DOWN IN FRIENDLY TERRITORY OR DAMAGED 1 - F/B 51 Totally
   Destroyed. No damage to other ships. (No. & type, reason of if known)
6. CASUALTIES: KILLED 1 WOUNDED 0 MISSING 0
7. TENTATIVE CLAIMS AGAINST ENEMY
   A. A/C None
   (Indicate whether in air, on ground, over water, whether single, twin or multi engine in each instance.)
   B. GROUND TARGETS Coord nates 1125 - 1516. Troops. Horse-drawn
   (Indicate no. & type, whether destroyed or damaged,
   field guns, half tracks.

8. BRIEF CHRONOLOGICAL NARRATIVE OF MISSION (omit information called for in subsequent paragraphs) Attacked ground troops with bombs scoring 4 direct hits in troops. Used rockets on trucks, half tracks and hillside village. Destroyed 4 armoured vehicles. Strafed troops in area. Strafed one horse drawn artillery pieces on road S from Naksong-dong 1127 - 1516. Returned to Base. Major Sebille in Aircraft number 394, sustained flak damage and made dive on half track, destroying target, aircraft and self and numerous enemy troops.

Sebille Mission Summary Report. *This is a copy of the actual Mission Summary Report prepared 5 August 1950 on Mission No. 26 for the three F-51 Mustangs of the 67th Squadron led by Major Lou Sebille. It became the basis for a Congressional Medal of Honor for Sebille, the first for the new U.S. Air Force. "Attacked ground troops with bombs scoring four direct hits in troops. Used rockets on trucks, half tracks and hillside village. Destroyed four armoured vehicles. Strafed troops in area. Strafed one horse drawn artillery piece on road south from Naksong-dong 1127-1516. Returned to Base. Major Sebille in Aircraft number 394 sustained flak damage and made dive on half track, destroying target, aircraft and self [in pencil] and numerous enemy troops." (NARA)*

they attacked nearby targets.

Sebille came down the slot for the second time. The Red gunners had a clear shot at him as he made his bomb run. Just before he reached the release point, Sebille called over the radio that he was hit, and pulled up sharply to the left once more. His flight heard a garbled comment over the radio that included, "I'll get those dirty bastards..." He continued his turn, diving straight toward the armored carrier, fired his six rockets in salvo, and held his finger on the trigger to keep his machine guns firing the whole way down. Instead of pulling up when he reached the 2000 foot danger level, he continued to bore in—1000 feet—500 feet—he dove his airplane and his remaining bomb into the target," Biteman recalled.

The Fighter-Bomber Final Mission Summary for Mission No. 26 of 5 August 1950 noted, "Major Sebille in Aircraft number 394, sustained flak damage and made dive on half track, destroying target, aircraft and self and numerous enemy troops."

Lou Sebille had, to be sure, "got the bastards...!"

"We pilots speculated at the time," Barber explained, "whether or not Sebille was mortally wounded or just stubborn and hard headed enough to crash his plane into the enemy. Most of us never thought much about being 'heroic' or 'saving America,' while we were on a mission. We just wanted

Major Lou Sebille, Commanding Officer, 67th Fighter-Bomber Squadron

to do a good job at hand."

"This should take nothing away from Lou Sebille's action. Very often, in fact mostly, we pilots were at the mercy of those

who wrote our citations. The good writers usually got theirs accepted. Being 'lucky' always trumps being 'good.'"

[Note: Lt. Col. Biteman prepared a series personal recollections entitled "Korean Tales, Unsung Heroes of the Korean Air War." As a founder and first President of the 18th Fighter Wing Association, Biteman placed many of these stories on the Association's web site: http://www.18thfwa.org/. Some of these stories and others by 18th Wing alumni may also be found in "Hot Shots: An Oral History of the Air Force Combat Pilots of the Korean War," by Chancey and Forstchen (Morrow).

The "story behind the story" of Lou Sebille's Citation for the Medal of Honor

by Lt. Col. Duane "Bud" Biteman, USAF (Ret.)

In mid-August, 1950, in addition to my duties as combat fighter pilot and 12th Sqdn Intelligence Officer, I was assigned the responsibility of Squadron Awards and Decorations Officer.

"It was logical," the boss had told me with a smile, because my "deep, probing interrogation" of returning pilots put me in the best position to identify and evaluate any meritorious acts which might have been performed on the missions. I could then write up a description of the details, complete with Citations flowery enough to convince higher-level headquarters to award the recommended decorations.

At that time there was already an existing backlog of some one-hundred Air Medals and twenty Distinguished Flying Cross awards waiting to be drafted and processed. I tried to insist that I could not do my Intelligence paper work (which, I had to admit, was by then almost taking care of itself, with the admirable help of Sergeant Dan Thornton), fly combat missions on a daily basis and draft awards--without the help of a couple of officers who would have, at least, a minimum flair for writing.

Tanks As Targets Near YongDong. North Korean tanks move along a valley road near Yong Dong on 3 August 1950. (NARA)

I specifically requested that First Lieutenant Don Bolt be assigned full-time to assist me, whenever he was not flying combat missions, and solicited the part-time help of Lieutenants Lee Gomes, "Chappie" James and 'Spud' Taylor, to help out whenever they were free. Capt. Harry Moreland, our Squadron C.O., even volunteered to help when he wasn't busy commanding the squadron or flying missions.

Lee, Chappie and Spud immediately went to work, getting practice by writing the almost "canned" citations for the Air Medals, but then, with the war going as badly as it was, they became too busy flying missions to provide much other help. I was disappointed, but not too surprised--flying combat is tough enough, without having the added paperwork of a tedious ground job; and the fact that they had written some citations relieved me of the need to do those few.

Don Bolt, on the other hand, jumped in with--not both feet, but "all ten fingers," and was a real help, as I knew he would be. I had enough confidence in Don's ability that, when asked by Col. Ike Wintermute, the Group C.O., to see what it would take to get approval for the Medal of Honor for Lou Sebille's last mission, I asked Don to do the legwork and I would help him with the formal write-up--which would eventually have to go all the way to the Secretary of the Air Force for approval.

Don Bolt was, if I recall correctly, a year younger than I, had graduated from flying training as a 2nd Lieutenant during mid-1945, just before the end of World War II, had gotten out of the Air Force in 1946 and had returned to college at the University of Maryland to get his degree in architectural engineering. He had then volunteered for recall to active duty in mid-1948, and after just a few months in the 'States, had been sent to the Philippines, to serve with me in the 67th Fighter-Bomber Squadron at Clark Field.

Don was a bachelor, about five foot six, and couldn't have weighed 125 pounds 'soaking wet.' His ground duty at Clark Field was Squadron Public Information Officer (PIO) at the same time that I was Squadron

67th *Fighter Bomber Squadron* officers gather around the Squadron logo, including: Capt. Joe V. Lane (far left), Lt. Don Bolt (upper left), Lt. Harold Edwards, Squadron Intelligence Officer (far right), and Lt. Bud Biteman (lower right). (Biteman)

Intelligence Officer, so we worked together on many projects and became social friends as well. Some squadron pilots thought Don not 'macho', or aggressive enough to be a good fighter pilot and, I had to admit, he wasn't much of a challenge in a good simulated dogfight. But he was a dedicated, hard-working officer on the ground, and I respected his journalistic and artistic abilities. In 1949 Bolt was caught up in one of the Air Force's recurring economy drives— "purges"—we called them, and was grounded; his pilot's rating was indefinitely suspended. Those so caught, were given the opportunity to be placed on 'inactive duty'--to become civilians again, or to remain on active duty in their current rank, but with no hope of regaining flying status. Such grounding was, of course, an automatic blemish on the victim's promotion records, through little or no fault of their own.

[Note: Col. Charles Schreffler notes that "Don was my observer on an instrument practice ride at Clark when I had a mid-air collision with Harry Dugan of the 44th Squadron. GCI (Ground Control In- *tercept) had vectored Harry and his wingman to bounce us and get our tail numbers. They did a good job and boxed us in. However, Don did not see either of their aircraft until too late, but called for a break anyway. Harry and I collided with Harry losing most of his tail surfaces and I suffered a bent prop and cracked canopy. Harry proceeded to belly in on the runway while I landed wheels down on our auxiliary runway. Naturally the brass had to find a scapegoat and decided to take punitive action against all but me. Harry and his wingman decided on the general courts-martial, while Don took an Article 104. Don was eventually grounded, while the others beat the rap. The prosecutors were not able to prove that their aircraft ever got off the ground. The case was eventually dropped for lack of evidence. I think the situation was a big factor in Bolt's subsequent grounding prior to Korea."]*

Despite all of the negatives, Don chose to remain on active duty as a 'groundpounder,' and continued to do a good job as Public Information Officer, for the 18th Fighter-Bomber Group. Then, with the coming of the Korean hostilities in mid-1950, and the subsequent shortage of fighter pilots throughout the theater, those grounded pilots who had remained in the Far East were offered the opportunity to regain their former flying ratings—provided they would "volunteer" for immediate combat duty in Korea!

Don Bolt headed the list of five names on a set of orders which included similar "volunteers" from all Far East Air Force units.

On July 30th Bolt was in Japan, enroute to Taegu, Korea, when he called to ask if there was anything he could bring over from Japan for me; at my request he promptly picked up two footlockers and filled them with canned beer (which I later used to expedite post-flight critiques, by offering a weather-cooled beer to the returned pilots, free, as long as they'd agree to sit and answer my questions until the can was empty!)

Don arrived at Taegu on July 31st, but because of our airplane shortage, he had to wait an additional three days before he could again check-out in the F-51. It had been a full year since he had flown an aircraft of any kind.

Finally, thanks to the arrival of airplanes from the USS BOXER, Don was at last able to take one short test hop--a familiarization flight, making sure that he remained south and east of Taegu, and well away from the front lines.

His next flight was a combat mission to the Chorwon area. By September 1st Don had successfully flown eight or ten combat missions, and said the old Mustang was beginning to feel comfortable again--he said he could "point the nose where he wanted the bombs to go, and for the guns to fire."

Then, that afternoon, while staging out of Taegu, flying wingman for Captain Jerry Mau, Don's airplane was badly hit by machine gun fire and he was barely able to limp to the deserted airstrip at Pohang for a crash landing. He was not injured, but he had to wait several nervous hours waiting to be picked up from the isolated airfield deep in the middle of "no-man's-land."

Lt. Donald Bolt (Frank and Erica Bolt)

He was not happy when he learned that Mau did not know that he'd gone in—it seems that they were using different radio frequencies when Don was hit.

Bolt's lack of self-confidence, the gnawing uncertainty about his pilot ability—and about his survivability in combat, was magnified at being shot down. To hide his concern, he tackled his ground assignment, helping me with the Awards processing with fervor. When told to find out all that would be needed in the line of paperwork for Sebille's Medal of Honor, Don dedicated himself to making sure that it would be a truly professional job. He persisted despite negative responses from the lower levels of Far East Air Force (FEAF) Headquarters, who gave the impression that Lou's death "...wasn't heroic enough" because there weren't more people involved--that he didn't wipe out an entire armored division single-handedly. But Bolt kept digging, collecting details about the flight and then, between us, we sat down to collaborate on the all-important descriptive Citation.

Periodically, Don began again to fly combat missions, and with each successful bombing or rocket attack, a small measure of his self-confidence returned. Following the Inchon landings, when the North Koreans were scattering to the four winds and racing for their lives toward the Manchurian sanctuary across the Yalu River, he told me that he finally was beginning to feel like a man again; that his flying efforts were beginning to pay their own way--that he no longer felt like an "albatross among the eagles."

Excerpted with permission from "Korean Tales, Unsung Heroes of the Korean Air War"

Bombed Tunnel. *Mission planners of the 18th Fighter-Bomber Wing have circled the area at center and noted, "Bombed Tunnel" near Waegwan, South Korea on August 16, 1950. Several spans of the railroad bridge in the background have been knocked out, as well. (NARA)*

We'll Have A Field Day

"Boy, we've got a hot one," Captain Arnold "Moon" Mullins told the assembled pilots in the Operations shack on Friday 4 August. Unable to restrain his excitement, he read from the "frag order" he had received moments before. Enemy transports were unloading troops up at Inchon Harbor (Seoul). "Man, oh man, we'll have a field day!" he said as the pilots completed the briefing and prepared to take off. Barber was to fly on Capt. Hoagland's wing, with Embery and Carter making up the "element." They took off almost immediately after the brief. Mullins' flight took off shortly afterwards.

When they arrived over Inchon, the sky was crowded with aircraft—"all kinds of planes, F-51's and Navy aircraft, making passes, bombing, strafing, firing rockets."

Barber's flight "sat up above until some of them cleared out of the way and then started in ourselves, Captain Hoagland first."

Barber dropped his bombs on his first pass, and was disappointed that they fell a little beyond the ships that were his target. "Flashes of fire could be seen from the warehouses on the docks as the enemy fired back."

Barber then fired his rockets one at a time at the same ship and hit with one of them at least. "We always strafe as we go in to shake 'em up and confuse their return fire. We then zig zag away low to the ground, flying as uncoordinatedly as possible to keep from getting hit. After dropping the 500-lb demolition bombs and firing rockets, I strafed warehouse on both sides of the causeway."

In the confusion, Barber lost sight of his flight and temporarily joined up with Mullins' flight. After making several more strafing passes at the now burning warehouses and ships, he looked at his fuel gauge. Dangerously low. Banking around to a new course of 130, he headed southeast hoping to "hit K-3 where I could land, fuel up, and return to Ashiya." Flying by himself, reading gauges, reading maps in the crowded cockpit, trying for radio contact "with anybody," he also remembered to try and "keep any Yaks off my tail."

Lt. Herbert C. Moore taxies into position for take off on a combat mission from Ashiya, Japan in August 1950. (Burns)

"Seoul City Sue"

Lt. Ken Barber reported hearing a broadcast on 16 August 1950 by "Seoul City Sue," the North Korean Axis Sally or Tokyo Rose. "In good English she told of the People's Army in their fight to liberate the South Koreans from the Capitalist, money-mad Americans, etc. etc. After a while she started reading out casualty lists (mighty old though)."

On 22 August, Lt. Barber was irritated to find that he had been transferred. "Doggone it! I'm transferred to Group Headquarters as Assistant Operations Officer. They must need someone else to stay up all night and get frag orders, but why did they have to pick on me when I have so little flying time." Like all fighter pilots, he wanted to rack up as many missions as possible and be in the best position to get back home when Air Force decided on a mission and rotation policy.

Barber flew a long mission on August 23rd that took him over Seoul to Pyongyang, "and hence around the railroads and highways through Chinnampo, Haeju and Seoul. We passed outside of Pyongyang, and there was a solid bank of flak puffs at about 2,500 feet. Others who went in earlier said there was a solid barrage from 3,000 to 6,000 feet. [Ross] Cree said, "I haven't seen anything like it since Cologne!"

A Group Commander should surround himself with a few capable men <u>who understand the working of a fighter squadron</u>. In this Group, several men are ground pounders and several more are bomber pilots, including Col. Wintermute. In order to rotate and act busy some of them dream up new ways of annoying the Squadrons who have their hands full already with the fighting. Col. Wintermute is OK tho."

Reaching the east coast of South Korea, he made radio contact with K-3, but couldn't find them in the increasing cloud cover. He decided to head down the coast to Pusan and try for a landing there. He was now trying to fly beneath the lowering cloud cover "to maintain visual contact." He was also on the emergency "D" channel. After getting erroneous radio direction bearings from someplace he thought was in South Korea, he questioned the suspicious directions that would have him head north and west—over enemy territory. New vectors were given—but still generally north.

Trying to lighten the tension, he told the unseen voice giving him the dubious vectors, "If I go down in Commie territory I'll never speak to you again. I sure hope you know what you're doing!"

He was down to about 35 gallons of fuel. Not much flying time left.

By that time he was "sweating blood, felt weak, and completely done in."

He told the DF station, "I think you're steering me wrong. I'm going to head SE and bail out in the drink when she runs out of fuel. Tell my wife I love her."

Trying to gain some altitude for a successful bail out, he was nursing the Mustang into a gentle climb. He was now at about 13,000 feet.

At that point, he was almost out of options.

"Moonshine" homer from Itazuke reached him on the emergency channel to tell him to turn on his emergency IFF. Actually, it was already on and "squawking."

Their "steer" was 140 degrees, "which sounded much more correct than those which Tsushima Homer gave me. Still, they would butt in when I was talking to Moonshine and try to steer me differently." Finally, Barber told Tsushima Homer to "shut up."

His fuselage tank was now dry. He had about five gallons in the left tank. It was dark and Barber decided to follow the Moonshine steers until his fuel was out completely, then bail out.

Suddenly, "the lights of Japan loomed up and was I happy." He called Moonshine to tell them that he saw Japan, but was sure

First Kill for Outfit. *Captain Arnold "Moon" Mullins, new Commanding Officer of the 67th Fighter-Bomber Squadron, 18th Fighter-Bomber Group is shown in this August 1950 Air Force publicity photograph--"Makes First Kill for Outfit"--pointing out "the location where he damaged three Yaks. These represented the first blood for the group." Airman First Class Joe Ruiz, an Armament Technician in the 18th Supply Squadron, recalled that "we served all the Squadrons of the 18th, including the Flying Tiger Squadron (12th FBS), the Blinker Nose Squadron (39th FIS), and the Red Scarf Squadron (67th FBS). One of the more charismatic pilots of the Red Scarfs that I remember was Major 'Moon' Mullins, an inspirational leader who led by example. Just watching him taxi down the runway and taking off to hunt enemy targets gave me a heightened sense of being part of a great war effort." (NARA)*

he would have to bail out anyway.

The gas gauge now read Zero.

Moonshine rogered his transmission and advised him to try and make it to Ashiya, "it's off your left wing."

Finally, Barber saw the runway lights.

His motor stopped. He was now virtually falling out of the sky in the barely controllable unpowered plane.

"There she goes," he radioed.

"Roger," Moonshine answered, "we have the rescue plane already on the runway."

"I'll try to dead stick it in," Barber called as he fought the mushy controls.

"Thank you, Moonshine. I love you," he added sincerely. "Never had I felt so relieved as I did when that airstrip loomed up. I was engulfed by such a wave of happiness to be back that the even greater danger of a dead stick landing didn't even enter my mind."

He circled the gliding Mustang and then "made a beautiful wheels down landing in the first third of the runway, coasted down, and turned off. She was completely out of gas—not even enough to fill a cigarette lighter."

A truck came tearing up to the now quiet plane as Barber got out. It was his own crew. "They had really been sweating me out—had heard that I had bailed out in Korea. Casey, my crew chief and a damn good man said, 'Am I glad to see you, Sir!' I was more glad to be back."

Barber made his mission report to the Intelligence Officer, and told "Moon" that he had dead sticked it in. Mullin's reply was "My God!"

It was Barber's first night flight and night landing in a Mustang.

"I was so happy to be back that nothing

else mattered," he noted.

Colonel Wintermute was holding a meeting at the Club, so Barber headed on over to learn what he could about schedules and plans. Wintermute shook Barber's hand and told him he was "sure glad" he was back. "Damn good job, Barber," Major Louis Sebille, 67th Squadron CO, added.

Barber felt good, but at the same time he "knew inside that I never should have gotten into such a predicament, especially in losing sight of my flight leader." The flight had landed at K-3, because several of its ships had been shot up.

Barber reported the suspicious "homers" to Intelligence. He was convinced that "the Communists were working Tsushima Homer, because their vectors were all taking me towards enemy territory."

"At any rate," Barber noted later, "I got all the excitement today that I need for the rest of my life. All I want is a pipe and slippers. How good that sack will feel tonight! Was I praying? You bet I was!!!" he said as he ended his diary on that Friday night.

He had survived his second combat mission.

Lt. Col. Kenneth Barber. Korean War Diary Number One (unpublished), 4 August 1950.

Barber Ordered To "Detached Service"

On Saturday, 26 August, Lt. Ken Barber's life took an entirely different turn. Major Stanley Chatfield, the 18th Group's Operations Officer, called him in and asked if he were "still interested in volunteering for a forward controller's job. It came as quite a surprise. I had mentioned it before when I first got into Group. I said, "Yes, Sir!""

Chatfield told Barber that he would leave the next day.

"Ken Barber had made the flight down to Ashiya with all of the other group pilots," Chatfield recalled, "and was looking forward to getting into battle. He was unfortunately made an Assistant Operations Officer in Group Headquarters, which changed the complexion of things."

From then on, Barber "would have to beg flights from the Squadron Operations Officers who were reluctant to short change any of their own pilots."

In spite of the obstacles, Barber had managed to fly regularly until the word came down that Chatfield "had to pick out someone to be a Forward Air Controller."

There "wasn't much of a choice," Chatfield recalled, "since there was no one else to call on, and Ken accepted this assignment with dignity and a sense of duty, which was characteristic of him."

Back at the barracks, Barber found that Lt. Dave "Marty" Martin and Lt. "Chappy" James were being assigned to similar duties.

Martin had his head under his pillow "bemoaning his fate."

"I entered the Air Force to be a fighter pilot! #$%$#$% I'm not the sturdy Infantry type."

"Of course," Barber noted with tongue in cheek, "we all did our best to make him feel good! Ha! What a razzing he got."

Later, they went to work fishing around in the storage room to dig out field equipment. Barber had to "scrounge a cartridge belt, holster and canteen from somebody else's equipment. After packing air mattress, sleeping bag, poncho, shelter halves, ground cloth, etc. etc., Dave and I headed for the Club for 'The Last Supper' in civilized country." Although it was already 2230, the kitchen staff cooked them up a fine meal of lobster and fried chicken.

Barber was not that unhappy with the new assignment. "Since I have been in Group I have been extremely restless sitting around and doing nothing, losing flying time and sleep. This will be a nice three week break, during which I will be able to

"Am I glad to see you." Lt. Ken Barber's (left) crew were worried. *"They had really been sweating me out—had heard that I had bailed out in Korea. Casey, my crew chief and a damn good man said, 'Am I glad to see you, Sir!' I was more glad to be back." (Barber)*

see the war first hand."

He had no idea of how long those "three weeks" would become, or how close he would see the war first hand.

"Since I cannot fly as I would like to, I would like to be out-of-doors with the Infantry. Secondly, it will be valuable experience, I believe. Last, and least, in three weeks time Group will probably have to find another Asst. Operations Officer and I may be sent back to the Squadron, even though Major Chat said he'd hold my job open for me."

On arriving at K-2 enroute to his new FAC duties, Barber ran into a West Point Classmate, Army Lt. Jack Osteen, who was serving in the 1st Cavalry Division, 7th Cavalry Regiment (George Custer's unit). After warm greetings, "we asked him during the conversation if they thought the fighters help any. Osteen was effusive in his assessment. "Man, we love you guys! I mean it. From 8:00 p.m. to 0600 a.m. we catch hell at night, but after that the Fighters are up and we don't hear a thing from the enemy as soon as they come over. Boy, we surely do love you!"

After reaching Fifth Air Force Headquarters, Barber was summoned back to Japan "for a special mission." When he arrived in Ashiya, he was handed a SECRET telegram that requests "a man with wide experience, combat missions, and good officer to be assigned on indefinite TDY to the 7th Division in Japan. *[His orders were later changed to 2nd Battalion, 31st Regiment, 7th Division.]* That's all they knew. I had been selected on account of my West Point experience, and my interest in such work."

"Frankly, it's more than I had expected," Barber noted. "I only wanted to get a job with some action—never meant them to think I was a hog for the Infantry. If I had wanted Infantry," the West Point graduate noted, "I'd have asked for it. They say this is a good deal, and that maybe it's something hot. Time will tell. In the meantime, I'm back in the Squadron." As he would find out in the not too distant future, the assignment was "hot."

On 31 August, Lt. Barber received orders sending him to Camp McGill for train-

Major Stan Chatfield queried Lt. Ken Barber regarding his interest in "volunteering" for a forward controller's job. (Chatfield)

"DS" vs. "TDY" for Barber

On 28 August, Col. Wintermute explained to Barber that he would be on "D.S."—detached service. That "worried" Barber because "D.S." implied that he would "be gone for a long time." [TDY— Temporary Duty—was seldom over 30 days. DS meant that Barber "could be kept a long time.]

Barber reported to the Colonel and "told him I didn't make it a practice to question jobs but that I was not desiring to spend the rest of my war career in the Infantry. If I had wanted it, I'd have asked for it. I also told him I'd been out of flight school only 11 months, two of which were taken up in furlough and in transit overseas. I said that while I wanted to get the experience of ground liaison work, my career was in the AF and I didn't want to get stuck."

Wintermute assured Barber that he wouldn't be "stuck," and made Barber "feel much better." Later, Major Cartwright told Barber that he would see that he was replaced in a month. "Now I feel OK about the job," Barber noted. "I just wish I could have finished my 35 missions required for the D.F.C. before I left. Hope I can!"

"It's getting cool around here. I'll have to get some winter clothing," Barber noted. He had no idea that the Chosin Reservoir in December was in his future.

---

ing as a forward air controller and then on to the Commanding General of the 7th Infantry Division.

When he reported to Camp McGill, Barber was told that he would go to a special four-day school "to try to make us more effective than the previous jeep controllers." He was advised that his D.S. "will be for some time, maybe until the end of the war." The briefer said "that while we probably now felt that we had been shafted out of a lot of good flying time (and most of us did), we would probably get very enthusiastic over the whole deal. We are to have a personal jeep, a radio jeep, and a trailer. We also will be given all sorts of field equipment plus binoculars, watches, carbines, etc. Makes me almost wish I'd left a lot of my own stuff at Ashiya," he noted.

Barber's team included PFC J. D. Mosley, Corporal J. B. Chandler, and Corporal William Wilkerson. They were "mechanics and radio men, tho I do not think they know anything about it as yet." Wilkerson, who would be promoted to Sergeant on Barber's recommendation on October 19th, was from Meridian, Mississippi and had been attached to the 49th Maintenance Squadron at Misawa AFB, Japan. Chandler was from Lucasville, Ohio, and had been assigned to the 3rd Communications Squadron at Yokota, AFB, Japan. Mosley was from Morris, Alabama and had also been assigned to the 3rd Communications Squadron.

"Rumor, and it's pretty reliable, indicates that we'll probably be in an invasion, the 3rd wave ashore, and the Major thinks the war will be over three weeks later."

"This should prove to be very interesting," Barber observed, "and will give me the opportunity to see war as it really is in all its raw grimness." He had no idea how grim it would actually be for the next four months.

The prospect "of being in on the invasion pleases me immensely," he noted.

On 2 September 1950 started TACP "school" at Camp McGill. Classes covered such topics as tactical air support in amphibious operations, radio equipment, tactical air support communications, coordination of supporting arms, speed map reading (signs and symbols), RT (radio telephone) procedures covering authentication systems, capabilities and limitations of close support, operations orders and air plans.

At one point, Barber doodled onto his class notes a list of things he planned to take with him in the jeep, including: blanket, poncho, ground cloth, underwear (1 change), socks (2 changes), fatigues (1 suit), rifle, small pistol and ammunition.

On 7 September 1950, Lt. Barber was given orders to report to Pier "A" in Yokohama, Japan. Barber, his men, his equipment and jeep were about to be loading aboard a Navy transport ship.

Lt. Col. Kenneth. Barber. Korean War Diary Number One (unpublished), 1950.

A Twenty on the Bar

By Lt. Col. Duane E. 'Bud' Biteman, USAF (Ret.)

During the early days of the Korean War, the holding actions of the 8th Army and Marines had failed to sufficiently slow Red troop advances and, despite the heavy pounding by our fighter planes on all three fronts encircling Taegu, even with a mass saturation raid by B-29s near Waegwan, we could not keep the enemy from crossing the Naktong River.

As the battle lines drew closer—as the noose tightened around Taegu—there were actually fewer Red supplies being intercepted because the Reds were 'holing-up' during daylight hours, and making their long moves at night, when our fighter planes were on the ground. It took them longer, but the supplies were still reaching the front. And, secondly, we were having to expend much more of our aerial resources at the front lines, supporting our troops. We didn't have time to go searching far behind the lines on interdiction missions.

But as the lines closed in on Taegu--from the west and from the north, our ground forces had to back steadily into an ever-shrinking defensive perimeter; we found it necessary to direct almost all of our mission effort to close tactical support of the frontlines, reducing the sorties we could send north to interdict their supplies. It was a "Catch 22"—we couldn't afford to slack off on our interdiction attacks because the armor coming onto the line would jeopardize our fragile hold on the perimeter's front lines—but if we didn't help our troops on the front, there wouldn't be any perimeter left to defend!

It is not possible to adequately describe the intense feeling of gratification we pilots felt when we could hit the Reds attacking our front-line troops. By August there were enough radio jeeps operating on our frequencies, and airborne T-6 Mosquito spotter planes, that we could work with reasonable safety within just a few hundred yards of our own troops.

When the verbal orders of the man on the ground were insufficient to tell us precisely where to strike, we'd ask the spotter to fire a smoke rocket, or the ground artillery to place a white phosphorus shell onto the target.

With positive target identification like that, we could work over the Red's dug-in positions with a venegeance. It was doubly gratifying because we were not only taking the enemy pressure off of our troops, but our men would often stand right up in plain sight to cheer us on.

We knew that our close-support efforts were deeply appreciated, so we would inevitably press our attacks a little harder—a little closer, or a little lower than was prudent for the safety of our own hides. But we knew too, that when we finally ran out of ammunition and had to head back over the hill to our base at Taegu, those poor characters below had to stay in their foxholes all night to protect our position and our lives.

Too often they didn't make it through the night, for that was when the Reds liked to attack—at night, when our planes weren't around to break up their thrusts.

But as the battle fronts closed in around our Taegu base, we soon had a steady flow of casualties passing through for medical air evacuation to hospitals in Japan, and for the first time we pilots had a chance to talk face-to-face with some of the Army and Marine people we'd been supporting during those close ground support missions along the front lines.

They had nothing but praise for the job we had been doing, and told us of the hundreds of 'kills' which we had been unable to see because we were moving too fast.

Little did they realize that it wasn't really our display of 'bravery' when we'd fly into those heavy concentrations of ground fire—it was just plain ignorance on our part!

We just couldn't see all the scores of enemy troops who were so busily shooting at us.

As the front lines neared Taegu airstrip, the stream of casualties increased proportionately. Seeing the maimed bodies of those youngsters quickly dispelled any remaining thoughts we might possibly have had about the war being a "game—a test of skills" among pilots.

I was especially touched one evening, after we'd been experiencing some especially rough close support missions just a short distance from Taegu, resulting in several severely damaged Mustangs and a couple of wounded pilots.

A young Army Captain hobbled into the little tent which we used for an 'Officer's Club'—he was bandaged from head to waist, had one arm in a sling and one bandaged foot—but he was managing. He made his way slowly and silently, with the aid of a makeshift cane, over to our packing-crate 'Bar,' as the few of us patrons moved aside to make room for him.

But instead of ordering a drink, he looked to both sides, laid a twenty-dollar bill on the bar, then said: "Thanks, men," 'turned around and hobbled out without another word.

My morale went up a thousand points upon hearing his appreciation for our risks.

Excerpted with permission from "Korean Tales, Unsung Heroes of the Korean Air War."

Stratemeyer Welcomed Back. *Lieutenant General George E. Stratemeyer, right, Commanding General of the Far East Air Forces (FEAF), is welcomed back to his command by Major General Earle E. Partridge, left, who acted in his absence. General Stratemeyer arrived at Haneda Air Base on September 6, 1950 from temporary duty in U.S. Air Force Headquarters, Washington, D. C. Also on hand to greet him were, left to right, Major General Victor E. Bertrandias, Director of Flying Safety, U.S. Air Force, who is in the Far East on an Inspection trip, and Brigadier General Edward H. White, Commanding General of the Air Transport Wing, Pacific Division, Military Air Transport Service, Haneda. (NARA)*

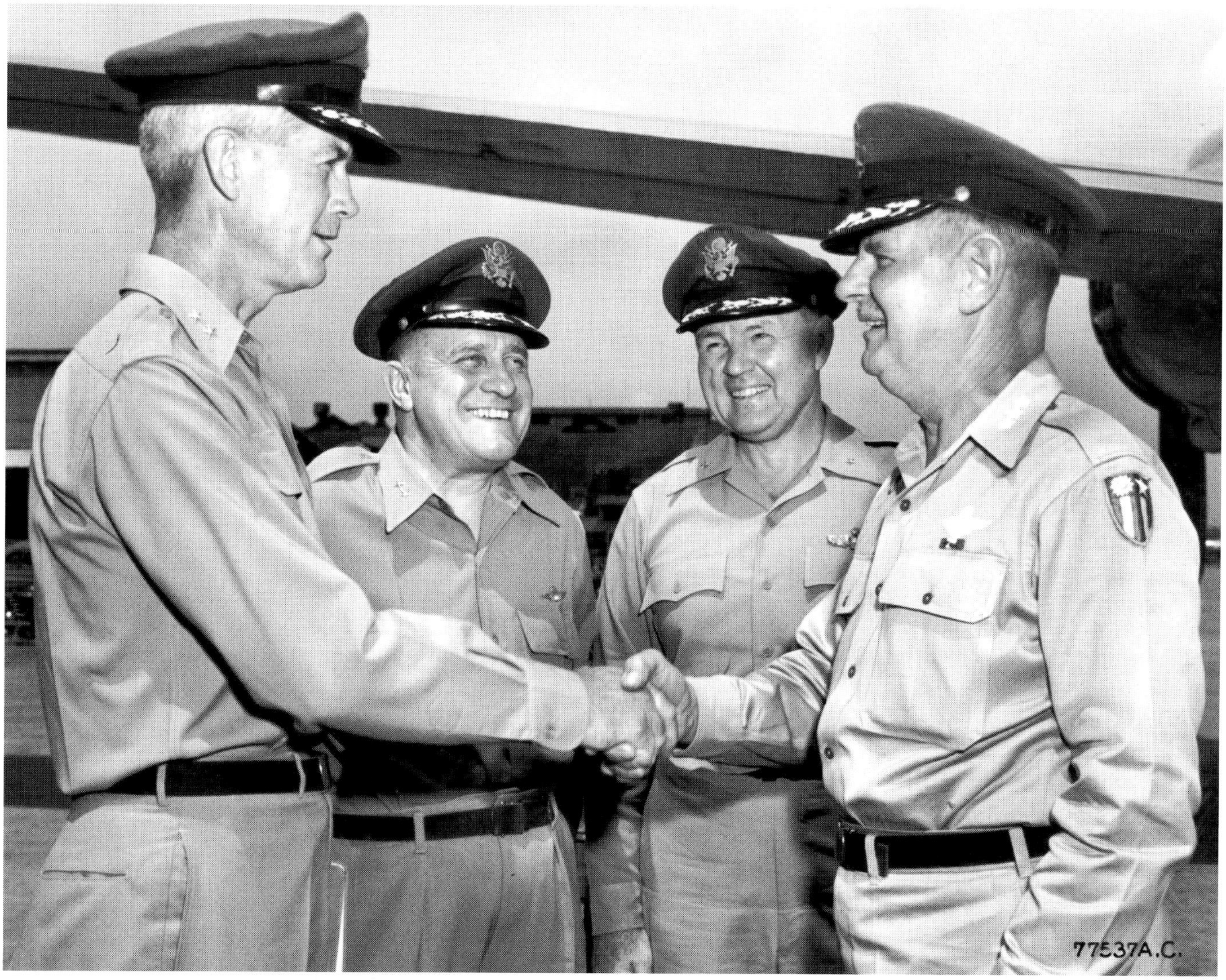

From Japan To "Dogpatch" for the 18th Group

During "the darkest hours of early September, when it appeared as though the 'last gasp' of the North Korean forces might carry their drive around Taegu and south to the port of Pusan," the 18th Fighter-Bomber Group "labored at peak efficiency, despite miserable flying weather and an untimely move from the comparative comforts of Japan to the newly-constructed airstrip in Korea designated, simply, K-9."

On September 7th the entire 18th Fighter-Bomber Group moved to K-9 airstrip near Pusan. This move to "Dogpatch," as the new base was immediately named, was the second such transfer for the 12th FBS, but it now placed the fighter-bombers, "within fifteen minutes flying time of the front lines and permitted ground-support operations, though limited, in even the foulest weather." [2]

Heat waves shimmered upward from rain pools alongside the airstrip at K-9, S/Sgt William J. "Sandy" Colton, a public in-

75

Major Bob Dow's Mustang is prepared for another mission from K-9 in September 1950. (Schreffler)

"that celebrities of the Bob Hope, Marilyn Maxwell and Jolson stature were usually met with banners and signs proclaiming proudly that the 18th was truly an airborne version of the popular stateside cartoon strip."

A letter dispatched through channels to Al Capp himself soon brought recognition from Li'l Abner's creator, who followed through by designing a Mustang motif patch with Nancy 0. and Abner astride a death-dealing F-51. This same insignia was featured on television and aroused such interest that the Texstyle Corporation sent along as a present full-color cloth patches for the Dogpatchers of the Fifth Air Force. By late 1951, Al Capp was an honorary member of the 18th and "would be amazed at the Dogpatch signs around the base," Colton noted. "Everything from the new control tower to the mess hall menus proclaim that the 18th is proud of its humble beginning in Korea, but more important we had a sense of humor that war could not lessen but only served to inspire everybody to greater efforts. In other words we could always eke out a laugh no matter how rough it was. Regardless of the hardships it may have been 'confoozin,' but it was still 'amoozin.'"

formation specialist attached to the 18th Wing Staff later reported. Colonel Curtis Low, Captain George Bales, and Colton surveyed the "uninspiring Korean landscape" from their ankle-deep vantage point in the mud. "Lower Slobovia or Dogpatch couldn't be worse than this," commented Low, while his two companions nodded weary agreement. Thus, Dogpatch received its Cappian title, which was to eventually be picked up by the state-side press and become a familiar label of the 18th Fighter-Bomber Wing.

Following the relocation of the 18th to K-9, Colton began datelining his news dispatches with the descriptive title and before long the 18th became identified as the "Dogpatchers of Korea." In fact the 18th became synonymous with Al Capp's comic strip village to such an extent, Colton noted,

Monthly Summary

At the beginning of September, North Korean forces were close to total victory. United Nations forces were squeezed into a bloody salient around the city of Pusan in Southeastern Korea. "A final desperate weeklong communist offensive along the Pusan perimeter failed to drive UN and ROK forces out of Korea. Relentless air attacks exacted a terrible price on enemy forces, and by mid-September, with the Eighth Army prepared to go on the offensive, UN forces confronted a starving enemy who was short of ammunition and other essential supplies." [1]

On September 15th, General Douglas MacArthur launched an amphibious invasion at Inchon, a port city west of Seoul and more than 150 miles northwest of the Pusan perimeter. While U.S. Navy and Marine Corps aircraft covered the invasion area, the

Air Force units endeavored to cut enemy lines of communication and patrolled enemy-held airfields to keep them out of action. The Inchon invasion forces drove a wedge between the North Korean Army in the south and its main supply routes in the north, threatening to cut it off and squeeze it against advancing Eighth Army forces from the southeast. Trying to escape the trap, the North Koreans retreated rapidly northward. By the end of September, U.S. forces from Inchon and Pusan had linked up near Osan. UN forces captured over 125,000 prisoners of war (POW). UN troops marched into Seoul and restored the ROK government there.

To support the UN Inchon landings, FEAF operations during September were conducted around the clock. Bomber Command conducted a major B-29 strategic

bombing campaign, attacking North Korean industrial facilities and troop training centers in such cities as Wonsan, Hungnam, Hamhung, Pyongyang, Songjin, and Chonjin, including marshalling yards and railroad junctions in North Korea. Fifth Air Force F-51s, F-80s, and B-26s destroyed large numbers of tanks and enemy troop concentrations, enabling UN and ROK forces to move northward to the 38th parallel. Combat Cargo Command, using newly recaptured airfields at Kimpo and Suwon, airlifted ammunition, rations, and other supplies to the fast-moving UN forces, then returned to Japan with casualties who had been airlifted from the battle area by H-5 helicopters.

Adapted in part from U.S. Air Force Historical Research Agency. January 2002. The U.S. Air Force's First War: Korea 1950-1953 Significant Events.

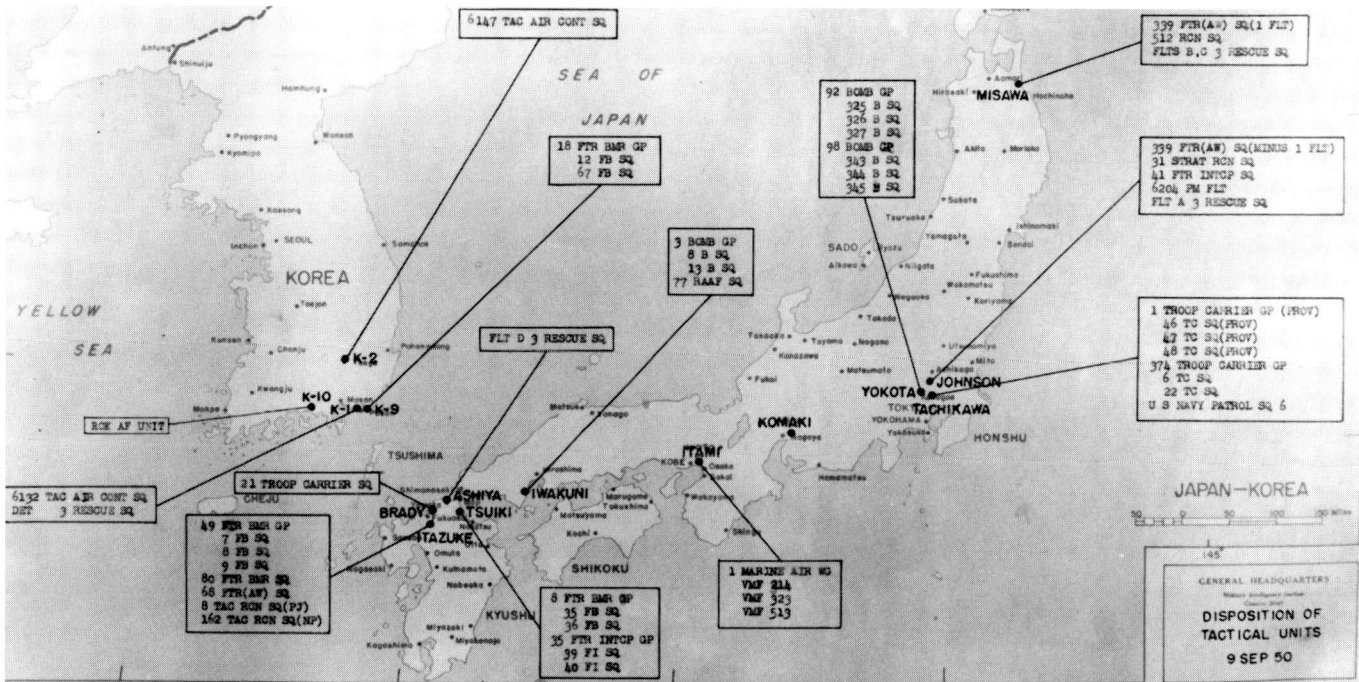

18th Group First Air Force Combat Unit Back to Korea. This Disposition of Tactical Units of 9 September 1950 reflects the return that day of the 18th Fighter-Bomber Wing to Korea. Based at K-9, near Pusan, the 18th was the first fighter or bomber Group to be based in Korea following the stabilization of the Pusan Perimeter. In less than a week, the Inchon landing would reverse the tide of battle. The return of the 18th also underscored the fact that FEAF planners were convinced that the Perimeter would hold and could be expanded with close air support near at hand. (NARA)

The runway at K-9 was basically a 6,000-foot long "steel mat, which had not been completed." There were "a handful of weather-beaten buildings to form the new base." The "officers and airmen immediately pitched a 'tent city' and set up housekeeping without a break in operations against the enemy. The move was planned and executed to "allow the Mustangs to take off from Ashiya, make their strikes, then stage from K-2 airstrip at Taegu. At the end of the day they landed at their new home and were ready for normal operations by the following day."

Gradually, "necessary supplies and equipment" arrived from Japan and the "primitive" living conditions were slowly im-proved. By the end of September, "most" of the tents had wooden floors and a "contract laundry" was available to personnel. A "belated shower arrangement" proved "immensely popular in spite of the cold weather." Fresh food was "limited but greatly appreciated." [3]

Squadron operations, armament, maintenance and communications were moved to the opposite side of the strip at K-9. The sections were then consolidated and housed in seven squad tents per squadron, centrally located near the respective aircraft dispersal areas but on the opposite side of the strip from the housing area. "This arrangement proved to be very satisfactory from all points of view." [4]

On 7 September, the 18th Fighter Bomber Group headquarters and the 12th and 67th Squadrons were moved to K-9, ten miles east of Pusan, Colton noted. "This airstrip, like K-2, utilized the dirt and steel runway mats. All personnel were quartered in 12-man tents, and many of the Wing, Group, and squadron offices also used these tents." [5]

K-9 was important as an air evacuation and staging area. The wounded were brought from the Pusan Evacuation Hospital to K-9 by rail transportation, loaded on ambulance and 6x6 trucks, and then to C-119, C-54, C-46, and C-47 aircraft for flights to Haneda and Itazuke Air bases in Japan. This field was bordered on three sides by

"Lower Slobovia or Dogpatch couldn't be worse than this," commented Col. Curtis Low, while his two companions--Captain George Bales and S/Sgt Sandy Colton--nodded weary agreement. Thus, "Dogpatch" received its Cappian title. Following the relocation of the 18th Group to K-9, Journalist Colton began datelining his news dispatches with the colorful title and soon the 18th became identified as the "Dogpatchers of Korea." Wherever the 18th was based in Korea was known as "Dogpatch."

Relocating to K-9/Pusan

Harbor near K-9 at Pusan, South Korean.
(Barber)

Aerial View of K-9

K-9 was the largest field in South Korea and the only one capable of handling jet aircraft. Marine Corsair, Navy Skyraider, and RAAF F-51 and C-47 aircraft of the 77th Squadron frequently operated from K-9. In addition, many high-ranking personnel of all nations passed through the field, and Generals Walker and Stratemeyer flew from K-9 quite often. K-9 was also important as an air evacuation and staging area. The wounded were brought from the Pusan Evacuation Hospital to K-9 by rail, loaded on ambulance and 6x6 trucks, and then to C-119, C-54, C-46, and C-47 aircraft for flights to Haneda and Itazuke Air bases in Japan. The field was surrounded on three sides by mountains just a mile away--and on the other side by the sea. (Barber)

mountains a mile from the field, and on the other side by the sea. South Korean laborers were used in the Mess, on the Flight Line, and in installation of the Base. This was the largest field in South Korea and the only one capable of handling jet aircraft. Marine Corsairs, Navy Skyraiders, and RAAF F-51's and C-47 aircraft of its 77th Squadron frequently operated from K-9. In addition, many high-

ranking personnel of all nations passed through the field--Generals Walker and Stratemeyer flew from K-9 quite often.

The first Flight of F-51's from K-9 occurred on 9 September. Brief close support sorties were followed by those utilizing napalm, in which operational contact with "Mellow' and 'Mosquito' were the same. The 12th eventually changed its Call Sign to TAMERLANE, but the 67th retained ELSEWHERE, as it was known at Clark Field. Engine cowlings of the 12th sported the familiar shark's teeth, while one side of the nose spinners of the 67th Fighter Squadron F-51's were painted red and the other white. The latter were soon called the "Blinking Squadron," and the former, the "Tiger Squadron." For this reason, they were associated with ground troops as the "F-51's with teeth" and the "Winking spinners."

[Note: When the 39th FIS was attached

to the 18ᵗʰ Wing in Spring 1951, the 67ᵗʰ gave up the winking spinners.]

The flying day usually began with briefing at 0500 hours, and ended with debriefing at 2000 hours, consisting of 15 hours' continuous support. Pilots could rest better at Taegu, but the aircraft were left alone only long enough to be refueled, rearmed, and considered in-commission. Quite often a two- or four-plane Alert Flight was stationed at the end of the runway with the pilot in the aircraft, the aircraft checked, engine shut off, merely waiting for a touch of the starter button.

The Air Controllers were "Mosquito Antidote" to the north, "Mosquito Mastiff" in the south, "Mosquito Vaudeville' in the East, and "Mosquito Wild West" in the remaining direction. "Mosquito Polygon: and "Amiable" were spares in the control slots.

Major Bob Dow, new Commanding Officer of the 12ᵗʰ Squadron, emerges from the Operations Tent at K-9. Major Dow was Commander of the 44ᵗʰ Squadron at Clark AFB when Lt. Ken Barber reported in as a 2ⁿᵈ Lt. in 1949. "He was highly respected by everyone--a quiet, nice man and extremely competent as a Commander. He was an excellent hypnotist too, and provided much fun at Squadron parties," Barber recalled. (Chatfield)

Mustang Operations From K-9

"With the advanced elements of the Squadron leaving for the shores of Korea the personnel of the Squadron all sat at Ashiya stewing in their own juice to get a little closer to the fight," the unit history report noted. On September 5, 1950, Fifth Air Force ordered Major Arnold Mullins, CO of the 67ᵗʰ via classified instructions to relocate the 67ᵗʰ from Ashiya Air Force Base, Japan to K-9, near Pusan. "The move was finally made on the morning of the eighth. The pilots took off on a mission and upon completion landed at K-9, and known to all as "Dogpatch." The move was complete with the arrival of the water borne supplies a few days later." 6

The relocation from Japan to Korea was "accomplished without cessation in tactical operations," with ground personnel being airlifted via C-47 type aircraft of the 21ˢᵗ Troop Carrier Squadron. TO&E material "peculiar to this type of unit was shipped direct from Clark Air Force Base to Pusan Harbor and transshipped to this location by rail and truck, with an initial stop at Ashiya Air Force Base. Transshipment from Ashiya was effected across the Sea of Japan by LST's of the United States Navy."

"Settling down to what was to become a normal routine, amid mud, rain and the confusion of setting up tents, the 67th Squadron continued to run its missions. With the ever encircling rain of enemy troops closing in on the "Pusan perimeter" flights were dispatched on a standby basis as fast as they could be reloaded and armed. In spite of the frequency of the missions over Korea, our weary armorers were able to keep up with the increased workload," Major Mullins reported in the September unit history.

"Four-ship close support was the order for the first two weeks of the month with long-range reconnaissance following when the landings at Inch'on became imminent. Reminiscent of the famous Patton's drive across France, our bomb line was an hourly change. Close support turned into four ship missions as the line progresses. The tempo did not let up but gained momentum as time over the target became earlier and earlier. Two hour pre-dawn take offs became a routine thing, while armament and engineering personnel lost knowledge of the days due to around the clock operations. Immeasurable credit for the success of the operation goes to these people," Mullins recorded.

The 67ᵗʰ would fly 255 missions in September—a total of 681 sorties—during which the Red Scarfers dropped 118 500-lb bombs, 881 canisters of napalm, and fired 2,113 rockets. Four aircraft were lost that month, and casualties included: Major Robert P. Scanlon, Captain Donald L. Plantine, 1ˢᵗ Lt. Jack L. Lightner and 1ˢᵗ Lt. Randolph C. Heard, who was wounded.

Targets for the 67ᵗʰ during that period included towns (23 1/2 destroyed, 65 damaged), buildings (164 destroyed, 41 damaged), troops (1225 killed), trucks (109 destroyed), field pieces, 36 destroyed, 21 damaged), railroad cars (20 destroyed, 10 damaged), supply dumps (20 destroyed), and tanks (11 destroyed).

18ᵗʰ Supply Squadron Missions

"The front line of the conflict was just to the north of Taegu," recalled Joe Roiz, an Armament Technician with the 18ᵗʰ Supply Squadron. "We were to be flown in as reinforcements to the air base there." Taegu was a important, strategic junction about fifty miles northwest of Pusan. "It was critical that the airfield be held. But before we could take off, intelligence reported that

Taegu had been overrun and taken by the enemy. Our destination was quickly changed to Pusan, which was located on the very southern tip of the Korean peninsula," Roiz remembered. "Things were not going too well for the UN Forces of which we were a part."

Roiz had been assigned to the 18th Fighter-Bomber Wing, which was en route to the conflict from Clark Air Force Base in the Philippines. As an Armament Technician, he had the "unglamorous job of helping to mix up 100 octane gasoline with a rubber compound to make napalm." He also "unpacked, prepared and armed the white phosphorus fuses that ignited the napalm bomb when it hit the target." Other duties for the AT's included hanging and arming rockets and loading fifty caliber machine gun ammunition in the wings.

[The napalm tanks were "cheap drop tanks manufactured for us in Japan out of thin tin metal so they would break open easily when dropped," explained Col. James Peek. "The napalm was pumped into these external tanks and before take-off the igniter's were inserted where the gas cap would normally be to keep the gas contained inside the tank. They were 75-gallon tanks and since gasoline weighs 6 pounds per gallon it weighed 450 pounds, then add some for the rubber compound and the tank weighs about 500 pounds. We always carried two and almost always dropped both at the same time."]

The 18th Supply Squadron, as a member of the 18th Fighter-Bomber Wing, "served all the squadrons of the 18th, including the Flying Tiger Squadron [12th FBS], the Blinker Nose Squadron [39th FBS, assigned to the 18th Group in Spring 1951], and the Red Scarf Squadron [67th FBS]."

The Army Corps of Engineers "had built a runway from perforated steel plates [PSP or Pierced Steel Planking] linked together and laid upon the graded soil. The length of the runway was minimal for the fully loaded F-51s taking off. At the north end of the runway was a mountain and the other end was the sandy beach into the Yellow Sea," Roiz explained.

"Pre-brief at squadron Ops," is Col. Stan Chatfield's inscription on the back of this snapshot. Mission pre-briefs could be highly informal at K-16, which the Group used as an advance operating base after the Inchon landings. (Chatfield)

The 67th Fighter Bomber Squadron began flying 'sorties' right away. "We would load them up with fifty caliber ammunition for the machine guns mounted in the wings, hang three-inch rockets under the wings and a five hundred pound napalm bomb under each wing. Off they would fly to the north to obliterate any targets they could find."

"First they would drop their napalm bombs, then fire off the rockets and finally strafe ground targets with their fifty caliber machine guns until they were out of ammunition or low on fuel. Tactical air support of the United Nations ground troops was their main role. Often they would come

back to base with ox carts registered as official kills. An enemy tank, the Russian built T-34, was a special kill," Roiz remembered.

The North Koreans "didn't have much in the way of anti-aircraft weapons in the front line areas except for rifles and machine guns. But often they were successful in shooting down one of our planes," Roiz recalled. He became friendly with one of the pilots, Captain Alexander Beck Padilla of the 12th Squadron, a Spanish-speaking native of California. Roiz enjoyed the handsome, 25-year old pilot's efforts to speak Spanish. Padilla was "a very lively guy with a good sense of humor. He wore a long white silk scarf which trailed out of the

Bill Slater emerges from his tent zipping up his flight suit and prepares for a briefing prior to his next mission from K-9 in September 1950. (Schreffler)

cockpit of his F-51 as he taxied on the runway—he was easy to spot among the other planes." Tragically, "on one of his sorties he never came back. I don't know exactly what happened to him. I assumed he was one of the casualties of the enemy ground fire. I thought about him a lot. The tragedy of war began to be more real and personal," Roiz remembered. *[Padilla was killed in action in October 1950 while serving as a Forward Air Controller.]*

Aside from the primitive living conditions, bad weather and long hours, "there wasn't much danger" for the airmen at K-9. There was, however, "Piss Call Charlie," a lone North Korean bomber "who would fly over the base at about the same time each night, just before midnight, and drop a bomb somewhere on or near the airfield." Roiz thought that his "visits were more for psychological reasons than for real destruction. They became a subject of a kind of nervous humor after a while. You never knew when 'Charlie' might score a direct hit some night. Occasionally he would cause a bomb crater in the runway which would quickly be repaired the next day," he recalled.

Checking Coordinates. Lts. Ray Carter and "Slide" Trumbo check their coordinates before a mission from K-9. (Chatfield)

Inchon Landings

Reverse Tide Of War

"Four-ship close support was the order for the first two weeks of the month with long-range reconnaissance following when the landings at Inch'on became imminent. Reminiscent of the famous Patton's drive across France, our bomb line was an hourly change. Close support turned into four ship missions as the line progressed. The tempo did not let up but gained momentum as time over the target became earlier and earlier. Two hour pre-dawn take offs became a routine thing, while armament and engineering personnel lost knowledge of the days due to around the clock operations. Immeasurable credit for the success of the operation goes to these people," 67th Com-

manding Officer Major Arnold Mullins recorded.

On 15 September, the U.S. Marines landed on the northwest coast at Inchon. A few short days later, the capital city of Seoul was taken. This was not highly significant for operational planning by the 18th Fighter Bomber Group—its primary mission was to support the Chinju, Taegu, and Pohang Sectors. From D minus 2 to D minus 10, the Group continued the rocket and strafing offensive against the Korean Red troops.

On 25 September, the Group received Frag Orders committing them to long-range reconnaissance of the area above the 38th Parallel. The area was divided into Recce Areas IV and V, or the Northeast and Northwest Sections. In the immediately following days, two pilots and three aircraft were lost, and on 6 October, rumors spread concerning a possible move to a Northeast airstrip near the seaport of Wonsan. When the Marines invaded Inchon, the Group exerted its maximum from D minus 4 to D minus 10. Major (Later Lieutenant Colonel) Kendal E. Carlson, who always caught flak in a mountain pass, was shot down in this pass, whereby it was promptly renamed Carlson's Alley." Captain Don Flentke was later killed in this same area. Major Carlson, however, was picked up by a Rescue H-5 helicopter when he bailed out of his burning aircraft, Colton recorded.

On 27 September, following the attack of the United Nations, a group of American infantrymen had been pinned down for five hours in the Chinju Sector. Weather at K-9 presented a ceiling of 15 feet, but Captain Howard I. Price and Lieutenant Castleberry, of the 67th Fighter-Bomber Squadron took off at 1105 hours in ELSEWHERE ABLE with two napalm bombs, six five-inch rockets, and a full load of .50-caliber ammunition and saved the day for the imprisoned men. Appearance of these aircraft, despite adverse weather conditions, provided a welcome sight for the infantrymen.

Significant Dates

September 1: As the NKA "noose" tightened on the Pusan Perimeter, Fifth Air Force units conducted relentless CAS and interdiction missions against NKA troops and armored columns attacking along the Naktong River front. Carrier-based aircraft from USN Task Force 77 also provided close air support to the perimeter defenders. General MacArthur directed General Stratemeyer to use all available FEAF airpower, including B-29s, to help the Eighth Army hold the "Pusan Perimeter," the southeast corner of the Korean peninsula that South Korea still controlled.

Headquarters EUSAK requested support missions from FAF to "attack and destroy hostile forces which have penetrated or threaten to penetrate our front lines." The Secret mission request orders called on FAF to support the defense of U.S. forces in South Korean and to be prepared to support a counterattack by blocking "enemy movement" with "particular attention to night movement across the Naktong River." [7]

On September 1st, a "miniature rotation plan" was established that would slowly begin to afford "a three day rest in Japan for officers and airmen who had spent a minimum of six weeks in Korea. Not more than four officers and seven airmen were placed on such duty at one time."

September 3: Task Force 77 withdrew its aircraft carriers from the Pusan area. It needed to conduct replenishment at sea operations and to move TF units north to strike communications targets. All close air support responsibility now rested with Far East Air Forces.

September 4: An H-5 helicopter rescued a downed U.S. pilot from behind enemy lines at Hanggan-dong. It was the first H-5 helicopter rescue of the war.

September 6: As North Korean forces approached Taegu, Eighth Army headquarters withdrew to Pusan.

September 8: The 18th FBG, which had departed Korea a month earlier, returned from Japan, settling at Pusan East (Tongnae). The 6002nd Fighter Wing moved to K-9 (Pusan).

September 9: North Korean forces attacking southeast of Hajang reached a point only eight miles from Taegu, their farthest penetration on the western front. FEAF

Deadly Eggs. *On the flight line at K-16, a re-arming crew maneuvers a napalm cannister into place as it readies a 67th Squadron Mustang for another mission. (Chatfield)*

Pre-Mission Conference with Armament Chief. *Major Stan Chatfield confers with the Armament Chief at K-16 before setting out on a combat mission. "Pineapple" as he was affectionately called by the pilots, was responsible for all the napalm, bombs, rockets and .50-caliber ammunition and for the loading of the aircraft. (Chatfield)*

Inchon Landings. *Four LST's unload men and equipment on the beach at Inchon, Korea on September 15, 1950. Ships include: LST-611, LST-745 and LST-715.*

Bomber Command began a rail interdiction campaign north of Seoul to slow enemy reinforcements, which might hinder the UN Inchon landing.

September 10: As a result of Task Force 77's unexpected withdrawal from close air support of the Eighth Army on September 3, General Stratemeyer persuaded General MacArthur to direct that all close air support requests must be routed through the Fifth Air Force. If Fifth Air Force lacked resources to meet the requests, they were to be forwarded to FEAF headquarters for coordination with the Commander, Naval Forces, Far East. [8]

September 13: Typhoon Kezia hit southern Japan, hampering FEAF operations and forcing some aircraft to move temporarily to Pusan and Taegu.

September 15: U.S. Marines invaded Wolmi-do in Inchon Harbor at dawn, occupying the island in less than an hour. The main U.S. X Corps landings at Inchon took place at high tide, in the afternoon, after a

forty-five-minute naval and air bombardment. U.S. Navy and United States Marine Corps aircraft from carriers off shore provided air cover during the amphibious assault. At the same time, FEAF air raids in South Korea prepared the way for the planned Eighth Army advance from the Pusan perimeter. [9]

The Inchon landings in the west central region of Korea were "indirectly supported" by the hard working Mustang pilots of the 18th FBW who "continued pressure against the enemy in support of the 24th Infantry, 25th Infantry, and the 1st Cavalry Divisions in the southern sector of Korea thus interdicting and possibly diverting forces to the north."

Mustangs of the 18th Fighter-Bomber Group "contributed their all-out support to the 24th and 25th Infantry Divisions and the 1st Cavalry Division along the Pusan perimeter thus indirectly aiding the landing at Inchon by diverting the enemy's attention from that area." [10]

September 16: U.S. forces secured Inchon and began moving toward Seoul. From the vicinity of Taegu, the U.S. Eighth Army launched its long-awaited offensive.

September 17: U.S. Marines captured Kimpo Airfield near Seoul. To support the Eighth Army offensive, Fifth Air Force F-51s and F-80s flew napalm attacks, reportedly killing over 1,200 enemy soldiers in Tabu-dong, Yongchon, and other strongholds near the Naktong River.

September 19: Supported by Fifth Air Force close air support missions, the 24th Infantry Division began crossing the Naktong River near Waegwan, and the 1st Cavalry Division broke through communist lines.

September 21: USAF forward air controllers in T-6 Mosquitoes equipped with air to ground radios spotted about thirty enemy tanks preparing to ambush the advancing 24th Infantry Division. They called USAF aircraft and USA ground artillery, which destroyed fourteen enemy tanks and forced

F-51 taxiing at K-9 in September 1950. (Barber)

the rest to flee.

September 22: North Korean resistance crumbled all along the Pusan perimeter. Lt. George W. Nelson, a USAF pilot in a Mosquito aircraft, dropped a note to 200 enemy troops northeast of Kunsan demanding their surrender. They complied, moving to a designated hill to be captured by nearby UN ground troops. [11]

September 23: HQ Fifth Air Force in Korea moved from Pusan to Taegu.

September 25: Far East Air Forces flew flare missions over Seoul all night that allowed USMC night fighters to attack North Korean troops fleeing the city.

September 26: U.S. military forces from Inchon and Pusan linked up near Osan, while ROK troops with Fifth Air Force support moved northward along the east coast toward the 38th Parallel.

Dogpatch Spa. *On September 5, 1950, Fifth Air Force ordered Major Arnold Mullins, CO of the 67th via classified instructions to relocate the 67th from Ashiya Air Force Base, Japan to K-9, near Pusan. "The move was finally made on the morning of the eighth. The pilots took off on a mission and upon completion landed at K-9, and known to all as "Dogpatch." The move was complete with the arrival of the water borne supplies a few days later." The spartan accommodations included primitive showers. (Barber)*

The "Secret" of Inchon

The week before General McArthur's famous landing at Inchon, during a flight debriefing, an intelligence officer told me all about it. The date, the time, place - everything! I flew several missions with this potentially compromising knowledge strapped under my helmet. I never understood how this dumb-ass intelligence officer had gained access to this information, or how he got a security clearance to begin with.

The Inchon landing came off without being compromised. It cut off the Commie troops around the Pusan perimeter and forced them to make a mad dash north to avoid being surrounded. This furnished us with lots of daytime targets for a couple of days. They, for the first time, did not have the prerogative of only moving at night and our Ferocious Four got our share.

Col. Howard "Scrappy" Johnson

(Above) **Tent City at K-9** *in September 1950. (Below)* **Outdoor chow.** *When weather cooperated chow was eaten outdoors at makeshift tables. (Schreffler)*

September 27: U.S. Marines drove enemy forces from Seoul and took control of the capital building. The Joint Chiefs of Staff ordered General MacArthur to destroy the North Korean Army, which involved crossing the 38th Parallel into North Korea. Only ROK troops were to be allowed by the UN Command in provinces bordering China and the Soviet Union.

September 28: ROK troops advanced into North Korea for the first time and General MacArthur officially restored Seoul to ROK President Syngman Rhee.

September 30: Throughout September, "bad weather, shortage of tents, bedding, and potable water provided much concern for officers and airmen alike" of the 18th FB Group. "There were no showers. Living conditions were, in a word, adverse. On September 30, 1950 a shower was installed in the Quarters (tent) area, however, living quarters proper were still over crowded." [12]

Combat Losses

Flentke, Capt. Donald L., 12th FBS pilot KIA in September 1950 near Wonsan, Korea. On Sunday, 7 October, Lt. Ken Barber wrote in his diary that he had "heard Bolt and Davis were shot down North of Pyongyang, and are walking back safely, we all hope. Also heard Flentke was killed. What a shame! He was in Mullins flight and they didn't miss him for thirty minutes...Mullins saw a flash out of the corner of his eye but thought nothing of it. Later, when they went

*MGen Earl Partridge, Commander Fifth Air Force, awards the Distinguished Flying Cross (DFC) to **Capt. Ed Mason** at K-9 in September 1950.*

back they found Flenthe's plane smeared all over the spot. They say Millie Flentke is about to crack up down at Clark Field."

Grisham, Capt. David Howard "Snowflake" 39th FIS pilot KIA on 3 September 1950 in the Sea of Japan. First Lieutenant Grisham (always known as "Snowflake"), was an ever-friendly Weather Officer, a forecaster who had at one time supposedly forecast a July snowfall at their central-Japan airbase and he turned out to be correct. It snowed enough to briefly close their airfield—hence his nickname "Snowflake," his friend and fellow pilot, Lt. Col. Duane

"Bud" Biteman recalled. "Grisham was caught up in the same Reduction in Force administrative "grounding" that had decked my friend, Don Bolt. In fact, his name was on the same set of orders returning him to flight status--provided that he "volunteer" for immediate combat duty in Korea. And, like Bolt and the others so named." Grisham had not flown any kind of airplane in a year. In Korea, Snowflake maintained his ground responsibilities as well, serving as one of only two assigned base weather forecasters, which meant that his combat flying had to be carefully integrated with his ground duties. "He couldn't fly very often--maybe once or twice a week, at most, and it meant that he had to fill in on many of the odd-ball scheduling times. For example, Grisham would often request the early, pre-dawn missions so that he could be back on the ground in time to meet his schedule as weather forecaster for the day; or he would take the last flight of the day for the same reason, so that he could finish his weather forecaster duties before going off on his combat missions. "Snowflake" Grisham was flying a pre-dawn mission from Ashiya, Japan, and while climbing his heavily-laden F-51 through night-weather conditions over the Sea of Japan, he disappeared from formation.

The 18th had been reassigned to Ashiya because the enemy had pushed the United Nations operations back to the Pusan perimeter, former Flight Leader Captain (later Colonel) James C. Peek explained. "The bomb line was just north of Taegu and for the security and safety of our airplanes we flew them to Japan each night after having staged out of Taegu during daylight hours. The procedure we followed was a fully loaded pre-dawn take off from Japan, fly across the Korea Strait (which is between the East China Sea and the Sea of Japan) and hit targets at first light in Korea."

After expending all ammo, napalm and/or bombs, the Mustangs "would land at Taegu, get refueled and rearmed, be briefed for another mission and go again. Usually we would fly three or more missions during the day, then on the last combat mission fly back to Ashiya instead of landing

Pusan Harbor aerial view near K-9. (Mason)

again in Korea. Fuel was not a problem because of the close proximity of the bomb line, which was only about 15 minutes from the airfield," Peek recalled.

The morning of September 3, 1950, Peek was assigned to lead one of the many flights of F-51D's being sent to Korea. "We were awakened about 0300, got dressed, obtained a bite of breakfast from the mess hall and went to Operations for our orders. In Ops I found my assignment was to be in Korea at first light with four aircraft and to attack enemy troops and rolling stock before they could hide themselves for the day. Operations had made up our sortie schedule and with me was a brand new 2nd Lt. by the name of Bader, he was the number 2 man on my left wing. I cannot remember the name of the element leader--the number 3 man--but the number 4 man was Grisham. I had never flown with Grisham before."

After the squadron briefing, Grisham mentioned to Peek that there was some weather over the sea en route to Korea. Peek replied that "we usually had to fly through some weather going over and for him just to glue himself to the number 3 aircraft and to never let that plane get out of his sight. Normal procedure was to leave all navigation lights on during the night flight until we reached Korea."

The take off and join up went smoothly, and the four aircraft set course for Tsushima Island climbing to 8,000 feet. "About 15 minutes from the coast of Japan we entered some light clouds," Peek recalled, "and I radioed my flight and told them to join up in close formation and hang in tight." The aircraft continued climbing and leveled off at 8,000 feet, then throttled back to cruise settings and proceeded on course. As the minutes passed the turbulence became rough and then extremely rough. "I kept talking to my flight telling them exactly what I was doing in order to keep them calm and abreast of this very serious situation. As the weather deteriorated I told them we would climb to 10,000 feet to get into smoother weather because by that time I was aware that we were in a typhoon or a thunderstorm of gigantic proportions. We then leveled

Hidden Pontoon Bridge Examined. *Before dawn, the night reconnaissance aircraft returned to Japan from Korea with the latest photographs of enemy movements and installations. Captain Herbert G. Spees and Sergeant John W. Cross examine photographs of a hidden North Korean pontoon bridge prior to sending a flash photo interpretation report to Fifth Air Force Headquarters where it will be used to schedule a strike by fighter bombers. (NARA)*

off at 10,000 still being buffered by the storm. At times while holding the needle and ball centered and the rate of climb at zero I watched the altimeter go past 11,000 and then down to 9,000 feet. The updrafts and down drafts in that air mass were something to write home about. We remained in straight and level flight but the updrafts would push us up a thousand feet or so and the down drafts would pull us down some 2,000 feet. It was an eerie feeling, fighting our way through this severe storm. Every few minutes I kept telling the flight on the radio to stick with me and keep tucked in so as not to become lost out there alone,"

Peek said.

The four planes flew in such weather conditions "for the better part of an hour and sometime during this period--unknown to me--Snowflake lost the formation. When we finally crossed the Korea Strait the weather cleared, we broke out of the clouds and saw Korea below us in the breaking dawn. We all gave great sighs of relief upon finally getting out of that storm. I then counted heads and found there were only three of us. I asked the element leader about his wing man and he said that because of the severe turbulence and the necessity to keep his eyes glued to the lead aircraft that he never noticed when Snowflake left the formation. I called and called for our number 4 man and never received a response. At this point there was nothing we could do for Snowflake so we pressed on with the mission hoping that he aborted and returned to Ashiya."

The flight of three Mustangs "continued north into our assigned target area and found many troops in the open who were in the process of camouflaging their tanks, trucks and other equipment. We burned 3 enemy tanks with napalm, strafed the troops with their trucks and left the area with many of those troops dead and much of that enemy equipment burning. We then flew to our staging base to land and refuel and rearm for the next mission. In our debriefing, we gave a full report of our mission including the loss of one aircraft and pilot. Operations checked by phone with Ashiya

Pursuing North Korean Forces. *Soldiers of the U.S. 24th Regiment pursue retreating North Korean forces after the Inchon amphibious landing. (NARA)*

Preparing for the Inchon Invasion

The process of loading his vehicles, equipment and team aboard the USNS Gen. Simon B. Buckner on 7 September 1950, was frustrating and confusing for Lt. Ken Barber and his men. After getting aboard the Buckner, Barber "got into a conversation with Lt. Hargrave, the billeting officer, which paid off in that I got a room with two bunks and a private bathroom." Hargrave fumed to Barber that "this loading was the worst mess of confusion and inefficiency he'd ever seen." And Barber added, "I feel the same way. If this outfit acts in combat like they do here in port, God help us all."

Loading went on "all day and all night. They even sleep on the dock. The story goes that one G.I. while asleep was run over by two half-tracks, but woke up long enough to fire four .45 shots at the half-tracks—and then died."

The next day, Friday, 9 September, Barber tried to check on his men, but couldn't find them. Barber observed a U.S. Sergeant admonish some ROK (Republic of Korea) soldiers. At first, Barber "was impressed by how impatient he could get with them, but later I could see why," he said. "They push and crowd, break into line ahead of others, crash the chow line twice, and are generally nuisances. One (ROK soldier) is supposed to go with each American soldier as a personal bodyguard and translator. What a fouled up bunch of people they are!"

On Monday, 11 September 1950, Barber's convoy left Yokohama and put out to sea "to avoid an imminent typhoon." By mid-week the effects of the violent storm were visited on the tossing ships. "The last two days have really been rugged. About noon yesterday the seas became heavy, climaxing last night in a terrific gale which took one of the jeeps overboard—and a couple of men." The "meter" broke at a wind speed of 79 mph. "We have been blacked out, and it's hard to describe the oppressive stuffiness of a closed up ship." Moreover, Barber "was cursed by a roommate who loves cards, whiskey and tobacco. As a consequence my room smells like the back room of a bar, and I am stifled every time I walk in. It is even worse with this black-out, and not being able to open the port."

The ROK personnel were "unbearable! They vomit, but still never miss chow call. It's incredible how they can do it! They have made the place very messy for the GI's. They were issued fine Officer's sleeping bags which they allow to lie on the decks, wet and unclaimed. I have no use for them at all!"

One of the passengers on the ships was 1st Lt. Al Haig (Class of '47), Barber noted. "Have talked several times with Al Haig, General Almond's aide. Al is a very smart person, has a lot of common sense, and I expect to see him go far in the service. We discussed the unfortunate situation that usually makes a man have to be old and burned out before he has an opportunity to express his opinions and put some of his ideas into effect. Like Al, I feel that I have lots of good ideas for the Air Force—but when will I ever be able to use any of them?"

[Eventually, Alexander Haig was promoted to the rank of General and would serve as Secretary of State during President Ronald Reagan's first term of office.]

Lt. Col. Kenneth Barber. Korean War Diary Number One (unpublished), 4 August 1950.

and found out that Snowflake had not returned to that base. My best estimate of where Snowflake went down is near Tsushima Island where I think we had the most severe weather," Peek concluded.

Hook, Capt. Robert, 12th Squadron pilot KIA in September 1950.

Lightner, 1st Lt. Jack A., 12th Squadron pilot KIA on 7 September 1950. 1st Lieutenant Jack Lightner was nursing his combat damaged Mustang back across the Sea of Japan to Ashiya after close air support mission near the Pusan Perimeter. That day, nine weeks after Lightner's arrival in Japan, the 12th and 67th Squadrons were moving back to the Korean Peninsula's newly refurbished base at Pusan. Jack, however, was busy flying with Capt. Robert R. Blank, attacking enemy trucks and tanks, engaged in desperate fighting just 20 miles northeast of our Taegu airstrip. "On that day (7 Sept.) I led a four ship flight out of Ashiya, at 9:30 a.m," Blank explained. "Jack Lightner was flying my wing. During the attack Jack destroyed two large enemy tanks, three trucks, and damaged another medium tank. We were being fired upon heavily, but Jack never said anything about his aircraft being hit. After expending all of our ammunition, we rejoined the flight for the return flight to Ashiya, Japan. We had passed over the southeast coast of Korea, and were about twenty miles over the Sea of Japan at an altitude of about 7500 feet when Jack called by radio to say his aircraft was on fire in the engine. He immediately turned back toward the Korean coast, hoping to reach an auxiliary base located about five miles east of Pusan. I turned with him, and remained in close formation, about 50 feet off his wing. His engine quit entirely after just 3 or 4 minutes and the plane began to rapidly lose altitude in a glide. I told him repeatedly that he should bail out no lower than 2000 feet, and that I would circle him until a rescue boat could pick him up. He answered in a calm voice and assured me that he would bail out at 2000 feet. When that altitude was reached, Jack said he was bailing out. The canopy came off, but Jack seemed to be having difficulty getting out of the plane. When the plane was

"An enemy tank, the Russian built T-34, was a special kill,"Joe Roiz remembered. Mute testimony of the accuracy of close support missions flown by FAF fighters is this North Korean tank, blasted out of the path of advancing 24th Infantry Division knits near Waegwan. The mangled shell of the jellied gas napalm bomb that knocked out the tank is shown in the right foreground. (NARA)

about 300 feet above the water, it suddenly nosed over into a 45-degree dive toward the sea. Jack at last got out of the plane at only about fifty feet, and never had a chance to pull the ripcord to open his chute. He struck the water at almost the same instant as the aircraft, hitting just behind the plane. I believe that he was killed instantly. It was then 11:20 a. m." Lieutenant Lightner was just four months short of his twenty-fifth birthday at the time of his death, noted Lt. Col. Duane E. Biteman, USAF (Ret).

Scanlon, Major, 12th Squadron pilot KIA in September 1950.

Webster, Capt. Harold Jr., 12th Squadron pilot KIA in September 1950.

Endnotes

[1] *U.S. Air Force Historical Research Agency. January 2002. The U.S. Air Force's First War: Korea 1950-1953 Significant Events. September 1950.*

[2] *History of the 18th Fighter-Bomber Group, July-October, 1950. USAFHRA.*

[3] *History of the 18th Fighter-Bomber Group, July-October, 1950. USAFHRA.*

Major Blume heads for his quarters in September 1950. (Regan)

[4] *History of the 18th Fighter-Bomber Group, July-October, 1950. USAFHRA.*

[5] *USAFHRA. "The Story of the 18th Fighter-Bomber Group in the Korean United Nations Police Action." 6002nd Tactical Support Wing, Public Information Office. S/Sgt Sandy Colton.*

[6] *USAFHRA. History of the 67th Fighter-Bomber Squadron, September 1950.*

[7] *EUSAK mission support memorandum of 1 September 1950 to Fifth Air Force. (NARA)*

[8] *USAFHRA. History of the 67th Fighter-Bomber Squadron, October 1950.*

[9] *U.S. Air Force Historical Research Agency. January 2002. The U.S. Air Force's First War: Korea 1950-1953 Significant Events. September 1950.*

[10] *History of the 18th Fighter-Bomber Group, July-October, 1950. USAFHRA.*

[11] *U.S. Air Force Historical Research Agency. January 2002. The U.S. Air Force's First War: Korea 1950-1953 Significant Events. September 1950.*

[12] *USAFHRA. History of the 67th Fighter-Bomber Squadron, September 1950.*

Moon's Conference. *Major "Moon" Mullins confers with his pilots in September 1950 at K-9. (Burns)*

Captain (later Colonel) Charles E. Schreffler pre-flights his aircraft prior to a mission from K-9 in September 1950. (Schreffler)

"Skid Row" returns to K-9 from a combat mission. (Burns)

First Daze At K-9

Sergeant William J. "Sandy" Colton, the assistant public information officer and staff journalist for the 18th Wing newspaper, *Truckbuster*, arrived at K-9 on 5 September 1950. He would spend nine challenging months with the 18th before he was transferred to an assignment for the *Pacific Stars and Stripes*.

Colton would "never forget" the pre-dawn flight from Ashiya, Japan to K-9 near Pusan, South Korea.

Each side of the lumbering C-46 had hammock-like bucket seats for the passengers. The center aisle was loaded chest high with tied down crates covered with huge tarps, leaving little aisle room at the sides except for an area near the exit door. "It was still dark when we boarded and picked our way around the lashed cases in the dim light to find a seat and strap ourselves in. The crew chief slammed the door shut and locked it. The engines coughed, sputtered and came to life."

"As we taxied towards the runway you could feel the apprehension in some of the men," Colton recalled. "Some of the others were just hung over from celebrating what they considered their last night out for a while. The plane roared down the runway and into the black sky until it reached cruising altitude and the engines settled into a steady drone. The men aboard tried fitfully to sleep. Some unbuckled their safety belts and crawled atop the packing cases or onto the floor. Others laid out in the hammock seat or just sat there, chin on their chest. A few smoked fitfully. One sat polishing his newly issued M1 carbine."

As the plane slowly crossed the Sea of Japan heading northeast towards Korea, "the sun rose, casting round beams of light through the starboard windows, illuminating the dust and smoke filled cabin and its weary passengers. Peering out the windows you could see small islands and then the Korea coast line."

"Christ! Who shit!," screamed someone from under the tarpaulins by the exit door. Out popped the head of Lieutenant Phil Conserva, one of the F-51 pilots en route to

Venison Rations. "*At K-9 in September 1950, the food was not gourmet by any stretch of the imagination,*" Allen Burns recalled. The food was mostly K-rations. "*A few of us--at spare moments--decided to go hunting up in the hills. We had heard there were deer up there. What we found were a lot of deer and a lot of pheasants.*" The gun Burns is holding is "*an old Japanese shotgun we liberated and used later to shoot pheasants. The deer were killed with M-1 carbines. Needless to say, we ate a little better because of this.*" (Burns)

Korea. Most didn't hear him above the roar of the engines. The crew chief, sitting by the door, with the heap that was Conserva at his feet, answered, "Welcome to Korea! The Koreans save their shit and spread it on their rice paddies. You can smell it as soon as you hit the coast line, even at this altitude!"

"A green light went on near the door and the crew chief picked up some ear phones to hear the pilot announce our approach to K-9. He got up and made his way carefully up the aisle waking the passengers and getting everyone back in their seats and buckled up for the landing. Sleepy eyes stared long and hard at the almost treeless hills, dirty brown rice paddies and a long strip of sandy beach. There was the twin thump of wheels locking down and then the thud as we landed on the steel runway mats and began our undulating rattling ride until we finally turned left and stopped in front of a tent marked base operations."

"Welcome To Korea..."

The crew chief opened the door, pushed it back against the fuselage, and hung an aluminum ladder from the doorway. The

apprehensive passengers, disembarked, one by one. They were met by a Lieutenant Colonel who introduced himself and announced, "Welcome to Korea, gentlemen. This is K-9 Air Base, some six miles north of Pusan, and roughly 80 miles from the Pusan perimeter and the shooting war! You are all part of the advance element. The rest of the wing will join us in a few days. It will be our job to prepare for their arrival. The first missions from this field are scheduled for tomorrow. Officers check into the BOQ tent behind operations. Enlisted men check into your billets, two tents up."

Once the enlisted men dumped what little gear they had brought with them, they were immediately put to work unloading the aircraft and setting up tents for the rest of the day. "There was no flooring in the tents so we scrounged left over steel landing mats on which to spread our sleeping bags. The area where we set up our tents had been a former rice paddy and, while not muddy at the time, was dusty dirt," Colton explained.

Colton could not remember what or whether he ate that night, although some "sort of primitive kitchen was set up." He did remember being "dead tired when we were finally allowed to turn in and go to sleep. The enlisted men had one tent, the officers another. There were probably a few more tents set up well off the edge of the runway."

Later that night the new arrivals "were awakened by automatic weapon's fire close by." A tense, scared voice outside shouted, "Don't turn on any lights and stay in your tents."

There was no electricity in any of the tents. It was pitch black. Colton could hear gun bolts being shoved back and shells loaded in the chambers of the carbines we carried.

To him and the others, "it seemed like an eternity just lying there in the dark, afraid and worried that now that we were in Korea at war, we were under attack. It seemed like hours in the dark silence before, exhausted from our day's labor, we finally fell asleep."

In the morning Colton was awakened by an incredulous voice—one of his tentmates—who said, "I'll be damned!"

"What's the matter," asked Colton, as he rose painfully from his "bed" of pierced steel planking, "feeling much like a waffle from the round holes in the metal landing strip planking we used as a bed, plus the after pains of the heavy work loads of the day before."

"Just look here," the voice answered as he held up his carbine . "When that gun went off last night I loaded a shell in the chamber and must have fallen asleep with the safety off! I had it pointed right at you all night!"

"He was a Master Sergeant," Colton recalled, "and even though he was a National Guard recall, he should have known better. I was ready to kill him right there."

This particular sergeant didn't last long with the 18th. "He excelled in politics and had himself transferred to an F-84 outfit that required cement runways for their opera-

Stirring Napalm. *"First, I found this long stick," Sgt. Strom appears to be explaining to Sgt. Charles Maynard (right), "then I stir it up real well--but very carefully," as they prepare to mix a seemingly endless supply of napalm. (Maynard)*

18th Group armament crew.

tions which also meant better housing and better food." Colton would meet the Master Sergeant again—"in a slit trench at Pyongyang West during a raid by Bedcheck Charlie. I was glad to see he wasn't carrying a weapon that time."

After spending yet another day unloading planes and setting up tents, Colton was glad to unload the Public Information Office (PIO) crates. He hovered over them as them were taken to "an old school building just off the main gate to the field. Col. Low met me when I entered the building and told me where our office would be— an empty room on the second floor. I un-

packed the crates and set up our office. Furnishings included a cot, which as ranking NCO, I confiscated as my own rather than return to tent city."

One of the crates contained many of Colton's personal belongings—a duffle bag that contained, besides extra clothing, his personal Webster's dictionary, a Roget's Thesaurus, Bartlett's Familiar Quotations, and, being a "romanticist," an old favorite, "Vagabond's Houses," poems by Don Blanding.

Office equipment included the shipping crate that also served as a desk. The crate also contained a folding chair, an old Un-

FAC "Winner"

by Col. Howard "Scrappy" Johnson

I was sent on forward air controller duty with a South Korean division. Our operations officer who did not like to make decisions selected me for the FAC tour. Cards with individual's names on them were drawn out of a hat and mine was the "winner." Mo would never have allowed this to happen. He was not negligent on making decisions and would have felt that drawing cards for an assignment such as this was passing the buck, or said differently, shirking responsibility.

I had flown 83 missions and since the squadron only furnished one FAC per month, I would have flown a hundred missions before the next quota. I departed Taegu driving a jeep and reached the ROK (Republic of Korea) Corps I was assigned to the next day.

Just prior to arriving at their position, I saw two Commie tanks lying in a ravine by a turn in the road. They were still smoking.

The previous night the South Korean troops had set a trap for them. They knew the tanks had been by-passed so they placed a 75-mm gun at a curve in a road. When the Commie tanks appeared they fired point blank at them from about 50 meters. The blast was so great it knocked the tanks off the road and into the ravine.

The ROK Division did not enjoy a high priority for air strikes. Consequently, I did not do a hell of a lot of controlling. As we moved north we had little need for air strikes because the opposition was very light. The North Koreans were still in disarray from the surprise of the Inchon landing. We moved about twenty miles each day. The South Koreans were accompanied by a group of American advisors led by a U.S. Army lieutenant colonel.

We advanced without opposition most of the day. Late in the afternoon the North Koreans would put up a defense. The South Koreans usually broke through after a short skirmish.

The U. S. advisory group had a master sergeant from the U.S. Corps of Engineers assigned to it. He had a small group of South Korean women that he sent ahead of our advance to bring him back information. After the ROK's had broken through one of the evening roadblocks, he told me his informants told him that, just prior to setting up the road block, several truck loads of recruits had driven up from Pyongyang. They were obviously very green and were singing and trying to boost their spirits.

Luckily for our side their skill did not match their enthusiasm.

I did not enjoy this tour as a forward air controller, and would have rather spent the time flying, the experience was interesting. It also provided me with some extra war stories later at the bar.

I was replaced prior to the Chinese entering the war. My replacement bought the farm when this and other ROK divisions collapsed from the Chinese onslaught which was launched on November 25th 1950.

---

derwood typewriter, some reams of paper, ink, pencils and erasers, scissors, glue, paper clips, a stapler and a few other office essentials.

Not long after, the rest of the PIO staff arrived—PFC Eugene McWhite and Cpl Bob Dumont. The Public Information Officer, Lt. Gallagher, to Colton seemed to have "absolutely no interest in the job and wanted to be a maintenance officer. That worked out fine for me. He pretty much turned me loose to do things the way I wanted which I did."

One of the first things Colton "did," was to get hold of a jeep and drive down to Fifth Air Force headquarters, then just a few miles down the road towards Pusan. He was determined to "find out just what I was supposed to write about. He had had writing jobs before, as a newspaper editor for the 20th Air Force on Guam and as the historian for the Air Materiel and Armament

Test Center at Eglin AFB in Florida, but he had never before been assigned to a PIO office.

"Just write about the exploits of your unit," Colton was told, "and bring them here."

There was no telephone or teletype communication with Tokyo from K-9 at that time. Then Colton's sharp eyes noted what actually happened to the stories that were delivered that way. For the most part they landed in a box pawed over by legitimate international correspondents. It was the intention by FAF that the journalists would see a story they liked and file it—or part of it—via their networks back around the world. Often the story would appear verbatim "under their own by-line! Oh well. It was our job to feed them material."

When Colton returned to the base that evening he made his way to the officer's tent. After getting permission to enter, he introduced himself as their PIO in search of stories. "Their reply surprised and almost scared me."

One of the pilots held up a copy of the *Stars and Stripes* and pointing to it said, "See this story? 'B-26's destroy oil refinery in Wonsan.' Hell, that wasn't B-26's, that was us!"

Another chimed in "I just got a letter from my mother. She wants to know what I'm flying. She says she sees stories about B-29's, B-26's, F-80's and F-84's but never sees anything about an F-51!"

"What conversation I had that day with those pilots,"

Capt. Frank Buzze

by Col. Harry Moreland

Frank Buzze was one of the original pilots to go up with the Dallas Project from Clark Field. Like all of the original pilots he was a volunteer. He joined the outfit after leaving the 44th Fighter Squadron in the Philippines and went to Japan with the first batch of pilots. Frank had lots of experience in the P-51 having flown it in the Pacific during WWII and was considered to be one of the best pilots.

After arriving in Japan we soon moved to Taegu where we were given 10 Mustangs to use that had been pulled out of mothballs and put back into shape—not too good of shape. Some of the instrumentation left much to be desired as the following tale will illustrate.

With only ten aircraft it was hard to mount much of a full days effort so we limited ourselves to two ship flights and spread them out through out the day turning them around as soon as possible. We developed an assembly line technique to speed up the turn around. Upon landing the airplanes would be towed to a line where they would be refueled, then to the next stop for .50-cal. ammo and then napalm. The crew chief would follow along to inspect the aircraft for the next pilot. Some times the same pilot would stay with the plane depending on the length of his previous flight. It was not unusual to get five sorties on an airplane in one day.

It soon became apparent that we were worrying the North Koreans during the daytime, but they had free access to the roads at night. It was decided that we would start night operations, as well as continue our daytime efforts—all this with ten airplanes.

None of us were trained for attacking night targets. Our tasks were to keep a constant eye on the major roads and to make passes at the vehicles as we spotted them. Because of the limited number of planes, we sent up single planes during this phase. The first few nights we encountered a fair amount of traffic running with their lights on and it wasn't too hard to make a firing pass. It was quite a blinding experience to fire rockets at night.

After a few nights the traffic became harder to locate, they were running without lights.

On one such mission Frank Buzze had to let down through an overcast to locate the road with the traffic. After attacking a convoy and making a sharp turn to avoid ground fire, he was horrified to see that his gyro compass was spinning and the magnetic compass was not working. Under the overcast it was impossible to tell which way to go. So he climbed over the cloud layer, located the North Star and reset his gyro compass while pointed at the North Star and then reversed course to fly back to the general vicinity of Taegu. He contacted the homer at the base and they steered him in for a let down—a most happy soul to be back on the ground. Our night operations did not last long and we soon received more aircraft and no longer continued the single ship operations. Later, I learned that if properly trained night work could be most rewarding.

Colton recalled, "was pretty much the same. They were discouraged that no one seemed to know what they were doing or going through. I left that tent challenged, determined to change that."

He would, too!

THE FEROCIOUS FOUR

by Col. Howard "Scrappy" Johnson

We were a flight of nicknames, "Scrappy," "Chappie," "Mother," and "Spud." There was me, the leader, Capt. Howard "Scrappy" Johnson, 1st Lt. Daniel "Chappie" James, 1st Lt. Ted "Mother" Baader, and 1st Lt. "Spud" Taylor. I never knew him by anything but "Spud."

We were formed in the summer of 1950 to fight the Commie bastards who were coming down from the north and attacking our good guys. I was the leader, not only by rank, but also by experience, and all those sneaky tricks I'd learned from Pappy Hood back in the PI. The four of us flew over 60 missions together. I don't remember who came up with the name. It was either Spud or Chappie, or probably me.

Ted Baader was nicknamed "Mother" because when he'd have more that one drink he'd say, "Mother wouldn't like this." I suspected that name was pinned on him by Danny Farr. "Spud" Taylor was a class guy, and one of the best saxophone players I ever heard play. His wife was the singer in the band he'd organized at Clark Field in the Philippines. I can still hear her and Spud singing, "Baby It's Cold Outside."

Chappie James was—well CHAPPIE JAMES.

We were fighting the North Koreans. They had little in the way of an Air Force, a few Yaks which were similar to our P-51s. When you compared pilots that's where the similarity ended.

Our pilots were so superior it was no contest. Any Yak sighted by an American pilot was promptly shot down. If you were lucky enough to see one, you had better not announce it on the radio, or you would have about 30 U.S. planes racing to beat you to it. We were not lucky enough to sight one, but I guarantee if we had, we'd have quickly

Capt. Howard "Scrappy" Johnson

1st Lt. Claude R. "Spud" Taylor

downed the SOB.

Here is a miniscule portion of the many missions flown by the Ferocious Four.

"Shooting Chappie Down"

I had trained the flight to make strafing passes individually (not follow in trail), when strafing a target. We made passes from different points of the compass. We were strafing a target near Pohang (K-3) in this fashion one day. I was making my last pass, and had just fired when an F-51 flashed in front of me at about a 90% angle. I did not think much of it until we were joining up the flight and Red Four (Chappie) was missing. We headed for K-2 to refuel before returning to our home base, which happened to be Ashya at the time. All the way to K-2 I was thinking to myself, My God I shot Chappie down.

Lt. Ted "Mother" Baader

After landing, while walking to de-briefing we were three dejected fighter pilots. At de-briefing we were told that number four had landed ahead of us. "Where is he?" "He's sacked out in a tent in area II." The de-briefing officer replied. With great sighs of relief, we were elated and mad at the same time. We raced over, rousted him out, and GAVE HIM HELL. He said he'd flown on ahead because his radio had gone out.

Hiding Tanks

One day we were bombing and strafing near a village between Taejon and Suwon when an enemy tank came racing out of a building in the village and sped north on a road toward Suwon raising a huge cloud of dust. We'd already dropped our bombs, so we took turns strafing it. After several passes, the crew must have grown weary of all those .50-calibers bouncing of their tank, so they pulled up under a small trestle, opened the hatch, climbed out and ran like hell. We continued to strafe it and with the hatch open we were able to start a fire and eventually its fuel started burning, and its ammo started exploding.

Driving a tank inside a building was one of the Commies favorite tricks. (After all it wasn't their building.) They'd drive them right through a wall to hide them from us. I saw several instances of this tactic later on when I served as a Forward Air Controller. Why that tank crew backed out of the building and raced up the road at that particular

time, I'll never know. They were perfectly hidden and would have been safe from us if they had stayed put.

"Die Like A Man"

For the most part U.S. pilots flew and died with honor. A good example is Major "Lou" Sebille of the 67th Squadron of our 18th group. He was killed flying into an enemy gun emplacement. He received the Medal of Honor for his heroic deed. However, another incident remains clear in my mind. One day when we were on our way home from a mission, ground fire hit a pilot from another group. He panicked and was shouting on the radio. "I'm hit, I'm going down, I'm hit and I'm going to crash." Another pilot got on the radio and calmly in a disgusted sounding voice, said, "Shut up fella and die like a man."

Seeing The Ground Fire

One evening just prior to dark we were strafing a position in a small town north of K-2, when I spotted machine gun fire coming out of the window of a house. The gunner was firing at Mother's airplane. I was in position to just lower the nose and let him have it with six .50-caliber's. Not only did I wipe the gunner out but several explosions came from the house, indicating he had a small arsenal in there. Had it not been near dark, I would not have been able to see the guy firing at us. Up to that time I'd flown in broad daylight and was not aware of how much they were shooting at us. As the darkness came the ground seemed to light up.

The General's B-17

Fifth Air Force moved its headquarters to Taegu. General Partridge, the FAF Commander had a personal B-17 parked at K-2. The Commies got within 7 miles of the base, and we began to get itchy about that. We made jokes like, "When that B-17 leaves, we're gitten in our Mustangs and hauling ass outa here." We finally were ordered to move to Ashiya, but I found out later that General Partridge had left several days before, leaving his B-17 there for morale purposes.

Mother Wants

To Hammer

After being run out of K-2, we flew out of Ashiya for a while then moved to K-9, near Pusan. Near the town of Pusan there was a UN hospital, which had a club. Some nights, if you were lucky, you might get to see a nurse there.

One night—no nurses in sight—Mother Baader, having downed a enough drinks to become pugnacious, got into a heated argument with a Marine Major, who was loudly declaiming that the Air Force didn't know how to fly close support. This did not wash well with us since we'd been fighting the war from the get go and the Marines had only arrived. We were particularly annoyed at this loud-mouthed fellow—Baader more than the rest of us. Nevertheless we got Ted safely out of the club. And, when on the way back to the base he told us the USMC Major was not even a pilot, not even an infantryman, but a public relations officer, we almost turned back to let Mother hammer the guy.

On a lighter note, I carried a single action Colt .45 all the time. It was in a quick draw spring-loaded holster that Mother's brother had sent him from Chicago. Chappie said, "Hey Scrappy, you've been carry-

An 18ᵗʰ Wing Mustang lands at K-9 in October 1950. (Myers)

ing that thing all this time, and I bet it won't even shoot." The others took it up and prodded me into shooting it. Since we were in an open weapons carrier, and in what we thought was an unpopulated area, I drew the Colt, pointed it to the sky, and fired it three times. After the laughter subsided, we soberly realized that we had just passed in front of the Fifth Air Headquarters building, when I'd fired my gun. We hauled out of there as fast as we could.

Delayed Ignition

While we were at K-9 the Commies had us closed into a small perimeter. We sometimes felt we needed to do desperate things to keep them from overrunning us completely. We four were flying a recce mission about 3000' east of the perimeter, when I spotted an artillery unit on a sandbar in a riverbed. They had six artillery pieces all lined up and were busy firing at our troops. We had four ships with two napalm bombs each. We couldn't believe they had allowed themselves to be so exposed. Normally they'd hide themselves better.

We came around and whoosh, dropped the napalm from tree top level. As happened a lot the fuzes did not ignite the napalm. It was all over and around them but it didn't burn. This happened so often it was standard procedure for us to make another pass, using the guns with API ammo, we'd set the napalm on fire. The artillery crew gave a sigh of relief when the napalm didn't burn, but this was short lived. On the next pass I strafed them and the whole area burst in flames.

Smoking Tunnel

We sometimes flew in two ship elements. We figured that two 12ᵗʰ Fighter Squadron pilots were good as four from most other

outfits. Mother was flying my wing we were recce-ing a segment of the north-south railroad in eastern South Korea. We came to a tunnel with smoke trickling out of the windward side of it. This was common procedure for the Commies. When planes were in the area, they'd hole up in the tunnels. They'd think they were safe there. This day they were badly fooled. We positioned ourselves so that when I dropped a napalm tank in one end, Mother slammed one in the other end. This removed the oxygen from the tunnel. And made breathing very difficult for any occupants.

A Quick Mission

We kept a two ship flight on alert so if something "hot" came up we could react in a hurry. This morning Mother and I were pulling the duty, when we were told to go to the assistance of an army division that was being held up by a road block about 50 miles to the northwest. The only problem was the weather. The ceiling was less than 1000' and the visibility was poor. The hills around the base were protruding up into the clouds. After takeoff we stayed below the clouds and managed to work our way west through a riverbed. After about 20 miles the weather got gradually better, and became clear when we reached the army division. They were strung out on a road headed west in about fifty trucks. The head vehicle was stopped around a bend in the road from a village about a quarter of a mile away. The Commies had some machine guns in a couple of the houses nearest them.

We flew in, made several strafing passes, and silenced the guns. We flew back and did a couple of rolls over the trucks, got thanked by the controller, and headed back to base. We were sweating out landing in the foggy weather, but luckily, it had moved out when we arrived home.

Chappie and Spud

While I was on FAC duty, Spud was shot down while leading the flight. Chappie took over, orbited two ships for RESCAP and called for a chopper. Even this early in the war there were rescue helicopters. After receiving no response, Chappie headed for the chopper base. He intended to lead the chopper to where Spud was down. His request for help was refused. The choppers were all being held on ground alert because General MacArthur was making a flying inspection over the battlefield.

Chappie went so far as to land at the base and plead with them to go get Spud out. They could not because of their orders. Time and fuel duly ran out and they had to leave Spud. He was later found dead on the spot. The North Koreans did not take pilot prisoners, at least any that I knew of. I doubt if General MacArthur knew about those orders to ground the choppers.

Some staff weenie probably conceived it. Known or not, a good man was lost because of it--and Chappie was devastated. I heard a couple of nights later he sang an emotional version of "My Buddy" in the Officers Club. I could understand this because I knew how much he loved Spud.

When I returned to the squadron from Forward Air Controller duty, I flew five more missions. I was told Chappie had been transferred to K-2 (Taegu) to fly a cameraman in a T-33. He'd lost it after seeing Spud shot down. Spud was gone, Chappie was gone and Mother and I were the only ones left of the Ferocious Four.

The Ferocious Four flew together, partied together, and were almost inseparable for a couple of months. Then I was sent on forward Air Controller, Spud got shot down, Chappie was transferred. Things were never the same. THOSE WERE THE DAYS.

Forward Air Control Team #7

When he reported to Camp McGill, Lt. Ken Barber was told that he would go to a special four-day school "to try to make us more effective than the previous jeep controllers." He was advised that his Detached Service "will be for some time, maybe until the end of the war." The briefer said "that while we probably now felt that we had been shafted out of a lot of good flying time (and most of us did), we would probably get very enthusiastic over the whole deal. We are to have a personal jeep, a radio jeep, and a trailer. We also will be given all sorts of field equipment plus binoculars, watches, carbines, etc. Makes me almost wish I'd left a lot of my own stuff at Ashiya," he noted.

Barber's team included PFC J. D. Mosley, Corporal J. B. Chandler, and Corporal William Wilkerson. They were "mechanics and radio men, tho I do not think they know anything about it as yet." Wilkerson, who would be promoted to Sergeant on Barber's recommendation on October 19th, was from Meridian, Mississippi and had been attached to the 49th Maintenance Squadron at Misawa AFB, Japan. Chandler was from Lucasville, Ohio, and had been assigned to the 3rd Communications Squadron at Yokota, AFB, Japan. Mosley was from Morris, Alabama and had also been assigned to the 3rd Communications Squadron.

"Rumor, and it's pretty reliable, indicates that we'll probably be in an invasion, the 3rd wave ashore, and the Major thinks the war will be over three weeks later."

"This should prove to be very interesting," Barber observed, "and will give me the opportunity to see war as it really is in all its raw grimness."

He had no idea how grim it would actually be for the next four months.

The prospect "of being in on the invasion pleases me immensely," he noted.

On 2 September 1950 started TACP "school" at Camp McGill. Classes covered such topics as tactical air support in amphibious operations, radio equipment, tactical air support communications, coordination of supporting arms, speed map reading (signs and symbols), RT (radio tele-

phone) procedures covering authentication systems, capabilities and limitations of close support, operations orders and air plans.

At one point, Barber doodled onto his class notes a list of things he planned to take with him in the jeep, including: blanket, poncho, ground cloth, underwear (1 change), socks (2 changes), fatigues (1 suit), rifle, small pistol and ammunition.

On 7 September 1950, Lt. Barber was given orders to report to Pier "A" in Yokohama, Japan. Barber, his men, his equipment and jeep were about to be loading aboard the USS (AP-3).

Inchon Landing For 18th Group FAC

Friday, 15 September 1950 was "D" day. Lt. Ken Barber and his Forward Air Control team were scheduled to land on D +5, the following Wednesday. "Patience is a wonderful virtue," he noted. "Wish I had more of it!"

"More and more as I travel through life I wonder just where we are going and what we are doing," he noted in his diary.

As he watched "a flight of Navy planes" passing overhead, heading for action, Barber "heartily wished myself back in the air. We are moving slowly in past small islands. I hope the Marines are lambasting them now. Our plan of action for the 7th Division is called Goldrush #4. We will land from D +3 to D +5. Wish it were sooner!!" He watched the "explosions of the Navy big guns as they pounded the shore, hearing the dull boom and feeling the vibration many miles away."

Two ROK "soldiers" were clapped into the ship's brig. "They were found with from 20-40 firing pins on them which they had swiped from rifles. Guess they are spies," Barber noted.

Lt. Al Haig went ashore and later returned to tell Barber that "it was all pretty well secured by now. The ROK's are still cleaning out Inchon, the Marines are bypassing it. About 300 POW's so far." Bar-

Controlling the Air War...from the ground

ber assumed that General Douglas MacArthur "was there too, tho no definite word is out that he was."

On Wednesday, 20 September, Barber and his team finally got ashore at Inchon. "It has been a long, tiresome wait and we'll all be glad to get ashore. Inchon is now secure, although there is still sniper fire from the houses. Kimpo AFB also has been secured, and Marine fighters and a transport group are already operating out of it. The Marines have gotten to the banks of the Han River and to the outskirts of Seoul against stiffening resistance. We will probably go in on the southern flank, the road to Suwon."

The Air Force was "getting all kinds of targets," Barber reported. "They caught over 200 trucks coming down from Pyongyang, destroying most of them and have knocked out around 10 tanks. They are probably having a field day. Sure wouldn't mind being in on it," the wistful fighter pilot sighed into his notebook.

Late on Thursday afternoon, in full field gear, Barber went over the side of the Buckner, down a rope ladder, and into an LCM that took him and many others over to Wolmi-do Island. The LCM threaded its way through the gaggle of ships, past "mud flats and stone break walls. The narrow strip of water between Wolmi-do and Inchon was full of LCM's, a hospital ship, small craft, sunken enemy ships and LST's marooned on the mud until high tide." Barber had removed his rank insignia and wings "so as to make a less conspicuous target for snipers."

"Inchon seemed fairly well off, although quite a few buildings were burned out and desolated by naval gun fire." (And perhaps as a result of his own prior air strike.) "Little, starved looking children stood along the road, eagerly grasping anything that the G.I.'s would give them. In the rubbish of burned out buildings, men, women and children searched for anything they could find." Barber passed "one little boy of about

six years with a pimply, sick, dirty, swollen face." He turned to Mosley and shook his head, "He's not long for this world."

Barber and his men hiked from Inchon down long miles of "dirt road" leading southeast, trying to reach the rendezvous point for this jeep and other equipment. They reached the "assembly area" shortly after midnight after hiking nearly 15 miles—"both infantry and AF were fagged out."

After a "C ration" breakfast on 21 September, Barber set out through "Georgia terrain"—small pines and red clay—to find the Command Post.

The next day his men arrived with a jeep, but no trailer. Taking the jeep, Barber and Wilkerson headed back to Inchon to try and find their precious trailer. They didn't find the trailer, but on the road he noted, "passed a Marine graveyard where 93 of our men were being buried."

Their Battalion formed up and began to move out, "the Infantry in columns down the road. Just as we turned a corner I noticed our trailer sitting over there by itself. How it got there I'll never know," Barber

wrote, "but we sure were happy to get it!" The Battalion continued moving in the direction of Suwon.

"As we progressed, we passed groups of men with their two hands folded atop their heads—prisoners of war, guarded by our men. All men and women refugees were inspected at various check points along the way." Hungry, Barber "pulled out a chocolate bar and began eating it. We drove on past bowing groups of people. At a blown out bridge, we detoured. At the end of the bridge I saw a dead Korean boy, about 12 years old, who lay there with dried blood on his face and shirt, his teeth white in a half smile—the first dead man I've ever seen. I continued eating my chocolate bar and was surprised that he didn't affect me. He reminded me some of squirrels, shot and stiffened, and I wondered at my own callousness."

When they reached Suwon, they passed "lines of bowing, clapping, laughing, smiling, crying Korean people, calling 'Banzai' (Welcome), and raising both arms in salutation. Some men even carried long Japanese rifles on their shoulders—apparently

Tactical Air Control Party (TACP) Team #7 completed its training at Camp McGill for the Inchon Landing and prepares to embark on their transport. (L-R) Cpl. James Chandler, Cpl. Bill Wilkerson, Pfc J.D. Mosley, Lt. Ken Barber and Lt. Melo. (Barber)

Convoy to Inchon *as seen from USAT Buckner on 15 Sept 1950. The naval units had departed Yokahama, Japan on Monday, September 11, 1950. "So far, the sea is fairly calm," Barber noted. However, two days later the "seas became heavy, climaxing last night in a terrific gale that took one of the jeeps overboard—and a couple of men. At a wind speed of 79 mph, the meter broke...we have been blacked out, and it's hard to describe the oppressive stuffiness of a closed up ship." (Barber)*

members of the South Korean underground or guerillas. Many waved South Korean flags, one man thrusting one into my hand,

attached to a stick as our jeep went by."

"One man grasped my hand as we drove by in our jeeps. I was riding "shotgun" in the cargo jeep. As we went by I smiled and waved at them, and experienced the same thrill with a catch in my throat that the liberating troops in Europe must have felt. My eyes even got a little moist, but I didn't get carried away so much that I didn't keep a sharp lookout for enemy troops. That town was far from secure!"

Late in the afternoon, the Regiment came under mortar fire. "I'm sure no hero," Barber noted, "It's the night of the 24th and I want to die of old age in bed just decided. What a horrible shuddering feeling to hear those things swish overhead and explode. We're dug in with Easy Company atop a high hill, on the very front lines. Machine guns are firing and the bullets hiss and whizzzzz by overhead. Oh, how I'd love for us to lay an artillery barrage on their positions. Let's

U.S. Air Force Lands At Inchon. *The U.S. Navy and Marine Corps were not the only military services landing at Inchon. The Air Force was represented by Lt. Ken Barber and his FAC Team, one of seven the Air Force created, trained and deployed with Army units. (Barber)*

"Aridn' Ole Jeep and a Leavn' Inchon." Corporal J. B. Chandler drives the FACF jeep and Lt. Ken Barber "rides shotgun" as they head north following the Inchon Landing--accompanying the infantry to ensure effective coordination of close air support missions. Barber cradles an M-45 "grease gun." Normally, the inaccurate but high rate of fire weapon was carried by Corporal Chandler. (Barber)

get this war over and get back to sensible, Christian living." Then he added, "and to Carolyn."

Later, he weathered another mortar barrage from "a too shallow two-man foxhole. I wish this were one man and six feet deep. Oh! Oh! There they go again, falling slightly short now. This old stuff is hard on the nerves and I ain't just a kiddin'. Man, no one's ever been to war unless he's been in the Infantry," Barber admitted. "Our tanks are firing back now, the machine guns are firing steadily and bullets whiz overhead with a long hissing sound. The tracers cut red lines right over our hole, dug near the top of the hill on a reverse slope."

Barber struck a conversation with a Captain Lashley, leading a tank column that was "passing through Suwon." Lashley told Barber that he "noticed Gook soldiers along the road but thought they were ROKs." Lashley shined his flashlight on one of them and saw a Russian Tommy gun, then shot the North Korean soldier with his .45 pis-

tol. "Then the water hit the fan," Barber recalled, "and bullets started flying everywhere. They all piled out of their jeeps and fought for about an hour, finally getting through the town OK."

A "recon party" had passed through Suwon earlier in the day "uneventfully," then returned to guide the tanks into the town. A Lieutenant Colonel from the Regiment "was in the lead jeep. He saw a tank silhouette moving down the road, climbed out of his jeep and stood in the lights to guide them. A machine gun rattled, cutting him down and the tanks, Russian-made T-34's, rolled over the Colonel, and four jeeps. The others apparently got out."

As Barber and his team arrived at the Suwon Airstrip then saw "North Korean prisoners, all dressed in civilian whites, their hands over their heads, guarded by ROKs while dead North Koreans lay on the ground, one with his pants missing."

Barber helped his men dig their foxholes, then he dug his own "long enough to

get my air mattress and sleeping bag in it. Good night's sleep."

Suwon Airfield

On Sunday 24 September 1950, Barber noted that "two Navy jets strafed George Company, killing five and wounding four. They were displaying panels [colored identification cloth placed on vehicles and equipment to identify UN forces from the air.] The Battalion has been jumpy all day. Every time an airplane passes over, Major Wood would get excited and call me telling me to contact them and keep 'em away from us."

About 1400 that day, Barber called for close air support—"a strike on a reported camouflaged tank. Three F-51's left from Suwon airstrip, contacted me. They were just out of sight over the hills when Major Wright ran up saying 'Call off the strike. They're friendly vehicles." Barber immediately contacted "Contour Sugar," and was

Pershing Tanks Guard Suwan Airfield. *Lt. Ken Barber and his FACP team arrived at the Suwon Airfield just south of the town after dark on 22 September 1950. "The looming, formidable shapes of Pershing tanks formed a perimeter defense around the airstrip. The 32ⁿᵈ Infantry Division was dug in among them." (Barber)*

greatly relieved when they actually heard him, because he couldn't hear them. He needed direct, line-of-sight for air-to-air reception on his SCR 522 transceiver.

When Barber drove his jeep back to the Suwon Airstrip to refuel, he escorted three prisoners. On returning to his Battalion, he recorded that Air Force planes had "strafed some 150 British Tommies. Some-

one better put a stop to this. Our planes are the Russians best allies." His note also indicated that he, and others, thought the Russians were ultimately behind the North Korean invasion.

That night, Barber and his team were ordered to dig in on a prominent hill in case "air strikes were needed in the morning." His position came under enemy fire that

night. "All of a sudden all hell broke loose under this beautiful full moon--our artillery is adjusting on the enemy positions now and their big stuff has shut up. They were using tanks and 4.2 mortars. One round landed about twenty feet from our hole."

By mid-week, September 25th, the jeep radio was inoperable and had to be taken to Division HQ for repair.

Prisoners of War taken by 1ˢᵗ Bn, 31ˢᵗ Infantry. *The small boy at left is "Mascot," whose mother and father were killed in Suchon. As Barber and his team arrived at the Suwon Airstrip they saw "North Korean prisoners, all dressed in civilian whites, their hands over their heads, guarded by ROK's, while dead North Koreans lay on the ground, one with his pants missing." (Barber)*

"The men in my team," Barber observed, "are all pretty good. They are all quite young. Chandler is quiet but pretty good. Mosley is easy-going, cusses like a sailor, and seems to be quite a hell-raiser. Wilkerson is slightly more serious-minded, but less quiet than Chandler. I'll probably put them all in for a promotion." [He did.]

The enemy were so close at times that "Major Smith told all the men not to use the word Lt. or Major but use the last names so the officers wouldn't get killed off—right away."

On top of the stress of operating in a combat environment, Barber was sick—"indigestion, sore throat, sore lips, cold--no decent sleep."

"Major Wood expects my radio to do impossible things," Barber noted, "and calls me all hours of the day and night to contact planes, etc. etc. which I cannot do most of the time with my limited equipment. The AF gave us radios that are old and not particularly good."

Because Barber and his team didn't get back to camp until 1900, they "missed the first hot meal" in several weeks. "Hot biscuits, coffee, and Mulligan stew. Yumm!" He recalled times from YMCA summer camp when "a long, cold hike in the rain" ended with a "delicious hot meal of Mulligan stew. I shall never forget it." There was no Mulligan stew that night for the hard-pressed radio team.

First Air Strike Operations

At noon on 26 September, Battalion called for an air strike. "We sent in the Air Request," Barber recorded, "and thirty minutes later the planes reported to me and I guided them in on the target, dug-in troops along the line marked by Hills 161, 113, and 92. The planes worked over a tunnel just east of Hill 92 where the enemy has ammo and supplies hidden. It sure looked good to us, and made us feel useful for a change! Until now we haven't been used at all. They worked over the area with rockets, napalm and .50-caliber. I asked them

U.S. Army howitzer shelling enemy positions near Suwon. *(Barber)*

to give us a buzz job on the way back, which they did. Sure wish I were flying again," the frustrated pilot noted.

Other Infantry units sent a nearby TACP jeep out with patrolling Infantry units. It was "knocked out" and the Air Force officer and team leader was injured. "Sure hope he's OK," Barber recorded. "That is certainly a poor way to use something so valuable as a TACP jeep. Now we'll have a heck of a time relaying messages back. Stupid brass again."

Moving Out to Attack

By dusk on 26 September, Barber's Battalion "got orders to move out to attack…why can't they move us in the morning instead of at dusk. I sure am getting ditch digger's hands…bet I can get a job anywhere when I get back. Only two more days and I'll be 25," he noted.

"G" Company lost three officers "and cannot remove all the wounded they are so pinned down with fire. Lt. Wagner from that Company came in shot through the heel, sobbing because he'd seen so many of his men shot. Lt. Dupre had a leg broken. Now, I hear that Col. Ovenshine, the Regimental Commander, who went forward with Lt. Col. Summers, was killed. [Later information determined that was false. It was Lt. Col. Summers who was "hit in the leg."]

"G" Company is pinned down on the approaches to Hill 113. A medic came back wounded in the arm, another grim-faced silent, old soldier shot in the shoulder. Chaplain Reynolds is everywhere trying to help make men feel better." Barber praised the Chaplain's serving with his outfit as "some of the finest and most consecrated men I know--any minister who looks down his nose at Chaplain's certainly doesn't have the big picture."

On Thursday, 28 September 1950, Barber was on hand to observe a heavy air strike on Hill 113 and 92. "G" Company had been thrown back with heavy losses—46 casualties—the day before and Battalion "wanted it worked over well." Strangely, Barber and his team were not asked "for our aid in controlling the strike." The air strike was controlled by "a cub," and lasted from 1200 to 1300. When it was over "the Infantry walked up and took it without firing a shot. They had been pinned down on the forward slope yesterday and couldn't make it. Many were killed. One Lt. got almost to the top and was shot in the back (killed) when he passed a camouflaged Gook foxhole."

Seeing Casualties First Hand

Barber took his jeep "over to Hill 113 with a Marine Sergeant name Terry. We walked up on the Hill to look around. Everywhere there were dead North Koreans. One lying half on his head must have been hit while diving for his foxhole. A full box of rifle ammo lay on his body. Nearby, another was dead in his foxhole. Atop the hill were five at a time, torn up by mortars, shrapnel, Air Force, etc. Earlier, two wounded prisoners had been brought in, one so weak from loss of blood he could hardly stand and did fall down once."

On their way back down Hill 113, they "saw the skull of an American G.I., apparently a member of the 24th Division, who was killed back in early July in their retreat. A combat boot with the foot rotted off inside it marked the spot where another G.I. had long ago been killed."

The sight of the "dead, lying there with their faces resembling wax, many with blood on their faces and always their bodies, holes through the head, mangled bodies hit by shrapnel, was not a pretty sight. What an end to life! Lying, dusty and dirty in a filthy hole with insects crawling over you, far from home, knowing before death that as vanquished no stone would ever mark where they fell, no wives or mothers would know where they were, that they would be relegated to their foxhole with a little dirt scraped over them—not very deep with perhaps a foot sticking out above ground."

The rumor was circulating on 29 September 1950 that "Joe Stalin has offered the U.N. four divisions to help defeat North Korea. That double-crossing S.O.B! Here we are picking up Russian guns, carbines, pistols, machine guns, howitzers that they have used against us, and now he's saying he'll help us. It looks to me like he wants a good excuse to move into North Korea again. That'll put things in the same state of affairs they were in after WWII."

Barber, Lt. Col. Kenneth. Korean War Diary Number Two (unpublished), 1950.

Tactical Air Control Overview

On July 14, 1950, General Partridge created the 6132nd Tactical Air Control Group (Provisional). By July 23rd the 6132nd was able to establish a Tactical Air Control Center (TACC) adjacent to the Joint Operations Center at Taegu. The TACC took over the operation of control station "Mellow."

In July 20, 1950 control of tactical support aircraft was assumed at Taegu by the Fifth Air Force—Eighth Army Joint Operations Center (JOC). Its radio control station at Taegu was given the call sign of "Mellow." Fighter aircraft were directed to the front by **Mellow Control** (Tactical Air Control Center) and **Mosquito Mellow**. When they arrived in the operating area, airborne Mosquitoes FACs directed them to specific targets.

Tactical Air Control Parties—TACP— provided liaison between ground and air, ground control of close air support in concert with airborne T-6 aircraft "Mosquitos." Each TACP consisted of an experienced pilot officer, who served as a forward air controller (FAC), and the airmen needed to operate and maintain the party's vehicular-mounted communications equipment. Troops on the ground could communicate directly with airborne forward air controllers via the SCR-300 "walkie-talkie" if necessary. Throughout the Korean War, combat squadrons were required to supply pilots for temporary duty with the TACPs. As one unit report from the 18th FBW noted, "TACP still necessitates the absence of three officers per each 21-day period on a TDY basis with ground force elements. Their duties in the main are concerned with the coordination of air strikes by fighter type aircraft in close support of such ground units." *[Note: TACPs for the Inchon invasion were assigned for up to four months.]*

TACP's were assigned at Battalion and Division levels and consisted of one Forward Air Controller (experienced pilot and team leader), two radio operators and one radio technician.

The TACC had authority to direct aircraft on strikes. However it "usually forwards them to the TACP's," Barber noted. The airborne controller, when they were available, usually flew an L-5 or a T-6. The airborne controller carried smoke rockets to mark targets.

FACs were required to "bring planes in parallel to the lines…to break away from lines…and to have positive control of the attacking aircraft."

The dangers of being hit by "friendly" ordnance were well understood. When bombs were being used, the controller would allow 1 yard of distance for each pound of explosive, e.g. 500 lbs = 500 yards of separation. Rockets required 150 yards of separation. However, if the targets "were dug in, even closer," Barber noted. Strafing runs could be conducted within 100-200 yards of friendly troops or positions. The final responsibility for ground strikes rested on the commander that was requesting support.

Having an attacking plane hit by friendly artillery was also to be avoided. Therefore, if the artillery trajectory was 1,100' high, the pilot was required to operate at 1,500', "leaving a 400' margin."

Potential targets were carefully evaluated to ensure that the appropriate ordnance and attack plan was used. FAC's were careful to "avoid duplication of missions" and not to "let one mission endanger the mission of another [supporting] arm." Missions were handled at the lowest echelon possible and coordinated at the highest effective echelon. All the "supporting arms" were to use a common system of target identification.

Call Signs:

Plantation 76	"D" Channel
Moonshine	"D" Itasuke
Mellow	Central Controller
Monologue	12th Squadron
Elsewhere	67th Squadron
Primary TADC:	"Devastate Baker"

The Battle For Hill 113

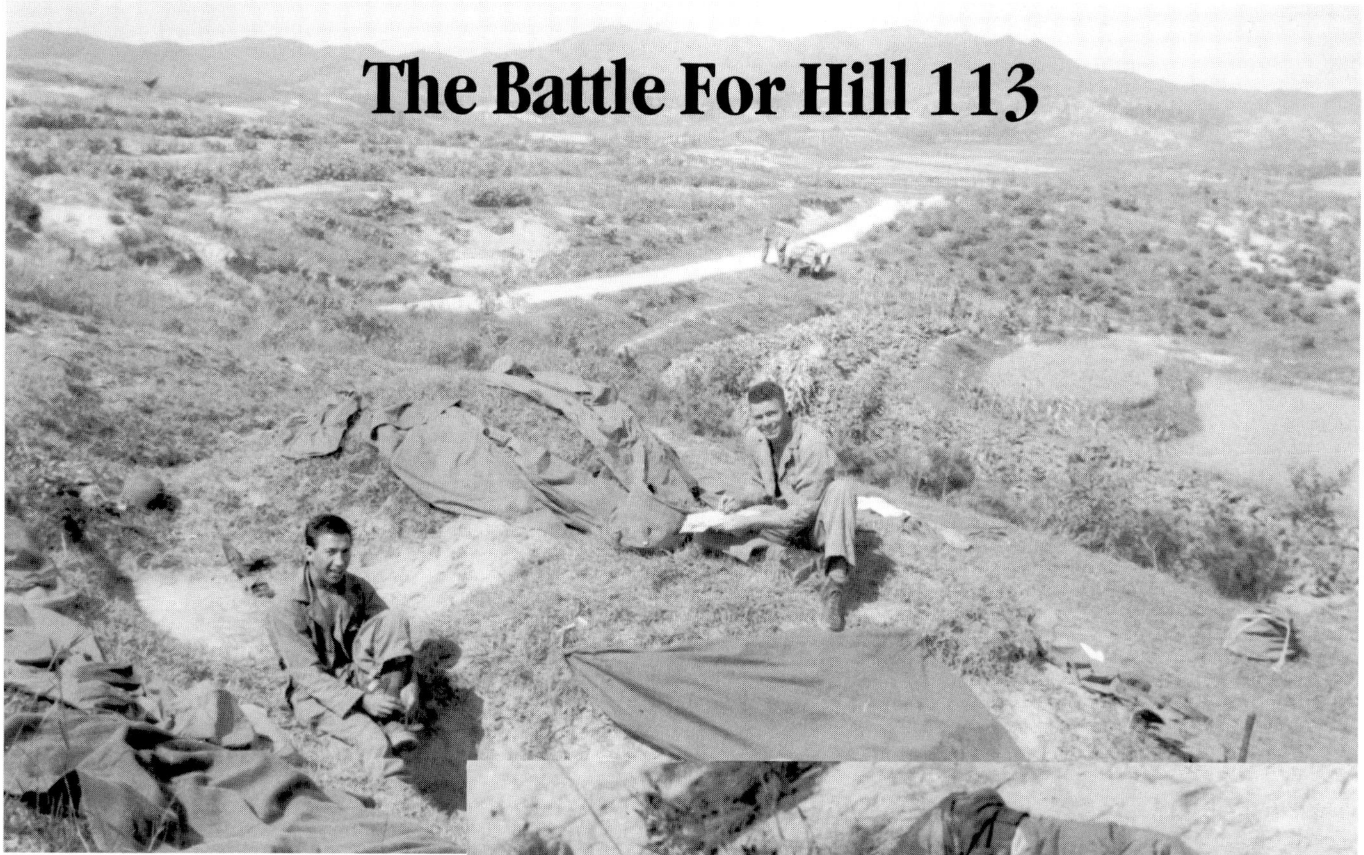

(Above) **Close Air Support Aftermath.** North Korean dead littered the top and slopes of Hill 133 after American fighter bombers spent an hour working it over with bombs, rockets and napalm. (Barber)

(Left) **American Skeletons.** On their way back down Hill 113, on 29 September 1950, Lt. Barber's team "saw the skull of an American G.I., apparently a member of the 24th Infantry Division, who was killed back in early July in their retreat. A combat boot with the foot rotted off inside it marked the spot where another G.I. had long ago been killed." (Barber)

North Korean Soldiers Killed in Action. Corporal Wilkerson and PFC Mosely on Hill 113 near Suwon on 1 October 1950. Their foxholes had to be dug on top of Korean graves. (Barber)

A Russian made machine gun on Hill 113 on 29 September. "Many rifles were lying around--much of it American stuff that had been captured and they were using on us. It was a gory sight. Many dead Gooks lay in their foxholes, clever, well-camuflaged holes dug down and back in and under. Scrub pines littered the hillside making good camuflage material." (Barber)

October 1950

Race To The Yalu

Sukchon Air Drop Cuts Off Escape. *"Angels" and equipment of the 187th Regimental Combat Team, "hit the silk" over the Sukchon Area to seal the Communist-led North Koreans' escape route from their fallen capital of Pyongyang, approximately 25 miles away. More than 4,000 of the 11th Airborne Division troops were dropped on an arc between the North Korean cities of Sukchon and Sunchon on October 20, 1950. (NARA)*

Monthly Summary

Within several weeks of the Inchon landings, few North Korean soldiers remained in South Korea. "General MacArthur prohibited further destruction of rail facilities south of the 38th Parallel unless the enemy was actively using them. UN and ROK forces advanced steadily into North Korea, taking Pyongyang and Wonsan and driving toward the Yalu River, which ROK troops reached by the end of the month. During October, most Fifth Air Force subordinate combat organizations, including four fighter groups and two reconnaissance squadrons-and

much of the support infrastructure moved from Japan to Korea. UN forces captured North Korean airfields at Wonsan, Sinmak, Pyongyang, and Sinanju, all of which became available to Far East Air Forces and Fifth Air Force aircraft."

The FEAF interdiction campaign against enemy bridges south of the Yalu River concluded, and as the daily number of fighter and bomber sorties declined, daily cargo sorties increased. During the month, FEAF aircraft transported 2,840 patients within Korea and 3,025 patients from Korea to Ja-

pan. To communicate a surrender ultimatum from General MacArthur, FEAF aircraft dropped 4,440,000 leaflets over parts of North Korea not yet in UN hands. Just as a united, non-communist Korea seemed within reach, over 180,000 Chinese Communist Forces (CCF) troops slipped over the Yalu River into North Korea.

USAFHRA. January 2002. The U.S. Air Force's First War: Korea 1950-1953 Significant Events. October 1950.

Combat Operations Move North

At the end of the first week in October, Colonel Curtis R. Low, the new Commander of the 18th Fighter-Bomber Group (then called the 6002nd), called Major Stan Chatfield in to tell him that he "was to head up a detachment to operate from a forward base in North Korea."

The 18th Fighter-Bomber Group was going to send a detachment to Wonsan "for a five-day staging operation," arriving on 12 October.

Chatfield had no idea how far north it was until he looked hard at the maps. Wonsan was above the 39th Parallel. *[Wonsan is on the east central North Korean coast.]* The Group would be using "a former airfield just captured by the Capital Division of the ROK Army."

After mustering a complete support group, Chatfield "loaded everything from food to jeeps and equipment on two C-119 transports." He did not really like the looks of the ungainly transport, "as it had only two engines to haul all of that stuff, but it was functional if not pretty."

Air Police to guard equipment, medical personnel (including a flight surgeon), cooks and bakers, maintenance men, armorers, and intelligence specialists were rounded up by Chatfield and put aboard the "Flying Boxcars." They loaded everything from fuel and napalm tanks, to rockets, and 500-pound frag bombs.

The detachment's arrival at Wonsan was "dramatic."

"The forward air controller used the base to direct strikes on enemy troops a few miles from the field. Indeed, it was for this purpose that we were brought in—to turn around F-51's from our Group after they had struck targets in the area, so they could strike again before returning to our southern base," Chatfield explained.

"The field was littered with shrapnel and spent ordnance from recent battles, and was unusable for us until it was cleaned up. Not to worry. The local Korean Commanders [ROK Capital Division] had several thousand prisoners of war holed up in a cave

"Air Force work"--a burned out train near Suwon on 1 October 1950. (Barber)

[actually an underground hangar] nearby to perform the clean up. And do the job they did, in very short order. They were lined up across the runway and taxiways, with buckets and they picked up all of the material that would keep us from using the field."

The North Korean "gook" prisoners were held in a very large WW II Japanese aircraft hangar built into the side of a steep hillside, recalled Col. (then 1st Lt.) James Peek. "It had huge armor plated doors on inoperable rail tracks. The smaller personnel doors worked. The prisoners seemed to be doing well and were happy as we fed them at noon chow. The next morning, Sgt. Shand and I, plus a few of my enlisted men needed to serve as prisoner chasers went over to the underground hangar to get another batch because we had plenty of work planned. The answer to my request was, "All dead. Not enough food. Need too many guards."

Captain Bill Myers, the Group Maintenance Chief, who was also a pilot and flew with the Squadrons when he could, joined Chatfield in putting "a tarp across a 'jungle gym' arrangement for a tent to keep the rain off of us. We had some canvas cots with sleeping bags." Chatfield kept his personal Smith & Wesson "close by as we were not too far from the fighting. In fact, Bill got up in the middle of the night to answer a call of nature. When I awoke and sensed motion, I had my firearm in my hands and ready. Bill let me know after then when he had to go."

Operations From Wonsan

On 14 October at 1505 hours, Major Arnold "Moon" Mullins led the first combat flight out of the newly occupied airfield at Wonsan. Other members of that flight included: Major Henry W. Lawrence, Capt. Alma R. Flake, and Capt. Herbert W. Andridge, Jr.

It was the first mission to be flown from that strip and the first North Korean airfield to be used by UN forces since the beginning of the Korean War the previous June. Just a few miles away, shelling and ground combat operations were still underway.

At the base, destroyed hangars provided mute evidence of previous combat operations at that base. Snipers were still active in the hills on both sides of the strip. ROK troops were busy clearing mines from the beaches and nearby areas.

Aircraft took off from K-9, flew their missions, landed at Wonsan, jumped off at noon for another mission, and returned to K-9. It was said that while the Group was present in the area, the Republic of Korea troops were still cleaning out stragglers of the occupying enemy and Navy dive bombers and Marine fighters were still napalming the bay across from the airfield, which was later coded K-25," S/Sgt Sandy Colton recorded.

The first day, "we had our first flight come in and we pointed out the targets from where we sat," Chatfield explained. "They were clearly visible, and there was no mistake about who and what they were. The ROK forces were shelling them, as well."

As the Mustangs were gassed and re-armed for the next mission, the pilots got a briefing and orientation by Chatfield and his Intelligence team.

"This move to Wonsan by the Air Force has been proclaimed by the pilots as the best arrangement for fighter-bombers since the beginning to the Korean police action," the *Air Force Times* of 1 November 1950, pointed out. "The aircraft are able to be at their targets just a few minutes after take-off. Close proximity enabled them to spend much time in the air over the enemy."

"The second day, we had a VIP visit. General Partridge, Fifth Air Force Commander arrived in his C-54 to see the operation and to tell us that we were to be relieved by the Marines who wanted to come over the beach and "Take the position." Here, all the time, I thought that the ROK Army and our guys had already taken it. We did indeed move out in a few days, and I guess the Marines got their photo ops. Just to satisfy my curiosity, I made a trip to the front lines with a ROK Army Officer who was with us at the time," Chatfield remembered.

S/Sgt Sandy Colton's report noted that "As the bombline and the front lines moved upward, more Controllers were added, and most of the 'Mosquitoes' operated from Seoul, Wonsan, and points north. By 15 October, the only Controller in the Taegu Sector was JOC itself, accounted for by the lack of targets of opportunity in the south. Ground forces there had only mopping up operations to conduct. A line was formed from the 40th Parallel to the Manchurian border, splitting Korea in half, thereby composing only two recce areas.

The Marines started north from Wonsan on 15 October 1951. The Navy continued its daily carrier-based operations on both sides of Korea, and shelled for two days off the coast of Recce Area II from the shore to 20 miles inland. By 17 October, tension and confidence had build up sufficiently within the Group that polls were being inaugurated to ascertain the day of the Group's arrival in Clark Field.

In Korea, the Flights were "Able," "Baker," and "Charlie," as per usual, but they were carried over until the alphabet

October Summary

by William J. "Sandy" Colton

The Group sent a few people to Wonson for a five-day staging operation which was later cut to one day. These men left K-9 on 12 October 1950 and returned 13 October 1951. Aircraft would take off from K-9 fly a mission and land at Wonson, jump off at noon for another mission and return to K-9. It is said that while the Group was there the ROK troops were still cleaning out stragglers of the occupying enemy and that Navy dive bombers and Corsair fighters were still napalming the bay across from the field. This field was coded K-25.

As the bombline and front lines moved northward, more controllers were added and most of the Mosquito's would operate from Seoul, Wonsan and points north. By 15 October 1950 the only controller in the Taegu Sector was JOC itself. The reason for this was the lack of targets of opportunity in the south. The ground forces had only mopping up operations to contend with there. Later the Recce Area's IV & V were rescinded and I & II substituted. Recce Area I was northwest and Recce Area II was northeast. A line was formed from parallel 40 to the Manchurian border and split Korea in half from those points.

The Marines started from Wonson on 15 October 1951. The Navy continued its daily aircraft carrier based operations on both sides of Korea. The Navy shelled for two days the coast of Recce Area II—from the shore to 20 miles inland.

By 17 October, optimism was so high for both Officer's and Airmen of the 18th Fighter-Bomber Group that polls were being taken to ascertain the day of the group's arrival in Clark Field.

In Korea the flights were "Able," "Baker," and "Charlie," as per usual. However, they were carried over until the alphabet ran out. It worked like this: if Elsewhere closed the day as Elsewhere George, the next day the first Elsewhere flight would be How. When Elsewhere Zebra Flight came up, the next flight would be Elsewhere Able. This applied to Tammerlane, as well.

Call signs, recce areas, control and mission numbers were changed for military security purposes every so often.

In a pose strikingly similar to those created by comrades in arms during the Civil War nearly a century before, Sergeants Maynard, Strom and Valentino smile for the camera wearing Air Force issue winter utility clothing. Valentino appears to be wearing a Korean quilted jacket with loops for fasteners over his Air Force utilities. (Maynard)

"Would You Like To Take My Picture?" *In October 1950, Air Force Chief of Staff Gen. Hoyt Vandenberg paid a visit to the Headquarters of the 18th F-B Group. "When it was known that he was arriving at our base," Lt. (later Colonel) Ed Mason explained, "several of us were rounded up to receive decorations that had not yet been presented. About seven of us got dressed up, got our cameras and asked friends to take our pictures with General Vandenberg. We were lined up outside the building when the door burst open, and the General rushed out all by himself and jumped into the back seat of his staff car. He had no idea who we were or why we were there. After a few minutes, we could hear other people getting ready to join him, and it became apparent that we would not get the anticipated presentation. One of the not too bright officers (me) happened to be looking in the direction of the back seat of the car and couldn't hold back his frustration, and said, 'Son of a bitch!' This is an expression that is easy to read, even by untrained lip readers. General Vandenberg promptly got out of his staff car, looked directly at me, and said, "Would you like to take my picture?" We all answered, "Yes, Sir," and this photograph is the result." (Mason)*

wore out, i.e. ELSEWHERE closed the day as ELSEWHERE GEORGE, and the following day, the first Flight was ELSEWHERE HOW. The ending with ELSEWHERE ZEBRA prompted the use of ELSEWHERE ABLE the next day. This also applied to TAMERLANE. Call Signs, reconnaissance areas, Controllers, and mission numbers were changed frequently to comply with military security measures.

The FEAF CHOPLINE was instituted on 15 October 1950, which limited the Group to action 20 miles south of the Manchurian border from longitude 12' degrees to the west coast. This was equally divided into three areas, Recce Areas I, II, and III. From 120 degrees to the east coast was "off limits" to the Group, but 'on limits' to the US Navy. [1]

Group Combat Operations

A comparison of the combat flight hours and sorties figures between September and October might have led some to conclude "that some measure of decreased efficiency is indicated," the 67th's unit report for October pointed out. "However, while the total time flown remained approximately the same as for September 1950, the sorties (by number) total was almost halved. This was due to the extended distances involved in flying from base to target and return— flights which ranged the entire length of Korea."

During October 1950, two-, four- and eight-aircraft flights were used in combat operations. Most flights by Mustangs of the 18th consisted of four aircraft flights, during which two of the aircraft would furnish "top cover" during armed reconnaissance or during strafing passes at enemy held positions and against enemy equipment or material.

Close support, armed reconnaissance and escort missions for B-26 type photographic aircraft comprised the bulk of missions for the 67th Squadron—"the entire length and breadth of Korea was ranged with the exception of those areas restricted. (Chop line, 35 miles south and parallel to the Manchurian Border, ranging its entire length) and those areas apportioned to other UN Forces."

Napalm again "proved to be the most effective weapon against the enemy, being equally effective against vehicles, tanks, ground positions, etc. High speed, low glide angle attacks from minimum altitudes provided for greater accuracy as well sustained effective operations under minimum weather conditions."

A shortage of M-16, internal fuses for the napalm tanks forced some battlefield ingenuity—wooden plugs took the place of the fuses; but, not for long. The "inherent vulnerability (inflammability) of napalm was underscored...It was discovered that the napalm tanks would ignite prior to release if a strafing attack were initiated prior to such release. Napalm seepage around the wooden plug was ignited by the gun blasts."

The 67th reported four "outstanding missions" that it felt "demonstrated the combat effectiveness of fighter bomber type aircraft during this report period."

Regiment Surrenders to F-51s

A four-aircraft flight led by 1st Lt. William G. Foster, napalm bombed, rocketed and strafed an enemy pocket of resistance in the vicinity of Chong-san, east of Taejon—with such effectiveness that an entire enemy regiment surrendered to UN Forces in that area. As reported in an undated *Stars and Stripes* article from "Dogpatch AB in Korea"—"Last week two pilots of the 18th Fighter-Bomber Group, a part of the 6002nd Tactical Support Wing, at this advanced Fifth Air Force Base, commanded by Col. Curtis R. Low, Needham Heights, Mass., captured 12 enemy prisoners from the air. More recently four more pilots of that same group were responsible for the surrender of an enemy regiment.

A flight of four F-51 Mustangs led by 1st Lt. William G. Foster, Franklinville, N.J., with

General MacArthur Flies In. *The Constellation (Connie) belonged to General Stratemeyer, FEAF Commander, accompanied by General MacArthur and numerous staff officers. They flew from Japan to K-9 where they refueled and prepared to observe the paratroop drop by the 187th Regimental Combat Team on Sukchon and Sunchon. These photos of the plane at K-9 were taken by Lt. Ed Mason, who explained that he "was on the ground instead of in the air, because the "old" 18th Group boys from Clark Field decided that they wanted this plum mission, so the new boys sat this one out." Gen. MacArthur "stuck his head out of the door occasionally." Mason noted that Gen. MacArthur "received the air medal for his part in the operation." (Mason)*

Suchon Para-drop. *This dramatic picture was made Friday, October 20, 1950 over the area of Sunchon, about 23 miles northeast of Pyongyang. It shows six Fairchild C-119 Flying Boxcars of Far East Air Force Combat Cargo Command about to paradrop troops of the 11th Airborne Division together with necessary equipment and supplies, in order to stop the northward retreat of North Korean troops who have been forced out of the enemy capital of Pyongyang. Paratroopers were dropped on an arc between the North Korean cities of Sukchon and Sunchon. (NARA)*

67 missions were out to assist the ground forces in cleaning up pockets of diehard enemy troops left in the wake of the fast moving United Nations offensive. Capt. Charles H. Spencer, Penn Yan, N.Y., was flying his first Korean mission as wingman for Foster. 1st Lt. George N. Olsen, Pennyville, Ill., with 64 missions was flying the number three position as leader of the second element, and Capt. Edward J. Mason, Brownsville, Texas, on his fourth mission, was flying as Olsen's wingman. The pilot of a Mosquito (spotter) plane called in the flight to relieve pressure on our troops attempting to take an enemy strongpoint on the west coast of South Korea. They were told to work over a city and a ridge nearby

that was swarming with enemy troops.

"It was good to find a decent target for a change," said Foster. "We saw groups of 50 or more troops standing all along the ridge," continued Spencer, "and gave each one a present!" By being able to see troops in their positions the four pilots were able to make direct hits causing considerable casualties. Once their napalm (jellied gas) had been dropped, the four F-51s with the 'Blinkin' noses went back to the edge of the city where they saw enemy troops running into houses. They fired at least 20 rockets into the area as well as made strafing runs.

After several passes Olson saw a white flag waving directly in front of him. "I cut off my attack," he said, "and made a tight

turn. About a block away I saw another white flag. I called the mosquito to tell him about it when I saw a third flag. The controller had us move back to the ridge." After working over the ridge for a while the pilots turned for home. As they left they saw a South Korean flag being raised on a flagpole in the center of the city. Total time over the target had been just about an hour. While en route home the pilots were called by an area controller who asked, "Did you guys hear about the regimental surrender?" "Hear about it?" answered Mason, "Hell, we did it."

On October 24th another flight of F-51 aircraft "engaged in an armed reconnaissance flight along the Huichon-Kangye highway in the vicinity of Mupyoug-ni, attacked an enemy vehicle convoy. A confirmed total of sixty (60) enemy vehicles laden with material, ammunition and personnel was totally destroyed; this despite the fact that due to gun malfunctions, only one gun in each aircraft was operative." The flight was led by Lt. Billie R. Cothern. Other members of the flight included: Capt. Richard H. Cassady, 1st Lt. Philip J. Conserva, and Major Mullins. Another Elsewhere flight was called in with napalm to complete this mission."

On 18 October 1950 another 67th Flight of four aircraft "demonstrated efficiency and teamwork in knocking out two tanks and one self-propelled field piece in enemy held territory." Lt. Philip J. Conserva, the flight leader, was "directed to the location of enemy tanks and a field piece and led the attack by scoring a direct napalm hit on one tank; a direct rocket strike on the second tank, followed by drop-tank (gasoline tank, externally hung) bombing by other members of this flight. Strafing passes successfully ignited the drop tanks which resulted in complete destruction of the tanks and field piece." Perhaps not surprisingly, "It was noted that there was a marked diminution in the intensity and accuracy of enemy anti-aircraft fire; enemy opposition was confined to small arms fire during this report period."

Keeping 'Em Flying

The Engineering Sections of the three Squadrons attached to the Group were able to keep an average of 14-15 Mustangs per Squadron per day in commission, a monthly percentage average of 61% in commission. Each Squadron flew an average of over 1,500 combat hours that month, slightly above September. Each Squadron expended nearly 300,000 rounds of .50-caliber ammunition, over 1,300 rockets, over 400 napalm bombs and about 25 fragmentation bombs that month.

The chronic shortage of personnel necessitated changes in rearming the hard working planes. A "more efficient operating system was established" during which the armorer's crews were "specialized" into rocket crews, ammunition crews, and bomb crews, "in lieu of individual armorers assigned per aircraft." The new system "worked exceedingly well. A Japanese-built napalm tank "worked well in comparison" to the Fletcher tank, which was of "flimsier construction."

The constant wear and tear on the guns and the "proximity to salt water corrosion" required the ground crews to use a heavier anti-rust oil. As the weather grew colder, the heavier oil "became congealed at low temperatures and hindered the thrust of the individual firing pins of the guns." The ingenious ground crews "rectified" the situation "by completing installation of gun-heaters" (which then allowed use of the lighter gun lubricants despite the cold weather), and constantly replacing the aging guns with new ones as they could be obtained. They also began to install gun cameras in the Mustangs.

The "blooding" of newly assigned pilot personnel was successfully accomplished. Mission level experience of such pilots is rapidly increasing. While no recognized intra-group rotation policy has been announced, the return of "high-mission" pilots to proper station remains a source of constant speculation.

Messing (food quality and quantity) was markedly improved during the latter part of the report period.

TACP (Tactical Air Control Party) still ne-

Craters, Downed Spans Show Fighter Bomber Visits. By October 31, 1950 FEAF mission planners were reviewing strike photography of targets in North Korea like this formerly classified view of a partially destroyed double railroad bridge at 38° 41' N Latitude 125° 45' E Longitude (near Sinch'on, North Korea, about 50 miles southwest of P'yongyang). The double span has been the subject of several "visits" by 18th Group fighter bombers judging from the number of bomb craters nearby. (NARA)

(Above) **Captain Gallagher, Lt. John Paller and Master Sgt. Johnson** *check out progress on an engine replacement at "Dogpatch" in October 1950. (Myers)*

cessitates the absence of three officers per each 21-day period on a TDY basis with ground force elements, the 67th reported. Their duties in the main are concerned with the coordination of air strikes by fighter type aircraft in close support of such ground units.

Perhaps the most significant issue noted by the 67th in October was "excessive mission length," meaning the long distances between "base-to-target and return-to-base." It was "a source of concern to all flying personnel." [2]

In a typical month for an 18th Group Squadron, in October, the 67th targeted towns (2 destroyed, 33 damaged), buildings (70 destroyed, 40 damaged), troops (870 killed), trucks (120 destroyed, 72 damaged), tanks (12 destroyed, 3 damaged), field pieces (8 destroyed, 4 damaged), railroads (40 cars destroyed, 12 damaged, 2 locomotives destroyed), warehouses (11 destroyed), barracks (3 destroyed), and ammunition dumps (13 destroyed).

K-9 Living

In early October, the Group continued to make improvements in billeting and messing accommodations. The 67th Squadron reported that "wooden tent frames and wooden flooring were installed, a marked improvement over previous Ready Room and Operation conditions," the unit report noted. "A similar flooring project for quarters tents for officers and airmen was accomplished during the period also. Fuel oil stoves, M-41 (two per tent) were installed in all quarters tents during the period 20 through 25 October 1950. This installation was welcomed without reserve by all personnel. Elimination of dampness and the partial alleviation of the early morning cold was a marked improvement in living conditions for personnel of this organization."

Significant Dates [4]

October 2: Captain Edward F. Hodges of the 67th Squadron was "forced to abandon his aircraft while in flight approximately 25 miles south of Pyongyang, North Korea. Engine failure occurred ostensibly due to enemy action. Captain Hodges was ob-

served abandoning his aircraft by the element leader, 1st Lt. Leake and his wingman, 1st Lt. Di Silvestri. As he left the aircraft after flying (gliding) as far south as possible, Captain Hodges was observed to strike the horizontal stabilizer of his F-51 type aircraft with his back. The aircraft struck the ground in a vertical dive, whereupon it exploded and burned fiercely. Captain Hodges jumped from an altitude of approximately 700 feet above the ground." [5]

Hodges Flight immediately established contact "with a Marine Rescue Unit based at Kimpo AB [Seoul, SK] and a Marine helicopter was immediately dispatched to rescue the downed pilot. A reconnaissance effected by the element leader and wingman disclosed enemy troops to the north and an orbiting pattern was established to fend off any threatening move on the part of the enemy. Approximately one hour and forty-five minutes later two marine F9F [Panther jets] aircraft entered the pattern and relieved the remaining members of the F-51 flight. Shortly thereafter the "windmill" (helicopter) arrived and the downed pilot was safely removed to Kimpo, AB."

October 3: China sent word through the Indian ambassador that it would send troops to defend North Korea if non-Korean UN troops moved north of the 38th Parallel.

October 4: Far East Air Forces were given operational control of all land-based aircraft in Korea. With the acquisition of enemy air installations in sight, FEAF stopped most attacks on airfields south of the 40th Parallel. The 2nd South African Air Force (SAAF) Fighter Squadron arrived in the theater and was attached to Far East Air Forces, 18th Fighter-Bomber Group. The aircraft assigned to the South African Squadron would be maintained in part by 67th Fighter-Bomber Squadron maintenance personnel. Of a total 15 aircraft assigned to the unit, South African Fighter Squadron #2, 8 would be so serviced and maintained.

October 5: The crowded aircraft conditions at K-9 required that changes be made. On October 5th, the Engineering and Armament sections of the 18th Fighter-

(Continued on page 115)

Bob Hope Show

When Bob Hope and Marilyn Maxwell arrived at Dogpatch Air Base, they were greeted by a large sign reading "Welcome Bing Crosby."

The sign brought gales of laughter from Hope's 40-member cast and the welcoming committee led by Col. Curtis Lowe.

After Hope and his troupe were made honorary citizens of Dogpatch, they "delighted a capacity crowd of over 600 troops with a wonderful show," the Truckbuster recorded.

"It was a cold, wet and miserable day at Dogpatch. In spite of it the mass of entertainment hungry GIs surrounding a makeshift stage set up in a field, were given a full two hours of the best in shows by a top notch cast. Miss Maxwell, the Taylor Maids and Judy Kelly were probably blue with cold but they stuck it out in thin gowns."

"Les Brown and his orchestra stamped their feet not only to keep time but to keep warm. The whole crew looked pathetically funny in their GI clothing."

Hope came prepared with his famous quips. In speaking of the cold, "We're on our way to Alaska. They just sent us here to get used to the weather."

As for Dogpatch itself, Hope noted, "It's the best dog kennel I ever played in. I never

thought I'd get so far east I'd get homesick for Japan."

By Wednesday, 18 October, Lt. Ken Barber had wangled several days of R&R in Japan, returned to K-9, then followed his Infantry unit to the harbor in Pusan, when he rejoined his team.

Still "sitting in the harbor," waiting for another amphibious operation on the east coast of North Korea to begin, Barber took one of his men to a hospital ashore to have a bad tooth repaired. While Chandler "went to the hospital, the rest of us went ashore in the afternoon to see the Bob Hope Show. It was very crowded, but by a little pushing and shoving I found a place to kneel down and take pictures," Barber noted. Les Brown and his band entertained for a while, "then Bob Hope came on—he was very good. Judy Kelly did some flips and splits, which brought howls of delight from the G.I. crowd. Then the "Tailor Maids" sang a few songs." Hope joined a tap dancing routine and "was pretty good, too." Jimmy Wakeley was up next and sang several songs, including "Slippin' Around," "Mule Train," and "Cool Water." As far as Barber was con-

cerned, "Wakeley could have kept on singing for an hour or so. He had a very nice, easy natural voice, which flowed out with no strain whatsoever. His act was just singing and he seemed to enjoy it. Everybody else did too. His renditions were excellent."

The final "act" was Marilyn Maxwell, "a beautiful blonde with a sweater which accentuated her [illegible illegible illegible] figure. She was platinum blonde, but I believe it would turn dark in a few months if left alone. In a couple of songs she revealed a mediocre voice but enough sex appeal to have the boys howling and cat-calling, with Bob Hope clowning around the stage."

"Hope is a natural! Everything he does is funny. He's not a wiseacre like Berle, but just genuinely and un-insultingly comical.

Acting like a cowboy, he sidles up to Marilyn and says, "Say, podner, I hyears theys been a lot of rustling on your place."

He grabs her around the waist, pulls her close, then adds, "And I want my share!"

Then he says, "Say, by the way, what ranch are you from?"

She answers, "The Rattlesnake. What can I do for you?"

"Bite me!" Hope says.

Then he comes out with, "Now see here Girlsohn!"

That brought the house down. Bob capered around and really got some good laughs. Everyone enjoyed the show," Barber noted.

Just before completing the show, Hope "dropped his guise as funny man and said it really was a nice place. It was a touch of home to hear him say in all sincerity, 'Get this over with and hurry home, fellows.'"

After the show, Barber noted it "was a bit of a let down to see squalid Korea again. Sometimes I wonder if these shows with girls are good or not. Shows such as Al Jolson and Bob Hope alone are very good, but the girls just get the troops all hot and bothered and they know there isn't a chance for them to be with the girls. If the girls date anyone, it's the Officers, which may bring a little added resentment. I wonder if it might be better to exclude the girls from wartime overseas shows, just to avoid that thwarted, let-down feeling. I like to see a good figure and nice pair of legs as well as the next man, but being married, they don't bother me much, while they sure do make the G.I. dissatisfied."

Before leaving for Pyongyang to continue the tour, the Hope cast spent the night at Dogpatch. By the next morning, a new sign had been erected outside the tent occupied by "Daisy Mae Maxwell," reading "Marilyn Maxwell slept here."

Excerpted from Barber, Lt. Col. Kenneth, Korean War Diary Number One (unpublished), 1950, and Truckbuster.

Thanks for the Memories

18th Wing Lament

Thanks for the memory,
A balmy survivor breeze,
Snipers in the trees,
Ice and snow at ten below,
And man-devouring fleas!
Oh, thank you so much.

Wasn't it grand down at Pusan?
And wasn't it swell up at Unsan?
And aren't we a fine bunch of crackpots...
To come this far—for this goddamn war?

Thanks for the memory,
Of Taegu's s downy beds,
Air-conditioned heads,
Briefing naps and interviews,
And infiltrating Reds!
Oh, thank you so much.

So, thanks for the memories,
Of mines along the shore,
Night soil evermore,
There never was a headache,
Like this bloody Korean War.
Oh, thank you so much!

Chemical Warfare Arrives in Korea? *The ("deodorized") skunk was named Chanel Number 5 by its owner Arnold Marcum, a North American Aviation technical representative ("tech rep"), an expert on the F-51 Mustang. Lt. (later Col.) Ed Mason "had known him several years earlier" when he was stationed in Japan and the Philippines. Marcum and other tech reps "were rotated among the Mustang groups to help with maintenance problems." Marcum brought Chanel to K-9 in October 1950, just in time for Bob Hope's visit with Marilyn Maxwell, Jerry Colona, and other members of a USO troupe, including Les Brown and his "Band of Renown." When Marcum tossed Chanel onto the stage, "Les Brown departed!" Mason remembered with droll understatement. Not content with his USO "coup," Marcum left Chanel with Mason "for nearly a week chained to my bed in our tent. It did not increase my popularity with my tent mates," Mason remembered. (Mason)*

114

Bomber Group were relocated "from the central portion of the field to the northwestern portion of K-9 Air Force Base." The move helped alleviate the crowded parking conditions, "as well as minimizing hazardous ground operations of aircraft and eliminating excessively long taxiing distances to the head of the runway"—"effective dispersion of aircraft, equipment and personnel resulted." As always, the move "was effected without interruption" in combat operations.

October 7: The UN General Assembly overwhelmingly approved a resolution authorizing General Douglas MacArthur to cross the 38th Parallel and move into North Korea. For the first time, U.S. troops crossed the 38th Parallel.

October 8: Two F-80s accidentally strafed a Soviet airfield near Vladivostok, USSR, on the coast northeast of the Korea border. General George Stratemeyer removed the group commander, reassigning him to FEAF headquarters, and court-martialed the two pilots.

Lt. Al Diefendorf and Lt. Alton H. Quanbeck were above the weather at 37,000 feet in their F-80 "Shooting Stars," when they started their "letdown" to find the target. Their target was the Chongjin airfield in the upper northeast corner of North Korea, very close to the Soviet Union border at Vladivostok. Unknown to them at the time, strong tail winds had pushed them past their intended target and over the Soviet airstrip at Vladivostok. Diefendorf and Quanbeck were about to attack the Soviet Union.

Passing through 10,000 feet they spotted a broad river valley lined with mountains which they proceeded to follow to the southeast. Soon they spotted an airfield loaded with targets, mostly of the P-39 and P-63 type aircraft built and flown by both American and Soviet pilots during WWII. Running low on fuel and with only seconds to make a decision, they decided to attack based on the similarity of the aircraft markings to those of North Korean planes. Also, they were being fired on.

As they whooshed down the line of parked aircraft, they sprayed them with machine gun fire. Later, they claimed one

aircraft destroyed and two damaged. It was a highly conservative report. Initial fires triggered more explosions that caused the airfield to burn for a week, according to reports.

The Soviets quickly protested. The U.S. quickly admitted responsibility.

Although Washington demanded a Court Martial for the pilots, they were found not guilty of all charges that included violating an order to stay clear of the Manchurian border and of making an attack without positive identification. The Court Martial was closed to the public and the results were never released. The pilots were reassigned to non-combat duties since the Air Force reasoned that they would be in jeopardy if they were ever shot down and captured.

October 10: A 3rd ARS H-5 crew administered blood plasma to a rescued pilot—while the helicopter was in flight. The crew members received Silver Stars for this action.

October 12: FEAF Combat Cargo Command began an airlift of ROK military supplies to Wonsan, which ROK forces had captured two days earlier. An advance party from the 18th Fighter-Bomber Group arrived at Wonsan airfield on October 12th. The equipment and personnel led by Major Stanley F. Chatfield of Minot, North, Dakota were flown into Wonsan on the following day by C-119s of the combat cargo command. This advance party included air police to guard equipment; medical personnel, including a flight surgeon; cooks and bakers; maintenance men; armored and intelligence men. Equipment, gasoline, ammunition, napalm and napalm tanks, rockets and 500-lb fragmentation bombs were also flown into the North Korean airstrip.

October 14: Two communist aircraft raided Inchon harbor and Kimpo airfield. Far East Air Forces believed they had come from Sinuiju, North Korea, on the Chinese border. Chinese Communist troops began to cross over into North Korea from Manchuria.

"A severe almost monsoon-like rainstorm inundated the Squadron Operations area" of the 18th Fighter-Bomber Group. The affected area included the Armament,

Communications and Engineering Sections that "had been relocated in the northwestern portion of the field." Many items of personal equipment, from parachutes to life vests "were rendered unusable by the heavy rain.

The entire Operations area was under approximately 12-inches of water. Drainage facilities were inadequate to carry off the excess water—a virtual quagmire resulted."

Mud and lack of transportation required that officers and airmen solve the problem of getting to and from their duty stations. The temporary solution was a "line taxi service to and from the messing and quarters area."

Over the next few days, the 18th trucked in "tons of clay surfacing and sandy topsoil" to raise and compact the affected area. Heavy earth moving and rolling equipment was used and "some measure of soil stabilization was achieved."

The unit history noted once again, "despite this situation, no squadron stand downs resulted. All scheduled commitments, Group and JOC directives, were complied with during this period."

October 15: General MacArthur, in a meeting with President Truman on Wake Island, predicted that the war would be over by Christmas and China would not intervene. Communist antiaircraft artillery for the first time shot down an F-51 over the Yalu River near Sinuiju. Fifth Air Force opened its Korean Headquarters in Seoul.

Mustangs of the 18th Fighter-Bomber Group flew their first missions from the newly captured North Korean Airfield at Wonsan. The planes were gassed and loaded by hand. A complete combat intelligence system was set up to brief the pilots on the latest codes and any troop positions.

Four Fifth Air Force F-51 Mustangs, led by Major Arnold Mullins, CO of the 67th, took off Sunday [October 15, 1950] from the newly occupied air field at Wonsan, above the 39th Parallel in North Korea, on the first mission to be flown from that strip," noted Captain Tom Baird in a *Stars and Stripes* article. "This was the first North Korean air field to be utilized by the UN

Pre-Flight Briefing. *"A routine pre-flight briefing by the 18ᵗʰ Group Intelligence and Operations staff," Col. Ed Mason explained. Briefing is Capt. Harold R. Edwards, 18ᵗʰ Group Intelligence Officer. Major John A. Kindig, infantry ground liaison officer attached to the 18ᵗʰ Wing, stands by to further brief the flight on recent intelligence reports. A weatherman will also brief the pilots on the weather situation over the target area. After the briefing, the flight will check out their personel equipment, including parachutes and helmets from the operations tents, check over their airplanes and "sweat out" the take off time. (L-R) (Seated) Lt. George Olsen, Capt. Ed Mason, 1ˢᵗ Lt. Ken Barber, and Capt. Charles Morehouse. (S/Sgt Gilliland photo courtesy Col. Ed Mason)*

forces since the beginning of Korea hostilities. Just a few miles from the airstrip an island was still being shelled. Fighter-bomber aircraft made their approach over the newly occupied strip. Puffs of black smoke were visible both on the island and on the mountain at the crest. The blasts shook nearby buildings. The base itself gave new evidence of previous bombings. Snipers were still active in the hills on both sides of the strip and, a party of ROK troops was clearing mines from the beaches and nearby areas."

The F-51s were from a squadron commanded by Major Mullins of the 18ᵗʰ Fighter-Bomber Group attached to the 6002ⁿᵈ Tactical Support Wing, based at Dogpatch and commanded by Col. Curtis H. Low, Needham

Heights, Massachusetts. Other members of the original flight were Major Henry W. Lawrence, Long Beach, California; Captain Alma R. Flake of Phoenix, Arizona, and Major Herbert W. Andridge, Jr., Pittsfield, Massachusetts.

"This move to Wonsan by the Air Force has been proclaimed by the pilots as the best arrangement for fighter-bombers since the beginning of the Korean police action. The aircraft were able to be at their target just a few minutes after take off. The close proximity of these targets enabled them to spend much more time in the air over the target. The first mission was devoted to destroying enemy troop positions in the mountains north of Wonsan. This was the 599ᵗʰ Korean mission for the Squadron in-

volved. They worked in direct support of the advancing ROK troops about miles north of the airstrip." [6]

Just 20 minutes after the first Air Force mission took off from this advanced base a Marine pilot from a nearby aircraft carrier took off on the carrier's first mission from Wonsan.

"Is This Your

Helmet?"

Meanwhile, 1ˢᵗ Lt. Owen T. Brewer of the 67ᵗʰ Fighter-Bomber Squadron was flying a close support mission for a UN Force spearhead "in the vicinity of Namchonjom."

Brewer was part of a four-ship flight—Elsewhere Able—loaded with rockets, napalm and .50-caliber ammunition. Their instructions were to report to Mellow Control at Seoul.

Lt. Conserva was the Flight Leader, followed by Lt. Patterson, Lt. Cothern and Lt. Brewer. Mellow Control directed them to Export 14, located in the Namchonjom area, approximately 40 miles northwest of Seoul.

Elsewhere Able loitered near the target for almost twenty minutes until Export 14 "requested the flight leader to utilize the full load of all aircraft in his flight to destroy enemy troops who had dug in on a hill south of Namchonjom and who were hindering the advance of a UN spearhead in the immediate area," Brewer noted in his after action report.

After making numerous passes at the designated hillside, Lt. Cothern called Brewer on the radio with alarming news—coolant was streaming from Brewer's aircraft. He would soon have to bail out.

Conserva recommended that Brewer pick "an easterly heading and bail out over the U.N. spearhead."

At 0930, Brewer headed east—towards the spearhead—climbing to approximately 3,000 feet and then jettisoning his canopy. As soon as the canopy had cleared the aircraft, Brewer immediately unbuckled his safety belt and unplugged the electrical connections from his helmet.

"With the throttle retarded and coolant temperature at 130 degrees and steady," Brewer noted in his report, he "left the cockpit from the right side at 110 MPH." He gripped the windshield and right cockpit ledge, and placed his right leg outside the cockpit with the bulk of his body behind the windshield. Then he popped his left leg over the side of the ledge. Now he was completely out of the cockpit and "clinging to the side of the aircraft." He immediately let go of the rapidly falling plane and after a free fall "of approximately five seconds the "D" ring was pulled and

the descent was made without incident."

Brewer landed on a steep, rocky hill about a half-mile from the UN forces column. Cothern's advice had been sound. When he landed, he heard someone calling him—by name. "I couldn't figure that one out," he related, "so I hid."

Soon, an Army corporal "came running up" with Brewer's helmet. "He said it had landed just a few inches from him. My name was on the back," Brewer explained.

Two UN patrols were immediately sent in his direction to bring him to the main road and the advance command post for First Cavalry Division where he was soon making a report "in person" to Lt. Col. Harris, Seventh Regiment, First Cavalry Division. "They treated me like a guest. Sure was a swell bunch!"

While with the Seventh Regiment, Brewer "got a chance to see for himself what happens when a napalm tank bursts. "It sure was horrible," he related, "enemy troops were just frozen in their foxholes—

Mission Briefing Format

Briefings prior to missions normally included detailed information on the tactical situation, weather, intelligence and special topics, e.g. start engine time.

The **Tactical Briefing** generally covered the following information and order of presentation:

Roll call (flights and pilots)
General nature of mission (often given by the Group Commander)
Type formation
Route out and back, including headings and mileage
Method of attack
Action to be taken in the event of an abort—ground or air
Evasive action
Emergency airfields
Rescue (land and water-methods of contact)
Armament load, including fusing
Communications
Call signs

Recall word
Frequencies used during flight
Controller
R/T procedures
Radio discipline
Place of landing
Special items

Weather Briefing, normally given by the Staff Weather Officer

Intelligence Briefing, normally given by Unit Intelligence Officer, included:
Bombline data
Situation, friendly ground forces
Situation—enemy ground forces
Target
Description
Recognition features and photographs
Vulnerability
Results of previous attacks
Last resort targets
Enemy defenses
Flak

Electronic
Camouflage
Other passive, e.g. cables
Aircraft
Type and number
Recognition
Characteristics
Armament
Vulnerability
Tactics
Description of recent encounters
Friendly air activity
Friendly naval activity
Escape and Evasion
Security
Special Data
Time Hack

Special Briefings included:
Start engine time
Take-off time
TTR
Designation of Deputy Leader

Major Ken Carlson, Commander of the 18th Maintenance Squadron "off for Sinanju" recorded Major Bill Myers in October 1950. (Myers)

burned to a crisp."

Seventh Regiment personnel explained infantry tactics to Brewer during his stay. "I never realized there was such close co-operation between the Air Force and the Ground Force," he exclaimed. "For instance our planes were working over an area just a couple of hundred yards in front of our troops. Those attacks have to be pin-pointed and timely. It's the cooperation that makes them that way."

The grateful Brewer stayed with Harris' unit for two days as a "guest AF observer at the end of which time the return trip was made back to K-9." [7]

October 18: Mustangs from the 18th Fighter-Bomber Group flew the first combat missions from the recently captured base at Wonsan. They were able to significantly increase the number of sorties to flying time as a result and "...demonstrated the necessity for advanced bases as well as the increased combat effectiveness of fighter-bomber type aircraft." The Group also provided air cover for the Sukchon and Sunchon para-drops and for SCAP (General MacArthur)."

October 19: After a battle at Hukkyori, approximately ten miles south of the North Korean capital, UN forces entered Pyongyang. Fifth Air Force fighters provided crucial close air support to U.S. 1st Cavalry Division troops during the battle.

October 20: FEAF Combat Cargo Command dropped the US 187th Airborne Regimental Combat Team thirty miles north of Pyongyang. Seventy-one C-119s and forty C-47s participated in the operation, dropping more than 2,800 troops and 300 tons of equipment and supplies at Sukchon and Sunchon.

October 21: UN forces operating from Pyongyang linked up with the 187th Airborne Regimental Combat Team in the Sukchon and Sunchon area. H-5s of the 3rd ARS evacuated some thirty-five paratroopers in the first use of a helicopter in support of an airborne operation.

October 24: General Douglas MacArthur gave U.S. troops permission to go all the way to the Chinese border.

October 25: FEAF Bomber Command temporarily quit flying combat missions. It was out of targets for its B-29s in Korea. Far East Air Forces authorized unrestricted close air support missions near the Yalu River, allowing fighter operations all the way to the Chinese border.

At K-9 a "stand down" of the 18th Fighter-Bomber Group was ordered for October 25th. On this day the Group took itself off the line for a few hours for a very special reason: Bob Hope and his troupe had arrived and were preparing a show for the tired, homesick airmen.

October 26: ROK forces reached the Yalu River along the Chinese border at Chosan in northwest Korea. Elsewhere, Chinese forces "severely savaged" a ROK battalion near Onjong. The first CCF prisoners were captured.

October 29: Medical evacuations were flown by C-47s from newly captured Sinanju, North Korea, the northernmost Korean airfield FEAF aircraft ever used, at the mouth of Chongchon River, some forty miles north of Pyongyang.

Combat Losses

Bolt, Capt. Donald, 12th Squadron pilot KIA on 2 October 1950. On that morning, Don Bolt flew an early, pre-dawn mission to Pyongyang, North Korea's capitol city, remembered his friend and fellow pilot, Lt.

Col. Duane "Bud" Biteman. His airplane was once again hit in the engine by ground fire, and he was able to glide just clear of a low ridge of hills southeast of the city before having to belly-in on a small, open rice field that was surrounded by a mile-wide ring of trees. After the Mustang came to a stop, Bolt jumped quickly out of the cockpit, onto the wing, then started running across the dry rice paddies toward the nearest trees. He stopped abruptly, after covering about a hundred feet, according to his flight leader who was by then circling overhead. Then, Bolt ran quickly back to the far side of his crippled airplane, ducking low as he ran. He pointed his arm toward the trees and the flight leader could see enemy troops jumping out of a truck alongside the trees. The leader made a strafing pass, firing his machine guns between Don's aircraft and the North Korean truck, making sure not to hit the troops but, at the same time, giving them notice to stay back and leave Bolt's airplane alone. He called Mellow Control for help, giving Don's position and the fact that he appeared to be uninjured. He would remain overhead to keep the enemy away as long as his fuel held out—perhaps another forty-five minutes—then requested other flights to take over the top-cover until a helicopter could be dispatched from Kimpo Air Base, 85 long miles southwest. It was by then approximately 7:30 AM on a crisp, clear autumn morning, when the air war over Korea stopped, 'seemed to come to a complete halt,' just to cover the downed Lt. Don Bolt. Every Far East Air Force fighter airplane in the area was suddenly dedicated to the protection of Don Bolt—who was by then sitting dejectedly on the wing of his downed Mustang, watching the ever-changing flights of fighters circling overhead. Ground targets took second priority as Mellow Control coordinated the air effort to keep a minimum of four fighters circling the immediate area at all times, watching to assure that no troops attempted to close in on Don Bolt. We did not know, until then, however, that the maximum range of those ancient, early H-5 helicopters was less than 150 miles. There was no way that they could fly from

Kimpo to Pyongyang to pick up Bolt, and have any chance of returning to friendly territory. Still, the combat air patrol (CAP) remained overhead all through the day, dipping low periodically to strafe between the trees and Bolt's ship, to remind the Red troops to stay away. By mid-afternoon there were enemy troops surrounding the entire field, and Don lay hunched low behind the wing; he had apparently been shot at while sitting on the wing. Each succeeding flight of circling fighters found it necessary to fire a burst of machine gun fire to keep the troops back behind the trees. Still, no means could be devised to pick Don out of his menacing circle. Finally, as dusk turned to darkness, after scores of combat sorties were diverted to protect him, Major "Moon" Mullins flew our last patrol—when Bolt was last seen alive, and still crouched beneath his Mustang. Moon said that he was sorely tempted to strafe the entire circle of enemy troops and vehicles, but didn't dare; surely such action would be the single act to trigger the killing, on the spot, of Don Bolt. He might just as well have strafed the Red troops. For, a week later, after our forces took Pyongyang, we received the rumor that the Graves Registration people had found Lieutenant Don Bolt's body buried in a shallow grave just a short distance from his airplane. He had reportedly been shot in the back of the head, execution-style.

Carlson, Major Raymond, 12th Squadron pilot KIA in October 1950.

David, 2nd Lt. Mike S., 12th Squadron pilot KIA 8 October 1950. During the third week of October 1950, just before the Marines were to make an amphibious landing on the east coast, near Wonsan, David was attacking targets along the coast near Hungnam when his airplane was hit in the engine by ground fire. He knew he had been hit, because he could see oil streaming up through the top of the cowling, and even though it was still running, he knew it would not be for long. He couldn't know how long the prop would continue to turn but, being a hundred miles behind enemy lines, he reasoned that his best chance for pickup would be with the Navy flotilla known to be steaming north; but it was still some fifty

miles south and east of Wonsan—with a lot of the Sea of Japan in between. Heading out over the sea to intercept them, David nursed his crippled Mustang as it gradually lost power and altitude. Mellow Control was alerted by radio, and they, in turn, notified the Navy, who were to arrange for a helicopter to be prepared for rescue. If David could keep his F-51 airborne for another 15 minutes, the helicopter could meet him and be ready to pick him out of the water the instant that he ditched. Despite the tenseness of the situation, things were beginning to fall into place; there was hope, after all. Seas were almost calm—just very gentle, long swells; the skies were clear, and even the water temperature was a mild 57 degrees, Biteman said. David could see the Navy formation off on the distant horizon, as his engine finally sputtered and froze, but the helicopter was just four or five miles from a rendezvous. Since Mike still had almost five thousand feet of altitude remaining, he'd have an easy glide down to the smooth surface of the sea, and the helicopter could by then be overhead; a few more minutes and he'd "have it made." The sun was beating in thru the Mustang's clear plastic canopy, and with the silence of the dead engine Mike was undoubtedly reminded more of the quiet sensation of gliding with a jet engine. But his dead-stick glide brought him closer and closer to the vast watery expanse. Finally, turning slightly left to head more directly into the wind, he raised his nose ever so slightly, as if to flare for landing on a long paved runway. Then, while the helicopter hovered several hundred yards off to the side, David' Mustang touched gently onto

the placid surface of the Sea of Japan. Instantaneously there was a great splash and spray of water as first the propeller hit, then the belly air scoop. Then, as if in slow motion, the Mustang's nose dipped under the surface, and with the continuing momentum of his landing speed, the entire airplane slid immediately under the water. From the air above, Mike could be seen trying vainly, and belatedly, to jettison his canopy. It was, by then, being held forcefully on by water pressure, and could not be budged. As the airplane settled deeper into the sea, its silvery outline was quickly changed to a darker and darker tone of blue-green. Soon it was gone from sight, and all that remained on the surface was an oil-slick to mark its passing.

Davis, Capt. Ramon Roderick, 12th Squadron pilot MIA October 1950.

Leake, Capt. Daniel D., 67th Squadron pilot KIA on 18 October 1950. The 67th FBS was flying its first 'three in one' mission that was led by Maj. 'Moon' Mullins, Lt. Col. Duane "Bud" Biteman recorded. The F-51s provided a fighter escort for the parachute drops—paradrops—at Sukchon and Sunchon, where the 187th Regimental Combat Team was being landed to cut off retreating North Korean troops. They then provided an escort home for General MacArthur's C-54, from which he had been observing the operation. They left the C-54 over the MLR, and then dove down to provide close air support for ROK forces near Wonsan, and finished up the day, after rearming and refueling, by providing a fighter escort for B-26s of the 3rd Bomb Wing. "During the course of the ground support portion of the day's efforts, Captain Danny Leake had to bail out after being hit by numerous rounds of small arms fire. His Mustang was being flown at maximum speed when it was hit, and the fabric control surfaces were seen by his wingman to have been shot away. Unfortunately, Leake was at too low an altitude when he cleared his Mustang, and his parachute just had time to blossom as he hit the ground with high impact. He was picked up by an air-rescue team, but died from his injuries," Biteman noted.

Longshore, 1st Lt. Lamar B., 39th Squadron pilot KIA in October 1950.

Padilla, Capt. Alexander Beck, 12th Squadron pilot KIA while serving as FAC in October 1950. When Lt. Ken Barber returned to K-9 from a mission on the afternoon of 9 October 1950, he "found out that Blank and Cothern had flown cover for Padilla who bellied his plane in, was hurt, and was captured when the helicopter was only seven miles away. What a heartbreaker! I hope he's OK, but so far, the North Koreans haven't taken any AF prisoners."

Sternard, 1st Lt. Robert E., 12th Squadron pilot KIA in October 1950.

Taylor, 1st Lt. Claude R. "Spud", 12th Squadron pilot KIA in October 1950 near Pyongyang, NK.

Endnotes

[1] USAFHRA. *"The Story of the 18th Fighter-Bomber Group in the Korean United Nations Police Action."* 6002nd Tactical Support Wing, Public Information Office. S/Sgt Sandy Colton.

[2] USAFHRA. *History of the 67th Fighter-Bomber Squadron, October 1950.*

[3] USAFHRA. *History of the 67th Fighter-Bomber Squadron, October 1950.* Historical Officer addendum to the monthly report that quoted from the "Stars and Stripes."

[4] Adapted from USAFHRA. January 2002. *The U.S. Air Force's First War: Korea 1950-1953 Significant Events. October 1950.*

[5] USAFHRA. *History of the 67th Fighter-Bomber Squadron, October 1950.*

[6] USAFHRA. *"F-51s Fly First Run From Enemy Air Strip." History of the 67th Fighter-Bomber Squadron, October 1950.*

[7] USAFHRA. *"Cav Support Pilot Drops In For Visit." History of the 67th Fighter-Bomber Squadron, October 1950.*

Lt. Mike David (left) and Lt. Ken Barber were good friends and roomed together at Clark AFB until Barber's wife, Carolyn joined her husband there shortly before the Korean War began. (Barber)

Barber Loses Friends...

On 3 October, Lt. Ken Barber and his team were operating near Suwon. On that morning he wrote a letter of recommendation for promotion for his men. Later than day he was told to expect a long motor ride to Pusan, "there to embark, probably for landings up around the 40th Parallel." He noted that he would be "going right by my unit at K-9 and am in a quandary as to whether or not I should try to be replaced at this time..."

On Saturday, 7 October, Barber was in Pusan and "went out to the field today, only two miles away. Saw Jim Allen, Joslin, Mike David, etc. Major Chat[field] and Major Cartwright said they would see about getting me replaced."

On Sunday, 7 October, Barber "heard Bolt and Davis were shot down North of Pyongyang, and are walking back safely, we all hope...Also heard Flentke was killed. What a shame! He was in Mullins flight and they didn't miss him for thirty minutes...Mullins saw a flash out of the corner of his eye but thought nothing of it. Later, when they went back they found Flentke's plane smeared all over the spot. They say Millie Flentke is about to crack up down at Clark Field."

Barber asked for and received permission to continue flying missions with the 18th as long he was in the area waiting for the next amphibious operation to begin. That afternoon, following a mission, he "buzzed the troops and gave 'em a slow roll. Sure was fun! Didn't get caught, either," he noted.

Burned out enemy tank on the road between Suwon and Pyongjom-ni. (Barber)

In Memory of Captain Danny Leake

I walked among the Crosses on the Hill;
I looked for names of those I knew.
Many crosses, white and still;
Until at last, I came to you.

Your name was there in letters small,
Day of birth and day you died.
In Memory Of, it said--that's all.
Not who cared, and not who cried.

Many things it does not tell,
That cross that's o'er you head.
Nothing there of why you fell;
In Memory Of, is all it said.

People will recall, each year,
On a certain day in May.
They'll kneel and maybe shed a tear,
And put some flowers where you lay.

But we will remember every day;
You, who gave his all.
Not just once a year in May,
Will we, your name recall.

For we who knew and called you friend.
For we who saw you fall.
We will remember--to the end,
That day you gave your all.

If only people could but see
Into our hearts they'd know,
Why your name will always be
With us, where e'er we go.

Burned upon our hearts they'd find,
If they could take a peek.
The mark that you have left behind.
In Memory Of...Captain Danny Leake.

by Master Sergeant Maynard A. Boynton,
his flight chief.

Soon after Captain Danny Leake was killed, his flight chief M/Sgt. Maynard A. Boynton brought this tribute to Journalist William J. "Sandy" Colton of the Truckbuster staff. Colton not only encouraged Boynton to complete the poetic tribute, but he worked with the photo lab to create the above montage of Leake and the silhouette of a Mustang. The montage and poem was released to newspapers across the United States as a "tribute to Captain Danny Leake, former Fifth Air Force pilot of the 18th Fighter-Bomber Wing, who gave his life fighting Communism with many other United Nations airmen that the goals of Democracy and Peace shall not have been in vain." The news articles credited M/Sgt. Maynard A. Boynton, "crew chief who serviced Capt. Leake's F-51 Mustang before each combat strike and regarded him not only as a friend, but as a symbol of our American way of life." (Colton)

Capt. Danny Leake with "Little Audrey." Note that at this stage of the Korean War, the 67th Squadron had painted its prop spinners half red and half white. When the engine was running the different colors appeared to blink, i.e. "winking spinners."

On Monday he awoke "to hear bad news. Mike David was killed yesterday. His engine quit just off of Wonsan. Potter was flight leader. Mike's engine quit, he couldn't get it started so he ditched it in a perfect 3-point stall, but his canopy wasn't off. It nosed right over and sank. For a half hour they flew overhead but only a few maps floated to the surface. Another of my good friends is gone."

Lt. Mike David was "from Los Angeles, of Hungarian parents, and a swell guy," Barber wrote in his notebook. "We roomed together at Clark until Carolyn came over and were in the play, "You Can't Take It With You" together. Mike had tried to resign from the Air Force, but couldn't and ever get his commission back if he were recalled. He only wanted a peaceful, easy-going life, in theatrical work, if possible. He loved to fly and was a top-notch pilot. What a shame to lose such a swell guy and good friend."

Barber, Lt. Col. Kenneth. Korean War Diary Number Two (unpublished), 1950.

Operations From Wonsan

Ruined Wonson. *The first combat flight from Wonsan by 18th Group Mustangs lifted off on 14 October at 1505 hours. It was the first mission to be flown from that strip and the first North Korean airfield to be used by UN forces since the beginning of the Korean War the previous June. Shelling and ground combat operations were still underway nearby. At the base, destroyed hangars (above) provided mute evidence of previous combat operations at that base. Snipers were still active in the hills on both sides of the strip. ROK troops were busy clearing mines from the beaches and nearby areas.*

(Right) 18th Group rearming crews combed the aptly named "bomb dump" for the right ordnance for the next mission. "This move to Wonsan by the Air Force has been proclaimed by the pilots as the best arrangement for fighter-bombers since the beginning to the Korean police action," the Air Force Times of 1 November 1950, pointed out. "The aircraft are able to be at their targets just a few minutes after takeoff. Close proximity enabled them to spend much time in the air over the enemy." (Maynard)

Homemade Shower. *(Right) Rearming and maintenance crews were without even the most basic of "facilities." M/Sgt Charles Maynard solved some of the challenges of keeping clean with this "homemade shower" he put together at K-26 by "borrowing" a heater originally intended to heat water at the mess hall. Maynard admitted to being "a good scrounge." (Maynard)*

The 6002nd Maintenance Squadron "swings an engine" in October 1950. (Myers)

1ˢᵗ Lt. Daniel "Chappie" James

1ˢᵗ Lt. Daniel "Chappie" James

"Spud" Taylor and Chappie James: An Exceptional Friendship

By Lt. Col. Duane E. 'Bud' Biteman, USAF (Ret.)

Following the North Korean invasion of South Korea on Sunday morning, June 25, 1950, we had gone into Korea in mid-July 1950 with the first increment of the 'Dallas Project,' a hastily-formed squadron of volunteer fighter pilots from the USAF's 18ᵗʰ Fighter-Bomber Group, then stationed at Clark Field in the Philippine Islands.

First Lieut. Claude R. "Spud" Taylor, was another unique example of the courageous band of Air Force pilots who flew early combat in the Korean War.

'Spud' had been one of the first to raise his hand when the 18ᵗʰ Group Commander, Col. Hank Norman asked for volunteers to go into battle; he went up to Korea as a "buck fighter pilot," I went along as the full-time Squadron Intelligence Officer and part-time combat pilot.

It didn't take either of us, or any of us, long to realize that our gallant, but feeble efforts, initially flying ten derelict F-51 Mustangs from the dirt airstrip at Taegu, South Korea, were having little effect in slowing the North Korean's relentless offensive drive toward Pusan. Things improved considerably in early August, with the arrival of a shipload of 150 'new' F-51 Mustangs and a batch of experienced fighter pilots fresh from the 'States on the USS BOXER.

But it wasn't until at least two months later, during September, 1950, that we honestly felt that we might be on the winning side. General Douglas MacArthur's audacious amphibious landing at the port of Inchon put a completely new perspective on what, until then, had been a purely defensive war.

The North Korean forces were soon forced into a complete rout; their offensive pressure around Taegu and the Pusan Perimeter was released immediately, and our attack efforts were simultaneously redirected toward support of our troops racing for the North Korean capitol city of Pyongyang.

Like so many of the World War II Army Air Corps fighter pilots, Spud had been released from active duty in the drastic RIF's (Reductions in Force) of 1946. Having been trained as a professional jazz musician, Taylor made a reasonable living playing with small combos at various nightclubs and cocktail lounges around the country.

But, also, like so many others of us, he too had been afflicted with the "fighter pilot bug" during the war and wanted very much to be flying again. He applied for Recall to Active Duty and was pleasantly surprised to be accepted for P-51 retraining during the Spring of 1948.

After a brief tour of duty in the 'States, he was transferred to Clark Field, Philippines, travelling across the Pacific by ship with his family. It was during the voyage from San Francisco to Manila that he met another fighter pilot with unusual musical talent—a singer with a pleasant deep bass voice, and it was only logical that they should share many pleasant musical hours en route.

Lieutenant Taylor stood about five foot seven inches and, soaking wet could not have weighed 150 pounds. He wore a well-developed bushy walrus mustache and affected a slouched, rhythmic walk—he played beautiful Dixieland Jazz on the saxophone and, well, he just looked the part of a jazz musician!

His new friend, another fighter pilot en route to Clark Field, First Lieutenant Daniel "Chappie" James, had a deep, well-trained baritone voice; and in contrast to Spud's slight stature, he was six foot four, and tipped the scale at about 220 pounds—he was built like a pro football lineman.

They made quite a combination. A study in contrasts—'Spud' Taylor and his new friend 'Chappie' James. Besides the other visual contrasts between the two, Spud Taylor was Caucasian and Chappie James was Afro-American, in the days when it wasn't popular to be a black officer—the only black officer in a recently-integrated all-white fighter squadron. Black or not, Chappie's personality was such that he was immediately accepted as a professional U.S. Air Force fighter pilot. James was assigned to the 12ᵗʰ Fighter-Bomber Squadron at Clark Field in late 1948. Taylor flew with the 44ᵗʰ Squadron until he volunteered to join the Dallas Project which later became the 12ᵗʰ Squadron.

In July, 1950, serving in the newly-redesignated 12ᵗʰ Fighter-Bomber Squadron at Taegu, Korea, flying combat missions together whenever the schedule would permit, they complemented each other in the air as well.

On October 20, 1950, following the Inchon Landings, Spud Taylor, while flying element leader, was hitting the Pyongyang airfield area as part of the "softening up" prior to an air drop by one of our Paratroop units, hoping to cut off a goodly number of the retreating North Korean Army.

During his dive-bombing and rocketing of the airfield, Spud's airplane was hit by ground fire—hit badly enough, apparently, that he was barely able to maintain control long enough to pull up a couple thousand feet and turn southerly toward our front lines. After just a few miles, however, the engine caught fire, forcing Spud to take to his parachute—he had to bail out while still several miles north of friendly territory. His 'chute' was seen to open, and he reportedly appeared to be conscious as he floated down, for he waved to one of his wingmen who flew by to check his condition.

Our ground troops came in by mass parachute drop early on the following morning, taking the area with but little opposition. Spud Taylor's body was found where he had touched down, still in his 'chute harness. He had been shot while descending in his parachute.

Spud's great friend, Chappie James, was absolutely beside himself with grief when told of Spud's fate. He had to be physically restrained from running out to one of our armed Mustangs with the intention of seeking single-handed retribution for Taylor's death.

Instead, he was ordered off to Tokyo for a week's Rest & Recuperation Leave, after which he returned to Korea to finish his 100-plus combat missions before returning to the United States in December, 1950.

Later, back at Clark AFB, Lt. Col. Ken Barber recalled, "Chappie sang in his nice, husky voice the song 'My Buddy,' at the O-Club. Everyone present knew it was for Spud Taylor and I heard there wasn't a dry eye in the house."

Daniel "Chappie" James was promoted to Captain before leaving Korea. He then went on to a highly successful Air Force career, rising rapidly through various command positions, with further combat responsibilities in Viet Nam, to become our nation's first black four-star General, as head of NORAD (North American Air Defense Command).

James did much to inspire hope among the black youth of our country, and he always "told it like it was"—he told the youngsters that they could not expect freedom and equality to be given to them as a "Right"— they had to "get their ass in gear and work for it"!

General 'Chappie' James died of a heart attack in 1978, at a young 56 years of age, and was buried with full military honors at Arlington National Cemetery, Washington, DC.

Excerpted with permission from "Korean Tales, Unsung Heroes of the Korean Air War."

A typical North Korean home at harvest time. (Barber)

Country

Comparisons

"It is very interesting to be in another country, seeing how others live," Lt. Ken Barber noted in his diary, "watching them at work, being amazed at how different they look from us as they do the same jobs our people do in America, wondering how they can possibly enjoy their life of poverty. I have often remarked that if I <u>had</u> to live in this land of Japan, Korea, Philippines, I would become a sailor because I could then have a certain amount of freedom—have my own boat, and be able to travel besides making my living probably by fishing. To be bound to a rice paddy would be a fate worse than death to me. And yet, the children play happily just as they do in America, the young girls flirt and the young men strut, the businessmen barter and the loafers loaf, and they all seem happy. I have frequently to remind myself that we foreigners are not used to this way of life, that they have been born to it, and it is as natural and happy a life to them as America is to us."

"It all boils down to the country in which one is born and raised. His land will always be the best to him—his way of life will seem quite superior, in most cases, to the ways of the lives of others. His home, his native land, take on more meaning as he leaves them behind."

"To try to say what a person's country means to him is a hard thing—an attempt which usually either falls flat, is stilted, or is too "gooey" with sentiment. It is impossible to describe such feelings as the tears of pride which fill your eyes as the flag is lowered at sunset over Clark Field to the inspiring strains of "The Star Spangled Banner," or the rush of feeling in your chest as you see the combat troops of America going off to war, or the flag flying over our ships, or the star on our airplanes."

"Sometimes you get the same feeling sitting in church, and you want to do something big; something bigger than yourself, something which will serve others.

This too, is America."

"When you leave the cities, take your rifle and dog, and hike through the pine woods and the fields—you camp under the stars and say your prayers. It's funny how you always say your prayers when you sleep out under the stars. You smoke rabbit tobacco, hunt buckeyes, go squirrel hunting—all this is the freedom belonging to youth and belonging to America. And then something comes to challenge this freedom and before long it becomes necessary to fight and many go off to war to fight for their country—their homes, and Freedom. I am one of them."

"Yes, I am one of them, and my freedom means more to me, by far, than my life. As soldier, it is my duty to serve, but it is more than just a duty. It is a <u>sacred trust</u> and an <u>honor</u> to preserve the freedom that is my birthright. We don't feel that we've done anything extraordinary when we chase a burglar off of our property, or when we kill rats invading our house. Our country

North Korean children play on the ice. (Barber)

Untae Kim

Many of the indigenous South Koreans were superb individuals and soldiers and contributed greatly to the success of the war. Such was Untae Kim!

On Thanksgiving Day, November 23, 1950 Lt. Kenneth Barber and his TACP team were transferred from the 2nd Battalion under Lt. Col. Reidy to the 1st Battalion, 31st Infantry, 7th Division commanded by Major Kermit R. "Red" Mason, so called because of his hair color. The 2nd Battalion was moved into reserve. Barber reported the food and new organization as much improved.

"The 1st Bn commander is Major Mason, a powerful looking young man. He has been in command for two months so I guess he must be pretty good. Major Rubottom is his executive officer." Later that day, Barber noted, "One of the interpreters named Kim seems to be a very smart Korean. He speaks and understands English very well. Upon later inquiry I found that he spent three years in medical school in Seoul, and speaks English, Japanese, Chinese (his home used to be in Manchuria) and Russian fluently besides being able to read German. He has a sharp, intelligent looking face, and I would like to know him better."

Barber did make it point to get to know Untae Kim much better.

Untae Kim's father was employed by the British in Maritime Customs in Antung, Manchuria (part of China) where Kim was raised and went to high school. His family had fled from Korea after the Japanese annexed the country in 1910. He was born around 1930. Shortly after graduating from high school, one week before Japan surrendered to the United States, Kim was drafted by the Japanese army to be sent to the battle front to make their last stand. Had World War II lasted a little longer, he probably would have been killed by Soviet or U.S. bombings. Korea was split in two at the end of WW II along the 38th Parallel with Russia installing a puppet Communist system in the north and the U.S. attempting to nurture a democratic government in the south.

is a public trust as much as our homes are our private trusts, and we owe to the whole as much as we owe to ourselves—otherwise we lose our private trusts by losing our government and our freedom."

"It is with the greatest contempt that I view those so-called men back home who gripe or worry about being recalled to military service, those who use wars as a method of self-aggrandizement, those who feel the government owes them a living, those who hoard sugar, nylons, gas, tires. These men and women are not fit to live our country and call themselves Americans. Even worse are those who hide behind the institutions of freedom, and enjoy all of our free country's advantages, while all the time they are trying to tear down the things for which our country stands. These people, to me,

are far worse than Benedict Arnold."

"Who would want to die peacefully in a bed, surrounded by nurses and weeping relatives? Who wants to pass on in groveling, sniveling fear of death? What could be worse? Who wants to die in some stupid bar brawl or some wretched hovel of old age, or even in a clean white hospital? Not I, sir. What better way can a man die than in fighting for his country, for his loved ones, and for those things in which he believes? What greater epitaph could he ask than, "This Soldier died fighting for his country." It is a proud way to live, and a proud way to die, in order that Freedom might have a better chance to succeed."

Barber, Lt. Col. Kenneth. Korean War Diary Number One (unpublished), 1950.

18th Wing air strikes in North Korea in November 1950. (NARA)

Lt. Kenneth Barber (right) and Untae Kim on 17 December 1950.

"As a member of Korean refugee groups trying to cross the 38th Parallel into South Korea," Kim explained to Barber, "we were caught by Soviet border guards, and would have been sent to Russian concentration camps in Siberia but for our wise group leader who bribed the Russian soldiers with a magnum bottle of strong Chinese liquor."

Kim entered medical school in Seoul, South Korea and had completed two years of studies when the North Koreans invaded on June 25, 1950. He decided to fight the invaders. Although a second year medical student he hastily put together a small group of like-minded medical students and physicians, volunteered to the South Korean Army and was dispatched to the front line at the northern outskirts of Seoul to set up an emergency medical aid station. By early the next morning the North Korean Army with tanks swept past all barriers and the volunteer medics dispersed.

Untae Kim hid in various places around Seoul, including hiding in the crawl space of two aunt's homes or in an attic or on a roof, avoiding house-to-house searches by the local Communist Youth Groups, eventually moving south to another relatives farm near Suwon. "After nearly a month of hid-

ing in Suwon, at last, Gen. Douglas MacArthur made the surprise landing on Inchon," he recalled.

The village of Suwon is not far from Inchon. Kim went to meet the UN landing troops and halfway to Inchon ran into the convoy of the 1st Battalion, 31st Infantry, 7th U.S. Division led by Major Kermit R. Mason who he greeted in English, to Mason's considerable surprise. Recognizing Kim's potential, Major Mason invited Kim to join him to fight the communists in the open. Knowing the medical school in Seoul wouldn't be open for several months, Kim enthusiastically joined him, Barber said.

"The 1st Battalion fought and convoyed south to Pusan via Taegu where they camped on Kimhae Beach," Barber explained. "The entire 31st Infantry was later loaded on ships, sent north again through the Sea of Japan to be landed far up north on the east coast of Korea at Iwon, and then to convoy north to the Chosen Reservoir (2nd Bn) and Pungsan (1st Bn) respectively. It was with the 1st Bn that Lt . Ken Barber met Untae Kim for the first time and it was in Pungsan that Kim, Captain Fred Keifer and Major Mason conducted the first "free" election of a town Mayor! Also, through his intelli-

gence work, Kim was one of the first to know that Chinese troops were about to enter the war, finding out from captured North Koreans."

Fierce battles were subsequently fought with the Chinese as the 1st Bn advanced to within about 20 miles of the Manchurian Border on the Yalu River. Unfortunately the "free" election in Pungsan was short lived because of the Chinese intervention and the ultimate need of the 1st Battalion to retreat back to Hungnam and Hamhung where ships evacuated the survivors back to South Korea, Barber noted.

Kim had been assigned to S-3 (Intelligence) as an interpreter under Capt Frederick J. Keifer, "a splendid soldier and 1944 West Point graduate," Barber recalled, "the S-3 of Red Mason's 1st Battalion, and also served part time as a medic because of his medical experience. He was an extremely valuable and courageous member of Mason's staff who lived and fought alongside the Americans in both North and South Korea."

Dr. Untae Kim came to the United States in 1952 where he finished his internship in Boston, Mass, specializing in cancer pathology, and in 1955 married, Priscilla Thomas and became an American citizen. He now lives in New York State, has five grown children and is active in Korean War veteran activities.

Close Air Support

Relieves Infantry

NORTH DOGPATCH AB Korea—Precision close support by Fifth Air Force F-51s of a fighter—bomber group of the 6002nd Tactical Support Wing, resulted in the relief of a United Nations infantry unit temporarily entrapped in the Ipsok area of North Korea recently.

The Mustangs, led by Lt. Col. Ira F. Wintermute, Salem, Ore., the group commander, departed from this advanced air base above the 38th Parallel in North Korea in response to an emergency call from a ground controller in an area approximately three miles north of Ipsok.

Upon arrival at the target Colonel Wintermute and his wingman, Capt. Thomas B. Meeker, Britton, Okla., dived down on a strafing run. The enemy had set up an ambush at a horseshoe curve in the road and were well dug in on two ridges to the right of it. Constant mortar and automatic weapons fire were keeping the infantry unit from rejoining their main body. Pilots claimed that approximately 150 vehicles were stalled by the ambush. Some of the lead vehicles, including an ambulance, had already been knocked out by enemy fire.

The second element of the flight, led by Capt. Richard H. Cassidy, Nashville, Ark., with wingman 1st Lt. Billie R. Cothern, Herrick, Ill, joined the attack.

"As we went in on a pass," said Cothern, "the enemy troops would stop firing. I guess the colonel noticed the same thing. He told the ground controller to get our vehicles through as soon as we started the strafing run."

The elements alternately went down to strafe, rocket and napalm the ridges, keeping up an almost continual fire against the enemy. On each run three or four vehicles would get through the temporarily silenced gauntlet.

After 55 minutes over the target the entire group had successfully escaped the combined roadblock and ambush.

Captain Meeker said, "Our support was so close that ground controller said he could feel the heat from the burning napalm. One time he called for us to hit closer to the road. Our napalm strike then was so close that he called back excitedly, 'Not that close'."

"As we left," continued Meeker, "he called and thanked us for what he said was the best souvenir he'd gotten so far. One of the empty shell casings, expended from our wing guns, had fallen into the back of his jeep. That's really getting close."

F-51's Get Field Day

DOGPATCH AB—What with the scarcity of targets these days, two flights of Dogpatch-based F-51s of the 18th Fighter-Bomber Group, 6002nd Tactical Support Wing, had a field day recently when they accounted for 80 or more enemy vehicles destroyed or damaged.

The first flight, led by 1st Lt. Billie R. Cothern, Herrick, Ill., was operating around Mupyong-ni about 35 miles above Huichon in North Korea. Capt. Richard H. Cassidy, Nashville, Ark., was flying wing for Cothern.

First Lt. Philip J. Conserva, Patchoque, N. Y., was leading the second element with Maj. Arnold Mullins, Phoenix, Ariz., commander of the squadron involved, flying wing for Conserva.

The four pilots had dropped their napalm and were looking for another target. Major Mullins called out, "Hey, come on over here—found some trucks."

When the other pilots checked they found two hillsides and the floor of a valley covered with closely spaced camouflaged vehicles.

"It was a phenomenal target," said Conserva.

The four pilots dove in for the kill. With 13 rocket and strafing attacks they destroyed at least 30 vehicles.

When their ammunition was expended they called in another flight. Capt. Charles H. Spencer, Penn Yan, N.Y., was leader of the second flight.

Number two was 1st Lt. William E. Hydorn Jr., Wooster, Ohio and number three Capt. Robert W. Ward, Marshaltown, Iowa.

"Every haystack was a vehicle," said Spencer. With three napalm bombs and nine rockets the pilots tallied 40 more vehicles destroyed or damaged.

"I never saw anything like it," said Ward. "One rocket would knock out four vehicles if you placed it right. Each vehicle must have been loaded with gas cans. The whole place was burning when we left. We had a field day."

November 1950
Pusan to Pyongyang to Suwon…In Four Weeks

At the beginning of November, the 6002nd Tactical Support Wing *[soon to be redesignated the 18th Fighter-Bomber Wing]* was operating from K-9, Pusan East Airstrip at Tongnae, South Korea as it had been since 7 September. By 21 November, the Group was moved "forward" to K-24, Pyongyang East Airdrome, Pyongyang, North Korea.

K-24 was located at "longitude and latitude 125 degrees, 49 minutes east; 39 degrees, minutes north; precisely one (1) mile south of the Taedong (gang) River and six (6) miles due east of P'yongyang, erstwhile capital city of North Korea. Grid, coordinates are YD (Yolk-Dog) 42-22." [1]

The 6002nd Tactical Support Wing reported that its Operations Section "continued to serve as advisor and liaison to the 18th Fighter-Bomber Group, which completed 839 sorties during the month of November. Close support, special interdiction, armed reconnaissance, airfield strikes, and escort missions were flown as directed by Fifth Air Force." [2]

18th Fighter-Bomber Group F-51 lifts off from K-9 on a combat mission. (Biteman)

The Tactical Support Wing's K-24 "office" was set up and operating at Pyongyang East by November 23. The next day "a TWX received from higher headquarters redesignated the 6002nd Tactical Support Wing…as the 18th Fighter-Bomber Wing."

At this point, recalled Col. Stanley Chatfield, then the 18th Group Operations Officer, the war in Korea was considered by the Far East Command to be all but over since UN forces were at or near the Northernmost borders of North Korea. "Col. Wintermute, the 18th Group Commander, received orders

to send a representative from the Group back to Clark AFB in the Philippines to plan and facilitate the return of the entire 18th Group to its 'Home Base.'" Chatfield was dispatched to Clark to work on the relocation plan, along with a spot promotion to Lt. Col. and a recommendation for a Legion of Merit.

Barely a week later, on November 30th, "a pincher movement of guerrillas and Red Chinese forced the Wing to begin the evacuation of K-24" to K-13 airstrip at Suwon, South Korea, about 30 miles south of Seoul.

Monthly Summary

UN forces occupied most of North Korea at the beginning of November. However, bomber strikes on enemy ports and bridges over the Yalu River could not shut off the flow of Chinese forces to North Korea. Pontoon bridges and thick ice that covered sections of the river by the end of month negated the loss of fixed bridges. Forbidden to over fly Manchuria, the B-29s attacked the bridges by following the course of the river. Their fighter escorts could only fly on the Korean side of the bombers. This enabled enemy fighters and antiaircraft guns based in China to threaten the bombers and finally resulted in a FEAF order that restricted flights in the area. "Following General MacArthur's orders, the command initiated in early November a two-week cam-

paign of incendiary attacks on North Korean cities and towns to destroy supplies and shelter for enemy troops."

The air war intensified. For the first time in three months, USAF pilots shot down enemy aircraft in Korea. Soviet-built MiG-15 swept-wing jet fighters, faster than any USAF aircraft in the theater, entered the war, operating with impunity from Chinese sanctuaries. A few of the MIGs were shot down by USAF F-80s, but some USAF fighters suffered heavy damage in these encounters. The Shooting Star was no match for the MIG 15. F-84 and F-86 fighters were en route to the Far East by sea, but they would not enter combat until December. "At the request of General Partridge, Commander, Fifth Air Force, FEAF Combat Cargo Command di-

verted airlift resources from the logistical support of ground forces to move three F-51 fighter groups from South Korea to bases in North Korea."

Units of the U.S. Eighth Army were concentrated along the southern bank of the Chongchon River in northwest North Korea to prepare for a final offensive. General MacArthur launched the attack the last week in November, but the Chinese Communist Forces responded with an almost immediate counteroffensive. All hope ended that the U.S. would have its boys "home by Christmas."

Adapted from USAFHRA. January 2002. The U.S. Air Force's First War: Korea 1950-1953 Significant Events. November 1950.

(Left/below) **K-9 Aircraft Maintenance Area.** *The open air maintenance area for the 12th Fighter-Bomber Squadron at K-9 near Pusan, SK in November 1950.* (Biteman)

(Right/below) **K-9 Aircraft Paking Area.** *The aircraft parking area for the 12th Squadron at K-9 in Pusan, SK in November 1950. Note the control tower on the top of the hill in the background.* (Biteman)

The Wing considered the move to Suwon "a temporary assignment, for tactical support of troops in Northern Korea, reassembly of troops, organizational supplies and equipment and Materiel and Supply." [3] The move from Pyongyang to Suwon was conducted from 1-4 December.

Forward Basing at P'yongyang East

On 8 November 1950 "an advance party established a tactical control center at P'yongyang (east) and the following day, tactical missions were flown from this field."

On 9 November 1950, information was received by responsible persons of this unit that the group and wing, *en toto*, would be moved to K-24 AFB, the 67th Squadron reported. This was announced by Major Arnold Mullins to the officers of his command. Plans were drawn up to effect this movement "without impedance and/or interfer-

ence with the tactical efforts of this organization. The advantages which accrued to combat pilots were most obvious in that the long hours of flying (base to target and return) were more than halved."

During this period, "K-9 AEB rapidly deteriorated as a tactical center and was rapidly turned into a Distribution Point for food and other supplies which were then airlifted by C-119, C-54 and C-47 type aircraft to various points of necessity in Korea. Air Evacuation aircraft continued to perform their vitally necessary duties from K-9 AFB."

On 18 November 1950, the barracks areas at K-9 where "permanent type shelters" were built, were occupied by Group and Wing personnel. The move was necessary in order to strike tents and to pack other necessary equipage for shipment to K-24. "Needless to say, the taste of "luxury" in occupying permanent type shelters was welcomed by all personnel. This situation lasted precisely three (3) days."

On November 20, 1950, all flyable tac-

tical aircraft assigned to the 18th FBG departed from K-9. A mission was flown and all aircraft landed at K-24 AFB (Pyongyang East). The 18th FBG had relocated to North Korea.

Living conditions at K-24 AFB, the 67th reported, "approximated those of K-9 during its early stages of development. No showers were available. Tentage was again resorted to as adequate shelter. The onset of cold weather made utilization of tent stoves (M-41) a constant burning necessity. Sanitary facilities were limited and quite primitive and open."

The TO&E materiel, "which had been loaded aboard LST's of the United States Navy," did not dock at Chinnampo until 29 November 1950. "Two airmen accompanied this unit property. Meanwhile minesweepers of the United States Navy continued their activities in clearing the mud-fringed channels approaching the harbor at Chinnampo and other areas so sown."

Ground personnel and personal baggage were airlifted by C-119 type aircraft of the 314th Troop Carrier Group stationed at Ashiya AFB, Japan.

Three echelons were used to conduct the move to K-24, including an Advanced Re-arming and Refueling Unit; Air Transported Party; and, LST Equipment Shipment. The initial R & R unit at K-24 consisted of

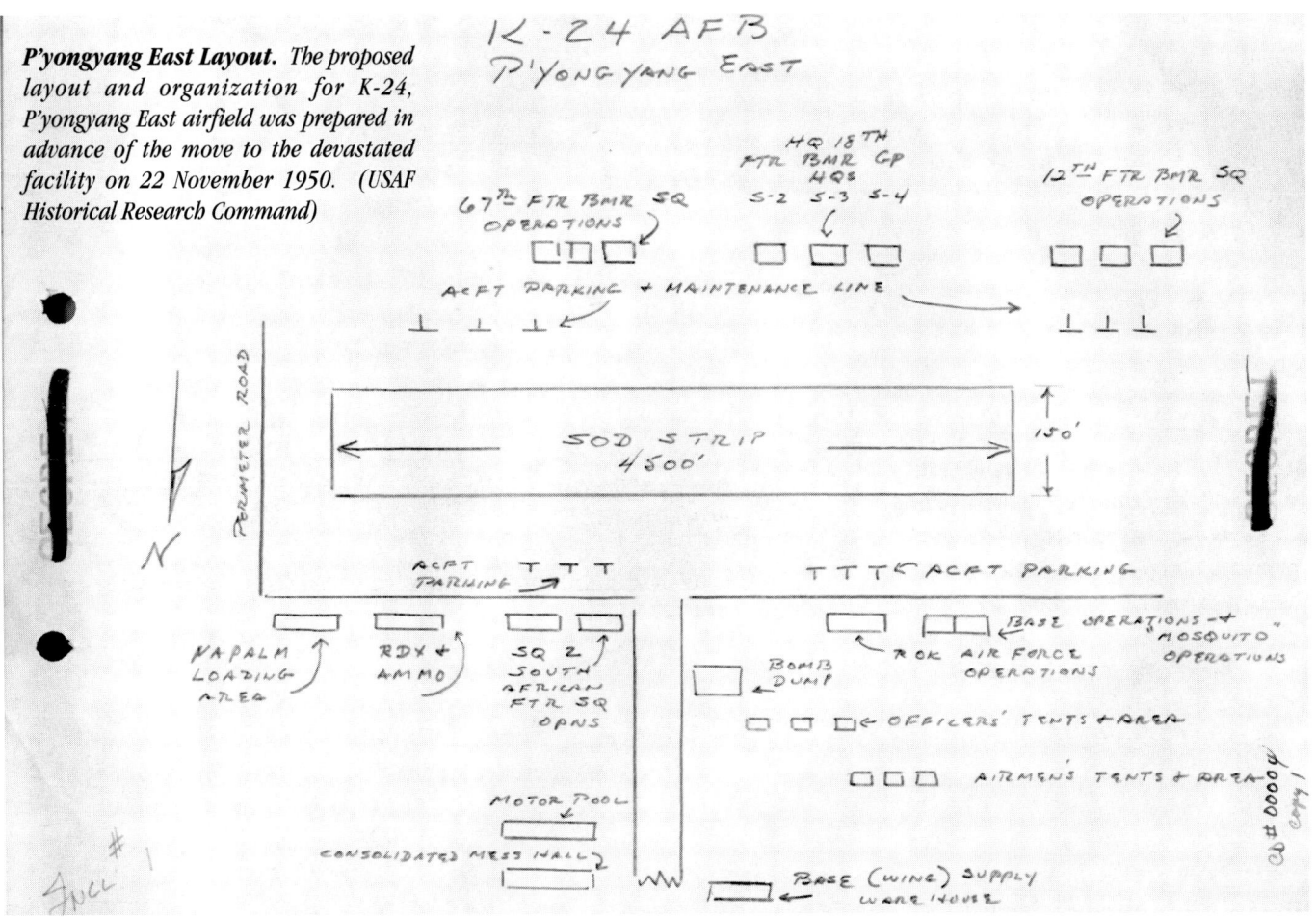

P'yongyang East Layout. *The proposed layout and organization for K-24, P'yongyang East airfield was prepared in advance of the move to the devastated facility on 22 November 1950. (USAF Historical Research Command)*

125 officers and Airmen sufficient to rearm and to refuel 36 fighter sorties per squadron per day.

The planned move embraced a 3-day period wherein combat cargo command aircraft airlifted 1420 tons on day one, 600 tons on day two, and 600 tons on day three. Additional tonnage was sent by LST.

R&R Attempts

Meanwhile, the Group continued "the miniature rotation plan previously established" in September, that provided a three-day rest for officers and airmen. Approximately four officers and seven airmen per squadron were "placed on temporary duty in Japan for rest and recuperation purposes." At the close of November, "this policy was temporarily suspended."

In the very little time during each day when essential combat operations were not being conducted, the men tried to find some "entertainment." At K-24 it "struck a new low in that the showplace utilized was the

mess hall which was unheated and drafty. In a sense however, this was a marked improvement over an "outdoor" theatre. However, only the most rigorously confirmed motion picture addicts attended these showings. Needless to say, the average attendance was approximately 50 to 100; the number varying with the temperature," the report explained.

Roiz Recalls Advance Liaison

The C-119 'Flying Box Car" was used to fly the advance liaison party north to Pyongyang East. Airman Third Class Roberts, turned to his buddy Joe Roiz, an Armament Technician assigned to the 18th Supply Squadron, as they waited in line to board the plane and said, "Damn it, if God wanted us to fly he would have given us wings." Roiz replied, "Well you know he didn't give us wheels either." Both the Airmen boarded the plane "somewhat reluctantly."

At that time, the airfield at P'yongyang was very close to the front line on the east coast. Because the Republic of Korea's Army was advancing so rapidly and trying to overtake the fleeing North Korean units, "there was no time for mopping up operations. As a result," Roiz recalled, "there were many enemy troops behind the front line. We could see and hear anti-aircraft fire from high areas around the landing strip. Some Marine F4U's and our F-51 fighter-bombers were still dropping napalm and strafing the hills surrounding the airfield."

Roiz, Roberts and the others on the lumbering "flying box car" had "a bird's eye view." For the first time Roiz saw "the terribly awesome effect of the napalm bombs. An explosion, white, yellow, orange, red, and black, forming an incendiary expanding cloud almost instantly. The splattering flaming napalm would stick to whatever it hit and burn tenaciously. Napalm was the most dramatically fearsome weapon used in Korea and the "Gooks" wanted no part of it. They stayed in their foxholes until the planes left the area." However, the F-51s and the F-4Us had much greater endurance than jet aircraft and "would hang around the area for as much as forty-five minutes, strafing targets with their fifty caliber machine guns until they were out of ammo or fuel.

Although the F-51s and F-4Us were providing the bulk of close air support, it was the newer jet aircraft that were being written up in the *Stars and Stripes* newspaper and in the news back home, Roiz remembered. Later, he became friendly "with a young Staff Sergeant who happened to be a *Stars and Stripes* reporter. *[The reporter was S/Sgt Sandy Colton.]* He explained that it was necessary to write up the F-80 jet because Congress and the people back home had to feel good about the millions of dollars that was being spent to build these new jets. But they were practically useless for tactical support because they used too much fuel at low altitudes. Although they were very fast, they couldn't maneuver close enough to the ground between the mountains and hills and their time over the target was too short to be efficient. They did participate in aerial dogfights effectively but they were very few and far between. They were soon replaced by the F-86 fighter plane," Roiz noted.

"After we had been there a week or so, the U.S. Marines made an amphibious landing on the eastern shore of Wonson bay (on North Korea's east coast, about 100 miles east of Pyongyang). We were there to give them a friendly welcome. They were late because of the unexpected quick advances of the ROK army had already made along the eastern side of the peninsula. The Marines landed without firing a shot. I was learning about the chaos of war. Nothing ever seemed to go as anticipated."

[Colton later noted that the Marines were "late" because mines in the harbor took longer to clear by Navy minesweepers than expected.]

"Some of the F-51s were being piloted by South Korean pilots who had been trained by the USAF. They could always be spotted because they would do ground

Flight From K-24. A "outgoing" flight of Lane, diSylvestro, Cothern and Olsen leaves Pyongyang Air Base in late November 1950. *(Myers)*

Flight Line at K-24. Several 2 Squadron SAAF, 12th Squadron and 67th Squadron Mustangs await their next mission at Pyongyang Air Base in November 1950. *(Myers)*

Upper Lower Slabovia. Lt. Edwards is joined by two pilots of the 2nd SAAF Squadron at "Dogpatch North." *(Myers)*

loops when landing. We spotted a few from our bird's eye view in the C-119 as we circled the airfield to make a landing."

"One of the C-119's engines was not controlling properly so the pilot had to make a landing at a much higher speed than the plane was designed to do. We bounced and used up all the runway. The plane was loaded to full capacity with fifty-five gallon drums of 100 octane aviation fuel, containers of a rubber compound used to make napalm, white phosphorous fuses, rockets,

fifty caliber ammunition, and about fifteen airmen. It didn't want to come to a stop. We went off the end of the runway into a sandy beach. The left landing gear sunk into the sand causing the left wing to dip into the sand and cause the plane to do a 180-degree spin before coming to a halt. We quickly jumped ship and ran for cover, not knowing if a fire would break out and start a deadly fireworks display. The pilot did an admirable job of landing the 'flying box car' under the worst of circumstances.

No one was hurt but the plane was out of commission with a broken wing and bent up propellers," Roiz remembered.

"During our short stay in Wonson some of us ventured into areas away from the airfield. This was not a safe thing to do because there were still snipers in the hills and other places. The enemy also had left land mines for us to find, the hard way. It was a stupid and unnecessary thing for us to do. It was mostly youthful curiosity, an eagerness to be part of the action on the ground. We imagined that we were making things safer by eliminating the snipers in the area and establishing our control. We heard sniper gunfire close by several times during our patrol but no one was hit. I saw and smelled dead bloated bodies floating in the small river which flowed slowly near the town. The stench was horrible. It was raining a fine misty steady rain. The buildings and houses seemed empty and gray in an unreal mystical haze. I had never experienced anything like the depressed, empty feeling I had at that moment. I had just reached my twentieth birthday," Roiz recalled.

Pyongyang Operations

Operations from the sod strip at K-24 "presented problems for flying personnel." The landing strip was "alternately extremely dusty and muddy," presenting "hazards on take-off and landing due to impaired visibility. No low visibility aids for landing and/or take-off were available." [4]

On one day alone, dust was responsible for the loss of two aircraft. A Mustang had suffered damage during a dusty, low-visibility landing. As it was being towed off the end of the runway by a truck, another Mustang piloted by Captain (later Major General) Frederick C. Blesse was attempting to land "under extremely low visibility conditions." Blesse's plane collided with the Mustang under tow and its truck.

The K-24 landing field was only 4500 feet long and "did not afford maximum take-off distance for heavily loaded aircraft." In trying to get air borne with a heavy combat load, Lt. Patrick J. O'Connell "lost a napalm

(L to R) **Captain Bill Myers**, **"Ole Joe" Lane** and **"Hells" Beals** *in between missions at Pyongyang East in November 1950. Myers is wearing an Army truck driver's coat "from a Combat Engineer Officer," he noted. "Many AF pilots had no winter gear...also same for Enlisted troops," Myers noted. (Myers)*

tank shortly after take off. The aircraft was totally destroyed." Fortunately, Lt. O'Connell was uninjured. [5]

The squadrons considered "planking the landing runway with the addition of overrun areas," but the "current military situation did not admit of the implementation of this plan."

Although the basic mission of the 18th "remained unchanged" during this period, the reports note the addition of numerous new missions for the hard pressed Mustangs, including: light bomber escort, armed aerial reconnaissance, minesweeper escort and constant air patrol, helicopter escort, strip alerts, and prisoner of war liaison coverage flights." The latter mission "concerned reports of United Nations Prisoners of War allegedly ready for release by the enemy. Unfortunately, this did not ma-

terialize positively. [6]

Preparing To Evacuate Pyongyang East

"The ground tactical situation took a turn for the worse during the opening days of the month in which elements of an "alien Communist" force crossed the Yalu River in strength. The situation called for and inspired a strategic withdrawal on the part of the United Nations Ground Forces from the gains outlined in the previous months narrative in order to consolidate these gains up to and including a line of stabilization north of the Chonchong (gang) river; the parenthesized "gang" indicates "river" in the Korean Language and is so indicated in this text to avoid redundancy."

Ken "Flip" Carlson's crash at Pyongyang in November 1950. (Myers)

"Accordingly, the bomb (battle) line was withdrawn from the boundary (Manchurian-Korean) perimeter and the "chop line" as a line of "no combat" demarcation was abandoned. The sum of the maneuvers briefly recounted, reflected a solid front from the western coast of Korea, embracing the waters of the Bay of Korea, to the eastern coast, to a point approximately eighty (80) miles north of Wonsan, including the waters adjacent thereto. This line ran across the "narrow waist" of Korea. By 27 November units of the 7th Infantry Division reached the banks of the Yalu river in the vicinity of Haesanginn."

"The events which resulted in the withdrawal outlined above stemmed in part from the attenuated lines of communications resulting from the successful thrusts initiated by paratroopers who were dropped in the Sunchon and Sukchon areas *[approximately 30 miles north of Pyongyang]*. These drops were supported (tactically) by Air-Ground elements mentioned in the previous month's narrative. Logistical support was sustained by aircraft (C-119 Type) of the Combat Cargo Command, based at Ashiya Air Force Base." [7]

Maximum effort was exerted in support of the United Nations Winter Offensive for the first 24 hours beginning on 29 November, S/Sgt Colton noted. Operations were smooth for the first day, but on the morning of the 30th, the Chinese Communists had broken the first line of attack in the 1st Cavalry Division sector. It appeared this enemy was not destined to be stopped. All supplies of napalm, rockets, and ammunition at K-24 were exhausted. There remained little hope of resupply since all transport aircraft were committed to evacuating wounded and transporting the mobile hospitals from the new battle areas. Aircraft of the Group were in the air an average of 20 in each 24 hours, and all other commitments were cancelled in this supreme effort to halt the breakthrough. Weather turned inclement when 500- and 1000-foot ceilings occurred; both Air and Ground Controllers were confused.

The situation had become so dire by 31 November that General Partridge declared

Allen Burns *stands next to the "Lower Slabovia" sign at K-24. He is dressed as warmly as possible to ward off the bitter cold. He wrote simply on the back of the photograph, "Cold!" (Burns)*

it 'serious,' to say the least. Personnel were compelled to dig foxholes and pull round-the-clock guard duty; Korean laborers were not permitted to enter the Base. K-24 was bombed one night, and F-82's and B-26's painted black provided cover for both air-

fields.

The 18th Group had been ordered to leave K-24 "around Thanksgiving," recalled Allen Burns, "and after a hard day of getting planes off on missions, we were asleep in the tent next to 'my hole' awaiting evacuation in C-119's. Around four in the morning we had a bombing raid, but they missed. However, the first bomb woke me up and while I was trying to figure out what was going on the second blast made me set new track records in diving into 'my hole'--right on top of another guy seeking shelter. A shocking blow to him, but we shared and survived. The raiders dropped four bombs and missed the field entirely. (Burns)

Move to Suwon

"After about two weeks or so the North Korean Peoples Army was pushing south," Roiz recalled, " and we were told to evacuate and to destroy all munitions and supplies that we didn't have time to take with us. This action was called a "strategic withdrawal". We were an advance temporary party and so we didn't have the niceties such as a mess hall or permanent buildings and stores supplies. We were roughing it military style. We lived in tents with dirt floors. Bathed out of our helmets--"bird baths"-- and ate C-rations. About that time I developed a crotch fungus from insufficient washing. I seriously began to wonder if I would ever get out of this "UN Police Action" as the War was called. Regardless of what you called it, people got killed every day. We loaded up our supplies and were flown south to a place called Suwon."

The 18th was compelled to move again, this time to a rear base at Suwon, or K-13. Whereas the Group was glad to leave this dangerous area, many tents were stuck in frozen ground and were burned--others were left standing. The night of the 31st was spent on the Flight Line in two tents remaining waiting for airlift to Suwon. In the movement of the Group from Pyongyang to Suwon, its personnel worked under hazardous living and operating conditions. When the first elements arrived in Suwon, no living or working facilities whatever were to be found. The latter did, however, possess a 6,000 ft. concrete runway, with a T-6 aircraft substituting as a control tower. Tents were immediately erected on frozen ground, and operations began.

The first day of operations found the squadrons with only the bare necessities for keeping their aircraft in the air. Air installations had no equipment with which to provide the group its necessities. There was no napalm, few rockets, and only enough ammunition to last approximately two days. On the last day at Pyongyang, the group had had 15 serviceable aircraft, and the enemy was advancing with lightning speed. The 24th Infantry Division had moved into the field to set up its command post and carry

Damaged city gates at Suwon in November 1950. (Burns)

out its mission of holding off the Communists until such time as the field could be evacuated and destroyed, thus denying its use to the enemy.

Chaplain Kept 'Em Flying

Fighting the war was not just for pilots, the Wing Chaplain was also on hand. When the squadrons moved to K-24 on the 20th, so did the Chaplain's Office. "A squad tent was pitched and outfitted with .50-caliber cartridge boxes for seats and on the floor for the altar. The altar and pulpit stand arrived at K-24 in good condition. Services were held at this station for only one Sunday, although daily Mass was said and one weekday Bible Study. The Wing was evacuated to K-13 on November 30th. [8]

Combat Operations

Summary

Flights from K-9 AFB [near Pusan, SK] ranged the entire length of Korea averaged 5:19 hours per sortie for the period 1-8 November 1950. Flights from K-24 AFB averaged 2:10 hours per sortie for the period 9 November to 30 November 1950.

November saw an "increased intensity in anti-aircraft fire as well as the appearance of enemy aircraft." In addition, "alien communist troops were encountered by ground elements north of Sinanju as well as along the entire northwestern front." [9]

In the space of a week, pilots of the 67th had "made the first contact with the enemy in the air since the early days of the war and accrued a total of five victories before any other units reported an engagement." [10]

Two-, four- and eight-aircraft flights were utilized during Group combat operations during November. However, a major portion of all flights consisted of four aircraft flights "wherein two aircraft furnished top (aerial) cover during armed reconnaissance flights or during strafing passes against enemy personnel, materiel and rolling stock." [11]

Napalm tanks continued to be "the most effective weapon against the variety of targets encountered, being equally effective against vehicles, tanks, ground positions, gun emplacements, etc. High speed, low glide angle attacks from minimum altitudes provided for greater accuracy when this weapon was utilized. The low accuracy being achieved by many pilots during this period caused serious concerns, especially when it dropped to approximately 45%. Investigation of the problem revealed that the napalm tanks were "hanging up" momentarily thus causing misses—overshooting the target. The bomb racks were "acknowledged to be unsatisfactory"—not stressed for weight carried and not stressed for weight point separation. However, cleaning the bomb racks after each mission with gasoline reduced the number of hang-ups. The deplorable operating conditions—excessive mud and dust—while operating from a sod strip, made it imperative that the racks be cleaned after each sortie. [12]

The Mustang pilots of the 18th learned that whether it was "aerial combat with conventional (propeller driven) type aircraft" or with enemy jet type aircraft, the "enemy would take-off from the sanctuary provided by the International Boundary (Yalu River; Korean-Manchurian Border) in the vicinity of Sinuiju (An-Tung)" and climb to altitude." All attacks pressed by enemy jet type fighters were made from altitude and a "yo-yo" pattern (i.e. Dive and Zoom) would be established. With conventional type aircraft an enemy peculiarity was revealed. Whether pressing an attack and/or fleeing from an attack, these fighters (Yak-9 type) would turn with great maneuverability and/or snap-roll—sometimes 3 or 4 snap-rolls—followed by a split "S". [13]

Pilots of the 67th FBS provided the first pictures (gun camera film) of enemy jet fighter type aircraft to FAF. The aircraft were identified as MIG-15s that "strongly resemble the F-86 American fighter aircraft."

Some improvements to operational tactics were made in November, including a new SOP that "for the most part," rocket fire was "rippled" off (automatic position) against armored targets and/or clusters of vehicles. The resultant pattern assured "a greater percentage of hits as opposed to singly-fired rockets." [14]

Strafing attacks were prohibited when the Mustangs had napalm and/or ferry (external tanks, 110 gallon capacity) tanks attached. This resulted in "clean" runs and minimized the hazards incidental to being struck by small arms and/or heavier caliber automatic weapons.

Take-off intervals between aircraft were changed from 5 seconds to approximately 1/2 a runway length and between flight elements as well.

Installing gun heaters cut the number of gun malfunctions. And, newly installed gun cameras "afforded a means whereby film exposed during combat runs could be assessed." Unfortunately, no facilities were

Train Under Attack. *A section of North Korean railroad passenger coaches just after being set afire by United Nations aircraft on November 22, 1950. These coaches were parked along a double-track railroad between Pyongyang and Chungwa, Korea. Also seen in this photo are two more sections which the Reds hastily dispersed up and down the tracks.* (NARA)

available to evaluate such films. To develop the exposed film required a "ferry flight" to Itazuke AFB. "This was not an ideal situation," the 67th reported.

Escape kits that were furnished by Group Intelligence were "inadequate"—not all pilots assigned and combat ready were furnished with the kits and the maps they contained did not cover the areas over which most flights were made. "By comparison with WW II standards these escape kits were woefully inadequate." [15]

Too often pilots of the 18th during a combat sortie would be contacted by in-flight controllers and asked to perform reconnaissance of areas that should have been surveyed by the controller "relative to spotting targets for combat aircraft."

Communications channels were overcrowded and overworked. Target strikes and results were both reported by pilots using the same channel, a practice that

"added to the ensuing communications snarl.

All too often the maps used by ground controllers and the Air Force charts used by the pilots on a combat mission "were so different as to cause confusion and non-identification of targets." The gridding of the Air Force charts in the north central portion of the Korean operating area near (Kunu-ri) was "very confusing to many pilots otherwise occupied with leading flights and/or planning strikes or reporting to a pin-pointed position—the gridding overlaps. Topographical features in many instances are erroneous." [16]

Four aircraft were lost in November by the 67th Squadron to enemy action and/or accidents, including 1st Lt. Bernard L. Pearson.

1st Lt. Edwin R. Henley "was apparently struck by small arms fire during an attack on enemy positions. Engine failure occurred approximately ten minutes after withdrawing from the target area (Anju area) and the aircraft was successfully landed with the landing gear retracted in a frozen river bed. This officer was successfully evacuated by helicopter to K-23 AFB—no injuries were sustained." [17]

During November, the 67th Squadron expended nearly 300,000 rounds of .50-caliber ammunition, 2,527 rockets, 816 napalm bombs and 6 fragmentation bombs. About one in six rockets failed due to deteriorated leads. "Since there is no way of determining this condition until the rocket is utilized, investigation and correction of this condition must of necessity be made at the level of procurement"—definitely beyond the capability of a ground crew operating with the bare minimum of equipment. [18]

The average number of aircraft in commission per day for the month of November was fourteen (14); this represents 66% in commission.

Total flying time for November, including test flights, ferry flights was: 1516:45.

The lack of shelter during the cold weather was a source of concern and discomfort to maintenance personnel. No facilities were available for the hangaring of assigned tactical aircraft. Engines had to be covered, then uncovered for maintenance. Lack of wing engine and canopy covers "resulted in delayed takeoff during early morning missions. The formation of hoarfrost on the wings and control surfaces required that they be de-iced prior to flight.

New Rotation Policy

Fifth Air Force Headquarters soon announced a new policy relative to the rotation of FAF Officer personnel: upon completing 100 missions, they would be reassigned to Japan. The new policy created more questions than answers for the pilots of the 18th. No provision was made "for extenuating circumstances relative to the noncompletion of the number of missions set forth. Additionally, project personnel who had not been scheduled previously for a foreign service tour, faced the possibility

of having to remain for the remainder of an uncompleted tour. No announcement of point credit accumulation was made by higher headquarters. [19]

As the "new blood" began to arrive, a new problem was created. Many of the new pilots, were not combat ready and "presented an additional operations problem." Heavy commitments meant "it was not possible to fly such pilots daily through to completion of the criteria established by Group policy." The "problem" was addressed by shipping the newer officers off to serve with tactical air control parties supporting ground forces elements. These five were "lost to combat duty" while they were TDY with the TACPs.

The "infusion of new blood" required that the Group create a "miniature training program" during which "officers who were recently assigned to this unit and had accrued only a minimum amount of time in the F-51 type aircraft, were entrusted to Captain Alma R. Flake. Since Captain Flake was an extremely stable person with the ability to impart instruction and caution to new personnel, his choice for this additional duty was considered a happy one." Although "progress in checking out new pilots was noted, "the shortage of aircraft due to operational and accidental losses sustained did not permit day to day scheduled training flights." [20]

Some South African fighter pilots were "blooded" by pilots of the 67th Squadron. Initially the "Flying Cheetahs" flew #2 and #4 positions during "combat transition" flights. Following completion of such flights, the South Afrikaners of the "Cheetah Squadron" flew missions on their own. They were an extremely personable and thoroughly trained group of officers. [21]

Endnotes

[1] USAFHRA. Unit History, 67th Fighter-Bomber Squadron, November 1950.

[2] USAFHRA. 6002nd Tactical Support Wing, Public Information Office. Unit History Report, November 1950.

[3] USAFHRA. 6002nd Tactical Support Wing, Public Information Office. Unit History Report, November 1950.

November Significant Dates [1]

November 1: The first enemy aircraft destroyed by the Group was accounted for by Captain Alma R. Flake, of the 67th Fighter-Bomber Squadron. ELSEWHERE BAKER, a flight of four aircraft, spotted three YAKS attacking a B-26 over Sinanju, close to the Manchurian border on the northwest coast of Korea. The B-26 shot down one, and the Flight of four fighter aircraft got a piece of one YAK, while the third got away.

On the same day, Wednesday, 1 November 1950, Lieutenant William G. Foster's Flight of four F-51's was jumped by "...six swept-wing, jet-type aircraft" late that afternoon. Foster could not ascertain whether any hits were inflicted upon any of these aircraft. The jets made hostile frontal passes, as well as a few from the side. It was concluded that the jets were either too fast or the pilots too inexperienced.

The fighters were "suddenly pounced upon by the jet-type aircraft while they were pressing their attack on ground targets at Yangsi, on the west coast of North Korea about 15 miles from the Manchurian border."

The flight of Mustangs was led by 1st Lt. William G. Foster of Springfield, Pennsylvania, with 1st Lt. George N. Olsen of Parkridge, Illinois, as his wingman. 1st Lt. Charles L. Morehouse, of Columbus, Ohio, led the second element with 1st Lt. Henry L. Reynolds flying his wing.

"Olsen and I went down and dropped our napalm," Foster reported, "and then went up to cover while Morehouse and Reynolds went down. While we were up I heard Olsen yell, 'They're on us.' I knew what he meant. There were two on my tail."

"I was pulling out of the attack on the deck," continued Morehouse, "when I saw a bogie come in at 11 o'clock. I saw blotches of red spurting from his wings as he fired at me. He flew about five feet under me and I got a good look."

"Upstairs, Foster and Olsen fought it out with six jets. Foster caught one in a turn, gave it a burst and it started smoking. The jet turned and ran off in a northwesterly direction."

"Olsen hit another in a wing during a head-on attack, and Reynolds joined the dogfight while Morehouse covered a Mosquito plane below."

"We didn't identify the markings for use," Olsen said. "They were going too fast to see much."

"In the end," Foster continued, "I was getting the planes regrouped when I saw two aircraft above me. One was Olsen and the other a bogie. I told Olsen about it and he peeled off to join us. The bogie turned for home. They were all gone then, and we turned back to the base." [2]

November 2: On Thursday, Captain Flake "encountered" another Yak-9 and shot it down. 1st Lt. William G. Foster was jumped by six MIGs.

November 3: In the face of strong CCF attacks, General Walker ordered the bulk of the Eighth Army to withdraw to the Chongchon River for regrouping and resupply.

November 4: B-26s providing close support for the Eighth Army attacked enemy troops near Chongju, killing an estimated 500 soldiers and providing hardpressed U.S. troops some relief.

November 5: Bomber Command began incendiary bomb attacks on North Korean cities and towns. Twenty-one B-29s of the 19th BG dropped 170 tons of fire bombs on Kanggye, located less than twenty miles south of the Chinese border. The attack destroyed sixty-five percent of the town's center.

November 6: On Monday, November 6th, Captain Howard I. Price "successfully engaged in aerial combat" with several Yak-9s, shooting down two of them "in a short fierce dogfight" approximately ten miles south of the Yalu River in the vicinity of Yangsi. [3]

November 8: In the largest incendiary raid of the Korean War, seventy Superfortresses dropped some 580 tons of fire bombs on Sinuiju on the Chinese border. Other B-29s attacked bridges over the Yalu River for the first time. When MiG-15s challenged F-80s flying in the same area, Lt.

Russell J. Brown, USAF, 16th Fighter Interceptor Squadron (FIS), shot down a MiG to score the first jet-to-jet aerial victory in history.

An advance party of the 6002nd Tactical Support Wing established a tactical control center at Pyongyang East.

November 9: A 91st Strategic Reconnaissance Squadron gunner, Sgt. Harry J. Levene, scored the first B-29 jet victory of the Korean War, destroying an attacking MiG-15. The damaged RB-29 limped back to Japan, but five crewmen died in the crash landing.

Major General Earle E. Partridge fired off a Letter of Commendation to the 67th Fighter-Bomber Squadron that singled out the "Elsewhere Squadron" for a special commendation. "Within the Joint Operations Center, the code name 'Elsewhere,' is fast becoming a legend. It appears regularly in conjunction with reports of downed enemy aircraft," Partridge wrote. "I wish to commend the officers and airmen of the 67th Fighter Squadron of the 18th Fighter-Bomber Group for their fine display of courage, aggressiveness, and determination to seek out and destroy the enemy in the air. The exploits of this unit reflect a spirit of cooperation that is exemplary of the best traditions of the United States Air Force. We are encountering an enemy who possesses aircraft of performance equal or superior to our own and who is daily growing bolder. We must depend upon the superior quality of our fighter pilots and the aggressive spirit exhibited by the "Elsewhere" squadron to maintain supremacy in the air over our Forces in North Korea."

The first tactical mission by the 6002nd Tactical Support Wing/18th Fighter-Bomber Wing was flown from Pyongyang East.

November 10: MiG-15s near the Yalu River shot down a B-29 for the first time. The crew, assigned to the 307th BG, parachuted behind enemy lines to become POWs. Less than thirty-six hours after its arrival in Japan, the 437th TCW began airlifting cargo on C-46s to Korea.

November 13: UN forces of X Corps, based in Hungnam, North Korea, began moving northward, with a regiment of the

1st U.S. Marines Division advancing into the Changjin Reservoir area.

November 14: Flying Cheetahs Arrive. The 2 Squadron, South African Air Force was assigned as a component command of the 18th Fighter-Bomber Group.

Major William E. May, relieved Major Arnold Mullins, as Commanding Officer of the 67th Fighter-Bomber Squadron, a unit of the 18th Fighter-Bomber Group, commanded by Lt. Col. Ira F. Wintermute. The Group was assigned to Headquarters, Fifth Air Force for Operational and Administrative purposes although still organically assigned to the Thirteenth Air Force, Clark Air Force Base (Luzon, Philippine Islands), as noted in the unit history. This was about to change, however.

Morale in the 67th took a turn for the worse following "the news that Major Arnold Mullins would be replaced as Squadron Commander by another officer senior in rank. To say that the officers and men took a 'dim' view of this situation would be treating it lightly," the unit report noted. However, "after three weeks under new supervision, it was generally conceded that the new squadron commander had succeeded in getting his feet on the ground, much to the satisfaction of all personnel." [4]

The report noted with unusual insight that the "relief of any commander during combat was fraught with reflection upon the ability and/or undetermined 'dereliction' of the old commander, as opposed to the ability and capability of the new commander. Administratively it was considered a necessary step; morally it was considered intrinsically wrong in light of various interpretations." The arrival of the new commander caused a "bump down" of one step for most of the more senior pilots of the 67th. Mullins moved to Executive Officer; Captain McGee from XO to Operations Officer; Captain Lane from Operations Officer to Flight Leader; and Lt. Conserva from Flight Leader to Assistant Flight Leader.

Despite some grumbling after the change in command, the 67th continued to perform its missions with the "esprit" and "élan" instilled "in a definitely superior manner."

November 18: For the first time, a USAF fighter group moved to North Korea. The 35th FIG, which had also been the first fighter group based in South Korea, settled at Yonpo Airfield, near Hungnam.

November 19: In the first massed light bomber attack of the Korean War, fifty B-26s from Japan dropped incendiary bombs on Musan, North Korea, on the Tumen River border with China. The attack destroyed seventy-five percent of the town's barracks area.

November 20: FEAF Combat Cargo Command air-dropped rations and gasoline at Kapsan, some twenty miles south of the Yalu River, to supply the 7th Infantry Division, the U.S. ground unit advancing the farthest north during the war.

The 6002nd Tactical Support Wing began its move from Pusan East/K-9 to Pyongyang East/K-24.

On 20 November 1950, the 18th Fighter-Bomber Headquarters Group, and the 2nd and 67th Squadrons, with the majority of their supporting elements, were moved to K-24 (Pyongyang) by C-54's and C-119's, Colton recorded. "The first plane was airborne from K-9 at 0630 hours, and upon their arrival it was found that the advance party of 8 November had done very little to set up the Base. Most of its time had been occupied with unloading aircraft. Here, as in Taegu and Pusan, the Base site was composed of rice paddies. Unlike the other strips, K-24 had no landing mats or concrete runways, but only a smooth grassy surface which supported the T-6, L-5, F-51, C-47, C-46, C-54, and C-119 aircraft. Nevertheless, the entire group had set up its facilities by 25 November." [5]

During the time spent at this very advanced airstrip, a total of three accidents occurred. On 10 November, Major Carleton had a rocket fire, which destroyed one flap and one aileron. On the same day, two aircraft dove into the sod of the strip. On 19 November, Lieutenant Ed Henley, 67th Squadron, nosed up an F-51, splattering it over the rice paddies 500 feet from the end of the runway.

"Plans were made to move an advanced party to the new location with sufficient personnel and equipment to set up housekeeping facilities, rearm and refuel the tactical aircraft with a minimum loss in operating efficiency. The move was started on 15 November and was completed on 20 November." The Wing at that time included 159 officers and 1,153 airmen. [6]

"The sparseness, lack of timeliness, of adequate intelligence information from Fifth Air Force Headquarters" during and following the relocation "continued to affect the [intelligence] section's operations. Such situation reports, estimates of the situation, and reports of enemy aerial combat tactics and capabilities as were disseminated were received too late to be of maximum value." [7]

November 23: The 6002nd Tactical Support Wing's K-24 "office" was set up and operating at Pyongyang East.

November 24: To support the UN offensive beginning this day, Fifth Air Force fighters intensified close air support missions, and FEAF Combat Cargo Command air-dropped ammunition to frontline troops.

A TWX received by units of the 18th Fighter-Bomber Group "from higher headquarters redesignated the 6002nd Tactical Support Wing, which is the parent wing of this organization, as the 18th Fighter-Bomber Wing. The administrative details relative to clarification of the status of tactical units under this wing were not available as of the submission of this report. [8]

November 25: Chinese Communist forces launched a major offensive and, with almost double the number of MacArthur's U.S. troops, stopped the UN offensive completely. The Royal Hellenic Air Force Detachment, a C-47 transport unit representing Greece's airpower contribution to the war, arrived in the Far East and was attached to Far East Air Forces.

November 26: USAF B-26s flew their first close air support night missions under tactical air control party (TACP) direction. The 3rd BG flew 67 B-26 missions along the Eighth Army's bomb line in a five hour period. Still, the enemy drove the Eighth Army in northwest Korea and the X Corps in northeast Korea southward.

November 28: The FEAF Combat Cargo Command began a two-week airlift of supplies to U.S. troops, whom the Chinese had surrounded in the Changjin Reservoir area. From Yonpo, North Korea, the 35th FIG flew intense close air support missions for the encircled forces. For the first time, B-26s, using a more accurate radar than previously, bombed within 1,000 yards of the front line. A small communist aircraft bombed U.S.-held Pyongyang Airfield, badly damaging eleven P-51 Mustangs on the ground. General MacArthur informed Washington that he faced "an entirely new war."

On 28 November 1950 an "alert" for evacuation was announced throughout the 18th Fighter-Bomber Group and a priority system was established: Priority One, Personnel. Priority Two, Personal Baggage. Priority Three, minimum necessary supplies and engineering. Priority Four, Aircraft. Priority Five, Other supplies and equipment.

November 30: The 6002nd Tactical Support Wing was inactivated and discontinued on November 30th at Pyongyang East (K-24) and its personnel "absorbed" following the arrival of the 18th Fighter-Bomber Wing "which was transferred to the Korean area from Clark Air Force Base, P.I.." The Wing Staff reported that its "main problem" was a "complete lack of information concerning the series numbers of orders, files, etc. of the 18th Fighter-Bomber Wing. The problem of not having the sequence of order numbers was solved by the use of unnumbered letter orders to execute directives concerning personnel matters." Wars are fought with "order numbers" as well as bullets and napalm tanks.

November Combat Losses

Capt. Malcolm Brodie Edens, 12th Squadron.

Capt. Fred Gray Hudson, III, 12th Squadron near Sinuiju, NK.

Capt. Bernard Lee Pearson, 12th Squadron. 1st Lt. Billie R. Cothern took off from K-24 airstrip on a pre-briefed mission with Lt. Patterson flying as his wingman. Lt.

Pearson and Capt. Solem were in the second element. On arrival at the target at 1400 hours, Cothern and Lt. Patterson proceeded to attack one target while Lt. Pearson and Capt. Solem worked the primary target. Ten minutes later, Capt. Solem called Cothern on the R/T and reported that Lt. Pearson had crashed. Cothern immediately proceeded to check the scene of the crash, inspecting the wreckage and the surrounding area for Lt. Pearson for 15 minutes. Captain Solem and Lt. Patterson made similar searches with negative results. Captain Solem informed Cothern that Lt. Pearson had napalmed two automatic weapons positions and observed intense small arms fire from a nearby ridge. He proceeded to strafe this ridge and when he pulled up from his pass he hit the top of the ridge and disintegrated.

2nd Lt. Howard R. Thompson, 12th Squadron.

Endnotes

[1] Adapted from USAFHRA. January 2002. The U.S. Air Force's First War: Korea 1950-1953 Significant Events. October 1950.

[2] USAFHRA. 6002nd Tactical Support Wing, Public Information Office. S/Sgt Sandy Colton. "Jet-Type Aircraft Appeared At Yangsi." Pacific Stars and Stripes, Thursday, November 2, 1950.

[3] USAFHRA. History of the 67th Fighter-Bomber Squadron, November 1950.

[4] USAFHRA. History of the 67th Fighter-Bomber Squadron, November 1950.

[5] USAFHRA. "The Story of the 18th Fighter-Bomber Group in the Korean United Nations Police Action." 6002nd Tactical Support Wing, Public Information Office. S/Sgt Sandy Colton.

[6] USAFHRA. 6002nd Tactical Support Wing, Public Information Office. Unit History Report, November 1950.

[7] USAFHRA. 6002nd Tactical Support Wing, Public Information Office. Unit History Report, November 1950.

[8] USAFHRA. History of the 67th Fighter-Bomber Squadron, November 1950.

November Summary

by William J. "Sandy" Colton

The first enemy destroyed (aircraft) in the air by the Group went to Capt. Alma Flake and the 67th Squadron. "Elsewhere Baker," a flight of four Mustangs saw three YAK '5 attacking a B-26 over Sinuiju, near the Manchurian border on the northwest coast of Korea. The B-26 got one of the YAKs and the whole flight got a piece of one YAK, while the third got away. On the same day, 1 November 1950, Lt. William G. Foster's flight of four F-51's was jumped by MIG-15 jets. Foster could not determine the number of hits inflicted by any of the aircraft. The jets made hostile front-on passes at the flights and a few from the side. The jets were either too fast or the pilots a little inexperienced.

On 2 November 1950, Capt. Flake's alert flight "Elsewhere Dog" met "Tammerlane" Peter"—also a flight of Mustangs—over the border city of Sinuiju and encountered two YAKS. Capt. Flake downed one and Lt. Jim Glessner of the 12th Squadron got the other. The Communist squadron flying those aircraft was having miserable luck.

The FEAF "CHOPLINE" was instituted on 15 October 1930 and limited us to action 20 miles south of the Manchurian border from longitude 120 degrees to the west coast. This was equally divided into three areas: Recce Areas I, II & III.

From 320 degrees to the east coast was cut off to us and was placed "on limits" for the U.S. Navy.

On 20 November 1950, the Headquarters, the 12th and 67th Fighter-Bomber Squadrons and the majority of the supporting elements were moved to King 24 (Pyongyang) by C-54's and C-119's. The first plane was airborne from K-9 at 0630 hours. When the men arrived at K-24 they found that the advanced detail which had been sent up on 8 November 1950 had done very little to set up the base. Mainly, because they were compelled to devote most of their time to unloading aircraft. There was the same setting up of tents in rice fields as there was at Taegu and Pusan. The only difference was that the strip had no landing mats, just a smooth grassy surface which took T-6, L-5, F-51, C-47, C-46, C-54 and C-119 aircraft. The Group was completely set up at K-24 by 25 November 1950.

During the time spent at this very advanced airstrip we had a total of three aircraft accidents. On 10 November 1950 Major Carlson on a go around had a rocket fire on him destroying one flap and one aileron. The same day saw two airplanes go down. Capt. Blesse went into a 2 ½ ton truck trying to pull a nosed up F-51 off the runway. On 19 November 1950, Lt. Ed Henley of the 67th Squadron nosed one up and splattered it over the rice paddies 500' from the end of the runway.

"Maximum effort" was the by-word on 29 November 1950 to support the United Nations winter offensive for the first twenty-four hours. It went along swell—for a day. On the morning of the 30th the Chinese Communists had broken the first line of attack in the 1st Cavalry Division sector. There was no stopping them. Napalm, rockets and .50-caliber ammunition ran out at K-24. There was little hope of supply, as all transport aircraft were committed to evacuating wounded and mobile hospitals from the new increasing battle areas. Planes of the Group were in the air 20 hours out of 24 hours. This kept up for three days in a attempt to stop them. All other commitments were rescinded.

The weather turned bad with 1,000 to 500' ceilings. Controllers were confused—both air and ground alike. The situation had changed so drastically that by 31 November 1950 it was declared serious by General Partridge.

Men were compelled to dig foxholes and stand guard duty. Korean laborers were not permitted to enter the base. K-24 was bombed one night. F-82's and B-26's painted black provided cover for both airfields. Then the 18th Fighter Bomber Group was compelled to move to a rear base at Suwon.

While the Group was glad to move, it meant that tents had to be struck down in frozen ground. Many tent pegs were left and many tents were burned. The night of the 30th was spent on the flight line in one of the two tents still left, waiting for an airplane to remaining personnel to Suwon. The K-24 airfield was bombed three straight days.

During the movement of the group from Pyongyang (K-24) to Suwon (K-13) on 31 November 1950, Group personnel were compelled to work under oppressive living and operating conditions. When the first group of men arrived in Suwon they were greeted by NOTHING. There was nothing at Suwon except a 6,000' concrete runway with a T-6 aircraft acting as a control tower. The men started the first day by putting their familiar twelve-man squad tents, up. The difference was that the ground was frozen and made it 200% harder to erect these tents.

The first day of actual operations found the squadrons with only the bare tools to keep the airplanes flying save any major damage or major inspections. Air installations had no equipment with which to provide the group with the basic conditions needed to keep the group or any organization going. There was no Napalm, very few rockets and about enough .50-cal. ammunition to last about two days.

The last day at Pyongyang found the Group with just 15 serviceable aircraft. The enemy was advancing with lighting speed and the 24th Infantry Division had moved in to the field to set up its command post with the mission of holding off the enemy until the complete airstrip could be evacuated and then to destroy the field.

The night of the 31st of November was a night that few men of the group will forget—especially, loading equipment on airplanes by flashlights.

A rear echelon of the 6002nd Fighter Wing was left until the last plane had ceased operations. The mess hall, base supply and the control tower were left burning when the last airplane tucked its wheels in the engine nacelles about 100 feet off runway 20 at K-24. This was at 1600 hours 3 December 1950. The field was taken by Communists forces on 4 December 1950. A truck convoy had been sent to Suwon and two freight trains. Two convoys got through and one railroad train. Guerillas harassed the

2 Squadron SAAF Mustang at K-24 in November 1950. *"The Second Squadron SAAF joined us at K-9 and stayed with us throught the entire war," recalled Allen Burns. (Burns)*

convoy and severed rail tracks in many places.

The War of Words

Staff Sergeant Sandy Colton's war was fought with words—had he been a pilot, he would have been an "Ace." Assigned to the Public Information Office of the 6002nd Tactical Support Wing, Colton prepared numerous well-written articles and radio scripts that were used by a variety of media.

During November the Wing's PIO (Public Information Office) prepared 234 news releases, including 167 "hometown" releases, 57 news releases and 20 pictorial releases. Collectively, the releases "netted approximately" 335 column inches of space in Far East news media, plus many of "our stories are being printed in whole and in part in stateside papers," 1st Lt. Marvin Gallagher reported. He noted that his office had stressed the "Dogpatch theme," and explained, "when the base moved to Pyongyang that base became 'North Dogpatch.' It is all paying off but how much can not yet be determined." One Airman told Gallagher that in a recent letter from his mother, "she had the radio tuned in to Arthur Godfry's nation wide radio show when Godfry mentioned and spoke of Dogpatch Air Base in Korea." [1]

Publicity in the main was considered to have been good during November. Approximately 2880 lines and 27 pictures as well as two *Stars & Stripes Review* supplements were garnered by the 67th Fighter-Bomber

Squadron alone. Hometown releases embraced all officers assigned to this unit; write-up in this regard was coordinated with the Wing Public Information Officer and direct releases were made. A "byline restriction" was imposed, by Fifth Air Force PIO in regard to publicity concerning this unit," although this "did not diminish news releases for publication."

Dogpatch Pilots

Describe Battles

With Red Airmen

On November 2, 1950, the Pacific *Stars and Stripes* ran one of Colton's accounts entitled: *"Dogpatch Pilots Describe Battles With Red Airmen."*

"A flight of four Dogpatch based F-51 Mustangs of the 18th Fighter-Bomber Group shot down a North Korean YAK-3 while operating west of Sonshon, North Korea Wednesday," Colton explained.

The encounter was the first reported with enemy aircraft in months and it would be the first enemy aircraft shot down by "Dogpatch F-51s."

The Flight was led by Captain Herbert W. Andridge, Jr., of Dallas, Texas, with 1st Lt. Harold J. Ausman of Beverly Hills, California, flying the Number 2 spot. Captain Alma R. Flake, of Phoenix, Arizona, led the second element, with Captain Robert D. Thresher, of Nyak, New York, as the Number Four man.

Flake was the first pilot to spot the YAK. "I saw it come down at six o'clock on the tail of a B-26…I told the others to watch for YAKs in the area," Flake was quoted.

"In the meantime, the '26 had shot down the YAK. I guess it was the turret gunner who got him. The YAK pulled up into what looked like a high speed stall, and then crashed."

The Dogpatch Flight had descended "to look at the wreckage when they heard a Mosquito (T-6 forward air control) plane call for help. They dropped their napalm and rockets and flew to his aid, and engaged the YAK."

"He kept diving and climbing," Thresher said. "We could outrun and outdive him, but he gave us hell on the turns and climbing. I finally got a shot burst into him and he started to smoke."

"Just about that time, I caught him peeling off to dive again. I got on his tail and followed him all the way to the deck, giving him short bursts all the way."

"He stopped smoking and fanned his prop, and I overshot him."

"I came in then," said Flake. "I pulled into on top of him and gave him a couple of short bursts. He burst into flame, did a snap roll and piled into the ground."

"He was aggressive and brave as hell," Ausman remarked.

"Yeah," said Flake, "but he sure was a lousy shot." [2]

Endnotes

[1] USAFHRA. 6002ⁿᵈ Tactical Support Wing, Public Information Office. Unit History Report, November 1950.

[2] USAFHRA. 6002ⁿᵈ Tactical Support Wing, Public Information Office. S/Sgt Sandy Colton. "Dogpatch Pilots Describe Battles With Red Airmen." Pacific Stars and Stripes, Thursday, November 2, 1950.

Communist Atrocities

S/Sgt William J. "Sandy" Colton diary entry

The city of Pyongyang was pretty much bombed out but a fairly nice place. We were situated across the Taedong river and east of the city. Just as the river leaves the city it forms a "U" and then straightens out again in another "U" only upside down forming a sort of "S" laying down curves.

Near the city, at the edge of the river, we found about two hundred Korean dead stacked up like cordwood. Followers of Kim Il Sung did their share of executing political prisoners. Kim Il Sung is the puppet premier of North Korea. His fame (or infamy) is well known as a sharpshooter. He got his start in Manchuria and did such a fine job that the Manchurians wrote a song about him that goes something like this: "Tell us you snow and wind in the Manchurian fields. Tell us you long, long boughs in the forest. Who is the greatest partisan ever born? Who is the greatest patriot who ever lived?"

The answer is Kim Il Sung.

From what I have been able to find out, Kim displayed his marksmanship in peculiar ways. His first hit was his first wife--while in their bedroom, he shot her in a fit a jealousy. After he murdered his first wife he married the daughter of one of his closest collaborators, a Mr. Hong Myung-Hi, a well known fiction writer in Korea. This time Kim shot his newly wedded wife while sitting across a dining table, angered by her advice to reconsider the policy of conscripting men from the ages of 16 to 42 to be recruited with compulsion into the so called "Righteous and Brave Volunteer Corps." (Literal translation)

Mr. Hong (last names come first over here and vice versa) committed suicide when he heard the news. Then Kim shot a Mr. Choi Young Kun, his right hand man and long standing comrade, during a cabinet meeting where Mr. Choi expressed his opinion of accepting the terms of the UN Security Council. That was when things were beginning to look rough for the North Koreans. In the last days before the fall of Pyongyang (also called Pengyang) he shot a

Mr. Kim Sonbong, the chairman of the so called "Highest Commissary of the people of the Chosen (Korea) Democratic Peoples Republic."

He also shot a Mr. Kang Nakok, his great grandfather and advisor during his six year reign!

His stool pigeons imitated him to the letter. Before they ran away from Pyongyang, they murdered all the political leaders, professors, artists, pastors, and others who had been arrested in the south during their three month occupation.

Those prisoners had been jailed, along with a number of North Korean political rivals of Kim. Some of the bodies that we saw were those people. The Koreans stayed clear of that spot.

Before leaving Korea they pulled one more stunt, too. They left with a big parade. After dark, when everyone thought that the Army had left, a number of political rivals and others who had been hiding in the hills, returned to town. The North Korean Army came back in the middle of the night, rounded them up, and shot them too. Even with the freezing weather, the corpses stunk.

Most of them had their hands tied behind their backs with a thin, pliable wire. They had been lying there for some time and obviously had been machine gunned. To one side was a pile of clothes and a partially dug trench grave. They apparently never had a chance to finish this crude grave. Next to them was a sandbar and the river. Their faces and chests were sunken in like mummies. They were well beyond the bloating stage and well into rotting.

The dogs were not as afraid of the place as the natives. Some of the bodies had parts chewed off while at least one was missing a whole leg. It was a miserable sight. The North Koreans were not friendly but more wary of us. They had been told that we would shoot them for sport and eat their meat! The kids were won over easily, but what kid won't when offered chewing gum or candy.

At first they ran from us screaming. But after we've been around a while they soon pester you with—"Hello! Choon gum, OK?"—over and over.

Driving into Pyongyang from the base

you come to a pontoon bridge which stretches across the river. Down river from this bridge is the main bridge with the center span neatly blown down. Since only military can use the pontoon bridge, the bombed bridge is swarming with Koreans in continuous lines crawling over the girders both ways. Many are refugees heading south. *[Max Desfor of the AP shot a picture of the bridge and refugees and won the Pulitzer prize for it.]*

Going into town you pass a huge temple like building. Once into the main section of town the streets widen out and stores become open shops. I tried to buy a clock but found that in each store I shopped they only had the face of the clock, no works to make it run. The only thing I did buy was a hammer, cheaply made of iron, as are most of the tools over here. I got a few dirty looks from the girls of approachable age. Money doesn't seem to mean much to them.

Rice will buy anything including a day's hard labor for a man, woman and child for one cup of rice a day.

Pyongyang is divided so that part of it is on the east side of the river. That section of the city was almost completely leveled by bombing.

There are a lot of coal mines around Pyongyang. At the end of our strip, which was nothing more than field, was a hill of debris taken from a coal mine. It was in that mine that they found a complete set up for manufacturing ammunition and weapons. Nice and deep in the ground, safe from bombs. Incidentally, they found a bunch of dead in there too.

Able Flight

The pilots and ground crews of the 6002nd Tactical Support Wing were busy fighting the new war by attacking enemy forces wherever they could be found. Staff Sergeant Sandy Colton, was very busy as well. Attached to the Public Information Office, Colton was doing his best to keep the folks back home informed about the deeds and accomplishments of boys from Dogpatch.

"Dogpatch Tower, this is Able Leader, number one position. Ready to scramble."

Colton led off a radio script in October 1950 with a "quote" from Captain Howard I. Price, who had recently shot down two YAK-9 fighters. The dialogue was as true to actual language and R/T (radio telephone) procedures as Colton could write it. Even with "dramatic license," it allows us to "listen in" on Able Flight as it goes hunting over North Korea. When the "show" was originally produced in Korea using whatever recording equipment that was at hand, Colton had called for background sound effects—"three aircraft engines running up and then down on pre-takeoff check—for eight seconds, then down until it maintained "a dull roar throughout as background."

"Roger Able Leader. This is Dogpatch Tower. Clear to roll. Winds seven knots from northwest."

The "engine noise" rises as the F-51's roar down the imaginary runway and take off, the noise facing into the narrative of the "narrator."

The sun was still hidden behind the ridge of mountains that surrounded this advanced air strip in Korea. Three Fifth Air Force F-51 fighter-bombers roared down the dusty strip and up through the early morning fog into the cold clear air above. Heavy with loaded guns, rockets, and external tanks, the Mustangs set course for the battle area.

The sun hit the top of the rugged mountains and slowly worked its way down to the shadowy lowlands.

It was the sixth of November 1950.

These three fighter-bombers of the 18th Fighter-Bomber Group, 6002nd Tactical Support Wing in Korea, were shortly to engage in aerial duel with enemy Yak-9 fighters near Sinuiju in North Korea—just across the Yalu River boundary from Antung in Manchuria. As a result of the battle, the flight commander, Captain Howard I. Price of Bradenton, Florida, claimed two Yaks destroyed.

Flying on his wing in the No. 2 position was First Lieutenant George N. Olson of Park Ridge, Illinois.

In the No. 3 slot was First Lieutenant Henry L. Reynolds from Jackson, Missouri.

The flight was assigned a mission to reconnoiter an area paralleling the Yalu River boundary in northwest Korea. They arrived at the city of Sinuiju at 0700 and spent the next two hours patrolling their assigned area searching out enemy troop movements. At 2 minutes after 9, enemy aircraft were sighted approaching them from the other side of the river."

" Able Leader. This is Able Two. Bogeys at two o'clock level. "

" Roger, Able Two. I have them spotted. Let's check them. "

The Mustangs turned at the approaching enemy aircraft to make a head on pass for positive identification, the Narrator explained.

" Able Flight. Able Leader here. Salvo tanks. They're Yaks. Let's go get them."

The Mustangs pulled into a screaming tight turn as they dropped their external tanks, the Narrator continued. They caught the Yaks halfway through their turn. Price lined up his sights on the number two YAK and pressed the firing button. The .50-caliber armor piercing incendiary bullets flashed like popping firecrackers as they struck the edge of the Yak's left wing.

The Yak snapped over on its back and did a split-S dive to escape the stream of fire. Instead of following him down, Price left him for the No. 3 man and picked on another, lined up his sights, and again pressed the firing button.

Hits flashed on the wing. Like the other, the Yak snapped and dived—this time Price stuck to his tail.

As the Yak pulled out of its dive Price scored again—hitting both wings.

Still trying to evade the blazing guns, the enemy fighter snapped and dived again.

Price followed him, reducing speed to keep behind and above him.

As the Yak turned to the right while pulling out of his dive, Price opened up on him once more.

The flashes ran across the right wing to the engine. Small pieces of fuselage were blown off by the exploding slugs. A heavy black smoke began to leave a trail behind the Yak.

Not until Price saw the enemy pilot jettison his canopy did he stop firing. Then he watched the pilot climb to the rim of the cockpit, bracing himself against the wind by holding on to the windshield, and then dive over the side.

The pilot made a slow turn and a half in the air before his square, dun colored parachute opened while the still smoking Yak spiraled crazily to the earth."

"Able Leader. Able Two here. Confirm one."

Price looked to the right over his shoulder to see Olsen still faithfully glued to the slot position protecting his tail."

"Roger Able Two. This is Able Leader. Let's check number three and see if he needs any help."

The two Mustangs turned to the left where they saw Reynolds chasing a Yak towards the Yalu River and Manchurian border. Pilots had specific instruction not to violate that border by crossing it, the announcer reminded the radio audience.

"Able Three, Able Leader here. Remember, do not cross the river."

"Roger Able Leader. Josephine Ammo."

[Note: "Josephine" was a pilot's code word meaning "running out of."]

Reynolds, on the tail of the other Yak called in that he was out of ammunition.

As Price and Olsen looked on they saw him make a desperate effort to down the Yak by shooting his rockets at it.

The Yak, apparently startled by the rockets flashing by him, made a steep turn, attempting to get on Reynolds' tail. As he came down again in the firing position on Reynolds, he also dove right into the sights of Price's guns. Price pressed his firing button and scored hits on the tail and fuselage.

The Yak, like the other, snap rolled and dived to avoid attack. Price followed him down and then up again.

As the Yak leveled off, Price, in an effort to conserve ammunition, fired four rockets at him, one at a time, each missing the enemy aircraft by only a few feet.

The Yak started a slight pull up.

Price fired his wing guns again, scoring hits on the tail and left wing.

The Yak pulled up sharply then and Price, behind and underneath, opened fire. The flashes from his hits splashed just in front of the tail section on the underside of the Yak and worked their way forward, like a slashing stream of lights, to the engine.

Strikes in the engine caused an explosion. Thick black smoke poured from the coolant scoop following by a greenish blue fire.

The Yak pulled up, stood on its tail hanging in the air, and then spun off on its left wing, its guns blazing, as it slowly twisted down to crash into the mud flats of an estuary of the Yalu River, just north of the North Korean City of Yongs.

"Able Leader. Able Two here. Confirm Two."

"Roger Able Two. Able Leader here. Join up. We'll do a 360 and recheck the area."

The fighter-bombers completed a slow circle over the area searching the skies for any additional aircraft. Four other Yaks that they had seen earlier had departed. They were alone."

"Able Flight. Able Leader here. Check in."

"Able Two here."

"Able Three here."

"Roger, Able Flight. Setting course for home."

Four hours and twenty minutes in the air. Two enemy aircraft downed in five minutes during a vicious two hundred and fifty mile an hour air battle. The tired pilots set course for home.

Price, who had downed two German aircraft in aerial duels during World War Two wondered if he'd get his third Yak soon to break that record.

The sun was high now. The rice pad-

dies formed their never ending varicolored jigsaw puzzle below—and then home."

"Dogpatch Tower, this is Able Leader."

"Able Leader, this is Dogpatch Tower. Over."

"Dogpatch Tower, this is Able Leader. Landing instructions for three chicks and permission to beat up the field and do a couple of victory rolls."

"Roger, Able Leader. Dogpatch Tower. Landing runway three three to northwest. Altimeter setting zero zero one. Winds twelve knots from northwest. Permission granted. Name of pilot please."

"Captain Howard I. Price. Peter-Roger-Item-Charlie-East." [26]

Splash Two Yaks: Mullins & Ausman

By Lt. Col. Duane E. 'Bud' Biteman, USAF (Ret.)

First Lieutenant Harold J. Ausman, of the 67th Fighter-Bomber Squadron, survived a rare aerial encounter with a pair of North Korean YAK fighter-bombers early in the war, and escaped unscathed.

In early November, 1950, Ausman was flying wingman with Major Arnold 'Moon' Mullins, who had assumed command of the 67th Squadron following the untimely combat death of Major Lou Sebille. They were returning from an interdiction mission north of Seoul.

Coming across a hole in the clouds a few miles northeast of Seoul, they let down through an opening in the clouds and unexpectedly found themselves overtaking a pair of single-engine airplanes directly ahead of them. With a quick 'double take', Mullins realized that they were not F-51 Mustangs—they were a pair of Russian-built North Korean YAKs—propeller-driven attack planes.

With their considerable speed advantage, descending unseen from the rear, Mullins quickly assessed the situation, and told Ausman to take the enemy YAK on the right, while he attacked the one on the left.

Their dive had caught the enemy completely by surprise. Mullins pressed his trigger and quickly the first enemy ship exploded in flame with his first burst of machine gun fire and saw it dive sharply to the ground. No parachutes were seen.

But Ausman was even more startled by their sudden, amazing stroke of luck; such a rare opportunity for an aerial 'kill'. He was so preoccupied with his extreme good fortune that he misjudged his high rate of closure on his target aircraft and, although firing his machine guns and getting a few hits, was not able to destroy the target on his first firing pass. Instead, to his utter dismay, he found the momentum of his dive was carrying him helplessly past the enemy, overtaking the target and drifting right into the sights of his quarry.

Where moments before he had been the attacker, he was suddenly and very unhappily becoming a sitting-duck target for the enemy YAK, who was about to be offered a beautiful straight-on, close-astern firing blast against his attacker!

Chopping his throttle completely off, and fanning rudder to skid the airplane in an attempt to dissipate excess speed, Ausman continued to slowly pass on the YAK's right side.

"Dive under," he heard Mullins shout over his radio, and Ausman immediately did as he was told.

Ausman hit the throttle, dove sharply and turned left under the enemy airplane as Mullins, who, fortunately, was still behind the surviving YAK was able to swing quickly and easily into trail position and shot down the second North Korean aircraft with a quick burst of machine gun fire, giving Major Arnold "Moon" Mullins two aerial victories in as many minutes—the first aerial encounters for the 67th Squadron and the first aerial victories for the 18th Fighter-Bomber Group in the Korean war.

Arnold 'Moon' Mullins, a P-47 veteran of WWII, where he had been shot down over Europe and evaded capture was, at age 30, promoted to Lieutenant Colonel soon after completing his Combat Tour and leaving the 67th Squadron in Korea. He was reassigned to a Tactical Air Command base in South Carolina in early 1951, developing air-to-ground communications procedures for

Close Support operations.

He was killed in the crash of a T-33 jet trainer aircraft in 1952 while demonstrating those tactical maneuvers.

Excerpted with permission from "Korean Tales, Unsung Heroes of the Korean Air War."

Mustang Attacks Allow Breakout

By Col. Harry Moreland

In late November 1950, we were flying from an advanced support base near Pyongyang, North Korea—the capitol. It was bitter cold, but our spirits were up—we had just heard that we could expect to be home for Christmas. And why not. Things were looking good because the North Koreans seem to be in full retreat.

I slept as close to the stove as I could—with all my clothes on to keep warm. My canteen would freeze solid at night. All of us felt lucky that we did not have to face the weather like our ground forces were having to do.

I was assigned a mission to lead a flight of four to reconnoiter the main road from Pyongyang that heads north to the Yalu River.

All of us in the flight could hardly wait to get into the airplanes—to get warm.

We were carrying two napalm tanks, plus the usual 1800 rounds of .50-caliber machine gun ammunition for the three guns in each wing.

After take off we formed up in our usual loose "finger tip" formation and headed north. About halfway up the highway—actually just a rather narrow road—I got an emergency call from a forward air controller (FAC) on the ground with one of the Army divisions. Lt. Mal Edens, from our squadron, advised me that the entire division was on the road in full retreat. The Chinese had entered the conflict and had taken the high ground on either side of the road. The division, he reported, was not moving because a large Army tank at the head of the column had been destroyed.

The road was blocked. The American troops were taking fire from hills on both sides. Edens' driver had been killed.

[The FAC was Capt. Mal Edens from Moreland's squadron. "He never made it out. I felt bad and lucky both because I had volunteered with him for that job and he was selected," Moreland recalled.]

We flew up and down the road to size up the situation. The entire division was on the road and not moving. They were sitting in their vehicles waiting for the roadblock to be cleared. There was no place for them to go. There was a big tank that had been destroyed at the head of the column and was blocking the road. About a half a mile in front of them was a strong check point. They were trying to push the tank off the road so the convoy could get moving. We decided it best to keep the enemy forces that were impeding the removal the tank under attack to allow the removal to take place. Rather than expend all our ammo at once we decided to work both sides of the high ground. We would strafe on one pass drop a single tank of napalm on another pass and do it one plane at a time. This would make the enemy keep their heads down for a longer period of time. So we worked both sides and before we finished the road block was cleared and the convoy started to roll again. We finished unloading all ammo and I don't know about the other pilots but I was cheering in the cockpit when I saw the first element reach the check point.

I sent the rest of the flight back and got on the radio to vector other fighters into the area to work over the high ground. Ground control was also notified of the situation with the recommendation they get all the help they could up to that area.

A few days later we had to evacuate K-24 and go to Suwon. So much for being home for Christmas.

Air Force Pilot Pipeline

Life As A Cadet

Six months after the Korean War began, the Air Force was moving fledgling pilots through the training pipeline as fast as possible. It was clear that the pool of available trained pilots in the various Reserve components would not be enough. Many of these pipeline pilots would eventually be assigned to the 18th Fighter-Bomber Group. Much has happened to those new aviators we first profiled in June 1950.

As a Fourth Classman, Aviation Cadets like Archie Connors and "Budd" Stapley, lived in wooden barracks and wore a very basic uniform that consisted of dungarees and a "fore and aft cap." When Reveille was sounded, they had to be ready to fall out in uniform literally within seconds of the "official" wake up alarm. Since shaving was impossible in the brief time allowed, they worked out a system of getting up before Reveille, then to quickly take turns shaving while classmates held a blanket over the window (to prevent any light from escaping from the officially still darkened barracks).

Meanwhile, Third Classmen, already up, shaved and dressed, were "patrolling" the areas outside the Fourth Classman barracks—looking for any lights. "If they spotted some light coming from your window, you had had it," Wilfred "Budd" Stapley remembered.

[Budd Stapley was Connors' roommate during part of his pilot training and later they flew combat missions together as members of How Flight of the 67th Fighter Bomber Squadron.]

They dared not get caught looking out of their room. Even a slight glance out of the window could earn the distracted Cadet another hour of military drill--EMI.

Just prior to Reveille, the shaved, uniformed Cadets would be poised by the door. At the sound of the wake up call, they would pour outside—"elbows over @$$holes"—and into ranks, ready for inspection by Third Classmen ever ready to find flaws in uniforms or bearing. These meant Extra Military Instruction or EMI in the form of "tours" that were marched off—one hour of marching for each tour. Too many "tours" and a Cadet was washed out permanently.

Ground School

The initial six weeks of pre-flight training was called "Ground school," and consisted of basic military subjects and introductions to subjects relating to aviation and aerodynamics. Pre-flight was pre-flight. The trainees were not even Cadets. "You are the lowest scum in the world," Stapley related.

Their days were spent mostly in school, with other periods devoted to keeping the old barracks clean and military drill instruction. The day lasted from about 0430 until 2030.

The T-6 Texan

The Texan had no armament and a range of just 750 miles. Its one 550-hp Pratt & Whitney radial piston engine would push it to a maximum speed of 205 mph and to an altitude of a little over 20,000 feet. However, over 17,000 of them were manufactured because it was the "Pilot Maker."

The AT-6 two-place advanced trainer became one of the most widely used aircraft in history—the aerial classroom for most of the Allied pilots who flew in World War II. Called the "SNJ" by the Navy and the "Harvard" by the RAF, the T-6 was designed as a transition trainer between basic trainers and first-line tactical aircraft.

Most AAF fighter pilots trained in AT-6s. During World War Two, many of the "Spitfire" and "Hurricane" pilots in the Battle of Britain trained in Canada in "Harvards," the British version of the AT-6. In 1948, the new USAF redesignated those Texans still in service as T-6s when the AT, BT and PT aircraft designations were abandoned. During the Korean War that followed in 1950, T-6s were pressed into service to meet the urgent need for close air support of ground forces. Flying "mosquito missions," the T-6s spotted enemy troops and guns, then marked them with smoke rockets for attack by fighter-bombers.

The Texan, "was a good airplane…you couldn't take the wings off it," former Truckbuster Wilfred "Budd" Stapley recalled.

Following six weeks of ground school, the new "Cadet" was advanced to Fourth Classman—when the hazing started in earnest, most of it conducted by those just a few weeks ahead of them in the training process. The Third Class was responsible for indoctrinating the fourth class into the cadet corps. Each class lasted about six weeks.

The "indoctrination" was intense and often mystifying to the Fourth Classmen.

The Aviation Cadets ate a "square meal"—perched on only the front three inches of their seats, backs ramrod straight, chests out, they kept their heads down as they brought food to their mouths from the plate, straight up to a point directly opposite their mouths, then in a straight line to their mouths.

This was the typical practice—until there was an "air raid." The cadet at the end of the mess table was the designated "tail gunner." Cadets sitting along the sides of the table were "side gunners."

At that time, milk was bottled in small half-pint glass containers capped with circular wax coated cardboard plugs that were removed or replaced by pull up tabs in the center of the plugs. Each time milk was drunk by the Cadet, the plug was to be removed and then replaced—tightly.

During an "air raid," upper classmen would start the show, upward wailing of an air raid "siren." The "tail gunners" would stand up and begin to fire their "weapons" loudly …boom…boom…boom… following the imaginary "bogie" around the room.

Fourth Classmen had to quickly grab their milk container and that of a nearby Cadet to form a set of "binoculars," that were then brought up to the eyes in order to spot the "attacking aircraft." Of course, if the Cadet had not replaced the plug tightly enough, the upended milk bottle immediately poured all remaining liquid all over the hapless Cadet. If a Cadet was caught "cheating"—sneaking his thumbs up and over the loose milk plugs—he was punished with a "tour," one hour of extra marching. The lesson being drilled into the Cadet by such "indoctrination," was attention to detail and that to survive you had to depend on your buddy.

The big thrill for Fourth Classmen was "starting to fly." That was what it was all about--why they had joined the Air Force. "You could take an awful lot of 'stuff' if every day you were able to get into the cockpit of an airplane," Stapley remembered.

Most Cadet washouts came while they were Third Classmen. Beginning with the Third Classman period, Cadets began to get enough flight time for the Air Force to determine whether that Cadet had what was needed to be a pilot.

After a Cadet's solo flight he was proud to go through the solo flight announcement ritual. At the next meal, the proud Cadet would turn to the upper classman serving as "Table Commandant" and request permission "to make a statement."

"Permission granted, Mr. Stapley," would come the response.

"Sir, I soloed today, I would like to make an announcement."

"Be my guest, Mr. Stapley."

The Cadet would then stand up and announce to the entire room: "Attention in the area. Attention in the area. I—Aviation Cadet Stapley, Wilfred C. of the supersonic second squadron--SOLOED TODAY!"

The entire mess hall would then cheer and clap. That was a day you remember for the rest of your life.

The solo for Stapley came after he had made about eight landings at a nearby practice field--"just greased 'em in." The flight instructor was writing in his clipboard and Cadet Stapley was writing in his notebook. Stapley was ready for the usual command: "OK Stapley, take me up again." Instead, the instructor said: "OK Stapley, let's see you take it up and around and land three times--by yourself."

After taking several deep breaths, Stapley took off, flew around the practice field and "greased it in" for a perfect landing. Took off, went around and again, greased it in for a beautiful landing. Only one more to go. Took off on the final leg, went around and "lost it." The instructor later told him: "I thought that you would either run out of gas, or that I would have to shoot you down."

The People of North Korea

by Lt. Ken Barber

The people of North Korea live in a land which, but for its lack of trees, might be termed a fertile mountain paradise. Beneath the steep, towering mountains lie fertile, rolling valleys, well cultivated and rich in wheat, rice, oats, cattle and hogs. In this autumn and early winter season one may see huge stacks of hay and oats, bright red or green peppers drying in the cold, daylight sun, sacks upon sacks of potatoes stacked inside the houses—fare for the cold winter ahead.

Near their homes the farmers may be seen beating their oats with a primitive flail. Women work with the men stacking up hay. Little boys help load hay on the ox sleds, leading their oxen from field to granary, while the little girls are given the charge of the babies. It is not uncommon to see little girls of six carrying around small children of two or three, slung onto their backs. At other times the little girls are expected to help around the house.

The homes are three room affairs built of hardened mud and sticks, the floors covered with grass mats. A large pit in the main room with fireplace and pipes running under all the rooms keep the floors warm at all times. The smoke is carried out by chimneys made from hollowed logs. Big pottery bowls of water over the fireplace furnish moisture in the air and serve to keep food warm at all times.

To enter the raised portion of these houses (the matted part) with shoes on is to commit great sacrilege. Often I have seen some tidy Korean women get angry as some careless G.I. walked across her nice, clean mats. It is not that they mind you occupying one of their rooms so much, but walking on their mats with shoes—Ach!—that is indeed verboten!"

The rooms of the houses open out into the yard. Each house is generally encircled by a thick brush fence, designed to keep snow and wind out of the house. A small outhouse near one corner completes the picture. If the house stands near a stream, you will probably see a crude sort of grain pounder worked by the running water. This same contraption is sometimes used for pounding their clothes clean.

The people dress in white clothes, many in rags. Tiny children run around almost naked, their feet and legs made chapped and red by the cold. Little boys have much more freedom than do the little girls.

In each small village stands the inevitable, long, wood schoolhouse, its immense stacks of cut firewood outside promising warmth to the pupils during the winter. Inside are wood stoves, maps, pictures of Stalin, blackboards, and tiny benches and desks.

This is Korea, a land which promises plenty but which has nothing. It is a land of happy, laughing children who grow up in the Oriental tradition of fatalism and futilism. Their needs are basic-food, shelter, clothing. Though they dearly love their families, they are brutal and cold-

blooded in their taking of human lives.

One feels sorry for these people. They are pawns in a game of chess, played by the larger nations of the world. Their allegiances must change with the flag of the victor who at that time occupies them. By the standards of Americans or Englishmen, these people are uncivilized and backward. The average G.I. considers them as inferior and two-faced, sticking with the power in power at the time.

They are people of bright smiles, friendly natures--and they are a people of great stub-

bornness and violence when so provoked. They are people whose national pride has been crushed by the tramp of Chinese, Japanese, Russian, and American boots. Their motto has of necessity become "Cooperate and live!"

These Koreans are backward. They have never had a chance, yet those who are educated are outstanding.

Barber, Lt. Col. Kenneth. Korean War Diary (unpublished), 1950.

Typical North Korean farmer. (Barber)

Keeping A Diary...

The next day, Wednesday, 29 November, Barber spent cleaning up the jeeps and getting them fueled and started. "We filled a couple of cans with gasoline and put them on each side of the wheels on Mosley's jeep, finally breaking them loose by pulling and pushing.

"The news is bad today. Sure hate to think of more war, but if it's to come, then let it come. We'll not lose our freedom to a bunch of dominating Communists."

"Keeping a diary," Barber noted, "can become quite a burden. You become a slave to it and cannot break away. Instead of writing the interesting letters you should write, you expend your daily writing interest on a book. And, once you begin, you cannot stop. You must write daily, and record the interesting events. I certainly hope these books get back home, and me with them."

Barber, Lt. Col. Kenneth. Korean War Diary (unpublished), 1950.

"Jealous Jackie" Set To Prowl. Corporal William Wilkerson, Corporal J. B. Chandler, and PFC J. D. Mosley and "Jealous Jackie" (the jeep) prepare to start out on patrol the morning of 27 November 1950. "They are mechanics and radio men, although I do not think they know anything about it as yet." They learned quickly, however. Soon, Barber was recommending them for well-deserved promotions. (Barber)

From Pusan to the Yalu

Sailing For Iwon. Lt. Ken Barber and his FAC team sailed from Pusan on 2 November 1950. Three days later they landed at Iwon, North Korea, about 70 miles south of the Yalu River. (Barber)

FAC Team En route to North Korea

Finally, on Thursday, 2 November, Lt. Ken Barber's ship "pulled up anchor from the pier (we had gone in for supplies and an exercise hike) and took off for North Korea, to the music of a port band." Once again, Barber found himself "on the wide-open, beautiful, blue, adventuresome sea. Once more I was filled with the fascination and adventure which the sea offers, with the delight and anticipation of seeing some new places, with the drunken roll and pitch of the ship, its motors vibrating on a deep roll, and with promise of new adventures." The ship soon arrived at Iwon, "far up in N.E. Korea."

"There has been much unconfirmed news lately. Reports indicate that Chinese Communists made a two-pronged attack near Hamhung, swarming over the ROK Divisions. Another report stated that a Regiment of the 1st Cavalry had been cut off or surrounded, although the news tonight did not mention it," he wrote.

The 32nd RCT is in Reserve this time, he wrote. "Our job will be to patrol and mop up from here to the Manchurian and Russian border. There are around 20,000 Chinese Communists supposedly fighting for the North Koreans. I rather suspect we shall run into a bit more opposition before this war is over. One important power plant that controls power in North Korea and in Manchuria seems to worry the Chinese considerably. Luckily for them, the Air Force has had orders to spare all bridges and power plants. I imagine the power plant will be a big bargaining point with the Chinese Communists because it lies on the North Korean side of the border."

Heading for the Yalu

On Sunday, 5 November, Barber and his team were finally landed at Iwon, North Korea, about sixty miles ENE of Hamhung. The Yalu River city of Hyesan was only about 70 miles NNW of Iwon, in a direct line. It was very cold. The next morning, they "moved out to the North, via the road through Pukch'ong." At 1000 when they started out, "it was warm enough for just a sweater and long handles [which he had put on that morning], but as we progressed it grew colder and colder, so cold that even a B-15 (AF) jacket, with fur collar up, and gloves would not keep me warm."

Barber began to notice, "with great amazement, little North Korean children running around barefoot, some of them dressed in rags, some of them naked. To such lengths had acclimatization taken them, while I rode past in a jeep, bundled up and cold. Perhaps when you live primitively, your body reacts more strongly to hardships," he thought.

The North Korean farms "seemed better laid out and much more prosperous than those of South Korea. We passed log cabins chinked with mud, well-sealed mud houses with log roofs, and some wooden houses. The roofs were waterproofed by bark shingles overlapping or some sort of shale shingles done the same way. A few had thatch-covered roofs, and quite a few more had roofs covered with stones. Beside every farm house stood huge piles of wheat or hay, tobacco hung in strips drying in the sun, a type of brilliant red pepper lay drying in the sun, while full baskets of rosy, red apples sat around the steps of the houses. Large piles of cut and stacked wood lay by every house.

In front of the houses we often saw a man or woman flailing their rice or wheat, then sifting it to separate the chaff from the grain. Here, the children seem much healthier, the children of the mountains I might call them, for we steadily progressed up into the mountains, looking back in the valleys on sheer drops and sheer beauty. At the beginning of one climb we saw the golden leaves of aspens, but farther up there were few large trees, just a few small pines, and much brush.

The North Koreans "cultivate way up on the hillsides. Indeed, the old story about mountaineers with one leg longer than the other must have originated here, because some of their fields were on slopes of a 45 degree angle."

Just before dark, the convoy "reached the top of our climb, a big, broad, fertile farm valley extending for many miles. The houses were well-built, the granaries full, the winter wood stacked high, the people dressed in fur vests and rabbit or other fur caps with ear flaps."

Monday evening, as the early winter dusk settled around them, Barber's team reached a road junction just south of Hwangsu won-ni, a small town about 50 miles north of Iwon on the Iwon-Pukch'ong-P'ungsan Road. They pulled off the road and lit fires to warm themselves and some food, while they awaited further orders from the Regimental Commander, Col. McLean. [Aboard ship McLean had made a speech "in which he said that the Chinese Communists were in North Korea and 'Our mission is to seek them out and destroy them; I repeat, to seek them out and destroy them, and I mean we're going to do it. Hubba! Hubba!' Of course, from that point on, McLean was known as "Hubba! Hubba! McLean by the troops. "He is not very popular," Barber noted.]

Barber retrieved his parka and "trigger-finger mittens" that were much warmer than the five-finger AF type, ate some supper and then "moved out" to drive another ten miles down the road. "We are about 50-60 miles south of the Manchurian border right now," Barber wrote. "It is extremely cold, way below freezing, in fact, down around 0 de-

grees Fahrenheit. There were evidences of a former snow on the ground, and ice in some places. Brrr, sure looks like a long, cold winter."

After spending a cold night sleeping on the frozen ground, Barber and his team arose on Tuesday, 7 November to learn their unit was to "attack a ridge line of hills not far away but hard to get to because of a river and lake."

Barber was soon asked to ensure that his radios were working—"Do so, right away and let me know," a Major told him. Before Barber had time to set up station or raise the aerial, the Major drove past shouting, "Follow me, Barber." He hadn't given the FACP even three minutes to set up.

Barber was not impressed with the "Bombast and stupid dunderhead," and decided it was more important to take his time and set up the radio equipment because "we're no good at all without our radios in order." Sure enough, they didn't check out, so Barber stopped at the Regimental Headquarters to find someone to repair them, after which he was soon on his way again. Barber determined that "air support here is a very tentative thing. A liaison plane is on CAP all day over this area, and if we need air support we contact him. There are also standby planes—Navy Corsairs—over the area most of the time."

The attack that had been in the works for many hours, was supposed to "hop off at 1500, but the mortars had set up out of range so we didn't move out until nearly dark, and then only "G" Company under Capt. Howard was where it was supposed to be, a typical example of this Battalion's status. Capt. Howard is outstandingly the best Company Commander in the outfit. Just before dark, with the mortars out of position and the artillery not zeroed in, Lt. Col. Reidy in desperation ordered "G" Company forward. Luckily, the enemy positions were deserted. A lot of shovels and some fires with many food supplies lay around. There had been about 200 enemy dug in. What a dunderhead Battalion!!"

Barber and his men spent the night in a deserted schoolhouse, "complete with stoves, and large stacks of wood outside. On the walls were North Korean flags and even some pictures of Joe Stalin, one of which Barber took with him and pasted in his journal.

'G' Company Was Surrounded

On Wednesday evening, 8 November, Barber advised that if his men slept inside (the commandeered schoolhouse), they had to go on guard duty. So, Barber "ups to Capt. Kyle, the S-1, and sez 'Sir, the Air Force is not supposed to go on guard." Kyle "ups and sez, "Ah, but if they sleep inside, they do." Barber "ups and sez "Taint so!" Kyle "ups and sez, 'Tis so." Finally, they compromised. Barber would "put it up to the men. They said they'd rather freeze lying down in their sacks than standing up on guard duty, so they would move out." As it turned out, Barber's men were assigned as "Supernumeraries" for guard duty that night—"so they stayed inside."

On Thursday, Barber and his men did "nothing all day. We cooked, washed our feet and some clothes, taught the children new words." The interlude was not to last very long. Barber was told to report to Regimental Headquarters at 0700 the next morning "to give them some technical advice about building an airstrip." He racked his brain "trying to remember various Take Off minimums and aircraft wing spans, wishing I had paid a little more attention in Air School classes. Finally, I had the perfect airstrip built up in my mind," he decided.

The next morning he arrived at the headquarters in time to confer with a "Major of the Combat Engineers" who was planning to "build the strip for C-47's. He just wanted to know if they could take-off and land in that area with no trouble." Barber's radio then summoned him "to hurry back to Battalion." He did, but not before he stopped once while he "fired at and missed (doggone it!) a pheasant. Sure would have tasted good." He was then stationed at the "top of the ridge line in case air support were needed by a platoon patrol going out from "G" Company."

Hearing from a G.I. that the "G" Company patrol "is surrounded—1 dead and 4 wounded," Barber knew that his TACP would soon be in action. "Sure enough, about two minutes later, Major Holland came tearing out called 'Barber!' We found out what the score was, called four Navy

Smoke rises from a burning supply dump near Pukchong on 5 December 1950. (Barber)

Corsairs that happened to be overhead, asked them to standby 25 minutes while we got to the top of the hill, and barreled up the hill in the radio jeep. At the top we found out where the enemy was with respect to our platoon patrol, called the Corsairs, gave them the coordinates, and had them identify our troops who were wearing parkas with the white side out. They really plastered the town of Yaksu-ri, virtually destroying it. The patrol called "E" Company on an SCR-300, who relayed to the Colonel's radioman who told me. I then directed the aircraft where the Patrol wanted it. We then directed the aircraft on the two hills from which the enemy was firing. After spending their ammo, the flight leader—'Jukebox Nehigh One'—called in another flight of three Corsairs who really plastered the hills, causing enemy fire to stop and enabling the patrol to withdraw. The Patrol said 'That's the most beautiful air strike we've ever seen.' Man, oh man, did we TACP's feel good We felt wonderful! We felt that at long last we had justified our being here."

"One man, Lt. Porter, had been killed—sawed in two by a machine gun. Two were shot in the arm, one in the hip, and one in the head. The one hit in the head was pretty bad off. He and one of the arm cases had to be carried. It was interesting to note that the North Korean civilians voluntarily carried the litter cases back in their oxcarts." Barber noted also that "G" Company had with them a Communist prisoner "to try to get the others to surrender." The prisoner was "first to sight the enemy and pointed them out. Then, when Lt. Porter was killed, he dragged his body back instead of running away. They made sure he had some cigarettes, food and a warm place to stay that night!"

Nahung-ni

On Friday, 17 November, Barber and Wilkerson "set out in the radio jeep to control an air strike, but could establish no radio contact. After a disgusting time with both radios, we told the Colonel that our radio was out, and headed back to Regiment." After getting the radios repaired at

North Korean farmer threshing oats. (Barber)

Regimental Headquarters, Barber and his team headed back out into the snow with a week's rations to "keep for emergency, so we're all set."

On Saturday, 18 November, Barber "woke up this morning to a world of snow. It must be almost a foot deep. We'll have much trouble getting back over that mountain," he correctly predicted.

He "hit the trail" with chains on his jeep, and began the "marathon climb" up the mountain that lasted three hours. When the trailer prevented the jeep from making the first hill, Barber had it "attached to a 6-by with 10 wheels, all with chains." Chandler was driving the cargo jeep and Barber was driving the radio jeep himself. "Try as we could the jeeps would spin their wheels and slide into ditches to be hauled out by hand. We had to resort to blood, flesh, bone and muscle—about 12 men—and at last reached the top."

Coming down was "fairly easy." Barber and his group "were the only ones to cross the mountain that day, and the sense of achievement certainly made us feel good!"

Near Naegi...Naiki

On Saturday, "a sniper shot at and narrowly missed one of the Communications men," Barber noted. Lt. Col. Reidy called in the headman of the town and "told him through his interpreter that he was the 'Military Commander' of this area. Ah, such

bowing and scraping, and 'Oh-ing!"

Colonel Reidy asked him if he knew what had happened to Yaksu-ri. He said that he did. Whereupon Col. Reidy told him that if any more pot shots were taken at him, he'd call in the airplanes and burn down Naegi as he had done to Yaksu-ri. [Yaksu-ri is the one Chandler and I burned down 10 November.] Such bowing demonstrations and reassurances of full cooperation with the Americans!. The town was ours!

Some fighters flew overhead and Barber ran for his radio jeep to try and contact them. Captain Mitchell, the new S-3, came running after Barber yelling, "Do you have contact, yet?" Barber considered it a "very stupid question to ask when he could obviously see I was running for the jeep to find out myself." However, out loud Barber answered, "No, not yet." Mitchell then yelled, "Why not." The second question seemed so stupid to Barber that he "didn't even bother to answer."

Meanwhile, Barber's Airmen had set up the radios and were trying to make contact with the nearby airplanes. They were not successful, although they could talk to each other on the jeep and mobile sets. "How disgusted can one be!" Barber asked himself. "How can we give air support when our radio is obsolescent and no good? I'm ready to back that fickle radio jeep up on a cliff and give it a shove," he recorded.

Shortly thereafter, a C-47 flew by, its cargo doors open, "buzzing up and down

Talking To Aircraft. *Lt. Ken Barber uses a convenient gully as a foxhole while calling in an airstrike for close air support on 17 November 1950. (Barber)*

Air Support Every Time From Now On...

Monday, 13 November, "has been very cold today. Last night it went down to around 9 degrees below zero. Today it has been around zero—with a cold wind blowing all day." Despite the temperature, Barber "for a short time toyed with the idea of a bath in an icy creek nearby, but gave up the idea when I got outside. I did strip down inside and wash in a hot and cold helmet liner, changed clothes, and took all my dirty clothes to a Korean house where I had them washed for a couple of cans of "C" rations."

On 16 November, Barber and his team were rejoining "F" Company after having their air control radios repaired. "Lt. Col. Reidy and Capt. Mitchell came roaring up in their jeeps saying they had been fired upon and even had a couple of holes in their jeep. They were pinned down on a narrow shelf by accurate machine gun fire. One man was shot through the fat of his leg—the million dollar wound—another broke his leg, one had his helmet creased by a bullet. Major Wood battered his knee against a rock wall several times, hurting it badly. Some Navy planes made a strike nearby which caused the Communists to stop firing temporarily giving the jeeps just enough time to get out one at a time, between passes." Lt. Col. Reidy "wants air support along every time from now on."

that valley at tree-top level like a misplaced fighter pilot." Barber ran for his camera and snapped several photographs, then reloaded the camera "as it began dropping rations to us in chutes of white, green, orange, purple colors—rations which we did not need because we are to move to Pungsan as Division Reserve at 0700 tomorrow morning." After dropping 19 chutes of 5-in-1 rations, the C-47 "made a low buzz job and left us. Quite a pilot! He was sure low in that valley. A couple of times I thought he would hit the sides of the mountain," Barber noted. Mosley was the first to reach the rations. Chandler had started out with

Mosley, but "pooped" out on the way. "The cold air is hard on one's lungs," Barber noted, "they burn very easily and your wind is short."

Colonel Reidy was not pleased with the air dropped supplies. To him, at that stage, it was "just more stuff to lug back over the hills."

Reidy sent out patrols to "find a new route to Pungsan, but failed to find more than a footpath."

The vehicles would go back over the mountains using the narrow roads, while the troops would hike via a path. The vehicles would have a 40 miles transit. The

troops would only have to hike 10-15 miles.

Cold Beauty In The Mountains

As the weather grew bitterly cold, Barber paid particular attention to his sleeping arrangements. He gave special attention to the pup tent, banking "snow over the edges of the tent and stacking hay inside to make a soft base" for his bed. The air mattress was not used because it lacked insulation—the air inside was frigid. "Hay on the ground is much warmer," Barber noted, who slept

152

Double Exposed...First Snow! *The first snow of 1950 in the mountains of North Korea arrived on 18 November. In this double exposure, Lt. Barber captures the scene of his TACP #7 jeep in a convoy passing a Korean mule train on the narrow road. TACP #7 "was the only group to get to three units that were isolated on the other side of the mountain." (Barber)*

on his sleeping bag "with three blankets folded double inside on top. Now I'm ready for the night."

Although achingly cold, Barber found beauty in the mountains. "After a supper of beef, sweet potatoes and bread, I went to my tent and turned in. It is a beautifully moonlit night outside, the light on the snow covered trees, pastures, fences, and bushes indescribably lovely. You breathe clear, crisp, cold air and look at the friendly shadows of this little village nearby, the houses with their rustic pens, stacks of hay, a few dogs roaming around and inevitably the big (usually red), one floor schoolhouse with its immense stack of winter wood behind it. It is hard to believe that behind this peaceful, lovely scene lie the horrors of war."

Buzzed Into Pungsan

On 20 November, Barber and his men struck camp and moved out down the valley, "catching up with the last vehicles of the convoy at the base of the west slope of

the mountain where they were encountering some difficulties." They "pulled up over the mountain, helping each other when one bogged down, repairing bridges, making delicious snow ice cream when we were stopped and had naught else to do."

At the top, the 31st Flyboys passed everyone, took the lead and buzzed into Pungsan around 1600 hours, an hour ahead of everyone else! We finally reached Pungsan, a fairly good-sized town. Battalion Headquarters in a bunch of one-story rooms (everything is one story in Korea that I've seen) surrounding a patio. Lt. Bill Colwell was here—he hadn't broken his arm but had strained his back, and had secured permission to remain in Korea with 2nd Battalion. He seems fine—good to see him!!"

The homes here are much nicer than those of the country cousins. They keep nice woodwork and pottery bowls, chests, etc. My men are set up in a nice house. I am staying on the board floor of a small, cold room in the headquarters which about seven of us call the B.O.Q."

On 21 November, 1950, Barber "got a package with six boxes of film from Mom yesterday evening. Now I can get "Takusan" ("many" in Japanese) pictures of this country. I hope to get some good portrait shots today and tomorrow.

Last night was rugged. I slept on the floor. The Chaplain's bad cough kept me awake a long time and people walking over my sleeping bag didn't help any."

23 November 1950

Thanksgiving

Barber and his men made sure they arrived at Regimental headquarters in time for a "feast" of a Thanksgiving meal.

"What a meal," he remembered. "Turkey—white or dark meat, mashed potatoes with giblet gravy, dressing, sweet potatoes, green peas, corn, hot rolls, mince meat tarts, pumpkin pie, olives, apples, coffee, candy and cigarettes. Everything except cranberry. When I left I was stuffed to the gills and couldn't have eaten another bite, but I didn't reckon on the appetites of my men so off we went to the First Battalion where, mustering up the hungriest looks they could, they went up to the chow line which had just closed. When asked if they had eaten, they said "No," very piteously. I walked into the kitchen after a cup of coffee, and seeing their predicament had to say, "No," when they asked me. So-o-o, a huge plate of peas, sweet potatoes, mashed potatoes, hot rolls, cranberry sauce, pumpkin pie and fruitcake was shoved in front of me. I protested using the excuse of an upset stomach, but they wouldn't hear of not eating a good Thanksgiving Dinner, so I, stuffed to the gills already, had to cram down another dinner. My men, sitting across the table stuffing themselves with great gusto, got a large charge out of my predicament, chuckling to each other and grinning like mules eatin' briars. Such is the fate of prevaricators!! I told 'em from now on, they could get out of their own scrapes. I was about to pop! It was quite funny! Anyway, Operation Turkey was a huge success, and the morale of all concerned was better afterwards by 100%."

That evening while Barber was writing a letter home to his wife, Carolyn, a man was brought in "who had been beaten, stabbed, kicked, and left lying in the far end of this village of Chang-ni. He had an ugly head wound just above the left eye, three stab wounds on his neck, and a slash wound across his throat not quite deep enough to reach the jugular vein. Under Dr. Stanley R. Lavietas supervision, the aide men sewed him up, doing a pretty good job. It was with some surprise that I learned that medics do most of the commonplace sewing in the Army. Personally, I'd sure rather have a Doctor working on me."

"He was badly beaten up. When he came to and could talk he said that his brother, a Communist, had been the cause of the death of three innocent persons of this village. The local police caught this man and worked him over—through the interpreter we gathered that this man, too, was a Communist.

The wounded man died the next day as he was being taken "to the rear" for further treatment.

The other officers kidded Dr. Lavietas about the man's death. "One man came in with a bruised foot," Barber noted. The other officers asked Lavietas, "Did he die, Doc?" Kidding him. "Nope," the doctor replied quickly, "just lost a foot." Barber chuckled in his diary at the doctor's quick sense of humor.

The temperature that day "hovered around zero—all day. Might snow tonight," Barber closed.

Under Attack...Air Cover

On Saturday, 25 November 1950, Barber was notified that the entire Regiment would be moving to Pukchong the next day, and then on to Hamhung. The ultimate destination was to be the Chosin Reservoir "to replace the Marines. Where they're going I do not know," he noted.

Since they were about to get on the road again, Barber and his men knew what they had to do next—get cleaned up. They immediately drove down the road "to a shower unit" that had been established. It broke down just as we were preparing to get in which necessitated a long wait. Finally, they fixed it. We nearly froze under ice-cold water until it finally warmed up. Then what

pure delight!!! I am sitting here in clean fatigues, feeling warm and happy," he wrote.

The happy feeling was not to last long, however. He was soon called into a meeting with Major Mason. "A bunch of about a thousand Communists have been reported about 12 miles down the road—heading this way. These medical officers have panicked but I can't see any reason sweating it out until it happens," Barber noted.

One of Barber's men, "Mosley picked up a puppy today—thick haired, he seems half chow, half husky and half sheep—that makes a dog and a half—but he's going to be a big rascal," Barber predicted.

The next day, Sunday, 26 November 1950, Barber led off with "What a day this has been! Wow! Last night the report came in that 1,000 Communists were in the villages about twelve miles South of here." Regiment was calling for close air support to attack the enemy columns. Barber and his men "went out with a patrol of about six jeeps this morning early—around 0630." An earlier patrol had found nothing to verify the reported enemy column.

About six miles down the road, the air cover Barber had requested arrived. As the jeep column headed down the road, the air cover would scout ahead and radio back the locations of groups of people traveling on the road. "In a small village about ten miles south of Chang-ni we stopped, saw

Beautiful Pungsan Valley Reservoir. Lt. Ken Barber took this photograph of the Pungsan Valley Reservoir on 20 November 1950. (Barber)

Air Drop By A Frustrated Fighter Pilot. *Cut off by the snow near Naegi (Naiki, NK), Army units call for supplies to be air dropped to them on 19 November 1950. The pilot of the C-47 barely skimmed the top of the mountain. Barber noted on his photograph, "a frustrated fighter pilot." (Barber)*

some people on a hill who quickly disappeared. Lt. Walker was in command of the patrol. He went off up the road to investigate the people on the hill while the rest of his men built a fire and gathered around it. The planes reported about ten men com-

ing up the road from the way we had come, so I sent about three men down there to cover them. Then firing broke out from the hill. Since Lt. Walker was nowhere around (and he should have been), I took over and dispersed the men in the village. My men,

all eager to get a Gook, had taken off after the bunch coming down the road towards us!. I finally got them back on the radio where they belonged. The enemy must have taken off over the high hill because we didn't see anymore at that place. I took Chandler

Racing For Supplies. *Colonel Reidy was not pleased with the air dropped supplies. To him, at that stage, they represented "just more stuff to lug back over the hills." As the unwanted supplies landed in the snow covered, isolated valley, the Army troops raced after them to keep them from falling into enemy hands and to see if there was anything in the bundles they really needed. (Barber)*

and the radio jeep a little further up the road, found Lt. Walker and had him take his ROKs off the hill, then directed the planes in on the hill for a strafing and rocket attack. We were receiving small arms fire and burp gun fire from back on the hill. Moving the jeep out in the open, we put 500-lb bombs and rockets not over 200 yards away from us on top of the hill. The explosion burst above us, so it couldn't hit us, even tho the textbook distances for ground support say one yard away per lb. of bomb—500 lb. bomb=500 yards away."

Lt. Walker did not want to risk any men to see what was on the hill and decided to return.

The Navy Corsairs also hit between 10 and 15 people a little farther west along the road to Fusen Reservoir.

Barber's men "were mighty curious to see what we'd hit on that hill, but not being in charge of the patrol, it was none of my

business. At the time, I didn't think much of Walker's patrol leading. He should have better deployed his men plus maintaining more contact with the main body of his patrol."

When Walker reported the results of the

patrol to Major "Red" Mason, Battalion CO, he was told that he should have "inspected the hill before returning. Therefore, another patrol must go out this afternoon to find bodies and bring back identification," Barber noted with some disgust.

"So-o-o, at 1300, off we went on another patrol, Capt. Keifer leading this one. Battalion had called for aircraft which preceded us down the road to the place where we had been this morning."

Wilkerson and Barber climbed the mountain, "puffing and blowing since we weren't in such good hiking shape as these Infantrymen." Barber had on a sweater, B-15 jacket, and a field jacket, and "began sweating. All that, plus camera (I was resolved to get some good combat pictures) and field glasses, carbine and .45 made up my load!" he noted.

They found nothing on the hill. Meanwhile, the CAS aircraft "had been circling overhead and had only about 15 minutes of gasoline and departed." The patrol continued along the road to the Fusen Reservoir. Captain Keifer told Barber "to lead the patrol to the place where the planes had

North Korean refugees uprooted by the heavy fighting in the bitter cold of the North Korean winter. (Barber)

strafed the enemy that morning. We found nothing but dug up ground and evidence of rocket blasts. Apparently, if any were killed, the Communists dragged them away. They usually do evacuate their dead if at all possible."

Finally, Capt. Keifer said, "They must have taken off. We might as well go back."

Barber's opinion was "let's look a little further. The Air Force strafed a little further up, too, I believe."

So, the patrol continued past a gold mine operation and started up a mountain road. Suddenly "as shots rang out we piled from our jeep to the sides of the road." Barber lay in a ditch firing his carbine, while Chandler got behind a wheel, firing his weapon. Capt. Keifer was "in the ditch behind us. Bullets sung overhead and whisked through the bushes behind us. It all seemed to be rifle fire," Barber noted.

The patrol hurried to get the jeep turned around and "sat there, bullets whizzing by, while Capt. Keifer calmly stood right out in the open examining the enemy through his glasses. We couldn't spot them so off we went back to a group of houses, where Capt. Keifer spotted several moving in the road through his glasses. He set his Springfield 1903 [rifle] for 1,500 yards and let loose a couple of rounds. They started running. We then headed back for the Command Post," Barber concluded.

"The planes left us five minutes prior to the ambush. They had no more fuel and could stay no longer. I sure can't see why Regiment couldn't have sent those planes an hour later, after we had inspected the hill. Then we could have had them when we needed them and really worked those birds over. As it was, they needlessly circled overhead while we checked that hill, probably plenty P.O.-ed at being wasted that way."

On the way back to Regimental Headquarters the jeeps had major problems getting back over two fords negotiated earlier in the day. "It was freezing cold and the road up from each side of the streams was a solid sheet of ice." Finally, one jeep got up the hills "and pulled the rest over."

Despite Barber's frustration, Major Mason "was quite pleased with the air support.

Attacking up the hill. *Elements of the 1st Battalion, 31st Infantry move up a snowy hill on the attack the morning of 26 November 1950. (Barber)*

Everything seems to be fine and we feel great after all that danger and action, and the good showing which the planes and the TACP made today," Barber noted.

A new change in plans was announced when Barber arrived with the patrol "just after dark." "Instead of moving to Pukchong, Hamhung, and Chosen Reservoir tomorrow, we are going out on another patrol to see how much stuff the Communists really have."

Those "plans" too, were changed. The aircraft had "scared the enemy away and they want definitely to locate them tomorrow. Ah well," Barber sighed, "tomorrow we rest!" After writing his wife a "long letter," he got a good night's sleep.

CAS...Too Late

"How wrong I was when I thought today would be a day of rest!!!" Barber noted on Monday, 27 November 1950. A jeep patrol went back down the road they had been on the day before, then "came hurrying back to report that the patrol had been pinned down a little closer to us than we were shot at yesterday afternoon." The enemy had returned and had moved closer to the American positions.

The Regimental XO arrived at Battalion Headquarters and joined Major Mason to prepare "a task force to go out and hit the enemy. Just as we were leaving, the planes report overhead. (Why can't they send 'em

Signal to move forward. *Captain Keifer signals his men of the 1st Bn, 31st Inf. to move forward on the attack. The men were under fire as this photograph was taken on 26 November 1950. (Barber)*

Body still warm. *A recently killed Chinese Infantryman lies where he fell. The American TACP noted that the body was "still warm." (Barber)*

to us after we get where we're going?!!)," Barber noted with great exasperation. He and his men were sent "ahead to contact the patrol and try to give them air support before the planes ran out of gas."

Arriving at the spot where the patrol had located the enemy, Barber "asked the planes to recce the road ahead and try to spot the patrol. This they did, reporting that the patrol was moving west toward Fusen Reservoir and was apparently in no trouble."

The CAS aircraft then left to fulfill other mission requirements. Barber asked them to "check back with us on their way home."

After meeting the patrol, they learned that it had "run into some gun runners with an ox cart—shooting one and capturing the other—and destroying the weapons and ox cart."

While Mosley took "Jealous Jackie" [the TACP jeep] up the hill to pick up Major Mason and escort the reinforced platoon, Barber took the other jeep and headed for the village. "Shots rang out from some woods

on our right and we answered their fire. About that time "Lovelace 41" reported back, saying that "Lace 65" would report to us in a few minutes." Wilkerson and Barber took the MAW mobile radio up into a gully atop the hill "where the bullets were singing all around us." The gully offered more cover. Barber snapped a picture of Capt. Keifer directing fire from the hilltop.

Barber then contacted "Lace 65" and "directed the planes on various haystacks to which we had seen the enemy run. We could see the enemy retreating across a valley and up a long ridge-like hill. Our location was just east of a tiny village (about 8 houses), one mile N.E. of the large village of Wonpung-ni and five miles S.E. of Fusen Reservoir."

It was so cold that Barber's hand nearly froze when he had to take his glove off to direct the air attacks.

As the Infantry moved out to attack the village, Barber "drove forward along with the scattered line of Infantry. Just as the Infantry was about to enter the small town, I told the planes to strafe it, going away from the troops. This they did, with Major Mason not over 150 yards away. It was a great show."

Two bodies were tied to the hood of the jeep to "carry back to where intelligence could examine them."

After returning to the village, they waited on the other platoon "which was still attacking and hadn't been given the word to withdraw. "Chandler told how he got his Gook. He was in the very front with Capt. Keifer when he saw the Gook lying in this road cut slowly raise up and slide his rifle forward from under him. When Chandler saw that he shot him in the shoulder with his carbine. The Communist jumped up about a foot and Chandler got him in the head with his .45. I believe the Gook must have been wounded by the planes or he would have run away. Well, Chandler had been wanting to get himself a Gook—now he had one. I don't envy him, even though I believe I could shoot one with no compunction. In my 36 missions I have probably killed many of them, but I have never seen any of them. I do not believe it is true—all the old sto-

Death by a haystack. *A mortally wounded Chinese Infantryman lies beside a burning haystack on the morning of 27 November 1950. "A little farther, just behind a burning haystack lay another man. He had apparently been hit by the planes strafing for his left foot was completely mangled, hanging by a thread at his ankle. A few feet away lay a heavy wool overcoat and carbine, which I appropriated. It turned out to be a German Mauser. The soldier was not yet dead. His chest heaved in a sudden jerky fashion as he struggled for air, bubbles of red blood forming on his lips and nostrils. I thought of putting a bullet through his head, as a gesture of mercy, but couldn't do it. I believe he was unconscious. Mosley returned and the Infantry was on its way back. I told Captain Keifer that the man was still alive. He got an interpreter to try to talk to him, but just then he died, his mouth opening with its blood-covered teeth in a ghastly grin, and his eyes slowly opening wide. No interpreter needed now!" Barber noted. (Barber)*

ries you hear of the men you killed coming back in your dreams, and bothering your conscience. I believe that only applies to those who kill unjustly. Killing is no fun at all, but when a man's trying to kill you or destroy your freedom, it seems right that you must kill in self-defense, yet kill is never really right. It's hard to explain."

A New War

"Living here with the medics," Barber noted on Tuesday, 28 November 1950, "we see all kinds of operations and ugly sights. Lots of frozen feet come in, their toes black and swollen with big blisters on the skin. One Korean came in with an ugly, infected gunshot wound in his stomach—a wound four months old. Tonight they brought in a ROK who had been accidentally shot through both legs just below his hips by one of his buddies while on patrol. His left leg bone was shattered (M-1 rifle) making that leg twice its normal size while the right leg was a clean flesh wound. That M-1 is a powerful weapon."

That night Barber heard that General MacArthur had said "We are now fighting a new war!" The Chinese Communists "are pressing hard in the west and on the other elements of the 7th Division or rather the 31st Infantry," Barber noted, "who are south of Chosin Reservoir. What terrible, discouraging news! It is hard to say just what we should do. What a strange reaction to this war! What can China possibly gain but the misery and agony of war? How can the Communists so delude those people that they would stand up against all the United Nations and fight them when they have been in no way provoked? How can they help but realize that we intend no aggression against them? How can they tell us that we are aggressors when we, along with the other United Nations are merely trying to keep the aggressor, North Korea, from destroying a free nation, South Korea, at their request? Had the North Koreans merely quit fighting and agreed to remain behind the 38th Parallel, the U.N. forces would never have crossed it. It sure beats me. Well, if they want war, they'll surely get it! I can't see bribing a nation to get them to lay off us. I just wish the evil minds in Moscow who wished this on a bunch of poor, misunderstanding people could receive their just desserts."

Barber, Lt. Col. Kenneth. Korean War Diary Number One (unpublished), 1950.

Bodies on the hood. *The bodies of several CCF troops lie on the hood of the TACP radio jeep on 27 November 1950 "at the very front lines." The vehicle was enroute from the "very front lines" back to Intelligence where they would be inspected. Chandler sits on the top, Capt. Keifer stands in front and Mosley at the rear. "We were still being shot at," Barber noted on the photographs. "My jeep alone crossed the river." (Barber)*

December 1950
Evacuating East Pyongyang...Retreating From North Korea

Last Flight From Pyongyang Airfield. *The last flight of North American F-51 Mustang fighters to use this airstrip at Pyongyang, North Korea, began their takeoff roll on December 4, 1950 as onrushing hordes of Communist troops force evacuation. Loaded with rockets and .50-caliber ammunition, the fighters continued to pound the enemy and enabled UN forces to withdraw to new defensive positions. (NARA)*

General Withdrawal

Once UN forces encountered Chinese Communist Forces (CCF) in force, they began to withdraw "to a tentative line of resistance north of P'yongyang." The line didn't hold for long.

Interrogation of Prisoners of War (POWs) established "that many units of Chinese Communist Forces had been com-

mitted to battle and that an entirely 'new war' confronted United Nations Forces." Estimates of enemy strength varied wildly, from 60,000 to 1.5 million troops. In addition to Chinese Communist troops, the North Korean army had grown to "an estimated eleven divisions." [1]

"A successful breakthrough in the Kunu-ri sector of central Korea made the positions of United National Ground Force elements in the North and Northwest as well as the eastern

coast of Korea untenable." A general withdrawal was implemented below P'yongyang "to a point approximately 30 miles north of Seoul extending laterally from the Haeju-Kaesong area to the Hwach'on reservoir area to the eastern coast of Korea in the vicinity of Chosanni..." The new line of defense "remained fairly static ostensibly due to the enemy's regrouping and consolidation of

Monthly Summary

To avoid being overrun by overwhelming numbers of CCF troops, the U.S. Eighth Army withdrew from western North Korea. Far East Air Forces played a critical role in this withdrawal by conducting a "reverse airlift" that allowed U.S. forces to take out most of their equipment and supplies. Food and ammunition was airlifted to encircled elements of the X Corps and their sick and wounded troops were evacuated. The X Corps' units concentrated at Hungnam, to enable UN forces to leave eastern North

Korea by sea. By the end of December, the UN line had fallen back to near the 38th parallel, and most of North Korea was back in communist hands.

Three USAF fighter groups deployed to North Korea withdrew to South Korea, reducing Fifth Air Force's ability to provide air support for US forces. However, effective Fifth Air Force attacks on Chinese Communist Forces forced them to avoid daytime movements. Far East Air Forces developed a new interdiction plan that divided North Korea into ten zones.

The zones made target destruction more systematic and allowed Far East Air Forces and U.S. Navy aviation to better coordinate their missions. F-86s and F-84s flew combat sorties into North Korea to challenge communist MiG-15s flying from Manchurian sanctuaries.

Endnote

Adapted in part from USAFHRA. January 2002. The U.S. Air Force's First War: Korea 1950-1953 Significant Events. December 1950.

territory and the establishment of line of supply and communications." Probing by CCF patrols "continued undiminished," the 18th Wing reported. [2]

Evacuating East Pyongyang

"During the last few days of November 1950, the enemy forces advanced rapidly southward down the Korean Peninsula and as a result, the 18th Fighter-Bomber Wing was forced to evacuate from K-24 Airstrip at East Pyongyang to K-13 Airstrip near Suwon, Korea. Evacuation was completed on December 4th by airlift, motor vehicle convoy and LST from Kyomipo Port. The Communist drive continued at a rapid pace necessitating a second evacuation during the month of December from K-13 to K-10, Chinhae Airstrip. Gradual movement of the 18th Fighter-Bomber Wing in small increments was carried out during December and by the end of the month only a skeleton force was in operation at K-13, with the mission of refueling and rearming organization aircraft." [3]

On December 1st, the 18th Fighter-Bomber Wing and its 189 officers and 1,360 airmen began their move from K-24 to K-13. "The movement to K-13 AB was engendered by the enemy's ground operations which jeopardized the continued effective sorties of this unit," S/Sgt Sandy Colton recorded. Nearly 100 tons of tentage, hand baggage, personal luggage and personnel were airlifted out of the airstrip that was now nearly surrounded by the enemy. A rear echelon of the 6002nd Wing had been left until the last plane had ceased operations. The mess hall, base supply, and control tower were left burning when the last aircraft tucked up its wheels at 1600 hours, December 3, 1950, Colton noted. "The last aircraft of personnel and equipment departed when the enemy was within three miles of the base," the 18th FBW unit history later recorded.

Evacuation of Pyongyang East was completed on December 4th by airlift, motor vehicle convoy and LST from Kyomipo Port.

The field was taken by the Communists on 4 December. Aiding in the evacuation were two truck convoys and one train, even though they were constantly harassed by guerrillas. Stalled vehicles were destroyed to deny their use to the enemy. [4]

Withdrawal To Suwon

"The 18th Fighter-Bomber Wing strategically withdrew to an abandoned airfield further south in Suwon [5]," remembered former Airman First Class Joe Roiz. At the time Roiz was an Armament Technician in the 18th Supply Squadron. He performed the "unglamorous job of helping to mix up 100 octane gasoline with a rubber compound to make napalm, which we pumped into 500-lb bomb shells, to be hung under the F-51's wings. I also unpacked and prepared and armed the white phosphorus fuses that ignited the napalm bomb when it hit the target. Other chores included hanging and arming rockets and loading fifty-

Got out of Pyongyang OK. Pyongyang West had already been evacuated when we left. It had been bombed and shelled for four nights. I watched the boys work night and day for three days. That's rough. I was with them so I know. Tearing down tents, packing things, loading airplanes, standing guard, burning and destroying records and equipment night and day. There was no perimeter of ground troops around us. They had already pulled back through us. In the end only a few men were left when night fell and the planes couldn't get in to land. It was a happy group of guys at sunrise when our C-46 landed to pick up those few while, as they left, a gigantic fire burned at the fuel and ordinance dump. A flight of 51s flew protection overhead. The North Koreans or Chinese could have easily taken the base that night but, fortunately, they didn't and we got all our men out safely.

I'm in a place called Suwon now...No mail since Sept. 20. They burned a big bunch of it at Pyongyang. Everything is fouled up here!
S/Sgt William J. "Sandy" Colton diary entry

caliber machine gun ammo into the wings. [6]

The runway at Suwon was a "concrete strip approximately 5,500 feet in length and 150 feet wide." A good portion of the field did not have landing lights, a "hazard to pilots taking off on early morning missions and/or returning from reconnaissance flights after darkness." Barrels of gasoline were "ignited at each end of the runway to make some light as well as affording beacon lights after a fashion."

New taxiways had to be constructed at both ends of the runway. "Numerous rice sacks were utilized to provide a base for steel (pierced planking) mats as they were laid down." Using rice sacking also "prevented excessive dust and mud from coming up through the planking as aircraft taxied to the parking area."

Conditions in Suwon

The living conditions at Suwon were as bad as those at P'yongyang. There were "no provisions made for the erection of tents in the assigned squadrons areas. The location selected was humped and furrowed, an old rice paddy which was alternatively very muddy and/or frozen according to the weather. There were no showers. There were no sanitary facilities whatever. The tentage utilized was not winterized. Installation of M-41 stoves in all tents was a necessity. This however resulted in thawing out the ground in the tents—mud was the end result. During this period officers and airmen alike resorted to the utilization of rice bags as tent or floor mats to alleviate this condition....There was no mess hall proper and food was eaten from any convenient ledge, shelf, jeep hood and/or 55-gallon fuel drums which were in the mess hall area in the open." [7]

"Conditions in Suwon were war torn," Roiz continued. "Three or four Russian T-34 tanks that had been put out of action by our own planes littered the area. Suwon was more of a village than a town. The rice paddies that surrounded the airfield survived and the few farmers that lived in the area continued to cultivate them. They used 'honey pots' for their fertilizer (honey pots are buckets filled with human dung), an efficient, if malodorous, way of handling the local sewage and at the same time providing nutrient for the rice paddies."

"Again we were forced to live in a place that we had essentially destroyed earlier in the war. The Army Corps of Engineers quickly repaired the damaged airstrip and leveled an area where we could assemble our eight man tents into a squadron village. I don't remember seeing a permanent building on the whole site except for the ammunition bunkers. These were bunkers of concrete and were semi-buried in the ground, covered over with dirt so as to not be readily visible from the air. They were like large tunnels with an entrance at one end and an exit at the other. We stored bombs, rockets, ammunition, and aviation fuel in these bunkers. Our tents were about two hundred yards away. It occurred to me that we were in that military classification known as 'expendables'."

One of the diversions that we invented was to play poker for money. We played everyday until we lost all our money. The money we used was military script. It didn't seem like real money and therefore I didn't mind losing so much because it was after all only script. I learned the hard way about the purchasing power of script after a while. An eighteen-year-old kid from Michigan was a real sharp at the game. We called him Hap because he was always smiling even when he had a terrible poker hand. He would often win the pot by sheer bluffing. Each month he sent home a sizable bunch of money."

"We were so desperate for entertainment that the guys actually asked me to sing for them, *a capella*. The only songs I could remember were *'I'm Going To buy A Paper Doll'* and *'Gloria'*. I sang them over and over. The guys really seemed to enjoy my singing. It was my first time to perform before an audience, four or five guys. One day we decided to hunt up a meal. We were tired of the rations we had been eating. We shot a large bird that was flying over the rice paddies. None of us had any experience in preparing food but somebody

*Capt. Mario di Silvestro, often the wingman for **Lt. Ed Mason**. Silvestro led both two-plane "elements" and four-plane "flights."*

Heading off on a napalm mission in late 1950, Capt. Ed Mason snapped a picture of his wingman, Capt. Mario di Silvestro on the way to the target, and (below), returning without the napalm tanks. (Mason)

162

thought it would be good to boil it. After cleaning the bird it looked much smaller. After boiling for about twenty minutes it turned dark, kind of a blue black. No one was brave enough to eat it."

"Again the North Korean Army was advancing south and we got word that we were to evacuate and to destroy everything, all the fuel and ammunition and equipment that we didn't have time to take with us. A handful of us were assigned to be the 'rear guard', the last to leave. As we were driving in a six or eight vehicle convoy south down the mountainous road we could see the flash and hear the bomb-dump explosions that we had set. I was riding shotgun in a four by four truck. It was dusk and visibility wasn't too good. Hap was driving the truck, driving like he never drove before. His eyes were big and fixed on the road. It was one of the few times that Hap was not smiling. We were really moving on. It was getting dark and visibility was not good. There were no white lines defining the pot-holed road. I wished that I had been one of those chosen to evacuate earlier by plane. We heard sporadic gunfire coming from higher up in the hills. Snipers were taking pot shots at us. The headlights on our vehicles made easy targets. Don't know who they were or how they got there but one thing we did know, they were not on our side. I was on the verge of losing control of my bowels. My mind was numb with anxiety and the knowledge that I personally could not do anything. The M-1 rifle and the forty-five-caliber pistol I had with me were useless in this situation. All I could do was hope that we made it to Pusan," Ruiz recalled.

18th Wing Operations

In early December, the Wing quickly established liaison with the 187th Airborne Division G-2 (Intelligence) at Suwon and made arrangements for quick telephone communications with that division "for aid in case an emergency security problem should arise at K-13 airstrip." The area around K-13 was hardly "secure."

The Fifth Air Force Situation Report was provided to the A-2 (Intelligence) section

via courier plane at the same time the Frag [Fragmentation] Order (list of assigned targets) was sent to the A-3 (Operations) section. All intelligence information was obtained from GLO "attached to the 18th Fighter-Bomber Wing."

A detailed map was "set up and posted with all overlay Recce Routes" sent to A-3 by Fifth Air Force.

More "routine" duties were also carried out, including "posting of bomblines, friendly and enemy ground and air information, of informing Group Interrogation Center of all current developments in the daily situation and passing on to lower echelons available intelligence material."

Maps were a major problem-specifically, obtaining "sorely needed maps of our fighter operation areas in Korea....A serious shortage of necessary maps of Korea was felt acutely by this organization. Much effort was expended to obtain these, such as repeated calls to 5th Air Force A-2 and A-4, calls to Itazuke, Tachikawa, Tokyo and Nagoya." [8]

Suwon to Chinhae

The Wing's assessment of the move to Suwon being "temporary," was accurate.

By December 10th the Wing was organizing "another move" from Suwon to Chinhae (K-10). The move to Chinhae, near Masan, SK began on December 11th. This move was not completed during the month in its entirety inasmuch as a small detachment remained at Suwon for the purpose of refueling and rearming staging aircraft."

The Communist drive continued at a rapid pace necessitating a second evacuation during the month of December from K-13 to K-10, Chinhae Airstrip. Squadrons were alerted to the move on December 16th. The decision to move to K-10 was not only due to the "deteriorating ground tactical situation," but because practically no facilities existed at K-13 "for the major repair and maintenance of assigned combat aircraft as well as the lack of shelter for squadron maintenance, armament, etc." [9]

Gradual movement of the 18th Fighter-Bomber Wing in small increments was carried out during December and by the end

of the month only a skeleton force was in operation at K-13, with the mission of refuelling and rearming organizational aircraft." [10]

The final phase of the move to K-10 was completed on January 5, 1951.

The move to K-10 was "regarded as highly desirable in view of its physical establishment with permanent type hangars, Quonset shelters, power and water systems, etc." The "drawback" was the "terrain was considered almost prohibitive" for flying heavily loaded F-51 aircraft on take-offs and landings during night and/or instrument conditions." [11]

"By using refueling and rearmament facilities and staging from the rear bases, both moves were completed with a minimum loss in the number of sorties flown. [12]

Humanitarian Services Continue

Incredibly, despite all the turmoil of three moves in a month from Pusan to Pyongyang to Suwon to Mason, in a day or so, the Wing reported that "contacts with the local civilian population have been gratifying. Clothes sent to Chaplain Shelton from the U.S. were given to a local Minister's family." The Wing's Medical Group "gave a large amount of clothes, food, and treats to the Chinhae Orphanage, under the direction of Reverend Lee. The N.C.O. Club also contributed candy to the orphanage to help make their Christmas and New Year Season a little brighter." Many of the Wing's "Protestant Personnel" went into Chinhae on Christmas Eve "and sang Christmas carols at several places" including the Chinhae Orphanage, the local Police Station, the Chinhae Presbyterian Church "as well as at the quarters of the Commandant of the Korean Navy." The Wing's Catholic Chaplain Westhoff "distributed clothes and food, contributed by men in this Wing, to the Catholic parishes in both Suwon and Chinhae, Korea." [13]

Using great ingenuity and organizational prowess, the Wing and the Group did their best to provide the support and information needed by the squadron Mustang combat pilots that continued to fly demanding missions regardless of the frequent moves made during that chaotic period. The Wing Staff's list of noteworthy actions during the December "bug outs," provides important insights into the variety of support services it provided the squadrons throughout the Korean War.

Flying Cheetahs

Operational

During December, the 2 Squadron of the South African Air Force (SAAF), became fully operational. The 18th FBW assumed operational control of the "Flying Cheetahs," although it was described, diplomatically as "continued to serve as advisory and liaison to the 2nd Squadron…and the 18th Fighter-Bomber Group." The Group completed 1,486 sorties during December 1950, providing "close support, special interdiction, armed reconnaissance, airfield strikes, and escort missions as directed by Fifth Air Force." [14] The basic mission of the squadrons remained unchanged, however "pilots engaged in a variety of missions which embraced escort at high altitudes (15,000 and 25,000) for RB-29 type aircraft, armed reconnaissance, visual reconnaissance, CAP for downed pilots, as well as close support missions." [15]

"A South African Squadron of F-51s shared the air field with us. You could always identify their F-51s, not only for the South African insignia on the fuselage and the wings but because their planes were always super clean and polished so that they glistened in the sunlight. Ours were not as bright." Roiz recalled. "The South Afrikaners looked and talked like Englishmen. They were fluent in English and Afrikan. They loved their beer and they drank it warm. They were a hard working bunch and a very effective fighting force," Roiz noted.

Crew Chiefs from the 67th Squadron huddle around a fire to thaw out numb fingers in December 1950 in "Suwon before the snow," recorded Major Bill Myers. (Myers)

Combat Operations

When the F-51's were escorting the B-29's, they were at the limit of their operational ceiling. "At this altitude the performance of the F-51 is definitely limited while jet aircraft are near their peak performance above 20,000 feet." When they were attacked by enemy jets, the "primary tactic" employed by the Mustang pilots "was to attempt to make head-on passes with the enemy aircraft. This maneuver offered limited protection for our fighters and no protection for the RB-29." [16]

The MIG-15's usually tried "to dive out of the sun, make a pass and climb back toward the sun."

Pilots were concerned that "evasion information was still inadequate and speculation continued as to the treatment that would be received in Manchuria if a pilot was forced to bail out in that area." [17]

Flak intensity remained fairly constant "with an increase in ground fire (small arms), however many points occupied by the enemy were equipped with anti-aircraft guns, usually of the 20-mm or 40-mm calibers."

Two-, four-, and eight-aircraft flights were used during December combat operations. Most of the flights consisted of four aircraft, two of which furnished "top cover" during armed reconnaissance flights and during strafing passes against enemy personnel, material and rolling stock. The interdiction tactics of 18th Mustangs "as well as that of other aircraft and organizations engaged in combat resulted in a paucity of ground targets such as vehicles, tanks, etc. The enemy resorted to heavy camouflage and night operations to preserve equipment and mobility." [18]

The enemy "continued to use camouflage as a principal means of hiding supplies and vehicles from air attacks. Their pattern remained the same and they continued to use dry creek beds, secondary roads and mountain passes." Haystacks and houses were also "a source of enemy subterfuge in hiding equipment. In areas of heavy snow fall the enemy began to cover vehicles and supplies with white tarpaulins." [19]

No matter, the Mustangs continued to inflict significant damage on vehicles, troops and supplies. In December, the 12th Squadron attacked vehicles (80 destroyed), houses (244 destroyed), buildings (318 destroyed), villages (13 destroyed, 31 damaged), troops (649 killed), field pieces (12

destroyed, 15 damaged), railroad rolling stock (two locomotives destroyed, plus 20 cars damaged), bridges (2 destroyed), supply dumps (65 destroyed), and trucks (63 destroyed). It took 353,330 rounds of .50-caliber ammunition, 1,841 rockets, 827 napalm bombs, and 74 fragmentation bombs to do the job. [20]

While based at Suwon, the pilots "had no problem reaching the bomb line, finding targets and returning with sufficient fuel…Approximately half the missions flown were armed reconnaissance missions deep into enemy territory." [21]

Several flights encountered enemy jet fighters (MIG-15) near the Manchurian border and sustained no losses. "Flight leaders and wingmen used excellent planning and judgment in warding off the attack and getting into position to attack the enemy aircraft when contact was broken off by the enemy. [22]

The Mustang pilots knew the roads the CCF were using to truck supplies to their troops, even without seeing the vehicles—it was winter and the heavily used roads "were clear of snow." However, "vehicles concealed in draws, ravines, under bridges, etc. along the main lines of communication" were "exceedingly difficult to spot and to destroy."

Somehow the 18th had kept its planes in the air providing crucial air support for the advancing—then retreating—UN forces, despite crushing shortages of almost everything. Lack of available transportation was the "prime factor." It was "difficult to transport personnel, supplies and equipment to and from as well as within the theatre of operations." There were acute shortages of "petroleum oils and lubricants, aviation ammunition, items of supply and other equipment to the point where it has been necessary in certain cases to transport these items of supply by means of motor vehicles often times over long and difficult road routes." Road transportation was not the answer, however, since there were "shortages of vehicular equipment and spare parts." Lack of sufficient numbers "of cargo type aircraft and ships have allowed stock levels of many supply items to become critically low and have causes shortages upon occasion." [23]

The "extreme cold weather" was another factor that "greatly affected normal maintenance operations." The ground crews and pilots virtually lived outdoors. In addition to the "usual personnel and material problems" associated with the cold climate, "a lack of sufficient aircraft engine heaters" further made "the already difficult job of cold weather aircraft engine starts" an ordeal.

Stratemeyer Praise

On December 16th, Lt. Gen. George Stratemeyer, Commanding General of FEAF issued a Letter of Commendation to his major component organizations, including FAF. "Our new foe," he noted, "has, since 25 November, deployed seven Corps against United Nations forces in Korea, has sacrificed one-seventh of this battle-wide, frontline fighting strength to the incessant air strikes of the U.S. Far East Air Forces, the Royal Australian Air Forces, the South African Air Force, the Republic of Korea Air Force and land based elements of U.S. Marine aviation." Approximately 33,000 enemy troops, "the equivalent of four of his full-strength divisions, are now dead or wounded, the result of coordinated strafing, rocketing, bombing and napalming by our combined air power." Stratemeyer summarized the efforts to resupply and withdraw UN troops using air cargo assets and the contributions of bomber command and material commands. "To you as airmen goes my sincere and heartfelt commendation for meeting the challenge in a superior manner. Your accomplishments during this trying period are in keeping with the finest traditions of our respective services."

Endnotes

[1] *USAFHRA. History of the 18th Fighter-Bomber Wing, December 1950.*

[2] *USAFHRA. History of the 18th Fighter-Bomber Wing, December 1950.*

[3] *USAFHRA. History of the 18th Fighter-Bomber Wing, December 1950.*

[4] *USAFHRA. "The Story of the 18th Fighter-Bomber Group in the Korean United Nations Police Action." 6002 nd Tactical Support Wing, Public Information Office. S/Sgt Sandy Colton.*

[5] *Roiz, Joseph. Memoirs. Unpublished manuscript.*

[6] *Roiz, Joseph. Memoirs. Unpublished manuscript.*

[7] *USAFHRA. History of the 18th Fighter-Bomber*

100 Mission Send Off. *Capt. Ed Mason (right) "sees off" Lt. George N. Olsen, "a fine officer and pilot" after Olsen completed his 100ᵗʰ mission. "As a Forward Air Controller he was recommended by the Commander 9ᵗʰ Infantry Regiment for the Distinguished Service Cross [America's second highest decoration]. It was not awarded," Mason noted. "Lost in the shuffle during our disastrous retreat of November 1950." When Mason joined the 18ᵗʰ, it was based at K-9, near Pusan. After an absence of two months while he served as a Forward Air Controller (FAC) and then recovered from wounds in a hospital and aboard a hospital ship, Mason rejoined the Group at K-10/Chinhae. (Mason)*

Wing, December 1950.

⁸ USAFHRA. *History of the 18ᵗʰ Fighter-Bomber Wing, December 1950.*

⁹ USAFHRA. *History of the 67ᵗʰ Fighter-Bomber Squadron, December 1950.*

¹⁰ USAFHRA. *History of the 18ᵗʰ Fighter-Bomber Wing, December 1950.*

¹¹ USAFHRA. *History of the 67ᵗʰ Fighter-Bomber Squadron, December 1950.*

¹² USAFHRA. *History of the 18ᵗʰ Fighter-Bomber Wing, December 1950.*

¹³ USAFHRA. *History of the 18ᵗʰ Fighter-Bomber Wing, December 1950.*

¹⁴ USAFHRA. *History of the 18ᵗʰ Fighter-Bomber Wing, December 1950.*

¹⁵ USAFHRA. *History of the 67ᵗʰ Fighter-Bomber Squadron, December 1950.*

¹⁶ USAFHRA. *History of the 12ᵗʰ Fighter-Bomber Squadron, December 1950.*

¹⁷ USAFHRA. *History of the 12ᵗʰ Fighter-Bomber Squadron, December 1950.*

¹⁸ USAFHRA. *History of the 67ᵗʰ Fighter-Bomber Squadron, December 1950.*

¹⁹ USAFHRA. *History of the 12ᵗʰ Fighter-Bomber Squadron, December 1950.*

²⁰ USAFHRA. *History of the 12ᵗʰ Fighter-Bomber Squadron, December 1950.*

²¹ USAFHRA. *History of the 12ᵗʰ Fighter-Bomber Squadron, December 1950.*

²² USAFHRA. *History of the 12ᵗʰ Fighter-Bomber Squadron, December 1950.*

²³ USAFHRA. *History of the 18ᵗʰ Fighter-Bomber Wing, December 1950.*

"Hi Sweet," Sgt. Charles Maynard wrote to his wife, Neva. "I have already sent you one Xmas card, but here's one from our outfit." (Maynard) [The Maynard's were married in 1948 and celebrated their 55ᵗʰ wedding anniversary in June 2003. "We still love each other," they noted in their notes for this publication.]

December Significant Dates [1]

December 1: The USS *Cape Esperance* arrived in Japan with F-86 fighters. Fifth Air Force headquarters moved from Nagoya, Japan, to Seoul, South Korea.

December 3: U.S. troops from the Changjin Reservoir area fought their way to Hagaru-ri, while a relief column from Hungnam fought its way toward them, reaching Koto-ri, about seven miles away. Communist troops prevented the two groups from linking and encircled them both, forcing them to rely on airlift for resupply. [2]

On this Sunday, the 18th Fighter-Bomber Wing Chaplain was "getting set up for services" following the move to K-13. There had been little time to properly prepare for Sunday services, but a "squad tent was pitched, heat provided, a make-shift altar arranged, and services held on a normal schedule that day. There were no seats available, as no .50-caliber boxes were available as yet." There would soon be "seats" aplenty.

December 5: UN forces abandoned Pyongyang, the North Korean capital, which they had held since October 19. Greek C-47s joined the FEAF Combat Cargo Command airlift to supply UN troops surrounded in northeastern Korea. The command evacuated 3,925 patients from Korea to Japan in the biggest day of the war for aeromedical airlift. Transports flew most of these from a frozen airstrip at Hagaru-ri. The U.S. Air Force suspended attacks on the Yalu River bridges, because enemy forces were crossing the frozen river on the ice.

December 7: B-29s bombed North Korean towns in the Changjin Reservoir area

Captain Bill Myers joins his Crew Chief next to his Mustang at K-13/Suwan in December 1950. The strange symbol on the side of the aircraft, Myers explained "was my grandfather's cow brand...now mine." (Myers)

to relieve enemy pressure on U.S. Marine and Army units attempting to break out from Hagaru-Ri and Koto-Ri. Troops in those two locations finally linked and built crude airstrips that allowed FEAF Combat Cargo Command airplanes to land food and ammunition and to evacuate casualties.

Col. Curtis R. Low, Commander of the 18th Fighter-Bomber Wing expressed his "very great appreciation to each officer and Airman of this Wing for the superhuman efforts put out by you during the period of our move from K-9 to K-24 and back to K-13. All of you have worked long hours above the normal call of duty. By your efforts we were able to continue heavy fighter operations against the enemy. During our evacuation of K-24 very little property of any value was lost to the enemy. Without the

extra drive that each of you exerted we would surely have lost much equipment which would hamper our operations in the future."

December 10: A two-week FEAF Combat Cargo Command airlift for surrounded U.S. troops in northeastern Korea concluded after delivering 1,580 tons of supplies and equipment and moving almost 5,000 sick and wounded troops.

December 15: The 4 FIG inaugurated F-86 Sabrejet operations in Korea. The Eighth U.S. Army withdrew below the 38th parallel.

1st Lt. Charles R. Morehouse started his takeoff run from Suwon after obtaining clearance from the tower. Just after lifting off, his aircraft struck a C-47 that was taxiing on the active runway, causing major

Grounded. *On 3 December 1950 these Marine Corps Corsairs were grounded by heavy snow. They were desperately needed by the Marines at the Chosin Reservoir. (Barber)*

Lt. Ken Barber prepares to take off on a mission from K-13 in December 1950. (Burns)

damage to both aircraft. "A successful pattern and landing was made by Lt. Morehouse."

December 16: Captain Joe V. Lane was strafing a target near P'yongyang when it blew up, causing major damage to his aircraft. The wings and control surfaces "had gaping holes blown in them and serious internal damage to oil lines, hydraulic lines, etc. resulted. The aircraft was successfully returned to base."

December 17: Lt. Col. Bruce H. Hinton, USAF, 4th FIG, scored the first F-86 aerial victory over a MiG-15 on the first day Sabres encountered communist jets. FEAF Combat Cargo Command abandoned Yonpo Airfield to communist forces.

December 22: One USN and five USAF pilots shot down six MiG-15s, the highest daily FEAF aerial victory credit total for the month, and the highest since June. A MiG-15 shot down an F-86 for the first time. Headquarters Fifth Air Force, Eighth U.S. Army in Korea headquarters, and the Joint Operations Center moved from Seoul to Taegu.

December 23: Three H-5 helicopter crews with fighter cover rescued eleven U.S. and twenty-four ROK soldiers from a field eight miles behind enemy lines. General Walton Walker, Commander, Eighth U.S. Army, died in a vehicle accident north of Seoul.

December 24: X Corps completed the sea evacuation of Hungnam. More than 105,000 troops and 91,000 civilians had departed since the exodus began on December 11. USAF B-26s and U.S. Navy gunfire held the enemy at bay during the night as the last ships departed.

December 25: Chinese forces crossed the 38th Parallel into South Korea.

December 26: Lt. Gen. Matthew B. Ridgway, USA, took command of the U.S. Eighth Army in Korea, as it absorbed X Corps.

December 28: A flight of four F-51's from the 67th FBS, led by Major Charles E. McGee, "engaged in a close support mission of United Nations Ground Force elements in the H'wachon Reservoir area. The effectiveness of very close support (the enemy occupied positions approximately 50 yards north of friendly troops) was heavily underscored, when approximately 125 CCF

troops surrendered following the attack by the F-51's." On the same day, a two-aircraft flight of F-51's led by Captain Herman Solem with 1st Lt. Edwin R. Henley, attacked enemy positions in much the same manner with precisely the same results. [3]

December 29: From Taegu, RF-51 aircraft began flying tactical reconnaissance missions in Korea for the first time. They had longer ranges than their RF-80 predecessors.

December 31: Chinese Communist forces in Korea launched an offensive against UN troops south of the 38th Parallel. General Ridgway ordered Eighth Army troops to a new defensive line seventy miles farther south.

Combat Losses in December

1st Lt. Harold J. Ausman, 67th Squadron.

Captain Zack W. Dean, 39th Squadron.

1st Lt. George E. Haines, 12th Squadron.

Major Kenneth Sherrill Hodges, 39th Squadron.

1st Lt. Ralph M. Olson, 39th Squadron.

1st Lt. Howard E. Smith, 12th Squadron.

1st Lt. John Shirley Starck, 12th Squadron.

Endnotes

[1] *Adapted from USAFHRA. January 2002. The U.S. Air Force's First War: Korea 1950-1953 Significant Events. October 1950.*

[2] *Adapted from USAFHRA. January 2002. The U.S. Air Force's First War: Korea 1950-1953 Significant Events. December 1950.*

[3] *USAFHRA. History of the 67th Fighter-Bomber Squadron, December 1950.*

Suwon Observations

by S/Sgt William J. "Sandy" Colton

Suwon, located about thirty miles south of Seoul, is an ancient walled city. The wall surrounding it is much like the wall in China. There are four gates leading into the city, one for each of the main points on a compass. The evidence of war around it is strong in the form of knocked out tanks, trucks and bombed out buildings. The gates themselves are very impressive. They were used as a sort of fort in the delaying action by our troops in the early part of this war.

The town is not much different from other small villages in North and South Korea. Just a group of thatched huts that look very much like something transplanted from Africa to here. It was at this place that we had one of the few chances of effectively using the A-bomb during the early part of this war. Suwon sits on a plain surrounded by mountain ranges. Very large masses of North Korean troops and equipment were spread out here then. Rumor has it that MacArthur wanted to use the bomb then but Washington said no. It might have ended things right then, if dropped. But, when you consider the consequences I think Washington was right. At least I think so.

Suwon is pretty barren. One thing I noticed that struck a bit of home in me and I think is very unusual. Trucks are parked along the main street in front of an all night eating place. It looked very much like the all night truck stop eating places you see back home. But these trucks were loaded with refugees. It was a pitiful sight to see, beat up Korean trucks loaded high with personal belongings and people sitting on top of them, moving south. Driving back from Seoul one night I passed bunches of them on the road. The richest moved in trucks. I guess they would all chip in to either buy or rent a truck, load it down and ride south. The trucks labored under their loads. I was cold in my winter clothing that night. I saw men, women and children, bundled up atop those trucks trying to keep warm.

Besides the trucks the road was jammed with ox carts and people walking.

On some of the ox carts a grandmother would sit on top of the bundle of family belongings, like an Egyptian queen, with her peculiar head dress, riding in regal splendor. Or a grandfather with his horse hair hat. The poorest carried what they owned on their backs and, heads down, trudged down the railroad tracks or roads, always south. It was the same all over Korea. Pilots came back reporting streams of them up to thirty and forty miles long on the roads leading south. It sometimes presented a problem. It is a well known trick of the North Koreans to infiltrate our lines and set up road blocks. They come through our lines dressed as refugees, pressing ahead of them men, women and children. They will put guns in the hands of men, women and children and then push them against us until we have nearly spent all our ammunition and then send in the combat troops.

In the roads, dressed in the traditional white peasant garb, they will wave their arms and shout as our pilots come down to strafe, surrounding themselves with innocent women and children. The big question is who is the peasant and who is the soldier? These guys are fighting a guerilla war, something supposedly outlawed by the Geneva Convention. How do you think you would feel if you were a pilot and knew that some of the people in those human masses waving at you on the road were really the enemy? The pilots have come back telling of uniformed North Korean troops just squatting in the road rather than running to the side for cover when they come down to strafe. Now using refugees for cover is very effective. There is a lot more to tell about this but it will have to wait until some day when I may write a book.

[Note: Colton noted that this entry "sort of took me by surprise in view of the recent hullabaloo about No Gun Ri and shooting innocent civilians. This technique was used by the NK so often it was tough to tell who was who. Sometimes the air controller would call in a strike on what appeared to be civilian refugees, and some may have been saying that they were being fired upon by such a group.]

"My ditch" at K-13 noted Allen Burns. On the way to the "chow tent," after getting his plane off on another combat mission, Burns was walking down this road. He looked up "and saw this swept-wing airplane" heading his way and flying "very low over the field." At the time, "the only swept-wing jet I knew of was a MIG-15, so I took a quick dive into that cold, slimy ditch." As the plane flew over, Burns looked up to see U.S. markings. "I cursed that pilot with everything I could think of for buzzing our field," Burns remembered. (Burns)

Effects of Napalm

Seoul, the capitol of South Korea, is pretty much bombed out too. The buildings in the main part of the city are very much like those in our town. Some are as high as five stories. Most stand as a shell with the floors and innards burned out. The windows are blackened from fire and the inside girders are twisted from the heat. At the center of town is the railroad station. On both sides of it are the yards where bombed out railroad cars sit rusting with their tops bent in. Imagine heating metal until it buckled. That's what happened to these cars when hit with napalm (jellied gas), the most horrible weapon we've used in this war, and the one the Koreans fear the most. The stuff (napalm) looks like cherry Jello with bits of tapioca mixed in it. It's actually gasoline with bits of a rubberized mixture mixed in with it so that it burns for a long time. It's carried in wing tanks and when dropped an igniter sets it off.

I've seen both it dropped and explode as well as the devastating after affects.

Just as an example of what it can do—one of our pilots said he strafed an ox cart for five minutes before he found out that the thing had already been hit by napalm and the ox, still standing, was burned to death but frozen standing up. The stuff works fast but I think this pilot was kidding me. I have seen what it can do to humans and it's not pleasant.

The capitol building in Seoul was pretty well bombed out. It had to be. The enemy was using it. One place did interest me, the Methodist church. I did a story about it and took some pictures I'll send you. Next to it was a school that had been completely destroyed by bombing and yet the church, which was only a few feet away, was undamaged except for a little scorching, some broken windows and knocked down plaster.

I'll say no more about Seoul now. I should tell you about Kimpo and Inchon too. The road to Inchon is winding and full of hills. It's littered with knocked out tanks and other evidence of a big battle. Inchon itself sits at the bottom of a hill on a bay.

Maintenance time for this Mustang at K-13 in December 1950. (Burns)

After seeing his bird off on a mission from K-13 in December 1950, Crew Chief Allen Burns could finally relax for a while until the plane and its tired pilot returned--if they returned. (Burns)

Pilots and Airmen line up in Suwon in December 1950 to wash their mess kits after chow. (Myers)

Calling In An Air Strike. Cpl. James Chandler uses the TACP radio to coordinate air operations. Chandler was operating as a member of TACP #7, Commanded by Lt. Ken Barber. The efforts of the TACP Teams were vital in helping U.N. forces retreat in good order following the intervention by Chinese Communist forces in November 1950. (Barber)

Strategic Withdrawal

On Monday, 4 December 1950, Lt. Ken Barber and his men moved to Pukchong "without incident" during a "strategic withdrawal." Disabled vehicles were left behind and destroyed. Ammunition and ration dumps were blown up "behind us as we pulled out. The day has been extremely cold." They arrived in Pukchong after dark and looked around for quarters. "One house upon whose door we knocked wouldn't open up. Upon finally finding an open door, a great weeping and wailing set up inside. We looked in to find some Korean women and children, apparently scared to death. We tried to calm them down—finally left them."

Barber received news that the CO and his replacement of the 1st Battalion, 32nd Infantry had been killed. "They saw the Chinese drag off Col. McLean's body the day he was killed. The 3rd Battalion has been cut to pieces up near Chosin Reservoir. Lt. Col. Deshon is now the 31st Regt. Commander. Capt. Robbins, Regt. (31st) S-1 was killed and the wire section almost annihilated."

On Tuesday, Barber's column resumed its slow crawl towards Hamhung. "It was a beautiful, seaside drive past coves in which were anchored small boats. Each cove had its small village. Between 1100 and 1400 it was fairly warm, the sun melting snow on the roads, turning them into mud."

Despite reports that the Chinese "were firing along the road, we met with no opposition. The convoy crept along the road past many overturned or damaged vehicles along the way. What a loss of equipment!! It was late at night when we pulled into Hamhung, a large manufacturing town, and were fed by the 2nd Battalion kitchens which had been left behind when the 2nd Bn. went to Koto-ri to relieve the pressure at the Chosin Reservoir. Heard much bad news tonight."

Snaking Out of Pukchong. A retreating U.S. truck convoy snakes along narrow, twisting, icy mountain roads as it departs Pukchong on 4 December 1950. (Barber)

Jeep convoy stops on the icy roads on 5 December 1950. Major Darden (left) Artillery Liaison Officer in the 1ˢᵗ Battalion, 31ˢᵗ Infantry and Lt. Barber. (Barber)

Planes Cutting A Path Out

On Wednesday, Barber slept in a tent for the first time in many weeks. "Kind of cold." He took Chandler with him to division headquarters to see Major Manch and try to get some radio equipment. First time I had met Major Manch. He is a very nice person, but still said there wasn't much immediate hope of our being replaced. I'll assure you that it brings me no joy to write that in my log."

Captain (Dr.) Galloway, the 31ˢᵗ Regimental medical officer "was shot in the eye and temporarily blinded." Captain Stamford, TACP with the 1ˢᵗ Marines, had his entire team with the exception of one man, wiped out. He crawled across the ice at Chosin and was captured with several others. The Chinks took a group of them into a house to warm up, but it was too crowded,

so they pushed them outside, telling them to leave. They expected to be shot but to their surprise, the Chinese just walked back into the house and shut the door. After four days of wandering around the hills, Capt. Stamford rejoined his unit at Hageru. He was out of his head—didn't even know his own name. They air evacuated him to the hospital ship Consolation. He came back

Strategically Withdrawing to Hungnam. American troops retreat south from Hambung to Hungnam Port on 10 December 1950. The troops were elements of the 1ˢᵗ Bn, 31ˢᵗ Inf. withdrawing. (Barber)

(Left) **Refugees crowd the roads** as U.N. columns move toward the safety of Hungnam and evacuation. (Barber)

(Below) **Ready for Demolition.** A bridge on the road from Hamhung to Hungnam awaits demolition by explosive charges seen here placed along the sides on right and left. (Barber)

today and apparently went back to his outfit to try and find his boys. No one knows where he is now."

"They are trying a breakout today, with planes cutting a path out. Sure hope they make it."

Hot dawg!!

Being Replaced

Overall, Barber was "pretty disgusted with the way they have treated us—not giving us any definite tour of duty, not making any apparent effort to relieve us."

"The war situation is not good," Barber noted on 9 December 1950. "Few believe that we can hold this beachhead for very long. The 2nd Battalion and 1st Marines have almost cut their way out and are on the way back to Hamhung. Fortunately, we will be supported by Navy aircraft and Naval gunfire. I guess the TACP's will see plenty of action and be among the last to board ships."

Major Callahan returned on 9 December "bringing wonderful news—we are to be replaced. Pilcher leaves in the next couple of days, Kessock second, and me third. Hot dawg!!! Maybe I'll be with Carolyn around Christmas after all. Oh, but I hope so, I miss that little gal terribly."

The next day, Sunday, 10 December, Barber reported they "pulled back from Hamhung almost to Hungnam. Rumor has it (pretty reliable) that we will board ships in order of 1st Marines, 7th Division and 3rd Division for Pusan. Sure will be good to return to Carolyn."

On 11 December, the X Corps began loading its men and equipment on ships in Hungnam Harbor. On 14 December, as Chinese forces approached, FEAF Combat Cargo Command launched an aerial evacuation from Yonpo Airfield near Hamhung. On 17 December, Combat Cargo Command abandoned Yonpo Airfield to the communist forces, having transported 228 patients, 3,891 other passengers, and over 20 tons of high priority cargo in just four days.

Fighting Chaplains

Chaplain Reynolds had reportedly killed about 3-5 of the enemy himself on December 12, 1950, Lt. Barber recorded. "That morning his assistant, Troy, had remarked

Refugees Turned Back...No Boats Leaving For South Korea. *American MPs had stopped this refugee train between Hamhung and Hungnam on 16 December 1950. On Saturday afternoon, after a trip to Hamhung, Barber "passed a trainload of refugees who were stopped by some M.P.'s and were piling off the train trying to get through to Hungnam port. We took a few pictures. The M.P.'s had to fire several shots before they got them back on the train. Poor people, but if they got in the port there's no telling how long it would be before the troops got off the beach. They finally got them turned back. The Communists had told them there were boats in Hungnam to carry them to South Korea with the express purpose of jamming our MSR's. They also use refugees as a mode of infiltrating our lines.*

That evening, Barber and the American troops "were all kind of tense. Navy big guns are firing all day and night, shaking the windows and harassing enemy attempts to regroup. They were hit hard at Chosin (estimate 25,000 out of 100,000 were killed), and are regrouping. A few enemy, dressed as ROKs, infiltrated, and hand-grenaded a couple of our troops last night." Barber slept with most of his clothes on that night. "We leave tomorrow." (Barber)

how he'd like to get a million dollar wound in the arm. [The "million dollar wound" meant a wound serious enough to bring evacuation out of the combat area for good,

i.e. to be sent home.]

As they were riding forward in jeep, the only jeep moving in a hail of fire, a bridge blew up right in front of them, Hollywood

style, and they had to desert their jeep and trailer. The bridge was mined, and a bullet had set off the charge.

Shortly thereafter, Troy was hit in the

Bombed out buildings *in the port of Hungnam on 7 December 1950. (Barber)*

shoulder and both hands, and little Chaplain Reynolds dragged him 300 yards down a ditch to the medics, then went back. He fired one shot from his .45; then it jammed. He threw it away saying "that thing's no damn good" (which was mighty strong for Chaplain Reynolds who is constantly preaching against profanity). Picking up a carbine, he shot three Chinks so he said, but those with him said he got at least five."

Another Chaplain, Father Hone, the Catholic Chaplain was considered "to be utterly fearless, leading attacks with an M-1 rifle in the very front and directing fire from atop the tanks. Later, while I was talking to him," Barber noted in his diary, "he said, 'That sure was fun, I'd like to be back there!' It takes either a fearless man or a fool to say that," Barber observed, "and he isn't a braggart."

"What this Army needs," Barber noted with only half a tongue in cheek, "is more fighting Chaplains and fewer soldiers. What an army it would make if it were composed of all Christain soldiers. Nothing could stop it!"

Operations

Near Hamhung

A Captain McKellop was "lying in a ditch when he was hit in the helmet by a bullet which pierced helmet and liner at the forehead, furrowed over his head without even cracking the skull or causing concussion, and went out the back of his helmet. Guess helmets are a good investment after all," Barber noted.

The temperature was around 29 degrees below zero some of the time, and below zero all of the time. Many cases of frostbite and frozen feet and hands."

"Al Haig, the other night, told me that General Barr broke down and wept when he heard Col. Faith had been killed. Faith was his fair-haired boy. I wonder if Bill Kempen (Class of '49) got out alive." [He had been killed.]

Hundreds of refugees were pouring out of Hamhung "down the road. The M.P's

Hungnam Destroyed. *The North Korean city of Hungnam on 7 December 1950 was largely destroyed. (Barber)*

(Below) ***Market scene in Hamhung*** *on 7 December 1950. Chickens were a popular item. Woman in foreground is carrying a child slung on her back. (Barber)*

War or No War...The Market Is Open. *Women were vending a variety of goods in the Hamhung markets on 7 December 1950 as American troops passed through during the withdrawal from the Yalu. (Barber)*

175

Ammo Dump Camp Out. *Lt. Barber spent the night of 16 December 1950 in the middle of this ammunition dump near Hungnam. The 700,000 pounds of ammunition had been "wired for demolition." (Barber)*

stopped them and sent them back. Apparently they heard of the Chinese approaching and also heard that there were boats at Hungnam to take them to South Korea. They were sent back."

Rotation...At Last!

Friday, 15 December 1950. "Got word to report to Division to Major Manch to get replacement. Yippee!!" After four months of grueling front-line, combat duty Lt. Ken Barber began to allow himself to expect that he would survive to return to his unit and his family. "I ran into Major Manch and Major Hidalgo, 7th Division Liaison Officer" in the hallway at Division Headquarters, Barber noted. Hidalgo, with a serious expression on his face, told Barber that there "had been a mistake." Just before Barber could react, however, Hidalgo and Manch laughed—"they were just kidding," Barber recorded, clearly relieved.

On Saturday, Barber briefed his replacement, Lt. Parker on "all the necessary information on TACP." Parker's team was experienced, having worked closely with Lt. George Olsen, of whom they "spoke enthusiastically," saying that "George got out just in time from the 2nd Division after doing a terrific job. The Chinese piled out of the hills and George worked the planes until the enemy were so close they had to leave."

Meanwhile, the units were "moving a little further back towards Hungnam to the south, where we set up in a tremendous ammunition dump. They say there are 70,000 tons here, much of which will have to be destroyed."

As he assessed the strategic location, Barber believed that "we could hold off the Chinese indefinitely and make them pay heavily for any attempts to drive us off. I don't mean our position tonight, for we are sitting on a veritable powder keg, but this Hamhung perimeter. With the 1st Marines, 7th Division, 3rd Division, ROK Capitol Division, plus Corsairs and Naval Gunfire, I don't see how they could ever evict us from North Korea unless they had air superiority. I believe that our move is mostly political. 'Well, Mao, we got out of North Korea. What do you plan to do now?'"

Barber Goes South

Sunday, 17 December 1950...The officers in the Battalion and Major "Red" Mason, Commander, 1st Battalion, 31st Infantry, "all feel that the only reason we were not cut off at Fusen Reservoir and then at Pungsan, is that we attacked the enemy on our 3rd patrol and they dug in, thinking we would be attacking from then on. The air daily reported lots of stuff dug in over there."

On the morning of Sunday, 17 December, Barber and his team "went to the Hun-gnam beach airstrip. It was bitterly cold. We arranged for a flight to Tachikawa; then waited around in the old, torn down buildings. A bunch of Greek pilots were standing around talking. They were all in the process of checking out in C-47's. After a while a fine looking, tall officer (field grade) in AF blues walked in. We found out it was General Partridge. He was very friendly, spoke to everyone, finally left in a jet, I believe. A high wind was blowing, windy and very cold."

About 1500, a Major Callahan "flew in in a VIP plane, and told us to report to Lt. Col. Goldenberg, 7th AF Forward in Seoul, before going anywhere else. He stopped the VIP plane just in time for us to get on, which we did. To my surprise, the pilot was Bill Vanaman, now a 1st Lt. He entered West Point in 1944, was turned back, and had a 2nd Beast Barracks and half plebe year in "F" Co. when I was a Yearling there. He resigned or washed out, got his commission, and was well ahead of us. He seemed quite bitter toward West Point. We flew to Seoul with me as co-pilot."

After four arduous months of front-line combat duty, Barber was heading back to his unit and his family.

Saying Goodbye

Reaching Seoul City Airport, Barber borrowed a jeep and "dashed into Seoul to 5th

AF Headquarters" to report to Lt. Col. Goldenberg, the ALO. Barber wanted to ensure that the orders issued to his men were changed. Otherwise, they might get reassigned to FAC duty. Barber did not wish "to get them involved in any more TACP's," and he emphasized that they were to return "to their former outfits."

Back at Base Operations, he arranged an aircraft ride for them to Itami, Japan "and saw them off. Being with them was a fine experience and after working together so closely for almost four months, it was pretty hard to say goodbye. They felt the same way too, I believe. We shook hands, paid each other a few compliments, and I left. If I ever should have to return as TACP, I'd want the same team with me. Fine men!"

"I feel that when I return to flying I will be a very efficient pilot from now on. A very efficient Killer Pilot. With 36 missions of experience behind me and the added benefit of acting as a ground controller, my effectiveness should jump considerably. In this war I have lost many good friends (Pat Gilliam, Art Truxes, Mike David) and even more acquaintances, and I am getting a slow, burning sort of anger—absolutely cold—toward the persons who make us have to continue this war. Vengeance is the Lord's and yet we think we are His tools. I often wonder what He thinks of all this— must make Him wish he hadn't created us the way we act like a bunch of fools, killing, lying, cheating, stealing and making sport of the sacred things in life. Yet, his promises are the hope to which we cling. I do believe them."

On Thursday, 21 December, Lt. Ken Barber finally connected with a direct flight to the P.I. He landed at Clark AFB about 1800. He had planned to surprise Carolyn. "I'm sure she didn't know I was coming. However, she called Base Ops and found out I was there. She arrived just as I was leaving and ran into Base Ops right past me looking right and left, then out to the ramp. I slipped quietly out behind her—then she turned around and saw me and with a little cry was in my arms. What a wonderful reunion! What a wonderful Christmas!"

Lt. Ken Barber and his TACP Team inspected this destroyed YAK fighter on the ground at Yongpo airfield. (Barber)

Leaving Hungnam

On 24 December, X Corps completed the sea evacuation of Hungnam. More than 100,000 troops and 91,000 civilians had been taken to safety since the mass exodus began on 11 December. "The Marines went first, and we were glad to see them go after their terrible ordeal in the north," wrote A.P. Correspondent Tom Lambert in a San Antonio Express article of 26 December 1950. "Then the South Koreans left; and after them the U.S. Seventh Division, which also fought its way out of the mountain trap. They went in a long series of truck columns, winding into the wide-flung jaws of tank-landing ships; in a long series of men shuffling down to the beaches or docks at night under spotlights; in a thousand whines of winches, lifting equipment aboard the freighters sharing the harbor with slender destroyers and the heavier bulks of cruisers."

Barber and his team have this view of Yongpo Airfield on 17 December as they circle once in a C-47 before heading south. "It is destroyed and burning." They were taken from Hungnam to Seoul to Taegu to Pusan. (Barber)

Chasing Wings and a Commission

While the 18th Fighter-Bomber Wing was moving in the direction of Chinhae/K-10 as its operating base in Korea, back in the Z.I. the Air Force pilot pipeline was moving fledgling pilots through their demanding training as rapidly as possible.

Brand new 2nd Lt. Wilfred "Budd" Stapley posed proudly with both his parents when he earned his shiny gold bars. (Stapley)

Aviation Cadet, soon to be Second Lieutenant 'Budd' Stapley, marches in formation as he completes cadet training. Most of the cadets in this picture, those that survived flight training, advanced single engine training, and combat crew training, would eventually be assigned to combat units in Korea.

Aviation Cadet William Timmons ("Tim") Urquhart.

As the new pilots pinned on their wings and moved into more advanced training, the Air Force publicity department distributed "hometown news releases" such as this one for Cadet Archie Connors of Jacksonville, Florida.

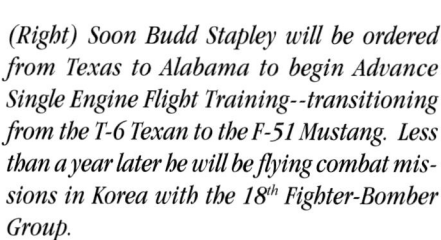

From Cadet to Lieutenant. *William Timmons "Tim" Urquhart enlisted as an Aviation Cadet in Class 51-G in September 1950. He went through basic training at Perrin AFB, Texas and was trained to fly the AT-6 Texan. He transferred to Craig AFB, AL for more AT-6 training and then transitioned into the F-51. "We were commissioned and sent TDY to Luke AFB, Arizona for Combat Crew Training in F-51s and then PCS-ed to Camp Stoneman, California as replacement pilots to Korea, arriving in March, 1952.*

(Right) Soon Budd Stapley will be ordered from Texas to Alabama to begin Advance Single Engine Flight Training--transitioning from the T-6 Texan to the F-51 Mustang. Less than a year later he will be flying combat missions in Korea with the 18th Fighter-Bomber Group.

January 1951

The enemy continued to use camouflage as a principal means of hiding supplies and vehicles from air attacks

12th Fighter-Bomber Squadron Mustang takes off from K-10 on January 30, 1951. (NARA)

The 18th Fighter-Bomber Wing completed its move from K-13 (Suwon) to K-10 (Chinhae) by January 4, 1951.

"The landing strip at K-10 is dirt and problems were immediately encountered. Large rocks on the runway were sucked into the propeller during run-ups, resulting in damage to numerous propellers and only extraordinary supply action kept such aircraft from become AOCP [Out of Commission for Parts]. [1]

Korean laborers were detailed to sweep the run-up areas and to distribute used engine oil on the runway to hold the dust down. The "solution" was almost worse than the "problem." The oil on the dirt runway took a while "to harden." Until it did, "it was thrown over the aircraft by propeller wash and became very difficult to remove. This added to the already long hours on duty required of the aircraft mechanics." At night the ground would freeze. During

1951 Summary

General Douglas MacArthur was relieved of the Far East command and replaced by General Matthew B. Ridgway. Following his relief, Gen. MacArthur addressed a Joint Session of Congress where he urged military action against Communist China. Gen. Ridgway sent North Korea a proposal to negotiate a cease-fire agreement.

Further attempts to negotiate an armistice failed.

UN forces captured "Heartbreak Ridge" north of Yangu.

Armistice negotiations at Panmunjom

began, but failed.

J. D. Salinger published "*Catcher in the Rye.*" Herman Wouk, "*The Caine Mutiny*" won the Pulitzer Prize novel. James Jones published "*From Here to Eternity*," a portrayal of Army life in Pearl Harbor, Hawaii just before the Japanese attack.

Rachel Carson completed "*The Sea Around Us*," effectively launching the ecological movement.

"*The King and I*" by Rodgers and Hammerstein opened on Broadway. Dave Brubeck formed the Dave Brubeck Quartet, including saxophonist Paul Desmond.

The new group was soon the most popular jazz combo in the world.

The first transcontinental television broadcast was made by President Truman from the Japanese Peace Conference in San Francisco. The new treaty with Japan authorized the U.S. to maintain military bases in Japan. The first commercial color television broadcast was produced by CBS from New York. A new video camera was developed that used magnetic tape on which to record both pictures and sound.

Electric power was first produced from atomic energy.

18th Fighter-Bomber Wing Chronology
1951

January-June

CCF Attack 11/3/50-1/24/51	First United Nations Counteroffensive January 25-April 21, 1951	Chinese Communist Army Spring Offensive April 22-July 8, 1951

18th Fighter-Bomber Wing and Group based at K-10/Chinhae, SK	18th FBG flies most combat missions from K-16/Seoul, SK

January   **March**   **May**

February   **April**   **June**

Mar. 24-Apr. 23: During K-10 resurfacing, 18th FBG aircraft operated from K-1 and K-13. The majority of organizational and field maintenance was performed at K-1.

Feb. 24: 18th FBWing 10,000th combat mission.
Mar. 4: MG Earle Partridge, CG, FAF honored Wing for 10,000 effective combat sorties.

Feb. 1: Col. T. C. Rogers assumed command of 18th Wing from Col. Curtis R. Low.

Jan. 15: Red CCF Tide begins to turn. CCF begin a limited withdrawal.

Jan. 4: 18th FBW completes move from K-13/Suwon to K-10/Chinhae.

May 12: 39th FIS operational at K-10.

May 9: 39th Fighter-Interceptor Squadron assigned to 18th FBG at K-10.

May 8: 18th FBG begins staging combat operations from K-16.

June 30: As of 30 June, the 18th FBG had flown 16,370 effective combat sorties during 36,758 combat flying hours.

Monthly Summary

On New Years Day Communist forces launched a powerful new attack that pushed UN forces out of Seoul and the nearby Kimpo and Suwon Airfields. Soon, Wonju, the north central crossroads of South Korea was engulfed in a see-saw battle. Air power, lots of it, was urgently called for—and delivered by FEAF. By mid-January, the enemy offensive had ground to a halt on a line between Pyontaek on the west coast and Samchok on the east coast. Overall air su-

periority by UNF played a critical role in stalling the bloody offensive. By late January, UN forces had regrouped and were again on the offensive. Enemy forces were being steadily forced northward toward Seoul.

FEAF Bomber Command raided enemy railroad marshalling yards, airfields, and supply centers. In an air campaign "intended to burn and destroy key North Korean cities, Bomber Command B-29s raided

Pyongyang, the North Korean capital, with huge formations dropping incendiary bombs on the city. Targets of other major incendiary raids in North Korea included Hamhung, Kaesong, and Komusan.

Adapted in part from U.S. Air Force Historical Research Agency.. The U.S. Air Force's First War: Korea 1950-1953 Significant Events. January 1951. http://www.au.af.mil/au/afhra/wwwroot/korean_war/korean_war_chronology/kwc_1951.html

K-10 Panorama. *Lt. Raymond "Mac" McKelvey, Jr. took these views of K-10 in early 1951. Placed side by side, they provide an almost panoramic view of the 18th Fighter-Bomber Wing base near Chinhae. (McKelvey)*

Arrival At K-10/Chinhae

the day it would thaw. "Large oil coated chunks of runway would be torn from the landing strip upon the aircraft's take off roll. The runway became, and still is, very rough," the maintenance history for January reported.

During pre-flight run-up of engines, "great clouds of dust envelope the entire aircraft parking area." The dust was "considered the primary cause for numerous abortive combat missions charged to rough

engines. The dust has a high silicate content and has a tendency to immediately foul the exhaust spark plugs."

The problems with dust, oil and cold did not stop the Wing's three flying squadrons from setting "new records" by dropping 871.78 tons of bombs and firing 7,366 rockets. The Truck Busters fired over a million rounds of .50-caliber ammunition in January, the greatest number since September. Napalm malfunctions were "cut by

more than half by careful attention to details of mixing, fuse assembly and fusing." [2] The demand for 500-pound General Purpose bombs was so great that it "necessitated daily truck runs to the 543rd Supply Depot for five days until a rail shipment arrived."

Living conditions at K-10 Air Base "have been far superior to any this organization has had yet," Lt. Col. William E. May, Commander of the 67th Squadron, reported in

(Below) **Pilot's lap map**. *Lt. Ken Barber annotated this portion of his pilot's lap map that covers the area near K-10/Chinhae. (Barber)*

January. "Adequate heat and food, combined with decent quarters for all concerned, has greatly boosted the morale of this unit."

Several "flying hazards" at K-10 "greatly hampered night and early morning operations. The airstrip is bounded on three sides by mountains 2,000' high that are within 3 miles of the strip. The fourth side of the airstrip is formed by a bay of water. Approximately 50 feet separates the entire length of the runway from the bay. A steel hangar is located at the south end of the runway and clears the runway by a mere 50 feet. Several Quonset quarters are located within 100 feet of the runway," May noted for the record.

Combat Operations From Chinhae

The ground tactical situation, which "directly affects the operations of this organization remained at a stalemate during the early part of the month," May reported. United Nations troops withdrew and established a fluid line of defense south of Osan on the West Coast and extended across the plains to the vicinity of Wonju. From Wonju to the east coast, the defense line extended north to Kangnung. The defense line allowed the air forces to work on enemy troops caught in the flat country north of Osan.

"At the time of this report, one defense line had moved north to the vicinity of the Han River on the western front. Enemy resistance had been apparently weak," May noted. "Contact with the enemy was through patrol action mostly. As a result, armed reconnaissance was the primary mission of

K-10/Chinhae airfield can be seen in the distance. The large hangar was a major landmark. Chinhae Bay lay right alongside the landing strip and posed a constant danger to departing or returning pilots. Proximity to deep water did help somewhat with supplies arriving by ship as well as by railroad. (Krakovsky)

Control Tower at K-10--"Dogpatch Korea."
(McLoughlin)

(Above) **Runway at K-10.** *Note how close it is to hangars and the bay. The south side of the airstrip was on the water. Approximately 50 feet separated the entire length of the runway from the bay. A steel hangar was located at the south end of the runway and was separated from the runway by just 50 feet. Several Quonset quarters were located within 100 feet of the runway. (Krakovsky)*

the squadron. Several dive-bombing missions were carried out against an enemy held airfield."

The basic mission for Truckbuster squadrons "remained unchanged" during January. However, combat sorties ranged from "escort at high altitudes (15,000 and 25,000 feet) for RB-29 type aircraft" to armed reconnaissance, visual reconnaissance, CAP for downed pilots, as well as close support missions," May explained.

Flak intensity "remained fairly constant with an increase around the Pyongyang area."

No enemy aircraft were encountered during January. However, while "there was no positive engagement with enemy jet type fighters during this report period," combat pilots "reported sighting such aircraft," May reported.

All take-offs and landings at K-10 were restricted to at least ten second intervals due to the heavy dust conditions. And, all take-offs and landings were "single ship."

The majority of missions for 18th Group Mustangs "were reconnaissance missions along the enemy's supply route. During the first part of the month, these missions were flown using four (4) ship flights carrying napalm and rockets. On the longer missions, external tanks were carried on all ships. These tanks are critical and all pilots were instructed to drop them only in an emergency."

"During the latter part of the month, a number of two (2) ship reconnaissance missions were flown. Many of these missions were flown with the aircraft loaded with rockets and without external tanks or napalm."

"Several dive bomb missions were flown carrying five hundred pound G.P. bombs with delay action fuses. The purpose of these missions was to drop the bombs on enemy airstrips. These dive bomb missions were very successful. The tactic most commonly used for dive bombing was to split S from approximately 10,000 feet and drop the bombs when in approximately a 70 degree dive."

The enemy "continued to use camouflage as a principal means of hiding supplies and vehicles from air attacks. Their pattern remained the same and they continued to use dry creek beds, secondary roads, mountain passes and white tarpaulins." [3] The 67th reported, "due to difficulties encountered in seeking camouflaged targets while carrying external tanks on low altitude reconnaissance missions, Squadron Operations gained the prerogative to recce without tanks on routes within 260 miles of

the base." [4]

Truckbuster pilots received a lecture by "a team of officers from higher headquarters" on "escape and evasion. They stressed the point of evading the enemy at all costs." The pilots were reminded that the "most important item to carry and use" was "a means of contacting friendly aircraft, such as a mirror or a flare." The unit reports are mute concerning pilot reaction to the receipt in January of new "escape kits." The new kits "contained items for bartering such as ball point pens and wrist watches," the 67th unit history noted.

Helicopters were able to reach "only a portion of the area covered by our fighters. Rescue aircraft were always standing by waiting to be called and others were airborne and flying a short distance behind the front lines."

A new D/F (direction finding) station "was installed atop a hill near the base at K-10 and all flight leaders were requested to request a steer when returning to base. The D/F operators improved with practice and gave accurate steers toward the end of the month." [5]

Squadron Activities

In January, Major William E. Bryan, Jr. assumed command of the 12th Fighter-Bomber Squadron. By the end of the month the veteran squadron had 41 officers and 137 Airmen assigned. Four of its senior pilots completed 100 combat missions and no pilots were lost to enemy action that month.

After the K-13/Suwon Air Base detachment was evacuated to K-10 on January 4th, the unit "remained intact" and focused on "improving the living quarters and offices. All departments were able to perform their duties more efficiently after the detachment at K-13 returned to K-10." [6]

The 12th Fighter-Bomber Squadron flew 500 combat sorties with its 26 Mustangs against enemy targets in January, a total of 1,452 combat flying hours during which they damaged 26 towns, destroyed six villages and damaged 47 others, destroyed 35 warehouses, destroyed 445 buildings and three factories, destroyed 55 trucks and 333 houses and reported killing 941 enemy troops. [7]

During January, the 67th accumulated 1,609 hours of combat flying time, the "second highest for this squadron since entering combat. The average number of aircraft in commission per day was 16.5, or an average of 70 percent. By January, the 67th had eight officers that had completed 100 combat missions.

Dusty Takeoff. *A 67th Squadron Mustang heavily loaded with rockets and napalm taxis toward takeoff in a whirl of heavy dust on January 30, 1951. (NARA)*

Endnotes

[1] USAHRA. *Monthly Historical Report, 18th Fighter-Bomber Wing*, January 1951, p. 4.

[2] USAHRA. *Monthly Historical Report, 18th Fighter-Bomber Wing*, January 1951, p. 5.

[4] USAHRA. *Monthly Historical Report, 12th Fighter Bomber Squadron*, January 1950, p 3.

[5] USAFHRA. *Monthly Historical Report, 67th Fighter Bomber Squadron*, January 1951, p. 4.

[6] USAHRA. *Monthly Historical Report, 12th Fighter Bomber Squadron*, January 1951, p. 4.

[3] USAHRA. *Monthly Historical Report, 12th Fighter Bomber Squadron*, January 1950, p 2.

[7] USAHRA. *Monthly Historical Report, 12th Fighter Bomber Squadron*, January 1951, p. 4.

(Above) ***Hangar At K-10.*** *A Mustang of the 12th Fighter-Bomber Squadron is towed out to the runway at K-10 on January 30, 1951, "prior to take-off on a mission to blast enemy installations." The hangar was one of the most striking landmarks at Chinhae, an incomplete skeletal hangar built by the Japanese during World War Two. The 18th Maintenance Squadron used the area for routine maintenance. (NARA)*

Napalm Attack. *Smoke rises following 18th Fighter-Bomber Group napalm attacks on a "Red held village somewhere in Korean" in January 1951. (NARA)*

Significant Events

January 1 FEAF redoubled attacks on enemy troop columns in an attempt to blunt a new ground offensive by almost half a million Chinese Communist and North Korean troops.

January 2 Forward-based F-86s were withdrawn from Kimpo Airfield near Seoul to the wing's home base at Johnson AB, Japan.

January 3 Seoul was evacuated before being overrun by massive numbers of Chinese troops that crossed the frozen Han River east and west of Seoul—the ROK government moved temporarily to Pusan.

January 4 CCF troops occupied Seoul—for the third time in six months.

The Intelligence Section of the 18th Fighter-Bomber Wing "departed from K-13 and landed at K-10 (Chinhae), with such office equipment as remained at K-13." The move to Chinhae Airbase was well underway.

January 8 A severe blizzard forced USN Task Force 77 carriers to suspend close air support missions. FAF took up the slack. U.S. forces in central Korea withdrew to new positions three miles south of Wonju.

January 10 Severe winter weather forced FAF to suspend close air support missions.

January 11 Improving weather enabled FAF to resume close air support missions for X Corps in north central South Korea.

January 13 FEAF flew the first effective tarzon mission against an enemy-held bridge at Kanggye, dropping a six-ton radio-guided bomb on the center span, destroying fifty-eight feet of the structure. While the Air Force had limited success with razon and tarzon weapons in Korea, they were the precursors of today's precision-guided weapons.

January 14 CCF reached their furthest extent of advance into South Korea when they captured Wonju.

January 15 The Red Tide began to turn—CCF began a limited withdrawal in some areas of South Korea.

7,000th Mission. *Major Charles McGee holds up seven finges to celebrate his return from the 7,000th mission for the 18th Fighter-Bomber Group on 28 January 1951. It was the 83rd mission for McGee, a WWII veteran and a former Tuskegee Airman. (McGee)*

(Below) Mustang from the 67th Fighter-Bomber Squadron is airborne from K-10 on January 30, 1951. (NARA)

January 17   F-86 operations resumed in Korea. "For the first time, the Sabres flew in the air-to-ground role as fighter-bombers, conducting armed reconnaissance and close air support missions."

January 19   FEAF launched a two-week intensive air campaign—fighters, light bombers, and medium bombers—to restrict supplies and reinforcements reaching enemy forces in the field.

January 23   A major air action day—33 F-84s staging from Taegu attack Sinuiju, provoked a furious half-hour air battle with MiG-15s from across the Yalu. The ThunderJets shot down three MiGs, the highest daily USAF aerial victory credit total for the month. While forty-six F-80s suppressed Pyongyang's antiaircraft artillery, twenty-one B-29s cratered the enemy capital's airfields. [1]

January 25: 18th FBW squadrons were "notified of a policy change on awards and decorations." The Air Medal "will be awarded every 30 missions and the Distinguished Flying Cross will no longer be automatically awarded at 30 and 75 missions. From now on, the DFC will be awarded only through meritorious achievement extraordinary." [2]

January 28   Hoengsong, a few miles north of Wonju, was retaken after USAF fighter-bombers dropped 8,000 gallons of napalm on communist positions within a 30-square-mile area.

Major Charles MeGee completes 7,000th combat mission for the 18th Wing.

Jan. 29   Eighth Army units moved several miles north of Hoengsong, SK, about 80 miles east southeast of Seoul.

January 30   The first USAF aircraft landed at the recaptured Suwon Airfield.

January 31: In Seoul, President Syngman Rhee signed a Presidential Unit Citation for the 18th Fighter-Bomber Wing. *[Note: the Citation did not reach the 18th until May 1951.]* "The 18th Fighter-Bomber Wing was transferred to Korea from another overseas station," the Citation noted, "coming thousands of miles to aid Korea in its conflict against aggression and iron-hand rule. The 18th Fighter-Bomber Wing is equipped with F-51's and has continuously

utilized this type of aircraft in coming to the air of the Korean government in its fight against the enemy. The Wing came to Korea early in the war and although forced to evacuate its base under enemy fire, it continues to fly large number of sorties against the enemy daily. The outstanding performance of duty by each individual member of the 18th Fighter-Bomber Wing, United States Fifth Air Force, is in accord with the highest traditions of military service." [3]

Combat Losses

Hutchinson, Capt. Arthur Earl, 12th Squadron pilot.

Jacobs, 1st Lt. Ralph E., 67th Squadron pilot.

Napalm Most Feared Weapon. *Interrogations of Communist prisoners by the Air Force established that napalm bombs were the most feared of all weapons used by the U.S. Far East Forces in Korea. Here the blast from a napalm bomb begins to envelop a building used as a military barracks by the Communists in January 1951. The jellied gasoline covers the building and is forced through open windows and doors by the blast. (NARA)*

Powers, Captain Joe E. Jr., 67th Squadron pilot KIA in January 1951. "In our Squadron we have lost two men—both in January," wrote Lt. Kenneth Barber on 12 February 1951. "One was Capt. Joe Powers of "A" Flight whose engine quit and he ditched just off Seoul, and sank, very similar to Mike David's case." Capt. Robert "Pancho" Pasqualicchio, Powers' wingman on that flight noted that he was credited with 14.5 victories in WWII.

Endnotes

[1] Adapted in part from U.S. Air Force Historical Research Agency. January 2002. The U.S. Air Force's First War: Korea 1950-1953 Significant Events. January 1951. http://www.au.af.mil/au/afhra/wwwroot/korean_war/korean_war_chronology/kwc_1951.html

[2] USAFHRA. *Monthly Historical Report, 67th Fighter-Bomber Squadron*, January 1951, p. 2.

[3] USAFHRA. *Monthly Historical Report, 18th Fighter-Bomber Group*, May 1951.

Combat Statistics January 1951

18th Fighter-Bomber Wing

Average No. A/C Assigned
Unavailable
Total Flying Time
Unavailable
Combat Sorties Flown by Wing
1,471
12th Squadron Sorties
500
67th Squadron Sorties
573
2 Squadron Sorties
478
A/C Lost to Combat
4
Pilots lost
3

Fuel Consumed
Unavailable

Ordnance Expended

.50-cal. Rounds
1,018,170
Rockets
7,366
Napalm Bombs
Unavailable
500-lb. GP Bombs
3,484 (est.)
Note: Figures and totals may differ in some categories due to differences in numbers provided by each component.

"Mayor of Chinhae"

One day while Sergeant Sandy Colton was walking down one of the main streets in Chinhae, someone called his name.

"I looked up and peering out of a second floor window was our amiable, cigar chewing Wing Sergeant Major Frank Fay. He invited me to drop up for a beer. Somehow he had found and was renting a very nice apartment in Chinhae. He seemed to have made friends with almost all the influential people in town, the mayor, the police chief and God knows who else and would use his apartment to entertain them as well as fellow airmen from the base. We called him the "Mayor of Chinhae.""

A New Species of Animal

"Have you homesteaders of Korea seen the new and happy faces wandering around the base?

Well, there are a few. Perhaps you were standing around, when a boyish and eager countenance pushed itself into your range of vision and asked, 'Say Sarge, where do they sell the ice cream around here?'

That, my friend, is a replacement, a species of animal which is heard about but seldom seen in Korea."

Ground Crews Set To Work At Sundown. *A striking sunset fades away behind distant mountains at K-10 in January 1951 as ground crews of the Two Squadron SAAF arrive to check these Mustangs whose engines are still warm from a close air support mission. (NARA)*

K-10/Chinhae, South Korea
New Headquarters for 18th Fighter-Bomber Wing

by S/Sgt. William J. "Sandy" Colton

The imminent potential loss of K-2 airbase at Taegu to rapidly advancing North Korean ground forces during the dark days of the "Pusan Perimeter" period, led to a hasty evacuation of the 12th Squadron on August 6, 1950, to Ashiya, Japan, where it joined the 67th Squadron and 18th Group Headquarters. However, reinforced U.S. and allied ground forces slowed the advance and then held their ground, despite enemy forces within artillery range on three sides, and the Taegu base did not fall.

A Refuel-Rearm operation, headed by 1st Lieutenant Harry Dugan, remained active at Taegu the whole time, to help overcome the logistical challenges of the extra added hour of flying time required from Ashiya to the targets surrounding the beleaguered base. Another airfield, named K-9, near the port city of Pusan, its paving badly deteriorated by heavily-laden transports early in the war, was quickly refurbished to enable minimal operation. Two squadrons from the 18th (12th and 67th) were able to move back across the Sea of Japan from Ashiya on September 8, 1950.

The return to primitive combat living conditions (following the relative creature comforts of Ashiya), soon caused the airfield designator "K-9" to become "Canine." Soon the field was unofficially renamed

T-6 "Texan" spotter aircraft lined up at K-10. (Krakovsky)

"Dogpatch" in recognition of the similarities to cartoonist Al Capp's then-popular comic strip village. 'Lil Abner and Daisy Mae' became part of the 18th Group's unofficial insignia.

The move to K-9 enabled the 18th Fighter-Bomber Group to redouble the relentless close air support for allied units around the Pusan Perimeter, without resorting to long-range auxiliary wing tanks as had been required for the combat flights from Ashiya.

The highly effective amphibious invasion of Inchon on September 15, 1950, produced an immediate and dramatic about face in combat operations in the Korean War. Within days the enemy in the South

was fleeing north in headlong retreat. Despite their retreat, many were still able to exact a heavy toll on the 18th's low flying Mustangs by concentrated pockets of heavy flak in the far north—pilot casualties continued to mount.

The months of October and early November 1950, were highlighted by almost continuous advances to the north by United Nations forces. Following the fall of Pyongyang in mid-November, 1950, the 18th Group, on November 21, 1950, was able to leapfrog its base of operations all the way to the former North Korean capitol city's heavily damaged airfield (K-24)—'Pyongyang East.' The period of operations there was very brief due to the intervention by Chinese forces in the war. Operations were moved back to Suwon in early December 1950, and then on December 2, 1950, back to the Pusan area to Chinhae (K-10), on the southern coast—subsequently renamed "Dogpatch."

At K-10 the Flights slept together in tents (with floors), steadily replaced the Air Installation Squadron with metal Quonset huts, marginally better accommodations than the tents they used "up North."

18th Wing Component Organizations "The Team"

"As a former 18th Group Commander, I needed the 'whole team' that was involved in combat," explained Colonel Ralph H. Saltsman, Jr. In early 1951 that included: the 12th Fighter-Bomber Squadron, the 67th Fighter-Bomber Squadron and the 2 Squadron SAAF, "plus all the supporting units." Later that Spring, the 39th Fighter-Interceptor Squadron joined the 18th F-B Group, bringing to four the total of combat flying squadrons.

The "entire 18th Wing played a part in what we now shall call 'The Combat Diary of the 18th Fighter-Bomber Wing in the Korean War," Saltsman emphasized.

The combat mission of the 18th Fighter-Bomber Group was "close support of United Nations Forces in Korean and other aerial combat missions as directed by higher headquarters. At this time the squadron reported that its "primary mission was subordinated to tactical interdiction of enemy rolling stock, personnel and other material. Armed visual reconnaissance comprised the bulk of all missions flown during this report period."

The 18thh Group continued to be officially based at Chinhae, but used K-46 near Hoengsong "as a forward combat operations base." Reloading and rearming was accomplished by the armament section at K-46.

The weekly newspaper for the 18th Fighter-Bomber Wing, *Truckbuster*, offered significant coverage and recognition not only to pilots and combat missions, but to the many types of ground and support personnel that made up the 18th "Team."

Up and down the "chain" it was clearly understood that everyone contributed to all missions--and everyone's contribution was essential.

As the 18th Wing and Group approached a year of demanding combat operations in Korea, many of the 18th Wing and Group component units took the opportunity to prepare profiles and summaries highlighting major events and accomplishments during the hectic year of operations. The writeups were highly individualistic and were written primarily for members or "alumni" of the component organizations, often noting an event or personage known only to members of that squadron or unit. Nevertheless, these summaries provide an important perspective on Wing operations as a whole. Many of them are reprinted on the following pages to give the reader a better understanding of the many units and in-

(Right) In this painting by Sergeant Dave McNichols highlighting the career of BG Turner C. Rogers, Commander of the 18th Fighter-Bomber Wing, an aerial view of K-10 is seen in the background, complete with an F-51 taking off.

dividual talents required to keep 75-80 aging Mustangs flying combat missions against an evermore prepared and equipped enemy.

While the combat squadrons received top billing for their achievements and sacrifices, we should never forget that the combat squadrons that made up the 18th Group depended on the absolutely vital support services provided by numerous other squadrons and units attached to the Wing. Certainly the Group respected these organizations greatly and expressed its gratitude frequently in the Truckbuster and other media.

The following pages reprint representative articles from a *Truckbuster* of this period that highlight some of the many squadrons and units of the 18th Wing that helped make it *"The Best Damn Fighter-Bomber Wing In The World."*

18th Fighter-Bomber Wing Headquarters at K-10

Flying Tiger Squadron

The Flying Tigers of Korea Squadron received its colorful label from President Syngman Rhee, who was impressed with the spirit and tempo of the veteran fliers on his first visit to the busy airstrip in July of 1950.

Reminiscent of Claire Chennault's famous AVG's the Tiger squadron has carried on the lofty traditions of its heritage and label. Not only has this unit accomplished near-miraculous results, but in the doing has been one of the most colorful groups to operate on the peninsula. People like "Migrate Willie" Bryan, Sam Wilkerson, Jerry Hogue, Fred Webster, J. K. Hall, John Rees, and many others have left their mark in the squadron archives.

"Truckbusting" as such came into its own under Bryan and Hogue leading their fabulous low-level strikes that were to become legendary. A good day's hunting always went over the century mark. Oldsters such as Jim Peek and Danny Farr could curl a replacement's hair with tall but true tales of the days of yore. The Tigers even had fraternities within its own ranks such as the "Foxy Few From Old Taegu."

The hubba-hubba of esprit hit a new high under John Roos' direction with operations and entertainment that has yet to be equaled around Dogpatch. Volunteers from the very first, the Flying Tigers with their familiar shark-teeth mustangs, have become an object of fear and dread to commie troops who have felt the Mustangs' leaden bite backed up with rockets and napalm.

When Communist North Korean forces invaded South Korea on June 25, 1950, the 12th was flying P-80C jets at Clark Field, PI, and was immediately ordered to Korea to counter the rapidly-advancing communist forces.

Many of the Foxy Few volunteered to form the 'Dallas Provisional Squadron' that immediately deployed to Korea. There they joined forces with the 'Bout One' pilots that had obtained 10 derelict Mustangs belonging to the fledgling South Korean Air Force. The combined unit became the '51st Provisional Squadron' and on July 10, 1950, began flying combat missions using those ten F-51s to slow the North Korean forces then advancing from the North.

The aircraft carrier USS BOXER arrived in late July 1950, carrying 150 F-51s collected from National Guard units in the United States and accompanied by scores of qualified Mustang pilots. The new planes and pilots, combined with the transfer of the 67th Squadron from the Philippines, enabled the '51st Provisional Squadron' to be reclassified as the '12th Fighter-Bomber Squadron'—a designation that it retained throughout the Korean War.

Following the move to Korea in July 1950, the 12th Fighter-Bomber Squadron became an amalgamation of personnel from the 12th, 44th, 67th, and several members

were recruited from Clark Base and other units. It was a 'new war', and its members wanted to replace the 'dirty dozen' with a fresh insignia.

'Knowing that it was almost impossible to secure timely official approval from USAF Headquarters, a few of the pilots sketched an early version of the "Foxy Few" logo, and as embroidered patches were ordered from different vendors in Japan and Korea, the shape of the Fox varied, but the basic shape--with bottle and scarf--remained essentially the same.

[1] 18th Fighter-Bomber Wing Album, October 1951, Flying Tiger Squadron.

12th Squadron esprit de corps in 1951 can be judged by this sign erected near its Operations Office at K-10. (Corley)

12th Squadron Flight Line. *Mustangs assigned to the 12th Squadron line up at K-10 in Spring 1951. (Pasqualicchio)*

*12th **Squadron** was known as the "**Foxy Few**," as well as the "Fighting Twelfth." This "foxy" Airman sign followed the Squadron around Korea from base to base. (Corley)*

***Lt. Melvin Corley** stands next to "Katy Bell" after a mission. Note the shoulder holster for his .45-caliber pistol. (Corley)*

193

18th Fighter-Bomber Group "Self Portraits"
From *Truckbuster*
In answer to the call we go...To hit the Reds once more

Red Scarf Squadron

The Red Scarf Squadron's welcome to Korea during the hectic "July Days" of last year sounds like overdrawn fiction from a best seller. Enemy artillery, crowded tents, eighteen-hour work days, men loading and servicing aircraft (regardless of MOS), and all the colorful staging that modern warfare is supposed to produce—and does.

Originally commanded by Major Lou Sebille, the first Air Force man to receive the Congressional Medal of Honor in the Korean conflict, the Red Scarf Squadron has continued its high operational efficiency under the leadership of Major "Moon" Mullins, Lt. Col. Bill May, Lt. Col. "Hank" Lawrence, and Major "Shorty" Colson.

These men have been typical of the aggressive commanders characteristic of the 18th. We have more than a few feats that we point to with obvious pride—first to operate from North Korea, first Squadron to win the Lou Sebille Bombing Award two months in succession, and many others.

Despite the mud, dust, snow, rain, and ice we had our share of chuckles. Remember how Lt. Lavin practically had a complex, because his ample bulk seem to encourage guerilla sharpshooters; Captain "Big Dog" Smith with his in-low-gear laugh; Col. Lawrence with his campaign-hat-plus-cigarette-holder program for becoming a four-star general overnight.

It isn't listed as TO/E equipment but a good stock level of humor and laughs was our most valuable asset. Sticky valves, weird mag-drops, hydraulic mysteries, and all the other gremlins that haunt a tactical unit were less nettling because we could laugh it off. All in all we feel that our spirit and our accomplishments are summarized in this simple stanza:

> *Be it fighters over Kimpo,*
> *Or to strafe Korea's shore;*
> *In answer to the call we go*
> *To hit the Reds once more.*

Following the North Korean invasion in June 1950, the 67th Squadron moved from Clark Field in the Philippines to Ashiya, Japan, reverted to F-51 Mustangs and on August 2, 1950, commenced combat operations. It was temporarily based at Ashiya, Japan because there was insufficient space to operate a second squadron from the rapidly-deteriorating sand airstrip at Taegu.

The 67th Squadron was the first to operate from North Korea, and the first Squadron to win the Lou Sebille Bombing Award three months in succession.

194

We'll not pass nor be forgotten like the rest!

(Above) **Col. T. C. Rogers** (left), Commander, 18th Fighter-Bomber Wing and **Lt. Col. Henry "Hank" Lawrence**, Commander 67th Squadron after a mission from K-10. (Pasqualicchio)

(Below) "Pancho" Pasqualicchio was soon in the cockpit of a 67th Squadron Mustang taxiing out for a mission from K-10. (Pasqualicchio)

(Above) **Capt. Robert P. "Pancho" Pasqualicchio** checking in at K-10 on January 1, 1951. (Pasqualicchio)

(Below) **1st Lt. Joe Burke** (left) and **Major Carl "Shorty" Colson** (center), Commander of the 67th Squadron following Lawrence, talking over aircraft maintenance problems with their line chief at K-10 in 1951. Burke penned the words to the Truckbuster's Song. (Pasqualicchio)

Truckbuster's Song

67th Fighter-Bomber Squadron parody of 'Whiffenpoof Song'

Busting trucks along the Yalu,
Blasting tanks along the Line.
It's the Mustang, mighty Mustang, every time.
We're the men who fly those Mustangs,
We're the Red Scarfs, and we're proud.
Sixty-seventh, head and shoulders o'er the crowd.
When those engines roar at daybreak,
Every crew chief on the Line,
Holds his head high as those Mustangs start to climb.

So we'll drink a toast to 'Red Scarfs,'
And our life and love shall last.
We'll not pass nor be forgotten like the rest.

CHORUS:
We are old fighter pilots and we're here to stay,
And fly, fly, fly.
Sixty-Seventh is the Squadron that will always lead the way
(and we're always in the fray)
To fly, fly, fly.

Mustang pilots all, are we.
Fly any bird through Eternity.
So God have mercy on such as we,
Who fly, fly, fly.

By 1st Lt. Joseph Burke, 67th Fighter-Bomber Squadron in 18th Fighter-Bomber Wing Song Book courtesy of William J. "Sandy" Colton.

18th Fighter-Bomber Group "Self Portraits"
From *Truckbuster*

"Ay Ziga Zumba Zumba Zumba. Ay Ziga Zumba Zumba Zay!"

2nd South African Air Force Squadron

"Aye Ziga Zoomba" may be just a song, but it will live forever in the hearts of the 18th as one of the many contributions from the hardy air warriors from the Union of South Africa. The Mustangs with the familiar roundel-and-springbok of "Two Squadron" have flown over five thousand bombline trips since last November.

Commanded by such veteran fliers as S.v.B. Theron, J.P.D. Blaauw, and B.A.A. Wiggett, the Flying Cheetah Squadron has been strictly "top line" all the way.

"Potty" Potgieter, Johnny Morris, Mike Frost, "Tank" Odendaal, "Tinky" Jones and a host of other Cheetahmen have become legendary figures for their courage, their wit, and their comaraderies.

Whenever hangar flying is in order at the club their exploits and deeds are rehashed in minute detail. The time Tinky actually "threw in the towel" as a token of his last combat mission, much to the chagrin of the tower operator. When Jan Blaauw capped his squadron mate and then crash-landed to help him until the rescue chop-

This 2 Squadron SAAF pin was among the personal effects of 1st Lt. Archie Connors.

per pulled them both out of enemy territory.

The 2nd Squadron story would be incomplete without such men as F/S Boyd, W/O Hendryck, and A/S Leach, who were typical of the Cheetah airmen.

Many of the gallant Fliers will never return to their homeland, but have a final resting place on the war-ravaged peninsula. To these valiant comrades-in-arms who sleep the eternal sleep beneath modest white crosses, we humbly dedicate our efforts.

Mustang of the Flying Cheetah 2 Squadron SAAF returns from a combat mission in September 1952. (Krakovsky)

18th Fighter-Bomber Group "Self Portraits"
From *Truckbuster*
"Helmets sans liners will always live in our mind as mobile bath tubs and as indispensable as a mess kit."

Wing Headquarters

Squadron

51st Provisional, Dallas, Bout One, Six-Double-O-Deuce are all terms that mark the progress of the 18th Fighter-Bomber Wing from a volunteer unit, hastily assembled in the Far East during the turbulent "July Days of 1950," to the present effective, well-known Wing that it is.

Originally commanded by calm, quiet-spoken Colonel Curtis R. Low from Needham Heights, Mass., the 18th was one of the first units to get into the Korean fray and has been part of the United Nations Team since that first hot July 15th when the first flight of F-51 Mustangs took off to strike an aerial blow for global peace and freedom.

From those first humble beginnings the 18th was destined to play a prominent part in the Fifth Air Force's role on the peninsula. Despite the fact that the Wing moved five times in as many months, the all-important sortie rate did not drop and its fighting spirit never flagged for an instant. Quite early, the TRUCKBUSTER tag was applied to the 18th, with 126 trucks destroyed in one day! This can be attributed to the "Pioneer" volunteers who evolved low-level attack techniques that today are SOP when attacking enemy equipment.

In mid-February of this year Brigadier General (then Colonel) T. C. Rogers succeeded Colonel Low as Wing Commander. It was through the wisdom, intelligence, and patience of these two commanders that the 18th was able to accomplish its enviable record in the Korean conflict.

The 18th has much to be proud of, such as being lauded in the Congressional Record. The Following "firsts" are indicative of its tempo and spirit: FIRST to fly com-

bat missions from airstrips north of the 38th; FIRST to encounter the MIG-15 in aerial combat; FIRST to use the tank-demolishing 6.5 rocket; FIRST unit to integrate another nation's air arm and forge a United Nations fighter-bomber wing when the 2nd Squadron South African Air Force joined the 18th in November of 1950; FIRST Air Force unit to have one of its members receive the Congressional Medal of Honor for action in Korea when Major Louis J. Sebille was awarded the Nation's highest award for crashing his battle-damaged plane into an enemy armored vehicle.

In the years to come when old 18th'ers assemble there will be one central thought coloring their nostalgic remarks: "THE 18TH WAS THE BEST DAMN OUTFIT IN KOREA!"

Air Installation Squadron

Hot showers, dust-less roads, stateside barracks, and Dogpatch real estate in general reflects this squadron's efforts for the past year-plus on the peninsula

If the Federal Housing Administration thinks it has headaches, one glimpse of a few of our home sites would have discouraged the most enthusiastic AIO'er.

Early blueprints for our combat-condition housing were starkly simple. Take one piece of canvas (non-rainproof), three poles (different lengths), five pegs (short & blunt), then erect on soft marshland (paddies) during calm wind conditions (gusts up to 50 knots). Once this was accomplished it was no problem to find a nice dry six-by in preference to the tired tents.

Helmets sans liners will always live in our mind as mobile bath tubs and as indispensable as a mess kit. But all this was the yesterday of 1950 and a visitor would find it almost impossible to credit the "below-zero temperature with two feet of mud" stories that combat veterans use to harass replacements today.

An AIO's work is never done, so we're as busy as ever with our various duties ranging from tedious maintenance to new structures. We're proud to be spiritual and actual stockholders in a construction "company" of the 18th Fighter-Bomber Wing.

18ᵗʰ Fighter-Bomber Group "Self Portraits"
From *Truckbuster*

"...we stormed the Korean beach head with spatula and skillet."

Air Base Group

Headquarters

Hewing closely to the "housekeeping" role the Air Base Group proudly points out that is many support functions have directly affected the morale and health of the entire 18ᵗʰ Wing. Relegated to near-drudgery tasks and lacking front-page glamour we are proud to have been a part of one of the greatest air units involved in the Korean conflict.

We started out as the six-double-oh-deuce with Major Bob Bonebrake and First Sergeant Charley Graves calling the plays. That was back in the famous "advance to the rear" days. Since then we've come a long way to our present stateside operation.

The dining halls, the barracks, our combination gym-theatre, the service club, and all the other elements that provoke the perennial term "fat," are mute testimony to the sweat and labor of our squadrons.

The ABG's roster is filled with such memory-jogging names as Powers, Pawlowski, Lavandoski, Wise, De Coursey, Wilson, and many other officers whose efforts have become history in the 18th.

Be it the Air Police or the Base Photo lab, we've been in there pitching from the very beginning. We're still rasslin' temperamental stoves, rotation, mail from home, and duty rosters, but in the main Dogpatch has taken on a streamlined "how-good-can-it-get" appearance. We can even boast a campus of our own with instructors from the University of California as part of Lt. Anderson's I & E Program.

In the pages that follow we give you a quick-take tour of our activities and squadrons. We may be the behind-the-scene little guys, but we've done our job. And we've done it well!

Food Service Squadron

It was early September of 1950 that we stormed the Korean beach head with spatula and skillet. Since those turbulent days of last year we've been putting out calcium, calories, and carbohydrates in the most palatable, edible manner that circumstances would permit.

Napoleon's bromide about the military traveling on its stomach never had a more practical application than the trials and tribulations of the 18ᵗʰ's Food Service Squadron. Old Timers in the 18ᵗʰ will recall with glistening eye the hardships of dust, mud, snow, sleet, and rain occurring within a twelve hour period—and they aren't kidding buddy.

Actually at times it seemed like a flashback to World War II days with a menu of corned beef, dehydrated potatoes (oh for the thrill of actually peeling a fresh spud), and the eternal spam. The small trickle of fresh vegetables from Japan's hydroponic farms was miserably inadequate.

Lest this narrative sound too much like a concert of wails, we had our share of laughs and gags. Many of you still remember when a man would hoard such items as canned peaches, pineapples, and other hard-to-get delicacies. They are commonplace at our stateside-quality mess halls today, but it wasn't many months ago that they were enviable luxuries.

Despite the fact that we set up and tore down stoves five times in as many months we still kept plugging or "grubbing" for the chow-conscious 18ᵗʰ'ers. Maybe our diet was a little monotonous at first, but visits by such personages as General MacArthur, Al Jolson, and Bob Hope made life a little less boring.

Of course there was that hectic struggle in October that turned out to be a three-way pull among the U.S. Marines, the North Korean forces, and ourselves. When the dust had finally settled in the Wonsan area, the Halls-of-Montezuma came off the victor. The enemy slunk northward and we once again packed up stoves, rations, captured enemy equipment (souvenir swords, etc.) and trekked south to our old base at Pusan.

And so it went. We yo-yo'ed up and down the peninsula with a lot of laughs, a few tears, and plenty of activity. Thanksgiving showed us a lot with all the turkey and trimmings. Somehow Christmas rolled around and we began to feel a sense of sta-

Airmen Krakovsky and Hoffman check out the Dogpatch General Store. (Krakovsky)

Airman Joseph Krakovsky took these photographs of the messing (food services) tent at K-10, probably for an issue of **Truckbuster,** *the Wing's bi-monthly newspaper.* (Krakovsky)

bility with permanent structures for mess halls, heated water, and FRESH VEG-ETABLES!

Now as our second Yuletide on the peninsula is just a few calendar pages away and we have much to be grateful for during our eighteen months in Korea. We've known some wonderful guys, a few not-so-wonderful guys, but in the main we're proud to say that we still HAVE THE BEST DAMN MESS HALLS IN THE FAR EAST!

The Chow Line

The chow line at night--"that was just about the best meal of the day," remembered Donald R. Smith. "Usually it was C-rations, but the Air Force did manage to put together a pretty good evening meal."

However, to Smith, "one of the best parts of the meal was the chicken noodle soup. It was thick, had lots of noodles and chicken and, to this day, every time I have chicken noodle soup I think of that soup in Korea. It was absolutely delicious."

In addition to hot food, everyone going through the line received a couple of candy bars, a package of cigarettes or two, and two beers."

"Usually, all the guys in the tent would put their beer together in a wooden case which bomb fuses or .50-calibre ammunition came in. Once the case was full of beer, someone would 'borrow' a fire extinguisher from the flight line and we would use that to cool the beer. That would only happen on days when there were no flights," Smith added.

Motor Vehicle Squadron

It was a blistering hot day, 4 July 1950, when the "Travelers of the Oxcart Highways" started churning the dust of the Korean peninsula The city of Taegu and vicinity was the christening point for these throttle jockeys and wrench pullers in the fight against communism.

Alter a brief regrouping, the mudgrips of the 18th Motor Vehicle Sqdn. once again started grinding over Korean mountains,

18th Fighter-Bomber Group "Self Portraits"
From *Truckbuster*

"We're sorry for the number of times we punctured you with dull needles!"

through rocky river beds and once in awhile, as conditions required, through marshy rice paddies. The mechanics usually worked in a bath of sweat repairing vehicles when mud covered the mechanism and parts were scarce.

As the "Fighters for Freedom" pushed the disintegrating Communist Army up the peninsula the need for frontline support drew the 18th Fighter Bomber Wing to the north. The Motor Vehicle Squadron played a most important role in the operation, as tons of supplies, material, and troops were transported to waiting aircraft and seaports.

When the very unexpected "New War" started, the Travelers struck their tents and commenced the long trek south, carrying a large part of the Wing's supplies and equipment. After weaving in and out of destroyed tanks and other equipment for several days a magnificent job was completed. This jaunt of several hundred miles was a considerable task under normal native circumstances, but this was accomplished despite the fact that all equipment and material had to be transported to the new operations site.

As the battle grew grim the 18th once again took the trails southward. During the trip south and upon arrival at the new airstrip a huge amount of vehicular operation

"Lil" Abner rides a giant flying syringe towards a presumably cowering patient on the sign marking the home of the 18th Medical Detachment. (Stevens)

was required.

The problem of subzero temperatures and adverse weather conditions confronted the outfit during all winter months of operation. Through the untiring efforts of the motor pool and maintenance section along with other units in the organization, the Motor Vehicle squadron played an important role in the build-up of the base and is doing a fine job of keeping the operation of the Wing at its outstanding efficiency level.

Medical Detachment

The 18th Medical Detachment is one unit of the Wing that needs little introduction. Mid agonized moans from mass inoculations we can still say that we have been more than vigilant towards the health and well-being of entire 18th.

Even our airborne hypo needle expresses a certain whimsical humor when it comes to designing distinctive organizational emblems and patches.

We've progressed from the dispensary-tent-and-that's-all state to our present deluxe crash ward, surgery, dental clinic, and base hospital set-up.

Speaking of caduceus characters. Where would you find a more colorful aggregate of personalities such as "Skipalong" Dozois, Major "Rudolph" Riley, and all the other medics whose sense of humor may not be listed as TO/E but is just as essential.

We're sorry for the number of times we punctured you with dull needles and all the other sundry crimes that we have thrown at us, but in all seriousness we can state that we've never unwrapped tongue-depressors

At K-10 the Flights slept together in metal Quonset huts, marginally better accommodations than the tents they used "up North" at K-46. (Pylant)

Life At K-10

Life for all 18th Wing personnal at K-10 in early 1951 was spartan. Airmen and officers alike lived in tents or Quonset huts. Note the Cushman motorscooter parked by the tent at right. (Krakovsky)

in a better outfit than the 18th Fighter-Bomber Wing.

(Below) The "goombo predictors" in the weather detachment launch a weather balloon. (Colton)

*(Above) **Airman Tom Patterson** poses in the door of his K-10 tent for fellow Airman Joseph Krakovsky . (Krakovsky)*

Barracks Life. *Photographer Joe Krakovsky captures life in the barracks at K-10. (Krakovsky)*

Air Postal, Weather, AACS & Combat Cargo

We were all members of the 18th's team and even though we were "attached" we never for a moment felt that we were otherwise than part of a good outfit.

Maybe the postman always rings twice, but there isn't a member of the Air Postal Squadron who didn't feel like ramming the canceling machine down someone's throat at the incessant chorus of "...what? No mail today!" Of course those days when there were takusan sugar reports, we were heroes.

18ᵗʰ Fighter-Bomber Group "Self Portraits"
From *Truckbuster*
"We've seen a lot real estate, strung miles of wire, wrestled with tempermental equipment, moaned, groaned, and griped—but we got the job done and we're still doing it."

Communication Squadron

We Combat Cargo-men had our little problems, too. Juggling manifests, rounding up stray luggage on the ramp, and patiently explaining that the R & R courier WOULD BE ON TIME so please don't leave after you've checked in for a flight! Sometimes we'd be so busy that even Captain Gillis would be actually talking FAST!

The goombo predictors in the Weather Detachment had bad moments when high stratus would drift across the crystal ball, but we usually managed to have enough millibars and adiabatic lapses to go around. There were even times when we were RIGHT, much to the amazement of all. Looking back on the year-plus we couldn't have signed clearances for a greater bunch of guys and we're proud to have been with the 18ᵗʰ.

Historically the AACS detachment hit the field almost before the advance party. Remember the time our makeshift hoist to the tower snapped and the transmitter lay in a thousand pieces before we could even get on the air. Captain O'Connor actually forgot about his trumpet for a moment, but in the months that followed we showed our true colors with a deluxe tower, stateside offices, and even helped form the first swing band in the area. Now O'Connor is wearing leaves and Lt. Adams has taken over, but we'll never forget that we are charter members of Dogpatch and take pride in our contributions to the 18ᵗʰ Fighter-Bomber Wing.

(Right) ***Flying safety cartoon*** *drawn by Sgt. McNichol that appeared in Truckbuster, the 18ᵗʰ Wing's weekly newspaper.*

Any historical flashback on the Communication Squadron requires the use of such names as Major Steele, Master Sergeant Branson, Staff Sergeant Williams, Major Livermore, and a host of other men who helped build the 18ᵗʰ into one of the greatest outfits on the Korean peninsula.

Lynch, Cotton, Short, Foster, Maeder, Embree, and Ritter would be on the honor roll too in summing up the personalities who were with us from the 51ˢᵗ Provisional Squadron phase up to our present stateside operation.

We've seen a lot real estate, strung miles of wire, wrestled with tempermental equipment, moaned, groaned, and griped—but we got the job done and we're still doing it. Collar ornaments have reflected increases in rank just as coveted stripes have been added to fatigue sleeves.

Remember the time Livermore and five airmen turned infrantrymen and practically played hide-and-seek with some guerillas for almost two weeks on that airstrip? And the time we bugged out a matter of hours before the commie avalanche from the north poured over one of our sites.

Now we have cradle phones, permanent structures, and all the many things that we didn't have last year during the "pioneer" days of the 18ᵗʰ. The mud, dust, snow and ice of our first winter in Korea only serve as reminders of just how "fat" we are now.

Today the old-timers can lean back in stateside chairs, quaff good American beer, and impress the replacements with accounts of Pyongyang, Wonsan, Suwon, and other locales that have become part of the Korean struggle. They were more than newspaper headlines to us. We were there.

Air Police Squadron

After months of wonderfully fragrant Korea, the members of "Dogpatch's Finest" can still be found marching through rice paddies and aircraft ramps on cold, dark nights with the same determination that was evident in July of 1950.

We'll never forget that November night when nine AP's were assigned to a "holding action" against the five-thousand enemy, who were supposed to attack "before dawn." Sgt. Bob Smith is still proud of his North Korean flag souvenir.

Our record sparkles with such incidences as Sgt. Kenny Hands proudly bringing in the first live guerilla to be credited to the Air Police. Unforgettable scene: Colonel Low appearing at guard posts all hours of the night with his cheerful grin and understanding words of encouragement.

Many faces and names have come and gone with only a few of the original Dogpatchers left, but our bright star of efficiency remains the same. Our motto, "Efficiency with Understanding" has been well appreciated by the 18th Wing.

Years from now when our men are old and gray they'll recall their part with pride in the "Police Action in Korea," with the accent on Air POLICE!

*(L to R) **Airmen Charles Patterson, Kolar, Redding and King** patrol the boundary of the K-10 Air Base near Chinhae in Fall 1951 in an armored vehicle. (Patterson)*

(Below Left) ***Airman Charles Patterson*** *stands beside an armored vehicle at K-10. One of his duties as an Air Policeman was to patrol the base perimeter and stop infiltration by guerilla forces that continued to operate in the area long after the base was officially listed as "secure." Patterson arrived in Korea in October 1951 and served with the 18th Air Police Squadron until November 1952. Patterson joined the Army in 1947 and was soon posted to Japan where he served as a member of the Sugamo Prison firing squad. In addition he was assigned to 18 of the 68 "hanging guards" squads that carried out the execution of convicted Japanese war criminals--"five at a time." In addition to base security, as a member of the 18th Air Police, Patterson served as a train guard on trips from K-10 to K-46. He volunteered to train dogs as a member of the K-9 unit. Upon selection, it would mean two weeks training in Japan. However, he was turned down for the job, probably "because I played softball-- third base," he recalled. (Patterson)*

18th Supply Squadron

One of the better things that come out of an operation of this type are the fine friends and memories that you collect. Many of us have forgotten some of the happenings so let's go back for awhile.

They had lots of names for that one— they all meant the same thing—you were dumped out in the Korean mud within a few days after the fighting had started. For those who don't know, Bout One boys came from Japan and hit this Land of Morning Calm on 5 July 1950—Dallas may be home to you but to the guys on the project from the Philippines it meant more of that Korean mud and dust—yes, they often came at the same time.

The mud wasn't the only thing either— remember the long days, when normal duty hours meant from 0700 to 2100 and then some—you worked anywhere and at anytime, doing whatever happened to be needed—nobody knew or cared what your spec was but the job got done. And how about that Korean cemetery we lived in— that was quite a deal, with the pup tents stuck up among the graves—but hell, you were so tired by the time you got in the sack that it would have been hard to tell the difference between the living and the dead.

Men like Sergeants Danvers, Whack, Odzana, Pastuszek, MacIntyre, Shimborski, Brim, Holt, Boone, White, Carter, Niemiec, Ryle and all the others will never forget those days—neither will Major Mills, he was the only officer in the supply setup then.

Remember Captain Bell and his LST's?—he left with them loaded with all the heavy stuff and just had them unloaded, when the word came to pull out and he had to load them back up again.

Remember the refugees? You would see a pile of people about twenty feet high and three hundred yards long down the railroad track at a good clip and you knew there had to be a train under them but it was hard to see—any train going south was dressed in white rags and the end the smoke came out of was the engine.

Then came ROTATION and a lot of the old guard went back to Japan and the Phil-

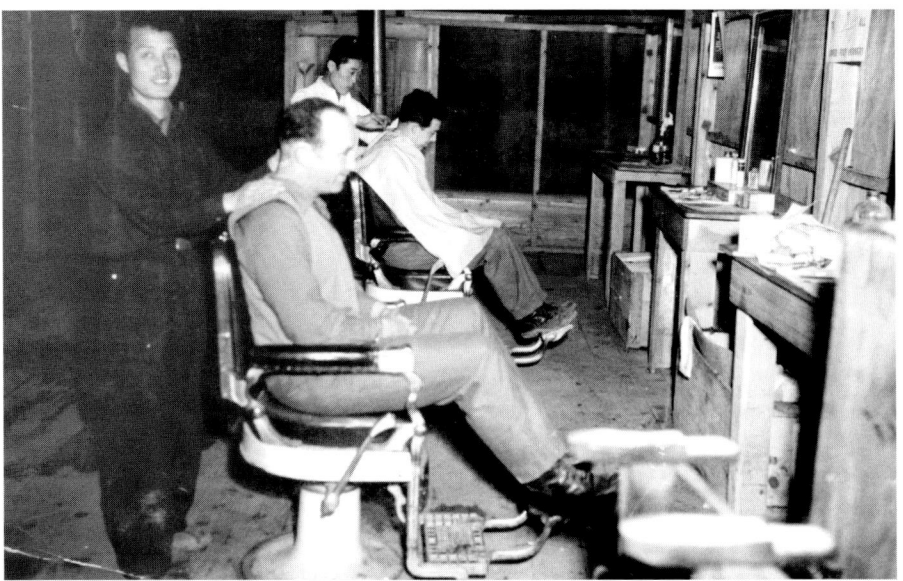

"Just a little off the top." Haircuts could be obtained at K-10 between missions. *(Krakovsky)*

ippines—Major Mills went back to Clark Field and was replaced by Captain Paul R. Williams, our new Base Supply Officer— Major Howard G. Beck took over the CO's slot from Major Rees. Under their direction we forged even further ahead and today the operation is practically Stateside—we have new offices and warehouses, good quarters and good chow—the living is good, that is if living in Korea can be good.

To the men of the 18th Supply Squadron past, present, and future goes the credit for our success and to them—this story is humbly dedicated.

"Water's Turned On NOW!"

204

Gun Camera Film. *Soon after these gun camera film packs were unloaded, they were rushed to the photo lab to be developed, processed and reviewed by Intelligence and Operations Staff Officers.* (Krakovsky)

Film Processing. *(Left) Airman Joseph Krakovsky, the staff photographer for the 18th Wing, processes film in the photolab.*

(Below) **Dogpatch/K-10 photo lab** *in September 1952. Built by the Japanese during their long occupation of Korea, the building was formerly an officer's latrine. Because it was one of the few buildings at K-10 with running water, it became the photo lab.* (Krakovsky)

Keeping Them In The Air At K-10

18th Maintenance

Squadron

Now that we look back on the year in Korea, it can be stated that the 18th's Maintenance Squadron certainly pulled their share in making our Wing the outstanding unit that it is today.

Major Tarr, Major Bill Myers, Sgt Shand and a host of other names are indelibly etched on our memories as the type of men who helped make us a great outfit.

We've set a few records, too. A complete wing change in 350 man-hours with M/Sgt Cowell and his crew humping every minute. Captain Vinson' mentoring our various teams netted us such titles as Dogpatch Softball Champs, Far East Badminton Champions, and so on down the line. Captain Duffy's Flight Test Section racked up 400 flying hours without an accident, and that's nothing but good!

Remember the time last winter when Major Bill and Sgt Shand's six-man salvage crew batted one thousand by pulling four stranded birds right from under the Commies' noses.

Of course we'll never forget Lt. Col. "Swede" Carlson, the World War II Ace, who had the honor of downing a MIG with his Mustang. Swede would sweep through the hangars like a whirlwind, alternately chewing out and passing out sincere "Damn good Job, Sarge."

Yes, the ol' 18th's broken a lot of records and set some new ones in the process. The pages that follow are just a small reflection of the personalities and activities of our squadron. With pardonable pride we can say that the Maintenance men helped make the Truckbusting 18th Fighter-Bomber Wing.

Flight Line at K-10 showing a mix of 12th Squadron, 67th Squadron and 2 Squadron Mustangs being serviced or rearmed. (Krakovsky)

That's My Story and I'm Sticking To It

T/Sgt Wylie Bryant, 39th Squadron, was"known throughout the Air Force as the greatest Mustang crew chief of all time," according to the always objective views of his fellow Blinker Nose Squadron correspondent, Lt. Richard Ward. "I like the F-51 becuz we have so little trouble with the nose gear and the only bucket we have to change is the pilot's seat," Bryant reportedly said.

When questioned "by a pretty service club hostess" as to the purpose of the "yellow tips on the F-51 prop?"

Sgt. Bryant reportedly replied quick as a Mustang, "To keep the black paint from sliding off in flight."

Any more questions?

Dogpatch Hospital for Sick "Birds" (Not Dogs)!

By S/Sgt Sandy Colton

The 18th Fighter-Bomber Wing in Korea has a base hospital for sick "birds"! Throughout the Fifth Air Force an aircraft is affectionately called a "bird" by the men who work and fly them. Occasionally these "birds" get sick from mechanical fatigue or—as will happen in any war—"lead poison" and must undergo a major operation to regain their health. These are the reasons for the 18th's Dogpatch Air Base "Hospital"—the base maintenance shops!

A crew chief on the aircraft will handle minor ailments, such as an engine adjustment, but it takes the specialists in the Maintenance shops to do some of the major repair work—an engine change for example.

Like the huge city hospital the base maintenance shops are staffed with many sorts of specialists. Although different types entirely from the city doctors, these maintenance doctors are concerned with saving or extending a life—the life of their mechanical patients—the birds that are flying tactical ground support missions daily against the enemy forces.

Instead of eye, ear, nose, throat, or heart specialists, the maintenance shop's staff includes instrument, sheet metal, woodwork, engine mechanical, paint, dope, and fabric specialists as well as many others. Each specialist has his part to play in the overall job of reclaiming and revitalizing the war weary little fighter—the F-51 Mustang—and other aircraft that come into the shops!

The 18th's hospital for sick "birds" has operated from many airstrips throughout the Korean peninsula where the shops usually consisted of little more than an open field.

Portable lights—even flashlights—were utilized for the performance of an "emergency operation" during the hectic "July days" last year when night work was a must. Many times unavailable parts were hand tooled in the portable base maintenance tool shops. Crashed aircraft were quickly "skeletonized" by eager maintenance personnel "cannibalizing" the valuable parts.

In a matter of days—and sometimes hours—a major repair work was completed on an aircraft and that aircraft was quickly returned to "duty" in the air war over Korea.

It is not at all unusual to see a team of specialists working on a single aircraft. The sheet metal men may be patching up holes from ground fire, while another group of mechanics are hoisting out the old engine to swing in a new one. At the same time a paint-dope-fabric specialist will be painting new insignia on the underside of the wing, a radio repairman working on the radio, an instrument specialist testing and replacing those vital "gauges," and right on down the line. Each specialist with his own job to do.

Primarily, the Dogpatcher's maintenance shops are concerned with the F-51 Mustang fighter plane, but they can, and have, worked on bigger jobs. Just recently they performed a 2,000 hour inspection on a base C-47—"surgery" usually performed in a well equipped factory. Everything on the C-47 had to be inspected and, if necessary, replaced. The entire aircraft was literally taken apart piece by piece, cleaned, inspected, repaired, or replaced.

Once an aircraft is ready to be released from this "hospital" another type of specialist goes to work on it. The inspectors fine-tooth-comb that aircraft. On a Mustang, the check list is six pages long and consists of 152 items. Each of these items leads to many others so that the sum total of items checked runs into the thousands and includes just about every nut, bolt and connection on that airplane. This is insurance that nothing will be overlooked in the "bird's" repair.

The final inspection ends with a test flight and if the "bird" comes through OK it is returned to the line where lethal fire bombs, rockets, .50-caliber ammunition and other accessories are attached. Once more it is a sleek, shiny, healthy weapon of war. Once more the "bird" becomes a welcome sight to the United Nations forces at the front and a dreaded sight to the enemy. Outstanding testimony to the efficiency of the Dogpatch hospital for sick "birds" are the 10,000 effective combat sorties against the enemy flown by the "birds" whose health these men look after.

*18th **Wing Mustang** taxies down the K-10 runway with Chinhae Bay just a few feet away. Numerous accidents involved planes ditching in the bay following problems on landing or take-off. Several pilots were lost in such accidents. (Krakovsky)*

The "Little Guy"

Tribute to the Crew Chiefs

Story and photographs by William J. "Sandy" Colton

Pre-Dawn Warmup. *A 12ᵗʰ Squadron Crew Chief warms up his bird to prepare it for a pre-dawn mission. (Colton)*

Imagine that you are visiting a fighter strip such as that maintained by the 18ᵗʰ Fighter Bomber Wing in Korea. Standing near a Squadron operations tent you watch an F-51 Mustang taxi into a parking area. A Little Guy wearing greasy coveralls signals the Mustang into its parking position. The engine revs up, coughs, then spits off while the Little Guy chocks the wheels and climbs up on the wing to help the pilot out of his harness.

"How'd it go, Sir!" he asks.

"Rough engine," answers the pilot. "I checked the mags. She almost cut out on left mag. Better check the plugs."

Before the pilot has left the airplane to turn in his personal equipment that Little Guy is tearing off the engine cowling to check the spark plugs.

Who is this Little Guy?

You rarely read about him but he is pretty important. You may read about some pilot shooting down an enemy aircraft but if it hadn't been for that Little Guy that pilot might not have come back. It may sound far-fetched but the pilot could have had engine trouble during his aerial battle and lost. Or, that Little Guy could have been lax in another way and the plane might not have got off the ground. Who is that Little Guy? He's the crew chief.

Go over and look at his hands. Under the grease and oil you'll see that they are scarred, chapped and cracked with skin

torn off at the knuckles. Those hands symbolize long hours spent working with a wrench—bare hands in cold, miserable weather. The crew chief's lungs are probably filled with dust blown up by the propwash of passing planes—his shop is an open field, the parking area. After a rain he may have to stand in mud over his shoe-tops and search for a fallen nut in deep mire.

At night you can see him working by flashlight. Yet, he's in love with his airplane and doctors it like a sick child to get it in the air again.

The Mustang crew chief is unusual in that he never gets to fly in his airplane, or "bird" as he calls it. The F-51 is a one-man airplane so there isn't room for him. Yet, that crew chief loves his bird so much that he wants it to be the best in the air—like a proud father shows off his son to friends.

You would have to be a crew chief to understand what it's like to be in love with an airplane; to give it human qualities and shower it with affection. The crew chief, pilot, and bird make up a close knit family. They have a bond of understanding that holds them together. When a pilot and bird have left on a mission over enemy territory our Little Guy "sweats out" their return. To ease the strain of waiting he will help another crew chief service his aircraft. He wants to work to keep from wondering "if

A crew chief loves his bird so much that he wants it to be the best in the air— like a proud father shows off his son to friends. You would have to be a crew chief to understand what it's like to be in love with an airplane; to give it human qualities and shower it with affection. Sandy Colton

Crew Chiefs anxiously watch their birds lift off on a combat mission. (Colton)

Crew Chief Hangout. Where do Mustang Crew Chiefs hang out? On a Mustang's wing, of course--as here at K-10. (Colton)

that mag holds up" or if his family is in trouble.

He will keep glancing at his watch and when it is time for his bird and pilot to come home he'll search the skies until he spots his aircraft. Then, a small, proud smile will show through the grease smeared on his face and he'll run over to the parking area to guide the pilot in.

His bird came home.

If the crew chief's aircraft is not with the returning flight he'll hurry to where the other planes are parking and wait eagerly for one of the other pilots to tell him what happened. If his pilot and bird went down there is no one more miserable than the crew chief—even though it wasn't his fault. The grief is as deep and real as that suffered from losing immediate members of your family.

Officially a crew chief's job is to service his aircraft with minor repairs, but when and if necessary, he'll work all night to get his bird in the air again and do major repair work, such as an engine change.

Major repairs are supposed to be performed by the maintenance shops. Visit one and you'll see the crew chiefs standing around, like husbands in a maternity ward, wanting to do something to help get their birds out and in the air again. Maintenance personnel sympathize with the crew chiefs and usually let them help to speed the repair work.

Normally, like those with the 18th in Korea, a crew chief's day in a combat zone starts before daylight and ends after dark.

At 0430 the crew chief is in his airplane turning the engine over and giving it a final check before it leaves on an early morning mission. Only after he's checked the bird's pulse will he get that first cup of hot coffee!

Each time the bird returns from a mission the crew chief refuels it and gives it another check. After the last mission he will give it a final "run-up" before putting it to bed. It is well after dark by then. The crew chief's hours depend on the amount of work to be done on his bird. If repairs are needed, he'll work through the night to have it ready by morning.

Pilots recognize the faithfulness of their crew chiefs and stand a little in awe of it. When a pilot returns from a mission he will discuss the airplane with the crew chief—always referring to it as "her." It's an affectionate her for a mutual love. Before he leaves, the pilot will let the crew chief know what "their" bird did to the enemy that day. The Little Guy gets a personal debriefing all his own.

Provided there is no work to be done at the end of the day, the crew chief will put his bird to bed. Then, the Little Guy with the greasy coveralls and the skinned up hands will wash up and "hit the pad" in preparation for an early morning warm-up and another day of sweating his family out.

The Little Guy is tired, but happy. His bird and pilot are home—safe!

*"**High Mission**" pilots of the 67th Squadron pose for a "football in cheek" photo lineup in late January 1951. (Front row) Capt. Marvin H. Castleberry (100), Capt. Lucien B. Schuler (59), Capt. Bill Myers (51), Capt. William Strand (54), Capt. Harold M. Powers (17), Capt. John H. Spencer (85) and Capt. "Smitty" (14). (Rear, L to R) Major Herman Solem (55), Major Charles E. McGee (82), Lt. Col. William E. May (48), and Major Arnold Mullins (86). "The pass in the background," noted Major Bill Myers on the back of this photograph, "is the route taken by the flights as they took off and landed. The name is really Chinhae. Masan is over the hill to the left. The area where the aircraft are parked is all former rice paddy ground filled in from dirt hauled from the small hill behind the tents. The tanks are all napalm tanks. Tent area belongs to the Runway Engineers." Several copies of this photograph exist, including ones provided by Bill Myers and Charles Morehouse, who noted on the back of his photograph the number of missions each pilot had at the time. Morehouse also noted that as of 26 January 1951 the 67th Squadron had completed 1937 combat missions with a total of 5,645 combat hours. (Myers)*

Technical Wizards

The ground crew personnel we had in the 18th Fighter-Bomber Wing that kept the aircraft in readiness to accomplish our missions were technical wizards," recalled Lt. Col. Peter Richardson, formerly a pilot with the 12th Squadron.

"They were ingenious, conscientious, and dedicated to their work of assuring the integrity and readiness of their aircraft to accomplish the assigned missions. In carrying out their responsibilities, in my experience with flying fighters, there was a singular comradeship, a closeness, between the pilot and the crew chief and his technicians."

In the 12th Squadron, the crew chief and usually other techs, would greet the pilot at the assigned Mustang, then the chief would do the walk-around with the pilot, usually accompanied by light banter and a laugh or two. The crew chief never failed to climb up on the wing to help the pilot strap in and then jump down to coordinate the engine start-up. As the fighter started out of the line, the chief would wave and salute, a confident smile on his face and a prayer in his eyes. What more could be expected?" Richardson asked.

The pilot felt "great confidence that the fighter would work well enough to accomplish the mission and get him home, barring being shot down—or my goofing," Richardson noted.

During his sixty missions with the 12th Squadron, Richardson recalled "no aborts nor a compromised mission. In the remaining forty seven missions with the 36th Squadron (8th Group) however, I had two aborts, one due to failure of the left landing gear to retract. The other abort was due to enemy fire, not maintenance."

The 18th Wing ground crews "earned a sky full of recognition," by 18th pilots.

Major Bill Myers is helped into his shoulder harness by his crew chief prior to a mission from K-10. (Myers)

Waiting for their bird to come home. Crew Chiefs of 18th Group Squadrons sit on tool boxes and anything else handy as they wait for their bird to return from a combat mission. (Colton)

K-10 maintenance hangar *on July 3, 1952. Three 2 Squadron and one 67th Squadron Mustangs undergo heavy maintenance. (Krakovsky)*

Inside the heavily damaged, but usable hangar at K-10, 2 Squadron SAAF mechanics could and did virtually rebuild the aging and damaged Mustangs. It was the efforts of highly skilled and dedicated ground crews that kept the vintage Mustangs flying well past the time when they should have been retired from combat flying. (Krakovsky)

Mustangs of the 67th Squadron *parked beside the maintenance hangar at Chinhae Air Base (K-10), South Korea.*

212

Flight Line Maintenance and Re-arming

2 Squadron Flight Line at K-10. The "Flying Chetahs" of South Africa's Two Squadron were attached to the 18th Fighter-Bomber Wing and were highly respected by their American colleagues for their professionalism and courage. (Krakovsky)

"The Beast" and other 12th Squadron Mustangs are readied for their next mission from K-10. (Krakovsky)

(Left) *Busy maintenance crew* services a Flying Cheetah Mustang at K-10. (Krakovsky)

Crewed and Rearmed. A Mustang of the 18th Fighter-Bomber Wing is hurriedly "crewed and rearmed" at K-10 for another mission on January 30, 1951.

High Velocity Aircraft Rockets (HVAR)

USAF fighter-bombers used the HVAR to knock out Communist tanks, trains, and bunkers. Originally developed by the U.S. Navy in World War II, the HVAR's TNT warhead sped to the target at 1,360 fps.

Two types of aircraft rockets were employed in Korea: the 5.0" HVAR and the 6.5" ATAR (anti-tank aircraft rocket). The 5.0" HVAR was the standard USAF and USN aircraft rocket and was used with a MK-148 nose fuse and a MK-149 tail fuse installed in the warhead.

The warhead was a blast type with approximately eight pounds of HE (high explosive) filler.

In July, 1950, when an urgent need was identified for a shaped charged anti-tank aircraft rocket, the 6.5" ATAR was developed and rushed to the theater in August 1950. The ATAR used the standard 5.0" HAVR and had a shaped charge warhead, with a filler weight of approximately 19 pounds.

Rearming 67th Squadron Mustangs at K-10. (Krakovsky)

NAPALM

NAPALM was an acronym derived from naphthenic and palmitic acids whose salts are used in its manufacture. NAPALM is a jellied gasoline used in flamethrowers, fougasses and aerial bombs. Napalm was used in two forms, the 110-gallon drop tank with one or two igniters and the AN/M-76 gasoline jel bomb using an AN/M-103 nose fuse and an AN/M-101-A2 tail fuse.

Normal loading for napalm was two tanks or bombs per fighter-bomber aircraft.

"Napalm destroyed or neutralized more T-34 tanks than all other airborne weapons combined," according to FAF operational analyses.

"Approximately 10 times as many tanks were claimed to have been destroyed (or 14 times as many hit) by rockets as by napalm...it can only be concluded that whereas relatively large effort has been expended in shooting rockets at enemy tanks, and apparently resulting in hits, actually only a small fraction were hits. Had actual hits been obtained, a much larger number of tanks would have been found [destroyed] due to rockets." [1]

Because napalm is generally used against relatively small targets, and because it must spread to a large area when dropped, it is released at a low altitude where the bomb will have a skipping effect on impact, the Combat Operations Manual for the 18th Fighter-Bomber Wing explained.

"The bomb run should not be a shallow one as you present much too fine a target for the enemy. A high angle dive with a level out before release at 50'-100' followed by a sharp break in either direction will prove to be the most effective while subjecting yourself to a minimum possibility of being hit. Be prepared for instability resulting from a "hung-up" bomb when at release altitude, as aircraft have been known to execute a roll if not properly checked."

[1] NARA. Fifth Air Force Operations Analysis Office Memorandum No. 35, March 1, 1951. CONFIDENTIAL Declassified.

Napalm was the fighter-bomber pilot's most feared weapon by enemy ground troops. The 18th Wing used hundreds of tanks of the jellied gasoline each month. (Krakovsky)

Firefighters Saved Lives
and Mustangs

Manuel V. Andujar, was ordered from the Air Force aircraft fire fighting school at Eglin AFB in Florida, to Japan, in 1950. After the rest of the 18ᵗʰ Wing personnel, equipment and supplies arrived, "we traveled by LST to Pusan, Korea. From Pusan we transported bombs and supplies to Taegu, and from there on it seemed like we were on our own," he remembered. "We followed the troops wherever they went all the way to the Manchurian border and the Yalu River."

"Then, we had to retreat and travel light. We destroyed our trucks and equipment, including our bags full of clothes. Finally, we settled south of Seoul at the airport."

"Our main job as firefighters and aircraft crash rescue personnel was to save lives and property. I thank the good Lord for looking after each and every one of us. I did not lose any of my men to the enemy or the elements. I am glad to report that everyone in my unit returned home safe and sound."

"Most of the aircraft that crashed came in and landed either shot up or on fire. However, many of the dedicated young pilots refused to abandon ship and instead brought their planes in regardless—hoping to give them another chance to take to the air one more time," Andujar recalled.

18ᵗʰ Wing fire crew member leans on the bumper of an 18ᵗʰ Wing fire truck based at K-46. *(Andujar)*

Front of the 18ᵗʰ Fighter-Bomber Wing Hospital at K-10. *(McLoughlin)*

Crash boats moored alongside the runway at K-10 are refueled. *(McLoughlin)*

The Air Force "Navy"

Crash Boats and Crews at K-10

Air Force Crash Boat Crews Wore Navy-type Uniforms. *Because the airstrip at K-10 paralled Chinhae Bay, which was just a few feet from the runway, crash boats and crews were stationed nearby and alerted whenever air operations were underway. The crews aboard the craft were Air Force personnel, but wore uniforms similar to U.S. Navy enlisted crews. Sleeve ranks however, were Air Force. (Krakovsky)*

217

At first glance this may look like the P-82 or "double P-51." Closer inspection reveals that this is a aircraft accident scene in which a 67th Squadron Mustang has hit and partially destroyed a Mustang belonging to the ROK Air Force. Manuel Andujar, a member of the rescue and fire fighting crew standing on the wing of the American Mustang, has written "me" on this photograph for his scrapbook. (Andujar)

The accident scene above seen from another angle illustrates the extensive damage to both aircraft. Andujar (white shirt) examines the aircraft for damage and fire. (Andujar)

This 18th Wing pilot did a good job with his "wheels up" landing. The maintenance crews will have this 67th Squadron bird in the air again very soon. (Andujar)

"Top of the Mark" Officers Club at K-10. *(Urquhart)*

To his squadron—informally—Major Carl C. Colson, Commanding Officer of the 67th Squadron in January 1952 was known as "Shorty." In person, "we knew him as 'Sir,'"recalled Wilfred "Budd" Stapley, a former pilot with the 67th.

During a party for new replacements at the K-10 club, "we were sitting around and singing songs. Someone, never identified or acknowledged, poured a drink over Stapley's head.

Getting up quickly…and perhaps, unsteadily…Stapley looked around for the culprit and spotted a stranger "with the most guilty look on his face that you ever saw," Stapley related later, "standing there with an empty glass."

Quickly grabbing him by the lapel with one hand, Stapley, a six-footer, poured a full glass of beer over the head of the guilty looking officer. Major Colson, all five foot five inches of the 67th's Commanding Officer, was "not amused." Nor, apparently, was he guilty of the "drink over the head" prank.

"Let's get him out of here!" Stapley's friends concluded.

Seeing the need for an immediate and hasty exit from the "party," two of Stapley's buddies grabbed him by the elbows and hustled him out of the Top of the Mark Club. Aptly named, the club was on top of a small hill. Patrons exiting the club came down the steps and made a sharp right turn— with no guardrail.

A very real danger for the unwary was a sharp drop for those who failed to "negotiate" the turn—into a canal—that also served as an open sewer drain.

Leaving the club hastily and in full retreat from an irate Major Colson, Stapley and his buddies "missed the turn" and found themselves going "elbows over @#$@#*$" down the embankment and into the stinking mire at the bottom.

Stapley remembered waking up the next morning "and I'm all beat up" (from the fall down the embankment) and my $450 uniform is piled in a soggy heap at the foot of my cot." Coming to, as opposed to waking up, Stapley asked, "What happened?" The answer he got from his buddies, who were not too happy about the malodorous trio, was full of foreboding for his relationship with "Shorty" Colson, "Oh Stapley," they told him, "you really F—ed up."

219

"Top of the Mark" Officers Club at Chinhae, South Korea (K-10).

The paintings

The fieldstone fireplace below the painting of the voluptuous girl in the K-10 Top of the Mark Club was often used for more than simply burning wood to heat the area.

From time to time, usually after some particularly serious "toasting," glasses would be hurled in the general direction of the fireplace where they shattered loudly into O'Club "flak." It was even believed in some circles that as Happy Hour progressed, accuracy might have been "off" somewhat. Generally, the flying glasses hit the fireplace.

It was a "tradition" at the Top of the Mark Club at K-10—sort of.

The Officer Club decorations eventually made seven moves, including: K-2, K-9, K-24, K-13, K-10, K-46 and K-55. Major Bill Myers took this photograph on one of those "moving days." (Myers)

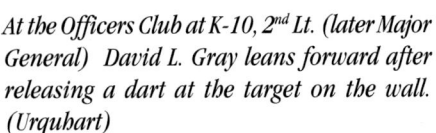

At the Officers Club at K-10, 2nd Lt. (later Major General) David L. Gray leans forward after releasing a dart at the target on the wall. (Urquhart)

220

Winter Wonderland

It was hot when the gooks came.
Then it froze when the Chinks came.
A helluva sight, Korea in white.
In our lousy winter wonderland!
We were pinned down, down at Ma-san,
A helluva fight, we never were right,
In Korea's winter wonder land.

Kim Il Sung was seeking a promotion,
Had us locked within the Naktong bend!
Then MacArthur had a better notion,
Ran Ned Almond clear around the end!

What a break! It was clover!
And the damned war was over!
It looked like a breeze—until the Chinese,
Smacked us in our winter wonderland!

*Anonymous, in 18th Fighter-Bomber
Wing Song Book courtesy William
J. "Sandy" Colton*

Ay Ziga Zumba!!

In the United States, disk jockies have "The Thing," S/Sgt Sandy Colton pointed out in an early 1951 article for Stars and Stripes. In Korea, they have "The Thing" in the form of a Zulu victory song that goes something like: "Ay Ziga Zumba Zumba Zumba. Ay Ziga Zumba Zumba Zay!"

The chant was introduced to American flyers by members of the 2 Squadron, South African Air Force. "The canticle has caught on like wildfire. The words to this haunting song echo over this advanced Fifth Air

Blues of Chinhae

From Chinhae to Pyongyang,
From Taegu to Seoul.
Wherever our Mustangs go.
I've dropped me some napalm.
I've fired me six rockets.
But there is one thing I know.
The Chinese are two-faced,
A worrisome thing, who'll
Leave you to sing
The blues of Chinhae.

(CHORUS)
Hear the Flak a-blown',
See the MIG's A-going'
WILDWEST, I can't get my tanks off.
Well laddie, you've had it.
But there is one thing I know.
You can't do a thing,
But sit here and sing,
The Blues of Chinhae.

We call into Mellow,
He thinks we are yellow.
But on to the target we go.
The weather is stinkin',

The engines are clinkin',
But there is one thing I know.
The 80's can't do it,
They're bungling things that leave you to sing,
The Blues of Chinhae.

(CHORUS)
Up and down the Yalu
Hear the pilots yelling—HEY YOU!
By Order of MacArthur,
We can't do a thing,
but sit here and sing,
The Blues of Chinhae.

We call a controller
He starts beating his molars.
His answer is "Stand by Please."
I'm working some 84's,
I do wish they'd carry more,
They' only fanning the breeze.
They'll be through in a minute,
Then you can come in,
And do the right thing,
For the Group from Chinhae.

(CHORUS)

Coming down the Nak-tong,
Pilots like to sing but one song,
I've finished my missions,
Let me go fishing.
But the first thing he does,
Is come in to buzz,
The strip at Chinhae.

Now this ends my story
Of Fame and of of Glory.
Together we've known hectic days.
We've had many good laughs,
The 18th and South Af's,
For whom we have nothing but praise.
Oh, I'm goin' to the ZI,
And tell one and all,
Of the deeds large and small,
Of the Group from Chinhae.

*Anonymous, in 18th Fighter-Bomber
Wing Song Book courtesy William
J. "Sandy" Colton*

Force airbase as both the Americans and South Africans chant the peculiar incantation during the nightly get togethers."

The music was supposedly adapted from a South African Zulu tribe's victory song—sung after the return from a successful war party or hunt. Colton found it "aboriginal and eerie."

The intent and the translation of the chorus "could aptly be applied to the part the colorful "Flying Cheetah" Squadron is playing in the air war over Korea," Colton pointed out.

"Hold him down you Zulu warrior," the chorus rings, "Hold him down you Zulu Chief!"

The South African flyers were indeed "holding them down" each time they came in contact with enemy forces.

"Although they arrived in Korea only last November to join the battle against Red aggression, the South Africans have already flown well over 1,000 combat effective sorties over enemy territory," Colton noted. "On many of these mission, SAAFs and Americans have flown side by side. The South African pilots drew high praise from the Americans both for their flying ability and their efficiency in spotting and destroying deceptive Communist targets."

Some difficulty was encountered early on, Colton said, "in the colloquial speech differences of the two countries. These however, were taken in stride and now it is not at all unusual to hear both SAAF and American pilots talking with a peculiar mixture of both American and South African slang."

When the 2 Squadron arrived in Japan in November 1950 for training, "many of the men had never before seen an F-51 Mustang, having worked with British Spitfires and Jet Vampires. The ground crews quickly became adept at maintenance while the pilots later proved their proficiency with the Mustang in the air over Korea."

Every member of the 2 Squadron was a volunteer. The South African Constitution has a Defense Act which prohibits any male from forced participation in any conflict outside of the Union of South Africa, Colton pointed out.

"Charley Tune" area of the K-10 "Top of the Mark" Officers Club in early 1952 where 18th Group pilots made "nail cuts" in the floor while singing Ay Ziga Zumba. The officer on the guitar is Lt. A. S. Van der Spuy--"Topper 6" or just "Topper," his call sign during WWII in Italy--a pilot with the 2 Squadron SAAF. Behind Topper is 2nd Lt. John W. Yingling. At right rear, Second Lt. Archie Connors of the 67th Squadron sings along.

Pilots for 2 Squadron, SAAF, were "big men with big moustaches and big hearts." They were physically bigger than most of the American pilots.

"Aye Ziga Zoomba" may just be a faintly remembered old song for some. But for veterans of the 18th FBW it will always be associated with the 2nd South African Air Force Squadron—the "Flying Cheetahs."

"We would form a circle at the Club," Budd Stapley remembered, "all of us wearing our heavy boots, and we'd start singing:

'Aye zigga zoomba, zoomba, zoomba, Aye zigga zoomba, zoomba, zay! Aye zigga zoomba, zoomba, zoomba, Aye zigga zoomba, zoomba, zay! Mow 'em down, you Zulu Warriors! Mow 'em down, you Zulu chief! After the verse was finished, we came to 'Chief, Chief, Chief'—and the boots would come crashing down on the floor boards. The first guy to actually break a floorboard with the heel of his boot was the hero for the evening.

Commander of the 2 Squadron SAAF Maj. J.P.D. Blaauw completed his missions in 1951 and was rotated home. (Pasqualicchio)

Behind "Dogpatch"

In the late 1920s, at the age of 19, Alfred Gerald Caplin ("Al Capp"), became the youngest syndicated cartoonist in America when he began drawing "Colonel Gilfeather," a daily panel for the Associated Press. In 1934, he took an idea for a new cartoon strip with a hillbilly theme to United Features Syndicate. At first "Li'l Abner" was carried by only eight newspapers. However, the hapless residents of Dogpatch struck a nerve in Depression-era America. In just three years it was reaching 253 newspapers

Tom Gilliland, the 18th's command photographer, hand colored a photocopy of the original line art drawing provided by cartoonist Al Capp who created the 'Lil Abner Truckbuster logo.

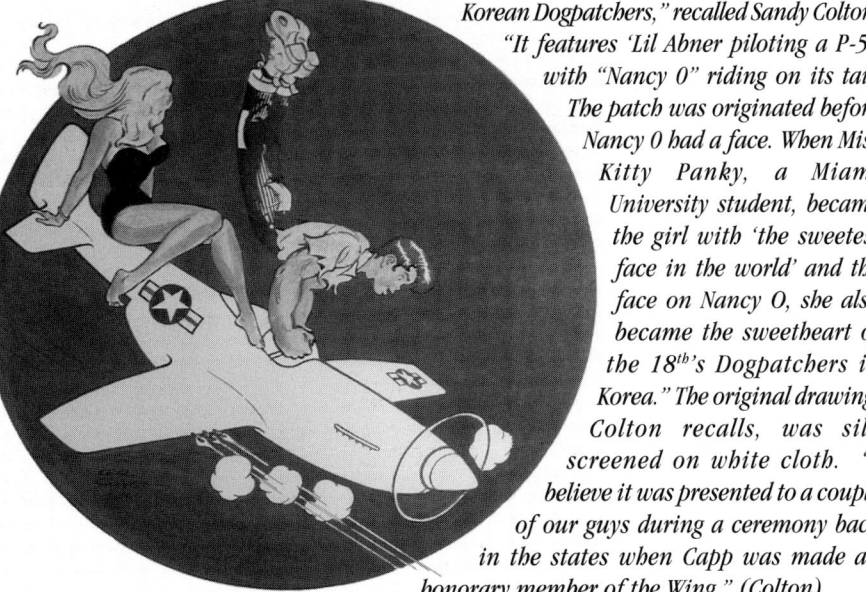

"A Cappian patch, drawn by Al himself, was the pride of the Korean Dogpatchers," recalled Sandy Colton. "It features 'Lil Abner piloting a P-51 with "Nancy O" riding on its tail. The patch was originated before Nancy O had a face. When Miss Kitty Panky, a Miami University student, became the girl with 'the sweetest face in the world' and the face on Nancy O, she also became the sweetheart of the 18th's Dogpatchers in Korea." The original drawing, Colton recalls, was silk screened on white cloth. "I believe it was presented to a couple of our guys during a ceremony back in the states when Capp was made an honorary member of the Wing." (Colton)

Sergeant Dave McNichol, a key member of the 18th Wing's graphics presentation section, completes the first copy of Al Capp's Nancy O insignia. Al Capp himself had chosen Ms Kitty Panky, the possessor of the "sweetest face" in the U.S., as the face for "Nancy O." Ms. Panky was chosen the sweet heart of the 18th Wing.

with 15 million readers. Soon it was reaching hundreds of newspapers with a circulation of over 60 million readers.

Capp's colorful characters and zany life in Dogpatch were changing popular culture throughout America. For example, in 1937 he introduced the annual Sadie Hawkins Day race into the strip. Soon real life girl-asks-boy dances were being held across the country. In 1948, Capp's lovable Shmoo characters became a national sensation— and the largest mass merchandising phenomenon of its era. [1] When Capp married Li'l Abner and Daisy Mae in 1952, it was an event that made front-page news.

The heartless capitalist General Bullmoose, the human jinx Joe Bfstplk (followed by his own rain cloud), Evil Eye Fleegle (owner of the double whammy that could melt skyscrapers), Lonesome Polecat and Hairless Joe (who lived in a cave and concocted Kickapoo Joy Juice, the ultimate moonshine), Fearless Fosdick (the fumbling detective with a bullet-riddled body), Moonbeam McSwine (gorgeous, but malodorous), and Mammy Yokum (a sweet old lady who could out box men).

Capp's Dogpatch was sadder and poorer than any stereotype of Appalachia. Its yokel residents were dumber than dumb, or else scoundrels and thieves. "Most of the men were too lazy to work, yet Dogpatch women were desperate enough to chase them. One preferred to live with hogs. Those who farmed their "tarnip" crop watched turnip termites descend every year, locust-like, to devour the crop. In the midst of the Great Depression, lowly Dogpatch allowed the most hard-up Americans to laugh at yokels worse off than they were. In Al Capp's own

223

words Dogpatch was "an average stone-age community" nestled in a bleak valley, between two cheap and uninteresting hills, somewhere. To old friends, the denizens of Dogpatch will be old friends. To strangers, however, they will probably be strangers."
[2]

In July 1950, "heat waves shimmered upward from rain pools alongside the airstrip" at K-9 near Pusan, South Korea. Colonel Curtis Low, Captain George Bales, and S/Sgt William J. "Sandy" Colton surveyed the "uninspiring Korean landscape" from their ankle-deep vantage point in the mud.

"Lower Slobovia or Dogpatch couldn't be worse than this" commented Low, while his two companions nodded agreement. So it was that "Dogpatch" began to eventually "seep through to the stateside press and become a familiar label of the 18th Fighter Bomber Wing.

Journalist Sandy Colton began datelining his news releases with the descriptive title and before long the 18th became identified as the Dogpatchers of Korea. In fact, "the 18th became synonymous with Al Capp's comic strip village to such an extent that celebrities of the Bob Hope, Marlyn Maxwell, and Jolson stature were usually met with banners and signs proclaiming proudly that the 18th was truly an airborne version of the popular stateside cartoon strip."

Dear Mr. Capp...We Is Your Boys!

On 6 January 1951, Colton, sat down at the rickety typewriter sitting at the packing crate that served as his "desk" in the public information spaces of the 18th Wing office and began putting together a letter to famed cartoonist, Al Capp from "South Dogpatch Air Base, South Korea."

"Some time ago our Commanding General [actually Col. Low] sent you a brochure of things along with a letter about our base, Dogpatch. I read the letter the other day and was tempted to write this letter to you because of it. The other letter from Colonel Low didn't tell you a lot of things about the outfit, nor did it tell you any of the things

that have happened since then."

Colton then brought Capp up to date regarding the Wing and its component Squadrons.

"The name of the outfit is no longer the 6002nd Tactical Support Wing. It was redesignated the 18th Fighter-Bomber Wing. The name of the base isn't the same any more either but that's because it isn't the same base," Colton explained.

"The original Dogpatch Air Base [K-9] was located near Pusan. It was from there that our "boss" wrote to you. Soon after we followed the war and moved. Being a tactical support Wing we had to stay right on the tails of the UN forces up front all the time. We operated out of Wonsan in North Korea and made history there. We were the first outfit to operate from an airstrip above the 38th Parallel and even beat the Marines into Wonsan! From Wonsan we returned to Pusan and soon after moved again to Pyongyang, the North Korean capital. This base became known as North Dogpatch. We gave the North Koreans hell from there up until the time of the reverses when the Chinese came in and pushed our forces back," Colton continued.

"Your boys didn't give out easily though. We stuck it out until the end. It was only four hours after the last of us left that strip that it was in Chinese hands. From Pyongyang we moved into Suwon, just below Seoul, the South Korean capital. That became

known as central Dogpatch. We stuck it out there until we got kicked out again, just a couple of days ago. Then we moved to Chinhae, down between Masan and Pusan in South Korea--this is South Dogpatch."

"This wing is what they call a "bastard" outfit," Colton continued. "We were born as a result of the Korean war. That type of outfit usually draws the rough end of things and we have certainly had our share. Excepting for Wonsan and this base, every one of our bases have been stinking, muddy, dusty, former rice paddies. Living conditions got worse rather than better after we left Pusan, those guys in this wing have worked miracles, gone through hell, and come out proud, Mr. Capp—proud of themselves, their record and their name—Dogpatch."

"We were the first outfit to go into action in this war. A group of volunteers from the 13th Air Force were rushed off to Taegu to give the first tactical ground support our boys got in this thing—and we've been at it ever since."

"Our pilots flew beat out, obsolete F-51's that should have seen a graveyard long ago. Some of those original planes are still with us. The ground crews improvised tools and everybody was putting in a normal day of from 12 to 24 hours a day. With that combination we did our part to hold them back at the Pusan Perimeter. Ask any G.I. who saw those planes overhead while he was in a foxhole up front. He'll tell you how much

General T. C. Rogers *(center) and* ***Col. "Curt" Low****, check out some Dogpatch art at K-10 in early 1951.* (Krakovsky)

they did."

"All this time an outfit was forming. We kept our airplanes going full strength in the air while we built this outfit up around them; in the field; in combat. We built the machine that keeps them going and supplied with bombs, ammunition, rockets, napalm, and repairs. Mr. Capp, we've got an outfit that is an outfit!" Colton added proudly.

"Our record will speak for us. It shows that we have flown more sorties than any other outfit over here, our list of kills is a big one too. The best—tanks, personnel, equipment, planes—we've knocked them all out and in big numbers. I believe the enemy knows who we are too. In November a bunch of Yak's started to come over from Manchuria to attack our boys. We knocked down seven in a week."

"All our boys drive are what the papers call "slow conventional type aircraft." The Russian jets that have been coming over this way are afraid of those slow conventional things though. For a while there they would attack our planes but the boys would shoot them up and they'd run for home across the border. We never even got a scratch. Our pilots are getting mad because they never see enemy aircraft any more, they are afraid of us. They seem to fight with other outfits but not the Dogpatch pilots. We're your boys, Mister Capp."

"We have three fighter squadrons under the Wing. One of them is called the "Flying Tigers of Korea." Syngman Rhee dubbed them that for being the first outfit here and voluntary."

"The planes with that squadron, the 12th, have the same sharks teeth painted on them that the old Flying Tigers in China used to have. The 2nd Squadron is the 2nd squadron of the South African Air Force, nicknamed the "Flying Cheetahs." The wings and fuselage, instead of the usual American insignia, carry their country's "Springbok" in the center of the British Circle. Also on the fuselage is a small Cheetah with the squadron motto—*"upward and onward"*—written in Latin, around it.

The last squadron is the 67th. Their mark of distinction is a red and white sort of hour glass painted on the prop spinner. They call them the "blinking noses," because when the prop is spinning it seems to wink at you as it blinks."

[Note: when the 39th FIS was assigned to the 18th Wing, its spinners were painted blue and white and "winked" when the engine was running. The 67th removed the hour glass from its spinners.]

"The pilots are a swell bunch of guys who fly as many as six missions a day. The fact that it is appreciated can be determined by what a general with the 2nd division said to one of our pilots on ground control with the outfit when our planes came over to help them out of an enemy road block. The general ran up to the pilot sitting an a radio jeep and said, "If I could meet one of those pilots I'd kiss him here and now."

"Whenever ground force personnel pass by our base they al-

ways stop by to look over the airplanes and tell us how many times they saved their necks. One time an infantry captain walked into the tent that had been set up for an officer's club, walked up to the bar, laid down ten bucks and bought drinks for all the boys. All he said was, "I owe it to you" and walked out."

Behind the pilots are the guys like us. We are the pencil pushers, the supply men, the ammo handlers and napalm mixers. We cover just about every field you can think of and we're all here to keep those boys in the air. To protect, as much as possible the boys in the foxholes up front. We think we've done a pretty good job. What do you think Mr. Capp?"

"We are mighty proud of this base and our name. Any place in Korea or Japan they know about Dogpatch air base."

The way we got our name was simple. The Pusan base was numbered K-9. Each air base in Korea has a different number. Colonel Low, our boss, twisted the K-9 to "Kay nine," then to dog, then took a look around and made it Dogpatch. The name stuck and became so famous that we held onto it."

"Most of the guys know that the Colonel asked you if you wouldn't draw us some sort of an insignia to wear on our jackets. I want you to know that here is one guy who would be mighty proud to wear that insignia. All the guys are eagerly waiting for it. The way we are working it's going to be a long time before people forget Dogpatch air-base in Korea or where ever we have to go from here. They won't forget the Dogpatch pilots or the men behind them. Sure we are proud but haven't we a right to be? We took a bum deal and set a record. Like I said, Mr. Capp, we is your boys. We even follow Li'l Abner in the *Pacific Stars and Stripes* whenever we can get copies and compare his exploits to our own lives."

"I hope I haven't offended you by becoming too personal," Colton closed. "Just thought that you would want to know what your boys are doing."

Dogpatcher Logo

The letters to Capp soon brought recognition from Li'l Abner's creator, who followed through by designing a Mustang motif patch with Nancy O. and Abner astride a death-dealing F-51. This same insignia was featured on television and aroused such interest that the Texstyle Corporation sent a present of full color cloth patches for the Dogpatchers of the Fifth Air Force.

The Wing made Capp an honorary member, and Dogpatch signs sprouted around the base. "Everything from the new control tower to the mess hall menus proclaim that the 18th is proud of its humble beginning in Korea, but more important we had a sense of humour [sic] that war could not lessen but only served to inspire everybody to greater efforts. In other words, we could always eke out a laugh no matter how rough it was. Regardless of the hardships it may have been 'confoozin,' but it was still 'amoozin.'" [3]

By March 27, 1951, Jerome Capp was writing to the 18th Wing

Public Information Officer, Captain Richard M. Maloney that "Al Capp is delighted and honored to receive a formal induction into the 18th Fighter-Bomber Wing....We are preparing an official insignia to be put on the fuselage of the F-51s. The insignia will carry the figure of NANCY O, arranged in a setting symbolic of the courage and daring of your outfit." Capp closed by noting, "We are trying to insert some of the 35-mm films taken by you at Dogpatch into a Paramount film entitled "Sadie Hawkins Day" for national and international release...We promise that we will use our best offices to publicize the exploits of the command...We are quite proud of you and the command and all that it stands for."

On April 17, 1951 Capp Enterprises was "air-mailing to you the insignia design of LI'L ABNER flying the F-51 with NANCY O as passenger."

By 21 May, Jerome Capp was forwarding "as a gift from us and our screen designers, some patches that we're sending to your men so that they can put them on their fatigues or uniforms."

"Was sorry to hear that you had to decline on the invite for our first-year-in-Korea ceremonies," Captain Maloney wrote to Jerome Capp on 20 June 1951. "The office is besieged all day long with men trying to get copies of the patch. Needless to say, they are practically collector's items by now."

On 23 August, Maloney had received Al Capp's "selections for the Daisy Mae Contest" and he heartily approved of his "artist's eye perspective on the pulchritude submitted."

Capp would be surprised "at the local interest in this contest," Maloney reported. "In fact, I have gone so far as to put Al's letter and selections in the adjutant's safe to keep the winner a secret until the base paper is printed." Maloney closed with a request for a photograph of Capp "looking into the camera with his pen just finishing

SIGNS of the TIMES

Montage of "Dogpatch art" used by 18th Wing components to identify their buildings and services. The originator, famed cartoonist Al Capp, fully approved the unusual compliment. (Krakovsky)

the long slash of his signature."

Maloney suggested that Capp inscribe the photograph with, "Best of luck to the 18th, the Truckbustin'est Dogpatchers in Korea."

Maloney got his photograph of Capp, posted to the 18th on 4 September 1951. "Undoubtedly your eagle eye will note that we've 'manufactured' this one for you," Jerome Capp explained. "You see, Al is still in Europe and we thought it best to send

this along to you rather than wait for his return."

1 Al Capp Enterprises. The Greatest Cartoonist of all time. January 15, 2002. http://www.lil-abner.com/index.html
2 Al Capp Enterprises. The Greatest Cartoonist of all time. January 15, 2002. http://www.lil-abner.com/dogpatch.html
3 18th Fighter-Bomber Wing Album, October 1951, Dogpatch.

Dogpatch, Korea

By Sgt. Sandy Colton

Nestled among the green and rocky mountains of South Korea lies a deceptively peaceful settlement called Dogpatch. Unlike the Dogpatch made famous by the cartoonist Al Capp, this mountain hamlet deals with the business of war.

F-51 mustang fighter-bombers commute daily from here to the battle front to aid, by direct support, United Nations troops in their fray with the North Korean Communist forces.

Dogpatch was hacked out of a Korean rice paddy by a group of aviation engineers. Just five days after work started transports began to deliver supplies and personnel to the base. A short time later the 6002nd Tactical Support Wing, commanded by Col. Curtis R. Low, Needham Heights, Mass., arrived and with them came the name—"Dogpatch." Attached to the 6002nd was the 18th Fighter-Bomber Group, commanded by Lt. Col. Ira F. Wintermute, Salem, Ore. The group is on detached service to the Korean front from their home at the 13th Air Force base at Clark Field in the Philippines.

Dogpatch Air Base is composed of not much more than a group of various sized tents erected around 877,000 square feet of steel runway mats. When it rains the roads become deep mires of mud. Sometimes the water rises so much that shoes laid under a bunk—if one is lucky enough to have a bunk—float away. When it doesn't rain, thick clouds of dust are blown up by the prop wash of the aircraft and passing vehicles until a dull brown cloud of it hangs over the field like a fog.

In the beginning the men used the steel mats to sleep on. After a night spent on one, the standard quip was always, "Now I know what a waffle feels like." As more men and supplies arrived, Dogpatch began to become more comfortable. Some of the tents got wooden floors. A few men got bunks. Everyone was scrounging a nail, here and a board there to make a cabinet, footlocker, or bunk. Then someone discovered a hot mineral bath only five miles from the strip and the Dogpatch citizens began to realize the luxury of a hot bath once again

Chow at first consisted of not much more than canned C-rations—three times a day, garnished with dust or water, depending on the weather. It was eaten outside—rain or shine—until some tents were erected to serve as dining halls. Then there was only dust to contend with.

Eventually a huge tank was built and a hot water shower was installed. Shifts were set up to keep the fire going under the tank all the time. The amusing part about the Dogpatch hot showers is that they usually run out of cold water! Then the showers became the Dogpatch Turkish Bath.

As time went on other modern facilities were installed. A small PX was activated where you could occasionally get a pack of cigarettes and a warm can of beer. A barber, who would gladly scalp you for a dime, set up his shop. A GI who knew something about repairing watches established a jewelry shop. Dogpatch became a municipality.

During the time that this building was going on the citizens of Dogpatch continued with their primary job of supporting UN troops at the front lines. Even here the Dogpatch theme played a big part. The paint, dope and fabric shop became known as the "Skonk Works" because of the odor of the doping mixtures. Men mixing the deadly naplam called the concoction "Kickapoo Joy Juice." Other signs came to light—"Dogpatch Municipal Airport," "Dogpatch Diner," "Dogpatch Aeroplane Repair Shop," "Dogpatch City Limits." Even the base chapel carried the sign "Dogpatch Chapel," and a "Dogpatch" sign was placed at the main gate to the base written in both Korean and English This was Dogpatch and the men were proud of it.

They labored night and day to keep their Mustangs in the air from dawn until after dark. The mechanics worked outside in the dust or rain and under flashlights when necessary. The Pencil Pushers in Supply and Headquarters burned the midnight oil to keep up with the rush. Tons of supplies were flown in by huge transports. The men were gratified to see the sleek Mustangs rush out loaded down with rockets and napalm tanks and return empty. The pilots were spending up to eight hours a day in the air. But they were returning with reports of enemy equipment destroyed. To date they have flown over 2,000 missions and 4,000 sorties in the Korean action.

Dogpatch pilots are probably the first ones to ever take prisoners from the air during the Korean War. At one time two pilots lined up 12 enemy troops in the road and marched them four miles to friendly ground troops by buzzing over their beads. Soon after that an enemy regiment surrendered to another foursome of Dogpatch Mustang pilots. That was followed by another group of enemy troops who formed a U.N. on the ground, including men who formed the abbreviating periods, as a method of surrender.

Sometimes pilots brought back amazing stories. Like the one who passed a field full of haystacks. When he returned the haystacks had moved to another field. He went down to check them and they started to move away. They were camouflaged Red tanks. They didn't move any more after that—they burned. Another time two pilots, fresh out of rockets and napalm, saw a Red tank next to a haystack. They set the haystack afire with .50-caliber bullets and then fanned the blaze with their propwash until the tank caught on fire and exploded.

February 1951

The 12th Squadron "made a name for itself" in February by destroying over 500 enemy vehicles during the month, including 108 vehicles in one day alone, a new record.

By the end of February, the 18th Fighter-Bomber Wing had 179 officers and 1,132 airmen operating from K-10 in southeastern Korea. Colonel Turner C. Rogers was the Commanding General and Colonel Edward F. LaClare was his Executive Officer.

The Wing Intelligence Officer reported a favorable notice by FAF (Fifth Air Force) as a result of the "continued excellent effective strike rate by this Wing, especially in uncovering and destroying camouflaged enemy vehicles on pre-briefed recce missions."

The Wing Operations Section "continued to serve as advisor and liaison" to the 2nd Squadron, SAAF and the 18th FBG. A total of 1,249 effective sorties were flown during February, of which 876 were flown by the Group and 373 by the Flying Cheetahs. The missions included "close support, special interdiction, armed reconnaissance, airfield strikes and escort missions" flown as directed by FAF.

Dallas Squadron Rotation

February was an eventful month for at least some members of the 18th Fighter-Bomber Group. "The rotation of personnel who first came to Korea as members of the 'Dallas' squadron commenced when the first increment of personnel from Clark Air Force Base arrived at K-10 as replacements. The same day, the first increment of 'Dallas' personnel boarded a C-54 bound for Clark Air Force Base and for many, a happy reunion with their families." A second increment departed for Clark AFB on February 23rd and others left on March 2nd and 9th.

Rotation of non-combatant personnel "who have been in Korea six months returned to Clark Air Force Base 70% of the enlisted strength of the 12th Fighter Bomber Squadron. These airmen had departed the Philippines 10 July 1950…approximately 20% of the total strength of the base was rotated, since the 12th Fighter Bomber Squadron, as "Dallas" Project, had brought separate squadron elements from Clark. The influx of fresh personnel had a morale effect analogous to a blood transfusion." [1]

This development "was quite a morale booster but the announcement of future plans for rotation to the Zone of Interior for those pilots who have completed 100 missions and also for personnel who had completed a normal overseas tour prior to 1 September 1950 added immensely to the increase in morale of all." [2]

Combat Operations

The ground tactical situation, which directly affects the operations of this unit," Lt. Col. William E. May, Commander of the 67th Squadron reported in February 1951, was stabilized as of the close of the report period. The bomb (battle) line ran, inclusively, from the west coast of Korea, slightly north of the Han River encompassing Seoul and thence to Masogu-ri; thence along the CS-DS grid line horizontally (E-W) to Changdong-ni and Y'uncho-ni, approximately due north to the 38th Parallel and extending to the eastern coast of Korea. Direct contact with the enemy was maintained solely through probing (patrol) activity following enemy reverses in the Wonju-Chochon area."

The movement to K-10 in early January "was engendered by the enemy's ground operations which jeopardized the continued effective operational sorties of this organization. Logistical problems as well as

---

Monthly Summary

UN ground forces advanced slowly but steadily northward along a line stretching from Suwon to Wonju and Samchok. By the end of February, U.S. troops had reached the Han River near Seoul.

Meanwhile, Communist forces were rebuilding and refurbishing airfields across North Korea—repairing runways and building revetments. FEAF attacks kept them largely free of enemy aircraft, however. Close air support operations were hindered by a combination of bad winter weather and mountainous terrain in central Korea. FEAF fighters on armed reconnaissance missions hampered enemy movement in daylight by road or rail.

Enemy aircraft activity had declined sharply in January. RF-80s on reconnaissance missions near the Yalu River occasionally attracted MiGs, and Fifth Air Force began calling northwestern Korea "MiG Alley."

Adapted in part from U.S. Air Force Historical Research Agency. January 2002. The U.S. Air Force's First War: Korea 1950-1953 Significant Events. February 1951.

maintenance difficulties compelled a regrouping of Wing support units." Unit equipment, personnel, luggage, etc. was airlifted by C-47, C-119 and C-54 type aircraft." Nearly 100 tons was airlifted, and more went by LST and by rail.

By the end of February, "progress against the enemy was proceeding in accordance with an attrition advance designed to inflict maximum casualties and losses upon the enemy with minimum attrition resulting to friendly forces," May reported. [3]

Fighter-bomber pilots were assigned to fly the same areas, hoping that the tactic would help them become familiar enough with the landscape to detect camouflaged enemy vehicles.

In late February, "armed reconnaissance of specific areas was given emphasis" by the 18th Group pilots. The various areas were assigned to the two squadrons and these areas became the squadron's responsibilities. As a result pilots became very familiar with areas after working them a few times and thus any small change in the terrain, roads or villages was noticed and investigated often disclosing camouflaged vehicles, supply or troop concentrations. This method of reconnaissance coupled with pilot meetings where camouflage techniques were discussed and evaluated resulted in the destruction of 728 enemy vehicles and heavily damaging 137 vehicles in the month of February alone." [4]

During February, the 18th conducted what May called "saturation" reconnaissance missions, "wherein an enemy-held area was thoroughly and constantly reconnoitered daily…" This tactic was judged satisfactory "in that many enemy vehicles and stores of material were destroyed. As a result of this technique a definite dispersion pattern and route selection on the part of the enemy was discerned." He reported that a "further refinement of this technique

was under discussion by responsible officers of this organization relative to the complete coverage of the entire assigned reconnaissance area by the various two-aircraft flights which were detailed to such duty. The dispersion pattern indicated above was indicated by a dearth of enemy vehicles in one area as opposed to the quasi-concentrated numbers in an adjoining area." [5]

Bad weather hampered operations during the month, and 18th pilots "used excellent judgment and technique in flying to and from the target area when the weather was marginal."

Propellers continued to be damaged "by rocks on the runway and in the parking areas. Rough engines are sometimes traced to a propeller thrown out of balance due to large rocks striking the propeller during high R.P.M. operation," the 18th Maintenance Officer reported in February. A new taxiway was put into operation during February "thus relieving the landing strip of much of its traffic." The runway itself was "still unsatisfactory. A small rain can cause serious damage to the runway and soft spots, bumps and excessive dust are a problem at all times."

Twice that month, 5-inch rockets exploded when fired, "causing substantial damage to the aircraft concerned." The cause was traced to "broken propellant which had resulted from rough handling in shipment."

After an hour or so in a target area, "each flight would be relieved by another two-aircraft flight." The .50-caliber ammunition "proved most effective against vehicles." The "standard two-ship reconnaissance flights were continued with excellent results. This system calls for one aircraft to fly at 100 to 350 foot altitudes, depending on terrains, while the second aircraft remained at 500 to 1,000 foot altitudes to provide top cover." [6]

During February the 18th FBG had 52 aircraft assigned that flew 876 effective combat sorties during which 787,082 rounds of .50-caliber ammunition were expended, 4,267 rockets launched, and 1,090 tanks of napalm dropped. Only 20 general-purpose bombs were used that month. Eleven aircraft were lost that month, four to combat operations.

Flak was encountered "in increased intensity in the P'yongyang and Kangdong areas. This included 20-mm and 40-mm automatic weapons fire, "as well as small arms fire." However, "flak busting" missions were prohibited, Lt. Col. May explained, because "the tactical results achieved were in no way comparable with the attendant risk and possible loss."

The well-known (to ground force units) "Elsewhere" call sign of the 67th Fighter-Bomber Squadron was changed to "Point" in February 1951.

During February, the majority of missions flown by the 12th Squadron were two-ship flights on armed reconnaissance missions searching out and destroying enemy vehicles and supplies. The 12th Squadron "made a name for itself" in February by destroying over 500 enemy vehicles during the month, including 108 vehicles in one day alone, a new record. Three of its pilots completed 100 combat sorties and no pilots were lost to enemy action.

Tactics Used Against

Camouflaged Targets

The enemy "continued to use the same means of camouflaging their vehicles and supplies. Primarily, the enemy parked their vehicles beside or between houses in small villages and covered them with straw. In areas of snowfall, white tarpaulins were

---

Many pilots "took time after each mission," the 12th Squadron reported, "to show their crew chiefs where they had been and what they had done. This policy seemed to give the airmen a boost and made them feel that they were not working in vain."

Combat Statistics

18th Fighter-Bomber Wing

February 1951

Average No. A/C Assigned
52
Total Flying Time
3,030
Percent of Aircraft in Commission
75%
Percent of Aircraft AOCP
1%
Combat Sorties Flown by Wing
876 (effective)
12th Squadron Sorties
468
67th Squadron Sorties
416
2 Squadron Sorties
Unavailable
A/C Lost to Combat
4
Pilots lost
5

Fuel Consumed

214,594 gals.

Ordnance Expended

.50-cal. Rounds
787,082
Rockets
4,267
Napalm Bombs
1,090
500-lb. GP Bombs
20

Note: Figures and totals may differ in some categories due to differences in numbers provided by each component.

---

used to hide the vehicles. The enemy also covered some of the vehicles with green branches and others are driven into a house." [7]

The squadrons held several pilot meetings in February, the 12th Squadron reported, "to work out a tactical doctrine for the squadron. At each of these meetings techniques in finding camouflaged vehicles were discussed which allowed the pilots to exchange ideas. The net result was increased proficiency of all pilots in finding enemy vehicles."

Survival Methods

By February the 12th Squadron was reporting, "helicopters were able to cover nearly all the area worked by fighters. The helicopters were placed as near the front lines as practical and could be alerted by calling any mosquito type aircraft or any front line controller." However, there was "still a critical shortage of essential items of survival equipment in the squadron."

In addition to "standard signals for in-flight procedures," an externally carried drop tank "properly modified was prepared for swift transport to a downed pilot. The contents of this tank were intended to supplement the normal escape and evasion equipment carried by the pilot in the event that rescue by normal means (e.g. beyond helicopter and/or liaison aircraft range) was not possible. Too, the possibility of a pilot being forced down behind enemy lines wherein a rescue could not be effected due to darkness, the high speed of an F-51 in transporting such additional emergency equipment improved survival percentages," May explained. [In March, the 67th would report that the "escape and evasion drop tank" contents included "a miniature VHF receiver and transmitter."]

Tactical Air Control Duties

Tactical Air Control Party duty, previously a 21-day period of TDY (temporary duty) of combat pilots to the front lines as controllers, was extended to sixty days TDY.

This was a serious blow to pilot morale, although it increased the number of pilots available for flying since the group quota was decreased from seven to five, and less time was lost in travel." However, increasing the TDY to two months had "serious drawbacks," including a loss of pilot flying proficiency and a further delay in completing the required number of combat missions before rotation. If a pilot missed out on TACP duty he could often complete his missions in about four months. With TACP duty a combat tour could take six months.

Lt. Col. Homer M. Cox, 18th FB Group Commander recommended "that mission credit be given for control duty" and that "pilots be assigned to controller duty when they complete 60 missions, and that their combat tour (normally 100 missions) be considered as completed after the sixty days. Not only would this improve morale," Cox noted, "but it would also result in a higher experience level among controllers"—the average pilot assigned TACP duty had completed 20-40 missions.

Enemy Jet Tactics

As the Mustangs were increasingly refocused on reconnaissance missions, "no encounters with enemy jet type aircraft were reported" in February. However, the 67th took no chances that tactics might not change again or that the constant danger of being jumped by the much more capable MIGs had really lessened. Pilots were briefed thoroughly on a summary of "Enemy Jet Tactics," that had been prepared by the FEAF Intelligence Staff on January 14, 1951.

"A review of the enemy jet attacks upon UN aircraft during the months of November and December reveals that the enemy employs standard fighter tactics very much like our own. The review indicates, also, that the enemy has not adopted distinctive tactics for attacks against F-51, F-80, F-86, or bomber aircraft," the SECRET document noted.

"Pilot interrogation reports have persistently carried the inference that the enemy has not fully exploited the apparent capa-

HEADQUARTERS
314TH AIR DIVISION
FEAF Operations Analysis Office
APO 710

PILOT'S ACCOUNT--AIR-TO-AIR COMBAT--IN KOREAN THEATER

1. Pilot Major Mullins   2. Unit 67th Ftr Bmr Sqdn
3. Place of Combat Pyongyang   4. Date of Combat 5 Feb 51
5. Time 0740   6. Altitude 1000'
7. Number of Aircraft Involved: Enemy 1   Ours 4   8. Weather CAVU
9. Type and Performance of Aircraft Involved:
   a. Enemy YAK - 9   Poor

   b. Ours OK
10. Armament (Gun, Rocket, Ammunition--Number, Type, Caliber):
    a. Enemy 1 20mm lower left nose and 2 or more light m/g's in wings.

    b. Ours 6 50 Cals
11. Enemy Tactics (Summary--Including items such as Angle of Approach, Estimated Ranges at open fire and breakaway, Aggressiveness, Effectiveness, Length of Bursts, etc:
    Aggressive. Long stray bursts. Vicious handling of a/c causing violent snaps.
    Good turning ability.

12. Own Tactics (Summary as for Item 11): Head-on pass, one short burst of
    less than 5 seconds resulting in immediate fire and destruction of enemy a/c

13. Malfunctions of Own Equipment NONE

OAO Form No. 1

Pilot's Account, Air-to-Air Combat in Korean Theater

14. Location and Number of hits noted on either aircraft E/A - Approx
    10 rds rear eng area and c'kpit. None on friendly
15. Resulting Damage to either aircraft E/A streamed white smoke, coolent
    fuel and went straight in.
16. Fires in own aircraft, if any None
    a. Location .
    b. Action Taken .
17. Wounds Received, if any--Location and Extent None

18. Effects of Aircraft Damage, Equipment Malfunctions, or Personnel Wounds upon Performance of Aircraft or Completion of Mission:
                              None

19. Final Results and Claims 1 YAK-9 Destroyed

20. Remarks, Comments, Suggestions Concerning Such things as Armor, Armament Equipment, Performance, etc.-
                              None

OAO Form No. 1   2

"Went Straight In..." Mission Summary report--front and back--covering YAK-9 "kill" credited to Major Arnold "Moon" Mullins on 5 February 1951 over Pyongyang. He described the YAK pilot as "aggressive," and firing in "long stray bursts." The aerial combat included "vicious handling of the aircraft causing violent snaps." Mullins shot the YAK down with a "head-on pass, one short burst of less than 5 seconds resulting in immediate fire and destruction of enemy a/c." The YAK aircraft "streamed white smoke, coolant, fuel and went straight in." (NARA)

bilities of the MIG-15. Whether this reluctance to profitably employ his aircraft is due to high command direction, desire to conserve the aircraft, or the inexperience of the pilots, is not yet apparent."

"Attacks have followed a similar pattern in the majority of the reported instances and generally conform to the following:

"The enemy pilot's initial attack is made from the rear and high, usually from 6 o'clock, although he has at times initiated the attack anywhere from 4 to 8 o'clock high. Only a few head-on attacks have been reported and those were ineffective. Attacks in general, have been by two-ship elements, elements remaining intact on the pass, splitting up on the breakaway. There have been instances of single-ship attacks, particularly in the first three encounters against B-29s in early November (on 10 November, one

B-29 was lost as a result.) For the most part, two passes have been the maximum, with attacks broken off by a steep climbing turn either right or left into clouds or towards the sun."

"The one significant departure from the above tactics occurred during the attack on an RF-80 and an escorting F-80 on 4 December. One MIG-15 stayed on the tail and high while two others flew in a wing position about 50 yards out, effectively boxing in the friendly aircraft. This is reminiscent of tactics employed by US fighters against the Japanese."

"Evasive action has consisted of sharp diving turns, vertical dives, chandelles, and rapidly executed acrobatics. Streaking for the border has been the most successful evasive action thus far," the report concluded.

The Shortcomings of K-10

The runway at Chinhae was a constant hazard to flying, especially in bad weather or in low-light conditions. "Runway conditions were unfavorable for take-offs in heavily loaded single engine aircraft, although constant work by air installations personnel was continuing during period of little or no traffic," Lt. Col. May reported in February. "The absence of a nature horizon to the north, obscured by a 2,500 foot mountain approximately 5 ½ miles north of the runway boundary, made recourse to instruments almost mandatory. The proximity of the lateral runway boundaries to Quonset buildings, tents and a steel framed hangar on the east and the bay on the west, made approaches and landing under unfavorable conditions extremely hazardous.

Night and instrument approaches and landings were, in the main, precluded."

Endnotes

1 USAFHRA. *Monthly Historical Report, 18th Fighter Bomber Group*, February 1951.
2 USAFHRA. *Monthly Historical Report, 18th Fighter Bomber Group*, February 1951.
3 USAFHRA. *Monthly Historical Report, 67th Fighter Bomber Squadron*, February 1951, p. 3.
4 USAFHRA. *Monthly Historical Report, 18th Fighter Bomber Group*, February 1951.
5 USAFHRA. *Monthly Historical Report, 67th Fighter Bomber Squadron*, February 1951, p. 4.
6 USAFHRA. *Monthly Historical Report, 18th Fighter Bomber Group*, February 1951.
7 USAHRA. *Monthly Historical Report, 12th Fighter Bomber Squadron*, February 1951, p. 3.

(Above) **Major "Moon" Mullins** *and* **Captain Bill Myers** *discuss a mission in front of "Moon's Folly XII." A close look at Myers left sleeve reveals a pencil and a large spoon stuck in the pocket. "All the mess tents had a shortage of eating utensels," Myers explained. (Myers)*

Just shows how much experience counts

On 13 February 1951, 1st Lt. Ken Barber "flew two missions…Major [Herman] Solem and I reccied the road between Kumwha and Kumsong. North of Kumsong we spotted six or eight tanks on the road and were getting ready to hit 'em when eight Navy Corsairs came in and cut us out of the pattern. Between Kumsong and Kumwha Solem hit a supply dump which billowed yellow smoke and I got a direct hit on a cluster of houses where he told me to put my napalm. He made several strafing runs until he was almost out of ammo. Farther down the road, he had me strafe two concealed trucks which I never did see but one of which started smoking. They were between a house and a row of trees. Upon reporting back in to Mellow at Taegu, he claimed 8 trucks and 1 P.O.L. dump. I was amazed—so that's what my napalm and all his strafing did in that village. Later, he said he had seen them all quite clearly. Just shows how much experience counts."

"A few days ago Major Solem picked up a 20-mm shell through his front windshield which pulverized the glass but glanced off. He received the first glass in his eyes but luckily had goggles which he pulled down over his eyes. He was recceing up near T 'Osan in C-1 area. He flew back home, had his eyes washed out and was OK, but a couple of days later his eye got bad (one of them) and he has now gone to Japan."

Solem was the Operations Officer for the 67th Squadron and was later killed in action.

Wondong Crash

On 9 February, four Mustangs of the 12th Squadron, out of fuel, were forced to land at K-7 airstrip at Won-dong. One landed safely, No. 177 "nosed up in mud," No. 654 "nosed up in a river at the end of the strip, and one was totally demolished "when it crashed into a house and an embankment during an attempted go-around." The unit report noted that Captain Myers and an Aero Repair crew under M/Sgt Shand, "drove to Won-dong the following day to reclaim the aircraft."

"Despite the airstrip at K-7 being extremely short and rough," the report noted, "and not intended for use by fighter type aircraft, Captain Myers sucessfully flew 073 and 177 out of this strip."

Dang! In February 1951 four 12th Squadron Mustangs made an emergency landing on an abandoned L-5 (small "Piper Cub"-like spotter aircraft) strip. The aftermath made for many long hours for the 18th Maintenance Squadron. Captain Bill Myers was able to fly two of the planes off the postage stamp strip after they were repaired and "stripped down." The others were hauled off by 6x6 trucks. (Myers)

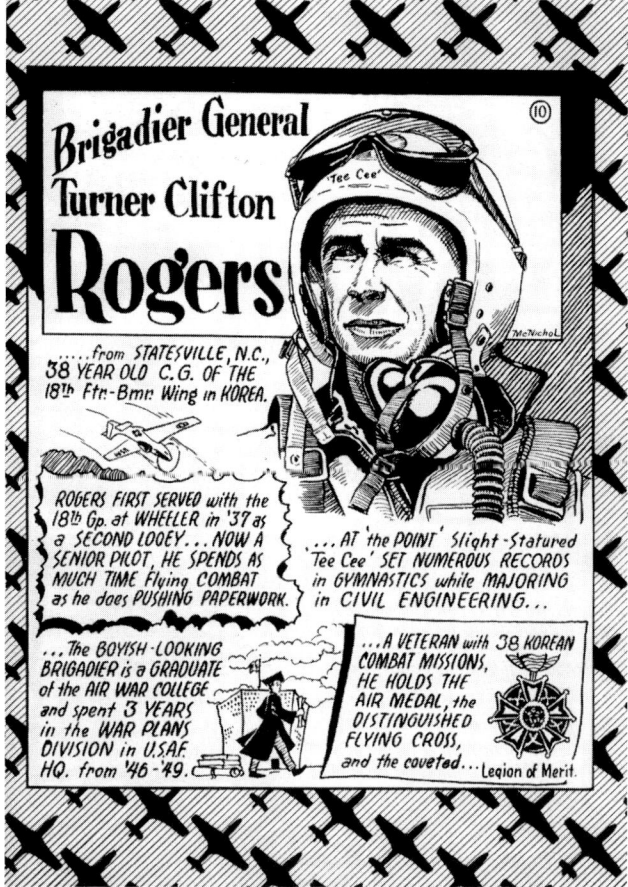

Brigadier General Turner Clifton Rogers

Tee Cee

.....from STATESVILLE, N.C., 38 YEAR OLD C.G. OF THE 18th Ftr-Bmr. Wing in KOREA.

ROGERS FIRST SERVED with the 18th Gp. at WHEELER in '37 as a SECOND LOOEY... NOW A SENIOR PILOT, HE SPENDS AS MUCH TIME flying COMBAT as he does PUSHING PAPERWORK.

...AT 'the POINT' Slight-Statured 'Tee Cee' SET NUMEROUS RECORDS in GYMNASTICS while MAJORING in CIVIL ENGINEERING...

...The BOYISH-LOOKING BRIGADIER is a GRADUATE of the AIR WAR COLLEGE and spent 3 YEARS in the WAR PLANS DIVISION in U.S.A.F. HQ. from '46-'49.

...A VETERAN with 38 KOREAN COMBAT MISSIONS, HE HOLDS THE AIR MEDAL, the DISTINGUISHED FLYING CROSS, and the coveted... Legion of Merit.

Colonel Turner C. Rogers was born in Taylorsville, N.C., in 1912, graduated from high school at Statesville, N.C. and attended Mars Hill College in North Carolina for one year. He graduated from the U.S. Military Academy at West Point, N.Y. and was commissioned a Second Lieutenant, Infantry in 1936.

The following fall, Lt. Rogers began flying training and graduated from primary and advanced flying schools at Randolph and Kelly fields in Texas. In March 1942 Lt. Col. Rogers was named chief of the personnel section in the Directorate of Air Defense at Army Air Forces headquarters, and a year later became chief of the fighter and reconnaissance section. He was transferred to the IV Fighter Command at Oakland, Calf., as assistant operations officer, and in March 1944 was appointed chief of the Fighter Division at Headquarters Fourth Air Force. He was promoted to colonel on May 12, 1944.

Following WWII he served as captain of the Fighter Evaluation Team, Air Evaluation Board, in the Southwest Pacific and as a staff planning officer in the War Plans Division at Air Force headquarters. He graduated from the Air War College at Maxwell Air Force Base, Ala. in June 1950.

"My first encounter with the 18th," General Rogers explained in a 1982 letter to his former Journalist, Sandy Colton, "came immediately after graduating from Flying School in 1937. I was assigned to the 18th Pursuit Group stationed at Wheeler Field, Hawaii. As I recall, the 18th then had two Pursuit Squadrons and one Attack Squadron. Believe it or not, we were still equipped with P-12's at that time—the last of the fabric covered, open cockpit, fixed landing gear, bi-winged fighter planes. It was fun to fly, but no match for the more modern fighter already appearing in Europe and Japan.

The next time Rogers met up with the 18th Fighter-Bomber Wing was in Korea. Rogers and Col. Curtis "Curt" Low were on their way to Japan when the Korean War broke out in June, 1950. They met en route and reported in to 5th Air Force Headquarters at Itazuke, Japan, in early July. Major General Pat Partridge was the commander of FAF. "The first night we were there," Rogers recalled, "he took us on a sight-seeing trip over Korea in a B-17. By that time the North Korean forces had advanced almost to Taegu. Curt Low was given command of the 18th and I was assigned as Assistant Operations Officer of 5th Air Force."

Soon after joining the FAF Staff, Col. Rogers "had a talk with Gen. Pat Partridge, explaining how I had missed out on WWII. I started the war in Washington, D. C. and never got below a major command headquarters. This time I wanted to see some combat. The general promised I'd get it, but for awhile in late 1950 I thought the war would end before I could get into it."

FAF soon moved into Taegu and established its headquarters in a school house, with living quarters in a Presbyterian mission. "The front lines were only a few miles away so it only took a few minutes for our fighter bombers to reach the combat zone," Rogers explained.

By the time Rogers assumed command of the 18th in February, 1951, the Wing had already traveled from Pusan to Pyongyang and back again to K-10/Chinhae—"the garden spot of Korea," Rogers remembered.

The Chinese intervention turned the UN command's expectations of a relatively quick victory into a full scale retreat back down the Korean peninsula.

In January, 1951, General Partridge called Rogers into his office and gave him "a choice of two fighter wings. I chose my old love, the 18th, and there followed the best year of my life."

When Rogers assumed command of the 18th "approximately 90% of the pilots were recalls from WWII. Some had come back in screaming. Some had just established small businesses or had become established with civilian companies when they were called back to active duty and shipped to Korea. I soon learned how fortunate I was to have these old timers. I did not fully realize just how good they were until we started getting in new graduates right out of flying school. During the year that I commanded the 18th in combat, I expect we had around 500 pilots rotate through the wing. Some would complete 100 missions in about 3 months or less. I had a front row seat in watching the greatest show on earth."

Rogers mentally put his pilots into one of three categories. He assigned himself "to the large middle category of pilots who really got a big thrill out of flying combat, but had to overcome a great deal of fear and tension prior to each mission."

At the top of the three categories "was a small elite group of pilots—maybe 10%—who were outstandingly good at their job, loved every minute of it and apparently did not suffer the qualms of fear...These were the men who always got their target. They probably did as much damage to the en-

Meet 1st. Lt. JOHN E. TAYLOR Jr.

From WASHINGTON, CONNECTICUT, the 18ᵗʰ FTR-BMR WING'S 27 yr. old 'FLYING ARSENAL'.

...HIS PERSONAL SUR-VIVAL KIT INCLUDES AMONG OTHER THINGS, a .45, CARBINE, BAYONET, a WAISTBELT and 2 BANDOLIERS of ASSORTED AMMO, and a SPARE FLIGHT JACKET.

...THE MUSTACHIOED BARNEY OLDFIELD HAS SPENT THE LAST FIVE YEARS BURN-ING UP TRACKS AROUND THE COUNTRY AS A PRO RACING DRIVER...BOTH IN STOCK CARS AND MOTORCYCLES!!!

...IN WW II, TAYLOR FLEW 36 MUSTANG MISSIONS with the 364ᵗʰ GROUP in the ETO... HE HAS ALREADY LOGGED OVER 133 MISSIONS WITH the 18ᵗʰ'S 'BLINKER NOSES' SQUADRON...AND WANTS TO SET an ALL-TIME RECORD by FLYING 200 COMBAT MISSIONS.... HOW EAGER CAN YOU GET!'

1ˢᵗ Lt. John E. Taylor, Jr. exceeded his personal goals. Eventually he would fly 160 missions in Mustangs, 60 missions in the F-84 and 47 missions in F-86 jet aircraft--a total of 267 combat missions--the most flown by an Air Force fighter pilot in the Korean War. Taylor would retire as a Major General.

Captain John Taylor, Jr. and Lt. Ernie Wakehouse stand still long enough for a photograph in front of the "Nest of the Cobras." Notice the ammunition Taylor has strapped around his waist for the various weapons he carried with him into combat, including a carbine. Wakehouse remembers Taylor showing him every rock and bush in Korea—at a very low level! (Cook)

emy as the rest of us put together. And an-other thing, they always came back. They were superior warriors who loved their work and took pride in being the best."

There was one pilot who truly stood out in Rogers' mind—a pilot who was "just a little bit different from every one else." Rogers said that he could "never quite un-derstand him."

Capt. J. E. Taylor, Jr.—"not a big man physically, maybe 5' 8", black hair and the bluest eyes you've ever seen. You could spot him a mile away because he wore several bandoliers of ammunition around his shoul-ders plus wearing a .45-cal. pistol and a small carbine."

Taylor explained that he carried his ar-senal so that should he ever be shot down he could fight his way out of enemy terri-tory. "I believe he would have," Rogers agreed, but "he was never shot down."

After Taylor completed his first 100 mis-sions, he came to Rogers and pleaded,

"Please now can I go and fly the jets?"

Rogers contacted 5ᵗʰ AF and arranged for his transfer to an F-84 unit. Later, after Taylor completed 100 missions in F-84s he asked for and was assigned to an F-86 wing. "Talk about some one who loves to fight!" Rogers remembered.

The third category of pilots constituted a very small percentage of the total. "These were the few who let fear or lack of confi-dence in their own abilities make them seek any route to avoid combat."

The South African Air Force played a major role in the history of the 18ᵗʰ Wing during the Korean war, General Rogers emphasized. "The second South African Squadron was attached to our Wing and if I'm not mistaken, the entire personnel of the South African Air Force rotated through the squadron during the war, with some pi-lots serving a second tour. There was never any doubt about the bravery and effective-ness of the South African Air Force. They

paid their way and always performed with distinction."

"Most of their pilots," Rogers recalled, "were very large men. I learned that some could barely squeeze into the Mustang and were actually going into combat flying cross-handed, i.e. operating the throttle with right hand and stick with left hand. I figured that was asking too much of any pilot and grounded those who were too large for the cockpit."

"Here is the true story of how the 18ᵗʰ picked up the Dogpatch name for its base," Rogers explained. "When we were ready to bring the 18ᵗʰ back from Japan, I called Curt Low to tell him the news. The unit was scheduled to operate out of K-9 at Pusan. I could not give him that number in the clear. So I told him he was moving to Dog Patch. The name stuck and was carried to all the many bases occupied by the 18ᵗʰ during the war."

Wing Commander's Diary

by Brigadier General Turner C. Rogers

On Friday, 23 February 1951, shortly after taking command of the 18th Fighter-Bomber Wing, Colonel T.C. Rogers began making entries in what he called his "Wing Commander's Diary." He continued the practice for the first three months of his tenure as Wing Commander. His entries provide a fascinating look into the issues he faced and the decisions he was making as he directed combat and support operations that affected the welfare and lives of over 1,500 men.

Rogers, like the other commanders of the 18th Wing, assigned himself combat missions. Unlike most of the other pilots in the Wing who had seen service in World War Two or had been trained as a fighter pilot since the war, Rogers had never been in combat and had to relearn the critical skills it took to fly the F-51 and to survive missions deep into heavily defended enemy territory.

The first mission for Rogers was in "The Pig," a piggyback version of the F-51. Major Solem was the pilot. However, the plane "developed [a] rough engine about Kumchon and returned to base." His first mission was a dud that took less than an hour to complete. That would not be the case on future missions.

Rogers returned from the aborted mission to reduce a courts martial sentence for a Private who had been AWOL for two months--a third offence--from two months and $200 fine to one month and $100 fine. Characteristically, Rogers took other factors into account. "Understand he drinks too much. May be making mistake but want to try experiment in rehabilitation. Now have nine men doing hard labor," Rogers noted. "It's a small percentage of the command, but still too many."

He also drafted a "letter of condolence to wife of airman who stole a truck on the night of 21 February and killed himself."

The next day, Saturday, the 18th Wing flew its 10,000th combat mission (sortie). "Capt. Hall of the 12th Squadron was the pilot. His flight destroyed 32 vehicles," Rogers noted. Following a symphony by an orchestra from the Korean Navy and a choral concert in the Airmen's mess, Rogers made his first address to the command and welcomed Korean visitors.

Although the 18th Group's missions were cancelled on Sunday due to weather, the Group flew its normal quota of reconnaissance flights—"recces." Rogers scheduled himself for a check out ride in the F-51 and made two landings. "Will take several more hours before I feel completely at ease in the plane," he noted. "Feels good to be back in a fighter."

> "After hearing what might happen should you go down behind enemy lines, I feel I'd just as soon have been left in the dark. Ignorance is bliss. Just the same, I think I'll do what the man says."

That evening, Rogers had dinner with President and Madam Rhee and Minister Shin at the President's summer home in Chinhae. The menu, he noted, included: beef broth, fish course, 2 kinds of fish—very good—barbecued chicken, rice, turnips and spinach. Dessert—sponge cake with peaches. After-dinner coffee with Korean cigarettes. President very old, but is smart and has sense of humor."

Rogers flew his second training flight on Monday, 26 February. For over 90 minutes, he "practiced gunnery on a small island in the bay" followed by two landings. He noted that he felt "more at home in plane, but still am not making proper landing pattern. Hope to fly combat after 3 or 4

more training missions." After he returned, he reviewed plans for an awards presentation by Gen. Partridge later in the week, then attended an escape and evasion lecture. "After hearing what might happen should you go down behind enemy lines, I feel I'd just as soon have been left in the dark. Ignorance is bliss. Just the same, I think I'll do what the man says," he concluded.

The next day, Tuesday, 27 February, he noted that a 67th Squadron Mustang "blew out tire on takeoff before becoming airborne, crashed and burned on end of runway. Pilot escaped with minor injuries. Fire Chief shot through leg and arm by exploding .50-cal. Aircraft completely burned. Tire had 16 landings—average life of tire 50 landings." He then inspected the Motor Maintenance Squadron and "found everything in good shape" although "lack of parts has 32 vehicles out of commission." Rain limited air operations to 14 sorties, during which 12 vehicles were destroyed. After reviewing proposed plans for the air base construction program, he approved the $49,000 in funds needed to complete the program.

Significant Events [1]

February 1: Colonel Turner Clifton "Tee Cee" Rogers assumed command of the 18th Fighter-Bomber Wing, succeeding Col. Curtis R. Low.

February 2: Captain E. J. Deschamps "crashed landed his F-51 Mustang in enemy territory and has been Missing In Action since that date. This brings to 14 the total number of pilots missing in action since Korean Operations began. Six pilots of this organization have given their lives in the Korean conflict." [2]

February 5: The U.S. X Corps advanced with strong air support near Hoengsong, northeast of Wonju in central Korea. The advance was conducted as part of Operation ROUNDUP, designed to disrupt enemy preparations for a new offensive,

Maj. Arnold Mullins, 67th Squadron, in an F-51 Mustang, shot down a YAK-9 seven miles north of Pyongyang to score the only USAF aerial victory of the month. Mullins was flying his 97th close support mission of the Korean War and leading a flight of three FEAF Mustangs. The flight also destroyed two locomotives and knocked out ten or more supply vehicles. "I was just pulling up from a strafing pass when I spotted the Yak directly above me. I let loose with a few bursts from my .50-caliber machine guns and scored direct hits in the cockpit and fuselage. The pilot must have been dead because the plane made a sloppy turn and just kept going. When he crashed it looked as if two napalm bombs were exploding." The dogfight lasted approximately 30 seconds. Earlier in his combat tour, Mullins had destroyed three Yak-9's while strafing an enemy airfield. [3]

February 8: Far East Air Forces using B-29s, B-26s, and fighters launched heavy attacks on rail lines in northeastern Korea between Hoeryong and Wonsan.

February 9: U.S. troops reached the banks of the Han River seven miles east-southeast of Seoul.

For the 12th Squadron, it was not a good day, however. Four of its Mustangs were forced to land at K-7 Airstrip (Won-dong), due to low fuel states. One landed safely, one "nosed up" in the mud, another "nosed up in a river at the end of the strip," and the fourth was "totally demolished "when it crashed into a house and an embankment during an attempted go-around." An Aero Repair crew drove to Won-dong the next day to reclaim the aircraft. Despite the airstrip at K-7 being extremely short and rough, and not intended for use by fighter type aircraft, Capt. Myers successfully flew 073 and 177 out of this strip." [4]

February 10: UN forces captured the port of Inchon and the important nearby airfield at Kimpo. Air raids had cratered the field so badly that it required extensive renovation before USAF aircraft could use it. On the east coast, ROK troops crossed the 38th parallel and entered Yangyang.

February 11/12: In central Korea approximately fifty miles east of Seoul, Chinese and North Korean forces attacked the ROK 3rd and 8th Divisions north and northwest of Hoengsong and in two days captured the town, forcing the UN forces toward Wonju, a few miles to the south.

February 13-16: Three CCF divisions surrounded UN troops, including members of the U.S. 23rd Regimental Combat Team and the French Battalion, at a crucial road junction at Chipyong-ni in central Korea. Despite heavy enemy ground fire, ninety-three transports dropped some 420 tons of food and ammunition to the encircled troops. Twenty C-119s dropped supplies at night over a zone marked by burning gasoline-soaked rags. Also, H-5 helicopters delivered medical supplies to the troops and evacuated more than forty wounded. Fifth Air Force flew close air support missions for the surrounded troops, who held out until relieved by a friendly armored column.

February 16: For the first time, the U.S. Army began using its own aircraft, the L-19 Bird Dog, for forward air control, artillery spotting, and other front-line duties, relieving Fifth Air Force of demands for these types of missions.

Captain Dolph G. Frantz "was forced to make a belly landing in his F-51 aircraft approximately three miles north of P'yongyang. He was engaged in an armed reconnaissance flight in that area and pre-sumably the coolant system of his aircraft was struck by small arms fire. A CAP mission was flown by flights from this organization [67th FBS] as well as one flight from the 2nd South African Squadron for approximately three hours at which time an Air Sea Rescue helicopter stationed at Suwon (K-13) successfully effected his rescue. He was uninjured." [5]

February 17/18: B-26s flew the first night bombing mission using shoran, a short range navigation system employing an airborne radar device and two ground beacon stations for precision bombing.

February 20: Lt. Col. Homer M. Cox assumed command of the 18th Fighter-Bomber Group from Colonel Ira F. Wintermute who was assigned to the Thirteenth Air Force.

February 21: The Eighth Army launched Operation KILLER to destroy large numbers of enemy troops while moving the UN line northward to the Han River.

February 24: The 18th Fighter-Bomber Wing completed its 10,000th effective sortie in the Korean conflict, according to the report filed by the 18th FBW Operations Officer. However, the 18th Fighter Bomber Group reported the same achievement for March 24, 1951.

February 27: Captain Richard H. Cassady of the 67th FBS "had initiated his take-off run and when at approximately mid-field his right main landing gear tire blew out at which time the take-off was abandoned. Two rockets, (5"HVAR) under the right wing came loose at this time and caused the aircraft to skid sideways, approximately 35 degrees right of the runway heading. Two externally hung gasoline tanks were ignited and the aircraft began to burn. Captain Cassady managed to escape from the aircraft uninjured despite initial difficulty in opening the canopy." [6]

February 28: UN ground forces eliminated the last communist presence south of the Han River.

Combat Losses

Captain Elzeard J. Deschamps, 67th Squadron, was presumed "missing in action" due to enemy anti-aircraft fire encountered over Kangdong airdrome," as recorded in the 67th's monthly unit report. Captain Deschamps "crashed landed his F-51 Mustang in enemy territory [2 February 1951] and has been Missing In Action since that date. This brings to 14 the total number of pilots missing in action since Korean Operations began. Six pilots of this organization have given their lives in the Korean conflict." Capt. Deschamps "went through flight training with me," wrote Lt. Ken Barber in his diary, "and volunteered for this Group when his Group changed to F-80's. He said he couldn't see flying a plane which could only do a "half ass" job in the air and the same on the ground. He said the F-51 could at least do a decent job of ground support. Deschamps was hit by flak while making a pass over Kangdong airfield east of Pyongyang. Nobody actually saw him crash. His mistake was circling in sight of the field before making his pass eliminating the element of surprise. Also, he made a low angle instead of high angle pass. Deschamps, an ex-paratrooper, was quite a boy!" Barber recorded. Capt. Bill Myers was Deschamps element leader on the flight which he described as a "stupid Frag from 5 (Fifth Air Force) Joint Operations Center to visually recce Kangdong at minimum altitude by every other mission. We were first mission of the day." After Deschamps was hit, Myers "called JOC and told them to cancel all subsequent missions, but again they failed to do so until Lt. Col. Gloesner was KIA on the next low pass over Kangdong Air Field. The only thing on it was plenty of 20-mm."

1st Lt. G.D. Doveton, 2 Squadron, SAAF pilot KIA on 15 February 1951. Lt. Doveton took off from K-10 on an armed reconnaissance mission of the Kaesong-Haeju-Sariwon area. After attacking several targets, they spotted a camouflaged vehicle near Kaesong. The vehicle finally caught fire on the fourth pass. As Doveton headed in on

"By dawn's early light" on January 30, 1951, an F-51 "Mustang" of the 18th Fighter-Bomber Wing synchronizes its take-off from K-10 with the first grey streaks of dawn. "The dark blobs under its left wing, stand out in sharp contrast with the light area of the clouded background, identifying its armament cargo of rockets, and bombs. Communist targets in North Korea, only a short flight from this Fifth Air Force airbase, will soon feel the "kick" of this sturdy "Mustang." the Air Force caption explains. (NARA)

yet another attack, his wingman Lt. McKellar saw the Mustang hit the hill, cartwheel and burst into flames. Later that afternoon, 2nd Squadron Commandant Theron and Captain Davis returned to the area. The wreckage was spotted, but there was no sign of Doveton.

Lt. Col. Milton F. Gloesner, Jr., 18th Fighter-Bomber Group pilot KIA in February 1951. "On this visit [to the University Club in Tokyo during a ferry flight stopover] I ran into Ken Skeen, a Captain I'd flown with in the 33rd Fighter Group in New

Mexico in '48," recalled Lt. Col. Duane "Bud" Biteman. "He told me that most of the old 33rd bunch were flying F-84s out of Taegu. Then I ran into Burke Gray, who I'd been stationed with in China in 1945; he was with the 1st Fighter Group at Johnson AFB, flying the hot new F-86 Sabre interceptors. We ran into a couple of the newer 12th Squadron pilots, over on R & R from Pusan; they told us that Lt. Col. Gloesner—the fellow who led my last mission up to the Yalu River in November, had been shot down and killed during the past week—

239

on the same day that his promotion to 'bird' Colonel had come through. What a shame; it was sad, sad news for me—I really liked the guy."

2ⁿᵈ Lt. D.R. Leah, 2 Squadron, SAAF pilot KIA on 7 February 1951. Commandant Theron led a four-ship flight on an armed reconnaissance of the Wonsan-Hamhug area on North Korea's east coast. Leah was flying No. 2. After they had used up their bombs during an attack on a supply dump, the flight located several camouflaged vehicles, which they attacked with machine gun fire, the only weapons they had left. Leah conducted two strafing attacks. While concluding the second attack, Leah turned and climbed sharply to the right. His starboard wing hit the ground— or something—causing the aircraft to cartwheel into flaming wreckage. No sign of Leah was observed during the subsequent search. No flak was observed, but the flight concluded that a flak-trap cable was possibly used to bring down the aircraft.

1ˢᵗ Lt. W. E. St. E. Wilson, 2 Squadron, SAAF pilot KIA on 2 February 1951. Lt. Wilson was leading a four-ship flight on an armed reconnaissance mission. They were briefed to patrol the roads north from Wonsan through Hamhung—as far as the Chosin Reservoir. Two of the Mustangs were sent home—one sick and the other to escort. Arriving over Wonsan, Wilson radioed that he was beginning his reconnaissance and descended to a lower altitude where he searched the roads north of Wonsan, then over Munchan. After two orbits of that area, he suddenly banked right and climbed, as his aircraft began trailing white smoke. His wingman, Lt. Gow, was told that his engine temperature was rising quickly and that he was heading out to sea to bail out. He then climbed to 3,000 feet and bailed out north of Wonsan. After making a successful parachute jump, the prevailing winds carried his chute out over the water—choppy and cold. Rescue units had been alerted and arrived within an hour. Meanwhile, Wilson was difficult to locate in the choppy waters. Eventually, a SA-16 "Dumbo" aircraft landed in four-foot swells and glimpses of Wilson's Mae West life pre-

server were reported briefly, but after about half an hour, that disappeared. Lt. Wilson's body was not recovered.

Endnotes

[1] Adapted in part from USAFHRA. January 2002. The U.S. Air Force's First War: Korea 1950-1953 Significant Events. February 1951.
[2] USAFHRA. *Monthly Historical Report, 18ᵗʰ Fighter-Bomber Group*, February 1951.
[3] USAFHRA. *Monthly Historical Report, 67ᵗʰ Fighter-Bomber Squadron*, February 1951, enclosure "certified true copy" of an undated article that appeared in Stars and Stripes.
[4] USAHRA. *Monthly Historical Report, 18ᵗʰ Fighter-Bomber Wing*, February 1951.
[5] USAFHRA. *Monthly Historical Report, 67ᵗʰ Fighter-Bomber Squadron*, February 1951, p. 4
[6] USAFHRA. *Monthly Historical Report, 67ᵗʰ Fighter-Bomber Squadron*, February 1951, p. 5.

What A Time To Take A Leak...

"Exciting day today!" 1ˢᵗ Lt. Ken Barber recorded on 15 February 1951. "We recced over snow covered Pyonggong airfield and Kumwha and finally started up the valley towards Singosan, with Wonsan just beyond. Just short of Singosan, I noticed Frantz streaming coolant and told him about it. He circled back just past Singosan, jettisoned his napalm and rockets and asked which way to go. I told him to go back up the valley, and called out a few instructions about bellying in. Especially, I told him to gain altitude if possible. Back up the valley he went. It sloped upwards, and I was really sweating him out to get out of those deep ravines to a place where he could belly in. He bellied in—a beautiful job in a perfect place and got out of the plane immediately—unhurt. I circled a couple of times looking for people, then climbed to 6,000 and called Thresher who got the helicopter on the way—then came over and joined me. We covered him until a Wild West (South African) flight came along to take over. The copter made a successful rescue."

Later that day, Barber flew up to Taegu in "The Pig," to pick Frantz up and return him to his squadron. "He was mighty glad to be alive—said no one fired a shot at him. The 'copter pilot—Lt. Clifford Brown, 3ʳᵈ Air Rescue Squadron, Detachment 1— landed, asked, "Anyone shooting at you?" Frantz said, "No." The 'copter pilot stepped out calmly to relieve himself. "What a time to take a leak!" said Frantz. "Guess his part of this war is over," Barber noted. "Anyone shot down in enemy territory and picked up is an 'evadee' and is not allowed to fly any more missions."

[Note: this statement was also made by other pilots. However, Col. Robert P. "Pancho" Pasqualicchio noted that he "was shot down behind the lines in April 1951 and returned to finish my missions."]

Journalist Goes On

Mustang Strike

by Staff Sergeant William J. "Sandy" Colton

It took a lot of begging and pleading but they finally let me go. To my knowledge, no one had ever written an eyewitness account of a Mustang strike and I wanted to do it. I'd been listening to and writing about the exploits of the Mustang pilots ever since I came to Korea. Naturally I dreamed of being able to take part in a Mustang flight, but the Mustang is a one-man airplane and there just wasn't room for me. Not until they got the Pig, that is. The Pig is a Mustang with the gas tank behind the pilot removed so that a passenger can squeeze in—and ride piggy back. When I heard about the Pig I really began to beg in earnest.

They finally told me that I could go on a strike with the F-51's and I was as excited as a kid with his first ice cream cone. I reported for mission briefing at 0600. I'd listened to Captain Charles E. ["Slide"] Trumbo, the Intelligence Officer, go through the routine dozens of times before; but this time the lecture seemed to be filled with things that I had to know and remember. After the briefing the Captain called me to one side to give me an escape and evacuation lecture. He told me the things to do if I had to bail out or was crash landed in enemy territory.

"If you go down," he said in closing, "bring that pilot back—we need him!" I was trying to keep up a brave front and his lecture didn't help things any.

After breakfast I was issued my escape kit, parachute, Mae West and a peculiar helmet that had earphones, throat mike, oxygen mask and a pair of goggles attached. All this gear fitted so tight that I thought I'd snap my neck before I could get into the airplane.

The parachute was the quick release type. One of the pilots asked me if I knew how to operate it "Sure," I said as I pressed the quick release button and the harness fell down around my knees. "No, no," he said. "I mean to open the chute. You pull the ripcord!"

I hope he didn't notice my embarrassment I meant to pull the ripcord but I'm glad I didn't. That would have been worse. I was really excited—too excited to think.

Major Charles McGee, the flight leader, briefed us just before we got into the planes. Lt. Colonel Ira G. "Ike" Wintermute, the group commander of the 18th Fighter-Bomber Group, was going to fly the Pig. The crew chief had to remove the canopy so I could get into the small back seat. As I squeezed into a comfortable position, the Colonel briefed me on what to do if I had to bail out.

"Duck your head down and I'll release the canopy," he said. "When it flies off unhook your belt, stand up in a crouch and

18th Group Commander Lt. Col. Ira Wintermute briefs Sgt. Sandy Colton before take-off. Colton, a journalist eager to write an eye-witness account of a Mustang strike against enemy targets in North Korea, got more than he bargained for during the mission. Loaded down with equipment, Colton was barely able to squeeze into the samll space behind the cockpit of the "Pig," an F-51 with the rear gas tank removed. (Colton)

dive for the leading edge of the wing. Keep your arms out in front of you and don't touch that ripcord until you're clear of the airplane!"

About then I was ready to back out of my ride. We hadn't even started the engine and I was already shaking like a leaf.

We moved out to the edge of the strip and I listened to the control tower operator clear each plane to take off. There were five planes in the flight, including the Pig. Once in the air the planes jockeyed into position and set course for the front. It was too late to back out now.

I amused myself by watching the other planes bounce up and down on our wing tip in the turbulent air. The Colonel called me on the intercom to check the connection. We were Baker Flight and the Pig was the fifth plane in the formation, making the Colonel Baker Five. I was Baker Five and a Half!

It was clear and bright until we approached the battle area. I'd listened to Baker Leader, Major [Charles] McGee, contact the central control which assigned us to a controller nearer the front. Colonel Wintermute pointed out the sandy Naktong River as we passed over it.

I thought of the first days of the war and the important part it had played.

The snow, which had only covered the mountain tops at the home base, worked its way into the lowlands as we moved north. A heavy overcast suddenly covered the sky and turned the white below to grey. It seemed to be some, sort of ominous warning and I begun to sweat with apprehension.

Near Wonju we contacted another controller. He had no target. Wonju came into view. The ground around the city was pock marked with bomb craters. In the center of the city three wide swaths of black ran parallel its whole length. Haze and smoke covered the area and in a little valley just north-west of the city a small village was burning, sending a white column of smoke hundreds of feet into the air. We spotted our own patrols on the mountain sides. They stood still and watched us. I wanted to wave at them.

The controller here had no target either. I was beginning to feel disappointed because we couldn't find a target. The controller did have a suggestion that made me feel a little better though. "Follow the railroad tracks to the northwest of the city," he said. "It's all fair game up that way." He went on to explain that enemy troops had been utilizing the buildings in the villages for shelter at night and for storing supplies. He asked us to seek out and destroy all the buildings which appeared to be in use.

The hunt was on! It wasn't the tanks or troops I had hoped for, but it was excitement just the same. We followed the tracks north. Snow covered mountain sides loomed up on either side of us.

Occasionally Colonel Wintermute would point out a friendly patrol. We came to a small village and Major McGee went down to take a look at the buildings. He picked out three large ones and came around on his napalm run. Before I could realize what was happening, Colonel Wintermute had gone into a screaming dive following McGee down. Then there was the chatter of the machine guns on the wings as we strafed McGee's napalm. Stretching over the Colonel's shoulder, I saw an ugly mass of red capped with a thick puff of black smoke flame flare up in front of us. I strained at my shoulder harness to peer over the side of the canopy as we passed over the target. At the same time the Colonel pulled out of his dive and I was forced back into my seat. The blood drained from my head down to my feet, taking all my insides with it. My jaw popped open and my cheeks sagged. I was carrying a camera and it weighed a ton.

Once upstairs we dove in again, this time behind the second element leader while he dropped his napalm. The wind screamed in fury. I felt some sort of exhilaration. There wasn't time to be afraid. The fire and smoke flared up in front of us again. This time I had a better look at the target. The buildings were near a river and several well used footpaths led from the buildings to the river and off into the mountains. Then we pulled out of our dive and I fought to keep my insides from popping out of my feet.

After that we stood off to one side while the other members of the flight went in and fired their rockets into the buildings. The four F-51's seemed to be playing follow the leader. They set up a pattern something like a figure eight—diving in to let go a rocket, pulling up and around into a dive from another direction. They call it yoyo-ing

After they had expended all the rockets we joined the formation and strafed. When we left, the three main buildings were completely destroyed while at least five others were pretty well torn up. The Reds wouldn't use those buildings for supplies or shelter anymore.

We regrouped and started for home.

Major McGee called the controller to let him know what we had done.

The snow worked its way back to the top of the mountains and the Naktong passed below. Then home. We made a run over the field in tight formation sort of strutting our colors. And then each plane peeled off to land. By that time I had grown to love that airplane. There was something nice and personal about it. Nonetheless, I sweated out the landing.

After I'd crawled out of the airplane, turned in my equipment and gotten stomach and heart adjusted, I checked into debriefing where the pilots gave an account of what happened to the Intelligence Officer. Every bone in my body seemed to ache with fatigue. Stomach muscles were painfully taut from the strain of the dives.

I couldn't help but wonder how the pilots could put in as many as six missions a day. All they did was kid me, 'Only 99 more to go before you're eligible for rotation,' they said. "No thanks," I answered,' I think I'll do it the easy way."

I meant it too.

Flying Mustangs with the 39th FIS

Boy! I'm glad I'm not in the Infantry.

Lt. Richard "Dick" Schiebel was the first National Guard pilot to arrive as a replacement in the 39th Fighter Interceptor Squadron (FIS) that was a component of the 35th Fighter Group based at Suwon/K-13. The 35th Group was about to be dissolved and merged with the 18th. When he wasn't flying missions, Schiebel kept a lively stream of letters heading back to his family. His observations as a Mustang pilot provide insights into what all those flying the F-51 were going through. The missions assigned to the 39th Squadron were virtually the same as the squadrons assigned to the 18th Wing based a few miles away. Although the pilots of the 39th could not know what lay ahead, they would be assigned as a unit of the 18th Wing in just a few weeks as the Air Force reduced its prop aircraft squadrons and consolidated all of the remaining Mustangs in squadrons assigned to the 18th Wing.

In early 1951, the 39th FIS was "split" between its home base at Pusan East/K-9 and the Seoul Municipal Airport (K-16), "with the bulk of the operational flying being from K-16, and the rear area base at Pusan being utilized for performing maintenance on the fighters," the unit report noted.

The 39th Squadron was notified on 5 May 1951 that the 35th Fighter-Interceptor Group, to which the 39th FIS had been assigned since January 1942, was being deactivated and the 39th Squadron would be attached to the 18th Group at nearby Chinhae/K-10 within several days.

Schiebel had just arrived in Korea when he began a series of letters to the folks back home about his missions, feelings and experiences.

13 February 1950

Well, I'm a veteran in the Korean War now with 3 missions under my belt. I checked out in an hour local flight Saturday, and became eligible for combat strikes. On Sunday my flight was the alert flight. We had to be on alert from 0600 to 1130. At 0900 we were scrambled and sent to Pohang, about 65 miles N.E. and told to contact a Mosquito plane for further instructions. We got up there and the Mosquito marked a hill with a smoke grenade where he said 50-100 guerillas were sleeping. There were four in our flight, each with 2 napalm gasoline jelly bombs, 6 rockets and 1800 rounds of .50-cal. machine gun ammunition.

We dropped the napalm and rockets first and then, raked the hill for about 4 passes with .50-cal. We were then told to rake a village where troops were suspected of hiding. We rocketed and strafed it and set it afire. I don't think there were any troops in there and I felt a bit bad tearing up homes while the inhabitants watched from South of town. Such Is War.

Yesterday 8 of us went 350 miles North to a town named Tokchore—about 65 miles N. E. of Pyongyang. That's way up in enemy territory, but everything went fine. Our target was a supply dump in the north section of the city. We had photos, so it wasn't hard to find.

We napalmed it first and then rocketed it and then strafed. We left it completely destroyed.

One of the fellows in our squadron was shot down by flak yesterday too. He was hit in the tail and had only aileron control. He got it back to Taegu and bailed out. He broke his leg when he hit the ground though.

A pilot in another squadron was shot down by flak Sunday up at Pyongyang and bailed out in the water. He was picked up by a corvette, but he died later of shock and exposure.

The loss rate in our squadron is very small.

I'm actually doing the same thing I was doing at Langley, but am getting credit for it. I'm very fortunate to be assigned to the 39th, because everyone in it is a prince of a fellow.

I have been appointed Athletic Officer and we have been having some hot games of volley ball behind our operations shack every afternoon. All the fellows call me Coach, and seem to like me very much.

My squadron C.O. told me Sunday at the Club, "Schiebel, I've never seen anyone accepted in this squadron so quickly as you have been." It made me feel very good.

Sunday after my first mission when I got back a Public Information man was waiting to take my picture. I am the first National Guard replacement in this area and was the first to fly a mission.

21 February 1951

Well, I now have 11 missions completed—only 89 more to go. That sounds like a lot doesn't it, but it will be only about four months and then I'll be finished. The latest word is that we will be rotated back to the States as soon as we finish our 100th regardless of time overseas—but nothing official has been sent out on that. They are going to use this theater as a training base because of the low loss rate and the lack of enemy opposition.

We lost 11 ships yesterday, and not one was due to enemy action.

I flew an early mission and was lying on my sack when a guy pops his head in the door and says "crash." I grabbed my camera and ran out toward the runway. The smoke was billowing up thick and black. It was an F-4U Corsair that had had a gear collapse on take off.

The pilot jumped clear just as three rockets cooked off and headed for our airplanes about a half mile down the line.

The rockets altogether accounted for six of our airplanes. One brand new one that had just been flown in the day before had

243

to be junked. The rocket went through the back just behind the cockpit.

Two others received major damage, and three received minor damage.

A 500-lb. bomb on the Corsair exploded just as I was taking a picture of it. I was about mile away and the concussion was tremendous. All the windows on the [flight] line were broken, and the only recognizable parts of the Corsair left were the engine and one wing. No one was hurt, or even scratched, which is slightly unbelievable considering the bomb, the rockets and about 50 rounds of 20-milimeter shells that cooked off.

Shortly after that, one F-51 overran another on the runway and chewed the tail & wing off the front one. The rear one burst into flames and was totally destroyed. Then, about 20 minutes later a F-51 landed with a flat tire and nosed up off the runway in the sand.

No one was injured in either of these accidents.

All in all it was a very successful day for the enemy.

Flew my fourth mission on Wednesday the 14th—a close support mission at Wonju. We contacted a ground controller and he zeroed us in on the side of a hill where the Reds were holed up. We could see the Reds on one side and our boys huddled on the other—less than 50 yards apart. We napalmed them first then rocketed and finally strafed with 1800 rounds each. You can't tell how much good you are doing, but the controller said we were right on the target and he estimated 100-125 killed.

Thursday the 15th was the 5th mission to Kumhwa—a 2-ship reconnaissance flight with my flight leader, Capt. Wright. We were to scout out enemy troop concentrations, supplies, vehicles, etc. We fly low looking for objects camouflaged by hay, trees, tarpaulins, etc. We found one truck but couldn't get it to burn. I dropped both my napalms in the mouth of a long tunnel that must have been loaded with supplies. It was burning furiously and smoking from both ends 30 minutes later. Capt. Wright said it was the most perfect hit he had ever seen and he's been here since November.

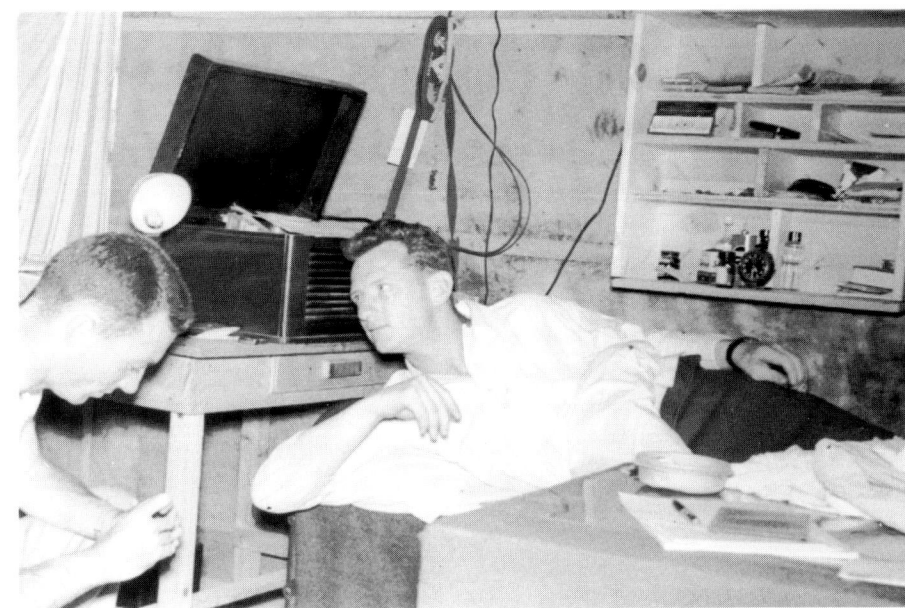

Home Sweet Quonset Hut. Lt. Col. Thomas D. Robertson, Commanding Officer of the 39th FIS and 1st Lt. Frank G. Bell relax in their corner of the Quonset hut that served as their home at K-9. (Schiebel)

Had a squadron party in the mess hall last night. Each month the Squadron has a party—one month given by the Enlisted men for the Officers, and the next month vise-versa.

We give next month and I'm on the program to juggle—as you probably already suspect.

The enlisted men put on a good skit epitomizing the life of a fighter pilot. (That's the wrong way to use epitomize isn't it?)

Anyway, they were funny as the dickens.

Our C.O. got his promotion to Lt. Col. that night and that caused a lot of mirth. He's only 28 years old and is a wonderful guy.

Number 6 on Friday was scheduled for close support at Inchon, but the weather over the target was snafu (Situation Normal, All xxxx-ed Up), so we went up the East Coast and worked over a village up there.

No. 7 and 8 on Saturday.

No. 7 was a 2-ship recce north of Seoul with the Squadron Exec. He only needs one more mission to finish his 100. I killed my

39th FIS pilots Dickman and Crouch gather their equipment and gear prior to a mission from K-9. (Schiebel)

244

first man on that trip. Two of them were on the road with packs on their backs. Maj. Bowers got one and I got one. It sort of preyed on my mind for a day or so, but it has worn off now.

No. 8 was a scramble when 2 pilots discovered a bunch of trucks camouflaged north of Seoul. We got 8 airplanes on the area and did a good job of shooting them up. I haven't accustomed my eye to picking up camouflaged objects, so I was just firing where my flight leader fired. We claimed 6 vehicles. I picked up a piece of rocket when I went in too low on a rocket pass. It hit in the scoop underneath. No serious damage. I'll watch those low passes in the future.

The weather socked in Sunday, so we didn't get any missions in. We played volley ball till 1030, and then I went to church. It was a good sermon on Pontius Pilate. Played 2 more games after church before lunch, and then hit the sack.

No. 9 on Monday was a recce north of Seoul, near Kumhwa. We discovered a 6 x 6 truck that was stuck in a culvert that had caved in across a road. It had been abandoned in a hurry that morning. They tried to hide it with a tarp, but it had slipped off. Tandy missed it with both his napalms, so I strafed it and it blew up. I fired 3 rockets at a bridge, and two of then went through the floor of the bridge. Good hits.

No. 10 yesterday was a 2-ship recce with another Captain in my flight. We got one truck that refused to burn. Nothing else worth mentioning.

Today I recced with Capt. Bright on an early mission. We briefed at 0540, and took off at 0640. Had the same area above Seoul toward Kumhwa. Tandy got a semi-trailer truck with napalm, I got 3 loaded pack animals. I let the man with them go.

We found a big bridge being rebuilt. I napalmed the buildings at the approach where we figured they kept supplies and equipment. It was a beautiful hit, and about 4 buildings went up. I then dropped the other napalm on the scaffolding of the uncompleted section. The darn thing went right through the scaffolding and hit the side of the gorge and burned. Only a little got on the bridge and it burned out in a few min-

utes. I should have dropped it at the bottom of the gorge and let it burn from the bottom. I missed it with my rockets too.

Our R.& R. leave has been cancelled until the 2nd of March because they want to count heads next week. I'm just as well satisfied because it gives me a chance to get in the shorter close-support missions while the troops are still in the Seoul area. The reccies are all over 3 hours. The close supports are usually 2-2 1/2 hours long.

Did you know that $200.00 of each month's pay over here is income tax exempt? All officers are that way, and the E.M. are exempt altogether. Also, our air mail is free.

We have a stage show at the Club tonight straight from the States—hillbilly stuff, etc. Gotta go eat and wash up. Don't worry about me.

27 Feb. 51

I've been lying around all day waiting for the weather to clear up so we could go on a sortie. My flight had early alert this morning and we had to be at briefing at 0545. After briefing we went over to our Ops shack and slept till about 0730 on benches. It has been raining hard all day, and it has shown no signs of slackening.

Things go along over here very rapidly. I lose track of the days and dates, and only have my diary to keep me straight.

Since I wrote you last I've only flown three sorties. I have a total of 14 now. I hope to get in a couple more before we leave for R & R in Tokyo Friday.

On the 22nd, no mission because of bad weather. We played a couple of games of volley ball, and then I played cribbage with Tandy. Came back to the barracks in the afternoon and built us a writing desk out of a bunch of old rocket and ammunition boxes. We built a rack for our bags so that they would be off the floor, and put up a bunch of nails to hang our stuff on. Also, built a bunch of shelves for my radio and shaving stuff.

On Friday the 23rd I got number 12. It started out as a recce flight up above Seoul toward Kuhmwa, but when we got in the Seoul area we were diverted by a Mosquito

T-6 for close-up support work. He zeroed us in on the northwest end of a bridge just East of Seoul about 2 miles, where enemy troops were dug in and firing on our boys on the opposite side of the river. I got three beautiful rockets on a building full of troops. It was the first time I've seen my rockets do any damage. The building was a brick and plaster affair, and when I looked back after I pulled out the dust and fire was spouting up.

My napalm was a good hit on the trenches and fox holes in the sand on the edge of the river. Don't know how many we got, but the Mosquito said we did an excellent job on the exact spot he wanted hit.

Number 13 came on Saturday, the 24th. It also started out as a 2-ship recce, but we got diverted again in the Seoul area. You see, the recces are all three hour flights, and we always do our best to get diverted as we go over the front lines to close support because you are finished in about 15 minutes and then you can go home. However, all these diversions were legal, and we didn't try for them, even though we hoped for them.

We hit a ridge on the South side of the Han about 20 miles southeast of Seoul where the river splits and goes northeast and northwest.

When you're working over a ridge with troop emplacements on it, you seldom see what you're hitting. All you do is spray the area with .50's after you drop your napalm on the spot that the mosquito tells you—just work in that general area.

That night Tandy and I went to the movie and saw Red Skelton in "Watch the Birdie." I had seen it in L. B., but enjoyed it as much the second time as the first.

Sunday we got to sleep late because we weren't scheduled until afternoon. I was planning to go to church at 1030, but at 0900 the Adjutant came in and asked me to take Tower officer duty till noon for one of the fellows in the squadron who got married on R & R and hadn't gotten back on time. I was glad to do it because the weather was bad & there was very little activity, and no fighter flying. I sacked out all afternoon, wrote a couple of letters, and went to the

Club in the evening.

Every night at 1700 we have a group briefing that brings us up to date as to the latest news from home, late war news, and a resume of the day's sorties. Each flight leader gives a narrative description of his mission that day. It is really very interesting, and it breaks the evening up pretty well. Most of the guys just sit around after briefing and drink and shoot the breeze, but not me. I just sit around & shoot the breeze.

Yesterday, Monday the 26th, I had my best mission.

We started out to recce, but when we got into the Seoul area we heard a Mosquito calling for any flight in the area with a full load. Well, we did, so we answered him. He said he had two tanks spotted, and would like us to work them over if we wanted to. We said, "Roger" and went to find him. He was just outside Seoul to the northwest about a mile, and the tanks were camouflaged behind a ridge.

It was in a cut through a ridge about 25 feet deep. The cut looked like it had been made with a bulldozer.

Tandy dropped his napalm on one, but overshot a little with one, and the other was a dud. It burned a little, but was only smoldering when I went in on mine.

I overshot a hair with my first napalm, but was determined to hit with the second, so I flew about five feet over it through the cut and hit it right on the nose.

We pulled away and strafed troops on a hill nearby for about five minutes, and then came back.

My tank was burning nicely, but Tandy's was just smoking, so he says, "Let's put a rocket into it."

I said, "OK," but have learned that putting rockets into a small target is a real job.

Well, he hit the thing right on top with his first rocket, and it exploded just as he pulled off.

About a minute later it must have hit the ammo because it blew up about 100 feet in the air. I saw parts of metal flying through the air that high.

Then we strafed mine a little more, and as I was going in on my last pass, it too exploded and blew flames and smoke about 100 feet high.

On the way home we heard an Aussie belly his ship in a rice paddle, and his wingman was calling for a helicopter.

The plane hit a 12 foot levee between paddies and the guy was killed. Too bad, too. They have lost 3 men since I got here. Two of them were in weather and spun in.

Just got back from briefing over at the Club. The Intelligence Officer says that the Reds are pulling back toward the 38th Parallel and are massing large numbers of troops for a suspected push in March. They are massing troops on the East coast for a flanking move, too. The roads have broken down under our heavy traffic, and we are at a stand-still now. The rice paddies are under five feet of water.

Boy! I'm glad I'm not in the Infantry.

March 1951

"The use of napalm has been more effective in destroying or neutralizing T-34 tanks in Korea than have all other airborne weapons which were used."

79608 AC

This candid shot of General MacArthur and members of his staff was taken on March 3, 1951 at an advanced U. S. Far East Air Forces Korean air base during one of the general's famous visits to the front for personal observation of the situation. Accompanying General MacArthur are (left to right), Maj. Gen. Doyle O. Hickey, Acting Chief of Staff, GHQ, Far East Command; Maj. Gen. Leven C. Allen, Chief of Staff, Eighth Army; Maj. Gen. Earle E. Partridge, Commanding General, Fifth Air Force, and Col. A. W. Tyer, commander of the 49th Fighter-Bomber Wing. (NARA)

Monthly Summary

UN ground forces continued to march back up the Korean Peninsula, advancing slowly and methodically—moving the front line an average of thirty miles northward. When UN troops crossed the Han River east and west of Seoul, flanking the former capitol, communist forces then abandoned the city.

The Communists were constructing new revetments and runways at major North Korean airfields, but their aircraft rarely appeared over the front lines. UN fighter bombers were threatened by significant numbers of new antiaircraft batteries being placed around such important North Korean cities as Pyongyang and Sinuiju, which UN aircraft frequently raided. B-29s returned to northwest Korea on interdiction missions that brought on MiG-15 attacks. Fifth Air Force flew F-86 fighters out of Taegu and Suwon to protect the heavy bombers. Air-to-air combat increased as a direct result, especially in the Sinuiju and Sinanju areas in northwest Korea.

Far East Air Forces began airlifting military cargo into a newly constructed airfield at Hoengsong (K-46), while U.S. Army engineers hurried to rehabilitate airfields at Seoul and Kimpo for transports.

For the first time, General Douglas MacArthur proposed a cease-fire. UN aircraft dropped 7,000 copies of his proposal over Korea during the last week of the month.

Adapted in part from U.S. Air Force Historical Research Agency. January 2002. The U.S. Air Force's First War: Korea 1950-1953 Significant Events. March 1951. http://www.au.af.mil/au/afhra/wwwroot/korean_war/korean_war_chronology/kwc_1951.html

Operations From Chinhae

Maintenance was difficult and flying was downright hazardous due to the K-10 airbase runway, which was originally designed and built by the Japanese for seaplane operations. Since mid-December when the 18th Wing relocated to K-10 from K-9, "if the weather wasn't wet and rainy causing runway operations to become dangerous, then it would be dry and dusty giving aircraft maintenance personnel many headaches. Large rocks on the runway were sucked into the propellers during run-ups, resulting in damage to numerous propellers. Great clouds of dust enveloped the entire aircraft parking area upon pre-flight run-up of the engines. This dust was considered to be the primary causes for numerous abortive combat missions charged to rough engines as it had a high silicate content which easily fouled the exhaust spark plugs," the monthly report noted. [1]

The engineers had tried putting oil on the dirt to combat the dust, but it too had major drawbacks. They had also tried to resurface the strip at Chinhae with decomposed granite, but "it did not stand the test of heavy rainfall during the early part of the month. We were forced to stand-down on two occasions because of ruts and soft spots on the strip," Lt. Col. Cox reported. Clearly, a brand new surface was needed. "A project which called for re-grading and leveling the existing airstrip to be followed by covering the strip with pierced steel planking was commenced on 25 March 1951. The estimated date of completion was 21 April 1951. It is felt that when the re-surfaced runway is completed many of the above mentioned problems which arise during dry as well as wet weather will be solved." [2]

While the K-10 strip was out of commission, "fighter operations were conducted from K-1 (Pusan West) Air Base," about 25 miles from K-10.

Construction was also started on "tropical buildings for living quarters, an officer's mess hall, latrines, airmen's mess hall and several other operational buildings."

Morale fluctuated "considerably" during the month of March primarily due to rotation plans that "were changing continually." Several different plans had been announced, followed by the details being "changed from day to day thus leaving with everyone a feeling of doubt as to the final outcome." [3] Those personnel who had come with the Group from Clark field and who had completed six months or more in Korea were "eagerly awaiting the arrival of their replacements from that station."

The plan to rotate combat pilots to the Zone of the Interior upon completion of 100 combat missions "seems to be functioning smoothly, however."

The Group's request for "mission credit" for pilots assigned to forward controller duty was now expected to be disapproved. However, Lt. Col. Cox again "strongly recommended" that officers who drew that duty "should have mission credit to compensate for the time lost away from Combat Flying."

Living conditions at K-10 were improving steadily and the arrival of spring weather "added to the environment, aiding morale considerably. The weather is almost perfect. Personnel can still remember the heat, dust, flies and mosquitoes of summer, and the bitter cold of winter, so the spring brings a feeling of well being," Lt. Col. Cox reported for the Group.

Base Planning Board

Rebuilds K-10

Soon after the 18th Wing was moved to K-10, Colonel Rogers established a "Base Planning Board," consisting of officers representing all major components that had a role in preparing the run down former Japanese seaplane base for sustained combat operations. The new board would have its hands full.

The meeting on 21 March 1951 was "convened to discuss proposed plans and specifications for the building of temporary housing and installations at K-10 Air Force Base..."

View of the flight line at K-10/Chinhae showing the proximity of the air field to the bay. A Mustang's engine quit on takeoff at K-10 and the plane bellied into the water, then flipped over as it sank. The divers went down to inspect quickly and found that the airplane was upside down in the mud. "We all thought it was over for him. He's gone west," remembered Wilfred "Budd" Stapley. "We had an old crane that was trundled out. Of course, this is taking time." Out to the end of the runway the recovery team went to set up the crane. Finally, the crane was in place and the divers went down to hook the winch line around the tail prior to pulling the plane out of the water—and the grim task of retrieving the body of the by now dead pilot. As they prepare to put the line around the tail, they are stunned to see a motion inside the cockpit of the inverted airplane. Incredulously, they realize—that someone—is waving at them—frantically. It was the pilot who was trapped in the cockpit, but still attached to his oxygen system—and still alive. Now working as fast as they could, the divers secured the airplane and pulled it up—just in time. The pilot's oxygen ran out soon after they pried open the damaged canopy. "Boy, I didn't know whether you guys were going to get there in time—or not," he said. (Urquhart)

Capt. James W. Lee and Lt. Ken Barber (right) just prior to Barber's 100th mission. Lee had just returned from a mission. Barber flew the mission in "Ferret," Danny Dillon's airplane. The three Lieutenants flew many missions together. (Barber)

Barber's Centurian Mission "Buzz Job." On 31 March 1951, Lt. Ken Barber completed his 100th mission. He and Capt Galyon as wingman, "hit some foxholes just across the bomb line south of Chorwon, and came right home. One of my rockets hung up, which made me mad because I wanted no obstruction to my 100th mission buzz job." Galyon landed, but Barber "went over to K-10 and buzzed it—then back to K-1 where I buzzed up the taxi strip and did a roll to the right—then landed." While landing the rear portion of the faulty rocket "fell off. The men said it was the lowest buzz job they had ever seen."

The Installations Officer reported that construction contracts had been "let" for 25 of the 41 proposed buildings approved by Fifth Air Force. The new construction included a wide range of new structures. A three wing 20'x108' Airman's mess, a two wing NCO mess, 9 fighter squadron operational buildings, and a T-shaped officer's mess were among the new buildings that were to be constructed.

Discussion for new buildings also included the merits of a combination Base Theater and Gymnasium. "The morale factor of Airmen is expected to be a problem throughout inclement weather. Present plans for utilization of theater for maintenance shops leaves no facilities for motion pictures or special services."

Other new buildings on the agenda included a Parachute Tower, Control Tower ("constructed of the cheapest possible material as soon as possible"), a Fighter Briefing Building to provide the "various offices necessary for the briefing and de-briefing of fighter group personnel," a Photo Lab (with the present facility converted into the

Post Exchange), an addition to the Communication's Center and Maintenance and Supply Offices. Four new Base Supply Warehouses, a Fighter Group Headquarters, an Air Terminal Building, Air Installations Shops, and a building to enclose the AACS Transmitter were also reviewed.

The lengthy session closed with a discussion of how to pave the runways and taxi strips with asphalt--not once, but twice. "Captain Wylie estimates a total of approximately 1,480 barrels of asphalt will be necessary to complete the taxi strips and parking areas. A total of approximately 300 barrels will be necessary to complete the road ways. Asphalt has been requisitioned, but at present there is none available on K-10 Air Force Base. Estimated cost of asphalt $13,518.00."

The Board concluded the meeting by recommending that approval be sought from Fifth Air Force to construct numerous new buildings, including: the Parachute Tower, Control Tower, a Fighter Briefing Building, the Fighter Group Headquarters, and the majority of the structures previously

discussed.

The 18th Wing not only had to fly challenging combat missions every day, keeping worn out Mustangs in the air, it had to design and build its own base and support facilities from scratch as it did so.

Polish Those Vehicles

Just ten weeks after the 18th Wing had been moved to the skeleton "base" at K-10, the 18th Wing Commander, Colonel T. C. Rogers received a tart letter from Major General Partridge signed out by the Deputy Fifth Air Force Commander, General E.J. Timberlake, Jr.

"During the period in which the Fifth Air Force has been engaged in Korean operations," the stuffy, formal letter began, "I have become increasingly concerned over the general appearance of motor vehicles and of the general standards of organizational and field maintenance of vehicles, auxiliary power equipment and ground powered equipment throughout the command. I feel that this condition is generally below acceptable standards."

"While I recognize that there are numerous difficulties incident to the basic problem such as shortages of spare parts, inadequate facilities, and difficult operating conditions I am particularly interested that commanders take action to overcome these problems rather than allowing the contributory causes to become a justification for the present state of maintenance of this equipment."

"The present rate of attrition together with the excessive number of deadlined vehicles are of such proportion that a continuation of this rate can only be detrimental to the effort of the command. The replacement supply of both general and special purpose vehicles as well as ground power equipment is such that present attrition cannot be sustained."

"It is my desire that commanders at all echelons take action to institute aggressive programs to eliminate operator abuse and insure thorough inspections and maintenance of all powered equipment. Personnel at all echelons must be impressed with the requirement to conserve and maintain these resources within the concept of established practices of sound management."

"I would like to have you acquaint me with what action you are taking to correct this problem," the letter demanded.

A week later, Colonel Rogers forwarded a three-page letter to General Partridge, that outlined "the program which has been established to raise our standards to the highest possible degree." He cited "definite progress" in the quality of maintenance and vehicle appearance with the "principal factor" being "the stable location of the 18th Fighter-Bomber Wing for the past three and a half months." Was he politely telling his boss, "Now that we're not driving up and down the length of the Korean Peninsula we are able to keep the vehicles clean and repaired?"

Rogers went on to outline other elements of the 18th Wing Vehicle Maintenance

The Mustang in these photographs taken seconds apart appears to be about 20-feet "off the deck" as its pilot "buzzes" the airfield at K-10 after completing his 100th combat mission in early 1951. A gaggle of 18th FBG pilots watch with envy as the F-51 literally kicks up the dust with a low, fast pass. (Mason)

Hundredth Mission Flight "Buzz Job"

The flying squadrons of the 18th Fighter-Bomber Group celebrated the tradition of a Hundredth Mission Flight for those finishing up their combat tour.

Early in 1951, 1st Lt. (later Lt. Col.) Peter Richardson of the 12th Squadron, "was scheduled with three other pilots to fly the hundredth. This included accomplishing a combat mission, which we carried out. On the way back to K-10 we practiced in-formation loops and barrel rolls prior to demonstrated at Chinhae 'by the sea.' To finish off the show, the flight leader put us in diamond formation with me in #4 position-- in the "hole" behind and below lead--with #2 and #3 on leader's wings, left and right, all in tight formation, for an on-the-deck run down the runway to peel up for landing."

At first as the tightly bunched Mustangs headed towards the K-10 runway virtually flying at ground level, Richardson "was concerned" for his coolant scoop. He was tucked in and below the lead, with planes above and on either side of him. He was "boxed."

However, the coolant became a distinct second to his worries when he "saw directly ahead the squadron C-47 looking as big as today's C-5 to me." His concern immediately "changed to fear." How would it "avoid hitting the gooney without hitting either wingman or chopping off leads tail section?" Just in the nick of time, the left wingman peeled up, then the lead, then the right wingman. The "box" expanded and Richardson clawed for some altitude to clear the cargo plane. "Later I heard that the gooney shook and wobbled from my wash," he reported.

Program that ranged from permanent drivers for each vehicle, improvements to the Motor Pool, requesting better logistical support from Fifth Air Force components, a washing and painting program, and the promulgation of a letter "directing that all personnel report any case of vehicle abuse." Rogers assured Partridge that any vehicle operator "found guilty of vehicle abuse will be subject to disciplinary action under the provisions of Article of War 83."

"I assure you that maintenance as well as care and operation of motor vehicles, auxiliary power equipment, and ground powered equipment will receive the proper emphasis, now, as well as in the future," Rogers closed.

Combat Operations

Operations for the 18th Fighter-Bomber Group "continued along the same pattern as established in the month of February," the monthly report noted. However, the "tempo has quickened and our two squadrons flew a total of 1302 effective sorties…" Over two thirds of these "were interdiction resulting in a record number of vehicles destroyed. The 18th Fighter-Bomber Group led all other groups in this activity. This achievement was recognized in several press releases in which the Commanding General stated that the 18th Fighter Bomber Group, "Ace Truck Busters of the 5th Air Force" again had destroyed a record number of vehicles." [4]

The Group reported the loss of four pilots in March, three to enemy action, one to an accident. 1st Lt. James D. Heath, 1st Lt. Gerald D. Heagney and 1st Lt. Willis R. Brown, crashed in enemy territory and are presently listed as missing in action. 1st Lt. Francis A. Holcolmb was killed on 15 March

What The… Captain Bill Strand, a 67th Squadron Flight Leader, awoke from a precious afternoon nap that started off in his tent, but ended on the runway thanks to some innovative pranksters in the spring of 1951. Strand was an outstanding flight leader who caught the eye of the new Wing Commander, Col. T.C. Rogers, who assigned himself to missions led by Strand so often, that he called Strand "my flying partner." (Mason)

Lt. Col. "Hank" Lawrence, CO of the 67th and Capt. Will Rogers, Operations Officer outside the Operations Office on 30 March 1951. (Barber)

when his F-51 crashed into the bay at K-10 after take-off." *[Additional information indicates a loss of eight pilots in March.]*

The 18th F-B Group implemented "a shift in armament loading from napalm to 500-pound General Purpose bombs was necessary in order to chop railroad lines and seal tunnels. In two weeks time, all tunnels in our areas have suffered severe damage as well as the supplies, engines and trains concealed inside these tunnels."

The Group was running out of truck targets—"there has been a definite scarcity of enemy trucks to be found in the usual camouflaged manner. It is no longer possible to find vehicles hidden in villages, in ravines, or disguised as straw stacks. It begins to appear that the enemy has learned a lesson and is now constructing bunkers in almost inaccessible ravines for the purpose of storing equipment and vehicles during the daylight hours. The ever increasing number of these log reinforced structures gives credence to the belief that the time is not far off when no trucks will be found in the open or protected by camouflage only. The cunning construction and location of these bunkers have, thus far, thwarted our efforts to destroy them or their contents. It appears that the enemy is aware of our inability to destroy vehicles safely hidden there and have made no attempt to camouflage or to protect them." [5]

Ammunition was a constant problem. The .50-caliber ammunition "is generally very old and of a very poor grade." Pilots were experiencing 30-60 percent "duds" when using the 500-lb General Purpose bombs "due to faulty primer-detonators-- there have been instances where bombs armed with this primer-detonator have detonated upon impact instead of detonating after the pre-set delay." [6]

"The use of napalm has been more effective in destroying or neutralizing T-34 tanks in Korea than have all other airborne weapons which were used." Napalm was the weapon of choice for fighter-bomber pilots in Korea the FAF Operations Analysis Office concluded in its March 1st Memorandum No. 35. The FAF based its conclusions on the findings of Weapons Effectiveness

---

Bill and Pancho Hunt MIGs

Flight leader Bill Strand and Robert "Pancho" Pasqualicchio had completed a naplam mission in North Korea one afternoon. The target was good and they felt confident that the mission was a success. The assigned target having been taken care of, the next order of business was to find another target--or targets. What the two former F-86 pilots had in mind was to "go get us a MIG." So they "waltzed" up to the Yalu.

Strand suggested that Pasqualicchio "stay low" at about 6,-8,000 feet and that he would try to catch the MIGs "at the top of their zoom," or about 16,000 feet.

No sooner had Pasqualicchio reached his assigned altitude, than he was "nose-to-nose" with eight MIG-15's. Thinking quickly, he pointed the Mustang at the MIGs, gave the bird full throttle, pulled the nose "up ten degrees and rippled off all six rockets into their faces." The MIGs "scattered to the four winds."

The aerial fireworks had caught the eye of 16 UN P-84s, led by Col. Don Blakeslee, who chased Pasqualicchio "around on the deck. They thought I was a YAK." Soon the U.S. pilots recognized the other planes as friendlies and called off the chase.

Pasqualicchio and Strand hoped the fracas was over. They were wrong.

They were soon summoned to Fifth Air Force headquarters in Seoul. Maj. General Frank Everest chewed on Pasqualicchio's butt for a while with Blakeslee standing by. Blakeslee added his opinion that the two Mustang pilots had "screwed up this whole air war."

As he dismissed the two pilots, Everest ordered them to the "stay the hell away from the Yalu River and you just shoot at trucks. Do you understand, Captain?"

The only answer that could be given at that point was "Yes, sir!" followed by a quick exit.

Pasqualicchio never did get to tangle with MIGs again, but he and the other 18th flyers were always anxious to get hold of any YAK or LA that they "could get their hands on."

Evaluation Teams—WEE Teams—that "followed the advancing ground troops and counted, photographed, and studied all possible armor and materiel." The WEE Teams also interrogated Koreans who had witnessed the attacks, where they could be identified. Each WEE Team was "a self-sustaining field unit and consisted of a team captain, an intelligence specialist, photographer, driver and Korean interpreter." [7]

The FAF used four major types of weapons against enemy armor: napalm, aircraft rockets, bombs, and .50-caliber machine guns. All bombing attacks during that period used the 500-lb GP bomb.

The WEE Team concluded that over 70 percent of the T-34 tanks were "killed" by napalm, 21 percent by rockets (including the 6.5" ATAR), 7 percent by machine gun strafing attacks and only 1 percent by bombing.

A significant finding was that "approximately 10 times as many tanks were claimed to have been destroyed (or 14 times as many hit) by rockets as by napalm...it can only be concluded that whereas relatively large effort has been expended in shooting rockets at enemy tanks, and apparently resulting in hits, actually only a small fraction were hits. Had actual hits been obtained, a much larger number of tanks would have been found due to rockets."

The hit probability of a pilot-aircraft-rocket combination "must have been very small on a target the size of a T-34 tank...What probably happened was that pilots thought they were hitting the tanks with their rockets; consequently, continued overemphasis and reliance was placed on their utility." The report noted that during tests conducted at Taegu in September, ground movies were taken of both napalm and rocket attacks on T-34 tanks. Due to the smoke and dust, observers believed many hits had been made. Actually, there was only "one hit out of 28 single rocket firings."

Another finding: "the aerial coverage obtained by dropping two 110-gallon tanks of napalm…is approximately 50 yards square."

The Group reported that for the month of March it had 51 aircraft assigned and that each aircraft flew 81 hours that month to complete 1,302 sorties and 4,086 hours of flying time. Fourteen aircraft were lost that month, including five in combat and 9 to other causes. Twenty-nine aircraft were damaged in combat. Nearly 300,000 gallons of fuel was consumed that month.

Combat operations required 1,894 napalm bombs, 458 GP bombs, 7,262 rockets and 1.3 million rounds of .50-caliber ammunition.

In March 1951, the 12th FBS was commanded by Major Sam C. Wilkerson, who led the 43 officers and 139 airmen of the squadron. The 12th set a new record in March by destroying over 600 vehicles and damaging many others, Wilkerson reported.

The majority of missions for the 12th during March were two-ship flights on armed reconnaissance to seek and destroy enemy vehicles and supplies. Late in the month, most of the flights were carrying 500-pound bombs "with delayed action fuses…to destroy railroads and highway tunnels," the unit report noted. The enemy was still using the "same means to camouflage their vehicles and supplies," but they had also "started building revetments in the side of hills to hide their vehicles. These revetments appeared in larger numbers this month than in previous months." [8]

Wilkerson pointed out that helicopters had been "moved forward along with the advance of our ground forces and were available for pilot pickup. From their advanced positions the helicopters were able to cover the area worked by our fighters."

Lt. Col. Lawrence reported that for the 67th Squadron, "the shortage of combat pilots due to casualties, completion of 100 missions…have severely hampered operations. Presently assigned pilots are rapidly accruing their prescribed total missions.

This workload (combat operations) has resulted in exhausting such pilots physically and mentally. Recognition of this problem resulted in the reassignment of one officer during the report period." Lawrence reported plans to "conduct a competitive program among the airmen and between the various squadron sections on a 'best job done' basis to stimulate additional interest and enthusiasm in the performance of assigned duties."

RESCAP procedures were being formulated. "Firsthand experience by rescued combat pilots indicated that: with two or more aircraft circling a downed pilot, on station aircraft are much more effective with a tight pattern in warding off potential attacks either by automatic and/or small arms fire. Keeping aircraft pointed (120 degrees Lufbery spacing) constantly in all directions tended to keep enemy fire interdicted. The unsecuring of small arms from a shoulder and/or hip holster prior to a parachute landing may result in its loss and/or becoming inoperative due to mud, etc. becoming lodged therein. All combat pilots carry two hand flares to be utilized for last minute spotting when rescue aircraft arrive. Premature utilization would enable the enemy to pin point a downed pilot's position." [9]

Endnotes

[1] USAFHRA. *Monthly Historical Report, 18th Fighter-Bomber Wing*, March 1951.

[2] USAFHRA. *Monthly Historical Report, 18th Fighter-Bomber Wing*, March 1951, p. 2.

[3] USAFHRA. *Monthly Historical Report, 18th Fighter-Bomber Group*, March 1951, p. 4.

[4] USAFHRA. *Monthly Historical Report, 18th Fighter-Bomber Group*, March 1951, p. 5.

[5] USAFHRA. *Monthly Historical Report, 18th Fighter-Bomber Group*, March 1951, p. 6.

[6] USAFHRA. *Monthly Historical Report, 18th Fighter-Bomber Group*, March 1951, p. 9.

[7] NARA. *Fifth Air Force Operations Analysis Office Memorandum No. 35*, March 1, 1951. CONFIDENTIAL Declassified.

[8] USAHRA. *Monthly Historical Report, 12th Fighter-Bomber Squadron*, March 1951, p. 4.

[9] USAHRA. *Monthly Historical Report, 67th Fighter-Bomber Squadron*, March 1951, p. 8.

Combat Statistics

18th Fighter-Bomber Wing

March 1951

Average No. A/C Assigned
51
Total Flying Time
4,086
Percent of Aircraft in Commission
69%
Percent of Aircraft AOCP
2%
Combat Sorties Flown by Wing
1,302
12th Squadron Sorties
468
67th Squadron Sorties
416
2 Squadron Sorties
373
A/C Lost to Combat
5
(29 planes were battle damaged)
Pilots lost
8

Fuel Consumed
295,294 or 72 gallons/flying hour

Ordnance Expended
.50-cal. Rounds
1,328,232
Rockets
7,262
Napalm Bombs
1,894
500-lb. GP Bombs
458

Note: Figures and totals may differ in some categories due to differences in numbers provided by each component.

Wing Commander's Diary

by Brigadier General Turner C. Rogers

"T. C. Rogers lost control on take-off and damn near flew through the fire station."

On Thursday, 1 March, Rogers reported "quite a day" during which the Wing had its "maximum sortie rate to date—87."

Lt. Col. William May, Commander of the 67th Squadron "was shot down just north of Seoul and picked up by helicopter. He is now aboard a cruiser slightly burned, I understand," Rogers noted. "Five planes from the 67th received battle damage from small arms fire and two from the 12th Squadron. Major Duff had engine failure on take-off and almost got it."

"T. C. Rogers," the General noted dryly in his own diary, "lost control on take-off and damn near flew through the fire station." Keeping tongue firmly in cheek, Rogers observed that "It was only through his superior skill and cool daring that he was able to take off and avoid a major catastrophe. (His landing wasn't so hot either!)," he added. Rogers fired his first rockets and recorded "with fair results." He concluded that he needed "an extra cushion behind me so that I can work rudder pedals. Am gaining confidence. Will be an old F.P. soon. It's still work though."

Friday, 2 March 1951 was "another rough day," Rogers noted. "Lost two South African pilots on a long mission into North Korea. Requested 5 AF not to assign any more such missions." He flew "another practice mission today and am ready to take on a combat mission any time. May be scheduled for one tomorrow."

That evening, he enjoyed a party at the K-10 Officer's Club—Top of the Mark. The party featured an orchestra and 16 Korean girls imported from Pusan. The "Officers acted like shy high school boys at first dance for about an hour," Rogers noted. "I took the first dance all by myself to break the ice. The girls were good dancers and officers were well behaved." Being Wing Commander, Rogers observed, "really puts a cramp on my party making. Must remain sober and sedate. T'aint easy. The price of rank and responsibility—must set a good example and all that rot," he noted.

"I might say I'm glad to be here making this entry tonight," Rogers noted on Saturday. "A few hours ago I faced the prospects of bailing out over enemy territory—not a pleasant prospect, I might add."

He had flown his first combat mission with Capt. Bill Strand of the 67th Squadron. Rogers' Mustang had developed engine trouble north of Wanju, but he "decided it was all in my mind. After clearing the engine, it sounded O.K." so he proceeded on mission.

Strand reported that "we got several vehicles," Rogers noted, "I shot where he shot. Buildings were all I saw but we did start several good fires. After we got rid of napalm and rockets and had made several passes with .50-cal. my engine really got rough. I immediately turned on emergency IFF and switched to "D" channel and started climbing."

Rogers lost track of his flight leader "which was a mistake since my radio was not working properly."

He then flew for half hour before he understood the instructions from the controller—Horseradish—to fly 160 degrees.

"After what seemed hours," Rogers spotted K-6, but then decided to try and make K-13—"another mistake." Unfortunately, K-13 "was in middle of a snow storm and by the time I found it, all [fuel] tanks read zero. I made a pass, overshot, and put it in anyway in the last 500 feet of field. Had less than 5 minutes fuel left. No field ever looked better." He then flew back to K-10 in a C-119. Empathetically, Rogers noted that "poor Capt. Strand was almost frantic and almost ran out of fuel himself."

Rogers "learned a lot from that flight. Must remember to write note of thanks to Horseradish (502nd Tactical Control Group). Must also remember to wear more clothes on next flight - imagine it's cold up in those hills at night. It's only by the grace of God that I'm here tonight. Dear God, I thank you."

On Sunday, 4 March 1951, General "Pat" Partridge arrived just before noon to present awards to 15 officers and Airmen and to present a plaque to the 18th Wing in honor of the 10,000th combat sortie. Each group was represented in the ceremony and Rogers accepted the plaque on behalf of officers and airmen. The event was covered by United Press International.

Following General Partridge's departure, Maj. Gen. Low, President Truman's special advisor, "dropped in for visit," Rogers noted, "just passing through."

Perhaps more important to Rogers, in light of his experience the day before, he "spent considerable time preparing maps and reading up on escape and evasion techniques—will fly prepared from now on. Have mission scheduled for tomorrow. I must go again at once. Even if I knew I'd be shot down, I'd have to go. Will be much better prepared psychologically on this one," he said.

On Monday, 5 March 1951, Colonel Rogers completed his second combat mission. The first plane he tried, "started off then ran rough on left magneto." He then changed to another plane which "still didn't run good, but flew it anyway." Captain Strand was again the flight leader and took the flight "to Recce area C-1. Load: rockets, 2 napalm and six .50-cal. Dropped napalm on village N.E. of Kaesong, started large fires. Flew out highway to N.E. and in small valley Capt. Strand picked up trucks. We got at least 10 vehicles in the area (identified by black smoke), possibly one ammunition dump and 3 A.A. guns (20 mm). I asked Capt. Strand later how he noticed guns. He said he picked them up when they were firing at me. Had I known, I'd have been scared to death. We dispersed the gun crews and shot up the gun positions. I noticed machine gun fire coming out of one house and really sprayed the area with .50-cal. I still can't pick out things on the ground the way Strand does—he is excellent," Rogers observed.

He then returned to make a thorough inspection of K-10 and found a "hell of a lot of work needed to clean up certain areas, especially the supply, mess and AIO areas. Also must get telephone and electric wires off the ground." He then appointed a Post Planning Board.

On Wednesday, 7 March Rogers contacted Fifth Air Force and requested they send an "expert on engines to come down and try to spot trouble with our F-5l's. We're having too many aborts and too many pilots flying missions on rough engines." Lt. Col. Homer Cox, Commander of the 18th Group, "had to land at K-l3 today with engine trouble. Col. LaClare had ground abort."

The venereal disease rates had increased "and all due to trips to Japan," Rogers noted. At the staff meeting, he "laid down a policy to deny R & R to anyone contracting V.D."

On his next combat mission—again with Captain Strand—Rogers headed to area C-1, north of Seoul. The flight "destroyed 4 vehicles, 30 or 40 buildings and fired on tank. Picked up moderate ground fire—small arms." The weather "was perfect and my a/c ran smoothly," Rogers recorded. "However, I must have used too high a power setting. I landed after 3 hours, 30-minutes with 4 gallons of gas, while Strand had about 30 gals. I was not taking any chances on a fouled-up engine."

"We lost 2 airplanes today," Rogers noted, "and one pilot." The first pilot, a member of the 67th Squadron, "got hit in coolant, overshot K-l3 and bellied it in. Plane is wash-out." The second pilot, a member of the 12th Squadron with over 50 missions, "strafed too low, hit tree and tore off wing tip. Wreckage scattered over considerable area -no chance of pilot's survival."

Lt. Col. May, Commander of the 67th Squadron, returned today," Rogers noted. "He was shot down in flames on 1 March, parachuted, was picked up by Navy helicopter and carried out to a c.v. He was burned in face and right hand, and his head was cut. He's very lucky to be alive. N.K. troops were shooting at him on the ground. He advises everyone to carry flares to assist rescue pilot in locating downed pilot."

"Can't say that I like flying combat," Rogers candidly told his diary, "frankly I'm scared. I'm about as scared of the airplane as I am of enemy ground fire. We're having too many engine failures. I feel tense before and during every mission and I sweat out that fuel load coming home. Our missions are running from 3 to 3 1/2 hours, which gives about 1 to 1 1/2 hours in target area."

"I still can't spot anything on the ground. Maybe I'll learn," Rogers noted.

The next day, Sunday, 11 March, Rogers visited K-3 and K-1 "looking for a spot to locate our three squadrons while K-10 runway is being repaired. K-3 is O.K. except for the runway which is breaking up. K-1 is ideal. However, Gen. Cushman says he can take only 30 planes," Rogers noted.

While he was traveling, General Timberlake visited K-10 unexpectedly. "Sorry to have missed him. He left note saying everything looked O.K," Rogers noted.

Monday, 12 March was "a beautiful flying day, but we only got off 60 missions—fuel trouble." One of the fuel truck drivers reported that morning "that the fuel was clear instead of green, as it should be," Rogers recorded. He called off flying and "got in some experts with testing equipment." The various fuels used by the Wing were dyed green, pink and purple. The lowest octane was clear. "We discovered that green gas, when exposed to sunlight, turns clear and then a purplish pink within 5 minutes. The discovery was a surprise to everyone, including the experts. We're having an octane test run just as an added precaution."

While the experts were sorting out the fuel problem, Rogers "covered the whole base today by foot. Took almost 3 hours. Still hell of a lot of work to be done." He then scheduled himself for a fifth combat mission.

Tuesday's mission for Rogers and Strand, was a "recce"—reconnaissance—mission to the Pyongyang area. "Shot up several camouflaged vehicles and several buildings. Got direct hit with napalm for a change, but was not so hot with rockets." When Rogers landed after the three hour and ten minute mission, he had less than five gallons remaining in his fuel tanks. However, he "felt more at ease on mission than previously."

Later than day he met with Captain Iseman, AAA Commander, who "complained about living conditions and food." Rogers then "issued instructions to supply him with lumber for tent floors and make equitable distribution of food - very legitimate gripe."

On Wednesday, 14 March, Rogers visited K-9 and K-1 "to firm up arrangements for move on or about 24 March." The South African 2 Squadron would move to K-9, while the remainder of the 18th Group would be based temporarily at K-1.

"Several planes of the 12th Sq. were shot up today. However, all returned safely," he noted, then added, "scheduled for dawn take-off tomorrow. I hate to get up that early, but will have more of day left for office routine."

The next morning, Thursday, Rogers was briefed for the mission at 0525, for a 0650 take-off on an armed recce mission to area C-2. After take-off the flight faced a "solid cloud layer from Chungju north. Found hole about Kumwa and spent 1 hr. and 20 minutes dodging mountains, clouds and bullets. Destroyed several vehicles and buildings. Lots of signs of enemy activity."

Later that afternoon, he reviewed runway construction with his air engineering officer, then pinned the Air Medal on Col. Theron and another SAAF officer who were returning to South Africa. At the farewell party that evening "the beer and brandy flowed freely."

On Saturday, Rogers flew "an armed recce with a Capt. Shuler who had a rough engine. We napalmed and rocketed two villages just north of bomb line and returned—1:55 min. shortest mission to date."

Col. T. C. Rogers, Commander of the 18th Wing at K-16 in 1951. (Pasqualicchio)

[Note: Capt. Lucien Shuler was a WWII Ace with seven kills credited to his P-38, recalled Lt. Col. Kenneth Barber.]

On Sunday, Lt. Holcomb, 67th Squadron "had engine failure on take-off and went into bay. He escaped from cockpit but drowned. He was not wearing Mae West and didn't get out of parachute—was probably stunned. Consensus was that he could have stopped plane on runway after engine started cutting out. Have made it mandatory that all pilots wear Mae Wests."

Rogers noted that he had "developed nose-bleed for no good reason—just starts without warning."

On Saturday, 24 March, the 18th Group had moved to K-1 and the 2 Squadron SAAF had moved to K-9. Rogers had remained at K-10 until Tuesday morning, at which time he drove to K-1.

Rogers was told by headquarters on Monday that the 18th Wing "would be expected to start R & R [Refueling and Rearming] from K-13 at earliest practical date after 35th clears out."

On Wednesday morning Rogers recorded that the weather was bad and that he was "standing by for take-off on reece on close-support mission. My flying partner, Capt. Strand, will soon finish his tour. He has 90 missions now. Heard rumor that time in Korea would count 3 points for rotation."

Col. Rogers did not mention in his diary that his pilots "were quite proud of the fact that unlike Col. Low, T.C. Rogers eagerly flew combat," recalled Col. Bill Myers. "We cheered when he only took 2 or 3 passes to land--and had a big bash when he made a landing on the first pass."

Wing Commander Flying Wing

by Major Raymond "Mac" McKelvey

Major Bill Greene was the 67th Squadron Operations Officer, and as the second senior officer in the squadron was the commander on any mission he flew. An excellent leader, his briefings were clear and concise leaving no doubt about what was expected of the men in his command.

The morning briefing brought out the full chorus of moans and groans when we saw the target—Pyongyang—the NK capital. To make things worse, our squadron, the 67th was leading the group in the heart of the city—napalm the target.

The 18th Group—67th, 12th, 39th, and 2 SAAF Squadron—was tasked to hit the main target. After the main briefing, Bill called me off to one side and asked, "do you realize who is flying my wing?"

I gave him my best "Yes, Sir."

He put his arm around my shoulders and completed his briefing as follows: "Your job is to ride herd on the general and make sure he stays as low as possible, and watch out for any gun pits that might show up. If anything happens to him, I don't even want to think what happens to us."

General Rogers flew quite a few missions with our squadron, but he let his most experienced pilots lead.

Major Bill Green, Operations Officer for the 67th Squadron at K-10 in 1951. (Pasqualicchio)

Significant Events [1]

March 1: FEAF Bomber Command B-29s launched the first mission of a new interdiction campaign, escorted by over twenty F-80s. The escorts, however, arrived at the rendezvous point too soon, ran low on fuel and departed. The B-29s over Kogunyong, North Korea, were attacked by MIGs. Ten were damaged, three of which had to land in South Korea.

Lt. Col. William E. May, CO of the 67th Fighter-Bomber Squadron, had succeeded Major Arnold "Moon" Mullins on 14 November 1950. On 1 March 1951, Lt. Col. May "abandoned his aircraft successfully after being struck by intense enemy ground fire behind enemy lines. He was rescued by a helicopter from the heavy cruiser St. Paul." May was hospitalized for burns. "Lt. Col. May was also shot down," Lt. Ken Barber recorded. "He was hit bad and flames were licking at his feet. He jettisoned his canopy and the flames really sucked up into his face, burning it, and he had to bail out—right over the enemy front lines. All four of the ships covering him were hit with small arms fire. The helicopter came in—then backed off. Capt. Croner told him to get the hell back in and pick up that man. This time the copter did, dropping a rope ladder up which Col. May scrambled! The 'copter had plenty of holes in it. Col. May is on a hospital ship—only burned around the face. Sure is lucky." [On 31 March 1951, Lt. Col. Henry W. Lawrence relieved Lt. Col. William E. May as Commanding Officer of the 67th FBS.]

March 3: A new shipment of tarzon (radio guided) bombs arrived in the Far East, allowing Far East Air Forces to resume raids, suspended since January 17, with the large guided weapons.

March 4: Major General Earle E. Partridge, Commanding General, Fifth Air Force visited K-10 to present decorations to members of the 18th Fighter Bomber Wing and to present the Wing with a scroll honoring it upon completion of 10,000 effective combat sorties as of 24 February. "This record was compiled by pilots assigned to the 18th Fighter-Bomber Group and 2 Squadron, South African Air Force. The ceremonies were very impressive in that, for the first time, an honor guard of officers and airmen were on hand."

March 6: The 334th FIS used Suwon as

Pre-Flight briefing for Major Herman Solem, Operations Officer, Capt. Bill Strand "A" Flight Leader, Capt. Lucian "Bob"--"Should be Major"--Shuler, "B" Flight Leader, and Lt. Col. William E. May, CO of 67th Squadron. Solem helped prepare Wing Commander Rogers for combat missions and was later killed in action. Strand was a particular favorite with Rogers and served as flight leader for many of the Wing Commander's early combat missions. (Barber)

257

a staging base from which F-86 Sabres began raiding the Yalu River area, where they had been absent for months.

March 7: UN forces launched a new offensive called Operation RIPPER to cross the Han River in central Korea east of Seoul, destroy large numbers of enemy troops, and break up preparations for an enemy counteroffensive. Fifth Air Force flew more close air support missions to support the operation.

READY TO ROLL The thumbs-up sign given by 12th Squadron Crew Chief Sgt. Toscano indicates to pilot Lt. Hall that the wheel chocks have been removed, and the sleek F-51 Mustang fighter is now free to taxi out to the take-off point. Sgt. John J. Toscano, Philadelphia, Pennsylvania, and 1st Lt. James K. Hall, Lebanon, Indiana, are members of the Fifth Air Force's 18th Fighter-Bomber Wing, 12th Fighter-Bomber Squadron, have previously talked over the general condition of the Mustang, its fuel, ammunition and other necessary details prior to this mission in March 1951. (NARA)

A typical scene in March 1951, according to the Air Force caption, "at this Fifth Air Force 18th Fighter-Bomber Wing base in Korea is the crew chief guiding the F-51 Mustang fighters to the desired parking area, and later giving the pilot the sign to kill the engines. The pilot, who has unloaded his rockets, napalm bombs, and .50-caliber machine gun ammunition on Communist targets, will talk over details of this flight with his crew chief." (NARA)

March 8: "Captain Lucian B. Shuler successfully made an emergency landing at K-13 Air Base (Suwon, SK). His aircraft lost coolant during a strafing attack on enemy troops near Kaesong, South Korea. By utilizing prescribed technique (1600 rps 32" hg, emergency coolant door release, primer switch), Captain Shuler nursed his aircraft back to friendly territory. While attempting an emergency landing at K-13 Air Base he was forced to retract the landing gear to avoid over shooting the runway."

March 9: The "Dallas" rotation of veteran personnel was completed March 9th. The "Fort Worth" rotation of Group Headquarters and 67th Fighter-Bomber Squadron personnel who had departed Clark AFB on July 30, 1950 was expected to begin "immediately after the Dallas rotation. Instead, it was delayed until April 12th, causing "great anxiety."

March 14: Communist forces abandoned Seoul without a fight after General Ridgway's troops seized high ground on either side of the city north of the Han River. At night B-26s began dropping specially designed tetrahedral tacks on highways to puncture the tires of enemy vehicles. They were more effective than the roofing nails dropped earlier.

March 15: UN forces entered Seoul, the fourth time the city had changed hands since the war began.

All units of the 18th Fighter Bomber Wing flew normal effort from K-10 on 24 March and landed at K-1 or K-9. The one-week relocation of aircraft was needed to give the engineers time to resurface K-10 with PSP—pierced steel planking. (Colton)

March 16: Far East Air Forces flew 1,123 effective sorties, a new daily record.

March 17: An F-80, flown by Lt. Howard J. Landry of the 36th FBS, collided with a MiG-15. Both went down with their pilots. Fifth Air Force lost no other aircraft in aerial encounters during the month.

March 20: Captain James Kuntz was forced to bail out after being struck by enemy ground fire near Kaesong, South Korea. Captain Kuntz "maintained sufficient altitude and airspeed to return to a point near Suwon, South Korea where he parachuted safely into friendly territory." Kuntz was hospitalized with a broken ankle.

March 23: Operation TOMAHAWK, the second airborne operation of the war and the largest in one day, involved 120 C-119s

and C-46s, escorted by sixteen F-51s. The 314th TCG and the 437th TCW air transports flew from Taegu to Munsan-ni, an area behind enemy lines some twenty miles northwest of Seoul, and dropped the 187th Airborne Regimental Combat Team and two Ranger companies--more than 3,400 men and 220 tons of equipment and supplies. Fifth Air Force fighters and light bombers had largely eliminated enemy opposition. UN forces advanced quickly to the Imjin River, capturing 127 communist prisoners. Some of the prisoners waved safe-conduct leaflets that FEAF aircraft had dropped during the airborne operation. Helicopters evacuated only sixty-eight injured personnel from the drop zone. One C-119, possibly hit by enemy bullets, caught fire and

Venison Stew for Chow. Major Charles Trumbo poses proudly with a deer on the hood of his jeep in March 1951. (Barber)

crashed on the way back. On the same day, twenty-two B-29s of the 19th and 307th BGs, protected from MiGs by forty-five F-86s, destroyed two bridges in northwestern Korea.

March 24: The 18th Fighter-Bomber Group reported completing its 10,000th effective combat sortie "against the enemy in Korea. In accomplishing this record number of sorties, aircraft assigned were flown a total of 26,177 hours."

For the first time, Far East Air Forces used an H-19, a service test helicopter, in Korea for the air evacuation of wounded troops. The H-19 was considerably larger and more powerful, with greater range, than the H-5s.

All units of the 18th Fighter-Bomber Wing flew normal effort from K-10 and landed at K-1 or K-9. The one-week relocation of aircraft was needed to give the engineers time to resurface K-10 with PSP—pierced steel planking.

March 24, 26-27: Fifty-two C-119s and C-46s dropped an additional 264 tons of supplies to troops at Munsan-ni, because they could not depend on surface lines of communication for supplies.

March 29: With fighter escorts, B-29s returned to the Yalu River to bomb bridges, which had become important targets again as the river ice thawed. Fifth Air Force light bombers and fighters, which had handled interdiction in the area during the winter, could not destroy the larger Yalu River bridges.

March 31: Elements of the U.S. Eighth Army moved northward across the 38th Parallel. 3rd ARS used the H-19 to retrieve some eighteen UN personnel from behind enemy lines, the first use of this type helicopter in a special operations mission. The 315th AD grounded its C-119s for modification and reconditioning.

Lt. Col. Henry W. "Hank" Lawrence relieved Lt. Col. William E. May as Commanding Officer of the 67th Squadron on 31 March 1951. Lawrence was relieved by Major Carl C. Colson in June 1951.

(L-R) Major Ed Jane, Lt. Col. Homer Cox (CO 67th), Capt. Harry Middleton (KIA) and Lt. Smith at K-1 in March 1951. (Barber)

Combat Losses

Captain W. J. J. Badenhorst, 2 SAAF pilot KIA on 2 March 1951. "Badie" Badenhorst was one of the four original Flight Commanders arriving in Korea with the squadron in November 1950. He was KIA leading an armed reconnaissance mission along a section of the MSR between Sinanju and Chonju. His plane was hit by flak when the flight at very low altitude drew heavy AA fire. His Mustang appeared to be out of control when it porpoised in after being hit, and then crashed in flames into Sinanju.

Captain Willis Ray Brown, 12th Squadron, "who crashed in enemy territory and is presently listed as missing in action," the

1st Lt. James Heath, Sr.

Squadron's monthly unit report noted.

1st Lt. James D. Heath, 12th Squadron, pilot KIA near Munsu-ri in March 1951.

1st Lt. Gerald D. Heagney, 9 March 1951, "crashed into a hillside deep inside of enemy territory when his heavily laden aircraft mushed into the ground following a strafing attack upon enemy positions." [2]

1st Lt. Francis A. Holcolmb was killed on 15 March when his F-51 crashed into the bay at K-10 after take-off. "The danger of operating with heavily loaded aircraft from a short strip terminating at waters edge was brought forcibly home this month." Lt. Holcomb "was killed by head injuries and drowning when his engine cut-out on take-off. His ditching attempt was unsuccessful." [3] Lt. Holcomb initiated a take-off to the south of Chinhae (K-10 AB) with a full load of napalm tanks (2) and rockets (6). During his take-off run his engine repeatedly cutout at which time both napalm tanks were jettisoned at a point approximately 2/3 down the runway. The aircraft was observed emitting white and black puffs of smoke as it became airborne. Approximately 2,000 feet south of the runway, complete power loss occurred at which time the aircraft was ditched. The altitude attained was estimated to have been approximately 90 feet; after being bellied in, the aircraft deaccelerated abruptly and swerved 90 degrees to the right of the flight path, hung momentarily tail high and almost immediately sank. The pilot's body was recovered the following day. Medical opinion disclosed that death was due to drowning. Salvage operations conducted by the ROK Navy retrieved the wrecked aircraft on 19 March 1951." [4] As a result of Holcomb's

Rearming. *Preparing a 12th Squadron Mustang for another combat mission from K-10. The napalm canister will soon join the HVAR rockets on the wing pilons. An armorer crouches on the wing while he replaces belted ..50-caliber ammunition in the three wing guns.* (Krakovsky)

death, new SOPs were put into place, including: all takeoffs were accomplished with 100% oxygen ON; all takeoffs would be made with 10-20 degrees of flaps to decrease load stresses as well as to increase the stability of the aircraft; tire changes were effected—8 ply nylon to 10 ply nylon on all aircraft."

1st Lt. D. A. Ruiter, 2 Squadron SAAF pilot KIA on 2 March 1951—a bad day for the SAAF 2nd Squadron—it lost two of its best, most experienced pilots, WWII veterans, Foxy Ruiter and Badie Badenhorst. While leading a four-ship flight during a combat mission north of Wonsan, Foxy's Mustang developed engine trouble—his coolant temperature was fluctuating. His wingman, Mickey Rorke (later KIA as well), checked the coolant shutter and reported that it was closed, then opened. Ruiter advised his flight that he had coolant prob-

lems and turned back toward base with Rorke flying on his wing. A few minutes later, the temperature fluctuation turned into white smoke just north of Wonsan Harbor. The white smoke was soon black smoke. The engine began to sputter. The

(Below) A crane on a barge recovers Lt. Holcomb's crumpled Mustang from Chinhae Bay at the end of the runway after he crashed on take-off when his engine quit. "Engine lost power on take-off," recalled former S/Sgt Richard "Dick" Joppru. "Pilot lost, could not get out." (Joppru)

Visit To The Front. *Lt. Gen. Matthew Ridgway, MG Doyle Hickey and General Douglas MacArthur, CINC UN Forces in Korea in a jeep at a command post near Yang Yang, Korea on April 3, 1951. MacArthur had less than two weeks before he would be relieved of command and sent back to the United States. In mid-April, President Harry S Truman shocked the world by replacing General Douglas MacArthur, who had publicly criticized the administration's Korean War policies, with Lt. Gen. Matthew B. Ridgway, USA. NARA)*

'D' Channel Controller was advised of the emergency and advised Ruiter that Yo-Do Island was in friendly hands. Looking for a landing site, the two Mustangs began a circuit of the island at about 5,000 feet. First, Ruiter signaled that he planned to bail out. Then, he changed his mind and reported he would try for a forced landing on the beach itself. He began a gradual turn to port at low altitude as he tried to line the plane up with the beach. While still over the water about 1,000 feet from the beach, his plane quit flying and the left wing hit the water. The aircraft floated briefly, then sank. Circling overhead, Rorke reported a brown object that floated away. Two nearby Corvettes searched the area without success. Ruiter's body was not recovered.

2ⁿᵈ Lt. Robert J. Thomas, 12ᵗʰ Squadron.

Endnotes

[1] Adapted in part from USAFHRA. January 2002. *The U.S. Air Force's First War: Korea 1950-1953 Significant Events*. February 1951.

[2] USAHRA. *Monthly Historical Report, 67ᵗʰ Fighter-Bomber Squadron*, March 1951, p. 3.

[3] USAFHRA. *Monthly Historical Report, 18ᵗʰ Fighter-Bomber Group*, March 1951, p. 7.

[4] USAFHRA. *Monthly Historical Report, 67ᵗʰ Fighter-Bomber Squadron*, March 1951, p. 4-5.

Losses and Damage to F-51D Aircraft

"Within the overall concept of aircraft vulnerability is included the ability of the aircraft to absorb enemy fire and continue to carry out its mission," a Secret Memorandum No. 40 prepared by the Operations Analysis Office at Headquarters, Fifth Air Force on 31 March 1951. The "scientific" language used by those drafting the report nevertheless reflected the reality that Mustangs were being damaged and loss. The report attempted to identify the types of damage being sustained so that tactics could be developed to off set the vulnerabilities of the increasingly obsolescent fighter plane.

"It is, in most cases, impossible to determine battle damage actually responsible for the loss of an aircraft," the report noted. "However, valuable information can be gained from aircraft that returned damaged. Knowledge of damage inflicted upon the various components and the effect of this damage on the operational capability enables estimates to be made of the damage amount and type, which will force discontinuance of a mission or cause the loss of the aircraft.

The report included some interesting summaries in the case of 18th Fighter-Bomber Group aircraft operations that offer important understandings regarding combat operations during the period of the report, June 1950-February 1951.

For example:

The 12th Squadron flew missions in close support, armed reconnaissance, escort, air patrol, and search. "The squadron became operational at K-9, Pusan, Korea on 10 September 1950. A total of 1,259 effective sorties were flown from K-9 from 10 September 1950 to 20 November 1950."

The typical distance to close support targets was approximately 150 miles from 10 September 1950 to 21 October 1950, due to the sudden advance of the United

The spinner on Major Bill Myers Mustang took the full brunt of exploding "hay." Meyers was lucky to get back to K-10 "after a large hay stack in a small field became a large explosion after I strafed it," he explained. (Myers)

Nations Forces, about 300 miles from 21 October 1950 to 20 November 1950. The typical distance for armed reconnaissance missions was from 200-400 miles.

From 20 November 1950 to 30 November 1950, the 12th Fighter-Bomber Squadron operated at K-24, Pyongyang, Korea. The average distance to close support and armed reconnaissance targets was usually 60 miles for close support and 100-200 miles for armed reconnaissance.

From 30 November 1950 to 18 December 1950, the squadron operated from K-13, Suwon, Korea, with missions primarily in armed reconnaissance. The average distance for these missions was usually 350 miles. A total of 432 effective sorties were flown from K-13.

From 18 December 1950 through 28 February 1951, the squadron operated from K-10, Chinhae (near Pusan), Korea. The typical distance to close support and armed reconnaissance targets was usually 180 miles for close support and 200-400 miles for reconnaissance. A total of 1,172 sorties were flown from K-10 through 28 February 1951.

The losses and damage to F-51D aircraft due to enemy action were very low for the number of effective sorties flown, the report concluded. Thirteen F-51D's of the 12th Fighter-Bomber Squadron were lost during combat missions between 10 September 1950 and 28 February 1951, of which four were known to have been due to enemy action; eight were operational; and one was to unknown cause. During the same period, approximately fifteen aircraft received battle damage.

No F-51D aircraft of this squadron were lost or damaged in air-to-air action. A total of eight air-to-air encounters were made with YAK-3 type aircraft by the 18th Fighter-Bomber Group. Six YAK-3 type aircraft were destroyed and two damaged.

Most of the damage on returning aircraft was to the structure and the engine, and indicates that the coolant system is the most vulnerable part of the F-51D. No known damage was inflicted upon the fuel system, cockpit section, or auxiliary systems of aircraft returning from combat missions.

The location of hits on damaged Mustangs from ground-to-air fire, included:

Nose section (8)
Mid-fuselage (0)
Aft fuselage (2)
Outboard left wing (4)
Inboard left wing (1)
Inboard right wing (1)
Outboard right wing (2)
Canopy (0)
Horizontal tail surface (1)
Vertical tail surface (0)
Total hits, 19
Total small arms hits (.30- and .50-caliber), 11
Total other ground-to-air hits (20-mm or larger), 8

1ˢᵗ Lt. Richard "Dick" Schiebel, a National Guard replacement pilot with the 39ᵗʰ FIS, earned a five-day R&R period in Japan in early March, 1951.

While we were gone [on R&R to Japan] they began sending one flight per day up to Suwon to fly missions out of there. One fellow got 17 missions in 3 days, and another got 8 in one day.

Due to shortages of some rockets, they have cut down to 2 ships a day, but we hope it will go back up after we get our ships back in condition. The Marine Corps accident cost us six planes, and we aren't back on our feet from that. Our day to go to Suwon is tomorrow. I hope the weather is good, because I want to get in as many as possible.

Saturday on the 10ᵗʰ of March I got 2 sorties in.

Number 16 was a recce with Capt. Sneed up to Kumhwa. We didn't see much, but I got a cow for sure.

Number 17 late in the afternoon was a "cutter" sortie up to Wonsan on the East Coast. We carried only .50-caliber, and all we did was recce the railroad from Wonsan inland about 75 miles, and there south. There is a locomotive that is still operative that runs at night, and holes up in one of the many long tunnels. They want to keep an eye out for it. I only fired about 200 rounds on the whole flight. We got a bunch of pack animals pulling loaded carts. I got a total of 6 hours in both flights, and I was really pooped.

Yesterday, Sunday the 11ᵗʰ, I also got 2 sorties in.

Number 18 was a 3-ship close support mission up near the Han River bridge-head. We hit a ridge loaded with enemy troops. We couldn't estimate the damage, but the controller said we were right on the target.

No. 19 was a special mission that was called when a ship reported many vehicles, guns and troops in the area near Kumsong.

Waiting to Scramble. *Captain Siegel M. Dickman, Captain Oscar R. Fladmark, and Captain Edward J. Slowinski wait beside the "Ops Tent" at K-16 for a "Scramble" message. (Schiebel)*

There were camouflaged objects all over the place. We got a tank and a couple of trucks, and were just getting to work on more troops when one of the guys got hit in the coolant radiator. He lost a good deal [of coolant] and it was touch and go for some time. We climbed and headed for the coast, thinking that if it didn't make it home he could bail out and be picked up by one of the many surface vessels in the area. However, the hole must have been a small one because after about ten minutes the trail of coolant stopped.

He landed at a base just south of the 38ᵗʰ at Kangnung called Coryo. He was picked up this morning by C-47. Again I got in six hours of flying in one day, and I was really bushed.

A bunch of us went to the show and saw "Kim"—it was very good.

This morning we briefed at 0455 and took off at 0600 on 2-ship recce to Kunhwa again. Tandy found a truck and gave it a short squirt and it burst into flames. We found a bunch of camouflaged field pieces beside a railroad track, and knocked out four of them and claimed 3 damaged. Also, got a machine gun nest with rockets and .50's.

The 40ᵗʰ Squadron lost a man today, and we don't know the complete story yet.

His flight mate didn't see him go down and does not know whether he bailed out, burned or what. He didn't even know where he crashed.

Yesterday a 40ᵗʰ man bellied in about 75 miles north of the bomb line. He hid beside his plane while they shot at him, but one of our pilots came over and strafed the enemy and kept them away from him.

He got in a ditch and was on the ground 54 minutes until a Helicopter picked him up. He was very lucky because a copter just happened to be in the vicinity when it happened.

I've got 33 missions in now—am really stacking them up.

Last Tuesday I got a flight at 1700 to Yongdu-ri. It was number 21 and was a close support sortie with [1ˢᵗ Lt. Orval H.] Tandy. We strafed, rocketed and napalmed a ridge and got a good word from the Mosquito plane.

Number 22 on the 14th was a close support West of Seoul under control of a Mosquito. We worked over troops in buildings just north of the Han River. The whole mission lasted only 30 minutes.

Number 23 a little while later was in the same area but further West. We hit 2 gun emplacements on the side of a hill with rockets and napalmed Red troops in houses. I squirted a shot at a suspicious looking hay stack and it burst into flames. It must have been a gasoline truck because it sure did spout. Tandy got a truck too. I got a 30-mm shell through the fairing doors covering the wheels. It went through the spoke and hub of the wheel and punctured the tube, so the right tire was flat when I landed. Luckily the wind was not too strong across wind, and I was able to hold it on the runway.

I missed the next mission while they repaired my plane, but while they were gone I had an interesting experience.

I was standing around mad because I missed a sortie and I noticed a large truck with some writing on the side. I investigated and found it to be a portable tape recording unit that goes from base to base and fox hole to fox hole and makes tape recordings of fellows—then sends the tape back home to the local radio station.

Naturally, I was the logical choice, so they chose me for an interview. I guess the expectant look I had on my face helped too.

He asked me where I was from and I said Little Rock because most of my friends are there, but I made sure he would send a duplicate copy to WFAA. They will call you when It is to be broadcast he said. We talked for a full six minutes, talking about the war and stuff. I said hello to all my friends in L.R.

After the interview I went into the Ops tent and was sitting reading a magazine, when this Captain came in who had interviewed me and asked if I'd mind doing another. It seems that be was asked to get some 2-minute talks from here on the morale, spirit, why we are fighting, and he liked the way I talked without prompting—so we did another one.

When the other three got back we went on number 24 which turned out to be sorry as the dickens.

We had trouble locating the Mosquito, and then when we found him he didn't know what he wanted us to hit. We wasted our ammo on houses which he suspected contained supplies.

We landed at K-9 after that mission, and we went to chow immediately after landing. We had a pilot's meeting at 1945, and they drew names out of a hat for two months of forward control. There were 6 names eligible, and three were to go. I was lucky and missed out on it this trip. If I'm lucky I may avoid going if I can build up 85 missions before the next request comes in. At the present rate, I may make it.

On Thursday I got 25 and 26.

No. 25 was a recce up near Pyongyang, but the weather was stinko, so we dropped our napalm on a village and brought back the rest of our load.

Number 26 was to the same area that afternoon, but my flight leader had a prop that threw oil all over his windshield, so we dumped our load just north of the bomb line and went home. He could hardly see out the canopy when we landed.

On Friday morning I took off at 0900 with our CO but immediately after take-off I lost my electrical system and began to get coolant out of the right side of the engine.

Col. Robertson saw it and we dumped our napalm in the river and, being just about over K-10, a Marine fighter strip about 35 miles from here, I landed there immediately.

[Schiebel was, at that point, unaware that K-10 was not a Marine air base, but the headquarters of the 18th Wing, of which the 39th FIS would soon be a part.]

I lost oil pressure when I was taxiing, but I don't know yet what was wrong. I called back here and they told me to get home the best way I could, so I caught a jeep ride into Pusan and caught a bus from there and got back here after a harrowing 35 miles of dusty riding at 1300.

I got another flight at 1400 with Tandy to recce B-3 area from Kumhwa south to the bomb line. We worked with a mosquito just north of the Han, east of Seoul where I

knocked out 2 gun emplacements with my napalm.

Our tanks were waiting at the bottom of the hill to go through the pass while we worked over the gun positions. The Mosquito called the ground controller and said, "OK, dogfaces, you can move up now, your hill is completely neutralized."

That makes you really feel like you're doing something toward winning this thing.

We went ahead and recced but found nothing.

I landed at Suwon. Tandy came back here, and I got in another mission with Col. Robie from Suwon. We reccied the same area and got a couple of 20-mm gun emplacements that fired at us as we went over—and a bunch of camouflaged supplies. We buzzed the Seoul area and gave the G.I.'s a thrill and landed at K-13 again.

Yesterday I got 4 sorties from Suwon.

Number 29 was a 3-ship recce of B-3. We napalmed a village and rocketed and strafed 2 gun positions.

No. 30 was a CAP (Combat Air Patrol) over K-13 for General MacArthur. He came in his 4-engine Constellation, stayed about 20 minutes and took off for Wonju in a C-47. We didn't know that he changed and when his C-47 took off we continued to circle until the Connie left and then trailed him for about 30 miles. Finally got released from him when we heard a guy say he was bailing out, and we high tailed it up to the coordinates he gave before he jumped.

By the time we got there he had a cover of 6 F-51's circling him, so we went back to K-13 and led the windmill up to him. The 'copter wasn't on the ground five seconds before he was aboard and they were off.

He reported receiving ground fire from a group of houses nearby, so we went back, gassed up and got two 500-lb. bombs apiece. We dropped six 500-pounders on the area where we knew the guns were that shot him (and 5 other planes last week) down. If we didn't kill him, he's got a mighty big headache, because all 6 bombs hit within a 300-yard radius. Eight more planes also hit him later, so we feel that we may have gotten him.

Then we went back to the area where

265

the pilot received the ground fire and really worked it over. We levelled the buildings with rockets and set a flock of others nearby afire with incendiaries, so we feel a bit avenged.

Number 32 was a late recce of all the main supply routes leading out of Central North Korea. We hit a truck and got it burning, but found nothing else. That keeps them holed up till after dark. We landed at K-9 at 1930, and I was completely bushed.

This morning I took off on No. 33 at 0700 & found our B-3 area socked in so we got hold of a Mosquito and he put us on a ridge full of trenches that were swarming with Chinks. We napalmed, rocketed and strafed them and then lit out for home.

We got back at 0900, and I went to church at 1030. Had an Aussie Padre give the sermon. It was really very good.

We have slowed down quite a bit since last Sunday. I got in only seven missions all week, and missed one day.

Number 34 was a special scramble of four ships up to Hwachon where we dropped our Napalm in the town and strafed and rocketed. We got more fires (12) going with 50's than we did with our napalm. I don't know what was so special about it, because we didn't see much activity.

Number 35, Monday the 19th, was an early take-off job at 0540. I was sure sleepy. I sat up late writing letters, not knowing that I was on the early flight. We were to CAP (Combat Air Patrol) the Imjin River from Munsan to Kumhwa to prevent the Reds from going either way across it. There was no activity, plenty of signs of activity though, so we hit a town with napalm that was putting up small arms fire. I had a test hop after I got back, but the prop slung oil all over the windshield so I brought it back. I really had to feel my way in too.

Number 36, Wednesday the 21st, was a 12-ship affair, which was supposed to go up and hunt out and destroy the hot-shot gunner that has been shooting an average of 1 plane a day down for 11 days. He didn't shoot any of ours down, but he put a lot of holes in them in that period. However, he must have moved his position because we tooled around at 1,000 feet trying to get him

to disclose his position but he didn't even raise his head. We dropped the Napalm on Munsan and then worked with a Mosquito plane on a ridge just north of Seoul where troops and guns were dug in.

I had fun working over one gun position that everybody else missed. That night I worked with the Colonel and a couple of other guys on the entertainment for our Squadron party. I'm in charge of the entertainment. Naturally, the star of the show will be a juggler, but we're also going to have a very cute skit, a couple of songs, a poem, an interview, and a couple of pantomimes. It should be pretty cute. The party is tomorrow night.

Number 37, on Thursday the 22nd, was another River CAP with Tandy. I can see now the reason for the CAP because it was a forerunner of the paradrop on Friday.

I napalmed a house with tracks leading into it and got a gun position on the top of a hill with my other one.

Tandy located another gun position and asked me to mark it for him with a short burst of .50's so I pounded in and made a short burst on it right on top of a hill. I must have hit a rock or something because just as I pulled up over the top of the hill something hit the canopy about 8" from my head on the left side. I ducked and closed my eyes, reflex action, and missed any of the Plexiglass chips that hit my face. It knocked a hole about 1 1/2" in diameter in the canopy and cracked it around behind my head. Well, when I settled down I made a rocket pass on some box cars and just as I punched the rocket tab the whole top of my canopy blew out. It made a hole about 20" in diameter and the noise was terrific. It sounded like a canon going off in my ear.

You can imagine how it startled me, and the suction almost took my helmet off.

We went right on home and you should have seen the faces on the GI's when I taxied by them waving at them through the top of the canopy.

The P.I.O. took a picture of me sticking my head and shoulders up through the hole, so I may be able to send one to you.

I went to church that night, which was Thursday, and took communion. There was

a show on at the club at 2030, but it was all Korean talent, and it was sorry, and I left about half way through it.

Good Friday I got No. 38. It was a four-ship flight that started out to be a close support mission for the paratroopers that dropped in the morning, but the smoke was so thick we could not see a half mile, so we reccied an area that was clear up near Kumsong. We didn't find a thing. In fact, it was the sorriest flight I've been on so far. I worked on the skit that night.

Yesterday I got No. 39, and led my first flight. It was a 2-ship Recce with Tandy in what is left of the B-3 area up to Kumhwa. We caught a truck on the road and made 3 passes each at it and left it burning nicely. We hit Kumhwa with rockets and .50's and destroyed 6 buildings—and I got one cow.

I have a little trouble keeping track of where I am and where the targets are on the map, so that I can report it to intelligence. But Tandy helped me a little and I got by in good shape. We went to see Jerry Lewis in "At War with the Army," but it was sorry. Worked on the skit till 2300 and came home and sacked out.

I went to church this morning about half way through this letter, and played the hand organ for the service . The Chaplain was leading all the songs previously without organ accompaniment, so I volunteered my feeble services. Everything went fine, but one of the pedals broke and I had to pump twice as fast on the other one to keep her going.

After church they came in and got the chaplain and said a C-54 had crashed on the field and they wanted him. I walked out to the runway and saw that a C-54 had overshot the end of the runway after landing and was in the rice paddies at the far end of the field. We caught a Jeep going that way and looked it over. The left wing looked like a chicken wing. It was bent back at about a 60 degree angle with both engines drooping to the ground. No one was hurt, luckily.

I missed the mission covering the paradrop, but Tandy said it was the most wonderful thing he'd ever seen. They had a field day killing Chinks who got panicky during the drop and ran out in the open. They

Blown Out Canopy

The FEAF News Security Division was soon approving a news release highlighting Schiebel's blown canopy mission.

A recent mission of the 35th Fighter-Interceptor Wing gave Lt. Richard H. Schiebel of Little Rock, Arkansas something to remember about the Korean Communist Army.

During an air strike near Kaeson, North Korea, Lt. Schiebel was flying as wingman in a flight of two F-51 Mustangs of this Fifth Air Force tactical support wing. He was strafing a gun position on a rocky ridge when according to his own words, "I must have run into some rocks flying from the ridge, as something hit my canopy and put a small hole in it. It cracked the glass into a half moon shape.

"I didn't want to get any speed up as I was afraid the canopy would fly apart."

"On the way back, my flight leader spotted some railroad cars on an auxiliary railroad spur and we both made a pass. Just as I hit the button to fire a rocket, I thought a cannon went off in my cockpit."

"A piece of the canopy, about a foot square flew off and if I hadn't had my safety belt fastened it would have pulled me out. I would have lost my helmet, too, if my chin strap had not been fastened."

His flight leader, Captain Tandy A. Wright of Devol, Oklahoma, stated "I threw the rest of my rockets into a village so I could escort the "Coach" (as fellow fighter pilots call Schiebel) back to the strip. We had to come back at about 10,000 feet as the weather was on the deck."

Lt. Schiebel added during debriefing, "It was really cold up there. My joints are still stiff."

Lt. Schiebel has completed over 40 combat sorties and Captain Tandy Wright has completed over 68. Schiebel was the first Air National Guard pilot to replace a 100-mission pilot of the 35th.

caught a bunch sitting beside their trenches watching the drop. General Ridgeway sent a very nice commendatory message to the C.O. of our Group that it was the best coverage he'd ever seen in his long years of service.

Conceived in strife, born in combat, nourished with blazing guns, and bred in battle—the story of the 18th Fighter-Bomber Wing in Korea.

By William J. "Sandy" Colton

On 31 March 1951, S/Sgt. and Journalist William J. "Sandy" Colton sat down at his packing crate "desk" at 18th Wing Headquarters at K-10 and hammered out the *"Born and Bred in Combat"* story that follows. He was trying to help the Mustang pilots of the 18th get some of the credit they had earned since they were thrown into the Korean War some nine months earlier. He released the story to the Far East Review, Air Force Times, American Weekly and "All Bureaus."

Like the infamous attack on Pearl Harbor, in that it came on a Sunday morning, the North Korean armed forces launched their attack against the South Koreans at 4 o'clock in the morning, Sunday, 25 June 1950.

Because it was an unprovoked attack against a legal government, the United States took immediate action by branding the invading forces aggressors and asking all nations to give assistance in repelling the attack.

Since the forces of the United States were the closest at hand, it became their duty to bear the brunt of the attack while other democratic nations were preparing to send such assistance as they could offer. As part of the immediate action taken by the United States, General Stratemeyer's Far East Air Forces swung into movement, quickly becoming an organized machine of war. The Fifth Air Force, under General Partridge, became the ground and tactical support air arm in Korea.

It was soon after President Truman's commitment of American troops and material to the Korean campaign that the Fifth Air Force sent out a call for volunteers to fly and maintain the obsolescent F-51 Mustang. At that time it was felt that the F-51 would in many cases be better than the more modern jet aircraft because of its greater range

and smaller area maneuverability. The enemy MIG-15 jet type aircraft had not as yet entered the picture. This request for volunteers was the seed of conception for the 6002nd Tactical Support Wing, later redesignated the 18th Fighter-Bomber Wing.

The Fifth Air Force was born and bred in combat. It was activated in Australia and bred through the bloody World War II campaigns of the South Pacific and Orient. Now, history was to repeat itself with this Fifth Air Force unit.

Those initial volunteers, recruited from both Fifth Air Force and the 13th Air Force, were rushed to the K-2 airstrip at Taegu to furnish some of the first real close tactical ground support of the Korean conflict.

Initially, the "six-double-oh-deuce" was little more than a volunteer squadron attached to an Air Base squadron at Taegu. Two groups of volunteers, then known as "Bout One" and "Dallas," formed the 51st Provisional Squadron and as such flew combat missions against the enemy forces day and night in an effort to slow down the North Korean offensive and offer some protection to our withdrawing, greatly outnumbered, troops. The efforts of this small volunteer unit were effective and drew praise from Syngman Rhee, the Republic of Korea President, who, because they were volunteers, later dubbed the unit "The Flying Tigers of Korea."

That volunteer squadron grew rapidly. Its designation was changed and another volunteer squadron joined it. Calm, quiet spoken, Colonel Curtis R. Low of Needham Heights, Massachusetts, took command and molded these squadrons, plus additional personnel that were arriving, into the 6002nd Tactical Support Wing. The Wing was born.

During the first six months of operations in Korea, from July through December 1950, that Wing moved its location a total of five times and operated from three dif-

ferent staging areas—that is flew out of their home base loaded down with the necessary armament and then, after expending their ammunition over the target, landed at an airstrip (staging area) nearer the front to re-arm and refuel. The planes operated from this advance strip throughout the day, returning to their home base only after the last mission of the day.

Young, new pilots and pilots who had stacked up long lists of combat hours during World War II flew side by side. During the less than six month period of operations in Korea they flew a total of 6,197 effective combat sorties totaling 17,831 flying hours. If it were possible to keep one airplane in the air continuously, twenty four hours a day, it would take that plane over two years to fly that number of hours.

That is quite a record considering the dust, adverse weather conditions, muddy strips, and other hazards encountered in Korea, plus the fact that it was compiled by two squadrons instead of the three which would normally be assigned to a Wing. In order to accomplish that record the ground crews, maintenance, supply, and even administrative personnel had to work often up to 18 hours each day. Each man in the Wing had to be a "Jack-of-all-trades." Dust clogged engines had to be cleaned; armament—napalm, rockets, bombs, and ammunition—had to be supplied and loaded to be dropped on enemy troops and equipment.

The fact that it paid off is shown in the record. To mention just a few of the items the enemy lost which are credited to pilots of the 18th through December 1950—16 enemy aircraft were destroyed, 1,282 trucks destroyed, 186 tanks destroyed, 10,153 enemy troops killed, and 76 locomotives destroyed. Remember that this count is only for the period up to December and does not count the kills made since.

In the latter part of 1950, the South African Air Force "2" Squadron joined the Wing as the third squadron and to date the Wing (including SAAF's) has flown almost double the number of sorties recorded at the end of last year. With the increased number of sorties has come increased skill. In one day alone 18th pilots accounted for an estimated 128 enemy vehicles destroyed.

The 18th Wing was the first unit to fly fighter planes on a combat mission from an airstrip above the 38th Parallel. On October 14th, shortly after it was captured, they flew out of the Wonsan airstrip—utilizing that former enemy air base as an advanced staging area until the arrival of a Marine Corps Air Wing, which took the air base over.

In line with their policy of keeping as close to the front lines as possible in order to have aircraft immediately available to UN front line troops, to keep those aircraft over those troops for longer periods of time, and because the F-51, unlike the more modern jet, needed no long and constructed runway, the Wing operated from fields that were not much more than former rice paddies. Rain or slushy snow converted these strips into rutted mud but even this did not keep the pilots from their aerial harassment of the enemy, or the protection—through close support—of UN troops. When one runway became too rutted for operations they merely moved the runway markers to the right or left to an area that wasn't rutted yet.

The 18th was operating from such a strip during the big enemy breakthrough last December, but throughout that period 18th pilots flew to and from enemy roadblocks, traps, and troop positions helping to clear the way for our withdrawing forces. When the pilots landed, their planes were refueled and rearmed while the pilots went through intelligence debriefing. As soon as their interview with the Intelligence Officer was over they would climb back into their waiting planes and return to the target area.

Last November, fighter pilots of the 18th encountered the first MIG-15 jet type enemy aircraft to be seen over Korea. In the first six days of that month, 18th pilots tore into the renewed enemy air activity and destroyed two YAK-3's, five YAK-9's, and probably destroyed two MIG-15's—the latest thing the enemy had to offer—all in aerial combat. When last seen the MIG's were smoking heavily as they streaked across the refuge of the Manchurian border where the Mustang pilots could not follow. The 18th pilots came out of those fights without so much as a scratch.

Pilots of the 18th Wing were the first to carry the new tank demolishing 6.5-inch rocket into combat. At Taegu, in the early part of the conflict, four 18th F-51's were constantly on alert loaded with this new weapon. The flight, led by Major Harry H. Moreland (Mobile, Alabama), was known as "Moreland's" Tank Busters—and lived up to that name. Three hundred of these new type rockets were flown over from the United States for this first combat test and passed it with flying colors.

Night flying was not uncommon with the original volunteer group. Although not equipped for night flying, the pilots flew their Mustangs frequently through the inky blackness searching out enemy troops of equipment to destroy. If they spotted headlights, fires, or other tell tale signs they dove their planes at the targets, covered their eyes with one hand to keep from being temporarily blinded by the flash of the firing guns, then pressed the firing button for wing guns or rockets. Only after they had released the firing button or the rockets had time to out distance the aircraft could they take their hand off their eyes and pull out of the dive. Although this was an extremely dangerous maneuver, the nervy volunteers made it an effective one.

These same pilots set a precedent early in the War by capturing and delivering enemy troops to UN forces although flying at over 250 mph and not firing a shot. Two pilots lined up twelve enemy troops in a road and by buzzing low over their heads marched them four miles down the road to UN troops. Later, more enemy troops—fearing the blazing guns, fire bombs, and low flying Mustangs—surrendered to the 18th pilots who notified ground troops to "walk in" and take over.

Mustang F-51's of the 18th Wing are readily familiar to the men on the ground up front. Often front line troops have dropped by the airstrip to "thank" the pilots personally for their close support.

These pilots pinpointed that close support by knocking out enemy positions as close as fifty feet from our own troops, dropping napalm fire bombs, rocketing and strafing. There is a classic story still going

Heavily loaded with rockets and napalm, a 67th Squadron Mustang turns into the wind prior to takeoff. (NARA)

the rounds of the pilots about the ground controller calling in an air strike at "Slaughter Pass," near Ipsok in North Korea. The 18th pilots were firing over the heads of our own troops but still the ground controller called "Closer, closer." The strikes came in closer until the ground controller called back excitedly, "Not that close. I can feel the heat from the napalm from here." When those pilots left, that same ground controller called in to "thank" them for a souvenir—an empty shell casing expended from the wing guns of one of the planes had fallen into the back of his jeep.

One of the 18th pilots was pulling a tour as ground controller at Kunuri during an air strike by other pilots of the Wing. He tells of the General who ran up to him and said, "If I could meet one of those pilots, I'd kiss him here and now."

Another time, a bewhiskered, fatigue-garbed, tired-eyed Infantry Captain, obviously just back from the front, walked into the make shift Officer's Club at one of the 18th's advanced strips, stood silently in the center of the room a moment looking around as though counting heads, and then walked up to the bar, plunked ten dollars on the counter and said, "I want to buy beer all the way around for these guys." This should cover it. I owe them a lot." Then he walked out before anyone could find out the story.

The pages of the 18th Wing history are filled with tales of humor, heroism and pathos. Flying obsolescent aircraft in all kinds of weather, day and night, under adverse conditions, these pilots established a record to be proud of. Early in the war they became well known as the "Dogpatchers"—Dogpatch being the name of their home base.

Although the 18th Wing is not a new organization, it was born and bred in combat anew as the 6002nd Tactical Support Wing. It was not until well after it had been organized that it was redesignated the 18th Fighter-Bomber Wing. There is mention of an 18th Wing back in the 1930's in the Hawaiian Islands.

The Wing's fighter organ, the 18th Fighter-Bomber Group, has a colorful history for the period of its activation in 1927 through World War II. It is interesting to note that Claire L. Chennault, famed leader of the "Flying Tigers" of China, was once a member of the 18th Group which now has the "Flying Tigers of Korea." During World War II, the 18th Group left a blazing trail behind them as they found their way from Hawaii across the Pacific to China. The Group's insignia, a Fighting Cock, and motto, "with talons and beak," is carrying on with traditional glory in the Korean campaign as the fighting element of the 18th Wing.

Colonel Turner C. Rogers of Statesville, North Carolina, recently took command of the 18th Wing, while Colonel Low moved up the ladder to a Fifth Air Force Headquarters assignment. Many of the original volunteer pilots have returned to the United States, their one hundred missions and overseas tours completed. However, some of the original pilots will always remain in Korea, having shed their blood and given their lives to the United Nations cause for freedom.

Conceived in strife, born in combat, nourished with blazing guns, and bred in battle. That is the glorious tale of the 18th Fighter-Bomber Wing in Korea.

T/Sgt John J. Casey, Crew Chief, congratulates Lt. Ken Barber as he sets out on his 100th mission from K-10. (Barber)

On 31 March 1951, Lt. Ken Barber completed his 100th mission.

He and Capt Galyon as wingman, "hit some foxholes just across the bomb line south of Chorwon, and came right home. One of my rockets hung up, which made me mad because I wanted no obstruction to my 100th mission buzz job." Galyon landed, but Barber "went over to K-10 and buzzed it—then back to K-1 where I buzzed up the taxi strip and did a roll to the right—then landed." While landing the rear portion of the faulty rocket "fell off."

The men said it was the lowest buzz job they had ever seen."

Sergeants O'Connell and Monte, among the crew chiefs who served aircraft flown by Lt. Barber. (Barber)

Pipeline Pilots
Learn To Ride "Mustangs"

The Mustang

On December 5, 1950 Airman Cadet A. H. Connors, Jr. had been ordered to the 3615th Pilot Training Wing, Advanced Single Engine, at Craig AFB, Alabama. The Air Force had established an Advance Flying Training School at Craig Air Force Base near Selma, Alabama on May 3, 1941. Over the 37 years and one week of its existence as an Air Force Base, Craig graduated over 30,000 student pilots after extensive training in fighter-type aircraft.

During six months of intensive training he had completed 135 flight hours in the T-6 aircraft, 57 of them solo hours. He had achieved an overall academic average of 77, with his best subjects being Aero Physics (92) and Flight Instruments (85). He earned a grade of only 69 in Principles of Flight early in the course of training. His scores improved as the training progressed.

Soon, like the other new pilots in his class, his fledgling skills as an airman would be tested to the limit as he moved from the slow, stable Texan to the legendary F-51D "Mustang."

Halfway through Advanced Single Engine Aircraft training at Craig AFB, Archie, Wilfred "Budd" Stapley and their buddies transitioned from T-6s trainers into true fighter aircraft. "It was a big change," Stapley recalled. "The T-6 was a trainer aircraft, very stable. Very forgiving. If you made a sloppy slow roll...it would do that for you. If you made a sloppy slow roll in the F-51 you might just end up in a spin or

a snap roll. I loved the '51, but it took a pilot to fly that bird," Stapley said.

When the new pilots of Class 51-D began to study the pilot training manual for the F-51 Mustang, the first paragraph they read let them know that they were joining an elite group of war fighters.

As the nervous pilots approached the F-51 they were to take on a solo flight for the first time, they kept in mind the background about the fighter that they had read in the pilot's manual.

"Like the Indian braves of the old southwest whose favorite in battle was the small, speedy Mustang, young fighter pilots today, with their newly won wings, almost without exception want to fly the famous namesake of that sleek and powerful war horse." [4]

The P-51[5] is truly a pilot's airplane, the manual explained. " In mission after mission it has proved that it can more than hold its own against any opposition. Its speed and range are tops. It operates effectively on the deck and all the way up to 40,000 ft. In maneuverability and load carrying capacity, it ranks with any other fighter in the

world."

The manual acknowledged that the original Mustangs were built for Britain's RAF. Flown by RAF pilots, Mustangs saw initial action in the summer of 1942. The British used the Mustang primarily for Reconnaissance and rhubarb missions—zooming in at low altitudes to strafe trains, troops, and enemy installations.

The new P 51s were the first American built fighters to take the war back across the English Channel after Dunkirk. They were so successful that the United States AAF decided to adopt the Mustang as its own. Eventually, the Allison engine was replaced by the more powerful Rolls-Royce Merlin engine with a two-speed blower. Along with other improvements, the prop was increased from 3 to 4 blades. The new model would prove to be an unquestioned success and eventually would become the most successful fighter plane of World War Two. The Mustangs were feared by their adversaries at any altitude and mission from escorting bombers all the way to Poland to low altitude interdiction as they tree hopped back to their bases.

For new pilots, however, mastering the P-51, and surviving to talk about it, would take plenty of hard work. "For being a first rate fighter pilot means being not only a pilot, but a whole crew—pilot, navigator, gunner, bombardier and radio operator—all rolled into one." [6]

The Mustang is a single-place, low-wing monoplane—a high-speed, long range, low and high altitude fighter built by North American Aviation.

The fuselage is a semi-monocoque, all

The P-51 was truly a pilot's airplane. It operated effectively on the deck and all the way up to 40,000 ft. In maneuverability and load carrying capacity, it ranked with any other fighter in the world. For new pilots, mastering the P-51, and surviving to talk about it, would take plenty of hard work--it meant being not only a pilot, but a whole crew—pilot, navigator, gunner, bombardier and radio operator—all rolled into one. (Below, right) These Mustangs were among those Aviation Cadet Connors and his fellow fledgling pilots used as they learned to fly--and survive--in the "hot" fighter. Twelve year old nephew Tracy Connors took these snapshots of the flight line at Craig AFB in January, 1951 with his new Brownie "Hawkeye" camera.

metal structure, with one of the smallest frontal areas ever placed around any high-powered liquid-cooled engine. The 12-cylinder Merlin was equipped with an injection-type carburetor, had two-stage supercharging, and developed over 1,400 hp on takeoff. The Supercharger Switch had three positions: Low, High and Automatic. Most of the time the supercharger switch was left on Automatic that allowed it to be controlled by an aneroid-type pressure switch—cutting into high or low operation as required.

Each new pilot went through his solo flight.

Reaching the parked aircraft, he climbed onto the left wing and looked into the already open cockpit. Before he began the exterior inspection of the aircraft, he needed to ensure that important switches were in the Off position, including the igni-

tion switch, gun safety switch, bomb arming switch, and the rocket release switch.

All were where they should be, and after checking the Form 1 to ensure the plane had been serviced properly, he got down off the wing and began to slowly walk around the plane clockwise. Before every flight pilots needed to conduct a thorough exterior inspection, starting with the left wing section, engine, right wing, right fuselage, tail section and left fuselage. The inspection was designed to identify problems on the

ground, before they became life or death matters once aloft.

The wings were examined for damage to air surfaces, lights, leading edge

First official photograph taken by the U.S. Air Force of Aviation Cadet A. H. Connors, Jr. as a pilot.

CONNORS AH JR

272

Soon after arriving at Advanced Single Engine School at Craig AFB, Alabama, Connors and his fellow Aviation Cadets began the transition into F-51s. It meant a lot of actual flying. However, there were still many hours of classroom instruction where they studied the "Flight Handbook for the P-51 Mustang" and "Pilot Training Manual for the P-51 Mustang." Connors (far left) listens to a fellow classmate in this photograph from the Class 51-D Yearbook.

(Below) There were also military duties to perform, including marching and calesthenics.

and gun bay doors, secure caps on fuel or drop tanks, leaks, and condition of the tires. The engine section was checked to ensure the cowl was secure, plugs over exhaust stacks were removed, the air scoops were unobstructed and that the propeller was in good condition. The right fuselage was scrutinized for cracks or leaks in the coolant door, that static-pressure vents were unobstructed and that the radio antennas were undamaged. The tail was checked for damage to control surfaces, and the tail wheel was examined for strut inflation and tire slippage. The last "stop" on the inspection tour was to ensure the fuel cap was secure on the left fuselage.

Sliding into the cockpit for the first time, he fastened his safety belt and shoulder harness, and then checked the operation of the shoulder harness lock. Then he adjusted his seat level to ensure he had full travel of the rudder pedals in extreme positions. The rudder pedals were where they should be for his leg length. Pulling the plunger on the side of the control stick, he unlocked it and checked the controls for free and proper movement, looking out of the cockpit to ensure the rudders and other surfaces were moving freely as he shifted the stick from side to side and back and forth.

He sat there for many exciting moments studying the cockpit and the lay out of its instruments and controls. Glancing slowly around the cockpit from left to right he began to put into his head the positions of the major instruments. On the left side of the cockpit he noted the location of the coolant radiator air control switches and the oil radiator air control switches, the mixture control, propeller control, throttle, the microphone (that was attached to the throttle control), the flight controls, rudder and aileron trim tab controls, bomb salvo releases, and the landing gear controls.

On the right of the cockpit were the plane's oxygen regulator, the emergency canopy release, the electrical control panel, the VHF radio control knob and control box, and the cockpit light.

Directly in front of him was the rate of climb indicator, the bank-and-turn indicator, the remote indicator compass, manifold pressure gauge, air speed indicator (tucked up in the left hand corner of the cockpit), and the directional gyro (sitting beside the artificial horizon). On the right side of the panel was his manifold pressure gauge, carburetor air temperature gage, tachometer, oil and fuel pressure gauges, oxygen pressure gauge, and the ignition switch. At the bottom center of the front panel were the weapons switches and fuel selector and shut off valves.

Finally, when he had completed his pre-flight checklist, his hands moved carefully across the switches and began to bring the powerful 1650-cubic inch Packard built Rolls-Royce Merlin engine to life.

Placing the ignition switch and battery-disconnect switch to Off and the mixture control to Idle Cutoff, he signaled for the ground control crew to pull the propeller through several revolutions.

The external power supply was connected.

He pushed the throttle control forward for about an inch (1500 rpm), set the oil and coolant radiator air control switches at Open. Checking to see that the propeller was clear, he held the starter switch at On. The propeller began to turn. After six blades had passed, he pushed the ignition switch to Both. Keeping his hand on the ignition switch and ready for emergency shutoff in case of a runaway engine, he moved the fuel booster pump switch to On.

As the massive propeller began to turn faster, the airframe wiggled slightly from the torque of the starter. The six exhaust stacks on each side of the engine cowling coughed deeply, at first barking roughly and then settling down into the Mustangs distinctive idling purr.

The acrid smell of burnt oil came rushing into the cockpit and he heard the plane's hydraulics start to close the large landing gear fairing doors and to raise the flaps. Slowly the powerful bird came to life under his hands. He sat there for a few moments savoring the moment as he allowed the coolant and oil to warm up. It had been a long, hard road from Woodstock Park to the bucket seat of this dangerous warhorse of an airplane. But he had made it this far

Members of Aviation Class 51-D march to class at Craig AFB, Alabama in Spring, 1951.

and he planned to go a lot further.

For Will Stapley, his first time in the F-51 he found he was very nervous, and his knees were shaking. Not because he was scared, but from anticipation. "This was what it was all about." As he headed down the runway on his first take off in the F-51, he thought to himself: "My God, I'm by myself…in a P-51." The "exaltation of flying that bird for the first time was something you never forget. I loved the '51," he remembered.

After getting clearance from the tower, the solo pilot taxied toward the end of the designated runway. He had already run through his head a number of factors that might affect his take off and subsequent flight. He knew the plane's gross weight was well within designed limits, and he had considered other factors such as wind, outside air temperature, type of runway, and the height and distance of the nearest obstacles. Considerations such as type of runway and obstacles were not really factors at a well-maintained field like Craig; however, he knew there would be other fields in the future where conditions would be far from ideal. It was good to mentally prepare himself early on for the challenges of he knew even then would almost certainly be combat flying.

He also realized something else: he was hot. Like other Mustang pilots, he was finding out that temperatures under the bubble canopy at low altitude could exceed 120 degrees F. And, after he reached higher altitudes, it would be freezing cold inside the cockpit. The roar of the engine was close to deafening. Noise levels exceeding 130 decibels inside the cockpit have been recorded. He was finding out why flying the Mustang for any length of time could be extremely tiring.

Reaching the end of the runway, he made sure the take-off area was clear and checked the final approach for other aircraft. Then he released the brakes and lined the bird up for takeoff using the steerable tail wheel. He knew not to jam the throttle forward, as the resulting torque from the 1250 horsepower engine might cause dangerous loss of control. He also knew that the 3000-rpm needed for the ideal take off run should be reached as quickly as possible after the take off run was started.

The sleek bird quickly gained speed as it responded to the throttle. "Careful," he thought to himself, "don't lift the tail up too soon." Lifting the tail would increase the effects of the considerable torque and could cause the plane to ground loop. Also, moving the stick forward to lift the tail would

"Magpie Flight" of Class 51-D. (L. to R.) Cadet Richard E. Chard of Rochester, Illinois, Flight Lieutenant Hulse, RAF, Cadet Archie Connors, and Cadet William E. Gibson of The Dalles, Oregon.. Flight Lieutenant Hulse was reported killed a year later in Florida when his aircraft "spun in." This photograph commemorated the Cadet's solo flight in the F-51.

unlock the tail wheel and make steering the plane more difficult. He maintained slight backpressure on the stick until he knew he had enough speed for rudder control. He tried to keep the tail on the ground as long as possible and let the ever-increasing lift fly the plane off the ground from a three-point attitude.

Once the plane was airborne, he watched the air speed indicator pass 100 mph, a few seconds after which he reached to his left in front of the aileron trim tab control knob, felt for the landing gear handle, and pulled inboard and up to retract the landing gear. He glanced quickly to check for any warning lights. He then raised the flaps to full up position and noted there was no noticeable sink (loss of altitude) when he did so. After lowering the nose slightly to allow airspeed to build up to the optimum climb speed of 170 mph, he scanned the gauges quickly to check the oil pressure and the temperatures for coolant and oil.

He squirmed in his seat a little to get as comfortable as he could, and allowed himself the momentary luxury of looking outside the aircraft not just to check his attitude or look for other "traffic" but to actually see and appreciate the view unfolding below him.

Pilots are taught to constantly scan the

Instructor's Lament... from the 51-D Classbook

The cadet is my pilot; Him I shall not want.
He makes me forced landings in rough pastures;
He leadeth me into trees and high-tension wires.
He destroys my confidence, he leads me into the paths of oncoming traffic.
Yea, though I ride through the air in the shadow of death, I fear all evil for he is with me;
His stick and rudder confuse me.
He prepares stalls and loops in the presence of
All planes in the air, my temper runneth over.
Surely goodness and mercy has followed me all
The days of my life and I shall be grateful if
You will spare my life and let this Yo Yo graduate.

instruments in the cockpit for orientation and safety. With the F-51 "you could not go around the cockpit quickly enough to maintain a straight and level flying attitude." In the very brief period of time when your eyes were in the cockpit and not looking outside to orient yourself and to make instant corrections to flying attitude using stick and rudder, the plane would start to wander or become unstable.

"I'm not saying that it wasn't possible to fly the F-51 under instrument conditions," Stapley explained. "It was possible, but we did that only when we were forced to by conditions, such as weather, over which we had no control," Stapley said.

After completing a short dog-legged indoctrination flight, the nervous pilot began to prepare himself and the plane for the approach and landing. Before he even entered the landing pattern, he turned the windshield defroster control knob to On, then made sure he switched over to the fullest internal fuel tank and checked the booster pump switch to make sure it was On. He adjusted the throttle to get the propeller rpm down to 2700 rpm, and watched his airspeed drop past 170-mph.

Without thinking consciously about it, he checked his harness. "With the '51 every time you landed you made sure your straps were snugged down tight because you weren't 100% percent sure you were going to make that landing," Stapley explained. The F-51 "was a pilot's airplane. I loved it. After I really learned how to fly it, I found that somehow you didn't just pull the stick back or kick the rudder…you just went wherever it was you wanted to go. Somehow the airplane went where you wanted it…almost as if the pilot just willed it. On the one hand you had to "fly" the '51 at all times, but after a while the pilot and the plane were melded." [7] Eventually, most of the F-51 pilots would achieve that feeling of oneness with the plane, but not for a while.

As he turned into the landing approach leg, he dropped the landing gear and lowered the flaps to 15 degrees. When he passed through 400 feet, he lowered the flaps to full down. He wanted to have his air speed at about 120 mph as he passed over the end of the runway and began his flare out. Using continuous backpressure on the stick to achieve a tail-low attitude, he felt the plane touch down at 90 mph. As the plane slowed down, he used the rudder control to control the plane's direction and lineup with the runway. Only when the plane had slowed almost to a walk as he turned off the runway did he touch the brakes.

He had done it, he had survived his first solo flight in the hottest fighter plane of its day. With a chuckle, he remembered his

This cartoon from the Class 51-D Yearbook sums up the goal in mind for all members of the Class--get your wings and your 2nd Lieutenant's Commission in the Air Force.

first solo flight not many months ago and his announcement to the mess hall crowd. There wouldn't be an announcement today, but he was certainly pleased that he had

done it…and that it was over. Overall, he thought he had done a good job without too many "dangerous tendencies."

At Craig AFB, Class 51-D was typical of the pilots the Air Forces was pushing through the "pipeline." Cadet Archibald "Archie" Connors was not pictured although he was a member of Class 51-D.

April 1951

"Those were truly the days! Never did I enjoy living each day as much as I did in those days as commander of Dogpatch,"

BGen Turner C. Rogers in a 19 February 1982 letter to William J. "Sandy" Colton

1ˢᵗ Lt. Mario diSilvestro, Captain Ed Mason's wingman, in "close and tight" returning from a mission over North Korea. (Mason)

Monthly Summary

At the beginning of April, UN ground forces were advancing steadily along the front with the exception of a small area near the Hwachon Reservoir in the central sector. Early that month, Fifth Air Force Reconnaissance aircraft identified new airfields and the rehabilitation of previously damaged ones. This development troubled senior leaders because it added up to the possibility of a major enemy air-ground offensive. Consequently, B-29 attacks against North Korean air fields were stepped up while B-26 light bombers attacked a railroads, bridges, airfields, and supply storage areas during daylight.

An all out Communist spring offensive with over 330,000 troops using "human wave" tactics reversed the hard-won gains. By the end of April, Communist forces were outside Seoul, but then the offensive ground to a halt—both men and supplies had reached their limits in the face of relentless UN ground and aerial assaults.

Fifth Air Force Sabre pilots, during counter air operations, destroyed fifteen MIGs without the loss of a friendly fighter. MIG pilots, while not as aggressive as UN pilots, were improving both flight discipline and tactics. New airfields were under construction in North Korea and previously damaged ones were being repaired. A major enemy air-ground offensive was a distinct possibility. General Stratemeyer, Commander, Far East Air Forces, therefore directed most B-29s against North Korean airfields.

The light bombers and fighter-bombers attacked rails, bridges, airfields, and supply storage areas during daylight. B-26 night operations were usually armed reconnaissance and interdiction of communications routes and facilities.

Prior to the Communist offensive, Fifth Air Force fighter-bombers flew an average of 250 armed reconnaissance and interdiction, and 80 close air support sorties per day. Once the offensive was in progress, Fifth Air Force increased its close air support sorties to an average of 140 daily.

Adapted in part from U.S. Air Force Historical Research Agency. January 2002. The U.S. Air Force's First War: Korea 1950-1953 Significant Events. April 1951. http://www.au.af.mil/au/afhra/wwwroot/korean_war/korean_war_chronology/kwc_1951.html

The 18th Fighter-Bomber Wing included 241 officers and 1,386 airmen on April 30, 1951. Wing level operations were heavily stressed that month because it was again dispersed from its home base. As runway repairs continued at K-10, Wing squadrons carried on combat operations and services from both K-1 (Pusan West) and K-9 (Pusan East).

The "main body" of aircraft operated from K-1 with an "advanced detachment of eight to ten aircraft operating out of K-13. The majority of organizational and field maintenance was performed at K-1."

The Wing was again reunited at K-10 on April 23rd "when the detachments at K-1 and K-9 returned."

A Company of the 811th Engineers completed laying pierced steel planking over the entire runway on April 22nd and the combat squadrons returned on April 23rd. "It is felt that the new runway will greatly reduce the maintenance problems which were caused by excessive dust, sharp rocks on the old dirt runway etc., as well as reducing the possibilities for aircraft accidents due to soft spots in the runway, irregular surfaces, etc.," the Wing's monthly report noted.

In addition to the runway, while the squadrons were gone, twenty-two separate major building projects were undertaken, from living quarters and mess halls, to latrines and a control tower. Much of the material used for the new construction was procured "on the local Korean market...because of their non-availability through normal supply channels."

"The last of the Fort Worth Project [personnel that had arrived in Korea immediately after the war began] departed during

Hidden Pontoon Bridge. *Before dawn, the night reconnaissance aircraft returned to Japan from Korea with the latest photographs of enemy movements and installations. Captain Herbert G. Spees and Sergeant John W. Cross examine photographs of a hidden North Korean pontoon bridge prior to sending a flash photo interpretation report to Fifth Air Force Headquarters where it will be used to schedule a strike by fighter bombers.*

the month which completes the last of the projected personnel rotations to the Philippines."

Combat Operations

During the month of April, the 18th Fighter-Bomber Group lost seven pilots to enemy action, including: Captain Graham Smith, Capt. Chauncey A. Bennett, 1st Lt. Harry R. Middleton, Capt. George E. Gray, Major Herbert W. Andridge, Jr., Capt. William T. Haskett and 1st Lt. Jack McConnell Wright. [1]

Despite the losses, "morale in the organization as a whole seems to be very high. One of the prime reasons for high morale is the way the rotation policy has been expedited. The move of all personnel into the prefabricated buildings lifted the morale...the only lack of morale seems to

be with the one hundred mission pilots for whom rotation policy seems to have broken down."

During April, the Group reported "practically a complete turnover of administrative personnel" as a result of "Fort Worth Project" being rotated back to the Philippines.

The 18th Fighter-Bomber Group had 48 aircraft assigned in April 1951, that compiled over 4,000 flying hours that month—an average of 85 hours per Mustang—to complete 1,444 sorties. In April, the Group lost 17 aircraft—8 to combat and 9 for other reasons. Over 1.3 million rounds of .50-caliber ammunition were fired at the enemy, along with 6,504 rockets, 1,532 napalm bombs and 862 500-lb GP bombs.

Missions flown by 18th Wing Mustangs during April included:

Armed reconnaissance, which made up the greatest portion of the Wing's combat effort;

Close support, giving direct relief to the ground forces at particular pressure points along the battle lines;

Counter Air Patrol, which "provided air cover for naval task forces, tank task forces, critical areas in the front lines and downed pilots";

Interdiction, which included "the cutting of roads and rail lines to impede or halt vehicular and rail traffic, and the bombing of railroad tunnels and trains; and,

Training, for newly assigned and attached pilots to bring them to a "state of combat readiness."

Actual Frag Order

SECRET: SEND IN THE CLEAR BY AUTH OF COL MEYERS DEPUTY FOR OPERATION

FROM: COMAF FIVE KOREA

EMERGENCY
~~Secret~~
FOR SPECIAL HANDLING

TO: **COMFTRBMRWG 18 KOREA K-10**
COMFTRBMRWG 18 KOREA K-13

OPC ~~3680~~

DTG ~~281000~~

THIS IS FRAG ORDER OF FIFTH AIR FORCE OPS ORD **ONE ONE NINE DASH FIVE ONE**

FOR **TWO NINE APRIL FIVE ONE** PD

H. 18th Ftr-Bmr Wg will:

(1) Dispatch 28 sorties effort to atk previously recommended tunnels on MSR fr Kaesong to Sariwon and perform armed recon in area indicated below. Acft w/b loaded at Gp CO's discr w/max ord and/or fuel to most effectively accomplish asgd mission. Acft w/ck in and out w/Mellow. All eny aflds w/i asgd areas w/b recon and personnel w/b atkd. Act rept req. JOC w/b notified of Mission no and TTRS.

Mission No	Area
Start w/1801	Area bounded by line fr YC-4080 to CT-1080, S to bb line, W along bb line and coast to YC-4010, N to YC-4080.

(2) Commit 2, 4 ship flts at K-13 for JOC alert fr 0530 until 30 min before sunset. Acft w/b loaded max nap, 5 in HVAR, and 50 cal ammo. Mission No to start w/1870. Acft w/ck in and out w/Greenhorn.

(3) Dispatch acft to Mellow to perform close spt w/TACPs as indicated below. Acft w/b loaded max nap, 5 in HVARs 50 cal ammo.

Mission No	No Acft	Aprx TTR	TOT	TACP
1850	4	1210	1250	Rakeoff CS-1767
1851	4	1450	1530	Rakeoff CS-1767
1852	4	1610	1650	Rakeoff CS-1767
1853	4	1635	1715	Shovel DT-2306
1854	4	1650	1730	Rakeoff CS-1767

PAR THREE XRAY PAREN ONE PAREN SEE EXTRACT FOR ANY PERTINENT INFOR-

MATION PD ACT ADDRESSEE UPON RECEIVING THIS MSG ACK RECEIPT TO ABLE

DASH THREE DUTY OFFICER JOC IMMN PD

OPC/STS/ /

~~Secret~~

GILBERT L MEYERS, COLONEL, USAF
DEPUTY FOR OPERATIONS

PAGE OF PAGES

Frag Order. This is a copy of an actual Frag Order for 29 April 1951. It originated from Fifth Air Force Headquarters and outlined missions for each Wing. Such messages were classified SECRET "Special Handling." (NARA)

Shortage of Pilots and Aircraft for 67th Squadron

The 67th reported that its "primary mission was subordinated to tactical interdiction of enemy rolling stock, personnel and other material. Armed visual reconnaissance comprised the bulk of all missions flown during this report period." [2]

The squadron was based at Chinhae, South Korea, known as "K-10," about seven miles southeast of Masan and about 15 miles west of Pusan at the tip of the Korean peninsula.

During April 1951 the 67th conducted combat operations from three different bases in Korea. At the end of March it had begun operating out of K-1, or Pusan West. This asphalt-paved field provided B-26, C-47 and F-86 type aircraft a 7,000-foot runway and over 60,000 s.f. of apron. Operating from K-1 gave the aviation engineers the ability to "commence long-needed repairs and improvements on Chinhae."

In early April, the squadron reinitiated an operations plan that called for one flight from the Squadron to stage out of K-13 (Suwon Air Base about 15 miles south of Seoul) for a two-day period, "such duty rotating between the four flights in the squadron." Operating from Suwon "placed part of the Squadron's striking power in much closer proximity to the battle lines and the enemy's supply build-up areas. It permitted full air strike effectiveness with a saving in flying hours and less pilot fatigue." [3]

Increasing losses of aircraft and pilots resulted in several important changes to combat tactics. Flight leaders reemphasized the need for more violent evasive maneuvers—"jinxing" the plane violently from side to side to make it more difficult to hit by enemy gunners. Combat sorties were rescheduled in flights of four aircraft rather than two. And finally, armed reconnaissance flights were briefed to fly 3,000 feet above the ground except during attack.

Another important change made by the 67th was to standardize the signals used in communicating with a downed pilot and the aircraft flying overhead. "Visual and coded

As a tank column rumbles towards a battle position on April 1, 1951, an H-5 helicopter of the 3rd Air Rescue Squadron answers an emergency call for aerial evacuation. (NARA)

radio signals were formulated to lessen the amount of radio transmission required during combat missions," Lt. Col. Henry W. "Hank" Lawrence, Commander of the 67th reported.

Squadron operations were hampered by the numbers of both pilots and aircraft assigned "in such limited numbers as to require the fullest effort of both." Lawrence was forced to reduce sorties. He only had an average of 16 aircraft in commission on any given day. However, he did gain eight new aircraft during the month. He was also dealing with the "rapid turnover of assigned pilots" that resulted in the "Squadron Staff positions being vacated more frequently than peak efficiency permits. Officer assignments," he noted "to fill such vacancies are

being made with a view to achieving maximum tenure and smoother continuity."

The rotation program (Fort Worth Project) set up to rotate airmen in the squadron with long service in Korea was a boost to morale, Lawrence reported. Pilot morale was suffering from several factors, including a shortage of replacements, the increase in losses to enemy ground fire, and "the lack of a clear cut policy by higher headquarters on rotation of pilots completing 100 missions to the Zone of the Interior [United States]. At present, 100 mission pilots are being reassigned to non-combat flying jobs in the Far East Theatre for an indefinite period of time." The combat effectiveness of the squadron was "holding its own but will probably decrease if more

Napalm demonstration at K-10 in Spring 1951. The 18th Group put on an airpower demonstration for the troops, dropping napalm "for effect." (Mason)

Wing Commander's Diary

by Brigadier General Turner C. Rogers

Colonel Turner C. Rogers arrived at K-1 on Monday, 2 April. On Tuesday, he flew up to K-13 and to K-16 "to deliver tents and stoves to the 35th Wing at K-16 in exchange for an equal number they are leaving for us at K-13." He discussed operations from K-13 with Colonel Schmidt, including the return of "our vehicles that they had on loan. There's room enough to operate eight F-51's at present. Hope to expand this to 12 in the near future. SAAF will not participate until we get back together at K-10. The Advance Detachment will move to K-13 on Friday, 6 April, and will start operations from that base on Saturday. Expect to get 32 sorties per day."

"Lost one pilot on 3 April," Rogers noted. "Lt. Wright apparently flew into ground. His left wing came off. No trace of pilot."

On 4 April, Rogers started on a dive bombing mission, but "aborted because of low oil pressure."

The next morning he took off with a four-ship "flight to go on road blocking mission north of Yul-li (near Pyongyang). Capt. Strand and Major Duff both aborted and I was suddenly in lead position," he recorded. "Had no radio contact with my wing man (Lt. Duffy). We missed the road with our bombs (near miss) and worked village north of Sin-ye. Did not start fires but silenced an anti-aircraft position near what appeared to be a barracks area. Road clogged with burned out trucks and tanks."

Note: Although Rogers would command the 18th Wing until February 1952, this was the final entry in his diary.

replacement pilots are not available. The assigned pilots are flying too often and do not have sufficient rest and relaxation."

"It is difficult to believe," Lawrence pointed out in his report, "that there is a USAF WIDE SHORTAGE of qualified F-51 pilots." Pilots were not the only Air Force personnel in short supply. On April 17, President Truman signed an executive order extending U.S. military enlistments involuntarily by nine months. It was an indication of just how severe manpower shortage was facing the military services during the war.

On April 22nd over 330,000 communist troops launched an all out spring offensive using "human wave" tactics. By the end of the month enemy forces were again threatened the capital of South Korea—Seoul. The communist advance finally slowed in the face of ferocious ground and aerial assaults by U.N. forces. Prior to the start of the Communist offensive, fighter-bombers from the Fifth Air Force flew an average of

250 reconnaissance and interdiction, and 80 close air support sorties per day. After the attack began, however, that Fifth Air Force increased its close air support sorties to an average of 140 per day.[4] Far East Air Forces were flying over 1,000 combat sorties every day, intent on inflicting heavy enemy casualties and destroying supplies needed to sustain the offensive.

Lawrence was also concerned about the "approaching bad weather season." He needed "up to the minute weather observations." During April, several missions had to be aborted because the actual weathers conditions en route to or over the target were worse than anticipated. "Missions aborted because of weather offer nothing but unproductive flying time on the aircraft and pilot and incur risk without gain," he noted.

A program was initiated to insure that each aircraft is equipped with properly functioning flight instruments. "All pilots are instructed to write up any unreliable

flight instrument, and repair or replacement will follow to the extent of available stocks and procurement means."

Conditions were primitive. During that month organizational supply moved to a new site adjacent to the orderly room and personnel office. "This section is still housed in squad tents. Rocket boxes were used to make up flooring in order that supply personnel may work platformed above the dirt floor which is usually damp and wet during the rainy weather and also to prevent items of supply from suffering damage through dirt and moisture."

The Fighting Cocks mustered 22 combat pilots assigned and five more were attached. By the end of the month three more pilots were assigned and ten were attached. They flew 722 effective sorties in April, a total of 1,736 combat hours—an average of 27 sorties flown per pilot available for this period. Nearly 3,000 rockets were fired at enemy targets and positions, plus 747 napalm bombs, 402 500-pound general-

Close Air Support. *Smoke and fires along a sharp ridge remain after Fifth Air Force fighter bombers have left the area in April 1951. "An operation that might have required weeks to dig out entrenched enemy troops has been accomplished in a single, well-coordinated strike by planes loaded with napalm, rockets and .50-calibre machine guns. It is in terrain such as this that Tactical Air Controllers work to best advantage in coordination with the ground forces. (NARA)*

purpose bombs and 260 fragmentary bombs were dropped.

During 1,700 hours of combat operations, the 27 pilots of the 67th that month destroyed 593 buildings, 600 houses, 588 troops, over 100 vehicles (including 14 ox carts), 12 gun positions, 3 warehouses, 2 bridges, and 4 boats.

Eight aircraft were completely lost in April and nine were damaged in battle.

Captain Carl Alexander was flying a combat air patrol (CAP) over the Imjin River to keep enemy troops from making a crossing. *[Following the course of the northeast-southwest Wonsan-Seoul valley, the Imjin River begins southwest of the North Korean city of Wonsan and flows south for 157 miles through North Korea until it crosses the 38th Parallel, then turns southwest.]*

During a strafing run his aircraft was hit in an oil line by ground fire. He was able to "nurse the aircraft back to friendly territory, north of Seoul, South Korea, before crashing landing in a rice field." He was not injured and was picked up immediately by friendly troops.

Captain Harry Hutton was forced to crash-land his aircraft in enemy territory northwest of Seoul, South Korea after being disabled by "intense accurate ground fire." Disregarding enemy sniping, he worked his way over to a nearby ROK patrol and was rescued.

Four pilots were injured, including:

Major Elmer Duff, who successfully parachuted from his aircraft after it had been hit by ground fire during a strafing attack near Yuli, North Korea (about 110 miles north west of Seoul). After spending four hours on the ground, he was rescued by a helicopter.

Duff's rescue "was from the deepest point in North Korea ever attempted by the Air Rescue Service," Col. Edward Mason pointed out, "and would not have been possible were it not for the bravery and resourcefulness of the helicopter pilot, Lt. Clifford Brown. Duff was forced to bail out in a remote, mountainous area just east of the North Korean Capital, Pyongyang, and landed in a narrow valley. His wingman covered him as long as he could, called for another Mustang flight to relieve him and requested a rescue helicopter even though he considered their location beyond helicopter range."

Then Captain Mason heard the call for help and vectored his flight over Duff's location and took up cover duties. Mason flew very low over Duff's position in a ground depression with some nearby cover.

Using sections of map, Mason wrote what was intended to cheer Duff--"Never fear. C Flight is here."--and threw them out of his opened canopy. Even though several came very close to Duff's hole, he did not venture out to retrieve them.

After about 45 minutes of covering Duff, word was received that a helicopter was on the way. Mason tore off one last section of the map, slowed his Mustang to low speed and dropped the message very near Duff, then climbed to rejoin his flight. Another 67th Squadron flight soon relieved "C" Flight, and not long afterwards the helicopter arrived and returned Duff to friendly territory.

Duff later told Mason that the reason he didn't retrieve any of the map notes dropped to him was because there were North Korean soldiers within visual range and he feared to leave his cover no matter

***Lt. Col. Henry "Hank" Lawrence** (left), Commander 18th Group welcomes **Lt. Joe Burke** back from R&R at K-10 . At the time, Lawrence was reporting a shortage of both pilots and planes that was affecting his ability to meet combat assignments. (Pasqualicchio)*

signed
9/28/08 Elmer H Duff Lt Col USAF Ret

Notes

Elmer H. Duffy
Lt Col USAF Ret

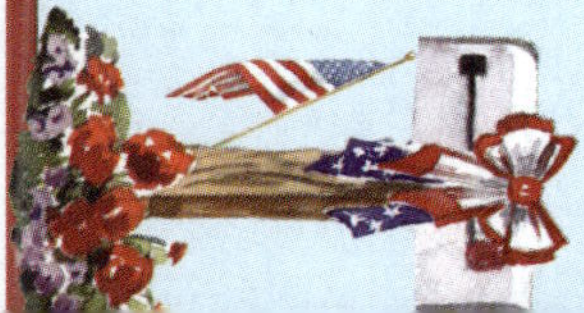

Lt. Burke's "Hole"

Lt. Walter Burke, a flight leader with the 67th Squadron, was "just pulling out of a strafing pass" on 10 April "when suddenly my plane lurched violently and began to tremble all over."

Burke's Mustang--"The Thing"--had been hit by anti-aircraft fire about ten miles southwest of Namchomjon, North Korea.

"I never felt so bad in all my life," Burke noted for the record, "when I saw that cra-

Get Outta My Hole. Captain Mario diSilvestro, jokes as he stands up in the two foot hole in 1st Lt. Walter Burke's left wing, the result of a direct hit by anti-aircraft fire. M/Sgt. John Casey (left) joins in the fun. Burke's tough Mustang--"The Thing"--brought him home again despite massive damage. (Burke)

ter in the center of my left wing, and right next to the ammunition, too."

If the shell--probably a 40-mm round--had struck just a few inches to the right it would have destroyed the plane's .50-caliber ammunition storage boxes in the wing, probably setting off some of the ammunition and blowing the entire wing off.

After he was on the ground, Burke's sense of humor returned when his wingman, 1st Lt. James W. Lee, asked him if he had "termites."

"Yeah," Burke replied, "the 40-mm type."

"Hope I get a chance to go back there," Burke said, "next time is my turn."

---

how badly he wanted to read Mason's messages. These soldiers were evidently familiar with the firepower of the Mustang and made no effort to interfere with the rescue.

That should have been the end of Duff's adventures for the day--but it wasn't.

During the return helicopter flight, Duff asked the pilot, Lt. Clifford Brown, how he got the long range out of his H-5 helicopter. Brown replied that he had carried with him a large number of 5-gallon cans of gasoline and had landed in North Korea, refueled himself by hand and left the cans there.

Sounded like a great idea to Duff, until Brown started a letdown--a long way from home.

"Why?" asked Duff.

"Got to recover those gas cans," explained Brown.

Duff offered to buy Brown all the gas cans he could want, plus a case of whiskey thrown in, just to call off this lunacy. How-

ever, Brown would not be deterred, so they flew to the spot where the gas cans were left, a small river island. When Brown saw that the gas cans were gone, did he give up on the idea? Not Cliff Brown.

He then tried to persuade Duff to accompany him on a raid into the nearby village to recover his stolen property.

Duff's logic and insistence finally persuaded Brown, and flight was continued to Seoul.

It had been a long day for Elmer Duff.

[Note: For Duff's 79th birthday, his children, without his knowledge, invited Cliff Brown for a visit and paid his expenses from Florida to Kalamazoo, MI for the party. Brown has visited Duff several times since and they call each other frequently.]

Captain Robert Smith was hospitalized for head injuries.

Captain James Corn had both legs broken while parachuting from his plane. He

was attacking front line enemy troops during a close support mission when his aircraft was hit and disabled by heavy ground fire. He bailed out "at an extremely low altitude" when he could no longer control the aircraft. Although injured when he abandoned his aircraft, he was "rescued quickly by a helicopter."

1st Lt. Robert Pasqualicchio was "hit while lining up for a skip bomb run to throw a 500-lb. bomb into a RR tunnel south of Sariwon," he explained later. "I was in North Korea, but made it back about 20 miles before the engine froze. I ended up about 30 miles behind enemy lines NW of Haegu."

Pasqualicchio's aircraft was struck several times by ground fire, injuring his eye, causing the aircraft to lose coolant rapidly. Luckily, he was just above "friendly territory" and crash-landed the aircraft in a rice field north of the Han River.

Capt. Ed Mason was leading a flight "just

crossing the bomb line when I heard over the radio about his bellying into a rice paddy not far from my position, so I took my flight there to see if we could help. I knew they would be low on ammo after their mission and we had plenty," he recalled.

When Mason's flight arrived on the scene, "Pancho was still in the cockpit waiting for a rescue helicopter. We later learned that he had hit his head on the K-14 gunsight and had suffered a hairline skull fracture. A group of about twenty-five North Korean farmers left their nearby village and were headed towards Pancho's plane. His flight leader did not like this development and made a very low pass directly in front of them. This stopped all but one old Papasan wearing his tall, black stovepipe hat."

The flight leader then fired a burst of .50-calibers from his six machine guns right in front of the old man, "who continued without apparent notice. The flight leader than asked Pancho if he wanted Papasan permanently stopped. Pancho said to let him continue, and he did. For the next several minutes, Pancho and Papasan had an apparent conversation, while two flights of Mustangs nearly spun in watching. The old guy then arose from the wing and rejoined the villagers."

"His flight leader asked Pancho what the

"Damn good!" *is how Capt. Ed Mason felt about completing his 100th combat mission. "At least until they notified me and about 25 others that we would not return to the States at that time, but go to a jet (F-80) squadron at Johnson AFB outside of Tokyo. They reactivated a Mustang squadron to which we were transferred--about a three month delay." (Mason)*

conversation was all about," Mason continued, "and was told the old man had invited Pancho to his house for dinner!"

"Papasan invited me to dinner," Pasqualicchio later explained to his flight leader with as much of a straight face as possible, "but since he wasn't having spaghetti, I declined his invitation."

Pasqualicchio was sent to Tokyo for debriefing and a few aspirins for his fractured skull. Upon return to K-10 for duty, Mason asked him what they really did talk about. "He said that the Papasan didn't speak a word of English!"

Combat Losses Degrade Aircraft Status for 12th Squadron

The 12th Squadron, commanded by Major John W. Rees, reported it had 40 officers and 135 airmen assigned in April. Six assigned and one attached pilots joined "the Dogpatch Century Flight," including Majors Jane, Watson and MacMillan and Captains Batsel, Webster, Farmer and Farr. "Four crews listed as MIA and two others were shot down but rescued." [6]

Combat losses and battle damage "wreaked havoc" on the 12th's aircraft status that month. "We started the month with twenty five aircraft and at one point were down to twenty one. ...Nine aircraft were lost in combat and this unit had twenty four aircraft with battle damage."

Endnotes

[1] USAFHRA. *Monthly Historical Report, 18th Fighter-Bomber Group*, April 1951, p. 2.
[2] USAFHRA. *Monthly Historical Report, 67th Fighter-Bomber Squadron*, April 1951, p. 2.
[3] Ibid.
[4] U.S. Air Force Historical Research Agency (USAFHRA). 28 July 2001. *The U.S. Air Force's First War: Korea 1950-1953 Significant Events*. http://www.au.af.mil/au/afhra/wwwroot/korean_war/korean_war_chronology/kwc_april1951.html
[6] USAHRA. *Monthly Historical Report, 12th Fighter-Bomber Squadron*, April 1951, p. 2.

Combat Statistics

18th Fighter-Bomber Wing

April 1951

Average No. A/C Assigned
48
Total Flying Time
4,063
Percent of Aircraft in Commission
60%
Percent of Aircraft AOCP
3%
Combat Sorties Flown by Wing
1,444
12th Squadron Sorties
714
67th Squadron Sorties
722
2 Squadron Sorties
Temporarily moved to K-9 and under operational control of 35th FIG while runway repairs were completed at K-10.
A/C Lost to Combat
8
Pilots lost
7

Fuel Consumed
289,049gals.

Ordnance Expended
.50-cal. Rounds
1,370,205
Rockets
6,504
Napalm Bombs
1,532
500-lb. GP Bombs
882
Note: Figures and totals may differ in some categories due to differences in numbers provided by each component.

HEADQUARTERS
FIFTH AIR FORCE
OFFICE OF THE COMMANDING GENERAL
APO 970

10 April 1951

Dear T.C.

"I have studied your letter on the subject of combat sorties for F-51 pilots and agree in part with what you say concerning losses as a result of enemy action. A balancing factor, however, is that the jet aircraft are experiencing such great operational losses that their personnel losses as a whole are very close to those of the F-51 wings.

As I told Colonel Low in a letter written previously on this subject, it is not believed feasible to establish a different combat tour for each type of aircraft.

You have undoubtedly received by now a letter written to all wing commanders indicating that we can no longer consider 100 sorties as a combat tour. There are many factors which require that pilots fly beyond this number of sorties and at the end of that time remain assigned within 5th Air Force on non-combat duty. A few of the factors effecting my decision are inadequate flow of replacement fighter pilots; furnishing T-6, B-26 and C-47 flare ship pilots from our own resources. We have never been up to strength on authorized pilots within 5th Air Force and it appears that the situation will not improve for some time.

While I am in sympathy with your feelings in this matter I know that you will be able to present the entire picture to both your wing staff and the combat group. I hope that some time in the near future our flow of qualified pilots from the ZI may be large enough to allow for the establishment of a suitable combat tour for all combat pilots in 5th Air Force.

E. J. Timberlake (for)
E. E. PARTRIDGE
Major General, USAF
Commanding

HEADQUARTERS
18TH FIGHTER-BOMBER WING
APO 970

15 April 1951

Dear General Timberlake:

First, I would like to state that I fully accept but do not concur in the wisdom of the decision to require F-51 pilots to continue combat beyond 100 missions. I believe that the 5th Air Force Comptroller will verify our statistics which show that F-51 losses from all causes exceed those of the jet units by 3 to 1. I also believe that you will find the ratio of combat hours per 100 sorties to be 3 to 2.

I know there is a feeling among many staff officers who flew combat in World War II that the Korean Campaign is like a gunnery meet in comparison. Not having flown combat in World War II, I can't make a comparison. However, approximately 80% of my pilots did participate in World War II. According to those with whom I have discussed the subject the mental hazard and combat fatigue are just as great as, if not more so, than were encountered in the European campaign. A surprising number of pilots who have completed 100 missions and returned to the U. S. have declared that they will never fly combat again.

With the number of pilots in the U. S. Air Force, it is impossible to convince these pilots that the shortage of pilots is so acute as to require a combat tour in excess of 100 missions. They feel that someone is letting them down. I feel that the situation can be partially alleviated by screening all units throughout the Far East Command for pilots with F-51 experience to bring us up to authorized strength.

The morale in this Wing is very high and the performance of the pilots I consider excellent. I am fortunate in having a very high experience level and I find that these officers take their job seriously. Despite the disappointment that news of the extended tour has caused, I'm sure the 18th Group will continue to perform meritoriously.

Sincerely,
T.C. ROGERS

Significant Events

April 3: The service test YH-19 helicopter with the 3rd ARS picked up a downed F-51 pilot southeast of Pyongyang, receiving small arms fire during the sortie.

April 9: "Major Elmer H. Duff successfully parachuted from his aircraft after it had been hit by ground fire near Yuli, North Korea. He was on a reconnaissance mission of the area and received the ground fire during a strafing attack. After spending approximately four hours on enemy soil, he was rescued by helicopter."

April 12: The heaviest concentration of B-29s against a single bridge across the Yalu River near Sinuiju brought on the largest and most determined enemy counter air effort of the war to that date. The 46 B-29s attacking the Yalu River Bridge at Sinuiju and one hundred escorting jet fighters encountered between 100 and 125 MiGs, which shot down three bombers and damaged seven others. Seven MIGs were shot down by B-29 gunners, and F-86 pilots downed four more, by far the highest daily MiG tally thus far. The bridge, despite numerous direct hits, remained standing.

At President Truman's direction, Lt. Gen. Matthew B. Ridgway, USA, replaced General MacArthur, who had several times publicly criticized the administration's Korean War and foreign policies.

April 14: Lt. Gen. James A. Van Fleet, USA, assumed command of the U.S. Eighth Army succeeding General Ridgway.

April 17: President Truman signed an executive order extending U.S. military enlistments involuntarily by nine months, an indication of the manpower shortage facing the military services during the war.

April 19: 1st Lt. Robert P. Pasqualicchio, while on a strafing pass on enemy troop positions near Kumchon, North Korea, received intense ground fire and his aircraft was struck in several places. The aircraft was losing coolant rapidly so a turn to a southerly direction was executed but he was unable to reach friendly territory and crash-landed the aircraft in a rice field north of the Han River. A helicopter from Seoul, South Korea rescued him within a very short

1st Lt. "Pancho" Pasqualicchio had to crash land in a rice paddy. Fortunately, he was in an area that allowed prompt pickup by a helicopter. "Ol' NaDSoB" stood for "Old Napalm Dropping SOB." Pasqualicchio)

time."

April 20: Captain James T. Corn was on a "close support mission attacking front line enemy troops when his aircraft was disabled by heavy ground fire. Loss of control of the aircraft made it necessary for him to bail out at an extremely low altitude. He was injured when he abandoned the aircraft but was rescued quickly by helicopter."

April 22/23: Enemy ground forces launched a massive spring offensive.

April 22: "With the completion of the runway [at K-10], the Wing's tactical aircraft landed at K-10 after performing their mission, and normal operations were resumed on 25 April 1951." [1]

April 23: Far East Air Forces flew some 340 close air support sorties, one of the highest daily totals prior to 1953. The 336th FIS began jet fighter operations from Suwon AB, South Korea, to enable its F-86 aircraft to operate for longer periods in MiG Alley near the Yalu River.

Captain Carl E. Alexander was "on a CAP over the Imjin River to keep enemy troops from making a crossing. During one of the strafing runs against the enemy troops his aircraft was struck in an oil line by ground fire. He was able to nurse the aircraft back to friendly territory, north of Seoul, South Korea, before crash landing in a rice field. He was not injured and was picked up im-

mediately by friendly troops."

April 23-26: Far East Air Forces flew over 1,000 combat sorties daily, inflicting enemy casualties and destroying supplies needed to sustain the offensive.

April 27: 1st Lt. Harry C. Hutton was forced to crash land his aircraft northwest of Seoul, South Korea, in enemy territory after it was disabled by intense accurate ground fire. He was rescued by a ROK patrol approximately one mile from his aircraft where he had finally worked his way despite continued sniping by enemy troops."

April 30: Fifth Air Force set a new daily record of 960 effective sorties. On separate sorties, two H-5 helicopters each picked up a downed UN pilot behind enemy lines. Small-arms fire damaged one helicopter. There was a "marked increase in anti-aircraft fire" experienced by pilots of the 67th, both in the rear areas of enemy territory and along the battle lines. Also very troubling was a report that on April 30th enemy radar-controlled antiaircraft guns shot down three out of four F-51s making an air-to-ground attack against a target at Sinmak. [2]

Combat Losses in April

During the month of April, the 18th Fighter-Bomber Group lost seven pilots to enemy action, including:

Major Herbert W. Andridge, Jr., 67th Squadron. Major Herbert Andridge, Jr. was pulling out of a steep dive from a strafing run when he lost control of the aircraft. His wingman lost sight of his aircraft momentarily and when he saw it next it was burning on a hillside. "Repeated attempts to locate the pilot were to no avail and he is listed as missing in action."

Capt. Chauncey A. Bennett, 12th Squadron pilot.

Capt. George E. Gray, 12th Squadron pilot.

Capt. William T. Haskett, 67th Squadron. On 14 April, Captain William T. Haskett, Jr. "abandoned his aircraft successfully north of Sohung, North Korea, after it had been struck by enemy ground fire during a strafing attack, resulting in the loss of the aircraft's coolant. He was observed by his wingman to parachute into a wooded section on a hill and a few moments later a star flare was seen from the same area. A helicopter was dispatched to the scene and searched the area thoroughly but no contact could be established and the helicopter withdrew because of heavy enemy ground fire. Numerous reconnaissance flights were made for the rest of the day and during the following day but no signs of life were observed. He is officially listed as missing in action."

1st Lt. Harry R. Middleton, 12th Squadron pilot.

Captain Graham Smith, 12th Squadron pilot.

1st Lt. Jack McConnell Wright, 67th Squadron. On 2 April, 1st Lt. Jack M. Wright, while making a bombing run deep in enemy territory crashed into the side of a hill. His aircraft was observed during the bombing run and he was unable to abandon the aircraft before it crashed."

Endnotes

[1] USAFHRA. *Monthly Historical Report, 18th Fighter Bomber Wing*, April 1951, p. 3.

[2] U.S. Air Force Historical Research Agency (USAFHRA). 28 July 2001. *The U.S. Air Force's First War: Korea 1950-1953 Significant Events.* http://www.au.af.mil/au/afhra/wwwroot/korean_war/korean_war_chronology/kwc_april1951.html

[3] USAFHRA. *Monthly Historical Report, 18th Fighter Bomber Group*, April 1951, p. 2.

Missions & Mosquitos

by Lt. Richard "Dick" Schiebel

Dear Folks, I got your wonderful letters, of last Sunday, last night after I got down from my 47th sortie. I was disappointed when I came in the room and found no mail, but my joy abounded when I learned that five letters had been delivered by mistake to another room. Pop, your letter was a masterpiece, and I have enjoyed reading it over and over to myself, and also to anyone who is fortunate enough to be near.

Tandy said, "He must be nuts," and I agreed wholeheartedly.

[Note: Walter J. E. Schiebel had been principal of Crozier Technical School in Dallas, Texas since 1932. All the Schiebel children attended Tech. At one time, when Dick was a Freshman, his brother Bill was a senior and sister Mary was a Junior. Walter dictated his son's handwritten letters home to his typing classes for practice, producing much more readable copies for the family and friends. It must have been fascinating for the high school typing students to be using a "play-by-play" account of the Korean War from a fighter pilot's point of view for typing practice sessions. Walter and his son shared a well developed sense of humor. Onnolee Schiebel, Dick's mother, was a highly active, civic-minded mother of four who also made time for her music, YWCA board, Cornelian Club, PTA, Silver Wings Club and her Lutheran Church Guild.]

I just got back from church, but I didn't play the organ today. They have gotten a Korean girl for the job, and she is really very good. I'm glad, because I enjoy singing hymns more than playing them.

The weather is socked in here today, and everyone and everything is at a standstill. It is getting warmer daily, and it won't be long before summer really sets in with its heat and dust.

Pop, I'm glad you enjoyed your scarf and p.j.'s and the house coat. I didn't expect you to wear it to school, but I guess I should have figured you for some crazy stunt like that. I'll try the jelly next opportunity I have. It should go over big. I've incurred a lot of enemies already with your bread-flipping trick, so that should really make me an outcast.

Pop, a Mosquito is usually a T-6 flown by an army pilot with a ground man in the rear seat. Both have strong binoculars with which they can pick out targets for the fighter planes. They are in radio-contact with a ground controller who in turn is in contact with the ground forces C.P. [Command Post]

Volleyball in bad weather. *When bad weather prevented air operations, the 39th would organize a game of volleyball to let off steam and get some much needed physical fitness training. (Schiebel)*

Flying Mustangs with the 39th FIS

"It was dark when we got back, and I almost pranged myself..."

The C.P. tells the Ground Controller what trouble they are having like say a pocket of dug-in troops on top of a ridge which is holding up our advance. So, the G.C. calls the Mosquito and tells him about it, and he shows the fighter planes the area by making runs over it, or by firing a smoke rocket, or by calling for a smoke mortar from the ground forces. Then we go in and work the general area over with Napalm, rockets and .50's.

One day, a Mosquito was trying to show some Navy F-4's a couple of trucks hidden under some trees. They wasted their load and never found it. Then the same thing happened with some Marine planes. Finally, the mosquito pilot got a bit P.O.'ed and said, "OK, I'll mark it this time with a smoke rocket." They carry only 6, and they try to save them. Well, he went in and fired the rocket and, yep, you guessed it, he hit the truck with the smoke rocket and it blew up.

Speaking of sorties, as I mentioned earlier, I now have 47, with only 53 more to go.

On Monday the 26th I got No. 40.

It was a 12-ship flight under our Group C.O., Col. [William P.] McBride, up near Pyongyang. We had received word that there were trucks and vehicles galore up there, so we went up looking. *[Note: McBride would soon be transferred to command the 18th Fighter-Bomber Group for a short period before he was severely wounded in the eye by flying glass.]*

I found one truck right in the middle of the road. We set it afire in quick order. Usually, the only ones you find on the road are break-downs or burn-outs, but this didn't seem to be either. It was a good truck and burned nicely.

We located camouflaged trucks or vehicles in ditches and got 2 to burn. We napalmed a town and rocketed houses. This was all by our 4-ship flight that I was in.

The other flights had similar luck. One located a switch engine and 4 trucks and had a field day on them. The mission was 3 hours and 40 minutes long, and we were really sweating gas when we landed. I guess I had maybe 15 gallons.

It was dark when we got back, and I almost pranged myself *["prang" was slang for crash landing or serious accident.]* and another guy on landing. He lost the guy in front of him in the pattern, and when he finally found him he was too close, so he made a big pattern and fouled me up behind him, putting me right behind him. I thought I had plenty of room, but when I got it on the runway the rate of closure was pretty fast, so I decided to go around. When the power took, the torque took me right across the runway toward him. I horsed back on the stick and staggered over him, missing him by about 2 or 3 feet. Luckily, I didn't have any load of armament or gas.

We had our squadron party at the mess hall about 2100 that night. Each month we have a party, with the responsibility of food and entertainment alternating between the Officers and the enlisted men. I was in charge of the entertainment and we had a lot of fun. Had a skit which was a take-off on Hairbreath Harry and Belinda Blinks of former comic fame. Had a couple of poems, songs, pantomimes and my juggling. All in all it went over very well. Everyone had plenty of beer and good eats, so that's all that really mattered.

On Tuesday the 27th I got Number 41, and I think it was one of my best ones. It was a 2-ship recce with Capt. Sneed up near Sanwon, South of Pyongyang. We were tooling along and saw a lot of tracks on the ground running all over the place. We went down to about 200 feet to investigate, and I flew right over a big 6 x 6 truck in a dry creek bed. It was covered with straw, but the contour was still there and easily recognizable.

I called it in to Capt. Sneed who looked it over and pronounced it a good one and told me to drop a napalm on it. I did and got a good hit.

Waiting to Scramble. 39th Squadron pilots Dickman, Fladmark, and Slowinski lounge beside the Operations Tent at K-16 on alert for a quick response mission. (Schiebel)

As I was pulling up off my napalm run I looked down and saw 6 more camouflaged vehicles in dug-in positions on the side of a hill. No attempt had been made to cover the tracks leading up to the position, so they were easy to see.

Capt. Sneed dropped napalm on one he found near my first one, and then together we got 2 of my others—got 6 to burn and damaged the other 4 but couldn't get them to burn.

The weather moved in that afternoon, so got no further missions.

That night we all piled into a GI bus and went over to the 14th Station Hospital about 10 miles from here. We went to the 0'Club and proceeded to take over. Everyone got stinko but me and we really had a time. One of the fellows took his guitar along and everyone joined in on every song they knew. The nurses were a lot of fun, and it was nice to have feminine company for a change. They all outranked me.

Number 42 on Wednesday the 28th was a 3-ship Close Support with the Operations Officer, Capt. Jones. We hit a ridge about 14 miles N.E. of Uijongbu with dug-in troop emplacements. We were hitting only about 75 yards in front of our tanks which were coming up the edge of the ridge. I landed at K-13 at Suwon on the way back, and after chow went to bed early. We have a small detachment up there with 4 ships from each squadron operating out of there.

Got up early Thursday the 29th for num-

Drawing Equipment Before a Mission. *39th pilots Siegel M. Dickman and Arthur B. Crouch prepare for a combat mission in the pilot's equipment room at K-9. (Schiebel)*

ber 43 with the C.O. of the 40th Squadron. It was a 3-ship Close Support in the same area above Uijoubu. We couldn't observe the results, but got good coverage.

Number 44 on the 29th was also a Close Support up near Chunchon. A marine L-5 spotter had seen enemy troops retreating across a river on a small foot bridge and going into a large camouflaged cave on the other side. We dropped 2 napalms right into the mouth of the cave, and the spotter estimated 75 killed.

I saw one run out of the cave just a mass of flames. He only got about 20 yards from the cave when he fell. Boy, what a way to die, huh?

Then we hit the other side of the hill and got 25 or 30 more with napalm and .50's. The spotter asked us to destroy the bridge, and so we rocketed it. I got the first hit with my second rocket. Another guy got another hit a minute later, and the entire middle section of the bridge floated down stream.

Number 45 late that afternoon was a 4-ship Close Support in the Uijongbu area on dug-in troops on a ridge. Negative results observed. Ate supper and went to bed early.

On Friday the 30th I took off with 2 others for a 3-ship recce, but something was wrong with my landing gear fairing doors—they wouldn't come up. I ran the gear through a couple of up and down cycles trying to get the doors up, but to no avail. Then only one gear would come down. Then the gear handle stuck in the down position and I couldn't get that gear up or the other one down.

Well, I tried all the emergency gear lowering tricks, but had no luck. I pulled 4 and 5 G's trying to get it down, but couldn't.

1st Lt. Walter E. Pittman and 1st Lt. Richard Schiebel of the 39th FIS celebrate Pittman's first combat mission at K-16. Pittman was killed 5 July 1951 on his 100th mission, long after Schiebel had completed his tour and returned to the Z.I. (Schiebel)

Finally, I tried pulling out and firing my guns at the same time, and that did it. The other gear came down so I flew back to K-9 with my gear down and landed OK. Don't know what caused it, but they fixed it right away.

I didn't get to go on any missions the rest of the day, probably missed out on 3 or 4 nice short ones out of Suwon.

Yesterday the 31st I had to get up at 0330 for a 0410 briefing on a 0510 take off. It was sure dark and cold.

We got to the bomb line just at dawn, and the entire area was covered with about 400 feet of ground fog. We hunted around till we found a hole big enough to work in and then wiped out about 15 houses with smoke coming out of them.

Captured P.W.'s say that the Red troops come out of the mountains at dawn and go into North Korean homes and cook their breakfasts, so we have instructions to hit houses with smoke coming out of them. I was strafing one when about 10 troops ran out and over to a gun emplacement. We hit them before they could get the gun going. We claimed 7 killed.

We got back at 0730, and played 3 games of good volley ball. The officers usually play the E.M., and usually skunk them pretty badly. Yesterday we played them with one hand in our pockets and beat them 21-4. They were humiliated.

[Note: Schiebel was a former All-City basketball star at Crozier Technical High School.]

At 1430 Tandy led 4 of us on a special 4-ship scramble to the Chunchon area where we hit a ridge with troops on it. Couldn't observe results because of the smoke.

Thanks again for the swell letters. Sure do enjoy them. We may move up to Seoul In a couple of weeks.

39th FIS pilots Edward J. Slowruski and Bodiford receive information about their next mission as they wait in the K-16 Operations Tent which was constructed at least in part from a parachute. (Schiebel)

Operating from K-16

We opened up operations at Seoul municipal [K-16] yesterday, and I was fortunate to be in the first eight to go up there.

The field is on a little island southwest of the main part of town, surrounded by the Han River. It is a pierced steel planking runway with 3,500 feet, and it isn't any too long when you take off with napalm and rockets on. The ramp is big enough to accommodate 16 aircraft easily, and the hangers will be usable for emergency repairs and stuff like that in a few days. The hangers are pretty well destroyed, but one or two are still semi-whole, with only one or two bomb holes in them.

I got in 7 missions yesterday and today, and now have a total of 60. I was scheduled to stay till tomorrow night, but my ship was overdue for a major inspection, so I had to bring it back after my 3rd mission today.

All but my last mission from K-16 were road cutters with 500-pound bombs, with a recce tied in with it after the cut.

We have been hitting the roads leading down out of Pyongyang—South and East. Our flights have been concentrating in the Sing-ye area between Yulli and Sibyon-ni. What we hope to accomplish, and I think

Aerial view of Pusan Harbor, a view seen often by 39th FIS pilots and also for 18th Group pilots when they were flying from K-9. (Mason)

Flying Mustangs with the 39ᵗʰ Squadron

Stars and Stripes says, "Little Damage"

It's no wonder the people at home are so apathetic toward this War.

already have to a great extent, is to make vehicular traffic along these main supply routes as difficult as possible. When 2 of these 500-pounders hit a road correctly, they cut a swath about 12-15 feet deep and about 20-25 feet across.

I've gotten some beautiful hits lately, although I threw 2 of them in the river next to the road today. I'll bet the Koreans went in and picked up a jillion dead fish after that explosion. Water spouted up about 200 feet.

To bring, you up to date on my missions…Number 48…was a recce of the E-2 area which starts at Namchoniom, just North of Kaesong, north on the road through Singye to Yul-li West on road to Chunghwa, and then South to Sariwon and then back East to the starting point.

We have been concentrating on the Southern and Eastern edges because these seem to be the places that the trucks dig in before driving all night to the front lines.

I was leading a two-ship element on No. 48. We got a truck and 7 buildings at Sibyon-ni and people on the road all the way up to Yul-li We have orders now to kill anything that moves. I try to avoid shooting women and kids, but sometime the men hide amongst the women and you can't help it.

Number 49 on the 3ʳᵈ was a 7-ship road cutter. I led an element with a Lt. Col. as my wing man. I got one good hit on the road, but the other one hung up and went out in the field.

I located a cache of dug-in trucks, and we had a regular rat-race around them. I got one to burn, the Col. got another. We damaged 4 others, and got a POL (Petroleum, Oil, Lubricants) dump which burned nicely.

Number 50 on the 4ᵗʰ was a 4-ship road cutter. I split the road with my bombs, but one failed to go off. We recced and got 3 vehicles, a supply dump and about 10 houses. I had tower officer duty all after-

Mixing Napalm. Ground crew of the 39ᵗʰ FIS prepare napalm needed to rearm the Mustangs that were staging combat missions out of K-16, considerably closer to the Bomb Line than the home base of the 39ᵗʰ at K-9 near Pusan. The 39ᵗʰ would soon be reassigned to the 18ᵗʰ Fighter-Bomber Group and move its operations from K-9 to K-10 near Masan. "Monday we had orders to burn out a 5-mile radius around Singye, and yesterday it was just North of the Injin river N. of Munsan that we were burning out. Today it is Namchomjom," Schiebel recorded in his letters back home. (Schiebel)

noon until 1830.

Got two missions on Thursday the 5ᵗʰ.

Number 51 was a napalm flight up to the Singyi area. Two of our boys had been shot down the day before in that area, and they wanted the area burned out. Both pilots were picked up, incidentally.

One bailed out at 500' and the other bellied in—were hit by small arms fire in the coolant radiator or oil radiator.

We hit a village, and must have killed 40 or 50 troops that were holding out there.

I was second to make a pass, right behind the leader, and when his napalm went off, they scurried out of the houses like scared rabbits, and all I had to do was punch the button and my napalm got most of them. I had a very rough engine, so I left the flight after I fired my rockets and went home alone. Found out that 2 of my plugs were not firing.

Number 52 late that afternoon was a 4-ship road cutter up near Sing-ye where the road splits. I had 6 hour delay fuses on mine, and I put them right in the middle of the road. They went off, because I saw the holes yesterday. We hustled home and got here just after dark. I got 2 missions and one test hop for a total of 6:45 for the day. I was pooped.

Number 53 on the 6th was a 4-ship [road] cutter with Tandy leading. Again got good hits and cut the road all the way across. The visibility was less than half a mile because of the smoke and haze, so we didn't do any strafing.

We hit a town with rockets and returned home. I was supposed to go up to Seoul on a later mission, but the weather socked in and flying was called off all afternoon.

Yesterday morning 8 of us got off at 0600, and flew a cutter up near Inchon, East of Sing-ye. We recced and then returned, landing at Seoul. I was very surprised at how efficiently things ran for the first day of operations. The mess hall was in operation when we got there, and so we had good hot coffee. The latrine was a little 3-holer with no siding on it. All four missions yesterday were cutters and recces in the Inchon area. We didn't find much except some supplies which burned. We wiped out 2 towns.

We got off at 0545 this morning and cut the road West of Sibyonni. We tried recceing, but the sun was so bright shining through the morning haze that we couldn't find a thing.

No. 59 was the same story—but No. 60 was really a dilly.

We took off at 1445 with napalm and headed for an area at Hwadong-ni, about 40 miles East of Pyongyang where a previous flight had discovered a rail center with supplies lying out in the open beside the railroad. He had come into intelligence earlier raving about it, so they sent a bunch of special flights up there. When we got there the smoke was terrific, and most of it was black, indicating oil fires.

There were many fires going brightly when we got there, and we had to wait about 30 minutes before we could work into the pattern there were so many ships there. The supplies were stacked in boxes, forming piles 45-50 feet long and 15 feet wide and 8 feet high. You couldn't miss them. In fact, one time as I turned on a pass, the smoke obscured my view completely. I knew the target was somewhere up ahead, so I just squeezed the trigger and something exploded.

When we left there were about 35 or 40 fires going, and some supplies were still untouched.

I figure that with the wind blowing as it was that the whole area would go up before morning. It was the best mission I've been on lately, and you may read about it. I think that was a marshalling point for supplies from the North and from Pyongyang, and because of our road cutting activities lately, the trucks have been unable to keep up their end of further transportation to the front, so the stuff piled up there. Before we began

our cutting missions, as many as 2,000 vehicles were sighted at night, but lately the most that have been sighted is 150, so it must be our cutting that is causing the hold up.

When I got back tonight I learned that my R and R has been cancelled, and that men with their 100 missions in and who have not been shipped out will remain here and fly until we get replacements. We now only have about 12 pilots who have not finished up, and it is putting quite a load on them. We expect 20 replacements in this week, but we don't know when. We haven't had any in over a month now.

Each Mustang carried 1880 rounds of .50-caliber ammunition. During 37 months of combat, the Mustangs and Sabrejets of the 18th Wing would fire over 32 million rounds of .50-caliber ammunition. (Krakovsky)

Mom, please don't offer any more of your friends stuff from Tokyo unless you send the money, because I doubt seriously if I'll have enough for everything now. I just looked over my gift list, and with yours and mine and Rose's all put together it amounts to more than 22, so slack off will ya? Tell anyone who wants a cloth like yours to send 21 bucks, and I'll send them one. Send it in a money order.

I'm sure pleased that the movies turned out well. I was a little worried when you sent me the new roll with the attached letter from the Kodak company. I got a kick out of your saying that grandma waved back at me. Could you read my lips when I said, "Hello, Momma?"

Successful Rescue

I only got in 9 sorties since last Sunday, and now have a total of 69.

On the 61st, I was on a 4-ship road cutter and recce up near Sibyonni. I was carrying 8-hour delay 500-lb. bombs, and I put

them right on the road.

On the way back the number 2 man was hit in the engine and had to belly in on a dry river bed west of Kumchon. He did a nice job, and the plane was hardly hurt at all. He scrambled out and ran over and crawled into a hole near a levee and hid there.

Tandy climbed up to 10,000 feet and put out a "May Day" distress call. Inside of five minutes we had 8 aircraft flying cover for him. In 10 minutes we had 15 planes.

We had a 4-ship gunnery pattern going around him, and we killed about 15 gooks that were firing on him. He hopped back and forth to opposite sides of the levee each time we found a new gook.

The helicopter came up from Seoul and picked him up uninjured in 80 minutes from the time he went down.

I had to leave before he was picked up, so I missed out on strafing his airplane. *[FAF policy at the time was to ensure that crashed aircraft were strafed to ensure they had no further military use to the*

Mustang loaded with napalm en route to a close air support strike. (Mason)

enemy, e.g. classified materials or intelligence.]

He is now listed as an evadee and is restricted from further combat flying, and will be rotated to the states.

We had to land at Seoul and get gas, and didn't get back here to K-9 until 2030.

When I landed at Seoul I found out I had a hole about 2" x 5" in the leading edge of my left wing. I must have gotten hit at the same time the man who went down was. They put masking tape over the hole, and I flew it on home.

No. 62 was a 3-ship road cutter and recce to Sibyonni.

I really got a beautiful cut this time. We had 8 10-sec. delay fuses, so I drove them right in at a pretty low altitude. They made a cut in the road at least 15 feet deep and 25-30 feet across the road.

When I got back and was in the mess hall a fellow came up and said, "Hello, Schiebel." It was one of the Texas boys from Langley Field. He and another guy were the first ones to volunteer for this deal, and they left about a week before I did. We all lived in the same barracks at Langley, and were pretty good friends. They had been to Las Vegas to gunnery school for 6 weeks, and had a couple of delays. They were really dumbfounded to learn that I had over 60 sorties in—in less than 2 months.

They were assigned to the 18th Group at K-10 about 30 miles from here. They spent the night here and I tried to get them assigned to our squadron. Col. Robie called all his friends at 5th A.F. and Tokyo, but the 18th was short of pilots just like we are, so they had to go.

That afternoon I had to stand a runway alert with Col. Robie.

It consists of 2 planes sitting at the side of the take-off end of the runway with the pilots strapped in and ready to go. They are scrambled by a phone from Operations to the runway control jeep.

I was sleeping when we got scrambled, but still we got cranked up and in the air in 15 seconds.

We flew around locally for an hour under the control of the radar net, and he vectored us into a number of "boggies."

We got in 2 replacements Monday, and both were assigned to our flight, since 2 of the other men finished last week. One of them is a real artist on the piano and accordion, and we had a good time Tuesday night singing in Col. Robie's room with guitar and accordion accompaniment.

On the 12th I got number 63.

It was what we call an "ass buster" because that's just what happens.

We are rigged with double drop tanks of 110 gallons of gas each, plus the 285 normal load. We were sent up to the Island of Senmido just South of Sonchon on the Western coast of Korea about 40 miles East of the mouth of the Yalu River—just East of Yongsapo on the peninsula extending down from Autun—about 380 miles N.W. of here.

Our mission was to CAP the island while a Navy amphibious plane picked up some paratroopers that had been landed there the day before to try to capture a MiG 15 pilot who bailed out and landed there.

They failed because the Reds landed 40 troops on the island and chased the paratroopers to an adjoining small Island.

While we were circling we heard a B-29 giving a "May Day" call and saying he was shot up and was going to ditch it in the ocean just off the coast of Chinampo.

We sent a flight down there and they located the wreckage but no signs of life.

Our flight escorted the "Dumbo" down and he landed and located the dead bodies of the crew floating amid the debris. He was heavily loaded with the paratroopers and the sea was heavy, so he only picked up one body.

We circled until we were low on gas and had to leave. I learned later that the bodies had gone down when a destroyer arrived.

We got home, and I was utterly miserable. We had been in the air 6 ½ hours, and my butt was really busted. I couldn't sit comfortably for 2 days.

All this happened on the 12th, the day that all the Migs were supposed to have been shot down with little damage to our planes. Only four B-29's went down that day, and the *Stars and Stripes* says—"little damage."

It's no wonder the people at home are so apathetic toward this War.

One of the B-29's landed on our strip at K-16 at Seoul and went off the end into the sand. His main gear buried up to his belly. They were the lucky ones, because two of the others were lost in enemy territory, and the other bailed out by Suwon.

Number 64 was a 3-ship road cutter to Singye.

We cut the road in 2 places with 6 hour delays *[delayed action fuses on the bombs]* and recced on the way home finding nothing.

Number 65 on Saturday the 14th was another "ass buster" to the same Island.

This time we covered a flotilla of 6 naval vessels and one LST with a helicopter on it. The copter went to the island and was searching for the downed MiG in the shallow water. He didn't find a thing, and we finally went back to K-16 with only a 4 hour and 55 minute flight.

Number 66 the same afternoon was a CAP for a downed marine pilot who bailed out and landed in No-man's land, between the lines. The Copter went in but was shot up, so came out without the pilot. We circled, along with about 15 other ships, for about 2 ½ hours while a ground patrol went out to try to reach him, but to no avail. We left before they tried a second copter, but they never did get him. My plane had an oil leak when I got down, so I missed the next mission which was a CAP for the Marine. I was just as happy because they were out 3 hours.

Yesterday I got 3 missions.

Number 67 was an early 0545 4-ship road cutter, but we couldn't claim much damage because the haze was so thick we couldn't get high enough to get a good dive bomb pass—so we tried to glide them in without much luck.

Number 68 was a 4-ship R.C. with instantaneous fuses. I split the road with mine, but with the instant fuses there isn't much penetration, so it didn't completely cut the road. It left a little ridge right in the center. We recced but found nothing.

Number 69 was the same type mission,

but by then (1530) the smoke and haze was 10,000 feet thick, and you couldn't see the ground from 5,000 feet. We rushed in and rushed out as it was Tandy's 100th mission, and we weren't taking any chances. I'm sure going to miss flying with him. I don't know who will take over the flight now. I'm sure I won't because there are too many Captains, and besides it is too much responsibility.

Today I had an early take-off on a local CAP that has begun since the enemy air force potential has arisen. We have to have 2 planes in the air an hour before Sun-up until 1 hour after—and the same at Sundown.

Tandy and I had tower duty all day, so we split it up 3 ½ hours apiece. I go again at 1530.

We are staging eight ships each squadron at K-16 now.

We send four up each day (morning) and 4 others come back each night after the last mission. That way you spend two days and one night up there.

I haven't gotten into Seoul yet, but may soon. We go up there 2 days out of 4 now because we're down to 4 flights now. We only have 14 pilots now who haven't finished up, and it won't be long before most of us are finished.

If they don't send replacements soon we'll really be sweating. The 100 mission men have been told they may be expected to fly beyond that number until we get replacements, but none have had to yet.

Just got back from No. 75 up near Sinanju, and we lost our leader. He was hit by flak at 300 feet—bailed out. His chute popped just as he hit the ground.

The flak was so thick you would run into it anyway you turned.

No. 2 man got hit in right wing and made a hole about 2 ft. across in the flap.

I was No. 3 and along with No. 4 was uninjured. I prayed long and loud and my prayers were answered. That makes 3 men in about a week.

I've bad a headache for about a week now, and I think it is a touch of the flu, along with nervous tension. Hope we get some replacements in soon so I can take a rest.

Got 3 sorties in yesterday, and now am three-fourths finished.

I'm sitting on the end of the runway in the cockpit of a ship on strip-alert. We maintain an alert from 0515 till 1945 of two ships—one from each squadron—and we usually catch it about every third day.

All of our flying is now being done out of here at K-16 [Seoul Municipal Air Field], with all major repairs and inspections being done at K-9, and the ships ferried up here. We are operating full blower, and yesterday the group set some sort of record by flying 113 sorties.

I have 84 missions in now, and will get another one this afternoon I think.

I hope to be able to go back to K-9 tonight and take a bath. I've been here since last Friday, and I'm pretty dirty. I take an Aggie bath at night out of an empty ammo can, but it doesn't do too good a job.

I had only 71 sorties in when I came up Friday, so you can see how we've been operating. I got in 3 Saturday, 1 Sunday, 3 Monday, and 4 yesterday; and I got 2 in this morning.

Most of the last three days have been short ones since the Chinks began their push.

Monday we had orders to burn out a 5-mile radius around Singye, and yesterday it was just North of the Imjin river N. of Munsan that we were burning out. Today it is Namchomjom.

The mission Sunday was really a tough one.

Four of us were sent up to Yongwon-ni, on the railroad N. out of Pyongyang just South of Kumeri to cut a tunnel. We were briefed to do just that and nothing else. Well, the flight leader had other ideas.

On the way up he took us over Pyongyang air field, one of the most heavily defended spots in N. Korea, "Just to see if they are awake this morning."

They were awake, and threw everything but the kitchen sink at us.

I was Number 3, and was scared stiff.

Well, he finally took us on the railroad leading north out of Pyongyang, and he lets down and starts reckying. I stayed up at 5000 feet as top cover and they began to pot shot at us at every bend in the rail-road.

We luckily missed all that stuff and got

up to our target. After we dropped our bombs, which incidentally missed, he begins reckying back south toward Sunchon on the deck. He found something and made a couple of passes and then went south from Sunchon.

I was still top cover at 5000, and thank God for that. Number One man went down in flames from 300 ft. He bailed out at 100 feet but his chute popped just as his body hit the ground.

As the No. 2 man went over the wreckage he got a 40-mm in the right wing which made a hole about two feet in diameter. A shell went through his left magneto and into his after coolant section and then into his induction system. He lost quite a bit of power, but was able to nurse it home.

I sent 2 and 4 home together and stayed up there trying to get rescue facilities going, but a flight that was in that area at the same time couldn't locate the wreckage, and No. 2 man said he didn't think there was a chance for the pilot, so I decided to come home.

Boy, you talk about praying. I strictly prayed hard when every way I'd turn I'd be headed for big puffs of black flak, right at my altitude. God was sure with me that day, as He has been every day. We were sorry to lose the man, but he knew better than to retrace his route over known flak positions.

That area is called "flak alley."

Friday, our late flights ran into weather up in the target area, and when one of our flights started to climb up through it, one of the fellows must have gotten vertigo because be went into a spin. His ship spun right through a flight below them, and he followed it through in his chute. He hit the ground, and before his flight could do anything the Chinks had him. He was assigned to my flight, and had just been back from forward control about 5 days. There's still hope for him as a P.O.W.

We got in four replacements [pilots] the other day, but the older men are finishing up faster than they are coming in. We are supposed to get in a big bunch this week, but so far none have shown up. One of the new boys is named Arnold—a West Pointer who played football with Blanchard, Davis and Tucker.

I was out on the side of the runway about noon today watching a couple of Navy planes land that had been in a mid-air collision. One had about 3 1/2 feet of wing missing, and the other had a badly ripped flap.

The one with the wing missing landed first and had to land so hot [fast] that he overshot the 3,500 feet of run-way. He had to pull up the gear to prevent plowing into a bunch of trucks on the road just off the end of the runway.

Incidentally, the trucks are bumper to bumper for miles and miles coming out of Seoul. They are usually loaded with civilians who are fleeing the city again. And on the other side going north are miles and miles of heavy equipment going to the front. The gooks are only about 30 miles north now, but everyone seems to be confident that we will hold them.

I sure hope I'm finished when the Chinks spring their Air Force.

One of the fellows in the 40th got a slug in his engine yesterday that cut the cam shaft on his left bank of cylinders. He was up about 50 miles north, and started limping home on about one-third power. He got to within 1000 yards of the runway and it quit on him, so be had to belly in on the sandy river bed about ¼ miles off the end of the runway. He did a marvelous job and with an engine, prop and coolant scoop change it will be ready to go again. The latest rumors concerning rotation aren't too good, but I think they are due to the pilot shortage, and as soon as it is alleviated, they will begin rotation again. There are so many rumors, it's hard to pick out one you like least—No rotation; rotation to Japan only; fly 150 missions.

Shucks! None of them sound very nice, but I'm not going to fly more than 100 missions unless it is a direct order from the Air Force. There are too many guys in the states goofing off who could be over here getting the good experience that is being offered for us to have to fly more than 100.

I finally decided on a name for my airplane: "Rossi's Revenge," in honor of my buddy who was killed on a X.C. [cross country] from Langley to L. R. I've got it painted in big Red Letters on the nose. I'll send you a picture of it when I can get it developed.

29 April 1951

The ground is just shaking from the artillery bombardment that is going on only about 2 miles north of here [Seoul/K-16]. It sounds just like a thunder storm in Texas in the middle of the Summer.

This is really a momentous day in my life—nearer to the War than I've ever been, or ever hope to be.

The Reds are within four miles of Seoul

on all sides, but all the ground officers are cocky about our ability to hold the line, but I don't see how they expect to do it.

The Reds have paid dearly for the miles they got in the last four days, and now we are ready to put up a real battle. We flew balls out today again, and I got four missions in. I now have 92, and if we hold out here a couple more days, I'll have my 100 in.

I don't know how many over 100 I'll have to fly, but I think I'll be able to get an R & R after 100, and maybe by the time I get back our replacements will be in.

I went to K-9 Thursday night after my last mission, and got 2 very nice days of rest. It rained both days, and that made it doubly nice to sleep and write letters.

Four of us left K-9 this morning and got in a mission and landed at K-16. I didn't get off again till about 1430, but I got in four altogether today.

The one this morning was a recce and we found a cache of trucks—destroyed 4 and damaged 2.

The second was a CAP. for a downed pilot whom they failed to rescue.

We unloaded on a ridge and went home and reloaded and got a close support east of Seoul, on a ridge and then went home and reloaded and did the same thing again.

One was 35, and the others 20 minutes long. Boy, that's the way I like them.

I must say I'm dog tired right now, and I feel like I can sleep through all the bombardment.

Boy! There goes a real salvo. I'll bet they fired 100 guns.

We could see the artillery fire--without field glasses

M/Sgt. Henry "Hank" Lunsford served with the 12th Squadron, "the Tiger Sharks of the Foxy Few," including a period of time at K-1 while the runway at K-10 was being repaired. K-1 was the home base of the 1st Marine Air Wing, then flying the F4U Corsair.

When the runway and other improvements were completed at K-10, the Truckbusters began to use K-16, west of Seoul, as an advance operating base.

"At K-16 we met a vicious attack from the Chinese that came close enough to our base we could see the artillery fire—without field glasses," Lunsford recalled. However, rearming and refueling at K-16, made "our pilots' missions approximately 15 minutes long."

"For a few days we — the Communication's Technicians—loaded ammunition, fuel, and any thing else we could get our hands on until nightfall when we would resume working on our aircraft's radios. If the radio went out during daylight hours the pilot kept his place in line, continued his missions without a radio. When it became too dark to fly and the planes were on the ground, we fixed the radios!"

"When I began to run short on replacement receivers and transmitters because of broken power output tubes in our replacement units I became suspicious mainly because their location in the center of the unit made it almost impossible to break unless it was done deliberately!"

When he determined that "all the units with broken tubes had the same final inspector stamp," Lunsford notified his commanding officer and explained his suspicions. "He told me he would be right over to the Communications Shop (tent)! When he arrived I told him what I feared was going on and how it might affect our operation. He completely agreed and said that he would leave the next morning for the depot on Okinawa! With nothing but an Inspector's Stamp number, he headed for Okinawa the next morning! "

When the inspector whose number was confronted with the fact, he "admitted we were right on the money and said he hoped he had helped North Korea's cause!!!" Lunsford had uncovered a major security breach by a Communist Sympathizer.

"After turning back the Chinese we moved to K-46 between Wonju and Hoengsong, a small base prepared just for us. I stayed at K-46 until going back to Chinhae in Dec. 51 for processing to return to U.S. as I now had more points than necessary for rotation!"

> ## Lunsford uncovered a major security breach by a Communist Sympathizer

Adaptability of "Wing-Base" Organization to Combat Conditions

Col. T. C. Rogers, 18ᵗʰ Wing Commander

The 18ᵗʰ Wing soon recognized the practicality of operating from air fields that were as close to the front lines as possible. A "Forward-Rear Base" operations strategy was designed to outline and explain both the advantages and disadvantages of splitting the Wing into the various components needed to take full advantage of closer proximity to enemy lines.

This staff study was not dated or signed. However, it was included in the personal papers of Brigadier General T.C. Rogers, covering the period when he served as Commander of the 18ᵗʰ Fighter-Bomber Wing from 1 February 1951-2 February 1952.

The Korean War has been the first opportunity the Air Force has had to evaluate the organization of Air Force Combat Wings under actual combat conditions. As stated in AFR 20-15 the operational concept of the Wing is to provide "an organization designed for both peace and war, combining into a single unit the combat and supporting elements necessary to carry out the mission of the combat unit." This writer will not attempt to analyze adequacies of personnel or material allocations as set forth in applicable T/O&E's, nor will the internal organization of the four main groups and related squadrons be examined in any other than in general terms. The purpose of this report is to consider the overall effectiveness of the "Wing Base" plan as applied to a Fighter-Bomber Wing under actual combat conditions.

The efficiency with which tactical aviation is able to perform its mission depends primarily on its mobility. The degree of mobility and the efficiency with which mobile forces are employed will be dependent entirely upon the suitability of equipment good training, good staff work, and a good organization. A Fighter-Bomber unit must

necessarily be mobile in that it accomplishes the following tasks from its operating bases to approximately 150 miles behind the enemy's front lines.

1. The establishment and maintenance of air superiority,
2. Reconnaissance.
3. Interdiction.
4. Direct support of ground forces.
5. Harassing action.

The rapidly changing ground situation in modern warfare, due to the large-scale employment of mechanized equipment requires rapid advancement and withdrawal of tactical air units so that the striking power of the jet aircraft may be best employed without sacrificing range and armament loads. In the initial stages of the Korean War, the movement of tactical units from one base to another presented a very difficult problem. At that time, the entire Wing-Base structure was physically transported from one air base to another 150 miles distant. The enormous quantities of equipment and personnel involved presented a most difficult logistical problem and affected the combat effectiveness of the mission group. From this demonstrated weakness in mobility a plan was devised which we shall designate as the "Forward-Rear Base" organization.

The Forward Base or operational base, consisted of a Wing Detachment and combat crews. All combat sorties were flown from this site and the location was 20-50 miles behind the front lines. Approximately 500 airmen and officers, including representatives of the service organization were located here and two-thirds of the assigned aircraft or sufficient to accomplish the sortie rate were on hand. Personnel other than air crews rotated to the Rear Base every 30-45 days, and air crews with "war weary" aircraft returned every *3-4* days.

All three combat squadrons operated from the Forward Base and only essential equipment was kept on hand. The entire

base to include personnel equipment and aircraft could be air-evacuated to either the Rear Base or another operating site in 4-6 hours, thereby providing the necessary mobility.

Inspection and field maintenance were provided at the Rear Base in addition to administrative and normal housekeeping functions. Fresh crews and aircraft were ferried to the Forward Base on a rotation basis. Facilities at the Rear Base were such as to permit combat operations out of this location without interruption should the situation dictate.

It might be pointed out that AFR 20-15 contemplated a "split-base" operation when it provided for separate squadron elements. However, with the introduction of Jet-Type aircraft into tactical aviation, the employment of separate combat squadrons as such are not normally considered economical for the following reasons:

1. Airfields: In the last War, Army engineers were required to construct airstrips 3,600 to 4,200 feet in length which usually involved 4 days time when P.S.P. was utilized. Present day jet fighters require an airstrip 6000-9000 ft. which takes from 10 to 14 days construction time. Apart from the increase in material and labor required suitable sites for airstrips over 6000 feet long having good approaches would be extremely difficult to find in some countries.

2. Transportation of Aviation Fuel: The conventional fighter bomber of World War II consumed about 60 gallons an hour. The jet fighter-bomber uses about 360 gallons an hour. This increase in fuel consumption will involve a large amount of rail and vehicle transportation in the areas just behind the front lines in order to support forward bases.

These two important considerations will limit the number of advance bases allocated to tactical aviation in future wars just as they did in Korea and necessitate the operation of two or more combat groups having similar type aircraft from one location. It is believed that the Rear Base could be organized along the lines of a Wing, Reinforced such as referred to in AFR 20-15 Par 6. The savings in manpower effected could be utilized to offset the personnel requirements at the Forward Base.

The Wing Reinforced organization would also counteract a deficiency noted in the function of the Wing Staff Operation Section. This particular staff section has an important function under combat conditions. However when only one combat group is assigned to the Wing, this section's responsibility for staff supervision of all operations constitutes a "bottleneck."

Normally, Operations Orders and Close Support "scrambles" flow from the Joint Operations Center at Air Force or Air Division level through the Wing A-3 to the Combat Group Operations Center. Unless coordination is necessary such as would be the case if two or more combat groups were under the Wing, a direct line between J.O.C. and Group not only would save considerable time but would assure a more efficient operation.

It was determined that a consolidated Refueling and Rearming operations at the Forward Base, organized as a Production Line and utilizing personnel from all three (3) combat squadrons in addition to the P.O.L. Section provided for maximum efficiency thereby contributing to a smoother operation. This same principle of pooling similar skills was applied to the Airborne Communication Section which was a consolidated unit, and the Group Intelligence Center where Intelligence Officers and clerks worked together with Group Intelligence personnel to accomplish necessary briefings and debriefings of combat crews. Each combat squadron was responsible for its individual operations and engineering section. Although it is conceded that consolidation will usually provide a more efficient utilization of personnel and equipment, this practice should be closely examined prior to adaptation in any combat unit for possible adverse effect on an

Rearming. *Mustangs of the 67ᵗʰ Squadron being rearmed at K-46.* (Cook)

organization's morale. Whenever in doubt it is well to remember that a good fighting spirit as exemplified by organizational pride will more than offset a production line operation.

Under the Wing-Base organization the groups are mutually dependent and as such there must be coordinated action among groups if the wing mission is to be performed with the maximum efficiency and effectiveness.

When employing a Forward-Rear Base setup, it was our observation that this mutual dependence feature often became a critical factor in the overall mission accomplishment. A majority of the combat group will be operating at the Forward Base, whereas the main support effort is located in the Rear echelon. Unless the Wing staff and support Group Commanders are alert to the telltale signs, support of the combat group is occasionally sublimated to that work-load incident to the operation of the installation. This situation is most undesirable under combat conditions and is attributed to the physical separation of combat operations and rear support troops. Those Korean units having rear bases in Japan experienced this problem much more than those outfits having both Forward and Rear Bases in Korea.

Conclusion:

It may be stated that the main weakness of the present Wing-Base organization as applied to the Fighter-Bomber wartime mission is that it lacks the inherent mobility desired of tactical aviation. However, by employing the basic organizational structure of a Wing, Reinforced to a split-base operation, rather than Separate Squadron Elements it is believed that the necessary mobility can be achieved without loss of efficiency. To achieve the organization required to man and equip two (2) bases it is necessary that a detailed analysis be made of the function needed to support a unit's sortie rate at an advanced base and the pro-rated shares of personnel and equipment therein allocated in that mobility is the prime consideration, maintenance at the Forward Base should be limited to that which can be accomplished by Squadron engineering personnel in not more than three (3) hours or sufficient to prepare an aircraft for a "one-time" flight back to the rear base.

To better prepare a Fighter-Bomber Wing for its wartime mission, it is strongly recommended that units and formation be trained to be mobile-minded in peacetime. This should include actual operations from satellite bases utilizing the required personnel and ground equipment with the assistance of suitable transport aircraft.

In conclusion, it may be stated that the two workloads involved in the operation of the Wing-Base organization are diametrically opposed in the peacetime mission. Necessarily, the workload incident to the operations of installation occupied is static by nature. The mission of a Fighter-Bomber Wing, is on the contrary, mobile. All peacetime training missions should consider this requirement and make plans accordingly.

A Truck Busting Tour

By Major Mario Prevosti, USAF (Ret)

1st Lt. Mario Prevosti arrived in Korea on 21 February 1951. He completed his 100 mission combat tour on 13 October with the 12th Fighter-Bomber Squadron—"Foxy Few"—based in Chinhae, Korea.

As a First Lieutenant in 1951, I joined the 12th Fighter-Bomber Squadron also known as the "Foxy Few" at Chinhae Air Force Base—also known as "Dog Patch" Air Force Base.

I was a pilot, and I engaged in "Truck Busting" early on. The Korean supply trucks going to the front came down through the valleys carrying their own fuel. The "Busting" technique was to first spot the trucks by identifying their appearance as bales of hay on the valley floor. The tip off was that the bales of hay were not squared off over the truck engines, so the lack of symmetry let us know that there was a truck underneath.

Once spotted, we attacked.

The initial attack consisted of a three-second burst of six .50-caliber machine guns. Then we would move on to another valley to search for more trucks. After fifteen or twenty minutes we would return to the initial target and give it another blast with our machine guns. The bales of hay would explode!

Truck Busters indeed: We were able to knock out twenty-five to thirty trucks a day.

It should be noted that at this time in the conflict, we were not being fired upon while delivering these ground-level attacks upon the supply lines. As time went on, we did begin to receive ground fire so we changed our tactics. The flight leader would search for, and identify, targets flying at low altitude while the element leader and the other aircraft would stay at six thousand feet ready to attack the targets identified.

Anti-Submarine Warfare?

One mission again complicated by heavy skies, left us holding our armaments. I had six 5-inch rockets for which no targets had been found. The whole North Korean peninsula above the 38th Parallel was fogged in to ground level by the thick smoke from the smoke pots the civilians burned. These fires were all built in the same manner throughout North Korea, and they produced an abundance of smoke to prevent us from finding targets.

I went out toward the sea near Inchon Harbor, west of Seoul, and let my rockets go into the sea. I didn't want to land in Seoul and have a 5-inch rocket blast out on the runway. By the time I landed, the phones were ringing off the hook at the base! Little did I know that the US Navy had submarines in the harbor!

Ground Pounder Departure

The night before an early first-light mission, at about midnight, I was trying to get some sleep in the Quonset hut where we were berthed. An engineering officer, a Cap-tain, was playing music on his radio, which kept me, a First Lieutenant, and other pilots wide awake.

I was the flight leader on the first-light flight. I asked him politely to please turn off the radio, as we had to get up at 4:00 AM.

My first request went unanswered.

About five minutes later, I asked him again to please turn off his radio. Still no reaction from the Captain.

The third time I asked him to turn off the radio, he again ignored my request. Thereupon, I reached down to the end of my cot where I had my shoulder holster containing a .45-caliber pistol, and I put a shell into the chamber.

To that Captain, the sound of the shell entering the chamber must have sounded like the loading of a 105-mm cannon.

The radio went off in a split second.

I can't imagine what went through that officer's mind when he heard that distinctive sound, but I did have all intentions of killing that radio for good.

The next day, the Captain, his cot, and his radio were gone and we never saw him again.

I had probably established a standard that ground officers should not be billeted with flying personnel for obvious reasons.

Yalu River Air Base Strike

A major operation was planned to obliterate a North Korean airbase just south of the Yalu River that divides North Korea and China. The Chinese airbase was just on the

Chinese side of the river and they flew their MIG's from there.

Our attack was a massive effort including jets from Japan, the 12th Fighter-Bomber Squadron, and top cover by F-86's based in Korea. Our squadron was led by a Captain, who took us in squadron formation at low altitude. Each flight was assigned a special target on this Korean air base.

My flight was assigned "Tail End Charlie" and a full Colonel Group Commander was my wingman. I told him before takeoff to stick with me and I'd get him home safely.

The Korean air base was surrounded by a large dike, about ten feet high on the perimeter, with a road on top of it. A large truck was parked on the road. A man dressed in white clothes leaned against it, looked up into the sky, and anticipated the show we were about to put on. As we flew over in formation, a signal went off in my head: Flak Trap.

I pulled off to my left and expected my wingman, the Colonel, to stay in formation to avoid the trap, but he hit the truck and destroyed it. I wanted to avoid this obvious flak trap because I don't believe the risk of losing a pilot and aircraft is worth the destruction of one truck, which was most likely bait, and was probably empty.

There was only one building on the airfield—a large building off from the center of the airfield, presumably housing operations, personnel, and officers' quarters. My flight was assigned to the destruction of the building, which my wingman and I accomplished effectively.

On our pass over the enemy base we received anti-aircraft flak that burst above us, which came from the China side of the Yalu River. When we made our circle passing the river, I responded with some of our fifty-caliber machine guns: Tit for tat.

Just after making the first squadron pass we received notice that our top cover, the F-86's, were leaving.

Our squadron leader decided to make a second pass and then exit over the Yellow Sea at an altitude of about 6,000 feet. I'm "Tail End Charlie" with a full Colonel on my wing and figure I'm about to be shot down by Chinese MIG's because our top cover was

gone and we were high enough to be seen on radar. If attacked by MIG's at this level we would be sitting ducks.

I decided at that point that if we were attacked I would want to be in a turn, either right or left, so the Colonel and I did lazy eights behind the squadron. I was ready to give an order to "Break right" or "Break left" if necessary.

I knew the squadron leader was aware that the Colonel was flying my wing, so I flew in front of the squadron leader and led him down in altitude to just above spray level over the water. If we were attacked now, the MIG's would have difficulty adjusting to our altitude while attacking at high speed.

We got back to base safely without further incident.

Note: Forty years later, Prevosti attended a reunion in Colorado. During a barbeque dinner and show, a shout rang out, "Hey! Prevosti!" It was one of the maintenance officers from the 12th Fighter-Bomber Squadron. He told Prevosti that when he had returned from the Yalu mission, the plane that his wingman, the Colonel, landed, had a huge hole in the wing! The Colonel never said a word to Prevosti about the hole in the wing. "I guess he was happy enough that I kept my word to him and got him back home safely," Prevosti explained.

Successful Rescue Mission

On mission in April 1951, I was flying as element leader when my flight leader was shot down. I assumed command of a flight of four F-51 aircraft.

It was about 4:00 PM and I saw his parachute going down. I followed his decent to the side of a small mountain covered with trees. A large ravine was to the east. Under heavy enemy fire from the ridges, I put my wheels and flaps down to indicate to the downed pilot the direction he should travel to reach the ravine. When the pilot reached the edge of the ravine, he had an unrestricted view of me and indicated to me his exact position by aligning his escape mirror with the sun and flashing me as I flew by.

I signaled back to him that I received his message by waving my wings. I used the

radio to alert those in control and nearby, "MAYDAY, MAYDAY, MAYDAY—Pilot down north of the reservoir!"

My flight was very low on fuel. In addition to that hazard, I realized that flying three aircraft in a Luftberry circle at low level with wheels and flaps down could be very dangerous for us. I sent the others back to Seoul to refuel, then to return to base at Chinhae.

About 15 minutes after the MAYDAY call I saw the rescue helicopter arrive near the ravine.

I explained to the helicopter pilot exactly where the downed pilot was, and the helicopter hovered over the edge of the ravine to extract the pilot from the location.

As I came around for another pass I saw the helicopter at the base of the ravine looking like a crushed mosquito, with blades and leggy metal pieces all over the area. The helicopter had been shot down, but the crew survived.

With no more than 200-to-300 feet of altitude I strafed the area as I flew in a circle to protect the pilot and helicopter crew until a second helicopter arrived and successfully completed the rescue.

My squadron commander arrived after I had called for the second helicopter and the commander relieved me. I just had enough fuel to reach Seoul. All personnel, including my flight and the helicopter crew returned to the base without loss of life.

[Note: for this life saving mission Prevosti was awarded the Distinguished Flying Cross.]

A Centurian At Last

The completion of 100 successful missions was required to finish the combat tour and return to the Unites States. After the 100th mission, the Officers' Club presented a bottle of Champagne to the very happy pilot. Three other pilots and I were honored on the same day. We were the perfect number to play a game of bridge, and we had a few bottles of Champagne in hand.

We played a game that lasted into the late afternoon, and we tallied astronomical bridge scores—we also tallied nearly as many empty Champagne bottles!

May 1951

"As we move into the month of June we anticipate another bad month for Uncle Joe's Boys!"

Major John W. Rees, CO of the 12th Squadron

A Surprise Merger

At the beginning of May, the 39th Fighter-Intercepter Squadron "continued its split operations from Pusan East Air Base (K-9) and Seoul Municipal Airport (K-16) with the bulk of the operational flying being from K-16, and the rear area base at Pusan being utilized for performing maintenance on the fighters," the unit report noted.

On May 9, 1951, however, the 35th Fighter Interceptor Wing was merged into the 18th Fighter-Bomber Wing—"a surprise" to the 18th. Fifth Air Force ordered the transfer of the 39th FIS to the 18th FBG "for operational control and support." The move came as "a part of the deactivation of the 35th Fighter-Interceptor Wing and Group, and the 40th Fighter-Interceptor Squadron." The 39th moved from K-9 (Pusan East Air Base) to K-10 where the 18th was based "with a complete TO&E of personnel and equipment.

"The unit was notified on 5 May 1951 that the 35th Fighter-Interceptor Group, to which the 39th Fighter-Interceptor Squadron had been assigned since January 1942, was to be deactivated and the 39th would be attached to the 18th Fighter-Bomber Group at nearby Chinhae Airdrome (K-10) within several days," the 39th reported in May. "A small advance party was immediately flown over to K-10 to reconnoiter the billet areas, flight line areas, etc. The people at K-10 were quite unprepared for the incoming unit. The airmen's billet area was not yet completed, their billets consisting of tents over winterized frames. The flight line area assigned the squadron was formerly the base's napalm dump and it was strewn with a multitude of napalm drums, drop tanks, tank crating and the terrain was entirely unsatisfactory for parking of aircraft due to many chuck holes and too soft a surface to support a fighter aircraft." [1]

The 39th Squadron "was ordered to be operational at K-10 by 2400 hours 12 May 1951." Motor pools at both K-10 and K-9 were alerted to furnish trucks to expedite the move. 1st Lt. Richard Schiebel was the officer in charge of "the first convoy of trucks rolled out of K-9 the morning of 10 May and after a hazardous 40 mile, three hour trip over mountainous roads the convoy rolled into K-10. Officers and airmen alike pitched in to set up the flight line area on a temporary site until the permanent area could be resurfaced and buildings constructed. Trucks rolled back and forth for the next two days, at most times driven by the squadron's mechanics and armorers. By 2400 12 May 1951 the bulk of essential equipment and personnel were set up and ready for operations as ordered."

The move from K-9 to K-10 "was accomplished with no loss in efficiency of the maintenance crews and all commitments for the operations at K-16 were met," the unit reported.

The airmen's billets "proved very unsatisfactory when it rained with moderate winds on the evening of 12 May. The tent-

Monthly Summary

For the first half of May, UN forces ground activity in Korea was limited, consisting mainly of patrols and preparations for another offensive against the enemy. Throughout the month of May the 18th Fighter-Bomber Wing's combat effort was largely focused on disrupting enemy transportation facilities. Far East Air Forces conducted heavy, continuous interdiction of enemy supply lines, which contributed largely to the complete failure of the communist offensive. However, the enemy increased anti-aircraft heavy guns and automatic weapons to approximately one thousand, at eighteen different locations in North Korea.

As expected, the communists launched the second phase of their spring offensive against ROK troops in eastern Korea—a last, vain attempt to drive UN forces from the Korean peninsula. Due to FEAF daytime aerial superiority and attacks, enemy forces were limited to nighttime assaults. "During the month of May we flew four ship flights on armed reconnaissance seeking out and destroying enemy troops, vehicles and supplies," reported the Commander of the 12th Squadron, Major John Rees in the May 1951 unit report. He noted that 500-pound bombs were used to posthole roads and railroads, he explained that "much napalm was used effectively against enemy troops, villages, railroad tunnels and supply dumps. It is believed that the success of tactics accounted heavily in halting the enemy's offensive push and putting him in full scale retreat all along the entire front."

Adapted in part from U.S. Air Force Historical Research Agency. January 2002. The U.S. Air Force's First War: Korea 1950-1953 Significant Events. January 1951. http://www.au.af.mil/au/afhra/wwwroot/korean_war/korean_war_chronology/kwc_1951.html

ing did not reach the floor sections of the frames and as a result the wind would get under the canvas and most of the personnel spent a very uncomfortable night. The next morning the 18th Air Installation Squadron was contacted and sufficient lumber was issued to board up siding of the tents, thus completing the job for making the airmen comfortable as possible."

"Officers of the unit were billeted in tropical style corrugated steel huts quite some distance from the airmen's billets."

New Group Commander

May also brought a new 18th Group Commanding Officer. Lt. Col. Homer M. Cox was transferred to Japan, and Col. William P. McBride was assigned as Group Commanding Officer. On May 4th, Lt. Col. Ralph Saltsman arrived from Clark Field to replace Lt. Col. Eugene Wilson as Group Executive Officer. The change in command "brought many new policies to the 18th and activities were temporarily bogged down until the unit could swing into step with the new commander. Colonel McBride's personal drive and magnetism pulled the organization together rapidly and turned the full force of the unit upon the enemy. [2]

The 18th Fighter-Bomber Wing personnel strength jumped from 182 officers to 318 officers and from 1,073 to 2,020 airmen as of 31 May 1951. Over 700 new personnel had been assigned to the 18th, "bringing our overall manning up to approximately 90 percent."

The addition of a new squadron boosted the number of combat sorties considerably. A total of 3,394 effective sorties were flown during May—567 by the 2nd Squadron, SAAF and 2,827 by the 18th Group. Missions included close support, special interdiction, armed reconnaissance, and airfield strikes flown "as directed by Fifth Air Force."

Unfair Rotation Policy

Jet fighter pilots with 100 missions "and less combat time" were being returned to the States. Pilots attached to the 18th and

Mustang of the 18th Fighter-Bomber Wing gets its .50-caliber wing guns lined up by two armament technicians, Cpl. Weldon S. Wilson of Alpine, California (in cockpit) and S/Sgt. Gordon McRea of Wichita, Kansas in May 1951. (NARA)

flying Mustangs expected the same policy to apply to them and for a short period of time it did. The policy of rotating all "Century" combat pilots home did not last. "The rotation of [18th] pilots to the Philippines and Japan upon completion of 100 missions has not had the desired effect. [In May, the 12th Squadron had six pilots qualify for the "Dog Patch Century Flight."] Although no permanent policy was established for rotation to the Zone of Interior upon completion of 100 missions, pilots did expect it since such a policy was temporarily in effect." The "problem" of unequal rotation policies "is affecting the operational effectiveness of individual pilots," the Group reported.

In addition, "pilots with over 100 missions are being retained until replacements can be secured. However, these pilots are assigned non-combat duties, such as ferry and test pilots, summary court officers and various other technical and administrative duties. No definite policy seems to be forthcoming on the 'who' and 'when' for rotation to the ZI."

The lack of a rotation policy was "affecting all of the personnel in the Group and morale is not high at this time. The pilots are without a goal to shoot for and the effect of the returning of pilots rotated to the Philippines last year was certainly for the bad. All of the men that have a long tour

behind them in the Far East want to know when they will see home again. The effects are visible with every report in the Stars and Stripes of another boat load of Army, Navy or Marines going home. An Air Force policy would help get our team in better spirits. The improvement of the messes, new housing, and all the beauties of our 'Riviera' in Korea are the main factors that keep the men happy."

Combat Operations

Operational assignments for the 18th Fighter-Bomber Group during May "were generally the same as the preceding month, the post-holing of roads, tunnel destruction, reconnaissance, and JOC alerts. Missions assigned while on JOC alert were generally close support or cover missions for downed pilots," the Group report noted.

When "post-holing roads with 500-lb GP bombs it was found that a dive angle of 30 degrees with an air speed of 300 mph and release points of 800 feet produced the best results. For destruction of tunnels, skip bomb tactics were used." [3]

Automatic weapons fire and flak were steadily increasing and necessitated "changes in our methods of reconnaissance." Attempting to conduct reconnaissance "with less than a complete flight is not advised. All members of a flight with

Lt. Gen. Otto P. Weyland (right) and Maj. Gen. Frank F. Everest (center), new commanders of the U. S. Far East Air Forces and the Fifth Air Force, are greeted by Lt. Gen. Earle E. Partridge at Haneda Airport, Tokyo, Japan, in May 1951, on their arrival from the United States. Gen. Partridge, former Fifth Air Force commander, had assumed temporary command of FEAF due to illness of Lt. Gen. George E. Stratemeyer. (NARA)

the exception of the leader maintain such an altitude as to minimize battle damage."

Bad weather during May—fog, stratocumulus cloud formations, and rain—decreased the overall effectiveness of the 18th's Mustang attacks. Another factor was that replacement pilots reporting from Nellis AFB had "not acquired the degree of proficiency expected." The Group recommended "more time be spent on formation and the various phases of ground attack. Four replacement pilots from Nellis have refused to fly combat either before their first mission or prior to their fifth. It is recommended that replacement pilots be more thoroughly screened so as to avoid such instances in the future."

The arrival of Spring was a big factor in helping maintain morale above rock bottom. The men "started their swimming and sunbathing" in May. In addition, "a lot of off-duty hours are going into fishing and manufacture of boats. This situation is a healthy sign that there isn't too much time to sit around and gripe," Lt. Col. Ralph Saltsman reported.

Group and squadron operations analysts designed "an extensive program" to render the main roads impassable. Flight leaders were directed to specific points along specified roads "where bomb craters positioned across the road could not easily be bypassed." The nature of the terrain was the chief consideration in choosing "critical choke points." It was found that "filled road beds through low, wet ground, such as rice paddies, were particularly vulnerable to effective cutting by bombs." Another element in mission planning called for "the dispersal of bomb strikes along a ten to fifteen mile distance." Planners believed "this would force the enemy to spread his construction crews thinly along his supply routes or be faced with the additional problem of transporting the crews as well as his military supplies." The effectiveness of this mission planning strategy and "other interdiction efforts" was confirmed by "responsible officers in the United States Army Ground Forces in Korea."[4]

On May 9th, pilots from the 67th joined Fifth Air Force and 1st Marine Air Wing fighter-bombers to fly over 300 sorties against Sinuiju Airfield in extreme northwestern Korea—"the largest mission of this sort in the Korean war to date." The objectives assigned to the 67th during this "spectacular fighter strike" were "important," Lt. Col. Henry Lawrence noted. "Excellent planning and intelligence" supported the effort. Each specific target was illustrated during briefings by reconnaissance photographs, and the pilots participating stated later that they had no difficulty in recogniz-

ing or locating their pre-briefed targets. All flights from this squadron reported excellent results from their napalm and strafing. The tactical efficiency with which their strike was conducted is evidenced by the absence of losses, either of pilots or aircraft."[5]

Col. Ralph Saltsman, at the time Deputy Group Commander, participated in this mission. "The target was just below the mouth of the Yalu River that bordered North Korea and Manchuria," he explained. "While our flights were circling the area prior to the attack, we could observe enemy aircraft landing at the airfield in Manchuria, where they refueled and rearmed without interference from Allied air units. This paradox was made possible by the UN sanction which prohibited Allied aircraft from crossing the Yalu into Communist China territory."

In addition to the Sinuiju Airfield, during that month 67th pilots destroyed or damaged over 1,500 buildings, 19 petroleum dumps, 27 boxcars, 3 entire villages and 737 troops.

Pilots were irritated and hampered in the cockpit by a shortage of maps. At the close of the month the "situation still existed with no relief in sight." Lawrence recommended that a "single sectional map be printed which would cover the area north and northwest of Seoul, thereby eliminating the four sectional maps now being used for that area. The mechanical difficulty in handling four maps in the cockpit of a fighter aircraft detracts from the pilot's efficiency," he said as a major understatement.

Pilots of the 67th "took an active part in inflicting the large number of casualities upon the Communist forces suffered by them during their unsuccessful offensive. Air strikes flown in close support of United Nations ground forces continued to dem-

Organization
Headquarters Fifth Air Force

as of 1 June 1951

**Commanding General
Fifth Air Force**
Maj. Gen. Frank F. Everest

Staff Judge Advocate
Lt. Col. R. B. Regan

Surgeon
Col. F. O. Kelly

**Adjutant
General**
Maj. J.L. O'Connor

**Vice Commander
Fifth Air Force**
Maj. Gen. Edward J. Timberlake

Operational Engineering
Col. J. D. Howe

Public Information Officer
Lt. Col. J.W. Ingram

Operations Analysis
Dr. Wade

**Asst. Vice Commander
Fifth Air Force**
Col. C. H. Scott, Jr.
Col. Robert S. Israel, Jr.

Inspector General
Col. J.L. Warren

**Deputy for
Materiel**
Col. M.M. Harvey

**Deputy for
Operations**
Col. G. L. Meyers

**Deputy for
Intelligence**
Col. B. Hubbard, Jr.

**Deputy for
Personnel**
Col. Curtis R. Low
(former 18th Wing Commander)

**Deputy for
Comm. & Elect.**
Col. J. Crawford

**Deputy for
Comptroller**
Col. M.E. Godfrey

**Deputy for
Installations**

onstrate a high degree of effectiveness." The squadron was flying 26 F-51's that month—gaining 16 aircraft and losing 19. Over 900 effective combat sorties were flown during May for a total of 1,608 combat hours, an average of 26 sorties per pilot assigned for the period. Nearly 650,000 rounds of .50-caliber ammunition were fired, plus 4,260 HVAR rockets and 1,246 canisters of napalm.

"Most of our flying time is...over the bomb line."

The "Foxy Few" or "Fighting Twelfth" "came through with a grand total of 1,048 sorties" requiring 2,039 hours of flying time. "We have been doing most of our flying out of K-16 which means that the majority of our flying time is chalked up over the bomb line," Major John W. Rees, Commander of the 12th Squadron reported in May. "As we move into the month of June we anticipate another bad month for Uncle Joe's Boys," he noted.

The 12th lost seven aircraft to enemy flak, and another 13 "incurred battle damage mostly from small arms fire.

The infusion of "extra" Mustangs upon the arrival of the 39th enabled the squadrons to "put them into combat condition"

and place them in a pool. "Now when the squadron has an aircraft that will be out of commission in excess of 24 hours it is turned in at the pool and another combat ready one is drawn out," the 12th reported.

The 39th Squadron reported destroying 185 houses, 18 vehicles, 36 trucks, 17 field pieces, 7 AA guns, 920 supply dumps, 3 gun positions and 22 fuel dumps. It expended 525 rockets, 50 napalm canisters, 106 bombs and 77,000 rounds of .50-caliber ammunition.

In May "it was finally decided that the dangers inherent in using 1,000 pound bombs on F-51's outweighed any possible advantage over 500-pound bombs so stocks of 1,000 pounders and their components were ordered back to the depot." [6]

In May, the Group flew 2,829 combat sorties, but lost 32 aircraft—24 to combat and 8 for other reasons. Over 1,200 500-lb general-purpose bombs were dropped, 4,070 napalm bombs dropped, 14,960 rockets fired and 2.4 million rounds of .50-caliber ammunition expended.

Operations From K-16

On May 8, 1951, the 18th began operations from the K-16 (Seoul Municipal Airport) airstrip and throughout the month of May conducted almost all of its combat ef-

Seoul Municipal Airfield. Fierce fighting that see-sawed back and forth in the Seoul region, there wasn't much left of Seoul's municipal airfield when the 18th Group began using it as an advance operating base. (Murphy)

Combat Statistics

18th Fighter-Bomber Wing

May 1951

Average No. A/C Assigned
77
Total Flying Time
2,829
Percent Aircraft in Commission
75%
Percent Aircraft AOCP
2%
Combat Sorties Flown by Wing
3,394 (approximately the "same number of sorties as the combined three jet groups flying F-80's in Korea.")
12th Squadron Sorties
708
39th FIS Sorties
Unavailable
67th Squadron Sorties
633
2 Squadron Sorties
567
A/C Lost to Combat
24
Pilots lost
5

Fuel Consumed

339,101 gals.

Ordnance Expended

.50-cal. Rounds
2,414,657
Rockets
124,960
Napalm Bombs
4,070
500-lb. GP Bombs
1,230

Note: Figures and totals may differ in some categories due to differences in numbers provided by each component.

Disposition of Air Force Tactical Units

as of 1 June 1951

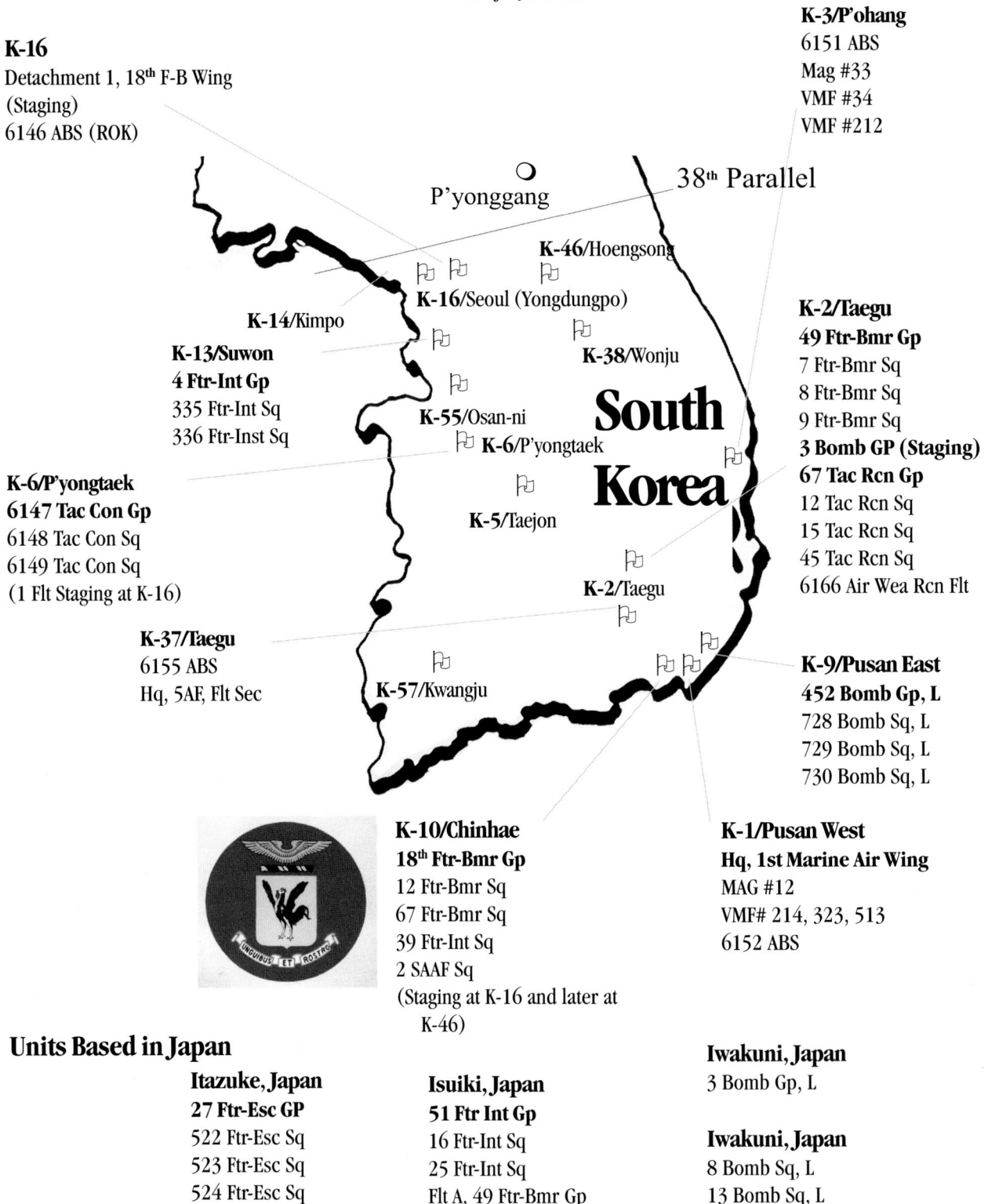

K-16
Detachment 1, 18th F-B Wing
(Staging)
6146 ABS (ROK)

K-3/P'ohang
6151 ABS
Mag #33
VMF #34
VMF #212

P'yonggang

38th Parallel

K-46/Hoengsong

K-14/Kimpo

K-16/Seoul (Yongdungpo)

K-13/Suwon
4 Ftr-Int Gp
335 Ftr-Int Sq
336 Ftr-Inst Sq

K-38/Wonju

K-2/Taegu
49 Ftr-Bmr Gp
7 Ftr-Bmr Sq
8 Ftr-Bmr Sq
9 Ftr-Bmr Sq
3 Bomb GP (Staging)
67 Tac Rcn Gp
12 Tac Rcn Sq
15 Tac Rcn Sq
45 Tac Rcn Sq
6166 Air Wea Rcn Flt

K-55/Osan-ni
K-6/P'yongtaek

**South
Korea**

K-6/P'yongtaek
6147 Tac Con Gp
6148 Tac Con Sq
6149 Tac Con Sq
(1 Flt Staging at K-16)

K-5/Taejon

K-37/Taegu
6155 ABS
Hq, 5AF, Flt Sec

K-2/Taegu

K-9/Pusan East
452 Bomb Gp, L
728 Bomb Sq, L
729 Bomb Sq, L
730 Bomb Sq, L

K-57/Kwangju

K-10/Chinhae
18th Ftr-Bmr Gp
12 Ftr-Bmr Sq
67 Ftr-Bmr Sq
39 Ftr-Int Sq
2 SAAF Sq
(Staging at K-16 and later at
K-46)

K-1/Pusan West
Hq, 1st Marine Air Wing
MAG #12
VMF# 214, 323, 513
6152 ABS

Units Based in Japan

Itazuke, Japan
27 Ftr-Esc GP
522 Ftr-Esc Sq
523 Ftr-Esc Sq
524 Ftr-Esc Sq
8 Ftr Bmr Gp
35 Ftr-Bmr Sq
36 Ftr-Bmr Sq
80 Ftr-Bmr Sq

Isuiki, Japan
51 Ftr Int Gp
16 Ftr-Int Sq
25 Ftr-Int Sq
Flt A, 49 Ftr-Bmr Gp

Iwakuni, Japan
3 Bomb Gp, L

Iwakuni, Japan
8 Bomb Sq, L
13 Bomb Sq, L
731 bomb Sq, L
(NA) (Staging from K-2)
77 RAAF Sq

fort from that field.

Each squadron kept ten aircraft and pilots at K-16. In addition "each squadron provided one more flight to fly missions from K-16 each day. Normally a flight would leave K-10 in the morning, land at K-16 and fly missions from there for the remainder of that day and the following two days, returning to K-10 on the afternoon of the third day," the Group reported.

"Although the use of this base has presented certain operational handicaps, such as a shorter, rougher runway and limited maintenance and living facilities, the tactical advantage of this location is patent.[7] Using Seoul instead of Chinhae, "reduced the average flying time per sortie from approximately two hours and twenty four minutes to an hour and thirty six minutes. The advantages accruing from this situation are likewise apparent," Lt. Col. Henry Lawrence, Commander of the 67th Squadron noted. "Statistically, the most tangible benefit is indicated by the 25% increase in the number of combat sorties flown by the squadron" during May. Another important benefit of operating almost two hundred miles closer to the "bomb line" was "the substantial increase in the striking range of the squadron, which may be translated into added staying power in the normal target areas should the mission require it. The northern extremes of North Korea are once again within easy reach of the squadron."

"The main body of aircraft fly from K-16 on combat missions using K-10 as a home base. Aircraft are rotated every three days so that proper maintenance can be performed," the Group report for that month noted.

The "split squadron" arrangement did pose some major problems, however. The "more troublesome problems arose out of the limited communications between the two strips. Occasionally more aircraft or pilots were needed at K-16 (Seoul), and such need could not be communicated to K-10 without undue delay."

About half of the squadron's armament personnel were relocated to Seoul and assigned to rearming and refueling returning planes. "Aircraft were rearmed, refueled,

Refueling and Rearming Ramp at K-16. *It wasn't long before 18th Wing and Group squadrons worked together to establish a virtual assembly line for Mustangs returning from nearby missions. In a matter of minutes the aircraft would be refueled and rearmed, ready for another mission. The pilot, meanwhile, had debriefed from his last mission, grabbed a bite to eat and drink, and obtained his briefing for the next mission. (Murphy)*

and minor maintenance accomplished immediately upon landing and dispersed for assignment to another mission." Pilots were "able to attack enemy troops and positions continuously and contributed greatly to the United National ability to first repulse and later attack the enemy."

Major maintenance was the primary task of armament personnel based at Chinhae. "Through new methods and efficient teamwork of available manpower, the two operations were coordinated successfully." Due to the increased volume of ordnance expenditures replacement of guns, bomb racks and related armament equipment was "at a new high." However, the "loading and arming of aircraft has been exceptionally fast and efficient, thereby adding to the success of the squadron's combat efforts. It is also a credit to the Engineering Section in that aircraft were kept in commission to a high degree, resulting in greater operating efficiency."

Another morale and efficiency problem was "the assignment to the squadron of

unqualified replacement pilots." This was an "added drain on personnel and aircraft which are needed for combat flying." Lawrence strongly recommended that a training program be established "in a rear area to bring these pilots to combat ready condition prior to their arrival in the squadron. This would allow full utilization of aircraft and personnel for combat operations."

Looking to future operations, Lawrence anticipated that the number of effective sorties "that will be flown during the coming month will be reduced considerably by the bad weather which is already setting in and which is expected to intensify."

On May 20th, General George Stratemeyer, FEAF Commander, suffered a severe heart attack. He was succeeded by Lt. Gen. Earle "Pat" Partridge, and MGEN Frank F. Everest, USAF, took his place as Fifth Air Force Commander.

By the end of the month, UN ground forces were on the move and had regained the initiative by advancing the front lines northward between 15 and 30 miles across the peninsula. Far East Air Forces were heavily engaged in conducting heavy, continuous interdiction of enemy supply lines, which "contributed largely to the complete failure of the communist offensive. But, the enemy increased anti-aircraft heavy guns and automatic weapons to approximately one thousand, at eighteen different locations in North Korea."[8]

Endnotes

[1] USAFHRA. *Monthly Historical Report, 39th Fighter-Interceptor Squadron*, May 1951, p. 3.
[2] USAFHRA. *Monthly Historical Report, 18th Fighter-Bomber Group*, May 1951, p. 2.
[3] USAFHRA. *Monthly Historical Report, 18th Fighter-Bomber Group*, May 1951, p. 3.
[4] USAFHRA. *Monthly Historical Report, 67th Fighter-Bomber Squadron*, May 1951, p. 3.
[5] USAFHRA. *Monthly Historical Report, 67th Fighter-Bomber Squadron*, May 1951, p. 4.
[6] USAFHRA. *Monthly Historical Report, 18th Fighter-Bomber Group*, May 1951, p. 3.
[7] USAFHRA. *Monthly Historical Report, 67th Fighter-Bomber Squadron, May 1951*, p. 2.
[8] USAFHRA. *The U.S. Air Force's First War: Korea 1950-1953 Significant Events*

Significant Events [1]

May 4: The change in the 18th Group's command to Col. William P. McBride "brought many new policies to the 18th and activities were temporarily bogged down until the unit could swing into step with the new commander. Colonel McBride's personal drive and magnetism pulled the organizational together rapidly and turned the full force of the unit upon the enemy.

May 5: An H-5 helicopter from the 3rd ARS rescued a downed F-51 pilot north of Seoul, escaping heavy small arms fire in the area.

The 18th Fighter Bomber Group is notified "that the 35th Fighter Interceptor Group, to which the 39th Fighter Interceptor Squadron had been assigned since January 1942, was to be deactivated and the 39th would be attached to the 18th Fighter-Bomber Group at nearby Chinhae Airdrome (K-10) within several days." A small advance party was immediately flown over to K-10 to reconnoiter the billet areas, flight line areas, etc.

(Tongue in cheek "Orders" issued for Dogpatch Officer's Club Party)

HINDQUARTERS
DOGPATCH AIR BASE
On The Korean Riviera
AFO 970
31 May 1951
LETHAL ORDER Number 1
TO:
You are authorized and will proceed on temporary duty to the Dogpatch Officers Club on or about 2000 hours, Saturday, 2 June 1951, for a period of approximately four (4) hours for the purpose of participating in a Naval Engagement without loss of Seamen (Dancing).

Upon arrival thereat you will partake of a minimum of one slug of saki for the purpose of enlivening the spirit.

These orders will be endorsed by appropriate staining of hooch upon arrival and departure.

Upon completion of duty you will return to proper place to carry or with the spirit of the occasion. Travel is deemed necessary and will be performed by ox-cart, honey-wagon or other inappropriate conveyance.

Capability of travel upon return will not be the responsibility of the command. Per Diem authorized with rate dependent on total saki guzzled. Copy of rate voucher will be forwarded to the nearest wastebasket without delay.

(Authority: Committee for Saturday Night Entertainment at the Officers Club, sponsored by the 18th Air Base Group and letter this hindquarters, subject: "Recreation for the purpose of I & I.")

BY COMMAND OF GENERAL BALLSOUT:
R. U. READY
Lt Col, U.S. Air Farce
Chief Wheel

"The people at K-10 were quite unprepared for the incoming unit," the Group reported. The Airmen's billet area was not completed and consisted of "tents over winterized frames." The flight line area assigned to

the squadron "was formerly the base's napalm dump and it was strewn with a multitude of napalm drums, drop tanks, tank crating and the terrain was entirely unsatisfactory for parking of aircraft due to may chuck holes and too soft a surface to support a fighter aircraft."

Not withstanding the difficulties faced by both commands, the first convoy of trucks "rolled out of K-9 the morning of 10 May and after a hazardous 40-mile three hour trip over mountainous roads the convoy rolled into K-10. Officers and airmen alike pitched in to set up the flight line area on a temporary site until the permanent area could be resurfaced and buildings constructed ...By 12 May 1951 the bulk of essential equipment and personnel were set up and ready for operations as ordered."

Despite the move and reassignment, the 39th FIS flew a total of 938 combat sorties requiring 1,495 hours of flying time.

Some procedures at K-10 were quite different than those at K-9. "The main change being the guns were kept charged at all times and rockets were plugged in on the taxiway instead of the end of the runway as was accomplished at K-9," the 39th FIS reported.

May 7: An advance party of four officers and eight airmen of the 18th FBW departed K-13 for K-16 to establish operations prior to operating from that strip.

May 9: In one of the largest counter air efforts so far, Fifth Air Force and 1st Marine Air Wing fighter-bombers flew over 300 sorties against Sinuiju Airfield in extreme northwestern Korea.

The 39th FIS was placed under the operational control of the 18th FBW.

May 12: Lt. Fred Thomas of the 67th Squadron flew "all day and into the night. The communists launched a big offensive in the eastern mountains and I flew three close support missions, and start on a fourth that is called back. I then flew back to Chinhae at night. Dog tired," he recorded in his diary.

May 15/16: As anticipated, the communists launched the second phase of their spring offensive against ROK corps in the east, a last vain attempt to drive UN forces from the Korean peninsula. As a result of air superiority, the Communists were forced to limit their assaults to night attacks.

May 17: Captain Verne M. Yahne, USAF was "returning from a local training flight" when his F-51 crashed into the bay near the K-10 airstrip. Yahne was stunned and trapped under water for a period of about three minutes. A crash boat was immediately dispatched to the scene, "but due to the proximity of the shoreline and an adverse tide condition the boat was unable to reach the scene," Colonel Rogers explained in a letter to the Commanding General of the First Marine Division. Sergeant Ralph Akers, USMC, a member of the Marine Cargo Detachment at K-10, "realizing that the pilot was stunned and in danger of drowning plunged without hesitation into the bay and swam to the aid of the stunned pilot. Upon reaching the pilot he was successful in keeping him above the surface of the water until the crash boat could maneuver into position to complete the rescue." After evaluating all the facts surrounding the accident, Rogers concluded that "Sergeant Akers prompt and heroic action probably prevented the drowning of the pilot." Rogers joined the Sergeant's Detachment Commander in recommended Sergeant Akers for the Navy Marine Corps Medal.

May 19: An H-5 helicopter rescued a downed F-51 pilot southwest of Chorwon in the central sector, sustaining damage from small arms fire during the pickup.

May 20: Capt. James Jabara, USAF, 334th FIS, destroyed his fifth and sixth MiGs in aerial combat, thereby becoming the world's first jet-to-jet ace. The Eighth Army successfully blunted the communist offensive, leaving the enemy overextended and under constant aerial attack.

On 21 May, General Partridge assumed command of Far East Air Forces. Maj. Gen. Frank F. Everest, USAF, took his place as Fifth Air Force Commander.

General Stratemeyer, FEAF Commander, suffered a severe heart attack.

May 21: General Partridge assumed command of Far East Air Forces. Maj. Gen. Frank F. Everest, USAF, took his place as Fifth Air Force Commander.

May 22: In close air support sorties, Fifth Air Force fighter-bombers inflicted some 1,700 casualties on enemy forces, one of the highest daily totals thus far.

May 24: The 136th FBW, one of two Air National Guard organizations sent to Korea, flew its first combat sorties of the war.

May 27-28: C-47s flew leaflet drop/voice broadcast sorties encouraging the enemy to surrender to elements of the U.S. Army's IX Corps. Some 4,000 enemy soldiers surrendered, many carrying leaflets. The captives reported morale problems among the enemy because of UN aerial attacks.

May 31: Fifth Air Force began Operation STRANGLE, an interdiction campaign against enemy supply lines in North Korea.

Combat Losses in May

Lt. Col. Leland P. Molland, 39th FIS.

1st Lt. Duncan Palmer, 39th FIS.

1st Lt. Michael H. "Mickey" Rorke, 2 Squadron SAAF pilot KIA on 15 May 1951. Lt. Mickey Rorke led a "vibrant life," his friend and fellow pilot, Lt. Col. Duane "Bud" Biteman remembered. Rorke "one of those who became vitally concerned with the wartime morale of his fellow combat pilots," Biteman noted, "who endured the loss of friends and narrow escapes which placed all of the No. 2 Squadron pilots and crews under considerable strain, and knew that something extra was needed to relieve the tension." That 'something' was the inspiration of the young SAAF officer from Eastern Cape, Mickey Rorke, who agreed that the USAF Officer's Club was comfortable and friendly—but it lacked South African atmosphere. With the help of Flt. Sgt. Bob Monroe, he borrowed a jeep, drove from Chinhae to a British NAAFI at Pusan, where he purchased ten dollars worth of bottled drinks. When he returned to base he built a bar next to his bunk from ammunition boxes. The original 'Rorke's Inn' was in business. He charged a paltry seven cents for a tot of Scotch whiskey, Biteman recalled, which was much lower than even the frugal costs at the American Club. Predictably, Rorke's venture was a great success. Rorke's Inn was then established in a tent, and later in a wood and iron building. The pub—and its proprietor Mickey Rorke—became an institution of the Cheetah Squadron until the end of the war. Winston Brent's book "*2 Squadron in Korea*" (Freeworld Publications, Nelspruit, SA) describes various aspects of Mickey Rorke's generous, outgoing life, and includes a full page and a half recollection by J. G. Willier, Brigadier, Ret., who was Rorke's flight leader and friend. It was Willier who was leading his final flight when Mickey was prematurely 'tossed into the air in a stalled condition' by K-16's notorious 'ski jump' at the 2200' point of the short 3200 foot runway. It was an early evening flight, Rorke's third of the day. A hurried refuel, re-armed and a take-off to the southwest, right into the setting sun. The haste was needed to get back to a previous target and finish off an enemy truck convoy and fuel dump discovered, but not completely destroyed, on the previous mission. It was a three-ship flight that lined up at the end of K-16's rough PSP—pierced steel planking—runway at 1855. Willers led the flight down the runway, one at time because the rough surface prevented formation take-offs. As the take-off plane rotated and became airborne, the next Mustang hit the throttle and began its run. About three fourths of the way down the steel planked runway, Rorke's aircraft was suddenly in the air, but it did not climb, just hung there briefly, nose high, then fell off steadily in a slow turn to the left, directly towards a damaged B-26 bomber parked just off the single runway. [Biteman remembered "that particular bump at Seoul's K-16 airport very well." It taught him "personally, quickly and regularly, the benefits of sudden rudder-exercise stall recoveries until adequate take-off speed could be accumulated in over-loaded, war-weary F-51 Mustangs."] As his left wing began to drop in the stall, Rorke attempted to lighten the war loaded bird and jettisoned the two napalm bombs. It was too late. His Mustang hit the bomber and both aircraft instantly became a holocaust of flame and flying debris. Lt. Rorke was buried in the UN Cemetery at Pusan, SK. "Rorke's Inn" lived on, an inspiration to the Flying Cheetahs until the end of the war.

1st Lt. Richard James Sequin, 39th FIS.

Captain Harry Melville Tyler, 12th Squadron pilot, was reported MIA on 25

12th Squadron engineering team poses proudly at K-16 in May 1951. The engine change they had just completed was accomplished in "six hours total from start to ready for test hop," reported S/Sgt Dick Joppru. Other members of the team included: S/Sgt Printz, Sgt O'Connel, Sgt Lundberg, and T/Sgt Roddy. (Joppru)

May 1951 and was soon the subject of a Congressional inquiry from Rep. Overton Brooks, M.C. to the 18th Wing Commander, Colonel T. C. Rogers.

Captain Tyler departed Seoul Municipal Air Base at approximately 1500 on the afternoon of 25 May, "as a member of a four ship flight on a pre-briefed close support mission against enemy troops and supply lines," Rogers explained. "Air control planes directed the flight to their objectives in a valley, and the flight had just dropped its napalm upon the enemy targets when the flight leader saw the right wing of Captain Tyler's aircraft hit a knoll. Thereafter, the plane bounced into the air and came down at a steep angle crashing into the side of the hill close to the point of initial impact. The aircraft was seen to disintegrate, but no fires results from the accident."

"After the crash, which occurred at approximately 4:00 p.m. in the area southwest of Yongpyong, Korea, the other pilots in the flight immediately began to patrol the area flying protective cover for the downed plane and pilot. They state, however, that no evidence of life was observed in the vicinity of the crashed aircraft. When friendly forces secured the territory his body was recovered, and the remains were taken care of by graves registration personnel."

Captain Tyler was interred on 10 June, 1951 at the Tanggok United Nations' Cemetery at Pusan. "The cemetery is well preserved," Colonel Rogers closed, "and properly cared for by attendants at all times, a fact which I believe his parents will appreciate."

Endnotes

[1] Adapted in part from USAFHRA. January 2002. The U.S. Air Force's First War: Korea 1950-1953 Significant Events. May 1951.

The Flight Line area at K-10 in May 1951. (L-T) S/Sgt Printz, Sgt Lundberg and Sgt O'Connel. (Joppru)

Gallant Rescue of a Flying Cheetah

On 11 May 1951, a 2 Squadron flight of four Mustangs attacked a bridge near Chorwon. Lt. V.R. Kruger, the flight leader, was soon in trouble—his aircraft had been hit by ground fire and had burst into flames. Despite wounds and burns from the flaming aircraft, Kruger bailed out and watched it explode into a ball of flame on impact as he floated down to a safe landing in an open area. He made himself as comfortable as possible while he waited for the helicopter and the remaining members of his flight circled overhead protectively.

Overhead, Major J.P.D. Blaauw, Kruger's wingman, contacted the rescue organization and continued to fly CAP. Kruger's crash had come near the end of their lengthy mission. There was not much fuel—or air time—left. When their fuel began to run low—"Josephine fuel"—Blaauw directed the flight to return to base. He would continue as CAP until his fuel ran out entirely, but would stay in the air until help arrived.

Blaauw "chose to cover the downed pilot alone knowing he did not have enough fuel to get back to friendly territory," explained Capt. Robert P. "Pancho" Pasqual-

icchio, a 67th Squadron Flight Leader who was heavily involved in the subsequent rescue operation.

Blaauw called for other "Friendlies" to help in the cover. Pasqualicchio, "heard the call and immediately along with several other flights raced to the area of the downed pilot. We did not get there in time to allow the Squadron Leader [Blaauw] to return home with his wing men, so we covered him while we were waiting for the chopper to arrive."

When Blaauw was about to run out of fuel, he "belly landed his machine next to

his downed pilot. After a short period the chopper arrived and plucked the two pilots out of danger and home. He should have received a very high award for his act of bravery and I'm sure he did. We celebrated the successful rescue with a few warm scotches neat back at K-10 that evening," Pasqualicchio recalled.

Blaauw would eventually be awarded the U.S. Silver Star for his bravery and gallant action.

Hanging By The Thumbs

by Col. Frederick Thomas, USAF (Ret.)

"Korea is a rather mountainous, beautiful country," 1st Lt. Frederick "Fred" Thomas recorded for his diary, "and, in 1951, is still clinging to much of its oriental traditions-rice paddies, thatched huts, and natives in traditional oriental garb." Thomas was "only in a major city once (Seoul) it was then mostly rubble."

Thomas was assigned to the 18th Fighter-Bomber Wing's 67th Squadron based near "the little town of Chinhae, right on the Sea of Japan. It is rustic, mostly dirt and mud, with a steel plank runway bounded by the sea on two flanks and mountains on the other. We live in a tent city, but do have an Officer's Club—a shack up on a hill. Four fighter squadrons are based here—three American and one attached South African. All are equipped with F-51 (nee P-51) Mustangs, the greatest fighter of World War II. Most of our combat missions will be flown in four ship formations doing close support of ground troops and interdictions of strategic targets. On several occasions we will go in a huge formation against Pyongyang and other major installations. We stage out of another rough forward base near Seoul—living there is really basic!

I am assigned to the 67th Fighter Squadron. After issuance of all of my personal gear (helmet, oxygen mask, parachute, survival vest, pistol, ammunition, life vest, etc.), I am assigned an F-51 with my name on it (although I rarely get to fly it, due to maintenance, rotation, battle damage, etc.). So, after a little local orientation flight, I am ready (?) to engage the enemy. Bravery is

1ˢᵗ Lt. Robert P. "Pancho" Pasqualicchio, a 67ᵗʰ Squadron Flight Leader, was among the American pilots flying CAP during the successful rescue efforts of Lt. V.R. Kruger and Major J.P.D. Blaauw of the 2 Squadron. Ol' NADSoB was short for "Old Napalm Dropping SoB." (Pasqualicchio)

really not my thing and to say I was filled with apprehension would be a huge understatement.

A tour of duty is 100 combat missions and I will attempt to picture a typical sortie. The fighter pilot — handsome, dashing with a white scarf—fearless! Reality is they are the usual mix of tall, short, fat, etc. and, if they reasonably understand the situation, very nervous!

A typical ground support mission is set up for four aircraft to take off at 9:15 a.m. The target is about 40 minutes flying time away.

I and my fellow pilots are up at 5:30 a.m—cold, dirty, unshaven and nervous. After a breakfast of powdered eggs and bad coffee, we go to the mission briefing.

The briefing officers identify the target and its grid coordinates, the route of flight and the ground situation. Then a weather briefing, intelligence update and areas of hostile fire en route and at the target.

We then do our preflight check—a careful inspection of our helmet, oxygen mask, survival vest, parachute, flotation gear, etc.—and finally, the airplane. A defect in any of these items could have serious consequences. On occasion, we run and jump in and leap off like you see in the movies—but that's mostly in the movies.

By 9:00 a.m. it's time to get all this gear on, get strapped in the plane and start engine at 9:08. After a pre-takeoff check, and radio checks, we line up and take off—two at a time. Our planes are heavily loaded—full fuel, six 50 caliber machine guns and ammunition, six-inch heavy rockets and two 110-gallon napalm tanks (or two five hundred pound bombs). By the standards of the day, quite a bit of fire power.

We roar off the short runway. The acceleration pushing G-forces on your back and neck and into the air at about 110 mph. We join up in combat formation and climb to altitude at 170 mph. We level off and cruise at 300 mph, keeping a constant lookout for possible enemy fighters, ground fire and flak. En route, black puffs of 40 mm flak burst around us and we take evasive action. Some are close enough to see the orange bursts and hear the explosion. I hunker down! (Like that's going to help). My mouth is dry, but as we approach the target area, the apprehension leaves and we go to work.

As a flight leader, I check in with a ground controller who has marked the target area, either by panels or smoke bomb. We now begin our runs on the target. On this mission, the target(s) is a concentration of artillery and gun emplacements on a ridge. We have learned that it is a mistake to peel off and follow each other in on the

Flak Bolter?

Returning from a second "R and R" after about 60 missions, 1st Lt. Fred Thomas was told to report immediately to headquarters. "Had I goofed up somehow?" he asked himself.

Because he was an attorney, he had been appointed the Defense Counsel for "a pilot who was charged with desertion in the face of the enemy. The defendant was a cocky guy who to some extent probably brought the charge on to himself--a fellow who told folks this tour was a piece of cake and he would be home in thirty days! It turned out that, at the first sight of flak, he did bolt for home (base, that is). When I interviewed him, he was a total mental and emotional wreck."

Thomas "got the charges dismissed, he was sent back to the USA and I returned to combat duty. Was I missing something here?"

enemy; it gives him a straight line of fire at our planes. Instead, we peel off from directions that are about 20 degrees apart and as one plane pulls up, the next is firing behind. Coverage works pretty well except for the last pass! Now I drop down to treetop level going about 350 mph and punch off my napalm about 100 yards from target. Ground fire is intense—red tracers all around and quad-50 antiaircraft guns blazing. We return with our six machine guns and make three or four more runs, firing our 5-inch heavy rockets. We continue strafing, the enemy fire abates and the target area is a mass of fire and smoke, eight napalm bombs having struck the area.

Early on, I devised my own method of attack—instead of making long, sweeping dives at the target, I will make steeper ones, give my machine guns a few squirts on the way down (get their attention) and jerk, slip and skid my plane until I get lined up on the target, my theory being that a deceptive flight path is harder to hit. It must have worked, as I sustained few hits. On the other hand, it is very tiring physically to be jinxing around at our high speeds. But, better tired than not!

Oftentimes, we are diverted or briefed to go to a second target for the rockets i.e., a railroad bridge, a tunnel, a supply depot, etc. As a rule, anything worth attacking is pretty well defended, so our flight is usually greeted with a variety of defenses.

Finally we re-form our aircraft and head back to the base. We slide into a tight echelon, peel off and land about 10 seconds apart. This mission has lasted about an hour and a half. We taxi in and line up the planes for re-fueling and re-arming.

After a debriefing conference with the intelligence officers, we go to the ready tent and wait for the next call.

Interdiction missions are much the same as I have just described, except instead of going in at treetop level we carry five hundred pound bombs and roll into a vertical dive from about fourteen thousand feet, releasing our bombs and pulling out at about six thousand feet in a high "G" turn. Ground fire from small arms is not a factor, but we are usually greeted with 20 and 40 millimeter flak.

On a few occasions, we are sent to some remote spot and don't see a thing. Seems like a piece of cake—but I'm sure someone down there is taking potshots.

And so it goes, day in and day out. The apprehension is there, but as the saying goes, "if you hang by your thumbs long enough, you get used to it."

Convoy From Pusan to Masan

On 12 May 1951, Dick Schiebel returned to K-9 from R and R "and found upon returning that our group [35th Fighter-Bomber Group] had been dissolved and our two squadrons merged into one and transferred to K-10 at Chinhae, 45 miles West of Pusan.

I was told I would lead a truck convoy to K-10 in the morning, so I got all my gear packed and ready to go. I loaded it into my jeep, and we took off at 0700 with 14 trucks and 3 jeeps. It took us 3 1/2 hours to go the 45 miles because of the rugged roads, but the scenery was beautiful. If you can stand the smell of the "honey-fed" fields, you can appreciate the views. After we got here, we unloaded the trucks and the men got into their quarters, so I went up to the BOQ and unloaded my stuff. The BOQ's are new, and were not finished yet, but we have moved in anyway. They are Quonset buildings with six large rooms in them. We will probably be 4 in a room. The showers and latrine are not quite finished, but will be in a day or so. The mess hall is about 20 yards from the and the BOQ and the Club is about 100. It sits right at the top of a little hill overlooking the bay and the runway, and the view is beautiful.

The reason for the move is to get all F-51's in Korea on the same base.

We are now attached to the 18th Group, but are still in the 35th, which moved by name only, back to Japan.

There are 3 U.S. squadrons and one South African squadron here now, and our squadron is made up of what's left of the 39th and 40th.

We got in a lot of replacements while I was gone, so we have about 40 pilots. We stop at 100 missions now, so I'll be done in a few days. We are still operating out of K-16 at Seoul for combat operations, and using K-10 as our home base for repairs and inspections.

I wasn't on the big show up at Sinuiju the other day, but the fellows who were say they had a gay old time. For once, the loss

A Ridin' Old Jeep and Aleavin' Pusan. Airmen and Officers from the 39th FIS threw their bags into a jeep and held on to their hats as they relocated on

rate was reported correctly at zero losses. Usually they report no losses in spite of quite a few.

The base here is on the side of the bay with the runway running parallel to the water about 75 feet away. If you should happen to ground loop to the west you would have wet feet. We are surrounded on 3 sides by very beautiful mountains, and on the South by the ocean. This used to be an old Jap seaplane base, and the swimming should be very good this summer. The town of Mason is also near here.

When I finish I think I'll volunteer to help down in Special Services till I get orders to go home or to Japan. We have a large hangar with lots of room for volleyball, badminton, ping pong, pool, reading room, hobby shop, theater and stage. It is very nice compared with what we've been accustomed over at K-9, which was nothing. One

of the old fellows from the 136th, who has been grounded because of his eyes, is special services officer, and he wants me to help him. It is a fat cat job.

The club here is very nice with plenty of lounge chairs, tables, a good bar, a snack bar where we can get wonderful steaks if we don't want to eat at the mess hail. They also serve a late breakfast here for those who sleep late. It is really a very nice existence, and should be very easy to take. I think I could take this place as easily as Japan until I get my orders home.

R&R Site. Re-arming and refueling at K-16 between missions. (Pasqualicchio)

Capt. Harry C. Moore:

F-51 Mustangs vs MiG-15 Jets = "No Contest"

Captain Harry C. Moore was assigned to the 67th Fighter Squadron at Clark Air Force Base and had gone north into Korea with Major Lou Sebille and the rest of the Squadron in early August 1950. His wife, Lois, remained at Clark with their one week old daughter.

In mid September, Moore was permitted to return to Clark Field because Lois and their daughter were preparing to return to the United States. In about one week's time they were prepared for their return and Harry saw them off safely and then returned to the 67th.

By the end of October he had completed almost fifty combat missions.

In May 1951 there appeared to be an extreme shortage of fighter pilots, caused by overly optimistic personnel forecasts during General MacArthur's "Home by Christmas" euphoria prior to the November entry of Chinese forces on the side of North Korea. This caused a panic in FEAF Headquarters which decreed that all fighter pilots who had flown any combat missions whatsoever in Korea must complete the full 100 mission tour before rotation to the 'States—no matter how long they had been in the theater or other extenuating circumstances.

The Chinese army's massive Spring Offensive of 1951 was just beginning. Until the entry of the Chinese into the war, in November and December of 1950 and the early months of 1951, Red air opposition had been almost nil. Then, with seemingly endless reinforcements streaming across from Manchuria, an occasional MiG-15 would venture a few miles south of its sanctuary north of the Yalu River.

Although the U.N. propeller-driven F-51 Mustangs were no match for the fast jets in air-to-air battles, it was known from simulated 'dogfights' between U.S. F-80 jets and the Mustangs that the '51 could survive a jet confrontation, but only if strict, disciplined defensive tactics were applied, with very precise timing of each defense maneu-

ver.

For example: the great speed advantage of the jets could be somewhat offset by the much tighter turning radius of the Mustang. So, when attacked by jets, the '51 pilot would have to keep a close eye on the attacking enemy fighter and make an abrupt tight turn into the attacker at just the precise moment before the jet came into firing range. In that way, the Mustang would have equal opportunity to fire at the jet in a head-on pass – trading gun for gun and, for the moment, eliminating the enemy's advantage of speed.

Then, when the jet sped past, swinging wide because of his excess momentum, the '51 pilot would have to immediately dive into a very, very tight descending spiral – racing to get down close to the ground as quickly as possible. If the jet set up for another attack before the Mustang could get down to the deck amongst the mountains, it might be necessary to synchronize yet more head-on passes to keep the jet from making clean, deadly stern attacks.

Finally, when the Mustang was able to get down into the mountain valleys, he could try to "scrape off" the high-speed, wider turning jet in the narrow canyons—still pulling up to meet each attack head-on, trading gun for gun, until ultimately the jet

must run low on fuel and return to base, leaving the '51 pilot with plenty of remaining fuel to high-tail it for home—badly shaken, but still safe and still flying.

Captain Harry Moore and his wingman, while flying at about 5,000 feet—just high enough to be out of range of most small arms fire, were jumped by a pair of Russian-built MiG-15 jets south of Yong-ju, near the mouth of the Yalu River. When they were attacked, for some reason, they were unable to turn to meet the attackers head-on, and use the defensive tactics that had been devised. They turned away and put their noses down, turning south as if to try to outrun the jets. The MiGs blasted both Harry and his wingman out of the sky on their first firing pass.

Captain Moore was shot down and apparently died within just minutes of the time that his friend and Squadron mate, Lieutenant Ross Cree was killed by ground fire just a few miles further south.

But Moore Was Probably Not Killed Then...Either!

On 7 August 2002, the Defense Department notified Lois Moore that recent interviews in Taganrog, Russia, with a Soviet veteran, "suggested that Captain Moore may have survived his shoot down."

The startling new information was developed through the auspices of the U.S.-Russia Joint Commission on POW/MIAs. Researchers from the Office of the Secretary of Defense, POW/Missing Personnel Office's Joint Commission Support Directorate were conducting research in the Central Archives of the Russian Ministry of Defense in Podolsk, Russia, and conducting interviews with Soviet veterans of the Korean War.

A 19 July 2002 Memorandum from the POW/MISSING Personnel Office to the USAF

Missing Persons Branch, contained documents that included Soviet Air Force reports documenting the shoot-down of an F-51 aircraft by Soviet pilots on 1 June 1951 and transcripts of interviews with Soviet Korean War veterans.

The USAF summary noted that "Captain Moore was a member of a flight of four F-51 aircraft dispatched to perform a reconnaissance mission on June 1, 1951, over North Korea. While en route to their assigned target, they were ordered to proceed north and provide close air support for a B-29 bomber crew that had bailed out in enemy territory. Moore's flight found itself off course and flying near the North Korea/China border. Moore and another pilot from his flight, Captain Hederstrom, were suddenly attacked by a flight of MIG-15 aircraft that were patrolling along the Yalu River. Moore and Hederstrom descended and were flying south along the coast in order to evade the MIGs. Hederstrom was unable to communicate with Moore during the time of the attack because of radio difficulties. Hederstrom turned east in the vicinity of Taehwa-do Island and continued inland. Hederstrom last saw Moore being chased by four MIG-15s."

The Soviet Air Force report stated that at 1230 hours, the First Squadron, consisting of eight aircraft, was ordered by the command post to fly a mission to destroy enemy bombers in the vicinity of Khajdzio. However, on arrival of the fighters in the designated area, the enemy aircraft had already departed.

The squadron, commanded by Captain Maznev, was despatched to the area of Rikakho, 35 kilometers southeast of An'dun, where they spotted "six enemy F-51 Mustang fighters in the area at 3,000 meters." Maznev observed "six unidentified aircraft to his left about three kilometers away and flying at a slightly lower altitude. In order to determine the type of aircraft he was seeing, Captain Maznev turned left and descended. When he determined that they were enemy aircraft, Captain Maznev ordered Captain Kalyuzhnij's flight to attack them."

From a distance of about 300 meters, he fired two long bursts at the enemy aircraft, which then banked hard to the right and descended into the hills in the vicinity of Rikakho. "The remaining enemy aircraft, having noticed our fighters, broke into pairs and single aircraft flights."

After pulling out of the attack, Russian pilot Sr. Lt. Shchukin "saw another F-51 that was to his front. Shchukin fired one long burst on an attack angle of 0/4 and from a distance of 300 meters. The enemy aircraft began to smoke and lost altitude and headed off to the south." It was Captain Harry Moore's Mustang that was under attack by the MIGs. Moore's plane was then attacked "in order" by three more MIGs, that "followed the enemy aircraft to where it crashed, the whole time attacking it. The enemy aircraft crashed into the Korean Gulf near the island of Dan-to, which is 60 kilometers southeast of An'dun."

Maznev attacked another F-51 that he encountered "head-on and fired on the aircraft from a distance of 800-300 meters. He fired two bursts and then passed over him. The enemy aircraft departed in the direction of the sea and descended. Guards Captain Maznev did not pursue the enemy plane because of a lack of fuel."

Former Guards Captain Aleksey Alekseevich Kalyuzhniy now lives in the Ukraine. During an interview conducted on 17 May 2002, Kalyuzhniy indicated he served as a flight commander in the 18th Guards Fighter Aviation Regiment (GFAR), 303rd Fighter Aviation Division, while in the Korean theater of war. The 303rd arrived in Korean in March 1951 and conducted combat operations from airfields in the Mukden Triangle (Mukden-West, Mukden-North and Mukden-East) from May 8, 1951 through February 20, 1952.

During this period, he claimed to have shot down seven aircraft. Documents at the Central Archives credit him with three shoot downs, including an F-51 on 1 June 1951.

In describing the 1 June battle, Kalyuzhniy noted that several MIG aircraft engaged the F-51, and it began to smoke and was quickly losing altitude. He said he personally followed the F-51 as it headed towards the bay losing altitude. The F-51

landed in the water 20-30 meters from the shoreline about 30 kilometers west of Anju, North Korea. Kalyuzhnig said the F-51 pilot "appeared to be in complete control of the aircraft as it gently landed on the sea. He did not see the pilot leave the aircraft but believes that the pilot should have survived the incident....Soviet archival records concerning this incident state that the F-51 crashed into the sea near the Island of Danto (Kado Island on contemporary U.S. Maps)."

The report noted also that in 1997 JCSD representatives "conducted an interview of Igor Ivanovich Shavsha, Soviet Korean War veteran from Kalyuzhniy's unit, who claims that Captain Harry Moore was interrogated by the Commander of the Soviety 64th Fighter Aviation Corps, Ivan Nikitovich Kozhedub."

A report covering the interview with Shavsha held on 15 November 1997, noted that Shavsha arrived in China in March 1951 as a Deputy Squadron Commander in the 18th Fighter Aviation Regiment. Although when he was questioned as to whether any American fliers were ever held at his unit, Shavsha responded negatively, this information was "at odds with the information provided by Vasily Nikolayevich Shalev...who stated that he personally had contact with a U.S. POW, as did other members of his regiment."

Later in the interview, Shavsha stated that "he had heard that an American flyer had been interrogated by Colonel Ivan Nikitovich Kozhedub, Commander of the 324th FAD. During a 1996 interview, Nikolay Nikolayevich Belyzkov stated that an American was interrogated by Kozhedub and was later sent to Moscow to serve as an instructor at the Soviet Air Force Academy at Monino, outside of Moscow."

The information was gratefully received by the Moore family, but it left them without any clear answers. It does seem probable that Captain Harry Moore did survive his crash landing in shallow water after all. The elusive reports suggest that he was probably interviewed by his Soviet captors and possibly sent to Moscow as a POW "instructor" at the Soviet Air Force Academy--until his military usefulness was exhausted.

June 1951

"Them YAK's are flown by a bunch of Yuks and there ain't no sweat."

Lt. J. B. Harrison on his 100th mission after shooting down a YAK with a "beautiful deflection shot."

Briefing for Italian Air Force Leaders. *Lt. Col. Alessandro Cerutti (left) and Col. Dante Bonifacio (center) of the Italian Air Force get an on-the-spot briefing on U. S. Air Force airborne armament as Col. T. C. Rogers, Statesville, N. C., 18th Fighter-Bomber Wing Commander, explains some of the finer points of the American high-velocity airborne rockets. The Italian fliers visited the forward staging base of the 18th Fighter-Bomber Wing in Korea in June 1951 to get first hand information on tactics and techniques used by this veteran Fifth Air Force fighter-bomber unit, the Air Force caption explained. (NARA)*

Monthly Summary

Struggling to overcome spring mud, UN forces recouped their losses from the communist spring offensive and broke into the Pyonggang-Chorwon-Kumhwa "Iron Triangle" fortified sanctuaries. This enabled them to deny enemy access to strategically important roads that traversed the Korean Peninsula just above the 38th Parallel.

FEAF concentrated on bombing Iron Triangle sanctuaries, experimenting with B-29s using the shoran bombing technique that combined radio navigation beacons and extremely accurate maps to aim bombs. The constant problem of defending B-29s against MiG-15s combined with successes in the shoran tactics would lead to the bombers operating almost exclusively at night. Meanwhile, interdiction attacks were being concentrated on enemy airfields in North Korea—construction crews were trying to reconstruct them to accommodate more aircraft.

Adapted in part from U.S. Air Force Historical Research Agency. January 2002. The U.S. Air Force's First War: Korea 1950-1953 Significant Events. June 1951. http://www.au.af.mil/au/afhra/wwwroot/korean_war/korean_war_chronology/kwc_1951.html

"Close support, special interdiction, armed reconnaissance and airfield strikes were flown as directed by FAF."

In June, the 18th Fighter Bomber Wing had 320 officers and 2,015 airmen assigned. During that month, six of its pilots were listed as missing in action. Eleven Mustangs were lost "to enemy action behind the bomb line," the Wing's monthly report noted. A total of 3,692 effective sorties were flown during the month of June 1951—552 flown by the 2nd Squadron SAAF and 3,140 flown by the 18th F-B Group. "Close support, special interdiction, armed reconnaissance and airfield strikes were flown as directed by FAF."

Dual Base Operations

The Wing continued to operate from two bases—K-10/Chinhae and K-16/Seoul City. All combat missions were being flown out of K-16, with the aircraft being rotated to K-10 "for maintenance and inspection."

"For all practical purposes, the operations of this Group are conducted from K-16 with only an occasional training flight being scheduled out of K-10," the Group report for the month noted. The staff had analyzed the split function operations between the two airfields and "decided to enlarge the K-16 operations to include all combat operations. All briefings and interrogations are handled in the combat sections at K-16. Squadrons, with a maximum load of 32 sorties, have found the operations smoother and more efficient." A "skeleton force" remained at K-10 to "assume the whole load of the work thrown into the base in case of an emergency such as bad weather or an enemy attack on K-16. Also, a provisional training flight has been established at Group level for the training of replacement pilots." The new pilots would "be given a thorough indoctrination in flying combat in Korea through lectures and actual flying." Training was conducted whenever possible by "pilots who have completed a combat tour…during their 'waiting on orders' period." Fortunately, the replacement pilots that were showing up in

June "were generally found to have a higher degree of proficiency than those of the previous month."

A new "production method" of loading and arming was put into place at K-16 during this period to "expedite the turn around time." All three squadron armament sections would work together as one unit, organized into an ammunition crew and a gun-camera crew. The new method was "found to be very efficient for the type of operation at K-16, the Group report noted.

The facilities at K-10 were constantly being "improved with the installation of oil-

---

"Christ" on Dog Channel

A massive air strike was planned for a military complex near Anju, No. Korea, about 40 miles north of Pyongyang in mid 1951, we had 48 P-51s of the 18th Fighter Group, along with about the same number of P-80s of the 8th Fighter Group. On the way up to the target things started to unravel when MIGs were called out by Mission Control.

F-86s, flying a high cover, jettisoned their drop tanks that rained through our formation of Mustangs. After we survived the drop tank "attack," the flak started, heavy 75-mm, 57-mm and 37-mm.

As one of the Mustangs was making his dive bomb run on his target, a burst of 57-mm AA exploded in front of him. He was about to make a call on his radio just as the flak exploded.

With his mike button down the burst startled him and he shouted, "Jesus Christ!" A few moments later an unidentified voice came over the radio and calmly stated, "You can get him on Dog channel" *["D" Dog channel was the emergency channel for all air operations.]*

That loosened everyone up and was the source of many laughs at beer call when we got back to base.

Col. Robert P. Pasqualicchio, USAF (Ret.)

---

surfaced parking areas scheduled for completion in the near future." Wash racks were under construction, plus run-up stands in each of the squadron parking areas.

The facilities at K-16 were downright primitive compared to those at K-10. Even getting to see an old movie was a challenge to the special services organization. Even water was a problem in the summer heat. "Efforts are being made to get ice to cool drinking water," the month report noted. "Most of the men at K-16 work hard all day and fall in bed at night. They look forward to changing off with the crews from K-10 at regular rotation intervals. K-10 is our luxury haven. At K-16, we just fight the war," Lt. Col. Saltsman noted in his first monthly report as Group Commander.

"We are improving," Saltsman observed. "A strong will to fight and even more pride in the unit continues. Our new sign in front of the new Group headquarters says, *'The Best Damn Fighter Group In The World,'* and we believe it," he closed.

The runway situation at K-16 was "not as good." The engineers were laboring to get the runway in shape, but it was "still the bumpiest strip of steel in Korea. Whenever the ground is softened by rains, the parking and taxiing problems are also a menace. The utmost caution is necessary to avoid mud-holes which could cause nose-ups or gear damage." [1]

June Combat Operations

During June the Group flew four ship flights "on close support and armed reconnaissance, seeking out and destroying enemy troops, vehicles and supplies." Five hundred pound bombs were used primarily for post holing roads, railroads, and airfields. These bombs were fused at different settings, depending on terrain and enemy activity. For the first time, this organization utilized five hundred pound 'butterfly' bombs, dropping them in or near

317

Rearming After CAS Missions. *Mustangs of the 18ᵗʰ Wing returning from close air support missions in July 1951, taxi into line to enable armament and refueling crews to ready them for more flights with minimum delays. Rocket carts pull up in front of the fighters as crew chiefs and mechanics busy themselves with other areas of the planes.* (NARA)

craters caused by the GP bombs." [2]

Combat missions flown by the 39ᵗʰ FIS in June "consisted primarily of road and railroad interdiction sorties, which also included armed reconnaissance, the results of which have become increasingly effective. Six hour delay fuses on 500-lb. bombs and 'Butterfly Bombs' were included in the ordinance load on these interdiction sorties in order to make repairs on the roads more difficult for the enemy forces." [3]

Although close support missions "were not as plentiful as in the past," the 39ᵗʰ FIS was "able to chalk up a remarkable record of 741 confirmed enemy troops killed," it reported.

Enemy airfields became particularly important targets and several were put out of commission." Enemy air activity "finally began to materialize" in June and accounted for the "first 39ᵗʰ pilot lost due to enemy air opposition since the unit's entrance into the Korean War."

The possibility of aerial opposition made pilots more "formation conscious." During armed reconnaissance missions three flight members would fly "top cover" with the flight leader "doing the actual reconnaissance work."

Due to the "vastly increased amount of flak utilized by the enemy," it was becoming "common practice" to use the tactic of "hit-and-run"—"striking those targets closely protected by the enemy no more than twice per mission. It is believed this effects a valuable saving in equipment and personnel while still accomplishing the assigned mission." [4]

In June 1951 Major Carl C. Colson, USAF of Cocoa, Florida, relieved Lt. Col. Henry W. Lawrence as Commander of the 67ᵗʰ Squadron. The 67ᵗʰ Squadron functioned as a unit of the 18ᵗʰ Fighter-Bomber Group, the "fighting arm of the 18ᵗʰ Fighter-Bomber Wing." The 18ᵗʰ Group was based at Chinhae (K-10) "a former Japanese Naval Air

Station, and using K-16 at Seoul as a forward combat operations base."

Averaging 20 aircraft in commission per day for the month, the 67ᵗʰ flew nearly 900 sorties in May, racking up almost 1,400 combat hours. It took nearly 540,000 rounds of .50-cal. ammunition, 4,494 5-inch rockets, 568 tanks of napalm and 986 bombs to destroy 750 buildings, 102 road cuts, 3 AA guns, 9 trucks, 43 railroad track cuts, 8 pieces of rolling stock and kill 255 troops.

In June the significant increase in anti-aircraft heavy guns and automatic weapons at many new locations in North Korea began to take its toll on 67ᵗʰ pilots. The early part of June "brought with it a severe about face from the fine record of no operational losses recorded by the 67ᵗʰ in May. The first two weeks of the month four 67ᵗʰ pilots and six aircraft were lost to enemy action. The sad losses included: Captain Ronald R. Cree of Garwood, New Jersey; Captain Harry C.

Combat Statistics

18th Fighter-Bomber Wing

June 1951

Average No. A/C Assigned
75
Total Flying Time
4,725
Percent of Aircraft in Commission
62
Percent of Aircraft AOCP
2
Combat Sorties Flown by Wing
3,187
12th Squadron Sorties
877
39th FIS Sorties
900
67th Squadron Sorties
858
2 Squadron Sorties
552
A/C Lost to Combat
13
Pilots lost
10

Fuel Consumed

339,101 gals.

Ordnance Expended

.50-cal. Rounds
1,874,379
Rockets
13,921
Napalm Bombs
1,845
500-lb. GP Bombs
3,251

Note: Figures and totals may differ in some categories due to differences in numbers provided by each component.

Moore of Wheeling, West Virginia; Captain Jack H. Hederstrom of Brecksville, Ohio; and 1st Lt. Francis W. Escott of Montpelier, Vermont.

"Five of the six aircraft losses were due to damage inflicted by heavy enemy ground fire; the sixth aircraft was last seen heading out to sea southwest of Sinuiju, pursued by four MiG-15 enemy jet fighters....The high casualty rate in the early part of June could be directly attributed to the heavy build-up of anti-aircraft weapons of all types now being concentrated along the enemy main supply routes." The enemy was "well aware that those routes were favorite 'hunting grounds' and that an efficient anti-aircraft organization could definitely hamper the effectiveness of air operations."[5]

Intense analysis of the combat losses due to ground fire revealed that none of the pilots "bailed out," although all of them had "ample opportunity to attempt successful bailouts." It was assumed that these pilots made their decisions in view of the successful belly landings in enemy territory during the previous four months. This belief "overcame the unfavorable conditions for a belly landing in a country with unusually rough terrain and also that the aircraft were placed in a very vulnerable situation in attempting to establish an approach for a successful belly landing."

Cree had been hit in the coolant and had plenty of altitude for a parachute descent "with the remainder of the flight immediately available for cover until Air Rescue could be brought to the scene."

Rough terrain was not the only danger pilots faced in making the decision to "bail or belly." In several instances a pilot who planned to belly land on what appeared to be a favorable spot slowed his aircraft down to approach speed. At the moment he considered "he had it made" his aircraft would be "blasted out of the air by automatic weapons covering the spot on which he intended to land."

Intelligence reports indicated that the enemy was "building up a very efficient organization of mobile anti-aircraft weapons and personnel, using a definite support fire system of several batteries under central

control." These units would be moved from time to time to "increase their effectiveness." The moving tactics on numerous occasions "caused flights to blunder into flak in areas where it would not have been expected because of intelligence flak position reports from previous missions as a guide."[6]

[Note: Intelligence responsibilities for the four squadrons were assigned to one officer and one airman who were then detailed to work with the 18th Group consolidated Intelligence Section. This method of operation was "by far more efficient in accomplishing the overall intelligence mission," the 67th reported.]

These shell game tactics cost 1st Lt. Vernon W. Burke of Boston his airplane and forced him to eat his words. He was hit by ground fire south of Yonan, NK at a spot "we had formerly considered fairly safe and had even jokingly referred to the area as 'The old lady's home.'" Fortunately, Burke was able to nurse his engine over the bomb line and close enough to a friendly island near Inchon to bail out successfully. He was picked up by a helicopter within 20 minutes of "landing in the mud." The helicopter pilot who picked him up turned out to be an old flying school classmate.

"The most spectacular rescue to that date..."

One of the "most spectacular rescues" of a 67th pilot was made in June. Captain Kenneth M. Stewart of Louisville, KY, was hit as he pulled up from a target just north of Sariwon on the Sariwon-Pyongyang MSR. "Keeping cool and playing it cagey," he pointed his dying Mustang straight west towards water. Reaching the estuary east of Chinnampo, about fifty miles north of the 38th parallel and 30 miles southwest of Pyongyang, he bailed out and landed in the water. So far, things were going as he planned.

Steward inflated his Mae West, crawled into his dingy and started to paddle down the river. Later debriefings revealed that he "was the only man on that flight who had

"Eggs Hatching In The Korean Sun." *A flight of 67th Squadron Mustangs taxi to take-off position for another strike mission on Communist targets in June 1951. Napalm tanks, ready for immediate installation on other Mustangs, cluster in the foreground like giant eggs "hatching in the Korean sun," notes the Air Force notes on this photograph. The Mustang at far left shows the effects on the propeller of a wheels up landing. (NARA)*

taken the time to fasten his dinghy snaps before take-off. Others have done this religiously ever since." However, this was not a day trip down a scenic river—"he soon found that he was not alone for he began to receive moderate small arms fire from the river shores to the east and west." Since his yellow dingy was a great target, he rolled over the side and "tried to keep nothing larger than his nose above water."

Meanwhile, his flight was calling for Air Rescue while strafing and rocketing gun positions nearby. A SA-16 "Dumbo" was airborne in minutes.

Lt. Joseph Babasa of Bridgeport, CT coordinated "very efficiently" the CAP overhead. He succeeded in "keeping ground gunners from connecting with Capt. Steward as well as planes overhead."

Steward, meanwhile, was drifting down the river, past the city of Kyomi-po. Spotting intense flak coming from a factory in that city, Lt. Babasa "led the flight down upon the gun positions and succeeded in silencing them with rockets and .50-caliber fire." Steward reported that "no more fire from the ground bothered him after Lt. Babasa's attack."

The low, slow Dumbo had to follow the coastline all the way around the Yonan peninsula to get to the rescue area. It took two excruciatingly long hours. It was now dark

and impossible to see Steward in the water. In another incredible series of lucky breaks for him that day, he had brought a small flashlight with him and "was able to signal his position to the 'Dumbo' who made a night landing near him on water completely unfamiliar to the pilot."

"The SA-16, although receiving fire from both sides of the river, made a landing approach without lights, avoiding low electrical transmission lines and rocks and debris on the river's surface. The pilot earned the Distinguished Service Cross for the rescue." [7]

"Thanks to his cool headed handling of the emergency, his dinghy being fastened, and his flashlight Capt. Stewart is still among us, flying combat with 'C' flight. It was the most spectacular rescue up to date in the group."

New Reconnaissance

Tactics

Following the tragic losses earlier in the month, "new tactics for reconnaissance" were adopted along with "a much more thorough appraisal of the changes in the flak map." After considerable discussion and appraisal of past experiences—"mostly bit-

ter"—the new tactics were adopted. Instead of having two men down low and other two high, it was decided, after making many passes over our friendly flak guns at K-16, that the number two man was a sitting duck trailing his leader at 500 to 1000 feet." A new method was adopted that proved "very successful." The flight leader would go in low—"flat on the deck"—to conduct the reconnaissance. The element leader, meanwhile, was at 4,000 feet "covering the leader and keeping him informed as to towns, flak areas, and other danger spots ahead." The number two and four men followed the element leader, "keeping a sharp look out for enemy fighters."

Testing the new tactic revealed that "the leader was in little danger from ground fire as long as he stayed very low and maintained his speed." A bonus was the "improved ability to see into wooded areas and ravines from close range. The leader's apparent speed on the deck in relation to observers on the ground was terrific, making the hand traverse of ground weapons very difficult if they were to successfully lead him and hit him." [8]

Hairy Missions

Captain William H. Strand, Assistant Wing A-3, "led a fine mission that destroyed one locomotive, burned one box car, made two complete road cuts on a main supply route, made several rocket rail cuts, destroyed a convoy of six trucks, and damaged one MiG-15." That mission was highlighted by "one of our 100 combat mission pilots," Lt. Joseph Babasa, almost shot down a MiG. He scored "effective strikes on it," but he ran out of ammunition "at the crucial moment." It would have been the first MiG to fall to an F-51's guns. Pilots began "conserving more ammunition after strafing passes."

First Lieutenant Robert P. Pasqualicchio of Washington, DC led another successful flight that destroyed three "live" trucks, starting very large fires.

"Able flight," led by 1st Lt. James B. Harrison of Atlanta, GA worked a close support mission and destroyed five trucks that resulted in fires and explosions.

"After these fine missions, the outlook of all pilots materially improved. Getting visible results with the weapons at their disposal took their minds off thoughts of ground fire and focused it on the finding and destruction of worthwhile targets. The fact that many sorties had been recently flown against active air fields, heavily defended by flak, and with absolutely no losses incurred—the flak spector faded."[9]

An unusual and very successful mission to some friendly islands off the west coast between Sinanju and Antung (about 60 miles northwest of Pyongyang, NK), provided another "morale boost." The mission was to "keep enemy fighters from supporting a Chinese invasion of two islands in that area." Everyone was "keyed up" for the mission and looking forward "to a possible air battle with victories for all." Twenty-four aircraft from the group took part, eight of them from the 67th.

As expected, they did "engage the enemy in air battle." Six IL-2's and two YAK-9's appeared and "offered immediate combat." Lt. J.B. Harrison, flying as number three man in his flight, shot down one YAK "with a beautiful deflection shot witnessed by the whole squadron." Soon after, Harrison completed his 100th combat mission. Upon his safe return from this highly successful mission he noted, colorfully: "Them YAK's are flown by a bunch of Yuks and there ain't no sweat."

An even dozen pilots completed their combat tours in May.

Bed Check Charlie

Late in the month, weary pilots and ground crews were rousted out of bed by night intruder raids and "Red Alerts" at K-16. "Bed Check Charlie" in a light biplane paid them frequent visits late at night "causing much mental unrest and sleeplessness, but causing no other damage." The purpose of the "raids" was harassment, trying to "keep us awake and jumpy and impairing the pilot's efficiency on the next day's missions." It worked—for a few nights. After that, "most of the pilots were too tired

Nearly A Year In Korea for the 18th

In June 1951, the 18th had been heavily engaged in combat for nearly a year. As the "First Anniversary" date approached, the Air Force Times noted, "when the Korean War broke the 18th Fighter-Bomber Wing of the Fifth Air Force was little more than a volunteer squadron attached to an air base at Taegu. The initial volunteers, recruited from both the 5th and 13th Air Forces, were rushed to the airstrip at Taegu to furnish some of the first close tactical ground support of the Korean conflict." [12]

"Two groups of volunteers, then known as "Bout One" and "Dallas," formed the 51st Provisional Squadron. They flew F-51s against the enemy forces during the early days in an effort to slow down the North Korean offensive and offer some protection to our withdrawing, greatly outnumbered, troops."

"Syngman Rhee, Republic of South Korea president, dubbed the unit "The Flying Tigers of Korea." The volunteer squadron grew rapidly. Col. Curtis R. Low assumed command and molded these squadrons, plus additional personnel into the 6002nd Tactical Support Wing. It was later redesignated the 18th Fighter Bomber Wing, the name it carries today."

"During the first six months operations in Korea, from July through December 1950, that wing moved five times and operated from three different areas."

"During the less than six month period of operations in Korea they flew more than 6,200 effective combat sorties totaling 17,800 flying hours. In order to accomplish that record the ground crews, maintenance, supply, and even administrative personnel often worked up to 18 hours each day. Each man in the Wing was a "Jack-of-all-trades.""

"Enemy losses credited to pilots of the 18th through December 1950 included 16 enemy aircraft, almost 1,300 trucks, 190 tanks and 75 locomotives destroyed, and

an estimated 10,150 enemy troop casualties. In one day alone 18th pilots destroyed an estimated 130 vehicles."

"The South African Air Force "2" Squadron joined the Wing in late 1950 as the third squadron. Since the first day of January the Wing (including SAAF's) has flown almost twice as many sorties as were flown up to the end of the year."

The 18th Wing claims distinction of flying the first combat fighter planes on missions from an airstrip north of the 38th parallel. On Oct. 14, shortly after it was captured, they flew out of the Wonsan airstrip."

The 18th was operating from such a strip during the big enemy break-through last December. Throughout that period 18th pilots smashed enemy roadblocks, traps, and troop positions, support our withdrawing forces."

"When the pilots landed, their planes were refueled and rearmed while they were debriefed. They then climbed back into their readied Mustangs and returned to strike at the enemy again."

"Last November fighter pilots of the 18th encountered the first MIG-15 enemy jets to be seen over Korea. In the first days of that month 18th pilots destroyed two conventional type YAK-3's, five YAK-9's, and probably destroyed two MIG-15's in aerial combat."

"Pilots of the 18th Wing were the first to carry the new tank-demolishing 6.5 rockets into combat. One flight of F-51's equipped with the new rocket and led by Maj. Harry Moreland, was known as "Moreland's Tank Busters" because of their feats."

Night flying was not uncommon with the volunteer group. The pilots flew their Mustangs frequently through the inky darkness searching out enemy troops or equipment. When they spotted headlights, fires, or other tell-tale signs they dove in for the kill."

321

Capt. Bill Crowell stands besides "Porky the Pig," the 18th Group's two seat (barely) piggy back Mustang used for training. From time to time, it also carried a Journalist--Sergeant Sandy Colton--and various ground crew members whose dedicated service in keeping the planes in the air was sometimes rewarded with a combat flight to show them what combat in the Mustangs was really like. (Cook)

to respond and just slept through the raids."

"Charlie" would arrive in the early morning hours, "dropping hand grenades, mortar shells, and strafing the area with a hand held sub-machine gun. No damage was inflicted by this 'bogie' other than a few barked shins, skinned elbows, caused when personnel stumbled over tent ropes en route to their fox holes," the 39th reported.

The Pig

A "big morale booster," the 39th reported in June, "in the maintenance section was the squadron's 'piggy-back' F-51. Many of the airmen had the opportunity to ride in this "T-51" and received the thrill of their lives when the pilot put the plane through a few aerobatics." [10]

In July, "The Pig" was sent to Base Maintenance for a complete reconditioning. "New landing gears, a new radio complete with intercom and a complete reconditioning of the engine put the "Pig" in excellent

condition. With the new paint job and two pigs, patterned after Walt Disney's "Porky" painted on each side of the cockpit, the squadron's "piggy-back" appeared as if it had just come off the factory assembly line."

Rotation Policy

Inconsistency

"Rotation of combat crews completing 100 missions remained its normal, haphazard fashion, some going direct to the Untied States, other going to the Philippines, and still others either remaining in Korea or going to Air Defense Units in Japan," the 39th Squadron reported. "There was no consistency in method of selection for return of these combat crews as in some instances those with only four or five months in the theatre would go direct to the US while others with 26 to 28 months would be required to return to Japan or the Philippines and assignments to a fighter unit there."

Group Combat Crew

Training

"Several officer pilots were assigned to the squadron from the Zone of Interior who where neither proficient in combat operations nor did they have the aggressiveness so necessary for a fighter pilot. So, after intensive training it was found necessary to have them grounded." By the end of June, it had been decided that "the best solution to training these inexperienced combat crews was to establish a Group Combat Crew Training Unit and those needed training would be put through the various phases required to round out their fighter tactics training before assigning them to a flight. This system would take the time and responsibility from the separate units and leave more aircraft available for actual combat operations," the 39th reported.

Instructors for the Group's CCT Unit were 100 mission pilots awaiting reassignment. Each squadron furnished several air-

craft. A gunnery range and bombing range were set up near K-10, the 49th Fighter-Bomber Wing offered the use of its camouflage training area, and "with films of actual combat strikes, the inexperienced pilots were given a well rounded course in tactical operations peculiar to this theatre," the 39th reported.

Morale

Morale "took a jump" following "all the talk of a cease fire," with "every ear bent around the speakers of the radios every time a news cast is on the air. The only glum faces were worn by the 100-mission pilots who still have no word or policy on rotation even though the Group has more pilots than has been seen around here before." The pilots were "particularly bitter" after hearing reports that jet pilots were being rotated. Understandably, they felt "a 100-mission tour in an F-51 type aircraft encompasses more combat time than does a jet tour." [11]

Morale was a big factor during June combat operations. "The flak increase had become oppressive, our losses were heavy as a result and the pilots began thinking so much about flak that it became the main topic of conversation. Everyone was getting nervous as they contemplated missions to areas heavily defended by enemy anti-aircraft weapons." The situation grew to serious proportions when it "brought on a reluctance to press home attacks as they would have in the past, without giving it a thought." Later in the month, as losses fell, the flak danger "began to take a more proper position in the minds of everyone."

Morale for the Airmen came in two flavors. Along working lines it was "excellent...no indications were brought to light during the period whereas anyone was at all dissatisfied with their jobs or working hours." While that generalization is highly suspect, morale is generally high when those fulfilling the mission know their assignment is important—that their buddies are depending on them.

The second flavor of morale involved "rotation." The basic complaint involved "displeasure over changes in policy or lack of a clear-cut policy. The rotation policy to the ZI (Zone of the Interior or Continental United States) still remains vague with automatic extensions of enlistments changing proposed return dates in many cases. The rotation effect on morale has become more acute in view of the new policy preventing rotation to Japan or other stations in the Far East."

The supply of pilots was "excellent"— at the beginning of the month. The 67th had 28 effective pilots exclusive of supervisory personnel. Within three weeks the squadron was down to 16 effectives and "the sortie load on these few became very heavy. Almost all pilots were flying three to four sorties per day at K-16 and the strain was beginning to tell." By the end of the month, the picture was "quite black. Word that many replacements were en route was reassuring, but did nothing to relieve the immediate situation."

The demands of the bureaucracy were also noted. "The immense work load caused by recurring and one-time reports has caused a great hardship on the administrative personnel of this organization. It is felt that many of these can be abolished, and the same results achieved from fewer and more compact reports," Major Colson recommended.

Morale was certainly not helped by continuing shortages in essential equipment and supplies. "Some pilots were required to fly in fatigues or woolen flying suits, which proved very uncomfortable in the warm weather. " One of the biggest reasons for planes being out of commission for parts "was shortage of wing flaps and often times it was necessary to move flaps from one ship to another in order to meet operational commitments," the 39th reported.

Endnotes

[1] USAFHRA. *Monthly Historical Report, 18th Fighter-Bomber Group*, June 1951, p. 3.
[2] USAFHRA. *Monthly Historical Report, 12th Fighter-Bomber Squadron*, June 1951, p. 4.
[3] USAFHRA. *Monthly Historical Report, 39th Fighter-Interceptor Squadron*, June 1951, p. 3.

[4] USAFHRA. *Monthly Historical Report, 12th Fighter-Bomber Squadron*, June 1951, p. 4.
[5] USAFHRA. *Monthly Historical Report, 67th Fighter-Bomber Squadron*, June 1951, p. 2.
[6] USAFHRA. *Monthly Historical Report, 67th Fighter-Bomber Squadron*, June 1951, p. 3.
[7] Adapted from USAFHRA. January 2002. The U.S. Air Force's First War: Korea 1950-1953 Significant Events. June 1951.
[8] USAFHRA. *Monthly Historical Report, 67th Fighter-Bomber Squadron*, June 1951, p. 5.
[9] USAFHRA. *Monthly Historical Report, 67th Fighter-Bomber Squadron*, June 1951, p. 7.
[10] USAFHRA. *Monthly Historical Report, 39th Fighter-Interceptor Squadron*, June 1951, p. 9.
[11] USAFHRA. *Monthly Historical Report, 18th Fighter-Bomber Group*, June 1951, p. 7.
[12] "Mustangs of 18th F-B Wing Nearing Year of Fighting." Air Force Times (Pacific). May 30, 1951, p. 10.

On a wing--
and right rudder

On 8 June 1951, 1st Lt. John Taylor, Jr. of the 39th "Blinker Nose" Squadron, was leading a flight looking for targets of opportunity after completing the pre-briefed mission of bombing a railroad target. In the vicinity of Siboni, he heard another squadron flight radio a message saying their flight leader had been shot down very close to Taylor's location. The other flight did not know if their flight leader had bailed out or not, since the canopy was seen on the ground very close to the burning aircraft.

The element leader and the other two wingmen were afraid to get near or fly by the crash site to find out the leader's fate and make a decision as to whether or not to call for air rescue support.

Taylor confirmed their position and led his flight to the location. "The Mustang was pretty much intact, but burning on both sides of the cockpit area," Taylor recalled. "I told my flight to orbit around 3-5,000 feet AGL [Above Ground Level]. The other element had departed upon the arrival of

Let's See...Parachute, Survival Pack, Carbine. Capt. John Taylor prepares to wedge himself into the cockpit of Lt. Rockmaker's Mustang prior to another mission from K-46. A close look at the unusual "rig" he is wearing reveals that in addition to his parachute, he has attached a survival pack that hangs below the parachute. A carbine nestles behind his right shoulder in a sort of vertical holster. Col. T. C. Rogers, 18th Wing Commander noted in his personal diary that Taylor "was just a little bit different from every one else." Taylor was "not a big man physically, maybe 5' 8", black hair and the bluest eyes you've ever seen. You could spot him a mile away because he wore several bandoliers of ammunition around his shoulders plus wearing a .45-cal. pistol and a small carbine." Taylor explained to Rogers that he carried his arsenal so that should he ever be shot down he could fight his way out of enemy territory. "I believe he would have," Rogers agreed, but "he was never shot down." (Cook)

Taylor's flight.

Taylor made a low pass at about 100 feet off the deck. He thought he saw the pilot still in the cockpit seat, but he could not be sure. He went back for another pass over the aircraft, this time at about fifty feet and "positively identified the pilot in the cockpit of the furiously burning F-51."

He chandelled up in a left climbing turn, clawing for altitude to avoid the guns that had downed the other flight leader. At approximately 1,500 feet, "the same gun position" had him in its sights and hit his Mustang in the left wing with a 37-mm shell. It nearly blew the Mustang out of the air.

Taylor was in a 60-70 degree bank at approximately 200 mph air speed when he was hit.

"I was in a difficult position with no left aileron and significant drag," Taylor recalled. A look at the photograph explains why--the left wing was virtually shot off--only a stub remained attached to the aircraft.

"The aircraft barely responded to my attempts to roll the aircraft level--full right aileron and full right rudder. I fired the six 5-inch HVAR rockets to reduce drag on the left wing and fortunately by then I was descending into a valley and was able to get my wings level about 300-500 feet AGL." With full right aileron and full right rudder the F-51 would roll very, very slowly to the right at 210-220 mph. "I could not maintain level flight below 200 mph and at 230 mph, the vibration became severe," he noted.

With full right rudder and the stick one inch from full right, Taylor "was able to maintain level flight with airspeed pegged at 220 mph." He returned to K-16, which had a 3,500 foot runway of PSP.

"I knew that it would be impossible to maintain level flight with the landing gear down, so that ruled out thoughts of going to K-14 (with 6,000 feet of hard surface runway). I decided that a belly landing on one of the smooth, level sandbars beside the K-16 air strip. It would be best to touchdown at 210 mph (soft sand and high drag conditions)."

Making a series of very cautious right turns, Taylor first made two "practice patterns" over what he considered the best landing area. He then "locked my shoulder harness, rolled the canopy full open, made my approach at 210 mph for best controlled airspeed, throttled to idle [when about ten feet above the sandbar], and slid to a fairly rapid stop."

Significant Events [1]

June 1: Maj. Gen. Frank F. Everest, USAF, assumed command of Fifth Air Force, replacing General Timberlake.

June 2: Captain Kuhn of the Foxy Few "was forced to belly land his aircraft after receiving damage inflicted by enemy ground fire. He was rescued by helicopter, hospitalized for observations, and subsequently reported to full duty status."

June 3: UN antiaircraft guns mistakenly shot down two 315th AD C-119's while the aircraft were attempting a resupply airdrop. This "friendly fire" or fratricide incident led to the adoption of new Identification-Friend-or-Foe (IFF) procedures for airdrop operations.

Lt. O'Briant of the Fighting Twelfth "was seriously injured in an attempted take-off from K-16 in a fully-loaded ship. The aircraft was completely destroyed and Lieutenant O'Briant was immediately evacuated to a hospital in Japan."

June 5: While leading a flight of four F-51s of the 67th Squadron, Col. William P. McBride, "who took command of the Group during the month of June, was struck in the face by automatic weapons fire and had to belly land at K-16. He has been in the Tokyo General Hospital since that date and has had to undergo several operations." [2] Lt. Col. Ralph H. Saltsman, Jr. assumed command of the 18th F-B Group on June 5 and Lt. Col. Henry W. Lawrence "was brought up from the 67th Squadron to serve as Group Executive Officer. Major Carl C. Colson moved from Group Operations to replace Colonel Lawrence as commander of the 67th."

June 7-10: To prepare for upcoming UN ground forces assaults, B-26 and B-29 aircraft conducted radar-directed area attacks against the Iron Triangle at night, dropping 500-pound bombs set to explode over the heads of the enemy troops.

June 10: Lt. Gen. Otto P. Weyland assumed command in Tokyo of Far East Air Forces, replacing General Partridge.

Lt. Col. Thomas D. Robertson, who had commanded the 39th FIS since 30 November 1950 was reassigned to Headquarters FAF as the ALO for the 10th Corps. He was succeeded by Major Murrit H. Davis, formerly of the 41st Fighter-Interceptor Squadron in Japan, an equally capable commander and fighter pilot. All personnel were saddened to lose Colonel Robertson, but the men soon recognized Major Davis' abilities and the unit retained its high level of esprit de corps under the new Squadron Commander.

June 11: An SA-16 of the 3rd ARS made a twilight pickup of a downed F-51 pilot

*The left wing of **Capt. John Taylor's Mustang** was virtually destroyed by a 37-mm anti-aircraft shell. This photograph was taken by a 2 Squadron "Flying Cheetah" pilot after the plane was picked up, returned to the "ramp," and had its landing gear extended. (Taylor)*

Two flights of 18th Wing Mustangs, each fully loaded with bombs, rockets and over 1800 rounds of .50-caliber ammunition, poised for a strike in July 1951. The target for this particular mission was "an enemy airfield which had its runways and revetment areas bomb-cratered and its overhaul workshops riddled."

from the Taedong River near Kyomipo, North Korea. The SA-16, although receiving fire from both sides of the river, made a landing approach without lights, avoiding low electrical transmission lines and rocks and debris on the river's surface. The pilot earned the Distinguished Service Cross for the rescue.

Captain John F. Thompson, E Flight Commander for the 39th FIS, "led his flight to the B-1 area, where the flight dropped 3 napalm bombs. After dropping his napalm, Captain Thompson and his number three man went down to low altitude for reconnaissance work. Captain Thompson started a turn at approximately 300 feet but his aircraft entered into a dive and never recovered, crashing and exploding on the side of a small hill near Choum-ni, Korea. Captain Thompson did not make any radio transmission prior to the crash, but it is believed he was struck and fatally wounded by enemy ground fire." [3]

June 14: When "capping a downed pilot," a Foxy Few pilot, Lt. Perey had to bail out over water. "He was picked up by an SA-16 flying boat and hospitalized for injuries sustained.

June 15: Fifth Air Force moved its headquarters from Taegu back to Seoul.

June 19: 1st Lt. Lee A Harper of the 39th FIS "received ground fire hits in his plane's coolant system while on armed reconnaissance in the B-1 area. Lt. Harper had sufficient altitude for a safe bail out, but for some unknown reason did not and attempted to belly-land his plane on the island of

Kyondong-do. Just before his ship crashed, the flight leader observed an object leave the ship, which was believed to be Lt. Harper but he was at such low altitude the parachute did not have an opportunity to open. A rescue helicopter arrived over the area shortly thereafter and Lt. Harper's body was returned to K-16."

June 20: Twenty-four pilots from the 18th F-B Group engaged 12 enemy aircraft in an air-to-air battle north of Pyongyang. Several pilots were credited with kills, probables and damage.

"B" Flight of the 39th FIS was "briefed to repulse the air support that was to be covering the Communist invasion of the Island of Senmi-do, which is three miles off the western coast of Korea and 75 miles south of the Yalu River. The flight was given top cover by F-86's and while this top cover was engaged in aerial combat with opposing MIG's, two MIG's slipped through and shot the wing off Captain John J. Coleman's F-51 and his plane went down in flames. Captain Coleman, the squadron Personal Equipment Officer, was not seen to jump from his plane prior to the crash." In his "Pilot's Account—Air-To-Air Combat—In Korean Theater," Captain Charles D. Sumner of the 39th reported that at 0655 hours at an altitude of 4,500 feet, ten enemy MIG-15's "came out of high clouds dead astern extremely fast" to attack the 12 Mustangs whose speed was 250 mph. The MIGs made one firing pass and pulled up to the right. The Mustangs "broke left and down keeping our nose pointed at the enemy a/c." The

MIG's firing pass produces "2 strikes on rt. Wing of F-51 at gun bay." The right wing then "broke completely off at the gun bay—destroying the aircraft." In the remarks section of the form, Sumner recommended that the 39th FIS "be equipped with jet a/c if we are to be sent against this MIG—the F-51 is too slow," he concluded as an understatement. [4] Lt. Ray Carter noted that the red nosed MIGs were "aggressive & effective" and fired in two-second bursts. He recommended that "tail radar should be installed." If an F-51 "is attacked from the rear," he noted, "the MIG will pull out in front. If the F-51 breaks up for 3 sec. & to the right (or left) for 3 seconds then completes a fast, barrel roll he will wind up on the MIG's tail between 100 & 300 yds behind." In using this maneuver to use the MIG's superior speed against them, he suggested, "caution must be used in case of an enemy wingman."

June 23: Jacob Malik, Soviet Ambassador to the United Nations, called for armistice negotiations between representatives of UN forces and the communist forces in Korea that would be based upon a demilitarized zone along the 38th parallel.

A "costume party" was held that evening at the Dogpatch Officers Club. A "hillbilly" motif was the highlight of the evening "carried throughout with the limited facilities available." The individual ingenuity displayed by members of this organization, both in costuming and decorating, played no small part in making the party a tremendous success," the Foxy Few monthly report noted. However, another not-so-secret ingredient was at work to improve the success of the party. "American Nurses were imported for the party—the first time in Dogpatch History." [5]

June 24: Two airmen of the 39th FIS armament section "were hurt quite seriously on 24 June at K-16 when one of the [Korean] laborers dropped a box of napalm igniters. S/Sgt Howard T. Heara and S/Sgt Niel D. Irving attempted to pull the exploding box of phosphorus igniters from the hangar to save the aircraft and other ammunition stored in the general area and received severe burns about their face, neck and arms. Both were immediately evacuated to a nearby hospital and are now in the Tokyo Army Hospital where they are reported to be doing very well. Both airmen are being recommended for the Soldier's Medal."

June 25: The 8th FBG moved to Kimpo Air Base in Seoul after completion of repairs to Kimpo's short runway. This marked the resumption of combat operations at Kimpo, although aviation engineers continued their work to restore the main runway.

June 30: A Foxy Few flight "pre-briefed to a road-cut north of Pyongyang, was engaged by a flight of six MIG's. As the friendly flight turned toward the enemy for a frontal attack the MIG's broke off and departed the area, with neither flight firing. The friendly flight continued on their mission as briefed." [6]

Captain Charles D. Sumner, B Flight Commander for the 39th FIS, received heavy damage to his fighter while over the enemy lines, starting a fire in his right wing and wheel well. He nursed the crippled plane back to K-16 and made a beautiful wheels-up landing and then found he could not get

Cobra on the Belly. *Lt. Greg James adjusts parachute straps prior to climbing into Capt. John Taylor's aircraft. Notice that Taylor has had a Cobra--symbol of the 39th FIS "Cobra In The Sky"--painted on the belly of the Mustang. He felt the belly cobra would clank [scare] the North Koreans and the Chinese Communists, recalled Jack Cook. James had previously served with the Oregon Air Guard's 123rd FIS. (Cook)*

Four "Cobras." *Lt. Ernie Wakehouse, Capt. John Taylor, Jr., Capt. Devol "Rock" Brett and Lt. Fred Rockmaker of the 39th FIS. (Cook)*

the canopy off to leave the burning ship. With the assistance of the K-16 crash crew, Lt. Col. Robertson, and several of the squadron's airmen, the canopy was pulled to one side sufficient to jerk Captain Sumner from the burning ship. Other than first and second-degree burns and a sprained back, Captain Sumner survived the close call very well. Lt. Col. Robertson, TSgt Coleman and SSgt Dick of the squadron are being recommended for the Soldier's Medal for their heroic actions in saving Captain Sumner from a seemingly inevitable death." [7]

As of June 30 1951, the 18th Group had flown 16,370 effective combat sorties and logged a total of 36,758 combat flight hours.

Endnotes

[1] USAFHRA 2001. *The U.S. Air Force's First War: Korea 1950-1953 Significant Events.*

[2] USAFHRA. *Monthly Historical Report, 18th Fighter-Bomber Group,* June 1951, p. 2.

[3] USAHRA. *Monthly Historical Report, 39th Fighter-Interceptor Squadron,* June 1951, p. 6.

[4] NARA. Capt. Charles D. Sumner. Headquarters, 314th Air Division, FEAF Operations Analysis Office Pilot's Account of Air-To-Air Combat in Korean Theater. 20 June 1951.

[5] USAHRA. *Monthly Historical Report, 12th Fighter-Bomber Squadron,* June 1951, p. 3.

[6] USAHRA. *Monthly Historical Report, 12th Fighter-Bomber Squadron,* June 1951, p. 3.

[7] USAHRA. *Monthly Historical Report, 39th Fighter-Interceptor Squadron,* June 1951, p.

Combat Losses in June

Captain John Joseph Coleman, 12th Fighter-Bomber Squadron. "B" Flight of the 39th FIS was "briefed to repulse the air support that was to be covering the Communist invasion of the Island of Senmi-do, which is three miles off the western coast of Korea and 75 miles south of the Yalu River. The flight was given top cover by F-86's and while this top cover was engaged in aerial combat with opposing MIG's, two MIG's slipped through and shot the wing off Captain John J. Coleman's F-51 and his plane went down in flames. Captain Coleman, the squadron Personal Equipment Officer, was

Captain Ross Cree, 67th Fighter-Bomber Squadron.

"A South African fighter squadron was also stationed at Chinhae," recalled Major Mario Prevosti, a former pilot with the 12th Squadron. "One of their pilots was a tall, fair-haired young man, who would run up and down the side of the runway for exercise. He did this to maintain his stamina, as he was an Olympic track and field contender for South Africa. Tragically, while he was piloting an F-51 on take off the propeller torque pulled him off the runway. He crashed into four parked Mustangs parked alongside the runway and destroyed them. Sadly, the South African pilot and Olympic contender was killed," Major Prevosti remembered.

not seen to jump from his plane prior to the crash."

Captain Ross Cree, 67th Fighter-Bomber Squadron pilot who was KIA 1 June 1951. "Ross did a helluva good job as a '51 fighter pilot for the 67th," remembered his friend Lt. Col. Duane "Bud" Biteman, "racking up close to 75 successful missions before he was finally sent back to the Philippines for a "rest break" early in January, 1951. Cree returned to Korea in May, 1951 when, as in Biteman's case, it was decreed that all fighter pilots must complete 100

combat missions before they could return to the United States. Cree immediately began flying with the 39th Squadron, out of Chinhae, and Seoul City Airport. Or. 24 May 1951 he was seriously wounded by a .50-cal. machine gun bullet in his arm, just above the elbow. "Fortunately, it tore into the fleshy, lower part," Biteman recalled, "but it made a nasty gash, and was undoubtedly very painful." It was Cree's 90th combat mission. After being in the Far East for almost a full year beyond his "normal" two year overseas tour, he fantasized that he

Rescue Mission Briefed to President Truman

In the summer of 1951, 1st Lt. Robert "Pancho" Pasqualicchio was on a mission with his wing man Max Haney. The pre-briefed target was "up in the Iron Triangle [area formed by Pyongyang, Chorwan and Kumhwa], west of the coastal city of Kansong." A radio call alerted them that "a Mustang was down and the cover pilot needed some more cover because he was running low on fuel."

Pasqualicchio was in the area and headed in the direction of the downed pilot. When he arrived he assumed command of the RESCAP over the downed pilot.

"We checked out the area, making several low passes to make sure the pilot was OK."

The rescue chopper was on the way and "as he went in to pick up the pilot the entire area exploded in machine gunfire that knocked down the chopper. He crashed in the immediate area of the downed pilot. Now we had five airmen on the ground!"

Pasqualicchio called for an additional chopper. Meanwhile, he "trolled the valley and ridge line looking for the machine guns as my wing man was watching the area for muzzle flashes from the enemy gunners. He was successful and we destroyed a least two nests. The next rescue chopper arrived and we extracted all five downed airmen safely."

The mission brought a DFC for Pasqualicchio--and a write-up in the Washington, DC newspapers.

Leonard H. Pasqualicchio of Washington, Pancho's proud father, had been in frequent contact with the White House on matters relative to post WW II Italian-American affairs. On his next visit to the see President Truman, the President asked him if the Captain Pasqualicchio referred to in the newspaper story, was his son.

"On my return home after finishing my missions," Pancho recalled, "I was summoned to the White House and the President asked me to retell the details of the rescue mission. It was a real HONOR. He was great to talk to--like talking to your Dad--he made me feel as comfortable as possible."

Pasqualicchio also recalled that during the Presidential visit, he "was scared sh..less!"

---

might be returned to the 'States' to recuperate. Biteman last saw Cree on May 25th, 1951, with his arm all bandaged and in a sling. He was a little perturbed because he had found that he would not be sent home, but he had resigned himself to going the full 100 missions, and the injury was keeping him grounded while the current Chinese Spring Offensive was underway. "They need me up there" he said, repeatedly, to Biteman. By June 1st, just one short week after being wounded, Cree apparently convinced the Flight Surgeon and the C.O. that his arm was no longer bothering him--it had "healed" enough for him to start flying again. Biteman found that incredibly hard to believe--after just one week on the ground! So Ross Cree, friend and contemporary, took off on another combat mission on the morning of June 1st--just because he thought--"they need me up there!" It was his 91st combat mission in Korea. He

was hit by enemy ground fire even before he could release his bombs or rockets; his airplane simply rolled over onto its back, and he drove his Mustang twenty feet into a fertile rice paddy of North Korea, Biteman explained.

1st Lt. Francis William "Scotty" Escott, 67th Fighter-Bomber Squadron, MIA on 16 June 1951.

1st Lt. A. G. Frisby, 2 Squadron SAAF, was KIA on 22 June 1951. Lt. Bob Frisby was the leader of a four-ship flight assigned an armed reconnaissance mission north of Hanp'o-ri. At a position approximately four miles northwest of Sibyon-ni he radioed that he had been hit and that he was bailing out. His flight saw the canopy come off and a brown object fall from the aircraft. No parachute was seen to open however, and no sign of the pilot was found during an initial and subsequent air search. His aircraft continued on for a period of time, losing height

and drifting to the left until it struck the ground and was destroyed.

1st Lt. Lee A. Harper, of the 39th FIS "received ground fire hits in his plane's coolant system while on armed reconnaissance in the B-1 area. Lt. Harper had sufficient altitude for a safe bail out, but for some unknown reason did not and attempted to belly land his plane on the island of Kyondong-do. Just before his ship crashed, the flight leader observed an object leave the ship, which was believed to be Lt. Harper but he was at such low altitude the parachute did not have an opportunity to open. A rescue helicopter arrived over the area shortly thereafter and Lt. Harper's body was returned to K-16."

Captain Jack Holly Hederstrom, 67th Fighter-Bomber Squadron.

2nd Lt. Terry Liebenberg, 2 Squadron SAAF. 2nd Squadron pilot who was KIA on 9 June 1951. Lt. Liebenberg was a member of a four-ship flight that planned to be wheels up at 0700 from K-10. The Chinhae airbase had a single runway with a nearby parallel seawall. Captain M.J. Uys, Operations Officer of 2 Squadron, asked Lt. Liebenberg whether he was fully prepared for his first combat mission. The answer was a strong affirmative. The last to take off, Liebenberg's Mustang began to drift to the left and finally veered off the narrow runway entirely, away from the seawall, but towards the Control Tower. After the aircraft hit a ditch, the undercarriage collapsed, and the plane hit a parked aircraft near the Control Tower. Lt. Liebenberg died in the immediate inferno. He was buried at the U.N. Cemetery at Pusan, SK.

1st Lt. Bernard D. Percy, 12th Fighter-Bomber Squadron.

1st James J. Schneider, 39th Fighter Interceptor Squadron.

Captain John F. Thompson, 39th Fighter Interceptor Squadron, was KIA on 11 June 1951. Captain Thompson, "E" Flight Commander for the 39th FIS, "led his flight to the B-1 area, where the flight dropped 3 napalm bombs. After dropping his napalm, Captain Thompson and his number three man went down to low altitude for reconnaissance work. Captain Thompson started a turn at approximately 300 feet but his aircraft entered into a dive and never recovered, crashing and exploding on the side of a small hill near Choum-ni, Korea. Captain Thompson did not make any radio transmission prior to the crash, but it is believed he was struck and fatally wounded by enemy ground fire."

Vermont ANG Hero

1st Lt. Scotty Escott

by
Brian Lindner

1st Lt. Francis Scott "Scotty" Escott, with his wife, Elinor and daughter, Patricia. (Lindner)

First Lieutenant Francis William "Scotty" Escott has the unfortunate distinction of being the only member of the Vermont Air National Guard to be Killed In Action in the Korean War. Escott became Missing In Action on 16 June 1951 and remained missing inside North Korea until a full two years after the truce was signed.

"Scotty" Escott was born in Binghamton, NY on 10 December 1924 as the middle son of five boys. In a short autobiography, he noted that except for one bad fall and the normal childhood diseases, it had been "an uneventful boyhood" growing up in Johnson City, NY.

In high school at Johnson City, he was inducted into the National Honor Society and held positions in student government. Eventually he became editor of the high school newspaper. Even at this age, Escott was highly articulate and already known as an excellent writer.

In February 1943, part way through his senior year, he entered the Army Air Force. On 04 August 1944 he was commissioned as a second lieutenant and transferred to flight school where on October 26th he was awarded his wings as a P-47 "Thunderbolt" fighter pilot. Prior to completing his combat training, the war ended and by October of 1945 Escott had returned to civilian life.

Earlier in 1945, he had been stationed at Andrews Field, MD where he met Elinor Lyman, a government junior statistician

from Northfield, VT. The young couple married in April 1946 in Boston, then moved to Johnson City, NY where Escott managed a small jewelry store until being accepted and beginning classes at Norwich University in the following September. Two months later, their only child, Patricia "Patti" was born.

The young family lived in a ramshackle trailer park that the university had set up for married students. Escott worked at the local veteran's home for extra money above and beyond what small amount the GI Bill was providing.

In January 1948 he was accepted as a fighter pilot into the 134th Fighter Squadron of the Vermont Air National Guard based at Ethan Allen Air Force Base in Burlington. In April 1949 he was promoted to First Lieutenant.

"Scotty was a nice, pleasant and well-mannered airman," his former commanding officer, Lt. Col. Rolfe Chickering, VTANG (Ret.), noted in a 1996 interview. "Everybody liked him."

Escott graduated from Norwich in 1950 with an honors degree in English. In January 1951, he received notification from the Air Force that he was being called to active duty and posted to Korea.

By February he was in California for training in the F-51 "Mustang" fighter-bomber. Once again, the Escotts were living in a trailer, but at least it was in a warm climate. When his training schedule per-

mitted, he enjoyed trips to the ocean with Elinor and their five-year old daughter, Patti.

Escott arrived in South Korea on 21 May 1951 and soon exchanged a brief series of letters with Elinor. "My dear thoughtful Scottie," she began and ended with "forever your own." On 22 May she sounded concerned, "the news [about the war] isn't too good. I just heard Lowell Thomas. Is it bad? Be careful my love. Don't take any wild chances."

He purchased some elegant Japanese coats and sent them home, but Elinor wrote him that both she and Patti would wait to model them upon his return. First, he had to survive the required 100 combat missions.

He decided to name his aircraft after his wife and daughter. "How does this sound—'Elie-Pat' To me it rings quaint and a little like gnomes or little fairies," he wrote. "Sounds like Lilliput, a bit," the English major noted, "I didn't want one of you slighted, so I thought the combination would keep you both from making war on me."

In a classic example of fighter pilot élan, he wrote Elinor, "Send me that red slip you have. One of the fellows up here has his wife's white slip around his neck and I'd like to go him one better."

Scotty and Elinor were still very much in love. "Oh, what a kiss—man, oh, man, that's what I'm looking for—more of that," he wrote. "Made my toes curl under and my breath stop—mmm, more please, my love, many, many more."

His letters told her something of a combat pilot's life, but he was careful not to detail the stress and pressure he was under. He was flying several missions a day and was counting each mission toward the day he could go home to Elinor and Patti.

Escott soon had more than thirty missions and on the morning of 16 June 1951, he lifted off with three other 67th Squadron pilots from Seoul's K-16 airbase on an armed reconnaissance mission.

"Following a strafing pass on enemy anti-aircraft positions in the vicinity of Chungham, North Korea, Lieutenant Escott's aircraft began to emit smoke," the Air Force report later noted. "He was warned of this condition and turned his aircraft southward. A short time later while above a fog covered area, he radioed that his engine had quit and he would attempt to reach a point of high ground visible above the fog. At approximately 1200 feet altitude, the canopy was seen to leave the plane. Lieutenant Escott again radioed stating that he would not be able to reach the designated point. The descending plane was then seen to go into a skid to the left in what appeared to be a deliberate maneuver to allow the pilot to abandon the aircraft. At an estimated altitude of 800 feet, a dark object left the cockpit, but, before it could be identified, it and the plane disappeared from view into the fog. Shortly thereafter the aircraft was seen to crash to the ground near Sariwon, North Korea, resulting in its complete destruction without its catching fire. Aerial protective coverage was provided over the area, but failed to locate the missing pilot and was greatly hampered by the prevailing fog condition. Since this accident occurred in enemy territory no ground search could be initiated."

Raymond D. McKelvey of Jacksonville Beach, FL later recalled Escott's downing and the efforts to locate him on the ground: "I never met Scotty, but he is a part of my personal remembrances of my time in the 67th, since I was his replacement in "B" Flight on the day he was shot down. My first mission was not the normal "cherry ride" into a quiet area but rather into the hot area where he was shot down so that we might search for him. I can only recount from the debriefing of flight leaders on his last mission the events of that flight."

"Bridges was the flight commander," McKelvey noted. "Burke flew his wing as #2; Foster led the element as #3; Scotty flew his wing as #4. They were on a low-level armed reconnaissance mission, as the early morning mission, near Sariwon--according to my records. The weather was clear with scattered middle clouds and early morning fog in the valleys. The hilltops were visible above the fog bank. While patrolling and searching for targets, the flight took moderate ground fire."

"The typical formation for such a mission had the leader as close to the surface as possible looking for targets, while the rest of the flight flew a crisscross pattern at about 500' altitude spacing each above the lead. Scotty would have been in an evasive "jinking" pattern at 1500 to 2000 feet over the terrain, changing altitude and direction to present a poor target while maintaining flight integrity."

"I cannot remember whether the flight was on the attack or setting up for attack when Scotty was hit. At the call that he was hit, the flight immediately broke toward friendly territory. Scotty's bird was streaming coolant, and he was forced to either bail out or belly in. He opted to belly in, and disappeared into the thinning fog. The others in the flight searched for his bird, but could not locate it in the poor visibility where he bellied in."

"As soon as the flight returned, I was assigned as Scotty's replacement and we immediately went to search for him in the area where he was last seen going into the fog. In the hour following Scotty's downing the fog had dissipated and we were able to see his bird. Each one of us made an extremely low pass to look into the cockpit. It was completely empty; even the parachute and attached dinghy were missing. We suppressed some ground fire and continued to search , but after about 20 minutes, with the ground fire steadily increasing, Bridges called off the effort, and we destroyed the bird by gunfire. There was no sign at all of Scotty - no 'chute' no flares, no emergency panel - nothing," McKelvey remembered.

The Air Force *Air Crew Casualty Report* concluded, "No sign of life at crashed aircraft or sign of bailout."

Escott's remains were repatriated in 1955 among those returned during Operation Glory. Documents provided by the North Korean government indicated that his remains had been removed from the wreckage and buried about 13 miles away until exhumed and returned four years later. He was buried in Arlington National Cemetery.

Escott continues to serve as an example of the true spirit of the Vermont Air Guardsmen who were called away from home, friends and family—and without complaint did his best on each and every combat mission.

Elinor never remarried and died in 1960. Patti still misses her father.

Wild Bill McBride: Too Close for comfort

By Lt. Col. Duane E. 'Bud' Biteman, USAF (Ret.)

I began to see myself finishing my 100 combat mission 'Tour' about the 1st of June, 1951 and, with a bit of luck, finally to return to the 'States after another ten days to two weeks.

My brief elation was soundly splashed that night, however, when I heard that my good friend Captain Ross Cree had taken a .50-caliber slug in his left arm, effectively grounding him in his race to complete 100 missions. It reminded me that not all hits were fatalities; several of the guys had been wounded pretty badly, and had managed to land their airplanes—many to recover and to fly again.

Colonel William McBride was one of them; he was hit while on a strafing pass—just a day or two after I'd returned for my second series of Korean combat missions. At the time, I wasn't even aware that he was the current 18th Group Commander—I'd just found my name next to his on the Operations Flight Schedule, and when we briefed he introduced himself simply as "Bill

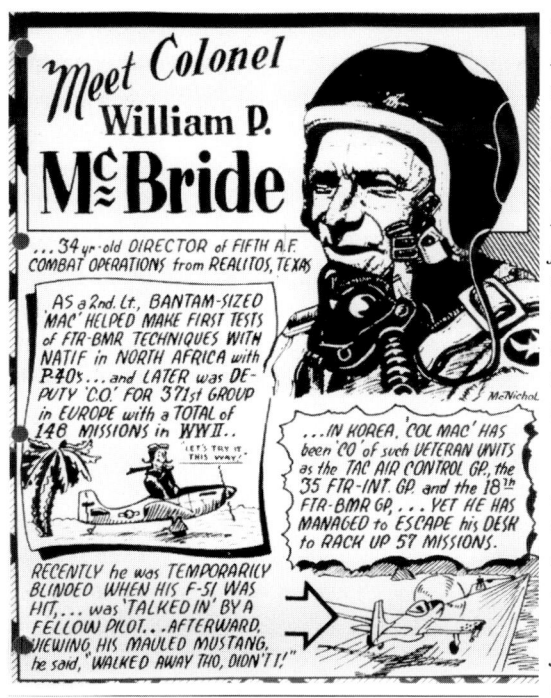

Col. William P. ("Willie Peter") McBride assumed command of the 18th Fighter-Bomber Group from Lt. Col. Homer M. Cox. The change in command "brought many new policies to the 18th and activities were temporarily bogged down until the unit could swing into step with the new commander," the Group's history recorded. The historian then noted, "Colonel McBride's personal drive and magnetism pulled the organizational together rapidly and turned the full force of the unit upon the enemy." His tenure as Group Commander was short. On 5 June 1951, while leading a flight of four F-51s of the 67th Squadron, Col. McBride was struck in the face by automatic weapons fire and had to belly land at K-16. Lt. Col. Ralph H. Saltsman, Jr. assumed command of the 18th F-B Group on 5 June 1951 and Lt. Col. Henry W. Lawrence "was brought up from the 67th Squadron to serve as Group Executive. Major Carl C. Colson moved from Group Operations to replace Colonel Lawrence as commander of the 67th.

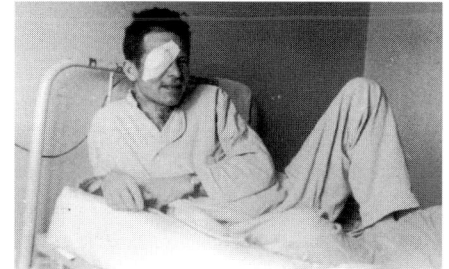

Lt. Col. William P. McBride was evacuated to a hospital in Tokyo for surgery on his eye. Several days later, he was visited in his hospital room by members of the 39th FIS, his former command prior to the 18th Fighter-Bomber Group. (Schiebel)

McBride's aircraft was heavily damaged, but he survived thanks to extraordinary airmanship by himself and his wingman, Captain Duane "Bud" Biteman. (Pasqualicchio)

McBride."

I was flying McBride's wing when it happened; or at least I was trying to fly his wing.

Like many old-time Colonels, McBride didn't seem to pay much attention to my position as his wing man; Colonels just naturally expected wingman Captains to do whatever was necessary to stick with them as they zigged and zagged at minimum altitude thru the narrow mountain canyons.

As a result, when I flew with 'Wild Bill' it was all I could do to manage to stay with him, and out of the way of his F-51 Mustang, because he was as apt as not, to turn right into me during his intensive search for targets, sometimes making me chop my throttle and pull-up into a sharp turn to keep from colliding with his airplane. Conse-

quently, on those few missions when I flew a Colonel's wing, I concentrated on my formation techniques, not on my own bombing or strafing attacks.

On the specific day in question, I was following Colonel McBride down a railroad track where we had seen a locomotive and a string of boxcars race into a short tunnel. As he prepared to skip his bombs into the tunnel, I decided to trigger my bombs off at the same time because, with the narrow canyon, I knew I'd have to pull up early to avoid flying through his bomb blast.

McBride made a good skip-bomb, right into the mouth of the tunnel, and I toggled mine off when I saw his release, then went into a steep climbing turn to the right. McBride climbed steeply straight ahead—

right over the top of a ridge above the tunnel, then made a wide climbing 180 degree turn to position himself for a rocket attack against the opposite end of the tunnel. He dropped low as he lined up with the track leading into the mouth of the tunnel, where he salvoed his six rockets right into the opening, then pulled up once again, directly over the top of the low ridge.

I tried to align my airplane to follow the same path down the track into the narrow canyon, but was caught swinging wide on the outside of the turn, and was not able to take satisfactory aim on the tunnel entrance, so I pulled off into a climbing right turn, preparing to make another pass to launch my rockets into the opening.

However, as McBride skimmed across

the top of the ridge at minimum altitude, he took a burst of small arms fire into the right panel of his windscreen, shattering the Plexiglass and stinging him alongside his right eye. He was wounded, but couldn't yet know how badly.

He immediately turned south, away from the target, and called to advise me that he'd been hit, and to confirm that I was still with him. I had him in sight and quickly pulled off of the target and added full power in an attempt to catch up with him, as he poured on full throttle, heading southeast for home at high speed. I was gradually able to overtake him, despite the fact that I was still carrying my rockets, which I quickly disarmed as I pulled into formation on his right wing.

We were only about twenty minutes northwest of Seoul's K-16 airstrip when McBride was hit, and close enough to the front lines to be fairly certain to reach friendly territory if he were forced to bail out. We climbed to about 4000 feet as Bill assessed his wounds.

He'd been hit with a relatively small caliber bullet, which went into the scalp next to his right temple and eye. He was bleeding profusely from the wound and could not see out of his right eye, but despite the beginning onset of a state of shock, he was still able to concentrate on keeping his airplane level and on a general course heading toward Seoul.

As we neared the airstrip at K-16, I pulled into close formation on his right wing, and asked him how he thought his eyes would be for a landing. He reported that he couldn't see a thing out of his right eye, and his vision from his left was somewhat blurred. He tried to read his airspeed indicator, but couldn't focus on the numbers. He would never be able to land by himself, I thought, so I slid underneath his airplane and pulled ahead on his left side. I then asked if he could see me well enough to fly formation on the final approach—he agreed that would be better than trying to make it on his own.

So, with 'One-eyed' McBride, half-blinded and losing blood from his wound, tucked in very close on my right wing, I verbally warned him by radio what I was about

to do, then slowly eased back on my throttle. He bobbled around a bit, once surging forward as if to chop my wingtip with his propeller, but managed to stay in close position on my wing. Then, when our airspeeds had dropped off sufficiently, I called, "Gear Down ...NOW." He bobbled around a bit once more, as his gear doors opened and his landing gear came out; then he tucked in close on my right wing once again. I called to tell him that he had three good gear, and told him to prepare to lower half landing flaps. By this time we were lined up about five miles southwest of the short 3200 foot K-16 airstrip. Because of a brisk northeasterly wind, we'd have to make our final

approach down between the maze of towering smoke stacks—we didn't dare try for a downwind landing from the other direction, which had a better, more clear approach zone; because the wind was too strong, and the runway too short.

I could see McBride trying to wipe the blood from his right eye with his throttle hand—his left hand; he had to keep his right hand on the control stick at all times to maneuver his airplane. Slowing to about 125 mph, I called, "Half Flaps—NOW!" Then, moved my flap handle down to the half-down detent.

McBride's airplane bobbled close to my right wing momentarily, and I had to again

Col. Ralph H. "Salty" Saltsman assumed command of the 18th Fighter-Bomber Group following Col. McBride's injury during a mission. Saltsman had been assigned to the 18th Wing in April 1951 as Executive Officer to Lt. Col. Homer Cox, 18th Wing Commander. Saltsman would return to the Philippines in early November 1951.

A Lowly Mustang

I'm only a lowly Mustang,
There are many virtues I lack.
I don't have the grace of an '80,
And my wings are not swept back.

I'm away from home in Korea;
A misplaced bastard at best…
For according to Hoyle and the "News Hawks,"
My bolts should be laid to rest.

"The jets are the hope of the future,"
The newspaper headline cries.
They won't waste a two-inch insert,
When a Mustang pilot dies.

But I can't understand the clamor,
That roars o'er Korea land,
When enemy tanks are sighted,
Or the Commies make a stand.

I never hear the word "Sabre,"
Or "Shooting Star" called in the hue.
It's always the same old story…
"Get those Mustangs into the Blue."

I think perhaps part of the answer,
And I'm sure you know what I mean,
Lies in the fact that my pilots
Never learned the word "Josephine." [1]

But by far the lowest blow came—
Broke my Packard [2] heart in two.
Was the day I staggered from '16, [3]
Carrying napalm to Sinanju.

"Jets strike the enemy's airfields,"
The papers screamed the next day.
They must have left ere I got there,
Is the only thing I can say.

There was hardly a building a-smoking;
The flak was heavy and true.
'Twas the only day I ever wished
To be smaller a foot or two.

But the heaviest blow came later.
'Twas the day I wished to have died.
I was sold out by the "world's greatest pilot,"
Also known as Colonel McBride. [4]

[1] Josephine—low on, as in Josephine Ammo or Josephine fuel.
[2] The F-51 Mustang had a Packard engine.
[3] K-16 airstrip near Seoul, the 18th's advance operating base until it moved to K-46.
[4] Col. William P. McBride, Commander of the 35th FIW.

Col. Ralph Saltsman considers "A Lowly Mustang," to have been written by someone in the 35th Fighter Interceptor Wing "to lament that Group's loss of the F-51's for the 'inferior' F-80 jets." Such a transition might have been engineered by the "feisty," somewhat diminutive Texan Colonel McBride prior to his leaving Japan. The 18th Group was proud of its Commanders, Saltsman noted, because they "were not desk bound brass, but pushed the throttle as good as the next zoomie." As the song suggests, if McBride considered himself the "world's greatest fighter pilot," then he certainly found the right home with the "world's greatest fighter Group," Saltsman said, closing the issue for history.

add power quickly to keep him from hitting the wing tip with his prop, then I saw him drop back suddenly.

He had missed the "half-flap" detent, and had put down Full Flaps. "No Sweat," I thought, that'll slow him down faster when he wants to reduce power. But I then heard the sudden roar of his engine as he jammed his throttle forward to catch up with me, just before I slowly started a long, gradual descent toward the short, rough airstrip on the little sand island in the Han River.

I called out my airspeeds as we gradually slowed our glide speeds: "140—135—135—130—130—One-twenty-five—120—120—120—One-oh-five—105—one-oh-five…" I did not dare drop the airspeed any lower until we were over the threshold of the runway and in a safe position for landing.

He was rough on his controls, trying to hold position on my right wing as I began a flare-out—off to the left side of the landing strip, so that McBride could fly over the center of the runway. Finally, as we slowed to ninety mph and he was in a nose high attitude over the end of the runway, I called him to, "CHOP IT," and pushed my throttle full forward to start my go-around.

Colonel Bill McBride was one of the very

lucky ones.

He'd been hit by a .30-caliber slug, which had penetrated the skin next to his skull, barely missing his right eye—and had lodged there. Stunned and temporarily blinded, he was able to bring his airplane back and, after but a week in the hospital, his eyes were again almost as good as new and he was out flying combat missions again.

Major General William P. McBride, USAF, retired with his wife Connie, in Austin, Texas, until his death at age 79 on 8 June, 1996.

Excerpted with permission from "Korean Tales, Unsung Heroes of the Korean Air War."

The End, Finis! Enough!
100 Low Altitude Combat Missions—Done!

By Lt. Col. Duane E. 'Bud' Biteman, USAF (Ret.)

We were greatly relieved then, on Monday evening, May 28th, when the skies finally began to clear, and the Weather Forecaster predicted that we would not have too much difficulty getting through to the bomb-line the next morning—as long as we stayed low, over the water, close along the west coast.

That's exactly what we did. 'Snuck under' the low scud all the way up to the North Korean transportation center of Chinnampo for some search and destroy attacks along the railroads, where they weren't expecting us so soon, while the rain and scud clouds were still hanging low in their areas.

After landing at K-16 for reloading, we went out again on our usual road-cutting ventures into the central mountains. The weather socked-in again on the 30th, seriously limiting the number of flights we were able to get out of our little airstrip near Seoul.

Then, after aborting a morning multi-flight mission to Sinuiju with a rough engine and poor radios (or 'jangled nerves,' I'm not too sure which, one of the very, very few aborted missions of my entire tour), I was unable to schedule another mission that afternoon, and had to chalk up the whole day as "wasted."

I made up for it on May 31st, however, by completing two long ones up to the Yalu River area of Sinanju and Anju—and, regretfully, bringing back unpleasant memories of my prior flight to Anju, in October, 1950, when I realized I was getting the "clanks" and was psychologically not able to lead three novice pilots into such a 'hot' target—an unpleasant memory that refused to go away!

But with luck, one more day should do it. I walked over to the Operations tent to verify the flight schedule for Friday, June 1st, making sure that the Ops Officer had me on deck for two, and possibly three missions.

He assured me that I could have two and, if I could keep my airplane running and flyable, I could have another while taking the Mustang down to Chinhae after the third—and my last—100th combat mission.

I was especially careful the next morning, during my preflight check of the dusty, dirty-looking old airplane; I checked it thoroughly from stem to stern. I didn't want to push my luck at that final stage of the game.

Our target was reported to be railroad traffic moving between Kyomipo and Pyongyang—which didn't enthuse me too greatly, 'thinking of the heavy flak concentrations in that area, and my vivid recollection of the polka-dot skies over Sinmak. We found our train, about halfway between the two cities, however, well out of the heavy flak areas, and proceeded to bomb, rocket and strafe it just before it could reach the protection of the nearest tunnel.

Despite the lack of any visible ground fire, I made sure that I "jinxed" my airplane around the sky every few seconds—like it might have had "St. Vitus Dance," to make sure that no eager gunner could get off a lucky shot at me.

Our second mission, just before 1000, took us over to the Haeju area, just north of the 38th Parallel, near the west coast, where one of our pilots was reportedly shot down by ground fire. His wingman had seen him bail-out, but was too low on fuel to remain with the downed pilot until he reached the ground.

We arrived in the vicinity he described, within just a very few minutes after the report, but, as much as we searched, we could find no signs of the parachute. Finally, after thirty minutes of looking, we had to give up and head north, toward Sariwon, to get rid of our load of armament.

We made some good road cuts in the hills south of the city, then rocketed some rolling stock in the rail yard on the outskirts of town. With that, we went back toward Haeju, hoping to see something of the downed pilot. Again, no luck. So we went back to K-16 for landing and reloading.

Upon landing, I was informed that Harry Moore, a good, longtime friend from the 67th days at Clark, had been jumped by four MIG jets, and had been shot down somewhere near Chongju. There was no hope that he could have survived, even if he had been able to bail out.

Then, less than thirty minutes later, we received word that Ross Cree, flying his first mission since having been wounded, was shot down while making his skip-bombing run. He'd 'just rolled over and piled into the ground,' was the way his wingman described it.

"What a shame—what a damn, damned shame," I thought. "A damned, damn filthy, dirty shame"!! Two good, close friends killed within just a few minutes of each other—neither of which should have been flying combat again in Korea!

They should have been back in the 'States training replacement pilots, or manning the new Air Defense squadrons—anything except flying additional combat missions in Korea.

I had to wonder, too, just who in the name of heaven, had cleared Ross Cree to fly again so soon after taking such a serious wound to his arm—it had been less than ten days; he could not possibly have healed enough. Surely, the Flight Surgeon must have known! Or had Ross even talked to the Flight Surgeon?

Knowing his eagerness to get back into the war, to finish his final 18 missions, it wouldn't have surprised me one iota if Ross had taken off his sling and simply faked recovery with the Assistant Operations Officer at Chinhae, to 'con' him out of an airplane and a slot on the mission.

After a bite of late lunch I was ready for my third mission of the day and, barring a "falling down of the heavens"—my final combat mission of the Korean War. The Ops Officer had set me up to lead a flight of two on a road-cutting mission a few miles north of Haeju—just barely over the front lines. I was to find my own targets, bomb them from whatever altitude that I chose, launch my rockets where-ever and when-ever I so desired, and, if I still felt brave, could strafe whatever I felt up to! In other words, the mission and its degree of danger, was being left completely up to my judgment—I could play it just as cool as my conscience and my nerves would allow.

As I fired up the big Rolls Royce Merlin engine that afternoon of June 1st, 1951, it didn't cross my mind for an instant that it was to be the last time I would go through that routine, nor that it would be the last time I would make my cockpit-check around that so-familiar little "office"—for that was to be the last time in my long career that I would be flying the venerable F-51 Mustang.

I probably should have thought about those little, but significant milestones in my flying career—but I didn't. And, at the time, if I had thought about it at all, I probably would have, instead, thought, "Good Riddance"!

"True", the Mustang had been good to me—carried me over the deepest of the oceans and around the highest of the mountains—from the 'Hump' of China to the unmeasured depths of the Philippine Sea—and had always brought me home safely, despite the holes I'd allowed into her—but on this last trip, my nostalgia was displaced by my concern for one last request...

"One more time, Lord; please, just one more time!

Weather conditions in my target area were close to perfect. Winds were gentle and coming from the west.

I had no reason to question the dive-bombing factors as I lined up over a road in a narrow canyon in the hills north of Haeju. At 8000 feet I rolled over, lined up on the road and, as I passed through 4000 feet, triggered off my two 500-pound GP bombs. As I pulled out, keeping well-clear of the nearby hills, I could see a good blast right in the middle of the steep mountain road. A good hit.

My wingman, a new replacement fresh from Japan, had a near miss, but I was not about to be critical—not on this mission. We wandered around over the hills, looking for possible rocket targets and, finding nothing of particular interest, I decided to launch my rockets into a tunnel on the railroad north of Haeju"—there's always something hiding in a tunnel."

I chose a tunnel with a nice clear, open approach, one that would not limit my 'jinxing' in and out, then, with one big salvo and a quick pull-up, the rockets exploded inside—hitting "I know not what"--but something, was sure.

We then dropped over to the nearby vicinity where the pilot had been reported down on the previous mission that morning, and, lo and behold, hanging from a tall cottonwood tree I could see a tall-white parachute. I thought sure that we had searched that same area on the previous mission, without seeing the 'chute. But, then again, maybe the long plume of the white nylon had been screened by the trees, and our search passes had come from the other direction.

On the other hand, there had recently been reported instances of the Chinese Reds purposely setting out decoy parachutes in an area where one of our planes had been shot down—for the sole purpose of snaring our low, slow-flying searchers as they came down to see if the pilot was still in the parachute harness.

The thought of a possible trap came immediately to mind, and I was leery of letting myself get caught in such a no-win situation on my 100th mission.

My first reaction was to remain above 3000 feet, make a good note of the location, and to simply report the 'chute sighting to 'Mellow Control.' They could send another flight in to look over the area again,

or maybe send a busy helicopter from Kimpo Air Base, and hope for a pick-up.

After all, if it was a trap, no small arms would hit me if I stayed up at altitude—and there probably would be no pilot in the harness, anyhow—or, if there was, he would probably be already dead—if it was a trap.

I tried my very best to rationalize in my own mind not going down to look closer--but my conscience wouldn't let me off the hook that easily. On the other hand, if the parachute was not a trap, the pilot could be still alive, and hanging in the harness, unable to cut himself free until someone came out to help him—and, until now, I was apparently the only person who knew the exact location of his 'chute.

I knew then that I had to go down for a look—trap or no trap.

Calling to my young wingman to stay high, and to keep a good lookout for small arms fire, I dove into a wide arc, looking for any signs of vehicles or troops as I dropped to treetop height, slowing my speed to about 175 mph over a cleared meadow which led over to the parachute tree at the edge of a wooded area.

Then, as I neared the 'chute,' I would pull up and roll over into a steep bank for a good view.

I did just that. And, as I pulled up to check the parachute, I could see clearly that the harness, which hung close to the trunk of the tree, about twenty feet from the ground—was empty. The pilot had undoubtedly been able to climb from limb to limb, and down to the ground. There was obviously nothing more that I could do for him at the moment, not knowing which direction he might have run to hide.

After a wide, easy climbing turn toward the south, we were soon over friendly lines again, and heading for Seoul. I called K-16 Tower and passed on to them the report of our sighting of the parachute, and its precise location, asking them to phone it to Mellow Control. I noted that no ground fire had been observed on my low pass, and that a helicopter should have no trouble getting into and out of the area—if they could locate the pilot, who had, no doubt, taken cover nearby.

Then I asked the tower for 'clearance to make a low pass over the runway for a "Hundred Mission Gear Check." They responded with an immediate "Clear for a high-speed gear check."

I pulled up sharply after missing the Operations tent pole by a scant ten feet, then, in a steep climb, I proceeded to barrel roll until my nose fell back to the horizon, at which time I rolled level and turned southward toward the Naktong River and Chinhae.

It was over—I had done it!

I was heading back for landing from my 100th Korean combat mission. All I had yet to do was to navigate the familiar hundred odd miles, over friendly territory, to our home base at Chinhae, where I must then land the F-51 without hitting the hangar, and without putting the landing gear over the seawall, taxi back to the parking area, shut down the engine and climb out— "finished"—"done"—"all through"—and most surprisingly, still alive!

My fuel supply was more than adequate, and the clear springtime sun was settling gently over the sea toward mainland China as the southern shore and its pretty coastal islands came into view. I toyed with the idea of requesting another "100 Mission Gear Check" at Chinhae, but by then I was beginning to feel awfully tired—that strange, anchor-dragging weariness that comes at the end of a long, tense period of stress.

By the time I had swung around onto my initial approach for landing, and had chopped the throttle and turned from downwind to base leg, I found it to be a major physical effort to reach down by my left shin to move the landing gear handle to the "Down" position.

The realization of my fatigue told me: "Hey there, Buddy, stay alert— you're not on the ground yet!"

And with that, I again became extra-cautious as I guided the frisky little airplane down onto the bumpy, steel-planked runway, with the sea-splashed seawall just a few yards to the left. My wheel-first landing was as smooth as the PSP surface would allow, and I made sure my tailwheel was centered as I lowered the tail with my decreasing

1951
18th Fighter-Bomber Wing Chronology

July - December

United Nations Summer-Fall Offensive
July 9-November 27, 1951

Second Korean Winter
Nov. 28, 1951-
April 30, 1952

18th Fighter Bomber Group based at K-10/Chinhae
Flying combat missions from K-16 /Seoul

18th Fighter Bomber Group based at K-10/Chinhae.
Flying combat missions from K-46/Hoengsong

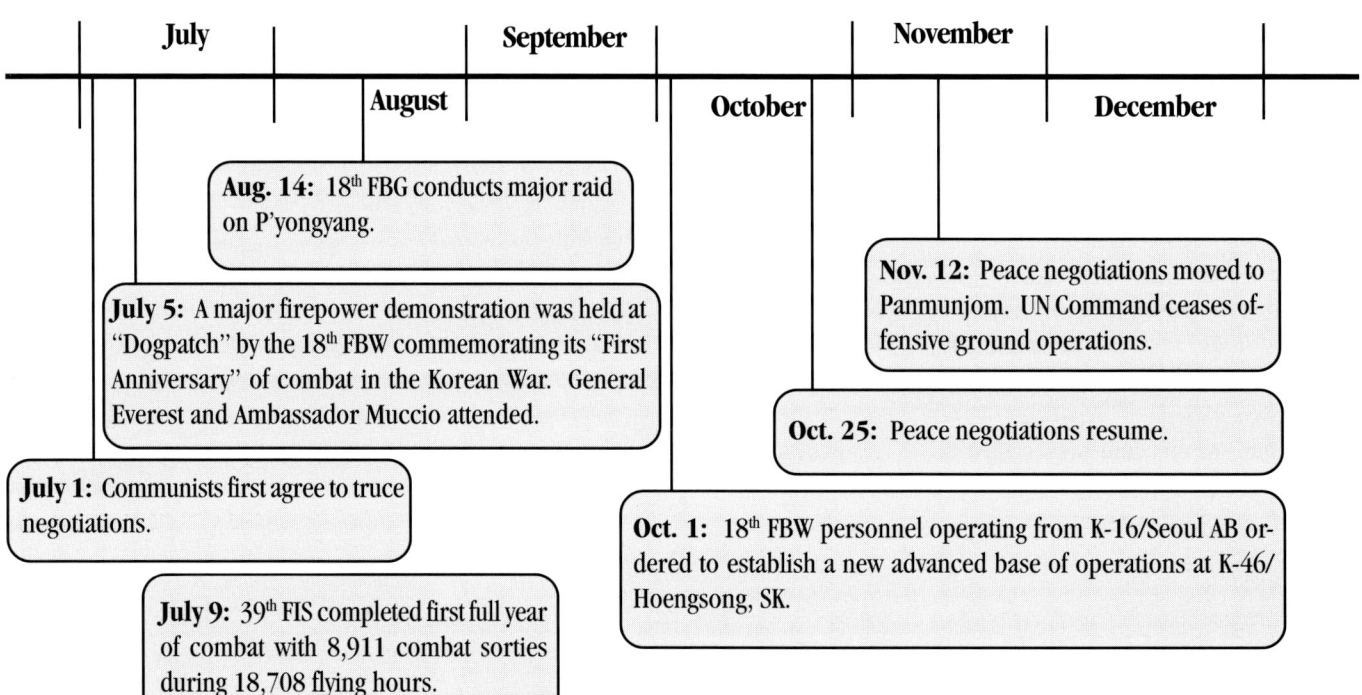

July   September   November

August   October   December

Aug. 14: 18th FBG conducts major raid on P'yongyang.

July 5: A major firepower demonstration was held at "Dogpatch" by the 18th FBW commemorating its "First Anniversary" of combat in the Korean War. General Everest and Ambassador Muccio attended.

July 1: Communists first agree to truce negotiations.

July 9: 39th FIS completed first full year of combat with 8,911 combat sorties during 18,708 flying hours.

Nov. 12: Peace negotiations moved to Panmunjom. UN Command ceases offensive ground operations.

Oct. 25: Peace negotiations resume.

Oct. 1: 18th FBW personnel operating from K-16/Seoul AB ordered to establish a new advanced base of operations at K-46/Hoengsong, SK.

Aug 29: 18th Wing completed 25,000 combat sorties, the first FEAF unit to reach this level.

speed. Then, testing my brakes lightly, I slowed and taxied carefully back to my designated parking space.

With a great sigh of relief, I pulled the Mixture control lever to Idle Cut-Off and, as the big prop stopped turning, reached over to turn off the Magneto, Ignition and Battery switches.

And there, at Chinhae, South Korea, on the evening of June 1st, 1951, I ended my final flight in North American Aviation's F-51 Mustang, after logging eight hundred and twenty career flying hours in what is probably the finest, most efficient little flying

machine ever produced.

As I climbed wearily from the cockpit with my total of 100 Korean combat missions (in 190 combat hours), I was greeted by the Crew Chief with a cold can of beer and a hearty, "Congratulations, Captain!"

It was over. I had done it. I had lived through it without a scratch!

Forty-five combat missions flown in just 19 flying days!

My very first stop, the first thing the next morning, was to be a visit to the Group Per-

sonnel Officer—they now had no more excuses for not printing a set of orders sending me back to the United States—and the sooner they got started on it, the better I would feel.

I walked to the Operations Office to check in. I needed to stretch my stiff legs. And with each step I felt better—and better—and better—and better!

DAMN, but it was GREAT TO BE ALIVE!!

Excerpted with permission from "Korean Tales, Unsung Heroes of the Korean Air War."

July 1951

"This is our greatest hope—that the blows struck here in Korea may help not only to win our war but also to prevent the next war."

President Syngman Rhee

A Year In Combat

The 18th Fighter-Bomber Wing had now been in combat for a year.

The 39th Fighter-Interceptor Squadron reported that it "rounded out a full year of combat against the North Korean and Chinese Communist forces in July, 1951. The squadron has had a complete turn-over of officer personnel in this one year period, changed from F-80C to F-51D fighter aircraft, has moved a total of eight times within Japan and Korea, and has become a tactical unit the Air Force could depend upon to put all its aircraft over the target area when called upon."

The four flying squadrons of the 18th FB Group were beginning to feel the pinch caused by the loss of key personnel to rotation and not enough replacements arriving. This was particularly true for those sections "required to maintain joint operations at both K-10 and K-16, the forward operating location since late March, 1951."

The problem of maximum utilization of manpower with a minimum of personnel was further aggravated by the all too necessary "rest and relaxation" program which allowed airmen three days pass in Japan every six to seven weeks. Engineering, Armament, Operations, Personal Equipment and Intelligence were required to keep sufficient personnel at both operating locations with no personnel augmentation for working at both bases. However, by constantly juggling personnel from one base to another to keep the "R&R" program in effect or to allow airmen to meet promotion or Career AFSC up-grading boards, the unit somehow managed to keep its expected high level of efficiency."

July Combat Operations

Overall, however, the month of July "was the most stable of any since the Group arrived in Korea."

Tactics during July "were little changed. Missions were flown with predominantly four ship flights, on close support and

Monthly Summary

After over a year of heavy fighting, July 1951 marked the beginning of a new phase in the Korean War. From that point on strategic military considerations for commanders on both sides would center on armistice negotiations that began in July. Strategies and operations for both sides would be focused on military actions designed and undertaken to bring about favorable outcomes in the negotiations. Colonel Ralph H. Saltsman, Jr., former Commander of the 18th Fighter-Bomber Group in 1951 noted, "the introduction of armistice negotiations at Kaesong definitely changed the tempo of all military operations in the Korean War, which would continue until the cease-fire in May 1953."

As a direct result of this strategic shift, FEAF increased the tempo of fighter and light bomber activities. It was named Operation Strangle and was directed in particular against vehicular movements and targets of known troops, supplies and installations. However, from the outset, Operation Strangle had problems getting "both hands" around the enemy's throat.

The numbers of MiG-15 aircraft operating over North Korea were increasing dramatically and their pilots were experienced and competent. Dodging US jet fighters escorting FEAF B-29s, the MiGs went after vulnerable fighter-bomber and reconnaissance aircraft operating north of Pyongyang. As the numbers of Communist aircraft increased, Air Force Chief of Staff Gen. Hoyt Vandenberg was telling FEAF Commander, General Weyland that he could not expect further augmentation in jet fighters. A general build-up in Europe required more aircraft. Also, General Weyland knew that other types of aircraft, including B-26s and F-51s, were not only experiencing high attrition rates, but they could not be replaced because they were no longer in production.[1]

On July 1st, the Democratic People's Republic of Korea Premier, Kim Il Sung agreed to participate in truce negotiations. The first conference of the armistice negotiations was held at Kaesong, thirty miles northwest of Seoul on July 10th.

Adapted in part from U.S. Air Force Historical Research Agency. January 2002. The U.S. Air Force's First War: Korea 1950-1953 Significant Events. July 1951. http://www.au.af.mil/au/afhra/wwwroot/korean_war/korean_war_chronology/kwc_1951.html

Preparing For Another Strike. *Mustangs from the 67th and 39th Squadrons returning from missions were met by highly skilled loading crews and mechanics to ready them for another strike. Carts of 5-inch rockets and .50-caliber machine gun ammunition pull up, and armorers will have the fighter bombers ready for another flight in an average time of seven minutes, according to Air Force sources. (NARA)*

armed reconnaissance against enemy troops, supplies, vehicles, and gun positions. There was still rail and road cutting, but caution was necessary in the reconnaissance areas due to the ever-increasing flak. The proportion of napalm to 500-pound bombs used increased during this month."
[1]

The number of combat missions flown in July was down by one-third from the previous month for all squadrons. The decrease was "attributed primarily to the monsoon season with resultant poor flying weather," the 12th Squadron reported. Eleven aircraft were lost that month, four in combat.

The delayed rainy season brought poor flying weather over the target areas during much of the month," the 39th Squadron re-

ported, "and at one time caused a three day stand-down, the longest let up in tactical operations since the unit entered the Korean War. In spite of adverse weather conditions the squadron was successful in meeting most of its commitments which consisted mostly of road cuts, armed reconnaissance missions and some close support missions. Limited ground force activity during the month reduced the number of close support sorties considerably."

In an effort to "improve the effectiveness of the unit and place more responsibility upon flight commanders," the 39th reported, "All flight leaders were held responsible for the assessing of their flight's latest gunnery film and to give other members of the flight constructive criticism when they returned to K-10 for a few days of rest.

Flight leaders were also required to closely coordinate the activities of their flight while at K-10 in order to schedule them for such details as Runway Control, Naktong Gunnery Range Officer, Firing-In Butt Range Officer, etc."

The main supply shortage for the Group "continued to be in personal equipment," the 39th Squadron reported, "summer flying suits. The only flying suit presently available was the very thick nylon suit, but was reported to be very dangerous as it afforded no protection against fire since it would burst into flames and fuze against the skin. A few cotton suits were substituted and the remainder of the pilots were required to either wear the nylon suit or herringbone twill one piece fatigues."

Nettled by "numerous cases of buzzing
(Continued on p. 340)

"Unique Mission..."

In early July, "what should have been an ordinary mission, turned out to be the most unique mission flown by the 18th Fighter-Bomber Wing since its arrival in Korea in the early part of July 1950," S/Sgt Dick Shingledecker enthused in the 30 July issue of *Truckbuster*.

Three F-51 Mustang fighter pilots of the 18th had flown 99 missions each and one South African Air Force pilot had 74 missions. Each flyer had one mission to go, Truckbuster reported. The required number of missions for American pilots in the Korean Theatre at that time was 100; while pilots of the 2 Squadron SAAF flew 75 before their combat tour ended.

The "interesting part of the flight," the Truckbuster article noted, "was the fact that each were members of different squadrons in the Group."

"Because of the bad weather that covered most of Korea recently, the four men were grounded for two days waiting for the mission that completed their tours. All four agree it did some talking to get the final okay to fly together."

The final "weather reconnaissance" flight leader was 1st Lt. Clarence L. Burke of Sweeny, Texas, a 25 year old member of the 67th Squadron, the "Fighting Cocks."

Flying wingman for Burke was 1st Lt. William I. Crowell of Charlotte, North Carolina, 34 (a bit old for fighter pilot), and a member of the "Blinking Nose" squadron. Crowell had arrived in Korea the first of the year and "wore a grin that covered his face" when he climbed from his aircraft and said, "I have been looking forward to this mission for six months." The "slightly graying" fighter pilot had previously spent two

months on the front lines as a Forward Air Controller, directing fighter strikes on enemy positions.

The last mission for the four flyers was primarily a "weather recce" during which they found a hole in the low hanging overcast and successfully made a road cut and three rail cuts southwest of Haeju, on the west coast of Korea.

The element leader was Captain Henry H. Livingston, Jr. of Columbia, South Carolina--a member of the "Tiger Teeth" Squadron, the Foxy Few. The 27-year old veteran explained the last mission "was one of the easiest missions of my tour, no ground fire or enemy aircraft bothering us while on our bombing and rocketing runs."

Commandant R.F. Armstrong, Commander of the 2 Squadron, flew Number Four position, better known as "the slot." Armstrong, of Pretoria, South Africa, was a WWII veteran with 125 missions. "I enjoyed flying with the American pilots very much. It was the first time I have ever flown with them but I have worked with them both here in Korea, and during the Second World War."

The joint operation, "the first of its kind in the 18th, came to a successful conclusion when the four ship flight came low over the airstrip prior to forming in the landing pattern. Each plane with its distinctive unit markings made a formal farewell salute to ground crews."

After the landing, ground crew personnel and fellow fighter pilots crowded around the flyers, "offering their congratulations before crew chiefs, armament and refueling crews took charge of the Mustangs, readying them for another mission against North Korean Communist armies."

After the press and VIP flurries were over, the entire operation was summed up by one of the Sergeants running the "cherry-picker," who looked over at Coomer's Mustang that still had the sign with the number of missions attached beside the cockpit. "Twenty five thousand," the Sergeant said, shaking his head in disbelief. "That's a hellofa lot of trips across that bombline!"

New Centurians. The four new Centurians from each squadron assigned to the 18th Group stride back to the post-mission briefing with well deserved grins. (L-R) Captain Henry H. Livingston, Jr., 12th Squadron, 1st Lt. Clarence L. Burke, 67th Squadron, Commandant R.F. Armstrong, Commander of the 2nd Squadron SAAF, and 1st Lt. William I. Crowell, 39th FIS Squadron. (Cook)

Napalm Hit On Railroad Yard. A railroad marshalling yard at Masen-ni, North Korea takes a napalm hit on July 11, 1951, setting a supply stockpile ablaze on a loading platform. Rockets and .50-caliber ammunition have started huge fires in other sections of the railyard. Interdiction strikes like this were the staples of combat operations for Air Force fighter bomber pilots and kept many thousands of tons of enemy supplies from reaching frontline troops. (NARA)

and low level acrobatics over the base," the 18th Wing "put out a letter concerning the violation of flying regulations to the units." The violations ceased.

Operating with WW II aircraft against jet propelled fighter aircraft

"Little may be recorded in the way of lessons learned as pertains to maintenance, armament, or supply of a tactical unit operating with World War II aircraft against jet propelled fighter aircraft," the 39th Squadron noted bluntly in its unit report for July. Tactical operations could be improved in that the aircraft utilized by this unit should be reserved for only close support missions and not for mass strikes over flak infested areas when medium or heavy bombers could do a more efficient job and with less risk to personnel."

The authors of this report from the 39th had no way of knowing that this assessment and warning would prove to be so tragically accurate within just a few weeks.

"Morale of officers and airmen alike remained on a fairly high level, but little can be said for the retarded rotation program in keeping the morale up," the 39th candidly noted. "Plenty of work, fair recreational facilities, average living quarters, and the idea they were contributing to a great extent in the defeat of the Communist invaders from the North seemed the only solution to the high morale. All personnel were more or less losing interest in the peace talks, casting a rather jaundiced eye on all the bickering, and seemed to think it would be better to get on with the war."

The "Airfield Period"

The 5 July issue of *Truckbuster* reported that Major Carl "Mighty Mite" Colson was to lead the Red Scarf Squadron. "Fighter pilots are axiomatically chosen for their short stature, but Major "Shorty" Colson is one pint-sized squadron commander who scorns elevators in shoes but loves them on Mustangs," the Truckbuster reported.

Colson, 31, was a native of Cocoa, Florida and had been flying for over ten years. While completing 121 combat missions in World War Two, he shot down ten enemy fighters in Europe. He already had over 1,000 flight hours in Mustangs and nearly 3,000 flight hours total.

"Colson is a pretty busy man," the *Truckbuster* reported, "and if he's not at his desk or flying missions he's certain to be on the line checking with the crew chiefs and mechanics."

For the 67th Squadron, the first two weeks of July brought good weather and good hunting. Over 300 sorties were flown. Squadron leaders called the first half the month the "Airfield Period." In the short space of ten days the squadron, in conjunction with other squadrons assigned and attached to the 18th Fighter-Bomber Group,

"Little may be recorded in the way of lessons learned as pertains to maintenance, armament, or supply of a tactical unit operating with World War II aircraft against jet propelled fighter aircraft..."

carried out attacks on nine enemy airfields. It was the first time the squadron had taken part in large fighter formations and "the first mass attack against enemy airfields." [2] As the attacks continued, mission planners feverishly evolved formation SOPs, tactics and procedures.

The first large strike was made against the heavily defended Suuchon airstrip. The 67th pilots led the group and sixteen aircraft participated. Despite intense flak and a misunderstood rendezvous point, "a quick 90-degree angle attack was made. The flights were in diamond formation with individuals within the flights flying fingertip formation. Only one aircraft received damage and that was minor."

On all succeeding missions, the 67th used "at least" a dozen aircraft to suppress flak. The flak suppression flights went in first, dropping two 500-lb GP bombs fitted with proximity fuses, then launching six 5-inch HVAR rockets with proximity fuses. This strategy "enabled the remaining aircraft to bomb the airfields, encountering only small arms fire and light anti-aircraft fire."

In addition, "great care was taken in explaining and pointing out all rendezvous points" on these missions. "Each man knew exactly where and at what altitude his flight was forming after the attack." The value of this strategy was confirmed on the second Suuchon raid "when six enemy MiG-15's

One "Probable" for Salty

"I don't see how that plane can fly," Lt. Col. Ralph H. "Salty" Saltsman, Commander of the 18th Fighter-Bomber Group was quoted in the *Truckbuster*. "I had all the oil from his plane on my bird. That was how close I was on him. I could only see out of the back of the left side of my cockpit."

Saltsman was credited with one IL-2 "probably destroyed."

"If I didn't destroy him, there are lots of repairs going to be done on that plane before it can fly again. I put 1700 rounds of ammo into him."

attempted to bounce our aircraft at rendezvous. The flights had joined up rapidly and the counter-measure of turning into the attackers was successful. The MIG's did not press home their attacks and were driven off."

Sadly, it was on this mission that the "gallant and experienced" 1st Lt. Joseph Babasa, disappeared. He was last seen "rolling into his dive." Babasa was flying number 3 in the lead flight whose mission was flak suppression of known positions around the airstrip. "He was an extremely aggressive and competent pilot who would have pressed home his attack with extreme disregard for his personal safety."

Other airfield strikes were "very much the same as far as procedures and techniques were concerned." During this period "every first class airfield in North Korea was rendered unserviceable and the 67th Fighter-Bomber Squadron can take credit for a large share of the success of the airfield attacks." [3]

Hot Missions for the Month

The last two weeks of July were almost impossible for combat operations due to weather. Operations "almost came to a stand-still. Attempting to get a handle on the weather—and to continue cutting roads."

Despite the awful weather, on July 30th the entire 18th Fighter-Bomber Group was sent out in a 64-ship formation to napalm Pyongyang, the second largest city in Korea. In the largest single mass attack during that month on targets in the Pyongyang area, 91 F-80s suppressed enemy air defenses, while a total of 354 USMC and USAF fighter-bombers attacked specific targets.

The "hot mission of the month was an all-wing show against the North Korean capitol of Pyongyang," Lt. Col. Saltsman reported in July. "Not one aircraft came close to being lost to the big flak nest. One pilot picked up a round in the tail section of his bird but reported it was as good as a miss.

Almost Ready for Another Strike. *Late afternoon at K-46 on the flight line of the 18th Fighter-Bomber Wing in July 1951. Even at this advanced hour of the day, some of the Mustangs are ready for another strike. At far left, a crew chief of a fully loaded F-51 makes a final check of the cockpit before it roars off for another strike on enemy targets. Meanwhile, mechanics, crew chiefs and armament technicians are busy at work readying other birds for a night or early morning mission.*

Wet Runway. At an 18th Fighter-Bomber Group airfield in Korea, 67th Squadron "Mustangs" heavily armed with bombs, rockets and .50-caliber machine-gun ammunition, prepare to take-off on July 27, 1951 from a water-soaked runway caused by torrential Korean rains. In spite of weather and terrain hazards, strikes by tactical aircraft continue on a daily basis against Communist targets, the Air Force caption noted. (NARA)

Results were excellent. We are still checking for official figures, however we know that a lot of enemy material went up in smoke."

To the great credit of its Engineering Section, the 67th had 100% of its aircraft in commission. Each of the 67th aircraft carried two 110-gallon napalm tanks and a full load of .50-caliber ammunition [rounds]. Pilots of the 67th flew through the bad weather and "demolished the assigned targets with precision timing."

The 67th squadron was assigned "a very small and difficult target in the center of town. Only four aircraft could attack at one time. The assault was made with aircraft line abreast and flights in close trail."

The "Foxy Few" 12th Squadron, led by Major John W. Rees, was "in the van during this napalm attack which resulted in many fires at the target with slight damage to the attacking aircraft."

The 39th reported that it "participated in a strike against an area which was reported to contain one of the largest flak concentrations in Korea and also some very lucrative targets. In spite of accurate and intense anti-aircraft fire, the squadron had excellent coverage on all assigned targets and all pilots returned to the forward base."

On this mission, 2nd Lt. James K. Gleoggler "received the dubious title of 'Luckiest pilot of the year' when he received a 20-millimeter shell through the side of the canopy, the missile plowing a shallow furrow along his back, into his parachute and then exploding. Although considerably shaken, Lt. Gleoggler returned his aircraft to K-16 and made a normal landing."

Unfortunately, the highly successful raid could not be talked about in public. In fact, the Joint Chiefs of Staff "withheld information on the strike from the news media" to avoid adverse world public opinion during the on-going peace negotiations. [4]

Major "Mighty Mite" Colson. The Truckbuster reported that Major "Mighty Mite" Colson was to lead the Red Scarf Squadron. "Fighter pilots are axiomatically chosen for their short stature, but Major "Shorty" Colson is one pint-sized squadron commander who scorns elevators in shoes but loves them on Mustangs," the Truckbuster reported. Colson, 31, was a native of Cocoa, Florida and had completed 121 combat missions in World War Two--shooting down ten enemy fighters in Europe. He already had over 1,000 flight hours in Mustangs.

The "Accident Period"

If the early part of the month was the "Airfield Period," the latter half was the "Accident Period."

1st Lt. Robert P. Pasqualicchio "led off by stalling out on the approach to K-16" after a test flight and "spun in," completely demolished his aircraft. Fortunately, he walked away with only a black eye. 1st Lt. Joseph Murray touched down at K-16, found he could not reduce power and ended up, nosed up at the end of the runway. Captain James Kuntz landed "slightly long in the rain at K-10 and slid off the end of the runway. There he hit soft dirt and was promptly flipped over onto his back." Finally, Major William J. Greene "nosed up" at K-16 while taxiing back to the parking area after landing.

Combat Film

July was also the month that "combat film" appeared in 67th Squadron reports. Major Michael Adams was the Gunnery Officer and was assisted by Captain Milton Taylor. Film developing machines were installed K-10 (Chinhae). From then on, within 48 hours of mission completion, the pilot could be looking at his film. The pilot's lounge in the operations office was converted "into a small theatre and frequent showings of combat film have been held." The showings were "quite successful and each pilot has a chance to criticize his own work with constructive criticism from flight commanders and supervisory personnel."[5]

Chronic Shortages

Reported

Despite the bad weather, the 35 assigned pilots of the 67th flew an average of slightly more than 15 sorties each for a total of 564 sorties and 830 combat hours. The squadron expended 341,447 rounds of .50-caliber ammunition, 2,466 5-inch rockets, 565 napalm tanks and 590 bombs to destroy nearly 300 buildings, 21 trucks, 30 AA guns, and 10 railroad cars; make 37 road or railroad cuts, destroy 14 bunkers and kill 298 troops.

The squadron was chronically short of "expendable supplies," and reporting that an excessive number of requisitions on base supply have been 'back ordered' on such items as flashlight batteries, coveralls, shoes, socks and mechanics caps. Even when they were available, the quality of supplies was not helped by "having to use tents in poor repair as storage for the unit supply. Mildewing of clothing and the added burden of constantly cleaning water and dust from the individual weapons of personnel are direct results of this lack of proper building space." Work orders for floors and tent frames were "disapproved," since permanent type buildings were "in the planning stage." There was "no adequate solution in sight."

All tactical missions continued to be flown from the "rearming base" at K-16 while K-10 served as the major maintenance base. Almost two thirds of the squadron's armament personnel were assigned to loading crews at K-16 with armorers "rotated from K-16 to K-10 for rest and relaxation." However, operation of the armament section was made "increasingly difficult as a result of a shortage of trained armorers." The squadron workload was staggering. Although the armament section had an authorized strength of 42, only 28 airmen were actually assigned.

One important morale item did improve—"a result of a newly constructed mail room."

At the end of July the squadron's strength was 139 Airmen and 44 officers. Although there was evidence of "some acceleration in the rotation of officers and airmen, there is still a shortage of housing brought about by new officers being assigned without authority to transfer the pilots who have completed 100 missions." Lacking authority to leave the squadron, despite having completed 100 missions in June, Lt. Babasa continued to fly combat missions and was killed in action in July.

"Morale suffers from the longer tour for Air Force personnel than is required by Army personnel in non-combatant duty."

Another problem was promotions—for the pilots. "Spot promotions have been few and far between due to the many Captains and Majors flying combat," the 12th FBS reported. The problem was "plaguing and difficult." It was hard for the pilots "to understand why support personnel can be promoted and they who carry the damage to the enemy cannot." Every effort was made at the squadron and group level to solve the problem, "including requests for assistance from the chain of command. This situation has been made doubly difficult due to the practically nil rotation of 100-mission pilots who are non-effective and charged to our TO&E." The veteran pilots were "hanging around from six to nine

(Right) ***Red Scarfers 8,000th combat sortie*** *was flown by Captain Ellis L. Fisher of Cumberland, Maryland. He was met at the ramp by Major Carl Colson "carrying a jumbo 'Eighter From Decatur' sign." 'True To Their Scarf' tradition Fisher and Colson insisted on posing with the familiar neckwear flying in the breeze."*

weeks" after completing their "Century Mission."

The surplus of pilots made for crowded living conditions.

The Wing Commander was "making every effort to replace Officers and Airmen who have dependents in the theatre and long terms of service in Korea and expired non-retainable dates. If this plan succeeds it will also be a boost in morale," the 12th noted.

Of course, the entire Wing was "waiting with great anxiety the outcome of the Cease Fire talks. Hope is high but most are skeptical." [6]

Were cracked ribs causing plane losses?

There was great concern when maintenance reported, "approximately seventy percent of the total assigned aircraft were found internally defective with cracked ribs." The old Mustangs were showing their age. The pilots were worried that the cracked ribs might be responsible for aircraft losses. "There was no evidence to link this with the reports of aircraft losing a wing and catching on fire in dive-bomb runs without the evidence of enemy ground fire," the Group noted in its monthly report. "We have had several peculiar incidents which are under investigation, thus far without results."

Life vests were in short supply, as were summer flying suits in smaller sizes. Even more worrisome was the new Escape and Evasion (E and E) equipment that was due in the theater on 20 July. Pilots come begging for the equipment after being given the E and E lecture and all we can give them is the same promises that higher headquarters gives us." Briefing teams visiting the base told the pilots "that they should have it and to get into contact with the Intelligence Section. The section goes to the home office of the team and gets a negative answer. This particular subject has been very weak in so far as help from the higher echelon is concerned," Lt. Col. Saltsman pointed out. "We are lucky to have a very effective program of our own."

"Best Damn Fighter Wing in the World!"

In the July issue of the *Truckbuster*, Colonel T.C. Rogers used the "medium of the press" to speak with all members of the 18th Wing. He thanked them for that "loyal support and the superb job that you are doing." There were many reasons, he explained that the 18th Wing was "The Best Damn Fighter Wing in the World."

He also commended them for the "manner in which you have upheld the principles of the United Nations. Here in our own community we are cementing relationships between nations that will pay dividends in the future. Only through tolerance and understanding of the other man's way of life can the ills of the world finally be cured," Rogers noted wisely. "Americans, in particular, quite often have the bad habit of alienating their friends and allies by ignoring customs of other nations and exhibiting a slightly superior attitude," he said, long before the term "Ugly American" was coined. "I note with pride," he continued, "the absence of any outward manifestations of such characteristics in our Wing."

With a nod to both South Korea and

South Africa, Rogers closed by wishing "that in the years to come the 18th Wing will be a cherished memory in the hearts of the Korean people—such as the memories that I know all we Americans will keep of those hard-fighting 'Zulu Warriors,' of the 2nd South African Air Force Squadron."

Distinguished Unit Citation

Combat operations from April to July 1951 can best be summed up by the Citation issued by FEAF nearly 18 months later, on February 21, 1953. In General Orders Number 95, FEAF promulgated a Distinguished Unit Citation Award for the 18th Fighter-Bomber Group for the period April 22, 1951 through July 8, 1951. In slightly less than four months, the Group, then consisting of four fighter-bomber squadrons, "engaged in uninterrupted daily combat operations against a numerically superior enemy in Korea, maintaining an exceptionally high daily sortie rate despite inadequate operations facilities and complex logistical problems.

Operating from sod, dirt-filled and damaged runways, F-51 Mustangs of the Group accomplished 6,500 combat sorties in

countering the Chinese Communist Forces Spring Offensive, flying constantly during daylight hours and mounting attacks against the enemy in support of hard pressed friendly forces regardless of limit-of-darkness factors. In addition to its ground support commitments, the Group relentlessly pursued an intensive, successful interdiction program against the enemy's northern supply arteries. Although the enemy widely employed natural and contrived camouflage techniques, the Group destroyed a record number of 683 vehicles, damaged an additional 532, and inflicted severe damage upon the enemy at strategic points and at a time when its benefit to United Nations ground forces was incalculable.

The combined efforts of the Group in establishing this high tempo of operations despite problems of logistical requirements and shortages of personnel evidenced the collective diligence, aggressiveness and singleness of purpose of all the officers and airmen of this organization. Through their courage, cooperative spirit and exemplary devotion to duty, the personnel of the 18th Fighter-Bomber Group contributed substantially to United Nations successes in Korea, and reflected great credit upon themselves, the Far East Air Forces, and the United States Air Force."

The enemy inflicted little battle damage on the 12th during July. "Two aircraft were lost due to enemy action and six damaged mainly by small arms fire," the monthly report noted. "One aircraft crashed on take-off from K-16. Another crash landed at K-16 from battle damage inflicted during the mission. Inability to lower the landing gear resulted in an aircraft crash near K-10."

Korean Orphans Find Home With 18th

In July 1950, the *Truckbuster* reported that four teenage boys "caught in the vicious backwash of an anonymous war," appeared at the 18th's Mess Hall in Taegu.

Chya Chul Choon's name was more impressive than his appearance, but his determination to become a member of the American Air Force struck the fancy of Mess Steward T/Sgt Randall F. Sims, who immediately dubbed the little boy "Jitterbug." The name stuck.

Sgt. Sims took over "parental" responsibilities for "Jitterbug's" appearance and education. "Before I knew it," he related in a June issue of Truckbusters, "there were four of them instead of just one. Still don't know just how or where we acquired them, but if anything were to happen to any one of those kids I'd feel just as badly as if it were one of my own children," he said.

Soon after Jitterbug arrived, "Mickey" or Choo Chant Kyun, decided that if two of his older brothers could be of service to the American Air Force as vehicle mechanics, then he should be with the 18th, too.

The 18th was then flying from the Suwon area, and before it moved it had acquired the services of a third "wanderkid"

in the form of Oh Song Moon, whose name was immediately shortened to "Moon" after the American comic strip character.

The last of the four boys to show up, did so just before Christmas, 1950. During a bed check of the other three, Sergeant Sims found that "Moon's bed had a suspiciously human lump at the foot." Chi Kwan Itoo, or "Little Pete" had joined the community, "but wasn't going to announce his presence for a while."

Actually, the three other boys had hidden and fed him for over a week. They were trying to keep "Little Pete" under wraps "until he could say in sing-song English, 'Georgia is the best state in the Union and the 18th is the best Wing in Korea,'" Sims recalled.

Sims cared for them and gave them English lessons. "Won't be long until they are speaking better than I am," Sims noted. "I can handle the English classes okay, but when they start asking me about aerodynamics, then I have to call in one of the pilots."

The pilots took up a collection and bought the boys bicycles and had them air lifted from Japan.

Endnotes
[1] USAFHRA. *Monthly Historical Report, 12th Fighter-Bomber Squadron,* July 1951, p. 2.

[2] USAFHRA. *Monthly Historical Report, 67th Fighter-Bomber Squadron,* July 1951, p. 2.
[3] USAFHRA. *Monthly Historical Report, 67th Fighter-Bomber Squadron,* July 1951, p. 3.
[4] U.S. Air Force Historical Research Agency (USAFHRA). 2001. *The U.S. Air Force's First War: Korea 1950-1953 Significant Events.*
[5] USAFHRA. *Monthly Historical Report, 67th Fighter-Bomber Squadron,* July 1951, p. 4.
[6] USAFHRA. *Monthly Historical Report, 12th Fighter-Bomber Squadron,* July 1951, p. 6.

July Significant Events [1]

July 1: Kim Il Sung, Premier, Democratic Peoples' Republic of Korea and General Paeng Te-huai, CCF Commander, responded to UN overtures and agreed to participate in truce negotiations. The Commander of the 67th Tactical Reconnaissance Wing, Col. Karl L. Polifka, USAF, was shot down and killed while flying an RF-51 near the front lines.

July 5: A major firepower demonstration was held at "Dogpatch" by the 18th Fighter-Bomber Wing to commemorate its "first anniversary" of combat in the Korean War. The 18th Wing monthly report noted that "General Everest and Ambassador Muccio arrived for the 18th Fighter-Bomber

Lt. Norman R. Mailloux remains in his aircraft while maintenance crewmen and armorers swarm over it as they refuel and rearm the Mustang for another mission from K-16. (Pasqualicchio)

"Every first class airfield in North Korea was rendered unserviceable and the 67th Fighter Bomber Squadron can take credit for a large share of the success of the airfield attacks."

Wing's ceremony marking the completion of one year participation in the Korean conflict. On July 5, 1950 "the first volunteers were alerted for movement to Korea. On that date this year the 18th held a ceremony commemorating a year's activity in the Korean War. Colonel Low received the Korean Presidential Unit Citation on behalf of the Wing" presented by Maj. Gen. Kim Chung Yul, chief of staff of the Republic of Korea Air Force. In a "fitting finale" a flight of four F-51's provided the spectators with "an on-the-spot assessment of the Mustang's lethal potential by attacking a nearby target island. Witnessing the potent demonstration one of the airmen in the 18th, T/Sgt. Earl B. Bos, summed it up as he left. "It's things like that," he said, "that make you proud to be in this outfit and mighty proud of what it's done." [2]

Lt. Gen. Otto P. Weyland, Commanding General of Far East Air Forces was invited by the 18th Wing Commander to attend but wrote that he regretted not being able to attend "because of the arrival of the Under Secretary of the Air Force and his party in Tokyo, on the same afternoon."

Weyland extended his "personal appreciation" to all members of the command "for the magnificent job turned in by the 18th Wing day in and day out, in good weather and bad. Regardless of enemy opposition and regardless of the losses you have sustained in accomplishing your mission, you have undertaken every task assigned and completed it with dispatch and distinction. Every member of the 18th Fighter-Bomber Wing may well be proud of the record which has been established during the Korean conflicts, and I want you to know that I share that pride."

Edward J. Cronin, Secretary of the Commonwealth of Massachusetts sent a letter to Col. Turner C. Rogers, Commanding General of the 18th Fighter-Bomber Wing.

"Would you kindly convey to the per-

South Korean President Syngman Rhee arrives at K-10 for the ceremony commemorating the 18th Wing's first anniversary of combat in the Korean War. (Newell)

July 28, 1951, the runways were still water soaked, a dangerous condition that a photographer crouching at left is trying to record as a Mustang from the 12th Squadron takes off heavily loaded with bombs and rockets. (NARA)

sonnel of the 18th Fighter-Bomber Wing from the Commonwealth of Massachusetts my personal greetings and good wishes for continued success. The people of Massachusetts may well be proud of the great fighting spirit and magnificent record of your Wing. The valor and bravery of their deeds will not be forgotten. They are carrying on a tradition of Patriotism that started here in Massachusetts at the time of the Revolutions. May God be with them in their mission."

July 7: 1st Lt. Howard B. Arnold, Jr., while leading "Baker Flight" on a mission over the Haeju area, was forced to bail out over the Haeju harbor when his fighter suffered heavy battle damage from enemy ground fire. Lt. Arnold bailed out, landing in the water, and was immediately rescued by the rescue "Dumbo" and returned to K-16. Since Lt. Arnold had been rescued from behind enemy lines, he was termed an "Operational Evadee," and required to proceed to Director of Intelligence, FEAF, for interrogation before flying further combat missions," the 39th reported.

July 8: One of the three C-47's assigned to the 18th Wing was lost when it had to ditch in Chinhae Bay. There were no injuries sustained by passengers or crew.

On February 21, 1953, FEAF would publish General Orders Number 95, a Distinguished Unit Citation Award for the 18th Fighter-Bomber Group for the period April 22, 1951 through July 8, 1951. In slightly less than four months, the Group, then consisting of four fighter-bomber squadrons, "engaged in uninterrupted daily combat operations against a numerically superior enemy in Korea, maintaining an exceptionally high daily sortie rate despite inadequate operations facilities and complex logistical problems. Operating from sod, dirt-filled

and damaged runways, F-51 Mustangs of the Group accomplished 6,500 combat sorties in countering the Chinese Communist Forces Spring Offensive, flying constantly during daylight hours and mounting attacks against the enemy in support of hard pressed friendly forces regardless of limit-of-darkness factors. In addition to its ground support commitments, the Group relentlessly pursued an intensive, successful interdiction program against the enemy's northern supply arteries. Although the enemy widely employed natural and contrived camouflage techniques, the Group destroyed a record number of 683 vehicles, damaged an additional 532, and inflicted several damage upon the enemy at strategic points and at a time when its benefit to United Nations ground forces was incalculable. The combined efforts of the Group in establishing this high tempo of operations despite problems of logistical requirements and shortages of personnel evidenced the collective diligence, aggressiveness and

singleness of purpose of all the officers and airmen of this organization. Through their courage, cooperative spirit and exemplary devotion to duty, the personnel of the 18th Fighter-Bomber Group contributed substantially to United Nations successes in Korea, and reflected great credit upon themselves, the Far East Air Forces, and the United States Air Force."

July 9: The 39th Fighter Interceptor Squadron "rounded out a full year of combat against the North Korean and Chinese Communist forces on 9 July, 1951. "The squadron had had a complete turnover of officer personnel in this one year period, changed from F-80C to F-51D fighter aircraft, had moved a total of eight times within Japan and Korea, and had become a tactical unit that the Air Force could depend upon to put all it aircraft over the target area when called upon," the 39th report noted. From 9 July 1950 to 31 July 1951, the 39th Squadron had flown 8,911 combat sorties that required 18,708.11 hours of flight time.

July 10: Vice-Admiral C. Turner Joy, USN, led the UN delegation that met the communists at Kaesong, some thirty miles northwest of Seoul and just south of the 38th Parallel, in the first conference of the armistice negotiations. A reconnaissance flight reported a long convoy of NKA trucks and tanks halted by a demolished bridge. Fifth Air Force diverted every available aircraft to attack with bombs, rockets, and gunfire, resulting in the destruction of over 150 vehicles, a third of them tanks.

July 21: An air intelligence detachment completed a weeklong effort near Cho-do Island to recover the most components ever salvaged from a MiG-15 aircraft. A combined operation, the effort involved Fifth Air Force aircraft providing high cover, British carrier aircraft flying low cover, and the U.S. Army contributing a vessel outfitted with a crane.

After circling K-10 for over an hour trying to lower the left landing gear of his Mustang, an 18th Group pilot "bailed out over the field."

July 25: Fifth Air Force directed that an air defense system for South Korea be established that used the resources of the 502nd Tactical Control Group and its subordinate squadrons.

July 29: UN jet fighter-bombers and reconnaissance aircraft operating near Py-

"I flew 12 missions this month," Lt. Fred Thomas recorded in his diary. "It is the rainy season, and our forward base is flooded part of the time, so we get long, tiring flights out of Chinhae. I also have to fly several engineering test hops and a few weather recce's.

This month, I lost my wingman. I am now a flight leader and a new replacement was assigned to me. I find that he tends to follow close behind me and I tell him to back off, as ground fire usually underleads and hits [the aircraft] behind the lead plane. On a relatively quiet flight, I look around and he is gone—no word or sound—we can only surmise that he took a direct hit and fell into the sea. A very personal loss to me.

Things continue to heat up. George Coyle loses his wingman on a close support mission. His wingman's plane is hit and just disintegrates. Then another fatality--in the landing pattern--one plane is too close to the one ahead, does not see him, and they collide, killing the lead pilot. Losses continue to mount.

ongyang encountered MiGs much further south than usual.

July 30: In the largest single mass attack for the month on targets in the Pyongy-

ang area, ninety-one F-80s suppressed enemy air defenses while 354 USMC and USAF fighter-bombers attacked specified military targets. To help avoid adverse world public opinion during on going peace negotiations, the JCS withheld information on the strike from the news media. "The entire group was sent out in a 64 ship formation to napalm P'yongyang, the second largest Korean city," the 67th monthly report noted. "Our aircraft carried two 110 gallon napalm tanks and a full load of .50-caliber ammunition. The mission flew through bad weather and demolished the assigned targets with precision."

Endnotes
[1] Adapted from USAFHRA. January 2002. The U.S. Air Force's First War: Korea 1950-1953 Significant Events. July 1951.
[2] USAFHRA. S/Sgt. William Colton. "Dogpatch Demonstration." *Stars and Stripes*, July 1951.
[3] USAFHRA. *Monthly Historical Report, 12th Fighter-Bomber Squadron*, July 1951, p. 2.

A flight of Two Squadron and 12th Squadron Mustangs heavy with full loads of bombs, rockets and .50-caliber ammunition prepare for takeoff as another F-51 returning from a mission lines up on the runway. Bombs were stacked near the runway to expedite rearming. (NARA)

Truckbusting Mission

On 14 July 1951, 1st Lt. Cassius C. Scott, a Flight Leader with the 12th Squadron with 84 combat sorties, led a flight of three Mustangs through marginal weather direct to the target area near Chiha-Ri, Korea.

"The weather en route and over the target was below marginal," recalled 1st Lt. Donald P. Reich. "We arrived in the target area near Chinha-ri, Korea just before darkness."

Although he was hampered by a low overcast and approaching darkness, he continued to search his assigned area and finally located a large convoy of enemy vehicles. He then led the flight in repeated gunnery attacks, through "a continuous barrage of enemy automatic weapons fire, and succeeded in destroying fourteen (14) enemy trucks loaded with supplies."

"We were subjected to enemy automatic weapons fire during the entire attack, but were able to destroy fourteen (14) trucks loaded with supplies before total darkness," Reich reported.

When he was forced to leave the target area because of total darkness, Scott then led his flight around a series of dangerous flak emplacements, "underneath a low overcast back to the home base, dodging enemy flak all the way back to the bomb line" and returned safely to the home base.

As a result of this highly successful mission, superbly executed under the most adverse conditions, the enemy suffered loss of vital transport and war materiel, his Commanding Officer noted in the report he prepared recommending Scott for the Distinguished Flying Cross.

Combat Losses in July

Capt. Joseph M. Babasa, Jr., 67th Fighter-Bomber Squadron who, in July 1951 was KIA near Pyongyang, NK. "Sadly, it was on this mission that the "gallant and experienced" 1st Lt. Joseph Babasa, disappeared. He was last seen "rolling into his dive." Babasa was flying number 3 in the lead flight whose mission was flak suppression of known positions around the airstrip.

Combat Statistics

18th Fighter-Bomber Wing

July 1951

Average No. A/C Assigned	**Pilots lost**
76	10
Total Flying Time	
2,665	**Fuel Consumed**
Percent of Aircraft in Commission	247,684 gals.
75	**Ordnance Expended**
Percent of Aircraft AOCP	**.50-cal. Rounds**
1	1,171,432
Combat Sorties Flown by Wing	**Rockets**
2,286	7,397
12th Squadron Sorties	**Napalm Bombs**
612	1,755
39th FIS Sorties	**500-lb. GP Bombs**
592	1,651
67th Squadron Sorties	*Note: Figures and totals may differ*
565	*in some categories due to differ-*
2 Squadron Sorties	*ences in numbers provided by each*
504	
A/C Lost to Combat	
4	

Wet Taxiway. *Not the most ideal runway, the Air Force caption explained, but still not enough of a hazard to stop operations is this miniature lake formed by torrential Korean rains at K-46. An 18th F-B Group "Mustang," heavily armed with bombs, rockets and .50-caliber machine-gun ammunition, plows through the water during take off on another mission against Communist targets on 28 July 1951. (NARA)*

"He was an extremely aggressive and competent pilot who would have pressed home his attack with extreme disregard for his personal safety." "Lt. Joe Babasa's name shows up in every citable action," recalled his close friend and fellow pilot, Major "Mac" McKelvey. "Joe was a superb pilot, and a natural leader who always showed up in the thick of the fight. It seems only natural when we remember that his heritage was that of an Apache Warrior. By July 1951, Joe had completed the magic 100, and he was awaiting rotation orders when his brother, with the 1st Marine Division, was KIA. Joe received permission to continue combat until his brother's body was ready for escort to the ZI. He was on his 106th mission, flying flak suppression when he rolled into his dive bomb run and disappeared. Gallant and experienced are minimal descriptions of Joe Babasa. Warrior-RIP."

1st Lt. F. N. Bekker, 2 Squadron SAAF, was KIA on 23 July 1951, during a weather reconnaissance of the West Coast. After successfully attacking and destroying a bridge over the Han Gang River, Bekker's aircraft was struck by ground fire, burst into flames and broke up.

Capt. Raymond J. Carlson, 39th Fighter-Interceptor Squadron, "was shot down near the Inchon area. His fighter plane was hit by enemy ground fire over the target area. Captain Carlson headed his disabled plane south towards friendly lines and started his let down over a reservoir near Pyonggang. He jettisoned his canopy and it appeared as if he had failed to duck low enough and the canopy struck his head as the plane continued straight on in in a 20 degree dive and crashed on the United Nations edge of the reservoir. Later reports from the Canadian troops who recovered his body stated that he had been hit five times from enemy quad fifty gun positions as he came over the north edge of the reservoir," the 39th reported.

1st Lt. R.M. du Plooy, 2 Squadron SAAF pilot KIA on 23 July 1951. Captain Freddie Bekker, 2nd Squadron SAAF and his flight were conducting weather reconnaissance of the West Coast of North Korea along the

Lt. Joe Babasa of the 67th Squadron. By July 1951, Babasa had completed the magic 100 missions, and was awaiting rotation orders when his brother, with the 1st Marine Division, was KIA. He received permission to continue combat until his brother's body was ready for escort to the ZI. He was on his 106th mission, flying flak suppression when he rolled into his dive bomb run and disappeared. (Pasqualicchio)

Han Gang River. Turning east at the mouth of the river the weather worsened, with low clouds and rain sweeping the hilly terrain. They were able to find and destroy a bridge across the Imjin River, but came under heavy AA fire. Captain Bekker's aircraft was hit and immediately began to break apart into flaming wreckage that required the other three pilots to take immediate evasive action. Losing sight of him for a few moments, the flight thought he had crashed. As Lt. Green made a pass over the area, amazingly a parachute went floating down past him. Another member of the flight, Lt. Halley had also descended to inspect Bekker's crash site. He, too, was hit by ground fire, bailed out and landed successfully. Now two Mustangs were down. The two pilots remaining in the air decided that Lt. du Plooy would CAP Halley, strafing until he ran out of ammunition. Lt. Green would climb to a higher altitude to establish radio contact with Air Rescue. Finding it hard to provide an exact location in that area, Green told the helicopter to rendezvous with him at a more definite location about ten miles away. While the helicopter was en route, he shuttled between the two points trying to avoid heavy ground fire. The helicopter arrived just as Lt. du Plooy reported that Lt. Halley had been captured.

Preparing to leave the scene, Lt. du Plooy himself radioed that he had been hit. His plane was later located, but there was no sign of Lt. du Plooy, who later became the first SAAF pilot to earn the Silver Star, according to Winston Brent in *2 Squadron in Korea*. Lt. Halley was repatriated in 1953. This weather reconnaissance mission went down in 18th history as one of the most expensive missions of the entire war—two pilots KIA, one pilot POW and three aircraft lost.

1st Lt. Eric Franklin O'Briant, 12th Fighter-Bomber Squadron. Lt. O'Briant of the 12th FBS was reported as MIA "when his aircraft exploded due to unknown causes over enemy held territory. [Pyongyang, NK] Lieutenant O'Briant had just returned to duty earlier this month, having been hospitalized after crashing on take-off at K-16." [1]

Major L. B. "Bunny" Pearce, 2nd Squadron SAAF pilot KIA on 9 July 1951. Major Pearce was flying No. 2 in a four-ship flight led by Lt. Marshall that was to ferry the Mustangs from K-10/Chinhae to K-16/Seoul. The weather conditions were marginal. They planned to fly VFR—Visual Flight Rules—or return to K-10. If weather conditions deteriorated to require flying by instruments, they planned to climb above

By the Light of napalm fires

by Major Raymond "Mac" McKelvey

One evening in mid-July 1951, my flight was standing JOC alert for the third time that day. We had already completed two good close support missions that day, but since it was so late in the day, we didn't expect to get another, since we didn't get too many late night missions.

So the four of us were thinking great thoughts—what's for chow, what time is it at home—and jointly decided that our work day was over, due to darkening skies and lowering clouds. We were relaxed and ready to stand down when the gods who are in charge preventing such relaxation struck. SCRAMBLE!!!

Previously briefed on tactics and emergency procedures, we were four Mustangs airborne in short order. As we neared the target area, my flight attempted to contact our AT-6 Mosquito, but without success.

Since I had radio contact, I took command under pre-briefed conditions. As we dodged around low scud clouds, the Mosquito made his marking run, asking for the napalm on a N-S axis, but warning us of the higher terrain at the North end. This meant that my "deaf" aircraft had to keep close formation with me and drop his napalm with me.

The enemy was showing his great displeasure at our presence, with "golf balls" coming from every which way.

One good napalm run, a quick 180 to get back out of the valley and home.

One gun pit showed up dead ahead and received full benefit from my six rockets. My flight mates caught quick targets for their rockets.

In the light of the napalm fires, I could see several trucks which I caught with my .50-caliber machine guns. As I looked back, I could see several trucks burning.

Along with the Quad 50 I had killed, I was well satisfied with the mission. We rallied for the trip home, but it was too dark to assess any damage that the aircraft had taken. We landed by the light of flare pots at each end of our runway. We deserved filet mignon dinners, but, gladly settled for SPAM.

Note: BDA (battle damage assessment) the next day after the strike indicated greater damage than was initially reported. McKelvey was awarded a DFC for this mission.

the overcast that was estimated to reach to about 8,000 feet. After take-off, near Masan, the flight ran into a rainstorm. The weather, plus the nearby mountains, delayed their turn around plan. Marshall advised them to climb, as planned. Soon after, Major Pearce could be seen having difficulty in maintaining formation, and then left the flight. During one more brief sighting, he was advised to climb above the overcast where the flight would rendezvous. The three planes left in the flight climbed above the weather and attempted to locate Major Pearce. He was not there. The wreckage of his aircraft was later found about 15 miles north of Chinhae, where it had crashed at high speed. Major Pearce is buried in the UN Cemetery at Pusan.

Capt. Walter Everett Pittman, 39th Fighter Interceptor Squadron, on 5 July 1951, "departed K-16 leading 'Charlie Flight' on a pre-briefed road cut and armed reconnaissance mission over the Hukkyo-ri area. Captain Pittman dropped his 500-pound bombers over the assigned target and when he started an easy pull-out his plane was seen to burst into flames and disintegrate. No explanation could be given for this accident and it was not known if his plane had been hit by heavy caliber enemy ground fire or if the explosion was caused by structural failure," the 39th Squadron reported.

Capt. Glenn E. Stewart, 67th Fighter-Bomber Squadron.

2nd Lt. Jessie P. Verster, 2 Squadron SAAF.

Staff Sergeant Fred E. Mack, 12th Fighter-Bomber Squadron. S/Sgt Mack, an armorer with the 12th Squadron, "was accidentally killed by .50-caliber bullets while checking the bomb release mechanism of an F-51."

Endnotes

[1] USAFHRA. *Monthly Historical Report, 12th Fighter-Bomber Squadron*, July 1951, p. 2.

18th Wing pilots George C. McLees, Jr., Plass, Magnus Francis and Raymond McKelvey prepare for their next mission.

Dogpatch Demons

Celebrate Year In Korea

By S/Sgt William Colton

At Taegu, KOREA, one year ago today, four F-51's led by 1st Lt. Frank Buzze bumped down a rutted, muddy runway and staggered into the air. A short time later they were on the east coast of Korea supporting elements of the 24th Infantry Division during their withdrawing action against over-whelming odds.

Buzze's gone from Korea now. So are the other three who were with him. But those four Mustangs were the beginning of a variety of airborne fraternities; the beginning of one of the most colorful fighter wings to come out of the Korean conflict—the 18th Fighter -Bomber Wing.

Most of the original pilots completed their 100 combat missions and were returned to the U.S. as was Buzze. A few will always remain in Korea. The remnants of their aircraft can be seen scattered here and there along the front—mute testimony of their sacrifice. Most of them were victims of ground fire because they dared to get close enough in supporting United Nations elements to be hit by enemy rifle and machine gun fire.

But their efforts have not gone unnoticed or unappreciated. Ask any infantryman who was pinned down by enemy fire when an air strike came in. He remembers and appreciates it and has shown his appreciation whenever he came in contact with an airman. The pilots bear that appreciation in mind when they are supporting the battle weary soldier.

Initially the 18th was a combination of two volunteer units known as "Bout One" and "Dallas." Recruited from both the 5th Air Force and 13th Air Forces, these units were rushed to Taegu to fly obsolescent F-51s and furnish some of the first real close air support of the Korean war.

Because they were volunteers, Syngman Rhee, Republic of South Korea president, called them the "Flying Tigers of Korea."

The name stuck and tiger teeth, reminiscent of General Claire Chennault's (former member of the early 18th) famed pre-World War II American Volunteer Group, were painted on the aircraft. This was the 18th's first airborne fraternity.

Col. Curtis R. Low (since promoted to a 5th AF staff position), the original commander of the 18th in Korea, molded those volunteer units, plus additional personnel, into the 6002nd Tactical Support Wing, later redesignated the 18th Fighter-Bomber Wing.

In order to understand an outfit you'd have to know something about the men who were in it. Those early "July days" were hectic ones for those men. They had little equipment, plenty of dust, mud and bad weather, and a big job to do. An 18-hour day was not unusual.

The pilots were flying continuous missions trying to knock a few of the enemy off the necks of our greatly outnumbered forces.

It's a pretty rough schedule to jockey an F-51 around for ten or more hours a day—bones ache and stomach muscles throb from the strain. That's one of the reasons that a fighter pilot is usually a "typed character" in most people's book. Actually they're crazy but wonderful guys when you get to know them.

Take Maj. Harry Moreland for example.

Harry wasn't too tall and sported one of those handlebar mustaches that became the fad with the pilots. It was Moreland who

started the second fraternity at the 18th— "Moreland's Tank Busters." He led a flight of four F-51's carrying the new tank demolishing 6.5-inch rocket into combat at the time when they were needed (the first unit to use the new rockets in Korea). His flight was on call 24-hours a day and their results earned them their name.

Maj. Lou Sebille is another you should have known. A good looking guy with blond, curly hair, a lot of people knew him as Lou Reynolds, night club MC around the Chicago circuit He could always draw a laugh from his men but at the same time was a tough squadron commander who loved to fly.

He always told his pilots, "If you have to go then take some of the enemy with you." On a close support mission near the Naktong River, Sebille was hit, probably fatally. He called his wingman, "I'm hit," he said. "I'm going back and get those bastards." Then he wheeled his crippled F-51 around and, with a 265-pound fragmentation bomb, hung up under his wing, dove into a vehicle loaded with enemy troops. That was Lou Sebille.

"Tamerlane Willie," Maj. William Bryan, started another 18th fraternity—"The Truck-busters." He had everybody guessing just how he managed to teach his squadron to find and destroy so many enemy vehicles. Willie's secret was simply skillful, daredevil flying at treetop level through the valleys and draws of North Korea—some-

times on wing edge when there was no other way to get through. At that height, it was easier to spot the expertly camouflaged vehicles.

"Pull in your mustache if you have to," he'd tell his men while twirling his own handlebar, "but get down there and look around."

For sheer spine tingling thrills you should try weaving in and out of draws on your wing edge sometime. Willie got the nation's second highest award for that one—the Distinguished Service Cross. The wing countered with as many as 128 enemy vehicles destroyed in one day.

Then there's 27-year-old Capt. Jerry Hogue, still with the 18th with 157 combat missions to his credit. Jerry's a good natured, thin, prematurely gray haired fellow whose clipped speech is almost as static as the wing guns in his F-51. Jerry and his three wingmen still hold the 18th's record for an individual flight by destroying 32 enemy trucks on a five-hour mission.

Lack of space precludes detailed mention of all the men. But there were: 1st Lt. Phil Conserva with his "Hotshot Charlie" brand of sophisticated wit; gangling Capt. Bill Slater with the scarf he wore always getting tangled up in his legs; tall, slim Capt. Howard Price with his pencil mustache and long cigar, plus that victorious smile he wore the day be knocked down those two YAKs; Maj. Moon Mullins—he used to do three barrel rolls when he came off his target; Capt. Charlie Moorehouse, always smiling,

one of the first members of the 100-mission fraternity; 1st Lt. Harry Ausman whose fellow pilots said was "one of the best damned wingmen in Korea"; and, Col. S. v. B. Theron, Commandant of the South African "2" Squadron, whose men insisted had "eyes like a hawk" because he was so good at spotting camouflaged vehicles.

The whole wing worked as a coordinated team with the airmen playing just as important a part as the pilots by keeping the "birds" in the air.

M/Sgt. Frank Fay, the 'wing Sergeant Major, with the big cigar continually clenched between his teeth and always was scrounging "reading material" when he could find time to read; M/Sgt. 'Pineapple" Burnsed, armament technician with one of the squadrons. He set up an assembly line to refuel and rearm the planes that was a whiz. You should have seen the goatee he had until Colonel Low kidded him into shaving it off. It wasn't a few who made the wing—it was every man in it. That combination made history in Korea as one of the biggest fraternities of all—the "Dogpatchers."

For awhile the Pacific Stars and Stripes carried daily headlines about the feats of the dauntless Dogpatchers (the first week in November they shot down 2 YAK-3s, 5 YAK-9s and possibly destroyed 2 MIG-15s in aerial combat). They were the first to encounter MIGs, the first fighter unit to utilize a fighter strip above the 38th Parallel—at Wonsan last October. They blew up tanks

with unorthodox methods, destroyed record numbers of enemy equipment, and captured enemy troops and even hills from the air. Almost everyone in the Far East knew about the Dogpatchers in Korea through these feats.

While all this was going on the Dogpatch theme began to seep into the United States via the American press. Today Al Capp, the originator of the cartoon strip "Lil Abner," is an honorary member of the wing.

A Cappian patch, drawn by Al himself, is the pride of the Korean Dogpatchers. It features Lil Abner piloting an P-51 with "Nancy 0" riding on its tail. The patch was originated before Nancy 0 had a face. When Miss Kitty Panky, a Miami University student, became the girl with "the sweetest face in the world" and the face on Nancy 0, she also became the sweetheart of the 18th's Dogpatchers in Korea.

The Stateside "Tex and Jinx" television show has already featured Miss Panky with the 18th's new patch. In the near future another TV show will tell the story of the 18th and at the same time Capp will receive his formal honorary induction into the wing.

The four fighter squadrons of the 18th, including the South African "2" Squadron have adopted the Dogpatch theme. Reproductions of Al's insignia are appearing on jackets and aircraft, and signs showing Lil Abner and Daisy May or Nancy 0 are being nailed up in front of everything from the base maintenance shop to the mess halls.

The 18th Wing history actually goes back to its activation in 1927 at Wheeler Field, T. H. In 1937 the present wing commander, Col. T.C. Rogers, was assigned to the unit as a "brand new" second lieutenant. He received some of his first fighter plane instructions from the then 18th operations officer, Capt. Frank Everest. Today the two officers are working together again—Rogers as the Commander of the 18th and Maj. Gen. Frank H. Everest as the Commanding General of the Fifth Air Force.

It was July 5 a year ago that the first volunteers were alerted for movement to Korea. On that day this year the 18th held a ceremony commemorating a year's activity in the Korean War. Colonel Low received

Two Squadron, SAAF Mustangs prepare to take off on a close air support strike against Communist frontline troops from K-46 in July 1951. Napalm bombs (center) were among the most feared weapons used by UN air forces. (NARA)

the Korean Presidential Unit Citation on behalf of the wing. It was presented by Maj. Gen. Kim Chung Yul, chief of staff of the Republic of Korea Air Force.

Also at the ceremony, Colonel Rogers presented to General Kim for Syngman Rhee, a huge oil painting depicting F-51's of the 18th in action. The painting entitled "Destruction from the Skies," was painted by Sgt. Dave McNichol. General Everest was on hand to decorate nine officers and airmen of the wing. He brought along a surprise package in the form of a Legion of Merit for Colonel Rogers for outstanding service earlier.

The Honorable John J. Muccio, U.S. Ambassador to Korea, spoke to the assembled group of airmen and officers. He recalled the first days in Korea when the unit was flying combat missions with few pilots, few men, and even fewer planes, from an airstrip where the grass grew "hip high." He congratulated the 18th for the "wonderful" job they bad done during their year's service in Korea.

For a fitting finale a flight of four F-51's on a rocket-napalm-training flight gave the spectators an on-the-spot assessment of the Mustang's lethal potential by attacking a nearby target island. Witnessing the potent demonstration one of the airmen in the 18th, T/Sgt, Earl B. Bos summed it up as he left.

"It's things like that," be said, "that make you proud to be in this outfit and mighty proud of what it's done."

Undated Stars and Stripes article, Pacific Edition. Approximate date, mid-July 1951. Probably prepared by S/Sgt William J. "Sandy" Colton.

Cracked Ribs Get Wing's Attention

During a major inspection on an F-51D, "it was discovered that the ribs in the wings were cracking," the 18th Wing monthly reported noted. "This was considered a serious situation as this Wing has experienced four wing failures as of this date. The aircraft affected were immediately grounded until further investigation could be made." Headquarters FAF was immediately contacted and a crew of maintenance inspectors was flown to the K-10 "to determine the seriousness of the cracked wing ribs." Eventually, the aircraft were released for flight and the aircraft having the most pronounced rib cracks were flown to Far East Air Materiel Command for "stress analysis tests." [1]

Meanwhile, construction work at K-10 was moving ahead rapidly. Two major projects were completed, including 37 prefabricated tropical buildings for both operational and troop housing and the rehabilitation of the maintenance hangar at the South end of the K-10 airstrip. Even though the Group staged combat strikes out of K-16 whenever possible, K-10 continued to be the Wing headquarters, the preferred location for most maintenance and continued to host combat sorties when needed. For ten days in August the "entire unit operated out of K-10" when flood waters "threatened to inundate the K-16 runway."

A major highlight of the month was Lt. Col. Saltsman's promotion to full Colonel. "Everybody was glad to see the Colonel have to dig into his purse for that kind of party and a big box of cigars. All agreed that the promotion was well deserved."

August Combat Operations

In mid-August 1951 the 18th Group was focusing the majority of its efforts "against the Communist forces" by assaulting their rail traffic. FEAF had refocused "Operation Strangle" against North Korean railroads. Planners believed that the CCF logistics system would quickly grind to a halt if the railroads could not be used to resupply troops. The overall intent was to prevent the buildup of supplies needed by the CCF for a sustained offensive or an effective counteroffensive. The FEAF established an overall division of labor for Operational Strangle forces: FEAF Bomber Command and U.S. Navy carrier aircraft worked over railway bridges and nearby rail lines. Fifth Air Force planes cut as many rail lines as possible. Meanwhile, the B-26s hunted trucks on the highways—at night.[2]

In August, the 18th Group was "still working on operations plan Strangle along with the regular commitments for close support in the form of column cover and JOC alerts. The column cover was highly successful, however, wasteful as much of the continuous cover was not needed," Lt. Col. Saltsman reported.

Monthly Summary

Armistice negotiations meant less active ground combat and thus, reduced the demand for FEAF close air support. However, negotiations at Kaesong went badly and then broke down entirely.

Planners concluded that the CCF logistical system would quickly break down if the railroads could be made unusable. Far East Air Command therefore initiated a rail interdiction campaign, carrying the same code name, Operation STRANGLE, as the short-lived campaign in June and July 1951. The objective of the new campaign was to prevent an enemy buildup of the supplies necessary for a sustained offensive or effective counteroffensive. Although bad weather reduced the tempo of air operations, Far East Air Forces stepped up the fighter-bomber campaign against North Korean railroads. Far East Command established a division of responsibilities among the Fifth Air Force, FEAF Bomber Command, and the U.S. Navy designed to keep North Korean railway bridges down and rail lines cut. Bomber Command knocked down key railroad bridges. Fifth Air Force and the Navy fighter-bombers cut the rail lines. Meanwhile, the B-26's shifted from daytime interdiction operations to nighttime truck hunting.

The commencement of armistice negotiations had reduced ground combat somewhat. The static ground situation did reduce the demand for FEAF close air support—for a while. Initial negotiations at Kaesong turned sour and then broke down after communist ground forces violated the Kaesong neutral zone. Talks were suspended on August 4th, resumed on August 10th and suspended again on August 22 following trumped up "evidence" that a UN aircraft had bombed Kaesong.

Adapted in part from U.S. Air Force Historical Research Agency. January 2002. The U.S. Air Force's First War: Korea 1950-1953 Significant Events. August 1951. http://www.au.af.mil/au/afhra/wwwroot/korean_war/korean_war_chronology/kwc_1951.html

> "Attacks on targets as heavily defended as Pyongyang by F-51's are not considered to be profitable when made under conditions which lessen the maximum striking potential of the airplane."
>
> *Colonel T. C. Rogers*

In the face of "intemperate weather," two types of missions were flown by 67th pilots, including "maximum effort missions against the rail yards" and "four ship assaults against rail lines themselves." The plan that was followed was to start off with "intense" strikes, "tapering off to three or four missions per week as the rail facilities are so damaged as to make immediate repair impossible."[3]

"It has been more than proven," the 39th reported, "that the type of aircraft used by this unit to wage war against the North Korean and Chinese Communist aggressors was very effective in close support and interdiction sorties; although the aircraft is highly vulnerable with its liquid cooled engine...The adaptability of the F-51 aircraft to the mountainous terrain has also been proven out in the past thirteen months. The aircraft's versatility and ability to stay over the target longer, to pin point enemy concentrations of troops and supplies, have shown that a reciprocal powered aircraft is much more effective in close support than its fighter counter-part, the jet propelled fighter-bomber."

The "Red Capital"—Pyongyang—received "considerable attention during the month." Three "maximum efforts" missions were sent this month to attack Pyongyang. "Maximum effort" missions were group mission, each squadron putting up sixteen aircraft for each mission. These missions were over and above the squadron's primary mission of "vigorous close support to the ground forces," during which it flew an average of 12 sorties per day.

Heavy Losses Bring Stiff Letter

Two of the maximum effort attacks on Pyongyang were made on 14 August. The heavy losses in pilots prompted a highly classified and uncharacteristically stiff letter from the 18th Wing Commander, Colonel T.C. Rogers to the Fifth Air Force Commanding General.

Rogers began by pointing out that the Wing was required to take off from its main base at K-10, a distance of 280 nautical miles from the target area. This necessitated reducing the normal load of two napalm tanks per aircraft by one, and so reducing each airplane's effectiveness correspondingly. "Attacks on targets as heavily defended as Pyongyang by F-51's are not considered to be profitable when made under conditions which lessen the maximum striking potential of the airplane," Rogers pointed out.

(Note: Lt. Col. Walter Burke pointed out that "we ALL carried TWO napalm bombs on this fighter sweep on Pyongyang." Photos on subsequent pages confirm his recollection.)

"Target #2 was attacked by the 2nd Squadron, SAAF, of this Wing on 30 July

Fusing HVARs. *S/Sergeant Elmer Strausheim of Denver, Colorado fuses a five-inch rocket on an F-51 at K-46. Note the steel matting (pierced steel planking) that was used for runways and ramps at the field. (NARA)*

1951," Rogers continued. "Pilot observations, as transmitted to Hq, 5th AF, on the mission report, indicated that buildings in the area had been previously damaged. Pilots further reported that no secondary fires or explosions were seen, as would have been the case had the storage area actually contained ammunition. This same target was attacked by the Wing's 12th Squadron on 14 August 1951. Virtually the same conditions as to previous damage and lack of secondary fires and explosions were observed on the occasion of the second attack as had obtained two weeks earlier," Rogers noted.

On the morning mission of 14 August, the 67th Squadron hit target #1, approaching from the southeast "as directed by the 5th AF operations plan. The attack along this axis was hindered by radio antennae or high tension wires which presented a hazard to low flying aircraft. An attack from the South would have avoided this obstacle," Rogers concluded.

"Very intense, accurate flak was encountered on the afternoon mission of 14 August, both into and out of the target area," Rogers continued. "This condition did not exist in the morning attack, where the element of surprise was present. Axes of attack were all as directed by 5th AF except for the afternoon attack on target #1 which was changed to avoid radio antennae."

Losses in the two strikes on 14 August for the Wing included two pilots KIA, three pilots MIA, six aircraft lost before returning to base, and four aircraft so heavily battle damaged that they were transferred to the 18th Maintenance Squadron.

Rogers concluded his letter by recommending that "maximum effort attacks against heavily defended areas be made only when the striking force is able to employ its maximum payload. Staging from any forward base might obviate the use of external fuel tanks, permitting each airplane to carry two napalm tanks or two 500# bombs."

Damage assessments and observations by pilots should be "given more weight in target selection," Rogers suggested. And, squadron or flight leaders should be "given discretion in the choice of axes of attack

against specific targets."

Rogers concluded by urging that "attacks against heavily defended areas be so planned and spaced as to afford the striking force the advantage of surprise."

Pyongyang received "considerable attention during the month."

Major Carl C. Colson, Commander of the 67th Squadron created a fifth flight, Easy Flight, "to permit more effective operations, and to permit one flight to return aircraft to K-10 where better maintenance facilities are available, and to take care of additional duties for a period of one or two days be-

fore being returned to the advance base." During that period the operations section was led by Major Michael E. Adams, Operations Officer, with 1st Lt. Harold K. Wimberly serving as Assistance Operations Officer. Flight Commanders included: 1st Lt. Walter H. Burke (A-Flight); 1st Lt. George N. Leitner (B-Flight); 1st Lt. James W. Lee (C-Flight); Capt. Robert P. Pasqualicchio (D-Flight); and, 1st Lt. George L. Coyle, Jr. (E-Flight).

Three pilots completed their 100 missions during the month and were "promptly returned to the ZI, with the exception of 1st Lt. Francis E. Lewis, who volunteered to fly another tour in F-84's. He was transferred to the 136th Fighter Interceptor Wing in Japan.

By the end of August, the 67th had flown

(Continued on page 360)

Weather conditions over the North Korean target area were always an important factor for 18th Wing pilots. Here two technicians and two pilots try to determine how weather will affect an upcoming mission on August 2, 1951. (Krakovsky)

Major Murrit Davis, Commander of the 39ᵗʰ Fighter-Interceptor Squadron in' "Sexy Sally" and another F-51 of the 18ᵗʰ ing (probably piloted by Captain Alphonzo T. Wagner), make a successful low-level napalm run over P'yongyang, North Korea on the morning of 14 August 1951. In this famous photograph from the Korean War, two napalm fire bombs head towards their targets just a split second after being released from shackles beneath Sexy Sally's wing. The bomb nearest the camera plummets earthward head first, while the other retains its horizontal position. During this "Group Gaggle" over Pyongyang, Major Davis suffered heavy damage to the right wing tip of his Mustang when the plane struck a cable over the target area. Captain Wagner's aircraft had a large portion of the right horizontal stabilizer shot away. However, both aircraft made it back to K-10 safely. The Truckbuster ran a photograph of Wagner standing behind a "practically non-existent elevator...ribs and little else." Wagner said he thought the fighter "acted a little funny" when he came in for a landing. "It's a good thing I didn't realize how badly pranged that elevator was or I'd probably have bailed out."

In the afternoon raid over the same target, Major Davis, Captain John L. Horn and Captain John F. Grossman failed to return. As noted in the Silver Star Citation prepared for Major Murrit Davis, "As squadron leader in a flight of twelve F-51 type aircraft, Major Davis displayed extraordinary heroism by leading his flight over the heavily defended target at Pyongyang...where his flight made a devastating low level napalm run against supply warehouses in that city. De-

(Left) This previously unpublished photograph, frame number 22, was taken by Horn during the morning raid shortly after the photographs taken over the Taedong River. It shows the devastation left by the low level napalm and rocket attacks after the morning raids on 14 August 1951, led by Col. Ralph Saltsman, Commander of the 18ᵗʰ Group. (Chatfield)

Captain John Horn, *Operations Officer for the 39th Squadron, was flying an F-51 equipped with a K-24C camera, and probably took these remarkable photographs. He was lost later that afternoon during a similar raid on Pyongyang.*

The "Sexy Sally drops napalm" frame is labeled 8 OL A 1863 18FBG 14 AUG51. The photographs at left and below are frames numbered 11 and 12, obviously taken just seconds after the napalm drop photographs as Davis and Wagner head across the Taedong River, swollen from recent heavy rains at the time.

These photographs were scanned directly from actual prints provided by Col. Stanley Chatfield, then Operations Officer for the 18th Group. (Chatfield)

spite heavy anti-aircraft fire which had critically damaged his aircraft, Major Davis without regard for his own personal safety, circled the target several times, attempting to locate and render possible assistance to two pilots who had been shot down by enemy fire. Fully aware that his aircraft had sustained critical damage from enemy fire, Major Davis unhesitatingly and courageously continued his search for the missing pilots thus jeopardizing his chance for a safe return to friendly lines. After an exhaustive search, Major Davis reassembled his squadron over the rendezvous point and led them toward the home base. Approximately ten minutes after leaving the target area, his engine failed." Although he "jettisoned his canopy," the aircraft "was seen to enter a spiral to the left, crash into the ground and explode."

Major Murrit Davis

These were typical missions for the "Truck Busters" of the 18th Fighter-Bomber Group. They were also extraordinarily hazardous to both planes and pilots. Enemy leaders anticipated such attacks on high value targets--cities, railroads, bridges and major highways. These areas were increasingly covered by concentrated, highly sophisticated anti-aircraft positions, many of them radar controlled. Fighter-bomber pilots faced such dangers daily, year round and in almost all weather conditions. Unfortunately, recognition in the Armed Forces Newspaper, "Stars and Stripes," was considered to be "small for all Air Force units in Korea." The general feeling was that the 'Sabre-jets' get the writeups and that there was a notation for courtesy's sake that the Mustangs 'also ran.'"

A last minute conference taking place between a crew-chief and a Mustang pilot of Two Squadron, South African Air Force prior to a mission in August 1951. The "Flying Cheetahs" were one of four squadrons attached to the 18th Fighter-Bomber Wing.

8,050 sorties during the Korean Campaign, 555 of them that month with nearly 1,100 hours of combat. The five Flights had expended nearly 400,000 rounds of .50-caliber ammunition, 1,338 5-inch rockets, 622 tanks of napalm and 494 500-lb bombs to destroy 115 buildings, five bunkers, six boxcars and one locomotive. Six gun positions, eight rail cuts and 287 troops had also been accounted for by the 33 pilots assigned. They had average 17 sorties apiece that month.

The hard work of the communications section had reduced the number of aborted missions due to communications equipment to just one during the entire month. However, the VHF radio sets were "getting old and many tubes have had to be replaced." Whenever possible, communications personnel replaced all the tubes in the radios as the aircraft were inspected.

"Expendable supplies" were still a major problem. Excessive numbers of requisitions were placed on "back-ordered" status. Storage spaces for supplies on hand were inadequate. As August turned into September, summer heat was rapidly replaced by "unseasonably cool weather at the advance base." Although winter cloth-

ing was now needed by early morning maintenance personnel and requisitions had been submitted for winter clothing in accordance with 8th Army directives, "no clothing has yet been issued." Colson believed that "Air Materiel Commands could more expeditiously provided both clothing and expendables for Air Force units as Army Supply channels seem to have been unable to fill our needs." The maintenance personnel worked in the cold, but they kept their planes in the air.

Up to this point, squadron dirty laundry was sent back to Japan "in bundles" to be cleaned. There were no laundry facilities at the base. There was a lot of laundry for a squadron of about 180 personnel. Frequently, bundles of laundry were lost, some temporarily and others permanently "due to the large amount of handling and transporting of laundry to Japan." In August, a "small laundry" was installed at the base and was "of great value in processing fatigue clothing."

The Engineering Section was keeping over three fourths of the squadron's 25 assigned aircraft in commission. Nine major inspections were performed that month, along with thirteen second intermediate inspections and six engine changes. This was in addition to routine daily maintenance work. Despite all the turmoil and relocations due to weather, flying time for the squadron jumped from 1,246 hours in July to 1,406 in August.

Pilots were not the only squadron personnel to face grave personal dangers in addition to constant fatigue. Staff Sergeant Vincent H. Brizzi, was changing the booster pump in the wing tank of aircraft #44-74592A when it exploded. He had to be evacuated to a hospital in Japan where he was treated for severe burns on the hands and face.

Morale went up that month when the 67th Squadron's Engineering Section was rated as "Excellent," following a Fifth Air Force inspection. "It is not often that an excellent rating is given out by an Air Force inspection team," Colson reported, "unless the section is far above average." Competition between Flights within the squadron

was "keen" and "morale generally remains high," Colson said.

Enlisted morale suffered as a result of promotions to Airman being "limited to TO&E vacancies. Only two Privates were promoted to PFC and one PFC to Corporal. "If this continues for any great length of time, it is felt that morale will be adversely affected by these policies," Colson warned.

[When reviewing this chapter, Col. Ralph Saltsman, former Commander of the 18th Fighter-Bomber Group observed that the "problems" with the 67th Squadron involving personnel and unit aircraft reported by Major Colson "are apparently personal observations." Saltsman did not view them as representing the 18th Group situation as a whole. "Colson is about to be reassigned after completing his tour in Korea," Saltsman noted, "and it would appear that he is making a final statement for the record."]

Strafing Runs With No Ammunition

"I flew twenty more missions in about as many days," Lt. (later Colonel) Frederick Thomas wrote for his diary, "and am beginning to see light at the end of the tunnel. Some of the missions are long, in an effort to influence the peace talks two all out missions are organized for the capital of North Korea, Pyongyang. Every plane in the Air Force that is available is utilized—fighters, bombers, flak suppressors...Pyongyang is heavily defended and we sustain some losses.

Next we hit airfields—the defenders turn the sky black with flak—talk about nervous!

Late in this month, I led my flight through some bad weather to an ammunition storage area in the mountains. No other flights get to the target area. Luckily, the sky opens up somewhat as we approach the target. We attack with napalm and rockets and score some spectacular hits. I run out of ammunition, but continue to make passes to cover my wingmen. "

[Note: Months later, back in the U.S., Thomas was awarded the Distinguished Flying Cross for this action.]

Re-Arming At K-16. *Stacked like darts in a box, rocket projectiles arrive for loading on Mustangs of the Two Squadron, SAAF at K-16 in August 1951. The engines have yet to cool down from the previous mission as the refueling and rearmament crews climb over and under the F-51s to ready them for another strike. (NARA)*

Tactics

Tactics remained essentially the same for August as for the previous month, Major John Rees, Commander of the 12th Squadron noted in his monthly report. "Four ship flights with napalm, rockets, and machine guns supported ground action along the bomb line. Armed reconnaissance of enemy MOR's and against his troops, supplies, vehicles and gun positions were flown as such and as the second objective of most bombing missions. A long range-bombing mission against enemy railroads, bridges and marshalling yards and a return reconnaissance along the MOR's was the order for the day usually. During August, as compared with July, there was considerable decrease in proportion of 500-lb bombs to napalm used," Rees noted. [4]

While overall tactics remained generally the same for August, "continuous work and study of large formations" was now a "must, since the squadron is now averaging two missions per day as a part of a large group formation." In the Pyongyang raids, for example, the 67th was assigned targets to be destroyed with napalm, making a low level attack necessary. "Each ship carried one napalm tank and one external fuel tank. Excellent results were observed, in spite of intense flak and the necessity for dodging cables which the enemy had stretched between hills and buildings," Major Colson noted in his monthly report.

Bombing accuracy continued to improve as a result of continuing emphasis on proper bombing techniques. Accuracy was improved also by an "important development"—the "decision to retard throttles upon entering the bomb run, to keep airspeed within 350 miles per hour, so that the aircraft could be controlled and aimed. Gun camera film is assessed by the pilots in the group at least once each week, and improvement is constantly noted." [5]

Eight new pilots reported on board during August, most of the recalled Reserve or National Guard Officers that possessed "a high level of experience." One of them, Lt. James F. Byers was a WWII Ace.

Mission to Pyongyang
weather be damned

On 14 August, 1st Lt. Walter H. Burke, led the second squadron of a sixty F-51 group formation in a low level attack as part of a "group gaggle" mission against the heavily defended North Korean capital city of Pyongyang. Burke was cited for "superior airmanship by navigating the formation through the most adverse of weather conditions and still maintaining a precise time-table to the target. When the formation arrived over the initial point exactly on schedule, the entire fighter force was immediately engaged by heavy, accurate, and intense anti-aircraft fire which persisted all the way to and through the attack route. The close proximity of hospital sites and a prisoner of war compound to the assigned squadron target complicated the navigation, demanding exact and precise pinpointing by First Lieutenant Burke."

Leading his squadron through the intense flak and at tree top level, Burke's napalm bombs were "observed to burst with deadly accuracy in the center of the assigned tar-get thereby causing maximum destruction and at the same time marking it for the three following flights that had no trouble completing the destruction of the assigned target area."

In all, ten warehouse type buildings were destroyed, one automatic weapons position was destroyed, and six office type buildings were severely damaged. Continuing on at tree top level, targets of opportunity were attacked as Burke led his pilots to the rendezvous point. Except for the same adverse weather hampering the return flight the mission was complete without further incident.

One pilot and aircraft were lost to enemy fire over the target.

"Such a record of destruction with no greater loss of life is a tribute to and the result of Lieutenant Burke's complete planning and superb execution of a difficult operation."

The Air Force recognized Burke's leadership with a second DFC.

Return to K-10

Bad weather hampered air operations during much of August. In fact, flood waters during the first week of August "forced the squadron to abandon our advance base at Seoul. We were forced to operate from the main base at Masan."

On August 9, 1951 the Han River began rising due to heavy rains and threatened to flood the runway at K-16. Five hours later the Group had evacuated to K-10 "due to the urgency of the situation."

Retreating back to Mason to avoid the weather "cut down the total effort of the squadron, since it added two hours flying time to each sortie." In some cases it was necessary to fit the F-51s with an external fuel tank to give them enough range to reach the assigned target.

The relocation was carried out "in rapid order fashion." Two C-54's carried 42 personnel and several tons of supplies first to K-9 (Pusan-East) on the first leg of the journey, than on to K-10 (Chinhae) the following morning." Combat operations continued "without a break, the aircraft flying from K-10. A week later the squadron resumed operations from Seoul "when the flooded Han receded."

No sooner had the advance base become serviceable once more than the 67th had to "abandon the rear base" to avoid Typhoon "Marge," then in the vicinity of Okinawa and moving towards Southern Korea at about eight knots an hour with winds reported to exceed 150 knots. All serviceable aircraft were flown to Seoul, and the southern base was secured against the expected winds. While operations continued unhampered at the advance base, the rear base was "kept secure for several days, prohibiting work outside hangers." At the same time mission commitments were increased because the bad weather grounded the bombers and "it fell our lot to maintain the tempo of the war without their aid." [6]

Just as the Group had set up operations at K-10, it was "met by the FAF Operational Effectiveness Testing Team" that proceeded to "very thoroughly analyze and inspect" the Group's operations. Just two days after returning to K-10, the Group "set up the big day of Pyongyang raids in which we sustained heavy aircraft and personnel losses."[7]

At K-10, the Operations Office had been "renovated and decorated with straw mats and bamboo strips; carpenters were busy building easy chairs to comfort the pilots during pre-mission nervousness and post mission relaxation, a side entrance was made in the ready-room in order to give pilots an easy access to the patio, which has been built beside the Operations Building; and a combat film library, designed by Captain Trumbull, has been established to put the latest film at the pilots' immediate disposal," the 12th reported.

After ten days of operating from K-10 in August, the Group returned to K-16 just in time to "operate through Typhoon 'Marge,' which passed to the west of the Seoul-Inchon area." The typhoon brought bad weather, but the Group nevertheless "performed a week of near maximum effort. Sorties were directed on rail cuts and JOC alert."

A "new type" of operation was begun. "Mass formations of thirty-six aircraft, working with all other fighter groups in Fifth Air Force set about on a program of rail cutting in 'MIG Alley.' This system of rail line destruction was to destroy all possible means of transporting supplies, equipment and troops by rail."

Personnel losses "were especially high" during the month "as the enemy continued to build up anti-aircraft weapon concentrations as their main counter-air measure," the Group reported.

Morale: Straight to the Top

Morale had improved somewhat. "With the departure dates rolling in to get rid of the 100-mission pilots and more and more replacement pilots coming in for the squadrons from the States, the morale has gone as we predicted—straight to the top," Col. Saltsman noted.

"There has been no tendency to let down because of Kaesong 'Peace' talks," Saltsman noted. "There have been indi-

Fires and explosions along dug-in enemy positions blocking the advance of United Nations ground forces in August 1951 were caused by rockets launched from Fifth Air Force fighter bombers. Enemy positions were spotted by T-6 "Mosquito" observation planes of the 6147th Tactical Control Group. The spotter planes marked the target site using smoke grenades. Fifth Air Force tactical aircraft then supplied "the knockout blow. These hunter-killer tactics have paid dividends in the mountainous terrain of North Korea in tactical support to Allied ground units," the Air Force reported. (NARA)

vidual instances of pilots who have a 'fear of combat' but this seems to be a combination of having to fly in F-51's and over consciousness (if possible) of enemy flak build up. However, a bad day of losses has little or no effect on the majority of pilots. The biggest factor behind this is the 'pick-up' program of the Third Rescue Squadron and more than one pilot, some former PWs of

Major Jack A. Davis assumed command of the 39th Fighter-Interceptor Squadron following the death of Major Murrit Davis on 14 August 1951.

World War II, have been heard to ask the question, 'Why didn't they have this in the last war?'"

As if to underscore Saltsman's report, the 12th Squadron noted, "2nd Lt. Ralph P. Clark parachuted from his airplane, which had been hit by ground fire, and was rescued in enemy territory by a 5th Air Force rescue team twenty-one minutes after he called for aid." The 12th lost three aircraft to enemy fire in August, and another that "crashed into the bay at K-10 due to unknown causes."

"With the rotation policy keeping in step with the plans, all of the Airmen are nose to the grind stone, ready to do their part for the time they are here. Our 'Gripes and Bitches' department has run out of big problems," Saltsman concluded.

Endnotes

[1] USAFHRA. *Monthly Historical Report, 18th Fighter Bomber Wing,* August 1951, p. 2.
[2] USAFHRA. *The U.S. Air Force's First War: Korea 1950-1953 Significant Events.*
[3] USAFHRA. *Monthly Historical Report, 67th Fighter Bomber Squadron,* August 1951, p. 2.
[4] USAFHRA. *Monthly Historical Report, 12th Fighter Bomber Squadron* August 1951, p. 2.

25,000 Missions. *The photograph to commemorate the 18th Fighter-Bomber Wing's 25,000th combat mission in Korea used "combined elements" to spell out the accomplishment, with members of the four Squadrons using themselves as the identifying numerals. The F-51 Mustangs parked in the background represented the tactical squadrons of the 18th, including the 12th "Foxy Few," the 67th "Fighting Cocks," the "Fighting 39th" or "Cobra in the Sky" 39th Fighter-Interceptor Squadron, and the attached 2 Squadron SAAF ("Flying Cheetahs"). Men of the 18th formed the numbers, while South Africans formed the lettering below. The veteran 18th Fighter-Bomber Wing, besides being the first Far East Forces Unit to fly 25,000 sorties, was the first Wing to fly from a Korean airbase after the outbreak of the war.*

25,000 Combat Sorties

On 29 August 1951, not quite fourteen months since the first Mustangs of the 18th Wing took off "to fight against the Commies from Taegu," the Wing was "still in there pitching," as it celebrated its 25,000th combat sortie.

The honor of flying the "25 grand milestone mission" went to tall, husky Captain Winott Coomer of the "Red Scarf" Squadron, who was also flying his thirteenth mission "which made the flight an event no matter how you look at it," the *Truckbuster* noted.

The first person to congratulate Coomer upon his safe return was M/Sgt M.J. Gardner, Det-One's Line Chief, on the "famous R&R ramp."

"I guess the first 25,000 are the hardest," Coomer said, "but I'll be glad when I hit that century mission mark personally." He spoke for every pilot that ever flew with the 18th.

Coomer had returned to active duty in April 1951 when he dropped his law studies at Denver University and "turned in his First Officer's uniform to United Air Lines."

"All I want right now is that one way ticket back to 2350 Niagra Street in Denver," he said.

As expected, the Wing set up a huge publicity photograph to celebrate the 25,000th mission, the first unit to fly that many missions in the Korean War.

The photograph used "combined elements " to spell out their accomplishment, using themselves as the identifying numerals. The F-51 Mustangs in the background represented the tactical squadrons of the 18th, including the attached 2 Squadron SAAF. Men of the 18th formed the numbers, while South Africans formed the lettering below. Captain Coomer was credited with the mission, "when he landed from a close support mission August 30th. The veteran 18th Wing, besides being the first Far East Forces Unit to fly 25,000 sorties, was the first Wing to fly from a Korean airbase after the outbreak of the war," the *Truckbuster* reminded its readers.

[5] USAFHRA. *Monthly Historical Report, 67th Fighter Bomber Squadron*, August 1951, p. 3.
[6] USAFHRA. *Monthly Historical Report, 67th Fighter Bomber Squadron*, August 1951, p. 3.
[7] USAFHRA. *Monthly Historical Report, 18th Fighter Bomber Group*, August 1951, p. 2.

Han River Flooding Drives 18th Operations Back to K-10

When the Han River flooded in August 1951, Manuel V. Andujar, an 18th Wing fire fighter and rescue squad member, was on hand to record the damage and disruption to operations in and around K-16. (Andujar)

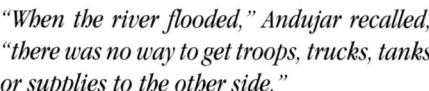

"When the river flooded," Andujar recalled, "there was no way to get troops, trucks, tanks or supplies to the other side."

The Han River bridge had been the target for numerous strikes by 18th fighter-bombers and was largely in the river and not above the river. Fortunately, the U.S. Army Engineers "were on the job to figure out the best way to get across the river," Andujar noted. "Their solution" was a pontoon bridge across the Han River over which the 18th moved many of its supplies as it 'bugged out' of K-16 until the waters receeded. (Andujar)

Significant Events

Members of the 2nd Squadron renamed their Club after Lt. Mickey Rorke, a young Port Elizabeth, South Africa flyer "who made the supreme sacrifice." Rorke had completed 64 missions in the Mustang when he crashed at a forward airstrip. A/M P.J.L. Swardt of Brzdasdorp, Cape Town installed the "Rorke's Inn" sign just outside the door of the 2 Squadron Club.

August 4: Communist ground forces violated the Kaesong neutral zone—truce talks were suspended.

August 10: Armistice negotiations resumed at Kaesong with North Koreans promising to respect the neutral zone.

At K-10, the 18th Fighter-Bomber Wing "Daisy Mae Contest" came to an end. Twenty nine photographs of wives, sweetheart and girl friends had been submitted. "The photos were sent to Al Capp, who will pick the winner," the Truckbuster announced.

August 13: "It was a pleasure and honor to be present at the Commencement Ceremonies for the Republic of Korea's first graduating class of Air Cadets from the Air Academy," Colonel T. C. Rogers wrote to Brig. Gen. Choi Yong Duk, Superintendent of the Academy. Rogers commended the Academy staff for their "success in training the first of many classes of military pilots. I am certain that the leadership and instruction which they have received will provide inspiration for the new graduate in their future years of service to the Republic of Korea. Only through such vitally essential training which you and your staff are providing can the free peoples of the world regard the future with calm determination of purpose. Determination that democratic nations can continue to exist as cultural and political entities, free from any threat of communist suppression and aggression," Rogers said.

August 14: "Activities around the squadron on 14 August were strikingly reminiscent of those on 30 July. The Group

Major Murritt Davis, Commander of the 39th Fighter-Interceptor Squadron

again struck Pyongyang with sixty-four napalm-loaded aircraft. Major John W. Rees, Squadron Leader for the morning strike, and Major Jack Davis, Leader in the afternoon, brought the Foxy Few home from both missions with no loss of personnel and negligible damage to the returning aircraft." [1]

"On 14 August 1951, a raid was scheduled over Pyongyang and Major Davis led the attack on rail yards and gun emplacements," noted Robert E. Sandlin in his unpublished manuscript "The Cobra in the Clouds Strikes Again." "That afternoon, the whole squadron was again scheduled for a second mission on Pyongyang to again strike military targets in the area. Major Davis led his flight in low over the target area and just after releasing their napalm were struck by a tremendous amount of ground fire. The results were tragic for the 39th. Major M. H. Davis, Captain John Horn, Operations Officer, and his wingman were all shot down and killed. Major Jack A. Davis assumed Command of the 39th Fighter Squadron."

August 18: Far East Air Forces began "Operation STRANGLE" against North Korean railroads.

August 22: The communist delegation trumped up evidence that a UN aircraft bombed Kaesong. Armistice negotiations were suspended.

August 24: General Hoyt S. Vandenberg, Air Force Chief of Staff, presented the nation's highest combat award "to the red-headed, 19-month old son of the late Major Louis J. Sebille." In early September,

the Truckbuster was reporting to its readers that the first Air Force Congressional Medal of Honor winner in the Korean Conflict was Major Lou Sebille. In the same paragraph, it noted that for most of its readers "it is probably just a name you have heard mentioned." Rotation in and out of the combat zone had meant replacement for most of those who had been part of the 18th in the earliest days of the way.

August 29: Capt. Winott A. Coomer, 67th Fighter-Bomber Squadron was credited with the 18th Wing's 25,000th combat sortie. "The veteran 18th FB Wing, besides being the first Far East Air Forces unit to fly 25,000 sorties, was the first Wing to fly from a Korean airbase after the outbreak of the war," the Truckbuster noted in its 9 September 1951 issue.

Combat Losses

Major Murrit Davis, Commander, 39th Fighter-Interceptor Squadron. "On 14 August the squadron joined in a group 'gaggle' over Pyongyang," the 39th Squadron reported. On the morning raid Major Murrit H. Davis, the Squadron Commander, suffered heavy damage to the right wing tip of his Mustang when the tip struck a cable over the target area and Captain Wagner's aircraft had a large portion of the right horizontal stabilizer shot away. However, both aircraft made it back to K-10 safely. In the afternoon raid over the same target, Major Davis, Captain John L. Horn and Captain John F. Grossman failed to return. Major Davis received battle damage in the coolant system while over the target and insisted on circling over the immediate target area to determine the whereabouts of the other two missing pilots. He finally left the area and started south, but his engine had overhearted and he subsequently crashed in enemy territory without bailing out. Captain Horn, the Operations Officer, was flying an F-51 with a K-25C camera and after his flight dropped their napalm he made a 180-degree turn back across the target to take photos of damage inflicted. No one saw him after he dropped his napalm and

"Never have I seen a group of pilots and men more grief stricken. They would have followed Dave anywhere. He has a living memorial in the hearts of his men."

BGen T. C. Rogers, Commander, 18th Fighter-Bomber Wing

turned back over the area, but it was assumed he was hit by the intense enemy ground fire and crashed in the immediate target area.

In early September, Colonel T.C. Rogers received a letter from Margaret Davis, writing about her husband, Major Murrit H. Davis, now missing in action. She expressed her appreciation and that of Davis' mother for the letters Rogers had sent them regarding their husband and son. "I am, of course, eager to know everything possible about the crash, and your letter contained much more information than the first sparse account received from Washington," she said. "Although I fully realize that the picture is very black indeed and offers very little encouragement for clinging to the belief that my husband survived the crash, I do have that belief and will hold to it. It is a comfort to know that the men of the 18th Fighter-Bomber Wing share my concern during this period of great anxiety. Major Davis was very proud to be a part of the 18th Fighter-Bomber Wing, and of the 39th Fighter-Interceptor Squadron. It makes me very proud to hear that in return he was admired and respected by all of his associates," she concluded.

Rogers replied to Margaret Davis on 16 September by noting that he fully realized "how difficult this war is for wives and parents. Sometimes I think it is worse for them than for the men actually engaged in combat," Rogers observed. "I have received other letters similar to yours," he continued, "in which wives cling to every shred of hope. I wish there were some assurance I could give you. As you probably know, unless positive proof of death can be established a man must be reported as missing in action. Dave's chances of survival are extremely slim," he pointed out.

"Mrs. Davis, your husband was a very gallant man," Rogers concluded, "his thoughts were always first for his pilots and men. I was waiting at his operations office

when his squadron returned from the mission on the afternoon of 14 August--never have I seen a group of pilots and men more grief stricken. They would have followed Dave anywhere. He has a living memorial in the hearts of his men. We all share with you the hope that he may have survived."

2nd Lt. C.L. de Jongh, 2 Squadron SAAF pilot KIA on 14 August 1951. Lt. de Jongh was flying No. 2 in a four-ship flight led by 2nd Lt. Denis Earp (later Lt. General and Chief of Staff of the SAAF). They were part of a massive, 64-ship formation that was attacking Pyongyang. As the flight pulled up following a low-level napalm attack, de Jongh radioed that he had been hit, was heading out to sea, but did not believe he would make it. The aircraft was streaming coolant fluid as it left the target area. His flight lost sight of him and he was never seen again. The target area was blanketed in heavy anti-aircraft fire and smoke at the time. *Winston Brent reports in "2 Squadron in Korea," that in 2000 a South African visitor to Beijing visited a Military Museum and saw the remains of 2nd Lt. de Jongh's Mustang, number 349.*

Captain David J. French, 18th Fighter-Bomber Group. Captain David J. French of the 18th Fighter-Bomber Group was lost during a close support mission. "His aircraft was hit and he was forced to bail out in enemy territory. He left the ship at about 200 feet and he was observed to hit the ground with his chute partially open. Rescue operations were hampered by enemy ground fire, and the helicopter pilot reported that he believed Captain French was dead and that it would be fruitless to attempt to recover the body."

Major William James Greene, 67th Fighter-Bomber Squadron. Major William J. Greene, the 67th Squadron's Operations Officer, was lost on the Pyongyang raids— "one of our best pilots." He had organized the operations section to a high degree of effectiveness and was "well versed in all

phases of fighter operations. His loss was a definite blow to the squadron."

Dorothy Greene wrote Colonel Rogers soon after receiving his detailed letter about her son's loss. "The smallest bit of news is so eagerly awaited in these anxious days," she told him.

"On the fourteenth of August--in this country--in the eastern newspapers, there was an account of a P-51 raid on Pyongyang on the previous day. The article stated that one aircraft had been shot down and that the pilot bailed out and was picked up. Can you tell me if there was another P-51 pilot missing on that date over Pyongyang?" Mrs. Greene asked. "Would it have been possible for some advanced patrol to have seen such a thing or perhaps the personnel in some other aircraft?"

"Here in my home in Ocean Springs, Mississippi I am only three miles from Keesler AFB and Major General Powell is in command there. He has been in communication with General Weyland about my son," she noted, giving Rogers a "heads up" that he might get another inquiry from further up the chain of command. "You see, Colonel Rogers, the Weyland, the Powells and Greenes all served together in the old days in Honolulu in the Thirties, and they have known my son since he was a small boy. General Powell assures me that it is quite all right to ask you to give anything that any one can find out, or any bit of information to General Weyland and he will get the message to General Powell and I will be told at once. If we could know that Bill did bail out even if he were a prisoner it would, of course, be a relief beyond all words of mine to describe. Thank you again for your kindness in writing," the grieving mother closed.

"I know how you must feel about Bill," Rogers responded, "and I sincerely wish I could give you some assurance on some positive information. Unfortunately we know nothing--except that he is missing."

"There was a raid [on Pyongyang] on the morning of the 14th in which we had one plane shot down and recovered the pilot. During the afternoon mission we lost a total of five F-51s and recovered only one of the pilots. I can find no one who was on the afternoon mission who actually saw Bill go down. So there is a big question as to his fate," Rogers explained. "I can only hope and pray that he managed to bail out of his aircraft. Of the remaining three missing pilots two were positively seen to crash."

[Lt. Col. Walter Burke notes that Major Green was shot down on the morning mission.]

"As you know Pyongyang is in the heart of enemy territory so there was no chance of friendly patrols being in the area," Rogers continued. "However, all the North Korean natives are not hostile so if Bill did manage to bail out he has a fair chance of evading capture."

"I do not want to build up your hopes," Rogers cautioned. "You probably realize that the odds are against him. But you can be assured that all the members of this Wing are showing that thin hope. I knew Bill very well--a fine officer and excellent pilot. I flew as his wingman on the first raid on Pyongyang on 31 July. We not only lost a fine officer and combat leader but I also lost a friend. I talked to Bill as he climbed into his airplane on the afternoon of 14th August and he was his usual jovial confident self. If any additional news concerning Bill comes in you will be notified immediately," Rogers promised.

Captain John Frank Grossman, 39th Fighter Interceptor Squadron. Captain Grossman, on his second mission, was hit on the way across the target and his aircraft went into an inverted dive and crashed into a small canal in Pyongyang city.

1st Lt. Grant D. Harkness, 67th Fighter-Bomber Squadron. "The entire squadron was shocked and grieved by the death of 1st Lt. Grant Harkness, who was killed in an accident while landing at our advanced base."

1st Lt. Richard Heilands, 39th Fighter Interceptor Squadron. On 18 August, 1st Lt. Richard G. Neillands "took off from K-10 on a napalm interdiction mission. Shortly after being airborne, his mission was cancelled by JOC due to inclement weather en route to and over the assigned target and was instructed by K-10 tower to salvo his napalm in the sea south of the base and return to home base. His flight leader stated they dropped the napalm as instructed and that was the last seen of Lt. Neillands. Search aircraft sighed napalm and oil slicks in the sea east of Koje-do Island but all search efforts for the pilot proved to have negative results," the 39th reported.

1st Lt. John David Hoke, 39th Fighter Interceptor Squadron. Lt. Hoke "was shot down on 31 August 1951 on a JOC close support mission. His flight had dropped napalm bombs and fired their rockets on the enemy troop positions and were commencing their strafing runs with Lt. Hoke's plane crashed into a small hill adjacent to their target. No radio transmission was heard from Lt. Hoke, but it was assumed he either sustained heavy battle damage to his aircraft or he misjudged his altitude, vision being limited due to impending darkness and cloud ceilings low over the target and mushed into the ground, his plane exploding on impact."

Captain John Lucas Horn, 39th Fighter Interceptor Squadron. Captain Horn, the Operations Officer, was flying an F-51 with a L-25C camera and after his flight dropped their napalm he made a 180 degree turn back across the target to take photos of damage inflicted. No one saw him after he dropped his napalm and turned back over the area, but it was assumed he was hit by the intense enemy ground fire and crashed in the immediate target area.

"The information was a great shock to us," Otto H. Horn wrote to Colonel Rogers on 9 September 1951. However, "it found us not entirely unprepared, for we realized as did 'Jack' that this is war and that such incidents would happen, even death. 'Jack' had a high patriotic motive in joining your ranks, an obligation to his Government and all free mankind. In the event he does not return, which now seems very remote, we wish that his personal effects be sent to us in due course." Mr. Horn concluded by thanking Col. Rogers for his "comprehensive and detailed information" regarding the loss of his son, "Jack."

[Note: Rogers prepared an internal memo asking for information on Captain Horn's personal effects to ensure they would be sent to his parents. The response noted the personal effects depot "holds effects on MIA personnel 120 days before shipment is made to Kansas City Depot.]

Captain Kenneth M. Stewart, 67th Fighter-Bomber Squadron pilot who "was reported MIA 25 August 1951 when his aircraft was hit by ground fire."

Major Jack A. Davis (right), Commander of the 39th FIS, *always tried to be down at the flight line when his flights returned from a combat mission. 1st Lt. Ernest "Ernie" Wakehouse was returning from a mission in which he had led the 18th Group. "Major Davis or Captain [Devol "Rock"] Brett always tried to welcome us back. Great People!," Wakehouse noted.*

September 1951

"There is a definite, aggressive fighting spirit with no consideration for the enemy's abilities. Our pilots feel they are as good as any in the business and are proving it every day,"

Col. Ralph H. "Salty" Saltsman, 18th Fighter-Bomber Group Commander

Combat Operations

"Tactical operations for the 18th Group in September continued to emphasize the rail interdiction program. The missions were flown as group missions with each of the squadrons furnishing eight or twelve aircraft with the exception of the squadron alternately furnishing close support flights on that particular day."

The results of the interdiction program "were graphically and interestingly explained by General Everest, Commanding General, Fifth Air Force, Colonel McBride and other officers from Fifth Air Force who visited K-16," the Group reported. The "distinguished visitors" reported the communists "are feeling the pinch in supplies reaching their front line troops in that with rail lines kept impassable they are forced more and more to rely on trucking their supplies and equipment. During the month

several camels were seen and attacked as well as horse drawn carts and wagons." [1]

After attacking a designated rail line as a primary target, the group formation—"gaggle"—would split off into squadron flights that would conduct armed reconnaissance on their way home.

The 67th Squadron reported that it continued flying maximum effort missions against rail lines, but also flew as many close support missions in conjunction with Allied front line troops as possible. In addition, its 37 pilots flew armed reconnaissance missions.

The primary mission of destroying rail lines would "continue to be a maximum effort until the Communist Forces rail lines are in such a condition as to prevent them from utilizing these facilities to arm and support their troops." Rail interdiction missions were performed as a group mission, with each squadron committed to fur-

nish between 8-12 aircraft. Close support and armed reconnaissance missions were flown as four aircraft flights. "First light" and "last light" periods of the day were best for armed reconnaissance missions. Armed reconnaissance missions were performed with four aircraft patrolling assigned MSR's before sunrise and after sunset "to seek out and destroy enemy vehicular movement." These missions "even if the enemy is not discovered and destroyed, limit the hours of darkness and prevent vehicular movement during the hours of semi-darkness." [2]

The squadron was also called on to perform "strip alert"—four or eight aircraft parked at the end of the take off runway in readiness for immediate take-off.

Weather was not too much of a problem during September, but did bring about two "stand-down" operational days.

Major Carl C. Colson, the 67th's Commander, reported that "tactics remain gen-

Monthly Summary

In the "Punchbowl" area of eastern Korea, the U.S. Army X Corps captured Bloody Ridge and Heartbreak Ridge, then successfully defended the new positions against enemy battalion-size attacks. The X Corps received fully two-thirds of Fifth Air Force's 2,400 close air support sorties for the month.

In air-to-ground activity, Fifth Air Force continued Operation STRANGLE against enemy railroads, although planners did not expect to stop all rail traffic. Basic repairs-involving earth, shovels, and thousands of unskilled laborers-were inexpensive for the enemy and often required only a few hours. While Fifth Air Force fighter-bombers made rail cuts by day, B-26 light bombers searched for trains and vehicles by night. In fact, the light bombers accounted for most damaged or destroyed enemy vehicles since they traveled mostly at night to avoid daylight attacks. The enemy made effective use of searchlights in conjunction with flak batteries to track and shoot down UN aircraft. Fifth Air Force lost nearly forty aircraft to enemy ground fire, reflecting the high cost of heavy interdiction efforts.

Personnel from the 18th Fighter Bomber Wing operating from K-16/Seoul Air Base were ordered to establish a new base of operations at K-46/Hoengsong and to "be in place and operating by 1 October 1951." The last three days of September 1951 were devoted to moving to the new location by "motor convoy and rail. Equipment required for winter operations was moved by rail from Chinhae to Hoengsong excepting necessary motor vehicles which were driven," the Wing's Monthly Historical Report noted.

Adapted in part from U.S. Air Force Historical Research Agency. January 2002. The U.S. Air Force's First War: Korea 1950-1953 Significant Events. September1951. http://www.au.af.mil/au/afhra/wwwroot/korean_war/korean_war_chronology/kwc_1951.html

Lethal Assembly Line. *By September 1951, rearming operations for the 18ᵗʰ Fighter-Bomber Wing had been studied and improved into a virtual assembly line process. Here a Mustang taxies up to a loading point, where napalm tanks will be slung under each wing. Rockets have already been attached at a previous station. Efficient loading techniques such as this permitted considerable savings in man-hour and equipment costs. It was one of the reasons combat operations could be sustained with a relatively few personnel. (NARA)*

erally the same," but there have been "great improvements by each individual pilot flying in the group formation. Efforts to improve group-flying skills were indeed necessary since "the squadron is now averaging two missions per day as part of a large group formation."

Dive bombing accuracy continued to improve after emphasis on proper sight pictures and proper bombing techniques was stepped up. Several factors contributed to the improvement. Controlling airspeed below 350 mph as the plane entered the dive-bombing run at around 6,000 feet was important. So, too, was releasing the bomb at about 1,500 feet indicated altitude. The "low release point was made possible by armament arming the bombs with 4-to-5 second delay fuses." Each pilot was required to "assess his combat film" at least once each week. [3]

One squadron in turn daily furnished the commitment of aircraft called for by JOC for close support. Such missions were "flown as four ship flights loaded with Napalm, rockets and full loads of .50-caliber ammunition."

"First and last light armed reconnaissance missions were also flown to search out and attack enemy vehicular movements on the main supply routes leading to the enemy's front," Col. Saltsman reported.

At K-10, intelligence activities centered around the group training program during which "newly arrived pilots were outfitted with maps and received their E and E lectures, indoctrination briefing on the Korean terrain features and the present military operations." [4]

Winter was on the way. "Stoves, sand

boxes and fuel drum stands have been procured...and are being installed in preparation for the forthcoming winter."

"There is a definite, aggressive fighting spirit with no consideration for the enemy's abilities. Our pilots feel they are as good as any in the business and are proving it every day," Saltsman concluded.

A change of command was held by the 12ᵗʰ Squadron. Major John W. Rees, was appointed 18ᵗʰ Group S-3 (Operations) Officer to replace Major Stanley Chatfield who was rotating in October. Major J.T. Crane, Jr. assumed command of the 12ᵗʰ Squadron.

Aircraft damages suffered by the 12ᵗʰ in September were reported as "slight," with only two aircraft lost "due to enemy action" and seven damaged by small arms fire.

In September, the 67ᵗʰ Squadron's pri-

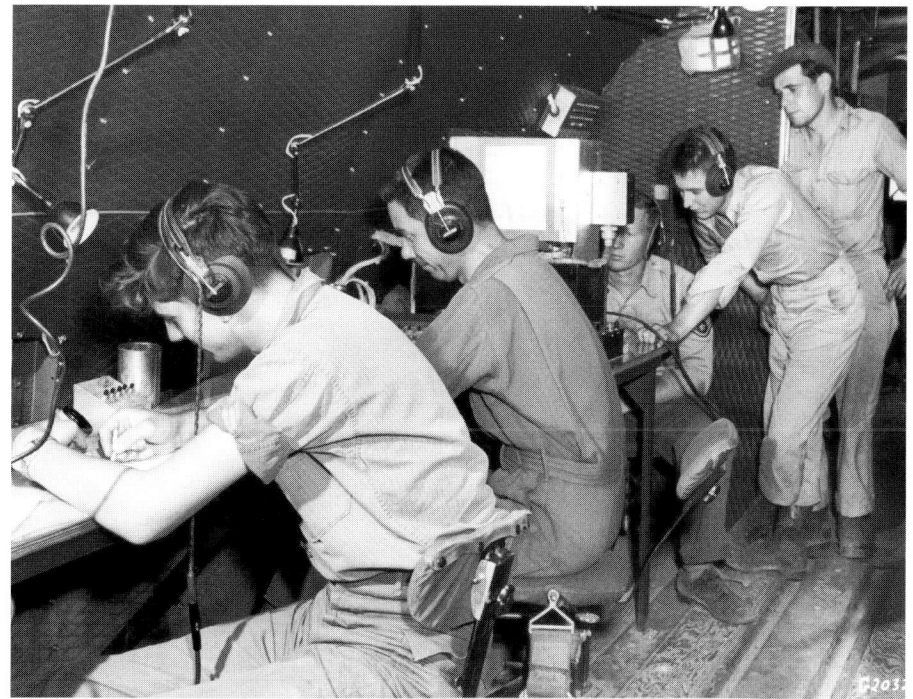

Mosquito Mellow. *Flying high over Korean front lines in an unarmed Fifth Air Force C-47 in September 1951, the crew of "Mosquito Mellow" from the 6147ᵗʰ Tactical Control Group carries on its work as though it were securely located in an office on the ground, the Air Force caption noted. Left to right: Sgt. James Fliege, Van Nuys, Calif., relays a message from a forward controller to Joint Operations Center as 1ˢᵗ Lt. Roy Todd, Hanover, N.H., officer in charge of "Mellow" operations, logs a T-6 "Mosquito" into a battle area. At the table at rear, S/Sgt. Gerald R. Gordie, Sneadi, Fla., monitors a transmission from the Kaesong conference as radio operator Cpl. Richard H. Webster, Salisbury, Md., listens in. Standing in the doorway is T/Sgt. James C. Glennister, Cos Cob, Conn., crew chief for the C-47. (NARA)*

HVAR In Flight. *This photo shows the path of a high-velocity rocket from the point of its release to within a few feet of its target. An F-9F "Pantherjet" of the 1ˢᵗ Marine Air Wing was summoned to the area by a T-6 "Mosquito" observation craft of the 6147ᵗʰ Tactical Control Group working with "Mellow" Control. The target was effectively neutralized. (NARA)*

mary mission of close support of UN forces in Korea or other aerial combat missions was subordinated "to tactical interdiction of enemy rolling stock, personnel and other material as well as the striking of enemy airfields to prevent enemy air buildup." Fifth Air Force maintained its pressure on interdicting enemy railroads. By then planners were not optimistic about stopping all rail traffic. Experience had shown that the North Koreans and Chinese were using thousands of unskilled laborers to begin repairing damage almost as soon as the fighter-bombers had cleared the area.

The 67ᵗʰ continued to be officially based at Chinhae, but used K-16 at Seoul "as a forward combat operations base."[5] Reloading and rearming was accomplished by the armament section at K-16. A steady rotation of personnel from Seoul to Chinhae and back was set up to provide R&R leaves, on the job training and medical and dental attention. Major maintenance was performed at Chinhae, as was cleaning of machine guns, bore-sighting, firing in of aircraft, OJT for armament technicians and pilot training. Ten aircraft were "fired-in" during the month on the "firing in butt" at K-10.

The armament section set up a training program at Chinhae that included classes on bombs, fuses, and other ordnance equipment handled by the section. Nomenclature, function, purpose and safety features were discussed and detailed drawings were used as training aids. A question and answer session was held after each class. The goal was to use the educational program to maintain "high standards of safety, apart from being instrumental in helping personnel who desire up-grading in rank and AFSC."

The squadron's intelligence officer, Captain Raymond P. Hutchinson had been reassigned pending rotation back to the states. That left the squadron with no intelligence personnel assigned that month. While Group Intelligence stepped up its efforts to help out, the squadron was "handicapped."

An important function of the Intelligence Section was to debrief pilots upon their return from a mission. These statements were used not only for mission planning, but also in substantiating a personal award based on mission accomplishments. As Major Colson noted in his report, "meritorious action against the enemy can more effectively be judged by personnel acquainted with actual accomplishments than by a combat pilot assigned the additional duty of Awards and Decorations." Statements that could be used to substantiate an award recommendation were obtained by the Intelligence Section during debriefing and could "contribute immeasurably to the immediate recommendation for an award for meritorious service."

During the month twelve new pilots reported to the squadron, most recalled Reserve or Air National Guard officers. This newest group of activated Reservists included Major Walter N. Burnette, a 1942 USNA graduate with 75 combat missions in "bombardment type aircraft in the Mediterranean Theatre of Operations during WWII." He was immediately made the squadron's Executive Officer.

Three pilots finished their 100 missions. One was sent back to the States. The other two were assigned to work with the Group and to help check out replacement pilots. Six officers were transferred to the ZI with no reason given for their change in assignment.

1st Lt. Harold K. Wimberley was now serving as squadron Operations Officer, assisted by Captain Roscoe L. Crownrich, Jr. Flights were being led by 1st Lt. Vernon L. Algood (A-Flight); 1st Lt. George N. Leitner (B-Flight); Captain Milton B. Taylor (C-flight); 1st Lt. Craig C. McCall (D-Flight); and 1st Lt. John S. Coleman (E-Flight).

The 37 pilots assigned to the 67th accounted for 721 sorties in September and 1,266 combat hours. A total of 167 "complete" rail cuts were reported, along with 29 "partials." Sixteen gun positions, 59 buildings, 19 box cars, 3 highway cuts and 850 troops killed were reported in September. 6 Squadron armorers loaded 340,000 rounds of .50 caliber ammunition, 1,607 5-inch rockets, 498 napalm bombs, and 856 demolition or fragmentation cluster bombs. Morale improved for at least four armament technicians—they were pro-

Old Napalm Dropping SOB. *Not the most ideal taxi-way, but still not enough of a hazard to stop operations is this miniature lake formed by torrential Korean rains in September 1951. An F-51 "Mustang" belonging to 1st Lt. Robert P. "Pancho" Pasqualicchio of the 67th Squadron plows through the water towards take-off position, heavily armed with bombs rockets and .50-caliber machine-gun ammunition. Regardless of weather and terrain hazards, strikes by tactical Fifth Air Force aircraft continued on a daily basis against Communist targets just a few miles to the north of K-46. (NARA)*

moted, three new staff sergeants and a corporal.

Faulty radio tubes and microphone adapters continued to affect operations, as did the empty communications officer billet since WOJG Blondell W. Staats had been returned to the States.

The Supply Section was severely undermanned, but did report moving to a better-protected building built by the section. Constructing the new building prevented the conduct of a required inventory and had to be reported to higher authority. "More suitable housing with bins and storage racks" improved "supply economy" but without more replacement personnel, "the section will be unable to properly perform its mission," Colson warned.

While Supply was building a new building, the Engineering Section was conducting 13 major inspections, 15 intermediate inspections, 8 acceptance inspections and 11 engine changes to maintain a 72% "in commission" status on the 26 aircraft assigned to the squadron. In noting an apparent drop of 5% in the "in commission" status from the August average of 77%, Colson explained that "The Pig," was sent to the 18th Maintenance Squadron for "rebirth" on 19 September 1951 "without benefit of a transfer." The Pig had, by itself, accounted for 288 hours of "out of commission" time.

S/Sgt Lloyd Bruce earned "high plane" of the month honors with 91 hours. "High Flight" was earned by M/Sgt Dorian Quinn's D-Flight with 458 hours. Sergeants Bruce and Quinn—along with all of D-Flight— were duly hosted at the monthly squadron party as "Guests of Honor" for outstanding efforts and devotion to duty.

Over 10,000 Korean War Sorties for the Cobra in the Sky Squadron

"Preparation for the movement from K-16 to K-46 (Hoengsong) continued," the 39th reported and "on the last day of the month everyone at K-16 was ordered packed for the movement by truck convoy and airlift to K-46 on the following day."

"The strength of the unit continued to dwindle away due to stepped up rotation of personnel to the Zone of Interior. A few airmen replacements were received from the 18th Maintenance Squadron but these served as a mere stop-gap since more personnel were alerted for stateside shipment shortly after arrival of the new personnel."

Two pilots, having proven unfamiliar with the F-51 aircraft and fighter operations in close support tactics, were reassigned to the 6147th Tactical Control Group and subsequent duties as 'Mosquito' T-6 pilots. It was felt such reassignment was necessary for these pilots survival and would further benefit the mission of Fifth Air Force, rather than attempt to ground them under circumstances over which they had no apparent control.

In September, the 39th completed 672 combat sorties requiring 1,222 flying hours. The Cobra in the Sky Squadron now had over 10,000 combat sorties in the Korean War.

Endnotes
[1] USAFHRA. *Monthly Historical Report, 18th FighterBomber Group*, September 1951, p. 2.
[2] USAFHRA. *Monthly Historical Report, 67th FighterBomber Squadron* September 1951, p. 10.
[3] USAFHRA. *Monthly Historical Report, 67th Fighter Bomber Squadron*, September 1951, p. 3.
[4] USAFHRA. *Monthly Historical Report, 18th Fighter Bomber Group,* September 1951, p. 4
[5] USAFHRA. *Monthly Historical Report, 67th Fighter Bomber Squadron* September 1951, p. 2.
[6] USAFHRA. *Monthly Historical Report, 67th FighterBomber Squadron* September 1951, p. 11.

Combat Statistics
18th Fighter-Bomber Wing

September 1951

Average No. A/C Assigned
72
Total Flying Time
4,421
Percent of Aircraft in Commission
74
Percent of Aircraft AOCP
1
Combat Sorties Flown by Wing
2,651
12th Squadron Sorties
708
39th FIS Sorties
672 (exceeded 10,000 total sorties in Korean War)
67th Squadron Sorties
721
2 Squadron Sorties
519
A/C Lost to Combat
8
Pilots lost
10

Fuel Consumed

301,168 gals.

Ordnance Expended

.50-cal. Rounds
1,267,330
Rockets
5,431
Napalm Bombs
1,540
500-lb. GP Bombs
2,408 (plus 24 M-29 500-lb Butterfly Cluster bombs)
Note: Figures and totals may differ in some categories due to differences in numbers provided by each component.

Chongchon Gang River*. Smoke from both flak and bomb explosions highlight this rare photograph of 18th Group Mustangs attacking the Chongchon Gang River railroad bridge crossing near Sinanju and Anju about sixty miles NNW of Pyongyang, North Korea on 4 September 1951. (McLees)*

Significant Events

September 9: Seventy MiGs attacked twenty-eight Sabre jets between Sinanju and Pyongyang-two MIGs were shot down.

September 10: A Wing Commander's conference was convened at K-10 hosted by MG Everest, CG, FAF. All Wing Commanders of the FAF assigned wings were present for the meeting, including representatives from the 314th Air Division and the 1st Marine Air Wing based at K-1/Pusan West. Following the conference "a picnic lunch was had on one of the nearby islands in the Chinhae Bay."

September 13: 2nd Lt. Elvin O. Wyatt, a pilot with the 12th Squadron "Flying Tigers," "flew their impressive ten thousandth effective combat sortie...and taxied into the famous R&R ramp at our advanced detachment," the *Truckbuster* reported. "Wyatt had a definite and monetary reason for grinning since he was able to share the $50.00 pool with his crew chief, S/Sgt. H. L. Grossley."

September 14: Capt. John S. Walmsley, USAF, 8th BS, on a night B-26 interdiction sortie attacked an enemy train, expending his ordnance. He then used a USN searchlight experimentally mounted on his aircraft's wing to illuminate the target for another B-26. Shot down and killed by ground fire, Captain Walmsley earned the Medal of Honor for his valorous act. [1]

September 24: Attempts to reopen peace talks at Kaesong failed.

September 25: In the largest air battle in recent weeks, an estimated one hundred MiG-15s attacked thirty-six F-86s flying a fighter sweep over the Sinanju area. Sabre pilots destroyed five MiGs in aerial combat, the daily high for the month.

September 27: In Operation PELICAN, a service-test C-124A Globemaster flew its first payload from Japan to Korea, delivering 30,000 pounds of aircraft parts to Kimpo Airfield.

September 28: On the longest flight to date for a jet aircraft using in-flight refueling, a Yokota-based RF-80 flew for fourteen hours and fifteen minutes on a Korean combat sortie, refueling multiple times from two KB-29M tankers.

Combat Losses

Grunder, 2nd Lt. M. O., 2nd Squadron SAAF pilot KIA on 1 September 1951. Lt. Grunder was flight leader of a four-ship flight assigned the mission of rail-cutting and reconnaissance of MSRs (Main Supply Routes). Anti-aircraft fire was heavy during the flight. Following completion of the rail and reconnaissance portion of the flight, Grunder saw something that he felt needed closer investigation from a lower altitude near Yongdong. While he was giving a close look to a wooded area, he radioed that he had been hit, but continued to press his rocket attack and to strafe the position he had identified. His wingman lost sight of him against the sun, but then saw a canopy and papers floating down past him. No sign of a parachute was seen. After a thorough search, the crashed aircraft was located, but no sign of the pilot or his parachute.

1st Lt. N. Biden, 2 Squadron SAAF pilot killed in action on 5 September. Lieutenants "Flash" Biden and Don Parks of the "Flying Cheetahs," were flying top cover for Lt. Willem van den Bos, downed near Sunch'on while trying to rescue an American pilot. Hit in the cooling system by small arms fire, the engine of Willem's Mustang failed at a low altitude and caught fire. He successfully belly landed it in a stream bed, jumped out and took cover in a ditch until the rescue helicopter arrived about 45 minutes later. After flying top cover during the rescue, Biden and Parker left the area for another target in the "Punchbowl" area where they were to napalm an artillery position. Biden was last seen in a shallow diving attack on the emplacement—a dive from which he never recovered. His plane crashed and burned. No sign of life could be seen by his wingman.

1st Lt. George L. Coyle, Jr., 67th Squadron, was on an armed reconnaissance flight when he was hit and then bailed out. His place of bail out "happened to be in an area where automatic weapons fire was intense."

Lt. Coyle was taken prisoner almost immediately upon his parachute landing. Colson added: "Lt. Coyle was a very aggressive fighter pilot and was flight commander of 'Easy' flight."

1st Lt. William Edwin Jackman, 39th Fighter Interceptor Squadron, "was shot down by Russian built MIG-15 jet fighters when he had entered into his dive bombing run on a rail cut near Sambong-dong, Korea. Lt. Jackman was flying Number Four position, last flight of a twenty-eight ship formation, when he flight was attacked by three MIG's. Evasive tactics were assumed by all other members of his flight and it was assumed Lt. Jackman did not hear his flight commander's warning of enemy aircraft. Lt. Jackman's ship suffered heavy hits from one MIG and crashed into the mud flats off shore from Sambong-dong. The pilot did not clear his aircraft before crashing and members of his flight reported it appeared the cockpit had received a direct hit by a 20-mm explosive shell from the attacking MIG."

1st Lt. Frank A. Montanari, 2 Squadron SAAF, killed in action on 12 September. Lt. Frank Montanari was Flight Leader of a four-ship flight on an armed reconnaissance mission from Inchon to Majon-ni and return. The cloud cover was dense and to get a closer look at the road they were patrolling, he descended rapidly along a sloping hill to an altitude of about 2,000 feet where it was hit by heavy flak. When he pulled up to about 3,000 feet his Mustang was leaking coolant rapidly. The plane began to spin, briefly recovered, then continued to lose altitude. Montanari attempted a crash landing in a river bed but the aircraft was destroyed on impact. No sign of the pilot was seen. Heavy flak prevented further investigation.

1st Lt. Orval H. Tandy, 39th Squadron "was shot down while leading 'D' Flight on a rail interdiction mission near Sonchon, Korea. He parachuted safely from his battle damaged aircraft, landed unhurt, and was last seen moving south and west into timbered land. Members of the squadron provided a 'CAP' over the downed flight commander but when the rescue helicopter arrived several hours later, Lt. Tandy could not be located.

1st Lt. Leland Harry Wolfe, 67th Fighter-Bomber Squadron. Close support missions were especially risky. 1st Lt. Leland H. Wolf was conducting such a mission when "his aircraft was hit by enemy fire and he was never observed to leave the aircraft." After he crashed, a mosquito pilot and his observer attempted to get a closer look at the wreckage and to see if Lt. Wolf was still alive. During their attempt, they too were hit by enemy fire and had to bail out. Now there were three airmen in trouble. A rescue effort was started to retrieve the men but "proved unsuccessful when the rescue helicopter arrived at the scene—and was also shot down. Rescue attempts were "abandoned.""

Royal Order of the Buffalo

One of the more unusual endorsements of the effectiveness of tactical air power was rendered to the "Flying Tiger Squadron" when its commanding officer and four of its pilots were inducted into the "Royal Order of the Buffalo."

On 4 September, Major John Rees, Commander of the 12th Squadron, and his flight "made a fast and accurate delivery of the usual quota of rockets and napalm" for a combat team of the 17th Infantry Regiment. The foursome waved an aerial good-bye to the ground troops with an "off the deck" roll as they headed homewards.

The Commander of the 17th, checked back with JOC to obtain the names and organization of the four Mustang pilots.

Soon, down through channels came a Citation that carried the 17th Regiment's famous Buffalo coin logo.

"This mission was the most effective delivered in our sector during the twelve months we've been fighting in Korea," McCown noted in the accompanying letter. "Its success contributed immeasurably to the accomplishment of our mission."

Blinker Nose Pilot of the Year

"A bunch of the boys were whooping it up just t'other day," 2nd Lt. Richard Ward wrote in his tongue-in-cheek style, "and decided 1st Lt. Jawn "Hairy" Taylor, Jr. should be selected as Blinker Nose pilot of the year. 'Hairy' has been with us a few short months and has decided he likes the Spamcan so well he is going to fly a couple hunert missions. The nickname 'Hairy' stems from his ample hirsute adornment, and he seems to believe his strength will be lost if he should succumb to the wiles of some tonsorial artist. Sort of a 'Samson and Delilah' complex. Jawn is from New Preston, Connecticut and when he isn't busy fighting wars in 'Stangs' he designs, builds and races motorcycles and cars. Perhaps you have seen him screaming down the taxi strip on his old, beat up motorcycle standing up on the seat!!!! Indeed, a fine example of our American manhood, devil may care, adventure seeking, etc."

"Admiration Dawg had his first rabies shot the other day and what he called the Doc wasn't worth calling. Sed he'd never had a sick day in his life and some people sure had a lotta nerve shoving needles behind his arm. He's got his shot record with him now and saw him talking to one of his friends the day after he got his shot, telling all about his 'operation.'"

The author, 2nd Lt. Ward had recently been promoted from Warrant Officer to Lieutenant and served as the Adjutant for the Foxy Few.

Meet 1st. Lt. JOHN E. TAYLOR Jr.

From WASHINGTON, CONNECTICUT, the 18TH FTR-BMR WING'S 27 yr. old 'FLYING ARSENAL'!

...HIS PERSONAL SURVIVAL KIT INCLUDES AMONG OTHER THINGS, a .45, CARBINE, BAYONET, a WAISTBELT and 2 BANDOLIERS of ASSORTED AMMO, and a SPARE FLIGHT JACKET.

...THE MUSTACHIOED BARNEY OLDFIELD HAS SPENT THE LAST FIVE YEARS BURNING UP TRACKS AROUND THE COUNTRY AS A PRO RACING DRIVER...BOTH IN STOCK CARS AND MOTORCYCLES !!!

...IN WW II, TAYLOR FLEW 36 MUSTANG MISSIONS with the 364TH GROUP in the ETO... HE HAS ALREADY LOGGED OVER 133 MISSIONS WITH the 18TH'S 'BLINKER NOSES' SQUADRON...AND WANTS TO SET an ALL-TIME RECORD by FLYING 200 COMBAT MISSIONS....HOW EAGER CAN YOU GET!'

"Admiration Dawg"

"...tell him to come on back and face the Flight Surgeon like a dog—er, man."

Major Jack A. Davis *assumed command of the 39th Squadron upon the tragic death of Major Murrit Davis on 14 August 1951.*

The Blinker Noses reported in early September that the "Squadron has not officially welcomed in the new Commanding Officers, Major Jack A. Davis. There was a little doubt in our minds when he first came over from the very Few Foxey," author, Lt. Richard Ward, wrote with tongue firmly in cheek, "but it was quickly ascertained he had not been with the very few foxey long enough for any to rub off on him and the Squadron is soaring along famously under his guiding hand."

"Cap'un 'this hyar is ole Tex' Hester is the Executive Officer, took over when Captain 'Spec' Sumner limped off for the States to fly F-82's (F-51's with built in wing man.)"

The Man of the Year for the 39th Squadron was Captain S. L. Ross, who "established something or other by being the only man from the Wing to complete 100 missions," Ward continued. "This signal honor has not turned Captain Ross' head, and he still maintains his usual jovial, understanding self. Other Century Club members are 1st Lt. Hamilton Reese White of the West B 'Gawd Virginia White, 1st Lt. James. Gleoggler, 1st Lt. Bert L. White and 1st Lt.

James W. Xuaennonbrrehc (Cherbonneaux spelled backwards). Lt. Cherr Bonneaux has also made some sort of a record in finishing 100 missions and still never allowed his bed to completely cool off," Ward continued, on a roll.

"Captain Hester was recently elected to the Officer's Club Board of Governors and nosed Admiration Dawg out by three votes to represent the Blinker Nose Squadron."

For those at K-10 who thought they saw several tents "gliding across the ramp area the other day" can "climb back off the wagon again—it's true," Ward explained.

"The Acey-Duecey Tent Moving Agency, Sergeants Porter and Horton, did what others claimed impossible—a usual feat with the Blinker Noses, and moved the Airmen's tents to another area so the Air Installations Boys can put up some new Quonsets in the billet area so when the snow is snowing the tents won't be blowing."

"Admiration Dawg was reading the Bulletin Board the other day and took off like a scalded ape," Ward noted. "The First Sergeant said 'Admire' saw the notice where

he had to take a rabies shot and when he asked how many in a series, he re-e-e-e-ly got clankey. If anybody sees that mutt up around the Bomb-line, tell him to come on back and face the Flight Surgeon like a dog—er, man. Besides, he can't get any more R&R to Chinhae unless his shot record is up to date," Ward explained with a grin.

Admiration Dawg *of the 12th Squadron led anything but a "dog's life." He was the pampered mascot of the Foxy Few who, it was reliably reported, was taken on at least ten combat missions. When the new Combat Support Group Commander barred dogs from the Officer's Club, all the pilots and most of the other officers voted "Admiration Dawg" as a member of the Board of Officers to ensure he was properly authorized to enter the Club, remembered Col. Bill Myers.*

Last Missions for Thomas

Lt. Fred Thomas flew his last 26 missions in 20 days.

"After landing from No. 100, I was met by the C.O. and given a warm reception," he noted in his diary. "After returning from No. 97, I see George Coyle's flight returning with only three planes. I hurry to meet the flight as they shut down their engines and learn that George has been shot down. His plane was in flames, but he was able to bail out and was seen being captured."

[Note: Coyle will "spend two grueling years as a prisoner of war, returning to Charleston in late 1953." Thomas immediately wrote to Coyle's wife, Julia, "to reassure her and his family as best I can." It was almost a year before they hear from Coyle.]

"More excitement," Thomas noted. "Returning from a mission, my wingman calls and tells me my plane is spewing oil out the nose. In the next 30 seconds, it is covered with oil, the coolant blows and the engine shuts down. I am now flying a powerless lump of metal. It's very quiet! I get my heart restarted and decide I have a chance of getting to an airfield at Taegu, about 30 miles away. If I see I can't make it, I'll just bail out."

[Note: Thomas did "make it," as the

An Engine's Final Moments. *Lt. Frederick L. Thomas of the 67th Squadron demonstrated superb airmanship in getting his Mustang back to a safe, dead stick landing at Taegu in July 1951. The ugly smear of oily residue down the side of the aircraft is graphic witness to the engine's "final moments." (Thomas)*

photograph of his "oil soaked bird on the ground at Tagu," attests. "I never found out the cause of the problem—malfunction or battle damage," Thomas reported, " but at least my plane kept going until I was back on our side of the line."*

"Lighter moments" for Thomas included:

"Returning from a mission that started off in the rain and mud, I am looking into the sun and can't see through the mud on my windscreen. I rolled back my canopy and tried to wipe off a spot that I can see through. The people on the base thought I was preparing to bail out and scrambled the fire truck and ambulance. Pandemo-

nium on the ground. (I landed o.k.)

"On another flight, my life vest accidentally inflated, rendering my head almost immobile. With all those straps and harness over it, I felt nailed to my seat. What if I had to bail out into the water with that thing inflated? Probably tear your head off, so I decided I would not try that. End of story--got back o.k."

"On a napalm run at treetop level, I punched off my tanks and only one of them released! I'm immediately almost inverted, looking at the trees. But I was able to roll out level after some struggle, I manually released the remaining tank."

"During a dive bombing mission on a marshalling yard deep in enemy territory: lots of action and we're all nervous. I started a screaming dive from about 15,000 feet and pulled out with a high "G" blackout. As my vision returned, I am inverted in the top of a loop and my engine quits cold! My heart stops next. I thought I had taken a direct hit. A few seconds later, I realized that in the heat of battle, I had forgotten to switch gas tanks. I changed tanks, the engine roars to life and it's back to business."

"George and I get up a bridge game with an engineering officer and I bid one no-trump. He replies with "seven no-trump" and I almost faint. He hasn't the foggiest idea about the game! I make him play the hand and he easily makes seven. A few minutes later, George and I are both off on another flight.

Frat Drag Praised by "Dean of Men"

The Foxy Few hosted a "Frat Drag" at the officer's club in September and invited their colleagues as well as squadron pilots.

"The party must have been good," the Truckbuster reported, "for all the pats on the back that Major Rees has been receiving the past couple of weeks.

"I particularly enjoyed my role as Dean of Men," Col. Rogers was quoted as saying for the Truckbuster. "The party showed the results of excellent planning and hard work. The Foxy Few whether in combat or at play, can be counted upon to turn in an excellent performance. All members of the Wing Headquarters join me in thanking you for a grand party."

Rotating Home?

Avoid Saying "Babysan"

The stepped up rotation plan during the summer of 1951, brought some tongue in cheek "advice by the Bard," writing in the Truckbuster. Making the assumption that some of the readers had not been back to the States in so long that they had forgotten "how to act when we get back there," the writer explained that the first "thing we'll do…is jump in the car and tear out for home." He then goes on to remind the American readers to keep to the right side of the road, "forget everything that was taught you about driving on the left side as in Japan."

"When you greet the wife," the Bard continued, "don't hail her as 'Ocksan' or 'Babysan' as some seem to take a dim view of such greetings. If you can't remember her name—if it has been that long—never mind as getting acquainted will come later any how. Several days later the problem of eating will no doubt arise."

"Try to recall what they called the food in the States. Don't call for 'Chop-chop,' 'Gohon,' or 'Kimshee' as they won't understand and you are apt to get fed a hand full of knuckles, a practice which has proven very remunerative to dentists."

"Should you be unfettered from marital ties," the Bard concluded, "when you refer to the gal friend, refrain from such endearing descriptive phrases as 'your moose' or 'your corbito.' They just don't understand and might cause a complete reversal of their affections for you. There will be a noticeable lack of 'A' frames back there, no more 'honey buckets,' no more 'Free Air Mail,' radio programs and something new—television. Your first impulse when you see Dagmar is to grab but all you'll get is a bunch of bloody knuckles and a bill for about 200 bucks for a new TV set. That's all the tips we can give you for 'survival in the ZI.' Now you are on your own."

Close Call. *Capt. Pancho Pasqualicchio holds the helmet worn by Capt. Bob "Big Dog" Smith of the 67th Squadron that was hit by small arms fire. (Pasqualicchio)*

Capt. James "Jimmy" Allen, *Aide de Camp for General Everest, Commander FAF, often flew missions with Pancho Pasqualicchio in 1951. Allen would later retire as a four-star general. (Pasqualicchio)*

Combat Crew Training for Pipeline Pilots

Luke AFB, Arizona

Staying Alive While Flying The

F-51 "On the Deck"

On August 8, 1940, President Roosevelt directed the military to produce 12,000 pilots annually. Responding to that order, the Army Air Corps conducted feasibility studies for the construction of new airfields. Phoenix City Manager Donald C. Scott announced on Feb. 13, 1941 that the War Department had approved a site two miles north of the town of Litchfield Park, Arizona, for the construction of an advanced single engine flying training base. The site not only had almost year-round flying weather, but it also enjoyed close proximity to vast stretches of desert ideal for bombing and gunnery practice. Two days later, Lt. Col. Ennis C. Whitehead arrived in the area to supervise construction of the base and to act as its first commander.

Ground was broken for Litchfield Park Air Base on March 31, 1941. On June 6, 1941, the installation was renamed Luke Field in honor of 2nd Lt. Frank Luke Jr., a Phoenix native who was a World War I ace and the first aviator to receive the Medal of Honor. The first student pilot class began training the next day.

During World War II, Luke Field produced 17,321 graduates from fighter training programs for the United States and its allies.

P-51 Mustang fighter training initially began at Luke Field in 1945 and ended in 1946. The program had produced only 280 graduates from its fighter training programs when it was terminated. The base closed Nov. 30, 1946. World War II was over.

Five years later, on February 1, 1951, Luke Air Force Base was reopened. The Korean War needed more fighter pilots than the Air Force could provide. The Mustang fighter-training program was one of the two programs conducted at the base. The other was the F-84 Thunderjet program.

By 1951, the "P" for pursuit designa-

tion that was common in WW II had been replaced by "F" for fighter and the P-51 became the F-51. The Mustang training program at Luke AFB began in 1951 and ended in 1953 after producing 624 graduates, including 2nd Lt. Archie Connors and 2nd Lt. Wilfred "Budd" Stapley.

On September 10, 1951, Connors and Stapley reported to Luke AFB, Arizona for intensive training in the F-51—Combat Crew Training. Their academic subjects included: armament, fighter attack, navigation, gun camera, recognition, climatology, geography, tactics, survival, flying safety, intelligence and physical conditioning.

Connors didn't do too well in rocket attack or low angle bombing, but scored high in angle strafing and dive-bombing. He completed 71 training missions totaling over 54 hours of airtime in the F-51.

The base was still in the process of being "reopened" in mid-1951—"there were still cement bags on the bar top in the Officers Club." A new "bird" colonel was arriving to take command at Luke.

As the new CO approached the Main Gate to the new base in his POV (privately owned vehicle), he noticed a movement almost at eye level directly ahead of him. Something was approaching his vehicle at an extraordinary rate of speed.

A moment later there was no mistaking the fact that an F-51 was streaking down the highway, virtually "on the deck," and

then whooshed over his car and out of sight down the road.

The new Colonel restarted his car and entered the base for the first time. Soon after, he called an "all hands" meeting. All the officers were required to attend.

At the meeting he related to the group the story of how he had been "buzzed." He also told them that had the pilot made another pass at him, he would have had his number, and he would have been grounded.

Everyone there knew, including the new CO, at that particular time of day there were only three or four F-51s in the air. It would have been relatively easy to find out the identity of the pilot. However, it was not his intention to nail the pilot.

"I won't have a fighter pilot that won't 'buzz,'" he told the assembled officers. "But when you attempt a risky maneuver like that—use your head. That pilot was really pushing his luck," the Colonel pointed out.

Low level cross-country flying was in the "curriculum" for combat crew training. Connors, Stapley and their fellow pilots were now being told to fly their F-51s in ways that would have had them grounded or dismissed as pilots just a few months earlier. However, low level cross country was the kind of flying that would better prepare them for the harsh realities of combat in Korea—the kind of flying that left trails behind the speeding planes...of dust.

One Luke pilot brought back gun camera film that showed a truck—at twilight—directly ahead—with his lights flashing on and off at the F-51 heading right at him on the highway. "That is low!!!" Stapley remembered.

Some of the pilots training at Luke had flown in WWII. The older (more experienced) guys flew somewhat higher than the "younger guys." Back at the Luke O-Club, Archie and Budd were treated to a "tongue lashing" from one of the older pilots, who yelled out for all to hear at the bar: "I saw you raise up to go over that cow." Of course, it was a compliment of sorts.

"Thank God," Stapley thought, "recognition." [8]

While undergoing combat crew training at Luke AFB, 2ⁿᵈ Lt. W. E. McShane's prop disconnected from the engine. Fortunately, he was able to bail out successfully. (Urquhart)

Target Fixation

Target fixation was always a danger, particularly for new pilots under pressure to learn their craft as quickly as possible. On one occasion, Stapley was making a practice "strafing run" and concentrating intensely on the "target"—the driver on a grader working on the runway. For a moments the new pilot was "in Korea, strafing the imagined enemy and pouring in 5-inch rockets"…then with a start, Stapley realized that he was boring in on a road grader now so close that "you could tell whether the driver had shaved that morning or not."

Stapley pulled back on the stick so hard that the resulting G's partially opened the wheel cover, causing a warning light to go on the cockpit. Close to blacking out, he hung on the stick and pulled out of the high-speed dive just over the head of the terrified driver.

Returning to base, Stapley found the driver had reported him—thinking the "buzzing" was deliberate. He claimed that Stapley's plane had come within 25' of the ground before it pulled out of the dive.

Stapley was let off with a warning when he explained how he had fixated on the "target" to the point where it had almost

cost him his life. It was highly realistic preparation for his months of combat in Korea.

Later, both Connors and Stapley would see the deadly results of target fixation from another point of view. During a trip to the Naval Air Station at North Island (near San Diego, CA), the C-47 carrying Connors, Stapley and other members of their Combat Crew Training Class, flew by an air-ground

2ⁿᵈ Lt. Wilfred "Budd" Stapley completed Combat Crew Training at Luke AFB in November 1951. (Stapley)

gunnery range for Navy and Marine Corps pilots (NAS Miramar). The Air Force pilots were treated to a grandstand seat from their angle and altitude at Navy and Marine Corps fighter bombers conducting low level bombing runs on the target area as the Air Force transport flew by in a safe, parallel heading transiting through the air space en route to San Diego.

Plane after plane made its attack to the cheers of the unseen gallery of fellow fighter pilots passing by above them.

Finally, a Marine Corps pilot in an F-4U Corsair began his attack, boring in on the target—closer, closer and closer—until his Air Force colleagues began to mutter "Pull out, pull out!" But he didn't. They watched in horror as the Corsair flew right into the ground near the target, the pilot concentrating on hitting the target to the point where he delayed his pull out too long—with fatal results.

The C-47 continued on to North Island with its now quiet, somber load of Air Force pilots. Real targets and real enemy ground fire were just days away.

380

October 1951

"Men, we're gonna win this h'yar war—in spite of the pilots!"

Tongue in cheek quote attributed to M/Sgt John Harris, Det One Blinker Nose line chief.

Group Combat Operations

The 18th Group and many of the maintenance and ordnance personnel were now operating out of K-46 "located approximately five miles southwest of Hoengsong and six miles northeast of Wonju."

"All personnel were very pleased with the new forward location," the 39th Squadron reported, "there being a longer landing strip surfaced with asphalt and gravel instead of the pierced steel planking utilized at K-16, better living quarters for all personnel, and excellent cooperation between the tactical units and the support elements," the 39th reported.

"There was little learned from the experience gained during the month of October 1951," the 39th Squadron concluded in its report. "The system of working from two locations was still proving to have many benefits, primarily in that it offered a change of scenery and a short rest from the intensified combat commitments for both combat crews and maintenance personnel. Lack of replacement maintenance personnel was rapidly becoming a serious problem and continuing losses to rotation would demand discontinuance of the two location systems to enable the unit to work from only the forward base. The only other solution to the manpower shortage would be to curtail or entirely discontinue the much needed 'rest and recreation' program to Japan."

In October, "the rail interdiction program was continued as the major effort of the group mission," Col. Ralph H. Saltsman, Group Commander reported. Tactical operations during October "were a continuation of the past months missions with the emphasis on two group missions daily attacking pre-briefed rail lines in North Korea. Following the bombing the formation would return to base by squadrons and attack targets of opportunity in assigned recce areas or would rocket and strafe pre-brief secondary targets in the enemy's build up area to the rear of his front. In addition, one squadron per day continued to furnish JOC with close support or call missions." [1]

However, the rail cutting operations were not living "up to the desired expecta-

Monthly Summary

Armistice talks resumed at Kaesong after a two-month suspension. UN ground forces in the western and central sectors had retaken territory up to six miles in some places along the front. To support the hard won advance, Fifth Air Force increased the number of close air support sorties. However, Operation STRANGLE, the rail interdiction effort, took the majority of Fifth Air Force's 20,000 air-to-ground sorties that month. As its rail lines were destroyed or damaged, the enemy responded by increasing use of motor vehicles for transporting supplies. Using flares dropped from transport aircraft, night-flying light bombers claimed damage or destruction of thousands of such vehicles. Fifth Air Force lost thirty-one aircraft to enemy ground fire.

Daylight B-29 strikes were continued against airfields, rail bridges, and marshaling yards. A few night sorties were dedicated to close air support, leaflet drops, and reconnaissance. Enemy anti-air artillery units refined their searchlight techniques, using more and higher quality lights to track UN aircraft almost instantaneously for flak or MiG attacks. Radar-controlled antiaircraft guns in northwestern Korea were endangering B-29s even at altitudes above 20,000 feet. When MiG-15s downed five medium bombers and damaged eight others in late October, the Air Force ended daylight B-29 raids.

In aerial combat, Sabre pilots downed twenty-five MiG-15s, an F-84 pilot destroyed one, and B-29 gunners shot down nine others. These thirty-five aerial victories represented the highest monthly total thus far in the war. Fifth Air Force lost five fighter aircraft in air-to-air battles.

The loss by rotation of "highly qualified aircraft mechanics within the squadrons" was beginning to be reflected by aircraft in-commission rates. The problem was worsened by the need to split available personnel between K-10 and K-46, a factor that limited the number of aircraft that could be inspected and maintained at any one time. Many Mustangs were Out of Commission for Parts as a result of landing gear failures that "were becoming a critical item of supply."

Five Mustangs were lost to enemy action in October 1951, plus four more to "flying accidents" and "operational causes not due to enemy action."

Adapted in part from U.S. Air Force Historical Research Agency. January 2002. The U.S. Air Force's First War: Korea 1950-1953 Significant Events. October 1951. http://www.au.af.mil/au/afhra/wwwroot/korean_war/korean_war_chronology/kwc_1951.html

tions" so Saltsman made some changes. The Group formation was eliminated and individual squadron formations were separated by a five-minute interval. This helped avoid "jamming up of aircraft over the target prior to starting the bomb run." In addition, the lead flight on flak suppression was given more time to search out and bomb flak positions.

Although Operation Strangle was initially successful, enemy efforts to overcome rail cuts were underway. "Not accounting for enemy reaction to Operation Strangle was another key lapse in the planning process," Kirtland explains. "Initially, the interdiction effort had been successful, destroying enemy supplies faster than they could be replaced. Combined with Eighth Army ground activity, the rail interdiction effort was hurting the enemy. There were even reports of food shortages in some areas. Realizing the need to maintain their supply lines, the Communists cannibalized existing double-track rail lines in order to assure that at least a single-track rail line would remain open. In many cases, trains were shuttled the short distances between rail cuts and the cargo unloaded and transferred to another existing rail line in order to complete the journey to the front. By October 1951, it seemed as if the rail interdiction effort would prove successful. But the enemy was beginning to overcome the difficulties created by the interdiction effort and FEAF proved slow to react to enemy tactical changes, signaling the eventual downfall of Operation Strangle." [2]

In addition, the bomb run altitude "was lowered to five thousand feet with an entry speed of two hundred ten miles per hour. The change kept the aircraft from building up excessive air speed in the bomb run and also lowered the torque effect," Saltsman noted.

The night landing tactical pattern was modified, as well. The pattern altitude was raised by 500 feet and splitting the four ship "flights" into two-ship "elements" prior to

86542A·C.

Trapped Communist Supply Train Cut To Pieces. *"Mustangs" of the Fifth Air Force's 18th Fighter-Bomber Wing trap a Communist supply train, powered by three locomotives hauling 28 bulging cars , and cut it to bits in October 1951. The train was spotted on the main rail line between Pyongyang and Wonsan, Korea. The Truck Buster pilots first stopped the train by knocking out rails both in front and rear, and then attacked it with bombs, rockets and .50-caliber strafing passes. One of the locomotives and two of the cars are ablaze in the foreground. Craters in the highway at right were made on previous interdiction strikes by US Far East Air Forces light and fighter bombers.*

Close Air Support Mission Prepares for Takeoff. *A "down the throat" view of a flight of 18ᵗʰ Fighter-Bomber Wing Mustangs taxiing into position for take-off fully loaded for a close air support mission in October 1951.*

landing. This change gave the pilots more time to orient themselves and provided "a great degree of safety in the pattern."

Those pilots who had completed their combat tours and were awaiting new orders were "used as instructors for training the replacement pilots." This gave the trainee "the benefit of getting first hand, from highly experienced pilots, the tactics used in bombing, strafing, rocketing and napalming," Saltsman reported.

"No problems arose during October," the 39ᵗʰ reported, "other than trying to conduct effective training of newly assigned pilots at K-10 while trying to meet combat commitments at K-46. The squadron commander and operations officers finally decided the only logical solution to this problem would be to conduct the pilot training program, with approval of Wing and Group A-3, at K-46 where they could more effectively utilize the aircraft in commission."

Group pilots showed "much interest" in new photographs provided by the GLO Team that depicted "the enemy fortifications of the "Heartbreak Ridge' and 'Bloody Angle' battles." The walls of the K-46 Intelligence Officer were used to "display to good effect photos of enemy equipment, camouflage techniques and a 1/250,000 plastic contour map, as well as photos of

specific target areas and bomb damage assessment (BDA) photos. BDA photos which give full rail coverage have been carefully screened and indexed and filed for immediate use and reference," Saltsman reported.

"Much time was devoted toward obtaining full photo coverage of all main supply routes in enemy territory," the 39ᵗʰ reported. "These vital photographs were being supplied by the 67ᵗʰ Tactical Reconnaissance Wing and it was anticipated full photo coverage would be received in several more weeks."

The AN/URC-4 Emergency Radio Set was in very short supply—only 13 were on hand "with no resupply in sight. The assistance the URC-4 afforded in the successful rescue of downed pilots makes it extremely important that more satisfactory supply action be afforded on this item," Saltsman noted. Due to the success of recent rescue operations in which these radios have been used there is an increasing demand for them by the pilots." 1ˢᵗ Lt. William Bryan of the 12ᵗʰ Squadron was put in charge of a project to design and produce a "carrier" for the radio consisting of a girdle supported by suspenders with two pockets that held the radio set and its battery. The pockets were positioned "over the stomach between the

parachute leg straps and below the harness release." The pilots liked it for its "comfort and handling qualities."

Group morale overall remained "very high with a notable exception among a very few pilots who have a fear complex. While the combat effectiveness of the enemy is not underestimated the pilots approach their duties with the confidence born of self-confidence and knowledge of full support by all elements," Saltsman noted in his final report as 18ᵗʰ Group Commander.

In-Commission Status

In the "front office," the Wing Commander was wrestling with how to improve the "in-commission status" of his combat weary, aging Mustang fleet. During October, the daily in-commission status of the Group's Mustang fleet ranged from a high of 78% to a low of 55%. The average for the month was an unacceptable 64%--only two thirds of the Wing's combat aircraft were available for missions on any given day. "We are on the low slope of a cycle that has been caused by battle damages and a number of major inspections becoming due simultaneously," the Wing A-4 (Chief of Material) reported on 23 October 1951.

The squadrons at K-10 and K-46 would

Strangle In Operation. *A Communist train gets "the works" from the F-51 "Mustang" of 2ⁿᵈ Lt. Denis Earp of the No. 2 South African "Flying Cheetah II Squadron" and gun cameras record the actual damage in 1 September 1951. [Note: Lt. General Earp would eventually serve as the South African Air Force Chief of Staff.] SAAF pilots joined the Korean war in October 1950, attached for operations to the U. S. Air Force's 18ᵗʰ Fighter Bomber Wing "a hard-hitting tactical Fifth Air Force unit," the Air Force explained. Corporal Ted Dickinson, 2 Squadron Photographer, prepared the above photo montage "with frames taken from the gun camera film," the Truckbuster reported. (NARA)*

"consider any airplane that is currently out-of-commission but may be readied for combat within a period of two hours," as a combat ready aircraft. The Wing would also evacuate aircraft to FEAMCOM for "depot assistance in those cases where aircraft are war weary and requiring many man-hours to return to combat ready status. In the past, we have completely reconditioned old aircraft here which is a depot responsibility. We undertook such work because we had the capabilities and the experienced personnel to accomplish the work," Lt. Col. Henry Laakman reported. "In the future we will divert our effort assistance to the squadrons in specific repair jobs."

"Emphasis is being placed on utilization of available manpower," Laakman noted. "Work will be pushed but quality will not be sacrificed. Seventy-five per cent of aircraft in-commission will be very difficult to maintain and no aircraft will be released for flight that is marginal simply to make the charts show a 75% rate," he said.

Rogers Requests Mission Priority Guidance

Four days later, on 27 October, Rogers acknowledged in a letter to Headquarters, Fifth Air Force that "we are not maintaining 75% of assigned aircraft in combat ready status." He pointed out that "we have for the most part fulfilled our operational commitments. There have been a few occasions

384

Truckbusters Rearm. *When U.S. Air Force F-51 "Mustangs" returned from a strike at Red targets in North Korea in October 1951, trailer loads of high-velocity rockets, bombs, napalm and .50-caliber ammunition are waiting to arm the sturdy fighters for another strike. "Mustangs" of the Fifth Air Force's veteran 18th Fighter-Bomber Wing in Korea have earned the name "Truck-busters and these long, dynamic rockets leave little to the imagination as to what happens when one makes contact with a truck, locomotive or tank. (NARA)*

after heavy battle damage wherein we could not furnish 32 aircraft for the interdiction mission and also meet requirements of close support and air defense."

"What is your desire on the priority of these 3 missions?" Rogers asked Colonel Gilbert L. Meyers, Deputy Chief of Staff for Operations. "In my opinion the air defense mission should take the loss. The two flights that are maintained on ground alert from 1 hours before to 1 hour after sunrise cannot be employed on the interdiction mission if it is scheduled for an early morning take-off," Rogers noted. "Another factor affecting our operational capability is the inability of the 2nd SAAF Sq. to mount more than two flights due to pilot shortage. Additional pilots are en route to the SAAF Sq. and they should be able to carry their full

load in the near future."

"I am convinced that we could maintain a higher combat ready status were we operating from a single base," Rogers pointed out. "But there are other advantages to the split-base operation that outweigh this factor. I am not yet convinced that we can't attain the 75% in commission figure, however, it is not going to be easy. Without battle damage I'm sure we could do it. What appears to be minor battle damage often take a full day or more to repair."

Rogers outlined the steps he was taking to improve the Wing's maintenance capability, including evacuating depot repair work aircraft to FEAMCOM. Also, the Maintenance Squadron would be required to "maintain a minimum of 2 combat ready aircraft in the pool at K-10." While empha-

sis would be "placed on utilization of available man-power-work will be pushed but quality will not be sacrificed," Rogers asserted.

Rogers closed by letting Meyer "know that we are not taking a complacent attitude toward our failure to meet the standard set by 5th Air Force. Unless battle damages increases, I believe another month will show a definite improvement in our combat ready status."

Combat Tactics

Combat tactics were "essentially the same," the 12th Squadron reported, "with UN close support missions being flown by four ship flights carrying maximum loads of ammunition, rockets and napalm or 500-

"I am convinced that we could maintain a higher combat ready status were we operating from a single base."

BG T. C. Rogers, 18th Wing Commander

pound bombs. Long-range interdiction missions directed against the enemy's transportation system were reported to have "greatly damaged his rail and highway facilities."

In October, however, as secondary targets after the railroads had been hit, the 18th squadrons were directed to "destroy villages and groups of houses or buildings containing troops or materiel. These secondary targets were usually close to the bomb line, and the destruction of them could have effectively injured the military potential of the enemy. Armed reconnaissance along the MSR's north of the bomb line accounted for many enemy troops, vehicles, gun positions and supplies." [3]

"A few changes in fighter tactics were initiated" during October, the 39th reported. "The first change was the method in coming off a bombed rail line. From an echelon right or left the flights attack the target simultaneously and upon his bomb drop, the leader makes a 180 degree turn and then a 90 degree turn off the target. The following aircraft make a 90 degree turn to join up with the flight leader. It was proven this new maneuver allowed for immediate air to air defense and for the leader to evaluate the effectiveness of the flight's rail cut."

Group gaggles "were discontinued" during October. Separate squadrons were airborne at intervals of five to ten minutes. "This greatly improved accuracy and effectiveness, provided better air discipline and defensive formations over the target as well as more time over the target," the 39th reported.

Casualty Reporting

Casualty reporting, always a special subject due to the time element involved, the 39th Squadron noted, "called for very close coordination between the personnel section and the operations section at the forward operating location. Usually the Adjutant was notified by Wing A-3 that one of our pilots was in a Missing or Killed in Action status. It was then necessary for him to call through several phone exchanges to K-46 for sufficient details to make out the initial casualty

Combat Pilot's Briefing. *General Omar N. Bradley (left), Chairman of the U. S. Joint Chiefs of Staff, and General Matthew B. Ridgway (right), Commander-In-Chief, Far East were special guests of Maj. Gen. Frank F. Everest (center), U. S. Fifth Air Force Commander, at a combat pilot's briefing on October 2, 1951, at an air base in Korea. General Bradley, accompanied by Gen. Ridgway, spent two days in Korea inspecting United Nations bases. Combat briefings are conducted before each tactical mission to familiarize pilots with their targets, the Air Force reported. (NARA)*

Top Quartet of Commanders. *This "quartet of top military commanders" was photographed following a tactical briefing held at Fifth Air Force headquarters in Korea in October 1951. Gen. J. Lawton Collins (left), U. S. Army Chief of Staff was accompanied by Gen. Matthew B. Ridgway, Far East Commander, Maj. Gen. Frank F. Everest, Fifth Air Force Commander and Gen. James A. Van Fleet, U. S. Eighth Army Commander in Korea. (NARA)*

New Century Club Member. 1ˢᵗ Lt. Walter H. Burke of Stockton, CA joins the "Century Flight Club" of the 18ᵗʰ Fighter-Bomber Wing in October, 1951. He poses with the lucky white horseshoe, the official emblem of the club as he completes his 100ᵗʰ combat mission with his F-51 Mustang.

wire. Within the next 72 hours it is a touch and go proposition in getting the eye witness statements down to K-10, obtaining accurate information for the Base Chaplain, etc. It would appear a solution to this problem of obtaining the initial data would be for Wing A-3 to request more details in the flash coded message from K-46."

Landing

Accidents

"You are hereby reprimanded for your negligence," General Rogers wrote in a Letter of Reprimand to a pilot of the 39ᵗʰ Squadron.

The investigation of a collision on 22 October disclosed that the pilot made a wheel landing with insufficient flaps, that he failed to clear himself on the runway even though he know there were other aircraft

on the runway, that he did not devote his full attention to handling his aircraft on the runway and that he did not comply with his squadron's standing operating procedure for night landings. As a result, the Mustang collided with another F-51 piloted by 1ˢᵗ Lt. Frederick Rockmaker.

"Two valuable aircraft" were lost "at a time when every weapon in our arsenal should be available for use against the enemy. It is of the utmost importance that all pilots operate their aircraft in such a manner that planes and pilots will be conserved so that the maximum weight of our arms may be used against the enemy," Rogers said. "Aircraft damaged or destroyed through carelessness and negligence are just as effectively lost for our purpose as they would be if the enemy shot them down."

"Landing accidents can be completely eliminated," General Rogers assured the Commander of Fifth Air Force on 29 October. The accident investigation report on a 22 October landing accident "determined that the primary cause of such accidents is the varying techniques employed by different pilots in landing. Our aim is to require all pilots to land at the same point on the runway in the same attitude at the same speed. With the rapid turn over of pilots this is a continuing problem," Rogers noted, "and one requiring the correction of bad habits acquired over many years."

Rogers directed Group and Squadron Commanders to periodically "perform the duty of runway control officer to detect and correct faulty technique in landings." He also assured General Everest that "the new

technique prescribed for night landings will eliminate the possibility of further collisions between landing aircraft."

Squadron Activities

October "was a good month for the 12ᵗʰ from the standpoint of total time flown and effective combat sorties completed." The number of sorties was up "substantially" over previous months.

More flying time meant more accidents and aborts during the month. One 12ᵗʰ Mustang crash-landed immediately after takeoff from K-46, another "ground looped" during landing. There were 14 aborts that month for maintenance reasons.

Morale in the 12ᵗʰ was "good" that month. "As usual the nearness of the date of one's rotation" was a major factor. Good food, usually excellently prepared and served, plus R&R leaves were other reasons. "Most of the airmen seem to believe that the mission of the squadron is a worthy one, that the conflict, of which they are an integral part, is a justified one, and that the squadron is accomplishing its assignment to the fullest extent with the equipment and personnel allocated to it," Major Joseph T. Crane, CO of the 12ᵗʰ Squadron, reported that month. "Morale of the Officers is generally high. They understand the mission, and the one hundred combat sorties tour is short," he concluded.

The morale of officers and airmen, both at K-10 and K-46, was improved considerably, the 39ᵗʰ Squadron reported. "This up swing may be attributed to several factors, namely the completion of barracks for airmen, the issue of winter clothing for flight line personnel, and the announcement of three credits per month for each month served in Korea. Rotation continued on its pre-announced schedule and few conversations around the Squadron excluded such comments as, "What's your non-retainable date?" or "When are you going home?"

High esprit de corps in the 39ᵗʰ Squadron "was very evident the latter part of the month when the blue and white silk scarves and Cobra jacket patches were delivered. Everyone in the Squadron had at least one

Mustang Mating? *When these two 18th Group Mustangs tangled at K-46 on 24 October 1951. It looked like a "coupling" that had gone terribly awry. (Cook)*

Toasting the Survivor. *1st Lt. Fred Rockmaker (foreground in cockpit with bandage over right eye), is "toasted" by fellow pilots Lt. Brown, Lt. Ned Frankart (later KIA), Capt. John Taylor, Lt. Richard Andrews and Lt. Davis. The occasion was Rockmaker's survival of a hairy runway collision the night of 24 October 1951. Rockmaker was not at fault. (Cook)*

scarf and patch and there was no question of their pride in wearing this visual identification of their Squadron."

"...without the loss of a single life"

Throughout September, "tactical interdiction of the enemy's transportation system" was the Group's primary mission.

Major Carl Colson noted that assigned personnel were "generally qualified in their specialties," but on-the-job training was still necessary in many cases. "Training in the theatre of operations leaves much to be desired," he reminded the 18th FB Group Commander. Personnel shortages were preventing supervisors from adequately supervising training—"the supervisors themselves must perform the work, along with and oftimes separated from the trainee, in order that combat commitments may be met." The training for administrative and supply specialists was "at a standstill" in that "there are no airmen who do not already have a full time job to train."

"Good food, acceptable although crowded living conditions and a high esprit-de-corps" were keeping the morale of the men high, although "some unfounded rumors of temporary cutbacks in rotation to the United States have hurt morale. "Every possible attempt is made," Colson noted, "to determine the truth and to pass it on to the men." A weekly briefing by the Wing Intelligence section was conducted on Monday nights in the base theatre "primarily to keep the airmen informed of the objectives and accomplishments of the wing."

K-10 did have an "adequate" Post Exchange, except that "recent" magazines were in short supply. There was some "mild bitterness" by "those airmen who have been in Korea for the longest time and have suffered some rather intolerable conditions get no relief from the change" of tour for Korean service that seemed to benefit those "more recently arriving in the theatre." In addition, while the number of pilots assigned was "slightly above authorized strength," enlisted strength "is below that deemed necessary to operate both the rear base and forward base in an efficient manner. Reports and other administrative functions are so numerous as to necessitate full authorized strength in both administration and supply sections under combat conditions."[4]

Overall, however, October marked a successful month of operations, as Squadron Commander Colson noted because it was "without the loss of a single life." A good month indeed. Nevertheless, it was a busy month for the 38 pilots and airmen of the 67th who flew an average of over 21 sorties each that month for a total of 818 sorties and 1,406 combat hours. The 67th was approaching 10,000 sorties thus far in the Korean Air War.

Captain James J. McCabe got off with a "badly sprained ankle...after he was shot down in enemy territory and then rescued by a helicopter. 1st Lt. Lyle E. Moore did even better. When his "battle damaged aircraft" gave out on him he made a successful "wheels up" landing in a rice paddy—with no injuries.

Artillery pieces (13), rolling stock (13), buildings (60), road cuts (19) were high on the priority list for "attention" that month. However, over 160 reported rail cuts were reported (Operation Strangle), along with attacks on 85 troop positions and over 230 enemy troops killed. Squadron armorers loaded over 510,400 rounds of .50 caliber ammunition, 2,3374 rockets, 494 napalm tanks and 1,127 500 lb. bombs.

The new dive-bombing procedures evolved during recent months continued, "to prove their soundness." So much so that the 67th was awarded the "Major Louis Sebille Plaque" for accuracy in dive-bombing. This sought after award was conferred by the 18th FBG to the squadron of the group attaining the greatest accuracy in dive bombing for two consecutive months. Colson noted that "it is fitting that the 67th should continue to uphold the tradition set by its first Commanding Officer in the Korean conflict."

Issues of Olive Drab winter uniforms were "inadequate"—not enough of them in the right sizes. While the winter flying clothing had been received and issued to flying personnel and line maintenance personnel, there were insufficient quantities in the large sizes. If you were a "large and heavy" pilot, you were in more danger of frostbite—personal equipment had been "unable to procure twenty-eight foot parachutes" needed by the larger pilots. "Adequate supply of these large parachutes would improve the state of mind of the large pilots," Colson noted dryly.

Inventories had been completed. Finally, enough bins to store and protect supplies had been completed. And, tool kits had been prepared for and issued to each mechanic. Progress, at last! Mechanics with tools.

A "whistling Mustang" was one challenge they couldn't seem to master. "A minor maintenance headache," was the way Colson described the musical aircraft. It seemed that to stifle the plane's whistle, would "involve disconnecting both hot and cold air ducts." Consequently, it was decided that the whistle was "the lesser of the two evils" and the wannabe Stuka was "flown with the whistle rather than without heat."

The biggest problem for maintenance was the chronic personnel shortage. The

Search and Rescue. *Two means of survival that played important roles in the successful rescue and evacuation of hundreds of United States Air Force and UN ground force personnel are represented here as an H-5 helicopter lowers gently for a landing near an SA-16 "Albatross" amphibian on October 17, 1951. Both types are assigned to the veteran U.S. Air Force 3rd Air Rescue Squadron, and often team their talents to perform spectacular rescues and evacuations. On many occasions, the tiny "wind mills" have rescued troops from rough terrain near the fighting lines, and speedily evacuated them to airstrips from which the longer-range SA-16s can take off to complete the journey to rear area hospitals. (NARA)*

biggest problem for the administrative section was reports, now felt to be "excessive." The morning report, for example, was fast becoming a "one-man, full-time duty." The report, like administrivia often does, was taking on a life of its own. "New additions to this report in addition to the myriad of administrative functions, personnel accounting, maintenance or personnel records, security clearances, reenlistment, finance matters, etc. will be a severe burden with anything less than the full authorization of administrative and personnel specialists." And, the problem was going to get worse. "New administrative personnel will have to accustom themselves with new procedures peculiar to this theater with little or no time in which to learn from the airman presently assigned and due to be rotated soon, his duties. [5]

In the 67th, "high esprit-de-corps and high effectiveness ratings, high rates of aircraft in commission are the main factors contributing to the high morale in the squadron." However, morale was not helped that month when a requirement was levied on the squadron to "furnish fifty two guards during the first eight days of the

month to supplement the Air Police Squadron Guard." That "had an adverse effect on the morale of the airmen," Colson said.

Perhaps in rereading the report before signing, Colson added: "It is to be noted that throughout this historical report, mention is made of personnel shortages. It is not the intent of these entries that an extreme emergency exists, rather, it is intended to show that a unit cannot comply with all of the directives and meet all of its commitments with less than a full complement of officers and airmen."

Colson closed his report by recommending that the "psychological conditioning for personnel in Korea" be improved. Intermediate goals and objectives, he noted, are necessary to establish a "will to fight." These goals and objectives are even "harder to define for the airman in as much as he cannot see the end result of his work."

Unfortunately, recognition in the Armed Forces Newspaper, *"Stars and Stripes,"* is "small for all Air Force units in Korea," Colson observed. "The common complaint is that the 'Sabre-jets' get the write-ups and that there is a notation for courtesy's sake that the Mustangs 'also ran.' [6]

Jets Get the Glory

Mustangs get the missions

Eventually it seemed that Colson's assessment was borne out by FEAF Headquarters some weeks later. On December 20, 1951 FEAF released a story that highlighted "Fifth Air Force interdiction-minded jet and conventional type fighter bombers" that had begun "to intensify their attacks against enemy rail lines." Since the advent on November 27 of the so-called "twilight truce" along the frontline in Korea, "fewer close air support sorties have been needed by UN forces. These bomb and rocket carrying planes are now adding their punch to the rail smashing program," FEAF noted.

The results, FEAF noted, "have been gratifying. Literally hundreds of miles of trackage and thousands of boxcars, flatbeds, steam engines and passenger cars, splintered and crushed, lie useless in marshalling yards and along the twisted and shattered rights-of-way. The enemy effort to punch southward his minimum required 10 to 15 supply trains a day needed to maintain his frontline forces has been practically nullified."

"A hard and dangerous job that has brought little enough glory is being performed daily by the energetic pilots of the 18th Fighter-Bomber Wing, flying F-51 Mustangs and by pilots of an F-80 Shooting Star unit, the 8th Fighter-Bomber Wing and pilots of the 136th and 49th Fighter-Bomber Wings, flying F-84 Thunderjets. They are currently smacking the enemy where it hurts. Unlike their glamorously publicized F-86 MIG-killing brothers, they are not becoming aces of the air war. However, along with maintaining air superiority, Far East Air Forces pilots also carry the responsibility of supporting the UN soldier by cutting his foe's supply lines. This job those pilots are doing."

The success with which they are handling the job is readily seen in these pictures. These recently taken low-level reconnaissance photos were exposed along a forty-mile stretch of track between Pyongy-

"Three great flight leaders," Lt. Col. Jack Davis, former Commander of the 12th Squadron noted on this photograph. (L to R) Captain John E. Taylor, Jr., 1st Lt. Ernest "Ernie" Wakehouse, and Captain William C. Norris in front of the Operations Office at K-10. (Wakehouse)

On 25 October, Captain John E. Taylor, Jr., was leading a flight of 39th FIS Mustangs, including Captain Eugene Z. Mazurak, Captain Robert D. Ramsey and 1st Lt. Ernest P. "Ernie" Wakehouse, element leader.

"Our target," noted Captain Ramsey in a mission report, "was a pre-briefed mission to an enemy supply and bivouac area near Pyonggang, North Korea.

Soon after arriving over the target, the flight was pressing home relentless dive bombing attacks with single bombs, indi-vidual rocket passes and successive machine gun attacks until all ordnance was expended.

The flight "accounted for the destruction of four enemy vehicles, three large secondary explosions, and the destruction of the entire supply and bivouac area. During these attacks intense enemy fire was encountered," Ramsey reported.

Every member of the flight was recommended for awards based on its persistence in the face of intense enemy fire.

ang and the once active Communist railhead at Sariwon. They illustrate dramatically a point recently made by FEAF Commander, Lt. General O. P. Weyland, who pointed out in a press interview that the inevitable outcome of the current interdiction program would be a virtual half of all enemy rail movement south of the Chongchong River."

7

Korean Air Police

Investigation

Wing Commander BGen Rogers was trying to deal with the findings of an investigation into illegal dealings by members of the nearby Korean Air Police. In a 6 October letter, Colonel Kim Duk Yong, Commander of the ROK Air Force Academy, reported to Rogers what he had "gained through a recent investigation of the Korean Air Police."

Colonel Yong "learned that the reason my men have acted in this manner, is that they have such a limited income and they sought to improve their financial condition in this way." This did not mean, he assured Rogers in the next sentence, "that I give sympathy to their actions in exhorting money or accepting bribes from contractors whom they should, as far as possible, protect." Yong promised that as soon as he learned of such dealings he would "relieve them of their position and disciplinary action will be taken against them."

Yong apologized to Rogers on behalf of the ROK Air Force and "for the actions of these people in committing such acts after the fine cooperation which we have received from you."

"I hear with regret," Yong added, "that some of your officers were so upset as to threaten one of my men about this matter and hope that your people will not be so angered again."

Yong closed by expressing the hope "that mutual respect, kindness, and cooperation will continue to further the cause of world peace between the U.S. Air Force and the Korean Air Force."

Driving Safety Measures

"Recently a member of your organization was driving a truck through a Korean village on his way to Pusan," Brig. Gen. Rogers wrote in a stiff Memo to Commander of the 18th Motor Vehicle Squadron entitled: "Safety Measures in Driving Vehicles." A Korean child had darted in front of the truck and was killed. The investigation determined that the driver was "not driving at an excessive rate of speed." However, Rogers added "when only the legal speed limit on that road is considered," and reminded the squadron commander that the driver was aware that there were children on the road and had, in fact, blown the truck horn as he drove through the village.

Capt. (later Lt. Gen.) Devol "Rock" Brett and Lt. Ernie Wakehouse in front of the 39th FIS Operations Office at K-46. The West Pointer and the National Guardsman became best friends in Korea and remain so after over 50 years. (Cook)

Rogers was not convinced that the driver had exercised enough "prudence and foresight." It was clear from the memo that he believed that every driver should anticipate "that children might suddenly run in front of their vehicle and they should drive at such a speed that an almost instantaneous stop could be made if necessary." Rogers noted that he had received many reports of rations truck drivers and buses "transporting indigenous laborers" driving at excessive speed on the road between this base and Chinhae and between this base and Pusan."

Rogers directed the squadron commander to instruct "all personnel driving vehicles belonging to your organization that excessive speed and careless and reckless driving are not to be tolerated. Persons violating speed limits or who drive recklessly will be brought to trial by court-martial," Rogers warned him.

Major William T. Hale, 18th Motor Vehicle Squadron Commander, assured Rogers soon thereafter that vehicular safety "has been brought to the attention of all persons driving vehicles in this organization." He went on to outline a variety of accident prevention measures and programs that had been "instigated" in recent months. The Wing had 752 licensed drivers, Hale pointed out, and only 144 of them were assigned to the Motor Vehicle Squadron.

Hale suggested that "all officers and senior noncommissioned officers be directed to make on-the-spot corrections, secure the driver's name, organization, and Vehicle Registration Number, and report all traffic violations to the respective organization commander for disciplinary action. He also recommended that Rogers appoint a group of six officers as "traffic spotters with authority to make on-the-spot inspections of vehicles for authorized dispatch, valid driver's license, Operator's Maintenance, and any other discrepancies which may be detrimental to safe and careful driving." Hale closed by noting that driving safety had also been the subject of a thorough indoctrination of driver personnel at K-46.

Rogers would agree with on-the-spot correction of traffic violations by officers and NCO's. He did not concur with the appointment of "spotters."

Bustin' Rails. *A 12th Squadron Mustang taxies out of the Rearm and Refuel area at K-46 to join others on a "rail buster mission coming up," recalled Lt. Col. George McLees. (McLees)*

Endnotes

[1] USAFHRA.
Monthly Historical Report, 18th Fighter-Bomber Group, October 1951, p. 3

[2] Kirtland, Michael A., Lt. Col., USAF. *Planning Air Operations: Lessons from Operation Strangle in the Korean War.* Aerospace Power Chronicles, DoDs First Professional On-Line Journal, Summer 2001, Volume XV, No. 2, http://www.airpower.maxwell.af.mil/airchronicles/apj/kirtland.html

[3] USAFHRA. *Monthly Historical Report, 12th Fighter-Bomber Squadron* October 1951, p. 2.

[4] USAFHRA. *Monthly Historical Report, 67th Fighter-Bomber Squadron,* October 1951, p. 2.

[5] USAFHRA. *Monthly Historical Report, 67th Fighter-Bomber Squadron,* October 1951, p. 6.

[6] Colson's note regarding one-sided credit for jet aircraft operations appears to have some basis in fact. "The remarking of the fact that the F-86's seemed to be the only one receiving publicity in the Korean war... that was only a slight exaggeration," noted Lt. Col. Duane "Bud" Biteman, USAF (Ret), a pilot with the 67th in 1951 and later the President of the 18th Fighter Wing Association. "As a matter of fact, the publicity was officially directed to include ONLY actions by JET AIRCRAFT (which then stretched to include F-80s and F-84s)," Biteman explained. He noted remarks by former Sgt. Sandy Colton, "who was our Stars and Stripes correspondent covering the 18th in the early days of the war, then went on to be a major network correspondent in later years." At an Association Reunion in 1994, Biteman asked Colton, "How come our
actions were not published." Colton told Biteman that Far East Air Force headquarters "had specifically ORDERED them to downplay the victories by the Mustangs because the new Air Force was brainwashing the public on the imagined advantages of an ALL JET AIR FORCE, and didn't want them to think the old WW-II birds could do the job better than the new

'blow jobs.'" As in "so many other instances, the "headquarters weenies" ignored the impact such actions had on the morale of those who were actually doing the work," Biteman noted.

[7] USAFHRA. *Monthly Historical Report, 18th Fighter-Bomber Wing,* December 1951. FEAF Press release of December 20, 1951.

Not all maintenance on 18th Group Mustangs was performed by its "official" maintenance crews. Here Lt. Melvin Corley poses with "YoYo" after they had completed "a little work" on "Katy Bell," his 12th Squadron Mustang. (Corley)

Combat Statistics

18th Fighter-Bomber Wing

October 1951

Average No. A/C Assigned
Unavailable
Total Flying Time
Unavailable
Percent of Aircraft in Commission
Unavailable
Percent of Aircraft AOCP
Unavailable
Combat Sorties Flown by Wing
2,976
12th Squadron Sorties
841
39th FIS Sorties
739
67th Squadron Sorties
570
2 Squadron Sorties
602
A/C Lost to Combat
6
Pilots lost
5

Fuel Consumed

Unavailable

Ordnance Expended

.50-cal. Rounds
Unavailable
Rockets
Unavailable
Napalm Bombs
Unavailable
500-lb. GP Bombs
Unavailable

Note: Figures and totals may differ in some categories due to differences in numbers provided by each component.

Significant Events

October 16: Fifth Air Force Sabre jet pilots destroyed nine MiG-15s in aerial combat, a record daily high.

October 19: The U.S. Army opened a 1000-bed hospital at Camp Drew, north of Tachikawa AB, Japan. Henceforth, C-54s flew medical evacuees from Korea to Tachikawa, then C-47s shuttled them to Camp Drew, thereby reducing transit time.

October 25: During an unusually effective close air support strike, F-51 Mustangs inflicted approximately two hundred casualties on enemy troops in the I Corps sector. Enemy small arms fire hit a rescue helicopter picking up a downed UN pilot. The H-5 made a forced landing in enemy territory. The next day, two other H-5s hoisted all four men to safety from the mountainside where they had hidden from communist troops during the night. At the request of the communists, peace negotiations resumed. [1]

October 27: MiGs flew approximately two hundred sorties, the high for the month. On a last medium bomber daylight raid, B-29 gunners shot down six MiG-15s, their highest number of enemy aircraft downed on any day of the war. A 3rd ARS H-5, with fighter escort, rescued a downed UN fighter pilot despite intense fire from enemy ground troops.

Combat Losses

1st Lt. Newman Camay Golden, 39th Fighter Interceptor Squadron. 1st Lt. Golden was "flying number four position in Mongoose Easy flight" when he was reported as missing in action on 17 October. "He failed to return from a napalm interdiction mission. He had radioed his flight leader he was hit and would bail out. He became separated from his flight in the heavy smoke over the target area and was not again sighted until the burning remains of his aircraft was sighted five miles south of their target. His flight and other flights of the group search the immediate area from crash back to the target for three hours on the theory Lieutenant Golden might have bailed out prior to his ship's crash, but had

negative results," the 39th reported.

1st Lt. George D. Jones, 39th Fighter Interceptor Squadron. Lt. Jones "was killed on a routine training flight. He was being trained in rocket firing on a small deserted island near K-10. The training supervisory pilot, a former flight commander with 100 combat sorties, stated he made his rocket run on the island to mark the target for Lieutenant Jones and then Lieutenant Jones stated he would fire his rockets. He entered into his rocket run and the plane started to snap roll and crashed into the water, exploding and burning. The cause for this fatal accident has not yet been determined," the 39th reported.

1st Lt. Oliver Eugene Jones, 12th Fighter-Bomber Squadron, was reported missing in action on 21 October.

1st Lt. H.T.R. Joyce, 2 Squadron SAAF. It was 'Theo' Joyce's first combat mission. He was flying No. 2 for Lt. Pretorious, who was flight leader on a rail interdiction mission at TD4893, approximately twenty miles north of the bomb line. No. 3 reported a coolant leak and was ordered, with No. 4 to return to K-46. Soon after, Joyce reported his engine was smoking, so he and Pretorious began their return to K-46, as well. A new report from Joyce indicated that his engine was running normally, once more, whereupon Pretorious decided they should attack the secondary target, Inchon, directly on their route back to K-46. Pressing in for the attack, Joyce was instructed to select and arm his bombs. After pulling away in a steep climb after the attack, Pretorious observed a large explosion on an Inchon hillside, an explosion that he knew was not from a bomb. Repeated calls to Joyce on the radio were unanswered. He concluded that Joyce had crashed into the hill during his bomb run. Subsequent searches revealed no sign of the plane or pilot.

1st Lt. Richard L. Olcott, 39th Fighter Interceptor Squadron.

Endnotes

[1] Adapted from USAFHRA. January 2002. The U.S. Air Force's First War: Korea 1950-1953 Significant Events. October 1951.

Truckbuster Reporter

Visits The Front

In October the 18th Fighter-Bomber Group began staging flights from Wonsan airport in North Korea. The 18th Wing owned a C-46 that was often used to fly supplies and personnel up from K-10. Sergeant and Truckbuster Journalist William J. "Sandy" Colton, decided to hitch a ride up to see what was happening.

When he arrived in Wonson, he met a Korean Military Advisory Group (KMAG) corporal attached to the ROK Capitol Division who was "dropping by the airport with a bunch of North Korean burp guns and other captured material that he routinely swapped for gallons of ice cream and steaks delivered by Navy carrier pilots based on a carrier off shore. When he left I decided to go with him to get a first hand look at things up front."

It was almost dark when the two left Wonsan airport looking for the ROK Capitol Division headquarters. On the way the Korean Corporal got lost. In the near darkness they saw another six-by coming down the road. They flashed their lights and pulled up next to it to ask directions as it stopped. "It turned out to be a truck load of North Korean troops. Apparently they were as surprised as we were as both trucks stepped on the gas and sped away in opposite directions."

A little later they found a group of Korean women making rice balls for the Capitol Division soldiers. "The corporal recognized them so we spent the night there and went on to the division HQ the next morning where I met the division CG and the rest of the KMAG advisors. From there I journeyed up to the front lines where I got to see some of our 51's in action. We later entered and area that had just been napalmed by them. A T-34 tank, knocked out by our planes, lay in the middle of the road. The South Korean army guys were all over it placing explosive charges to blast it off the road." Colton moved about 50 yards away and aimed his Speed Graphic camera to get a good picture of the blast. "The blast was so big I was almost knocked off my feet. There was nothing left on the road and when I processed my film later I had nothing but a blurry white flash."

Heading back to Headquarters and the air field, Colton noticed that captured enemy weapons were stacked up all along the road. "I asked if I might have some to take back with me. We wound up loading the six by with every type of weapon we could find from burp guns up to and including anti aircraft guns."

Back at division headquarters "the commanding general was interrogating North Korean prisoners, among them a number of camp followers. At one point he pointed to me and I noticed that they looked at me and shook their heads 'Yes.' When I left to return to the airstrip at Wonsan, one of the camp followers followed me and tried to get into the truck. When I asked what was going on the general laughed and came over to explain. He said that he asked the girls which they would prefer, going to prison or taking care of me. They all volunteered to go with me he said, so he picked out what he thought was the prettiest one. You'll need her to keep you warm at night, he told me."

Colton thanked him for the weapons they were taking back but told him that he could not take the girl and left.

"The weapons were loaded onto our C-46 and we dropped them off at Fifth Air Force in Seoul for their museum."

Colton then returned to K-9. He had seen "what was happening."

Colton's Jeep "Evolves"

After the 18th Wing had settled in at Chinhae it soon established "the very finest officer's and top three clubs in Korea," recalled Sandy Colton.

The secret, as he understood it, "was that one of our men had been a produce buyer in Tokyo before being recalled and assigned to our outfit. Our Wing C-46 made a weekly visit to Tokyo where the buyer would then purchase fresh vegetables, fish and meats, among other things, for the clubs."

Men from other units in Korea used to fly or drive in just to get a decent steak dinner.

After Colton left the 18th and returned to Korea as a *Stars and Stripes* correspondent, he would make it a point to get back to Chinhae "as often as I could for a good meal. Whenever I did I would complain to the manager of the top three club about my having to hitch hike all over Korea. The Stripes had no vehicles assigned to them."

On one of Colton's visits "the boys at the top three club presented me with a jeep! It seems that nearby, in Mason, was a U.S. Marine salvage and scrap yard. The Mason Marine sergeants were frequent visitors to the club. Somehow the club officers convinced the Marines to find a jeep in their scrap pile for me. It had no hood, windshield or bumpers with identifying numbers. There was only one seat, for the driver. There were no headlights and no spare tire but it did run. Oh, there was a little problem! There was a leak in the radiator that sprayed water into the motor fan that then blew it back on the driver. It was necessary to stop frequently to keep the radiator filled with water."

As Colton happily left the club to drive his "new" jeep into Pusan, about 30 miles

away

The site of a *Stars and Stripes* bureau office, the members of the club deposited a box containing a half dozen bottles of good scotch into the jeep. Bargaining material, they said.

In Pusan, on the black market, Colton bought headlights for the jeep and hooked them up. He then got ready to set off for Seoul, some 300 or so miles to the north. One of the "Stripers was going to accompany me but chickened out at the last minute, saying he didn't think I'd make it."

Dressed in a swim suit to protect himself from the water spraying back from the engine, a duck billed cap with a flying fish across the front of it on his head, and rubber zori on his feet, Colton set off for Seoul by himself with a duffle bag and the booze in the back of the jeep.

A few miles out of Pusan on the road to Taegu, Colton came upon a farmer pulling along a baby deer with a rope tied around its neck. Colton stopped and, bargaining with the farmer, bought the deer for three packs of cigarettes. He then headed towards Taegu, marked out on the MSR (Main Supply Route) map he was carrying to guide him to Seoul.

"I held the deer in my lap with his front hooves on the steering wheel," he recalled. "My feet were up on the dashboard most of the way as I drove with the throttle pulled out rather than use the gas pedal. We were quite a team, the deer and I, and also quite a sight at each village we dropped by to get water. The kids would flock around to pet the deer."

Everything went fine until, past Taegu, Colton came to a fork in the road.

A group of ROK Army troops, some in a tank, were at one side of the road near a bridge that had been destroyed.

Colton stopped and asked in his "very poor Japanese if this was the way to Chungju, the next stop on my way to Seoul.

They pointed to the road on the other side of the destroyed bridge. I saw where other vehicles had gone down the side of a hill, forded the stream and then went up the other side to the road so I took that road as they kept shouting something to me in Korean I assumed was good luck or something. I drove on for an hour or more, passing nothing, seeing no one, until I came to a small village and stopped to get water. A flock of children soon surrounded me to pet the deer. Finally an old man came, I asked for water for the engine and he brought me some. I then drove on until dark, worried now because it didn't appear Chungju was that far away on the map."

Finally, Colton came to a town and was stopped by a Korean MP at a traffic stop who spoke some English. When Colton asked if this was Chungju he said 'Yes,' but asked me to wait for a moment while he called in my presence. Soon an American Army major showed up in a jeep and asked me where I'd come from. I told him and he asked me to follow him to his headquarters. Going in he pointed out a number of bullet holes around the place, saying they'd been under attack recently by guerrillas."

The Major showed Colton a map of Korea and asked him to again show them where he came from. Colton did so, and was told "that's impossible." When he asked if this wasn't Chungju he was again assured that it was, "but not the one you want."

The town Colton wanted was pronounced "Choongju."

The town Colton was in was pronounced "Chongju."

It was soon apparent that the ROK unit that Colton had passed by at the bridge was part of a battalion of ROK military and police trying to take North Korean guerrilla headquarters in South Korea, which Colton had just driven through.

The Major suggested that Colton spend the night and take a different route up to Seoul in the morning.

"I can only believe that the sight of this American in a bathing suit, driving a junk jeep with a deer in his lap must have convinced the bad guys I was crazy so they let me go on through," Colton recalled.

"The next morning, as I entered the outskirts of Seoul, there standing on a corner hitch hiking was the Striper who was going to ride up with me from Pusan. He was hitch hiking into Seoul from the airport. Inside the city, en route to the correspondent quarters across from the capitol building, I was stopped by some English MP's. Where is my registration, they asked. I had none, I explained and went on to tell them how I came to have the jeep. I then told them to look in the correspondent billet's compound and they would see a number of other jeeps belonging to the correspondents that started out like mine.

"You mean to say the American Army condones such things?" they asked.

When I said yes they said "Oh, very well. Carry on," and let me go. I drove on to the correspondents billets for the night and the next day drove on up to Uijongbu, a major Army repair depot where I talked to the sergeant in charge. I left the jeep with him along with four bottles of scotch.

Two days later I returned to pick up my jeep. The water leak was now repaired, hood, windshield, extra seat in front and back and a spare tire and bumpers installed. Later I painted Stars and Stripes under the windshield. I was now the proud possessor of the only *Stars and Stripes* jeep in Korea and used it to travel from unit to unit while there.

Congratulations, General!

Congratulations poured into 18th Wing Headquarters at Chinhae Air Base following Col. Turner C. Rogers' promotion to Brigadier General in October 1951.

Rogers drafted numerous personal notes of appreciation for their thoughtful congratulations.

"I had the privilege of meeting you on your visit to Korea," Rogers reminded Air Force Secretary xxx "and am happy to report that the 'Mustangs' of the 18th Fighter Bomber Wing are still striking fear in the hearts of the enemy."

"I wish to thank you for the great honor that been bestowed upon me and the trust you have placed in me, Rogers told Air Force Chief of Staff General Hoyt S. Vandenberg. "I feel that my promotion reflects great credit upon the officers and Airmen of the 18th Fighter-Bomber Wing who have so loyally and ably supported me during the Korean conflict. The entire command joins me in expressing our appreciation of the recognition of our combat record in Korea."

"I am recovering slowly from a state of shock occasioned by an entirely unexpected promotion to the rank of general officer," Rogers admitted to Lt. Gen. Otto P. Weyland, Commander of Far East Air Forces. "I fully realize that I have largely to thank you and General Partridge. I am extremely grateful and highly honored that you have placed such trust in me. I shall endeavor to justify that trust," Rogers promised. He closed by again giving credit for the promotion to the efforts of the Wing.

One letter was from Maj. Gen. John H. McCormick, who would serve in senior roles throughout the Korean War in the Air Force Office of Personnel in Washington. For much of the war, McCormick had the sad duty almost on a daily basis of signing out telegrams to the families of KIA and MIA personnel, as well as a constant stream of followup letters providing as much infor-

'Tee Cee'

mation as the Air Force had regarding the circumstances surrounding the fate of the serviceman. Rogers, who spent many years in various personnel billets, asking McCormick to "give my regards to General Wetzel and my friends in Personnel."

"I'm sure that no one was more surprised than I when my name appeared

---

A Tie Between Nations

"I wish to thank you for your letter of congratulations on my nomination for appointment to the grade of Brigadier General," Colonel Rogers wrote to Commodore Kuk Mo Chung, Commander of the Chinhae Naval Base. Rogers gave "full credit for this promotion to the Officers and Airmen of the 18th Fighter-Bomber Wing who have so loyally supported me during my tour of office."

After thanking Commodore Chung "for the generous support and cooperation of the Korean Navy," Colonel Rogers closed by saying "it is my sincere desire that we establish, here in Korea, a tie between our nations that shall endure long after the United Nation's Forces have departed.

---

among those selected for promotion to B.G. (and I know there were a lot of surprised people!)," Rogers chuckled in a letter to "Casey and Peggy" Vincent. BGen Vincent was then Commander of McChord Air Force Base. "Any advice you could give as to the pitfalls awaiting the new general would be greatly appreciated. Over here running a combat wing, life is fairly simple, but I anticipate complications upon reassignment to the Z.I."

"I must confess to a feeling similar to that when I received my commission as a 2nd Lieutenant and reported to my fist assignment," Rogers admitted to Maj. Gen. Roger M. Ramey, then serving in the Pentagon.

One of Rogers' last letters on the subject of his promotion was, characteristically, to T/Sgt Robert S. Hutcherson of the 18th Food Service Squadron. "The cake that was presented to me last Saturday evening at the Officer's Club came as a very pleasant surprise. It was a masterful job and tasted delicious. I wish to thank you for myself and for the Command for your contribution to our well-being in Korea."

At the October Wing Commander Conference, Major Gen. Frank Everest, Commander Fifth Air Force, pinned on Rogers' shiny new stars. "I would like to thank you for the stars you presented me at the latest Wing Commander's Conference," Rogers wrote. "I shall endeavor to live up to the trust that has been placed in me."

That same day, Rogers dictated a Memorandum for Major Rackham on the subject of "Flying Safety." "As a means of making all units accident conscious, it is suggested that we put up a bill-board in a conspicuous place and post monthly and cumulative accident rates of each squadron including the 2nd SAAF." It was his first directive as a General Officer.

November 1951

Combat Operations

Tactical operations did not change for the 18th Group in November, and continued to follow the pattern established in previous months. The rail interdiction program remained as the primary group mission. After performing rail cuts, squadrons would "return to base individually and expend rockets and .50-cal. ammunition on pre-briefed secondary targets in enemy supply buildup areas close to his front lines. One squadron a day continued to furnish JOC with close support missions." [1]

"Missions in close support of the Ground Forces were flown by four ship flights carrying maximum loads of ammunition, rockets and napalm or five hundred pound bombs," the 12th Squadron reported. "Long range interdiction missions against the enemy's transportation system again, as in previous months, greatly damaged his rail and highway facilities. Buildings, villages and groups of houses immediately behind the front lines were attacked in November as secondary targets after the rail interdiction missions."

In November the 12th Squadron flew escort for the Vice President "while he made an inspection tour of the Theater." Armed reconnaissance along the MSR's north of the bomb line accounted for many enemy troops, vehicles, gun positions and supplies," the 12th FBS reported.

The 12th Squadron concluded that enemy anti-aircraft activities had "increased if battle damage is an indication." More 12th aircraft—five major, 13 minor—were damaged in November than in many months. Fortunately, no 12th aircraft were lost or damaged due to flying accidents.

The 18th Group found it was necessary to establish a new training program at K-46 that covered "all phases of combat flying in F-51 type aircraft. Although the majority of replacement pilots required little training prior to being assigned to flights, it was found that some pilots had not graduated from CCTS [Combat Crew Training School] before coming overseas. A brief course, approximately that of CCTS training given at Luke AFB, was initiated at K-46. A survey of new pilots revealed that very few had experience with napalm, rocket firing or high angle strafing." [2]

Due to the "sudden and large influx of new pilots" during November, the 39th Squadron reported that the K-46 pilot training program was of necessity stepped up in scope and intensity. After determining the degree of pilot proficiency in the F-51, training flights for the rooky pilots were "scheduled under the supervision of veteran flight leaders to insure that new pilots are well acquainted with all phases of combat flying in the F-51 type aircraft."

The most difficult problems for the

Monthly Summary

The UN Command was generally limiting offensive operations to short, vigorous probing actions and aggressive patrols during November. This strategy was intended to keep the CCF off balance, deny its forces favorable terrain, retard the build-up of potential offensive forces, and to effect as much damage and loss to personnel and equipment as possible. FEAF aircraft were making around-the-clock attacks on enemy installations and positions across North Korea. Late in November, peace negotiations moved to Panmunjom, a village about five miles east of Kaesong. It was located in a brand new demilitarized zone on the 38th parallel. [1]

Far East Air Forces flew many sorties, bringing on air-to-air duels between FEAF jet fighters and MiG-15 interceptors. Although hampered frequently by poor flying weather, FEAF warplanes made around-the-clock attacks on enemy installations throughout North Korea, placing the greatest emphasis on interdiction, airfield neutralization, and close support of Eighth Army front-line units. Fifth Air Force fighters and fighter-bombers provided napalming, strafing, bombing, and rocketing attacks on enemy troop concentrations and artillery positions. Later in the month, Allied airmen increased nighttime close support of Eighth Army ground troops.

Fifth Air Force fighters, fighter-bombers, and light bombers, together with attached SAAF, ROK, and USMC aviation units, interdicted enemy supply and communication routes incessantly to prevent or hinder the resupply of front-line Communist troops. Fighter-bombers worked systematically to destroy the enemy's rail network. During daylight hours, fighter and fighter-bombers attacked railroad rolling stock, while night intruder aircraft struck at vehicular traffic along highway supply routes. Fifth Air Force light bombers and FEAF Bomber Command B-29s nightly attacked key rail bridges and marshalling yards. [2]

[1] Adapted in part from USAFHRA. January 2002. The U.S. Air Force's First War: Korea 1950-1953 Significant Events. November 1951.

Fast Turnaround. *Mustangs from 67th Squadron, 12th Squadron and Two Squadron SAAF line up for assembly line armament reloads at K-46 in November 1951. Trailers of high-velocity rockets, and bomb-laden dollies await the returning aircraft. "In an average of seven minutes the scrappy little fighter-bombers are refueled, re-armed and ready for another combat flight," the Air Force caption noted.*

squadrons were "encountered with newly assigned pilots…that had no previous F-51 time to their credit." Overcoming that situation entailed "a long, arduous period of training for these pilots, particularly in view of the cold weather, combat commitments and lack of aircraft."

Bad weather in November dropped the number of combat sorties, but the Group report for the month pointed out that "effectiveness…of sorties was maintained at its previous high level and it is expected in spite of the great influx of relatively inexperienced pilots that the training will enable the Group to maintain its usual high degree of proficiency and effectiveness."

The overall decrease in sorties during November was "attributed primarily" to two factors. The weather was frequently bad and unsuited for combat flying operations. And, the "members of the cease-fire conference

in the Kaesong area were for a time in much accord, and this condition was accompanied by a corresponding decrease in the overall war effort," Major Joseph T. Crane, CO of the 12th Squadron reported in November.

Note: *Colonel Ralph H. "Salty" Saltsman, Jr., former Commander of the 18th Fighter-Bomber Group, pointed out another factor that contributed to the lower sortie rate. "The static bomb-line," he noted, "reflects little if any movement of ground forces by the enemy such as to require close-support missions by the Group."*

The 12th Squadron reported an "uncertainty" in the squadron "arising from the Status of the cease-fire conference" that it concluded was behind a "slight lowering of spirits in November. The approaching winter also contributes to this condition," it

reported.

"Unexpected progress of the Kaesong meetings during the month has also given new hope to those just arrived in Korea, presenting the possibility of an early cessation of hostilities and speedy departure," the Group reported with unintended irony in November.

Morale among the pilots "remains high, in spite of the rapid turnover of pilots. As new pilots are absorbed into flights and gain first hand knowledge of enemy capabilities, self confidence usually reasserts itself quickly and affects pilot morale proportionately," Lt. Col. Lawrence concluded in November. The extensive turnover, particularly among maintenance personnel generated problems. The "experience level" of the replacements was quite low. "On-the-job training programs now in progress are heavily taxing the small number of quali-

INTERDICTION BLOW. This photo, taken by a low-flying reconnaissance plane, reveals dramatically the destruction of the Hwangju marshalling and switching yard located on the Communist rail line between Pyongyang and Sariwon. Battered and burned boxcars and passenger coaches lie amid the debris of a four track walk-over and the empty shells of storage sheds, testifying to the effectiveness of bomb and rocket carrying fighter bombers of the Fifth Air Force. (NARA)

fied supervisory personnel available and can only in part accomplish the task of retaining efficiency at a high level."

"The commitments of an organization cannot be met by less than the authorized strength if that strength is composed of only partially qualified personnel..."

The Executive Officer of the 12th Squadron, Major Julian F. Crow was reassigned in November as Commanding Officer of the 67th Squadron succeeding Major Carl C. Colson, USAF.

It was another busy month for the 67th, not only for the fortunate pilots none of whom were lost to enemy action, but for the ground crews who had to repair eleven aircraft that were damaged by enemy ground fire. Two aircraft were totaled in crashes.

The squadron was operating with about 50 officers and 139 Airmen—above strength in pilots and continuing below strength in enlisted personnel. The "overage" in pilots Crow considered necessary "in order that combat commitments may be met and that pilots may be given Rest and Relaxation Leave." Enlisted strength was a major concern for Crow. In fact, in his view "enlisted strength has reached the danger point in operating two bases, especially in view of qualification of personnel replacing those being rotated to the United States. All sections of this unit are seriously handicapped by below authorization manning," he said. 3

"The commitments of an organization cannot be met by less than the authorized

strength if that strength is composed of only partially qualified personnel," he noted in his first report.

November also marked a period of "heavy rotation" of squadron personnel. Those leaving the squadron had "spent from six to seventeen months in Korea and are well qualified, having gained valuable experience in adverse conditions, one of these being the operation of a section undermanned." The replacements, Crow noted, with few exceptions, had only "recently completed an Air Force school and have no experience." Not only were the new personnel right out of school with no practical experience, they were arriving in the 67th and being provided by their orders "with a maximum of two or three days to learn from the airmen whom they are replacing their duties." The situation was worsened by the

fact that even when a qualified person was available to teach the replacement their duties, "that person must cease his own activities while teaching. When this situation occurs, supervisors become workers, in-as-much-as the work has to be done. It seems hardly fair that the squadron receives an apprentice while shipping out a senior specialists technician or supervisor," Crow pointed out.

The armament section was now up to its authorized strength and was conducting an excellent training program. However, personnel shortages in other sections "have created the rather pitiful situations partly explained" in the Personnel Qualification section of the monthly report.

Lt. Max Tomich was forced to bail out in the traffic pattern at Hoengsong during a night landing when his engine failed. For-

Sebille Plaque Earned by 67th Squadron. New dive bombing procedures helped the 67th win the Major Louis Sebille Plaque in November, 1951. This highly sought after award was conferred by the 18th Group on the squadron achieving the greatest accuracy in dive bombing for two consecutive months. Brigadier General T. C. Rogers, (left), Commander of the 18th Fighter-Bomber Wing and Col. Ralph H. ("Salty") Saltsman, Jr., Commander, 18th Fighter-Bomber Group present the Sebille Plaque to Major Carl C. ("Shorty") Colson, Commander of the 67th Squadron. (NARA)

tunately, he was not injured. Lt. Carl B. McCamish was involved in three major accidents that month—but escaped injury. Two were wheels up due to battle damage, the third aircraft crashed and burned on takeoff.

Crow kept the squadron focused on rail interdiction and accurate dive-bombing. The 67th again won the "Major Louis Sebille Plaque," the third consecutive month the squadron had led the Group in this combat capability. The plaque now belonged to the 67th. In addition, the Squadron received a letter of appreciation from Headquarters 32nd Infantry Regiment, 7th Infantry Division for its "excellent close support strikes" conducted on November 2nd. The 67th flew 570 sorties that month during which it expended 611,920 rounds of .50-caliber ammunition, 1,865 rockets, 404 napalm tanks, and 664 500-lb. bombs to destroy 25 artillery pieces, 161 buildings, 325 troops, 79 troop positions, 13 ammunition dumps, 9 supply dumps and 18 bunkers. In addition, their accurate dive bombing accounted for 47 railroad cuts.

On November 16th Fifth Air Force fighter-bombers were successful in cutting the railroads between Sinanju and Sukchon and between Kunu-ri and Sunchon in over 100 places. Many bridges were damaged, gun positions knocked out, supply buildings destroyed, fuel dumps lit up and enemy rail cars destroyed.

Five pilots completed their 100 mission

tours and were sent back to the States. Their loss was more than covered by the arrival of thirteen replacement pilots from the ZI. November had shown that "the combat effectiveness of the squadron is at a high point and with the present pilot replacement program now in effect it should remain so," Crow observed.

The Squadron lost its Awards and Decorations Officer, Captain James G. Kuntz in October and then its Awards Clerk, S/Sgt Kenwood R. York in November. It took a month to clear the backlog. There were 70 Air Medals, and three recommendations for the Distinguished Flying Cross to send forward. "Awards and decorations are a big factor in morale," Crow noted. "Despite knowing this to be true, progress toward

A New Brigadier General

"As your new Commanding General," the recently promoted T.C. Rogers wrote to the Wing in the Truckbuster, "I wish to thank you for the honor and for the many sincere expressions of congratulations I have received.

I can truthfully say that my appointment to the rank of Brigadier General reflects great credit upon the officers and airmen of the 18th Fighter-Bomber Wing. I suppose I can thank the old Roger's luck in falling heir to a command so ably manned and administered plus the 18th phenomenal fighting spirit."

the goal of being able to have the individuals awards presented before his departure continues to be slight, due to unqualified administrative personnel and those in insufficient number," he said.

Olive Drab winter clothing remained in short supply. In fact, at the end of November, the second winter of the Korean War, there were 65 airmen from the 67th that "cannot be issued winter olive drab clothing." The tents were cold, as well. The burners for tent stoves could not be obtained in sufficient quantities.

The larger pilots were still lacking the 28-foot parachutes they needed for a safe descent. Crow described them as "impatient," but "eager to perform their duties but with the proper equipment to insure their chance of living to a ripe old age." 4

The Supply Section was then manned at a pathetic 50 percent. "The supply personnel are attempting to perform their mission," Crow noted dryly, "with success commensurate with their strength."

The serious personnel shortage had also "seriously affected the efficiency of the Engineering Section in performing the maintenance mission." Early in month, turnover was minimal; however, during the last two weeks of November, eight airmen were gained, "half of which were at the apprentice level in skill and experience." At the end of November, the Engineering Section was 25 Airmen below authorized strength. The Squadron's average "in commission" status dipped to 68 percent for the month.

The heavy turnover in Administrative Section personnel reduced "the unit orderly room to a personnel processing unit" and prevented "adequate research for accurate reports and routing administrative duties. "Administrative personnel arriving are inexperienced and are slow in learning procedures," Crow observed.

By changing the barrels of the .50 caliber machine guns more frequently and stressing, "short bursts," Crow had helped reduce the number of split barrels or "explosions within the wings."

"The commitments of an organization cannot be met by less than the authorized strength if that strength is composed of only partially qualified personnel," Crow stressed. "The separate under strength sections have maintained a high standard of efficiency during the past months by having extremely well qualified personnel who went about their duties with no lost motion. As these qualified personnel are replaced by recent school graduates there must be a slow down in all operating sections in order to acquaint the replacement with duties. Since there cannot be a slowdown, the result is inaccurate reporting, poor personnel records, less excellent maintenance and inability to maintain directives current. Combat operations continued to be successful and commitments met during November," Crow reported. "It is doubtful that the same will be true in months to follow," he concluded his report pessimistically, "without additional qualified replacements, in view of the large turnover expected in December, January and February."

Rogers Decoyed. *M/Sgt Fay presented the oil portrait created by Sergeant Dave McNichol to BGen Rogers in a surprise ceremony on 3 Nov 51 at the base gymnasium. "If I could, I'd take the entire 18th back to the States with me," claimed General T.C. Rogers during a surprise portrait presentation. Rogers was decoyed to the Base Gym by Col. Ralph Saltsman, Jr., Commander of the 18th Group, who used a pretext of looking at "a radio-controlled model plane powered by a miniature jet engine." "I didn't suspect a thing," General Rogers admitted, "Salty really did a selling job that time. I was dumbfounded when I stepped into the Gym and saw Sergeant Fay on the stage. Thought for a minute we had interrupted a meeting of some sort."*

Note: *"It is somewhat apparent to a reader of the Monthly Reports," noted Colonel Ralph H. Saltsman, Jr., former Commander of the 18th Fighter-Bomber Group, in reviewing this chapter, "after the departure of Major Carl Colson from the 67th Squadron that his replacement, Major Julian Crow, is more oriented to the technical aspects of the 67th than was Colson."*

"Facilities available there can be relied upon to provide maximum comfort and operating efficiency during the long winter months to come."

In November, the 39th Squadron completed its sixteenth month of combat in the Korean War. The forward operating base at K-46 had "now been improved to the point where facilities available there can be relied upon to provide maximum comfort and operating efficiency during the long winter months to come.

Twenty new pilots joined the 39th in November, bringing pilot strength to a new high.

The most difficult problem encountered with newly assigned pilots during November "was that four of the new pilots had no previous F-51 time to their credit. This will entail a long, arduous period of training for these pilots, particularly in view of the cold weather, combat commitments and lack of aircraft. Of twenty new pilots assigned to the squadron during November the majority have completed their training and have been assigned to flights."

The pilot training program begun the previous month at K-46 had "definitely proved itself superior to the type of training conducted at K-10. Aircraft can be utilized to a greater extent than was possible previously. New pilots are able to assimilate a more easily understandable working knowledge of combat requirements with no loss of time," the 39th reported. "At K-46 the newly assigned pilot feels and is a more integral part of the Squadron than was the case while undergoing training at K-10."

Although no new changes in fighter tactics were initiated during November, "emphasis was maintained on good battle formation to prevent effective enemy air-to-air attacks. Line abreast formation is utilized with the elements spread wide in order to maintain complete maneuverability as an effective combat unit. Stress was also placed

Duffy's Tavern. *"A Well Done is in order for our buddies from the local Navy base," the Truckbuster reported. "They've taken the bull by the horns and opened up a club in town. It's a nice little affair. We checked it out the other night and found the beer to be good and cold, and, naturally, delicious. It's under the supervision of our good friend and general manager, Petty Officer 1/C Duvall, who is well known around the Top Three Club. It's set up for Navy personnel and AF Top Three, so let's give them some down-town business and help them out."* (Krakovsky)

on the importance of having wingmen keep well up in order to allow flight leaders to keep them easily in sight and to forestall enemy attacks on them as laggers."

Navigation proficiency continued to receive special attention by all pilots. Flight leaders would designate a member of the flight to navigate on return from target to base."

The increased turn over of pilots required more detailed and exact briefings and interrogations as well as numerous pilot meetings to insure complete understanding of all operational procedures by new pilots.

The Squadron "bid farewell to one of its most outstanding and colorful pilots, when Captain John Taylor completed his one

Barracks for the 18th Wing Medical Group at K-10. (McLoughlin)

hundred and sixtieth F-51 mission and departed--not for home--but to a new Combat Group where he hopes to complete one hundreds and sixty more missions," the 39th reported.

Endnotes

[1] USAFHRA. Monthly Historical Report, 18th Fighter-Bomber Group, November 1951, p. 3
[2] USAFHRA. Monthly Historical Report, 18th Fighter-Bomber Group, November 1951, p. 4.
[3] USAFHRA. Monthly Historical Report, 67th Fighter-Bomber Squadron, November 1951, p. 2.
[4] USAFHRA. Monthly Historical Report, 67th Fighter-Bomber Squadron, November 1951, p. 6.

"Zulu Warriors"

"One night our South African pilots painted themselves black," Lt. Fred Thomas recorded in his diary, "dressed up as warriors with spears and shields and had a 'Zulu Warrior Night.'"

"Upon arriving, a 'Witch Doctor' gave out a mandatory strong brew, and it was downhill all the way after that. The warriors screamed and danced and sang wild Zulu songs."

A USO lady fainted (or passed out).

"It was a moonlit night, and for some reason not clear to me, I stepped in a drainage ditch thinking it is a path. It was two days before anyone flew."

Significant Events

November 1951

November 6: Eleven enemy twin-engine, light bombers (probably TU-2s), bombed Taehwa-do, a UN-controlled island. This raid was the first confirmed report of air-to-ground action by an enemy light bomber formation since the Korean War started.

November 10: "The Republic of Korea Navy has added immeasurably to the success of the United National Forces fighting for the freedom and sovereignty of the Korean Nation," General Rogers said in a letter to Commodore Keung Mo Cheung, Commandant of the Chinhae Naval Base Command, to recognize the Republic of Korea Navy Day of 1951. "The tradition of bravery established by your forces in this conflict will live long in the hearts of your valiant people and will always reflect the greatest credit upon you and your forces. I sincerely hope that the celebration of this meaningful day will be an outstanding success and that the Republic of Korea Navy Day celebrations of the future will be with peace and freedom from aggression for your nation."

November 12: Peace negotiations moved to Panmunjom, a village less than five miles east of Kaesong, in a newly established demilitarized zone on the 38th Parallel. The UN Command ceased offensive ground operations.

November 16: Fifth Air Force fighter-bombers made over one hundred rail cuts between Sinanju and Sukchon and between Kunu-ri and Sunchon. They also damaged bridges, knocked out gun positions, destroyed supply buildings, fired fuel dumps, and took a toll of enemy rail cars.

November 28: Representatives of all intelligence gathering organizations in Korea met at Far East Command, Liaison Division, to discuss how to coordinate their activities. The conference resulted in the establishment of the Combined Command for Reconnaissance Activities in Korea.

November 30: In one of the largest aerial battles of the war, F-86 pilots engaged 44 enemy jets over the island of Taehwa-do that were flying south to bomb a UN target. The Sabre pilots destroyed twelve and damaged three others. Maj. George A. Davis Jr.,

At K-10, near a air gunnery range, Air Force salvagers found children living in unusable F-51 drop tanks. A volunteer policy regarding the bar tab was instituted to ensure that at least ten percent of the money "passing through the bar" went to the local orphanage. In addition, Budd Stapley reported, "we'd always throw our loose change in the donate jar for the orphanage and the kids."

USAF, achieved Korean War ace status by downing a TU-2 and a MiG-15. He was the first to be an ace in two wars, since he had been an ace in World War II as well. Enemy forces attacked Taehwa-do, north of Cho-do, forcing friendly forces to retreat to Cho-do. Fifth Air Force aircraft dislodged the enemy, enabling friendly forces to retake the island.

Colonel Seymour M. Levenson, assumed command of the 18th Fighter-Bomber Group from Colonel Ralph H. Saltsman, "the ever popular and efficient Group Commander," who departed for the States. Lt. Col. Henry W. Lawrence was assigned as Group Executive Officer.

Adapted in part from U.S. Air Force Historical Research Agency. January 2002. The U.S. Air Force's First War: Korea 1950-1953 Significant Events. November 1951. http://www.au.af.mil/au/afhra/wwwroot/korean_war/korean_war_chronology/kwc_1951.html

Combat Losses

1st Lt. Ned Charles Frankart, 39th Squadron, "was reported missing in action on 3 November 1951. Lt. Frankart was flying Number Two position in a flight of four F-51 aircraft. He was last observed going in on a rocket pass on a tunnel. After failing to respond to a radio call by his flight leader, the remains of his aircraft were observed burning on the ground following a huge explosion. Although the flight search the area thoroughly after the incident, no sign of Lt. Frankart was found."

Captain G. H. Krohn, 2 Squadron SAAF, KIA on 24 November 1951. George Krohn was flying as No. 3 on rail interdiction mission led by 2nd Lt. Grobler. A radiator defect on take-off forced Krohn to abort his take-off and pull off the runway. After a delay of ten minutes, he managed to take off and tried to catch up with his flight, a fact that was observed by two USAF flights. His earlier flight completed their mission prior to his arrival, and he radioed that he was going to attack a position with the Americans, which he did. After his bombs exploded, the last American pilot leaving the scene reported seeing a "Cheetah" turning south. Nothing further was heard from

Lt. Donald O. Lynd

Lt. Krohn.

1ˢᵗ Lt. Robert J. Lucas, 12ᵗʰ Fighter-Bomber Squadron.

2ⁿᵈ Lt. Donald O. Lynd, 39ᵗʰ Fighter-Interceptor Squadron, was "killed while attempting to land at K-10 after flying an F-51 down from K-46. After making a normal approach, his aircraft was observed to fall off to the left while on final approach. His aircraft crashed and was almost completely destroyed. The cause for this fatal accident is being made the subject of an extensive investigation," the 39ᵗʰ reported. Lynd arrived in Korea several weeks before his friend Wilbur "Budd" Stapley, who had known him as a student officer in Cadet Class 51-D at Craig AFB, Alabama in 1951. "We got word that Don had spun in turning onto final at K-46," Stapley remembered. "This was late in November 1951." Lynd was a student officer at Craig and "had already escaped the grim reaper once while in flight training. A group of student officers (a.k.a. 'stupid officers') were out reccing on the country roads at night and Don was in the lead. He had a '50 Mercury Convertible that was fast and Don could horse it around the curves like no one else. He took one curve too many and went off the road and the car rolled over 6 or 7 times before coming to a stop upside down. His buddies ran up to the wrecked car bemoan-

ing the loss of poor old Don. Out of the darkness staggered a somewhat disheveled Lt. Lynd who had been thrown through the canvas roof," Stapley recalled. Lynd had played linebacker in college and his rugged physic had served him well on that occasion. "Too bad his luck didn't hold out," Stapley said. "I remember Don as a nice guy who didn't try to impress us cadets with his rank. We were all just a bunch of guys trying to get our wings."

1ˢᵗ Lt. Critton J. Pappas, 2 Squadron SAAF pilot KIA on 4 November 1951. Lt. Pappas was flying his first combat mission with Lt. Pretorious. The four-ship flight—with full combat loads of bombs, rockets and machine gun ammunition—was on a rail interdiction mission in the YD area. After successfully attacking the primary target with bombs as planned, they proceeded to the secondary target, which they attacked with rockets. During the attack, Pappas disappeared and the flight reported seeing a bright, silver flash at about the location where Pappas was pulling out of his dive. Although a search was conducted for some period of time, no trace of the plane or pilot was found.

Captain A. Janse Van Rensberg, 2 Squadron SAAF pilot KIA on 20 November 1951. Captain van Rensburg was leading four-ship flight a railroad interdiction mission. Each of the Mustangs was loaded with a full complement of bombs, rockets and .50-cal. machine gun ammunition. After completing a successful attack on the primary target, the flight headed for the secondary target, a village with a hidden supply dump. After bombing, rocketing and strafing the village, Lt. Parsonson observed a long burst of flak tracers flash between him and van Rensberg. The flight leader's aircraft immediately began streaming coolant and pitched toward the ground. It appeared to be out of control and as Lt. Parsonson took quick evasive action to avoid being hit by van Rensberg's aircraft, he saw its pilot slumped forward over the controls. The aircraft exploded in flames as it crashed.

Combat Statistics

18ᵗʰ Fighter-Bomber Wing

November 1951

Average No. A/C Assigned
67
Total Flying Time
3,505
Percent of Aircraft in Commission
73
Percent of Aircraft AOCP
7
Combat Sorties Flown by Wing
2,315
12ᵗʰ Squadron Sorties
602
39ᵗʰ FIS Sorties
579
67ᵗʰ Squadron Sorties
590
2 Squadron Sorties
541
A/C Lost to Combat
5
Pilots lost
6

Fuel Consumed
230,703 gals.

Ordnance Expended
.50-cal. Rounds
1,743,085
Rockets
5,762
Napalm Bombs
1,206
500-lb. GP Bombs
2,408
Note: Figures and totals may differ in some categories due to differences in numbers provided by each component.

"Drive Carefully! The Man You Run Over May Be Your Replacement."

"What have I gotten myself into?"

It was late November that Airman Clarence Frownfelter boarded a C-119 of the Green Hornet Squadron at an Air Base on the southern tip of Japan and "headed out across the Japan Sea to a small fighter strip on the south tip of Korea called K-10."

As the lumbering "Flying Boxcar" touched down at K-10, he was asking himself, "What have I gotten myself into?"

Frownfelter just turned 18 the previous July. He was "very fascinated with being a member of a fighter squadron and around airplanes."

Frownfelter's father, "was a pilot from the 1930's and I had learned to fly from him between ages 12 to 17 in a 40 HP and later 65 HP Piper Cub." Frownfelter talked his dad into giving parental permission for him "enlist in the Air Force because the Recruiting Office had led me to believe that I would probably get to fly. Well, I did get to fly--a desk.' I was told I would need to be 19 years old to be eligible to go to Flight School. Anyway, I made the best of it."

"It was a single landing strip with one end butting up to the Japan Sea with about a 20-foot wall down to the water. The first thing I noticed was F-51's parked on the flight line. We were greeted by a "six-by" as transportation to the main part of the base. From this vehicle I saw a sign that read, 'Drive Carefully. The Man You Run Over May Be Your Replacement.' This was my introduction to "Dogpatch."'

Airman Clarence Frownfelter stands outside his office, the Orderly Room of the 67th Fighter-Bomber Squadron at K-10. (Frownfelter)

67th Orderly room Gang. Corporal Miller, Pfc Miller, Corporal Frownfelter, Sergeant Sexton, 1st Sergeant Glenn and Lt. Shockley in front of the 67th Squadron Orderly Room at K-10 in 1952. M/Sgt. Glenn was referred to as "the one and only," by Frownfelter, who noted at the time, "He sure is a swell guy." (Frownfelter)

Within a few hours, Frownfelter had been welcomed and processed as a member of the 67th Fighter-Bomber Squadron, a part of the Truckbusters of Dogpatch Korea. "We were called the 'Red Scarf' Squadron and our slogan was "*The Fighting Cock Tops Them All*." The Mustangs of the 67th Squadron "were trimmed with red around the canopy, rudder tip and wing tips and the side of the nose bore a painting of the fighting rooster in boxing gloves."

Frownfelter was assigned to the Orderly Room where he worked closely with the Commander of the 67th, Lt. Col. Julian D. Crowe. The "Orderly Room Gang" also included: Lt. Shockley, Captain Crosby, Sgt. Glenn (First Sergeant), A. F. (Frank) Massey, Sgt. Golden, Airman Miller, Airman Edick, and Sgt Sexton.

Lt. Col. Julian Crow "was my idol," Frownfelter recalled. "He didn't know it at the time, but I watched and admired him daily. To me, he looked like Steve Canyon in that blue flight suit, the red scarf around his neck with the silver lined officer field cap."

Being assigned to the Orderly Room allowed Frownfelter "to see, know, and be around our pilots. I processed the daily morning report, and typed many of the reports put together by Lt. Col. Crow and later Lt. Col. Stanley Long.

The sounds of early morning F-51 run-ups to this day remain a vivid memory to Frownfelter. "Those 12-cylinder piston engines had a sound of their own and then there were the daily morning take offs," he remembered.

December 1951

"Pride in the squadron and the knowledge that its success or failure depends on each one's individual performance tends to give each man pride in having a sense of responsibility toward the successful completion of our missions."

Three 18th Group Mustangs taxi down the airstrip at K-46 prior to taking off on a mission in December 1951. (NARA)

Combat Operations

Rail interdiction was still the "major objective" for the 18th Group in December and its squadrons "continued cutting rails on the tracks running east out of Sunchon." The frequent "visits" by napalm-loaded Mustangs "became increasingly costly as the enemy continued to build up his defenses along this line under constant and repeated daily attacks. Three aircraft were lost as a result of attacks on this rail line and one aircraft was lost attacking the rail line from Sunchon to Pyongyang."

The Group was varying its tactics "in an attempt to suppress flak but flak damage and losses continued until the assignment of the rail line south of Pyongyang between Kyomipo and Sariwon was made after mid-month," Levinson reported.

The greatest number of CAS missions was "flown in the vicinity of the British Commonwealth Division in the western I Corps sector where the enemy was most active. Several close support missions in support of ROK units engaged in wiping out guerrilla and bandit forces in the south central portion of Southern Korea south of Taejon were flown from both K-10 and K-46" that month.

However Fifth Air Force fighters, fighter-bombers, and light bombers destroyed numerous troublesome enemy artillery sites and continued its rail interdiction program. "Enemy artillery positions and supply and troop areas were constantly attacked un-

der the direction of one or more recce ships from the 67th Tactical Reconnaissance Wing," the 18th Fighter-Bomber Group reported that month.

"Due to the heavier flak concentrations," the 12th Squadron reported, "many interdiction flights carried VT Bombs and Rockets for purpose of flak suppression. The usual method being used is for 2 lead aircraft in each of 2 flights of 8 aircraft to be loaded with VT ordnance. This method has proven effective."

Although hampered by frequently poor flying weather later in December, Far East Air Forces maintained a high interdiction sortie rate against enemy resupply activity. Fifth Air Force attacked enemy rail and highway transportation routes, frequently bomb-

Monthly Summary

As 1951 ended, negotiators at Panmunjom dickered over concrete arrangements for an armistice and provisions pertaining to prisoners of war. Meanwhile, ground forces of both sides conducted small-scale patrol actions that sometimes escalated into vicious firefights. Overall, the Eighth Army maintained a vigilant readiness in case of a general enemy attack. [1]

Inactivity on the ground activity did not extend to the same degree among UN naval and air forces. UN warships and naval aircraft interdicted the enemy's supply network, bombarded strategic coastal targets, and maintained the blockade of the Korean peninsula.

Far East Air Forces cut back on close support for ground troops along the generally static front lines. "With the continuation of the static front line situation there was little call for close support missions during the month," the 18th Group Commander reported. "Fewer close support missions were flown probably as a result of stalemate in the battle line," the 12th FBS reported. In main, the missions were interdiction against transportation lines, supply concentrations, and artillery positions. In all cases, heavier flak is being encountered."

Adapted from USAFHRA. January 2002. The U.S. Air Force's First War: Korea 1950-1953 Significant Events. December 1951.

ing, rocketing, and strafing bridges, marshalling yards, and rail and vehicular rolling stock.

At night, B-26 light bombers and Marine fighter-bombers, aided by flare-dropping aircraft, made interdiction assaults on enemy road traffic.

After the communists released locations of Allied POW camps, Far East Air Forces stopped air strikes in those areas until the camps could be pinpointed.

During December the enemy increased the challenge to UN air supremacy by flying more MiG-15 sorties from Manchuria, moving more aircraft near the Yalu River border, bombing and strafing UN ground installations and front-line positions, and increasing night interceptor attacks against UN aircraft. The 18th Group reported that it maintained the "normal strip alert both morning and evening" but that the Mustangs were not scrambled. The Group did report "several missions, counter air in nature, were flown in support of naval units in the Chodo Island area west of Chinampo and patrolling over shipping in the Inchon Harbor area." [1]

Failure Meeting Operational Commitments

Throughout the first week in December, General Rogers had been "expecting a blast" from Headquarters, Fifth Air Force "on our failure to meet operational commitments." He thanked them for "being so patient."

"We are in a slump," BGen T.C. Rogers explained in an 8 December letter to Fifth Air Force Operations, "brought on by many factors some of which are in our power to correct. I have compared our operations now with a year ago and tried to analyze our troubles. We flew more hours with 2 squadrons in November 1950 than we did with three in November 1951. A year ago we flew 2 & 4 aircraft flights and could naturally get off more sorties than under the present system of operation."

Rogers outlined the problems faced by the 18th Wing that contributed to the dismal performance records.

A shortage of aircraft limited the number that can be made available for maintenance at the rear base and increased the periodic inspection rate on the available aircraft.

Exceptionally cold weather at the forward base "with its attendant increase in maintenance problems."

Lower quality of maintenance personnel. The Air Force was sending replacements that were "largely jet-trained men and must spend a long period of apprenticeship."

Lack of incentive on the part of maintenance personnel due to split operations and to the cease-fire talks.

Failure on the part of 18th Wing leadership "to get a full days work out of available personnel."

Rogers said he fully realized "that many of the above factors are a reflection on leadership." He explained that he had launched a "Fall back-up" from the Wing Commander on down.

"For the first time since I took command of this Wing," Rogers noted, "we have pilots running out our ears--about 40 per squadron." This

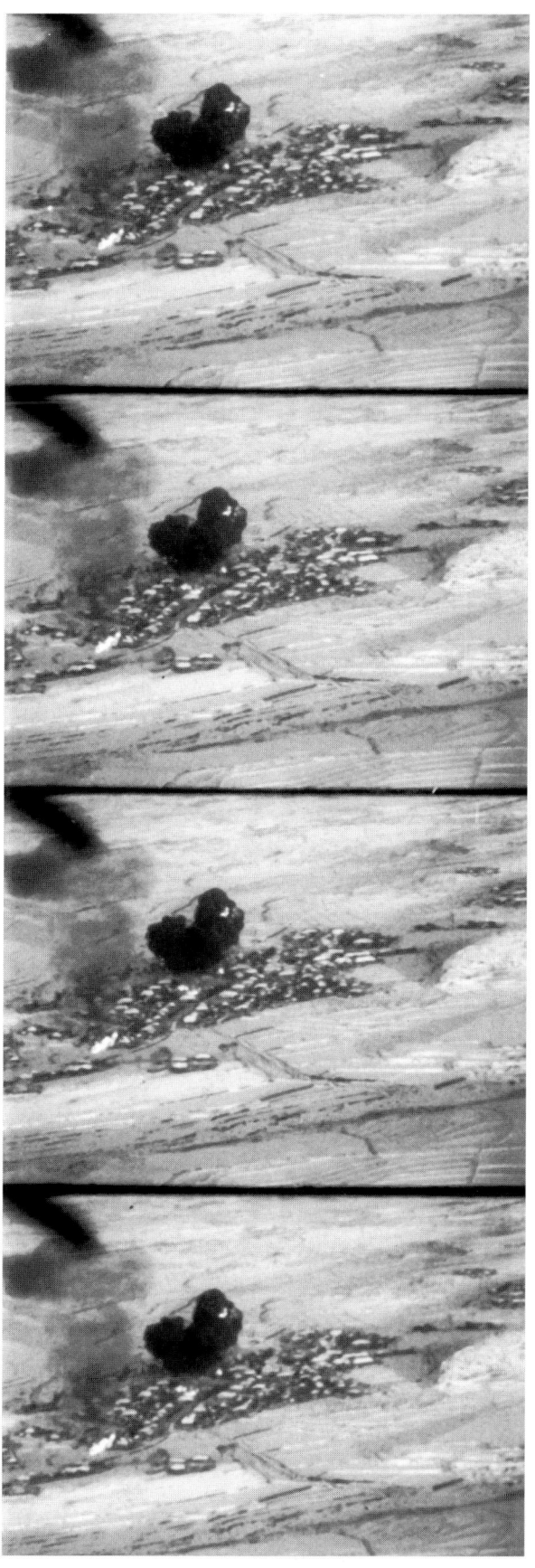

Gun camera strip *showing attack by USAF planes on a "Communist Military installation in a small village somewhere in Korea." (NARA)*

407

Combat Statistics

18th Fighter-Bomber Wing

December 1951

Average No. A/C Assigned
66
Total Flying Time
3,688
Percent of Aircraft in Commission
69
Percent of Aircraft AOCP
9
Combat Sorties Flown by Wing
1,932
12th Squadron SSorties
514
39th FIS Sorties
470
67th Squadron Sorties
566
2 Squadron Sorties
420
A/C Lost to Combat
8
Pilots lost
10

Fuel Consumed

237,732 gals.

Ordnance Expended

.50-cal. Rounds
864,485
Rockets
3,968
Napalm Bombs
576
500-lb. GP Bombs
2,037

Note: Figures and totals may differ in some categories due to differences in numbers provided by each component.

Thanks for CAS. *Mustang pilots of the 18th Fighter-Bomber Wing in Korea received a verbal pat-on-the-back when four members of the Eighth Army's Second Division stopped at this advanced air base in December 1951. "We had some anxious moments on Heartbreak Ridge and really appreciated the close support missions flown by these "Mustangs" of the Fifth Air Force," stated one of the front line veterans, "They really did a good job and made our job easier." 1st Lt. Elvin O. Wyatt (right), Baton Rouge, La. talked to the men prior to take-off on his 100th combat mission. "Makes us feel good to know that we are doing a good job on close support," stated Wyatt. "Usually we are directed by a ground or air controller and never know our results." The Second Division veterans who visited the base were: (left to right) Cpl. Frederico A. Garcia, San Benito, Texas; Pfc. Rohiyung Yong, Seoul, Korea; M/Sgt. Charles Starks, Portageville, Mo. and T/Sgt. Louis Sambuco, Waterbury, Conn. (NARA)*

did not apply to the South African squadron, however, who could not "meet their commitments now due to pilot shortage." Rogers pointed out that impending rotations among both airmen and key officer personnel would hit the Wing "hard during the next two months...By the end of March this will be an entirely new Wing so far as personnel go. I sincerely hope we can retain the fine cooperative spirit that has characterized the command in the past," Rogers said.

Win-Win Bomb Storage Agreement

General T.C. Rogers worked out an agreement with Rear Admiral Son Wun Il that enabled the Wing to use bomb storage facilities at the Korean Naval Academy. Son had originally opposed the plan, believing that the Wing would be "hauling to and from the bomb dump daily." Rogers "assured him that it would be a permanent storage area to be drawn upon only in the event of an emergency." The Admiral changed his mind and sent a message to Headquarters, Fifth Air Force withdrawing his previous objections.

The negotiations were a "win-win" for the two organizations. The Wing would not have to bear the cost of "constructing another bomb storage area and will avoid the necessity of confiscating rice producing land in this area," Rogers wrote in a thank you letter to Commodore Jung Kyun Mo.

Targeting

As the second Korean winter of the war took hold, "snow generally covered most of these targets in the vicinity of the enemy's

Pyongyang Airfield. *This reconnaissance photo taken on December 16, 1951, by a "high flying" photo reconnaissance jet revealed the non-serviceable condition of the Pyongyang (main) airfield. Well-aimed 100-, 500- and 1,000-pound bombs "made it impossible for the enemy to stage any flights from its runway," the Air Force noted. (NARA)*

rear and along the bomb line." Aircraft from the 67th Reconnaissance Squadron did not have "rockets for target identification" and were attempting to mark targets with "API" or Armor Piercing Incendiary rockets. Flight leaders of the attacking squadrons were "usually unable to see the API strike the target due to the snow." Even when the flight leaders joined the recce flights to fly in formation with them, "while targets were marked pinpoint was still nigh impossible." This lead to the attacking squadrons "spending an undue amount of time circling the target area alerting the enemy to the impending attack and thereby increasing his antiaircraft fire effectiveness. This was reflected in the increased battle damage and aircraft lost on these particular missions," the Group reported.

A brief attempt to correct the situation included selecting three pilots, one from each squadron, to attend 67th Tac Recce Group briefings and then to fly a mission with the "Hammer" aircraft. "The pilots were then thoroughly briefed on the target and were able to mark the target with one or more of the six rockets each carried." The new system "worked well," but mysteriously "due to circumstances beyond the control of this group could not be continued."

Navigation

The Group established a new course in map reading and Korean Pilotage. New pilots and those having fewer than twenty missions over North Korea were required to complete the seven-hour course. "The course covered map scales and the grid system employed, prominent terrain features, air fields and emergency strips and frequently used check points on mission

routes. The pilots learned the navigational features in a procession of steps and upon completion of the course could "plot these features from memory on a blank outline map of Korea." As snow and ice covered much of North Korea and northern target areas and check points were increasingly obliterated, the useful course received "much favorable comment." [2]

Survival

In mid-December an E&E team visited K-46 and demonstrated new survival equipment to 18th Group pilots. The pilots, understandably, were very interested in the equipment that could easily save their lives if they were forced down in enemy territory. They were particularly interested in the "Hornet" rifle. The problem lay in the fact that very "little or no equipment was being made available to them." Group Commander, Col. Seymour Levenson immedi-

ately visited FEAMCOM and after his return another "Survival" meeting was held. He returned with some new equipment that was displayed and demonstrated. Much of it required adaptation to the "peculiarities of F-51 pilots." Also during December, "Kits, Emergency, Subsistence, Very cold climate, Seat type A-1, Spec. #20105, Stock No. 8330-559136-55" were ordered and received. Because the Kits, Emergency, Subsistence were too large for the F-51's due to limited cockpit and headspace, "dinghy packs were ordered without dinghy with the idea of converting the large kits into smaller dinghy type kits which would be suitable." [3]

Parachutes with red or orange panels were also requisitioned because "it has been proven that white chutes cannot be seen on the snow now covering North Korean target areas."

Morale in the 18th Group remained high despite winter weather and the relatively

cease-fire conference. The fact that a cease-fire might come at any time is not conductive for top efficiency on combat missions. The old axiom applies in that no one wants to have the dubious honor of being the last casualty. However, despite the general feeling, the pilots the 12th are continuing to do an outstanding job," the Commander of the 12th Squadron, Major Joseph T. Crane, Jr., reported in December.

The Airmen being received by 18th Wing squadrons were far from adequately trained. "All airmen received were either recruits who possessed only technical school training or airmen of the top three pay grades who had been on recruiting duty or away from normal operations for a period of several years. Intensive on-the-job training materially assisted in improving the qualifications of airmen but at the cost of decreased efficiency" for the squadrons. Group Commander Colonel Seymour Levenson, cited a PFC whose primary AFSC was Assistant Fire Control Systems Mechanic who was assigned to the Group as a Draftsman.

"All sections of this organization," Major Julian Crow led off in his December report, "with the exception of pilot strength, continue to be below authorized strength. Enlisted strength has risen above the low mark reached at the beginning of the period covered by this report. However, enlisted strength is hardly over the danger point, in view of overall personnel qualifications and losses due to rotation." 4

Replacements continued to arrive "with little or no experience in their specialty fields." The lack of qualified specialists and supervisory personnel "had an adverse effect upon all squadron activities during December." Strong emphasis by Crow and

high loss rate in early December. "The high percentage of successful helicopter rescues of downed pilots in the 18th has had a marked effect upon morals (sic)..."

Sebille Trophy

The Major Lou Sebille Award had been established to recognize the squadron that at the end of each month "had done the most outstanding and accurate bombing," the Truckbuster reported. The winning squadron retained the trophy for thirty days. At the end of the thirty day period, the trophy was moved to the next winning squadron, until one squadron earned it for three consecutive months, then it would become the "permanent property of the squadron."

In December, after winning the coveted trophy for three consecutive months, the

"Red Scarfers" of the 67th Squadron were awarded the trophy to "retain it as their permanent property.

Major Julian Crow, the new Commander of the 67th Squadron, accepted the Sebille Trophy from General Rogers and 18th Group Commander Colonel S. M. "Sy" Levenson. The original plaque was then "forwarded to the widow of the late Major Sebille."

Squadron Activity

"Pride in the squadron and the knowledge that its success or failure depends on each one's individual performance tends to give each man pride in having a sense of responsibility toward the successful completion of our missions. The biggest determiner to morale, especially among rated personnel, is the uncertainty of the

squadron leaders helped improve personnel qualifications during the latter part of December, and the statistics reflected a slight improvement. However the improvements in qualifications were "attributable to the long hours of work and instruction on the part of the few "old-timers" remaining in the squadron," Crow explained. He noted that in the administrative and supply areas "the replacements are making rapid progress but are unable to perform their duties efficiently. It is anticipated that a period of two months will lapse before any degree of personnel stabilization can be realized. Personnel stabilization can only result when the 'heavy rotation' ends."

While Crow was trying to stabilize personnel rotation, negotiators at Panmunjom were arguing over concrete arrangements for an armistice and provisions pertaining to prisoners of war. On the ground, both sides kept up the pressure with aggressive patrols that sometimes evolved into vicious firefights. Overall, the Eighth Army kept itself in a state of vigilant readiness for any enemy offensive operations, up to a general attack.

The standoff on the ground was not mirrored in the air or at sea. UN warships blockaded the coast while naval aircraft paid special attention to strategic coastal targets and interdicted enemy supply networks. Static front lines did not require as much close air support by FEAF fighters, although bothersome enemy artillery sites were heavily targeted.

During December the 67th lost two aircraft in crashes and one received major damage during attacks on highway transportation routes, bombing, rocketing and strafing bridges, marshalling yards, and rail and vehicular rolling stock. First Lieutenant Max Tomich was forced to bail out behind the front lines on December 1st. His injuries were minor and he was successfully rescued by helicopter. Second Lieutenant John P. Streit was involved in a major accident when he nosed-up his aircraft on landing at K-46.

Six pilots completed their combat tour of one hundred sorties during December. Based on medical recommendations, two pilots were certified as completing their sorties just below the "Century Mark."

A number of pilots were assigned in December who were not qualified currently in the F-51 type aircraft. "Their training has been a function of the 18th Fighter-Bomber Group Training Section," Crow noted.

Combat commitments were not met during some periods of December "because of shortage of aircraft and inability to keep those assigned in commission. The same situation has occurred in all supporting sections largely due to inadequate number of qualified airmen," Crow noted. The squadron redoubled its efforts and maintained an average in commission status of over 76%, with some 1,089 combat hours flown during 566 combat sorties.

While expending over 351,000 rounds of .50-caliber ammunition, 262 napalm tanks, 1,558 rockets and 748 bombs, the 67th accounted for 25 artillery pieces, 11 pieces of rolling stock, 128 buildings, 36 troop positions, 18 small boats, 99 rail and 2 road cuts, and

Rocket Attack in progress. *Gun camera film of a rocket attack on a small village. The white spots in the foreground are HVAR projectiles heading for the target. (NARA)*

411

End of the Line. A smashed Communist tank rests forlornly at the end of the line between Pyongyang and Sariwon. Interdiction fighter bombers of the Fifth Air Force blasted the rail bridge and stranded the tank which then became easy prey to sharp-eyed rocket-firing pilots on December 22, 1951. (NARA)

136 troops KIA. Eight recommendations for the Distinguished Flying Cross were submitted that month alone.

The supply section was hampered by the lack of wool jackets to replace those same items they had been required to turn in the previous summer. It was now so cold that "armament malfunctions have been attributed to congealed lubricants causing stoppages." Those problems were dealt with by "continued oiling of parts and use of the gun heaters."

The two replacements for S/Sgt. Elmer Zametz had "so little supply experience that their presence does not offset the loss of Sergeant Zametz" who had been returned to the States.

Lack of flyable aircraft to meet tactical commitments as well as train newly assigned pilots continued to be a chief trouble

In December, the 39th Squadron completed its seventeenth month of combat operations. In December the hard working "Cobra in the Clouds" Squadron flew a total of 672 combat mission requiring a total of 1,124 flight hours. "Due to the shortage of aircraft, maintenance personnel were very busy all month keeping as many aircraft in commission as possible so operational commitments could be met. Eleven aircraft suffered battle damage, three were lost over the target area and one demolished in a take-off accident. Five aircraft were gained from 18th Maintenance shops during the month.

The Squadron "continued maintaining three flights at K-46, one on Rest and Relaxation pass in Japan, and one flight at K-10, rotating every six days from forward location.

No insurmountable problems arose during December for the 39th, although "training of newly assigned pilots continued to be the one headache. Lack of flyable aircraft to meet tactical commitments as well as train newly assigned pilots continued to be a chief trouble."

The 39th "continued to operate singly as group gaggles were discontinued in October. This has proven to be a much improved operation as it give the squadron more time over the target and provides better offensive and defensive formation over the target."

"It is highly evident," the 39th concluded in its December 1951 unit report," that proper training of replacements by older members of the squadron is a necessity. Lack of an adequate number of supervisory personnel for the new replacements has proven to be a point that cannot be overlooked in the future."

In its 1951 Christmas Card from "Dogpatch" (K-10), the 18th Fighter-Bomber Wing took note of its twenty eight years of service and expressed pride in having established "a fine array of precedents and won for itself a proud position on the roster of great military outfits. In keeping with the tradition of American spirit and sacrifice during time of war, the Wing has contributed enormous quantities of human effort and achievement to every emergency which faced its homeland."

> "F-51s have given the Air Force its strongest contender for top place in the annals of military aviation, and the deeds of their pilots have won the profoundest admiration and respect of military men the world over."
>
> *Christmas Card from 18th Fighter-Bomber Wing… "Dogpatch" 1951*

Happy Centurian. A very happy Captain Richard W. Palmer poses with 2nd Lt. Donald Drage outside the 67th Squadron Operations Office at K-46 after completing his 100 missions in December 1951. Other 67th pilots completing 100 missions that month included: Captain Wynn A. Coomer, Captain Richard D. Anderson, Major Ellis L. Fisher, 1st Lt. John J. Nibert and 1st Lt. Edward G. Murphy. (Drage)

"While it is now the sleek and colorful jet which dominates the headlines and directs traffic in historical MIG Alley, the 18th, with its slow and obsolete fighters, is the hero of the front line soldier for whom it operates. The once famed F-51 Mustang, strafing bunkers and implacements [sic] and playing havoc on battle-line supply lane, has become the Air Force's closest relation to the ground troop."

"The 18th fought side-by-side with the doughboy in the early, tragic days of the Korean War. It sent its fighters out with the Army and Marine patrols, when the seas were crowding the UN's bloody patch of territory. It followed the lines as they were slowly pushed up above the 38th, and was the first Air Force outfit to operate from a Base above that Parallel. No other Wing in Korea should feel justified in making any claims for glory without checking the records and pitting its feats with those of the 18th. Our proudest claim is our saddest memory, Major Lou Sebille, who died in a blaze of glory, and was awarded the Air Force's only Congressional Medal of Honor in Korea.:

"Not even considering the competition with which it must vie for honors, the F-51s have given the Air Force its strongest contender for top place in the annals of military aviation, and the deeds of their pilots have won the profoundest admiration and respect of military men the world over."

Endnotes

[1] USAFHRA. *Monthly Historical Report, 18th Fighter-Bomber Group,* December 1951, p. 8
[2] USAFHRA. *Monthly Historical Report, 18th Fighter-Bomber Group,* December 1951, p. 9
[3] USAFHRA. *Monthly Historical Report, 18th Fighter-Bomber Group,* December 1951, p. 10.
[4] USAFHRA. *Monthly Historical Report, 67th Fighter-Bomber Squadron,* December 1951, p. 2.

Captain Jim Byers, the 12th Squadron Grenidier Love Flight Leader, poses for his Century Flight photo on 15 December 1951. Byers and his brother, Capt. Bill Byers had also flown combat during WW II. In the European Theater, they were probably the only brother combination flying wing for each other. Byers had been recalled to active duty from the 123rd FIS of the Oregon Air National Guard at Portland. (Bill Byers flew 115 missions in F-80's for the 49th FBW) (Cook)

Lt. Ernie Wakehouse of the 39th FIS celebrates his Centurian Flight on 22 December 1951. Wakehouse was considered one of the best Flight Leaders in the 39th by his squadron commander. Note the shamrock on his helmet and the banded spinner on his Mustang that when rotating at high speed gave them the "blinker nose" squadron label. Wakehouse was one of eight Oregon Air Guards pilots who flew combat missions with the 18th Wing, noted Jack Cook. (Cook)

Significant Events

December 3: Enemy jets made their first air-ground attack of the war, bombing and strafing UN ground positions near Chorwon, almost sixty miles northeast of Seoul.

December 13: Twenty-nine F-86s encountered seventy-five MiG-15s over Sinanju, and in a wild melee the F-86 pilots shot down nine MiGs, giving USAF pilots a total of fourteen aerial victories for the day.

December 21: Fifth Air Force units flew 530 sorties, making thirty cuts in the main rail line between Sinanju and Sukchon and attacking a supply complex near Kunu-ri.

December 27: FEAF aircraft flew 900 sorties, the largest number of the month, damaging or destroying locomotives, railcars, buildings, vehicles, and gun positions.

December 31: "Information has come to me that on the night of 27 December 1951 a motorbus from K-10 Air Base struck and injured Second Lieutenant Kim Nak Kyu of the Korean Air Academy," General Rogers wrote to Brig. Gen. Yung Duk Choi, Superintendent of the Korean Air Academy. "I deeply regret that such injuries were caused to a member of your command by reason of a defection on the part of a member of my command. Charges in courts-martial have been preferred against the driver of the motorbus for striking Lieutenant Kim and for leaving the scene of the accident without rendering assistance to Lieutenant Kim. Please accept my apologies and those of the officers and airmen of this Wing for the incident," Rogers closed, wishing a Lt. Kim "our sympathy and our wishes for his speedy recovery."

Combat Losses

1st Lt. Thurston Richard Baxter, 39th Fighter Interceptor Squadron, "flying Number Two in a flight of four was reported Missing In Action on 21 December 1951 when he failed to return from a rail interdiction mission. His flight was assigned flak-suppression, to commence dive at 11,000 feet and pull out at 6,000 feet. He started his dive at 11,000 and never recovered. A complete search of the area for pilot or parachute had negative results. Tactics for these missions are being carefully studied to see if some improvements can be made."

1st Lt. Harold S. Forster, 12th Fighter-Bomber Squadron.

1st Lt. Donald Edward Hoffman, 12th Fighter-Bomber Squadron. Lt. Hoffman and Lt. Wilfred "Budd" Stapley were roommates for a while as cadets in Class 51-D at Craig AFB, Alabama. Hoffman was from Chicago and Stapley was from Hammond, Indiana, a "suburb of Chicago, so we drove back and forth to base several times." Hoffman "had played center on his college football team and could be a stand-in for Superman anytime." Stapley remembered later that he had "the bad habit of smoking a cigarette in bed after lights out. Don tried to get me to quit by talking to me several times. One night he decided to take things in his own hands and he grabbed me by the shoulders and sat me up in bed. It was the last time I did that—while we were roommates," Stapley recalled. "Other than that once incident, we were good buddies." Hoffman "had the bad luck to have a napalm tank hang up on his plane as he tried to zoom up out of a valley. The weight of the tank threw his plane into a spin at low altitude and he hit the side of a hill," Stapley recalled. "I believe this was in late December 1951 or early January 1952."

1st Lt. Lyle Earl Moore, Jr., 67th Fighter-Bomber Squadron, was "hit on a dive-bomb

1st Lt. Donald E. Hoffman

run on 15 December 1951, and has been listed as missing in action."

1st Lt. P.I. Norman-Smith, 2 Squadron SAAF. (See below entry for Lt. Ken Whitehead)

Captain Robert Douglas Ramsey, 39th Fighter-Interceptor Squadron, was "flying lead position in Mongoose Zebra flight" and was reported as Missing In Action on 10 December "when he failed to return from a rail interdiction mission. No radio transmission was heard from the pilot. Witnesses stated dived straight into the ground on his initial attack. A search of the heavily

Early Christmas Dinner in Japan. *How Flight, 67th Squadron enjoys a dinner on December 21, 1951 at Johnson Air Base (Japan) Officer's Club during a much needed R&R period. (L-R) Captain Glenn E. Stewart, Lt. Shirley B. Tubbs, Lt. Clyde O. Armstrong, Lt. Donald D. Drage, Lt. Wilfred C. "Budd" Stapley and Captain John W. Gerwig. (Drage)*

defended area resulted in no visible trace of parachute or pilot."

1st Lt. Robert Leslie Smith, 39th Fighter-Interceptor Squadron, was "flying Number Two in a flight of four" when he was reported Missing In Action on 14 December 1951, "when he failed to return from a close support mission. He radioed that he was hit in the engine section and would bail out. At approximately 5,000 feet over the terrain his canopy was seen to come off, his airplane go into a steep spiral, crash and burn. A search of the area near the scene proved negative....All pilots have been advised to roll the canopy back manually if possible in emergency case (sic) to preclude any possible chance of the canopy from striking the pilot."

1st Lt. John A. Swanson, 12th Fighter-Bomber Squadron.

Captain Harry M. Tyler, 12th Fighter-Bomber Squadron.

1st Lt. Ken R. Whitehead, 2 Squadron SAAF pilot KIA on 3 December 1951. Lt. Ken Whitehead was flying No. 3 in a four-ship flight that had successfully attacked its primary target and was proceeding to the secondary target. Clouds hid that target, so they turned for home. After about twenty minutes of flying time, the leader advised the flight that he was preparing to let down through the clouds. Once below the overcast, the flight reformed and tried to determine exactly where they were. Determining they were over Wonju, they asked Control for a "steer" to K-46. However, an emergency was in progress and they were asked to stand by. Both K-14 and K-16 were asked for directions with No Joy. Now down to about 1,000 feet flying below the clouds, the flight recognized the Han River below them and began to follow it to Seoul. As they approached Seoul, Lt. Whitehead's aircraft suddenly collided with Lt. Norman-Smith's aircraft, which immediately rolled over and crashed into the Han River. He was killed instantly. Lt. Whitehead's aircraft had lost its propeller and engine. It followed the stricken Mustang into the river, as well. Whitehead is buried in the UN Cemetery at Pusan.

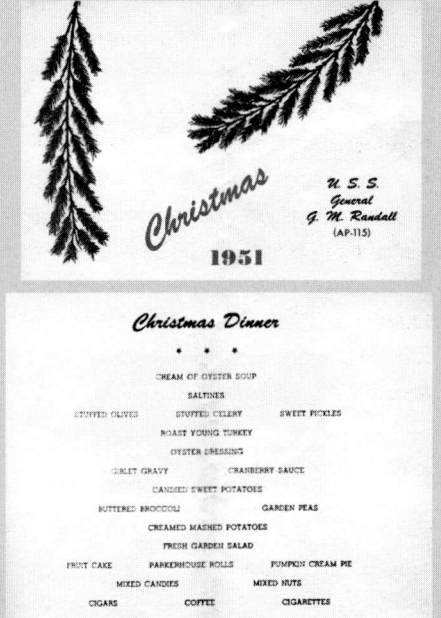

USNS General George M. Randall (AP-115) was launched 30 January 1944 and sailed from Norfolk four months later with nearly 5,000 troops headed for Bombay, India and returned bringing home to California over 2,000 wounded veterans. Until the end of World War Two the RANDALL continued to shuttle troops to war theaters and to bring wounded home. After the war, she was part of the "Magic-Carpet" fleet, making voyages from San Francisco and San Diego to the Far East. She was assigned to the Navy's Military Sea Transportation Service (MSTS) in October 1949 and made scheduled runs between the West Coast and the Orient until the Korean War began in June 1950. In September 1950, she participated in the amphibious assault at Inchon which routed the North Korean Army and forced Communist evacuation of South Korea. After Chinese Communist troops poured into Korea and trapped American forces, she helped evacuate Hungnam, saving countless embattled G.I.'s. On December 18, 1951, she got underway from San Francisco, CA with troops headed to Korea. "Dear Mom," wrote Airman First Class Bob Cranston, "will leave today for Japan. Will take app(roximately) 14 days. Will write you as soon as I dock. I used to say I wanted to travel. Well, now I am. Love, Always, Bob." Cranston was soon assigned to the 67th Fighter Bomber Squadron of the 18th Fighter Bomber Group at K-46. In 1958, the RANDALL was still "on station" putting troops of the 35th Tank Battalion ashore at Beirut, Lebanon on the morning of August 3, 1958. The RANDALL was decommissioned on June 2, 1961. (Cranston)

1952
18th Fighter-Bomber Wing
Chronology

Second Korean Winter November 28, 1951-April 30, 1952	Korean Summer-Fall 1952 May 1-November 30, 1952
18th Fighter Bomber Group officially based at K-10/Chinhae, SK Flying combat missions from K-46/Hoengsong, SK	18th FBW based at K-46

January February March April May June

18th Group Mustangs penetrated deep into enemy territory. Communist rail lines, bridges, storage dumps, troop emplacements and vehicles suffered heavy losses. F-51's attacked 30 supply buildings near Sibyon-ni, rocketing and napalming until the entire area "was crackling in flames."

"We have been hitting, with the entire 5th Air Force, a small section of rails each day. The results have proven very satisfactory."

June 1: 18th FBG moves operations from K-10 to K-46.

June 24: FEAF flew 1,043 sorties, the highest daily total for the month FAF fighter-bombers flew over 250 sorties against North Korean targets.

In January, the rail interdiction program continued as a focus for combat operations. Most flights directed against railheads, communication lines and highways.

April 19: 39th FIS reassigned from 18th FBG to the 51st FIW.

Close support, interdiction, rail cutting, and rescue missions account for the largest number of sorties to be flown by the 18th FBG.

Operation Strangle. *The twisted and battered skeletons of two Communist supply trains litter a switching center somewhere between Pyongyang and Sariwon. Note that the through line terminates abruptly at bomb crater in lower right of picture. Note also upended locomotives. This low level aerial photo is another excellent example of how "Operation Strangle" has disrupted Communist rail movement of supplies to their battle line forces in Korea, the Fifth Air Force claimed in January 1952. (NARA)*

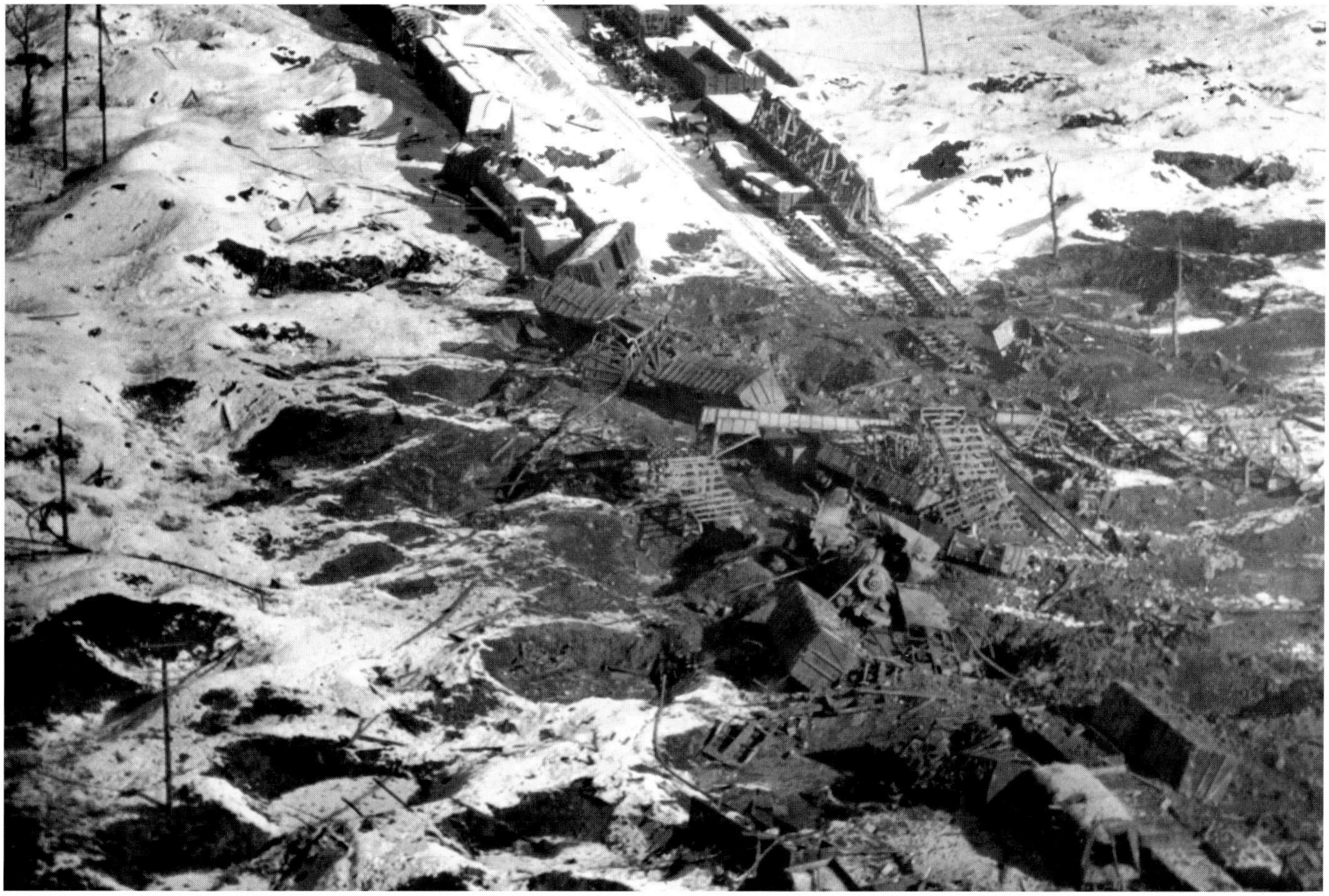

1952 Summary

King George VI of England dies and is succeeded by his daughter, Queen Elizabeth II. Prime Minister Churchill announces the Britain has made an atomic bomb. In the U.S., scientist Edward Teller successfully tests a hydrogen bomb, the world's first thermonuclear weapon.

President Truman signs a "G.I. Bill of Rights" for veterans of the Korean War that provides benefits similar to those given to World War II veterans.

Dwight D. Eisenhower resigns as Supreme Commander in the Europe and is elected President of the United States. His Vice President is Richard M. Nixon. Gov. Adlai E. Stevenson of Illinois and Sen. John J. Sparkman of Alabama oppose Eisenhower.

UN General Assembly adopts Indian proposal for Korean armistice, which China rejects.

The Pulitzer Prize is won by Ernest Hemingway for "The Old Man and the Sea." Edna Ferber publishes "The Giant." Herman Wouk publishes "The Caine Mutiny." A British film based on C.S. Forester's 1935 novel, "The African Queen," stars Humphrey Bogart and Katharine Hepburn.

"The Revised Standard Version" of the Bible is published for Protestants.

More than 2,000 new television-broadcasting stations are built and put into operation throughout the United States. About 65 million people watch the presidential nominating conventions.

"Due to heavier flak concentrations and ground fire only one firing pass will be made on secondary targets."

Lt. Col. Joseph Crane, Commander, 12th Squadron

Combat Operations

In January, the rail interdiction program continued as a focus for combat operations, as well as "attacking specific enemy 'build up' areas of supply, troop and vehicle shelters pinpointed through aerial photos and often attacked under the direction of tactical reconnaissance aircraft."[1]

"From the standpoint of flying," the 12th Squadron reported, "January is the worst month the 12th Squadron has had since October 1950. Bad weather, lack of airplanes seemed to be the contributing factors."

Lt. Col. Gilland became CO of the 39th FIS.

The "increased percentage of battle loss and damage during the month of January necessitated positive and corrective action," the 18th Group reported. To lessen the loss of aircraft and pilots on secondary targets, "pilots were briefed to make only one pass on secondary targets."

"Tactics remained essentially the same as in previous months," Lt. Col. Joseph Crane, Commander of the 12th Squadron reported in January, "except that due to heavier flak concentrations and ground fire only one firing pass will be made on secondary targets. There were fewer close support missions flown probably as result of stalemate in the battle line."

To further lessen losses and battle damage, pilots were urged to notify their flights when they were "in trouble." Flight members were encouraged to "check damage aircraft to determine extent of damage and to decide on necessary action."

Fire and damage inflicted on assigned targets was enhanced by providing each flight with "photographs and maps of assigned targets." The flights then "directed their own attacks against these targets." Fuse settings were changed from "instantaneous" to one-tenth second delay."

Training was stepped up, with more emphasis put on the map course, the pilot's information file, D.F. (radio direction finding) steers, the location of emergency airfields and a gunnery program.

The map course covered prominent topographical features in Korea "found useful by the experienced pilots." The pilot's information file included a compilation and revision of all existing group training tests including engineering, communications, tactics, intelligence and armament. Direction finding steers "are conducted by new pilots in returning flights with K-46 'Bromide' and 'Hothouse.' New pilots on return flights also are shown emergency landing fields." [2]

Two pilots had to bail out in January immediately over the front lines—and "actually within mine fields." It brought to the attention of the 18th planners that "more information was needed" regarding the location of mine fields in event of future bailouts."

The number of both air and ground aborts increased in January and flying time

---

Monthly Summary

Static, defensive-type ground warfare continued into January 1952. United Nations warships and naval aircraft worked closely with Far East Air Forces to interdict Communist supply networks.

UNF air attacks were countered by active air opposition and increasingly heavy anti-aircraft fire from Chinese Communist and North Korean Forces.

At Panmunjom, UN negotiators labored to achieve an armistice; however "communist intransigence, evasiveness, and procrastination thwarted their efforts."

UN jet fighters provided protective aerial cover for fighter-bombers and inflicted costly losses on hostile MiG-15s, which made only sporadic attempts to interfere. There was a strong perception among fighter-bomber pilots that they were frequently used as "bait" to entice MIGs into battle. During the month, UN pilots shot down thirty-two MiGs and damaged twenty-eight others.

Although Far East Air Forces "lost only five jets in aerial combat, it saw enemy ground fire destroy forty-four other aircraft. These had been engaged in low-level bombing runs and strafing sweeps."

The official Air Force chronology makes frequent mention of actions in which jet fighter aircraft, heavy bomber aircraft or rescue helicopters were engaged, but rarely mentions actions by fighter-bomber squadrons flying the now outdated F-51 Mustang aircraft.

Fifth Air Force tactical strikes were directed primarily against railheads, communication lines, and highways over which the communists moved supplies and equipment to front-line positions. Fighter-bombers concentrated on rail-cutting missions but also provided vital close air support (CAS) for Eighth Army ground forces that included bombing, napalm, and rocket strikes.

Adapted from U.S. Air Force Historical Research Agency. January 2002. The U.S. Air Force's First War: Korea 1950-1953 Significant Events. January 1952. http://www.au.af.mil/au/afhra/wwwroot/korean_war/korean_war_chronology/kwc_1951.html

increased due to the severe cold weather at K-46. Coolant leaks put additional "heavy work loads" on squadron maintenance personnel.

Requisitions were put into place for "Seat type, quick release, multi-colored parachutes, back packs and E&E (Escape and Evasion) equipment. Fifty were requisitioned and received. Twelve each will be issued to the three squadrons and 2 Squadron, SAAF."

Six, .38-caliber revolvers were received "for service testing." Revolvers were issued to each squadron commander, group commander and two operations officers at the advanced base." A report on their use was requested in thirty days.

"Continued improvement in transportation to the advanced base, a general improvement in living accommodations there despite the extreme cold and the fact that each individual within the unit has a full day's work to accomplish also tend to keep morale at a high level," Col. Seymour Levenson reported. "The cessation of using 67th Tactical Reconnaissance ships to lead

the 18th Fighter-Bomber Group strikes against pre-briefed targets allowing our own tactics to be employed against these targets has resulted in lessening the time over target with a corresponding decline in battle damage and battle loss. This was the outstanding factor affecting morale of the pilots during the period."

"More publicity by radio and newspapers other than service publications would be a morale booster to the organization as little is published to give the true story of the tremendous job the F-51 Mustang has done and continues doing to harass and interdict the enemy," Levenson concluded.

"Minor Miracle" For Maintenance Section

The primary mission of the 67th Squadron continued to be the "tactical interdiction of the enemy's transportation system."[3] Commanding Officer Lt. Col. Julian Crow was directing most of his flights against railheads, communication lines and high-

ways—all badly needed by the communists to move supplies and equipment to front-line positions. 67th Squadron fighter bombers flew nearly 500 sorties in January concentrated on rail and road-cutting missions and reported 99 rail cuts and 3 road cuts, along with the destruction of 13 pieces of enemy artillery, 48 buildings, 18 troop positions, 9 vehicles and 12 bunkers. Over 200 enemy troops were reported KIA by the 42 pilots flying combat sorties that month.

The squadron gained 18 new officers and lost 17, leaving it with 52 officers assigned by the end of the month. Enlisted strength was 145 at the beginning of the month and 143 by February—"all sections of the organization, with the exception of pilot strength, continue to be below authorized strength." While replacements "arriving later in the month" appeared "better qualified than previous replacements and hold more rank," the volume of new men was "below the anticipated number in view of the many men from this organization who are to be ro-

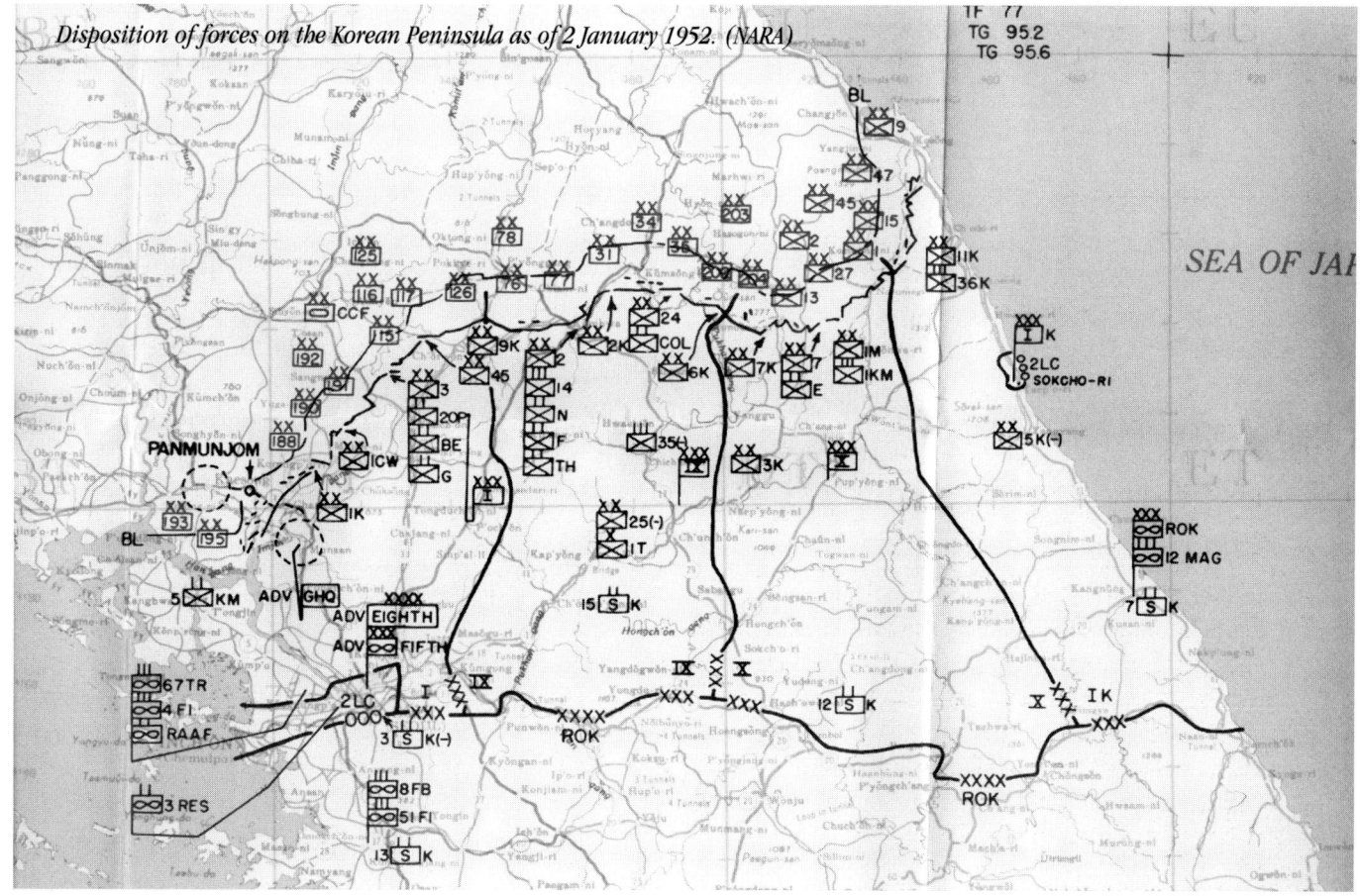

Disposition of forces on the Korean Peninsula as of 2 January 1952. (NARA)

Precious Stationery. *Among the first "pipeline pilots" the Air Force had been training since the beginning of the Korean War a year and half before, 2ⁿᵈ Lt. Archibald "Archie" Connors arrived in Korea in January 1952 to join the 67ᵗʰ Squadron after a brief assignment with the 35ᵗʰ Fighter Interceptor Squadron in Japan. The box he is carrying appears to be one usually containing stationery. In one of his letters he mentioned how scarce writing paper was at the time. (Connors)*

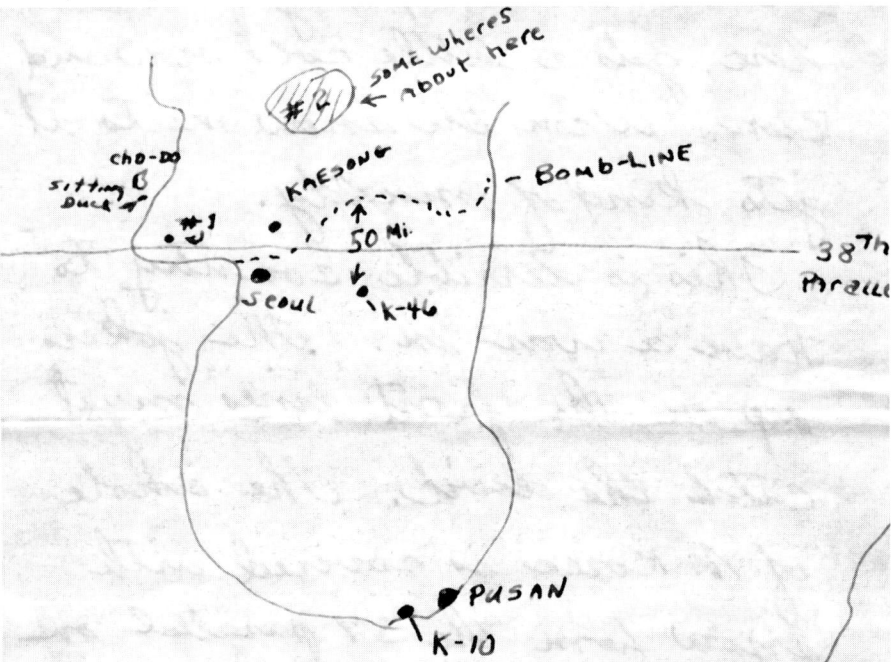

"Sitting Duck." *Lt. Connors drew this rough map for his mother, Eva, of his first combat mission in Korea in early January 1952. "Here is what the situation looks like: #1 was my first mission," he explained. Note "sitting duck" reference near Cho-do Island. (Connors)*

tated in February and March," Crow pointed out.

Squadron veterans were still carrying "dual workloads," performing their own jobs plus the additional duties of training the new arrivals and "keeping them under close job supervision."

During the month of January, the Awards and Decorations Officer, 2ⁿᵈ Lt. Raymond T. Plevyak prepared 17 recommendations for the DFC, and one for a Silver Star. These awards came with a heavy price tag that month.

Four aircraft were lost due to enemy ground fire and two received major damage.

Two pilots survived the flak nightmare and completed their 100 missions: Captain James T. Davis and 1ˢᵗ Lt. Lyman F. Weaver.

After extensive On the Job Training (OJT), Airmen were being upgraded to Air First Class. Personnel shortages continued to "prevent supervisors from doing top supervisory work," primarily "because they themselves must perform much of the work." Crow optimistically predicted that "with the influx of more experienced specialists there will be a decided increase in the amount and quality of the training rendered."[5]

The Maintenance Section accomplished a minor miracle in January: the average "in commission" status was over 86% for the 18 aircraft assigned (plus "The Pig"), ten percent over the December average and eleven percent above that required by Fifth Air Force. This major improvement in commission status required ten engine changes, fourteen major inspections, and fifteen intermediate inspections. It had "become an established policy of this section to accomplish a major inspection upon completion of an engine change. This being considered conducive to better maintenance." The engine changes were required due to five cases of coolant leaks and a low compression starter clutch.

Rotation of Line Chief Kubilis and Chief Inspector Willard continued "to rob this section of its supervisors," Crow noted.

420

Although replacements were arriving to bring the total assigned men in the Engineering Section to 65 at the end of month, it was still 28 men below authorization.

Master Sergeant Mains "A-Flight" racked up the highest total flying hours in January with over 217.

The new Armament Officer was 1st Lt. Donald D. Drage and operations for the section "have run smoothly," Crow reported. There were a total of "12 armorers carried." However, four members of the section were rotated to the States and only three replacements received. "All loading, including training missions, is now being carried out by armorers at Det #1."

"Rotation remains the biggest single morale factor, with morale rising and falling as policy changes (and accompanying rumors and speculation) effect rotation," Crow reported.

The food remained "relatively the same," Crow observed, "usually adequate, generally unbalanced; sprinkled with incongruities such as Iced Tea, Iced Coca and Ice Cream on the coldest days." The stoves in the Lower Four Mess Hall were not kept lit, making "for a cold atmosphere, not conducive to good digestion."

Living was better. "Hot water is con-

North view of K-46 showing operations areas. At far right, the living areas. (Holmes)

stant in the Main E.M. latrine, where the addition of two stoves has aided in comfort considerably." The P.X. had been enlarged and was operating under "obviously better management." All these factors "aided positively in troop morale together with an excellent Service Club and movies at the base theatre six times a week."

"Complaints are still forthcoming from all quarters that publicity concerning the activities of this Wing should be much more widespread than at present," Crow con-

cluded as he praised the hard work and sacrifices of his men. "It is felt that even while working with a several shortage of qualified personnel this unit has met its combat commitments only because of the determination of the few qualified personnel still assigned and the eagerness of the new men to learn."6

Operations offices at K-46 of the 12th Squadron "Foxy Few," 67th Squadron "Fighting Cocks," and the 2 Squadron SAAF "Flying Cheetahs."

Endnotes

1 USAFHRA. *Monthly Historical Report, 12th Fighter-Bomber Group,* January 1952, p. 1.

2 USAFHRA. *Monthly Historical Report, 12th Fighter-Bomber Group,* January 1952, p. 5.

3 USAFHRA. *Monthly Historical Report, 67th Fighter-Bomber Squadron,* January 1952, p. 1.

4 USAFHRA. *Monthly Historical Report, 67th Fighter-Bomber Squadron,* January 1952, p. 1.

5 USAFHRA. *Monthly Historical Report, 67th Fighter-Bomber Squadron,* January 1952, p. 5.

6 USAFHRA. *Monthly Historical Report, 67th Fighter-Bomber Squadron,* January 1952, p. 8.

(Above) Capt. Joe Peterburs beside his 12th Squadron Mustang in January 1952. (Peterburs)

(Left) "Main Street" at K-46 in January 1952. (Peterburs)

(Below) Major Vern Holmes recorded this view of the K-46 base from the nearby hill on which the DF (direction finding) equipment was sited. (Holmes)

Combat Statistics

18th F-B Wing

January 1952

Average No. A/C Assigned
61
Total Flying Time
2,666
Percent of Aircraft in Commission
74%
Percent of Aircraft AOCP
5%
Combat Sorties Flown by Wing
1,699
12th Squadron Sorties
396
39th FIS Sorties
636
67th Squadron Sorties
467
2 Squadron Sorties
404
A/C Lost to Combat
7
Pilots lost
7

Fuel Consumed

290,353 gals.

Ordnance Expended

.50-cal. Rounds
245,605 (by 67th Squadron alone)
Rockets
1,446 (by 67th Squadron alone)
Napalm Bombs
202 (by 67th Squadron alone)
500-lb. GP Bombs
734 (by 67th Squadron alone)
Note: Figures and totals may differ in some categories due to differences in numbers provided by each component.

Napalm bombing attack on a Communist occupied Korean village. (NARA)

Significant Events

Jan. 17 Captain Glen E. Stewart, 67th Squadron, had his landing gear collapse while attempting a landing at K-46/Hoeng-song.

Jan. 25 2nd Lt. James A. Pryor, 67th Squadron, reported engine trouble on take off from K-46, followed by a major accident.

Jan. 27 2nd Lt. George V. Patton, 67th Squadron, nephew of a famous Army General, was hit by ground fire while over his target and forced to bail out. He was picked up and returned to K-46 with minor injuries.

Combat Losses

2nd Lt. John P. Streit, 67th Squadron, was listed as missing in action on 1 January 1952 due to enemy ground fire.

2nd Lt. Medon Armin Bitzer, 67th Squadron, was listed as MIA on 7 January 1952 after being hit by enemy ground fire during an interdiction mission. Bitzer, USMA Class of 1950, was on a combat mission, when his aircraft received a direct hit by anti-aircraft fire, burst into flames and crashed.

1st Lt. George Baylor Eichelberger, Jr., 67th Squadron pilot reported as KIA on 15 January 1952. Lt. Eichelberger, a native of Norfolk, VA and a USMA graduate Class of 1950, was listed as MIA due to enemy ground fire while attempting to knock out transportation assets--his aircraft received a direct hit by anti-aircraft fire and crashed. Lt. Eichelberger and Corporal Clarence Frownfelter whose assignment was in the 67th Orderly Room, "became very good friends. He was a Christian and was very open about it. He met with several of us for Bible Study and Prayer in the evenings. Included in these meetings were members of the 67th Fighter-Bomber Squadron, the 12th Fighter-Bomber Squadron and the Second Squadron SAAF. I remember how our Squadron Commander [Lt. Col. Julian Crow] was affected the day that we lost Lt. Eichelberger. As it was with other pilots we lost, it was a very somber experience."

Capt. Tedrick G. Irwin, 12th Squadron pilot KIA 31, January 1952. "The following officers were reported MIA," the 12th Squadron noted in January. "**Lieutenant Bill Elson** on the 6th of January 52 and Captain Tedrick G. Irwin on the 31st of January 52." Captain Irwin was the pilot of a F-51D Mustang night fighter with the 12th Squadron, 18th Fighter-Bomber Wing. On January 31, 1952, while on a combat mission, his aircraft was hit by anti-aircraft fire, caught fire and crashed into the crest of a ridge.

1st Lt. Morton D. Britten, 67th Squadron.

1st Lt. Thomas C. Lafferty, 39th Fighter Interceptor Squadron, while making a strafing run on enemy positions on January 31, 1952, his aircraft was shot down by ground fire. He dove into his target.

1st Lt. L. W. "Jimmy" Parsonson, 2nd Squadron SAAF was KIA on 6 January 1952. Lt. Parsonson was leading 'A' Flight on an interdiction mission. Enroute to the target area, a railroad yard, he was informed that his No. 4 man had engine problems. Parsonson then instructed both No. 4 and No. 3 to return to base. Since another 2nd Squadron flight led by Major Lyon was heading to the same target, Parsonson requested permission to join in the attack with his two remaining aircraft. The six Mustangs attacked the target and then

1st Lt. George Eichelberger returns from one of his final missions before being killed in action on 15 January 1952. (Frownfelter)

moved to hit the secondary target, which they attacked with rockets and machine guns. During this attack, Lt. Parsonson radioed that he was hit, and was told to head south. Before he could reach friendly territory, he radioed that he was on fire and crashed soon after. His flight searched the area for any sign of him or his aircraft without any success.

"Captain Glen E. Stewart, was involved in a major accident on landing at K-46 on January 17, 1952. Reported that landing gear collapsed on landing," the monthly report for the 67th noted. (Stapley)

424

The New Debriefer

by Wilfred "Budd" Stapley

Debriefings were conducted after every combat mission. No mission was really "typical." Many involved facing—and surviving—hails of radar directed anti-aircraft fire, enemy fighters, and the vagaries of worn-out airplanes. As they gathered in the debriefing tent after returning from yet another dangerous mission, the pilots could look forward to some "help" in unwinding. They would be offered a big "coffee mug" and a couple of fifths of whatever was available. A slug of the "coffee" would be followed by a slug of water.

Reportedly, some of the missions "got a little hairier" the longer the "coffee" had to take effect. "They did that to loosen us up," Stapley reported. "Quite often we would end up floating away from a debriefing." Of course, if a pilot knew he would be flying again that day, the "coffee" was real. Sometimes the pilots knew they were on the flight list for the day, sometimes the news came in the form of an "oh, by the way, Stapley…"

On average, pilots were flying about 12-15 missions per month.

On one mission, we went up, hit the target, a little flak you know, then we came back and we didn't have the regular Intelligence Officer debriefing us. It was a new guy, a very new guy. While the regular debriefer, a Captain, was present he introduced the new arrival and made it clear he wasn't going to say much if anything.

How Flight looked at each other with The Look. With straight faces they began to "fill in" the new—and gullible—debriefer.

"We saw this row of big tanks so we made a low level bomb run on 'em…blew up maybe ten or twelve of them…then the Migs jumped us…forty or fifty of 'em…we were jinxin' all over sky, but we knocked down two or three of them before we got out of there…"

The How Flight guys looked at each other out of the corner of their eyes…asking without saying anything out loud: "Do you think this guy's buyin' this

Air Intelligence Office (left) and Briefing Room (right) for the 18th Fighter-Bomber Group at K-46. (Urquhart)

stuff?"

The debriefer, meanwhile, has his head bowed over the clipboard, scribbling away furiously, nodding his head and muttering: "Wow, incredible, jeez…"

The Captain leans back in his chair with a "you've got to be kidding" smile on his face, fully aware of the "initiation" How Flight is giving the new debriefer.

On a roll, the How Flight spokesman continued, "And about that time I shot down two more Migs…" Nodding vigorously the rookie keeps on scribbling. "Yeah, yeah, unbelievable! Oh man!"

Finally, the Captain had had all he could stand and leaned forward in his chair. "Alright, you sons of bitches, now tell us what REALLY happened." The new debriefer, still not realizing he had been had, sat upright. "Huh?"

Finally, after the laughter died out, How Flight provided a more accurate, if "typical" report on the combat mission. "Just another bomb run. Just the usual flak."

"Flak" Stapley

Second Lt. Wilfred "Budd" Stapley was the number four plane in a four-plane bomb run, when he saw tracers heading towards his buddies that were completing their bomb runs. Calmly he keyed the microphone and announced: "How Leader.

How Two, here. There's flak at the top of the pattern."

Seconds later, his plane was over the target and "boxed" by several streams of "golf ball" anti-aircraft tracers that were scything the air all around him. "Chewm, chewm, chewm…right over the canopy," the tracers were about to cut him in two…or three…it seemed. The calm of the previous transmission vanished in an instant: "Holy S—, How Leader, How Four, flak all over this @#$@#$ place." ["It was comical…later…if you got back…and began to think about it," he remembered .]

"That's OK kid," a laconic voice responded on the radio. "One of the rules of the game over here is that they are allowed to shoot back."

At the debriefing…there were about sixteen pilots present…one veteran pilot looked around the room with disdain and asked, sarcastically: "Who the hell yelled, 'Flak!'"

Sheepishly, Stapley a "veteran" of his third mission, "had to admit" that he was the one who had, shall we say, announced the in coming rounds with extra adrenalin adding to his volume.

"Don't you ever YELL, Flak, again, do you hear me, Stapley?" The veteran grilled him. "You damn near busted my eardrums…I could get a Purple Heart out of your damn radio transmissions," he smiled—finally—defusing the dress down somewhat. Lesson learned: the difference between announcing and yelling of information on the radio.

From that moment on, Stapley's nickname was "Flak."

"No Harm Done"

"While under the influence of intoxicants," General Rogers letter explained, a Marine Corps Second Lieutenant had "wandered into the senior officer's billets and created a disturbance by acting in an obnoxious manner toward Major Ragsdale and frightening Miss Lillian Lewis." Rogers was writing to the Lieutenant's Commanding Officer, Colonel Russell Jordahl, Commander of the 1st Combat Service Group to "give you the true facts in case you have received any rumors concerning an incident involving one of your officers."

After being ordered out of the quarters by Major Ragsdale, the tipsy Lieutenant "continued to prowl around the area, particularly near Miss Lewis' and the Special Service girls' quarters. Subject officer was ordered to remain in his quarters for the duration of the night by the undersigned [General Rogers]. There was no attempt made to force entry into either of the girls' rooms nor to force attentions upon any of the girls."

"Apparently," Rogers explained with empathetic candor, "the sight of American girls and too much whiskey got the best of the Lieutenant."

"No harm was done," Rogers assured the Colonel, "and I hope that this incident will not cause you to curtail visits to K-10. We enjoy having your officers and would like them to feel welcome to visit our club at any time." With perhaps a gentle reference to younger Marines who might drink too much and not be able to return to their base, Rogers added "we have sufficient transient facilities to accommodate over night guests. Hope you will pay us a visit soon."

Ready for a mission in Linda Lee II. 1st Lt. Wilfred C. "Budd" Stapley (left) and 1st Lt. George V. Patton (right) sitting on the wing of "Linda Lee II" (Stapley's aircraft) prior to a mission. Note 500-lb bomb secured to the port wing bomb rack. Patton, the namesake and nephew of General George Patton, was also an Army brat. His father, Stapley recalled, was a career army officer. The young Patton had flown a combat tour during WWII as a tail gunner on a B-17. (Stapley)

Luckiest guy...alive!

On 27 January 1952, 1st Lt. George Patton was on a close air support mission when he was hit by ground fire, his friend former 1st Lt. Wilfred "Budd" Stapley recalled. Wrestling the badly damaged Mustang for control and trying to gain enough altitude to bail out, Patton also tried to get "disconnected" enough to bail out—but he was "hung up" on his equipment, straps, cables and harness. As he fought to keep the plane in the air and to get himself clear enough to bail out, the plane continued heading south—closer to the no-man's land between the UN and Communist forces.

Finally, when he was clear, he bailed out—and landed literally between the lines—in a minefield.

Friendly troops were trying to tell him he was in a minefield, but he didn't hear or understand the warnings.

"Stay down. Stay down," they yelled, "we'll come out and get you."

Caught in the middle of a combat zone,

Patton was in no frame of mind to sit there and wait to be rescued. After all, he was so close to friendly forces that he could see and hear them—almost. All he had to do to be rescued was get over to them...as fast as he could run. And run, he did, right through a mine field that he was later told was designed to ensure no person on foot could get through—alive.

"You are the luckiest guy...alive," they told him when he reached friendly troops south of the "bomb line."

To calm his nerves, they offered him a drink...and then another. By the time he had been picked up by a helicopter and returned to K-46, his "nerves" were much better.

"George said after he found that out, it took about a pint of Kentucky's finest to settle his nerves," Stapley remembered.

"Top Kick How Flight" poses for a snapshot on January 2, 1952. (Bottom row, L to R) 1st Lt. Wilfred Stapley, 1st Lt. Donald D. Drage, 1st Lt. Clyde O. Armstrong. (Top row, L to R) Capt. John W. Gerwig, Capt Glen E. Stewart, 1st Lt. Shirley B. ("Wash") Tubbs. (Drage)

(Below) 1st Lt. Donald D. "Lucky" Drage arrived at K-10 on November 25, 1951 and flew his first mission, a MSRCAP, three days later. The leader of How Flight at that time was Captain Gerwig, who was succeeded by Captain Stewart in February following Gerwig's rotation to the Z.I. Following Stewart's rotation several weeks later, Drage was appointed How Flight Leader. (A. H. Connors, Jr.)

Smoking in the cockpit

1st Lt. Wilfred "Budd" Stapley smoked—quite heavily by his own later recollection. On one mission he was at a safe altitude heading for an IP [Intercept Position] up north and puffing away on his cigarette. In the midst of a heavy drag on the Pall Mall, he smelled gasoline—in the cockpit.

Looking down quickly to check things out, he saw "about an inch of gasoline on the floor of the cockpit"—the source of the fumes. In the F-51 the gas gauges came "right up off the main tank." One of the gauges had broken off and gasoline was sloshing around his feet. And there he sat, rumbling along at altitude, 130-octane aviation gasoline swirling his feet, enjoying his cigarette.

"Oh S—," he said to himself, realizing that at any moment the lighted cigarette in his hand could set off the fumes now filling the cockpit. Years later, he recalled: "You never saw a cigarette put out as quickly—and safely—as that one."

Stapely carefully ground out the cigarette in the palm of his gloved hand knowing that if even one of the dying emberettes got loose, he would almost instantly be just a ball of flames and twisted aluminum falling out of the sky.

The cigarette now safely out, Stapley had other problems. He needed to advise the Flight Leader that he had "troubles." However, in order to do that he would have to use the radio and run the risk that the minute spark it gave off when transmitting would itself set off the gasoline. Rolling back the canopy he "aired out" the cockpit until the fumes were thinned out. Keying the mike, he sent the shortest radio transmission of his life: "Gasoline in the cockpit. Got to go back!"

Turning south, Stapley was told that he would be accompanied by a F-51 with no radio. Typically, planes returning from north of the Bomb Line were not allowed to return singly, but were assigned in multiship groups. This allowed pilots lacking some vital instruments to use those of nearby planes to get home. On the way back, Shirley Control would have to be contacted and the flight identified, otherwise it would be intercepted.

Stapley still had the problem of the gasoline fumes…and the potential sparks from a radio transmission. But, he had the only functioning radio in the group. Another "micro" transmission from Stapley: "Shirley Control, Filter How. In-bound. Two birds."[1] End of transmission—and Stapley was still in the air and in one piece.

[1] *The 18th Fighter Bomber Group radio call sign was "Filter." The call sign for a 16-ship "gaggle" was "Filter Leader." All other Flights used "Filter" plus the name of their Flight, e.g. How, Item, George.*

18ᵗʰ Wing Mustang Combat Tactics

Early in 1952, the 18ᵗʰ Group published a "manual" of combat tactics for the F-51. The single spaced, mimeographed pages spelled out for the new pilots the basics of how to stay alive until they could complete their required missions and go home.

Tactics in the target area

Subject to the desires of the flight or unit commander, normal formation while en route to the target area will be a battle formation, which will afford not only maximum defense from air attack, but will also offer more opportunity to observe ground action. Evasive action, upon anticipating or encountering enemy anti-aircraft fire should be accomplished by irregular

changes in course and altitude in order to add greater tracking error to Group Gun Crews. Known areas of heavy anti-aircraft fire should be circumnavigated, unless that position is designated as the target area, or is adjacent to it. [1]

Normal Finger Formation

Close Finger Formation

Close Support Tactics

Upon reaching the target designated by the TACP, the flight leader should observe the terrain and other conditions in order to establish the best axis and method of attack. The objective is to deliver maximum fire power to enemy positions while absorbing a minimum of return fire from them. To accomplish this, the method of deploying aircraft to attack at different angles and altitudes has been proven highly successful. These aircraft, evenly spaced will provide almost continuous fire on enemy positions, while in the target area. After completing a bomb, rocket, or firing run, evasive action should be taken by a series of sharp turns, or a change in direction, or by hitting the deck. Aircraft making rocket-firing and gunnery runs at a high angle present a more difficult target for ground gun crews and at the same time provide a more effective concentration of fire against ground personnel and equipment. This type of attack is best utilized under good weather conditions, however, it is difficult to adapt to low ceiling conditions. [2]

Armed Recce

Formation to the target area will be battle formation flown at an altitude of 7,000 feet or at an altitude practical to avoid known anti-aircraft guns, small arms fire and overcasts.

The Flight Leader should be on the

428

Echelon Formation

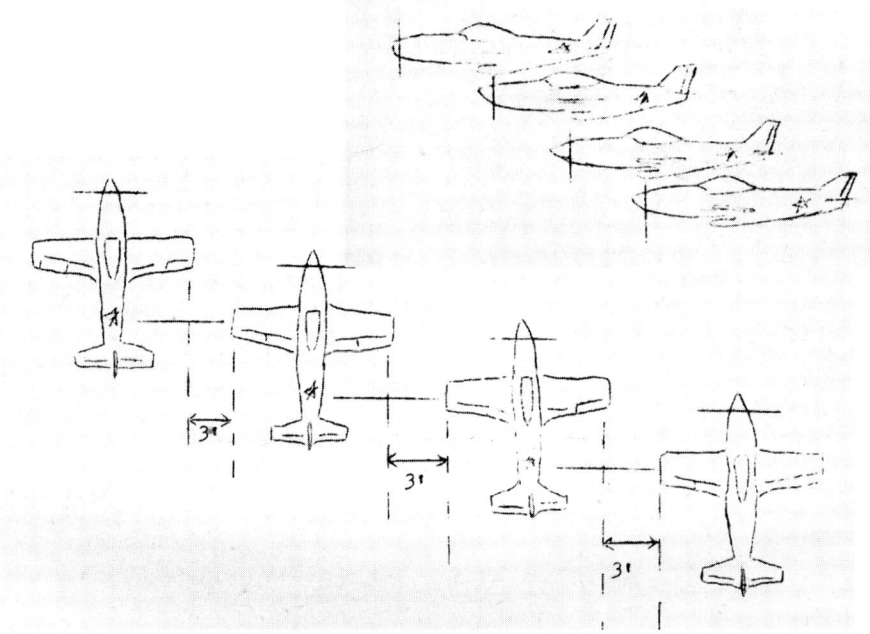

deck, flying at an indicated air speed of at least 300 mph. He should pull up occasionally (above 3,000') in order to orient himself and to regain his low level air speed. The leader's wingman should fly up with No's. 3 and 4, who should be flying at least 4,500' above the terrain. These three aircraft will fly a spread formation, weaving for mutual protection as well as flak evasion. The element leader will advise the flight leader of known flak positions, towns, villages, railroads, etc., that the Flight Leader cannot see. When a worthy target is found, the flight leader will determine whether to utilize two or four aircraft in the attack. In either instance, spacing between aircraft should be such that the most difficult target is presented to ground fire. This is usually accomplished with four aircraft in the form of a Clover Leaf Pattern with one aircraft always in a firing position. With two aircraft in the attack, the wing man should make his pass at least 45 degrees off from the axis of the leader's attack. At the completion of the last pass, the Flight Leader will so inform the flight.

Power settings for aircraft on the deck will be kept at 44'hg 2700 rpm or higher. Power settings of the cover flight will be whatever is necessary to stay over the leader. Aircraft on the deck will be constantly turning to present a difficult target for enemy ground fire. Do not "Stooge" at low air speed, straight and level, or in one small area. Make a few turns then move down on a road a few miles farther over this area, then move to another road. Don't follow one road from town to town, if you do, the enemy will be waiting for you with everything they have. Find targets for your napalm early so you'll have a more responsive aircraft. It is almost impossible to see small arms fire unless you see the flash or the person shooting, so assume that you are being fired at continuously and make yourself hard to hit. Fire your guns until you reach your tracer ammunition, the rest of your .50-caliber ammunition is a reserve to fight you home if you are jumped. After you have completed your reconnaissance and have expended your ordnance, climb to a safe altitude and proceed Home. Use tactical formation from the target area to your home base. Don't go to sleep going Home! Keep looking around.

Pre-briefed Targets

Targets that are of such a nature as to warrant assignment of a specific mission before take off are pre-briefed targets and generally include bridges, rail and road cuts, flak batteries, marshalling yards, etc. As the primary mission is the destruction of a particular target, the most direct route to that area should be taken, circumnavigating flak areas, which could cause disruption of the mission. The armament load will be determined by the particular type of mission, which in turn will have a direct bearing on the type of tactics employed.

Upon completion of the assigned mission, the flight will return to base, providing all armament has been expended. If the flight has not expended all armament and has sufficient fuel, they will perform an armed reconnaissance of the area en route to the base.

Bombing, Rocketry and Gunnery

Dive bombing: Dive bomb runs must originate from an altitude so that the aircraft can be aligned with the target long enough to make an accurate release of bombs and still recover from the dive and break away without entering the area of bomb blast. This entry altitude is usually above five thousands feet and varies with the steepness of the dive. The aircraft should be trimmed for the dive as soon as possible after entering bomb run in order to make a more effective alignment on the target. The point of release depends on the steepness of the dive. The greater the angle of dive, the less correction will be necessary for the bombs' trajectory. The high angle dive bomb run is the most effective means of pinpointing a target. In breaking away from the target after the bomb release, it is recommended that the break be made down and away from the target to the deck, taking evasive action.

Glide and Skip Bombing

These two methods of bombing attack are adaptations of dive-bombing and require more technique that does dive-bombing. The bomb in both instances is released from a lower altitude and should incorporate a delayed fuse. In glide bomb

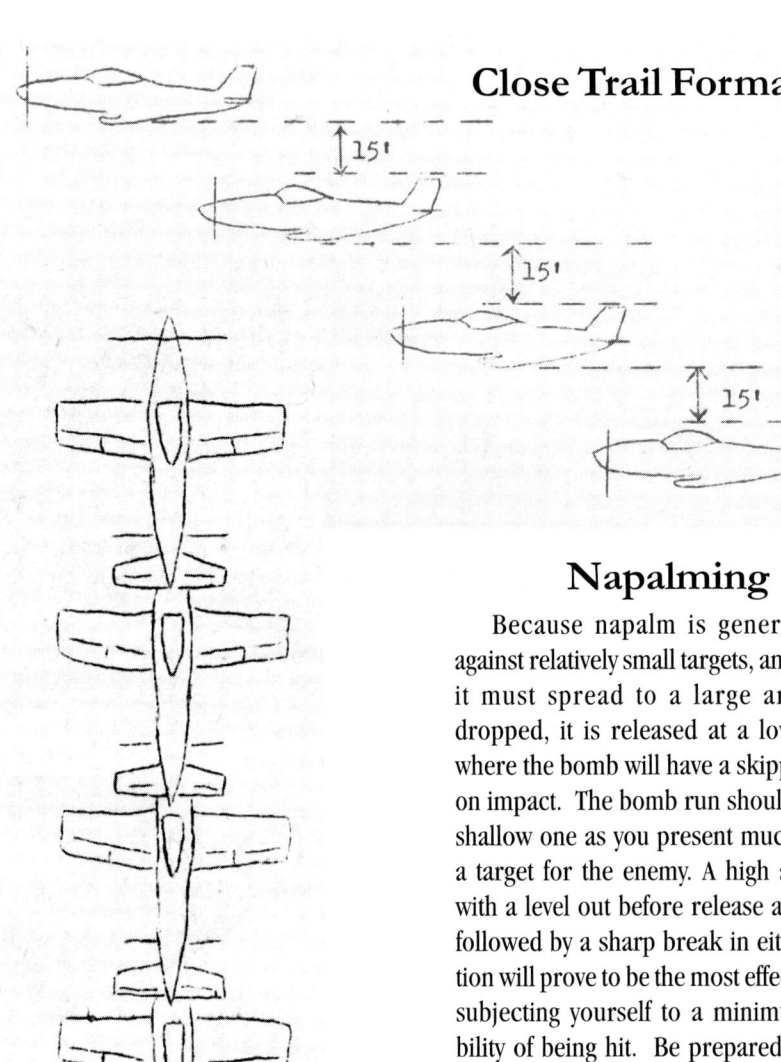

Close Trail Formation

15'

15'

15'

Napalming

Because napalm is generally used against relatively small targets, and because it must spread to a large area when dropped, it is released at a low altitude where the bomb will have a skipping effect on impact. The bomb run should not be a shallow one as you present much too fine a target for the enemy. A high angle dive with a level out before release at 50'-100' followed by a sharp break in either direction will prove to be the most effective while subjecting yourself to a minimum possibility of being hit. Be prepared for insta-

bility resulting from a "hung-up" bomb when at release altitude, as aircraft have been known to execute a roll if not properly checked.

Gunnery

The common error in air-to-ground gunnery is allowing the burst of fire to travel from the first point of fire, through the target and beyond. The most destructive fire is that which is held on the desired target for the length of the time actual firing is accomplished. There are occasions when a dispersed fire is desired, however, most targets are stationary and by "walking" your rounds through your target only a small percentage of them are effective. Here again a steep angle of attack is desired, with the subsequent break-away for evasive action. Depending on the nature of the target, the number of passes will be made to be most effective, that is if it is a heavily defended area a second pass should not be made whereas close support attacks can be pressed.

Rocketry

The 5" rocket is most effectively fired from an F-51 in a high angle of attack. Quite

runs, allowance must be made for a bigger arc in bomb trajectory than was true of dive-bombing. Skip bomb runs are made from low altitudes with the aiming point in front of the target. A hit can be scored by either skipping the bomb into the target or by driving the bomb directly into the target. The most common error in skip bombing is aiming short of the target and skipping over it. In the case the aiming point should be moved back. As was the case in other bomb runs, accomplish evasive maneuvers at all times except while on the alignment run prior to bomb release.

430

obviously there are two types of error in firing: vertical and horizontal. Vertical error is minimized by using a high angle of attack and the correct mil depression. The horizontal error is minimized by firing the rockets when the line of flight of the aircraft coincides with the longitudinal axis of the aircraft. Regardless of what direction the rocket is pointed at the instant of release, its vertical line of trajectory will parallel the line of flight of the aircraft.

The optimum release point for the 5" HVAR rocket is at a slant range of about 2,500 feet. (When using the 5" rocket equipped with the VT fuse, a minimum slant range of 3,200 feet will be observed as a release point). If a dive angle of 60 degrees is used a sight depression of 10 mils will cause your rockets to hit at the aiming point you had at the instant of release.

The problem now is to get the aircraft at the release point in the correct, coordinated attitude. Proper coordination can be accomplished in the following manner. Trim the aircraft for the speed you wish to release (about 315 IAS). Coordination can be checked on the firing passes by the following methods:

1) Set the sight selector of the K-14 sight in the "both" position. Make sure the cross and "Pipper" are in the same vertical plane.

2) Check your needle-ball indicator to assure that the ball is in the center.

3) When you reach your release point (with proper IAS) you should have equal rudder pressure.

Always break away sharply after firing so as to avoid the rocket blast. Clear the point of impact by at least 500 feet.

Air-to-Air Tactics

Attack by enemy aircraft is to be expected at any time. If an attack is made by conventional aircraft, the speed, firepower and rate of turn of the F-51 will keep you out of trouble if you keep your eyes open and deprive them of the element of surprise.

If the attack is made by enemy jet types, the Mustang still has many very definite advantages if the pilot remains calm and uses them. To panic and try to outrun or outdrive [sic] a jet is inviting disaster. Keep the flight intact and use your tighter turn-

ing radius, low fuel consumption and greater rate of fire. At altitudes below ten thousand feet the jet will use his fuel so fast that he'll soon have to break off and head for home.

Defensive tactics are a vital part of any combat flying. Although it may sometimes be necessary, because of our slower speed, to go on the defensive, we must never lose our aggressiveness. We can't force the enemy into a fight, but if he wants one we can make him fight against a TEAM rather than an individual aircraft, and we can choose our altitude. Only through teamwork—as a flight, section or squadron—can we accomplish our mission. We must be ready at all times to go on the defense.

Our first and best defense against enemy jet aircraft is to see them before they start the attack. Therefore we must fly the formation that enables us to visually cover the greatest area. Our present, fingertip, combat formation gives us the most visual coverage, but lacks a certain amount of flexibility and maneuverability for mutual support against attacking jet aircraft. The combat fingertip formation will be flown at all times going to and from the target. Upon sighting enemy aircraft, the respective wingmen will close in on their leaders to about 45 degrees, where they can best hang on during hard, sharp turns in either direc-

tion. All breaks should be into and under the supporting element in order that they may protect your tail by turning into the enemy. Do not break until the enemy has committed himself on the attack. After the elements cross, they will reverse their turns to come out on the original heading as before. If the enemy attacks from 6 o'clock it will be necessary to continue to turn a complete 180-degrees and then make another 180-degree turn back to the desired heading. A weave or scissor should then be started for mutual support.

Since jets climb at higher speeds than the cruising speed of the F-51, attacks can often be expected from the six o'clock low position. It is imperative that these attacks be discovered before they are within firing range. The weaving formation affords you the best opportunity to cover that position.

As a general rule it is best to work the flight down to an altitude where the jets can not make overhead passes and their fuel consumption is greatly increased. Four thousand feet, depending on terrain, is considered a good altitude because it gives you room enough to maneuver without fear of running into the ground.

Covering A Downed Pilot

When a member of a flight declares that he will crash-land or bail-out over enemy territory the following procedure will be accomplished:

The flight will change from its common frequency to the emergency frequency.

One man of the remaining flight will assume command of the flight and climb for altitude.

The other two members of the flight will keep the downed pilot pinpointed and commence to give him cover.

The leader of the flight will declare an emergency and contact rescue control through available facilities giving pertinent data such as location, condition of downed pilot, etc. He will also require additional cover. It may be possible to contact other flights immediately by calling "in the blind" on all VHF channels. As soon as it is deter-

mined that the pilot is alive or could possibly be alive, the leader of the cover flight will request rescue control to scramble the helicopter or SA-16.

It is important that one man control the rescue. It will be his responsibility to establish high and low cover and to neutralize the ground fire in the vicinity of the downed pilot prior to the arrival of the rescue aircraft.

When the rescue aircraft reaches the location of the downed pilot, a luftberry should be established around the rescue aircraft so as to discourage ground fire and keep the rescue operation under con-

stant observation. Once the pilot has been picked up the downed aircraft should be destroyed and the helicopter or SA-16 provided with cover on the return journey.

If it becomes necessary to relieve the cover flight a new leader of the operation must be designated and the pin-point position of the downed pilot and other pertinent information must be passed on.

Endnotes

[1] 18th Fighter-Bomber Group. Standardized Procedures for Combat Operations. 1952. p. 14.
[2] 18th Fighter-Bomber Group. Standardized Procedures for Combat Operations. 1952. p. 8.

Crew Chief Paul Richards stands proudly next to "Sweet Ethel," named after his girlfriend. "We wrote all that time," Ethel Richards recalls, "and fell in love through our letters to each other. He asked me to wait for him. I did and he asked my Dad if we could be married. I held my breath as my father--after many questions--said 'Yes.' Thank God we had 42 years together and we miss him more than we can say. But, we have many wonderful memories."

February 1952

Tactics remained "essentially the same," although the 18th experimented with skip-bombing of railroads for a short time "with generally unsatisfactory results."

In February the 12th Squadron flew just 350 effective combat sorties—594 combat hours—"the lowest figures to date, according to the reports on hand, the cause being due to a shortage of available aircraft and inclement weather." Also a factor that month was "the long missions the squadron had an abundance of this month. Many of the sorties, such as MSR caps and Chodo Island caps, lasted three hours or longer." [1]

Tactics remained "essentially the same," although the 18th experimented with skip-bombing of railroads for a short time "with generally unsatisfactory results."

Fifth Air Force directed a change in rail cut bombing that "consisted of glide bombing specific rail embankments, rather than dive bombing a rail area." The change

was accomplished over a ten-day period, but then was apparently suspended. "After reverting back to our normal practice of dive bombing," Lt. Col. Julian Crow, Commander the 67th Squadron, reported, "pilots were briefed to facilitate a relatively steep dive, thus creating a more pronounced crater effecting more damage." [2]

As Operation Strangle continued, FAF was searching for new tactics to cut the railroads and to keep them out of commission. The targets "were fills on a stretch of railway at BU 5335," the Commander of the 18th Fighter-Bomber Group, Col. Seymour Levenson reported in February. "These fills are frozen solid and nestled between two ridges of 200 foot mountains. It was discovered that 8-15 sec[ond] delay fuses were inoperative and that a flat

pass would cause the bombs to skip over. It was decided that a glide bomb pattern was probably best using our old, dependable 4-5 sec delay fuse. A dive angle of approximately 30 degrees causes the bombs to enter the fill at a 90-degree angle. Furthermore, it requires about three 500-lb GP bombs at one spot to get a complete cut; so pinpoint targets were assigned. The Group did better work, however, using dive bombing tactics due primarily to experience with these tactics," Levenson reported. [3]

A new target area for rail cuts was assigned to 18th Group squadrons, "with the reconnaissance of MSR's more or less replacing the secondary targets formerly given flights returning from rail cuts. Interdiction missions against the enemy's

Monthly Summary

The "bomb line" remained unchanged, "running generally from Hungwang-ni northeast to Chungdong-ni, eastward to Schui-ri, and northeast to the vicinity of Kosong on the east coast."

Ground action consisted "primarily of small-unit reconnaissance patrols and raids into hostile positions, particularly along the western sector of the front. These operations generally encountered determined enemy defenses and prompt counteraction."

Communist jets made only sporadic attempts to engage UN fighters; however, communist air power based north of the Yalu River was still a major threat to UNC air, ground, and naval operations in Korea. USAF pilots destroyed thirteen MIGs, damaged thirty-eight, and probably destroyed five more. The MIGs shot down two friendly jet fighters, while seventeen other UN warplanes of various types fell to enemy ground fire.

Most FEAF sorties were daytime counter-air sweeps, day and night interdiction of the main communist supply routes, and airlift of high priority supplies.

Meanwhile, FEAF reconnaissance aircraft secured intelligence information on enemy ground dispositions, air targets, vehicle movements, airfield status, and weather. Cargo planes and medium bombers also dropped psychological warfare leaflets over North Korea. Bad weather reduced the number of sorties flown during the month.

Fifth Air Force fighter-bombers, "under the protective cover of jet fighters, penetrated daily deep into enemy territory. The fighter-bombers also supplied limited support for Eighth Army front-line troops, permitting them freedom of movement not enjoyed by the enemy and destroying lucrative enemy targets near the battle area."

Operation SATURATE, an intense rail interdiction campaign, "became a race between U.S. airmen trying to destroy rail lines and North Korean laborers repairing them. During a given night as many as forty B-29s might hit a bridge and fighter bombers would drop some 500 bombs on a single length of track, only to see the bridge and track repaired within a day or two." [1]

Adapted in part from U.S. Air Force Historical Research Agency. January 2002. The U.S. Air Force's First War: Korea 1950-1953 Significant Events. February 1952. http://www.au.af.mil/au/afhra/wwwroot/korean_war/korean_war_chronology/kwc_1951.html

"No missions this day for these planes" of the 67th Squadron, explained former Crew Chief Robert Cranston. *"One of the many days that we were snowed in at K-46" during the winter of 1952. "Life on the Flight Line,"* remembered Cranston, *"was seven days a week from 0500 preflight until post flight--weather permitting."* During winter months *"the planes had to be covered--wings, engine and canopy areas--due to the heavy snow."* Pre-flight in winter months included *"uncovering the plane, checking for leaks, visual check and run up."* Any liquid puddles under the plane *"could be fuel, oil, coolant--or melted snow."* To determine the exact source of the liquid--and potential problems--*"you would stick your finger in the puddle, then feel, smell or taste it. You could smell the fuel, feel the oil, and the coolant tasted sweet."* The *"taste the liquid"* problem solving routine also provided an opportunity for some good natured *"fun"* on the Flight Line. *"Sometimes, if you beat your 'neighbor' to preflight you could relieve yourself under his plane--then watch him check for coolant leaks."* Cranston admits that he *"fell for it"* once himself...but only once. (Cranston)

transportation system, supply concentrations, troop billets, and artillery positions primarily remain our targets as in preceding months," the 12th Squadron reported in February.

"Our rail area was switched to a different sector south of BU 5335," Col. Levenson noted, "for the last half of the month. This area has been beaten by dive-bombing with fair results. The good results are primarily due to using pinpoint targets, dive-bombing, and changing the pinpoint target every few days. Pinpointing the target and changing it frequently negates enemy flak capabilities and allows pilots to make longer, steadier passes. Good passes, plus experienced high angle bombing ensure hits," he concluded.

Formerly scarce "bail-out type radios," were now more plentiful, so much so that "a comparatively new plan of escape and evasion, based on these radios, has been formulated and is now being discussed among the squadrons. The plan came about as a result of the intensity of automatic weapons and flak fire, which has made the rescue of downed pilots behind the enemy's lines increasingly difficult and often hopeless. A new escape and evasion

back-pack, reinforced to carry these radios as well as the usual emergency items, has been designed is now available to the pilots. It is strapped to the pilot rather than the parachute, as has been the case in the past. The back-pack, containing all emergency items, presumably enables the pilot to leave the vicinity of his landing to seek cover, and work independent of his capping flight until such a time that he can direct his own rescue by means of his radio." [4]

"The Airmen are in high spirits..."

Although morale was reported as "very good," the 12th Squadron conceded "there is no denying of the damaging effect of the fluctuating cease fire talks, the shortage of aircraft, and the bad weather. The resulting slow process of building missions because of these effects, however, is the chief cause of what dissatisfaction there is among the pilots and that is far from detrimental to the mission itself."

"Working long hours under poor conditions, the Airmen are nevertheless in high

spirits and show pride in their work and their Squadron. Contributing factors are the comparatively good food, rest and recreation leaves, and rotation to the Zone of Interior."

"Each man in the Squadron knows that he is doing his utmost in his contributions towards world peace."

The 39th Fighter Interceptor Squadron completed its 19th month of "active duty" in the Korean conflict in February 1952.

"Due to extremely cold weather conditions encountered in February it was found impossible to keep the stoves at K-46 operating at all times." [5]

The policy of rotating flights between K-10 and K-46 every three days has proven quite successful during the month of February. Each pilot has more time to work on his secondary duty while still being able to fly the same number of missions as before," the 39th reported.

Training of new pilots was less of a problem in February. The fact that "all new replacements were graduates of an F-51 CCTS eliminated the problem of instructing combat procedures to pilots who are not familiar with the F-51 type aircraft," the 39th FIS reported.

Lack of available aircraft "imposed a great problem in trying to meet tactical commitments as well as train newly assigned pilots."

Aggressive action was often needed to ensure that combat commitments were met. Usually, the needed action was taken by pilots—but not always. "Captain Becraft, supply officer, has been tied down to various other additional duties throughout the month but has given generously of his off-duty time to help this section in many ways. He has made several trips to Pusan Army Depots in an effort to obtain needed items, which are not available through out normal supply sources. He has proved himself a 'Scrounger Extraordinary,' a title usually reserved for men with less scruples," the 39th FIS reported.

Morale in the 39th "continued on its upward trend during the month of February. Each section is taking pride in their own individual accomplishments as well as those of the Squadron as a whole. Although it is hard for us to compete with other outfits of the 'Jet Arena' for the lime light, a decided amount of pride goes along with every combat sortie the Fighting 39th completes. Each man in the Squadron knows that he is doing his utmost in his contributions towards world peace."

Tactical Interdiction

The primary mission of the 67th Squadron during February remained "the tactical interdiction of the enemy's transportation system."[6] The defensive positions of UN and communist forces remained about the same, running generally from Hungwang-ni northeast to Chungdong-ni, eastward to Schui-ri and northeast to the vicinity of Kosong on the east coast.[7] Small unit reconnaissance patrols and raids to feel out hostile strength and positions were met with determined enemy defenses and prompt counter attacks.

The 67th was still using K-46, "located approximately five miles southwest of Hoengsong, as a forward combat operations base."

Almost every day, Fifth Air Force fighter-bombers, protected by jet fighters, penetrated deep into enemy territory to attack supply system routes.

The 67th began the month with 52 officers, but was down to 45 by early March. Enlisted strength at the beginning of February was 143; however, it gained 44 and lost 23, raising total enlisted strength to 164 at the end of February. This was an improvement but it raised enlisted strength "hardly over the danger point, in view of overall personnel qualifications and losses," Lt. Col. Julian Crow noted.

It was also much the same story regarding training and qualifications. Overall qualifications of the new arrivals were better than previous replacements and

Almost Mission Ready. *An armorer checks below the wings of this 12th Squadron F-51 being readied for a mission from K-46 in February 1952. Note 500-lb bombs on wheeled racks in the foreground. (Stapley)*

held more rank. However, their numbers were "below the anticipated number" needed in view of those Crow knew would be rotated in March. The remaining few veterans "must do their own work as before plus the additional one of training the new arrivals and keeping them under close job supervision."

Six pilots completed their one hundred mission tour, including: Captain John W. Gerwig, Captain Roscoe L. Crownrich, Captain Clifford J. Whitham, Captain Robert A. Nolan, 1st Lt. Lawrence T. Dowd and 1st Lt. Walter E. Rueger. Four new pilots were assigned to the Squadron during February, while 29 others departed the squadron for the States, to be replaced by 24 new men. The total assigned to the Engineering Section was up to 62, but that was still a whopping 31 men below authorization.

The squadron was able to muster only 15 F-51s and one T-6, 10 below authorization for combat aircraft. The 43 pilots reporting combat sorties during February completed 459 sorties during 842 combat hours. The squadron expended 186,549 rounds of .50 caliber ammuni-

tion, 48 napalm tanks, 1,009 rockets and 669 bombs to destroy 205 buildings, 4 vehicles, 1 bridge, 39 rail cuts, and 205 enemy troops.

Fortunately, it was a good month in that no pilots were lost to enemy action or accidents.

M/Sgt Ritter took the honors that month for having the flight with the highest total flying hours of over 208 hours that month. The caliber of the squadron's enlisted men "was very high," Crow reported. "Their inexperience is overcome by their spirit, eagerness and willingness to learn and get the job done. There should be no reason why the Fighting Cock cannot continue to top them all."

Operations in the Armament Section ran smoothly in February. T/Sgt Jack S. Smith took over as Armament Chief and nine new men were added to the Section. Crow reported a strong correlation between an increase in "malfunctions of caliber .50-machine guns" and "insufficient personnel." He attributed the reduction that month of machine gun malfunctions to the assignment of new men.

"The combat commitments of this or-

Although it is hard for us to compete with other outfits of the 'Jet Arena' for the lime light, a decided amount of pride goes along with every combat sortie the Fighting 39th completes. Each man in the Squadron knows that he is doing his utmost in his contributions towards world peace."

39th Squadron Monthly Report

ganization have been met through sheer determination to see a job well done even in the face of heavy losses of aircraft and a definite shortage of personnel," Crow summed up.[8]

Endnotes

[1] USAFHRA. *Monthly Historical Report, 18th Fighter-Bomber Group,* February 1952, p.7.
[2] USAFHRA. *Monthly Historical Report, 67th Fighter-Bomber Squadron,* February 1952, p. 4.
[3] USAFHRA. *Monthly Historical Report, 18th Fighter-Bomber Group,* February 1952, p. 4.
[4] USAFHRA. *Monthly Historical Report, 12th Fighter-Bomber Squadron,* February 1952, p. 3.
[5] USAFHRA. *Monthly Historical Report, 39 FIS,* February 1952, p. 1.
[6] USAFHRA. *Monthly Historical Report, 67th Fighter-Bomber Squadron,* February 1952, p. 1.
[7] U.S. Air Force Historical Research Agency (USAFHRA). 28 July 2001. *The U.S. Air Force's First War: Korea 1950-1953 Significant Events.* http://www.au.af.mil/au/afhra/wwwroot/korean_war/korean_war_chronology/kwc_february1952.html
[8] USAFHRA. *Monthly Historical Report, 67th Fighter-Bomber Squadron,* February 1952, p. 8.

Capt. Joe Peterburs leaves 12th Squadron Operations at K-46 in full winter mission gear en route to his Mustang for a combat mission over North Korea in February 1952. (Peterburs)

(Below) **Mission ready pilots** waiting in front of 12th Squadron Operations Office include Major Stanley A. Rollag and Lt. Harry J. Tyndale. (Peterburs)

Combat Statistics

18th F-BWing

February 1952

Average No. A/C Assigned
59
Total Flying Time
2,640
Percent of Aircraft in Commission
56%
Percent of Aircraft AOCP
2%
Combat Sorties Flown by Wing
1,437
12th Squadron Sorties
Unavailable
39thh FIS Sorties
Unavailable
67th Squadron Sorties
Unavailable
2 Squadron Sorties
263
A/C Lost to Combat
7
Pilots lost
6

Fuel Consumed

183,652 gals.

Ordnance Expended

.50-cal. Rounds
451,170
Rockets
2,032
Napalm Bombs
118
500-lb. GP Bombs
1,649

Note: Figures and totals may differ in some categories due to differences in numbers provided by each component.

Significant Events

Feb. 7: 2nd Lt. Ralph L. Michael reported engine trouble during take off, followed by a major accident when he tried to land the sick bird at Hoengsong.

February 17: Fifth Air Force flew 695 sorties, "cratering rail tracks in over fifty locations, damaging a locomotive and fifteen rail cars north of Huichon, strafing a convoy of trucks near Sinanju, and destroying supply buildings and dumps between Kumsong and Sibyon-ni." [1]

Feb. 19: 2nd Lt. Owen S. Nibley's engine failed shortly after take off and he had to crash land his plane in a river bed adjacent to the Hoengsong airstrip.

The communists flew approximately 389 MiG-15 sorties, the largest aerial effort to date. USAF pilots destroyed three enemy aircraft.

Feb. 22: Lt. Col. Julian Crow, Commander of the 67th Squadron, was forced to make an emergency landing in a rice paddy within friendly territory after he was hit by enemy fire during an interdiction mission.

Combat Losses

1st Lt. James E. Clay, 39th Fighter Interceptor Squadron on 5 February 1952, was "flying lead position in Put Put Victor Flight was reported Killed In Action on the 5th of February 1952. Lt. Clay's aircraft was seen to lose all of its coolant after he had made a low-level reconnaissance flight over enemy gun positions. The number two man in the flight followed his aircraft to an altitude of 3,500 feet over the friendly island of Sol-Te. At this time Lt. Clay transmitted that he would bail out. The aircraft continued to lose altitude and he was seen to leave the ship at an altitude of approximately 500 feet. Due to the low altitude the chute failed to open and Lt. Clay was killed on impact. The body was later recovered." Clay, a decorated WWII veteran was a native of Lararie, Wyoming. [2]

1st Lt. Robert H. Hammer, 39th Fighter Interceptor Squadron, flying Number Two position in Put Put William Flight on 18

This 2 Squadron SAAF Mustang "creamed" on landing in February 1952. (Peterburs)

February, was reported Missing in Action. The Put Put Willie

Flight was on a mission searching for a downed pilot when he called Willie leader and stated that his aircraft was leaking coolant. Lt. Hammer climbed his ship to an altitude of approximately 4,500 feet and bailed out. Willie leader observed him reach the ground safely and 100 feet to a drainage ditch. Lt. Hammer contacted William leader on his bailout radio and informed him that he was all right. A helicopter was in the area at the time and came over Lt. Hammer at 700 feet and remained there for about 20 minutes. Due to intensive ground fire he was unable to pick up the pilot. Soon afterwards five enemy troops were observed at the position of the downed pilot. The CAP was called off at approximately 1750 hours and all aircraft returned to K-46." [3]

Captain R.A. Harburn, 2 Squadron, SAAF pilot KIA in February 1952. Prebriefed to bomb a target at CT062459, Captain Dicky Harburn flew as No. 2 with 'C' Flight led by Lt. Baransky. During the flight, Harburn radioed that his aircraft was leaking fluid, a fact that Baransky confirmed—the entire starboard side of the fuselage

was covered in oil. After sending the other element to complete the mission, Baransky and Harburn turned back towards K-46. They were instructed to salvo their ordnance prior to landing. Harburn was directed to drop his bombs into the river, which he did, then asked Baransky whether or not the bombs had left his aircraft. Since Baransky had not seen the bombs fall, he suggested that Harburn do a fly-by of the Control Tower for a visual inspection. Soon after, the Tower reported that Captain Harburn's aircraft had crashed. The accident report concluded that his engine had finally seized from insufficient oil pressure, and that Harburn had been struck in the head by the canopy as he prepared to bail out. His body was recovered and buried at the UN Cemetery at Pusan, SK.

Captain Bruce Cram, 39th Fighter Interceptor Squadron, was flying lead position in Put Put X-Ray flight when he was reported Missing In Action on 18 February 1952. "Captain Cram was leading his flight on an armed reconnaissance mission after cutting rails in North Korea. Witnesses stated that he spotted several trucks in a small town and went down to a low altitude to identify them. After he completed his pass the other members in his flight stated they saw white smoke coming from the right side of the aircraft. At this time he called and said (very calmly) that he was going to bail out because he was leaking coolant. The flight immediately went to D channel and started rescue procedures. Captain Cram was seen to make a successful jump and he called from the ground and stated that he had landed safely and was all right. At no time was Captain Cram seen on the ground and when the helicopter arrived he could not be located any where in the area. He was listed as missing in action." [4]

1st Lt. J. N. Lellyet, 2 Squadron SAAF pilot KIA in February 1952. Lt. Jack Lyllyet was flying No. 2 to Captain Leathers, who was leading a four-ship flight on a training mission—a simulated interdiction strike on a rail bridge over a river. The flight arrived in the area and Leathers formed the flight into Echelon Port, radioing "No. One going in," as he conducted his attack. After diving from about 10,000 feet in a 60 degree dive and pulling out at 3,000 feet, Leathers glanced back to see an explosion that took place short and to the right of the target. The No. 3 pilot reported that No. 2 "had gone in." The flight leader returned to the crash site and conducted a search. Eventually, it was speculated that Lt. Lellyet had not used up excess gasoline from the fuselage tank, and did not compensate for the aft-center-of-gravity condition. Lt. Lellyet is buried in the U.N. Cemetery at Pusan.

1st Lt. Robert L. Staats, 2 Squadron SAAF pilot KIA on 17 January 1952. Lt. Bob Staats was in the middle of his second combat tour. On a previous mission, his Mustang had been badly damaged by ground fire near Wonsan. He bailed out over Wonsan Harbor, inflated his dinghy, and was rescued by an U.S. destroyer after only twenty minutes in the water. After his first combat tour, Staats volunteered for a second tour with the 2nd Squadron. The veteran pilot was testing Mustang 374, following a period of maintenance. The flight was only planned for about half an hour. Everything appeared to be normal. He was last seen circling K-10—the Chinhae airstrip was built alongside the bay. A belated message was received that reported a Mustang crashing into Chinhae Bay. Korean divers recovered his body. Staats had returned to Korea for a rare second combat tour just twelve days prior to this flight.

Endnotes
[1] U.S. Air Force Historical Research Agency. January 2002. The U.S. Air Force's First War: Korea 1950-1953 Significant Events. February 1952. http://www.au.af.mil/au/afhra/wwwroot/korean_war/korean_war_chronology/kwc_1952.html
[2] USAFHRA. *Monthly Historical Report, 39th FIS*, February 1952, p. 5.
[3] USAFHRA. *Monthly Historical Report, 39th FIS*, February 1952, p. 6.
[4] USAFHRA. *Monthly Historical Report, 39th FIS*, February 1952, p. 6.

"My God! He crashed!"

Early in 1952, 2nd Lt. Wilfred "Budd" Stapley was sent out to the air gunnery range to help orient and train newly arriving pilots. His assignment was to last about a week, and during the period the range experienced a guerilla attack. Even in supposedly "safe" areas under UN control, small groups of Communist soldiers or sympathizers continued to conduct very small-scale hit-and-run attacks. Damage or injury was minor, but it meant that detached units had to be alert and on guard.

After some local Communists "took a couple of pot shots at the place," Stapley remembered, "we got a little closer than normal."

To further break the monotony of range duty and to demonstrate his flying skills, Stapley told the range crew not to put up any new wires while he was gone and he would give them a world class "buzz job, one that you won't forget." Returning to K-10, Stapley checked out his aircraft and headed over to the air gunnery range.

Spotting the tents used by the range crew as temporary living quarters, he got down "on the deck" and headed for them—actually flying in between the tents. Coming back around for another pass, he approached the guard post on a platform that was called the "control tower," at high speed. His eye level was below the platform of the "tower."

As he passed the tower he kicked the rudder and went into a slow roll—a maneuver he had done countless times—al-

A flight of 12th Squadron Mustangs prepares for take off from K-46 on a combat mission. (Peterburs)

though always at considerably more altitude. As the plane turned upside down, Stapley's seat belt slipped—not completely—but enough to drop him instantly several inches toward the top of the canopy—in a plane that is hurling along just above the ground—upside down.

For the plane to continue to fly upside down, the nose had to be "kept up" and that was done using "top rudder." Hanging upside down in his loose seat belt, Stapley could not get enough rudder pedal leverage to hold the nose up. The plane began to sink toward the ground flashing by just inches below his helmet. Squirming in his harness as best he could and "standing" on the tips of his size twelve boots, he "kicked top rudder" with just his toes and rotated the aircraft as fast as he could back to level flight.

In several—interminable—seconds the crisis was over as the silver bird streaked down the range by the tower—flipped over on its back—then quickly rolled back to normal flight attitude—and disappeared into a cloud of dust.

The plane had been so low when it rotated from its inverted position to normal flight that it kicked up thick swirls of dust. The ground crew was aghast. For several seconds they thought Stapley had crashed.

As he fought to pull the Mustang up and over the nearby hills, Stapley heard the gunnery range air controller exclaim over the radio: "My God, he crashed!" No sooner had the transmission been completed, than Stapley's plane darted out of the dust cloud, climbing for altitude.

"Stapley, Stapley, we thought you crashed!" the controller blurted out, disregarding call signs and RT procedure. In the cockpit, Stapley heard the transmission—but he couldn't talk—not for a while. It was all he could do to get his nerves together and try to make a safe return to K-10.

Later, the range ground crew went out to the area of Stapley's dust cloud. A neat oval had been mowed through the underbrush and scrub grass by Stapley's prop. At one point it was only 18-inches from the ground.

"My own damn foolishness," he later related. "If I hadn't had big feet, hadn't rotated when I did, if everything hadn't gone the right way, I would have bought the farm. Boy, was I cussing that seat. To this day I don't know why I would do something like that. But then, I was a fighter pilot."

Bomb Hangup

On one skip bomb mission, only the left bomb on 1st Lt. Budd Stapley's plane came off and he headed up a valley after the run. At the top of the climb out he realized that he had applied full left aileron and full left rudder—without even realized he was doing so—compensating for the added weight of the unreleased bomb. By the time he reached the crest of the ridge the weight of the unreleased bomb was bringing the aircraft close to a stall. "If the crest of the ridge had been even a few feet higher…" he remembered, his voice trailing off.

Cresting the ridge, he dropped down into a valley, trying to get the bomb off with several "high G" pull outs as he sped down its length, glancing from side to side for any evidence of anti-aircraft fire. No dice, the bomb would not release.

As he headed back to K-46 he wondered what would happen on touch down. The attempted release had converted the bomb from "safe" to "armed." If it jarred loose on touch down, it would immediately explode under the aircraft.

Landing "hot" to avoid a stall situation that could possibly jar the bomb loose, he couldn't get his aircraft slowed down enough to avoid running off the paved portion of the runway. The still almost airborne Mustang reached the section of (barely) paved runway and bounced back into the air, the left wing dropping rapidly from the weight of the unreleased 500-lb. bomb. Instinctively, Stapley applied hard rudder to get the wing up…and jammed the throttle forward for a moment to use the powerful Merlin engine's high torque to force the wing back up. Had it "caught" or dug into the turf, the plane would have

cart wheeled—with a live bomb. Not a "walk away landing" scenario.

Moments after full throttle, Stapley chopped the throttle and applied forward rudder to "force" the plane onto the uneven runway. Somehow, the almost loose bomb remained on its rack…a major problem for the armorers to deal with, but a lifesaver for a lucky pilot who had lived…at least that day…to fly another mission.

"I beat the odds again," was about all he could think of mutter to himself as he unhooked and climbed out on the wing.

Bombs on the runway

by Wilfred "Bud" Stapley

On one 16-plane 18th Group mission flying out of K-46, the first aircraft took off and, as usual, his prop wash kicked up swirling clouds of dust from the barely "paved" runway. He was followed by 15 other aircraft from the 18th, each roaring down the runway at full throttle into the dust and grit—following the leader.

Picking up speed down the runway, pilots would watch the lights flashing by on each side to approximate their position. At the right airspeed they would "rotate" and lift off—air borne. They were unaware that the during his take off run the first pilot had reached up to adjust his goggles that had fallen down over his eyes, and in the process he had brushed his bomb release. Immediately, two 500-lb bombs were dropped on the runway. Because they had been dropped "safe," they did not explode. However, they were lying on the runway directly in the take off runs of the remaining 15 aircraft taking off behind him and blinded by the dust.

No one noticed the bombs on the runway, not even runway control—the dust was too thick. Only after all 16 aircraft were airborne and the No. 2 position pilot notified the No. 1 pilot that he didn't see any bombs on his aircraft, were the "missing" bombs found on the runway after the dust had settled. How all sixteen planes missed the bombs was considered to be a miracle.

Betty Hutton Plays Dogpatch

Colonel Lambert welcomes actress Betty Hutton to "Dogpatch" Korea, home of the 18th Fighter-Bomber Wing on February 27, 1952. (Krakovsky)

There's No Business Like Show Business

"There's No Business Like Show Business," was the theme of the laugh packed, rhythm filled, Betty Hutton show that visited Dogpatch earlier this month," the Truckbuster newspaper reporter enthused. In the true spirit of show business, though plagued by the loss of her voice, Miss Hutton went "On with the Show."

The "number one" block entertainer kept the jammed

Actress Betty Hutton poses with Col. Ira Levenson following her arrival at K-10 on Februry 27, 1952. (Krakovsky)

packed gym in stitches as she rendered songs from her hit films, "Somebody Loves Me" and "Annie Get Your Gun." The crowd of satisfied Airmen and Officers whistled, yelled and applauded for more as she joked and danced her way across the stage.

Supporting the Hollywood star were the Skylarks, one of the nation's top vocal groups, accordionist John Kiado and Bill

Betty Hutton signs an autograph during a "Welcome to Dogpatch" lunch at the K-10 NCO Club. (Krakovsky)

Howe, pianist and master of ceremonies.

After the show the Top Three Club played host to the troupe and provided them with one of their tasty meals."

Many of those in the audience at Dogpatch remembered beautiful Betty Hutton as "The Blonde Bombshell" from her billing during World War Two. Ms. Hutton was only two years old when her father abandoned her mother and sister. Three year old Betty Hutton began singing for patrons in the speakeasy opened by her mother to make ends meet. By age 13, she was singing professionally with local Detroit bands. Her big break into show business came when she was heard and hired on the spot by orchestra leader Vincent Lopez.

Just before World War Two she appeared in several musical film "shorts" and was given a role in a Broadway musical review, Two for the Show. She went on to make 14 films in eleven years.

Betty Hutton was a remarkably talented singer with a powerful range that included comedic asides. She could croon ballads and love songs with the best of the Forties vocalists. She could also "yonk and squawk" her way through show tunes that enabled her to showcase her comedic dexterity. She could and did veer from "straight" singing into a tune like "I'm Just A Square (In A Social Circle)" or "Can't Stop Talkin' About Him" to delight her audiences with swinging, tongue twisting dynamics accompanied by facial mugging and easy going physicality.

By the time she performed for the Dogpatchers, Betty Hutton had been a leading star for over a decade that included hard living and demanding schedules. She was facing a major disagreement with Paramount in 1952 that would cause her to walk out on her contract, effectively ending her Hollywood career.

By the end of the Sixties, Ms. Hutton was trying to overcome bouts of drug abuse and alcoholism, ending with a suicide attempt. With help from a priest she began to pull her life back together while working as a cook and housekeeper in a Rhode Island Rectory. She went on to earn a Master's Degree and to teach acting at two New England colleges.

She lives today in Palm Springs, California.

Actress Betty Hutton (nee Elizabeth Thornburg) flashes a brilliant smile for Lt. Don Drage during a USO show tour at K-10 in February 1952. Ms. Hutton was nicknamed "The Blonde Bombshell," as a tribute to her energy and presence on stage and in film. She had appeared on Broadway in the early 1940s and then moved to Hollywood, where she was best known for her comedic and musical roles, including starring roles in The Perils of Pauline (1947) and Annie Get Your Gun (1950). In 1952 she became embroiled in a contract battle with Paramount Studios that effectively endered her Hollywood career. In the 1970s she turned to a Rhode Island priest to help her deal with an unhappy personal life, earned a Masters degree and taught acting. She lives in Palm Springs, California. (Drage)

442

(Above) **1st Lt. Budd Stapley**, *How Flight, 67th Squadron, en route to the target in April 1952. How Flight is using Echelon flying formation. Note the locked down tail wheel. Most American F-51s in 1952 had their tail wheels locked in the down position due to mechanical problems. The extra drag took about 10 mph off cruising speed and burned more fuel. (Stapley)*

MIG Bait. *Mustang pilots were convinced that on occasion they were sent into "MIG Alley" as bait for FEAF F-86s. Sometimes the friendly jets were "late," and the Mustangs would be "jumped" by the MIGs and have to fight their way out of the trap.*

"Sleek U.S. Air Force F-86 "Sabre" jets of the 51st Fighter Interceptor Wing form this pattern of power as they patrol skylanes high over "MIG-Alley" in northwest Korea," an Air Force caption reports on May 22, 1953. (NARA)

Getting Jumped by 75 MIGs

by Wilfred "Budd" Stapley

In February, 1952...up by the Yalu...we were inbound on the target, when I saw these "golf balls" going by my cockpit. [The "golf balls" were the tracer rounds from ground to air or air-to-air gunfire. From the ground it was called "flak."] I was used to them coming up at me, but these were going by from above and behind my plane.

"What in @#@#$%" and about that time the MIG goes diving past my aircraft. We had no idea that they were anywhere around. He had been shooting at me, but remember, I never flew my aircraft in a "straight and level" attitude once I passed the Bomb Line. [Pilots called the constant weaving and bobbing "jinxing."]

He had not been able to hit me, even thought I didn't even know he was there. Up until then, I hadn't even looked for another airplane...an enemy airplane--coming up behind you. After that I did. We had a mirror in the cockpit, but it didn't give much field of view. The best "mirror" was your own eyeballs, as you kept looking left, right, up, behind. It's the guy you don't see that shoots you down.

There were 16 of us and about 75 of them. Their attacks on us were very well coordinated. They formed themselves into three loops so that there were three guys shooting at us at all times. We tried to stay in formation. We went into a "sissors"...two guys weaving back and forth. The object is to try and suck the attacking plane into a diving turn that brings them across the guns of the other wingman.

We kept that up and tried to make it out over open sea. The sea belonged to us (UN forces). They didn't follow us out over open water. Probably thought that if we shot down one of their planes that we would capture a Russian pilot.

Before we reached the water, about 36 F-86s jumped the MIGs and chased them away. I was never so happy to see 86's in my life.

They didn't actually tell us that they were sending us into a particular area as "bait" for the MIGs, but we strongly suspected that was the case.

When we would be sent into "MIG Alley," they would tell us that was "a possibility of intercept by MIGs...but a lot of the time the 86's weren't there!

K-46 Images and Recollections

K-46 Overview. *The hill beside K-46 provided an almost panoramic view of the base and flight operations. The row of painted buildings at right center included the operations offices for the four flying squadrons and the 18ᵗʰ Group. At this time, the 18ᵗʰ Wing was preparing to transition K-46 from an advanced operating base to the home base for the Wing. "The 18ᵗʰ had moved to K-46 from K-16 (Seoul) just a few months before I arrived in November 1951," explained R. F. Titus. "The 18ᵗʰ Wing Headquarters was at K-10, but most combat was flown from K-46. I was in the 39ᵗʰ Squadron and we kept one Flight on R&R, one at K-10 and the rest at K-46. We rotated every week or so." (Titus)*

*(Right) **18ᵗʰ Group flight line at K-46** in late Winter 1952. "The K-46 flight line was shared by all the Squadrons." This photo shows more "red tails" [67ᵗʰ Squadron "Fighting Cocks"], but the birds were parked in single file by Squadron." The "box" in the center forground served as the latrine for flight crews. (Titus)*

Winter of '52

"My most vivid memory," recalled R. F. Titus, of the winter of 1952 was of the bitter cold. "At K-46 we slept in tents. We had oil fired stoves, and the fuel tanks were outside. At night, water in the lines would freeze, and by morning the one gallon cans that we heated water in were solid ice. As the Squadron Assistant Operations Officer I had to be first up and got to re-start the stove in the tent and shiver down to Operation to do the same thing there."

"We were severely short of flying gear--parachutes, helmets, etc.--so those items were pooled. Find a helmet that fit and go fly. We had no oxygen so the oxygen masks were worn because the microphones were in the masks. The K-46 strip was short and covered with gravel, so we made single ship take-offs to avoid rock damage."

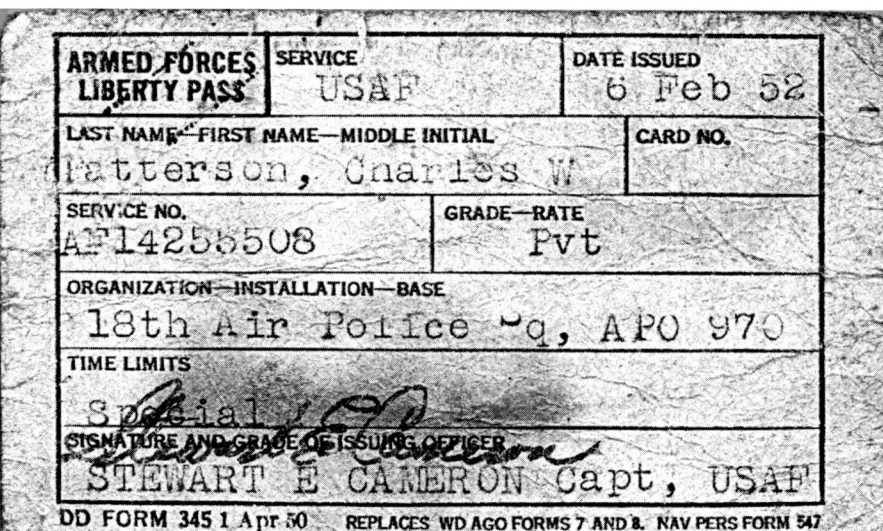

Charles Patterson's Armed Forces Liberty Pass issued on 6 February 1952. As a member of the 18ᵗʰ Air Police Squadron, Patterson would normally be checking such cards as base personnel left on off-duty recreational visits. (Patterson)

444

Truckbusters "Pipeline"

William Timmons "Tim" Urquhart was typical of the young officer candidates the Air Force was pushing through the pilot pipeline by late 1950.

He enlisted as an Aviation Cadet in Class 51-G in September 1950 and went through basic training at Perrin AFB, Texas--trained to fly the AT-6 Texan. He transferred to Craig AFB, Alabama for more AT-6 training and then transitioned into the F-51. "We were commissioned and sent TDY to Luke AFB, Arizona for Combat Crew Training in F-51s and then PCS-ed to Camp Stoneman, California as replacement pilots to Korea, arriving in March, 1952.

"Upon arriving in Korea as a junior 2nd Lieutenant, I was given a local check out in the F-51. I flew my first combat mission with a grand total of 349 hours in my logbook. Don't get me wrong, I felt then and now that I was well prepared. After all, we had been intensively trained for about 18 months. We used to joke about our "free" $50,000 government flying education—"they stick it up your tail a nickel at a time." Urquhart finished his required 85 missions in September 1952 with a total of 510 hours flying time.

Urquhart was assigned to "H" (How) Flight, 67th Fighter-Bomber Squadron, 18th Fighter-Bomber Wing at K-10 and K-46 Korea. "Our combat operations were flown out of K-46, and our real headquarters and maintenance were at K-10 [Chinhae, SK]. Until we combat pilots wore out our

welcome at K-10, we would stage out of K-46 for almost five days then catch a C-47 down to K-10 for two days of rest. I use the word 'rest' lightly, because we would do

our level best to demolish the Officer's Club at K-10."

Barracks 14-2 at Perrin AFB-- "Home" *for Class 51-G-3. (Urquhart)*

(Below) **Aviation Cadet Class 51-G-3** *stands in snowy sleet to have its picture taken at Perrin AFB, Texas in February 1951. In a matter of months, many of them would be flying combat missions in Korea. (Urquhart)*

445

March 1952

"Combat commitments of this organization have been met through sheer determination to see a job well done even in the face of heavy losses of aircraft and a definite shortage of personnel."

Lt. Col. Julian Crow, Commander, 67th Squadron

Maximum Effort. *When intelligence analysts and tactical planners determined that a particular target was important enough to justify a major strike, the 18th Fighter-Bomber Group was tasked to "hit a target with all its available resources-- "maximum effort"--Col. Joe Peterburs explained. "The Group would put together a force from all four squadrons and we would get from 30-50 birds in the air all hitting the same target at the same time." In this photo, Mustangs from all four of the 18th F-B Group squadrons turn up prior to taking off on a maximum effort mission in March 1952. (Peterburs)*

The operational effort of the 18th Fighter-Bomber Group improved considerably during March, even facing a loss in average aircraft assigned, from 66 to 57 for the Group and down to 14 for the 2nd Squadron SAAF—18 aircraft short of authorized strength of 75 for the Fighter Group. The "in-commission" rate (based on aircraft hours on hand versus aircraft hours In-commission) dropped to just 42 percent, or approximately 24 aircraft (an average of eight per squadron). The number of combat crews assigned, however, rose to 137 in March—more than 17 above authorization. The average sorties per pilot dropped to a low of 8 per month as compared to a 20 per month average in 1951—despite the fact that the total flying time increased for March and total effective sorties increased 6.7 percent.

There were too many pilots for the number of flyable Mustangs on hand…or there just weren't enough of the aging birds for the number of pilots that the Air Force was shoving through the pipeline. In January 1952, 14 pilots of the 18th completed their combat tours and went home. In February, that total dropped to three and in March just one pilot became a Centurion.

The Wing reported that the average experience level for its combat pilots dropped from 37 missions in January 1952 to 31 in March. The experience level reflected the comparative glut of pilots with fewer planes to fly.

"The main disturbing morale factor,"

Monthly Summary

Ground combat in Korea during March consisted mostly of "patrols and raids against determined enemy opposition" and fending off widely scattered, small-scale enemy exploratory attacks. "The front lines remained essentially the same, with U.S. Eighth Army units - U.S. I Corps, U.S. IX Corps, U.S. X Corps, and ROK I Corps - deployed from west to east across the peninsula."

In the air, the war was anything but stalemated. FEAF aircraft, in one of the busiest months of the Korean air war, "mounted more than 1,000 sorties almost every day." Air superiority over the battlefront by UN aircraft, enabled ground forces to operate with complete freedom from Communist air attacks. Primary tactical air missions included interdiction, close support, and counter-air, supported by routine aerial reconnaissance, airlift, search and rescue, and flare and leaflet drop missions.

Fifth Air Force fighter-bombers, B-26 light bombers, and other tactical warplanes "concentrated mainly on interdiction missions against enemy rail and highway facilities to choke the movement of enemy supplies and equipment to front-line areas. Other targets included marshalling yards, bridges, and traffic choke points." [1]

1 Adapted in part from U.S. Air Force Historical Research Agency. January 2002. The U.S. Air Force's First War: Korea 1950-1953 Significant Events, March 1952. http://www.au.af.mil/au/afhra/wwwroot/korean_war/korean_war_chronology/kwc_1951.html

Repair Crew on the Run. *This dramatic photograph by a low-level reconnaissance flight on March 27, 1952, shows Communist rail repair crews scurrying for cover--the circled figures. The striking photo also reveals how cratered roadbeds were restored to serviceability within a few hours of the damaging cuts. Materials were hauled in on cars. Rail ties, steel rails, sandbags and tools were made readily available, and manpower was recruited as needed. Three rail lines blend easily into two parallel tracks by a system of simple switches. Section in right foreground shows how the ties were laid, and later wedged by additional ties. White parallel lines at left foreground and extreme background indicate recent repairs to damaged track. Labor crews encircled have one objective at this point--to escape from the overhead aircraft. (NARA)*

Major James M. Todd, new CO of the 39th Fighter Interceptor Squadron reported, "concerns pilots only and has to do with the limited number of aircraft in the squadron and prevalent feeling that the future won't be any better on that score and will likely become worse." [1]

"The merciless flogging handed the enemy has achieved the goal for which it was designed..."

In March, the rail interdiction program remained the major focus of combat operations for the 18th Group. The Wing newspaper, *Truckbuster*, reported that "18th fighter pilots play key role in Operation Strangle." On August 18, 1951, the Fifth Air Force kicked off the concentrated interdiction program, code named Operation Strangle. Since then, "fighter bombers of the 18th Ftr Bmr Wing, under the protective umbrella of Allied Sabre-Jets, have been carrying this program out twenty-four hours a day denting Red supply routes, knocking out rail lines and causing the enemy its biggest supply problem since the outbreak of the 'police ac-

tion.' The merciless flogging handed the enemy has achieved the goal for which it was designed," the *Truckbuster* claimed. "With no safe way of transporting troops, ammunition and badly needed food and clothing, the Reds have been forced to retaliate in the air, to give up their previous ground plans, and to place their greatest emphasis on a defensive air War."

"The job of the Fifth Air Force is to make the Communists pay as high rent as possible for their stay in Korea," explained Lt. Gen. Frank F. Everest, CG FAF. "Operation Strangle" has done just that, and "it might just possibly go so far as to 'evict' the Com-

mies," the *Truckbuster* noted.

In mid-March, Mustangs from the 18th struck "at ammunition dumps northwest of Chorwon. Explosions following the strikes shattered the entire area of concentration. Napalm bombs splashed on enemy troops, bunkers, bridges and gun positions," the Truckbuster explained. [2]

Kaesong, Kumhawa and Ando-ri were "hard hit" as well; the F-51's "pulverized gun positions and troop supply bunkers. Eight more mortar and artillery positions, 10 troop and supply bunkers knocked out, and 20 more Reds killed. The next dawn was brightened by the flames from

"The job of the Fifth Air Force is to make the Communists pay as high a rent as possible for their stay in Korea."

Lt. Gen. Frank F. Everest, CG FAF

Thanks for keeping 'em in the air. Lt. Col. Julian Crow, Commanding Officer of the 67th Fighter-Bomber Squadron poses with senior NCOs of the 67th, including (L to R): Technical Sergeant Roy Pylant, 1st Sergeant Gleen, Master Sergeant Rose (line chief), and Sergeant Holt. (Pylant)

two front-line supply dumps which Mustangs attacked. The fighters wheeled for home after the area was a blazing inferno."

The necessity of maintaining two operation locations in a combat theatre almost doubles the need for supervisory personnel in the fields of aircraft maintenance, operations, armament, intelligence and communications, Group Commander Col. Seymour Levenson pointed out.

Combat film assessment was now a "program" headed by 1st Lt. Leonard R. Miraldi. He had been working for months to improve the quality of combat film, its assessment by the Intelligence Section, and analyzing the film to substantiate mission claims. In addition, he began scheduling "film showings for the various squadrons." All the combat film was viewed by each squadron the day after a mission. In emergency situations, the film could be ready for viewing within two hours of a completed mission. An edited selection of the week's "outstanding film" was forwarded to K-10 for viewing by the Wing staff at each Monday morning staff meeting. [3]

> **"We learned once again that conventional aircraft are much superior to jet aircraft on close-support type missions..."**

As the number of "junior" pilots grew, the need for training programs was obvious. "A new training program was initiated which requires more flying time for each new pilot before he is declared, "combat ready."

The tactics of the Group returned "to the group gaggle principle," Levenson noted. "We have been hitting, with the entire 5th Air Force, a small section of rails each day. The results have proven very

Airman Don Hall plays "Dr. Strangelove" on a 500-lb. bomb at K-46. (Black)

satisfactory. Each pilot of the Group flew close support missions in order to "keep their hand in. The close support business is very well liked by all pilots and a welcome change from rail cutting missions." [4]

"No new tactical lessons were learned during the month," the 39th FIS monthly reported observed, "though from statements made by ground force officers we learned once again that conventional aircraft are much superior to jet aircraft on close-support type missions. The future appears to have a need for conventional or turbo-prop fighters but as yet there hasn't been any assurance that the future will provide these aircraft."

The biggest negative morale factor in March was the crowded quarters at K-46. "At the present time, 14 men are quartered in one tent," Levenson noted. "Additional construction has been given high priority in the building program outlined for this location, and it is indicated that the crowded housing situation will be alleviated early in April."

"...sheer determination to see a job well done..."

"Combat commitments of this organization have been met through sheer determination to see a job well done even in the face of heavy losses of aircraft and a definite shortage of personnel," recorded Lt. Col. Julian Crow, Commander of the 67th Squadron.

There were too many pilots and not enough enlisted personnel assigned to the 67th. All sections, with the exception of the pilot section, continued to be below authorized strength. The overage of pilots caused individual pilots to feel that they were not being utilized to the fullest extent of their capabilities.

At the beginning of March officer strength for the 67th was 45, but up to 47 by the end of the month. Despite the number of pilots, the 67th accounted for a scant 307 sorties in March with only 730 combat hours flown. No bombs were reported dropped that month at all. Railroad cuts

(44), buildings (54) and enemy personnel (64) led the list of "claims" that month, among the least impressive reports provided by the squadron to that point in the conflict.

Going to war every day certainly wasn't "business as usual" for the 67th, but the squadron's report for March 1952 devoted far more attention to the business side of operations than to the operations themselves. There were too many pilots and not enough enlisted personnel.

"As long as the 'Fighting Cocks' remain in Korea, rotation will probably continue to be the largest single factor affecting morale," Crow predicted. "Morale in the enlisted ranks depends a great deal upon the work load. As long as the men are kept busy with their jobs, they feel that they are important enough to the effort in this theatre to justify their presence in the 67th. To date, the shortage of enlisted personnel causes all EM to be kept very busy. Consequently, their morale is very good. Conversely, morale in the Pilot ranks is not good. This section is over manned and missions have come too slowly to the pilots during the last month," Crow reported.

Although enlisted strength at the beginning of the month was 163, there were only 19 gains against 44 losses, leaving total enlisted strength at 138 at the end of the month. Personnel shortages prevented supervisors from doing top supervisory work, "primarily because they themselves must perform much of the work. It is anticipated that with the influx of more experienced specialists there will be a decided increase in the amount and quality of the training rendered," Crow reported. [5]

The Armament Section was operating "smoothly and successfully" perhaps as a direct result of an "extensive OJT program" that had been initiatives. All the Airmen were now being placed on OJT for the next higher AFSC, complete with new function charts and status boards to track training progress.

Better maintenance was also cited for a decrease in the malfunctions of the .50 caliber guns during that month. "Improvements in the Armament shope (sic) are

taking place rapidly with two cabinets with doors being built in the gun cleaning room and the room being painted also." [6]

It was a different story in the Maintenance Section that month. The average "in commission" status achieved for March was just 49.37%—32.26% below the February figure and 25.63% below that required by Fifth Air Force. High turnover of maintenance personnel seems to be the leading factor behind the low percentage of planes that were combat ready. Six men departed, and eleven arrived; however, four supervisory personnel were lost and two experienced supervisors checked on board that month.

The 67th Squadron could only muster 77 maintenance personnel that month, 16 men below authorization. The workload on those present that month was staggering. Seven new aircraft were received, but eight were lost for various reasons, leaving the total number of combat aircraft assigned at 15—ten below the squadron's authorization for combat aircraft. The Maintenance Section completed 9 engine changes, 9 major inspections, 22 intermediate inspections and 6 acceptance inspections that month. Every inspection was "very rigid regardless of the type." Morale was "moderate" for the section that month.

"With the arrival of warm weather, spirits have been zooming!"

Major Stanley Long took over as Executive Officer of the 12th Squadron after Major James M. Todd moved up to Commanding Officer.

The weather was getting better. "With the arrival of warm weather, spirits have been zooming," the 12th reported in March 1952.

"Interdiction missions against the enemy's transportation system, supply concentrations, troop billets, and artillery positions primarily remain our targets as in preceding months," the 12th reported. "However, we are again taking an active

Kicking the Tires. *Capt. Joe Peterburs "kicks the tires" on his 12ᵗʰ Squadron Mustang prior to a mission in March 1952. (Peterburs)*

Ready for Action. *A rearmed Mustang from the 12ᵗʰ FBS leaves the parking area at K-46. (Peterburs)*

"Gear in the well." *Capt. Joe Petersburs lifts off from K-46 on a combat mission in Spring 1952. (Peterburs)*

part in close support missions after several month during which we have very few."

"Some experimentation was done in regard to a number of Group gaggles on rail strikes," the 12ᵗʰ reported. "This concerned mostly the type of formation utilized to and from the target and the type pass to be used on the target itself. Those gaggles involved a group formation of twenty planes, more or less, and it was a turn around affair. Also, the entire group had a chance to fly a few close support missions for the first time in several months," the 12ᵗʰ explained. "A great deal of valuable experience has been gained through these missions, exceptionally valuable in the case of pilots who have been assigned within the past four months." The targets for CAS missions included "mostly bunkers, gun positions, and troops."

Mosquito planes of the T-6 and L-10 type controlled the CAS strikes. "The flights for the most part preferred the T-6's over the L-10's because they marked the target much better using smoke rockets."

Another "new development" reported that month was the "so-called M.A.C. line, which follows the bomb line ten miles to the north. Any strikes within this line must be controlled by mosquito or radar. MIG sightings have been more numerous and attacks against our planes more frequent."
[7]

Signing the Log. *Capt. Joe Peterburs signs his log after completing another combat mission from K-46 in March 1952. (Peterburs)*

Endnotes

[1] USAFHRA. *Monthly Historical Report, 39 FIS,* March 1952, p. 8.

[2] USAFHRA. *Truckbuster. Vol. 1 No. 19 March 31, 1952. p. 1.*

[3] USAFHRA. *Monthly Historical Report, 18th Fighter-Bomber Group,* March 1952, p. 5.

[4] USAFHRA. *Monthly Historical Report, 18th Fighter-Bomber Group,* March 1952, p. 7.

[5] USAFHRA. *Monthly Historical Report, 67th Fighter-Bomber Squadron,* March 1952, p. 5.

[6] USAFHRA. *Monthly Historical Report, 67th Fighter-Bomber Squadron,* March 1952, p. 9.

[7] USAFHRA. *Monthly Historical Report, 12th Fighter-Bomber Squadron,* March 1952, p. 3.

Crew Chief S/Sgt. Elbert D. Black *readies his Mustang for yet another mission from K-46. (Black)*

Combat Statistics

18th F-BWing

March 1952

Average No. A/C Assigned
57

Total Flying Time
2,736

Percent of Aircraft in Commission
42%

Percent of Aircraft AOCP
2%

Combat Sorties Flown by Wing
1,141

12th Squadron Sorties
385

39th FIS Sorties
636

67th Squadron Sorties
Unavailable

2 Squadron Sorties
404

A/C Lost to Combat
4

Pilots lost
4

Fuel Consumed

192,472 gals.

Ordnance Expended

.50-cal. Rounds
590,656

Rockets
1,972

Napalm Bombs
102

500-lb. GP Bombs
1,646

Note: Figures and totals may differ in some categories due to differences in numbers provided by each component.

A very soggy flight line at K-46 in March 1952. "It was the rainy season," remembered S/Sgt. Elbert Black. "We couldn't fly for days. We had to sandbag the Han River to protect the planes. It rained so hard the tents leaked badly." (Black)

Bullet Through Prop. *(Below) A close call for Capt. Joe Peterburs when his prop was hit by a anti-aircraft round. The prop got him home to K-46 but the damage required some major "surgery" by the maintenance crew. "On one of my close air support missions I got a .50-cal. through one blade of my prop as I was coming off the target. There was a flash and then the bird started vibrating real bad. I didn't know what or where the damage was. I nursed the bird back to home plate (considered bailing out a couple times), landed and when I shut down the engine the blade with the hole in it was right in front of my face. I did not realize that such a little (?) hole would cause so much vibration."*
(Peterburs)

1ˢᵗ Lt. Ray Plevyak

1ˢᵗ Lt. Wilfred "Budd" Stapley was on Runway Control duty when his friend 1ˢᵗ Lt. Ray Plevyak (left) took off on his last mission. (Holmes)

Significant Events in March

March 1: 1ˢᵗ Lt. Edward F. Borsare was forced to make an emergency landing at K-46 as a result of damage inflicted to his aircraft by enemy fire while on an interdiction mission.

March 6: 1ˢᵗ Lt. Marvin Satenstein "was involved in a major accident during take-off at K-46 due to mechanical failure of landing gear."

Mar. 11: Fighter-bombers dropped 150 tons of bombs and approximately 33,000 gallons of napalm on a four square mile supply storage and troop training area near Sinmak. Fifth Air Force operations officers reported this to be "the most intensive napalm attack on a single area in the war." [1]

2ⁿᵈ Lt. Melvin Sousa "was forced to make an emergency landing in the double bend of the Imjin River as a result of damage inflicted to his aircraft by enemy ground fire while on an interdiction mission.

Mar. 14: 1ˢᵗ Lt. Jacob B Armstrong was "involved in a major accident while taxiing at K-46 due to a hole in the taxiway."

Mar. 25: Fifth Air Force flew 959 sor-

A fully loaded 67ᵗʰ Squadron Mustang prepares for take off in Spring 1952. (Peterburs)

ties, concentrating on interdiction of the rail line from Sinanju to Chongju and making approximately 142 cuts in the track. Some aircraft struck the Sunchon-Pyongyang highway, scoring twenty-seven hits.

March 26: Captain Victor E. Bocquin, was "forced to execute an emergency landing at K-14 as a result of damage inflicted to his aircraft by enemy ground fire while on an interdiction mission."

Combat Losses in March

2ⁿᵈ Lt. Floyd B. O'Neal, 67ᵗʰ Fighter-Bomber Squadron was lost on 4 March 1952.

2ⁿᵈ Lt. Raymond Thaddeus Plevyak, 67ᵗʰ Fighter-Bomber Squadron from Carbondale, Pennsylvania, was lost on 1 March 1952. "Ray was lost during a rail cut mission," his friend and fellow pilot in How Flight, 1ˢᵗ Lt. Wilbur "Budd" Stapley remembered.

"His fellow flight members said he had

453

dropped his bombs and fired his rockets all in good order. He lost contact with his flight on the way back to the I.P. and was never seen again. His flight made serveral sweeps of the area but could find no trace of him. I had been out on runway control when his flight had taken off and had joked with Ray," Stapley recalled. "His loss hit me pretty hard."

Plevyak planned to be married when he returned to the States and Stapley had agreed to be his best man. "Does that tell you where he was in my heart," Stapley asked.

Stapley and Plevyak had also been roommates all through Advanced Flight Training at Craig AFB. "We had been at the same basic school at Perrin AFB in Denton, Texas," Stapley recalled, "and I'm afraid we arrived at Craig as 'losers.' Ray had been moved back from 51-B to 51-D for some infraction of the rules and I had been caught with a beer can in my room with only four days left to graduate. I had 50 tours to walk off when I arrived at Craig AFB at Selma, Alabama. Ray still had a few himself. The Cadets walking tours agreed to tell the Airmen asking why we were walking, that we had flown under the Edmund C. Petus Bridge in downtown Selma. An official notice in the base newspaper exposed our heinous fabrication."

After training at Craig, the newly commissioned 2ⁿᵈ Lieutenants moved on to Combat Crew Training at Luke AFB. They were heading to Korea. Meanwhile, they wangled some leave and headed for New York. One of their friends had been killed in a crash and they were delivering his "canary yellow Olds 98 convertible" to his widow in New York.

But first they had to get out of Texas.

They packed the car with their B-4 bags and other gear, including their pistols. "Ray had purchased a .38-caliber pistol to carry in combat while I figured an Air Force issued .45 was good enough—couldn't hit anything with it anyway." Stapley was planning to ride with Plevyak as

far as Chicago, his home, and then Plevyak would take the car on to New York. At about 0300 in the morning the two young pilots were steaming along the Texas highway "doing about 80 mph, when a semi suddenly pulled across the road and blocked our way. We screeched to a stop just short of the truck and both Ray and I were going to leap out and show the truck driver the error of his ways."

The canary yellow convertible was immediately surrounded "by a small army of cowboys and state troopers" who rushed their car "with guns galore at the ready and ordered us to freeze—and freeze we did," Stapley recalled.

The troopers asked them where they were going. "To Chicago," replied Stapley. "To New York," replied Plevyak.

Were they armed? "No," replied Stapley. "Yes," replied Plevyak.

Did the car belong to them? "Yes," said Stapley. "No," replied Plevyak.

"We were digging ourselves deeper into a hole we didn't even know we were in," Stapley explained. The reason for the traffic stop and grilling by the troopers was an armed robbery and murder. "It seems that two guys about 21 or 22 (that's us)," Stapley said, "about 5'11" tall (that's us) about 165 pounds (that's us) with brown hair (that's us) had robbed a bank, killed a guard and escaped in a (you guess it) canary yellow Olds 98 Convertible!! And these boys figured they had their men."

About an hour later and following a "not too gentle frisking," and tearing the car apart looking for the missing loot, the cops began "having a few doubts." Stapley and Plevyak produced their "orders, uniforms, and the pistol" that was packed

in an inaccessible place, and "we finally had a chance to tell our story."

The two scared pilots finally "convinced the state trooper in charge that we were as innocent as new born babes—well, maybe not that innocent." Finally, the trooper said they had him convinced, but that just in case, he was going to keep them in custody until the "real criminals were caught." And he did—for about two hours—when the radio reported that the two real felons had been captured. Stapley and Plevyak were allowed to proceed on their way. "I've often wondered," Stapley recalled, "just how many canary yellow Olds 98 Convertibles there were in that part of Texas. I just wish that Ray was still around to back me up when I tell this story. I know it sounds like a whopper but sometimes truth is stranger than fiction."

1ˢᵗ Lt. David L. Taylor, 2 Squadron, SAAF pilot KIA on 20 March 1952. On 25 February, Lt. Taylor had a close call during an attempted landing at K-10. After his Mustang stalled on final approach, it cart wheeled into Chinhae Bay. He was rescued by Air Force Sergeants S.M. Starts and R. Renaud, the latter risking his life to pry Taylor from the now submerged cockpit. On 20 March, Taylor was a member of 'Able' and 'Dog' Flights that were taking part in three strikes by the 18ᵗʰ Group aircraft—hitting the Sunch'on-Kuadon-ni portion of the North Korean's railway. Two flights—eight aircraft—from 2ⁿᵈ Squadron took off for their third strike of the day. Enroute, two aircraft were sent back to base with engine problems. At the assigned target, heavy flak was encountered as the Cheetahs headed in on the attack. As they pulled off the target in a climbing turn—looking back to check results—they were jumped by MIG-15 enemy jet fighters. Taylor's plane was immediately hit by cannon shells—badly—coolant and black smoke streaming behind the doomed Mustang. The flight formed up tightly around Taylor, trying to protect him until they could hide in a nearby bank of clouds. The lead aircraft turned into the attacking jets, and lost sight of Taylor's plane. One of the flight—Lt. Joubert—spotted and attacked a MIG trying to get into firing position. The flight broke hard to port, and the MIG was hit by a long burst of .50-cal. machine gun fire—verified by gun camera film. The MIGs left the area and the flight immediately returned to searching for Lt. Taylor's aircraft. No sign of Lt. Taylor or his aircraft was ever found. He was the first SAAF pilot to be shot down by MIGs during the Korean War, one of only two.

2ⁿᵈ Lt. Harry Eugene Rushing, 39th Fighter-Interceptor Squadron, USMA Class of 1950 from Montgomery, Alabama, on 3 March 1952, was flying number two position in Put Put Willie flight. Lt. Rushing's plane developed engine trouble about three minutes north of the bomb line and he immediately turned back toward friendly islands. The engine began to smoke and caught fire before the coast was reached forcing Lt. Rushing to bail out immediately. He bailed out at 8,000

feet altitude and drifted south landing in the water of the Han Estuary just off the enemy coast. His wind filled chute dragged him on the surface of the water toward a sand bar to the south and he appeared to be working with the shroud lines of his chute. Meanwhile the flight leader had alerted rescue facilities and Lt. Thomas F. Casserly flying number three followed him down. Upon learning that there would be

Lt. Marvin Satenstein used all his skills as an airman and as a savvy survivor to "walk away" from this spectacular crash. (Peterburs)

a 30-minute wait for a helicopter and noting that Lt. Rushing's chute had collapsed a short distance off the sand bar, Lt. Casserly bellied his plane in on the sand bar and began searching the water where the chute was last seen. After searching unsuccessfully for fifteen minutes in the freezing water, Lt. Casserly was forced to give up the search and return to his plane, which was now practically submerged by the incoming tide. Lt. Casserly was soon picked up by the helicopter and returned to K-46. Lt. Rushing's body was not recovered."[2]

Endnotes

[1] The U.S. Air Force's First War: Korea 1950-1953 Significant Events. March 1952.

[2] USAHRA. Monthly Historical Report, 39th FIS, March 1952, p. 4-5.

Satenstein's Crash with drop tanks

by W. C. "Budd" Stapley, Tim Urquhart and Col. Joe Peterburs

The runway at K-46 was one of the shortest runways in Korea—just over 4,000 feet long. The first 1,000 feet of the runway surface was pierced planking. The rest of it was unpaved, resulting in numerous instances when planes would literally "get stuck in the mud."

In April 1952, as Lt. Marv Satenstein was taking off on a long mission with external gas tanks his engine malfunctioned. The heavy aircraft hit hard at the end of the runway. The rough surface of the runway and the hard bounce combined to "wipe out" his landing gear.

In an instant, his Mustang belly flopped onto the runway, skidding along at high speed—the two 150-gallon tanks full of high-octane aviation gasoline. Almost immediately the tanks were ripped open and the gasoline sucked out and around the aircraft that skidded off the end of the runway. The resulting explosion was spectacular. The flames reached some 500' in the air as the plane continued to skid down and then off the runway. Awed observers shook their heads and muttered prayers for the hapless pilot who was either dead or being fried alive in the cockpit.

"Our runway was built alongside a riverbed and we had Army anti-aircraft emplacements nearby," Tim Urquhart explained. Near the end of the runway, an Army truck with quad .50-caliber machine guns mounted on the rear was parked where it could provide any cover needed against marauding enemy aircraft. A nearby tent provided some shelter—sleeping and living quarters for the anti-aircraft crew.

It was winter and their tent canvas had

455

about zero insulation value. To slow down the transfer of heat that took some of the chill off from the pot bellied stove to the Korean countryside, the crew had built a framework out of scrap wood and basically paneled the inside of their tent. Hearing a loud crash outside the reinforced tent, a crewman threw back the flap to see what was going on.

What they saw was truly amazing—Satenstein's F-51 sliding by on its belly tanks about ten feet outside the tent flap—and humongous flames engulfing the plane—and everything else nearby. The flaming plane was too close to the front flap for the crew to escape from the tent that way and the back "exit" and sides were now boarded up to help them stay warm.

A few weeks before, a quick jab with a sharp knife, a pull, and they would have been out of the burning tent in a flash. In fact, this crew did get out safely—and in the process, set a record for dismantling tent paneling.

Budd Stapley, somewhat safer "up the hill" at his own tent, was watching the spectacular crash and fire. Shaking his head in mourning for his friend—he muttered to himself "Sayanorra boysan--that kid's had it—he's gone west."

When the plane finally stopped it was hardly visible at the center of a roiling mass of gasoline fed red-on-black flames. After not more than a few seconds, out of the towering holocaust of flames a small black dot appeared, a figure plunging directly out of the flames—"hauling butt out of the flames and away from that airplane," Stapley remembered.

It was Lt. Marv Satenstein, still very much alive—and running for his very life. Miraculously, Satenstein had had the presence of mind to keep his oxygen line connected in the cockpit as the flames soared around him—then jettison the canopy—disconnect his wires and lines—dive out of the cockpit and run to safety—keeping his thumb closed over the oxygen hose as he ran to keep from sucking any smoke or flames into his lungs as he ran.

Quickly reaching a relatively safe distance from the totally engulfed airplane,

1st Lt. Marvin Satenstein shows how much damage flak could do to low flying Mustangs. (Krakovsky)

he fell on the ground to help put out the flames trying to take hold of his clothing.

During the few seconds he was trapped in the cockpit, the massive amount of fuel released had saved him by creating so much fuel vapor that the actual combustion took place slightly outside a "vapor bubble" that surrounded his cockpit. The bubble gave him just enough time to disconnect his lines and get free of the cockpit and run to safety.

Satenstein had saved his life by calling on extraordinary airmanship skills and his wits. As the plane was skidding to a halt, he was unhooking himself from his parachute and radio connections inside the cockpit, with the exception of the oxygen system. When the plane had stopped, he found that the ripped open tanks had released so much gasoline, that there was not enough oxygen directly around the cockpit to support combustion—until the fumes were several feet beyond the cockpit and canopy. Inside the plane, still breathing oxygen, he was inside a huge bubble of gasoline vapor that was actually combusting some distance from the cockpit.

When the plane stopped and he was

unhooked, he vaulted out of the cockpit still wearing his oxygen mask tightly strapped on—and holding the now open end of the connecting hose closed with his gloved thumb as he ran for safety outside the flames.

His injuries included burns around his eyes where the skin was not protected by the helmet or mask. He probably would not have had those injuries were it not for the fact that on the previous mission his goggles had been broken and had not yet been replaced.

"Lt. Satenstein was not killed—a miracle," remembered Airman Clarence Frownfelter, "but ended up in the base hospital that night with severe burns on his face. The only thing that did not get burned was his 'walrus' mustache, which was protected by his oxygen mask. He had received a letter from home which I took to him that evening. He asked me to read the letter to him since he was unable to see with all the burns around his eyes."

Marv Satenstein and Joe Peterburs first met at Camp Stoneman, California on their way to Korea. When their orders included a layover of several days in Hawaii, they rented a car and toured Honoluly. When

456

they arrived in Korea, Satenstein was assigned to the 67th Squadron and Peterburs to the 12th.

A few days before his accident, Satenstein was involved in a "very high stakes poke game," Peterburs recalled. "He was not doing well and he hit me up for a loan of about $300--a lot of money in those days." When Peterburs heard that "Marv was in a flaming accident on the runway, I thought poor Marv, however, no matter how crass it sounds, I also thought 'Goodbye, $$$.'"

"Marv came out of the ordeal with flying colors," Peterburs continued, "and I took a few pictures of him with the weird burnt look around his eyes. Of course, after things settled down and Marv got his old self back in shape, he repaid the loan. In fact, I think he did pretty well in the poker game after I provided him with a stake. We finished out tours together and went back to the States on the same route we took coming over. This time we distinguished ourselves by being kicked out of the Royal Hawaiian."

Staff Sergeants Tom "Red" Ryder and Robert Marquis, *crew chiefs, worked together closely while on duty with the 67th Squadron at K-46. (Pylant)*

Crew Chief Recalls

by Thomas "Red" Ryder, Master Sergeant, USAF (Ret.)

Sergeant Thomas "Red" Ryder arrived at K-10 to join the 67th Squadron January 1952 after spending two weeks aboard the USS Randall. "After traveling on the troop ship, K-10 was a luxury. Our quarters at K-10 were Quonset huts comparable to the old open bay barracks."

K-10 was where battle damage to the aging Mustangs was repaired and major inspections were performed. "At this time the wing was experiencing a shortage of F-51's so no time was lost when an airplane was received." Ryder was assigned to perform aircraft inspections and "our work day lasted up to 18 hours or more. You really didn't mind though because there wasn't any thing else to do. The airplanes were needed and we got them ready."

"While at K-10 I got blood poisoning in my foot and spent about four days in the hospital. The Doc said I was not to get out of bed for anything and I spent the first two days catching up on sleep and eating. Then it got boring," he recalled.

In mid-February 1952, Ryder was transferred to K-46, near Hoengsong, the Wing's advance operating base, for flight line duty. "Parts and supplies were scarce and you made do with what you had, but I do not believe any plane was ever sent out that was not ready. We were very proud of our work and knew that the pilots depended on us. There were many times that I had pilots offer to help if nothing more than to hand me wrenches."

Quarters at K-46 "were large tents with wood floors and frames. There were two oil heaters per tent but at times you needed more. We had about 12 men to a tent. We used the heaters to boil water for coffee and it really didn't taste bad—after you got used to it. As mechanics, we found ways to regulate the fuel valves to get the most out of the heaters, but you still needed a good sleeping bag and blankets."

The showers and latrines were very different, Ryder remembered. "The latrine area was like a very large outhouse with a flushing system quite different. A fifty gallon half of a drum was installed off center. When it became off balance it would dump the water down the trough under the seats. When this happened you did not need paper, you needed a towel. All water was trucked in once or twice a week. It was not unusual to be taking a shower and be all soaped up and run out of water."

At K-46 the enlisted men were allowed a beer ration of two cans a day. "This beer had to be purchased from the officers section and distributed through the squadron. If you bought it you got to keep or share the beer that the others didn't want. This made for some very good beer busts. Later in the year a club was built about half way between the tents and the mess hall. There were an awful lot of liquid dinners served thereafter."

"When the 39th Fighter-Interceptor Squadron transferred to F-86's I think that I was a crew chief for the shortest time on record. The 39th sent the airplane off on a mission and then handed me the forms. That plane never came back. After the 39th left they would periodically come over and

Mustang FF 643 of the 67th Squadron gets refueled at K-10 in 1952. (Krakovsky)

buzz the field. Scared the hell out of us."

"At night, Bed Check Charlie was known to come over and drop a grenade or two. A new arrival told us he had found the perfect place to be. We said where and he said behind those sand bags. We told him that was the napalm dump."

"About the middle of the year we received more F-51's. I was assigned plane #064, which I crewed until I left in December 1952. [*Note: just several weeks later, the Mustangs were withdrawn from combat and the 18th Group shifted to F-86 Sabrejets.*]

"One very exciting job we got to do besides crew the planes was base guard duty." Ryder recalled. "With extensive guerilla activity around the base we would pull guard duty on the perimeter. We were given a clip with three rounds of ammo and instructions to fire them in the air if we had any trouble."

"One exciting incident that I remember was during a group gaggle. All the aircraft were taking off, when a pilot popped his coolant, did a 180 and landed against the flow of other aircraft taking off. Luckily, no one was hurt or any planes damaged but it was sure an exciting few minutes."

"On another occasion, my plane was loaded with 500-lb. bombs. That night I was told to reload with drop tanks. I could not find the line guard although I hollered for him, so I proceeded to change the load. After dropping the bombs, I was bringing the drop tanks to the plane when the guard

hollered halt and slammed the bolt home. I stopped!!"

"My plane was assigned to an early mission. During the pilot's preflight of the controls I heard something rubbing when he moved the rudder. I told the pilot that I had to check it out before it could fly. He said, 'I'll take it.' I told him that this airplane is not going and if you're going on this mission you will have to get another airplane. After repairing what I thought was the problem, the plane went out on a later mission. Later, I heard that he was coming back—with control problems. I got on another radio and listened in. Whenever he lowered the speed to put his gear down he didn't have enough aileron control. They told him to bail out but he elected to bring it in wheels up. He brought it in with very little damage. The problem was found to be shrapnel lodged between the wing tip and the aileron, but I sure sweated that one out."

The planes that were ferried back and forth from K-46 to K-10 for inspections would carry cargo drop tanks. "One pilot was returning with a load of officer's liquor and accidentally dropped the tank. He was not well received when he arrived."

Ryder did get to go on R&R to Japan one time. "At K-46, when any guns fired you hit the dirt. During this R&R there was some kind of Japanese holiday and they were shooting firecrackers left and right. I spent half of the time under the table, instead of at it."

"When maintenance was low we played

a lot of pinochle. We'd sent the planes off and head for the line shack—a dollar a game and a penny a point. It was even though and passed the time, especially on long drop tank missions."

"We rotated performing early flight preflights. We would preflight—including engine run-up—up to 4 or 5 aircraft. One morning as I finished the last aircraft the regular crew chief arrived and said he would finish up. I headed to the tent to warm up and as I was sitting on my cot taking my shoes off the flight chief came in. He asked me if I had preflighted a/c number such and such, and I said, 'Yes.' He asked me to sign off the forms and I did. Then he said 'I don't think that you have any sweat but it went in at the end of the run way on take off.' It was determined that the pilot had failed to turn on the carburetor heat and the carb iced up."

Another time a crew chief was preflighting an aircraft. When he turned on the pitot heat switch all six guns fired 1800 rounds of .50-cal. ammunition before he could think to turn it off. No damage except for the replacement of gun barrels for over heating."

In December 1952, a group of us that had arrived a year before were supposed to leave in time to be home for Christmas. President-elect Eisenhower made his promised inspection tour of Korea. All flights of returning personnel were grounded while he was in the area. This put us behind so that we did not get back until January."

Tents Burning Down

by Wilfred "Budd" Stapley

It got so cold there that the fuel oil for the pot bellied stoves that tried to heat our tents would actually freeze. Also, we kept 4-5 buckets of water close around the stove to use in case of fire.

One night someone got the bright idea—"let's use aviation gas in the stove—it doesn't freeze." So, they replaced the regular diesel fuel oil in the tent stove with aviation gas. Later, as the high-octane gas worked its way through the stove, we were awakened by a strange noise and a new "light" in the tent. Flames were whistling, roaring up the stove's exhaust stack—which was white hot—glowing brightly in the dark tent. Sparks were being blown high into the cold night air, only to begin landing on the paraffin coated canvas of the other ten or so tents that made up our "compound."

Thinking quickly, one of the occupants quickly grabbed one of the fire extinguisher buckets and heaved the contents at the white-hot stove. In an instant, a new law of physics was reinforced—water freezes even faster than low grade fuel oil—a conically shaped block of solid ice flew out of the bucket and hit the stove full force.

Up north, at K-46 in the winter, we never got out of our clothes. We tried to sleep on the cots—fully dressed in our flight suits—inside a sleeping bag—with several more blankets thrown over us—and we were still cold. I remember trying to hop out of the now burning tent to safety. It was quite a sight—about twenty guys—many of them still zipped into their sleeping bags—and it was simply too cold to get out of them—trying to hop between and over the cots and out of the burning tent.

The squadron CO was so mad at the unknown perpetrator(s) that he took his time in replacing the heavily damaged tents that were now "air conditioned" with big holes. "After that, as you were trying to go to sleep, you could look up at the stars—and really see them"—through the somewhat porous tent roof.

Home Sweet Tent. *Airman First Class Robert Cranston, a Crew Chief for the 67ᵗʰ Squadron from January 1952 until Novmeber 1952, prepares to enter his tent at K-46. "COLD, WET & HOT," he remembered, "to the extreme. I have never been so cold in my life as I was from January through March. We lived in canvas tents with wooden floors with "heat" provided by two oil stoves that were gravity fed by 55 gallon drums of diesel fuel. It would get so cold that the fuel would freeze in the lines," he recalled. Each tent slept twelve men. "We would put layers of paper between the canvas of our cots and our blankets to help keep out the cold." (Cranston)*

On March 28, 1952 "How Flight," 67th Squadron prepares to leave combat and head out from K-10 to Japan for a much needed R&R. (Bottom, L to R) Assistant Flight Leader 2nd Lt. Wilfred C. ("Flak") Stapley, 2nd Lt. Archie ("Clanky") Connors. (Top Row, L to R) Acting Flight Leader 1st Lt. Shirley B. ("Wash") Tubbs, 2nd Lt. Melvin ("Crash") Souza, Flight Leader 1st Lt. Donald D. ("Lucky") Drage, 2nd Lt. Joel O. ("Jeff") Rives, and 2nd Lt. William E. ("Mutt") McShane. They were about to find out that O-Club "etiquette" in war torn Korea was quite different than O-Club etiquette in Japan. (Stapley)

From Toasting to Namedropping

The fieldstone fireplace below the painting of the voluptuous girl in the K-10 Club was often used for more than simply burning wood to heat the area. From time to time, usually after some particularly serious "toasting," glasses would be hurled in the general direction of the fireplace where they shattered loudly into O'Club "flak." It was even believed in some circles that as Happy Hour progressed, accuracy might have been "off" somewhat. Generally, the flying glasses hit the fireplace. It was a "tradition" at the Top of the Mark Club at K-10—sort of.

After five or six weeks of combat flying, a Flight was taken "off the line" and sent off for R&R. At the end of March 1952, following a hard month of combat flying, the 67th Squadron's How Flight was sent to Japan for a week of R&R at Johnson AFB at Tachikawa, near Tokyo.

Most of How Flight consisted of relatively new pilots who had survived their first 8-10 missions. They were "combat veterans"…had been "blooded" and were sure that the "peace talks" that had recently begun at Panmunjom would be successful and that they would soon be heading home. Thank goodness, they congratulated themselves, we got over here just in time. A few more weeks and peace would have broken out—and we might have missed the war.

How flight now included 2nd Lt. Archie Connors who had joined them in Decem-

ber after a very short posting to the 40th Fighter-Interceptor Squadron that was attached to the 35th Fighter-Interceptor Wing at Tachikawa Air Base.

Following their arrival in Japan, How Flight headed for the base O-Club to begin the winding down process. After some liquid refreshment at the Tachikawa O-Club, How Flight ran into some of its former classmates who were just arriving in theater. "War stories" for the brand new, never been in combat pilots were the order of the evening. Drinks were ordered, then reordered.

Eventually the very relaxed, very happy How Flight pilots were giving and receiving toasts of the "here's to you, here's to us, here's to them" variety. After a particularly vigorous toast, someone remembered the "glasses in the fireplace tradition" at K-10. In moments the air was filled with glasses sailing towards the O'Club fireplace. The crashing and tinkling of the broken glass and the shards flying in all directions brought cheers and laughter. It also brought the now highly irate, non-aviator Captain who managed the club.

Getting more and more agitated and worked up as he dressed them down, he advised them, floridly, that they didn't throw glasses at the fireplace in HIS O'Club. What's more, he began to demand to know the names and units of those responsible. Some form of punishment or official chastising was just around the corner.

How Flight was incredulous. OK, so some glasses were broken. Tell us the damage and we'll pay for it and get out of here. But, it wasn't going to be that easy.

The Captain's tirade got worse and worse. He didn't back down until Lt. Connors injected the names of the commanding officer of the squadron to which he had been attached so very briefly a few weeks before. Later, How Flight concluded—with a twinkle in their eyes—that it might even have been possible that the way Connors described things, the Captain could have come to the conclusion that the glass throwing miscreants were attached to the 40th squadron.

The Captain seemed to be backing down as Connors, sensing that the name dropping gambit might just get them out of this broken glasses scrape, laid it on thick and heavy. He was so close to the Colonel, it seemed, that he was very nearly family. Unfortunately for How Flight, as they later found out, the pilots from the 40th Fighter Interceptor Squadron had a bad reputation with the Club Manager Captain. Now he sensed that he had "the goods" on the squadron's commanding officer. He stopped chewing out How Flight and began making mental notes…lots of them.

After the Captain had apparently been suitably cowed by the heavy mention of the Colonel's name, Connors, Stapley and the rest of How Flight got out of the club as quickly as possible. After spending the rest of the night peacefully in the "Transient

Barracks," they got up early and dressed for an exciting day on the town-Tokyo. The temporary unpleasantness of the night before was now just a distant memory-to them.

The Captain, meanwhile, had been busy tying a noose, of sorts, around the hapless Colonel's neck. He was out to get those so-and-so troublemakers from the 40th and called the base commanding general to give him a highly detailed account of what the Colonel's guys had done. The way he related things raised the General's blood pressure considerably.

The General called the Colonel at "oh dark thirty" in the morning to demand an explanation. The mystified Colonel assured him that none of the names of the glass throwers were from his squadron. When the name "Connors" was mentioned to the Colonel, however, he vaguely remembered that a 2nd Lieutenant by that name had been in his squadron for a very short period a month or so earlier, and then transferred to the 67th FBS in Korea. Now the Colonel was steamed. Some troublemaker of a 2nd Lieutenant had tried to pass himself off as a member of the 40th—after trashing the Club.

That explained why, at 0630 in the morning, the residents of the transient barracks were rousted out of their warm cots by a squad of Air Police conducting a bed-to-bed check to find Lieutenants Stapley, Connors and others from How Flight. How Flight, ever the early risers (since they had been thrown out of the O'Club the night before while still relatively sober), were almost out the Main Gate of the air base to find a taxicab that would take them into town-and all the interesting things they would find to do.

Their progress through the gate was arrested, literally, by the arrival of several jeeps—complete with sirens—full of Air Police, an agitated Colonel and a steamed up General.

The Captain O-Club Manager was also in one of the vehicles. Seeing How Flight about to head through the Main Gate, he stood up and gestured theatrically at Connors: "That's the man!" If it had not really happened, the scene could have been a

In Japan, Lt. Archie Connors was assigned for just a few weeks to the 35th Fighter-Interceptor Squadron, before being transferred to the 67th Fighter-Bomber Squadron. It was at the Johnson AFB Officer's Club a few weeks after this photograph was taken, that Archie and his fellow pilots were involved in a glass throwing "misunderstanding" that resulted in his being put in the brig.

brainchild of writers for McHale's Navy or No Time for Sergeants.

The last time How Flight saw Connors that day he was being "escorted" by two burly Air Policemen, one holding each elbow as he was taken into custody. "We didn't stay around to fight for his honor," Stapley laughingly recalled much later.

There was nothing they could do and after all, Connors had brought much of the trouble down on his own head. Periodically, they did make calls back to the base, trying to determine what was going on

Meanwhile, back at the base, Connors finally had a chance to explain the full circumstances to the Colonel and the General. Using all his "reasoning" abilities, Connors finally got the "brass" cooled down and himself released from custody—after he agreed to pay for the glasses. Eventually, he was able to rejoin How Flight later in the day to enjoy Tokyo before heading back into combat.

One of How Flight's R&R destinations in Japan was the Fujiya Hotel at Miyanoshita Spa. The hotel's food was positively heaven for guys used to being impressed when the organic concoctions given them to eat at K-46 were "warm," much less tasted like food. The accommodations in the Chrysanthemum Bed Room helped them forget for a few hours the hard cots and freezing temperatures of their tents and Quonset huts. (Urquhart)

The "Engel Bath" (right) would help relax muscles sore from countless hours in a cramped, cold cockpit.

(Left) The Baca bomb was a popular "Hi Ma" location for a souvenior photograph. 1st Lt. Archie Connors poses by the familiar landmark.

1st Lt. Wilfred Stapley with his crew chief beside "Linda Lee II," named after Stapley's sister. (Stapley)

Smoke on Runup

How Flight was taxiing out to the end of the runway, preparing to takeoff on a mission. At the end of the runway, the procedure was to "run up" the engine to close to full power momentarily, to help reduce the chances that a pilot would try to take off with an engine that was not air worthy. Along with the others in the Flight, 1st Lt.

Wilfred "Budd" Stapley kept his feet on the brakes and ran the engine up while he checked the instruments to detect any signs of trouble.

"Number Three, you're on fire. There's smoke coming out of your engine."

The transmission was almost unnecessary. Smoke surrounded Stapley's plane and was swirling around inside the cockpit. The smell was almost unbearably acrid. The cockpit was still open although the outside temperature was about zero.

Thinking quickly and worried that if he plane was on fire he could explode in the midst of his flight—and possibly set off their ordnance—Stapley gunned his engine and taxied—quickly—out into the middle of a nearby parking area. The heavy smoke kept him from noticing that he had stopped the heavily smoking aircraft close to a C-46 transport aircraft that was loaded—with infantry troops. The C-46 pilots had seen the F-51 taxi by, start its run up, begin to belch heavy smoke, and then taxi quickly with its load of bombs and rockets, right over to a spot adjacent to their aircraft.

Stapley got out of the "burning" aircraft in record time, bounded down the wing, jumped onto the paved surface, and

legged it away from the smoking aircraft as fast as he could..

The C-46 pilots decided to evacuate their aircraft—on the double—and run down the aisle toward the door yelling: "Get out of here. That plane's on fire and might blow up any second."

The reaction by the troops was immediate—and predictable—a hell-for-leather exodus in the direction of the rear door that normally needed a wheeled step ramp for entry and exit. The "contents" of the C-46 poured down the aisle, paused only momentarily at the door, then leaped "lemming-like" onto the tarmac. There could have been many injuries, but aside from scrapes and bruises, only one trooper broke his leg as a result of the panicked exit.

Meanwhile, Stapley had reached a safe distance and turned around to watch his plane burn or explode. But with the engine stopped, the smoke quickly dissipated and then was gone entirely. Cautiously, he and the ground crew checked out the bird and eventually found the problem: coolant had overflowed onto the hot manifolds; hence, the smoke. The run up prior to take off had heated the manifolds up enough to cause the spilled oil to smoke.

The Operations Flight Line at K-46 where a C-46 and two C-47s are parked. The 18th Fighter-Bomber Wing used the cargo planes to shuttle supplies, equipment and personnel back and forth between K-10 (Chinhae) and K-46 (Hoengsong). "Once in a while, they would haul a group of pilots up from K-10 to K-46 instead of having them fly a plane up themselves," Budd Stapley recalled. The take off would be relatively uneventful for the unsuspecting C-47 pilot. Once in the air however, the F-51 pilots would begin to have a little fun with the C-47 pilot. "We would slowly...slowly...get together in a group and slowly...slowly move towards the tail of the aircraft." The unsuspecting C-47 pilot would begin to twirl the knob of the trim tab setting to help keep the aircraft's tail up. About the time the pilot had finished trimming up the cargo plane, the 67th pilots grouped in the tail would begin working their way towards the front of the aircraft, again forcing the pilot to constantly retrim the aircraft. Usually, about the time the fighter pilots had arrived in the forward part of the aircraft the C-47 pilot would finally "get it." Sometimes they retaliated by waggling the stick to make the tail of the aircraft flop up and down, back and forth, throwing the miscreants all over themselves and down the aisle of the airplane. It was all part of trying to have some fun in the face of the harrowing reality of war. (Urquhart)

Gooney Bird Forgot Call Sign. *"One morning, right around day break, everyone was awakened by the anti-aircraft guns firing," Donald R. Smith recalled. "We had 20-mm and 40-mm anti-aircraft stationed on the hills around K-46. Needless to say, everyone ran outside and headed for the trenches. After a few minutes, we realized there were no aircraft in the area but someone did see a lonely Gooney Bird (C-47) flying in circles a mile or so north of K-46. Seems he had forgotten to turn on his IFF or had forgotten the call sign for the day. Anyway, he stayed out there until he was identified."*

Captain Joe Peterburs catching up with the news after a mission in March 1952 at K-46. (Peterburs)

Capt. Joe Peterburs poses at K-46 with house boy Kim at "Home." (Peterburs)

In the Spring of 1952, Col. Joe Peterburs recalled, *Stars and Stripes* Newspaper published an article about a couple of Russian YAK's—World War Two propeller-driven fighters. The article described how the YAK's flew into South Korea on a combat mission—and were promptly shot down. "The article went on and on about the stupidity of the enemy in sending these old WWII aircraft against us. I guess *Stars and Stripes* didn't know that we were sending old WWII aircraft into battle every day—all the way to the Yalu," he recalled.

Captain Joe Peterburs, a 27-year old fighter pilot, arrived in the Korean theater on 26 December 1951 and was assigned to the 12th Fighter-Bomber Squadron until 6 July 1952.

After passing through Japan for "processing," he was ordered to report to the 12th Squadron, then based at K-10, Chinhae, near Pusan, SK.

Peterburs had not flown a P-51 since the day he was shot down over Germany on 10 April 1945, nor had he flown any other type fighter aircraft since that date. Yet, here he was reporting to a fighter-bomber squadron flying an average of 500-700 combat missions each month in F-51 Mustangs.

"I guess like riding a bike you don't forget how," he recalled. He flew three solo flights in the F-51 of about six hours flying time and then began flying combat missions. "Our forward operating base was at K-46—at Wonju—close to the DMZ."

When the wing found out that Peterburs family had two brothers that had been killed in action they tried to relieve him from flying combat and assigned him to the finance office. "I strongly objected and got my way," he recalled, and went on to fly 76 combat missions over North Korea—many to the Yalu River bordering China.

"At K-10 we got a room in a barracks where most of my belongings were kept. I don't think I spent more than two or three weeks total time at K-10. At K-46 [Hoengsong] it was tent city—an almost exact duplicate of the setting in the TV program "mash." I shared a tent with two other guys and the tent was heated by a pot-bellied stove. I spent almost all of my more than six months in Korea at K-46. A big change from the open barracks I lived in during WWII and a far cry from what the pilots lived in during Vietnam."

On several missions, Peterburs sustained heavy battle damage, including being wounded in the face by small arms fire on 28 May 1952. "I was strafing enemy troops in trenches. On my rocket run a small caliber bullet came through the canopy, grazed my helmet and bounced off the armor plate behind my head. It shattered my canopy, which in turn splattered my face with pieces of Plexiglass, and my face was bleeding profusely. My wingman had lost his radio so I could not contact him. I had him join up on my wing and we headed back to base. Not knowing of my difficulties he peeled off and landed first. Of course, I had notified the base of my difficulties so when my wingman landed they thought it was me and the ambulance and fire engines were following him. I landed without fanfare and taxied to my parking spot. I had my head down in the cockpit after I parked. When my crew chief got on the wing (not knowing anything was wrong), I looked up and he saw my face covered in blood. He was so startled he almost broke something falling off the wing. Eventually things got squared away and the flight surgeon spent the next several hours picking Plexiglass out of my face. I was flying combat again by May 31st."

Combat missions for the 18th Group were usually one of three types, Peterburs recalled.

Interdiction—"Going after known targets such as rail lines, troops in trenches, artillery, and supply depots."

Close air support—"Supporting our troops in contact with enemy troops, usually under the control of a forward air controller."

Combat air patrol/rescue support—"We were airborne 4-5 hours at a time

Capt. Joe Peterburs and *Lt. James Hambrick* survey wreckage from a Mustang crash in Spring 1952. (Peterburs)

Captain Joe Peterburs prepares for take off on a mission from K-46 in April 1952. (Peterburs)

On the ground the crew chief owned the Mustang. Lt. James M. Hambrick of the 12th Squadron signs off a mission with his Crew Chief. (Peterburs)

465

A pilot from the South African Two Squadron returns from a mission with empty bomb and rocket racks. (Stapley)

waiting for targets of opportunity, unexpected close air support, or support of choppers doing rescue work. It was not unusual to fly two or three missions a day. I had one two week period during which I flew two missions each day—and one day I flew three. We were fairly close to the front lines so our missions were short (between 1 and 2 hours) except for CAP. My longest mission was four hours and 50 minutes. It was a CAP that turned into rescue support during which one of the members of my flight was KIA. My total combat time for 76 missions was 140 hours and 20 minutes while in Europe it was 266 hours and 45 minutes for 49 missions," he remembered.

Another type of mission flown by the 18th Group, Peterburs remembered was a "hammer" mission. "The 67th Tactical Reconnaissance Wing was also flying F-51's for photo reconnaissance. When they would pick up a lucrative target they would have the guy that did the photo recce rendezvous with one of our flights and lead us to the target. Of course, they were unarmed but they would bring us right into the target, low level and all. I would say that of all the missions I flew these were the most productive."

"Another type of mission we flew was really the pits—Main supply route (MSR) patrol," Peterburs recalled. "There were several MSR's leading to Panmunjom and we got the job of patrolling them. The Communists were allowed to drive convoys of trucks down the MSR's as long as they were flying a red flag (what other kind). We were not allowed to attack the convoys flying the red flag. Instead, we were supposed to go down and check for the flag. However, there was no rule that they couldn't fire at us. We lost several pilots on this misadventure. They also placed a restricted zone around Panmunjom that we were not allowed to fly through under any circumstance. Anyone entering the area regardless of reason (plane shot up etc.), would be court-martialed," Peterburs explained.

To Peterburs and other pilots who had fought in both WWII and Korea, there were major differences between their experiences. "In pictures of WWII fighter pilots you can see the air of jauntiness and bravado exude from their faces," explained. "They were invincible—the best training and equipment that one could ask for. We were ready and able to engage the enemy at any time and place and we did."

In Korea, the F-51 pilots were a different lot, he said. "Older, more serious about the tough job they had to do (all guts and no glory). Most had no close air support, bombing, napalming or rocket training. We were flying probably the most vulnerable piece of equipment in the inventory for the job it was doing. Whoever decided that the F-51 with its vulnerable air/coolant system would be an acceptable close air support aircraft was nuts. In addition to its vulnerability, it had no significant weapons carrying capacity. They tried strapping two, 1,000-lb bombs on once—it was a disaster. I would watch Navy SBD's on a bomb run and they couldn't get rid of their entire load in one run. I, for one, would have been a hell of a lot happier, more effective, and safer with my ass strapped to a P-47 with its radial engine, multiple and heavy bomb carrying capability and especially the eight .50-cal. guns," he said.

Pilot-to-Combat Process "Totally Unacceptable"

Within the first month that Captain Joe Peterburs was a part of the 12th Squadron, "it became painfully apparent that the way pilots were introduced to Korean combat was totally unacceptable. We were getting

---

"We were flying probably the most vulnerable piece of equipment in the inventory for the job it was doing. Whoever decided that the F-51 with its vulnerable air/coolant system would be an acceptable close air support aircraft was nuts." Col. Joe Peterburs

guys with minimum to no time in the F-51 or jet pilot school graduates, as well as guys like me that had not flown a fighter in years. They would get a minimum check out, and then off to combat. As a result, our non-combat and combat losses were running much too high for new pilots.

In his first several months in the Squadron, Peterburs' flight "got a guy that had several hundred hours in the F-51 but hadn't flown it in a number of years. On his second flight he was doing some aerobatics and the bird got away from him and he went in (was killed). He had a fuselage tank that was half full and I guess he forgot the instability this caused."

Three other pilots "let the torque get the best of them and pranged on take off." A young Second Lieutenant joined the Foxy Few right out of F-84 transition. "After a long check out—over 15 hours, I turned him loose. On his first mission I observed him on his bomb run. He looked like he was in a 45 degree slip. Bombs and rockets were going all over the place—except on target."

When Peterburs debriefed him after the mission he said, "Well I put my feet on the floor – off the rudders when I started my run, like I would in an F-84."

Back to training!!!

After Peterburs gave him several more rides in the "piggy back"—the two seated F-51—they "turned him loose again. He pranged on his next solo take off when he let the torque get the best of him." Peterburs was able to get him transferred to administrative duty flying C-47's. "After that I knew I had to do something to help these guys," Peterburs related.

He set to work and developed an "introduction to combat" flying training program for the Group and sold it to the group commander. The program consisted of ten flights that included, low-level navigation, aerobatics, rocket firing, dive-bombing and napalm drops. The last two flights were actual combat missions that either Peterburs or his training officers would select and get cleared by higher headquarters. The combat flights included one trainee in a flight of experienced combat

Gear Up. A "Flying Cheetah" Mustang takes off from from K-46. (Peterburs)

pilots. One was a dive-bombing mission, the other a low level napalm drop. As a result of this program, both combat and non-combat losses in the Group were significantly reduced. For his efforts in creating and managing this life-saving training program, Peterburs was awarded the Bronze Star.

The armament carried by the Group's Mustangs was either two 500-lb bombs and 4 high velocity 5-inch rockets, or two 650-lb napalm tanks and 4 high velocity 5-inch rockets. "Of course, we always had a full load of .50-cal ammunition for our six machine guns," Peterburs recalled.

The combat tour in mid-1952 was 75 missions. Captain Joe Peterburs flew 76 missions and returned home on 15 July 1952. During his tour with the 12th Squadron, Peterburs served as a flight commander, assistant group operations officer, and group-training officer. As Group training officer he developed a training program of ten missions that would familiarize new pilots with our tactics as well as dive bombing, napalm dropping and rocket firing techniques. Their last 2 train-

ing missions were combat missions with an experienced combat pilot. The program significantly reduced the losses being suffered by the 18th Group with new pilots.

After completing his combat tour, Peterburs was rotated to Tyndall AFB, Florida, where he served as Operations Officer for a support unit flying F-51H's. He flew the Mustang into 1954 and eventually accumulated over 800 hours in the bird.

A 39th Squadron Mustang touches down after a mission in Spring 1952. (Peterburs)

Even the roar of Merlin engines could be temporarily overcome by bagpipes. Here Flight Lieutenant Bobby Locke, 2 Squadron SAAF leads an impromptu parade down the street in front of the K-46 Operations Offices. (Holmes)

Flighing Cheetahs. *Two flight officers with the 2nd South African "Flying Cheetahs"Squadron, probably taken at the K-10 passenger terminal. (Left) Lt. A.S. Van der Spuy--"Topper 6," his call sign during WWII in Italy. At right, Lieutenant Colonel R. "Dick" Clifton, Commanding Officer of No 2 Squadron. The pilot in the background is 1st Lt. Melvin Sousa, 67th Squadron. The "Flying Cheetahs'" were attached to the 18th Fighter-Bomber Wing. "Dick was a regular officer and after retiring he went to live at the coast in Knysna where he continued with his favourite sport, fishing," recalled Brigadier Jock Lello. Clifton died on July 1, 1993. Following his combat duty with U.N. forces in Korea, Van der Spuy joined South African Airways and would eventually retire as a Boeing captain. "He was a very popular person at parties as he was an excellent guitar play and had a host of air force songs." Brigadier Jock Lello remembered years later. Van der Spuy died on December 1, 1996. The "Flying Cheetahs" were highly regarded by their U.S. Air Force comrades in arms. "Good men, all," summed up 67th pilot Wilfred "Budd" Stapley years later. (A. H. Connors, Jr.)*

April 1952

"The "ever growing intensity and accuracy of enemy flak has taken a heavy toll in aircraft and pilots recently."

12th Squadron Monthly Report

Gen. Matthew Ridgeway is greeted by Lt. Gen. Frank F. Everest, Commanding General of the Fifth Air Force, upon his arrival at an air base somewhere in Korea on April 3, 1952. (NARA)

18th Group Combat Operations

In April, the 18th Group's "continuing effort" remained the rail interdiction program." Also continued was the tactic of "flying group formations on interdiction missions as initiated in March..."

The 12th and 67th Fighter-Bomber Squadrons were approximately 16 percent over authorized strength in pilots. At the time the 39th Fighter Interceptor Squadron was transferred, 45 pilots were assigned to each squadron. However, there were fewer than 16 aircraft per squadron. Pilots were averaging only nine sorties per month. With the departure of the 39th, "all aircraft were distributed between the two

remaining (U.S.) squadrons, giving an average of 23 each. In addition, an administrative request was initiated to halt the flow of new pilots."

The Group lost eight aircraft in April, with four pilots listed as MIA. "All losses were due to small arms fire and automatic weapons, or to unknown causes with ground fire as probable cause. There were no minor casualties," the Group reported.

The Group was preparing to detach the 39th Fighter Interceptor Squadron and to deal with the personnel issues the transfer would bring, including a shortage of 55 men from the maintenance section.

The "on line maintenance" was now excellent. Improvements had been made in forecasting repair completions. The

Group needed the more accurate estimates for mission planning.

As spring progressed, the days were lengthening and that necessitated establishing a shift schedule for all airmen working in the Intelligence Section. "Early morning missions and last light recce's put the Intelligence Section on a working basis from 0300 to 2300 hours daily." However, the Group now had sufficient enlisted personnel for the first time to cope with the extended day's activities in all three of the divisions, including: target, operational intelligence and administration. [1]

The Group's target section was busy cataloging photographic reports "on all special rail targets." FAF began assigning targets by code designation on specific sections of rail covering rail complexes in North Korea. The Target Section prepared each target in an individual file "complete with annotated photographs, flak reports and detailed maps. The advance preparation made it possible to furnish sufficient information for operational planning shortly after receipt of the early warning on the day prior to the mission."

The reassignment of the 39th Squadron did help alleviate "the critical shortage in Evasion and Escape materials." The Group set up procedures for a monthly inventory of all E and E equipment. Seat type parachutes were replaced in April for two primary reasons. The first was the difficulty a pilot encountered with leaving the aircraft in an emergency. The other was the inability to attach a life raft to a seat type parachute.

Warmer weather brought problems with tar. As the days warmed up, the tar was "slung on the shock strut by the wheels," then collected grit and dust which

Capt. Joe Peterburs taxies toward a take off position from the R&R ramp at K-46, his Mustang fully loaded with bombs and rockets. (Peterburs)

wore the packing rings and scratched the polished surface of the strut." This problem was handled locally by manufacturing "strut boots of canvas." By the end of April,

about half the Mustangs had strut boots.

On April 9, 1952, Production Line Maintenance (PLM) with the 18th Group was begun at K-10. The 67th Squadron's

Monthly Summary

Two major ground engagements were brought on by communist forces that attacked positions held by the 1st Marine Division south of Panmunjom, and later assaulted the 1st Commonwealth Division north of Korangpo-ri. Friendly units held their ground during both night attacks, and ground activity tapered off for the remainder of April.

The FEAF rail interdiction campaign—Operation Saturate—continued with missions "concentrated on two main railroads from Manchuria, the Namsi-dong-Sinanju and the Huichon-Kunu-ri lines. Far East Air Forces rendered the Sinuiju-Sinanju line unserviceable for most of April. In response to rail interdiction efforts, the enemy erected formidable antiaircraft defenses, especially along the Sinanju-Pyongyang line."

[On Feb. 25, 1952, FAF director of intelligence strongly recommended the implementation of "Operation Saturate," an around-the-clock concentration of available railway-interdiction effort against short segments of railway track, including Kunu-ri to Huichon, Sunchon to Samdong-ni, Sinanju to Namsi-dong and Pyongyang to Namchonjom. Operation Saturate was put into effect on March 3rd. Attacks were sustained throughout April and May. Soon after the operation began, flak batteries had been put into place along nearly all rail lines. Losses of tactical aircraft were high.]

Fifth Air Force F-51, F-80, F-84, and B-26 aircraft "generally flew daylight armed reconnaissance and interdiction sorties against enemy railroads, vehicles, bunkers, and troop concentrations, and a smaller number of close support sorties. At night, B-26s of the 3 BW and 452 BW hit enemy railroads and vehicles. Other fighters under Fifth Air Force's operational control included ROK Air Force and SAAF F-51, RAAF MK-8, and USMC F4U, F7F, F9F, and AD-2 aircraft. These concentrated on armed reconnaissance and interdiction but also flew search and rescue and close air support, assisted by T-6 spotter aircraft. Fifth Air Force lost seventeen aircraft to enemy ground fire."

Sabre jets flew daytime counter-air and escort missions…and "destroyed thirty-seven MIGs in aerial combat. Fifth Air Force lost four F-86s and one F-80 in air-to-air engagements. The 6160th ABG rescue boat detachment performed 128 missions.

Citing "shortages of fighter-bombers," the FEAF announced it was assigning "Sabres of the 4th FIW and 51st FIW a new commitment - the armed reconnaissance of enemy lines of communication." [1]

Adapted from U.S. Air Force Historical Research Agency. January 2002. The U.S. Air Force's First War: Korea 1950-1953 Significant Events. April 1952. http://www.au.af.mil/au/afhra/wwwroot/korean_war/korean_war_chronology/kwc_1952.html

then follows it down to K-10 to help work on it when it goes into the PLM hangar," the unit report noted.

[Note: Master Sergeant Thomas "Red" Ryder, a 67th crew chief at the time, recalled that "this did not happen."]

The Group reported that morale was "generally improving." The highest morale detriment was the "crowded quarters at K-46." However, the condition was reported as "corrected" with the construction of sufficient housing "to make comfortable facilities available to all personnel."

"Bomb Dump" *at K-46. (Peterburs)*

Radio Shop was enlarged and re-designated as the PLM Communications Maintenance Section. Personnel were re-shuffled for maximum maintenance efficiency both at K-10 and K-46. Equipment, spares, and personnel were "pooled" to help overall efficiency.

Each aircraft now had a "permanent Crew Chief" who followed the airplane back and forth between K-46 and K-10. "The man crews the plane while it is at K-46,

Rearming Mustangs *of the 67th Squadron at K-46. (Black)*

Operational Tactics

Operational tactics for the 18th Fighter-Bomber Group remained "essentially" the same in April. However some "relatively new SOP's devised in Fifth Air Force and the 18th Group" were reported that "directly affected" the squadrons and were "worthy of mention."

"Excessive combat damage" brought about a change in SOP that restricted flight flights to only two passes at a target during close support missions—a "bombing and strafing pass followed by a rocket pass."

Downed pilot capping procedures were also changed "in hopes that the change will cut down the losses suffered on capping missions. The "ever growing intensity and accuracy of enemy flak has taken a heavy toll in aircraft and pilots recently," the 12th reported, "and our tactics have taken a more cautious course as a direct result. The actual capping of a downed pilot must remain to the discretion of the capping flight." However, the flight was being asked to "circle at a safe altitude, keeping an eye on the downed pilot's position and keeping contact with him over the bail-out radio which every pilot must carry." No attacking passes were to be made "unless the capping flight has complete command of the situation." The 12th reported taking part in several successful capping missions in April using "similar tactics."

Group rail cutting missions had become the "rule of the day as a result of a comparatively new policy of the Fifth Air Force which has proven quite effective." A small section of railroad track would be assigned as a target and then "bombed all day long until there is virtually nothing to bomb other than the bomb holes already there." The missions were in Group strength and proved "very effective." Railroads that had been out of commission for only a few hours at the most, were now being knocked out for many days. "Our missions have extended much farther north than in the recent past and last an average of about two and a half hours apiece. The intense damage to a relatively small section of track rather than indi-

(Above) The Control Tower at K-46. (Holmes) (

(Above) A 67th Squadron Mustang prepares to take off on a combat mission from K-46. (Holmes)

Headquarters of the 18th Fighter-Bomber Group at K-46. (Cranston)

vidual cuts over a large section has thwarted the enemy's very efficient repair system," the 12th Squadron noted.

"Truly the fabulous Fightin' 39th"

The 39th Fighter-Interceptor Squadron had been assigned operationally to the 18th Fighter-Bomber Wing since May 14, 1951. As it completed its 21st month of combat in Korea, it was told to turn over its weary

Mustangs to the 12th and 67th Squadrons as of April 19, 1952. On April 21st all aircraft assigned to the 39th FIS were transferred to the 12th and 67th Squadrons.

Morale in the 39th FIS "was at an all time high. The men were very thrilled and excited with the idea of becoming a jet outfit," the 39th reported that month. The Squadron was taking with it a "vast storehouse of knowledge the flying and maintaining the F-51 has given us. The F-86 is a great aircraft. We feel certain that with the fine Esprit de Corps and 'Yankee' inge-

472

nuity the organization has we will continue to prove the 39th Fighter Interceptor Squadron is truly 'The Fabulous Fightin' 39th.'"

"The morale of the enlisted men rises and falls with the work load..."

"Through sheer determination and the excellent leadership throughout the squadron, the 67th was able to get the most out of the equipment on hand."

Captain Victor E. Bocquin and Lt. Col. Julian Crow were two of the happiest pilots that month. Both completed 100 missions during April. Crow was soon succeeded by Major Stanley A. Long as Commander of the 67th Squadron, which now included 45 officers. During the month, a major influx of enlisted personnel took place. Thirty-one airmen arrived and only six departed, leaving a total enlisted strength for the squadron of 158 at the beginning of April. Despite the increase in enlisted strength and a decrease in pilot strength, "neither one as yet, is at a suitable point," Major Long reported. 2

The overall qualifications of the reporting replacement personnel were "improving," however the "squadron veterans are still working double time in doing their own job and teaching, and supervising the work of the newer men."

Rail cuts (105) were clearly a high priority target during April. Artillery (18 pieces), buildings (12), bunkers (54), roads (3 cuts), tunnels (1), rolling stock (3), and troops (119 KIA) rounded out the claims made by the 43 pilots flying combat missions that month.

Transportation was another problem Long mentioned in his monthly report. "There is a definite lack of transportation at K-46 Air Base. The increase of assigned planes and personnel at this base has brought about this situation. At this date the Engineering Section has been unable

Warming Up. 67th Squadron Mustangs prepare to take off from K-10 in Spring 1952. (Ramsdell)

to obtain additional transportation. The maintenance section changed four engines, completed eight major inspections and 22 intermediate inspections. To "better utilize the maintenance equipment and to get the most out of the maintenance personnel," all Squadron personnel in this section are now at K-46. Any rear echelon maintenance is done by the Group PLM system at K-10."

Rotation was still the biggest morale factor in any of the units, Long reported. "The morale of the enlisted men rises and falls with the work load. The more recognition for their efforts and achievements the higher the morale." Long reported that the "maintenance personnel have been shown the pilot's combat film. This gives them a better idea of the good results of their effort." In turn, the pilot's morale

was greatly increased "when the number of assigned aircraft increased from 10 to 19" as a result of an additional nine aircraft acquired from the 39th Squadron when they left the group.

New uniform regulations at K-10 "tended to lessen the morale of the pilots." This vague wording reflected the pilot's unhappiness with strict enforcement of uniform regulations. Many of them had adopted combinations or items of apparel that were most certainly not within uniform regulations.

The Post Exchange at Chinhae was "adequate," but "the P.X. only comes up to K-46 once every other week. P.X. facilities at least once a week at K-46 would greatly improve the morale of the enlisted personnel."

Six pilots of the 39th FIS make final preparations for a mission from K-46 in April 1952. Their helmets--blue with a white 3-leaf clover--mark them as pilots of the "Blinkernose Squadron." (Krakovsky)

Combat Damage

Restricts 12th Squadron Flights

In April 1952, the 12th Squadron was flying its combat missions from the K-46 "staging base" near Hoengsong, Korea.

The Commanding Officer of the 12th was Lt. Col. Joseph T. Crane, Jr. Major Stanley Long left that month to become the CO of the 67th Squadron.

At that time, the 12th had a total of 25 Mustangs assigned, somewhat more than usual "due to the departure of the 39th Fighter Interceptor Squadron and the subsequent pooling of its aircraft among the remaining squadrons."

Some changes in tactics were noted that month that were "worthy of mention." Due to "excessive combat damage in the past, our flights are restricted to only two passes at a target on close support missions, a bombing and strafing pass followed by a rocket pass."

Missions for the 12th (and other squadrons of the 18th FBG) "have extended much farther north than in the recent past and last an average of about two and a half hours apiece. The intensive damage to a relatively small section of track rather than individual cuts over a large section has thwarted the enemy's very efficient repair system."

Like other squadrons in the 18th Fighter-Bomber Group, the 12th relied on a training program that "has been taken over entirely by the Group…a thorough training program has been established. A new man now receives an average of six training missions with ample practice in gunnery, bombing, aerobatics, cross-country and night flying. All indications show that this training should prove quite effective and the pilots should be thoroughly competent before joining a combat flight."

During April, the "Foxy Few" flew a total of 414 sorties, averaging nearly ten sorties per pilot. In the process, some 900

Mustangs being repaired at K-46. The lighter areas pocking the hills behind the mix of 67th and 12th Squadron F-51s are shell holes, Earl Ramsdell noted on this photograph. (Ramsdell)

combat hours were logged, or approximately 22 hours per pilot during that month. Because K-46 was so near the "bomb line," most of the hours were logged "on the enemy side."

The 12th lost two pilots that month, including: Lt. Allan S. Bettes (sic) and Lawrence Wolfe. The unit history report notes that "Lt. Bettes (sic) was lost on a rail-cutting mission" on April 15th and Lt. Wolfe "went down diving a close support mission" on April 26th. It also notes that Lt. Bettis was "rescued by SA-16 after crash landing his aircraft on a mud flat in North Korea on April 23.

"In all we lost three aircraft to combat and one to reasons other than combat. We suffered an unfortunate number of minor accidents during the month, only one serious enough to destroy a plane completely, however."

"Morale, never a problem in the 12th, has, if anything, improved with the assignment of additional aircraft to the Squadron and the arrival of Spring and warm weather," the report concluded. "All show high spirits and pride in their work and their Squadron. The working hours are long and living conditions are poor, especially at K-46, where the comforts of home are sadly lacking. However, rest and recreation leaves and three points a month toward rotation more than suffice to keep spirits alive."

Endnotes

[1] USAFHRA. *Monthly Historical Report, 18th Fighter-Bomber Group,* April 1952. p. 5.

[2] USAFHRA. *Monthly Historical Report, 67th Fighter-Bomber Squadron,* April 1952, p. 1.

Staff Sergeant Robert T. Clark and Technical Sergeant Roy Pylant, Jr. at K-46. (Pylant)

474

Combat Statistics

18ᵗʰ F-B Wing

April 1952

Average No. A/C Assigned
47

Total Flying Time
2,687

Percent of Aircraft in Commission
50%

Percent of Aircraft AOCP
5%

Combat Sorties Flown by Wing
1,027

12ᵗʰ Squadron Sorties
414

39ᵗʰ FIS Sorties
465

67ᵗʰ Squadron Sorties
417

2 Squadron Sorties
347

A/C Lost to Combat
6

Pilots lost
7

Fuel Consumed

187,985 gals.

Ordnance Expended

.50-cal. Rounds
442,769

Rockets
998

Napalm Bombs
72

500-lb. GP Bombs
1,622

Note: Figures and totals may differ in some categories due to differences in numbers provided by each component.

Significant Events

Apr. 5 Captain Charles L. Tabor was forced to make an emergency landing at Chodo due to damage to his aircraft while on a search mission.

"While on a low level search mission, Lt. Grover C. Crocker, flying number three position in 'Put Put Willie' flight, was hit by 20-mm and .50-cal. AA fire at the coast just north of the Chinnampo Estuary. Coolant sprayed back over his canopy as he climbed out toward the sea and after about three minutes the engine froze. Lt. Crocker bailed out, at 2,000 feet, and landed safely on the mud flats about 300 yards from shore. His plane crashed about 100 yards from him and he moved over behind it directing 'Willie' One and Two against enemy troops and AA positions with the URC-4 radio. An F-84 flight was diverted to assist in capping the downed pilot, while 'Willie' One and Two, both of which had also been hit by enemy ground fire, left the area to escort the helicopter in to pick up Lt. Crocker. The helicopter picked up Lt. Crocker and returned to Chodo. 'Willie One and Two made it back to K-46 and landed safely. Total losses: one F-51." [1]

April 21: Capt. Jack Shepard was flying as the element leader in a four-Mustang flight escorting a rescue helicopter near Sonchon back to friendly territory. As he attacked an enemy gun position, his right external napalm tank was shot off. "Disregarding the damage to his aircraft, he pressed his attack at minimum altitude, successfully dive-bombing the enemy position with his remaining external tank." Shepard continued pressing his minimum altitude attacks on additional enemy positions--making several mock attacks even after expending his ammunition "in order to protect the helicopter on its return flight." Shepard was awarded the Silver Star Medal for this mission.

Apr. 22 Citing shortages of fighter-bombers, Fifth Air Force assigned Sabres of the 4ᵗʰ FIW and 51ˢᵗ FIW a new commitment - the armed reconnaissance of enemy lines of communication.

Also in April, Major Stanley A. Long succeeded Lt. Col. Julian Crow as Commander of the 67ᵗʰ Fighter-Bomber Squadron. Born in August 1918, during WWII Long flew with the 11ᵗʰ AF in the Aleutian Theater as CO of the 54ᵗʰ Fighter Squadron flying the P-38 Lightning aircraft. During 100 missions in the Lightning, he scored

Major Stanley A. Long, Capt. Kelly and Capt. Elliot D. Ayer in a jeep in front of the 67ᵗʰ Squadron's Quonset headquarters at K-46. Ayer was selected as How Flight Leader for the 67ᵗʰ Squadron in June 1952. He distinguished himself in that role until he was killed in action on July 25, 1952. (Photo courtesy Ione R. Lenhart)

three kills on Japanese aircraft. Between WWII and the Korean War, he was the owner and operator of "Long's Air Activities" and taught flying courses to civilian pilots.

Combat Losses in April

2nd Lt. Gus J. Baransky, 2 Squadron SAAF, was KIA on 20 April 1952. Lt. Baransky was flying as No. Three man a rescue flight—FILTER RESCUE"—of four F-51s that had been circling Cho-do Island for about three hours. The Flight was led by 1st Lt. Wilfred "Budd" Stapley, of the 67th Fighter-Bomber Squadron.

During this mission, Stapley's No. 3 man, a South African pilot with Two Squadron—1st Lt. Gus Baransky— "went down in flames…I never saw an airplane blow up so completely like that…it just became a mass of flames…all you could see was the wingtips…for a moment…we were right on the deck and he didn't have a chance."

Stapley found a fire in the vicinity of where Gus Baransky had been circling, and not wanting to lose sight of the earlier pilot they were 'capping', he went down to inspect the fire and found no sign of life, nor did he observe a parachute. They circled the area and were unable to find any sign of Lieutenant Baransky.

1st Lt. Allen Shields Bettis, 12th Fighter-Bomber Squadron. Lt. Col. Joseph T. Crane, Jr., USAF, CO of the 12th FBS wrote to Lt. Bettis' family on 15 April 1952, "I know that you are terribly upset and in an effort to relieve some of the uncertainty and anguish I will attempt to reconstruct as well as possible the events leading up to Al's accident. Al departed K-46 Air Base in Korea at 16:45 on April 13, 1952 with a flight of four aircraft. Their mission was to bomb rail lines 6 miles Southeast of Chongju on the Northwest coast of North Korea. The flight to the target was uneventful and the dive bomb run was started. From pilot reports Al's aircraft was seen, apparently hit by anti-aircraft fire and out of control. The aircraft was observed to crash with no evidence of parachute. The

pilots with him immediately searched the adjoining area of the crash but no signs of life were observed."

Another account was written on 14 April 1953, by Major General John H. Mc-Cormack, USAF, Director of Military Personnel, noted, "The review just completed concerning your son discloses that he was a member of a four plane flight of F-51 aircraft which departed Hoengsong Airdome, Korea, on 13 April 1952, for a rail cutting mission in the vicinity of Chongju, North Korea. The flight arrived over the target without incident and began the attack. Lieutenant Bettis' plane was seen as he started his bombing pass, but continuous observation of his F-51 was not maintained because of the prevailing conditions. As the flight leader pulled up from his pass, he noticed your son's aircraft in an inverted spin at an altitude of 5000 feet. He immediately radioed Lieutenant Bettis to bail out but received no response. The F-51 momentarily appeared to be under control but upon descending to 2000 feet, it began spinning again and crashed to the ground, exploding upon impact. An aerial search of the crash area by the accompanying pilots failed to find any trace of your son or his parachute and to date no further information has been received which might clarify his status." Another account specified Major Bruce R. Clark as the group leader that day.

Captain John Adams Dille, Jr., 18th Fighter-Bomber Group pilot from Roanoke, Virginia was KIA on 13 April 1952.

1st Lt. J. O. Holtzhausen, 2nd Squadron SAAF was KIA on 10 April 1952. 'Holtsie' Holtzhausen was flying No. 2 in a pre-briefed flight of four aircraft whose mission was to attack railroad stock at YE5004. As the flight neared the target it was formed up in starboard echelon, and Flight Leader Mouton noted that both his No. 2 and No. 3 pilots were in their proper positions.

Low clouds and haze required the flight to bomb from a lower than usual altitude.

Following the attack, as the aircraft headed to the designated rendezvous point, Mouton radioed for them to check-in. Only No. 3 responded. Finally, No. 2 responded that he was joining a nearby U.S. Air Force flight. Upon his return to base, Mouton was advised that Lt. Holtzhausen had not returned with any other flight. Neither pilot nor aircraft were ever found.

1st Lt. Joel Orlander Rives, 67th Fighter-Bomber Squadron pilot from Birmingham, Alabama, was KIA 27 April 1952. While on a combat mission, his aircraft received a direct hit by anti-aircraft fire, crashed and burned.

1st Lt. William Charles Sankey, 67th Squadron pilot from Gettysburg, Pennsylvania, was KIA on 17 April 1952. First Lt. William C. Sankey, Jr., was "wounded in action when forced to abandon his aircraft while on a rescue mission. He "made a successful bailout near Chodo after his aircraft sustained major damage from enemy fire while returning from a RESCAP mission." His status was changed to MIA on April 27th.

1st Lt. Lawrence Ervin Wolfe, 12th Fighter-Bomber Squadron from Americus, Georgia was KIA on 26 April 1952--while on a combat mission, his aircraft dove into the target.

Endnotes
[1] USAFHRA. Unit history of the 39th FIS. April 1952. p. 4.

K-46/Hoengsong Air Field
Evolution of an advanced operating base into a permanent base

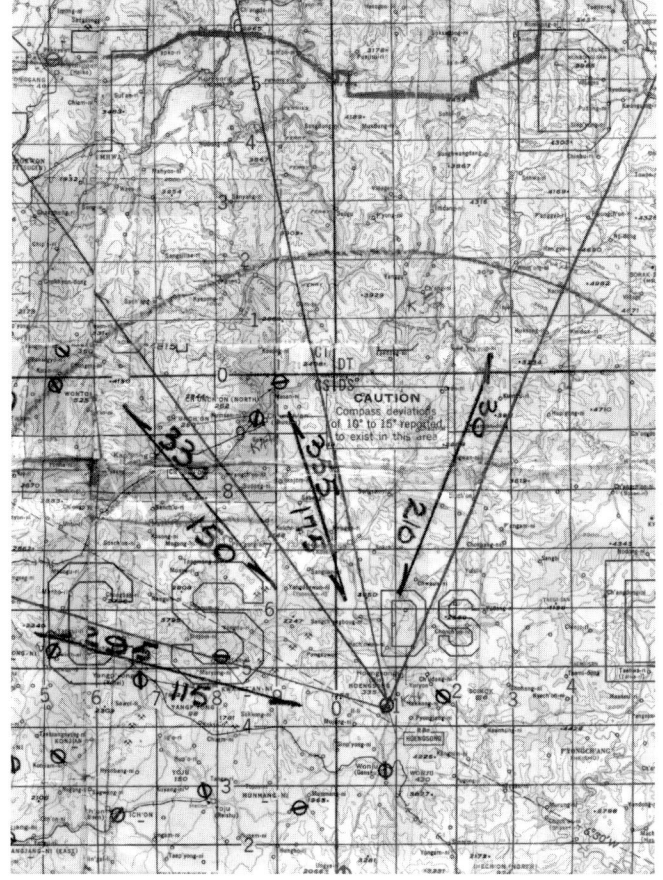

"Dead Man's Gulch" leading to K-46. (Peterburs)

K-46 Air Base near Hoengsong, SK was about ten miles north of Wonju in the central highlands of South Korea. (Above) Pilots flying from K-46 annotated their lap maps with lines of bearing to and from the base. Note the "Bomb Line" that zigzagged across the Korean Peninsula.   K-46 was ringed with mountains ranging from 2,000-3,000 feet. Pilots called the valley approach to the K-46 strip "Deadman's Gulch." (Corley)

An Air Policeman sentry at the K-46 front gate salutes Lt. Tim Urquhart as he crosses the road to the living quarters--tent city. (Urquhart)

"Aerial view" *of K-46 from a nearby mountain. (Cranston)*

Operations Complex *for the 18th Fighter-Bomber Group at K-46. The large building in center foreground is Group Operations. Other buildings (l-r) include: 39th Squadron Operations, 12th Squadron Operations, 67th Squadron Operations, and SAAF Operations. The sand bagged building is the briefing/debriefing room. (Peterburs) (Right inset) Operations Office of the 67th Fighter-Bomber Squadron at K-46 . (Cranston)*

When 18th Wing personnel were leaving the operations area and crossing the street to their living quarters (tents), they were greeted by numerous children--many orphaned by the war--who were there in hopes of some money, some candy, a cigarette or other item they could barter for food or necessities. "We would always have a candy bar for them, a meal (C- or K-rations), or something like that," Budd Stapley related years later. Korean children, many of them orphans, tried to survive the war years by living together in small bands near both K-10 and K-46. At K-10, near a air gunnery range, Air Force salvagers found children living in F-51 drop tanks that had been jettisoned and were no longer air worthy. That was when 18th Wing pilots decided to take a more direct role in helping the children.

A volunteer policy regarding the bar tab was instituted to ensure that at least ten percent of the money "passing through the bar" went to the local orphanage. In addition, Stapley reported, "we'd always throw our loose change in the donate jar for the orphanage and the kids." (Urquhart)

478

Panorama of living quarters area for the 18th Fighter-Bomber Wing at K-46 in Spring 1952. (Peterburs)

Officers Quarters at K-46. *Capt. Joe Peterburs stretches out on his bunk. (Peterburs)*

Officers Quarters *at K-46 were large tents with wooden floors. The tents were "conveniently" located on either side of the latrine--the large building in the center. "Got up at 5:30 to fly a plane back up here [K-46] from down south," Lt. Archie Connors wrote his mother, Eva. It sure was nice down there [K-10]. No snow and sheets to sleep on, even running water in the commodes. Speaking of commodes, it is just a trough with a box over it and a hole in the box. If you have to go early in the morning the smell knocks you out." (Urquhart)*

479

April Headlines from Truckbusters

Communist's Supply Lines Again Hard Hit by Mustangs

F-51 Mustangs of the 18th Fighter-Bomber Wing continued to direct their firepower toward the North Korean communists in the last two weeks and have marked up new records in the way of rail destruction. Our propeller driven 51's have concentrated their attacks on Red rail supply lines and for several days straight blasted the main lines between Chongju and Sinanju. Rail traffic in this area has been virtually paralyzed by the repeated attacks. Dive bombing planes of the 18th and other 5th AF Wings have severed rails in more than 250 separate places and knocked out

all rail bridges along the 22-mile stretch of track.

Other Mustangs of the 18th swept up the west coast to strike once again at the Unden Station area. The communist rail junction was already badly battered from continued bombings but pilots of our fighter squadrons claimed seven new rail cuts.

Near the end of last month our fighter-bombers were almost daily hampered by extremely poor flying weather and operation was more or less limited to close support work. Heavy anti-aircraft fire was thrown up in front of the low-flying close support fighters across the entire front but our pilots managed to pound front line enemy positions.

Operation Strangle

Fifth Air Force's "Operation Strangle" was designed to "cut off the main arteries of the enemy's supply and logistical system," the Truckbuster reported on April 15, 1952. Strangle, it claimed, had "continued unmolested since its initial mission."

The Mustangs of the 18th's squadrons had concentrated chiefly on rail interdiction roles in the overall scene, and "have met with continued success." When weather permitted, Mustang pilots had participated in strikes "beginning in the pre-dawn hours and extending into the last light of day."

On a recent mission into Northwest Korea, the Mustangs had hit rail line districts that had been "left alone by UN Air Forces for several weeks. Surprising the enemy, the Mustang jockeys rode in on the target, dropping 500-pound bombs and high velocity rockets that jarred honey-buckets for miles around. Twenty-nine effective cuts were counted, but delayed fuzings on other missiles precluded the possibility of other claims. In strafing actions, pilots brought back a log toll of eight KIA, and nine WIAs. On the coastal areas, several large sampans were attacked and one sunk. Four surface vessels sustained heavy battle damage. An interfering gun position was hit hard."

The advent of clearer skies and warmer, longer days held the "unspoken promise that the 18th will continue to bring back large claims of destruction on Communist targets. Fight-bombers attack Red positions all the day long, and night marauders take up the task when the sun has set," the Truckbuster explained.

Returning from a mission over North Korea in Spring 1952 (l-r) 1st Lt. David Merrill, Unknown, 1st Lt. Shirley B. Tubbs, 1st Lt. John Yingling and 1st Lt. Jack Shepard. (Shepard)

New record...

Crew Chief S/Sgt Norman Brousseau, A/2C Harold Hudren and A/3C Freeman Finley worked for two months on refining and improving the process followed to change the engine on an F-51. The usual time for the complex job was approximately 125 hours. Finley and his team "whizzed through the job in the breath taking time of 40 hours and 30 minutes." The men were honored by the Group and lauded by Capt. William Wakeham, maintenance supervisor. "I defy any other three men to perform the same job in a comparable length of time."

The *Truckbuster* noted, "The teamwork exhibited by these men, each of whom was from a different Squadron, reflects the attainment of cooperation that is possible at Dogpatch. The squadrons represented were the Foxy Few, Blinker Nose and the Red Scarfers."

New Titles...

In a "sweeping change designed to increase the dignity and respect accorded to its senior airmen," the Air Force restricted its non-commissioned officer status to the top three grades and revised the nomenclature of the lowest four enlisted ranks.

On April 1st, grades from sergeant to private were changed to:

Sergeant: Airman First Class
Corporal: Airman Second Class
Private: Basic Airman.

The change cut the noncom status from five grades to three and sliced the over-all percentage of requirements for noncoms from 77.45 percent to 34.11 percent. Under the former policy, three out of four airmen were noncoms.

The Air Force was attempting to return prestige and respect to noncom status.

Armorers align Mustang prior to boresighting machine guns. "Boresighting," explained former armorer Earl Ramsdell, "is to fire the guns to see if they are sighted in properly." (Ramsdell)

Five pilots from How Flight, 67th Squadron return from a mission in April 1952. (L-R) 2nd Lt. Joel O. ("Mutt") Rives, 1st Lt. Don ("Lucky") Drage, Capt. Shirley ("Wash") Tubbs, 1st Lt. Wilfred ("Flak") Stapley and 1st Lt. ("Mutt") McShane. "Strictly a publicity photograph," Stapley later recalled. Rives and McShane were "Mutt" and "Jeff" from the cartoon characters and their differences in height. Lt. Rives was KIA on 27 April 1952. (Krakovsky)

Jet Jockey Learns About Torque

by Wilfred "Budd" Stapley

We had a jet jockey that had been assigned...temporarily as it turned out...to our squadron because he couldn't handle high altitudes. He hadn't flown a prop aircraft since his days in the T-6. Although we kept telling him...warning him...'the '51 has torque'...he looked down his 'noses' at us because after all he was a 'jet jockey' and we were 'props.' He didn't listen to us.

On one of his first takeoffs, he put the power on too fast. The aircraft went out of control, veered to the left, hit an embankment, wiped out the gear, skidded along until it hit—and went through—a gas refueling truck, split it wide open, and went on to hit a big rock...I mean a rock so big we had an anti aircraft gun emplacement on top of it. It was about the size of a house, you know. When he finally spun around and stopped, his wings were off, the engine and tail were torn off, and it was only the cockpit lying there.

He got out of the aircraft somehow, ran away from it, turned around...and fainted.

**"My God, he's on fire," someone said
on the radio.**

In the midst of a dive-bombing run in early April, Stapley felt the "boot in the fanny" shock that meant the aircraft had taken a substantial hit in the tail section. Instantly dismissing the thought of aborting the bomb run, he regained control of the plane and lined up on the target. If the controls had been damaged to the point he could no longer control the aircraft, he knew he was "dead anyway." On the other hand, if the plane was flyable and he was able to pull out of the dive, he "might as well go ahead and complete the bombing run successfully."

Completing the run with a direct hit on the target, he pulled up to check his instruments and controls. When everything checked out, he went around again and commenced a rocket attack on the probable position of the flak battery. Only after he had completed that run, when the adrenaline had subsided somewhat, did the inner dialogue begin: "Wait a minute, I'm flying around doing bomb runs and rocket attacks in an airplane that's been beaten up pretty badly; and, I'm flying it as if everything's OK." Breaking off another attack, he gained some altitude and asked his wingman to check him out.

"Your tail wheel is completely shot off," the wingman replied as he flew slowly around the banged up Linda Lee II.

In addition to tearing off the wheel, the hit had cut the control cables to his rudder trim and elevator trim tabs.

He then turned Linda Lee II southward and prepared to make an emergency landing at K-46.

"K-46 tower, this is Filter How Three here. Request clearance for a straight in approach after How Flight lands."

"Roger, How Three, do you have an emergency?"

"Roger, battle damage. Took a forty in the tail. Tail wheel shot off and trim tabs shot out. This will be a squeek job."

"How Flight, clear the air, we have an emergency."

"Negative. Negative, How Flight, go ahead an land," Stapley countered. "This

bird has gotten me back this far, it will keep me up. I need to check it out for slow flying, any way."

How Flight made an uneventful landing, but all eyes were on Linda Lee II as Stapley tried to "grease" her in for a smooth landing. Although he had tried to hold the rear wheel off the runway for as long as possible until the stick was completely forward, as soon as the tail section—sans wheel—touched down Stapley's plane yawed violently back and forth, spewing sparks, smoke and dust into the air.

"My God, he's on fire," someone said on the radio.

But it was just sparks and dust. Linda Lee II skidded to a stop and when the dust cleared somewhat, How Flight was relieved to see Stapley exiting the aircraft—just a little faster than usual. At that moment, Stapley remembered he was "very aware of man's mortality."

RESCAP Missions

All too often, the mission facing 18th Group pilots would be a RESCAP [Rescue Combat Air Patrol]. Drop tanks would be installed to give the Mustangs additional range. "These missions could be as long as seven hours," Budd Stapley remembered. The rendezvous for RESCAP would

be Chodo Island, held by UN forces and a staging point for rescue helicopter flights into North Korea to pick up pilots who had been forced to bail out or ditch in enemy territory.

At about noon on April 20th, 1st Lt. Harry L. Winberg, an F-80 pilot with the 35th Fighter Bomber Squadron of the 8th Fighter-Bomber Wing, was briefed for a "routine" rail-cutting mission over North Korea. He was to fly in the number three position of the lead flight in a squadron of twelve aircraft. Each of the F-80s carried two 1,000-lb general-purpose bombs and 1,200 rounds of .50-caliber ammunition. His flight took off at 1355 and flew to its IP, a "bow-tie" bend of a river near Songch'on. By 1420 his squadron was turning into the target, diving from East to West at 10,000 feet. He released his bombs at about 3,000 feet and was at 2,000 feet when he completed the pass and remained "on the deck" heading West and weaving through the low hills to avoid anti-aircraft fire. At Sunga-san Mountain the flight turned southeast and started to climb for the flight home.

Shortly after starting the climb, Winberg saw two "golf balls" pass his left wing, and then felt a severe jolt to the aircraft. His wingman radioed immediately that he was on fire. Winberg could see a red glow in the rear view mirror and when he looked outside the base of the left wing and the entire fuselage aft of the cockpit "was in flames." Barely reaching 2,000 feet, the F-80 lost elevator control. The cables had burned or melted. The jet began to "porpoise" wildly. Winberg knew he had to get out—immediately.

Reaching down to the T-handle, he fired the canopy and was immediately engulfed in smoke and dust stirred up by the 330 miles per hour air speed. The violent buffeting of the airplane at that speed jerked his head above the slipstream, which immediately tore off his helmet and oxygen mask. By the time he had gotten himself back into position to fire the ejection seat, he was at an altitude of 600-feet, when he cleared the aircraft. The chute opened immediately and he saw that he was about

482

to hit the ground. He "tried to relax" as he landed on his back and slid about seventy feet until the "canopy snagged on some brush and small tress and stopped my sleigh ride." He was down…on a spur about halfway up a large hill. It was 1425.

Starting up the hill with his Evasion and Escape seat pack, he looked back and "saw a group of about twenty men, carrying rifles or carbines, turn off a road there and start up the hill toward where my parachute lay." He had not had time to hide it. Although the group below had not spotted him—yet—he knew it was only a question of time. Meanwhile, he could see his Flight making low passes all over the area—"apparently searching for me." Groping in the seat pack, he found a smoke flare and set it off as he tried to move as rapidly as he could up the 60-degree slope of the hill. His flight saw the smoke and began to orbit over his position. The infantry also saw the smoke and began heading up the hill.

Winberg worked his way up the hill as rapidly as he could looking for cover and for a better location for what he hoped might be a pickup by a helicopter. The incline, rocks, bushes and trees made for an exhausting climb. After finding a somewhat level area near the top of the hill, he heard voices and had to jump over the rocks and slide about 15 feet back down the hill, where he found a large, overhanging rock to hide under. He heard voices just above him, that finally, faded away. Finally, he had the time and opportunity to use his portable radio to contact his flight, still orbiting above him. After telling them he was OK, they replied that they would stay in the area as long as possible, but that they were running low on fuel. However, a RESCAP was on the way. "A short time later, four F-51s arrived in the area.

On the afternoon of April 20, 1st Lt. Wilfred "Budd" Stapley was the Flight Leader for "Filter RESCAP," a flight of four F-51s that had been circling Cho-do Island for about three hours. He and his wingmen were bored…among other things, he was thinking about his 24th birthday, only two days away. Stapley's luck "had been running badly." About a week before, on Easter Sunday morning, his bird had taken a direct hit on the tail wheel from a 40-mm shell.

Suddenly, "D 'Dog' Channel burst with chatter." Stapley was given the coordinates for an F-80 pilot "in trouble," and immediately turned his flight in that direction and moved out from "loiter" speed to "combat" speed. En route, Stapley contacted "Shirley, our controller" and informed them that I thought the helicopter would need an escort to the area as it was a well known hot spot, and asked if they could divert any F-51 flights in the area to Cho-do." Shirley had bad news for Stapley. "There were no fighter aircraft available of any kind."

When Stapley arrived over the area, he contacted the F-80s in the flight to pin point the position of the downed pilot. They assigned Winberg a new call sign: "Downed Pilot." Filter RESCAP was so far from friendly territory, that Stapley could not contact Shirley control from a low altitude. To maintain radio contact, he had he No. 2 man, who was on his first mission, climb to about 10,000 feet to establish radio contact. Then, Stapley led his flight in a "couple of strafing passes to clear out several groups of enemy soldiers from the area."

Winberg could only talk to the RESCAP when they were directly in "line of sight." In addition, he had trouble helping them pinpoint his exact location. To expose himself, as they requested at one point, might mean giving his position away to the growing number of uniformed searchers that were combing the slopes. Instead, he asked them to orbit over the next hill over from his—"as I was afraid they were attracting too much attention to my hill."

The news that Shirley control had for Stapley once he had reestablished radio contact was not good. Shirley advised him that "due to ground fog at Chodo, the helicopter could not take off." Stapley was "astounded by this news because just fifteen minutes before when we left Cho-do the conditions were C.A.V.U." [Ceiling and Visibility Unlimited] He had his "doubts" about the veracity of Chodo's weather report. The real reason for the "unavailability" report was that the chopper had to be fitted with an extra fuel tank in order to have enough fuel to make the attempt.

Throughout the afternoon, the RESCAP continued to orbit over the adjacent hill, even strafing it to fool the searchers into thinking they were protecting the American pilot who was hidden somewhere on THAT hill.

Ground fire for the RESCAP was "as we were wont to say: 'Intense to Unbearable' and my flight started taking hits," Stapley recalled. His No. 3 man, a South African pilot with Two Squadron—1st Lt. Gus Baransky—"went down in flames…I never saw an airplane blow up so completely like that…it just became a mass of flames…all you could see was the wingtips…for a moment…we were right on the deck and he didn't have a chance."

[Much later, after he had returned, Stapley counted ten bullet holes from small arms fire in his bird and his No. 4 man had several more holes in his plane.]

Stapley was now well into the RESCAP extraction effort, except for the fact that it was looking increasingly like no chopper was going to be sent out that afternoon, he now had only three aircraft and was rapidly using up both fuel and ammunition. It soon got even worse.

"A new burst of radio chatter on D Dog informed me an F-84 being shot down in our vicinity. Sure enough, a chute was sighted coming down about 2 or 3 miles east" of Winberg's position. Stapley circled "the new member of our little party and recced the area to see if I could see any hostiles on the ground." Seeing no enemy troops near the downed F-84 pilot, Stapley decided to "loosen" his cover "in the hope of not attracting attention to a specific spot." He started circling an area about three miles south of the downed pilots. He radioed Winberg and informed him of the new plans and advised him to take cover.

As the afternoon lengthened, Stapley's RESCAP tried to conserve its fuel as it circled south of Winberg's position. They made frequent "strafing passes to make it seem like we were applying close cover at that spot." About every ten minutes or so, he would lead the flight back to Winberg's position "to discourage any ground search by large groups." After one of these forays, he "spotted the F-84 pilot in the custody of several armed soldiers."

Late in the afternoon, Stapley had to tell Winberg that low fuel and darkness was about to send them back to base. Stapley and his flight had been airborne for over five hours. He "had not been on cruise control for quite awhile." He "waited for the news of the chopper coming to no avail" and when he calculated he "barely had enough fuel to make it back to K-46," he requested permission from Shirley Control to break off the cover and return to base." Shirley approved the request.

It broke Stapley's heart to have to tell Winberg that they had to leave, but they promised him they would be back first thing in the morning.

"I cannot describe to you the feeling I had when I was forced to leave you on your own," Stapley later wrote Winberg. "I wasn't much of a Christian then but I prayed for divine assistance like I hadn't before and seldom have since." Subsequent events have convinced Stapley that his prayers were heard.

Winberg was now all alone on the enemy hill, hiding under a rock. After dark, he climbed back up to the level area and "tried to figure out where the best place for a helicopter pickup was located." He decided the best pickup location was the level area and settled down to wait for dawn—sleep was not an option. Sitting on the hill during the night he could observe railroad trains and truck convoys passing in the valley below.

After returning—barely—to K-46, Stapley pinpointed Winberg's position for the team that was coordinating the rescue and offered his recommendations as to the best way of getting him out. He specifically "requested an escort of fighters for the chopper, both for the chopper's safety and to avoid the chance of a convenient ground fog goofing things up." Stapley volunteered for the mission, but was refused.

Shortly after dawn, the RESCAP returned—a mix of F-80s and F-51s. After two hours of orbiting, they escorted the rescue helicopter to Winberg's hill. He used his rescue radio to vector the helicopter pilot to his location. The activity attracted Communist ground troops who began moving rapidly towards the area in large numbers…firing at the helicopter and RESCAP as they approached the rescue location. The helicopter pilot was flying the bird by himself and trying "to work the winch," the winch. On the second pass, Winberg finally was able to get one leg in the sling and hang on desperately as the pilot tried to get the bird back in the air—riflemen were shooting at them from about 100 feet away. Winberg hung on to the sling as the incredibly brave and dexterous pilot got the helicopter in the air and operated the winch to bring his rescued pilot closer to the plane. As the heavy bird mushed slowly into the air, a shot creased Winberg's forehead—"shocking" him, but he "was able to hang on."

When the winch had pulled Winberg up to the access door, he found that it was closed, the slipstream had forced it shut. He had to "bang on the window to attract the pilot's attention. He was still busy trying to fly the helicopter and work the hoist, but when he saw my predicament, he managed to push the door open a little bit and I got it open the rest of the way."

The heroic helicopter pilot and relieved fighter pilot climbed up to 6,000 feet and headed West—for the coast. But it wasn't over yet.

The helicopter had been hit in the gas tank and it was losing gas. Just as worrisome was the heavy flak they encountered while crossing the Sunan Railroad. The pilot called "Filter RESCAP" ["Filter" was the call sign for units of the 18th Fighter Bomber Wing.] and asked them to strafe the flak positions which they did repeatedly and successfully as the guns all became quiet."

The crippled helicopter couldn't gain much altitude and was losing fuel. Meanwhile, the F-51's had been busy strafing and bombing enemy positions to provide enough protection for the helicopter to effect the rescue and to get away safely with the now wounded pilot. The Mustangs "were all out of ammo" when they spotted a twin 40-mm flak position on the last hill before the rescue helicopter would make it safely to the sea. "One of the flight still had his drop tanks on and made a low pass, putting the flak position out of operation with his drop tanks." The pilot, Stapley reported later, "was put in for the Silver Star but it was refused."

Thinking he would have to ditch the helicopter, the pilot gave Winberg ditching instructions as they finally reached the coast where they were joined by another helicopter and a "Dumbo," a rescue flying boat.

They made it to Cho-do at about 1130, where "the medics" cut Winberg's hair and dressed his scalp wound. He was then taken by C-47 to Paengyong-do and on to K-16, arriving at about 1300—overall, an incredible 24 hours of desperation and heroism of his own and by many other pilots dedicated to getting him out safely.

"I wasn't much of a Christian then but I prayed for divine assistance like I hadn't before and seldom have since."

"Tank" in the haystack

The 67th Squadron's How Flight was returning from an April mission. All bombs and rockets had been expended, but there was still some .50-cal. ammunition left.

Jinxing through farmland, they spotted what looked like tank tracks going into and beneath a large haystack. The "natural" conclusion by an inexperienced pilot is that a tank was beneath the hay stack and to immediately launch anattack. But, more experienced pilots knew that quite often, the "hay stack" was a trap.

Korean farms and outbuildings were often built in a large circle that was then connected with fencing to create a central enclosure for farm animals. Outside of the enclosure was the land they farmed. The "hay stack" was near one of the "storage buildings."

The trap would then be sprung by Communist gunners who were watching the skies overhead. When a fighter-bomber was spotted beginning its "run," the gunners manning the quad mount anti-aircraft guns concealed in the building waited until the attacking plane was both committed to the run and within range of the guns. At that point the false walls of the buildings would be dropped, clearing the 40-mm guns for action, and tables turned on the attacking aircraft.

Knowing the tank tracks might be a trap, the tactic used by the fighter-bombers in a four-plane flight was to take the haystack under fire with the Leader and No. 2 plane. The Number Three aircraft, following right behind the first two and slightly lower, would keep his guns aimed at the farm house and outbuildings throughout the run. Should the "walls" drop, he would immediately strafe the hidden gun emplacement.

Following the Leader and No. 2, 1st Lt. Wilfred "Budd" Stapley had the logical out building in his sights—ready to fire in a split second. As he approached the target at approximately 250-mph something inside the compound caught his eye…just a speck at that distance.

Meanwhile, the first two aircraft laced the haystack with enough rounds to set it on fire. No tank, just a haystack.

With his thumb poised over the firing switch on his joy stick, Stapley was just milliseconds away from strafing the farm compound…but he hesitated…just for a moment…the "speck" in the compound was now getting larger and beginning to have some shape.

For several more brief moments as the plane bore down on the compound, Stapley held his thumb over the switch, ready to toggle the six wing guns into hundreds of rounds in a split second.

Then the shape made sense…to his horror he realized that it was a baby sitting on the dirt in the middle of the compound.

Suddenly, another shape materialized from under the roofline of the building he was aiming at. It was running in the direction of the baby.

Racing to retrieve her baby and somehow find some safety from the attacking planes, the mother swept the baby up in her arms and ran for cover, even as she looked over her shoulder at Stapley as his plane roared by overhead.

Turning the plane on its wing as he aborted his strafing run and pulled up, the scared pilot and the terrified mother and baby were, for a brief moment, almost eye-to-eye.

Then,in an eye blink, the plane roared by the farm at roof top level, and was gone.

The mental picture of the brave North Korean mother and frightened child burned itself into Stapley's mind and would be there for the rest of his life.

Low Level CO: Lt. Col. Julian Crow

Most fighter bomber pilots on an MSR interdiction mission, would look for targets from about 1,500-2,000 feet. If they saw any target worth going after, they would complete a bomb, rocket or strafing run, then return to the previous altitude.

That wasn't the tactic used by Lt. Col. Julian Crow, Commanding Officer of the 67th.

Crow liked to look for his targets "right down on the deck."

Crow and 1st Lt. Wilfred "Budd" Stapley were on the deck looking for targets, when Stapley saw a 40-mm tracer round barely miss his engine. Letting his eyeballs instinctively calculate a reciprocal bearing for the round, he looked quickly in that direction and spotted the likely position for the AA fire. Peeling off, he strafed the 40-mm position, and rejoined Crow. Stapley was highly agitated at what he considered highly risky—unnecessarily risky—flying. As he poured on the power to rejoin Crow, still on the deck, he questioned himself aloud about Crow's flying

(Below) At K-46 the "view" from the Officers Quarters was the runway and the flight line. A close look at this photograph shows two T-6 Mosquito spotter aircraft landing in formation. (Urquhart)

tactics: "What's got into him? What in the world are we doing down here?"

At the time, Stapley is not aware that while he was adjusting a helmet wire on the way to rejoin Crow, he was bumping the R/T button and broadcasting his rhetorical musings to all pilots in the vicinity—including Crow, who had a good idea of what was going through Stapley's head.

"Say again, Number Two," Crow requested, as if Stapley's transmission had been garbled.

"Disregard my last, Sir," Stapley had the presence of mind enough to answer as they hurtled down yet another valley looking for likely targets.

The Weather Reports

Targets "came down" from Fifth Air Force to the 18th Group. After a decision was made regarding the proper squadron to which the target should be assigned, the squadron then decided who was going to be included on the mission.

Prior to a mission, pilots received several briefings, recalled Budd Stapley.

Part of the briefing prior to any mission included a "weather report," that was a "comedy" to the pilots. Just prior to the "weather man's" report, the pilots being briefed would look around for scraps of paper, which they would then wad up tightly—and then wait. As soon as he starting outlining his prognostications of weather over North Korea, the pilots would loose a barrage of paper wads at him. Since the weather over North Korea generally originated over Siberia and China and other Communist territory, reliable weather reports were scarce. The science of weather prediction at that time was rudimentary. Consequently, the only weather reports or projections the pilots trusted were those that came from previous UN flights that had been through the area—recently.

It was rare that a flight would make a straight run on a target. The usual procedure was to select an "IP" or Intercept Point several miles from the target. The flight would "hit" the IP at a pre-planned time and altitude, then "turn in" to launch its strike. Once at the IP, pilots would make final preparations within the cockpit for the imminent strike. Intensifying, if possible, the "jinxing" of their aircraft, the flight would turn towards the target and prepare for action. "If an enemy gunner were ever to have aimed in front of me—success-fully—I would have moved from that heading, if only slightly, and altitude. I never flew straight and level once I crossed the Bomb Line," Stapley said.

The F-51 had markings on the wing denoting 30 degrees, 50 degrees, 60 degrees. As you approached the target, as the location went under the wing and "hit" that mark—I liked sixty degrees—you rotated the aircraft upside down until you were looking directly up at the target and that would give you about a sixty degree dive. After we had dropped the bombs, we switched over to rockets and went back attacking with rockets. With me, if I dropped the bombs on the target, that was as good as it gets. As I came back around, I was looking for flak positions. I hated flak positions. Experience taught you—if you survived—where they usually put the flak positions. If I saw one, I would put some rockets on it. A lot of our guys felt the same way.

"How Flight" of the 67th Squadron in Spring 1952. (Left to right) 1st Lt. Wilfred C. Stapley, Capt. Shirley B. Tubbs (seated, hand on sofa arm), 1st Lt. Donald D. Drage, (unidentified), and 1st Lt. Melvin Souza. Pilot at center rear is 1st Lt. William E. McShane. Souza was KIA soon after this photograph was taken. (Stapley)

1st Lt. Wilfred "Budd" Stapley had some explaining to do to his crewchief who will not be pleased about the flak damage to "his" aircraft. (Stapley)

May 1952

"Sorties flown cutting rails still account for most of the missions...for the most part...in the far northern portions of Korea, far outside the range of our jet competitors."

12th Squadron Monthly Report

High Endurance CAP Mission. *Mustangs of the 67th Squadron at K-46 loaded with auxiliary fuel tanks (drop tanks) and ready for a high endurance Combat Air Patrol (CAP) mission "usually for a pilot that was down behind enemy lines," noted Robert Cranston, a former Crew Chief in the 67th. "During post flight we would perform any needed maintenance, refuel, load ammo, rockets and two 500-lb. bombs or napalm. If the upcoming mission was to fly CAP for a downed pilot, we would change the bombs for extra fuel tanks. This would add about four hours flying time. We usually flew two flights per day--if you could keep your plane together." (Cranston)*

Monthly Summary

The FEAF Commander recommended that North Korea's hydroelectric power facilities be the focus of major attacks as "the least costly means of impressing on enemy leadership the increasingly high costs of communist recalcitrance in armistice negotiations.

In May, FEAF aircraft flew 30,000 sorties, the highest monthly total in the war up to that period. Fifth Air Force and attached units lost twenty-two aircraft to enemy ground fire.

Use of the F-86 in air-to-ground missions was resumed for the first time since January and February 1951. "The F-86 aircraft in the fighter-bomber role showed decided advantages in comparison with the F-80 and F-84. The F-86 could maintain a higher dive angle without exceeding its critical mach number and was more accurate in bombing and rocketry. Moreover, the Sabre could penetrate and withdraw from defended areas better than the other jets and required no separate air cover. In aerial combat Sabre pilots, four of whom attained ace status during the month, destroyed thirty-two MiGs and two other enemy aircraft. Well-trained MiG pilots, operating with ground-controlled radar, increased friendly aircraft losses. Fifth Air Force lost five F-86s and five other fighters." [1]

The 18th Wing provided a warm welcome and needed training for Navy Commander MacKenzie, plus three other Navy officers in aerial photograph and map reading. "They expressed their appreciation and gratitude for the course." MacKenzie was the Senior U.S. Naval Officer advisor to the Korean Navy and would soon be providing the course to Korean Naval Officers.

The 39th FIS was detached from the 18th Fighter-Bomber Wing and attached to the 51st Fighter-Interceptor Wing. It had been an integral and important unit of the Group since May 12, 1951. In May 1952 it was entering its 22nd month of combat in the Korean War, and had flown 13,535 missions with a total of 27,337 combat flying hours. In May 1952, however, it flew no combat missions for the entire month due to preparations to move the squadron.

Adapted in part from U.S. Air Force Historical Research Agency. January 2002. The U.S. Air Force's First War: Korea 1950-1953 Significant Events. May 1952. http://www.au.af.mil/au/afhra/wwwroot/korean_war/korean_war_chronology/kwc_1951.html

More Crews Than Craft

Excess combat crew pilots and a shortage of combat ready aircraft created problems for morale in the 18th Wing in May. A partial solution was achieved by convincing FAF to give the 18th the authority "to deplete excess combat crews in three months by earlier forecast, i.e. less than 85 missions." [1] It would now be possible for pilots to complete 85 missions and go home instead of 100 combat missions.

During May the rail interdiction program was carried out as the main continuing effort of the unit.

Sorties and flying time were increasing "due to the arrival of warm weather and additional aircraft," the 12th FBS reported. "Tactics have been improved to meet new situations and have proven more than satisfactory. Rail interdiction missions and close support missions remain our primary targets and the Squadron is accomplishing its mission successfully."

18th Group Moves Headquarters to K-46

Plans were underway to move the Fighter Group Headquarters, plus all squadron activities from K-10 to K-46. When completed, it "would be the first time in many months that the Group would be operating as a combined unit instead of operating a split base." The move was initially approved by Colonel Levenson, however, a final decision was saved for Colonel Brinson when he assumed command on May 17th.

The move also presented may technical problems in logistics and administration between the Wing and its supporting groups.

Initial construction had begun early in the month on the office buildings and quarters needed at K-46 to accommodate the "influx" created by the move.

The move was completed by air and rail. "The Squadron is on the move again," the 12th recorded in its monthly report. "This time we are moving to K-46 near Hoe-

Damaged, but back. This badly damaged Mustang at K-10 brought the pilot back in May 1952. The armament shack "was next to the radio shack on the flight line," explained former Armorer Earl Ramsdell, "enabling us to hear when a damaged plane was returning and to prepare for the worst if armaments were still aboard." Note the Korean guards in this photograph. (Ramsdell)

ngsong, Korea. By the second of next month it is to be completed."

The new Production Line Maintenance program was "proceeding effectively" with a few exceptions. Duty hours for the PLM crews continued from 0700 through 2300 hours seven days a week "depending upon the work load on hand."

Even at this point in the war, supplies were hard to obtain. "Four-inch scotch tape is still a critical item and is needed for covering of combat pilots flight maps. China marking pencils of all colors are needed for annotation targets. Clear ac-

etate is an item that has been virtually impossible to obtain. This acetate is needed for covering maps for briefing purposes."

Even more critical was the shortage of personal equipment items, including: "Glasses, Smoke Rose; Kit, Bartering; Watch, Air Crew; Raft one-man type C-2-A; Parachute, Back type 28 ft; Jacket aircrew type L-2; Kit, sea water desalting; Paddle, life raft."

Mustangs from the 12th and 67th Squadrons undergoing maintenance at K-10 in Spring 1952. (Ramsdell)

Combat Operations

Close support, interdiction, rail cutting, and rescue missions account for the largest number of sorties to be flown by the Group in several months, the 18th Group reported.

During several days of close support missions "over 80 effective sorties were flown per day and 111 effective sorties were flown in one day by the Group and the 2nd SAAF Squadron. Close support operations were utilized to keep pilots current in this type of mission rather than in support of large scale ground activities."

Interdiction missions were flown "deep into enemy territory and enemy jet (MIG) aircraft were encountered. One MIG was damaged by two of our pilots and no damage was inflicted by the enemy. Our tactics used were of a defensive nature only after being bounced by the MIGs," the Group reported.

The longer hours of daylight and the "almost flawless weather" enabled the 18th squadrons to fly more sorties in May than in previous months. "Sorties flown cutting rails still account for most of the missions," the 12th reported. "These missions for the most part have been in the far northern portions of Korea, far outside the range of our jet competitors." The time for these long missions averaged from 2 ½ to 3 hours. That far north, the pilots found portions of the rail system that "were virtually unprotected when the Group first attacked, but have since moved in heavy and accurate anti-aircraft defense equipment." Vehicles, the Foxy Few's "first love" were not spotted but very few times that month.

"All of the sorties were flown north of the bombline," the 12th reported, "although one flight of four was alerted for a patrol over the prison camps on Koje-do Island during the time General Dodd (now Colonel) was held prisoner."

The only change in battle tactics in May was the "elimination of flights in trail from the rendezvous point to a section of track. Too many times during the end of the month, the enemy jets have driven from the last flight to the lead flight, firing all the

Pilots congregate outside the 67th Squadron Operations Office at K-46 in May 1952 to compare notes on recent missions. (Urquhart)

way. The flights now stagger themselves on each side of the lead flight."

High Missions=Rotation

Morale was improving steadily within the 67th. The "new high" in morale was reached when "the ten men with the highest number of missions in the Group were reported for rotation. This boosted all pilots hope of going home." Officer strength climbed from 45 to 59, and 52 of them were reported as flying combat missions.

The Air Force pilot pipeline was pushing so many pilots into the Group that even without a full 100 missions, some of the lucky ones were going home.

"With increased morale and better leadership, the 67th was better able to accomplish the assigned missions during the month of May," Major Stanley Long reported.

Long also noted that the "qualification of replacement personnel, especially among the pilot personnel was higher during this period than it has been the last few months." 2 Nevertheless, Long noted that

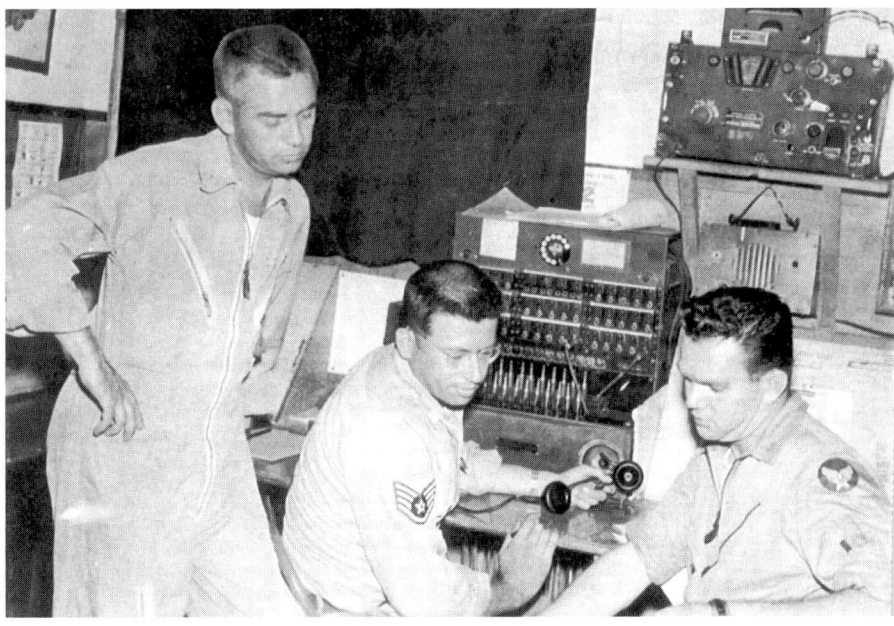

18th Group Operations Office. (Left to right) Major Warren T. Lenhart (standing), S/Sgt. George Falder and Capt. Ernest Woodrick. (Photo courtesy Ione R. Lenhart)

Captain Shirley Tubbs completes pre-flight checkout on "Ridge Runner" and puts on his parachute as he prepares for a mission in May 1952. (Shephard)

"pilot training has been stepped up to give the pilots more combat preparedness. More use is being made of the Air to Ground Gunnery Range."

At the beginning of the month, there were 158 enlisted personnel on board, still below that authorized. During the month, 18 Airmen were gained and only 3 lost, bringing the enlisted total up to 173 at the end of May.

The bitter Korean winter was winding down, the second the squadron had spent in Korea. "Winter clothing was turned in during the month of May." According to an inventory conducted by the Supply Officer, supplies were adequate to perform the mission. Even the "transportation shortage at K-46 has been alleviated some." Still there was a "need for more transportation, especially by the maintenance personnel."[3]

The greater number of qualified enlisted maintenance personnel enabled them to keep the planes in better flying condition—the in-commission percentage jumped to an average of 82.33% for the month. Eight engines were changed out, six major and twenty-nine intermediate inspections were conducted during the month.

Morale in the enlisted ranks was steadily improving. "The main factor in this was pride in their work and their desire to see a job well done. A competitive spirit has developed among the Airmen to see who does the best job," Long reported.

Another factor, perhaps the most significant factor in the improved morale, was

(Below) Maintaining as many planes in flying and fighting condition as possible would not have been possible without the spirit and professionalism of the ground crews of the 18th Fighter-Bomber Wing whose invaluable contributions to sustained combat operations were frequently pointed out in unit monthly reports. Technical Sergeant Roy Pylant, Jr., 67th Squadron with "The Ridge Runner" flown by 1st Lt. Jack Shepard.

Crew Chief Technical Sergeant Roy Pylant checks out "Ridge Runner."

"the opening of a new and larger Service Club. Beer and Whiskey sales across the bar were made, available to the Airmen."

Morale was improving, but the combat losses and damage continued.

Air Medals and Oak Leaf Clusters were being awarded to numerous pilots.

Significant Events

May 1: 2nd Lt. David L. Gray made a wheels up landing at K-14 (Kimpo).

May 2: The "Flying Cheetahs," 2 Squadron South African Air Force, flew its 8,000th combat sortie against the Communists in North Korea. Lieutenant Alan "Shadow" Gardiner-Atkinson, 27, of Melville, Johannesburg, "smiled as he climbed down from his cockpit to learn that he had had the honor of bringing the Squadron's total to 8,000 strikes. He had just led a flight of four Mustangs through a barrage of heavy flak in a raid on vital Communist rail supply lines near MIG Alley, deep behind enemy lines." [4]

May 7: On take-off Lt. Paul Kniss' tail wheel lock snapped at about 40 mph. "I burned off my right tire trying to stay on the runway, but to no avail. I bounced about ten feet into the air, and then the base motor pool filled my entire windscreen. I cut my batteries, mags, checked my shoulder harness--which was unlocked because I could never reach all of the necessary switches while it was locked--and dove into an open area about twenty feet square. I landed on a search light, bounced off a fuel truck and sheared off the fuselage behind the armor plate, then slid into a Quonset hut. A young airman sitting at a desk stood up and left his body's impression in the steel covering of the Quonset. My prop had stopped about three feet short of his desk. I suffered a black eye from my head's contact with the gunsight, and the airman needed a change of underwear before he could return to duty." Robert Cranston, a crew chief at the time, happened to be standing at the fence between the runway and taxi ramp watching his ship take off. He then noticed Kniss as he put it in a tongue in cheek e-mail

Bring 'em back with flying safety. *Major Robert L. Holsomback (right), Houston, Texas, displays his flying safety kit on a taxiway of the 18th Fighter-Bomber Wing in Korea. As flying safety officer for the wing in May 1952, Major Holsomback devised new methods for restricting aircraft accidents at his base. Here he explains a few of the items to 2nd Lt. Walter A. Smyk, of Sisseton, S. Dak. (NARA)*

years later, "having a MINOR problem on take off. If I remember correctly, all that was left of your plane was the cockpit and the engine." When the emergency crew arrived, Kniss was sitting on the side of the hill next to a road, smoking a cigarette.

May 8: In the first of four major interdiction strikes, Fifth Air Force fighter-bombers "flew approximately 465 sorties against the enemy supply depot at Suan, located about forty miles southeast of Pyongyang, in the largest one-day attack since the war began. Over a thirteen-hour period, the UN pilots damaged or destroyed over two hundred supply buildings, personnel shelters, revetments, vehicles, and gun positions. Enemy antiaircraft fire downed an F-86 on a dive-bombing strike against the Kunu-ri marshaling yards, the first loss of a Sabre on a fighter-bomber sortie." [5]

May 12: Gen. Mark W. Clark, USA, replaced General Matthew B. Ridgway as Commander, UN Command.

Several pilots of the 6149th TacConSq were flown to K-10 to conduct "surveillance of Koje-do Island. Their missions

were directed by a controller from 5th Air Force Operations, while Intelligence did the briefing and debriefing. A total of seven missions were accomplished, during the course of which one of the planes was fired upon and many meetings, rallies and considerable unrest were noted in the prisoner compounds," the 18th FBW reported.

May 13: 1st Lt. Melvin Sousa made an emergency wheels up landing at K-14 after his plane had received major battle damage.

May 15: Fifth Air Force fighter-bombers flew 265 sorties during attacks against a vehicle repair factory at Tang-dong, north of Pyongyang. Thirty-nine buildings and a power plant were destroyed.

Major Richard E. Steckel was reported as MIA.

1st Lt. Harry E. Steffensen had a major accident while taxiing to the parking ramp after completing a combat mission.

May 16-17: Rioting POWs at Koje-do necessitated a emergency unit movement by the 315th AD that used C-119, C-54, and C-46 aircraft to transport 2,361 members of the 187th Regimental Combat

Paperwork at the office. *Airman First Class Robert Cranston was "caught" by the photographer as he filled out the "paperwork" that while it was essential for maintenance and proper upkeep of the aging Mustangs, was a pain in the butt for the air crews. (Cranston)*

Team, plus combat equipment, vehicles, and supplies from Japan to Pusan, Korea to put down an insurrection by POWs.

Colonel Sheldon S. Brinson, assumed command of the 18th Fighter-Bomber Group, relieving Colonel Ira Levenson, who was transferred to Headquarters, FAF.

On take-off Lt. Paul Kniss' engine failed. "The only options were straight ahead into the 11th evacuation hospital, or over a ridge into a box canyon, which looked to be only about ten feet long. Inspired by the small desire to save my ass, I bellied in (again with a black eye from the gunsight for not having my shoulder harness fastened). I had attracted small arms fire, which stopped when his three wingmen made a few low passes over the area. About five minutes later his "hero" arrives with a chopper. "On his first pass he almost hits the only tree within fifteen miles, and goes around. On pass number two, he's too high and goes around again. On pass number three he makes a 'controlled crash' next to my airplane. 'Hurry up,' the chopper pilot yelled at me, 'There are guerillas all over the place.' "Bullshit," Kniss yelled back, "they're not trying to hit us...not as long as our CAP aircraft are in the area, and after that flying exhibition of yours, I know it would be safer to walk ten miles through guerilla territory than take a chance on a ride with you." After the helo pilot shoots him "the finger," Kniss changed his mind and agreed, "Let's get the f--- out of here!"

May 22: Nearly 500 fighter-bomber sorties by the Fifth Air Force destroyed more than 90 percent of the Kijang-ni industrial area southwest of Pyongyang. The complex produced hand grenades, small arms, and ammunition. 1st Lt. Cleyburn L. McCauley successfully bailed out after his plane received major damage from ground fire.

May 23: Another 275 fighter-bomber sorties, the last of four major interdiction strikes by the Fifth Air Force, destroyed 80 percent of a steel factory complex in the Kijang-ni area.

May 28: Capt. Joe Peterburs sustained heavy battle damage and wounds to the face while strafing enemy troops in trenches.

May 30: Lt. Gen. Glenn O. Barcus, USAF, replaced General Frank Everest as Commander, Fifth Air Force. Barcus had served as commanding general of the Tactical Air Command at Langley Air Force Base, Va., from July 1950. He remained Commander, FAF until the end of May 1953, when he returned to the United States to become vice commander, Air Training Command. He was succeeded on 31 May 1953, by Lt. Gen. Samuel E. Anderson, USAF.

May 31: The 39th Fighter Interceptor Squadron was detached from the 18th Fighter-Bomber Group. "About half the pilots were reassigned to the 4th Fighter Interceptor Wing and the remainder went to the 51st Fighter Interceptor Wing. Airmen with less than four months retainability were kept in the 18th Fighter-Bomber Wing while the rest of the organization went to the 51st Fighter-Interceptor Wing." [6]

By the time the 39th Squadron was detached in May 1952, the 18th Fighter-Bomber Group "had worked out a unique system for the four squadrons, the 12th, 67th, 39th and 2nd South African Squadron," explained Robert E. Sandlin in his history of the 39th Fighter Squadron "The Cobra in the Clouds Strikes Again."

"On a rotation plan, one squadron would fly close support missions for one day and then fly interdiction missions for the next three days, which worked out great. The whole group had always worked well together, and now were the only Mustangs still operating as fighter-bombers."

One of the last group efforts together before the 39th was transferred in late May involved a strike at a high value target.

An RF-51 from the 45th squadron "had located a large cache of enemy supplies in bunkers, near the base of a hill." The 12th squadron scrambled four Mustangs. Captain Elvin Wyatt was the flight leader who took his group to the target, near a small village, east of the Imjin River. Enemy forces "responded with a great amount of ACK-ACK but several firing passes were made, trying to get something to blow. It was getting dark, so they headed back to K-46. At the de-briefing, it was realized something of importance was there because it had been so heavily defended."

The 18th Group was asked for permission to hit it again at first light.

A plan for all the squadrons to attack as a unit was suggested by Captain James Byers. "The 12th and 67th would hit the area with air burst of VT fused 250-pound frag bombs to knock out the gun positions and 39th squadron would come in on low level passes with napalm on the supply area. The plan worked to perfection, and with the enemy fire knocked out the 39th made a perfect run. The entire storage area was flamed with 100% coverage. The best part was, all the Mustangs returned to base without damage. A classic example of teamwork by a great wing of "Tang" pilots," Sandlin noted.

"If you could love an airplane, there was much affection for the F-51 Mustang, because it had been a part of the 39th for so many years. From April 1945 through mid-June 1952, with the exception of five months when the 39th had flown the F-80-C's, the Mustang was our aircraft. It had been called names, The Tang, Spam Can, a tail-dragger, ol'e reliable, and many more than could not be written, but always a wonderful fighter, acclaimed by all, as the best prop aircraft ever built."

Combat Losses

1st Lt. Robert Stanley Fluhr, 12th Fighter-Bomber Squadron from Glen Rock, New Jersey, was KIA on 6 May 1952, while on a combat mission, his aircraft's engine failed and the plane crashed inverted in the sea near Paengnyong-do, Korea.

1st Lt. Leonard Stanley Olson, 12th Fighter-Bomber Squadron. "Lt. Leonard S. Olson, who had just arrived early in May, was killed on his first training mission." On 14 May 1952, while on a combat mis-

"My Baby." During his tour of duty with the 67th Squadron, Airman First Class Robert Cranston served as Crew Chief for two Mustangs, 484627 and 484916. "Marguerite" was the name of his girl friend "at the time." Note "Lefty" painted on her right wheel cover. That was Cranston's way of reminding folks that he was left handed. On the back of the snapshot showing FF 916 he wrote just two words that summarized and symbolized the pride and professionalism of all ground crewmen of the 18th Fighter-Bomber Wing. "My Baby," he wrote proudly, capturing the essence of "ownership" and protectiveness the ground crews felt towards their planes--and pilots. "Thank GOD I never lost a plane or a pilot from mechanical failure or enemy fire." Many pilots thanked him, he recalled, "upon their safe return from a combat mission. But they were the real heroes, I was just doing my job." Cranston's only regret "is that we didn't finish the job. So many died in that war, Korea is still divided after more than 50 years, and we still have American troops there." (Cranston)

sion, his aircraft received a direct hit by antiaircraft fire, exploded and crashed a half mile northwest of Ultin, Korea, according to the American Battle Monuments Commission.

2nd Lt. Melvin Souza, 67th Fighter-Bomber Squadron from Oakland, California. Lt. Sousa had been tapped to be How Flight Leader for the 67th Squadron in mid-May 1952 and to assume leadership of the Flight upon Stapley's departure from Korea after completing his required number of missions. But first, Souza needed a check out flight led by 1st Lt. Wilfred "Budd" Stapley.

A four-plane formation from How Flight set out from K-46 on a mission that would help Sousa transition into his new Flight

Leader shoes. Stapley was flying No. 2 that day. "Sousa was already fully qualified," Stapley later related. It was to have been Stapley's last combat mission.

As we approached the Bomb Line my engine temperature kept going down. I put the temperature control on manual to try and hold the temperature up, but that didn't work. The engine temperature kept falling—"below the green." Pretty soon the engine was going to be either running very rough or even shut down completely. I didn't dare head into enemy territory with the engine in this condition.

Reluctantly, he radioed Sousa to report he had to abort and was turning back. The closer he got to K-46, the warmer the engine began to run. Stapley was incredu-

Combat Statistics

18ᵗʰ F-B Wing

May 1952

Average No. A/C Assigned
36
Total Flying Time
2,733
Percent of Aircraft in Commission
67%
Percent of Aircraft AOCP
7%
Combat Sorties Flown by Wing
1,371
12ᵗʰ Squadron Sorties
385
39ᵗʰ FIS Sorties
Detached and assigned to 51ˢᵗ FIS
67ᵗʰ Squadron Sorties
Unavailable
2 Squadron Sorties
365
A/C Lost to Combat
6
Pilots lost
3

Fuel Consumed

222,373 gals.

Ordnance Expended

.50-cal. Rounds
700,256
Rockets
1,933
Napalm Bombs
558
500-lb. GP Bombs
2,182
Note: Figures and totals may differ in some categories due to differences in numbers provided by each component.

What's The Scoop? *The Bulletin Board outside the Orderly Room at K-10 was where important information was posted for 18ᵗʰ Group Airmen. (Ramsdell)*

Time for R&R. *In May 1952 this group of tired, but happy, Airmen prepare to board the plane taking them to Japan for three days of R&R. Note their ties are already tucked in their belts. "After putting in 12+ hours per day, seven days a week under often stressful and dangerous conditions, these three day R&R periods were most welcomed and appreciated," remembered Earl Ramsdell.*

lous at the turn of events. He knew he wasn't "that clanky," and did not abort the mission north of the bomb line out of concern for his own safety at the end of his required missions. Prior to landing, he headed into the bomb drop area south of K-46 *[planes returning with unexpended bomb ordnance were not allowed to land with them. Instead, they were dropped prior to landing at a designated area—the bomb drop—where they would dropped on "safe."]* As Stap-

ley made a low level, he "made a sloppy turn—maybe 25-30 feet off the ground—and dropped my bombs on "safe."

Two 500-lb bombs were instantly released from beneath the wings and because of his extreme low altitude, they landed almost immediately. The supposedly "safe" bombs exploded on contact. The effect was like a major "kick in the @#$@," Stapley remembered.

Thinking the aircraft had been damaged, even as he marveled that he was still in the air, Stapley climbed quickly to survey his plane and to have enough air below him for a (relatively) safe parachute drop should it be needed. The plane checked out well enough for him to make a safe landing. After taxiing to the parking area, he inspected the plane and found rock holes and dents "all over the plane" from the exploding bombs.

Meanwhile, Souza and his two other pilots—both recent arrivals to the 67th—continued on their mission. During his bomb run, Souza was struck by a 40-mm anti-aircraft round and lost three feet off one wing. Nursing the barely flyable F-51 back into friendly territory, Souza made a belly landing on an "emergency landing strip" at K-16. This was the designated "belly landing" strip for the region. F-51 pilots who were badly shot up would try to make it to K-16 and put a sick bird down on the emergency strip instead of attempting a risky landing at K-46 where an accident would shut down flight operations entirely until the debris was removed and the air strip repaired.

Souza's belly landing at K-16 was successful, but as often happened the extraordinary stress and trauma of facing—and

1st Lt. Melvin Sousa

surviving—such life threatening situations, he was too jittery to fly combat for a while.

Pilots in that condition were said to be "flak happy." They would be taken temporarily off combat flying missions to let their "nerves" settle down. They were not grounded necessarily, but taken off the combat mission list.

Souza was grounded for combat missions, but not for other types of flying.

Several days later, Sousa was asked to

ferry an F-51 from K-10 to K-46. Heading north with his wingman, Sousa flew into "weather." His wingman followed Souza's lead, but as he later reported, his airplane "felt like it was going too fast."

Taking his eyes off the "soup" and Souza's wingtip for a moment, he glanced down at his instruments and noted that his air speed indicator was much too high. As a snap decision, he decided to "go on his own gauges" and not follow Souza's lead. He would find his own way to K-46.

Keying the mike, he advised Souza that he was "in a dive, in a dive, spiral, pull up."

Souza replied, "No, I'm OK."

No further radio transmissions were ever received from Lt. Souza.

Wreckage of his airplane was later found on a mountainside. "Mel Souza was too good a pilot—an excellent pilot—to have misread his gauges. They must have been wrong," Stapley believes.

While at Luke AFB in the Fall of 1951, Souza was flying a night training flight when his engine quit and he was forced to bail out, his friend "Budd" Stapley remembered.

After making a successful exit from the falling Mustang in the middle of the desert,

he landed without injury. Gathering up his parachute, he noticed the glow of a camp-fire not far away. Slinging the parachute over his shoulder, he set out in the direction of the fire. When he reached the area, both he and the campers were shocked: he, because it was a group of picnicking doctors and nurses from a local hospital. Knowing Souza, Stapley remembered, he probably said something like: "Hate to drop in like this…"

Endnotes

[1] USAFHRA. *Monthly Historical Report, 18th Fighter-Bomber Wing,* May 1952. p. 2.

[2] USAFHRA. *Monthly Historical Report, 67th Fighter-Bomber Squadron,* May 1952, p. 2.

[3] USAFHRA. *Monthly Historical Report, 67th Fighter-Bomber Squadron,* May 1952, p. 5.

[4] USAFHRA. *Truckbuster. Bi-weekly newspaper of the 18th Fighter-Bomber Wing.* May 16, 1952.

[5] U.S. Air Force Historical Research Agency. January 2002. The U.S. Air Force's First War: Korea 1950-1953 Significant Events. May 1952. http://www.au.af.mil/au/afhra/wwwroot/korean_war/korean_war_chronology/kwc_1952.html

[6] USAFHRA. *Monthly Historical Report, 18th Fighter-Bomber Group,* May 1952, p. 4.

Airman Joseph Krakovsky was able to visit his brother, Robert, at the front lines in May 1952. Robert was serving with the 457th Field Artillery Battalion, 2nd Division near Chorwon, Korea. The "conditions were bad," at the forward artillery base, but "it wasn't as bad as the infantry," he recalled. The NCO in charge of the battery asked Joe if he "would like to fire the howitzer. He told me, 'Hey, on the next fire mission, stand with your back to the weapon and pull the lanyard when I yell, Fire.'" It might have been the only time during the Korean War when an Air Force Airman fired an artillery round at the enemy. (Krakovsky)

Krakovsky found bodies washed ashore in the nearby river. (Krakovsky)

A Nasty Surprise for a Communist General

by Wilfred "Budd" Stapley

Late May 1952—we were going up on a close air support mission on the East Coast. We had a salient up there that was pretty narrow—too narrow in fact to use artillery for support. So, they used a Navy heavy cruiser for "artillery."

The problem there was the flat trajectory of the Navy 5-inch and 8-inch guns. They were very effective on the sides of hills and mountains towards the water, but much less so on the other side of those ridges. In other words, they were "rifles" and not "howitzers."

Our first rendezvous point was over the heavy cruiser. As we approached the cruiser, we became increasingly worried about "friendly fire." I had never seen so many anti-aircraft batteries on one ship before. The entire superstructure seemed to point up at us…and to rotate as these batteries followed us as we circled the ship prior to beginning our mission. We tried to give the ship an extra wide "berth," keeping our distance. They told us over the radio, do not drop your nose below the horizon. Those Navy boys are "trigger happy" and they will start shooting.

I was flying Number Two, checking out another new flight leader. Our objective was a Communist command post and our intelligence analysts were saying that our strike was being called in because they had indications that the CP was being visited by a very senior Communist officer—a general—and his staff. They not only wanted to get the CP, but to do so with him and his staff in there.

The Forward Air Controller—flying a mosquito aircraft (T-6)—put a smoke rocket into the area to mark where they wanted our bombs and rockets to land. The new flight leader had never flown a close air support mission before. He began to lead his flight into the target coming from a direction over enemy held territory and then pulling out over friendly territory.

When I saw where he was heading, I yelled "Negative, negative—any long bombs could hit friendlies." I recommended a bomb run that would be parallel to the line.

The flight leader responded by asking me to lead the flight in. So I had the T-6 put another smoke rocket into the target area and we went around again on the new course. On the way in I debated on whether to use a skip bomb release or a glide bomb release—and decided on more of a glide bomb approach. How Flight put it right in the entrance to the CP.

Photo-reconnaissance after the mission showed total destruction. The mosquito pilot reported 37 bodies in and around the target. We estimated that from 180-200 people were inside at the time and were probably killed. If the General was in there, it was Sayonara. That was the last mission I flew.

Happy Hour. *(Left to Right) Lt. Rexford R. Baldwin, Capt. Warren W. Mills, Major Stanley A. Long, Lt. James E. Camp, Capt. Kimball, Lt. Joseph E. Williams and Capt. Knight. (Photo courtesy Ione R. Lenhart)*

CHODORESCAP

Mission

Besides rail, communications cuts and close air support for front line troops, Lt. Col. Donald Drage, a former Flight Leader with the 67th Squadron in early 1952 explained, "we flew other interesting missions."

Off the west coast of North Korea is the small island of Chodo. UN forces maintained a small airfield there equipped with helicopters and SA-16s.

When the FAF was planning major missions into northern North Korea, the 18th FBG would be tasked to furnish a four-ship flight (CHODORESCAP) composed of "one bird and a pilot from each squadron" (67th, 12th, 39th and 2 SAAF), that would "loiter" off the coast near Chodo ready "to respond to any emergencies." When a pilot declared an emergency, "we would establish contact, find the troubled bird, escort him if necessary or CAP him if he was down and set up a rescue. A very rewarding and satisfying mission," Drage remembered.

One such mission on April 21, 1952 was particularly memorable and resulted in a commendation from Lt. Gen. Frank F. Everest, Commanding General of the FAF. General Everest included both the 18th FBG and 2 Squadron SAAF for "the highly efficient manner in which they performed their mission in the rescue of a downed pilot." The nature of the operation "was not only hazardous but demanded the closest timing and the highest degree of airmanship." Both the downed pilot and the helicopter pilot had been "outspoken" in their "praise of the outstanding performance" by the F-51 pilots and had declared that "without their constant cover and strafing attacks against the many gun positions encountered" during rescue it "would not have been successful." Everest concluded his message by particularly commending the "pilots who contacted the downed pilot and escorted the helicopter. It is evident that they used sound judgment

and excellent flying technique in their operations." [1]

Main Supply Route Combat Air Patrol

Another interesting mission was the MSRCAP (Main Supply Route Combat Air Patrol). During the peace talks "the North Koreans would occasionally send some vehicles carrying negotiators along the main highway between Pyongyang and Panmunjom. These vehicles would be marked with a white cross on top. Our responsibility," Drage explained, "was to provide a CAP over the convoy to prevent any UN aircraft from attacking the cars." The protective air cover "was a nice gesture on our part," Drage believed, "but it did not deter enemy troops on the ground from firing at us along the route."

On May 5, 1952, How Flight had an especially "good day," as reported by the 18th Wing's Public Information Office. The brief news release reported that "South African and American airmen of the 18th Fighter-Bomber Wing flew only a minimum of sorties yesterday, but this time a big thing came in a little package. F-51 pilots, in short but devastating encounters with the enemy, destroyed three personnel shelters, four bunkers, two artillery emplacements, 50-feet of trenches, and inflicted four rail cuts."

One four-plane flight, "jockeyed by Lt.

"Lucky" Drage, Salt Lake City, Utah, Lt. Melvin Souza, Oakland, California, Lt. Ray Zeliadt, Des Moines, Iowa and Lt. Tim Urquhart, Houston, Texas, found hunting especially rewarding and destroyed two Red trucks, damaged two more, and splashed fiery napalm over trenches, but were unable to observe the charred results. Lt. Drage, Flight Leader, topped off the mission in a big way by demolishing a Communist tank that got in his way." [2]

Endnotes

[1] Fifth Air Force msg DTG 230700Z (1952) from CG Fifth Air Force to Commanding Officer, 18th Fighter-Bomber Wing.

[2] 18th Fighter-Bomber Wing Public Information Office release May 5, 1952.

Pilot to POW...

in two hours

On the morning of 31, May, 1952, the 18th was conducting an interdiction mission north of Namsi, Korea. It was a "group gaggle," attempt to cut the railroad lines in that area. All the flyable aircraft in the Fifth Air Force and Navy joined to bomb the same section of track three times on one day. In addition to using 500-lb HE bombs with contact fuses, the armorers added time delay fuses to many of the bombs ranging from 12-72 hours that would explode during the time when the repair crews were working to repair the earlier damage. The

time delay fuses helped ensure the rail line was closed to traffic for periods of 4-7 days.

The Group Flight Leader of about 20 Mustangs for the mission was 1st Lt. John Carlton, formerly a fellow flight instructor with 1st Lt. Paul Kniss at Craig AFB in Selma, Alabama.

The Flight Leader for Love Flight that afternoon was 1st Lt. Paul Kniss of the 12th Squadron. Kniss was training an alternate leader for the flight. Lt. James Massey led the flight that day and Kniss was flying as his No. 2.

As the gaggle approached Sinanju, it was jumped by Mig-15's and were soon advised by Shirley Control to abort the mission and return to K-46. Love Flight prepared to dump ordnance and began return to base. Kniss noticed that Carlton had not responded to the controller's directions. In a very short period of time, most of the 18th Group was heading south and Carlton had only Massey and Kniss—with him. Massey's No. 3 had aborted north of the bomb line and No. 4 had pealed off to escort him home.

Massey and Kniss decided that they could not let Carlton proceed on the mission alone, so Massey and Kniss would fly as his wingmen.

Soon, Kniss heard Massey's voice over the radio warning, "Love 2, break, there is a Mig on your ass." After a few seconds spent looking around to identify "Love 2," and see whether he was doing as Massey had ordered, Kniss realized that HE was "Love 2."

It was too late. His Mustang was being torched by the Mig and was on fire. As Kniss turned toward the ocean—and safety—another Mig made a pass at him from about the ten o'clock position. Kniss continued his turn and held his trigger switch down as the Mig flashed past. Kniss saw hits, but had too many problems of his own to make more than a quick mental note of the fact.

As he opened his canopy and went through the drill of detaching himself from the airplane, Kniss knew that the plane was never going to make it to the ocean. As he stood up in the cockpit, the tail burned off,

(Above) Squadron Operations Offices at K-46. Early on the morning of 31 May 1952, 1st Lt. Paul Kniss and other members of the "Foxy Few" pilots who were penciled in for missions that morning, departed from the 12th Squadron's Operations Office at K-46 to pre-flight their aircraft. The mission that morning was a "group gaggle," of over 20 Mustangs hitting the same section of railroad track repeatedly and using time delay fuses. The target that morning was a section of track just north of Namsi, North Korea, northwest of P'yongyang--in the heart of "Mig Alley." (Kniss)

the nose headed for the ground and Kniss was catapulted into the air—hitting both the vertical and horizontal stabilizers with his head and his butt. Although one Mig came so close to him that it almost hit him as he swung in the parachute, none of them actually fired on him in the chute.

While he was parachuting from his flaming aircraft, Kniss looked down and knew he was going to land in a group of trees. While this would have hidden him temporarily from the Communists, it would have precluded his rescue by helicopter. While he still had enough altitude, he slipped his parachute so as to land in the middle of a huge rice field near the inter-

Last Korean War Mission for Kniss. 1st Lt. Paul Kniss smiles for the camera prior to departing on a rail cutting "group gaggle" mission on 31 May 1952. Two hours later he was in the middle of a North Korean rice paddy, surrounded by angry civilians, and staring down the muzzle of a rifle. Soon after, he was a prize being fought over by Chinese and Soviet troops, who wanted to hang him on the spot. (Kniss)

499

section of two irrigation ditches.

Moving as fast as his injured back would let him, he jumped into the irrigation ditch and buried his classified information under the mud and rocks. "My first obligation once I was on the ground in North Korea, was to destroy or hide any classified information. I had with me our combat map which showed the location of every forward controller close to the battle line and other classified information. I hid this in the mud under the water level of the irrigation ditch that I was in," he explained.

To his great relief, he found that his escape radio was working and he checked in with Massey, maneuvering overhead and told him to get a chopper up to the area ASAP.

Kniss was now aware that he was drawing small arms fire, although it seemed to him that the aim was not to kill him but to hold him in one spot.

Massey asked him if he was OK. Kniss could detect concern, even fear, in his voice as he told him that the Migs were still on them.

Kniss knew that if he ordered his flight away that he "was courting disaster, and most probably death." However, he did so for their own safety. "I felt that command was a duty, not a right, and I could not have lived with myself if someone else had lost their life while trying to save mine."

Kniss had never lost a wingman and as bad as his own situation was at the time, he did not want to lose Massey by holding him in the area—under attack by Migs—while they waited on the chopper. He ordered Massey and the remained flight members out of the area. Even as he did so, he knew that he was probably sealing his fate—at the hands of the North Koreans and Chinese.

"According to our Military briefing, if we were shot down over North Korea, we were to try to escape. If that was not possible, we were to try to surrender to the Chinese army. If you could not do this, you were to surrender to the North Korean army, and told to expect some rough treatment. Also, that your chance of survival was severely reduced. Under no circumstances

should you surrender to the civilians, as there was slim to none of a chance of survival," Kniss recalled.

There might be more cover in the trees, Kniss decided as he soon began to take small arms fire from several different directions as the enemy ground troops converged on him down the irrigation ditches. He tried to make a hobbling run for whatever safety the trees might offer. He had to cross 1,000-2,000 yards of open rice paddy. He ran as best he could, trying to dodge the rifle fire. He could not make it. His right hip gave out and he fell into the mush. He struggled to get back onto his feet, but it took some moments before he could get them to do what he was willing them to do. Finally, as he lurched onto his feet, he "was looking down the barrel of a very large rifle."

It was 0930 in the morning. Kniss was now a POW. He had no idea for how long— the duration could be measured in months --or longer.

During escape and evasion briefings back at K-46, Kniss and other 18th Group pilots had been warned not to surrender to civilians. The reason was starkly simple: they would most likely kill you on the spot.

Kniss had no choice in the matter. As the eager hands stripped him of all his personal possessions—watch, wedding ring, pistol, etc.—he tried to prepare himself for whatever happened next.

The Korean who had taken the pistol then fired a round into the ground near Kniss' foot—perhaps by accident, since he was holding the gun near his leg "and in accidentally firing a shot, nearly took his foot off." The incredible stress and bizarre turn of events, brought an involuntary laugh from Kniss—a big mistake. The enraged Korean began to hit Kniss in the face with his own gun.

Kniss was taken to a Korean village. The Korean who had captured Kniss, "made a game of placing a pistol in my ear, pretending to shoot, then removing it and laughing with the crowd that was standing nearby. This lasted for ten minutes, or ten years, depending on your position in the drama," Kniss explained. Whatever reac-

Paul Kniss had lost over 50 pounds during more than 15 months as a Prisoner of War. (Kniss)

tion Kniss exhibited at this "mock execution" must have pleased the crowd. The Korean gave Kniss on of his own cigarettes and everyone then smiled at him.

Chinese soldiers soon arrived and took Kniss away from the civilians. Even as Kniss was being led away from the civilians towards an anti-aircraft position manned by the Chinese, a group of about eight Russian soldiers appeared on the scene and demanded that Kniss be surrendered to them for hanging.

At that time, Kniss spoke neither Russian nor Chinese. He did not need to. The life or death drama "was all done in a very clear pantomime. My Chinese captors said 'No.' The Russian then released Kniss' arm and "proceeded to hit me in the face several times."

The Chinese took several steps back from the assault—and cocked their rifles. The Russians, startled, armed their air-cooled machine guns. Kniss, in the middle of the standoff, stood there "with a stupid look" on his face. Eventually, the two "allies" allowed cooler heads to prevail. The Russians hopped back on their truck and left.

The march continued. Suddenly, someone halted the group of about 6-10 Chinese soldiers.

Kniss was then blindfolded and pushed

against a tree. The next sound he heard was that of bayonets being placed on rifles.

During WW II, Kniss had lied about his age three or four times while attempting to enlist in the Navy. He finally succeeded and entered the Navy in 1944, a few days after his seventeenth birthday. Before the war was over, Kniss had served in the Pacific theatre and received seven battle stars for various engagements in which the ships he served on saw action, including: Okinawa and Iwo Jima.

In the late Forties, only a year and a half of formal high school education, he had managed to pass the two year college test and enter Air Force air cadet training. After cadet training, he had so impressed his command that he was appointed a flight instructor. After he saved an aircraft at Craig Field, he was sent to Command and Staff school as a First Lieutenant. He was the only officer of that rank in that program.

He was eventually ordered to duties in Japan—as an AT-6 spotter. However, the personnel officer was a classmate, and Kniss talked him into sending him on to the 18th Fighter-Bomber Group that was flying F-51's. His friend warned Kniss against this action due to the high losses being suffered by the pilots who were still flying the capable, but vulnerable, Mustang. [In the three months Kniss was in the 18th, the Wing lost 30 aircraft.] However, Kniss insisted, and was posted to the 18th Fighter-Bomber Group, 12th Squadron.

After just 18 missions Kniss was designated a Flight Leader, a position of great responsibility, ahead of several Captains. On the day he was shot down—his 29th mission—he had been asked by Col. Crane to become the operations officer of the 12th squadron.

Kniss was a very determined and courageous fighter pilot, whose plane had suffered battle damage four or five times during his missions.

Kniss had destroyed two F-51's that month. One had its tail wheel lock fail on takeoff, and the resulting crash "demolished the aircraft in the motor pool. I landed on a searchlight, struck a fuel truck,

and ended up in a Quonset hut." Kniss received a chipped tooth, bruises and abrasions. The cockpit was all that remained intact. The engine of the second Mustang failed over the 11th evacuation hospital. Rather than belly in on a road in the area, "I took the aircraft over a ridge and landed in a dead-end canyon about 1000 feet long. In this canyon, I was subjected to small arm fire from guerillas. The canyon was so small, that the rescue helicopter could only land on his third attempt." Kniss was treated for another chipped tooth and bruises. There was no pilot error in either case.

In April, Kniss had only flown seven combat missions; therefore, he had to fly twenty one or twenty two in May.

As he heard the bayonets being fixed to Chinese rifles, Kniss knew he was going to need all of his determination and courage to face what was ahead. He was very well aware of the World War II Japanese practice of using blindfolded captives for bayonet practice. He braced himself for the pain—and waited.

Suddenly, the blindfold came off, the bayonets were removed, and without explanation, he was moved to a hut, where he was left until nightfall. The Chinese took away his flight suit. Eventually, it was returned. Someone had washed it. Throughout the day Kniss was the object of great curiosity. Both Russian and Chinese soldiers paraded by him all day.

Later that evening, he was taken from the hut by the Koreans and driven a few miles to another location where he was interrogated by a Korean officer who would ask a question, then shove his gun into Kniss' face and scream for emphasis.

Kniss was soon moved into the town of Sinanju—where the real interrogations began—and continued the entire time of his captivity.

Kniss was to be a Prisoner of War for over 400 days, enduring most of it in solitary confinement "in a mud cell." He was "allowed to bathe twice during the entire period of over four hundred days, but unable to brush my teeth at all. My only clothing consisted of a padded Chinese suit, my

old pair of silk flying socks, and a pair of tennis shoes they gave me from which I cut the toes because they were too short. This was all I had to protect me from the cold Siberian winter." Kniss jogged in his cell to keep from freezing. In addition to enduring the solitary confinement, upon his release in September 1953, Kniss was covered with lice, and suffered from severe malnutrition—he had lost 50-60 pounds.

During his hellish time as a POW, he "was treated as an animal, held up for public ridicule, and was used for propaganda purposes by enemies of this country." During one public session during which the Chinese publicly displayed American POWs whose death sentences were reduced to life imprisonment. The photograph shows Kniss, allegedly signing a "confession," with his head in the palm of his hand, and fingers strategically placed in the universal sign of derision and disdain. If the Chinese had noticed the gesture at the time, it would likely have led to his execution. "I felt that I had an obligation to my country and friends to get a message out," he explained.

His whole "ambition was to fly 100 missions in the P-51, and then fly 100 missions in the F-86 for some air to air combat.

My whole world was shattered when I was shot down, as I only ever wanted to be a fighter pilot, and fly air to air combat. I knew that this was my only chance, and this proved to be true," Kniss explained.

June 1952

The major air attack against hydroelectric power plants called for "maximum air effort." Two squadrons of the 18th Group—12th Squadron and 67th Squadron—made "one of the greater efforts produced by this Group on one mission."

Main Street for the 18th Fighter-Bomber Wing at K-46. From right to left is the Communications Center and the Operations Offices for the Two Squadron SAAF, the 67th Squadron and the 12th Squadron. (Urquhart)

Monthly Summary

Elements of the United States 45th Infantry Division in the central sector near Chorwon launched two successful attacks to gain high ground and repulsed determined enemy counterattacks. Otherwise, ground action remained light.

Fifth Air Force, FEAF Bomber Command, and Naval Forces Far East aircraft "flew over 1,200 sorties against North Korean hydroelectric power facilities, rendering eleven of thirteen power plants unserviceable and destroying over ninety percent of North Korea's and twenty-five percent of Manchuria's electric power potential. Previously, the Joint Chiefs of Staff had forbidden attacks on the Sui-ho, Changjin, Pujon, and Kyosen complexes. Despite the destructiveness of the raids, the communists failed to move toward an armistice. Moreover, British Labor Party opposition and U.S. congressional inquiries diminished the political effectiveness of the strikes, signaling that the United States was conducting a limited war. The hydroelectric power plant strikes represented the major exception to the daily FEAF sortie pattern of the previous two months' operations. Also, Fifth Air Force and attached units flew 2,859 close air support sorties to thwart enemy preparations for another offensive and to maintain pilot proficiency in such operations. Fifth Air Force lost fourteen aircraft to enemy ground fire." [1]

F-86s destroyed 21 enemy aircraft, eighteen of them MiGs, while losing two Sabres.

Adapted in part from U.S. Air Force Historical Research Agency. January 2002. The U.S. Air Force's First War: Korea 1950-1953 Significant Events. June 1952. http://www.au.af.mil/au/afhra/wwwroot/korean_war/korean_war_chronology/kwc_1951.html

From K-10 to K-46

The move from K-10 to K-46 was completed during June and "for the first time in many months, the 18ᵗʰ Fighter-Bomber Group began operation as a complete unit." The only personnel left behind at K-10 were the 100 who were attached to the 18ᵗʰ Maintenance Squadron PLM program.

The move from K-10 to K-46 was successful, but "quarters were not immediately available upon arrival and personal property had to be temporarily stored in a tent. This resulted in the loss of a few personal items. Closer coordination with the Air Base Group could have eliminated this situation," the 18ᵗʰ Group reported.

The move was completed mostly by airlift on June 2ⁿᵈ. "An earlier shipment of the operating facilities, such as desks, chairs, cabinets, etc. was made by rail transportation. The airlift was highly successful and was accomplished with such rapidity that this section [Administration] missed only one day of operation."

During half the month, the Wing Office was not receiving the 5ᵗʰ AF Operational Summary, which was "our only reliable source for briefing material on that subject," the Wing history recorded.

Base defense plans were updated on the basis of reports of "possible Guerrilla activity in the Chinhae-Masan area." More stringent defense and security measures were implemented to "protect K-10 from possible attack or acts of sabotage. Meetings were held, and the situation was discussed with recommendations given." The result, after study, coordination with CO's and staff officers of neighboring organizations, was what the Wing "considers to be one of the best base defense plans existing in Korea."

The Wing Chaplain's Office, during its last weeks at Chinhae, continued its religious and morale enhancing programs for Korean Protestant and Catholic personnel, plus servicemen from the South African Air Force. In addition, it provided services for the Korean Air Force Academy during which 574 attended from the five services. During June, attendance at the Base Chapel total 2,606 for Catholic Services and 2,622 for Protestant Services. An important component of the Chaplain's service was "assisting needy Koreans by disbursing won and used clothing through orphanages and schools. The Chaplain employed three Koreans to serve as music director, organist and gardener. [1]

"Maximum Air Effort" Against Hydroelectric Plants

A major air attack against hydroelectric power plants called for "maximum air effort" and on the day of the attack, two squadrons of the 18ᵗʰ Group—12ᵗʰ Squadron and 67ᵗʰ Squadron—made 37 effective sorties out of a total of 38 aircraft airborne. "This was one of the greater efforts produced by this Group on one mission. Subsequent attacks on the power plants were made but with fewer aircraft," the Group reported.

Interdiction and close support missions accounted for the majority of effective sorties for the Group in June. Rail-cutting missions were fewer in June than in May. The combat missions "consisted mainly of rail cuts and close support," the 12ᵗʰ reported. "The outstanding sorties of the month were the hammer job done on 'Ping Pong East Airfield' which was thoroughly clobbered on the 14ᵗʰ by the 18ᵗʰ Group and the power plant raids at Chosen #2 and Fusen #4 on the 23ʳᵈ, 24ᵗʰ, and 28ᵗʰ." [2]

Lights out. *This photograph, looking directly down at what remains of Kyosen Power Plant No. 3, discloses heavy structural damage to the plant in July 1952. The penstocks, leading from the reservoir to the power plant, were cut by bomb bursts (note spray from escaping water). At least one direct hit and two near misses were scored on the generator house (near dark shadow), and the control building probably suffered a direct hit and three near misses. Severe damage was done to the transformer yard. Photo was made by 67th Tactical Reconnaissance Wing. (NARA)*

The maximum effort on June 14th to hit Pyongyang East airfield was noted tersely in the Daily Summary of Operations filed by the 18th Group. The 12th Squadron put 22 aircraft in the air on target during three interdiction efforts and claimed 10 direct hits on the runway at YD 4721. The 67th Squadron put 24 Mustangs on target to score 11 direct hits on the YD 4721 runway. The Two Squadron SAAF, during three missions, with 21 aircraft claimed 14 direct hits on the runway at YD 4721, one building destroyed at CT 1740 and one secondary explosion at DT 1966. [3]

The excellent results achieved during the hydroelectric raids brought the 12th Squadron "a commendation from the Commanding General of the 5th Air Force. One of its flights, 'Nan' Flight, led by Lt. Baxter, was commended in a letter from Colonel Brinson for its outstanding work east of Pohyon-ni, where in cooperation with controller 'Marlin' they inflicted great damage to the enemy while working only 1,000 yards from friendly troops," the 12th reported in its monthly history.

Combat Statistics

18th F-B Wing

June 1952

Average No. A/C Assigned
50
Total Flying Time
2,345
Percent of Aircraft in Commission
55%
Percent of Aircraft AOCP
14%
Combat Sorties Flown by Wing
1,138
12th Squadron Sorties
549
67th Squadron Sorties
586
2 Squadron Sorties
430
A/C Lost to Combat
3
Pilots lost
3

Fuel Consumed
177,524 gals.

Ordnance Expended
.50-cal. Rounds
693,420
Rockets
1,740
Napalm Bombs
224
500-lb. GP Bombs
2,035
Note: Figures and totals may differ in some categories due to differences in numbers provided by each component.

"Typical Combat Missions"

The Operations Summary during this period provides important perspective about combat missions conducted during this period.

On June 23rd, the 12th Squadron Daily Summary of Operations, reported one interdiction mission with 18 effective sorties; one RESCAP mission, and negative aborts. The 18 aircraft it had in the air that day "bombed, rocketed, and strafed a power plant (hydro-electric) and a switching station with two direct bomb hits, seven rocket hits, three near misses on the power plant and one direct bomb hit and one rocket hit on the switching station." The flight claimed "one power plant and one switching station destroyed" at target CV 802561.

The 67th Squadron reported two missions on the 23rd--one interdiction with 18 effective sorties and one RESCAP with one effective sortie. It too, had 18 Mustangs in the air that day to bomb, rocket and strafe the hydro-electric power plant and switching station with eleven direct bomb hits, four rocket hits on the power plant. Three bombs and six rockets found their mark on the switching station. Two large secondary explosions were observed on the generator plant. The 67th claimed a power plant, switching station and generator plan destroyed.

Two Squadron was also heavily involved in the raids with 14 aircraft taking "part in the missions with the other two squadrons." It pilots found the mark with six direct bomb hits on the power plant, followed by two secondary explosions. In addition, six direct bomb hits were made on buildings and four hits "on the power plant at CV-766503" the same target hit by the 67th.

On 24 June, the 12th Squadron hit the hydro-electric power plant at CV 573473, with 10 direct hits on the plant, six on the switch yard and seven near misses. The 67th Squadron also hit the same plant with four direct hits on the power house, two direct hits on the west end of the building,

one direct hit on the east portion of the building, followed by three secondary explosions.

The results achieved by the pilots also reflected great credit on the part of the much appreciated, but often inadequately credited ground and maintenance crews who redoubled their efforts prior to the "hammer jobs." As a result of their extraordinary efforts, the "in-commission" rates for that period approached 100%.

The 12th Squadron reported "no casualties" in June, nor damage to any aircraft. "This streak of good fortune can be attributed to the scarcity of flak as well as the absence in our areas of our *bete noir*,' the MIG-15."

The number of sorties by the Group was up, but as the 12th Squadron noted, "it is the results that matter. Here the picture becomes slightly murky. It seems that the accuracy of the Squadron, particularly in dive bombing pin point targets, leaves room for improvement." Intense critiques pointed out such areas for improvement, including: "no definite procedure for dive bombing, i.e., dive angle, entry into dive and sight picture, and failure on the part of wing man to recognize the target clearly before entry into dive." However, the 12th took comfort in "the credit side of the ledger," and mentioned, "frequently flights in the Squadron have been credited with 100% coverage and 100% effectiveness on close support missions."

June, the 12th Squadron reported, "was a pretty good month from the standpoint of total sorties flown. The weather was unusually fair for a month which threatened to be quite wet according to forecasters." There were only five stand-down days in June due to bad weather. The ideal conditions enabled the 12th to "rack up" the considerable score of 549 sorties and 838 combat flying hours—an average of 19 hours per pilot.

Three aircraft were lost during the month, two of which were in the combat area. Two 18th pilots were MIA and one KIA.

No enemy aircraft were observed in June, on the ground or in the air. "Friendly

jet aircraft were pre-briefed to provide close top cover on all missions within operational range of enemy jet aircraft," the Group reported.

The Group training program continued with all new pilots being given a complete indoctrination in Escape and Evasion, Map Study, Navigation, Bombing and Gunnery, and were given a demonstration of personal flying equipment and all accessories. The course in map reading and the lectures on escape and evasion "delivered by Captain McKay of the Second South Africa Squadron were of particular interest and value," the 12th reported.

"Emphasis on training was made to standardize bombing and rocket tactics, utilizing the 'wing line' method to determine angle of dive and slant range. New pilots were given two combat training missions over the bomb line, with the formation led by experienced pilots who critiqued the mission after its completion." The "aerial phase" of the training course included transition, formation, in-trail aerobatics, full load missions and work on the dive bomb and gunnery ranges.

Pilot Information Files were set up in every squadron ready room. To augment these files and to disseminate information to all pilots, Group Operations established a writing of 'PIF' Memos which call items of flying safety, pilot techniques, and operational conditions to the pilot's attention in brief and concise form." [4]

Some essential equipment was still very hard to get and keep. The AN/URC-4 Survival Radios "became an urgent need as supplies were relinquished and could not be immediately replaced," the Group reported. "There were not enough of these valuable radios and every pilot was not equipped with one on the maximum air effort against the hydro-electric power plants during this reporting period, as he should have been." [5]

On June 25th, the 67th had five missions, two interdiction with 20 effective sorties, two RESCAP with eight effective sorties, and one armed reconnaissance with two effective sorties. Despite all the firepower represented by 30 Mustangs with combat loads, the 67th counted only one bunker destroyed that day. One terse sentence told a far sadder loss for the Squadron. "A/C 363 LOST due to ground fire on mission 1890." 1st Lt. Archie Connors was declared MIA.

"The work load remained heavy due to the movement of Squadron Headquarters from K-10 to K-46."

During the last week in May and the first few days of June, the 67th Squadron moved its headquarters from K-10 (Chinhae, South Korea) to the former "forward combat operations base" at K-46, near Hoengsong, South Korea.

Officer strength dropped from a high of 57 early in June, to 44 with the loss of 24 officers and gains of eleven. Enlisted strength remained at 175 with gains equaling losses.

The 67th was on the move…at least its headquarters. For over a year the squadron's official headquarters had been at K-10 (Chinhae, South Korea). After much preparation, the split squadron operation was coming to an end. The "forward combat operations base" at K-46, near Hoengsong, South Korea would be home to the entire squadron. On June 2nd squadron supply was moved by train and air from K-10 to K-46, in two phases. First, all property and equipment other than combat cargo was moved by train. The second phase included all combat cargo and was moved via air transport. By June 5th, the supply operation was operating at full capacity.

Officer strength peaked at 57 early in June, then dropped to 44 with the loss of 24 officers and gains of eleven. Enlisted strength remained at 175 with gains equaling losses.

The Maintenance Section increased the average in-commission status of the squadron's planes to 95.78 %, a significant accomplishment that enabled the pilots to fly 586 combat missions and report 1,114 combat hours.

Based on the claims reported that month, the 67th had a very successful month of combat operations. In addition to the "typical" entries for buildings (131), gun

"Deluxe quarters" for the 67th Squadron's How Flight at K-46. (Drage)

The 67th Sqadron How Flight "Hilton" at K-46 in Spring 1952. (Urquhart)

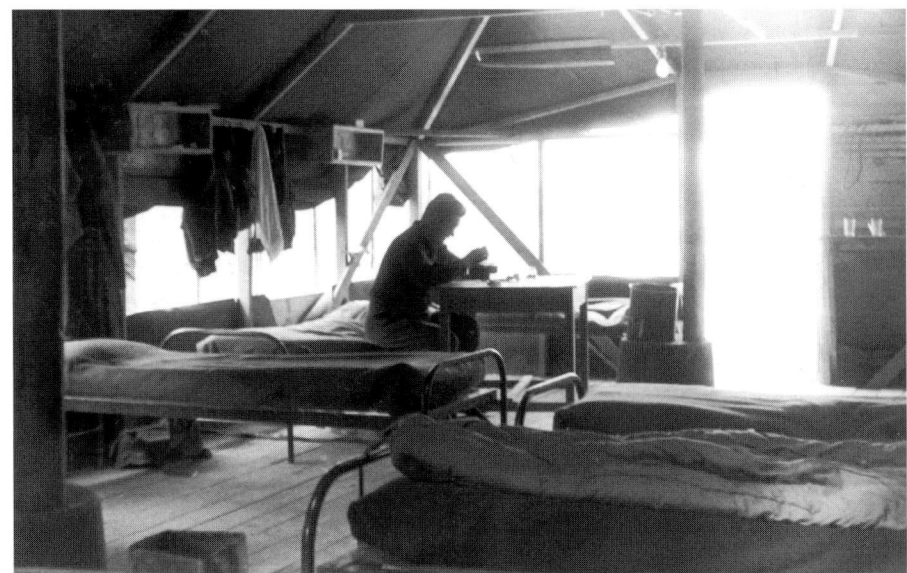

Interior of How Flight "Hilton" at K-46 during warmer Spring weather. 1st Lt. Tim Urquhart works at a table building model cars. The "infamous" diesel oil heater and flue can be seen at right center of photograph. (Urquhart)

positions (7), artillery pieces (13) rail cuts (46), road cuts (15) and bunkers (33), the 67th reported other significant targets, including sampans (10), "comm." Trench (200), "trench" (820), hydroelectric plant buildings (4) and runways (11). The 67th had been hunting different targets in June.

The price had been high.

Endnotes

[1] USAFHRA. *Monthly Historical Report, 18th Fighter-Bomber Wing,* June 1952, p. 2.
[2] USAFHRA. *Unit history of the 18th Fighter-Bomber Group.* June 1952. p. 2.
[3] NARA. *Daily Summary of Operations, 18th Fighter-Bomber Group,* June 14, 1952.
[4] USAFHRA. *Monthly Historical Report, 12th Fighter-Bomber Squadron,* June 1952, p. 7.
[5] USAFHRA. *Unit history of the 18th Fighter-Bomber Group.* June 1952. p. 9.

Significant Events

June 1: The 39th Fighter Interceptor Squadron was reassigned to the 51st Fighter Interceptor Wing.

June 2: All Squadron supplies were moved by train and air from K-10 to K-46, in two phases. First, all property and equipment other than combat cargo was moved by train. The second phase included all combat cargo and was moved via air transport. By June 5th, the supply operation was operating at full capacity. The move "marked the first time in many months in which the Group began to operate as a complete unit, thereby eliminating many of the problems that were inherent in the divided operation," the Group reported that month.

June 7: During an air refueling test, code named Operation HIGHTIDE, thirty-five F-84 ThunderJets took off from Japan, refueled from KB-29M aircraft over Korea, and attacked targets in the north. 1st Lt. Joseph Spinnenweber (67th Squadron) blew a tire while landing at K-46, resulting in a major accident. 1st Lt. David Gray (67th Squadron) hit a cable due to "marginal visibility" in a T-6 en route to K-46.

June 10/11: Eight B-29s from the 19 BG attacked the rail bridge at Kwaksan, North Korea. Enemy MiGs, operating in conjunction with radar-controlled searchlights and flak, destroyed two B-29s and badly damaged a third. This new development in the enemy's air defense system prompted Far East Air Forces to improve electronic countermeasures (ECM) to jam and confuse enemy radar.

June 12: 1st Lt. Russell Bunn (67th Squadron) and 1st Lt. David Baker (67th Squadron) had to make emergency landings at K-46 due to heavy battle damage.

June 13: 1st Lt. George V. Patton (67th Squadron) was MIA.

"Dear Mom," Airman Robert Cranston started out with a new letter to his mother in Hogansville, Georgia. "Yes, this is Friday the 13th and not such a lucky day. We lost another pilot [Patton] and airplane this afternoon. The airplane was Boone's. He is pretty hurt about it but not near as hurt as we all are about the pilot because he was so close to us. He would come out to where we were working and laugh and cut up and act like one of us. He was due to go home in a few days. He had flown his prescribed number of missions and was waiting for orders. It just doesn't pay to get to know these guys. But, outside of that, everything is OK. They made us turn in all of our ammo (bullets), so I guess things are getting better, huh. Old Korea is still the same. Nice weather and cool nights. We don't work as hard as we used to. Will get R&R some time this month. No date is definite, yet."

June 14: After reconnaissance flights revealed repairs at the Pyongyang Airfield, Fifth Air Force fighter-bombers cratered the runways during 150 sorties, rendering them unserviceable during approximately 150 sorties without a loss.

June 15: 1st Lt. William "Tim" Urquart (67th Squadron) hit a cable while on airborne search.

June 18: Major Frank L. Orth succeeded Lt. Col. Joseph T. Crane, Jr. as CO of the 12th Squadron. Orth had "considerable World War II fighter experience to recommend him for the job," the 12th reported. Col. Sheldon S. Brinson succeeded Major Orth as Commander of the 18th FB Group. Orth "for a short period, was Commanding Officer of the Group."

June 23: Fifth Air Force fighter-bombers, with F-86 cover, flew approximately 250 sorties against North Korean hydroelectric power plants. The Sui-ho complex sustained seventy percent structural damage, rendering it non-operational.

June 24: Far East Air Forces flew 1,043 sorties, the highest daily total for the month. Fifth Air Force fighter-bombers flew over 250 sorties against North Korean hydroelectric power plants, four of them having been targets the previous day. 1st Lt. John A. McAlpine (67th Squadron) was KIA.

June 24/25: Fifth Air Force fighter-bombers "rendered temporarily unserviceable" the Samdong-ni rail complex, the choke point of the east-west and north-south rail lines in North Korea. Night-flying B-26s seeded the area with delayed-action bombs to hamper repair efforts. [1]

June 25: 1st Lt. Archibald H. Connors, Jr. (67th Squadron) was MIA (later declared KIA) during Mission 1890 during which How Flight was assigned to fly cover for a helicopter rescue mission to extract a downed Navy pilot from a heavily defended area of the infamous "Iron Triangle." On the third try, the helicopter pilot, Captain Leslie Wayne Lear, was successful in rescuing Ensign Ronald Eaton, but was then shot down. Lear and Ensign Eaton were killed. The medical technician, S/Sgt Bobby Holloway survived and was a POW for 14 months. Connors was shot down minutes later while flying at tree top level, attempting to determine the fate of those on board the downed helicopter. It was one of the most heroic, and expensive, aerial rescue attempts of the Korean War.

Airman Robert Cranston wrote his mother on 26 June 1952 from Sleepy Hollow Korea, K-46 Air Base that he was "back in old Korea again (darn it)." Cranston had just returned from a short, three-day R&R leave in Japan. The more he went to Japan, the more he liked it, he reported.

"Nothing new around here," he reported. Then added, "We lost two planes a couple of days ago. Yes, pilots too." [McAlpine and Connors]

Airman First Class Bob Cranston stands beside the World Memorial Bridge constructed by the 434th Engineering Construction Battalion and dedicated to "United Nations Military Personnel who died here in the battle against Communist aggression." (Cranston)

"An oriental building in the area of WonJu," noted Airman Bob Cranston in May 1952. (Cranston)

Cranston told his mother about the "big damn near the Manchurian border on the Yellow River. We were in on that and will be until it is completely destroyed."

June 27: 1st Lt. David Gray (67th Squadron) had to make an emergency "belly landing at K-46 due to battle damage." This was Lt. Gray's "third aircraft to belly in,"

During infrequent trips out of the K-46 compound, 18th Wing personnel looked for souvenirs in the WonJu market. (Cranston)

recalled Master Sergeant Thomas "Red" Ryder, a 67th Squadron crew chief at the time, "another F-51 and a T-6. This was my airplane--064--and I guess his experience helped because we only had to replace the prop, engine, wing tip, scoop and radiators. This all happened at K-46 (the advance operating base, where heavy maintenance or repairs were not usually performed) within a week and it was flying again."

Combat Losses

1st Lt. Archibald "Archie" Connors, Jr., KIA 25 June.

1st Lt. John Matheson McAlpine, 67th FBS pilot KIA on 24 June 1952. McAlpine was born in Union, South Carolina, on 23 May 1927, the second youngest of six children. He lost his father at an early age and was reared by his mother, Mrs. Joe Ketchin McAlpine, of Union, South Carolina. His early school years were spent in Union where he graduated from high school in 1944. He attended Georgia Tech for a year but the quiet and friendly "Johnny Mac" joined the cadet corps at West Point in 1946. A good description of Johnny Mac during these years is furnished by one of his roommates at West Point who wrote the following for the HOWITZER. "Johnny Mac is one of those people who has never been dejected for a second even at West Point. He's never been too busy to help a classmate. Lucky at everything, a lot of fun, considerate of everybody, and a hive at everything." This is the same Johnny Mac who always had a smile and a helping hand for everyone. Upon graduation McAlpine chose the Air Force. He entered flight training at San Angelo, Texas, and then followed the usual route to Selma, Alabama, for completion of flight training. In August 1951 he went to St. Louis where he married Carol, the girl he had met during his third year at West Point. The newly married couple traveled to Luke Air Force Base for their first station, but it was only a short time later that Johnny received orders for Korea. John M. McAlpine, 1st Lt., USAF, while flying as a fighter pilot with the 67th Fighter Bomber Squadron, 18th Fighter Bomber Group, was killed in action as a result of participation in the Korean operations on 24 June 1952. Earlier, he had successfully completed numerous combat missions in an F-51 type aircraft from 10 February to 25 April 1952. His citation says in part: "While participating in aerial flights against forces of the enemy in the Korean Campaign, First Lieutenant John M. McAlpine distinguished himself... by flying at dangerously low altitude in adverse weather over enemy held territory, rocketed, strafed, and bombed enemy supplies, troops, equipment, and transportation facilities. By his aggressive leadership, and courage, and by his superior judgment and flying skill, First Lieutenant McAlpine has brought great credit upon himself and the United States Air Force."

1st Lt. George Vernon Patton, 67th Squadron pilot from Washington, D.C., was KIA on 13 June 1952. "On June 13, 1952, while on a combat mission, his aircraft received a direct hit by anti-aircraft fire, hit the ground at a 45 degree angle and exploded," the American Battle Monuments Commission records.

"I was in Japan awaiting transportation home," 1st Lt. Wilfred "Budd" Stapley recalled, "when I got word that George had been shot down on his last scheduled mission. It was during a mission to Ping Pong [Pyongyang, NK] and his wingman said a 90-mm shell hit his aircraft in the cockpit. The aircraft fell in pieces." Patton, the namesake and nephew of General George Patton, was also an Army brat. His father, Stapley recalled, was a career army officer. The young Patton had flown a combat tour during WWII as a tail gunner on a B-17. While they were roommates at Craig AFB, Alabama during Advanced Single Engine flight training, Stapley recalled Patton "as the most dedicated person to doing the best job possible that I ever saw. The Air Force lost a future General when it lost George Patton."

"For some reason, he and I became friends," remembered Donald R. Smith, at the time a Corporal in the 18th Wing. "Here I was a lowly Corporal and he was a fighter pilot and an officer. Didn't make much difference to him. I asked him one time if he was related to the General George Patton of WWII fame. He said he didn't want to talk about it. He came to me one day and said he was flying to Seoul and if there was anything I wanted or needed, he would get it for me. There wasn't a thing I could think of except maybe if he could get a bottle of whisky," Smith recalled, "it sure would taste good. Sure enough, a few hours later he came back with a fifth of Canadian Club. It cost me $1.50." Patton and Smith "would sit around occasionally and have a drink or two. He was shot down in June 1952. His wing man saw no parachute and nothing on the radio and no activity after the plane crashed."

Endnotes

Adapted in part from U.S. Air Force Historical Research Agency. January 2002. The U.S. Air Force's First War: Korea 1950-1953 Significant Events. June 1952. http://www.au.af.mil/au/afhra/wwwroot/korean_war/korean_war_chronology/kwc_1952.html

Hit by .30-caliber

How Flight was on a mission in late June 1952 just before R&R, led by Capt. Elliot

Sergeants Weaver and Cory haul a load of 250-lb bombs. (Black)

Ayer. First Lieutenant William E. McShane was flying No. 3, and a visiting Major was flying No. 4.

The flight was further organized into two elements. The most senior pilot, Capt. Ayer, led the flight. It was called a "finger formation" of four. The Flight Leader flew in the "middle finger" position. No. 2, 2nd Lt. Tim Urquart, flew in the "index finger" position. Numbers Three and Four were flying in the "ring" and "little" finger positions.

How Flight's mission was "routine"—armed interdiction on targets identified during the flight and attacked with bombs, rockets, napalm and .50-caliber machine gun strafing. "We came in four abreast—side by side—separated by about 50 yards," when Urquhart's plane was hit by ground fire. A .30-caliber round grazed the fuselage, missed the armored glass windscreen and shattered the side glass. The round nicked his head.

At the same time, he saw a fireball on his right. "It was the Major crashing and burning. He just blew up." The three survivors pulled up, aborting the mission. Procedure at that point required that they begin a search of the area to determine whether the missing pilot was alive or not.

Urquhart knew his plane had been hit at least once and might have taken ground fire in the plane's liquid cooled engine cooling system. "It had plumbing pipes all over the aircraft. I didn't know where else I might be hit and perhaps leaking coolant." If so, he knew his engine would have only a limited amount of flying time left before it would overheat and bring him down in enemy territory.

Watching his instruments closely, he circled over the area, searching for any sign of life and "waiting for the rescue flight to relieve us."

Urquhart had another problem. He was lost. "Visibility was god awful. All you could see by looking straight down was a cone-shaped view of the ground that was only about a mile across." He knew he could not make it home again "without being led" by an experienced member of the Flight.

"So, I stayed with the Leader—because I had to and because I had nowhere else to go," he recalled.

After the Flight returned to K-46, Urquhart went to "sick call" to have the "scratch" over his right eye looked at by the Flight Surgeon, a young First Lieutenant right out of medical school. He asked Urquhart if he could "see the hill" right outside the window on which was located a radio direction finding unit. "Yes, sir!" Urquhart answered the doctor. "OK, you can go on back to work," the doctor replied and returned him to a duty status.

Attacking AA gun

"We were attacking and bombing a target in North Korea—some buildings that we soon learned were protected by anti-aircraft guns," recalled former 1st Lt. Tim Urquhart.

On the way down Urquhart noticed a gun firing at them from a position very close to where he knew the bomb release point would be. He "eased over" during the Mustang's approach to the target during the dive. As he kept the gun literally in his sights, he saw "a gigantic smoke ring come out of that gun" as it fired directly at him.

"About that time I decided that getting that particular gun was not quite as important to me as it had been a few moments before," he remembered. He readjusted his approach and dropped his bomb on the targeted buildings a few seconds later and "got on out of there."

1st Lt. William Timmons "Tim" Urquhard receives the Distinguished Flying Cross. (Urquhart)

The lost magneto...

A magneto generates the spark for a spark plug. The F-51 had two magnetos, a primary and a backup "to get you home."

Mustang pilots had an expression that when you crossed the "bomb line" the engine goes into automatic "rough." This referred to the effect that crossing into hostile territory had on the pilot's alertness, or some would say, to his imagination. Anxious eyes would scan the instruments constantly alert for any sign of potential trouble that might jeopardize his chances of getting back to base.

The 67th's How Flight was "chugging along" on the last mission before a five-day period of R&R in late June. About the time the flight cross the bomb line, 2nd Lt. Tim Urquhart's engine began to run rough.

"Shoot," he thought to himself. "It's just my imagination. I'm getting nervous in the service and maybe a little clanky." He decided not to abort the mission, even though the engine seemed to be running "mighty rough."

How Flight finally reaching the target and made its attack. "We missed the target," Urquhart remembered, "and returned to base."

He still thought his perception of the engine running rough was more imagined than real, so he didn't "write up" the aircraft upon returning to K-46. Instead, he parked it and "went off to his tent to relax after the mission."

The next pilot in the airplane pre-flighted the aircraft and ran up the engine to check its performance. In doing so, he discovered that one of the two magnetos had failed. Urquhart had flown an entire mission with only one...barely adequate...magneto.

"Pedro Tare" and "Filter RESCAP #1"
Into the "Iron Triangle"

The USS BON HOMME RICHARD (CV 31) had gotten underway from Yokosuka, Japan on Saturday morning, 21 June 1952 en route to its assigned operating area. The next day it joined Task Force 77 off the eastern coast of Korea near the 38th Parallel. TF 77 was a powerful armada of four U.S. aircraft carriers, including in addition to the BON HOMME RICHARD, the USS BOXER (CV 21), USS PHILIPPINE SEA (CV 47) and USS PRINCETON (CV 37), supported by various heavy support and screening ships.

The "Bonny Dick" was home to Carrier Air Group SEVEN, commanded by Commander G.B. Brown, USN. CARGRU Seven included seven squadrons and detachments of jet, propeller and helicopter aircraft. VF-71 and VF-72 had a total of 32 F9F-2 "Patherjet" fighters. VF-74 was flying 16 F4U-4 "Corsairs." The 25 pilots of VA-75 flew 16 AD-4 "Sky Raider" attack fighter-bombers.

On Wednesday, 25 June, unfavorable weather over most of North Korea hindered carrier air operations. However, "coordinated jet-prop strikes were made on troop concentrations, supply storage areas and truck parks in the CT sector south of Wonsan," CV-31 reported.

Shortly after noon, about two miles east of present day Simp'o, North Korea, Ensign Ronald Dow Eaton and his wingman were en route to a strike mission in their F4U-4s flying at about 10,000 feet. It was Eaton's third combat mission. Eaton's wingman reported anti-aircraft fire in the form of large black bursts.

Eaton was soon telling his wingman that he was losing oil pressure rapidly. His first reaction was to head for water—and safety. However, his engine was in no condition to get him that far—about 25 miles.

"A few minutes afterward Ron radioed that he was abandoning his plane and the pilots who were accompanying him saw him parachute to the ground and run to take cover in some trees some distance from where his parachute landed. The planes in the air observed numerous enemy troops in the area."

On the morning of June 25, 1952, Captain Wayne Lear and Medical Technician A/1c Bobby Holloway (later MSgt.) were on call at an advanced "strip" just behind the bomb line. They had flown to the site early that morning from the 8055th MASH. This was only the second time that Holloway had been on call for pilot rescue duty—"pilot pickup" they called it. They were on "stand by" pending a call from the Joint Operations Center in Seoul alerting them for a rescue mission.

Fifth Air Force Joint Operations Center immediately contacted 18th Fighter-Bomber Wing Operations at K-46 when it was notified that Eaton was down. Soon after, two 67th Fighter-Bomber Squadron RESCAP (Rescue Combat Air Patrol) flights

(Continued on page 513)

Captain Leslie Wayne Lear *(standing at far left) participates in a March AFB briefing that explains the air rescue capabilities of the H-5 helicopter. (Della Holloway)*

Captain Leslie Wayne Lear

Ronald Dow Eaton *was born in North Reading, Massachusetts on December 22, 1929. When he was about 15, the Eaton family moved several miles away to Wilmington, Massachusetts, on Silver Lake.*

Eaton had blue eyes and wavy brown hair. He packed 152 muscular pounds on a wiry 5'8" frame. He was strong, agile and had fast reflexes—all good qualities for high school athletics and later, for service as a Navy fighter pilot.

"Ron worked every job he could get as a teenager—from shoveling snow off the railroad tracks to cutting ice from local ponds or washing off the bay and straw they used to insulate the precious ice from the summer heat," remembered his sister, Joyce. Ron called her "Joy."

On 27 February 1947, even before he graduated from Wilmington high school, Ron Eaton enlisted in the Naval Reserve. In some respects, his choice of military service was preordained—all his brothers had chosen the Navy, as well. One of his brothers, Everard, explained with tongue in cheek that he had chosen the Navy because if he ever had to die, at least he would die clean.

In 1951 he graduated from Acadia University in Nova Scotia, Canada. Almost immediately, the Navy sent him down to Pensacola, Florida to earn his Navy "Wings of Gold."

Ensign Ronald Dow Eaton *of Wilmington, Massachsetts.*

USS BON HOMME RICHARD (CV 31), *a 27,100-ton* Essex *class aircraft carrier, was built at the New York Navy Yard, Brooklyn, New York. She was commissioned in late 1944, just in time to join other new, fast carriers in the Pacific combat zone in March 1945 that were to take part in the final raids on Japan. With the end of hostilities in mid-August,* BON HOMME RICHARD *continued operations off Japan until September, when she returned to the United States. "Magic Carpet" personnel transportation duties occupied her into 1946. She was thereafter generally inactive until decommissioning at Seattle, Washington, in January 1947.* BON HOMME RICHARD *was recommissioned in January 1951 for Korean War service and deployed to the Western Pacific that May, sending her planes against enemy targets in Korea until the deployment ended late in the year. A second combat tour followed from May-December 1952, during which she was redesignated CVA-31.*

Airman First Class (later Master Sergeant) **Bobby D. Holloway** *was the Medical Technician aboard "Pedro Tare."*

were notified and briefed by the 18th Fighter-Bomber Group Operations and Intelligence Duty Officers at K-46, Hoengsong, SK. "Filter RESCAP #1" was led by How Flight Commander, Captain Elliott D. Ayer. Flying as his wingman was 1st Lt. Archie Connors, who had recently returned to the squadron from a 45-day period of emergency leave. His wife, Frankie, had almost been killed in an automobile accident. Their daughter, Sharon Lee, had been still-born.

A radio call was received from JOC and relayed to Capt. Leslie Wayne Lear that a Navy pilot was down. All the information known to FAF was passed along to the pilot and crew. "Everything they knew about the situation and area, they passed along to us," Holloway related.

"One of the Army L-19 spotter plane pilots showed us a map of the area. The locations of known anti-aircraft guns were noted with a small black circle or dot. The map in that area was almost solid with black dots. He told us that he didn't think we should go in." However, Lear was ordered to proceed with the mission by headquarters.

"We were told to go...and we did," Holloway explained.

They made a quick take-off and headed toward the downed pilot at about 50 mph.

Weather conditions in the pickup area were not favorable. The visibility and ceiling were "limited," with winds approaching 45 mph in the pick-up area, approximately 22 miles NNE of Kumhwa, Korea. "We flew northeast at about 4,000 feet. Flak was popping all around," Holloway said.

The rescue helicopter was given the code sign of "Pedro Tare."

"Pedro Tare" was an H-5H Sikorsky helicopter attached to Detachment One of the 3rd Air Rescue Squadron. At the controls was 27-year old Captain Leslie Wayne Lear from Santa Anna, California. His medical technician was A/1c Bobby D. Holloway from Dubach, Louisiana.

"Pedro" was flying from a "power air strip" at CT 3426 (approximately 20 miles WSW of Kumhwa, SK), a forward operating strip between Old Baldy and Cholwan.

The 3rd Air Rescue Squadron was stationed at Seoul City Air Base, about 45 minutes from the bomb line. However, to cut response time to a minimum, the helicopter spent most of its time when assigned pilot pickup duty on standby at the forward strip.

At approximately 1500, the Mustangs

of "Filter RESCAP Special #1" located the slow, low helicopter. "Rendezvous was affected between 1500I and 1510I." ["I" or "India" was the time zone for the Korean theater of operations.]

Captain Ayer directed his No. 3 and No. 4 Mustang pilots to proceed immediately to Eaton's last known location at CT 8274. Ayer and Connors stayed with "Pedro Tare" to protect the vulnerable helicopter as it approached the pickup point.

"Filter RESCAP joined up with us...they were circling over us because we were so much slower. I know we were in contact with them. It took us about 45 minutes to arrive over the location. They kept directing us into the area," Holloway noted.

When the two escorting Mustangs and the helicopter arrived in the pickup area, Ayer's second element of Mustangs Nos. 3 and 4, were "orbiting" at 10,000 feet. They were providing "high cover" for "Filter RESCAP Special #2," four additional Mustangs from the 18th that were preparing to suppress any ground fire and flak. The "high cover" fighter-bombers were watchful for any enemy aircraft in the area, but more importantly, trying to spot muzzle flashes from the AA guns and then direct the "low cover" aircraft in successfully attacking the numerous emplacements.

Captain Ayer was not only directing the air covering and fire suppression operation for eight Mustangs, but doing so while his own plane was exposed to significant danger due to his assigning to himself and Lt. Connors the most vulnerable, low-level covering position for the helicopter.

Captain Ayer directed a softening up strafing run by four of the Mustangs while he guarded the helicopter by circling at low altitude. "The rescue team waited until a covering force of four F-51 fighters had softened up the pickup spot. There were no enemy sighted, but before the rescue helicopter went in one of the fighters buzzed the area a number of times, flying just above ground in an attempt to draw enemy fire (and thereby exposing the enemy positions so the other fighters could attack them). No enemy fire was encountered, so the helicopter started to land." (CILHI/REFNO # FSC 548-A)

"We approached the location at about 6,500 feet and immediately they begin lobbing anti-aircraft at us. We were in the mountains and it was hard to make out anything below in the maze of rugged hills and valleys," medical technician Bobby Holloway remembered.

"He's on the tabletop," one of the fighter RESCAP pilots said over the radio. He meant that Ensign Eaton was somewhere on a flat topped mountain below us. As Pedro Tare began its descent towards that location, puffs of flak smoke began to erupt in the sky around it.

"When we arrived in the area," Holloway recalled, "the downed pilot signaled us with a survival mirror."

After "Filter RESCAP #2" had strafed the area and drawn no enemy fire, "Pedro Tare" made its first approach to Eaton's position.

1ˢᵗ Lt. Archie Connors at K-10/Chinhae shortly after his arrival in Korea in January 1952. Stationery was hard to obtain and was worth carrying around to prevent "borrowing" by fellow pilots.

"We then proceeded to go in," Holloway said, "to make the hoist pick up. Since he was on the side of a hill, we first attempted to make a running pick up, but with no success."

"We did see that he was on a hillside, not a steep hillside, but enough that trying to hover a helicopter was very delicate. The first time we went in to make a running pickup—maintaining some forward motion with the helicopter, while we lowered the sling "O"-ring and dragged it by him—virtually trolling for the pilot. If the sling was on target the downed pilot could break from cover, grab the sling and put one arm, then the other through the "U"-shaped harness, and be winched aboard the helicopter even as it tried to gain both speed and altitude. The pilot would be dangling in mid-air as the helicopter pulled away from the pick up site," Holloway explained.

Unfortunately, on the first attempt Eaton did not break cover in time to grab the dangling sling. Holloway provided directions and vectors as Lear worked the controls feverishly to gain some speed, hold his altitude and make another pass at the hillside that was alive with hostile fire—from small arms to anti-aircraft emplacements, Holloway said.

It was a trap. Capt. Lear in "Pedro Tare" reported to his RESCAP that he was under heavy machine-gun fire and worse, that he had been hit." The situation was deteriorating rapidly.

Second Attempt

As Captain Lear circled the heavily damaged helicopter, Airman Holloway provided directions based on Eaton's mirror signals. The flak was much heavier and closer now as the guns zeroed in on the lumbering, awkward helicopter.

As Holloway tried to vector Lear to the location they had last seen the mirror signal, something else caught his eye on the ground. It appeared to be an enemy bunker—probably a communications bunker, he thought, since wires and two antennas stuck up from the emplacement. He could see two Chinese soldiers down in the bunker "moving around."

Quickly reaching for his M-2 Carbine, Holloway "emptied a 30-round clip into the bunker as fast as the semi-automatic rifle could fire. "After that I didn't see anyone moving around in that bunker."

"We had started to come around for another attempt when we were hit in the nose of the helicopter," Holloway explained. "From what I could see most of the 'glass' was gone and the instrument panel was leaning at an angle—to the right. Captain Lear and I were cut by the flying shards of Plexiglass and debris. I was cut on the head, face, and hands."

Lear asked the Mustangs for strafing attacks to suppress the ground fire. All six

Mustangs, including Ayer and Connors, then strafed the ridges where enemy gunners were hidden. The six Mustang CAP made three strafing passes at the ridges before Lear determined to make another rescue attempt.

Captain Lear circled the heavily damaged helicopter until they again spotted the mirror signal. The flak was much heavier and closer now as the guns zeroed in on the lumbering, awkward helicopter. Captain Lear "was working that chopper like a man possessed," Holloway reported.

"We then attempted another running pick-up. We dropped steadily from about 1,000 feet to less than 500 feet, but I still couldn't make out the pilot's position. Machine guns opened up on us as we came down out of the fire line."

The helicopter was now almost hovering at about 30 feet above the brush. "Eaton stood up and began jumping up and down—waving us in." As the helicopter moved over the ecstatic pilot, the sling did not quite reach the pilot and the helicopter passed slowly over Eaton.

"As we were coming out of the second attempt we were hit in the left side [Plexiglas] bubble by AA fire. It came in the bottom and exited the top without exploding, showering the interior with shards of plastic and pieces of instrument panel. This was approximately a foot to my left," Holloway said. "The concussion momentarily stunned me. When I came to, I was learning forward, hanging by my seat belt."

For a moment, he wondered if Captain Lear had survived the blast. Wind was howling around and through the now open nose of the aircraft. Captain Lear was wounded again, but still maneuvering the aircraft. "Are you OK," Holloway yelled. Lear nodded his head in the affirmative as he fought to get the now heavily damaged helicopter under control and back up to about 80 feet.

Third Attempt

Now making his third attempt, Captain Lear changed his approach. Even though coming to a full stop—at a hover—in mid air—required extremely delicate manipulation of the helicopter's controls, and would place him in even more danger from enemy fire, he decided that it would give Eaton a better chance to grab the sling and be hoisted aboard. Trying to keep the damaged helicopter in the air in a hover about 75 feet above the hiding pilot required not only courage, but also extraordinary airmanship.

"We were not moving--absolutely stationary," Holloway recalled.

There was a brief let up in the machine gun and small arms fire "until after we turned around and began to slow into a hover at about 30 feet over the Navy pilot...Captain Lear somehow hovered the helicopter over the hillside to give Ensign Eaton time to get into the hoist sling. Everything was perfect this time. Eaton reached out and caught it with both hands," as Holloway motioned frantically

for him to get into the sling. As soon as Holloway saw that Eaton had the sling around him, he yelled into the microphone, "I've got him, I've got him. Let's get the hell out of here."

As Holloway operated the hoist that was slowly winching the downed Ensign toward the hovering helicopter, Captain Lear began to climb away from the exposed position, nursing the battered chopper forward, struggling to gain altitude as Eaton was towed through the air, up and away from his brush hideout. Now the dangling Naval pilot and the helicopter were just one big target for any of the countless gunners and ground troops that were shooting at them.

The hoist started up—dragging Eaton up towards the struggling helicopter. "It seemed like forever, but it was more like a minute," Holloway recalled.

Ignoring his wounds, Captain Lear maneuvered the heavily laden and badly damaged helicopter as it slowly gained altitude and speed. Airman First Class Holloway pulled Ensign Eaton, now without a parachute, through the helicopter door.

As "Pedro Tare" began to climb away from the pickup area and to gain speed, escorted by "Filter RESCAP Special #1," Captain Ayer was escorting the helicopter so closely that he reported he was seeing "parts flying from Pedro Tare." (3ARS Incident Report 26 June 52)

"Ensign Eaton had just gotten into the helicopter when we were hit the third time. He didn't have time to put on the spare

parachute that we carried. The helicopter just seemed to be coming apart," Holloway said. The helicopter had been hit "in the rotor head." Other reports from the RESCAP Mustangs seemed to indicate the tail rotor had been shot off.

"The helicopter was going down in a diving spin (presumed loss of tail rotor)." (ARS Detachment 1 Incident Report 26 June 52)

"The way it was hit—you know it—you don't wait around. It was more like an explosion. A jolt. I believe we were hit in the rotor head from the jolt and the sound. The helicopter was not spinning, then, but it soon rolled to the right and that's when Eaton and I went out of the aircraft through my door on the left hand side," Holloway said.

They had just seconds to get out the door of the plummeting helicopter.

"Captain Lear continued to yank on the controls trying to keep it under enough control" for Holloway and Eaton to exit with enough altitude for their chutes to open," Holloway recalled.

"We both went out...at the door I grabbed him and he grabbed me and we went out the door as best we could holding on to each other."

There was no time for Holloway to explain to Eaton that their only chance was to ride the one chute down together. He didn't stop to think that in doing so he would jeopardize his own life. He simply grabbed Eaton and held on. As they fell clear of the spinning helicopter, Eaton reached around to the left side of Holloway's chest and they pulled the D-ring—together.

"As we cleared the door, we pulled the D-ring. We both pulled the D-ring. They told me later, after I got back, that we cleared the aircraft at 800 feet."

"Face to face...we had hold of each other."

"I never thought about the consequences...I knew he didn't have time to get a parachute on. I had mine on. I hoped we could make it together...on one chute."

The parachute opened moments later. The "snap" was violent and despite the efforts of both men to hang on to each other,

it jerked Eaton free from Holloway's grasp. "It was so quick that you had no time to react. There was no time for anything. One instant he was there, then an instant later he was gone."

"Sergeant Holloway bailed out of the helicopter at an altitude of approximately 800 feet. His statements indicate that the emergency occurred so suddenly the Navy pilot had not time to put on a chute and therefore bailed out with Sergeant Holloway. The shoulder strap he was holding broke when the chute opened and the Navy pilot fell almost 800 feet to the ground. Sergeant Holloway's statements further reveal that Captain Lear...bailed out at such a low altitude his chute did not have time to open before hitting the ground." (AFPMP-12-E-3/RT 42755 of 19 January 1954 ICO Lear, Leslie W. AO 932234 Determination Case #191)

[Note: The broken strap referred to in the Report of Death was not the parachute strap, but a strap on the survival vest Airman Holloway had reattached below his waist. He was unable to wear a parachute and a vest and still have enough mobility to operate the helicopter hoist.]

"The first man left the helicopter from the right side [*Holloway reported the left side*], and successfully parachuted to the ground. He was seen removing his chute.

1st Lt. William Timmons "Tim" Urquhart, a native of Houston, Texas, "dreamed of being a fighter pilot just like my older cousins." He entered Aviation Cadet Class 51-G in September 1950 and graduated in October 1951. His entire class of 25 new Lieutenants was assigned to the Air Force "pipeline" to Korea. Three of his classmates were killed at Luke AFB and three more in Korea.

The other chutes did not open..." (ARS Detachment 1 Incident Report 26 June 52)

Ayer and Connors stayed with the helicopter as its passengers and pilot attempted to bail out. They were themselves in greater danger as they now attempted to determine the fate of the downed airmen. In fact, they flew so close to the helicopter that Ayer *[as Flight Leader he would make radio reports]* was able to report the approximate altitudes at which the pilot and crew left the spinning helicopter and the fact that one parachute had opened.

Enemy fire continued to be intense and accurate.

Shortly after the helicopter had been shot down, Lt. Connors radioed his own "Mayday," after being hit by ground fire and crashed. Captain Ayer continued making "passes" over the crash sites only a mile or so apart, subjecting himself to grave danger in the process as he attempted to determine what could be done. He continued to patrol the area at low altitude for over 15 minutes before being ordered to return to base.

The sole survivor from the helicopter, Airman Holloway had landed on a berm that separated two dry rice paddies and immediately took cover. Firing was very intense all around him even though the helicopter was now down. He soon realized why—the fighter bomber escorts—Ayer and Connors—were still over head trying to provide cover and to determine the condition of the men they had seen bail out of the plunging helicopter.

"There were no bullets hitting near me that I could tell—but I wasn't standing up to look around, either," he reported in a recent interview.

Struggling out of his parachute, he stayed as close to the ground and tried to stay hidden in the brush. Above the "popping" of small arms, machine guns and heavier anti-aircraft cannon now at a crescendo, Holloway heard another sound—a Merlin engine at full throttle right overhead. Captain Ayer and Lt. Connors had stayed close to the helicopter to provide cover. After the helicopter had crashed, they dropped below 500' and circled the area trying to determine the status of the three helicopter airmen.

After Holloway was on the ground and out of his chute, he looked up to see one of the RESCAP Mustangs circling "right where I was"—directly overhead in a tight left bank—a tight circle standing up on his left wing. He was no more than 150'-200' above me. I could see the pilot looking down, searching for me and the oth-ers," Holloway remembered.

Moments later, as 1st Lt. Archie Connors' searched the brush for wreckage and signs of life, "he came around where I could see him right in front of me, and a puff of smoke came out of the engine," Holloway said.

"Mayday, Mayday, I'm hit," Connors radioed to Ayer and Filter RESCAP pilots. His Mustang began a slow, flat spin to the right from approximately 200-feet. There was not enough altitude to bail out. He would have to dead stick the plane into a belly landing—just seconds after he was hit.

The Mustang "rolled over, went right down and I didn't see him after that," Holloway reported. Holloway dared not raise up to try and see the crashing Mustang. Doing so would give away his position and make himself more of a target than he already was.

Back at K-46, Crew Chief Barry Agovino and his team waited anxiously for "Filter RESCAP Special #1" to return. "Of the four pilots on that mission, I knew and remember Capt. Ayer," he said. "I recall the day we waited for Capt. Ayer and Lt. Connors to return from the mission. We would wait out in the parking area with the crewchiefs whose planes were late for their hoped for return. The wait would sometimes last for hours beyond the time when we knew that the plane must long before have run out of fuel. Somehow we were the last to receive notice that the plane was officially missing or had been seen going in. The feeling of emptiness and helplessness cannot be described."

On August 3, 1952 1st Lieutenant John E. Hill, USAF explained in a letter to Connors' wife, that "we were in a flight of four (4) aircraft on a RESCAP Mission to cover the helicopter while it made the pickup. Lieutenant (William) McShane and myself were top cover while Archie and Captain Ayer were bottom cover with another flight that had covered the helicopter while he made a successful pickup, and were escorting him out when Archie was hit. He flew about one mile when we saw his ship crash on the side of a knoll in a flat position. The aircraft did not burn and was intact when Captain Ayer made passes over it, but there was no movement at all in the area of the crash."

"At this same time #2 man of FRS #1 was hit and crashed at CT 905695. The #2 man [Connors] had called "Mayday" twice, but crashed and it appeared as no chance of survival." [USAF Third Air Rescue Squadron, Report of Incident 26 June 1952 (SECRET/Declassified)]

As soon as he could get refueled and rearmed back at K-46, Captain Ayer was again airborne with How Flight—Hill, and McShane were joined by 2nd Lt. Tim Urquhart. The operations summary called his mission "1 Armed Recce w/4 effective sorties." How Flight headed directly back to CT 905695.

"A little while later, I heard airplanes in the distance. I sneaked a quick look in the direction of the engine noise. It was the F-51's coming back to look for us," Holloway related.

When How Flight arrived over the crash site, they made several low altitude passes over the scene looking for any signs of life. There were none. The cockpit of aircraft 363 was empty. Following standing orders in such cases, How Flight made a final pass and regrouped in an in-trail formation. One by one they made a firing pass at 363, now a target that would have no future military use to the enemy. Before that mission was completed, the report would include: "2 artillery positions destroyed, 2 bunkers destroyed, 2 KIA at CT0818; 3 bunkers destroyed, 3 active artillery positions destroyed and 1 secondary explosion at CT819539…"

Top Secret Deal

Following two weeks of intensive refresher training in combat flying--he had been on emergency leave in the Z.I. attending to his wife who had been seriously injured in an automobile accident--by June 19th, Lt. Connors was again flying combat missions with the 67th Squadron. At 1630 that afternoon, he sat down in the ready room at Hoengsong, South Korea to write his older brother, Woodrow. He had al-

ready flown two missions that day. Having cheated death twice that day, his letter alternated between sophomoric humor and prophetic insights.

"How is the elder son of the clan? Still elder? Oh well, guess my high level of humor is way above your thin head uh, hair that is."

"Now 4:30 p.m. and already have two missions today. What's better than that. The flak on the second wasn't intense, it was unbearable! What a pity it would be for the world to lose my genius at such an early age.

"How is A. H. & Sons?" [A. H. Connors & Sons Construction Company.]

His letter of June 19th was interrupted, and then continued on June 20th. He explained: "before I could finish this sentence they came and got me for a big top secret deal. Now am at K-10 (Chinhae, South Korea), about 170 miles south."

The "big top secret deal" probably referred to planning for raids conducted by the 18th FBW from June 23rd through June 26th on the North Korean power plants at Suiho, Choshin and Fusen. The first was on the massive hydroelectric plant at Suiho, a fork of the Yalu River. Pyongyang, Chinnampo and much of Manchuria got their electricity from the Suiho plant. The attack was a success.

Another plant at Choshin was hit on June 24th. Lt. John McAlpine was killed during the action.

"…I will be making around 5 ½ bills per month," Archie continued the letter a day later. "Guess with the old lady working we should be able to save around $500.00 per. About a year of this and we will be able to make a good down payment on a home. With this new G.I. bill, have been thinking seriously of going back to school and getting a degree." He had earned an Associate of Arts Degree from Jacksonville University.

"The Migs are getting worse and worser (sic)," he noted, switching subjects abruptly. "So by the time you hear from me again I may be an ace. They use us as decoys to bring them out where the glory boys in 86's can take a shot. As it now

stands we will have them (the 67th would transition into the F-86 in October, 1952) before fall. What could possibly be better than that."

"Well, guess I'll close for now with 72 to go."

"P.S. Tell Jim (Cox) that the fishing over here is limited to suckers. Who won the election and by what majority?" [9]

Last Letter

On June 21st, shortly before the start of the power plant raids, Archie wrote: "Dearest Frankie, Still south but go back tomorrow. They are flying taksan missions now your husband gets shafted as usual."

[*"Taksan is Japanese for large or many," Will Stapley explained years later. "Apparently they were getting lots of missions up north (K-46) and Archie was sitting down south (K-10) upset that he wasn't getting in on the action."* Like all the pilots, he wanted to fly as many missions as possible and get back home.]

Archie had had "a long talk with one of the South Afrikans," who gave him "a lot of good advice on marriage…just hope I have sense enough to use it," he said.

"Sure will be glad to get back up to K-46 (Hoengsong) as I should have a lot of mail. Three days since I heard from little fat wife. Love you."

"The mail has been pretty good these last few days, but I had better quit bragging."

"Only need 2:10 for my flight pay and will get about :50 of that tomorrow morning."

"Will close for now hon. Be good and write often. You (and only yours) husband, Archie."

"P.S. Still hope to finish by September." It was his last letter.

1952
18th Fighter-Bomber Wing
Chronology

Korea Summer-Fall 1952	Third Korean Winter
May 1-November 30, 1952	Dec. 1, 1952-Apr. 30, 1953

18th Fighter-Bomber Group officially based at K-46/Hoengsong, SK

July   August   September   October   November   December

September: FEAF directed most air attacks against enemy industrial remnants and troop concentration areas. Many targets were in border areas, which had been virtually untouched by FEAF attacks.

Nov. 10 18th FBG records 50,000th combat sortie. Honor given to 2 Squadron SAAF pilot.

Aug. 29: FEAF conducted the largest air attack to date against Pyongyang as a dramatic military action during a visit by China's premier, Chou En-lai, to the Soviet Union.

October: Close support sorties increased during October to represent more than one-half of the effort for the month. Armed reconnaissance, rescue air patrol, and road reconnaissance were the other types of missions flown by the 18th FBG.

July 11: Highlight for the pilots when "a maximum effort was directed at Ping Pong (Pyongyang East)."

Nov-Dec: 18th FBG's principal interdiction efforts "were directed against enemy troop concentrations and supplies. Close support again accounted for the largest portion of the effort. Armed reconnaissance and rescue combat air patrols were the other types of missons flown."

July 9: Capt. Elliot Ayer, 67th FBS, completes 45,000th combat mission for 18th FBG.

Close support, interdiction, road recces, and RESCAP missions were the main types of missons flown during July.

Dec. 26: The 18th FBW transferred its headquarters from K-10/Chinhae "to the new base at Osan Airdrome (K-55)."

On 26 December components of the 18th Fighter-Bomber Wing relocated from K-46 (left) and K-10 to K-55, near Osan-ni, South Korea.

519

July 1952

Hangar space is a luxury which is simply non-existent at K-46...space of any kind is dear at our diminutive field where the Mustangs are parked wing tip to wing tip. Most of the work on the planes has to be done right on the line. The wind and dust from the aircraft being run up render working conditions on the ramp pretty disagreeable at times.

Captain Elliot D. Ayer is congratulated by Colonel Sheldon Brinson, Commander of the 18th Fighter-Bomber Group, after flying the 18th Fighter-Bomber Wing's 45,000th mission on July 14, 1952. Ayer, Flight Leader of the 67th Squadron's How Flight, was killed in action just two weeks later on July 25, 1952. (Krakovsky)

"During the month of July this station underwent a six-day deluge of rainfall which seriously hampered the operation of all units and sections," the 18th Wing reported in July. "Parts of the living and operational areas of the base [K-46] were inundated by heavy drainage and floodwaters from the river. Flood control crews were organized and were on an almost

Monthly Summary

The heaviest ground fighting took place in the eastern sector near the coast, near Hill 266 (Old Baldy) in the U.S. 2nd Infantry Division sector, following attempts by an enemy battalion to seize it. After changing hands several times, it remained under friendly control at the end of the month. U.S. troops inflicted heavy casualties upon the enemy.

Flying weather was so bad in July, that for eleven days Far East Air Forces ordered a "stand down" (no flying). Marginal conditions existed for an additional nine days. Photographic reconnaissance was severely limited and affected target selection.

Air-to-air combat was relatively low in July. Fifth Air Force pilots destroyed sixteen MiGs at a cost of four Sabres. Fifth Air Force lost only nine aircraft to ground fire, the lowest in 1952, as a result of the decrease in rail interdiction and the unusual number of "stand down" weather days.

Adapted in part from U.S. Air Force Historical Research Agency. January 2002. The U.S. Air Force's First War: Korea 1950-1953 Significant Events. July 1952. http://www.au.af.mil/au/afhra/wwwroot/korean_war/korean_war_chronology/kwc_1952.html

continuous duty call. At the peak of the flood, group headquarters building was under three inches of water."[1]

Combat Operations

During July the 18th Fighter-Bomber Group "was assigned various types of targets, including rail line bridges, factories, supply areas and ammunition storage areas in the Pyongyang sector, transformer yard and, all across the front lines, personnel and supply targets were attacked. Close support, interdiction, road recces, and RESCAP missions were still the main types of missions flown during the month."[2]

The "inclement weather with low clouds covering the local area, as well as the combat area," was a major operational issue during July.

"It is an accepted fact," the 12th Squadron noted in July, "that rain has an adverse effect on the state of mind of human beings. The men at K-46 are human beings (perhaps an invalid premise), therefore the gloomy weather made them grumpy. At any rate there was much grumbling as the deluge burst upon us."

Another factor was a recent ban against "the flight caps which had more and more become innocuous symbols of squadron and flight pride."

First Extensive Use of Radar Controlled Bombs

"Despite the low cloud cover over and ahead of the bomb line, successful missions were flown against known troop concentrations and supply areas," the Group reported. "The bombing was done by use of MPQ-2 radar sets located in the front line areas. Radar controlled bomb drops are not new innovations but this was the first time extensive use was made of this type of operation. The aircraft were vectored over the target by a radar controller who told the pilot when to release the ordnance. Effective bombing was done with as little as 200 feet error from 11,000 feet altitudes. This type mission can be

flown only when base weather is forecast to remain good enough for the flight to return."[3]

With the increase of supply area targets being assigned to the Group, a new briefing aid was prepared—"complete coverage of the entire bomb line was accomplished" with 1:50,000 scale maps—including the bomb line, location of friendlies, mine fields, and known enemy flak and machine gun positions." When a

A ground crew of the SAAF Two Squadron works on a Flying Chetah Mustang at K-10 in July 1952. (Krakovsky)

target was assigned, it was plotted on the new map and reconciled with a photograph. With the new briefing aid "it was possible to brief the pilots on practically every possible condition existing around a specific target. It also gave the pilots a better perspective of the target, the surrounding areas, and terrain features with respect to the assigned target." Pilot's briefings were further improved by changing the Escape and Evasion Map, which was covered with acetate and "more clearly annotated. A new panel was constructed depicting all restrictions encountered in flight," the Group reported.

During the latter weeks of July, "low ceilings and continuous rain kept the airbase inoperational." However 854 effective sorties were flown by the two squadrons of the group. Aircraft and pilot losses were much lower than in previous months with one pilot MIA and two aircraft lost. One aircraft was lost in the combat zone and the other was bellied in during a ferry trip," the Group reported.

Night flying training was conducted during July "with stress on every pilot achieving at least one night take-off and landing. One flight of four aircraft com-

pleted a close support mission, taking off after official sunset time, rendezvousing with a mosquito control airplane, and releasing bombs and rockets on a target in almost complete darkness. Other last light recce missions were flown with no difficulties encountered in returning to the airbase."

When the pilots were grounded due to weather—operational stand-down periods— "a continuing training program for the pilots" included "lectures and discussions held on such subjects as standardized bombing and rocketing procedures, atomic warfare, maintenance, care and use of machine guns, tactics, etc."

For the first time in seven months, the Group used 500-lb M-67 'fire bombs' against supply center targets and buildings. The bombs were not as effective as napalm "but afford better opportunity for dive-bombing tactics and more safety to the pilot from ground fire."

Pull Altitude Raised

Tactics changed in July. The minimum altitude for all action above the bombline was raised to 3,000' above the ter-

Combat Statistics

18th Fighter-Bomber Wing

July 1952

Average No. A/C Assigned
33
Total Flying Time
1,419
Percentage of Aircraft in Commission
84%
Percentage of Aircraft AOCP
7%
Combat Sorties Flown by Wing
1,208
12th Squadron Sorties
Unavailable
67th Squadron Sorties
419
2 Squadron Sorties
344
A/C Lost to Combat
1
Pilots lost
1

Fuel Consumed

116,946 gals.

Ordnance Expended

.50-cal. Rounds
409,927
Rockets
1,871
Napalm Bombs
94
50-lb. GP Bombs
1,432

The 18th Wing Flight Line at K-46. (Pylant)

Staff Sergeant Robert Marquis rests on a pile of 500-pound bombs at K-46. (Pylant)

The 18th Wing Flight Line at K-46. (Pylant)

In this Air Force Hometown News Release photograph taken on July 9, 1952, Lt. William "Tim" Urquhart (left) is seen with Lt. Russell Bunn, Lt. McAreaey, Lt. Spinnenwebber and Lt. John Yingling. (NARA)

rain and it "paid dividends in fewer losses and fewer instances of battle damage to aircraft. The change in pull-out altitude and entry altitude necessitated additional training on the ground-gunnery range. The training paid off in increased effectiveness and less damage to friendly aircraft," the Group reported.

Fifth Air Force has "from time to time recommended in its frags that the 18th do its dive bombing from an altitude which would enable a pilot to pull out no lower

than 3,000 feet," the 12th noted in July. "Last week Wing became more explicit when it made the 3,000 foot minimum a part of the Wing's operational SOP's. While this action was necessary to reduce our losses and to prevent battle damage from flak and small arms fire, it gave rise to a problem. In a dive bombing run the higher the release point the great the chances of missing." Almost immediately, squadron pilots "began speculating on the best method of dive bombing with accuracy

from 9 or 10,000 feet." Lt. Taylor of the Group Training Section solved the problem by increasing the dive angle to 60 degrees and "throwing in a proportional increase of depression in the sight." The proponents for a 90-degree dive angle saw the solution as "merely pointing the nose of the airplane straight down and releasing the bombs." They argued that no sight depression was necessary, "a fact which eliminates the danger of forgetting to turn the sight back to zero for either air to air or ground firing." They also pointed out that it took "less time to line up and release using this method than it does the other which would serve to eliminate the danger of target fixation and its attendant late pull out." [4]

"At this writing nothing has been definitely decided on. It is the sincere hope of all the pilots who are sacrificing their time and effort that something effective be decided. If it is worth being here at all, it is for the damage we can inflict on the enemy. It is for our little share in eliminating the war-making potential of the aggressor," the 12th Squadron report noted.

Maintenance Woes

"It has been said," the 12th Squadron reported in July, "that the more worthwhile the endeavor, the more difficulties encountered. That axiom certainly holds true for our maintenance section. Keeping a high number of airplanes in commission is a difficult task in the States where facilities, equipment and training personnel are abundant. The maintenance crews at K-46 and of the 12th Squadron, although they are not generously blessed with any of those ingredients, continue to do a commendable job."

The success of the squadron as a whole "depends directly on the effectiveness of the work done beyond the bomb line and the indispensable support of the ground elements such as engineering, armament, supply and administration. Problems we shall encounter," the 12th explained, "the insoluble ones, never—well, almost never."

"Hangar space is a luxury which is simply non-existent at K-46," the 12th noted for the record. "Indeed, space of any kind is dear at our diminutive field where the Mustangs are parked wing tip to wing tip. Most of the work on the planes has to be done right on the line. The wind and dust from the aircraft being run up render working conditions on the ramp pretty disagreeable at times," it noted as an understatement.

Survival radios--AN/URC-4--were in short supply, necessitating "the flying of missions without each pilot possessing a radio. Unsatisfactory supply letters were written by each squadron and the group supply office." It took the Group three more months to "overcome" the shortage.

18th Wing 45,000th

Sortie

In July, the 67th Squadron reported that it was located at K-46 Air Base, South Korea, approximately 7 mi. north north east of Wonju—127 degrees 57 minutes 30 seconds longitude west, 38 degrees 26 minutes 30 seconds North—or approximately 5 mi. southeast of Hoengsong, Korea.

The stated mission of the 67th Fighter-Bomber Squadron was "close support of United Nations forces in Korea and/or other aerial combat missions as directed

Second Anniversary Cups

When the 18th Wing passed its second year of continuous combat, these commemorative mugs were created to mark the occasion.

by higher headquarters. During the period covered by this report, the primary mission has been the tactical interdiction of the enemy's transportation system."

The 67th Squadron, commanded by Lieutenant Colonel Stanley A. Long of Marquette, Mich., is a unit of the 18th fighter-bomber group, which is commanded by Colonel Sheldon Brinson.

Heavy rains in July heavily damaged the bomb dump area and also the rocket and napalm storage areas, the 67th Squadron reported. Although the "situations" were quickly cleared up, the Service Club was "closed for a while due to necessary billeting of men there while repairs were being made to their permanent quarters which suffered damage during the heavy rains of this month." Also, "the extreme heat has played an important factor in the discomfort of the troops." [5]

Total officer strength at the beginning of July 19th 1952 was 44. Officer gains numbered 6, and losses five, leaving a total of 45 officers assigned at the end of July. The total enlisted strength at the beginning of July was 177.

The total number of sorties flown during July 1952 was 419.

Claims: Destroyed Artillery Positions 13 Rail bridges 2 Rail cuts 10 Road bridges 2 Box cars 4 Bunkers 56 Mortars 25 Gun positions 2 Machine guns 7 Secondary explosions 15 Self-propelled gun 1 Supply shelters 4 Caves 2 Buildings 39 Village 1 Factories 1 Trucks 3 Transformer yard 1 (damaged) Ox cart 1 (damaged) Trench 720' KIA 9

Losses to personal and aircraft: Other than the above-mentioned MIA on Captain Ayer, there were no other losses to the squadron this month.

The training program was considerably more pronounced this month due to more than usual poor weather days which allowed the squadron the opportunity to stress navigational and instrument flights.

During the month of July there have been considerable rocket malfunctions due to bad plugs and bad motors. July's gun malfunctions have dropped to 12,480 rounds per malfunction as compared with June's rate of 10,000 rounds per malfunction.

Due to daily flying reports being filled out both at K-46 and K-10, an accurate total of flying time is impossible at this writing. The approximate total was 839 hours and fifty minutes.

Morale: In the airmen, there was no obvious change in the morale from last month. Extreme heat has played an important factor in the discomfort of the troops. The service club was closed for a while due to necessary billeting of the men there while repairs were being made to their private quarters which suffered damage during heavy rains of this month.

Pilot morale also remained about the same. Capt. Elliot D. Ayre completed the 45,000th combat sortie for the 18th Fighter-Bomber Wing, thereby setting the record for the most sorties to be flown by a combat outfit in Korea. Also, our Commanding Officer was given a promotion from Major to Lieutenant Colonel, this had a definite lift to the morale of the Squadron as a whole.

The 67th Fighter-Bomber Squadron was able to complete its mission and accomplish its assigned duties because of its high morale and Superior leadership, it reported.

Weary Mustangs

The "weary Mustangs of the 18th Fighter-Bomber Wing are ending their second year in Korea," the Truckbuster noted, "and are looking back at all the good work they have done. We can't help but shower them with praise. The boys up front always give the most credit to the Mustangs for their close support missions. We have a statement in which one boy on the front lines said, 'the Mustangs flew so close to us today that the hot .50-caliber shells were falling on us.'"

"45,000 combat sorties. Mull the words over a bit. By themselves, they don't mean too much. Just another statistic. But consider the enormous amount of men, money and materiel that went into that simple figure and the picture takes on an-

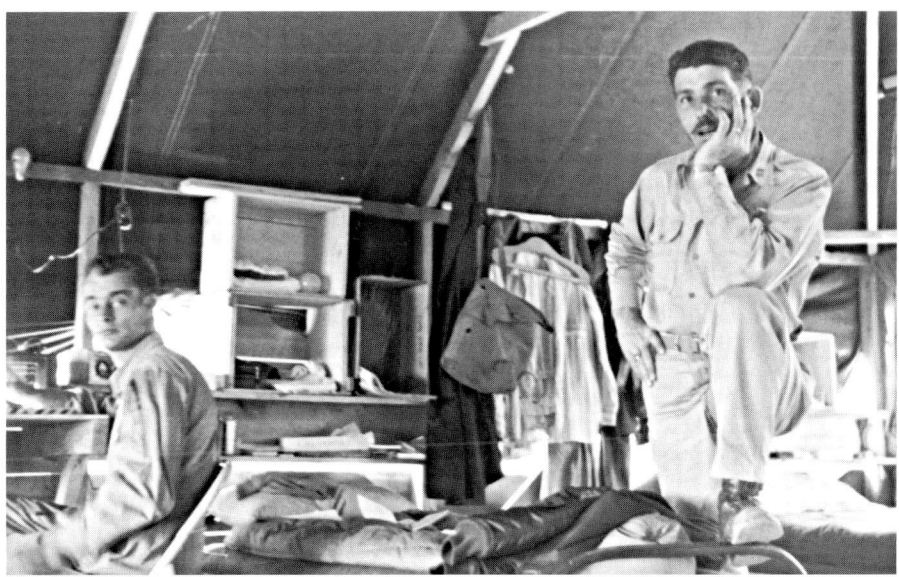

Inside the How Flight tent at K-46 in July 1952, 1st Lt. John E. Hill and Capt. Charles T. Hudson await their next mission. It was probably from this desk that Hill wrote his thoughtful letter of condolences to Frankie Connors following the death of her husband, 1st Lt. Archie Connors on June 25th. (Urquhart)

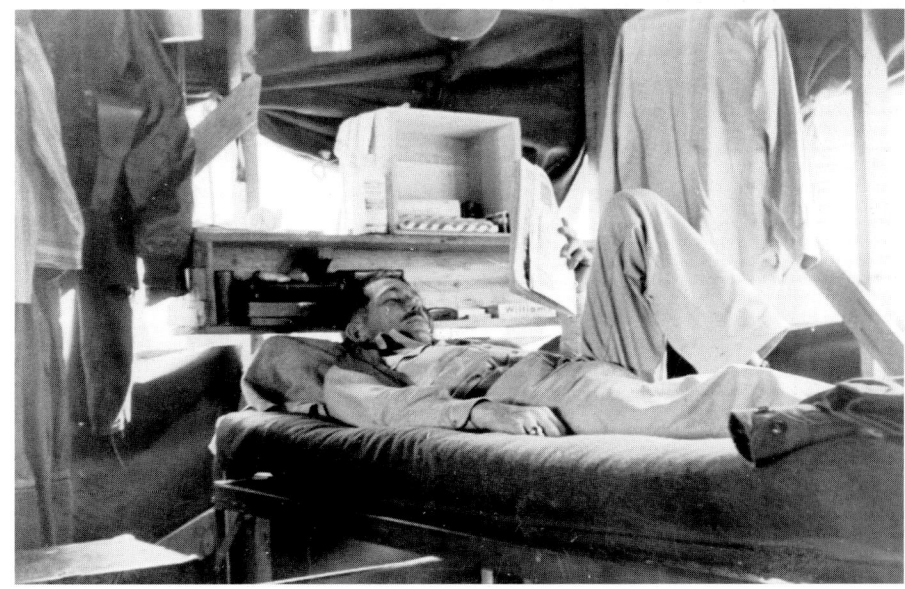

Shortly before 5 p.m. in the How Flight tent, Capt. Charles T. Hudson lies on his cot reading a magazine between missions. (Urquhart)

other hue," *Truckbuster* reporter continued. "Of the men who have made it possible, the bulk have rotated, others remain; many are living, many have died. It is to the men and machines that give meaning to the 45,000 combat sorties that this and every issue of the Truckbuster is dedicated."

"Although rumors are flying rapidly and thickly about a new location and a new aircraft, the 12th is still at K-46 flying its slightly superannuated birds on tactical support and other missions sent down by JOC," the 12th reported in July.

Sorties "were not exactly overabundant during the month," and came to the squadron "in dribbles." The squadron flew only 405 sorties in July, down 144 from the previous month. The "unwelcome advent" of rainy weather "forced the squadron off operations for nine days." The weather up to that point had been unusually fair, "but when the rain did come, it came down by barrels full, turning our field into a quagmire." Plans were made to evacuate the aircraft. With tongue firmly in cheek, the 12th reported that "Wheels" were drafting plans "for a huge ark in the form of an aircraft carrier."

The pilots were not happy over their enforced inactivity, illustrated by "the piddling 16 combat hours per pilot for the month to which old Pluvius restricted them. They spent most of their time trying to keep themselves dry in their perforated tents," the 12th noted for the record.

Those missions that were flown consisted of close support.

The highlight of the month for the pilots came on the 11th when "a maximum effort was directed at Ping Pong (Pyongyang East)." Pin point accuracy was not required for this extensive target, so "the boys could hardly miss, and they didn't as is attested by the estimated 13 buildings left blazing. The flak, which was moderately heavy, did not seem to be tuned to our frequency that day. Only Captain Kimball picked up battle damage when his Mustang was hit in the wing by a twenty millimeter shell." [6]

Endnotes
[1] USAFHRA. *Monthly Historical Report, 18th Fighter-Bomber Wing,* July 1952. p. 4.
[2] USAFHRA. *Monthly Historical Report, 18th Fighter-Bomber Group,* July 1952. p. 11.
[3] USAFHRA. *Monthly Historical Report, 18th Fighter-Bomber Group,* July 1952. p. 15.
[4] USAFHRA. *Monthly Historical Report, 12th Fighter-Bomber Squadron,* July 1952, p. 4.
[5] USAFHRA. *Monthly Historical Report, 67th Fighter-Bomber Squadron,* July 1952, p. 6.
[6] USAFHRA. *Monthly Historical Report, 12th Fighter-Bomber Squadron,* July 1952, p. 2.

Significant Events

July 4: Over 50 MiGs, some piloted by Soviets, attacked an equal number of F-86s and seventy F-84s during a raid on the North Korean Military Academy at Sakchu near the Yalu. Fifth Air Force pilots downed thirteen MiG-15s at a cost of two Sabres.

July 9: A four-ship flight of the 67th Squadron "returning from a close support mission landed at K-46 airbase. The fourth airplane of the flight completed the 45,000th effective combat sortie of the 18th Fighter-Bomber Wing, six days short of two years of combat flying in the Korean conflict. This number of sorties was the greatest among completed by any combat fighter bomber wing in Korea." [1] Captain Elliot Ayer, How Flight Leader, was credited with the 45,000th combat sortie.

July 11: FEAF flew 1,329 sorties, the highest daily total for the month. In the first raid of Operation PRESSURE PUMP, nearly every operational air unit in the Far East attacked thirty targets in Pyongyang, in the largest single strike so far of the war. Attacking aircraft destroyed three targets, including the North Korean Ministry of Industry. Most others sustained heavy damage. [2]

July 13: FEAF initiated a new general warning leaflet drop program over enemy territory that identified specific towns and targets to be destroyed by air attacks.

July 15: FEAF fighter-bombers flew approximately 175 sorties against the Sungho-ri cement plant and a nearby locomotive repair facility.

Adapted in part from U.S. Air Force Historical Research Agency. January 2002. The U.S. Air Force's First War: Korea 1950-1953 Significant Events. July 1952. http://www.au.af.mil/au/afhra/wwwroot/korean_war/korean_war_chronology/kwc_1952.html

Combat Losses

Captain Elliot Dean Ayer, 67th Squadron How Flight leader was listed as MIA on 25 July 1952. Ayer was born in Greenfield, Massachusetts on 30 April 1921. He grew up to be a rugged handsome, muscular 200 pound young man over six feet tall with brown hair and brown eyes.

When Japanese forces attacked Pearl Harbor, Corporal Ayer manned his anti-aircraft gun as a member of the 19th Infantry. When he applied for appointment as an Aviation Cadet on 24 July 1942, he was accepted by the Army Air Corps for flight training. Corporal Ayer earned the shiny gold bars of a Second Lieutenant on 3 November 1943. When he was promoted to Captain on 7 August 1946, his records noted under "battles and campaigns," European African Middle Eastern Campaign Medal, Northern Apennines, Italian Campaign, Southern France, Po Valley, Rome-Arno." In addition to many service awards, Captain Ayer had been awarded the Distinguished Flying Cross and the Air Medal with three OL clusters.

His heroism wasn't enough in the post-war demobilization period for the Army to keep him on active duty.

When demobilization policies were announced, the Army gave Captain Ayer an extraordinarily difficult choice to make—leave the Air Force or continue on active duty—as a Master Sergeant. He chose to stay in the Air Force. From 1946 until 1951, Master Sergeant Ayer served as an Aircraft Approach Controller GCA. His Enlisted Record and Honorable Discharge on 1 October 1949 mentions only a Good Conduct Medal, American Defense Service Medal and a World War II Victory Medal. On 2 October 1949, Master Sergeant Ayer reenlisted in the U.S. Air Force for three

There I was...

by

William Timmons "Tim" Urquhart

We were How Flight of the 67th Squadron, led by Captain Elliot D. Ayer. I was flying his wing in a four Mustang formation. It was a routine interdiction mission against North Korean rail lines. Everything went well and according to plan until we were almost home.

We were told by ground control that a South African F-51 was lost returning to our base at K-46. Our instructions were to fly low above river valleys and search for him, which we did with gusto.

My flight leader flew very low above a river bed. I was in low level spread formation, slightly above him, when out of the corner of my eye there was a power line stretch across the valley directly in front of me.

I pulled the control stick back in my lap and firewalled the throttle by instinct and luckily hit the cable dead center on the prop spinner.

The wire was cut cleanly by the prop, throwing the left half over the left wing and the right half down into my right wing, hitting the .50-cal. gun barrels and knocking a crease across the leading edge of the right wing.

That's when the V-1650 Merlin engine quit.

I had about 250 mph airspeed and 200 feet altitude climbing.

My first thought was obvious, I'd ruined the engine. Our single engine out procedure was to throttle back, change fuel tanks, fuel boost pump on, and throttle forward.

Nothing can describe the joy of hearing that Old Merlin come back to life.

I'd drained a fuel tank at a bad time.

This actually happened in the Summer of 1952 in Korea to a very young and inexperienced 2nd Lt. There's an expression that fighter pilots use--you're never dead 'til you run out of altitude, airspeed--and ideas."

---

more years at Eglin Air Force Base.

After the Korean War broke out on 25 June 1950, the new U.S. Air Force was hard pressed to find enough qualified pilots for combat duty, especially for the rapidly aging, already obsolescent "prop jobs" such as the F-51 Mustang. When the "system" relocated Master Sergeant Ayer and made him an offer, he accepted. Ayer was "discharged" on 13 May 1951 to "accept active duty as a commissioned officer." On 14 May 1951, he was reappointed a Captain--AO 758 753.

He celebrated the restored rank and new duties with his wife, Marguerite Savage Ayer, who lived with their two young sons in Tallahassee, Florida.

By 25 June 1952, Ayer was Flight Leader of How Flight, a unit of the 67th Fighter-Bomber Squadron, 18th Fighter-Bomber Wing based at K-46, Hoengsong, South Korea. His Squadron Commander rated Ayer as "a well experienced Flight Commander who has demonstrated qualities of good leadership throughout his tour

under my supervision. He has an excellent flying safety record. I would recommend further assignment in positions of great responsibility for this officer. He exercises a high degree of judgment in the economical management of personnel and resources under his supervision, commensurate with his responsibilities."

Endnotes

[1] USAFHRA. Monthly Historical Report, 18th Fighter-Bomber Group, July 1952. p. 14.

[2] U.S. Air Force Historical Research Agency. January 2002. The U.S. Air Force's First War: Korea 1950-1953 Significant Events. July 1952. http://www.au.af.mil/au/afhra/wwwroot/korean_war/korean_war_chronology/kwc_1952.html

Captain Elliot Dean Ayer

August 1952

"A particular source of irritation as far as the combat pilots are concerned is the shortage of coveralls. Most pilots have only one pair which in many instances does not fit properly. Helmets are scarce also, and since there are just enough to go around, a man is obliged to wear a helmet whether it fits him or not."

Combat Operations

During August and September, the 18th Fighter-Bomber Group "was assigned various types of targets, including troop concentrations, supply shelters, gasoline storage tanks, and artillery positions. Close support and interdiction missions were the main types of missions flown during this period." [1]

Missions flown during August include close air support, interdiction, armed reconnaissance, recap and for the first time in several months, the Group provided a "sweep patrol from Seoul to the North. There was an unidentified aircraft spotted on this mission with negative results."

The number of missions in August left much to be desired by the pilots. "Missions were a rare commodity during this month of relative inactivity," the 12th Squadron reported. "Only 299 sorties were flown. To compensate "for this dearth of missions" the 12th stood down for five days of training, "all of which made the pilots stamp their feet with joy," the report noted somewhat sarcastically.

Three aircraft were lost in August. "One pilot was killed due to weather conditions," the Group reported. "One pilot bailed out after canopy of the aircraft came off shortly after take-off, striking him on the head. The bailout was successful, but the pilot was not conscious of the conditions under which he bailed out. He was later picked up approximately 12 miles east of Hoeng Song. The other aircraft was lost after receiving major battle damage on an interdiction mission. The pilot made a successful belly landing at a forward air strip and was later picked up and flown to K-46."

Enemy aircraft "became more prevalent and aggressive" in August. "Their radius of action on several occasions during the month extended as far

Monthly Summary

Toward mid-month the enemy in reinforced-battalion strength attacked UN positions in several sectors. Hills in the 1st Marine Division and in the II ROK Corps sectors changed hands several times, but UN forces retained control while inflicting heavy losses on the enemy.

Far East Air Forces continued B-29 and fighter-bomber attacks against communist supply and production areas, although FEAF intelligence concluded that North Korea had no remaining strategic or economic targets suitable for strategic attack. The medium bombers struck Pyongyang on five nights in some of the most massive attacks of the war. B-26s flew more daytime interdiction than in previous months, mainly against enemy supply areas and airfields.

Fifth Air Force increased voice broadcast sorties, flying a total of thirty-seven, to encourage defections among enemy troops and civilians. It also flew 182 leaflet sorties with emphasis on warning civilians of impending attacks and impressing the North Koreans of their government's inability to prevent the bombings.

Following the loss of three B-26s in four nights, General Barcus ordered an operational standdown for the 3 BW. He concluded that light-bomber crews were not adept enough at low altitude night operations and directed that B-26s generally should not operate below 4,000 feet. Ten days later, following a change of command, introduction of new tactics, and intense training, the 3rd BW returned to operational status and did not lose another aircraft to enemy action until December. The new tactics had fighter-bombers at last light to bomb highway intersections, then at first darkness B-26s dropped butterfly and delayed-action bombs on adjacent roads, and through the night individual light bombers searched the roads for stranded vehicles to attack. As a result the B-26s destroyed greater numbers of enemy vehicles.

The tempo of the air-to-air war increased as MiGs entered North Korean skies more frequently during daylight hours. Sabre pilots destroyed thirty-two MiG-15s while losing one F-86 in aerial combat. However, other causes resulted in the loss of five more F-86s and one F-84. Fifth Air Force lost fourteen additional aircraft to enemy ground fire.

U.S. Air Force Historical Research Agency. January 2002. The U.S. Air Force's First War: Korea 1950-1953 Significant Events. August 1952. http://www.au.af.mil/au/afhra/wwwroot/korean_war/korean_war_chronology/kwc_1952.html

Inside the 67th Squadron Operations Office, 1st Lt. C. J. Gossett (left) and 2nd W. T. Urquhart stand the duty. The number of combat missions in August left much to be desired by the pilots. Missions were a rare commodity during this month of relative inactivity. Training was stepped up and "made the pilots stamp their feet with joy," a unit report noted somewhat sarcastically. (Urquhart)

south as the Haeju area."

Morale had taken a steep dive in late August, "shot up considerably when the unpopular uniform regulations imposed upon the squadron were abrogated when Col. Perego assumed command of the Wing. The pilots and other members of the squadron immediately donned their weird assortment of headgear which are so important to their individuality," the 12th reported.

The challenge of achieving accuracy during high altitude release bombing was "slowly resolving itself. No specific method has been adopted. Some pilots drop their bombs from a very steep dive using the nose as an aiming device while others use the method advocated by the training section of throwing in 120 mil and bombing from a 60-degree angle," the 12th reported.

Practice dive bombing training methods at the Naktong range came in for harsh criticism as being "at worst detrimental to a pilot's dive bombing skills. It is folly," the 12th noted, "to send out a flight which has been dropping bombs daily on regular missions on a practice mission to a dive

bomb range where conditions are vastly different from those encountered over the bomb line. The run made on combat targets is not rigidly controlled to an nth degree turn of the base leg as it is at Naktong. If the dive bombing range were simply a series of concentric circles and one could enter the run from any direction as is the case on combat missions, then at least it could be said that the training missions had the value of providing just a little more practice. Even so, it would be analogous to the proverbial busman's holiday. Training, it would seem at times, has been somewhat of a fetish," the 12th concluded.

Pilots were also hacked off because flying equipment remained inadequate. "A particular source of irritation as far as the combat pilots are concerned is the shortage of coveralls. Most pilots have only one pair which in many instances does not fit properly. Helmets are scarce also, and since there are just enough to go around, a man is obliged to wear a helmet whether it fits him or not," the 12th reported.

"Field equipment" was inspected. Recommendations were offered "that

more effort be made to repair equipment locally, wherever possible, due to the shortage of replacements in this command." Life raft containers were inspected and condemned. Many of the 24-foot back parachutes were over seven years old. They were turned in to Fifth Air Force. After inspecting the vehicles, many discrepancies were corrected. However, "due to a critical shortage of motor vehicle parts and the heavy work load of the Motor Vehicle Squadron, it will be some time before all write-ups can be corrected.

Finally, the squadrons and the Group were "authorized to requisition 50 percent more winter flying clothing so that proper sizes could be obtained. Authority was also received to requisition two OD [olive drab] army uniforms for each pilot."

"Each week the Group Intelligence and Ground Liaison Sections delivered an indoctrination lecture to airmen based at K-46. These lectures covered the highlights of the previous week, claims of the unit for that week, and in general covered our entire program. Each week a special training aid was prepared, usually consisting of bomb damage assessments of targets hit that week, types of missions flown, and illustrations of our effectiveness against the enemy. Interrogations continued to reflect the aggressiveness and increasing effectiveness of the combat pilots in this Group. The bombing skill and accuracy of the pilots have greatly improved, due to the intense training program being conducted."

The 18th Group Supply Officer travelled to K-14 in August, September and December "to obtain information on special tools, equipment, spare parts and TO&E authorized property" as the Group prepared "for the conversion to jet aircraft.

Better Effectiveness

"Every month that we fly teaches us just a little bit more about dive bombing and the tactics required of a fighter bomber pilot. Problems directly concerned with combat flying are slowly resolved by experience and practice. The problems of

Combat Statistics

18th F-B Wing

August 1952

Average No. A/C Assigned
52 (excluding 2nd Squadron SAAF)
Total Flying Time
1,943
Percent of Aircraft in Commission
65%
Percent of Aircraft AOCP
16%
Combat Sorties Flown by Wing
1,124
12th Squadron Sorties
U
67th Squadron Sorties
343
2 Squadron Sorties
389
A/C Lost to Combat
2
Pilots lost
1

Fuel Consumed

151,082 gals

Ordnance Expended

.50-cal. Rounds
272,692
Rockets
762
Napalm Bombs
20
500-lb. GP Bombs
1,028

Note: Figures and totals may differ in some categories due to differences in numbers provided by each component.

morale and spirit are perhaps ironed out more slowly, but with the proper attitude and professional pride on the part of the pilots and men and with the proper balance between discipline and understanding on the part of the supervisory personnel, these too cannot escape solution. All this effort toward improvement has but one aim--better effectiveness against the enemy," the 12th concluded.

Endnotes

[1] USAFHRA. *Monthly Historical Report, 18th Fighter-Bomber Group,* August 1952. p. 12.

Significant Events

August 2: Captain Charles M. Sargen, bailed out near K-46 after sustaining a major injury to his head when his canopy came off in flight.

August 5: Lt. Col. Albert J. Freund succeeded Major Frank Orth as Commanding Officer of the 12th Squadron . "Col. Freund came to the unit from the Pilot Training Center at Luke AFB, while Major Orth went the way of all happy warriors to his Valhalla in the states," the 12th noted in its report.

August 6: Fifth Air Force pilots observed an estimated 250 MiGs, the largest daily total since April 1. In the major air-to-air battle of the month, thirty-four F-86s destroyed six of fifty-two MiG-15s.

August 8: Fifth Air Force fighters flew 285 close air support sorties, the highest daily total for the month. Indicative of FEAF's increased use of propaganda, at night B-26s flew three voice broadcast sorties totaling almost four hours over enemy-held positions near the east coast.

August 12: On Sunday, August 17th at K-10 over 1,500 airmen, "fueled by high octane exuberance," jammed the Lower Four (18th Fighter-Bomber Wing Airmen's Open Mess) to celebrate the official opening of the club's new patio. Before the evening was over the *Truckbuster* reported, "they were flying fifty thousand feet over everywhere without benefit of wings."

August 15: The 315th AD transported 300 medical evacuees, the highest

daily total for the month.

August 19/20: FEAF aircraft dropped general warning leaflets over Pyongyang concerning the next night's attacks.

August 20/21: Thirty-eight B-29s bombed supply areas of the enemy's capital, the highest number of medium bomber sorties against a single target this month.

August 22-23: On successive nights, three C-47s flew sixty-minute voice broadcast sorties near the front lines, indicating a greater emphasis by UN Command on psychological war.

August 29: At the request of the U.S. Department of State, Far East Air Forces conducted against Pyongyang the largest air attack to date as a dramatic military action during a visit by China's premier, Chou En-lai, to the Soviet Union. The State Department hoped that the attack might lead the Soviets to urge the Chinese to accept an armistice rather than expend further communist resources in the war. FEAF aircraft, protected by USAF Sabres and RAAF Meteors, flew approximately 1,400 air-to-ground sorties. The thirty-one targets sustained moderate to severe damage, but Fifth Air Force lost three aircraft to ground fire.

"A major air attack against military targets in the Pyongyang area highlighted air action against the enemy for the month of August," the Group reported. "The two squadrons of this group were committed for a total of 89 sorties and flew 86 effective sorties. Six of the effective sorties were rescap."

"Ping Pong was revisited last month," the 12th reported somewhat laconically in its monthly report. "The uninvited guests received a rude welcome on the first mission, but they failed to take the hint and came back five more times during the day. Much destruction was claimed. All one had to do was fly over the city to hit something."

[1] Adapted in part from U.S. Air Force Historical Research Agency. January 2002. The U.S. Air Force's First War: Korea 1950-1953 Significant Events. September 1952.

"The only place one could get a cold beer in Korea," remembered Joe Krakovsky who took this photograph of Duffy's Tavern. Although Navy personnel "attached it," and brought over a refrigerator from Japan, the tavern's location so close to K-10 and the 1,000+ airmen and NCOs of the 18th Fighter Bomber Wing meant that "usually there were more Airmen than Navy customers." (Krakovsky)

Combat Losses

Captain R.P.G. Kotzenberg, 2 Squadron, SAAF pilot KIA on 22 August 1952. 'Piet' Kotzenberg was Deputy Commander of the 2nd Squadron. His four-ship flight, led by Captain 'Jan Bal' Bolitho, was briefed for a dive-bombing mission against enemy artillery positions at CT154343. Kotzenberg was flying No. 4. The bombing run was started at 10,000 feet and pulled out at 4,000 feet, a new FAF rule designed to cut pilot losses by mandating higher release altitudes. Following the attack all flight members checked in except Kotzenberg. Returning to the bombed target, Captain Bolitho could locate only a secondary fire. The higher search altitude requirements made it impossible for him to determine whether the secondary fire was the missing aircraft. After 45 minutes of searching, he returned to base. No sign of the pilot or aircraft were found.

1st Lt. Trevor C. Scott, 2 Squadron, SAAF pilot KIA on 9 July 1952. Lt. Scott was leading the attack on a target at CT2711. While over the target, Scott reported problems with his radio and delegated leadership of the attack to Lt. Singleton. The No. 4 pilot, Lt. Austin saw flames coming from Scott's aircraft. Pieces were breaking off. Scott's plane did not recover from the dive. His Flight circled the wreckage, now a mass of flames, and determined that it was not possible that Lt. Scott had survived.

Interdiction Tactics

By Ralph Waterman

The mission of the 18th included close air to ground support, interdiction and rescap. Of these, interdiction included road cuts, rail cuts, the bombing of bridges, military storage facilities, etc. One of the more clever tactics used with road cuts involved action against roads used by the North Koreans for resupply of frontline positions. Troops, equipment, spare parts, food, and munitions all were resupplied by trucks using roads known to us to be used for those purposes. Due to our limited sophistication compared with today's air tactics, the enemy knew that traveling their supply routes by nighttime cover of darkness would provide them with a greater degree of protection and safety from aerial attack.

We of the 18th never flew night missions. We were, however, instrumental in implementing a tactic that was used in conjunction with another WWII airplane, the B-26. This tactic proved to be quite effective in disrupting nighttime travel on those supply routes. It worked like this. We would fly out at what we termed "last light", just before dark. Usually there would be two flights of four with a total of sixteen 500-lb bombs. These bombs would be a "mixed load". By that, it meant that the fusing on the bombs would be varied to provide a combination of instant contact and delayed explosions. The delayed fusing would be set for a variety of time intervals after armed release.

We would fly to a predetermined supply route location and drop our "mixed load," making a road cut, preferably where there could be no easy way to detour around the damaged road. Since we had

Planning To Leave K-46

"It finally quit raining this morning," Airman Bob Cranston wrote his mother in Hogansville, Georgia on 21 August 1952, "and we are flying again although my plane hasn't flown yet." He could hear the Mustangs taking off from K-46 from his tent as he wrote. He would go on duty in the afternoon. "Some are going over now, maybe it is mine."

"We may leave K-46 by the first of October and go to a new base somewhere else in Korea. We are supposed to get jets. I don't know what they will do with guys like Boone and I who are so close to rotation--but it won't affect us coming home any. Will leave here the last of October or first of November."

Returning From Patrol. On August 24, 1952 Airman 1st Class Joe Krakovsky got permission to visit his brother, Steve, an Army Infantryman serving at the front with the 160th Infantry Regimental Combat Team near Kapyong, South Korea. When Krakovsky arrived at Kumwa, he found that his brother was "on patrol." As Steve Krakovsky returned to the forward position tired and wet from the rain and mist, he was amazed to see his brother, Joe waiting on him. "Are you crazy," he said, shaking his head, "what the hell are you doing up here?" After visiting with the Army unit, Joe remembered that it made him "realize how fortunate I was being in the Air Force...I was glad to get to see him and I know my Mom was glad when I wrote to her and said that he was alright," Krakovsky recalled.

(Right) The soliders had recently received their "beer ration." A nearby mountain stream provided just the chill needed for the brewskies. (Krakovsky)

taken this action just prior to darkness, and the supply trucks would begin rolling at about that time, it wouldn't be long before the first truck would arrive at an impassible road condition as a result of our bombing. Having learned that we would often make such road cuts, their first trucks would often carry troops along with shovels, picks, etc. to enable repairs to be made to the roads. As this work progressed an unexploded bomb's fuse would reach its preset time and explode resulting in further delay of repairs. Continued disruption would occur, as each succeeding delayed fuse bomb would explode.

Meanwhile, along the route, the trucks that had been started with wide spacing to make any aerial attack of the convoy more difficult would begin to pile up. This would occur, as there was no communication ability from truck to truck. So, while traveling at night, sometimes without lights, there was not a great deal of advanced notice that one truck was approaching another and the pileup of trucks would occur.

With the trucks of the convoy thus bunched up, our "hard nosed"* B-26's from the 13th Bomb Squadron would go to the site of the road cut, come in at low altitude and bomb and strafe the much easier concentrated targets. This tactic proved somewhat difficult for the enemy to defend against and was quite effective as long as the road cuts were made at strategic locations and weather conditions permitted its use.

* A hard nosed B-26 was an attack version that had formerly been designated the A-26 and one that did not have a Plexiglas nose or bombardier station, but rather, had in its place an aluminum alloy nose housing six or eight .50-caliber machine guns, or sometimes in various other combinations with 20-mm cannons mounted there. These aircraft also had 3 additional 50's in each wing. This version was built by Douglas Aircraft, whereas original versions of the B-26 were built by Martin Aviation.

September 1952

"More pilots for the squadron! They kept coming in droves while hardly any left due to the sparsity of missions."

In September, "attacks against enemy supply centers, close-in interdiction and close ground support missions were stressed. The increasing enemy build-up in the front line area was met by continued persistent air attacks by this and other Fighter Bomber Groups. During September the Group flew 1,355 effective combat sorties, of which the 2 Squadron flew 241 missions. The South Africans had to devote much of that month to training a large number of replacement pilots who had recently arrived.

The use of radar controlled MPW-2 bombing "increased the effectiveness of the Group and permitted operations to continue during marginal weather conditions. Assessed results indicated a high rate of effectiveness," the Group noted in its monthly report.

Over 60 combat MPQ-2 sorties were flown in September--"varying results, dependent on the time of day, communications, weather, and controller. The main difficulty encountered was the limitation on communication caused by the four channel VHF set, which made available only one channel which could be used, "Red," and

Korean Bomb Crew. *Korean civilian laborers were hired to help move supplies, equipment and even ordnance at K-46. This group posed with a 1,000 lb. bomb at Wonju in September 1952. (Bist)*

often the controller had closed down on that frequency, which caused loss of time or an abort because of lack of control. Three times the mission had to be worked on "White" because the controller's "Red" was inoperative. Luckily, one of the aircraft in the flight happened to have one of the few 8-channel sets on board. This put the leader on one channel and the remain-

der of the flight on another, depending solely on visual signals for control. For late evening flights this was unsatisfactory. Unforeseen weather conditions over the target caused undesired weather penetration and high altitude flying which, again during the late evening, was unsatisfactory. Loss of control by the controller several times during a single mission also caused

Monthly Summary

The heaviest ground activity centered in the II ROK Corps sector with intense see-saw fighting but little change in the front lines. The enemy suffered high casualties, for example, losing in one four-day period an estimated eleven hundred soldiers.

Far East Air Forces directed most air attacks against enemy industrial remnants and troop concentration areas throughout North Korea. Many targets were in North Korea's border areas, which had been virtually untouched by FEAF attacks. For the first time, FEAF Bomber Command employed a few B-29s solely in an ECM role. The command flew its usual small number of close air support sorties at night. Light bombers continued day and night attacks primarily against enemy supply targets and vehicles. Fifth Air Force flew ninety-six flare-drop missions in the interdiction campaign.

In air-to-air combat, F-86s destroyed fifty-eight MiGs, the highest monthly total so far. Two Sabre pilots attained ace status, but Fifth Air Force lost nine Sabres and at least five F-84s. The 22nd Crash Rescue Boat Squadron performed eight rescue missions, saving one life and recovering three bodies.

U.S. Air Force Historical Research Agency. January 2002. The U.S. Air Force's First War: Korea 1950-1953 Significant Events. September 1952. http://www.au.af.mil/au/afhra/wwwroot/korean_war/korean_war_chronology/kwc_1952.html

extended close formation night-time flying....Analysis of the unsatisfactory flights led to early morning and early afternoon sorties which proved much more successful."

With the passing of "the monsoon season" flying weather improved considerably, "with only a total of eight days out of the month being non-operational. Flying was safer, as well. "No aircraft accidents occurred."

"There were no combat aircraft losses" in September. It was the first 30-day consecutive period since April 1951 that no aircraft losses were sustained by the Wing.

"The recent change in tactics, whereby the minimum altitude for all action above the bombline was raised to 3,000' above the terrain, has paid dividends in fewer losses and fewer instances of battle damage to aircraft. The change in pull-out altitude and entry altitude necessitated additional training on the ground-gunnery range. The training paid off in increased effectiveness and less damage to friendly aircraft," the Group reported.

"With the coming of good weather and a resulting high combat sortie rate the morale and effectiveness of the entire Group reached a new high."

The Group was notified in September "that future pilot replacements would have jet experience, and it was anticipated that incoming mechanics, electricians, armorers, etc. would be similarly trained in the new equipment. Nonetheless, 22 F-51 pilots reported in September."

Squadron Level Developments

"More pilots for the squadron!," the 12th reported in September. "They kept coming in droves while hardly any left due to the sparsity of missions."

Early in September the 12th Squadron's Mike Flight "had a brief but hairy encounter with some MIGs. The only damage incurred, other than to the flight member's nerves, with suffered by Bill Dursteler who caught a direct hit on the wing by a 37-mm shell. Everything turned

out well. Dursteler and his wingman, Dick Kempthorn, landed at K-14 while Laird Guttersen and his wingman, Greg Costello, landing at K-16." Bill Dursteler's aircraft "had a hole big enough to permit a man to stand in it when it landed at K-14."

The supply of flying clothes remained "in a pitiful state. The pilots are reduced to the sorry state of having to procure their own equipment or improvise. In the matter of shoes, if a pilot's shoes wear out he cannot go to supply even to buy a pair of shoes, but must either wait until he goes on R&R or until a friend brings a pair from Japan," the 12th noted.

"Hollywood films about flying notwithstanding," the 12th noted, "a fighter outfit is a peculiar organization which, to a very great extent, runs on esprit de corps. A fighter pilot can be ordered into the air, but nobody is going to be with him in the cockpit to see that he makes a determined effort to put his bombs on the target, which in the case of a fighter-bomber is the reason for existence of the pilot and airplane. A certain amount of carefree abandon is necessary if a pilot is going to approach his target with nerves steady enough or a determination strong enough to make his dive bomb run effective," the 12th concluded. "This peculiar mental state can be nurtured in a pilot, by instilling in him a devastating pride in his work which will overcome any psychological or material obstacle which might arise."

Combat

Operations

"Pilots Hit High For Bombing Accuracy During Strikes on Red Supplies, Shipping," the *Truckbuster* reported on September 30, 1952. Twenty-two aircraft of the 18th FBW "recently planted 43 of 44 bombs dropped directly into a North Korean troop concentration in a magnificent display of fighter-bomber accuracy which accounted for 18 buildings destroyed and 10 damaged."

"Carrying general purpose and fire

Captain Howard R. Ebersole stands by his F-51 prior to another combat mission in September 1952 while he was assigned to the 12th Squadron at K-46. He would soon be heavily involved in planning the transition of the 18th Fighter-Bomber Group from Mustangs to Sabrejets. (Ebersole)

bombs, the 22 Mustangs barely missed a perfect bombing record when one bomb hung in its rack and was released late. It was a pilot's field day as the six flights, led by Captain Warren N. Mills of Westfield, N.J. found freshly constructed buildings with metal roofs where they had expected grass huts for a target."

"When we dove in, Captain Mills said, "I could hardly believe my eyes. There were all these buildings, lined up in about five neat rows, just like an airfield. There was freshly dug earth around the area that showed the construction was new—we couldn't miss."

1st Lt. Earle T. Carothers, Jr. of Dallas, Texas, who led the last flight into the target, had a good view of the damage inflicted. "The first squadron in dropped the general purpose bombs, and we carried the fire. There were already fires going, with huge clouds of reddish smoke billowing out. When we dropped our stuff, there was a secondary explosion, and the whole target area practically disappeared in the smoke."

"A flight of four Mustangs of the 18th struck Red shipping along the west coast

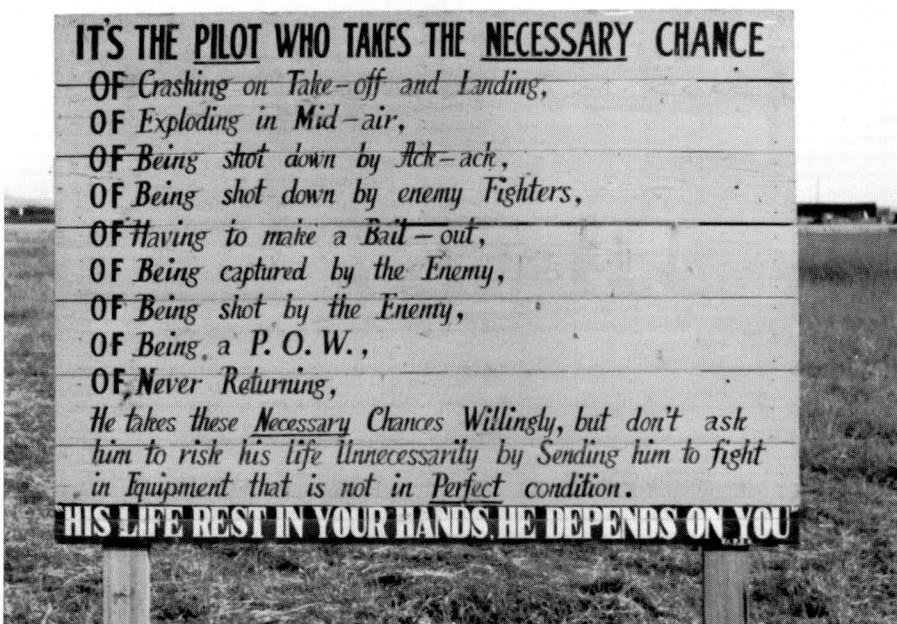

*"It's the Pilot who takes the **necessary** chance,"* this K-13 sign points out. *"He takes these **Necessary** chances willingly, but don't ask him to risk his life unnecessarily by sending him to fight in equipment that is not in **Perfect** condition."* (Ebersole)

A 2 Squadron SAAF Mustang prepares to take off from Wonju/K-46 on a combat mission in September 1952. (Bist)

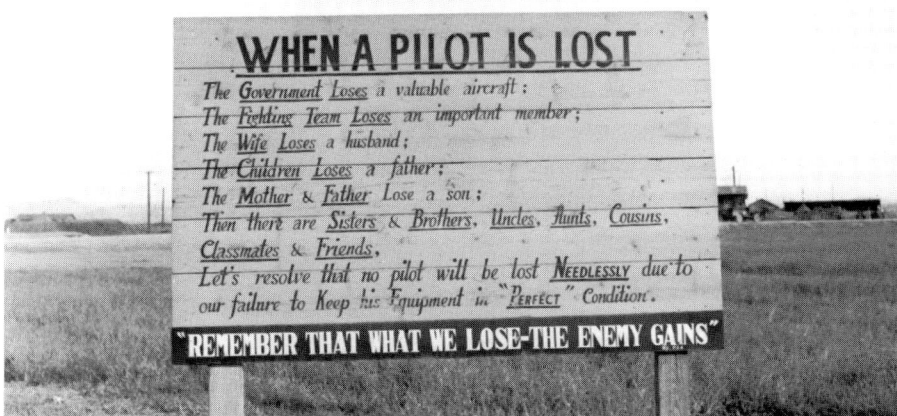

What We Lose—The Enemy Gains. *"Let's resolve that no pilot will be lost **Needlessly** due to our failure to Keep his Equipment in "**Perfect**" Condition,"* this inspirational sign at K-13 says. (Ebersole)

Combat Statistis

18th Fighter-Bomber Wing

September 1952

Average No. A/C Assigned
36
Total Flying Time
2,328
Percent of Aircraft in Commission
85%
Percent of Aircraft AOCP
6%
Combat Sorties Flown by Wing
1,361
12th Squadron Sorties
Unavailable
67th Squadron Sorties
566
2 Squadron Sorties
247
A/C Lost to Combat
0
Pilots lost
0

Fuel Consumed
170,951 gals.

Ordnance Expended
.50-cal. Rounds
467,237
Rockets
1,548
Napalm Bombs
0
500-lb. GP Bombs
1,664
Note: Figures and totals may differ in some categories due to differences in numbers provided by each component.

535

recently in a sitting duck mission that lived up to its name."

Small craft used for shipping Communist supplies along the estuary of the Taedong River west of Chinnampo were the target of the bombing, rocketing strike that resulted in three boats destroyed, and five more damaged. Returning pilots reported the boats didn't appear to be of the usual wooden construction.

"1st Lt. Thomas G. Cestello, of Los Angeles, California said, "When our bombs lit in among them, they didn't disintegrate like the wooden junks…They just hopped and skipped around down there like a bunch of sand fleas."

Captain Richard D. Kimball, of Detroit, Michigan, said, "As I was pulling out of my pass, I saw two sets of bombs and some rockets blast into the middle of the cluster." The former WWII transport pilot continued, "It was a sitting duck mission—that is, we go up there and take whatever targets are given us. And that's just what those boats turned out to be: sitting ducks."

"In another blow at enemy troop and supply concentrations, the pilots of the 18th again demonstrated their marksmanship as they blasted targets just west of the Kaesong restricted area in one of a series of successful dusk assaults. Twenty four aircraft participated in the fire bomb raid which left a string of fire visible against the night sky for miles around."

The first two waves into the target area destroyed 21 buildings and left such fierce fires burning that the third wave diverted to a nearby target where it destroyed another six buildings and damaged four more."

Returning pilots reported some flak in the areas they went into their passes.

Airman Third Class William Ackeridge loads .50-caliber ammunition into a 12th Squadron Mustang at K-46 in September 1952. Airman Third Class Stanley Bist (left) observes. (Bist)

Captain Arthur L. Flowers of Darlington, S.C. said the tracers arced through the sky in gentle curves. "The stuff didn't seem to be going fast, and it looked like the 4th of July—till some heavy stuff burst right off my wing. Somehow, it didn't look so pretty then, but when we pulled off the target, it looked like all the blast furnaces in Birmingham going at once, there were so many fires."

Captain Herschell G. Larrick, Jr. of Solana Beach, California, who led the third wave in, said, "We started in, and made one pass, and then took off. There wasn't any use putting any more stuff in that target. It was obliterated. So we went to a nearby target and dumped our stuff in there. I've never seen better bombing than that."

Significant Events

September 3/4: B-29s flew fifty-two effective sorties, the monthly high and all but two against the Chosin hydroelectric power plant complex.

September 4: Seventy-five fighter-bombers flew well north of the Chongchon River to attack targets, flushing out an estimated eighty-nine MiGs from their Manchurian bases. The thirty-nine Sabres screening the F-84s engaged the MiGs, destroying thirteen, to equal the one-day record set on July 4. Four F-86s fell to the MiG pilots. Maj. Frederick C. Blesse, USAF, 334th FIS, destroyed his fifth enemy aircraft to become an ace. An H-19 from the 3rd ARS rescued a downed fighter pilot and two crewmen of a USN helicopter, which had lost power and crashed in the water while attempting to pick up the pilot.

September 5: In two daylight strikes, Far East Air Forces flew over two hundred sorties against an ore and processing plant located northeast of Sinanju, damaging or destroying approximately seventy buildings and repair shops.

September 9: Protected by F-86s, forty-five F-84s attacked the North Korean Military Academy at Sakchu. Of approximately sixty-four MiGs in the area, some penetrated the Sabre screen, shot down three ThunderJets, and forced several flights to jettison their bombs. The F-86s suffered no losses during the aerial combat and destroyed five MiGs.

September 12/13: Twenty-five B-29s attacked the generator building at the giant Sui-ho power plant. Prior to and during the attack, USAF B-26s and USN aircraft dropped low-level fragmentation bombs to suppress enemy searchlights, rendering eight of approximately thirty unserviceable. At the same time, four B-29s orbiting to the east jammed enemy radar. Enemy fighters shot down one medium bomber and flak damaged several others, but the B-29s dropped their bombs on target, again rendering the plant unserviceable. Far East Air Forces concluded that searchlight suppression and ECM probably had saved the B-29s from greater losses.

September 15: To improve air-ground coordination and mutual understanding between the U.S. Air Force and the U.S. Army, General Barcus began sending groups of fifteen pilots at a time on three-day tours to the front lines.

September 16: Fifth Air Force flew 110 B-26 sorties, the high figure for the month, mostly night armed reconnaissance and interdiction. Using the recently-developed roadblock tactics, the light bombers damaged or destroyed over one hundred enemy vehicles.

September 19: In the first daylight medium bomber raid in eleven months, thirty-two B-29s with F-86 escorts attacked an enemy barracks and two supply areas southwest of Hamhung. An RB-45 preceded the B-29 formation, and an RB-29 orbited in the assembly area, providing weather information.

September 21: Sabre pilot Capt. Robinson Risner, USAF, 336th FIS, destroyed two MiG-15s to become an ace when the enemy responded to an attack on the Pukchong munitions plant by forty-one F-84s.

September 27: At night, three B-26s flew in the central sector loudspeaker sorties totaling three and one-half hours, an unusually high amount of broadcast time.

September 29: Fifth Air Force fighter-bombers flew against enemy bunkers and gun positions 207 close air support sorties, the highest figure this month and well above the daily average.

Adapted in part from U.S. Air Force Historical Research Agency. January 2002. The U.S. Air Force's First War: Korea 1950-1953 Significant Events. September 1952. http://www.au.af.mil/au/afhra/wwwroot/korean_war/korean_war_chronology/kwc_1952.html

Combat Losses

None

Airman Second Class Bobby Danner (right) prepares to "double clutch" the towing vehicle that he and *Airman Third Class Stanley Bist* (left), armorers for the 18th Fighter-Bomber Wing, use to tow loads of rockets and bombs out to the flight line to load onto waiting Mustangs at K-46 in September 1952. (Bist)

October 1952

The major factor affecting morale "is the indecision as to when we are to transfer to jet type aircraft. The move has been postponed so many times many are wondering if it will ever come."

During October, the operational effort of the Wing increased, with the combat components flying the most sorties since June. The 18th Group flew a total of 1,584 sorites, of which 2 Squadron flew 326, the 12th 631 and the 67th 627. The Group focused its principal interdiction efforts against enemy troops and supplies. "Close support sorties again increased during October to represent more than one-half the effort for the month. Armed reconnaissance, rescue air patrol, and road reconnaissance were the other types of missions flown," the Group reported. However, close support, interdiction and rescue missions accounted for the majority of the sorties flown.

From 9-18 October, FAF conducted "an intensified air attack program" that attempted to achieve a fifty percent increase in the effort of FAF activities. "Principal targets were troop concentrations, communications centers, and centers of military activity along MSR's. In support of this operation, Group attacked selected targets on interdiction and armed reconnaissance missions. During the period, in addition to this accelerated program, the Group flew 372 effective close support sorties, 70 effective rescue and combat air patrol sorties and 26 effective reconnaissance sorties."

Ground fog hampered combat operations in October, restricting early morning flying on 13 days that month. Adverse

Transition to Sabrers...Finally. *By October 1952 the 18th was preparing for the long awaited transition to F-86 jet fighters. Captain Howard "Ebe" Ebersole was selected to become an "IP"—Instructor Pilot—who would play an important role in the challenging training program that lay ahead for the "Truckbusters." (Ebersole)*

Monthly Summary

Between October 6-15, Chinese ground forces attacked mainly in the western IX Corps area northwest of Chorwon in a vain attempt to improve their position before the onset of winter. In mid-month, Eighth Army launched Operation SHOWDOWN to seize critical high ground in eastern IX Corps northeast of Kumhwa, but it became a seesaw contest to retain dominating terrain. In conjunction with Operation SHOWDOWN, Naval Forces Far East conducted in the Kojo area of northeast Korea a live amphibious demonstration intended to lure enemy forces onto roads where they could be attacked. Fifth Air Force and Bomber Command intensified air-attacks against troop concentrations, key communication centers, vehicles, and rail lines south and east of Pyongyang, while 315th and 403rd Troop Carrier Wings concentrated C-46 and C-119 aircraft at Taegu AB for a paradrop exercise. Disappointingly, intelligence noted little enemy response; either the hoax did not deceive the enemy, or he could not respond to the threat.

Fighter-interceptors flew combat patrols over northwest Korea daily as weather permitted. Fighter-bombers struck enemy supply points and other lucrative targets, including bridges, gun positions, vehicles, repair shops and troop concentrations. Fifth Air Force concentrated on targets south of a line from Pyongyang to Wonsan and on close support to assist UN ground forces, especially in the IX Corps area. F-84 Fighter-bombers, usually escorted by F-86s, initiated first-light reconnaissance of the rail line between Huichon and Kanggye to catch locomotives before they could be hidden in tunnels. The fighter-bombers also attacked enemy rail bridges and rolling stock. Enemy fighter opposition during October was meager and non-aggressive.

Reconnaissance could not determine if the Sui-ho hydroelectric plant was still operational but did find more antiaircraft guns in the vicinity. Reconnaissance units gave particular attention to locating prisoner of war camps.

The 502rd Tactical Control Group opened an air-direction center on Cho-do off North Korea's western coast. This facility gave UN fighter-interceptors ground-control intercept vectors of the same kind that the enemy had enjoyed for several months.

Adapted in part from U.S. Air Force Historical Research Agency. January 2002. The U.S. Air Force's First War: Korea 1950-1953 Significant Events. October 1952. http://www.au.af.mil/au/afhra/wwwroot/korean_war/korean_war_chronology/kwc_1952.html

weather grounded the Group for eight more days.

The Group lost five aircraft in October—four to combat operations and one to a training flight. Of the four that were lost in combat, "one was shot down by enemy MIG-15's, one by automatic weapons ground fire, and two were lost due to mechanical malfunction. A mid-air collision on a training flight resulted in the death of one pilot," the Group reported.

Group rescue flights "succeeded in locating and capping two downed pilots were rescued due to the high degree of coordination and resourcefulness displayed by the capping flight."

Three damaged aircraft returned from napalm missions. The subsequent investigation indicated that napalm had either leaked out of the tanks and was ignited by a gun flash, or was caused by incendiary projectiles from ground fire. Armament sections were ordered to use "only those napalm tanks pressure tested by napalm area personnel, cleaning of napalm mix that may have been found on the outside of the tanks, and ascertaining that the filler cap well was tightly fitted."

One pilot from the 67th Squadron ran into difficulties on take-off and headed for the bomb drop area to get rid of his bombs. The bombs were supposed to be dropped "safe" to ensure they would not explode on impact. Fortunately, the bomb disposal personnel working in the area were not harmed by the explosions. Another pilot attempted to salvo his bombs safe, but improperly set the switches and they were dropped, armed, from 200 feet. The bombs exploded on impact, causing major damage to the aircraft. The Group report noted with some understatement that a "flying safety meeting was held and pilots were again instructed as to the proper method of dropping bombs safe."

Also that month, on four occasions, .50-cal machine guns were fired from aircraft while they were parked on the R&R line. One firing was the result of a gun malfunction. The other three were "attributed to carelessness on the part of line personnel. A new SOP was published giv-

The next to last replacement class of F-51 pilots for the 18th, included (L – R) "Deacon" Wright, Ortega, Cottrell, Carmichael, Lanning and Iverson. Front row (L – R) Hathaway, Mason, Smotherman and Smith. Carmichael, Smotherman and Smith, stayed on and flew combat in the F-86. "Smo" was KIA on 31 May 1953. "Smitty" was hit on a dive bombing run at dusk on 15 June 1953. (Ebersole)

ing detailed instructions to line personnel in regard to safe positions of switches."

Squadron Level Developments

The major factor affecting morale in the 12th during October "is the indecision as to when we are to transfer to jet type aircraft. The move has been postponed so many times many are wondering if it will ever come. There are those who would like to fly the jet and are therefore standing down and those who want to do anything but fly jets, and are consequently pushing for missions. Couple this circumstance with the fact that no one has the slightest idea as to when the move will commence and you have a perfect setup for poor morale."

A 12th Squadron armorer prepares this Mustang for a winter mission from K-46 with rockets and napalm in October 1952. (Bist)

539

Combat Statistics

18th F-B Wing

October 1952

Average No. A/C Assigned
54 *(excludes 2nd Squadron and is one short of authorized strength)*
Total Flying Time
2,357
Percent of Aircraft in Commission
87%
Percent of Aircraft AOCP
5%
Combat Sorties Flown by Wing
1,583
12th Squadron Sorties
631
67th Squadron Sorties
635
2 Squadron Sorties
332
A/C Lost to Combat
2
Pilots lost
2

Fuel Consumed

181,571 gals.

Ordnance Expended

.50-cal. Rounds
586,275
Rockets
1,391
Napalm Bombs
32
500-lb. GP Bombs
1,650

Note: Figures and totals may differ in some categories due to differences in numbers provided by each component.

The weather was getting much colder. "Pilots were instructed to wear heavier clothing on missions and the wings of the aircraft were covered at night to avoid frost."

"Let us hope that soon we will be enlightened as to the future of the Foxey Few. Until that time comes, the squadron will continue in its quest for perfections--perfection not only in aerial warfare but in all other endeavors it is associated with as well."

Significant Events

September 30/October 1: Including five ECM flak suppression aircraft, forty-eight B-29s from all three units--19th BG, 98th BW, and 307th BW-destroyed the last strategic-type target in Korea, the Namsan-ni Chemical Plant located 1,300 feet from the Yalu River and near the Sui-ho Dam. During the bombing, seven B-26s swept in at low altitudes to suppress eight of some forty searchlights.

October 5: Fifth Air Force combined attacks with USN aircraft against barracks and supplies of the Chinese 67th Army at Loeyang.

October 7: Fifth Air Force fighter pilots and USN airmen attacked the CCF 26th Army at Yongpyongni.

October 8: In support of the amphibious hoax, ten B-29s of the 98th BW conducted a rare daylight visual bombing mission on the supply area at Kowon in eastern Korea in coordination with USN fighter-bomber attacks. Truce talks at Panmunjom recessed over the issue of forced repatriation of prisoners of war. The UN delegates proposed to allow enemy POWs to choose repatriation or not; the communist delegates insisted on the repatriation of all POWs at the end of the war.

Captain Charles R. Riggs, of the 67th Squadron, made a successful emergency landing at K-46 when he could not lower one landing gear.

During the period 9-18 October "an intensified air attack program was conducted by Fifth Air Force. The concept of the operation was a fifty percent increased in the effort of Fth Air Force Activities."

October 9: Fighter-bombers attacked widely scattered communist communications centers from Huichon in North Korea south to the bomb line. Fifth Air Force aircraft inflicted heavy casualties on a communist regiment, delaying its commitment to the enemy attack underway.

October 12: An SA-16 pilot, 3rd ARS, participated in two rescues within thirty minutes and over one hundred miles apart. After directing a helicopter pickup of a downed Sabrejet pilot, the SA-16 pilot landed in the Haeju harbor and, while overhead fighters suppressed ground fire from the shore, picked up from a dinghy a 69th Squadron pilot who had parachuted from his burning F-84.

The 18th Group flew 125 sorties on this date, "the largest effort mounted for several months. Excellent results were achieved on all missions which included close support, interdiction, rescue, armed rescue and recce."

October 12-14: The 315th AD conducted paratroop-drop exercises with the US 187th Regimental Combat Team as part of the Kojo deception.

October 12/13: Twenty-six B-29s from all three medium bombardment units struck nine separate troop concentrations on Haeju Peninsula.

October 13: In preparation for the Kojo amphibious demonstration, FEAF and USN aircraft hit enemy positions around Kojo, and USN surface craft shelled the beach area. After a respite of almost a year, the enemy, using small fabric-covered biplanes, hassled Cho-do and the Seoul area with "Bedcheck Charlie" raids.

Airman Third Class Stanley Bist and Airman Second Class Richard Abernathy outside their tent "quarters" at K-46/Wonju in October 1952. (Bist)

October 15: For the amphibious Kojo hoax, assault troops climbed down to assault landing craft, which made a pass at the shore then returned to the ship. In addition, thirty-two C-119s, 403rd TCW, flew to Chorwon, let down to paradrop altitude of 800 feet, then returned to Taegu AB.

October 16: North Korea sent a strongly worded protest to Far East Command concerning the recess in armistice negotiations but continued to insist on total repatriation of Chinese and North Korean prisoners of war.

October 24: Fifth Air Force and Eighth Army completed a successful thirty-day test in IX Corps area of a new flak-suppression technique that allowed friendly artillery to continue firing while close support strikes were in progress.

October 27: Fifth Air Force aviation engineers completed a heavy-duty runway for combat cargo operations at the Seoul Municipal Airport.

October 31: North Korea presented a new POW camp list.

Adapted in part from U.S. Air Force Historical Research Agency. January 2002. The U.S. Air Force's First War: Korea 1950-1953 Significant Events. October 1952. http://www.au.af.mil/au/afhra/wwwroot/korean_war/korean_war_chronology/kwc_1952.html

Combat Losses

For the Group "there were three accidents in the month of October, one of which resulted in the death of Lt. Col. Brewer. In addition, two aircraft were lost to enemy action. One of the pilots was safe in friendly hands and the other is listed as MIA."

Captain John G. Woliung, 12th Squadron pilot. "A mid-air collision on a training flight resulted in the death of one pilot," the Group reported.

(Above) "Item Flight" of the 67th Squadron in October 1952. Left to right: Rexford R. Baldwin, 1st Lt. Richard H. Deihl, 1st Lt. C. J. Gossett, Capt. Charles M. Sargen, Captain Warren W. Mills and Lt. Joe B. Dishongh. (Above, right) 1st Lt. Richard H. Deihl.

Meanwhile, back at K-10

The 18th Fighter-Bomber Wing moved the majority of its combat operations from K-10 to K-46 in June 1952. A significant amount of maintenance was still performed at K-10, however. The 18th Air Installations Squadron ensured that K-10 remained in satisfactory operational condition. If the war took a turn for the worse, the Wing might have to move back to K-10. Anthony "Tony" Falo arrived in Korea in September 1952, straight from Engineer School at Fort Belvoir, Virginia. When he arrived at K-10 as an architect/engineer for the 18th Fighter-Bomber Wing, he was assigned to the Air Installation Squadron.
The Air Installation Squadron operated from this corrugated steel building at K-10. (Falo)

Two Airmen from the Air Installation Squadron solve a "water supply problem" at K-10 in their own, creative way in October 1952. (Falo)

November 1952

"Every person in this squadron is looking forward to the proposed transition into F-86 type aircraft and when this conversion becomes a reality morale will greatly improve.

In early November 1952, General Mark Wayne Clark, Commanding General, Far East Command, arrived at K-10, still the official headquarters for the 18th Fighter-Bomber Wing, to participate in ceremonies honoring the ROK Military Academy in nearby Chinhae. Clark had been named Commander-in-Chief, U.N. Command, and Commanding General, U.S. Army Forces Far East on 30 April 1952, succeeding Lieutenant General Matthew B. Ridgway. Clark served as commander of United Nations (U.N.) Forces in Korea until 7 October 1953, signing the Military Armistice Agreement on behalf of the U.N. Command with the Communist forces at Munsan-ni, Korea, July 27, 1953. Here, Clark cooperates with Airman Earl Ramsdell in having his picture taken "with some of the fellows" of the 18th Wing. (Ramsdell)

Principal interdiction efforts for the 18th Group in November were directed against troops and supplies. Close support missions again represented more than one-half of the effort for that month. Armed reconnaissance and rescue combat air patrols were the other types of missions flown, the Group reported.

The 18th FBW reached its 50,000 combat sortie--flown by a SAAF pilot.

"The Fifth Air Force intensified close air supports during the month. Approximately 75% of the missions flown were close air supports," the Group reported. "Napalm was used primarily on interdiction work."

The Group's combat operations were restricted for a period of eight days during the month due to bad weather. During the month three aircraft were lost due to combat operations. One was killed in action, one was missing in action and the third pilot bailed out successfully and returned to combat the following day."

During the month of November, three aircraft were lost due to combat operations, including one pilot killed in action, one listed as missing in action and a third pilot who bailed out successfully "and returned to combat the following day."

Three aircraft that month returned

Monthly Summary

After mid-November the scale of ground actions declined as the enemy replenished supplies and reinforced troops. Fifth Air Force increased close support in IX Corps sector where enemy ground forces pressed attacks on ROK outposts.

Reconnaissance revealed little activity on North Korean airfields. However, FEAF intelligence found that the Chinese had stationed one hundred of the latest-model Soviet-built IL-28 light jet bombers in Manchuria, thus increasing the possibility of aerial attacks upon UN front lines, air bases in Korea, and installations in Japan.

Fifth Air Force units continued operational pressure on enemy rail systems, troop concentrations, supply areas, and headquarter areas. Destruction of two small hydroelectric facilities at Kongosan left virtually no hydroelectric facilities functioning in North Korea. Fifth Air Force rail interdiction sorties dropped some two hundred tons of bombs on the Sinuiju-Sinanju line with two heavy attacks on the Yongmi-dong bridge. Yet, the line remained serviceable to through traffic through November, except for three days.

Although hampered by bad weather, Fifth Air Force obtained good results against enemy supply routes, following an interdiction plan called "Choke." At last light, fighter-bombers attacked selected road bridges and shortly after dark B-26s hit similar objectives. During the night other B-26s reconnoitered and bombed vehicles stalled behind the blown-out bridges.

Late in the month, Fifth Air Force began scheduling F-80 and F-84 fighter-bombers on night, armed reconnaissance missions, patrolling the highway and rail line from Sinanju through Pyongyang to Sariwan. Fifth Air Force also placed F-86 flights south of MiG Alley for ground-controlled interceptions of MiG-15s whose pilots had evaded the main Sabre screen and attempted to attack Sabre patrols returning south and low on fuel.

Adapted in part from U.S. Air Force Historical Research Agency. January 2002. The U.S. Air Force's First War: Korea 1950-1953 Significant Events. July 1952. http://www.au.af.mil/au/afhra/wwwroot/korean_war/korean_war_chronology/kwc_1952.html

from missions with damage from napalm--"either the napalm had leaked out of napalm tanks and was ignited by gun flash, or was caused by incendiary projectiles from ground fire."

On two occasions, aircraft returned to base with flap damage due to burning of leaking napalm. Since all the tanks were pressure tested and all the igniters were secured with rubber gaskets and then checked for tightness, "it is probable that the leaks were due to small arms fire."

Movement Orders

The long anticipated "movement orders" for the 18th Fighter-Bomber Wing arrived on 29 November from Headquarters, FAF. "Take necessary action for which you are responsible to move the 18th Fighter-Bomber Wing, and the 2nd South African Air Force Squadron from present Station to K-55, Korea, APO 970. The units will be moved on or about 15 December 1952 and be in place no later than 31 December 1952. The move from K-10 and K-46 affected the following units:

Headquarters, 18th Fighter-Bomber Wing

Detachment #1, 18th Fighter-Bomber Wing (at K-46)

Headquarters, 18th Fighter-Bomber Group

12th Fighter-Bomber Squadron

67th Fighter-Bomber Squadron

Headquarters, 18th Air Base Group

18th Air Police Squadron

18th Communications Squadron

18th Food Service Squadron

18th Installations Squadron

Headquarters, 18th Maintenance & Supply Group

18th Maintenance Squadron

18th Supply Squadron

18th Motor Vehicle Squadron

18th Medical Group

2nd South African Air Force Squadron

The 18th Wing Commander was ordered to leave enough personnel at K-46 to "maintain, operate and secure" the air base until 1 January 1953 at which time the 6155th Air Base Squadron came into existence and assumed the responsibilities of the base.

The move would be made by water, motor convoy, rail and air as required.

MIGs Fly "Cover" For 18th Pilots

"There is nothing more conducive to a fighter-bomber pilot's peace of mind than the sight of a flight of jets flying top cover for him to keep the MIGs off his back as he goes about his work," the *Truck-buster* reported on November 17, 1952.

"A flight of four Mustangs, ranging into North Korea recently in search of a target as fighting erupted along the front, were heartened to see high-flying, swept-wing jets wheeling and circling lazily thou-

Armorer Airman Third Class William Ackeridge opens the access panels on a 12th Squadron Mustang while rearming the plane prior to its next mission. In the background, similar operations are underway for F-51s of the 67th Squadron. (Bist)

sands of feet over their heads." The Mustangs picked up a controller and prepared for their targets.

"It felt great," Lt. Robert L. Taylor said, "there we were, loaded for bear, juicy targets all over Korea, and plenty of protection."

It felt great until one of the jets peeled off and dived from around thirty thousands feet to investigate the Mustangs. That was when "shock set in. The three high-flying jets were MIGs."

"About then, we decided that discretion was the better part of valor," Taylor said, "and we headed for the ground. The MIG broke off his pass and went back to join his buddies. We evidently were too low for them to dive on us and recover, so they never did fire on us. There are tactics to meet all kinds of situation—even when it's a MIG against a propeller-driver plane. It's a matter of training and knowing in advance what to do under a given set of circumstances. Nevertheless, it doesn't do much for the digestion when your top cover turns out to be the enemy." [1]

Squadron Activities

A major change occurred in the 12th Squadron when Lt. Col. Albert J. Freund, Jr. "was elevated to Group Commanding Officer and Major Vernon Harwood assumed leadership of the Foxey Few." Harwood had been the 18th Group Training Officer and had been attached to the 67th Squadron.

The combat mission of the Foxey Few was modified to include "interception...it is not interception in the true sense of the word but rather identification of unknown aircraft operating on the front lines. Teams of two are sent out to patrol specified sectors of the front, and working in conjunction with T.A.D.C., strive to maintain air supremacy," the 12th reported.

The 12th lost two pilots in November. "One never pulled out of a dive on a close support mission and the second went under on a low level bombing mission. Another officer was temporarily put out of commission when he picked up a thirty caliber in the buttocks."

[The unit reports did not name these pilots. However, Richard Deihl, a former Mustang pilot with the 67th Squadron, noted that one of them was "Lt. Warren Hull, who was captured and became a POW--later released on the last day of prisoner exchanges."]

The 12th reported that "experienced F-51 mechanics rotating to the Z.I. were being replaced by jet mechanics directly out of school with no practical experience in aircraft maintenance whatsoever."

A boost in morale took place when the "wearing of squadron caps again came into practice. Airmen will also be parading around in squadron fedoras in the near future which should give quite an impetus to squadron morale."

The 67th report noted, "All officers and enlisted men in the squadron were encouraged to wear red hats and the traditional 'Red Scarfs,' which definitely increased the feeling of pride in the section."

"Every person in this squadron is looking forward to the proposed transition into F-86 type aircraft and when this conversion becomes a reality morale will greatly improve. The personnel in this squadron are the best, and with new, up-to-date equipment the squadron will be unexcelled anywhere," the 67th promised.

For the 12th the month came to an end "with the question of jet transition still left dangling. Although rumors are flying wildly concerning jets it isn't impairing the efficiency of the outfit in the least."

Attack At Dusk

"The Ridges Were Alive With Flashes…"

A bird's eye view of the front lines at dusk was "an awesome thing," according to four pilots of the 18th in November 1952 who "attacked and destroyed an automatic weapons position and a troop concentration" in the Pyonggang area of North Korea, the Truckbuster reported.

"The ridges were alive with flashes in the gathering dusk as the Mustangs went in on the targets."

"There was a hell of a fire-fight going on down there," Capt. Jack Hawley, of Bridgeport, Mich., said, "and they weren't all firing at each other. Some of them were firing at us. Golf balls were going by us from all angles. I think that's when rigor mortis of my trigger finger set in."

With help from a Mosquito controller, the flight first attacked the automatic weapons position. Lt. Earle T. Carothers, of Dallas, Texas, who led the flight, said, "The Mosquito asked me if I could see it. I'll say I could see it. It was looking right down the barrel of it, and he was looking right back up the barrel at me. My bombs went right into the position and he quit firing. We went down to have a look at it and the weapons was quiet and listing over at a strange angle."

It was almost dark when the flight left the area. "It was an awesome thing to see," Carothers said, "along the ridges the firing looked like thousands of flash-bulbs. During the daytime there's a lot of firing you never see, but at night you begin to realize just how much stuff they're throwing at each other." [2]

Strip Alert

"Cold, Cramped Cockpits…"

"It's one of those mornings again," Lt. J. H. Kriele, SAAF explained in the *Truckbuster* on November 17, 1952, "Baker Flight is on 'Strip.' Our trusty flight commander comes around to wake up the other three members of his team. The time is 0400 hours, the temperature outside below freezing. The stoves in our tents add a lot to our comfort, but once out from under your pile of blankets, you are strictly on your own."

"We get into our winter underwear, thick socks, boots, and flying overalls. A scramble to the ablution building for a very quick wash with a delicate finger, and we

Combat Statistics

18th F-B Wing

November 1952

Average No. A/C Assigned
39
Total Flying Time
2,022
Percent of Aircraft in Commission
89%
Percent of Aircraft AOCP
4%
Combat Sorties Flown by Wing
1,316
12th Squadron Sorties
106
67th Squadron Sorties
542
2 Squadron Sorties
297
A/C Lost to Combat
1
Pilots lost
2

Fuel Consumed
161,667 gals.

Ordnance Expended
.50-cal. Rounds
434,755
Rockets
191
Napalm Bombs
216
500-lb. GP Bombs
1,474
Note: Figures and totals may differ in some categories due to differences in numbers provided by each component.

An Honor Guard of ROK troops awaits the arrival of dignitaries in early November 1952 at K-10. The VIPs, including General Mark Clark, Korean President Syngman Rhee and Ambassador Robert D. Murphy, were taking part in ceremonies recognizing the first anniversary of the ROK Military Academy in nearby Chinhae. (Ramsdell)

General James Alward Van Fleet, Commander, U.S. Eighth Army leads President and Mrs. Syngman Rhee and General Mark Clark following their arrival at K-10. After duty as commander of the Second Army in the United States, Van Fleet was sent to Korea in April 1951, to command the American Eighth Army as the replacement for General Matthew B. Ridgway, who had succeeded General Douglas MacArthur as Far East commander. (Ramsdell)

(Far left) U. S. Ambassador to Japan Robert Daniel Murphy (1894-1978), had previously served as U.S. Ambassador to Belgium (1949-1952. During his diplomatic career which began in 1920, he had helped to negotiate with Vichy France (1940). Later, he was President Eisenhower's personal representative in Lebanon (1958). General Mark W. Clark, reaches out to greet a member of the arrival team as General James A. Van Fleet, Commanding General U.S. Eight Army smiles at the photographer, 18th Fighter-Bomber Wing Airman Earl W. Ramsdell.

General James Van Fleet (center) looks over at Korean President and Mrs. Syngman Rhee confer as they wait for their vehicle to transport them to the nearby ROK Military Academy near Chinhae. (Ramsdell)

are set for breakfast. The silent walk up the hill to the mess does everybody a lot of good, and by the time we get there, everybody seems more or less awake."

"Two eggs, 'over and easy,' some bacon and grapefruit juice and we are on our way to 'Ops.' There we have a small briefing, get our aircraft numbers, and put on our flying kits. First the gunbelt with .38 and bayonet. Then the radio vest, which is our most valuable piece of safety equipment. Then the bulky but necessary E&E vest with its multitude of pockets filled with vital items necessary to sustain life behind enemy lines. I am sure that with a bit of ingenuity one can almost have a good time with all those things carried in that vest. Then over all that goes the 'Mae West,' which, when inflated, makes the origin of the name quite obvious. The item was designed to save the wearer from drowning, but not from freezing."

"After that, it's just a matter of struggling into your parachute, getting your 'electric listening hat,' and map. By this time you have worked up a nice sweat, and this, coupled with the icy drive down to the flight line makes you a fair candidate for pneumonia."

"Every man to his plane now. The erks are scraping the ice off the windscreens and cockpit canopies while you make a hurried inspection to see that all the essential parts; airscrews, engines, control surfaces, etc, are all there. Then up onto the wing, where the erk awaits you with your dinghy. This thing must save your life when you fall into cold water with sharks, and also serves as a cushion to sit on, since all parachutes are of the back type.

[Note: The 67th Squadron had seat chutes, noted Richard Deihl.]

This 'Cushion' is about a soft as sack full of broken bricks. A brief skirmish between you and the erk and the dinghy, and then you can climb into the cockpit. Once you have made yourself as comfortable as your bulk will permit, you must resign yourself to the fact that there will be no stretching of cramped muscles. Sign the book, put on your helmet, attach oxy-

gen and radio connections, fasten oxygen mask, and you are all set."

"There! The leader is starting up already. With a mighty heave, you contort yourself to go thru the action of starting up. A few nice encouraging words to the old engine, a rattle, a few wheezes, a couple of bangs, and there she goes. Radio on, a few more vital actions, a bit of sweat to get all the lights on, and the leader's voice over the air makes you jump as far as the straps will allow, which is maybe half an inch."

"Baker Flight, check in."

"Baker 2, 3, and 4."

"Roger, 5-5, go red and check in."

"Just a word about the radio at this stage. It consists of a little box situated somewhere in the region of your right elbow. In daylight, it somewhat resembles a typewriter with the keys marked in different colours. This was devised by the boffins to confuse the enemy as well as the pilot himself. Anybody with ten fingers and a night-seeing eye on his right elbow won't have any difficult in operating the radio at all."

"Anyway, everyone has checked in on all channels, and the boss has received permission from the control tower for taxi-clearance, so away we go. Grim shadows weave their way through the darkness over miles (it seems) of tricky taxi-strip. An occasional glimpse of a red or green navigation light ahead, that horrible feeling of being lost in the dark, a few 'look-sees' with the powerful landing lights, and, one by one, the aircraft take up position. Then for the next minute or so the hills reverberate with the roar of four mighty Merlins (Packard-built, of course) being tested. Every pilot makes sure that everything is in good order, one final cleaning at '30' boost…and then, to those foreign with the procedure, a very strange thing happens. One would have expected to see these metal monsters go hurtling into the air one by one, bent on death and destruction. But no…the mighty air screws slow down and come to a stop. Then the lights wink out, and perfect quiet once more descends upon the airfield." [3]

"The reason for this phenomenon

is quite simple. This is 'Strip Alert,' or a 'Runway Standby,' and found bleary-eyed pilots have to sit on the side of the runway in cold cockpits for an hour and half—just in case."

"Up in the billets, a young pilot stirs and shakes off the four MIGs that have been chasing him all night, curls himself into a tighter ball under his blankets, and with a happy smile grins to himself: 'Hell, I'm glad I'm not on 'Strip' this morning!'" [4]

Endnotes

[1] USAFHRA. *The Truckbuster. "Mistaken MIGs Fly 'Cover' for 18th;* November 17, 1952, p. 1.

[2] USAFHRA. *The Truckbuster. Pilots Term Front 'Awesome' at Dusk."* November 17, 1952, p. 1.

[3] USAFHRA. *The Truckbuster. Pilots Term Front 'Awesome' at Dusk."* November 17, 1952, p. 2.

[4] USAFHRA. *The Truckbuster. "Strip Alert."* November 17, 1952, p. 3.

Significant Events

November 1: Fifth Air Force fighter-bombers attacked three railroad bridges at Yongmi-dong.

November 4: Dwight D. Eisenhower, having campaigned on a promise to seek an end to the Korean War, was elected President of the United States.

FEAF photographic surveillance showed the three railroad bridges at Yongmi-dong again in serviceable condition and two by-pass bridges nearing completion.

November 6: On a return attack against the Yongmi-dong railroad bridges, one-hundred fighter-bombers found that the enemy had moved in antiaircraft artillery and begun to build a fifth bypass bridge.

November 10: The 315th AD air evacuated the 250,000th patient from Korea to Japan.

On 10 November, Lt. Moir flew a challenging close support mission against artillery and infantry positions near ROK troops east of Kumsong. The Mosquito controller having been forced to leave the area, Moir made contact with a ground controller. Artillery shells were used to mark the target. It took two bomb runs before the bombs actually left the racks, during which Moir's aircraft and his wingman's plane were hit by flak. Both planes were lucky to make it back to K-46 with oil pressures well below normal. A large crowd was waiting for them, a fact they associated with their damaged aircraft. In fact, the group was there to celebrate the 50,000th combat sortie by the 18th Fighter-Bomber Wing in the Korean Campaign, the sortie they had just flown. The 18th was the first fighter-bomber wing in Korea to reach this total, of which the Flying Cheetahs had contributed 10,000 combat sorties.

Note: On 10 November, the 18th Wing reached its 50,000th sortie--flown by a pilot from the SAAF 2nd Squadron. When the Wing reached the 10,000th, 25,000th and 45,000th sortie marks, ceremonies were held and photographs taken. Significantly, for the 50,000th sortie there was no known ceremony to mark the occasion.

November 12/13: Six B-29s of the 98 BW knocked four spans out of Pyongyang's restored railway bridges.

November 16: USMC aircraft attached to Fifth Air Force attacked hydroelectric facilities at Kongosan.

November 17: USAF fighter-bombers attacked hydroelectric facilities at Kongosan. Col. Royal N. Baker, USAF, Commander, 4th FIG, flying in MiG Alley with the 335 FIS, scored his fifth MiG kill.

November 18: When USN Task Force 77 attacked the North Korean border town of Hoeryong in the far northeast, unmarked but obviously Russian MiG-15s flying from Vladivostok attempted to attack the fleet. Carrier-based F9F aircraft engaged several MiGs and downed one of them.

November 18/19: Six B-29s from the 98th BW attacked the Sonchon supply center, thirty-five miles from the Manchurian border. On this night, weather in the target area was clear, and enemy interceptors used new tactics to shoot down one B-29. The enemy dropped flares so that searchlights could lock on the bomber, and four fighter passes riddled it, forcing its crew to abandon ship over Cho-do.

November 19: The 49th and 58th Fighter-Bomber Wings, in two separate strikes totaling 179 aircraft, attacked a troop and supply concentration at Kanggye. An Eighth Army-Fifth Air Force indoctrination team completed a tour begun in late October to brief key Eighth Army officers on the nature and functioning of the air-ground system.

November 21: Major Vernon Harwood assumed command of the 12th FBS—the Foxey Few.

November 22: The 8th FBW lost two F-80s to ground fire during close support missions in IX Corps. One of the pilots, Maj. Charles J. Loring, Jr., USAF, leading a flight of four F-80s, was hit near Sniper Ridge by enemy ground fire. He deliberately crashed his aircraft into the midst of enemy gun emplacements, destroying them completely. Major Loring was posthumously awarded the Medal of Honor.

November 23: 1st Lt. Damon Reeder, of the 67th Squadron, made an emergency landing at K-14, due to battle damage.

November 25: Lt. Col. Albert J. Freund, Jr., who previously commanded the 12th Fighter-Bomber Squadron, assumed command of the 18th Fighter-Bomber Group, relieving Col. Sheldon S. Brinson, who returned to the Z.I.

November 28/29: All three medium bomber units at forty-five-minute intervals hit at Sinuiju and Uiju targets defended by approximately 116 heavy guns, ninety-four of which were radar-controlled, and forty searchlights as well as enemy interceptors. Preceding the attacks, five B-26s flew flak suppression missions. Fourteen B-29s bombed Sinuiju Airfield, six struck the Sinuiju locomotive repair facilities, ten hit the Uiju Airfield, and four attacked the Uiju communications center. In spite of clear weather, using ECM equipment and chaff, the B-29s escaped losses in a generally successful mission.

Adapted in part from U.S. Air Force Historical Research Agency. January 2002. The U.S. Air Force's First War: Korea 1950-1953 Significant Events. November 1952. http://www.au.af.mil/au/afhra/wwwroot/korean_war/korean_war_chronology/kwc_1952.html

Combat Losses

"In the month of November," the Group reported, "there were two aircraft lost and both pilots are listed as MIA."

One of the two pilots lost "on a low-level bombing mission," noted Richard Deihl, "was Lt. Warren Lull, who was captured and became a POW. He was released on the last day of prisoner exchanges later in 1953. Later, he visited my wife and me in Del Rio, Texas (Laughlin, AFB)."

December 1952

"The majority of pilots are brimming with happy expectation of things to come. The 86's are almost within their grasp and before long they will have those stove pipes running red hot."

The Escorts Got No Photo-Ops. During a visit to Korea in December, 1952, President-elect Dwight D. Eisenhower stopped at the U. S. Air Force F-86 "Sabre" jet 4th Fighter Interceptor Wing. With the President-designate during the tour of the "MIG killers" base were Lt. Gen. Glenn O. Barcus (left), Commanding General of Fifth Air Force; Col. Russell A. Berg (center), Commander of the 67th Tactical Reconnaissance Wing and 1st Lt. Ira A. Porter (right background), a "Sabre" jet pilot with the 4th Wing. When it came to VIP "photo opportunities," the available records reveal very few poses in locations other than jet aircraft or heavy bombers. Few celebrities ever visited Dogpatch to be recorded for posterity by USAF photographers. Ironically, 18th Fighter-Bomber Group records note that its aircraft provided the escorts for President-elect Eisenhower. (NARA)

Monthly Summary

Ground fighting slowed to a near halt during December. UN Command implemented across the entire Eighth Army front the new flak-suppression technique tested in October. It allowed friendly artillery to continue flak suppression while fighter-bombers prosecuted their frontline attacks, thus reducing Fifth Air Force losses to enemy antiaircraft fire.

In Geneva, the League of Red Cross Societies recommended that the combatants exchange sick and wounded prisoners of war in Korea before a cease-fire.

Since the Chinese were augmenting their ground forces and increasing supply traffic in North Korea, communist troop concentrations, supplies, and equipment became main objectives of UN air attack. Fifth Air Force fighter-bombers focused on known military headquarters, troop concentrations, and supply areas. B-26 light bombers, usually escorted by RAAF Meteors, attacked many of the same targets. The fighter-bombers struck rail lines in northwest North Korea leading from Manchuria and the Pyongyang-Sariwon line. They made roadblocks at Inchon, Chaeryong, and below Pyongyang. In combined attacks, fighter-bombers made road cuts at dusk, light bombers attacked vehicle concentrations during the night, and fighter-bomber sweeps at dawn sought out vehicles not under cover. Fifth Air Force claimed destruction of 2,321 vehicles during December, although it devoted about half of its effort to close support of the UN ground forces.

The 315th AD airlifted the 18th FBW headquarters from Chinhae to Osan-ni AB and its attached 2nd SAAF Squadron from Hoengsong Airfield to Osan-ni, the largest airlift of an USAF unit up to this time. Early in the month the newer C-124 Globemasters assigned to the 22nd TCS developed leaks in their gasoline tanks, and by the end of the month all were grounded.

Adapted in part from U.S. Air Force Historical Research Agency. January 2002. The U.S. Air Force's First War: Korea 1950-1953 Significant Events. December 1952. http://www.au.af.mil/au/afhra/wwwroot/korean_war/korean_war_chronology/kwc_1952.html

During the period 3-5 December, FAF conducted a special escort operation. The 18th Group flew 90 effective sorties in support of this operation. *[The "special escort operation" was the visit to the Korean front by President-elect Dwight Eisenhower.]*

From 20-25 December, FAF directed an intensified air intercept patrol along the front lines. The Group flew 54 effective sorties to support the operation.

In December, "as in November," the Group's principal interdiction efforts "were directed against enemy troop concentrations and supplies. Close support again accounted for the largest portion of the effort. Armed reconnaissance and rescue combat air patrol were the other types of missions flown.

The 18th Group "was committed to a large number of front line support missions in lieu of build-ups by the enemy. The Group struck in numbers ranging from 26 to 36 ship missions," the Group reported.

The operational effort of the 18th Fighter-Bomber Wing decreased in December due to poor weather.

Replacements from Luke AFB, Combat Crew Training School, "continued to show a lack of training in the methods of dive-bombing, rocketry, and strafing used in this theater. Those with previous TAC and ADC time were quicker to adapt themselves to the change in techniques than those who had recently graduated from flying school."

"New pilot personnel," the 67th Squadron reported, "do not have the high experience level found in previous replacements, who came from National Guard and Reserve units. Most of the pi-

Just prior to a mission in December 1952, Lt. John Staring, Lt. "Tex" Beneke and Captain "Ebe" Ebersole stand outside the Operations Offices of the 67th and 12th Squadrons at K-46. Six months later, Staring was a passenger on a C-124 that crashed in Japan. "Tex" Beneke, brother to the famous band leader, was killed on 31 May 1953 during a take off crash in an F-86F. "Both were WWII combat fighter pilots," Ebersole noted. (Ebersole)

lots received during this period were recent graduates of flying school and required more training and closer supervision."

Three T-6 "Texans" were attached to the advance detachment at K-46 to provide "the heretofore unavailable means for increased and supervised training in all phases of instrument flying."

The AOCP [Out of Commission for Parts] rate for the Group "reached an all-time high during December," varying from 20-40 percent. "Shortage of radiators, spark plugs, brakes, and hydraulic fluid, in that order, caused the high rate. Considerable liaison was conducted by the S-4 Section" to alleviate the shortages and increase the "in commission" rate of aircraft assigned to the Group.

Squadron Activities

The number of interdiction missions increased considerably while the close support missions fell off proportionately," the 12th Squadron reported in December.

The shortage in missions--349-- "was due partly to the fact that the squadron stood down six days while President-elect Eisenhower visited Korea. Weather and AOCP aircraft were also contributing factors to the scarcity of missions."

The 12th "fared well in that no casualties were suffered and no aircraft were destroyed. Going even further, there were no aircraft that picked up battle damage during this happy month. Santa was very good to us," the 12th reported.

The majority of pilots are "brimming with happy expectation of things to come," the 12th noted. "The 86's are almost within their grasp and before long they will have those stove pipes running red hot. The airmen are as elated over the conversion as the pilots. Steps have been taken by the squadron commander to encourage the airmen to feel the kind of pride in the organization that comes easily and naturally to the pilots. One of the tangible moves which was made was the ordering of the

yellow and blue baseball cap for every single man in the outfit."

As 1952 came to a close, the 12th looked back on another year of combat in Korea. "The squadron experienced heartfelt sorrow when comrades were lost. It underwent unpleasant and sometimes frustrating episodes, which in retrospect somehow seem less unpleasant. There were probably times when airmen and officers asked themselves, is this worth my trouble, my discomfort. But in the light of work accomplished and of the job still to be done not only are they comforted but a new determination, a new enthusiasm rejuvenates their tired spirits and prepares them for what promises to be a greater and fuller year."

Significant Events

December 2-5: President-elect Eisenhower toured the front in Korea and met with South Korean President Syngman Rhee.

December 3: F-86 pilots engaged enemy swept-wing jets in strength in the Pyongyang area for the first time since August 9.

December 4: Captain Jack Hawley, was involved in a major accident at K-46 due to engine failure on take-off.

December 5: Shortly after 2100, enemy aircraft dropped three bombs on Chodo, causing no damage in the fifth reported attack on this installation.

December 6: New flak suppression technique across the Eighth Army front became effective for close support sorties.

December 11: A fully loaded B-26 of the 3rd BW caught fire at Kunsan Airfield and exploded. The accident soon destroyed three other B-26s and caused major damage to six F-84s of the co-located 474th FBW.

December 17: Two F-86 Sabre pilots claimed the first sighting of the enemy's IL-28 twin-jet bombers, one having

Anthony Falo designed the K-55 Airman's Club, the NCO (seen here, at right, while under construction) Officer's Clubs, and the Mess Hall, The night before the mess hall was to open, "the Japanese boiler blew up and it burned to the ground." (Falo)

Long before the 18th Wing relocated from K-46 and K-10 to K-55, it had its architects like Tony Falo and Walter "Wally" H. Bauer designing the runways and buildings it would need to be fully operational from Day One. Fallo drew up the plans for the first jet runway at K-55 and Bauer, a surveyor, ensured it was properly laid out for the Army Engineers who arrived to perform the actual construction. At right, an F-86 of the 2 Squadron SAAF is rearmed and refueled on Falo's runway in February 1953 after a light snowfall. (Falo)

Combat Statistics

18th F-B Wing

December 1952

Average No. A/C Assigned
35
Total Flying Time
1,512
Percent of Aircraft in Commission
82%
Percent of Aircraft AOCP
9%
Combat Sorties Flown by Wing
900
12th Squadron Sorties
333
67th Squadron Sorties
374
2 Squadron Sorties
212
A/C Lost to Combat
0
Pilots lost
2

Fuel Consumed

118,903 gals.

Ordnance Expended

.50-cal. Rounds
200,543
Rockets
141
Napalm Bombs
0
500-lb. GP Bombs
1,182
Note: Figures and totals may differ in some categories due to differences in numbers provided by each component.

crossed the Yalu River a few miles south of the Sui-ho Reservoir, escorted by two MiG-15s, while the other remained over Manchuria.

December 19: Photo-reconnaissance of the Pyongyang main airfield revealed the presence of three aircraft, the first observed there since October 1951.

December 22: A SA-16 crew landed in an inlet near Haeju, a North Korean port just north of the 38th parallel on the Yellow Sea, and rescued a downed HMS Glory Seafury pilot in his dinghy. The only fatal aero medical evacuation accident of the war occurred when a Royal Hellenic Air Force C-47 transporting patients collided with an F-80 jet fighter-bomber at Suwon AB, South Korea.

December 26: Two Squadron, SAAF left K-46 for K-55 for the first transition into the F-86 type aircraft for the 18th Fighter-Bomber Group.

The 18th Fighter-Bomber Wing transferred its headquarters from K-10/Chinhae "to the new base at Osan Airdrome (K-55)."

December 27-31: The 18th Wing issued Operations Order 362-1 to the Group. The mission of the Wing under this Operations Order was to "stand down from F-51 operations and move to K-55 as required to accept and convert to F-86 type aircraft." The mission of the Wing was to: a) move to K-55 and assume control of that Base, b) operate F-51 type aircraft until conversion to F-86F type aircraft can be made, c) convert to F-86F type aircraft." An informal directive was issued to the 12th Squadron to stand down on January 12th, move to K-55 and to withdraw their F-51 equipment to K-10.

December 28: A SA-16 crew of the 3rd ARS picked up a downed pilot in the Yellow Sea north of Cho-do. He was in the water less than three minutes.

December 30: As a part of Project SPOTLIGHT, an RB-26 located five locomotives in one marshaling yard, and two B-26 light bombers destroyed four and damaged the fifth.

December 30/31: 19 BG bombed the Choak-tong ore processing plant near

Captain Ebersole's "corner of the tent" displays 1952 Christmas cards, presents, books and hot chocolate mix. (Ebersole)

"Pappy" Juhrs, Stan Wells, Ed Aubuchon and John Staring in their tent at K-46 in December 1952. A homemade Christmas tree and presents is the focus of their attention. (Ebersole)

the Yalu. Aided by a full moon and a signaling aircraft, enemy interceptors downed one B-29 and damaged two others so badly that they were forced to land at Suwon AB.

Adapted in part from U.S. Air Force Historical Research Agency. January 2002. The U.S. Air Force's First War: Korea 1950-1953 Significant Events. July 1952. http://www.au.af.mil/au/afhra/wwwroot/korean_war/korean_war_chronology/kwc_1952.html

Combat Losses

In the month of December, a 2 Squadron, SAAF pilot was killed in action, the Group reported.

1st Lt. John Moir, 2 Squadron, SAAF pilot KIA on 25 December 1952. On Christmas Day Lt. Moir and Captain Nortje were over Chorwan at 10,000 feet conducting bomb-line patrol. After patrolling to the double-bend of the Imjin River, they returned to Chorwan, and continued to Kumwha and a position near the Hwachon reservoir. A light aircraft below them was identified as an ROK L-19 spotter aircraft. A second unidentified aircraft was spotted. Nortje followed the "bogey," which they identified as a U.S. Navy Skyraider. Moir followed his wingman and dropped behind the Bogey—Navy aircraft. Behind Moir, a second Skyraider immediately took position on him and immediately opened fire. Moir's Mustang went down in flames. He did not survive the crash. As Brent sadly notes in "2 Squadron in Korea," Captain Nortje immediately called for help, only to hear the Skyraider pilot radio the controller aircraft that he had just shot down an aircraft that was making a pass at them. After returning to base, the Navy pilots visited the SAAF quarters to offer their respects and condolences, "which were accepted in courteous good spirits by Moir's shaken comrades."

Capt. Robert L. Russell, 12th Squadron.

"Christmas" For A POW

by Paul R. Kniss

By Christmas 1952, 1st Lt. Paul R. Kniss, formerly of the 18th Fighter-Bomber Group's 12th Squadron, had been a Prisoner of War for seven months. Although he did not know it at the time, it would be over eight more months before he would be repatriated.

For much of his captivity, Kniss was in solitary confinement—locked in a confiscated North Korean farm house built of clay, logs and corn stalks. When there was wood for a fire—an infrequent occasion since there were shortages of everything, including firewood—a fire would be built by the "host" farm family in a clay firepit in what had formerly been the farmhouse kitchen. The smoke and heat from the fire would try to follow a serpentine crawl space beneath the three more rooms in the house. By the time it reached the end of the house—where the prisoner(s) was confined—there was virtually no heat left. Temperatures in North Korea reached 20-30 degrees below Zero.

The rooms were Spartan, with mud walls and floor. The window was just a piece of rice paper, as was the skeletal door. That was all there was between the prisoner and the Siberian winter.

The floors had a bamboo mat and felt like ice, due to the construction of the house. Occasionally, the farmers decorated their walls with a piece of newspaper stuck to the wall by wetting it.

Kniss describes his "Christmas" of 1952.

"Along one wall there is a pile of rags. Dirty and vermin-infested, it is curved in a fetal position. Suddenly, the rags move, and a face and hand emerge, and it almost looks human. The face is haggard from lack of sleep, and other indignities. It is unshaven, the teeth a filthy yellow, the hair is so dirty that you can run your hand through it, and your hands are filthy black from dirt. The odor emanating from this thing would gag a maggot. His breath is like the North end of a South bound skunk. You can see noth-

ing in the eyes but despair, agony and a questioning look.

He has been beaten with gun butts, spit on, had a pistol in his ear and mouth and dry-fired, dug his own grave, faced a firing squad, and interrogated for days on end. Ending only when they could no longer keep him awake and then quickly resuming again once he regained consciousness. There are many blank days in his memory to the point that he has no idea when or where he was interrogated.

The Russians tried to hang him when the Chinese soldiers pulled him from their grasp.

His clothes consist of a blue quilted Mao suit, light cotton padding, no belt, jacket open at the bottom, so his stomach can freeze. On his feet is a pair of tennis shoes with the toes cut out back about 3 inches. Toes protrude about an inch past the shoes. On his feet is a pair of silk socks that he has nursed for 7 months. These are well worn, and provide little or no protection from the cold.

This person or thing has no underwear, or toothbrush, or soap or water for weeks on end. The teeth have not been brushed for 7 months—and will not be, for at least 8 more months.

He grunts to his guard, and the guard motions for him to come outside. The POW walks about 10 yards to a slit trench to relieve himself. When he goes to the bathroom, he must straddle a slit trench at 20 to 40 below zero, with all of his private parts exposed. When he has finished, there is no such thing as toilet tissue, so after a weeks, he takes on an odor of his, alone. Rats run when they hear him coming, and the only things that can tolerate him, are the lice.

If the guard is in a good humor, he will motion the POW outside of the compound and give him a hatchet. Behind the compound, runs a stream about one foot wide by 6 inches deep. It has run through ground that, for several centuries, has been fertilized with human waste, so by the time it arrives at this location, aromatic is not the word that comes to mind.

He takes the hatchet and chops into

the ice. About five inches into the ice, he sees a trickle of water. Putting two fingers in the water, he puts the finger in each eye socket. With this, his morning toilet is finished. In a few weeks, there will be no water, as the creek freezes solid.

He is returned to his cell to wait for his breakfast.

To kill time, he goes on a lice hunt to catch them and pinch them. If you don't like your guard, sometimes you plant them on him. He runs constantly in his cell to keep from freezing. He hurt constantly, from cold and hunger.

Then the big moment—his breakfast comes—a cup of rice and a cup of fried onions. This goes on for 8 months. "Breakfast" is followed with a big cup of boiled water which is almost frozen when you receive it.

A guard feeling sorry for him brings a bucket of charcoal—if he is a nice guy. He sits down and tries to wrap himself around it, his face over the life saving bucket. Later in the day his head explodes from all of the carbon dioxide he breathed. The bucket will last about 1 or 2 hours, and that is it for the day. Lunchtime passes, and no food, or he gets a half cup of bean curd.

In the afternoon the Chinese interrogator arrives with his daily dose of propaganda. He casually mentions that he should be with other POWs, kept warm, fed properly, and about 100 other violations of the Geneva Convention. The interrogator replies, "you have your own private room." It sounded like solitary confinement to the POW.

The interrogator leaves and it is back to cold and lice. He tries to sleep, but the cold precludes it, so he runs—and kills lice.

Dinner arrives—rice and boiled cabbage—another 8 month item. Finally, a cup of water and Chairman Mao's restaurant is closed.

With dark creeping in, he seeks the slim warmth of his filthy blankets—one under him, one over him. He assumes the fetal position trying to stay warm, but he knows he must wake and run. He dreams of home, warmth and family, and wonders if this was his last day on earth, as he and all other captured pilots were war criminals under sentence of death.

The bugs crawl on him and he can't stand his own smell or health.

He's cold, bone numbingly cold—and hungry. But then he remembers, "I'm alive!," even as he prays for the souls of the more than 1,000 pilots killed in the Korean War.

The B-29's bomb a little long this night, and they land just over the hill from him—shaking the hut and the ground. "God, it's cold, and I'm so hungry."

Dawn arrives and he congratulates himself on surviving for another day. Then he remembers. Today is Christmas. Peace on Earth Goodwill to Men. If he weren't a grown man he would cry."

1953
18th Fighter-Bomber Wing Chronology

Third Korean Winter December 1, 1952-April 30, 1953	Korea Summer-Fall May 1-July 27, 1953

18th Fighter-Bomber Group officially based at K-55/Osan-ni, SK

January	March	May	July
February	April	June	

3 February: 18th Wing started its F-86F training program with 56 USAF and 28 SAAF crews--"plus the need to retrain all our maintenance people."

14 April: 18th Group makes it first fighter-bomber attack with F-86 a/c against troop concentrations.

Jan. 20-30 March: Squadrons preparing for combat flying the F-86F jet fighters.

Mar: 31-Apr. 17: Squadrons flying air-to-air combat sorties in the F-86F.

July 27, 1953: Armistice takes effect.

23 Jan. Major Jack Hawley, 67th Squadron XO, led last F-51 mission for 18th Wing.

Jan. 1-23: F-51 "Mustang" aircraft phased out. Mustangs transferred. Movement to K-55 completed.

Jan. 10: 18th Wing Staff moved from K-46 to K-55

18th Fighter Bomber Wing operations in 1953 can be organized into four periods, including:
1 January – 19 January
F-51 aircraft phased out
Aircraft transferred
Movement to K-55 competed
20 January – 30 March
Squadrons preparing for combat flying the F-86F fighters
31 March – 17 April
Squadrons flying air-to-air combat sorties in the F-86F
18 April – Armistice
Squadrons flying both air-to-air and fighter-bomber combat sorties.

January 1953

"In January, immediately following the movement and consolidation of this Wing at K-55, a conversion from F-51 aircraft to F-86F aircraft was accomplished."

January 1953

Other than a few patrol clashes, little ground fighting occurred during the month. The U.S. Eighth Army and Fifth Air Force experimented with joint air-ground support tactics, and the 18th Fighter-Bomber Wing got good results using a pathfinder to lead its twenty-four aircraft close support strikes. The wing recommended the use of pathfinder aircraft in all large close-air support strikes.

Fifth Air Force interdiction continued the second week of the month with six days of intense activity against the Sinanju area. Fighter-bombers flew 1,166 sorties, 453 against bridge targets and 713 in flak suppression. Fifth Air Force aircraft also struck bridges, rail lines, highways, repair installations, and gun positions in the Sinanju-Yongmi-dong vicinity to deny the enemy the use of this important transpor-

Significant Events 1953

Joseph Stalin dies and is succeeded by G. M. Malenkov; L. P. Beria is tried and executed.
Ian Fleming publishes "Casino Royale," the first of 13 novels that will feature a secret agent, 007, named James Bond.
A struggling young writer and editor named Hugh Hefner, publishes the first issue of a new magazine he calls "Playboy."
Arthur Miller publishes "The Crucible."
"Kismet," a musical based on Borodin's music for "Prince Igor," opens on Broadway.
Popular songs include: "I Believe," "Ebb Tide," "Stranger in Paradise," and "I Love Paris."
Hillary and Tenzing become the first to climb 29,028-foot Mount Everest.
Alfred C. Kinsey publishes "Sexual Behavior in the Human Female."
Lung cancer is first attributed to cigarette smoking.
Major Charles E. Yeager achieves a record air speed of 1,600 miles per hour in the Bell X-1A aircraft.
Men's clothes become the interest of fashion designers who create and promote Bermuda shorts for summer season wear.

Monthly Summary

Besides a few patrol clashes, little ground fighting occurred during January. The U.S. Eighth Army and Fifth Air Force tested and evaluated joint air-ground support tactics, and the 8th FBW achieved good results using a pathfinder to lead twenty-four aircraft in close support strikes. The wing recommended the use of pathfinder aircraft in all major close-air support strikes.

Fifth Air Force interdiction was stepped up during the second week of the month with six days of intense activity against the Sinanju area. Fighter-bombers flew 1,166 sorties, 453 against bridge targets and 713 in flak suppression. Fifth Air Force aircraft also struck bridges, rail lines, highways, repair installations, and gun positions in the Sinanju-Yongmi-dong vicinity in an attempt to deny the enemy the use of this important transportation hub. Light bombers and fighters flew nightly to prevent repair of facilities knocked out by the daylight raids. Fighter-bombers also attacked supply dumps in the Sariwon and Sinmak areas and struck troop concentrations in the central sector of Korea. Fifth Air Force gave special attention to the railroad line between Pyongyang and Sariwon and the branch lines from Sariwon to Chongyon and Haeju.

Fifth Air Force took advantage of an increase in vehicular traffic, claiming 2,582 enemy vehicles destroyed in January. In spite of the magnitude of the flak suppression effort, enemy ground defenses shot down seven fighter-bombers and inflicted major damage on twelve others. Fighter-interceptor pilots sighted over North Korea a record for the last year of the war of 2,621 MiG-15s—engaged 333 of those sighted, and destroyed thirty-two.

Adapted from U.S. Air Force Historical Research Agency. January 2002. The U.S. Air Force's First War: Korea 1950-1953 Significant Events.

Welcome to K-55. *Major Howard Ebersole poses in front of the 18th's new Welcome sign at K-55. There were many weeks of back breaking work ahead before the new base had even the rudiments of comfort or efficiency previously enjoyed at K-46. (Ebersole)*

tation hub. Light bombers and fighters flew nightly to prevent repair of facilities knocked out by the daylight raids. Fighter-bombers also attacked supply dumps in the Sariwon and Sinmak areas and struck troop concentrations in the central sector of Korea. Fifth Air Force gave special attention to the railroad line between Pyongyang and Sariwon and the branch lines from Sariwon to Chongyon and Haeju.

Fifth Air Force took advantage of an increase in vehicular traffic, claiming 2,582 enemy vehicles destroyed in January. In spite of the magnitude of the flak suppression effort, enemy ground defenses shot down seven fighter-bombers and inflicted major damage on twelve others. Fighter-interceptor pilots sighted over North Korea a record for the last year of the war of 2,621 MiG-15s—engaged 333 of those sighted, and destroyed thirty-two.

The Wing Operations Office reported "immediately following the move-

ment and consolidation of this Wing at K-55 a conversion from F-51 aircraft to F-86F aircraft was accomplished."

Wing Operations In 1953

18th Fighter-Bomber Wing operations during 1953 can be organized into four periods, including:

1 January – 19 January
F-51 aircraft phased out
Aircraft transferred
Movement to K-55 completed
20 January – 30 March
Squadrons preparing for combat flying F-86F "Sabrejet" fighters
31 March – 17 April
Squadrons flying air-to-air combat sorties in the F-86F
18 April – Armistice
Squadrons flying both air-to-air and fighter-bomber combat sorties.

Combat missions continued in F-51s until 23 January in the 67th Squadron, Richard Deihl pointed out.

Move to K-55

At the beginning of 1953, the three combat flying squadrons of the 18th Fighter-Bomber Group were located at K-46, "situated in the valley between Wonju and Hoengsong in central Korea," the 12th Squadron reported in January. "The front lines were 30 miles or 18 flying minutes to the north and our rear base, at K-10 on the southern tip of Korea near Chinhae, was 150 miles to the south."

The 18th Group had transferred its entire operations from K-10 to K-46 late in 1952, after which "the base had gradually developed from a forward staging base into the primary operational base of the Wing. The support Groups of the wing had, by January 1953, well-established detach-

A Last Mission For The Mustang. *This faded, grainy, fuzzy photograph is one of the last ever taken of 18th Wing Mustangs taxiing out of the rearming area prior to a combat mission. The venerable, but tired, F-51 was soon to be replaced by the sleek F-86. This combat mission was among the last for this legendary aircraft--arguably, the most famous of all single-engine, propeller-driven combat aircraft. The excellent results of the last two missions, the Group noted "were a fitting tribute to the end of another phase of aviation development." Like these fuzzy images from "the Forgotten War" the Mustang was about to fade into history. (Bist)*

ments at K-46 and the Wing Commander and his Operations Staff Section were established with the Wing Detachment there. Much of the logistical support for the Squadrons was drawn from the Wonju supply area so that the major items of supply required by the squadron and obtained from K-10 were practically limited to aircraft parts. Major inspections were being taken care of at K-10 by the 18th Maintenance Squadron, which had been augmented by the Fighter Squadrons for this purpose. Other than personnel for this, the entire Squadron was located at K-46," the 12th noted.

The now comparative comforts of K-46 were about to be lost.

The base at K-55 was located near Osan-ni about 30 miles south of Seoul. "Being situated in the plains of western south Korea it was in a considerably different type of terrain from the mountains surrounding K-46," the 12th reported.

K-55 was "an airbase designed for fighter use," recalls Lt. Col. Vi Bielefeldt, at the time a pilot with the 67th Squadron. "The runway was the standard of that day, 150-feet wide by 10,000 feet long. There was a chain barrier at each end with the nose wheel web catch system, designed to stop jet aircraft if they were unable to take off or stop on the runway. There was a taxiway the full length of the runway, with four diamond shaped taxiways situated off

the main taxiway, but touching the taxiway at a point, to accommodate the aircraft parking pads. There were no revetments for protection of the aircraft from the weather, but there were steel fences on three sides of the parking spaces for some protection from enemy action."

K-55 at Osan-ni, Korea, near Suwon, was located "in a flat rice paddy valley," the 18th Air Base Group reported. "The base was still under construction and everything was makeshift. Heaters were still being uncrated and barracks were damp and cold and overcrowded; wiring had not been completed in most buildings; only two dining halls were operative, which necessitated standing in line thirty to forty minutes for each meal; there were no recreational facilities; mail was being routed everywhere in Korea but to us; the base was not fenced and the local Koreans roamed the base stealing, almost at will. It was quite a comedown from the lush living at K-10 on the 'Korean Riviera.' There was little here more than work—long, weary, uncomfortable hours for everyone. At first time dragged; we had one mail delivery in two weeks; the weather became more bitter and we started into a mental slump." [1]

Wing and Group leaders "were quick to act." They redoubled their efforts "to spark and encourage and praise each good effort." Movies were shown in the dining halls at night. Mail deliveries

were expedited. Beer was sold by the case out of a tent. The Fighter Group began flying missions in the F-86 Sabrejets. "We" got a MIG. Another dining hall was opened. All the clubs were completed and opened. The base laundry began functioning. "We were on the way up—we were going places."

By the end of June, the Air Base Group reported that "we had one of the best bases in Korea and were still working, still amazing people who came from 'the States' or even other bases in Korea, with the things we had accomplished. Those of us who were here worked hard, very hard, and were proud of what we did." That said it all...for everyone.

"The long talked-about move to K-55 became a reality on 11 January 1953. It was in every respect well coordinated and smoothly executed, with the lion's share of the credit going to personnel of the Maintenance and Supply Section for their detailed planning and close supervision of the operation," the Group reported.

"This move brought all groups of the wing together for the first time since June, 1952." K-55 was located approximately 35 miles south of Seoul City, and approximately ten miles inland from the Yellow Sea.

The Fighter Group Headquarters was located "next door" to the Wing Headquarters. "After having been at separate

Combat Statistics

18ᵗʰ Fighter-Bomber Wing

January 1953

Average No. A/C Assigned
Unavailable
Total Flying Time
Unavailable
Percentage of Aircraft in Commission
Unavailable
Percentage of Aircraft AOCP
Unavailable
Combat Sorties Flown in F-51 Aircraft
400

Interdiction	71
Close Support	221
Rescue CAP	105
Recce	3

12ᵗʰ Squadron Sorties
Unavailable
67ᵗʰ Squadron Sorties
Unavailable
2 Squadron Sorties
Unavailable
A/C Lost to Combat
Unavailablen
Pilots lost
Unavailable

Fuel Consumed

Unknown gals.

Ordnance Expended

.50-cal. Rounds
Unavailable
Rockets
Unavailable
Napalm Bombs
Unavailable
500-lb. GP Bombs
Unavailable

locations for seven months the 'next door' arrangement made possible the establishment of new and improved administrative policies and procedures. Whereas in the past distribution was as often as not delayed, we were not able to take immediate action on matters requiring expeditious handling. It was not possible to place into operation a practical, workable suspense and priority system." [2] In fact, the move to K-55, plus the transition to F-86F's "necessitated the rewriting of most of the Group Regulations and Standing Operating Procedures."

By the end of January, the transitioning program was well under way with the majority of personnel either undergoing or scheduled for training," the Group reported.

In February, FAF announced plans to make K-55 its next headquarters in the event it should be "driven out of Seoul by enemy forces. It was necessary to tie their communications plan to that of K-55," the Wing noted. The Wing surely remembered the old saying, "When given lemons, make lemonade." The Wing took care to ensure that while it "worked out" its support for FAF, that "we were able to strengthen some of the weaker points in our communications system, notably the HF radio and VHF radio links."

Wing planners had to plan for and complete such "passive defense" projects as a personnel sandbag shelter in the housing and working areas, aircraft revetments and POL camouflage.

"Mammoth Task"

Conversion "In the Field" From Mustangs To Sabrejets

Immediately following the movement and consolidation of the 18ᵗʰ Wing at K-55, "a conversion from F-51 aircraft to F-86F aircraft was accomplished." [3]

The 18ᵗʰ Fighter Bomber Group at the end of 1952 "was an F-51 unit composed primarily of recalled Air Force Reserve Officers, none of whom were jet qualified," the 18ᵗʰ noted.

"January and February of this reporting period presented the Group with the mammoth task of conversion in the field," the Group reported.

During initial planning sessions "it had been agreed that the 18ᵗʰ Wing would be given twenty pilots, ten each from both the 4ᵗʰ and 51ˢᵗ Fighter Interceptor Groups" when they began the conversion to jet fighter-bombers.. As per the agreement, in early January the Wing Commander made "personal direct requests" for the promised twenty jet pilots and also "requested a Fifth Air Force plan and authority for disposing of the F-51 pilots for whom transition was not economical."

Instead of the twenty pilots promised, the Wing received just four on temporary duty. At no time were more than three of these qualified pilots actually available to the Wing. Later in the spring, eight "combat ready F-86 pilots" were reassigned to the Wing from Fighter Interceptor Wings. These quickly completed their missions and "rotated" by June 30ᵗʰ.

In a series of FAF progress reports on the "Conversion and Movement of 18ᵗʰ Fighter-Bomber Wing and 2 Squadron South African Air Force," goals were finally established at between 85-90 crews "based on completion of 60-65 missions and theatre retainability beyond 1 April 1953. There was no indication of possible release of pilots with less than fifty missions," the Wing reported.

The retraining process was launched in early January with the activation of the 18ᵗʰ Combat Crew Training Flight (Provisional) whose function was to instruct, "assigned pilots in the operation of jet fighters. Three jet-experienced pilots of the Group formed the nucleus of the flight with five additional instructors being assigned later on a TDY status from the 4ᵗʰ and 51ˢᵗ Fighter Interceptor Wings.

Pilots from the 2 Squadron SAAF were the "first to undergo transition train-

Armorers tow a 12th Squadron Mustang over to the bore sighting range before calibrating its six .50-cal. machine guns. (Ramsdell)

Tired Mustangs. *In January 1953, Earl Ramsdell recorded this line up at K-10 of 12th Squadron F-51s that were being returned to "combat shape" prior to turning them over to the ROK. "The 18th was getting F-86 Sabres," Ramsdell noted, "to be flown out of Osan/K-55. These F-51s were among the very last Mustangs to see combat action with the U.S. Air Force." Not long after this, Ramsdell "was one of the last 18th Wing personnel to be flown out of K-10 to K-55." It was a short lived tour for Ramsdell. After a year of Korean duty, Ramsdell was returned to the Z.I. a week later. (Ramsdell)*

ing. Each of these pilots received a minimum of one transition flight in the T-33 aircraft and a minimum of two instrument instruction flights with USAF instructors." After completing training for the SAAF pilots, the training flight moved over to train 12th Squadron pilots in the T-33 jet trainer aircraft, while simultaneously "acting as instructors for the South African pilots who were checking out in the F-86." They then moved on to the 67th Squadron.

The period from New Years 1953 to the end of June "was very eventful," the 67th reported. "During this period, the squadron changed from F-51 to F-86 aircraft, moved to a new base and almost had a complete turn over in flying personnel. The change to the new jet type aircraft also required pilots to be proficient in fighter interceptor as well as fighter bomber missions and made the training program even more difficult."

The conversion process was daunt-ing in more than its scope. The weather was extremely cold, there were "no indoor facilities, and an absolute lack of supplies for maintenance severely hampered the maintenance activity and rarely were more than two of the five aircraft in commission at the same time."

The "urgency of the program" necessitated that flying training "be conducted early and late and in marginal weather conditions." The fact that accidents were "held to a minimum" was a testament to the "superior airmanship and instructor ability of members of the Combat Crew Training Flight," the Group pointed out.

"Converting a flying organization from one type of aircraft to another type aircraft is a difficult proposition under optimum conditions," the 18th noted in its monthly report. "The task of conversion under the conditions with which this Wing was faced proved to be tremendous. We had just competed a move to an unfinished air base in the middle of the winter. Construction of buildings and hangars in the flight line area had not commenced. The entire area of the base with the exception of the concrete runway, taxi strips and hard stands was one big mud hole. Maintenance of aircraft had to be accomplished in the open and this proved to be a serious handicap because of the cold weather. Exposure to the weather causes many persons to become sick. Effectiveness of aircraft maintenance suffered as a result. Living quarters were over crowded. There were no clubs or other activities available to occupy what spare time the men had. They ate, they slept, and they worked if they were physically able. Despite the terrific hardships encountered, the personnel of this Wing did the job and the conversion was a success." [4]

Conversion from F-51's to F-86's "made it necessary to set up completely

(Left) ***Changing Markings.*** *The first F-86 aircraft to be turned over to American units of the 18th Fighter-Bomber Wing were transferred from the 2nd Squadron SAAF in mid-January 1953.*

(Below) American crews begin removing the SAAF squadron markings and prepare to repaint the jet with American colors.

new service stocks; technical order files; prepare new flying regulations and SOP's; train pilots, maintenance and support personnel. New tactics and techniques had to be devised since this Wing was pioneering use of the F-86 as a fighter-bomber. Training of the pilots involved a double training load. They had to receive transition and become proficient in jet aircraft and had to master fighter-interceptor tactics since this Wing was to have the dual capability of fighter-bomb operations primarily and fighter-interceptor operations when needed." [5]

An intensive training program for 18th pilots was initiated using four F-86 pilots transferred in from the 4th and 51st Fighter-Interceptor Wings as instructor pilots. Three T-33 jet trainers were acquired for transition flying and an F-86 Mobile Training Detachment arrived at K-55 on December 27th 1952.

The Wing also faced a critical shortage of qualified jet mechanics and specialists. Only by the end of January did the needed personnel begin "to trickle in," and these men "were recent school graduates with little or no line experience," the Group reported.

Four T-33's were assigned to the 18th Group. "The maintenance of these aircraft at first presented a myriad of problems, primarily because we had no jet mechanics assigned, no one familiar enough with jets to anticipate part needs and, too, the planes needed much work when assigned."

Only by the end of February did the

Group report approximately 90 percent manned with jet mechanics; however, "the experience level was extremely low. Adding to this problem was the shortage of electrical, hydraulic and instrument specialists."

"One squadron at a time," the Wing explained, "phased out of F-51's and into: F-86 MTD Ground School; T-33 familiarization and transition; F-86 checkout and local training missions; and finally fighter-interceptor training missions to MIG Alley." The decision to schedule the fighter-interceptor missions prior to engaging in fighter-bomber missions was "based on the fact that the pilots of this Wing were already experienced fighter-bomber pilots and only lacked the fighter-interceptor training to become proficient in both roles. This dual pilot proficiency is necessary to fully exploit the F-86 aircraft."

The 12th Fighter-Bomber Squadron was ordered to "stand down" from flying combat missions and was first to start conversion to F-86s while the 2 Squadron South African Air Force and the 67th Squadron continued flying combat missions from K-46. Shortly thereafter the 2 Squadron SAAF "ferried their F-51s to Japan and returned to K-55 to commence conversion." On January 15th the 67th Squadron flew a maximum effort mission, taking off from K-46 and landing at K-55. Four F-51s were turned around upon landing at K-55 and flew a JOC Alert mission the same day. The last F-51 mission was flown from K-55 on 23 January 1953. At this time it was decided to 'stand down' the 67th Squadron for logistical reasons due to the short time remaining to effect complete conversion. The 67th Squadron subsequently ferried their F-51s to Japan and

F-86 Markings for 18th Wing. *The nose and fuselage band are yellow, the tail stripes red, white and blue (the vertical stabilizer design was used by the 18th Group for all three squadrons). "At first we had a blue field with four stars on the horizontal stabilizer, and later went to what is shown here," Howard Ebersole explained. (Ebersole)*

started conversion training prior to the end of January."

The promised F-86's for American Squadrons were delayed. Wing leadership decided that to expedite the training program, two of the F-86's would be transferred from the 2 Squadron, SAAF to the 12th Squadron. They could then be used "by the then currently proficient American pilots in chase rides for checking out the South African pilots."

By the end of February the 12th, 67th and 2nd Squadrons had completed their MTD, the T-33 transition training and were "well into F-86 training." The training curriculum included aircraft familiarization, formation flying, gun camera, instruments, navigation, night flying and combat indoctrination flights. Over 1,200 training sorties were made, of which the SAAF pilots flew 682, the 12th flew 340 and the 67th flew 270.

In late January, Headquarters, FAF sent a letter directing that the conversion training curriculum be "revised to place initial emphasis on fighter-interceptor tactics, with emphasis to shift to fighter-bomber work after all pilots had attained fighter-interceptor proficiency."

Bitterly Cold Weather

As if moving the entire Wing to a new air base and converting from prop driven aircraft to jet fighters weren't enough, the weather was bitterly cold. Throughout most of January and February, the temperature hovered near zero. The ground crews and pilots took a beating since the hangars and facilities were "non-existent." Linemen in particular were affected. At one time during this period, three out of four linemen "were ill from over exposure."

Working outside in zero degree weather was not the only difficulty. The "only poles available were power poles already installed. All of the ducts under the roads, runway, taxi strips and parking diamonds were filled with water and mud and frozen solid. Most of the culverts were in a similar condition, consequently laying wire across roads and runways presented a major problem. Often a mile of wire (critically short) had to be expended to reach a telephone a quarter of a mile away," the Wing reported. Finally, in April, the "ground thawed enough so that it was possible to open most of our ducts and make permanent installation."

In the midst of relocating, changing aircraft and coping with bitter weather, the rotation policy suddenly kicked in and experienced officers and NCOs began hemorrhaging out of the Wing. For example, about 65 percent of the Communications Squadron personnel including all its officers were rotated in January and February. "This forced an almost complete rebuilding of the organization during and imme-

diately after change of station," the Wing recorded.

"The efficient and orderly manner in which the 18th Fighter-Bomber Wing accomplished the move from K-10 and K-46 to K-55 reemphasizes the basic concept that all tactical organizations can and must be capable of maintaining a maximum mobile capability at all times," the Wing noted in its report.

"Conversion from F-51 aircraft to F-86 aircraft under adverse conditions can be accomplished without the loss of a pilot if a thorough and well supervised training program is used as was done by this Wing. The F-86 is superior to all other aircraft in fighter-bomber operations. Fighter-bomber combat missions flown by pilots of this Wing during the period of this report prove that the F-86 has excellent stability on the bomb run which is necessary for high bombing accuracy. It has a low vulnerability to ground fire because of its great speed. Although the enemy air force has not attempted to disrupt our fight-bomber operations it is reasonable to assume that the F-86F does not need fighter-interceptor escort for protection while engaged in dive-bombing missions since it has the capability of defending itself."

[Note: 18th Fighter-Bomber Group pilots accounted for nine MIG's destroyed, three probably destroyed, and six damaged from January through June 1953.]

"The versatility of the F-86 is limited only by the capabilities of the pilot. Maximum utilization of the F-86 fighter-bomber pilot can be realized only if he is allowed to participate at regular intervals in fighter-interceptor missions. These fighter-interceptor missions should be scheduled in areas where contact with enemy aircraft is most likely to occur. Defensive sweeps are fine for formation training purposes, however, unless the fighter-bomber pilot engages the enemy in air to air combat on these missions much time is lost in gaining the fighter-interceptor proficiency and experience he should have." [6]

Combat Operations

The last F-51 mission was flown from K-55 on January 23rd. Four hundred sorties had been flown in the outdated and worn out Mustang by 18th pilots since January 1st—91 flown by the 12th Squadron and 309 by the 67th Squadron. The 67th continued to fly combat in the old F-51's until January 23rd; however, "maintenance and combat operations were made difficult by the extremely cold weather. An excessive number of aborted missions resulted in a request for a maintenance stand-down. The stand-down became permanent on 23 January, the day that marked the end of combat operations for the 18th Fighter-Bomber Group in conventional fighter type aircraft."

Close air support and interdiction missions predominated, with a proportionate number being RESCAPs. The 67th Squadron lost one aircraft to combat during the month when the pilot bailed out Northwest of Sariwon because of engine failure. He was picked up by helicopter and returned to base with only minor injuries.

The first F-86 aircraft received by the Group "was assigned to the 2 Squadron, SAAF. The first transition flight was made by Commandant Gerneke of the 2 Squadron, ushering in a new era in jet type operations for the 18th."

The Group was also called on in January 1953 to fly sorties for "sitting duck" missions. "On these missions, a flight of four aircraft was dispatched to Chodo Island where they contacted the Naval forces stationed there. They were then directed, usually by the Fire Control Section of one of the destroyers, into attacks on observed shore batteries or activities across the straits from Chodo Island."

For six days in January, the Group was committed as JOC alert aircraft. When on alert, the "pilots stood by in Squadron Operations awaiting word from Combat Operations that they were to scramble. Fifteen minutes was allowed to obtain the 'flims' [7] (which gave controllers, coordi-nates, time on target and mission number) and the authentication sheets, to brief, and to get airborne. As soon as the four or eight aircraft committed were landed from a mission, the same number was expected to be ready to go again. There was normally at least an hour or so between each 'scramble.' However, because the missions were rotated among the three Squadrons, forty minutes was allowed normally between receipt of the mission information at combat operations and the time on target, since the front was 18 minutes away at the closest point and 25 at the furthest," the 12th reported. [8]

67th Squadron Last To Remain Operational During Move to K-55

The 67th Fighter-Bomber Squadron was the only 18th squadron to "remain operational during the move to K-55." On January 11th, the day of the move, the squadron took off from K-46, flew a combat mission and landed at K-55 after completing the mission, thereby "effecting the move without any loss of combat capability," the Group reported.

During the conversion, 67th pilots were given two rides in T-33 type aircraft "to become familiar with jet aircraft flying characteristics and techniques. This was a very short time to learn so much but by much hard work it proved enough. The next step was to check out in F-86's with an experienced jet pilot following in another plane to help in case of an emergency." Two more practice missions followed the checkout rides to "become familiar with new aircraft and to get the 'feel' of high speed and high altitude flying." Each pilot was then given seven formation-training missions to become familiar with the techniques required in high altitude flight. At least two instrument flights were required and five camera gunnery missions to become familiar with the new radar sight," the 67th reported.

As each pilot progressed through the program, new problems arose that had to be solved. New tactics had to be learned and mastered, even as old tactics were changed and modified. At the completion of this abbreviated training program "each pilot was considered combat ready and began to fly combat missions with Major [James P.] Hagerstrom and Lieutenant [Archie P.] Buie, "who were the only experienced jet combat pilots at that time."

Shortages Hamper Move and Combat Operations

The 12th Squadron reported many problems during the transition, including "the lack of special tools for the F-86 aircraft when the first aircraft arrived. Maintenance was performed with the tools of the mechanic's toolbox. Long, frustrating hours were spent on the major problems which arose as the aircraft began to accumulate flying hours. Oxygen regulators, fuel control valves, fuel flow regulators and the hydraulic system presented the greatest difficulties," the 12th reported. [9]

External loads were another major problem. "The bomb racks and the fuel tank racks were not the same as they had been on the F-51 aircraft. The best configuration had to be determined by flying and the accompanying adjustment of racks. The early missions were flown with the 120-gal. fuel tanks on the inboard stations and the bombs outboard, but the configuration reversed as more combat missions were flown." Then there were the fuel tanks themselves. The speeds achieved by the F-86 required that the tanks be specially designed and well constructed. However, "of the three types used at first, only one proved to be able to withstand the forces on it and several incidents occurred before methods of flying with them were developed."

Another problem was finally solved by a "pilot's experiment." When released, the tank would "swing out and along the leading edge of the wing—the right one

Navy LST's were able to bring personnel and supplies right up to the runway at K-10 in January 1953. By that time the 18th Wing had moved north to K-55 near Osan-ni, south of Seoul. (Ramsdell)

not infrequently taking the pitot tube boom with it as it slid off the wing tip." The pilots worked out a "release technique" that decreased the incidence, but it still happened occasionally. Also, "until the pilots learned to leave the tanks pressurized, there were several collapses during rapid descents."

The average shortage of footwear throughout the winter was 40%. The heavy socks arrived in February.

Improper sizes of G-suits and oxygen masks were the "most critical items" in very short supply.

"Spartanized"

During the first month of operations at K-55, "all maintenance was done in the open," the 67th reported. "Tents were erected on one of the hardstands for the Engineering Office and the Specialist shops. With just these barest of facilities, all the F-51's were given transfer inspections and ferried to Japan."

The 18th Air Base Group reported that "due to the static condition existing in this Korean Police Action we settled down, and so did numerous tenant organizations, so that we found ourselves servicing an average of 5,700 troops instead of the one wing. *[Note: the 18th wing averaged about 1,700 Airmen and 175 officers.]* "We needed clubs—three of them....our Post Exchange did an average business of $150,000 each month and was authorized one officer and one Airman...Personnel Services, prior to Project Spartan, was au-

thorized four officers and nine Airmen to carry on a program including movies every night at two different locations, publishing a newspaper twice monthly, running a hobby sales store that did $5,000 a month business, processing 200 personnel a week for R&R leave, conducting organized sports, handling live talent shows, running the hobby shop and conducting an Information and Education program including testing."

Project Spartan cut them back to one officer and four Airmen with which to accomplish these and other duties. "Indigenous personnel" (Korean nationals) were used extensively. However, experience convinced the 18th Air Base Group that they could not be used in the Exchange, although forty slots were authorized. "People who are desperate for the very rudiments of life, food, clothing and shelter, simply cannot be entrusted with money and/or merchandise, regardless of supervision," the 18th reported.

Project Spartan cut the overall strength of the Air Base Group by 69 personnel. While the report noted that it was "a much needed step in the right direction, in most instances, trimming excess fat," in "isolated cases it was not believed the reductions were the outgrowth of sage study and foresight for operations peculiar to Korea."

"Our Personnel Services Section was confronted by every imaginable obstacle," the 18th Wing reported in early 1953, "the most serious of which was the skimpy per-

sonnel authorization, especially after we were 'Spartanized.' We were able to develop a full, well-rounded program only because of the tenacity and caliber of the personnel we were fortunate enough to have assigned. These men, all of them, worked a 12- to 14-hour day, not once in a while, but every single day of the period covered by this history [six month]. They gave unstintingly of their time, their efforts, and their talents. All of us who reaped the fruits of their labors are, indeed, indebted to these few men." [10]

Endnotes

[1] USAFHRA. *Monthly Historical Report, 18th Air Base Group,* January-June 1953, p. 1.

[2] USAFHRA. *Monthly Historical Report, 18th Fighter-Bomber Group,* January-June 1953, p. 3.

[3] USAFHRA. *Monthly Historical Report, 18th Fighter-Bomber Wing,* January 1953, p. 3.

[4] USAFHRA. *Monthly Historical Report, 18th Fighter-Bomber Wing,* January 1953, p. 4.

[5] USAFHRA. *Monthly Historical Report, 18th Fighter-Bomber Wing,* January-June 1953, p. 6.

[7] Slang for "flimsies," the extremely thin paper used as 2nd, 3rd or 4th carbon copies.

[6] USAFHRA. *Monthly Historical Report, 18th Fighter-Bomber Wing,* January-June 1953, p. 14.

[8] USAFHRA. *Monthly Historical Report, 12th Fighter-Bomber Squadron,* January-June 1953, p. 17.

[9] USAFHRA. *Monthly Historical Report, 12th Fighter-Bomber Squadron,* January-June 1953, p. 33.

[10] USAFHRA. *Monthly Historical Report, 18th Fighter-Bomber Group,* January-June 1953, p. 20.

Significant Events

January 6: The advance echelon of the 18th Fighter-Bomber Group moved from K-46 at Hoengsong, Korea to Osan Airdrome/K-55. The main body followed on 11 January. "This move brought all groups of the Wing together for the first time since June, 1952. K-55 is located approximately 35 miles south of Seoul City, and approximately 10 miles inland from the Yellow Sea.

January 8: The 12th Fighter-Bomber Squadron was withdrawn from combat operations and ordered to ferry its F-51's to Kisarizu, Japan by way of Itazuke AFB, Japan. A landing accident at Itasuke "marred the otherwise well executed move. Two aircraft were completely destroyed and two pilots suffered minor injuries," the Group reported.

January 9/10: Seventeen B-29s kicked off an air campaign against the Sinanju communications complex by bombing rail bridges at Yongmi-dong, antiaircraft gun positions near Sinanju, and two marshalling yards at Yongmi-dong and Maejung-dong.

January 10: FAF fighter-bombers followed up the B-29 night attacks with a daylight 158-aircraft raid against bridges, rail lines, and gun positions.

The 18th Fighter-Bomber Wing Operations Office was moved from Hoengsong Airdrome, K-46, to K-55. The move was completed via airlift and the office was back in operation the following day.

The 12th Fighter-Bomber Squadron flew all its F-51 aircraft to K-10.

The 67th reported its move to from K-46 to K-55 "without loss of operational commitments and continued to fly F-51 (Mustang) type aircraft. Due to very poor conditions at the new base, this was a very great achievement and much credit must be given to everyone involved for the smooth operation."

January 11: Battle damage assessment indicated that all rail lines in the Yongmi-dong area were unserviceable.

The 18th Fighter-Bomber Group moved to K-55--"the long talked-about move to K-55 became a reality." The move "brought all groups of the wing together for the first time since June, 1952." K-55 was located approximately 35 miles south of Seoul City, and approximately ten miles inland from the Yellow Sea.

January 12: Two Mustangs collided and burned on the runway at Itazuke when one overran the other during landing. Although neither pilot was seriously hurt, Lt. Rock in the first aircraft was trapped until rescued by Lt. Kempthorn. 2nd Lt. Richard J. Kempthorn ran to one of the planes in which a pilot was trapped—and burning. "Disregarding the intense heat, he tore off the canopy and carried the pilot to safety." He was awarded the Soldier's Medal for "his courage in risking his life to save another." *[Lt. Col. Howard "Ebe" Ebersole noted that Kempthorn "tore out the gun sight and carried Lt. Rock to safety."]*

January 12-15: Following a day on the ground due to bad weather, FAF fighter-bombers continued around-the-clock attacks in the Sinanju area.

January 13: Headquarters, FAF sent a message to Col. Frank Perego, Commander of the 18th Fighter-Bomber Group, stating that due to "recent developments in enemy capabilities, it is desired by this headquarters that initial emphasis in F-86 training in your organization be placed on fighter interceptor tactics. When all pilots in a squadron have been completely training in fighter interceptor tactics, and have flown sufficient interceptor missions to be considered proficient, training in fighter bomber tactics will be instituted."

January 14: Keeping up the pressure created by B-29 attacks the night before, fighter-bombers struck gun positions, railroads and bridges in the Sinanju area.

On this date, 1st Lt. Richard Deihl "was on an amazingly similar rescue operation to that involving Harry Winberg (see). This mission was successfully completed with Lt. [Charles R., Jr.] Cottrell as the happy survivor. The tactics of RESCAPs, although varying to some extent depending upon weather, the time of day, the terrain and so forth, were very similar, often successful and were a great morale factor in the minds of the combat pilots. We knew that everything that was humanly possible would be done to rescue downed pilots before we were captured," Deihl recalled.

January 15: Photo intelligence photographs detected a new camouflaged yard at the Sui-ho hydroelectric dam and two of the four generators working.

"Beginning the middle of January movies were shown nearly nightly in both the Officer's and Airmen' Dining Halls. Attendance average 800 men per night," the 18th Personnel Services Section reported.

January 17: Twenty Mustangs from the 12th Fighter-Bomber Squadron flew from Itazuke, Japan to Kisarazu, Japan where they were turned over for disposition. The pilots returned to K-55 for training in the F-86F.

January 18: The 12th Squadron reported that its move to K-55 was completed.

January 20: Pilots of the 12th Squadron started their transition program into the F-86 aircraft. Initial training was conducted by the 18th Combat Crew Training Flight, a provisional unit of the 18th Fighter-Bomber Group. "Pilots were scheduled to attend a 10-day MTD course consisting of 40 hours of instruction and a short ground school course conducted by the CCTF unit. Concurrently, they started flying in the T-33 for jet familiarization and progressed into the F-86 early in February," the 12th reported. Three flights were made in the T-33, "the rest was done in the F-86. The entire program was conducted without an accident."

January 22: The 18th Wing prepared to withdraw its remaining F-51 Mustangs from combat and prepared to transition to Sabres, thus ending the use of USAF single engine, propeller-driven aircraft in offensive combat in the Korean War. "The arrival of the first F-86 aircraft in January," the 18th Group reported, "brought to light a desperate need for qualified jet mechanics and specialists."

January 23: The last F-51 mission was flown from K-55. Four hundred sorties had been flown in the outdated and worn out Mustang by 18th pilots since January 1st—91 flown by the 12th Squadron and 309 by the 67th Squadron. The 67th continued to fly combat in the old F-51's until January 23rd; however, "maintenance and combat operations were made difficult by the extremely cold weather. An excessive number of aborted missions resulted in a request for a maintenance stand-down. The stand-down became permanent on 23 January, the day that marked the end of combat operations for the 18th Fighter-Bomber Group in conventional fighter type aircraft. "

"As a final effort, two close support missions of eight ships each were flown by the 67th Squadron. At 1505 hours on 23 January, eight aircraft, "Easy" and "Item" flights, led by 1st Lt. George W. Hartwig took off on a mission from K-55 and attacked bunkers, automatic weapons and mortar positions from CT792552 to CT798551. This attack resulted in 100% coverage and 100% effectiveness with 10 bunkers damaged, one mortar position damaged, two automatic weapons damaged, two secondary explosions, and one fire left burning. At 1520, Major Max King, Commander of the 67th Squadron, led eight aircraft, "George" and "How" flights, on a mission that attacked an enemy strong point from CT479444 to CT483443. The results were 20 personnel shelters destroyed, four mortar positions destroyed, six bunkers destroyed, three command posts destroyed, and one secondary explosion. The above aircraft were the last USAF single engine, propeller-driven aircraft to be flown in offensive combat. The excellent results of these two missions were a fitting tribute to the end of another phase of aviation development." [1]

Major Jack Hawley, Executive Officer of the 67th Squadron, "won the distinction of completing the last combat sortie." Hawley "was given the honor of leading the last F-51 mission because he had been a member of the squadron longer than anyone else. This ended the era of the famed Mustang. The Mustang was gone but would never be forgotten," the 67th accurately predicted.

January 24: Colonel Maurice L.

Martin assumed command of the 18th Fighter-Bomber Group, relieving Lt. Col. Albert J. Freund, who was reassigned to Headquarters, FAF.

January 25: The UN Command limited immunity from attack for only one communist convoy each way per week between Pyongyang and the Panmunjom area. The enemy could no longer use the armistice negotiations as a pretense for sending supplies and reinforcements unthreatened by UN air power to the front lines.

January 28: In addition to interdicting enemy transportation targets, fighter-bombers attacked a troop concentration near Pyongyang.

January 29: FAF fighter-bombers followed up the previous day's attack near Pyongyang.

The 18th Group Commander, Col. Frank S. Perego, sent a message to FAF noting that 25 [F-86] aircraft will be delivered to the Wing by 15 February 1953. Based upon that assumption, he "anticipated that the 18th Fighter-Bomber Group will be combat ready by 15 March 1953 for interceptor tactics. The 2nd Squadron SAAF, this Wing, will be combat ready for interceptor tactics on 1 March 1953." In addition to 36 training flights of approximately 33 hours in the F-86 as part of each pilots' transition program, Perego wanted all assigned pilots to "fly enough interceptor missions to acquire a minimum of 70 hours F-86 time prior to resuming air-to-ground operations"—in other words, prior to resuming fighter-bomber roles.

January 30: Four F-86 aircraft were assigned to the 12th Squadron "and 10 more arrived during February. The additional work load caused by inexperienced personnel was added to by the fact that there were many discrepancies in the aircraft on their arrival," the 12th reported. "The condition of replacement aircraft and

F-51 Pilots Eager To Fly Jets

Mustang pilots were "anxious to swap their prop-driven fighter-bombers for jet aircraft," an undated Stars and Stripes article by S/Sgt. Bob McNeill noted. "If and when the time comes, they will have trouble in making the conversion," McNeill predicted, quoting Maj. Glen R. Hall, the flying safety officer for the 18th Wing.

"As a whole," Hall explained, "they'd rather fly jets. But, there are some exceptions among the pilots who have been flying propeller driven craft since the last war." Hall noted that the F-51 Mustang, one of the best fighters to appear in World War II is a good plane for the job it is doing--interdiction and close support. However, it could not stand up to the MIG in aerial battles.

Hall said that UN Air Forces "need a fighter-bomber that can act as a bomber and still be capable of striking fear into the hearts of MIG pilots." A jet is "so much simpler to fly than a conventional plane," Hall noted, "that there is no comparison. It's the simplicity that gives the jet the advantage. There is no manual labor in flying a jet because much of the pilot's work is done by mechanical means."

The pilot, he continued, must "be more familiar" with the airplane. "You can make some mistakes in a prop-driven plane and live to correct them, but make the same mistakes in a jet and there will not be a second chance."

"Teaching a man to use his engine properly on landings is the biggest problem," Hall said. Before the Wing's pilots could switch to jet, "the boys would have to learn to think a lot faster." He point out that jet speed is about double the speed of ordinary airplanes and that calls for pilots to make decisions twice as rapidly.

The 18th Wing pilots would rather fly F-86's "of course," than any other type of jet. Propeller driven aircraft, particularly as fighter planes, had lost much of their effectiveness due to their inability to protect themselves against enemy jet interceptors.

aircraft returned from major inspections at the REMCO unit was not what would have been expected."

Combat Losses

None.

Endnotes

[1] USAFHRA. *Monthly Historical Report, 18th Fighter-Bomber Group,* January-June 1953, p. 8.

Adapted in part from U.S. Air Force Historical Research Agency. January 2002. The U.S. Air Force's First War: Korea 1950-1953 Significant Events.

Going the Chapel

And We're Gonna Get

Court Martialed

By MGen Walter D. Reed, USAF (Ret)

Most of the headquarters of the 18th Fighter-Bomber Wing moved from K-10 and K-46 to K-55 at Osan, South Korea. The runway at K-10 was not very long and on one side there was a hill or large mound about half way down the runway, with the sea on the other side. Also, the runway started at the sea wall on one end by a large hanger built on the edge of the runway.

It was arranged that C-119's would be available to load up the Wing material and deliver us to our destination at K-55. We packed our office desk, filing cabinets, and other equipment, and as I recall not a lot of attention was paid to weight and balance. When the pilot said that was enough, we closed the doors and climbed aboard. Because of the short runway, the aircraft was backed up to the end of the runway, and I believe the tail booms were over the edge of the sea wall, to give the maximum distance for take off. It was a good move for the Wing, and as I recall, it all took place without incident.

THE *BELLY*

...an army travels on!

This historic quote takes on new meaning in the Air Age. For in the belly of the rugged Fairchild C-119 transport, the air and ground armed forces can move with a mobility not believed

C-119 "Flying Boxcars" like these helped air lift 18th Wing headquarters personnel from both K-10 and K-46.

K-55 at Osan was a nice spot built by the engineers. We lived in tropical shells, had a nice chapel, mess hall and medical unit. The headquarters building was an open shell. Our separate offices were marked out with chalk on the concrete floor. Very shortly after we arrived it became necessary for us to hold a Special Court Martial--but we had no court room.

To improvise, we turned some of the benches around in the back of the Chapel. There we held our Special Court Martial. It is perhaps the only time an Air Force trial by Special Court Martial was ever held in a Chapel. I recall that one of the charges against the accused was bigamy. Perhaps the Court appropriately considered those charges in the Chapel and received, I am sure, divine guidance in its deliberations.

Not long after we arrived at K-55,

the consolidated mess hall was completed. The very day it open, the mess hall burned to the ground. Our investigation revealed the cause of the fire. It seems that the ovens were fired by gasoline that was piped from elevated barrels near the mess. The baker was anxious to start his work, and it appeared that the ovens were ready to go. He turned on the gas at the elevated drums, but unfortunately, the maintenance people had not hooked the gasoline lines up to the ovens. The result was that gasoline ran onto the ground and ignited--the conflagration spread to the entire installation. It was indeed a very sad evening for the Commander, Col. Perego, to see this fine installation burn to the ground on the day it was opened.

February 1953

Upon arrival of the first F-86's, the aircraft were assigned to the men with the most experience…the first month of operation with the new aircraft was slow due to the lack of trained personnel.

Transition Continues

By the end of February the 18th Fighter-Bomber Wing possessed 76 combat crews. Of these, however, only eight percent were combat ready, twenty –eight percent were in training and sixty-four percent were not combat ready for other reasons.

In February, "new buildings were readied for operations," the 67th reported. "Due to the lack of skilled personnel for jet aircraft, personnel were sent to Mobile

Monthly Summary

Ground activity along the front was slow, consisting mostly of patrol engagements and minor enemy probes. Intelligence determined that the enemy had built twelve new bypass rail bridges. Fifth Air Force reconnaissance focused on the area from immediately behind the enemy's front lines back to some twenty miles in the rear gave very little evidence that the enemy was preparing to attack. However, it did locate more vehicles moving up to replace those destroyed during weeks of FEAF attacks.

Enemy antiaircraft weapons had decreased to the lowest total since the end of 1951; however, radar-controlled guns made up a greater proportion than ever before. MiG fighters would frequently penetrate south of Chongchon, but then immediately withdrew when interceptors headed out to meet them. Intelligence assumed they were possibly probing UN radar defenses and testing the scramble time of the Sabres. At a cost of two F-86s lost in air combat, the Sabre wings destroyed twenty-five MiG-15s.

Fifth Air Force and FEAF Bomber Command kept most North Korean airfields cratered and out of service. Most fighter-bomber interdiction strikes were directed against the enemy's transporta-tion network, and Fifth Air Force claimed 2,850 vehicles destroyed in February. When transportation interdiction mission assignments were light, Fifth Air Force aircraft attacked hostile concentrations of troops and supplies.

Light bomber attacks against locomotives traveling at night continued during Operation SPOTLIGHT, which maintained locomotive kills at the same high level as in January.

Adapted in part from U.S. Air Force Historical Research Agency. January 2002. The U.S. Air Force's First War: Korea 1950-1953 Significant Events.

"Beware of Jet Blast." Ground crews prepare an 18th FBW F-86 for its next mission from K-55 in Spring 1953. The Sabre in the foreground is flown by Lt. Hook—"The Hooker"—as noted below the gun ports. The F-86 behind The Hooker belonged to Lt. Bat Masterson, Dodge City, Kansas, grandson of the famous Sheriff. The signs at right foreground warn bystanders to "Beware of jet blast." (Bist)

Combat Statistics

18ᵗʰ Fighter-Bomber Wing

February 1953

Average No. A/C Assigned
17
Total Flying Time
592
Percentage of Aircraft in Commission
57%
Percentage of Aircraft AOCP
13%
Combat Sorties Flown by Wing
12
12ᵗʰ Squadron Sorties
311
67ᵗʰ Squadron Sorties
Unavailable
2 Squadron Sorties
Unavailable
A/C Lost to Combat
0
Pilots lost
Unavailable

Fuel Consumed

252,578 gals.

Ordnance Expended

.50-cal. Rounds
5,519
Rockets
0
Napalm Bombs
0
500-lb. GP Bombs
0

Checking Out "New" F-86s. Airman Third Class Stanley J. Bist checks out the "new" F-86s at K-55 in February 1953. (Bist)

Training School to get a little knowledge about the F-86. Upon arrival of the first F-86's, the aircraft were assigned to the men with the most experience…the first month of operation with the new aircraft was slow due to the lack of trained personnel."

"During fighter interceptor operations, damage was suffered by drop tanks hitting the wing and damaging the leading edge and wing tip when being jettisoned from the aircraft."

The maintenance "challenges" facing all the 18ᵗʰ squadrons during the transition from prop to jet aircraft were daunting—probably unparalleled in U.S. Air Force history.

"No one was actually familiar with the F-86," the 67ᵗʰ reported, "and the majority of the personnel had little experience with the electronics equipment used in this type aircraft." The only answer was the "establishment of a thorough OJT program." Mobile training units were used wherever feasible and Airmen were sent TDY to Japan to service schools there.

Electronics supplies were critically short. "By borrowing and trading equipment from base to base and squadron to squadron, exchange of equipment from aircraft to aircraft and improvising equipment when necessary, a good percentage of aircraft was kept in condition. This shortage of equipment made it necessary for personnel of this [Electronics] Section to perform third and fourth echelon maintenance."

Throughout January the Electronics and other Sections were "very poorly located in a 15x20 foot tent. We had no mock-ups, little or no test equipment and an insufficient amount of supplies. Through the perseverance, determination and initiative of personnel in this section, we designed and built portable mock-ups, work benches, office equipment and storage space for spare parts and test equipment. As a result of many hours of hard work and training we now have the finest Squadron Electronics Section in the Far East and possibly only a few of the ones in the states will equal it."

The Armament Section reported, "The transition from P-51 type aircraft to F-86 jet aircraft went smoothly, belying the schooling and training necessary for such

"Urban Renewal"...Korea Style. *"After our F-86 training period," Howard Ebersole noted, "we became a tactical squadron and went about improving our buildings by building a lounge. 2ⁿᵈ Lt. Dick Kempthorn sparked the project and all hands helped. The Engineers received a T-33 ride up toward the Front and we, strangely enough, received building materials with no paper work." (Ebersole)*

a change. Armament mechanics that were old hands on the F-51 aircraft soon became proficient on the new aircraft. The praises of the new jets were soon being sung whenever a willing ear could be found," the 67th reported.

To enhance safety during maintenance on the .50-caliber machine guns, the Armament Sections designed "useful devices" such as a circuit breaker puller and placed barrels filled with sand and sand bags in each revetment "directly in front of the guns of each aircraft when parked in the revetment. This has proved every effective in preventing any accidental discharge of rounds from endangering life and property." [1]

R & R Leave

In Korea, "we worked seven days a week from 0730 to 1700 hours, and into the night as needed," Special Services reported. That entitled personnel to five day leaves, not chargeable as leave, to Japan. Early in 1953, an officer or Airman could take three unchargeable leaves, if he could obtain approval from the chain of command. About 200 18th Fighter-Bomber Group personnel per week were flown to Japan for much needed rest and recuperation. While it was R&R for the personnel participating, it was a full time job for one Airman to manifest the R&R personnel, make hotel reservations, answer their questions and brief them prior to departure.

On February 14th the R&R service was "enhanced by a direct flight from K-55 to Tachikawa Air Base, Japan, on a weekly basis—a C-124, known as the 'Cocktail Courier.' We enjoyed this deluxe service until all Globemasters were grounded and R&R's cancelled as a result of the C-124 that crashed near Tachikawa on 18 June 1953, carrying 129 service personnel to their death—the world's worst air disaster to date." Other sad losses to the Wing to be killed in the C-124 crash, were Captain John H. Staring, the Assistant

Buttering Bricks for a Pet Project. *Sergeant McElroy (left) of the 12th Squadron Engineering Section, "butters" bricks with mortar as the new lounge nears completion. Lt. Richard J. Kempthorn (right) keeps a sharp eye on construction of his "pet project." Just a few weeks before, on 12 January 1953, two Mustangs collided and burned on the runway at Itazuke when one overran the other during landing. Although neither pilot was seriously hurt, Lt. Rock in the first aircraft was trapped until rescued by Lt. Kempthorn. 2nd Lt. Kempthorn ran to one of the planes in which a pilot was trapped—and burning. "Disregarding the intense heart, he tore off the canopy and carried the pilot to safety," the unit report noted. Lt. Col. Howard "Ebe" Ebersole suggested the report was incorrect. In fact, Kempthorn "tore out the gunsight and pulled Lt. Rock to safety. As they both rolled off the left wing, the ship blew up." Kempthorn was awarded the Soldier's Medal for "his courage in risking his life to save another." (Ebersole)*

Personnel Services Officer and Lieutenants Sam Hyde and Bill Church of the 12th Squadron.

Flying the Real Aircraft in Combat...Wasn't Enough. *(Left) Captain H.R. Ebersole holds a model aircraft that was soon to be pitted against other models in the squadron. "I didn't build this model," he told his son, "Tex" in a note on the back of the photograph, "I was just looking at it." Lt. Henry Rock (Right) holds up the remains of one model airplane and another named "Kimchee Komet." A few weeks earlier he had been pulled from a burning aircraft in Japan by Lt. Kempthorn. (Ebersole)*

"OK, Who Was Supposed To Bring The Nails?" In March 1953 the 18th Wing was still moving into temporary quarters at K-55/Osan. Here Airman Third Class Stanley Bist (left) and Airman Second Class Bobby Danner lay out the floor for a tent to house the armorers at the new base. (Stanley J. Bist)

What, No Gloves? Hands in pockets signaled how cold it was at K-55 in February 1953 as Airmen Bist and Tripp erected tents and sorted out gear, much of which like that in the background, was still on pallets and exposed to the elements. (Stanley J. Bist)

Significant Events

February 2: One hundred Fifth Air Force fighter-bombers struck a troop billeting area located six miles south of Kyomipo, destroying 107 buildings.

February 3: On February 3 the 18th Wing started its training program with 56 USAF and 28 SAAF crews to be converted, "plus the need to retrain all our maintenance people."

Major Harry "The Horse" Evans assumed command of the 12th Fighter-Bomber Squadron from Major Vernon Harwood, who was reassigned to the Wing Staff as Inspector General.

The 12th Squadron commenced checking out its pilots in the F-86F.

Major James P. Hagerstrom assumed command of the 67th Squadron succeeded Major Max J. King, and "started the transition program to train pilots to fly the F-86 Sabre jets. "The transition in a combat zone was very difficult and with only a few experienced jet pilots, was accomplished very efficiently," the 67th reported. "The

"We Called It, Home!" Airman Stanley Bist stands outside the "Foxy Few" tent at K-55 in February 1953. (Stanley J. Bist)

571

squadron received very few of the new F-86 aircraft and time was critical. Most of the pilots had never flown a jet aircraft and this made the job seem almost impossible."

February 9: At Kyomipo, Fifth Air Force fighter- and light bombers leveled the former steel mill being used as a munitions factory and locomotive repair shop.

February 11: Lt. Gen. Maxwell D. Taylor took command of the Eighth Army.

February 14: R&R service for the 18th Wing was "enhanced by a direct flight from K-55 to Tachikawa Air Base, Japan, on a weekly basis"—a C-124, known as the "Cocktail Courier."

February 16: The 1st Marine Air Wing led a 178-aircraft formation, including Fifth Air Force fighter-bombers, in a major attack against troop billeting and supply storage in the Haeju-to-Sariwon region of western North Korea.

February 18: In one of the most adrenaline pumping actions of the Korean air war, four F-86s attacked a formation of forty-eight MiG-15s just south of the Sui-ho Reservoir, shooting down two enemy aircraft. Two other MiGs, attempting to follow an F-86 through evasive maneuvers, went into unrecoverable spins and crashed.

February 19: Lt. Col. Glenn A. Stell, was assigned as 18th Group Executive Officer on 19 February 1953.

February 22: In a letter to Kim Il Sung, Premier, Democratic Peoples' Republic of Korea, and General Paeng Te-huai, CCF commander in Korea, the UN Command affirmed its readiness to repatriate seriously ill and wounded POWs who were fit to travel and asked whether the North Korean and Chinese leaders were prepared to follow suit.

February 25: The first combat mission in the F-86F type aircraft was flown by 18th Wing pilots during a four plane flight on a Yalu sweep. Major James P. Hagerstrom, Commander of the 67th Squadron and flight leader, "shot down one MIG-15 type aircraft," the Group reported. "By the end of February this Wing possessed seventy-six combat crews. Of these, eight percent were combat ready, twenty-eight percent were in training and sixty-four percent were not combat ready for other reasons." In February, the Wing flew 12 effective sorties in F-86F type aircraft.

February 26: Fifth Air Force instituted routine armed daylight reconnaissance over northwestern Korea in response to the enemy's vehicle movements.

Adapted in part from unit history records and U.S. Air Force Historical Research Agency. January 2002. The U.S. Air Force's First War: Korea 1950-1953 Significant Events.

"About That Nose Wheel Tire Pressure." The new F-86s at K-55 in February 1953 get a full inspection by 18th Wing armorers Airman Second Class Mills (left) and Airman Second Class Stanley J. Bist. Looks like the tire pressure in the nose wheel may need attention, as well. (Bist)

March 1953

The combination of pilots new to jet aircraft but with a great deal of combat experience and pilots with jet training but no combat experience proved very good.

Monthly Summary

Frozen diplomatic initiatives began to thaw in late March when communist negotiators expressed a willingness to exchange sick and wounded prisoners of war and to discuss placing prisoners of war who did not wish repatriation in the temporary custody of a neutral nation.

In the ground war, the overall stalemate continued through March. During the first several weeks of the month the CCF attacked in company strength in several areas, particularly along the central front in the Kumhwa and Kumsong regions. Later, the communist attacked in regimental strength in the central and western sectors. Intelligence analyses determined that enemy military strength was increasing, with from one to three Chinese divisions en route or entering the Korean peninsula. The buildup suggested a possible enemy offensive might be planned to seize as much territory as possible before an armistice.

UN air strategy was thus focused on destroying targets in areas that curtailed the flow of enemy supplies to front-line units and to apply pressure to end hostilities. Far East Air Forces devised Operation SPRING THAW, a brief, intense interdiction campaign to cut off front line infantry from distant depots, forcing the enemy to use up stockpiled supplies. Far East Air Forces used medium bombers against bridges to create choke points, followed by fighter-bombers against roads leading to the bridges to destroy backed up traffic. Bad weather reduced the effectiveness of SPRING THAW, but the campaign did succeed in slowing supplies by forcing enemy vehicular traffic onto boggy secondary roads and makeshift bridges.

By March, Fifth Air Force had equipped four squadrons with new F-86F interceptors. With higher thrust engines and solid leading edge wings the F-86F differed from earlier versions and matched the MiG-15 in performance. Increasingly confident in F-86F capabilities and highly trained pilots, Fifth Air Force aggressively sought to engage and destroy enemy fighters, reasoning that heavy losses of the expensive MiG would encourage the enemy to end the war.

Communist pilots were spending more time in Korean airspace. During March, UN pilots sighted 2,032 MiGs in the air, an increase of twenty-nine percent over February. Late in March, the MiG pilots aggressively sought aerial combat. As a result of their inferior training and experience, they suffered heavy losses. UN pilots downed thirty-four MiGs while losing two in aerial combat. The very high kill ratio of 16.6:1 that had prevailed since January was maintained.

Adapted in part from U.S. Air Force Historical Research Agency. January 2002. The U.S. Air Force's First War: Korea 1950-1953 Significant Events.

Lt. Col. Glenn Stell (left), 18th Group Executive Officer and Lt. Col. Carroll Stanton, the new 67th Squadron Commanding Officer following Major Jim Hagerstrom's departure after completing his missions in Spring 1953. (Ebersole)

(Left) **Going Home!** *Finished our missions and "were going HOME" in March 1953. Lieutenants Ralph Waterman, Damon Reeder, Richard Deihl, Harold Cadwell and Merle Hower, "wear the red 'Fighting Cock' hats of the 67th Squadron and all were F-51 pilots," Richard Deihl notes.*

(Below) *Col. Frank S. Perego, Commander of the 18th Fighter-Bomber Wing in 1953 at K-55 from 1 January 1953-15 June 1953, succeeding Col. William H. Clark. Unit reports noted that morale had taken a steep dive in late August 1952, "shot up considerably when the unpopular uniform regulations imposed upon the squadron were abrogated when Col. Perego assumed command of the Wing. The pilots and other members of the squadron immediately donned their weird assortment of headgear which are so important to their individuality," the 12th reported. As this photograph illustrates, Perego set a good example for his men in wearing "non-regulation" head gear. (Ebersole)*

The 18th Wing Commander was "unsatisfied with progress or future of our training program" and made a personal visit to Commander, Fifth Air Force on 3 March 1953. As a result of that meeting General Barcus authorized a "purge" and the following day, 21 pilots were reassigned within the theatre and nine were rotated. "All of these pilots had participated in and some had completed the training program. Much time had been expended in the training of these personnel that could have been better utilized had these pilots been reassigned earlier," the Wing reported.

Sixteen new pilots reported to the 67th from the Z.I. on 4 March 1953. "These pilots were all new and inexperienced but were the first of many to arrive with F-86 jet training at Nellis AFB. As soon as more aircraft were received, the new pilots were trained by the end of March and were flying their first combat missions. The combination of pilots new to jet aircraft but with a great deal of combat experience and pilots with jet training but no combat ex-

perience proved very good," the 67th reported. "By exchanging knowledge and much 'hangar flying', a very effective team developed as the squadron combat record proves."

Developments in March

The 67th Fighter-Bomber Squadron reported erecting and using a storage tent in March, and that it established a Tool Crib on the flight line, thus eliminating the previous shortage of hand tools among flight line personnel. The accomplishment of these tasks required long hours of labor on the part of Supply personnel."

"Conversion from F-51's to F-86's made it necessary to set up completely new service stocks," The 18th Wing reported, "technical order files, prepare new flying regulations and SOP's, train new pilots, maintenance and support personnel. New tactics and techniques had to be devised since this Wing was pioneering use of the F-86 as a fighter-bomber. Training of the pilots involved a double training load. They had to receive transition and become proficient in jet aircraft and had to master fighter-interceptor tactics since this Wing was to have the dual capability of fighter-bomber operations primarily and fighter-interceptor operations when needed."

During this period the Communications Office was "fighting desperately to keep the communications lines open and at the same time try to build up communications" on the new base at K-55. "If was a difficult task," the 18th Wing unit report noted, "with supplies few and far between. The Communications Squadron, planning ahead, had accumulated a supply of expendable items to carry them over the first phase of the move, until supply could be in a position to function again…It wasn't until late February or early March that supplies began arriving in any quantity and by May the supply situation became normal again."

"Passive Defense"

During this period the 18th Fighter-Bomber Wing unit report contains some unusual references to various "Passive Defense" initiatives.

An average of three "special weapons defense lectures" were given during that period, the first reference to special weapons in any of the unit reports. In addition, a Base Defense Plan, an Active Air Defense Plan, a Mobility Plan and a K-16 evacuation plan were prepared. There were two practice air alerts, twenty actual Red Air Alerts and twenty-five Yellow Air Alerts from January-June 1953. "No enemy air attacks have materialized from these alerts."

The housing areas were protected by a "personnel sandbag shelter project." However, construction on aircraft revetments and POL camouflage had not started by June. Camouflage was in short supply and the 934th Aviation Engineer Group had changed the design for the aircraft revetments.

Significant Events

March 5: Good weather permitted Fifth Air Force to complete 700 sorties. Sixteen F-84 ThunderJets attacked in northeastern Korea an industrial area at Chongjin, just sixty-three miles from the Siberian border, destroying buildings and two rail and two road bridges, damaging seven rail cars, and inflicting several rail and road cuts. Fighter-bombers flying ground support missions reported damage or destruction to fifty-six bunkers and gun positions, fourteen personnel shelters, and ten supply stacks.

March 9: Responding to press reports that U.S. pilots routinely pursued communist jets across the Manchurian border, Commander in Chief Far East asserted that UN pilots broke off engagements at the Yalu River boundary, enabling many damaged MiGs to escape, although some border violations might have occurred in the heat of combat. Informing the U.S. Joint Chiefs of Staff that air operations in Korea were conducted strictly within limitations established by appropriate authority, he also directed Far East Air Forces to comply with directives concerning violation of the Manchurian border.

At K-55 the "dread word 'Fire' flashed across the base. In the darkness of that cold, windy evening we watched one wing and the kitchen of the recently completed Airmen's Dining Hall go up in smoke and flames. This was a disheartening development for both morale and from a

A Fifth MIG Kill. On 27 March 1953, Maj. James P. Hagerstrom of Tyler, Tex., an F-86 'Saberjet' jet pilot of the 18th Fighter-Bomber Wing, shot down his fifth MIG-15, becoming the 28th jet ace of the Korean conflict. This series of dramatic photos taken from his gun camera film, shows the underside of the MIG and the first belch of smoke as Major Hagerstrom's bullets start to score hits. (NARA)

supply standpoint," the 18th Air Base Group reported.

March 13: Colonel Maurice "Marty" Martin, 18th Group Commander, engaged two MIGs while leading a two Squadron SAAF flight and shot down one.

Major Howard "Ebe" Ebersole noted in his diary that on his 44th F-86 mis-

gan receiving "combat commitments" on 18 March, "but since the change in mission was not accomplished officially until the 31st, there are considered as part of

sion, Col. Martin, Lt. Pierson, and Capt. Gerneke reached the Yalu River. "Hagerstrom got 1 1/2 MIGs, Dunlap got 1/2 and Col. Martin got a probable destroyed. Gerneke saved my butt!" Then added, "I got a bath today and a shave!"

March 14: To provoke aerial engagements with communist fighters, Fifth Air Force combat crews dropped leaflets asking, " Where is the Communist Air Force?" over each ground concentration they attacked.

For Major Ebersole and his flight, the answer was "on our tail." Ebersole's diary noted "Hag & Buie were trapped by 16 MIGs--got out OK."

March 18: The 12th Squadron be-

576

the training missions."

March 21: North Korean truce negotiators expressed their willingness to observe the provisions of the Geneva Convention and exchange sick and wounded prisoners of war. At the same time they hinted that the exchange might lead to a resolution of other issues hindering an armistice.

March 27: MiG-15s equipped with external fuel tanks jumped two RF-80s and two RAAF Meteors between Sariwon and Sinmak, only thirty-eight miles north of the front lines. This was one of several MIG forays close to front line positions, seemingly in response to UN leaflet drops goading the enemy air forces to come out and fight.

Maj. James P. Hagerstrom, CO of the 67ᵗʰ Squadron, destroyed his fifth MiG to become the twenty-eighth Korean War jet air ace—the first 18ᵗʰ Fighter Bomber Group jet ace.

March 28: Capt. Mann of the 12ᵗʰ Squadron arrived in his patrol area, but was forced to return due to fuel difficulty.

Last Mission for Locke. SAAF pilot Bobby Locke after his last mission. After flying with the 51st Fighter Interceptor Group to "check out" in the F-86, Captain Ebersole returned to the 18th Group and flew 26 more missions in the F-51. Following the move to K-55 in January, 1953, Ebersole helped set up a "college" and "gave ?!! sold the SAAF's two rides each in the T-33 and then checked them out in the F-86 and they took over from there. They were wonderful guys, aggressive as heck, and excellent pilots."

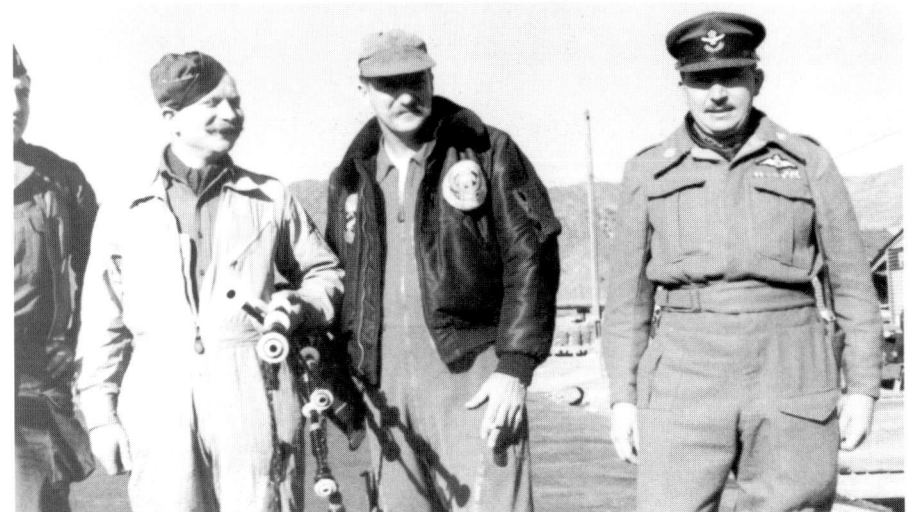

His wingman, Lt. Jeangerard, became separated. "They were on courses to the Suiho Dam for rendezvous when Capt. Mann sighted six MIGs which he engaged. One of the six 'spun out' and the rest disengaged toward the Yalu. The one MIG recovered at about 27,000 feet but could not be overtaken short of the Yalu. Capt. Man was able to fire at this aircraft and observed hits. It was claimed as damaged," the 12th reported.

March 30: Chou En-Lai, Foreign Minister, Peoples' Republic of China, suggested that POWs not desiring repatriation might be placed in the temporary custody of a neutral nation until negotiations determined their final status. Prior to this proposal the communists had insisted on the repatriation of all POWs. Their new flexibility on this issue provided an opportunity to resume truce negotiations.

March 31: "The part of the mission assigned on 31 March for which the Squadron was actually committed prior to 17 April was to destroy enemy aircraft (an average commitment of 10 sorties for patrol or air alert per day was given)," the 12th reported.

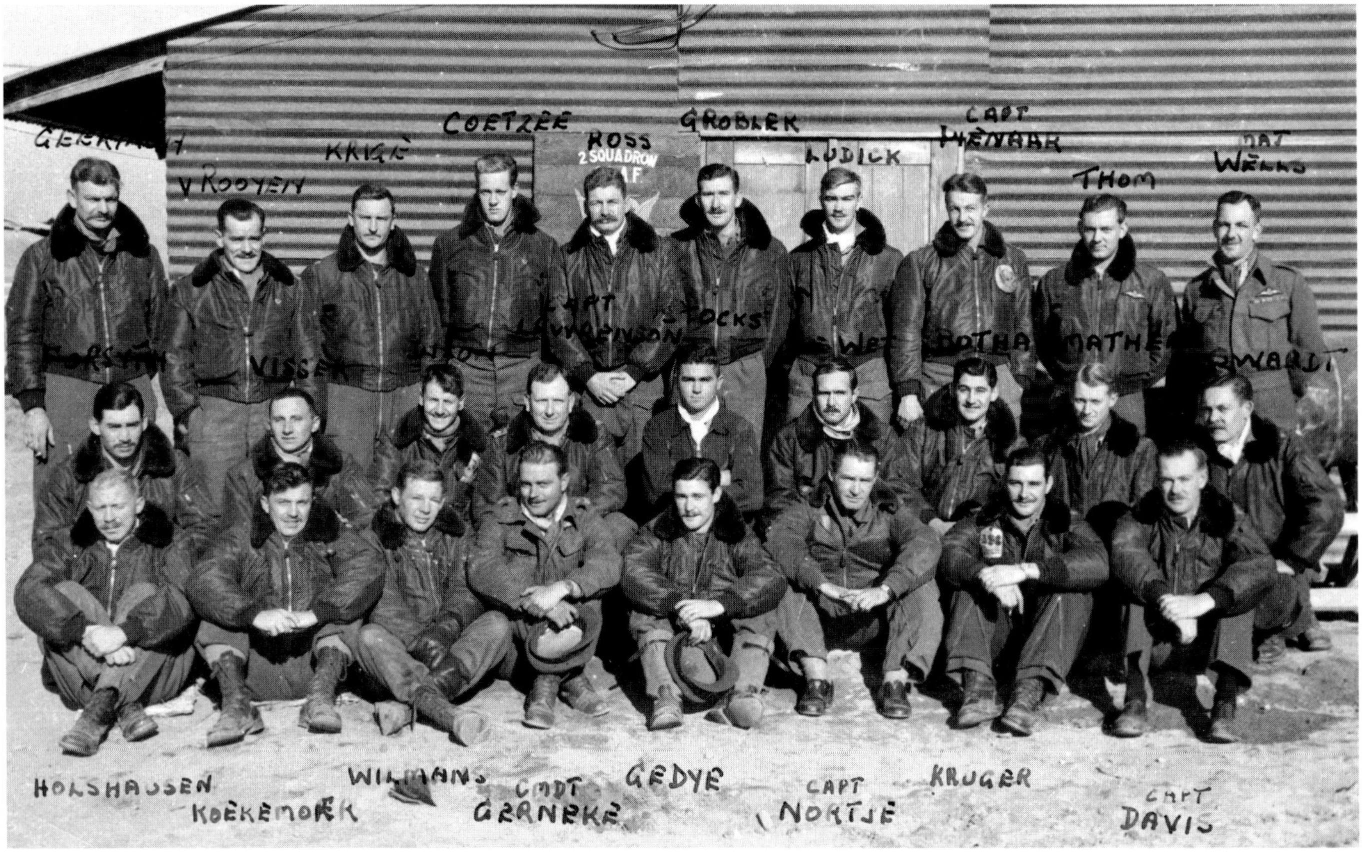

The "Flying Cheetahs" pose outside their Operations Office at K-55 in spring 1955. (Ebersole)

From California to Choong Ang
California Women's Club Clothes the Children

Nearly 40 boxes of children's clothing gathered by the Women's Club of Pico Rivera, California is distributed to hundreds of children. (Below) 1st Lt. Richard H. Deihl and Lt. Cadwell played Santa Claus to primary school kids at the Choong Ang School in Pyungteak. (Deihl)

The pilots and Airmen of the 67th were not always "raining death and destruction" on the enemy. Long before the days of "community relations" and "outreach," the 67th was trying to help others in the war torn country that were suffering. One such initiative was the "California Clothing" drive on behalf of the Choong Ang Primary School at Pyungteak Kyunggi-Do, South Korea.

In January 1953 1st Lt. Richard H. Deihl, a member of the 67th "Item Flight," became aware of a primary school and orphanage at Pyungteak, Hyunggi-do "that had children ill-clothed for the harsh winters in Korea."

Deihl mentioned this to his mother, Wilma Deihl, a resident in Pico Rivera, California and a long time member of the Women's Club. An energetic humanitarian, Mrs. Deihl immediately gathered the members of the Women's Club and led a clothing drive. A few weeks later, in February, the post office at K-46 (Wonju) received 37 boxes of clothing sent by the thoughtful ladies of the Pico Rivera Women's Club.

Deihl remembers that the numerous boxes "did not endear me to the airmen in the post office," but they did help him "load the chaplain's jeep with the help of another pilot of the 67th, Lt. Cadwell." (Cadwell is now deceased.)

1st Lt. Richard Deihl hands warm winter clothing to a Korean girl whose face reflects many emotions--from gratitude to fear. The clothing drive put a more personal face on the Korean war for the pilots and Airmen of the 67th. (Deihl)

It took several trips to the school with a loaded down jeep to deliver and distribute the clothing to the children.

Several weeks later, Deihl received a letter from the Principal at Choong Ang Primary School thanking him for the clothing. The labored English syntax still manages to explain how much the school and its children appreciated the thoughtful gesture.

"Dear Sir: We are greatly appreciated for that you donated to us such valuable goods. This school was damaged by the war very badly so that we always tasked to rebuilding for the kids but as you know the situation is so poor, please advise to us for the school's rebuilding. Thanks lot. We wish you always good health."

"I always felt good about this part of my Korean campaign," Deihl remembers, "since it was a welcome departure from some of the boredom of aerial combat assignments and added a much-needed positive note to the primary mission of "raining death and destruction" on the enemy."

Deihl completed his combat missions successfully (including the award of the DFC), fulfilled his active duty military obligation and left the service to pursue a highly successful business career. "It is strange," he recalls, "that although I am now a retired CEO and Chairman of a national financial institution...I probably remember more vividly the months I spent in Korea than most of the events I experienced in the 40 years of my business career."

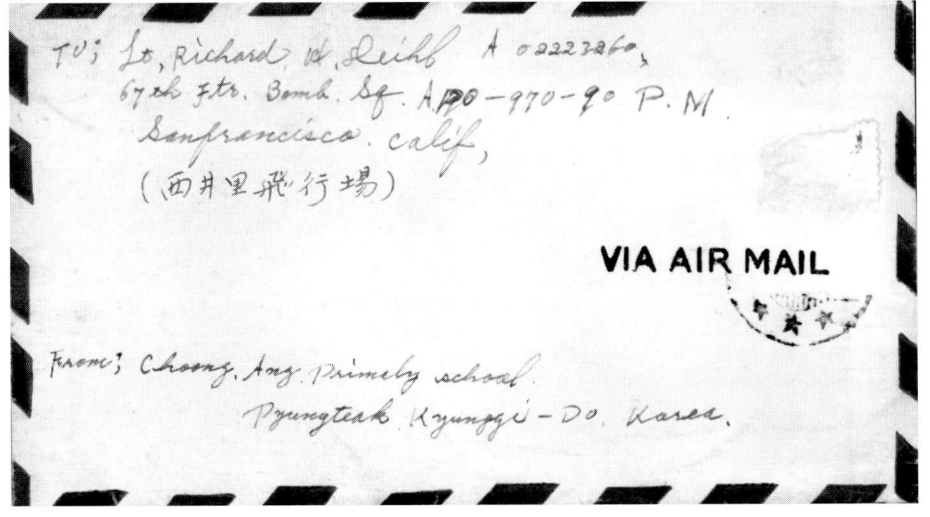

VIA AIR MAIL

April 1953

Combat Operations

Flap damage caused by loose bomb arming wires was a major problem—literally a million dollar problem annually. Fortunately, the 18th had a very savvy Airman Second Class Short of the 12th Squadron. [Unfortunately, the unit history reports did not include his first name.] He gave the problem some thought and recommended a attaching the ends of the arming wires to the bombs permanently so that the wires were pulled loose from the racks, whether the bombs were dropped safe or armed. "This method eliminated all flap damage caused by the arming wires and the saving in materials could be estimated in the neighborhood of $1 million annually." In addition, the "increase in the availability of aircraft added directly" to the accomplishment of the mission." Airman Short was recommended for the Bronze Star.

A boresight range was constructed at the west end of the runway for use by all

three squadrons. Each squadron boresighted its aircraft every third night (to ensure the aircraft would be available for daylight combat operations). Five ground crewmen—and the pilot—were required for the process. Boresighting was started

at 1800 and continued until 0430, during which four aircraft would be completed. The Airmen assigned to the duty were given the afternoon before and mornings after off. *[No mention was made in the reports regarding "off time" for the pilots.]*

Monthly Summary

During the continuing truce talks in Panmunjom, communist and UN representatives haggled over details of POW repatriation. In Operation LITTLE SWITCH the adversaries exchanged seriously wounded and ill prisoners, including: 6,670 Chinese and North Koreans for 471 South Koreans, 149 Americans, and sixty-four other UN personnel.

As warmer weather brought the spring thaw, ground combat tapered off to small-scale probes and raids. Bomber Command B-29s and Fifth Air Force fighter-bombers delivered coordinated attacks on railroad complexes and trans-

portation arteries to disrupt the flow of supplies from Manchuria to enemy forward areas. Later in the month, troop concentrations and supply areas again became primary targets. MiG-15 activity remained sporadic, and UN pilots sighted only 1,622 MiGs. However, the CCF and Russians deployed between four and five hundred fighters, an abnormally large number, to two Chinese airfields near the Yalu River, within easy sight of UN counter-air patrols. FEAF intelligence officers interpreted their presence as an intentional display of defensive strength. Far East Air Forces initiated Project MOOLA in an attempt to ac-

quire the latest communist jet aircraft. Anyone who delivered a MiG or other jet aircraft to UN forces in Korea would receive political asylum, resettlement in a non-Communist country, anonymity, and $50,000. An additional $50,000 would go to the first person to take advantage of the offer. In September 1953, after the ceasefire, a North Korean MiG-15 pilot defected, flying his aircraft safely to Kimpo AB, South Korea.

Adapted in part from U.S. Air Force Historical Research Agency. January 2002. The U.S. Air Force's First War: Korea 1950-1953 Significant Events.

Nose Art. The maintenance painter sketched the outline of Major Howard Ebersole's "nose art" before actually painting the aircraft. "Gus-Gus" was his youngest son. "Tex" was his oldest son (born in Greenville, Texas, of course). "Miss Marie" was Ebersole's wife. Thus the "nose art." (Ebersole)

Living quarters were extremely cramped with up to 26 Airmen living in a "building designed for a maximum of 21. Officers were crowded as well three barracks being assigned until April when a fourth was assigned."

The overworked generators broke down during much of May and June. "Only enough power was available to supply either the line area or the quarters area at one time and, since much work had to be done at night on the line, this left the quarters in darkness. Most of the water heaters were electric and therefore the lack of hot water was very depressing," the 12th reported. Water, itself, was a problem throughout early 1953 "and only during June was the supply adequate to allow water all day."

Mess facilities, particularly for the Airmen, were "extremely unsatisfactory until concerted efforts brought a gradual betterment of conditions in May and June. A standard complaint, and rightfully so, was that they were not being given enough to eat. This situation still existed at the end of the period [June]."

Long hours on the flight line were necessary to fulfill the work load and because so many of the personnel were inexperienced. "The increase in air raids during May and June did not help this situation as they cut into either working or

The Airmen in the Maintenance Section worked long and hard to keep us flying. Boys like Willy—and M/Sgt Nye (Line Chief), and Flight Chief Lloyd E. Wynn, M/Sgt Barr, Borrego, Beaven, Crooke, Hinton, Hirschfield, Howard, Moffat, Pinkston, Sanders and many more," Ebersole remembered gratefully. (Ebersole)

sleeping hours. The muddy conditions, which increased at the end of the period as the rainy season approached, made moving about difficult. The dampness which pervaded everything increased in like manner."

The Airmen and NCO Clubs "developed slowly" and gradually improved from February to June "to the point where they are now used primarily for fraternization and relaxation with a lessened emphasis on the consumption of alcoholic beverages."

Sports were available…if time permitted. Volleyball, softball and horseshoes were played, "but the Airmen generally had little time off in which they felt like athletics. The horseshoes games on the line were the most utilized and the officers kept a ping pong table busy."

By late Spring, K-55 was becoming almost habitable. "We had a Herculean task under adverse climatic conditions to make K-55 operational and livable," the 18th Air Base Group reported. "It was the kind of situation where the 'old army' would have said, 'this is where we separate the men from the boys.' We didn't do that. We rose to the occasion and made men out of everyone, and got the job done. We were fortunate. We had good leadership, men who, for the most part, worked together throughout the entire period and, by the grace of God and the strength of the United Nations forces, we were unmolested by the enemy."

Combat Statistics

18th Fighter-Bomber Wing

April 1953

Average No. A/C Assigned
45
Total Flying Time
1,933
Percentage of Aircraft in Commission
83%
Percentage of Aircraft AOCP
6%
Combat Sorties Flown by Wing
626
12th Squadron Sorties
328
67th Squadron Sorties
Unavailable
2 Squadron Sorties
Unavailable
A/C Lost to Combat
0
Pilots lost
Unavailable

Fuel Consumed

819,145 gals.

Ordnance Expended

.50-cal. Rounds
23,631
Rockets
0
Napalm Bombs
0
500-lb. GP Bombs
569

(Left) "A" Flight of the 12th Squadron in spring 1953. (Ebersole) "Allston was shot down on a strafing pass on 16 June 1953. (Ebersole)

(Right) 12th Fighter-Bomber Squadron poses for a group photo at K-55 in the spring of 1953. (Ebersole)

Captain Van Hellen (below) served as "B" Flight Commander.

Lt. Chad Smith, 67th Squadron was killed in action on 15 June during an armed reconnaissance mission.

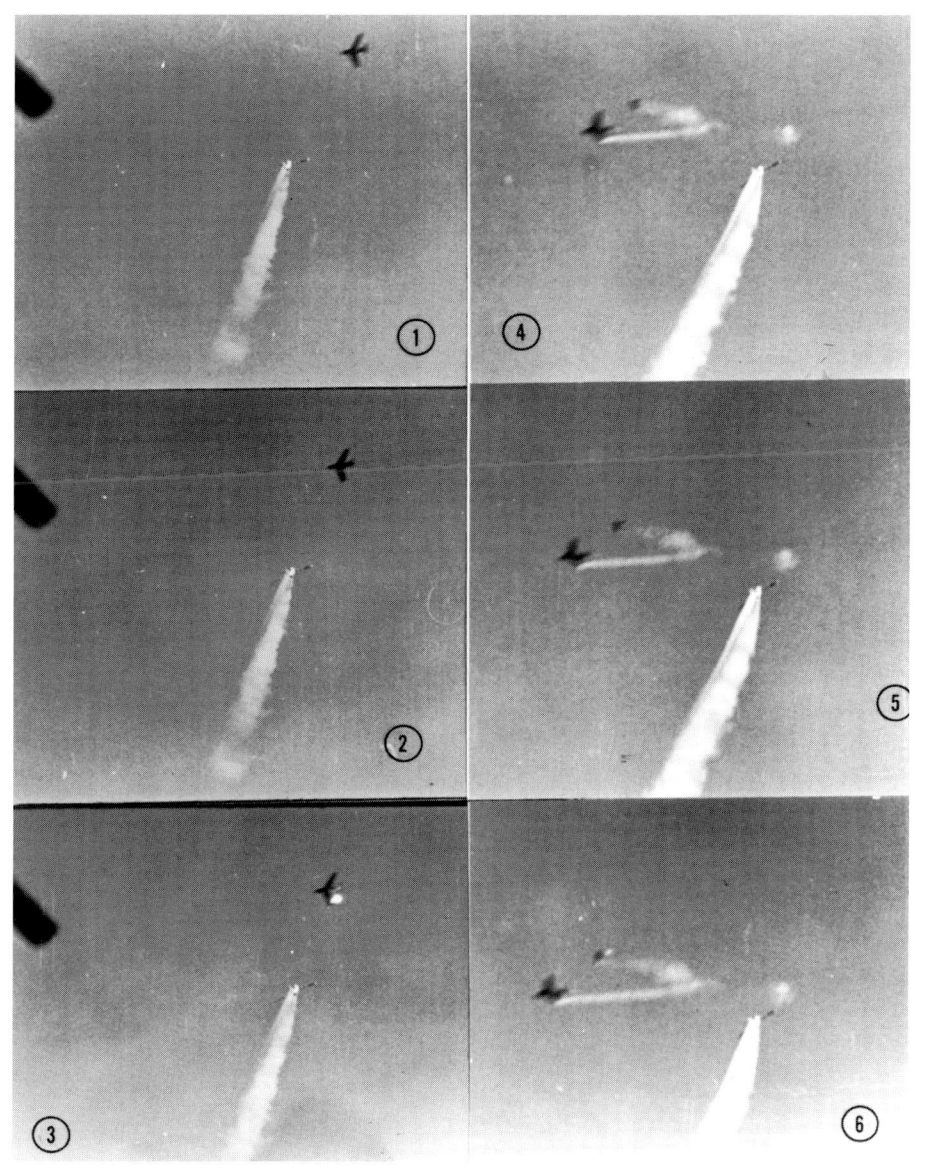

A flight of four F-86s was flying cover for fighter bombers in North Korea at an altitude of about 10,000 feet when MIGs were sighted. Two F-86 pilots started in on the MIGs. The No. 1 man hit one of the MIGs in the left wing but the F-86s speed was excessive and he overshot. The No. 2 pilot started firing at the MIG, hitting him. (You see the No. 1 F-86 at top of all pictures in gun camera frames taken by No. 2 F-86. The MIG, smoking is at center of all frames. Overrun indicator on frames 1, 2, and 3 indicates that No. 2's guns are not firing). The MIG, fired approximately three rounds. The No. 1 F-86 pilot pulled his Sabre" jet hard in front of the MIG in an effort to get back on the offensive. One hit was apparent on the left wing of the F-86 and it appeared to be from a 37-mm gun (frame 3). F-86 sheared off (frames 4, 5, and 6). MIG was seen to crash and explode seconds later. The kill was shared by the two pilots, but unfortunately the No. 1 man didn't come back to share the glory. May 1953 Issue of **Air Intelligence Digest**. (NARA)

(Below) 18th Group F-86s leave the maintenance and rearming area prior to take off on a combat mission from K-55. (Bielefeldt)

Significant Events

April 1: The 18th Fighter-Bomber Group flew its first practice dive bomb mission in the F-86F, using 500-pound GP bombs. The results were cited as "excellent." The Group immediately launched a training program "to qualify all pilots as combat ready in fighter-bomber operations using the Suwon Gunnery Range.

April 4: Col. Harry "The Hoss" Evans flight encountered MIGs on a Yalu river patrol. The first encounter was a head on pass with seven MIGs with no opportunity to engage. Col. Evans than broke right with his Wingman and Capt. Mann, with Lt. Jeangerard, broke left. Capt. Mann was immediately fired on by another MIG and engaged in a scissor maneuver with all aircraft firing. The MIG disengaged and withdrew north with no damage to either side. Col. Evans and his wingman, Major Shelton, encountered six MIGs after the break. Five withdrew across the Yalu, but one was cut off and engaged at 21,000 feet. Col. Evans closed on the MIG's tail and followed him through eight loops, getting hits in each of the two bursts he fired. He then disengaged in the Sinuiju area and the MIG was last seen entering the clouds in a descent and emitting intermittent black smoke. The MIG was claimed as destroyed. Major Shelton became separated during the melee and found two MIGs at 16,000, which he immediately attacked. However, his sight filament had burned out and the MIGs withdrew before he could get close enough to fire without it.

April 6: Major Ebersole's flight conducted a "wx recce" up to the Yalu. He also noted in his diary, "12th started dive bombing in F-86 today (practice)."

April 7: While on airborne alert over Chodo Island, Col. Evans encountered eight MIGs. The enemy planes "came right to the flight in its orbit and the controller didn't know they were there until informed by Col. Evans. They were first sighted at an eleven o'clock position. When approximately four miles away, the MIGs evidently sighted the F-86's and four of them began to climb. The other four continued on course and were lost to sight while the flight concentrated on the ones that were climbing. These split into two elements, one of which Col. Evans and his Wingman, Lt. Jeangerard, attempted to engage but these MIGs withdrew. The element leader, Major Shelton, with his Wingman, Lt. Stotts, engaged the other element but overshot them. One MIG disengaged and withdrew. The other reversed his turn and made two head-on passes with Major Shelton before the engagement was broken off. There were no claims or evident damage on either side." [1]

April 6/7, 7/8, 11/12: At night Bomber Command B-29s raided the three serviceable railroad bridges spanning the Chongchon River at Sinuiju. The following mornings, FAF fighter-bombers struck traffic backed up on the approaches to the damaged bridges.

April 13: Captain Encinias of the 12th Squadron encountered ten MIGs during a Yalu sweep. His flight engaged four MIGs soon after reaching the sweep area, but the flight was unable to close to firing range as the MIGs withdrew. A few minutes later a flight of four MIGs flew through the flight without firing and withdrew across the Yalu. Just as the flight was about to leave the area, two MIGs engaged from 9 o'clock high making firing passes on Lt. Crocker, the number four man. He was not hit. The enemy fighters immediately disengaged and withdrew across the Yalu.

April 14: The 18th Fighter-Bomber Group made its first fighter-bomber attack with the F-86F against troop concentrations.

April 15: The communists completed approximately seventy-five miles of railroad linking Kusong with Kunu-ri and Sinpyong-ni. Built in less than seventy days, the new line bypassed numerous bottlenecks created by USAF bombing of the Chongju, Sinanju, and Sunchon railroad complexes.

The 12th Squadron dispatched two flights on a Chong Chong sweep. Capt. Mann and Capt. Masterson led the flights.

Masterson's flight was diverted to the Yalu River where it sighted numerous MIGs but could engage none of them. Capt. Mann's flight divided into two elements, with Capt. Dee Harper, leading the second element. Capt. Mann and his Wingman, Lt. Bellow, encountered eight MIGs just north of the Chong Chong River, and a several firing passes were made but no damage inflicted on either side.

April 16: Captain Pienaar of the 2 Squadron SAAF completed his 100th sorties, bringing his operational tour to a close. He was the first South African to complete an operational tour in the F-86 aircraft and the first pilot to complete a tour at K-55.

April 18: The 12th Squadron reported "major commitments were to conduct interdiction of enemy ground lines of communications and provide close support of United Nations Ground Forces." The 18th Fighter-Bomber Group was now qualified enough in the F-86's to fly both fighter interceptor and fighter-bomber type missions.

April 20-3 May: During Operation LITTLE SWITCH, communist and UN forces exchanged sick and injured prisoners.

April 26: Suspended for six months, armistice negotiations between communist and UN forces reconvened. Armistice talks begin again.

April 26/27: A B-29 medium bomber dropped leaflets over North Korea to kick off Project MOOLA, the FEAF effort to obtain an operational MiG-15.

April 27: The 18th Fighter-Bomber

Aerial rockets were an important part of the F-86 combat load. (Bielefeldt)

Group flew its first close support mission in the F-86F. "Results of operations in April ranged from excellent to satisfactory," the Group reported. "The aircraft has proven itself a very capable fighter-bomber. An attack from any altitude or air speed is possible when using dive brakes as the speed stabilizes at approximately .85 Mach, making possible very accurate bomb releases. Control characteristics of the aircraft at high speed are excellent, aiding in the accuracy of bomb runs."

Endnotes

[1] USAFHRA. *Monthly Historical Report, 12th Fighter-Bomber Group,* January-June 1953, p. 22.

Adapted in part from 18th Fighter-Bomber Wing unit histories and U.S. Air Force Historical Research Agency. January 2002. The U.S. Air Force's First War: Korea 1950-1953 Significant Events.

Russian-built MIG-15, with markings changed to those of the U. S. Air Force, is ready for test flight on Okinawa in October 1953. The Communist fighter plane, which was flown to Kimpo Air Base in Korea in September by North Korean Pilot Ro Kum Suk, was dismantled, flown to a U. S. Air Force installation on Okinawa, and reassembled for tests by American technical experts. Maj. Gen. Albert Boyd, commander of Wright Air Development Center, Wright-Patterson Air Force Base, Ohio, headed a team of test pilots that also included Major Charles Yeager, the first man to fly faster than the speed of sound, and Capt. Tom Collins. After a week of testing which included simulated combat with F-86 "Sabre" jets, they said the MIG-15 did not measure up to the F-86. (NARA)

Lieutenants William L. "Curly" Church and Lt. Jim Bellows. Church was killed in a C-124 crash in Japan on 18 June 1953. Bellows "was killed on a mission dive bombing the front lines" on 18 June 1953. "He crash-landed on the friendly side of our lines, but did not survive," Ebersole noted. (Ebersole)

May 1953

"Sleek U.S. Air Force F-86 "Sabre" jets of the 51ˢᵗ Fighter-Interceptor Wing form this pattern of power as they patrol skylanes high over "MIG-Alley" in northwest Korea," an Air Force caption reports on May 22, 1953.

Monthly Summary

The front lines were generally quiet until the last week in May, at which time the CCF launched a major ground offensive against UN positions on ridges dominating the U.S. I Corps sector--approximately ten miles northeast of Panmunjom.

Armistice negotiations were faltering over disagreements regarding the repatriation of prisoners of war. The communists wanted North and South Korean prisoners unwilling to return to their homelands detained indefinitely, in effect, punishing them for their decision. The UN Command wanted to release all prisoners to civilian status on the day the armistice became effective.

The stalled truce negotiations had a direct and immediate effect on the air war. Faced with the prospects of a protracted war, General Mark Clark decided to attack previously untouched sensitive targets, including dams critical to North Korea's rice production. It was hoped that from the dip-

lomatic perspective, the raids would demonstrate that continuance of the war would bring about ever greater political and economic costs. The attacks on the irrigation dams, previously spared from destruction for political and humanitarian reasons, also had a psychological impact. Asian populations associated the "empty rice bowl" with starvation. Militarily, destruction of the irrigation dams would disrupt communist preparations for a ground offensive by flooding out rail and road networks.

FEAF Bomber Command strikes were concentrated on supply storage and troops. The most important target was the Kuwonga Dam, which B-29s hit twice. Fifth Air Force light bombers switched from night armed reconnaissance to close support missions as enemy ground activity increased. FAF fighter-bombers launched heavy attacks on supply and troop concentration areas. The single engine jets also made deep penetrations to keep North

Korean airfields unserviceable and to strike reservoirs and hydroelectric dams.

In the most intense air-to-air combat since September 1952, UN pilots sighted 1,507 MiGs, engaged 537, destroyed fifty-five, and damaged twenty-four. Enemy pilots seemed even less experienced than previously, sometimes bailing out when engaged by UN aircraft even before their aircraft sustained hits. On other occasions their inept maneuvers destroyed their own aircraft. Also during May, H-19 helicopter pilots flying search and rescue missions rescued ten airmen, six of them between May 16 and 18.

Adapted in part from 18ᵗʰ Fighter-Bomber Wing unit histories and U.S. Air Force Historical Research Agency. January 2002. The U.S. Air Force's First War: Korea 1950-1953 Significant Events.

Pilots from the 12ᵗʰ Squadron sit outside their Operations Office at K-55 waiting for a mission. They are looking up as they watch another flight return from a mission. (Ebersole)

Combat Operations

The weather was awful in May and "played a decisive part in the curtailment of operations for the 18ᵗʰ. On seven days during the month, fewer than 10 sorties per day were flown, due to inclement weather. On ten other days, 50 sorties or fewer were flown due to "non-operational weather." Nevertheless, in May the 18ᵗʰ flew a total of 1,606 sorties, an increase of 720 over April.

More importantly, the "effectiveness of the unit's bombing was "steadily improving. Ratings on close support missions by the controller, and bomb damage analysis photos confirmed this trend."

In May, one aircraft was lost to enemy action and the 18ᵗʰ suffered three major accidents, two of which were fatal to the pilots. One aircraft, an F-86F equipped with 6x3 leading edges, "failed to become airborne and crashed and burned off the end of the runway." The cause was attributed to an "excessively nose-high attitude on take-off. All pilots were briefed as to the low angle of attack necessary on take-off with this aircraft." [1]

Another pilot was killed because his instrument proficiency was inadequate to the weather conditions.

Endnotes

[1] USAFHRA. *Monthly Historical Report, 18ᵗʰ Fighter-Bomber Group,* January-June 1953, p. 15.

Significant Events

May 1: May Day was "celebrated" by both UN forces and the North Koreans. FAF fighter bombers struck Radio Pyongyang. Screened by the 4ᵗʰ and 51ˢᵗ FIWs, the 8ᵗʰ and 18ᵗʰ Fighter-Bomber Wings briefly headed toward the Yalu River then abruptly swooped down on North Korea's capital to bomb the broadcasting facility and its power supply. Monitoring the battle from the air, General Glenn Barcus promised that his aircraft would return every time the communists broadcast "filthy lies" about Fifth Air Force.

The 12ᵗʰ Squadron "was in full swing on its mission of ground attack by 1 May."

For Major Howard Ebersole and his flight, it was a busy, eventful day as he noted in his diary. During a mission against the "Ping Pong Radio Station," Dick Kempthorn "had 0^2 trouble...battle damage from a .30 in wing...[Lt. Col.] Marty had a fire warning light @ pullout"...and ended with "Dick had a flameout...headed for water...relit OK per our 4/9/00 talk."

May 2: "Musical Madcaps," the first of only two USO shows to visit the 18ᵗʰ in 1953 took place at K-55, due "to the lack of proper facilities." Over 1,200 personnel attended the show that was "very well received." Live talent shows "were a great success."

May 13: In the first attack against previously excluded irrigation dams, fighter bombers attacked the Toksan Dam holding the Potong River's water twenty miles north of Pyongyang. Floodwaters swirling from the breached dam washed out six miles of embankment and five bridges, destroyed two miles of the major north-south highway, rendered Sunan Airfield inoperable, and ruined five square miles of prime rice crop.

May 14: Communist and UN truce negotiators recessed indefinitely following differences concerning POWs who refused repatriation.

May 16: Lt. Gen. Glen Barcus presented the Distinguished Unit Citation to the 18th Fighter-Bomber Group "in recognition of the Group's outstanding contributions to the cause of the United Nations during the period 22 April 1951 through 8 July 1951."

May 17: Lt. Ted Dorris of the 12th had become separated from the rest of his flight during an interdiction mission and was attempting to rejoin his flight when two MIGs dove on him. He turned into them and they withdrew, but now he had only 400 pounds of fuel left. While regaining altitude, two unidentified planes approached and he dived to gain speed, and lost them. After obtaining "a steer to Chodo Island" he bailed out with only 100 pounds of fuel remaining. Bailout was successful and he was "picked up immediately by friendlies."

Major Ebersole noted in his diary, "Lt. Dorris, Ted--bailed out over Chodo--picked up OK. Lt. Bellows dead sticked into K-14--hit the barrier and is OK...Harry the Hoss dead sticked into ___?" The 17th was also Masterson's last mission #85.

May 18: An H-19 helicopter rescued two members of a B-26 crew twenty miles inside enemy territory by using tactics presaging those of later conflicts. The helicopter scrambled from its base and flew to a small island off the Haeju Peninsula to await fighters to clear the path to the downed airmen. Penetrating enemy territory at 5,000 feet, the helicopter followed the fighter pilots' directions until it located the survivors who were signaling with a mirror. After the survivors set off a flare to indicate wind direction, the helicopter landed and rescued them, staying on the ground for approximately thirty seconds.

May 19: "Good hits" at CT 383557, Howard Ebersole recorded in his diary. "Best JOC I've been on...all in target area...secondary explosions."

May 21/22: Tests were conducted with napalm tanks on the F-86's now being flown by the 18th. "Eight tanks of napalm were dropped successfully at speeds

12th Squadron briefing in Spring 1953. Standing (L-R) Lt. John Dawson, Lt. George Trayer, Lt. Col. Evans, M.G. Davis, Lt. John Bartholma, Lt. Charles Beaver, and Lt. Haskins. Seated (L-R) 18th Wing Commander Martin, Lt. Jack Debois, and Major Howard Ebersole, 12th Squadron Operations Officer. (Dawson)

Lieutenants John Crocker, John Putty and George Trayer prepare for their next mission. (Dawson)

up to 400 knots with no damage to aircraft or racks. The empty tanks were loaded by hand then filled with the mixed napalm jelly," the 18th Group reported.

May 25: The UN Armistice delegation vainly attempted a compromise with the communists, proposing that non-re-patriate prisoners of war remain in neutral custody for up to 120 days after the armistice until their governments could confirm their attitude toward repatriation.

May 27: Aerial reconnaissance discovered communist preparations for a major ground offensive.

Heading for the target somewhere in North Korea at 40,000 feet. (Dawson)

A busy day of three missions for Capt. Ebersole and fellow pilots: Haines, Waggoner, Westcott, Crocker, Bartholoma, Hyde, Rosse and Kearnan. On Ebersole's mission #82 a bridge destroyed north of Long Dong and east of Sinuiju would eventually bring a DFC. Mission #83 was credited with destroying 200 yards of trenches, and five personnel shelters. Mission #84 resulted in 100 yards of destroyed trenches, four of six bunkers destroyed and three of five mortars damaged.

May 28: The communists launched a series of company to regimental sized attacks that lasted into early June. Gen. Duk Shin Choi, the senior ROK Army delegate to the UN Armistice delegation, informed negotiators that his government considered the May 25 proposals by the UN Command unacceptable and announced that he was boycotting future negotiations on the instructions of his government.

May 29: General Clark warned the Joint Chiefs of Staff that the South Korean government might release POWs unilaterally.

May 31: Lt. Gen. Samuel E. Anderson, USAF, assumed command of Fifth Air Force, replacing General Barcus.

"Tex Beneke went in on T.O. [Take Off]," Ebersole noted in his diary. "Col. Pappie Stell pulled one of the guys out of the wreckage--don't know which," Ebersole continued, "think it was Tex--badly burned." "1/Lt. Smotherman bought it on instruments," he added.

Combat Losses

Airman James J. Barrett of the 67th Squadron was killed on 3 May, 1953, on the Harmozation (sic) range by the accidental discharge of a .50-caliber machine gun."

Captain Walter C. Beneke, Jr., 67th Squadron, became the first combat casu-

Last 12th Squadron Flight Commander's Party prior to departure for Z.I. Lt. Perciville Gates, Lt. Dick Ludwig, unknown, unknown, Lt. John Dawson, Flight Commander Van Hellen, Lt. George Trayer, Lt. John Paulk and unknown. (Dawson)

Combat Statistics

18th Fighter-Bomber Wing

May 1953

Average No. A/C Assigned
44
Total Flying Time
2,054
Percentage of Aircraft in Commission
91%
Percentage of Aircraft AOCP
3%
Combat Sorties Flown by Wing
1,234
12th Squadron Sorties
630
67th Squadron Sorties
Unavailable
2 Squadron Sorties
Unavailable
A/C Lost to Combat
1
Pilots lost
2

Fuel Consumed

942,069 gals.

Ordnance Expended

.50-cal. Rounds
104,780
Rockets
0
Napalm Bombs
4
500-lb. GP Bombs
982
1,000-lb. GP Bombs
1,116

591

alty suffered by the 67th of the year. His F-86 crashed and burned on take-off and he died a few hours later." Captain Beneke was the brother of Tex Beneke, the band leader who formerly sang with the Glenn Miller orchestra, explained former S/Sgt Louis J. Cain. Beneke was also known as "Tex" by his fellow pilots.

It had been raining continuously for several days, Cain explained, and "it was feared that the earth would wash out from under the runway." Lt. Col. Harry Beamer, Personnel Officer, "ordered us to get down there, shovel sand into bags, and pile them along the edge of the runway. The planes took off in flights of four, and we naturally viewed the action from that vantage point. We could see a plane tumbling over and over far down the runway. We learned later that it was Captain Beneke who had crashed."

An F-86 aircraft, fully loaded with bombs and machine gun ammunition, began its take-off from K-55 for a combat mission, the 18th Wing reported. "The aircraft failed to become airborne and crashed." Lt. Col. Glenn A. Stell immediately ran to the burning plane to attempt a rescue of the trapped pilot. "Fully aware that the aircraft's armament and fuel might explode at any moment," Stell disregarded his own personal safety as he tried to save the pilot's life. "Approaching the aircraft he found the canopy smashed and the cockpit in flames with the pilot still trapped in his flaming cockpit. Despite the searing flames and danger of explosion," Stell removed the pilot from the burning wreckage. "With the help of others he carried the pilot to a safe distance away from the shattered aircraft and then stripped the burning tatters of clothing from the pilot's body." Stell was awarded the Soldier's Medal.

1st Lt. Marion K. Smotherman, was KIA on 31 May, 1953. Following the take-off crash of Captain Beneke, the other members of the flight continued with the mission and became separated while flying in weather. "Two of the aircraft returned to this base and during landing were unable to stop on the very slick run-

Crash On Take-Off

Captain Walter C. Beneke, Jr. was the brother of Tex Beneke, the bandleader who formerly sang with the Glenn Miller orchestra, noted Louis J. Cain, a former Staff Sergeant with the 18th Wing.

"He was also known as 'Tex' by his fellow pilots. I was a member of a group that was piling sandbags at the take-off end of the runway when the crash occurred," Cain recalled.

"At the time, I worked in the Wing personnel Office as a classification specialist performing myriad duties. Lt. Col. Harry R. Beamer was the personnel office, and he also did double duty functioning as the Wing Executive Officer. I was an Airman First Class then, which was unfortunate when working for Col. Beamer. Airmen of the lower four grades were regarded as an instant detail force, and he would order us out of the building to do his bidding despite that fact that we were overloaded with our daily work which was seven days a week while the war was going on. But I understood the old codger (he must have been at least forty), because I know where he was coming from--there was a job to do, and you better do your share).

K-55 was known as a super base, and we had the only concrete runway at the time. Rumors of a truce were rampant, and the line of separation between North and South was proposed to be roughly the 38th Parallel, base based on territory held. Thus, each side wanted control of the high ground and the 18th Fighter-Bomber Wing was flying dawn to dusk sorties to support the ground troops in their efforts to hold the line.

It had been raining continuously for several days, and it was feared that the earth would wash out from under the runway. The good Colonel ordered us to get down there, shovel sand into bags, and pile them along the edge of the runway. The planes took off in flights of four, and we naturally viewed the action from that vantage point. We could see a plane tumbling over and over far down the runway. We learned later that it was Captain Beneke who had crashed. The casualty clerk would work with us, and I could have recorded all the events in a diary. I never took pictures or wrote anything down which is unfortunate--simply did what I was ordered to do and moved on."

Lieutenants George Trayer and John Dawson show off Trayers "home" in their Quonset hut at K-55. Trayer's wife, Alma Jane, occupies a place of honor on his "dresser." (Dawson)

way resulting in one aircraft receiving minor damage and the other receiving major damage result in Class 26. Both pilots escaped without injury. Soon after these accidents, a report was received that First Lieutenant Marion K. Smotherman had crashed into a hill north of Seoul and was killed."

Adapted in part from unit histories of the 18th Fighter-Bomber Wing and U.S. Air Force Historical Research Agency. January 2002. The U.S. Air Force's First War: Korea 1950-1953 Significant Events.

(Above, right) 12th Squadron parking ramp at K-55 in Spring 1953. Note mountains and control tower at left. Ground crew members appear to be involved in a pickup game of catch between maintenance tasks. At the far end of the taxi way is the squadron's operations building. Silver drop tanks and bombs are lined up at right in readiness for the next close air support mission. (Dawson)

(Right, center) In this double exposure, Lt. John Dawson "relaxes" in the intake of his F-86, "Naughty Nellie" at K-55 in Spring 1953. (Dawson)

Lt. John Dawson works with his crew chief to pre-flight "Naughty Nellie" prior to a mission. Dawson is already wearing an emersion suit, survival vest, Mae West, and his flight suit with "G"-suit arrangement. Before heading out on another combat mission, he will also don a parachute and a dingie. (Dawson)

Lt. John Dawson waits at the rearming area to have his 500-lbs bombs loaded on his F-86 prior to a mission in spring 1953. (Dawson)

Lt. John Dawson heads out on a combat mission wearing helmet, gloves, oxygen mask, flight suit, parachute, Mae West, "G" suit and boots. "Naughty Nellie" was the name of his fiance' to whom he was married when he completed his tour and returned home in December 1953. (Dawson)

Lt. John Dawson straps into his F-86 prior to a mission over North Korea from K-55 in Spring 1953. After completing Aviation Cadet training in Class 52G, Dawson was sent to Nellis AFB for gunnery training in the F-86. He was assigned to the 12th Squadron--"Foxy Few" and arrived in Korea in January 1952. By the time 1st Lt. Dawson rotated back to the Z.I. in Decmeber 1953, he had flown 78 combat missions and had been awarded the first of several Distinguished Flying Crosses. (Dawson)

Air-to-air gunnery training was conducted by having an F-86 tow a "sleeve" target behind the aircraft while flying at 20,000 feet. "The .50-caliber ammunition was dipped in paint," explained former pilot John Dawson. "Red, green, yellow and blue colors were assigned to specific squadrons and flights so that when the round passed through the 'banner' or 'rug' they left a color mark. Each pilot in a Flight of 2 or 4 knew what color ammunition had been loaded into his magazines. The pilot then counted his color marks for the score. All unmarked 'holes,' went to the lucky pilot whose ammunition had not been dipped in paint," Dawson recalled.

A Commander's

Perspective

by Col. Glenn A. Stell, Deputy Commander, 18th Fighter-Bomber Wing, 1953

After completing ten weeks of aerial and ground gunnery flying the F-86 Sabrejet at Nellis, AFB, Lt. Col. Glenn A. Stell was posted to Korea.

Since he had to fly five and a half days a week, "the only time we could go into Las Vegas was on Saturday nights. We would get a baby sitter and we participated in the gambling. I only played blackjack and each Saturday night I won enough to pay the baby sitter and for our evening out. At that time all the shows were free and as a result we got to see some good ones."

When he arrived in Korea, much to his surprise, he was assigned to the 18th Fighter-Bomber Wing, then still flying the F-51 Mustang. "I thought surely after all the jet training I would be assigned to an F-86 unit."

For a few weeks he was flying combat missions in the F-51, "then after a short time we were stood down and the F-51's were taken away. The Wing and its squadrons were transferred from K-46 to K-55— Osan. Here a new concrete runway had been built and brand new F-86 jets were flown in. The only facilities were Quonset huts. These were open metal buildings with concrete floors. I lived in one with nine other Lieutenant Colonels. We slept on metal cots and there was no privacy. Only two of the ten officers were pilots. The others were in supply and support functions."

Stell and Col. Carroll Stanton "were the only pilots at Osan that had any time in jet aircraft. We took two of the new planes up just to fly around and bore holes in the sky. With just internal fuel the F-86 could stay airborne for about fifty minutes."

"Stanton called and said he was getting low on fuel and was returning to base. I looked at my fuel gauge and as it indicated 500-lbs. I told him I was going to stay up a little longer. However, when I looked at my watch and then at the fuel gauge and knew that something was wrong so I started for the base. I got within about five miles when the engine quit. I was at 5,000 feet and going like a homesick angel. I started my glide after calling emer-gency—trying to stretch the glide to reach the base."

"I knew that at a certain altitude I had to decide to land or bailout. The seats of the F-86 were fitted with a cannon shell that the pilot could fire. When fired, the explosive will shoot the seat and pilot straight up out of the plane. The pilot then released the seat belt and shoulder harness and kicked away from the seat before deploying the parachute. I did not want to do this and lose a plane."

"The base got closer and I thought I could make it. Just as I got real close to the end of the runway I let the gear down and as I passed over the end of the runway I let the flaps down and opened the speed brakes. I then shut everything down including ignition and fuel switches. I made a perfect dead stick landing and when slow enough I turned off on a taxiway. Stanton had heard me call an emergency so he sat in his plane to watch" the show."

"When my plane was checked there was not enough fuel to fill a cigarette lighter and the fuel gauge still indicated 500-lbs."

It became Stell and Stanton's responsibility to check all the Mustang pilots out in the F-86. Since the Sabrejet was a single seated aircraft they could not be checked out with an experienced pilot actually in the plane with them.

Because those being checked out were "all experienced pilots," there were no accidents and soon the entire Group was checked out in the jet fighter-bomber.

Stell was appointed deputy wing commander. The Wing Commander was Col. Maurice L. Martin, with whom Stell had served in Germany and "who had gotten married in our house there."

The Wing's primary responsibility "was to bomb targets assigned to us by higher headquarters. Each airplane was armed with six .50-cal. machine guns, two 1,000-lb. bombs, and two fully loaded external fuel tanks. This made the plane rather heavy and it took quite a long roll for take off. When the temperature was hot I sometimes felt the plane was not going to fly. Jet engines performed better in cold damp air.

"We would use the external fuel to climb to 40,000 feet. By the time the altitude was reached the external fuel was exhausted so we jettisoned the empty tanks hoping they would hit a North Korean. When we got to our target we would open the speed brakes, roll over, go straight down, release the bombs, close the speed brakes and zoom to 45- or 48 thousand feet. We would then patrol the Yalu River that divided North Korea and China hoping a Mig would try to enter our patrol area."

"Just across the river in China we could see as many as 24 Migs lined up on the ground at a Chinese airbase. We were not permitted to go down and strafe them—we were to wait until they flew across the border. I decided right then that the Korean War was not worth getting killed for."

"We would patrol along the river

(L-R) Lt. Col. Carroll Stanton, 67th Squadron Commander and Col. Maurice L. Martin, 18th Group Commander review a combat mission. Officer at center is unidentified. (Stell)

until we got low on fuel before heading back to our base. The only thing that broke the monotony of the patrol was when the Mig pilots had a graduation class. Then they would send a flight of Migs across the border in a 100-mile sweep. When this happened the Americans had a field day. The Mig pilots that got back across the border graduated. The kill ratio was about 10 Migs for every one American."

"Our radar was located on a small island adjacent to South Korea and kept us informed as to enemy aircraft activity. When Migs came across the border, we were advised as to number, location and altitude. Flying back and forth along the border became rather boring so I thought of something to liven things up."

"We knew the Russians, Chinese and North Koreans had a flying school at Mukden, China about 100 miles into China. Prior to one of our missions I decided to take four aircraft and fly into China, hoping to catch some students airborne. Eight of the twelve aircraft in the flight were to screen four of us from the radar and we broke and went into China."

"Apparently the flying school had a fuel shortage as no aircraft were flying. We headed back to Korea and the radar called

us out as bandits and F-86's converged on us from all directions. When the American pilots recognized us they were so disappointed they even used some ugly language. Later on I got to thinking how stupid we had been flying into China against all regulations, I decided not to do that anymore. I knew that if something had happened to any of us while over in China, our government would have disowned us."

Stell acknowledge doing "another foolish thing while in Korea." A North American Aviation Company "Tech. Rep." [technical representative, a highly knowledgeable expert on that particular type of aircraft], "came to our base to put on a flying demonstration to show the excellent flying characteristics of the F-86. His name was Bob Hoover and he was test pilot for the North American Aircraft Company that built the F-86. He put on an excellent show and did things that we had not realized the plane was capable of. Then Bob asked to go on a combat mission into North Korea. Without checking with higher headquarters, I told him he could go. My thoughts were—wouldn't it be something if a Mig jumped him, since Bob was one of the best pilots I had ever met."

"The mission turned into a regular

bombing and patrolling mission and no Migs. When we returned I asked higher headquarters if Bob Hoover could go on a combat mission. Of course I did not tell them he had just returned from one. They told me in no uncertain terms that he could not go on a combat mission. So much for that. I lucked out again as I could have been fired."

"The Mig pilots on the whole were taught to do certain things in certain situations. The difference between them and American pilots was the American was taught to do anything he was capable of. We learned early on that when we got into a dog fight (aerial combat) with a Mig was not to go into a loop. We had one pilot that had been on the Air Force aerobatic team and a Mig got on his tail. This fellow's name was Harry ["The Hoss"] Evans. Harry put his plane into a very tight turn, as we knew the Mig could not turn with the F-86. When they tried the Mig would go into a stall then start spinning. Harry got on the Mig's tail and the Mig pilot tried to loop and when he did Harry shot him in the top of the loop."

"We were never sure of the nationality of the enemy pilots—they were probably Koreans, Chinese or Russian. They seemed to be taught by rote and the American pilots had superior training and were very successful against the Mig—most of the time."

"One flight that turned out differently. One of our more experienced flight leaders, a Captain, got on the tail of a Mig and was all set to shoot him down. The Mig pilot pulled his plane into a violent turn and got behind the Captain's plane. The American pilot did everything he could think of and some things he had never done before. He even went to the deck (ground) twice and this was never done in a jet as the fuel consumption increases. Finally, he knew he could not shake the Mig so he just flew straight and level knowing he was a goner. The Mig pilot flew up along side of him, saluted and headed back across the border. To this day we do not know the nationality of that Mig pilot. We figured it had to be an American or German getting

Lt. Col. Harry ("The Hoss") Evans, *Commanding Officer of the 12th Squadron in 1953, stands in front of his F-86 at K-55. (Ebersole)*

paid to train the enemy pilots. Whoever he was, he was good. In a two weeks period the Captain flight leader's hair turned completely gray."

During this period, General Glenn O. Barcus, Commander Fifth Air Force, "while flying on a mission and knowing our radio frequencies were monitored, made an announcement. He broadcast that the Air Force was going to bomb a certain city on a certain day and at a certain time. In fairness to the General, I assumed he was warning the civilians to evacuate. I do not know whether the civilians evacuated or not. I do know that the North Koreans and Chinese assembled all their anti-aircraft guns. There was so much ground fire they must have used the boy, girl and cub scouts, as well. There were so many aircraft involved, that altitudes and times over target had to be assigned. There was so much ground fire you could almost walk on the flak. Stanton was my wingman and he called that he was hit. He started climbing so fast that I called to him to slow down so I could check his plane. I see where a shell had gone through the fuselage. He said his tail pipe temperature and air speed gauge were inoperative. I told him to get on my wing and that I would lead him to our base. I told him to put the

gear down, then I checked to see that they were down. As he had no air speed indicator, he followed me until he flared out for landing, then I went around to land."

"The F-86 had slats on the leading edge of the wings. When the air speed dropped to a certain figure the slats would automatically extend, lowering the stalling speed and assisting the pilot in controlling the aircraft. Here again to give another insight to the brilliance of some of the people in higher command, we were ordered to take the slats off all aircraft and replace them with a hard leading edge. Inside this hard leading edge was to be installed a rubber bladder to hold additional fuel. This idea probably would have been good—only the rubber bladders were not shipped."

"Without the slats we had to change the take-off attitude of the plane. With the slats we could pull the nose up as high as we wanted to and the plane would take off. With the hard leading edge the nose could not be raised above a 30-degree angle, as the airplane would not fly off the runway regardless of the speed. This angle of take off characteristics was hammered over and over to the pilots."

"I had a radio in my office and I could monitor radio transmissions from the planes. One day it was raining lightly when I heard a pilot, returning from a mission, call an emergency as he had sustained damage from enemy ground fire. I decided to go to the fight line to watch the emergency come in. As I walked out of the office to get in a jeep a Lieutenant was walking by. He asked if he could ride to the flight line as he had a mission coming up. He was carrying his raincoat in his hand when he got in the jeep. When we arrived at the flight line there was twelve aircraft lined up for take off. They were loaded with two 1,000-lb. bombs, a full load of external fuel and ammunition for six machine guns"

"The leader was a very experienced pilot and he and his wingman started their roll for take off. The two of us sat in the jeep watching the planes take off. The flight leader raised the nose of the plane like we used to prior to the wing modification and I knew if he kept the nose up as he was doing the airplane would not fly. As I had no radio in the jeep, all I could do was sit there and watch. Then the pilot lowered the nose of the plane and I let out a sigh of relief as now the right altitude of the plane was attained, the plane would fly; Then, I guess the pilot saw the end of the runway coming closer he got anxious and pulled the nose up again. By this time the wingman was airborne and he pulled to the side so he would not be over his flight leader. The other planes in the flight were already committed so they were on their take off roll. The flight leader was probably going 200 mph when he ran off the runway and hit the dike surrounding a rice paddy."

"Seeing the plane was going to crash I had already started driving to the end of the runway. When the plane hit the dike both wings came off, the two bombs came off, the two fuel tanks ruptured and sprayed fuel over everything including the bombs and the plane fuselage. Then everything caught fire."

"When I stopped the jeep the Lieutenant started running through the rice paddy to the plane. When everything came off the plane, the fuselage began to roll and fortunately stopped right side. The canopy had been torn off. I could see the pilot trying to get out of the cockpit with fire all over him."

"When the Lieutenant saw the two bombs burning he stopped and when I went by him I jerked his raincoat out of his hand. When I got to the pilot I put the raincoat over him to put out the fire."

"All pilots were required to wear Mae Wests (life preservers) on all flights so that in an emergency they were to bailout over water to be picked up by helicopter. When I reached down to release his safety belt I put my hands in burning rubber. The fuselage was so hot it burned my legs as I leaned in to pull the pilot out. The pilot weighed more than I did, but I lifted him out with what seemed apparent ease."

"I got him away from the plane and by this time the ambulance and fire-fight-

ing equipment had arrived. Two corpsmen were running towards the plane with a stretcher and they also stopped when they saw the burning bombs. I yelled for them to come on, as the pilot was still alive. They got him and put him in the ambulance."

"By this time the fire was being extinguished so I asked the Lt. to drive me to the hospital. All the burned skin that was hanging from my hands was cut away. I do not know what was put on my hands prior to bandaging but it worked. When I recovered I had no scars on my hands and the doctors as well as I thought it a miracle."

"You certainly find out who your friends are when you lose the use of both hands—especially when going to the bathroom. The pilot involved in the crash was conscious the entire time. He knew who had pulled him out of the crash and kept saying he wanted to be sent to Honolulu, Hawaii, as his wife was a nurse there. He joined his wife but a few days later shock set in and he died. It was a pretty good while before I was able to fly combat again."

After the "fiasco in Korea finally ended," Stell was transferred to Tokyo, Japan and assigned to war plans. "It was my job to formulate contingency plans for Far East emergencies. I had the responsibility of anticipating actions by foreign governments and then planning American reac-

tion. This was an interesting assignment and I spent two years in that job. The only problem was everything was Top Secret and I was restricted from going anywhere since I might be kidnapped."

June 1953

Monthly Summary

UN forces fiercely contested the enemy's continued ground assaults, but eventually yielded the Nevada outpost complex--possession of which would facilitate the communist offensive and provide leverage in the final stages of the armistice negotiations. The communist assault largely fell upon ROK and U.S. forces in the eastern and central sectors of the front rather than weaker positions in western Korea.

The UN Command elected not to counter attack--minimizing its own losses--and the communists soon captured high ground despite heavy losses. The UN Command coordinated heavy artillery barrages and close air strikes that prevented the enemy from exploiting the costly gains, while the communists shifted their offensive to the ROK II Corps and USA X Corps forces holding the central sector.

Following savage fighting, the enemy had gained an average of 3,000 meters along a 13,000 meter front. After pausing for six days, the communist offensive resumed, this time targeting ROK forces al-most exclusively, perhaps hoping to convince the South Korean government that continued fighting would be extremely costly. This final communist offensive coincided with the final stages of the armistice negotiations.

By mid-June both sides had agreed to the establishment of a Neutral Nations Repatriation Committee. The South Korean government, which was boycotting the truce conference over the repatriation issue, released 27,000 prisoners of war, describing the event as a "mass escape." This action severely undermined the UN Command's negotiating ability. With communist delegates doubtful that South Korea would respect any armistice, truce negotiations stalled once again.

During most of June the UN Command directed air strikes against communist forces attempting to penetrate the UN main line of resistance and against North Korean airfields near the Manchurian border. To dampen communist ground offensives, the UN employed medium bombers, light bombers, and fighter-bombers in close air support missions. Raids on enemy airfields sought to ensure they could not be used by reinforcements of jet aircraft that the Chinese Communists might fly into North Korea in days, or even hours, preceding the signing of an armistice. Far East Air Forces employed both B-29s and fighter-bombers to bomb the airfields, even striking nearby dams in an effort to flood the runways or otherwise render them unserviceable.

Air Force fighters maintained overwhelming air superiority in MiG Alley. For unknown reasons the MiGs sought combat at altitudes below 40,000 feet, the Sabrejets most effective combat environment. As a consequence, the USAF pilots broke all previous records, sighting 1,268 MiGs, engaging 501, and destroying seventy-seven without suffering a single loss in air-to-air combat.

Adapted in part from U.S. Air Force Historical Research Agency. January 2002. The U.S. Air Force's First War: Korea 1950-1953 Significant Events.

Combat Operations

In June 1953. Col. Maurice L. Martin, commander of the 18th Fighter-Bomber wing, completed a Secret classified monthly analysis of the Wing's combat operations.

Of the total of 1526 airborne sorties. There were 14 non-effective sorties. The wing had an effective sortie rate of 99.08%, he noted. Sorties per aircraft had increased by 6.9 per aircraft over at the previous month.

The majority of the missions flown that month—52%—were "close support." The remaining 48% of the wing's missions that month included: interdiction; counter air; armed reconnaissance; rescue; and, reconnaissance.

The wing shot down one MIG-15 jet fighter, and damaged two others. Of the 14 MIG-15's sighted, only four were actually encountered. The colors of the enemy jets were silver, olive drab, green and blue. No distinctive markings were observed.

Weather had prevented flying on five days that month and caused slack operations on two additional days.

There were five major, and one minor aircraft accidents that month. The 200-gallon wing tanks had been found to cause unstable operations, when aircraft operated at altitudes above 35,000 feet. An average of 1.31 tons of bombs per effective sortie were expended in combat that month.

Ammunition expenditures in combat of .50-caliber machine gun ammunition had increased 43% over May to a total of 165 rounds per effective sortie.

A total of 193 wing tanks had been dropped at a cost of $53,770.96. This was a decrease from the month of May during which 358 tanks had been dropped at a cost in excess of $100,000.

The release and accuracy of the 56 napalm tanks dropped during the month of June was very good. However, the Wing reported that it took considerable time to reservice an aircraft for a napalm mission, "and the turnaround time at present is very high."

During June 1953, 1038, 500 pound general-purpose bombs were

dropped. In addition, 1420 1000-pound general-purpose bombs and two 500-pound incendiary bombs were expended in combat. This was an average of 1.31 times per effective combat sortie for the wing.

During the month of June, there were no problems reported regarding taking off or landing with bombs. One aircraft lost a bomb on take off, and four aircraft landed with bombs. One of these had a full fuel load and ran off the end of the runway, but there was no damage to the aircraft. The practice of landing with bombs was not recommended, and was considered to be an emergency procedure only.

The loss of seven aircraft, due to

enemy action that month, resulted in a high aircraft of attrition rate of 4.58%.

The wing had no air pressure gauges for aircraft tires that were calibrated above 160 pounds. Finally, the wing fabricated a high pressure gauge at K-55 and began testing it.

Ground Fire Brings Bail-out

Major Flamm D. Harper, Number 2 man of mission Expire 01, was airborne at 1601 from K-55 on an interdiction mission to skip-bomb a rail bridge at YC423963. After pulling off the target, he experienced a "definite vibration in the nose section" and noted high tailpipe temperature readings. While he reported that he was not positive his aircraft had been hit by ground fire, in view of the events that followed, the Air Force investigation noted, "it can be assumed that he was definitely hit."

Harper reduced power to approximately 80%, but the tailpipe temperature remained at 700 degrees centigrade. Major Harper then climbed to approximately 16,000 feet where the engine froze at which time the throttle jerked back to the rear stop and the wing flaps went to the full down position. He retracted the wing flaps and established a glide path to the west. However, smoke filled the cockpit and his wingman reported fire was coming from the underside of both wing roots.

At approximately 8,000 feet Major Harper elected to bail out due to the extensive smoke and fire. He suffered a painful back injury received when he struck a rock upon landing. Air Rescue reported that the pilot was on the ground approximately 30 minutes before being picked up by an H-19 Helicopter. Major Harper was taken to Chodo Island and from there to the 121st Evacuation Hospital. On July 3rd he was transferred to the 18th Medical Group Hospital for further treatment.

The Group dropped napalm in June with "approximately 90% effectiveness. On the first drop, where excessive airspeeds for optimum utilization of a napalm run were used, 80% effectiveness was realized. The napalm spread out so fast as not to allow the igniters to start burning reaction. On the second drop the pilots held airspeeds down, resulting in 100% effectiveness," the Group noted.

Significant Events

June 1: Twelve aircraft, led by Major Howard Ebersole, attacked personnel and supply shelters just north of Kumwha. Other members of the flight included: Lieutenants "Ike" Iglehart, Alva Branch and Bill Hagood. "We were attacking some warehouses near a village named "Long Dong." Bomb release was lower than current policy, but "it paid off," Ebersole recalled. "The warehouses literally blew up in our faces after we obtained excellent hits." At the debrief following the mission Col. Harry Evans thought that Ebersole had pressed the attack "too close." Was Ebersole getting reckless or just "flacky." Evans suggested that Ebersole "go on R&R."

June 2: 1st Lt. Lyle R. Krause, 67th Squadron, was taking off from Kisarazu, Japan on 2 June 1953 to bring a new aircraft to the squadron when he crashed. His injuries proved fatal and he died on 19 June 1953." [1]

June 10: Fifth Air Force and Bomber Command made coordinated strikes against North Korean serviceable and near-serviceable airfields.

The 12th Squadron suffered its first pilot loss of the year. Ebersole led an interdiction mission into the Charlie Tare ("CT" on the grid map) area. Ebersole led the D Flight, Capt. Robert A. Coury led the element. "A damned good head with experience," Ebersole remembered of Coury. "Bob had won $5 from me doing three more vertical rolls than I had on a flag pole run two weeks earlier."

Combat Statistics

18th Fighter-Bomber Wing

June 1953

Average No. A/C Assigned
43
Total Flying Time
2,211 (1,886 in combat)
Percentage of Aircraft in Commission
92%
Percentage of Aircraft AOCP
2%
Combat Sorties Flown by Wing
1,526
12th Squadron Sorties
736
67th Squadron Sorties
Unknown
2 Squadron Sorties
Unknown
A/C Lost to Combat
7 (4.58 a/c attrition rate=high)
Pilots lost
5

Fuel Consumed
959,684 gals.

Ordnance Expended

.50-cal. Rounds
241,452 (165 rounds/sortie)
Wing Tanks Dropped
193 ($53,770.96)
Napalm Bombs
56
500-lb. GP Bombs
1,038 (1.31 tons/sortie)
1,000-lb. GP Bombs
1,434

[*A WWII veteran pilot, Coury had flown 28 missions as a B-17 pilot with the 92nd Bomb Group, 8th Air Force from late 1943 through May 1944, during a period when finishing 25 missions was against all the odds. Coury flew 28 and survived.*]

Lt. Sam Shattuck was Ebersole's wingman. Lt. Rick Westcott was on Coury's wing. It looked "like a typical mission, but it didn't turn out that way."

After locating the target, Ebersole's flight lined up with the sun at their back, rolled over into a 45 degree dive, put their manual pippers on the target and one after the other "pickled" their bombs (pushed the bomb release--pickle button--on the B-8 stick grip). As his wingman pulled off the target, Ebersole noted some secondary explosions caused by his bombs. However, as Coury dove in, one of the flight warned him to "watch the flak Bob, it's getting close." Just as Westcott went into his bomb run, D Flight heard, "Caddy three here, I've got a problem."

Fire was streaming out of Coury's tail pipe for at least one hundred feet, Ebersole recalled. He looked like a torch. After getting a "steer to the nearest friendlies," Coury turned due South and headed for Old Papa-San, a large mountain on the front lines near Khumwa. While the North Koreans and Chinese held the mountain, the area just south of it was flat and under UN control.

Coury cleared the mountain, barely, then bailed out just before the plane exploded. It crashed at the foot of the mountain and Coury landed nearby. Ebersole had followed him down, virtually as a wingman. When he saw Coury land, Ebersole switched his radio to the emergency channel. "Caddy three, Caddy lead...do you read?"

"Roger Caddy Lead, loud and clear." Then, the radio was silent.

Area where Coury had landed was "pocked with openings" and several gun emplacements. As Ebersole went to full throttle, banked left, circled over the top of the mountain, and came around for another look, cutting back the throttle until

Target Claims June 1953

Target	No. Attacked	Damaged	Destroyed
Personnel Shelters	63	20	43
Mortar Positions	45	35	10
Bunkers	89	64	25
Trenches *	2,286 yds	980 yds	1,506 yds
Buildings	157	67	70
Bridges	24	11	13
Rail Cars	16	16	0
Tanks	2	1	1
Trucks	38	21	17
Revetments	7	4	3
Heavy Guns	2	2	0
Machine Guns	3	2	1
Gun Positions	7	5	2
Automatic Weapons	9	6	3
Vehicles	19	11	8
Caves	17	17	0
Artillery Positions	10	8	2
Artillery Pieces	3	0	3
Firing Bays	8	8	0
Box Cars	32	13	19
Concrete Abutments	1	1	0
Hard Stands	1	1	0
Troops	170	0	0

Note: the totals for "damaged" and "destroyed" trenches add up to more than the number of yards of trenches "attacked." However, those are the exact figures quoted on page 6 of the 18th Wing Monthly Analysis of June 1953.

he was virtually gliding. Things looked quiet, until his third pass. As he topped the hill, he saw a large man run from a cave and "jump on a quad-fifty." As the guns began to turn toward him, Ebersole fired a short burst from his .50-cal. machine guns. The man and quad-fifties "just exploded."

UN artillery began to "powder" the hill, trying to keep the North Koreans in their holes long enough to effect a rescue. A Mosquito (T-6) was now overhead directing the artillery fire while he was vectoring in a flight of Aussies in Meteors. "What a gutsy guy," recalled Ebersole. Ebersole was low on fuel and turned over the CAP to the Australian pilots. As he vectored in on K-14, his engine flamed out. No fuel. After a harrowing glide back to base, "slipping to lose altitude after the low key point," he touched down at mid-field

and rolled to a stop just off the runway. A bullet had gone through the gun camera and there was another hole just behind his head in the canopy. A much larger hole was found in the vertical stabilizer.

As noted in the 18th Wing monthly report, Capt. Coury, flying Ebersole's element lead, had been hit by flak, which caused a small fire in the aft section of the fuselage. Although hit while breaking off the target but was able to climb to 14,000 feet before his engine flamed out. He then tried to reach friendly territory, but was forced to bail out over "no man's land" because the fire in the aft section had made staying with the damaged plane impossible. Major Ebersole "expended all his ammunition on enemy positions before withdrawing, when another flight arrived to take over the CAP." Capt. Coury was seen to land safely, but the CAPing pilot lost sight

of him and could not locate him for the helicopter when it arrived on the scene. A ground patrol started out but was unable to contact him. He was listed MIA and presumed captured," the 12th reported. Ebersole's diary noted, "Coury went down this trip...I capped him...went to K-14...hole in nose, hole in tail, hole aft of canopy, in canopy, about 6" back of my head."

[On the ground, Coury had no sooner responded to Ebersole's radio call than he felt a rifle in his back. He was immediately moved to a cave collection point for POW's. After an unsuccessful escape attempt, he spent three weeks in a farm house guarded around the clock. Eventually, he was moved to Sinuiju in extreme northwestern North Korea and kept in solitary confinement under very harsh conditions. After unsuccessful attempts to interrogate him,

June 1953 was "a rough month" for the 12th Squadron. *"The Red's were bargaining for peace at Panmunjom and at the same time launching a ground offensive campaign. Fifth Air Force Headquarters removed the minimum altitude restrictions, and we were to hit anything that we saw move, north of the bombline. The 12th Squadron Tigers were turned loose, and a few had mishaps. Then we lost three pilots on a transport in Japan on 18 June. That same day, Jim Bellows was killed. Bob Coury was MIA on 10 June. Chad Smith was KIA on 15 June and Ed Dillon was MIA on 15 June. On 16 June Lt. Allston was KIA, and Don Forbes crashed. Fortunately, he got out OK. Spirits weren't too high. Then the South Africans invited us to their Club and threw us a real wing-ding of a party. I shall never forget that gesture. Each South African Air Force pilot took a 12th Squadron pilot as a guest and nothing could have done more for morale than that party," Ebersole remembered. (Ebersole)*

the North Koreans were "displeased" with him and threatened to shoot him. "I was awfully run-down at the time and my attitude was 'have at it,'" he recalled years later. Coury was finally released three months after the armistice in July. He weighed 100 pounds.]

June 11: Fighter-bombers made their deepest penetration of the war when thirteen F-84s attacked Chunggang-jin Air-

other two MIGs did not engage. One MIG was probably destroyed.

June 12: "Rhythm Review," the second of only two USO shows to visit the 18th in 1953 took place at K-55.

June 13-18: In order to flood airfields at Namsi and Taechon, F-84s, B-29s and Marine F4U Corsair fighter-bombers struck irrigation dams at Toksan and Kusong. The raids failed to breach the

was implemented as a means of speeding up the time element between landing and debriefing, thus enabling Intelligence personnel to interrogate pilots before various events claimed their interest, as well as serving to disseminate the debriefing information to other interested units with greater dispatch." [2]

Lt. Chadwick B. Smith and Lt. Iglehart of the 12th Squadron were hit by

field located mid-way on the North Korean-Manchurian border. Pilots reported that the raid had rendered the runway unserviceable.

June 13: Col. Martin of the 12th Squadron, led six, four-aircraft flights on a Yalu sweep. The 12th had the three leading flights in the formation. Starting the patrol up the Yalu River at 40,000 feet, Martin soon sighted three MIGs below them at about 10,000 feet. They engaged and made a firing pass, during which the MIG pulled up to the right and then dove away. The MIG was smoking as it dived. As it pulled up, Martin scored more hits before breaking off the engagement due to "considerable flak at this altitude." The

dams, because the communists had lowered water levels to decrease water pressure on the dams.

June 15: The three squadrons of the 18th Fighter-Bomber Group "established a new record of 190 sorties. This record surpassed the old record of 155 sorties set by four squadrons of F-51s in May 1951.

After nearly three years of combat, the 18th Fighter-Bomber Group revised its debriefing policy for its pilots. "Group Intelligence Officers were dispatched to the fighter squadrons to conduct debriefing sessions, rather than wait for the pilots to report to the Intelligence Office in accord with previous custom. The new procedures

flak during a napalm mission. Lt. Smith's damage was minor; however, Lt. Iglehart's gear collapsed on landing.

Lt. Edward Dillon was Number Two man on mission Expire 48, airborne at 1635 on an armed reconnaissance mission. Numbers 3 and 4 separated from Numbers 1 and 2 to cover the target area. Lt. Dillon's aircraft was hit by enemy AAA fire and he had to eject. Within ten minutes after the pilot was on the ground, enemy troops were observed in the immediate area. Number 1 man circled the area until 1745, but was unable to establish contact with the downed pilot. Col. Martin provided the initial RESCAP and was relieved by Major Ebersole. "Pilots were briefed on tactics to be used on reconnaissance mission," the Group reported, "areas of known AAA activity were stressed."

"Lt. Dillon was lost while attacking camouflaged trucks south of Wonsan. He was flying Col. Evans' wing at the time. He was hit by small arms fire, bailed out, and was surrounded by enemy troops within 5-10 minutes. He was declared missing action presumed captured," the 12th reported.

Later that evening, Lt. Smith led two wingmen north of Wonsan to bomb six boxcars. He led the flight to the target and started a bomb run from 15,000 feet. Intense automatic weapons and small arms fire was encountered and Lt. Smith's aircraft was not observed to pull out of the dive. A "severe explosion occurred in the target area although it was not observed whether the explosion was actually caused by Lt. Smith's aircraft. There was no evidence of ejection or parachute and no communication. The remaining aircraft circled the target area for some time but it was too dark to find the aircraft. Lt. Smith was declared MIA, presumed killed. Major Ebersole's diary noted, "Lt. Chad B. Smith went in on bomb run."

June 16: Setting a single day record, Fifth Air Force flew 1,834 sorties. More than half were close support missions against enemy troops in the Pukhan Valley area.

"Lt. Forbes crash landed in no-man's land--got out OK," Major Ebersole noted.

June 17/18: The South Korean government unilaterally released 27,000 anticommunist POWs.

June 18: Two 18th Group pilots, 2nd Lt. Samuel Hyde and 2nd Lt. William Church, were aboard the "ill-fated C-124 that crashed on take-off from Tachikawa AFB, Japan…killing all aboard. Another fatality was Captain John H. Staring, Assistant Personnel Services Officer for the Wing.

Two Airmen of the 18th Air Installation Squadron based at K-55 were supposed to be on board the Globemaster that crashed. Anthony "Tony" Falo and Walter "Wally" Bauer were coming off R&R and worried sick that we would not make the flight. "The taxi driver got stuck in traffic," Falo recalled, and we arrived at the airport just in time to see our plane take off without us." They were devastated. If they didn't make it back in time, they would have a lot of explaining to do or be listed as AWOL. "Just a minute later, we also saw, in horror, the plane crash with all aboard. Helping to remove bodies is still with me in memory," he explained over fifty years later. It was fifteen years before Falo could talk of this horrific tragedy. "Because Wally and I were listed on the plane's manifest," Falo said, "we were reported dead--until an officer asked us who we were." When they gave him their names, he advised them to call the 18th Wing immediately "to clear it up. Otherwise, we would have been listed as casualties and our families would have been notified as such."

1st Lt. James Mayo Bellows, Jr. of the 12th Squadron was flight leader on Mis-

sion Expire 17, airborne at 1830 on MPQ mission on 18 June 1953. The Number 4 man, Lt. Sprague, could not release his bombs so the flight turned North to attempt to salvo the bombs. After jettisoning bombs and again turning south, intense and accurate automatic weapons fire was encountered, some of which hit the lead in the engine section. Lt. Bellows aircraft was hit in the aft section and flamed out. The flight went to the emergency channel. The last transmission received by the flight was, "I'm at 3,000 feet and am being shot at. I'll have to get out soon." The pilot crashed in the aircraft. The flight stayed in the area until low on fuel and then withdrew. The pilots did not sight Bellows but a ground party recovered his body. The primary cause of the loss was due to enemy automatic weapons fire. The Air Force investigation recommended "that briefings stress avoidance of known AAA areas and that aircraft fly at altitudes where the guns are least effective."

June 20:

"SAAF's invited us to a party," Ebersole noted in his diary. It was a much appreciated gesture of good will from the Flying Cheetahs to the other squadrons of the 18th Group that had lost good friends in the days before.

June 23: With all North Korean airfields but one inoperable, General Weyland, advised his air forces to limit attacks to follow-on raids to damage the airfields sufficiently that another series of air raids could knock them out in four or five days.

June 25: 2nd Lt. Maxwell Shipp "was killed when his F-86 flamed-out and crashed off the end of the runway at K-55" on 25 June 1953. It was Lt. Shipp's first transition flight, "at this base, in an F-86 aircraft. Lieutenant Shipp encountered a flame out on base leg and failed to make the runway. He crashed just short of the runway and received fatal injuries."

June 29: Major Howard "Ebe" Ebersole completed his 100th combat mission--a Chodo alert. "Hooray," he noted in his diary. "Col. Martin says 'Major, you're grounded.' Guess Hans and I were suspected of beating up the field!!"

June 30: Sabres set a record by destroying sixteen MiGs in a single day. The previous record, fourteen kills, had been set on December 13, 1951. Flying with the 25th FIS, 1st Lt. Henry Buttelmann became the Korean War's thirty-sixth jet ace.

The 18th Wing listed 127 "combat crews." Of these, 82 percent were combat ready and only 18 percent were in training.

Combat Losses

2nd Lt. James Hartford Allston, 12th Squadron, was Number 2 man on Mission Expire 52, Ford Flight, armed reconnaissance mission in Area 1 on 16 June 1953. He followed the leader in on the dive bomb run during which the target was a truck. The leader sustained damage on the run and crashed south of the bomb line. Lt. Allston was hit and crashed during the attack. "Lt. Allston went in north of Kidney Lake--north and east, I guess," Major Ebersole noted in his diary.

1st Lt. James Mayo Bellows, Jr. of the 12th Squadron was flight leader on Mission Expire 17, airborne at 1830 on MPQ mission on 18 June 1953. The Number 4 man, Lt. Sprague, could not release his bombs so the flight turned North to attempt to salvo the bombs. After jettisoning bombs and again turning south, intense and accurate automatic weapons fire was encountered, some of which hit the lead in the engine section. Lt. Bellows aircraft was hit in the aft section and flamed out. The flight went to the emergency channel. The last transmission received by the flight was, "I'm at 3,000 feet and am being shot at. I'll have to get out soon." The pilot crashed in the aircraft. The flight stayed in the area until low on fuel and then withdrew. The pilots did not sight Bellows but a ground party recovered his body. The primary cause of the loss was due to enemy automatic weapons fire. The Air Force investigation recommended "that briefings stress avoidance of known AAA areas and that aircraft fly at altitudes where the guns are least effective."

1st Lt. Lyle R. Krause, 67th Squad-

ron, was taking off from Kisarazu, Japan on 2 June 1953 to bring a new aircraft to the squadron when he crashed. His injuries proved fatal and he died on 19 June 1953." [1]

2nd Lt. Maxwell Shipp "was killed when his F-86 flamed-out and crashed off the end of the runway at K-55" on 25 June 1953. It was Lt. Shipp's first transition flight, "at this base, in an F-86 aircraft. Lieutenant Shipp encountered a flame out on base leg and failed to make the runway. He crashed just short of the runway and received fatal injuries."

Captain Chadwick B. Smith of the 67th Squadron was flying Number 3 position on mission Expire 48A, airborne at 1940 15 June 1953 for armed reconnaissance. The flight leader aborted on take-off and Smith led the mission to the target area and commenced a bomb run from 15,000 feet. No communication was received from Smith during the dive. Small arms and automatic weapons fire was encountered during the dive, and Captain Smith failed to pull out of the dive. A severe explosion was observed in the target area. However, it was not determined whether the explosion was caused by Smith's plane crashing, since visibility was limited due to the late hour. The primary cause of his loss was due to enemy automatic weapons fire.

Endnotes

[1] USAFHRA. *Monthly Historical Report, 18th Fighter-Bomber Group,* January-June 1953, p. 17.

[2] USAFHRA. *Monthly Historical Report, 18th Fighter-Bomber Group,* January-June 1953, p. 10.

Adapted in part from unit histories of the 18th Fighter Bomber Wing and U.S. Air Force Historical Research Agency. January 2002. The U.S. Air Force's First War: Korea 1950-1953 Significant Events.

Million man Chinese attack stopped in its tracks. The 18th Group had destroyed its ammunition.

Late in the afternoon of 15 June 1953, Lt. Col. Harry "The Hoss" Evans, Commander of the 12th Squadron, hit the door of the 18th Group Operations Office at K-55. He had been in combat for about a year and by now was almost unflappable--but not that afternoon. Lt. Col. Carroll L. "Stan" Stanton, Commander of the 67th Squadron had never seen him so excited.

Evans had just returned from a mission during which the entire flight had expended most of its ammunition and bombs. On the way back to K-55, Evans had seen an ammunition train that had broken down not far from the protective cover of a tunnel just north of the 38th Parallel. As many as 100 box cars full of ammunition were heading south with ammunition needed by the Communist forces for a big offensive prior to a truce. Although a few of the box cars were destroyed with the very last of the flight's ammunition, a nearby marshalling yard held even more cars. Evans reported that everything they shot at exploded. It was the target of a lifetime. But it wouldn't last for long. Time was of the essence--even if nightfall was rapidly closing in on the "daytime" squadrons.

Communist troops were feverishly trying to unload the train by hand and to haul the precious ammunition into the tunnel.

The time to act was right now. A command decision had to be made. But who was there on board to make it?

Col. Frank Perego, the 18th Wing Commander and Col. Maurice "Marty" Martin were in Toyko at a conference. Lt. Col. Glenn Stell was the Acting 18th Group Commander.

By 1700 that afternoon, all 92 sorties had been completed, although two flights were still north of the MLR. In the Combat Operations Center, the duty staff was almost through closing up operations for the day.

Evan's news electrified the Group Staff. Major Dee Harper, the Group's Operations Officer, contacted the Combat Operations Center at Fifth Air Force Headquarters. While he was on the telephone, the Operation's Center duty officer was busy "scrambling" every available plane for the urgent mission. Harper stressed the need for immediate action and advised the FAF Duty Officer that he was in the process of launching the alert flights while requesting the necessary permissions. It never entered Harper's mind that the needed permissions would not be given.

Fifteen minutes later, the 18th Group alert aircraft were ready to launch. Harper's call to FAF Headquarters brought the news that the commanding general was at dinner. His staff did not want to disturb him. Harper advised the duty officer that the 18th Group would launch the flights that were ready and prepare the ground crews for rapid turn around of the returning flights.

By now, the K-55 air base was pulsing with activity. Bombs and munitions were hustled from the dump to the flight line. The Intelligence Office had prepared maps and photography to support the mission. Every component on the base was helping support the mission in any way possible.

Harper, meanwhile, was in mental agony--he was the only one on the base who knew that the strike had not--yet--been approved by Fifth Air Force.

The Group continued launching flights into the now dark skies. Reports from the target were riveting--the fires and explosions at the target site were so extensive that the pilots could read their instruments without their cockpit lights. The entire valley in and near the target area looked like daylight. Pilots en route to the target reported they didn't need the maps given them prior to launch--they could see the fires well over the horizon. As the flights shuttled back and forth from the target, clouds began to move in.

The Commanders of the 12th and 67th Squadrons took turns controlling the attacks as they orbited over the target. After several hours of constant attacks, a C-47 arrived on scene with a forward air controller to coordinate the maximum effort.

Lt. Col. Stell, the 18th Group Executive Officer was not aware of the delay in FAF approval. In the press of events, Harper had not advised him of the delay. Harper was completely confident in ultimate approval and kept at his other duties. Both Stell and Harper were both grounded for medical reasons at the time--both recuperating from recent injuries. Stell had pulled Capt. "Tex" Beneke from his burning aircraft several weeks earlier and had received burns. Harper had bailed out of his burning Sabrejet over North Korea and had been seriously injured. He was just out of the hospital.

Periodically, over the next several hours, Harper contacted FAF Headquarters to request a status report on the permission process. He even requested at one point that they order him to stop or grant permission. Silence. Finally, he surmised that the FAF Staff had not told the General during the dinner, and now with the reports being fed in by Harper of the magnitude and success of the unauthorized mission, no one on the Staff wanted to be the one to tell the General that one of the biggest and most successful missions of the Korean War had been organized and locally approved by the 18th Group.

Harper began to believe he was being hung out to dry, even though it was the only real target anyone in the Group had seen during their combat tours in Korea.

Finally, about 2100 and no permissions on the horizon, Harper decided to finish the job. Rather than expose anyone else to what he felt was going to be a Court Martial, regardless of the successes achieved, he determined to keep quiet about the permissions.

The shuttle flights to the target continued.

Shortly after midnight, Lt. Don Forbes was hit and bailed out in No Man's Land. Two planes were lost to ground fire. With these losses, it was now a certainty that the mission could not be kept secret. In the wee hours of the morning of 16 June the unauthorized combat operation was shut down. Of the Group's 212 sorties, 120 had not been authorized by FAF.

About 0300 Harper obtained the FAF Frag Order from the courier. A terse notation directed Colonels Martin and Perego to forego returning to K-55, but to proceed directly to FAF Headquarters. Harper knew the meaning of the directive--an investigation was already underway. As he fell into his rack exhausted by the day's events and stresses, visions of a court martial and a stretch at Leavenworth were burning holes in his thoughts.

Note: In 1993, Col. Martin confirmed the details of this mission "with real pride." When he and Col. Perigo arrived at Fifth Air Force Headquarters, "staff and command embarrassment were covered neatly with a good 'chewing'--Perigo and Martin retaining the teeth marks." Martin noted the significance in the fact "that we were ordered to Tokyo together--Wing and Group CO's--speaks volumes for the mind set in those last days of the War."

Col. "Pappy" Stell "proved his qualification for command by knowing when not to ask questions," Martin added. "Dee Harper did what had to be done. God, don't we hope that in this day of instant communications and micro-management that such initiative-leadership does not perish. Had Dee not acted there is no way to evaluate the consequences. There were hoards of Chinese obviously headed South," Martin noted.

About 1400 on 16 June, Harper was back in the Group Operations Office when Col. Martin walked in. With a funny half-grin on his face, he told Harper that he knew he had had a pretty busy day the day before. After a long pause, he added that Air Force officers had to make decisions and that Harper's decision had been the right decision. And, he added, if he never had to make another decision again in his career, he had earned his pay for the rest of his career.

Harper was as surprised as he was delighted to hear Martin explain that the 8th Army had hard intelligence that the Chinese intended to launch a million man offensive prior to finalizing any truce agreement. The 18th had destroyed the munitions needed for the offensive the night before.

Harper was relieved to hear that he was not going to be court martialed. Neither was he to be decorated. For over four decades, it was all he ever heard about the mission.

It was, in fact, one of the most important missions of the Korean War. It stopped a million man offensive before it started and had a significant impact on the peace talks. While it is impossible to evaluate the effects of an operation that never happened, it seems clear that the ammunition train mission on 15 June 1953 saved many lives and hastened the signing of the final truce agreement.

For Dee Harper the buck truly stopped on his desk.

Epilogue: Louis J. Cain, a former Staff Sergeant with the 18th, worked for years to get the Air Force to acknowledge the accuracy of the ammunition train mission and Harper's role. At Cain's suggestion, General Ronald R. Fogleman, Air Force Chief of Staff, directed the Air Force History Support Office to confirm the details. A 9 October 1997 letter from AFHSO indicated "we verified the story..." The information was forwarded to Air Force professional military training organizations for possible use in developing lesson plans.

"It must have been an act of providence that he [Harper] occupied the position he had because he was in a non-flying status due to an injury, and a command structure vacuum existed because the Wing and Group Commanders were summoned to a conference in Tokyo in anticipation of the forthcoming truce," Cain pointed out. "I submit that Dee did everything possible to get approval for the mission in which 120 sorties were flown. I doubt if anyone of equivalent rank ever made a decision of more momentous potential," Cain concluded.

Truce Headlines. *The headlines scream "Truce Signed," and provide the best reason possible for a celebratory photograph of 18ᵗʰ FBW armorers at K-55. (L-R) Wilbur Short, Thomas Greene, Merle Keaton and an unidentified Airman. In front, Airman William Ackeridge (right), joins Airman Stanley Bist (left) in their widest grins as they hold the long awaited news. The folded bedroll at left might be a sign someone was ready to head back to the States and home. (Bist)*

Monthly Summary

Chinese Communist Forces pounded ROK positions at Arrowhead and drove Americans from positions on Porkchop Hill in early July. In mid-July they struck hard at ROK units along the central sector of the front, making significant penetrations. To halt the advance, U.S. units relieved ROK units or took up blocking positions behind them. An ROK counterattack regained some territory, but in late July the communists were left with considerable gains. Their final effort had driven UN forces back six miles along the central front, eliminating the Kumsong salient and straightening out defensive lines.

During July, truce negotiations reopened but were stalemated. The commu-

nists were marking time, awaiting the outcome of their final offensive. They began to negotiate seriously later in the month, as their forces assimilated recently conquered gains. At that point technical specialists determined the line of demarcation and the demilitarized zone, the place of delivery for POWs, the inception of activities for the armistice implementing committees, and the physical arrangements for the actual signing of the cease-fire.

During July, poor weather hampered air operations, reducing sorties. Most of the UN air effort was focused on providing support for UN ground forces, interdicting communist supply lines, and neutralizing North Korean airfields. Forty-three

percent of FEAF sorties directly supported UN ground forces. As the communist offensive drew to a halt, Fifth Air Force aircraft shifted from ground support to airfield neutralization. During the month, FEAF Sabres flying air superiority missions destroyed thirty-two of 200 MiGs encountered. The median altitude at which the engagements took place was 20,000 feet, where Sabres were most effective.

The Korean War ended with the signing of the armistice on July 27, 1953.

Adapted in part from unit histories of the 18ᵗʰ Fighter Bomber Wing and U.S. Air Force Historical Research Agency. January 2002. The U.S. Air Force's First War: Korea 1950-1953 Significant Events.

Significant Events July 1953

July 6-11: General Maxwell. Taylor abandoned Pork Chop Hill, a 7th Infantry Division outpost, to the Chinese as not worth further fighting.

July 10: Fifth Air Force fighter-bombers began raiding rail bridges at Sinanju and Yongmi-dong to hinder the build-up for the final communist assault.

July 11: South Korean President Syngman Rhee agreed to accept a cease-fire agreement in return for promises of a mutual security pact with the United States.

July 12: Reconnaissance aircraft detected heavy concentrations of anti-aircraft artillery opposite sectors of the front held by the U.S. IX Corps and the ROK II Corps, providing warning of an enemy offensive.

July 12-20: Close air support sorties by FEAF aircraft contributed significantly to halting the communist onslaught against ROK II Corps.

July 13-19: CCF launched a major, six-division attack against ROK II Corps and U.S. IX Corps south of Kumsong. After retreating some eight miles to below the Kumsong River, UN forces regain the high ground along the river.

July 16-20: FAF Fighter-bombers completed a series of attacks on the Chongchon bridges rendering them unusable.

July 19:. The final session of armistice negotiations at Panmunjom convened. After meeting one day the senior negotiators agreed to adjourn while technical experts worked out the cease-fire details.

July 22: Combat between USAF Sabres and communist MiGs ended with an air battle between three 51st FIW and four communist jets. During this engagement, Lt. Sam P. Young, 25th FIS, scored the last MiG kill of the Korean War.

July 27: At 1000, Lt. Gen. William K. Harrison, Jr., USA, the senior delegate for the UN Command, and Gen. Nam Il, the senior delegate for the Korean Peoples Army and the Chinese Peoples Volunteers, signed the armistice agreement to produce a cease-fire in the Korean War. Armistice agreement was signed at 1000; all fighting stops twelve hours later; both sides have three days to withdraw two kilometers from the cease-fire line.

In the final hours before the cease-fire, Fifth Air Force fighter bombers hammered North Korean airfields. Post-strike photography from 67 TRW aircraft confirmed that every airfield in North Korea was unserviceable for jet aircraft landings, indicating the successful conclusion of the airfield neutralization program.

As the Korean War formally ended, by 10:01 p.m. all FEAF's aircraft were located either south of the front line or more than three miles from North Korea's coast.

As outlined in the Armistice Agreement, in August, prisoners of war were exchanged in Operation BIG SWITCH-77,000 communists for 12,700 UN men, of whom 3,597 were Americans.

Adapted in part from unit histories of the 18th Fighter-Bomber Wing and U.S. Air Force Historical Research Agency. January 2002. The U.S. Air Force's First War: Korea 1950-1953 Significant Events.

18th Fighter-Bomber Wing in the Korean War:
Integrity, Selfless Service and
Professional Excellence

Foundation for U.S.A.F.

After 37 months of intense, deadly combat the Korean War was over—if not totally over then at least active hostilities had ceased as part of the armistice that went into effect July 25, 1953.

The men that had served in the 18th Fighter-Bomber Wing knew that they had made a significant contribution to the United Nations effort in the Korean War. However, as it turned out no comprehensive assessment of the Wing's combat operations would be completed until publication of this book.

After the armistice was in place, veterans were busy preparing their new base at K-55 for the jet operations. Soon, however, the 18th Wing was transferred from Korea to Kadena Air Force Base on the island of Okinawa. During that transfer, many of its records from the Korean War were lost or misplaced. There was also a rapid turnover in the Wing's personnel. Those that had been in combat for many months were anxious to return to the United States or to move on to their next duty assignment—to resume some normalcy in their lives. Many important sources for a comprehensive review of the 18th Fighter-Bomber Wing's Korean War service would remain sequestered in file cabinets and behind the barriers of classified information for decades to come. A better understanding of what that great Wing had accomplished would have to wait until the records were unclassified and until its veterans were better organized to share their personal stories of combat operations.

Brigadier General Turner C. Rogers, 18th Wing Commander in 1951-1952, noted in a message to the Wing when it concluded a year of combat in 1951, "that in the years to come the 18th Wing will be a cherished memory in the hearts of the Korean people—such as the memories that I know all we Americans will keep of those hard-fighting 'Zulu Warriors,' of the 2nd South African Air Force Squadron." There were many reasons, he explained that the 18th Wing was "The Best Damn Fighter Wing in the World."

The assessment of the Wing's Korean War combat operations, the focus of research for *Truckbusters From Dogpatch,* confirmed that what this unit had accomplished during its Korean War service should rank it alongside other legendary military units of the United States Armed Forces.

Rogers' assessment rings even truer after the passage of over half a century. There are many reasons to support his opinion of the 18th Fighter-Bomber Wing during its Korean War service. As the record reveals, during the Korean War, the 18th Wing played a critical role in determining the outcome of the war on many occasions, in the process establishing an unsurpassed combat record. Less evident perhaps, but also significant, were its many contributions to the fledgling U.S. Air Force in what are now referred to as "core values." During its 37 months of Korean War combat, the 18th Wing and its component commands epitomized integrity, selfless service and command excellence. Long before those critical values were codified

and incorporated into the official U.S. Air Force Core Values of today, the 18th Wing lived by them, exemplified them, and established them as its legacy to the brand new Air Force. As such, the 18th Wing and its Veterans can take great pride in laying the foundations for what was—and remains—the greatest Air Force in the world.

When the Communists invaded South Korea, the war that followed put the brand new U.S. military service on trial. The strange, come-as-you-are conflict in an inhospitable land was going to test the men, equipment and organization of the new, independent U.S. Air Force—to their limits, as it turned out. Far East Air Forces (FEAF), the senior Air Force Command in the region, had much to learn during the three years of a conflict that was a challenging mixture of the last of the "conventional wars" and the first jet air war. However, when the shooting finally stopped on July 27, 1953, FEAF had much to be proud of regarding the record it had achieved. As Futrell summarized in *"The United States Air Force in Korea,"* in general, FEAF had acquitted itself with honor during its three years in combat. [1]

FEAF was never a large force, yet its units flew a total of 720,980 sorties—including 66,997 counter-air, 192,581 interdiction, 57,665 close support, 181,659 cargo and 222,078 miscellaneous sorties.

FEAF aircraft delivered 476,000 tons of ordnance against the enemy.

Between June 26, 1950 and July 27, 1953 Air Force, Marine and friendly-foreign aircrews claimed to have destroyed 976 aircraft, 1,327 tanks, 82,920 vehicles,

"The Best Damn Fighter Wing in the World."

Brigadier General T.C. Rogers, Commander, 18th Fighter-Bomber Wing

18th Wing Korean War Statistics

Manning: averaged about 1,700 personnel from a variety of squadrons and support groups. Generally, there were about 250 officers assigned and between 1,600-1,700 enlisted personnel, usually dispersed between the official home base and a forward operating base.

Flying Squadrons Assigned: From July 1950 through November 1950, the 12th and 67th Squadrons comprised the 18th Fighter-Bomber Group, the combat flying arm of the 18th Wing. In November 1950, they were joined for the duration of the conflict by 2 Squadron ("Flying Cheetahs") of the South African Air Force. From May 1951 through May 1952, the 39th Fighter Interceptor Squadron was attached to the 18th Group.

Planes Assigned: Generally, each squadron had between 15-20 F-51D Mustangs assigned.

Monthly Flying Time: Averaged about 4,000 (4,023) hours per month in 1951, 2,283 per month in 1952 and 1,659 hours per month in 1953—the changes reflecting the addition or subtraction of squadrons and later, in 1953, the conversion from F-51 to F-86 without standing down from combat mission requirements.

Combat Flying Hours by pilots from 18th Wing squadrons from July 1950 through July 1953 totaled 103, 635 hours— 4,318.125 days or 11.8 months of around the clock flying.

Pilots and Airmen Killed in Action: 163 (best estimate based on records review and other sources)

Fuel Consumed: 11,741,693 gallons during 37 months of combat.

Machine Gun Ammunition Expended: 32,043,545 rounds of .50-cal. machine gun ammunition were fired from 1950-1953.

High velocity aerial rockets (HVAR): Average of 6,520 per month in 1951, decreasing to 1,268 per month in 1952, and were not reported used at all in 1953. Total: 135,504 rockets reported fired at enemy targets during the war.

Napalm bombs: 20,447 in 1951, 1,566 in 1952. By 1953, napalm was not being reported as expended.

General Purpose (GP) Bombs: 21,204 General Purpose bombs in 1951, 19,844 in 1952 and a combination of 500-lb and 1,000-lb bombs in 1953—2,589 500-lb bombs and 2,550 1,000-lb bombs from January to July.

963 locomotives, 10,407 railway cars, 1,153 bridges, 118,231 buildings, 65 tunnels, 8,663 gun positions, 8,839 bunkers, 16 oil-storage tanks and 593 barges and boats. Enemy railroads were cut 28,621 times.

18ᵗʰ Wing Combat Record

The men of the 18ᵗʰ Fighter-Bomber Wing and its component commands, made many significant contributions to FEAF's overall achievements in the Korean War, many of which are only now able to be understood.

The 18ᵗʰ Wing strength throughout the war averaged about 1,700 personnel from a variety of squadrons and support groups. Generally, there were about 250 officers assigned and between 1,600-1,700 enlisted personnel.

From July 1950 through November 1950, the 12ᵗʰ and 67ᵗʰ Squadrons comprised the 18ᵗʰ Fighter-Bomber Group, the combat flying arm of the 18ᵗʰ Wing. In November, they were joined for the duration of the conflict by 2 Squadron ("Flying Cheetahs") of the South African Air Force. From May 1951 through May 1952, the 39ᵗʰ Fighter Interceptor Squadron was attached to the 18ᵗʰ Group. Generally, each squadron had between 15-20 F-51D Mustangs assigned.

Monthly flying time averaged about 4,000 (4,023) hours per month in 1951, 2,283 per month in 1952 and 1,659 hours per month in 1953—the changes reflecting the addition or subtraction of squadrons and later, in 1953, the conversion from F-51 to F-86 without standing down from combat mission requirements.

Although the unit records have gaps in places and were not totally standardized for reporting categories, a conservative estimate of the combat flying hours by pilots from 18ᵗʰ Wing squadrons from July 1950 through July 1953 totaled 103, 635 hours—4,318.125 days or 11.8 months of around the clock flying.

Futrell reports that FEAF units flew a total of 720,980 combat sorties, of which 181,659 were cargo missions, clearly beyond the capabilities of the F-51 Mustang. Subtracting the cargo missions from the total leaves 539,321 combat sorties. Reviews of unit histories from the 18ᵗʰ Wing, Group and component squadrons conservatively indicated a total of 62,162 sorties for 18ᵗʰ Wing units from July 1950-July 1953. This allows us to conclude that 18ᵗʰ Wing squadrons flew in excess of 10 percent (11.5 percent) of all FEAF combat sorties for counter-air, interdiction, close support, reconnaissance, air control and training missions.

FEAF reported a total of 1,466 aircraft lost in combat during the Korean War. In air operations FEAF sustained a total of 1,841 officer and airmen casualties during the war, including 1,144 dead, 306 wounded, 30 missing men who returned to military control, and 214 POW's who were repatriated.

While all losses are regrettable, and FEAF lost many of its finest young men, as Futrell notes, "considering the destruction wrought upon the Red aggressors by air attack, FEAF's loses of men and planes were amazingly light."

Of the 1,144 dead reported by FEAF, at least 163 (14.3%) were pilots and airmen from the 18ᵗʰ Fighter-Bomber Wing.

[This figure includes both pilots and airmen and is based on a review of various records, some of which are not in agreement. It represents the author's best estimate of combat causalities to 18ᵗʰ Wing personnel during the Korean War.]

During more than 62,000 combat sorties, 18ᵗʰ Wing aircraft delivered a staggering amount of ordnance to targets that ranged the length and breadth of the Korean Peninsula.

The 18ᵗʰ Wing consumed nearly 12 million gallons of fuel (11,741,693) during 37 months of combat. Interestingly, the reported monthly fuel consumption more than doubled in 1953 following conversion to the F-86.

More than 32 million rounds (32,043,545) of .50-cal. machine gun ammunition were fired from 1950-1953.

High velocity aerial rockets (HVAR) were heavily used early in the war—an average of 6,520 per month in 1951—but that average decreased to 1,268 per month in 1952, and were not reported used at all in 1953. Nevertheless, a total of 135,504 rockets were reported fired at enemy targets during the war.

Napalm bombs were also heavily used early in the war—20,447 in 1951—but then were significantly reduced in 1952—1,566. By 1953, napalm was not being reported as expended. Early in the conflict napalm destroyed or neutralized more T-34 tanks than all other airborne weapons combined, according to FAF operational analyses. Approximately ten times as many tanks were claimed to have been destroyed (or 14 times as many hit) by rockets as by napalm. While a relatively large effort was expended in shooting rockets at enemy tanks, and apparently resulting in hits, actually only a small fraction were hits.

The 18ᵗʰ reported using 21,204 General Purpose bombs in 1951, 19,844 in 1952 and a combination of 500-lb and 1,000-lb bombs in 1953—2,589 500-lb bombs and 2,550 1,000-lb bombs during seven months of combat prior to the Armistice.

Surprise Attack—Come As You Are, War

18ᵗʰ Called to Action

As the sheer numbers attest, the 18ᵗʰ compiled a remarkable record for missions and ordnance. However, the records established by the 18ᵗʰ Wing and its component squadrons seem even more remarkable when we consider where it was and what it was doing when the Korean War broke out unexpectedly in June 1950.

In 1949, the 18ᵗʰ Fighter-Bomber Group, based in the Philippines, finally got its chance to fly the jet aircraft it had been waiting on for four years. The Group converted to the new (to them) P-80C's in late 1949. Soon after that, they flew the old Mustangs down to Manila and gave them to the Philippine Air Force. They did not realize it at that time, but the pilots and those venerable aircraft would soon cross paths in a country called Korea.

One of the first decisions made by the US Air Force after the North Koreans invaded South Korea, was to shift from defense to offense by attacking the supply train and combat units of the North Korean army. It was quickly apparent that jet aircraft could not provide the time on station needed when conducting close support operations.

The runways in Korea could not handle high-performance jet aircraft. However, if these aircraft were based in Japan, they could not stay on station long enough to be effective. While the Jets might perform adequately for short periods of time, the Mustangs had far greater range and could loiter over targets for hours and use shorter and rougher runways. It was obvious that every Mustang that could be rounded up in the Far East and from the United States would be needed as soon as possible.

Squadrons that had already converted to the P-80 "Shooting Star" aircraft were hurriedly retrained to fly the prop-driven Mustangs once again.

At the outbreak of the Korean War in June 1950, the 18th Fighter-Bomber Wing was based at Clark Air Base in the Philippines "in a cadre state." [2] Within a week of the North Korean assault, it was ordered to supply a single fighter squadron for duty in Korea. A volunteer contingent was identified and given the name "Dallas Project," which became the "Dallas Squadron" upon its arrival in Japan at Johnson Air Base on July 10, 1950. The first priority was to cross train the pilots from F-80s back into F-51s to satisfy Air Force mission requirements. After just four transition sorties, "new" F-51 pilots were flying combat missions.

The first Korean War combat mission for the "Dallas Squadron" of the 18th Fighter-Bomber Group was flown on July 15th—making the Dallas Squadron one of the first U.S. Air Force units to go into combat in Korea. "They flew F-51s against the enemy forces during the early days in an effort to slow down the North Korean offensive and offer some protection to our withdrawing, greatly outnumbered, troops," the Air Force Times reported. [3]

By July 27th, the squadron was based at Taegu Air Base, Korea. "The initial volunteers were rushed to the airstrip at Taegu to furnish some of the first close tactical ground support of the Korean conflict." [4]

The "51st Provisional," "Dallas," "Bout One," and "Six-Double-O-Deuce" were all terms that marked the progress of the 18th Fighter-Bomber Wing "from a volunteer unit, hastily assembled in the Far East" in June-July 1950 until December 1, 1950 when it was moved "on paper" from the Philippines to Pyongyang, North Korea, absorbing the personnel, F-51 aircraft, and combat responsibilities of the 6002nd Tactical Support Wing.

"Syngman Rhee, Republic of South Korea president, soon dubbed the unit 'The Flying Tigers of Korea.' The volunteer squadron grew rapidly. Col. Curtis R. Low assumed command and molded these squadrons, plus additional personnel into the 6002nd Tactical Support Wing. It was later redesignated the 18th Fighter-Bomber Wing..." [5]

[Note: Master Sergeant (Retired) Thomas "Red" Ryder pointed out that the 18th Wing has had two name changes since the Korean War. In 1958 it became the 18th Tactical Fighter Wing and in 1993 it was designated the 18th Wing.]

In November, 1950, the South African government dispatched its "2" Squadron, with a full complement of F-51 Mustangs and personnel. The first United Nations air wing was a reality.

Typical Combat Operations

Combat operations for Mustangs of the Group revolved around "the use of four-ship flights on close support mis-sions." This tactic was "found to be the most effective and the most efficient." Two-ship flights were also used when needed "due to the requirements of the situation."

In general, the two-ship flights operated as a team, "often making simultaneous strafing runs from different directions in order to diffuse enemy fire. Passes were varied as much as weather and terrain permitted, taking advantage of the sun and natural cover to minimize the danger from anti-aircraft and small-arms fire."

Four-ship operations "were much the same" except that "while two of the ships were working over the target the other two ships would remain at a high altitude, affording top cover against air attack and spotting ground-fire sources, artillery and troop positions."

With time, as air operations became "more stabilized" the four-ship flight became the predominant type and "was very effective on ground support, reconnaissance and other type missions."

Most armed reconnaissance flights were flown carrying napalm, rockets and .50-caliber rounds. The great majority of the time rockets or machine-gun fire would be used to attack the target instead of the napalm.

In close support missions the speed of the aircraft was not an essential factor, but rather the fact that the plane was capable of short field landings and takeoffs and could carry a great deal of ordnance. Although the Mustang did have the advantage of an armored cockpit, it was vulnerable to small arms fire, and that vulnerability would continue to cost the lives of Mustang pilots throughout the Korean War.

The 18th was destined to play a prominent part in the Fifth Air Force's role on the peninsula. It was certainly omnipresent. "During the first six months operations in Korea, from July through December 1950, the wing moved five times and operated from three different areas." [6]

In less than six months of operations in Korea, the new Wing flew more than 6,200 "effective combat sorties totaling

17,800 flying hours." It required that ground crews, maintenance, supply and "even administrative personnel" often worked up to 18 hours each day.

From November 1950 through January 1951, it earned a Distinguished Unit Citation for destroying roughly 2,400 enemy vehicles and severely damaging almost 500 more.

In November 1950, pilots of the 67th Squadron provided the first pictures (gun camera film) of enemy jet fighter type aircraft to FAF. The aircraft were identified as MIG-15s that "strongly resemble the F-86 American fighter aircraft."

Major General Earle E. Partridge fired off a Letter of Commendation to the 67th Fighter-Bomber Squadron in November 1950 that singled out the "Elsewhere Squadron" for a special commendation. "Within the Joint Operations Center, the code name 'Elsewhere,' is fast becoming a legend. It appears regularly in conjunction with reports of downed enemy aircraft," Partridge wrote. "I wish to commend the officers and airmen of the 67th Fighter Squadron of the 18th Fighter-Bomber Group for their fine display of courage, aggressiveness, and determination to seek out and destroy the enemy in the air. The exploits of this unit reflect a spirit of cooperation that is exemplary of the best traditions of the United States Air Force. We are now encountering an enemy who possesses aircraft of performance equal or superior to our own and who is daily growing bolder. We must depend upon the superior quality of our fighter pilots and the aggressive spirit exhibited by the "Elsewhere" squadron to maintain supremacy in the air over our Forces in North Korea."

From early 1951 until January 1953, the 18th Group and its tactical squadrons, moving from base to base in South Korea, operated separately from the rest of the 18th Wing. The Group earned its second Distinguished Unit Citation from April 22 to July 8, 1951, when it flew 6,500 combat sorties while operating from sod, dirt filled and damaged runways to counter the enemy's 1951 spring offensive.

The 21 June 1951 issue of *Truckbusters* noted, "the 18th Fighter-Bomber Wing…has sought out and pursued the elusive enemy in the air and on the ground. In the first eleven months of the Korean Action it destroyed 1,420 enemy trucks."

By July 1952, the 18th Wing had completed over 45,000 combat sorties. Throughout the Korean War the 18th Wing was first in the total number of effective combat sorties. It remained in combat until the Armistice was signed in July 1953.

Tactical Accomplishments

The 18th Group was one of the first Air Force combat units in country and could provide the critical close air support and armed reconnaissance mission support so desperately needed if UN forces were to escape being forced out of Korea in a replay of Dunkirk. It played a critical role in reversing the tide of North Korean troops that had poured across the 38th Parallel and down the peninsula, pushing UN forces into what was called the "Pusan Perimeter."

Although the Inchon Landing—and therefore Gen. Douglas MacArthur—is generally given credit for the dizzying tactical turnaround in September 1950, in fact it had actually begun weeks before as a direct result of the relentless aerial assault on North Korean troops, positions, and supply lines by fighter bombers. Being one of the few such units actually based in Korea during that period, the 18th Fighter-Bomber Wing played a pivotal role in changing the direction of the Korea War in August 1950. Without its contribution, it could be argued that the outcome of the Korean War would have been seriously in doubt.

North Korean POW's reported that air action destroyed more than 70 percent of their tanks, trucks and artillery pieces and inflicted 47 percent of the casualties they sustained. We must not overlook the fact that "decisive air attacks against the enemy's rear and strong Eighth Army de-

fensive actions had already destroyed the effectiveness of the North Korean Army" as the prelude to the successful landing at Inchon, Futrell points out in his authoritative history of U.S. Air Force operations in the Korean War.. [7]

By failing to recognize the significant contribution to initial "victory" in South Korea made by Air Force interdiction efforts, General MacArthur made "a fateful decision" in October 1950 to press forward to the Yalu. As the UN supply lines grew long, those of the Communist forces grew shorter and were less exposed to air attack. With the sudden appearance of Chinese Communist troops in large numbers along a narrow zone up to the Yalu, UN air forces could not conduct decisive attacks. However, once UN forces were in the process of being forced back down the peninsula. UN air forces, particularly the fighter bombers, greatly delaying and harassing CCF movements, gave the Eighth Army time to withdraw in a more orderly fashion and prepare defenses, and inflicted some 40,000 casualties on the Chinese—the equivalent of removing five Chinese divisions from the conflict. [8]

Extraordinary Mision Capability

The Truckbusters of the 18th Fighter-Bomber Wing flew every possible type mission that could be undertaken by a fighter aircraft and on almost a daily basis, as noted by Lt. Gen. Brett in the Foreward to this book. Most combat sorties involved fulfilling several different missions and using different ordnance. "I honestly believe that no other Fighter Wing during the Korean War even came close to performing such diverse, challenging and tough missions, as did the Truckbusters," he notes. "If one statistically measures the cost effectiveness of all types of ground targets destroyed, the Truckbusters would come out clearly on top. Case in point, unlike the fighter bomber Jets, we Mustang drivers on almost every mission hit more than one target and frequently two, three or more with our bombs, rockets and .50-caliber ammo and rarely came home with any ordnance on board having expended it on either the assigned target or targets of opportunity. For us Mustang drivers North Korea was always a target rich environment, as we could take the time and get down low to find targets and then work them over with deliberate skill."

The Wing was the first U.S. Air Force unit to have one its members receive the Congressional Medal of Honor for action in Korea (Major Louis J. Sebille), who, when mortally wounded, deliberately crashed his Mustang into an enemy armored vehicle and troops on August 5, 1950.

By the end of August 1950, all Air Force tactical units, including the 18th Group, had been withdrawn from Korea to Ashiya, Japan, but were still flying lengthy missions to stabilize the Pusan Perimeter. Significantly, the 18th Group was the first Air Force tactical combat unit to be returned to Korea. By September 9, 1950, the 18th Group was relocated to K-9 near Pusan. Clearly, the Pusan Perimeter had been stabilized, it would hold and it could be expanded that much more rapidly with close air support at hand. Of course, during the Inchon Landing about a week later, the 18th Group played a key role in providing air cover for the landing forces and interdiction of enemy supplies and reinforcements.

Early in its combat role, the "Truckbuster" tag was applied to the 18th after its squadrons destroyed 126 trucks in one day. "This can be attributed to the 'Pioneer' volunteers who evolved low-level attack techniques that today are SOP when attacking enemy equipment." [9] Enemy losses credited to pilots of the 18th from July through December 1950 included 16 enemy aircraft, almost 1,300 trucks, 190 tanks and 75 locomotives destroyed and an estimated 10,150 enemy troop casualties.

The 18th was the first unit to integrate another nation's air arm into its attached squadrons, thus forging a United Nations fighter-bomber wing when the 2nd Squadron South African Air Force joined the 18th in November 1950. The collaboration between the South Africans and the Americans would be extraordinarily effective, harmonious and would last to the present day.

Early in the Korean War, the great majority of Truckbuster pilots were Regular officers and enlisted airmen. However, by early 1951, these veterans, particularly the pilots were in the process of being rotated out of the combat zone as they completed their missions--or were wounded or killed. Increasingly, the replacements would be Reserve Officers and Enlisted personnel. As noted by General Brett, "My first experience with Reserve and Air National Guard personnel was upon being assigned to the 39th. To me this was then and is now very important, as the Reserves, both officers and enlisted, made up the majority of Wing Personnel." In addition to being the first unit to integrate another nation's combat squadron into its operations, the 18th would fight during most of the war with the majority of its personnel being Reservists from Air Reserve and Guard units. In so doing, the Wing was among the very first Air Force tactical units to prove that a superior combat team could be forged from units and personnel with vastly different backgrounds.

"In every respect they [Reserve and Guard personnel] were absolutely superior individuals," noted General Brett, "not only being incredibly dedicated and patriotic, but their experience and professional skills made the never-ending exceptional performance of the Truckbusters possible. In modern terms they made the outstanding performance of the Wing a 'GIVEN'!"

Following the collapse of the North Korean Army and its precipitous retreat after Inchon, the 18th was the first Air Force unit to fly combat missions from airstrips north of the 38th Parallel. Four 18th Fighter-Bomber Group F-51 Mustangs, led by Major Arnold Mullins, CO of the 67th "took off Sunday [October 15, 1950] from the newly occupied air field at Wonsan, above the 39th parallel in North Korea, on the first mission to be flown from that strip," noted Captain Tom Baird in a *Stars and Stripes* article. "This was the first North Korean air field to be utilized by the UN forces since the beginning of Korea hostilities."

Eighteenth Wing Mustangs were the first to encounter the Russian MIG jets in combat over Korea. "Last November fighter pilots of the 18th encountered the first MIG-15 enemy jets to be seen over Korea. In the first days of that month 18th pilots destroyed two conventional type YAK-3's, five YAK-9's, and probably destroyed two MIG-15's in aerial combat," the unit history reported.

The Dogpatchers, as they were already being called, of the 18th Fighter Bomber Group attached to the 6002nd Tactical Support Wing, continued to press home their attacks even when UN forces were driven back down the peninsula by the intervention of Chinese Communist Forces that month. Again, it can be argued that without the support offered by the 18th Wing and its three Mustang squadrons, the "strategic withdrawal" might well have become a catastrophic military disaster.

Pilots of the 18th Wing were the first to carry the new tank-demolishing 6.5 rockets into combat. One flight of F-51's equipped with the new rocket and led by Maj. Harry Moreland, was known as "Moreland's Tank Busters" because of their feats.

Improbably, an 18th Wing flight was the first Air Force unit to capture enemy troops while flying aircraft during a combat mission. Night flying was "not uncommon with the volunteer group. The pilots flew their Mustangs frequently through the inky darkness searching out enemy troops or equipment. When they spotted headlights, fires, or other tell-tale signs they dove in for the kill. These same pilots set a precedent early in the war by capturing and delivering enemy troops to UN forces while flying overhead at more than 250 mph, and without firing a shot. Two pilots lined up 12 enemy troops in a road and by buzzing low over their heads marched them four miles down the road to UN troops. Later, more enemy troops—fearing the blazing guns, fire bombs, and low flying Mustangs—surrendered to the 18th pilots, who notified ground troops to 'walk in' and take over." [10]

In early 1951, the CCF launched two massive ground attacks against UN forces designed to drive them back down the peninsula to the sea. In both attacks, the contributions made by 18th Mustangs were significant in stopping the advances.

The second phase of the CCF spring offensive against ROK troops in eastern Korea was a last, vain attempt to drive UN forces from the Korean peninsula. Due to FEAF daytime aerial superiority and attacks, however, enemy forces were limited to nighttime assaults. "During the month of May we flew four ship flights on armed reconnaissance seeking out and destroying enemy troops, vehicles and supplies," reported the Commander of the 12th Squadron, Major John Rees. He noted that 500-pound bombs were used to posthole roads and railroads, and explained that "much napalm was used effectively against enemy troops, villages, railroad tunnels and supply dumps. It is believed that the success of tactics accounted heavily in halting the enemy's offensive push and putting him in full scale retreat all along the entire front." [11]

At the beginning of April 1951, United Nations ground forces were advancing steadily along most of the front. Soon after, Communist forces launched an all out spring offensive using over 330,000 troops and "human wave" tactics. By the end of April, Communist forces were outside the capital city of Seoul. But there the offensive ground to a halt in the face of unrelenting UN ground, and perhaps most importantly, aerial assaults.

The 18th Wing was heavily involved in close support and interdiction operations throughout the month of April that played a major role in stopping the Chinese offensive. The Wing's operations were heavily stressed, because it was not even operating from its home base. And, because runway repairs were still being made at K-10, its squadrons had to conduct their combat operations from several other bases in south east Korea. It used the Seoul municipal airport (K-16) as an advance operating base. The Chinese offensive almost overran the air base.

"At K-16 we met a vicious attack from the Chinese that came close enough to our base we could see the artillery fire—without field glasses," Henry "Hank" Lunsford recalled. However, rearming and refueling at K-16, made "our pilots' missions approximately 15 minutes long….For a few days we—the Communication's Technicians—loaded ammunition, fuel, and any thing else we could get our hands on until nightfall when we would resume working on our aircraft's radios. If the radio went out during daylight hours the pilot kept his place in line, continued his missions without a radio. When it became too dark to fly and the planes were on the ground, we fixed the radios!"

The challenges faced by the 18th Wing in April 1951 (just one of 37 months in combat) in conducting its combat operations illustrate what its commanders were faced with throughout the war. Even though it was then short of pilots, operating from three different bases throughout South Korea, and faced with the perennial challenges of topography and weather, it nevertheless successfully completed nearly 1,500 combat sorties that month and flew over 4,000 combat hours. The ability to overcome so many obstacles to conducting successful combat operations was clearly a major factor in helping United Nations forces stop the 1951 spring offensive and eventually to push the Communists back above the 38th parallel. No matter what was happening on the flight line or in the maintenance hangars or in the operations shack, the Fifth Air Force could always count on the 18th Fighter-Bomber Wing to fulfill its assigned missions.

Wing-Base Organization

The Korean War was the first opportunity by the new military service to test the concept of Wing-Base organization. By April 1951, it was clear that the "main weakness of the present Wing-Base organization as applied to the Fighter-Bomber wartime mission is that it lacks the inherent mobility desired of tactical aviation."

The solution employed by the 18th Wing in Korea was to employ the basic organizational structure of a Wing, but to modify operations and personnel assignments to create a split-base operation. Basing much of the headquarters and heavy maintenance functions at K-10, but staging combat missions out of bases much farther north and closer to the front lines enabled the 18th to achieve the necessary mobility "without loss of efficiency." However, the Wing was required to man and equip two (or more) bases. This made it necessary to reevaluate the entire Wing organization plans for personnel and equipment—plans that had been created and funded in peace time. Maintaining effective sortie rates at an advanced base required "pro-rated shares of personnel and equipment" provided "that mobility is the prime consideration." Maintenance at the forward base was limited to that which could be accomplished "by Squadron engineering personnel in not more than three hours or sufficient to prepare an aircraft for a "one-time" flight back to the rear base."

A fighter-bomber wing had to prepare for its "wartime mission" by training "to be mobile-minded in peacetime," including conducting "actual operations from satellite bases utilizing the required personnel and ground equipment with the assistance of suitable transport aircraft."

The lesson was clear to Gen. T.C. Rogers and other senior Air Force commanders in Korea, "the two workloads involved in the operation of the Wing-Base organization are diametrically opposed in the peacetime mission." The workload incident to the operations of an installation in peace time is static by nature. "The mission of a Fighter-Bomber Wing, is on the contrary, mobile. All peacetime training missions should consider this requirement and make plans accordingly." [12]

On May 8, 1951, the 18th Group began operations from the K-16 (Seoul Municipal Airport) airstrip and throughout many months thereafter conducted almost all of its combat effort from that field.

Each squadron kept ten aircraft and pilots at K-16. In addition "each squadron provided one more flight to fly missions from K-16 each day. Normally a flight would leave K-10 in the morning, land at K-16 and fly missions from there for the remainder of that day and the following two days, returning to K-10 on the afternoon of the third day," the Group reported.

"Although the use of this base has presented certain operational handicaps, such as a shorter, rougher runway and limited maintenance and living facilities, the tactical advantage of this location is patent. 13 Using Seoul instead of Chinhae, "reduced the average flying time per sortie from approximately two hours and twenty four minutes to an hour and thirty six minutes. The advantages accruing from this situation are likewise apparent," Lt. Col. Hank Lawrence, CO of the 67th Squadron noted. "Statistically, the most tangible benefit is indicated by the 25% increase in the number of combat sorties flown by the squadron." Another important benefit of operating almost two hundred miles closer to the "bomb line" was "the substantial increase in the striking range of the squadron, which may be translated into added staying power in the normal target areas should the mission require it. The northern extremes of North Korea are once again within easy reach of the squadron."

About half of the squadron's armament personnel were relocated to Seoul and assigned to rearming and refueling returning planes. "Aircraft were rearmed, refueled, and minor maintenance accomplished immediately upon landing and dispersed for assignment to another mission." Pilots were "able to attack enemy troops and positions continuously and contributed greatly to the United National ability to first repulse and later attack the enemy."

Major maintenance was the primary task of armament personnel based at Chinhae. "Through new methods and efficient teamwork of available manpower, the two

operations were coordinated successfully." Due to the increased volume of ordnance expenditures replacement of guns, bomb racks and related armament equipment was "at a new high." However, the "loading and arming of aircraft has been exceptionally fast and efficient, thereby adding to the success of the squadron's combat efforts. It is also a credit to the Engineering Section in that aircraft were kept in commission to a high degree, resulting in greater operating efficiency."

Joint Operations

Joint military operations are today considered so fundamental that it is difficult to imagine a time when such operations were rare. However, the 18th Wing was in the forefront of what are today called "joint ops." It was Capt. Harry Moreland, Commander of the "Dallas Squadron" who led the first joint Air Force-Navy-Marine Corps fighter-bomber mission.

In November 1950, the 67th and 12th U.S. Air Force Squadrons were joined in the 18th Fighter-Bomber Group by 2 Squadron SAAF, creating the first joint command for UN forces.

On May 9, 1951, for example, pilots from the 18th F-B Group joined Fifth Air Force and 1st Marine Air Wing fighter-bombers to fly over 300 sorties against Sinuiju Airfield in extreme northwestern Korea—"the largest mission of this sort in the Korean war to date." The objectives assigned to the 18th during this "spectacular fighter strike" were "important," Lt. Col. Henry W. Lawrence reported. "Excellent planning and intelligence" supported the effort. Each specific target was illustrated during briefing by reconnaissance photographs, and the pilots participating stated later that they had no difficulty in recognizing or locating their pre-briefed targets. All flights from this squadron reported excellent results from their napalm and strafing. The tactical efficiency with which their strike was conducted is evidenced by the absence of losses, either of pilots or aircraft." 14

Rescue CAP missions were frequently

joint operations. For example, on June 25, 1952, Mission 1890 from K-46 was directed at protecting a helicopter from ARS 3 that had been dispatched to pick up a Navy "Corsair" pilot flying off the USS Bon Homme Richard (CV 31).

Radar Controlled Bomb Drops

Radar controlled bomb drops are not new innovations by today's standards, but in July 1952 the Wing reported "this was the first time extensive use was made of this type of operation. The aircraft were vectored over the target by a radar controller who told the pilot when to release the ordnance. Effective bombing was done with as little as 200 feet error from 11,000 feet altitudes.

End of an Era

Finally, the 18th Fighter-Bomber Wing was the last American combat unit to fly the P/F-51 "Mustang" in combat—ending an era during which the Mustang reigned supreme as the world's best fighter plane. Only in January 1953 was the 18th Wing converted to the F-86 fighter-bomber jet aircraft. "The above aircraft were the last USAF single engine, propeller-driven aircraft to be flown in offensive combat. The excellent results of these two missions were a fitting tribute to the end of another phase of aviation development."

"F-51s have given the Air Force its strongest contender for top place in the annals of military aviation, and the deeds of their pilots have won the profoundest admiration and respect of military men the world over."

Christmas Card from 18th Fighter-Bomber Wing "Dogpatch" 1951

As a tribute to its leadership and adaptability, the 18th Wing is the only known Air Force flying unit to be asked to convert from one type of aircraft to another—while engaged in combat and without "standing down" from required combat mission completions—not once, but twice and while operating from "forward operating bases." In July 1950, 18th Wing squadrons were ordered to convert from F-80 "Shooting Star" jet aircraft to the aging F-51 "Mustang" fighter-bomber. In January 1953, 18th Wing Squadrons converted from the F-51 "Mustang" to the F-86 "Sabrejet"—again while in active combat and while meeting all operational commitments.

In a 9 October 1997 letter to Lt. Col. Flamm D. Harper, USAF (Ret.), the Air Force History Support Office noted "you stated your interest in gaining some recognition for the unique accomplishment of the 18th Fighter-Bomber Wing in converting from piston-engine F-51's to high performance jets (F-86F) at a new base, in winter, and in a combat zone." "We agree," wrote Col. Christine L. Jaremko, "in fact, we cannot find another example of a similar conversion in the history of the Air Force."

Interdiction Led To Armistice

Throughout 1951, it was UN air-interdiction attacks, led by the fighter-bombers that applied disruptive force in the rear of Communist forces that "were a decisive factor which enabled the Eighth Army to hold its positions against Red assaults and finally to force the enemy back north of the 38th Parallel." [15]

In August 1951, UN air forces began full-scale interdiction attacks on the railway system. The objective was to interfere with and to disrupt the enemy's lines of communications to such an extent that he would be unable to contain a determined offensive by UN forces or be able to mount a sustained major offensive himself. After ten months of such "attention," the North Korean railway system was badly shattered. While it could not support a sustained Communist ground offensive, the enemy was always able to get just enough materiel up to the front line to sustain basic operations. Not enough UN air power could be focused on the system to bring it to full collapse and force the Reds to ac-

cept UN armistice terms.

By effective use of manpower and while suffering enormous casualties, the Communists were able, periodically, to bring together enough supplies at dispersed front line stockpiles to support intensive periods of all-out ground combat. In every case, when they launched these ferocious attacks, they did so in the face of heavy, even catastrophic losses of manpower and materiel inflicted by air firepower—predominately delivered by fighter-bombers. Thus, each attack, while bloody and initially effective, would be short, attrited to the point of exhaustion by the napalm and bombs during CAS by the fighter-bombers. No Red offensive could ever bring enough of its superior manpower to bear for long enough to achieve a lasting ground victory. Finally, with no hope for victory, nor any realistic prospects except to continue suffering enormous losses of men and equipment, the Communists agreed to an Armistice that took effect on July 27, 1953.

A Legacy for U.S. Air Force Units

A thorough review of the record established by the 18th Fighter-Bomber Wing and its component organizations provides the perspective needed to understand that in addition to its unsurpassed combat record, the 18th Wing's service and dedication served as an important benchmark for subsequent Air Force units. During its arduous, sometimes grueling 37 months of combat in Korea, one of the most important legacies the 18th bequeathed to those U.S. Air Force units that would follow in later years was that its Korean War service epitomized the core values needed by the fledgling military service—integrity, selfless service and professional excellence.

Integrity

Throughout the Korean War, the pilots and ground crews of the 18th Wing

demonstrated consummate adaptability in the face of constant obstacles that ranged from old equipment, weather and topography to being far down on the Air Force list of priorities and at the end of a supply chain on the other side of the world. They were professionals who knew their jobs and performed their duties diligently.

Improvisation and Adaptation

Creative adaptation and resourceful, ingenious improvisation were hallmarks of 18th Wing squadrons.

Early in 1951, in one of countless examples from the record that could be cited of the Wing having to fend for itself in improvising much of its own equipment, in addition to "standard signals for in-flight procedures," an externally carried drop tank "properly modified was prepared for swift transport to a downed pilot. The contents of this tank were intended to supplement the normal escape and evasion equipment carried by the pilot in the event that rescue by normal means (e.g. beyond helicopter and/or liaison aircraft range) was not possible. Too, the possibility of a pilot being forced down behind enemy lines wherein a rescue could not be effected due to darkness, the high speed of an F-51 in transporting such additional emergency equipment improved survival percentages," the Group Commander explained. The "escape and evasion drop tank" contents even included "a miniature VHF receiver and transmitter.

The ability to accept rapid change without losing organizational effectiveness or morale was virtually an every day occurrence to Truckbuster units.

Wing leadership down to the flight line never knew what to expect in the way of missions, assignments or orders. However, it always seemed to be able to take them in stride, make any changes or adjustments needed, and get on with putting ordnance on targets.

For example, the Wing was notified

on 5 May 1951 that the 35th Fighter-Interceptor Group, to which the 39th Fighter-Interceptor Squadron had been assigned since January 1942, was to be deactivated—AND—the 39th would be attached to the 18th Fighter-Bomber Group within several days. Obviously, the billet areas, flight line areas, and "the people" at K-10 were quite unprepared for the incoming unit. [16]

Notwithstanding the short notice, 39th Squadron "was ordered to be operational at K-10 by 2400 hours 12 May 1951." Motor pools at both K-10 and K-9 were alerted to furnish trucks to expedite the move. "The first convoy of trucks rolled out of K-9 the morning of 10 May and after a hazardous 40 miles three hour trip over mountainous roads the convoy rolled into K-10. Officers and airmen alike pitched in to set up the flight line area on a temporary site until the permanent area could be resurfaced and buildings constructed. Trucks rolled back and forth for the next two days, at most times driven by the squadron's mechanics and armorers. By 2400 12 May 1951 the bulk of essential equipment and personnel were set up and ready for operations as ordered."

Personal courage was an everyday expectation for both pilots and ground crews.

Truckbusters were well aware of the dangers they faced. As the war progressed, the Chinese continually improved the quality and quantity of their anti-air defenses. Despite the clear and obvious dangers, 18th Wing pilots fulfilled their missions even as they worked to change tactics and doctrine to counter the increasing dangers.

The first warning of enemy radar-controlled antiaircraft guns came with the loss of three out of four F-51s making an air-to-ground attack against a target at Sin-mak in April 1951. There was a "marked increase in anti-aircraft fire" experienced by pilots, both in the rear areas of enemy territory and along the battle lines. [17]

"Five of the six aircraft losses [in June 1951] were due to damage inflicted by heavy enemy ground fire; the sixth aircraft was last seen heading out to sea south-west of Sinuiju, pursued by four MiG-15 enemy jet fighters….The high casualty rate in the early part of June could be directly attributed to the heavy build-up of anti-aircraft weapons of all types now being concentrated along the enemy main supply routes." The enemy was "well aware that those routes were favorite 'hunting grounds' and that an efficient anti-aircraft organization could definitely hamper the effectiveness of air operations. "[18]

Intelligence reports indicated that the enemy was "building up a very efficient organization of mobile anti-aircraft weapons and personnel, using a definite support fire system of several batteries under central control." These units would be moved form time to time to "increase their effectiveness." The moving tactics on numerous occasions "caused flights to blunder into flak in areas where it would not have been expected because of intelligence flak position reports from previous missions as a guide." [19]

The possibility of aerial opposition made pilots more "formation conscious" in June 1951. During armed reconnaissance missions three flight members would fly "top cover" with the flight leader "doing the actual reconnaissance work." [20]

Following the tragic losses earlier in the month of June 1951, "new tactics for reconnaissance" were adopted along with "a much more thorough appraisal of the changes in the flak map." After considerable discussion and appraisal of past experiences—"mostly bitter"—the new tactics were adopted. Instead of having two men down low and other two high, it was decided, after making many passes over our friendly flak guns at K-16, that the number two man was a sitting duck trailing his leader at 500 to 1000 feet." A new method was adopted that proved "very successful." The flight leader would go in low—"flat on the deck"—to conduct the reconnaissance. The element leader, meanwhile, was at 4,000 feet "covering the leader and keeping him informed as to towns, flak areas, and other danger spots ahead." The number two and four men followed the element leader, "keeping a sharp look out for enemy fighters."

Testing the new tactic revealed that "the leader was in little danger from ground fire as long as he stayed very low and maintained his speed." A bonus was the "improved ability to see into wooded areas and ravines from close range. The leader's apparent speed on the deck in relation to observers on the ground was terrific, making the hand traverse of ground weapons very difficult if they were to successfully lead him and hit him." [21]

Countless examples could be cited of pilots pressing home attacks in total disregard for their own safety, sometimes even when no ammunition was left. During rescue missions trying to save fellow airmen, all thoughts for personal safety were forgotten in the fierce determination to do whatever possibly could be done to extract the downed pilot. During Mission 1890 of June 25, 1952, for example, helo pilot Capt. Leslie Lear made three pickup attempts—all under heavy fire—to rescue the downed Navy pilot, Ens. Ronald Eaton. In between attempts, 18th Mustangs commanded by Capt. Elliot Ayer, made repeated, low-level attacks on the heavily defended area. After the rescue was completed and the pilot on board the now badly damaged helicopter, a lucky shot in the rotor brought it down. As Lt. Connors made several low-level passes over the helicopter attempting to determine the fate of those that had bailed out, he too was shot down, fatally crash landing from an altitude of about 150'. Three pilots were lost that afternoon, one medical crewman survived. However, their bravery was unsurpassed, even when compared with countless other heroic acts of aerial combat during the Korean War.

Duty before self

Truckbuster pilots and airmen set extraordinary examples of mental and physical stamina and toughness, while putting mission accomplishment ahead of their own needs.

Throughout the Korean War, the 18th Wing was moved frequently, was assigned to primitive bases with few creature comforts, and forced to operate from several locations simultaneously, thus forcing the undermanned wing to spread its personnel even further. The records reveal the constant struggle at every level of the Wing's organization to cope with providing even the basic necessities.

None of the air bases assigned to the 18th Wing in Korea were adequate. In fact, operating the heavily loaded and sometimes damaged Mustangs from K-10 and K-46 was risky and dangerous.

Shortly after the Wing was posted to K-10 in early 1951, units reported that several "flying hazards" at K-10 "greatly hampered night and early morning operations. The airstrip is bounded on three sides by mountains 2,000' high that are within 3 miles of the strip. The fourth side of the airstrip is formed by a bay of water. Approximately 50 feet separates the entire length of the runway from the bay. A steel hangar is located at the south end of the runway and clears the runway by a mere 50 feet. Several Quonset quarters are located within 100 feet of the runway," the record noted.

"The landing strip at K-10 is dirt and problems were immediately encountered. Large rocks on the runway were sucked into the propeller during run-ups, resulting in damage to numerous propellers and only extraordinary supply action kept such aircraft from become AOCP [Out of Commission for Parts]. [22]

Conditions were primitive at K-10, despite efforts to improvise and "make do." During April 1951, for example, organizational supply moved to a new site adjacent to the orderly room and personnel office. "This section is still housed in squad tents. Rocket boxes were used to make up flooring in order that supply personnel may work platformed above the dirt floor which is usually damp and wet during the rainy weather and also to present items of supply from suffering damage through dirt and moisture."

"Expendable supplies" were still a major problem in August 1951. Excessive numbers of requisitions were placed on "back-ordered" status. Storage spaces for supplies on hand were inadequate. As August turned into September, summer heat was rapidly replaced by "unseasonably cool weather at the advance base." Although winter clothing was now needed by early morning maintenance personnel and requisitions had been submitted for winter clothing in accordance with 8th Army directives, "no clothing has yet been issued." Major Carl C. Colson believed that "Air Materiel Commands could more expeditiously provide both clothing and expendables for Air Force units as Army Supply channels seem to have been unable to fill our needs." The maintenance personnel worked in the cold, but they kept their planes in the air.

Up to this point, squadron dirty laundry was sent back to Japan "in bundles" to be cleaned. There were no laundry facilities at the base. There was a lot of laundry for a squadron of about 180 personnel. Frequently, bundles of laundry were lost, some temporarily and others permanently "due to the large amount of handling and transporting of laundry to Japan." In August, a "small laundry" was installed at the base and was "of great value in processing fatigue clothing."

Shocking Shortages of Essential Gear and Equipment

Throughout the Korean War, the 18th struggled to fulfill its vital role as a Fifth Air Force unit that was depended upon for a wide variety of missions. The formerly classified records reveal shocking shortages of manpower, equipment, air craft, supplies, aviation gear, part and basic necessities such as living quarters.

Bad maps were cited not only in November 1950—"were so different as to cause confusion and non-identification of targets"—but six months later the problem was still an issue when the record noted that pilots were irritated and hampered in the cockpit by a shortage of maps.

At the close of the month the "situation still existed with no relief in sight." The Group Commander recommended that a "single sectional map be printed which would cover the area north and north-west of Seoul, thereby eliminating the four sectional maps now being used for that area. The mechanical difficulty in handling four maps in the cockpit of a fighter aircraft detracts from the pilot's efficiency," he said as a major understatement.

Throughout the conflict the Wing and its squadrons were chronically short of "expendable supplies," and reporting that an excessive number of requisitions on base supply have been 'back ordered' on such items as flashlight batteries, coveralls, shoes, socks and mechanics caps. Even when they were available, the quality of supplies was not helped by "having to use tents in poor repair as storage for the unit supply. Mildewing of clothing and the added burden of constantly cleaning water and dust from the individual weapons of personnel are direct results of this lack of proper building space." Work orders for floors and tent frames were "disapproved," since permanent type buildings were "in the planning stage." There was "no adequate solution in sight."

Ammunition was a constant problem, even in mid-1951 unit reports noted that the .50-caliber ammunition "is generally very old and of a very poor grade." Pilots were experiencing 30-60 percent "duds" when using the 500-lb General Purpose bombs "due to faulty primer-detonators…there have been instances where bombs armed with this primer-detonator have detonated upon impact instead of detonating after the pre-set delay." [23]

In June 1951, nearly a year into the war, life vests were in short supply…as were summer flying suits in smaller sizes. "Even more worrisome was the new Escape and Evasion (EandE) equipment that was due in the theater on 20 July. Pilots come begging for the equipment after being given the E and E lecture and all we can give them is the same promises that higher headquarters gives us." Briefing teams visiting the base told the pilots "that they should have it and to get into contact with the Intelligence Section. The section goes to the home office of the team and gets a negative answer. This particular subject has been very weak in so far as help from the higher echelon is concerned," Lt. Col. Saltsman pointed out. "We are lucky to have a very effective program of our own." Time and again the Group would report that the Wing was improvising to supply its own equipment and training when the system failed to do so.

In November 1951, the AN/URC-4 Emergency Radio Set was in very short supply—only 13 were on hand "with no resupply in sight. The assistance the URC-4 afforded in the successful rescue of downed pilots makes it extremely important that more satisfactory supply action be afforded on this item," Saltsman noted. Due to the success of recent rescue operations in which these radios have been used there is an increasing demand for them by the pilots." Improvising once more, 1st Lt. William Bryan of the 12th FBS was put in charge of a project to design and produce a "carrier" for the radio consisting of a girdle supported by suspenders with two pockets that held the radio set and its battery. The pockets were positioned "over the stomach between the parachute leg straps and below the harness release." The pilots liked it for its "comfort and handling qualities."

Issues of Olive Drab winter uniforms were "inadequate" as the Wing moved into its second winter of the war—not enough of them in the right sizes. While the winter flying clothing had been received and issued to flying personnel and line maintenance personnel, there were insufficient quantities in the large sizes. If you were a "large and heavy" pilot, you were in more danger of frostbite—personal equipment had been "unable to procure twenty-eight foot parachutes" needed by the larger pilots. "Adequate supply of these large parachutes would improve the state of mind of the large pilots," Colson noted dryly. Squadron Commander Crow described the pilots as "impatient," but "eager to perform their duties but with the proper equipment to insure their chance of living to a ripe old age." 24

Olive Drab winter clothing remained in short supply. In fact, at the end of November, the second winter of the Korean War, there were 65 airmen from the 67th Squadron that "cannot be issued winter olive drab clothing." The tents were cold, as well. The burners for tent stoves could not be obtained in sufficient quantities.

The Supply Section was then manned at a pathetic 50 percent. "The supply personnel are attempting to perform their mission," Crow noted dryly, "with success commensurate with their strength."

Over two years into the war, in September 1952, the supply of flying clothes remained "in a pitiful state. The pilots are reduced to the sorry state of having to procure their own equipment or improvise. In the matter of shoes, if a pilot's shoes wear out he cannot go to supply even to buy a pair of shoes, but must either wait until he goes on R&R or until a friend brings a pair from Japan," the 12th Squadron reported.

High Morale Despite Inadequate Credit

Truckbuster squadrons generally maintained high morale in the face of a perceived and palpable institutional bias towards other, more politically popular squadrons and despite an overall lack of public credit for extraordinary achievements.

It was a commonly held perception that recognition in the Armed Forces Newspaper, "Stars and Stripes," is "small for all Air Force units in Korea," but even less for those flying the venerable Mustangs. "The common complaint is that the 'Sabre-jets' get the writeups and that there is a notation for courtesy's sake that the Mustangs 'also ran.'" 25

In the Spring of 1952, a squadron commander was noting that "Complaints are still forth-coming from all quarters that publicity concerning the activities of this Wing should be much more widespread than at present," even as he praised the hard work and sacrifices of his men. "It is felt that even while working with a severe shortage of qualified personnel this unit has met its combat commitments only because of the determination of the few qualified personnel still assigned and the eagerness of the new men to learn." 26

The lack of a rotation policy for the first half of the war was another threat to morale. In mid-1951, Lt. Col. Ralph Saltsman noted that the lack of an adequate rotation policy was "affecting all of the personnel in the Group and morale is not high at this time. The pilots are without a goal to shoot for and the effect of the returning of pilots rotated to the Philippines last year was certainly for the bad. All of the men that have a long tour behind them in the Far East want to know when they will see home again. The effects are visible with every report in the Stars and Stripes of another boat load of Army, Navy or Marines going home. An Air Force policy would help get our team in better spirits. The improvement of the messes, new housing, and all the beauties of our 'Riviera' in Korea are the main factors that keep the men happy."

However, Saltsman closed his report on a characteristically positive tone. "We are improving," Col. Saltsman observed in June 1951. "A strong will to fight and even more pride in the unit continues. Our new sign in front of the new Group headquarters says, 'The Best Damn Fighter Group In The World,' and we believe it," he closed.

Pursuit of Excellence

Truckbuster reports indicated that leadership typically saw problems as opportunities—units frequently reported new approaches that improved the way they went about doing their jobs.

Typical was an entry in October 1950, in which the 67th Squadron reported that a chronic shortage of personnel necessitated changes in rearming the hard working planes. A "more efficient operating system was established" during which the armorer's crews were "specialized" into rocket crews, ammunition crews, and bomb crews, "in lieu of individual armorers assigned per aircraft." The new system "worked exceedingly well. The constant wear and tear on the guns and the "proximity to salt water corrosion" required the ground crews to use a heavier anti-rust oil. As the weather grew colder, the heavier oil "became congealed at low temperatures and hindered the thrust of the individual firing pins of the guns." The ingenious ground crews "rectified" the situation "by completing installation of gun-heaters" (which then allowed use of the lighter gun lubricants despite the cold weather), and constantly replacing the aging guns with new ones as they could be obtained."

The ingenuity of the ground crews was noted frequently throughout the 37 months of combat. Time and again the guys with greasy hands and dirty overalls would bring about near miracles of improvisation, process improvement, or sheer "work until they're flying again" dedication that would enable the Wing to keep enough of the old, shot-up Mustangs in the air to meet mission requirements.

A continuous improvement philosophy for tactics and work processes was clearly evident, even when it was often necessitated by critical shortages of supplies, parts and equipment.

For example, in November 1950, improvements to operational tactics included a new SOP that recommended rocket fire be "rippled" off (automatic position) against armored targets and/or clusters of vehicles. The resultant pattern would assure "a greater percentage of hits as opposed to singly-fired rockets." [27] Strafing attacks were prohibited when the Mustangs had napalm and/or ferry (external tanks, 110 gallon capacity) tanks attached. This resulted in "clean" runs and minimized the hazards incidental to being struck by small arms and/or heavier caliber automatic weapons. Take-off intervals between aircraft were changed from 5 seconds to approximately 1/2 a runway length and between flight elements- as well.

Unit reports were replete with examples of attempts to more effectively manage the mission, the men, and the resources that were provided—despite persistent shortages and inadequate supplies. Their reports detail efforts to overcome the awesome difficulties that lay in the path of mission accomplishment.

Group and squadron leaders understood the importance of training—that a pilot or an airman's life depended on good training. However, for the first 18 months of the war the "training pipeline" for Air Force units in Korea was inadequate for the task based on unit reports. All too often the reports cite shortages of adequately trained personnel or training that was not germane to the mission.

November 1951, for example, marked a period of "heavy rotation" of squadron personnel. Those leaving the squadron had "spent from six to seventeen months in Korea and are well qualified, having gained valuable experience in adverse conditions, one of these being the operation of a section under-manned." The replacements, Lt. Col. Julian Crow noted, with few exceptions, had only "recently completed an Air Force school and have no experience." Not only were the new personnel right out of school with no practical experience, they were arriving in the 67th and being provided by their orders "with a maximum of two or three days to learn from the airmen whom they are replacing their duties." The situation was worsened by the fact that even when a qualified person was available to teach the replacement their duties, "that person must cease his own activities while teaching. When this situation occurs, supervisors become workers, in-as-much-as the work has to be done. It seems hardly fair that the squadron receives an apprentice while shipping out a senior specialist technician or supervisor," Crow noted.

Operational excellence was a point of pride and the objective sought in every day's operations—from combat missions to engine inspections.

For example, in late February 1951, "armed reconnaissance of specific areas

was given emphasis" by 18th Group pilots. The various areas were assigned to the two squadrons and these areas became the squadron's responsibilities. As a result pilots became very familiar with areas after working them a few times and thus any small change in the terrain, roads or villages was noticed and investigated often disclosing camouflaged vehicles, supply or troop concentrations. This method of reconnaissance coupled with pilot meetings where camouflage techniques were discussed and evaluated resulted in the destruction of 728 enemy vehicles and heavily damaging 137 vehicles in the month of February alone." [28]

Major Carl C. Colson, the 67th's Commander, reported in September 1951 that "tactics remain generally the same," but there have been "great improvements by each individual pilot flying in the group formation. Efforts to improve group-flying skills were indeed necessary since "the squadron is now averaging two missions per day as part of a large group formation."

The 18th Wing had and used many different types of internal communications, from weekly newspaper to frequent briefings. Unit reports had many entries such as this one from February 1951, that reported the squadrons held several pilot meetings "to work out a tactical doctrine for the squadron. At each of these meetings techniques in finding camouflaged vehicles was discussed which allowed the pilots to exchange ideas. The net result was increased proficiency of all pilots in finding enemy vehicles."

Many pilots "took time after each mission," the 12th Squadron reported, "to show their crew chiefs where they had been and what they had done. This policy seemed to give the airmen a boost and made them feel that they were not working in vain."

When some "unfounded rumors" of temporary cutbacks in rotation to the United States hurt morale, "every possible attempt is made," Colson noted, "to determine the truth and to pass it on to the men." A weekly briefing by the Wing Intelligence section was conducted on Monday nights in the base theatre "primarily to keep the airmen informed of the objectives and accomplishments of the wing."

Every effort was made by 18th Wing leaders to use every possible resource as efficiently and effectively as possible. However, from the moment the 18th Wing and its pilots were ordered into combat, and throughout the course of the Korean War they would have to overcome an enormous range of challenges in order to fulfill their combat missions and responsibilities. These challenges, not only included the topography of the Korean peninsula, which was rugged, mountainous and affected by wide ranges of inclement weather; but they also included simply trying to survive and conduct their mission at the end of a U.S. Air Force supply line that stretched halfway around the world. Although shortages of basic provisions, supplies and ammunition early in the war can be understood and forgiven, similar shortages would plague the 18th wing and its support components and personnel throughout the war.

Air Power Lessons

Learned

Even as UN forces began an uneasy truce that exists to this day, there were many lessons to be learned—and applied in future conflicts—that were bought with blood and sacrifice—much of it by 18th Fighter-Bomber Wing personnel.

Propeller-driven aircraft were obsolete—the jet age had truly arrived.

As Futrell noted, although propeller-driven aircraft were successfully employed for a time in Korea, such equipment was not suitable for global conflict in a jet age. This was no surprise to the Mustang pilots of the 18th who paid the price with many lives of having to use a fighter plane designed to intercept the Luftwaffe over Europe to fly close air support and armed reconnaissance missions during the Korean War.

Air superiority was absolutely es-

sential. Without control of the air by UN forces, the Korean War would have been lost.

The successful outcome of the Korean War would have not happened had the U.S. domination of the air been reversed by the Communists.

FEAF fully understood the intent and significance of Communist efforts to rebuild their air bases in North Korea. Periodically, they were reminded that they could not hope to rebuild their air operations bases without air superiority—something they never quite achieved.

Political and military restrictions greatly complicated combat operations.

Politico-military restrictions that kept active hostilities on and above Korean soil, also allowed the Communists to rebuild and operate an air order of battle that became powerful enough to threaten the survival of UN forces in Korea. While the Communists generally did not use their aircraft against UN ground positions, it was probably because they were fearful that such use would bring reprisal raids on Chinese territory. [29]

Success of ground action depended on close air support and interdiction by fighter-bomber aircraft.

UN ground forces were always facing numerically superior Communist ground forces in Korea. Successful UN ground action required every possible assistance that UN air forces could provide that prevents the enemy from massing the full potential of his men, equipment and supplies on the battlefield.

Interdiction efforts, particularly by the fighter-bombers, used airpower to prevent, delay or destroy enemy men, supplies and equipment. The successful strategy was doubly effective: the enemy was easier to attack while he was concentrated en route to the front, and the more men and materiel destroyed away from the front lines, the less effective the enemy's battle efforts would be.

Interdiction worked best when active ground conflicts—battles—were underway. During such periods, heavy interdiction efforts help drain men and mate-

riel from both the front and elsewhere simultaneously.

It was airpower, particularly the Interdiction and Close Air Support missions flown by fighter bomber pilots that had been the decisive factor in the outcome of the ground battle in Korea. It was the relentless and effective attacks by the fighter-bombers on the Communist logistical system that had, finally, caused it to virtually collapse and had inflicted enormous casualties on its ground forces, casualties that not even they who thought so little of sacrificing human lives, could ignore.

Unrelenting interdiction eventually brought about armistice.

Finally, after a year of air attacks against their rear areas, the Communists decided that the war was too expensive for them to continue.

During the three years of the Korean War, air interdiction against the rear of Communist ground armies and close air support against its front line units had made a decisive difference in the outcome of the War. The combination of UN air superiority and the application of air power through fighter-bomber operations were, finally, what brought the Communists to the truce table.

When the United States is perceived to be militarily weak, enemies see aggression or war as a viable instrument of national (sectarian) policy.

Another important lesson was learned in Korea, one that has stood the test of time, as they say. America's weakened military forces after World War II had directly led to the Korean War. Our perceived weakness, in military arms and strength of purpose, tempted the Communists to exploit war as an instrument of national policy. They came very close to being successful.

The American people began to see that world peace does not come by unilateral disarmament or weakness, but through strength. In Korea the 18th Wing and other combat units bought with their blood and taught the American people—and the world—the lesson they must learn, it seems, over and over again—that the price of peace is eternal vigilance—and readiness to defend freedom—for us and for our allies.

Freedom is not, nor has it ever been, free. It comes with a price. Veterans of the Korean War paid that price for America and the world half a century ago.

The price of their dedicated, heroic service in Korea was steep, it was emotionally draining, at times it was tragic—but history had shown that it was worth it. Their sacrifices and enormous achievements on the ground and in the air saved a nation and its millions of citizens from lives of unimaginable bleekness, restored an ally, stopped Communist aggression, saved tens of thousands of American and Allied lives, and contributed significantly to the emergence of the United States and its brand new Air Force as a power for freedom that was better able to maintain peace through preparedness.

Endnotes

[1] Futrell, Robert F. The United States Air Force in Korea. (Washington, D.C.:U.S. Government Printing Office, 1991 Rev.), p. 693.

[2] 18th Fighter Bomber Wing Album, October 1951, Foreword.

[3] "Mustangs of the 18th F-B Wing Nearing Year of Fighting," Air Force Times, May 30, 1951, p. 10.

[4] Air Force Times, May 30, 1951, p. 10.

[5] Air Force Times, May 30, 1951, p. 10.

[6] Air Force Times, May 30, 1951, p. 10.

[7] Futrell, Robert F. The United States Air Force in Korea. (Washington, D.C.:U.S. Government Printing Office, 1991 Rev.), p. 700.

[8] Futrell. p. 701.

[9] 18th Fighter Bomber Wing Album, October 1951, Wing Headquarters Squadron.

[10] Air Force Times, May 30, 1951, p. 10.

[11] USAFHRA. Monthly Historical Report, 12th Fighter-Bomber Squadron, May 1951, p. 3.

[12] Fifth Air Force "Forward-Rear Base Operations" staff study (unsigned and undated) found in the personal papers of Brigadier General

T.C. Rogers, covering the period when he served as Commander of the 18th Fighter-Bomber Wing from 1 February 1951-2 February 1952.

[13] USAFHRA. Monthly Historical Report, 67th Fighter-Bomber Squadron, May 1951, p. 2.

[14] USAFHRA. Monthly Historical Report, 67th Fighter-Bomber Squadron, May 1951, p. 4.

[15] Futrell. p. 702.

[16] USAFHRA. Monthly Historical Report, 39th Fighter-Interceptor Squadron, May 1951, p. 3.

[17] U.S. Air Force Historical Research Agency (USAFHRA). 28 July 2001. The U.S. Air Force's First War: Korea 1950-1953 Significant Events

. http://www.au.af.mil/au/afhra/wwwroot/korean_war/korean_war_chronology/kwc_april1951.html

[18] USAFHRA. Monthly Historical Report, 67th Fighter-Bomber Squadron, June 1951, p. 2.

[19] USAFHRA. Monthly Historical Report, 67th Fighter-Bomber Squadron, June 1951, p. 3.

[20] USAFHRA. Monthly Historical Report, 12th Fighter-Bomber Squadron, June 1951, p. 4.

[21] USAFHRA. Monthly Historical Report, 67th Fighter-Bomber Squadron, June 1951, p. 5.

[22] USAFHRA. Monthly Historical Report, 18th Fighter-Bomber Wing, January 1951, p. 4.

[23] USAFHRA. Monthly Historical Report, 18th Fighter-Bomber Group, March 1951, p. 9.

[24] USAFHRA. Monthly Historical Report, 67th Fighter-Bomber Squadron, November 1951, p. 6.

[25] Far East Air Forces headquarters had specifically ORDERED Stars and Stripes to downplay the victories by the Mustangs because the new Air Force needed to convince the public regarding advantages of an all jet Air Force. "The policy ignored the impact such actions had on the morale of those who were actually doing the work," Lt. Col. Bud Biteman noted.

[26] USAFHRA. Monthly Historical Report, 67th Fighter-Bomber Squadron, January 1952, p. 8.

[27] USAFHRA. History of the 67th Fighter-Bomber Squadron, November 1950.

[28] USAFHRA. Monthly Historical Report, 18th Fighter-Bomber Group, February 1951.

[29] Futrell. p. 694.

Suggested Readings

Blair, Clay. *The Forgotten War.* New York: Times Books, 1987.

Cleveland, W. M. *Mosquitos in Korea.* Portsmouth, N.H.: Peter E. Randall Publisher, 1991.

Cline, Maj. Tim. "Forward Air Control in the Korean War." *American Aviation Historical Society Journal,* Winter 1976.

Dorr, Robert F. and Warren Thompson. *The Korean Air War.* Osceola, Wisc.: Motorbooks International, 1994.

Futrell, Robert Frank. *The United States Air Force in Korea, 1950—1953.* Washington, D.C.: Center for Air Force History, 1981. (Revised edition)

Grant, William Newby. *P-51 Mustang.* London : Arms and Armour Press, 1980.

Hallion, Richard P. *The Naval Air War in Korea.* Baltimore, Md.: Nautical and Aviation Publishing Co. of America, 1986.

Jackson, Robert. Air war in Korea, 1950-1953. Osceola, WI : Motorbooks International, 1998.

Lewis, Michael, Maj., USAF. *Lt. Gen. Ned Almond, USA: A Ground Commander's Conflicting View with Airmen over CAS Doctrine and Employment.* Maxwell AFB, Ala.: Air University, 1997. (A School of Advanced Air-power Studies thesis.)

Marion, Forrest L. That Others May Live: USAF Air Rescue in Korea. Montgomery, AL: USAF Historical Research Agency, 2004.

—. "'The Dumbo's will get us in no time': Air Force SA-16 Combat Operations in the Korean War Theater, 1950-1953." *Air Power History* (Summer 1999), 16-29.

McLaren, David R. *Lockheed P—80/F—80 Shooting Star: A Photo Chronicle.* Atglen, Pa.: Schiffer Publishing Ltd., 1996.

—. *Mustangs over Korea The North American F—51 at War, 1950—1953.* Atglen, Pa.: Schiffer Publishing Ltd., 1999.

—. *Republic F—84, Thunderjet, Thunderstreak, and Thunderflash: A Photo Chronicle.* Atglen, Pa.: Schiffer Publishing Ltd., 1998.

Millett, Allan R. "Korea, 1950—1953." In *Case Studies in the Development of Close Air Support,* edited by Benjamin Franklin Cooling. Washington, D.C.: Office of Air Force History, 1990.

Momyer, William W. *Airpower in three wars.* Montgomery, AL: Air University Press, 2003.

Moore, Dermot Michael. *South Africa's Flying Cheetahs in Korea* Johannesburg : Ashanti Pub., 1991.

Rottman, Gordon L. *Korean War Order of Battle: United States, United Nations, and Communist Ground, Naval, and Air Forces, 1950-1953.* Praeger Publishers, 2002.

Sherwood, John Darrell. *Officers in Flight Suits: The Story of American Air Force Fighter Pilots in the Korean War.* New York: New York University Press, 1998.

Toland, John. *In Mortal Combat Korea*, 1950-1953. New York: William Morrow, 1991.

Wilson, David. *Lion over Korea: 77 Fighter Squadron RAAF, 1950—1953.* Canberra: Banner Books, 1994

Warnock, A. Timothy, ed. *USAF in Korea: A Chronology, 1950-1953.* Washington, D.C.: Air Force History and Museums Program/Air University Press: 2000.

Y'Blood, William T., ed. *The Three Wars of Lt. Gen. George E. Stratemeyer: His Korean War Diary.* Washington, D.C.: Air Force History and Muse-ums Program, 1999.

—. "The U.S. Air Force in Korea, 1950-1953." *Air Power History* (Summer 2000), 38-39, 42-43.

Glossary

.50-Caliber guns

The F-51D carried six free-firing .50-caliber machine guns, three in each wing. The guns were manually charged (loaded) on the ground, and fired simultaneously when the pilot pressed the trigger switch on the front of the control stick ("joy stick") grip. The maximum ammunition capacity was 400 rounds for each of the inboard guns, and 270 rounds for the center and outboard guns—a total ammunition load of 1880 rounds. Typically, the guns were aligned to converge at a range of from 250-300 yards.

38th Parallel

The 38th degree of north latitude as it bisects the Korean Peninsula became the arbitrary demarcation line between North and South Korea from 1945 to 1948 and the border between the Republic of Korea and the Democratic People's Republic of Korea from 1948 to 1950.

500-pound bomb

AN/M64 general-purpose bomb used by USAF fighter-bombers in Korea. It was normally fused with an AN/M-103 nose fuse and an AN/M-101-A2 tail fuse.

51st Fighter Squadron (Provisional)

On July 8, 1950, General Timberlake named Taegu as the destination for the "Dallas" Squadron, which the 13th Air Force was forming from a nucleus provided by the 12th Squadron. "In response to the North Korean invasion of South Korea on Sunday morning, June 25, 1950," Lt. Col. Duane "Bud" Biteman recorded, "this reporter had gone into Korea in mid-July 1950 with the first increment of the **'Dallas Project'**, a hastily-formed squadron of volunteer fighter pilots from the U.S. Air Force's 18th Fighter-Bomber Group, then stationed at Clark Field in the Philippine Islands." The **"Dallas"** squadron arrived at Johnson Air Base on July 10th and by July 15th, was flying combat missions from Taegu, South Korea. Prior to the arrival of the "Dallas" fliers at Taegu, Fifth AF on July 10th organized the 51st Fighter Squadron (Provisional) at Taegu to take over the American personnel from **"Bout-One"** (See) and the **"Dallas"** pilots. To provide logistical support for the provisional new fighter squadron, Fifth AF organized the 6002nd Air Base Squadron and dispatched it to Korea.

A/A

Air to Air

A/C

Aircraft

A/G

Air to Ground

A/W

All-Weather

AAA

Antiaircraft Artillery

AACS

Airways and Air Communications Service, a global command that provided airways-communications facilities, navigational aids and flight services for the Air Force.

AB

Air Base

ABG

Air Base Group

Able Mable

Pilot slang for the Navy-Marine Corps AD-1 "Sky Raider"

Abn

Airborne

Absolute ceiling

See **Ceiling**.

AC&W

Aircraft Control and Warning

Ace

In aerial warfare downing five enemy aircraft qualifies a fighter pilot for the unofficial designation of "ace." There were 40 American air aces from action during the Korea War alone. Thirty-eight were from the Air Force and one each was from the Navy and Marine Corps.

Act

Action

AD

Air Division (Combat Cargo); Destroyer Tender; Douglas "Skyraider": single-engine attack plane (USA).

Air Depot

ADC

Air Defense Command

ADCOM

Advance Command and Liaison Group in Korea (Army). See **EUSAK**.

ADF

Auto Direction Finder

ADVATIS

Advanced Allied Translator & Interpreter Section

ADVON

Advance echelon

AERO

Aerobatics

Aeromedical Battlefield Evacuation

One of the major innovations of the Korean War was the use of helicopters for evacuating the wounded from the battlefield.

AF

Air Force

AFB

Air Force Base

AFF

Army Field Forces

AFFE

Army Forces Far East

AFOOP

Director of Operations, USAF

AFPMP

Director of Military Personnel, USAF

AFR

Air Force Regulations

A-Frame

A load-carrying device frequently seen in Korea. It consists of a simple wooden backpack frame built roughly in the shape of the capital letter "A" with shoulder straps of woven straw. Using this pack frame, Koreans could carry surprisingly heavy loads over the most rugged terrain.

AFSA

Armed Forces Security Agency, founded in 1949.

AFSC

Air Force Specialty Code, a serviceman's job classification.

AG

Adjutant General

AGL

Above Ground Level

Aircraft Component Parts

Structure: includes the skin, control surfaces and structural members making up the airframe.

Engine: includes the power plant and those items mounted upon the power plant including accessories, fuel lines, etc.

Fuel System: includes the fuel tanks

and the fuel lines external to the engine section.

Cockpit Compartment: includes the pilot, the canopy, and that equipment in the cockpit provided for the survival or convenience of the pilot (oxygen system, heating system, pressurization system, etc.)

Auxiliary Systems: include the hydraulic, control, armament, and other integral systems of the airplane actuated by the pilot for the functioning of the aircraft. (Memorandum No. 40, Operations Analysis Office, Hq. Fifth Air Force, 31 March 1951)

Air Medal
First authorized in World War II, the Air Medal was awarded during the Korean War in the name of the President of the United States, recognizing single acts of merit or heroism for aerial flight. Also awarded at times early in Korean War for a given number of combat flights.

Airfields
During the Korean War, the U.N. Far East Air Force (FEAF) used some 15 air bases in Japan to support combat operations in Korea. In Korea itself, the Air Force either improved or constructed some 55 airfields. These air bases were all numbered and some became better known by their number than by their name. The more important of these airfields included: **K-1** Pusan West; **K-2** Taegu; **K-3** Pohang; **K-5** Taejon; **K-6** Pyongtaek; **K-8** Kunsan; **K-9** Pusan East ; **K-10** Chinhae; **K-13** Suwon; **K-14** Kimpo; **K-16** Seoul; **K-40** Cheju-do Island; **K-46** Hoengsong; **K-47** Chunchon; **K-55** Osan.

Air-to-Air Tactics
"Attack by enemy aircraft is to be expected at any time," 18th Fighter-Bomber Group Standardized Procedures for Combat Operations explained. "If an attack is made by conventional aircraft, the speed, firepower and rate of turn of the F-51 will keep you out of trouble if you keep your eyes open and deprive them of the element of surprise. If the attack is made by enemy jet types, the Mustang still has many very definite advantages if the pilot remains calm and uses them. To panic and try to outrun or outdrive [sic] a jet is inviting disaster. Keep the flight intact and use your tighter turning radius, low fuel consumption and greater rate of fire. At altitudes below ten thousands feet the jet will use his fuel so fast that he'll soon have to break off and head for home. Defensive tactics are a vital part of any combat

flying. Although it may sometimes be necessary, because of our slower speed, to go on the defensive, we must never lose our aggressiveness. We can't force the enemy into a fight, but if he wants one we can make him fight against a TEAM rather than an individual aircraft, and we can choose our altitude. Only through teamwork—as a flight, section or squadron—can we accomplish our mission. We must be ready at all times to go on the defense. Our first and best defense against enemy jet aircraft is to see them before they start the attack. Therefore we must fly the formation that enables us to visually cover the greatest area. Our present, fingertip, combat formation gives us the most visual coverage, but lacks a certain amount of flexibility and maneuverability for mutual support against attacking jet aircraft. The combat fingertip formation will be flown at all times going to and from the target. Upon sighting enemy aircraft, the respective wingmen will close in on their leaders to about 45 degrees, where they can best hang on during hard, sharp turns in either direction. All breaks should be into and under the supporting element in order that they may protect your tail by turning into the enemy. Do not break until the enemy has committed himself on the attack. After the elements cross, they will reverse their turns to come out on the original heading as before. If the enemy attacks from 6 o'clock it will be necessary to continue to turn a complete 180-degrees and then make another 180-degree turn back to the desired heading. A weave or scissor should then be started for mutual support. Since jets climb at higher speeds than the cruising speed of the F-51, attacks can often be expected from the six o'clock low position. It is imperative that these attacks be discovered before they are within firing range. The weaving formation affords you the best opportunity to cover that position. As a general rule it is best to work the flight down to an altitude where the jets cannot make overhead passes and their fuel consumption is greatly increased. Four thousand feet, depending on terrain, is considered a good altitude because it gives you room enough to maneuver without fear of running into the ground."

Albatross
SA-16; amphibious rescue aircraft. See **Chodo**.

ALO

Air Liaison Officer

ALT
Altitude; Alternate

ALTN
Alternate

Aluminum overcast
See **Globemaster**.

AM
Amplitude modulation

AMC
Air Materiel Command

Ammo
Ammunition

AMS
Army Map Service

an.
Annex

AN/ARC-3
Transmitting and receiving equipment designed to provide air-to-air or air-to-ground communications. The set could be operated anywhere between 100 and 156 megacycles. Frequencies of this range are characterized by line of sight distances. Average communications distances are 30 miles at 1,000 feet above terrain and 135 miles at 10,000 feet. These distances vary depending on atmospheric conditions and on intervening terrain and other obstructions.

AN/M64
General purpose bomb. See **500-pound bomb**.

AN/URC-4
The AN/URC-4 Emergency Radio Set was in very short supply—only 13 were on hand "with no resupply in sight. The assistance the URC-4 afforded in the successful rescue of downed pilots makes it extremely important that more satisfactory supply action be afforded on this item," Col. Saltsman noted. Due to the success of recent rescue operations in which these radios have been used there is an increasing demand for them by the pilots." 1st Lt. William Bryan of the 12th Squadron was put in charge of a project to design and produce a "carrier" for the radio consisting of a girdle supported by suspenders with two pockets that held the radio set and its battery. The pockets were positioned "over the stomach between the parachute leg straps and below the harness release." The pilots liked it for its "comfort and handling qualities."

Anak
Area south of Chinnampo.

ANG

Air National Guard

ANGLICO

Air and Naval Gunfire Liaison Company (Navy-Marine)

AOA

Angle of Attack

AOCP

Aircraft Out of Commission for Parts. "The landing strip at K-10 is dirt and problems were immediately encountered. Large rocks on the runway were sucked into the propeller during run-ups, resulting in damage to numerous propellers and only extraordinary supply action kept such aircraft from becoming AOCP." [1]

AP

Armor-piercing

API

Armor Piercing Incendiaries

APU

Auxiliary Power Unit

ARG

Air Rescue Group

Armd

Armored

Armed Reconnaissance

"Formation to the target area will be **battle formation** flown at an altitude of 7,000 feet or at an altitude practical to avoid known anti-aircraft guns, small arms fire and overcasts," 18th Fighter-Bomber Group Standardized Procedures for Combat Operations explained. "The Flight Leader should be on the deck (i.e. close to the ground), flying at an indicated air speed of at least 300 mph. He should pull up occasionally (above 3,000') in order to orient himself and to regain his low level air speed. The leaders' wing man should fly up with No's. 3 and 4, who should be flying at least 4,500' above the terrain. These three aircraft will fly a spread formation, weaving for mutual protection as well as flak evasion. The element leader will advise the flight leader of known flak positions, towns, villages, railroads, etc., that the Flight Leader cannot see. When a worthy target is found, the flight leader will determine whether to utilize two or four aircraft in the attack. In either instance, spacing between aircraft should be such that the most difficult target is presented to ground fire. This is usually accomplished with four aircraft in the form of a Clover Leaf Pattern with one aircraft always in a firing position. With two aircraft in the attack, the wing man should make his pass at least 45 degrees off from the axis of the leader's attack. At the completion of the last pass, the Flight Leader will so inform the flight. Power settings for aircraft on the deck will be kept at 44'hg 2700 rpm or higher. Power settings of the cover flight will be whatever is necessary to stay over the leader. Aircraft on the deck will be constantly turning to present a difficult target for enemy ground fire. Do not "Stooge" at low air speed, straight and level, or in one small area. Make a few turns then move down on a road a few miles farther over this area, then move to another road. Don't follow one road from town to town, if you do, the enemy will be waiting for you with everything they have. Find targets for your napalm early so you'll have a more responsive aircraft. It is almost impossible to see small arms fire unless you see the flash or the person shooting, so assume that you are being fired at continuously and make yourself hard to hit. Fire your guns until you reach your tracer ammunition, the rest of your .50-caliber ammunition is a reserve to fight you home if you are jumped. After you have completed your reconnaissance and have expended your ordnance, climb to a safe altitude and proceed Home. Use tactical formation from the target area to your home base. Don't go to sleep going Home! Keep looking around."

Armistice Agreement

Agreement between the United Nations Command and the military forces of the North Korean People's Army and the Chinese Communist Forces (CCF) that went into effect July 27, 1953.

Armor

Mustang pilots were partially protected by armor plate at three points: behind the pilot's seat, for protection from the rear; at the firewall in the opening between the engine and the fuselage; and, behind the spinner, in front of the coolant tank. They were "further protected by the bulletproof glass windshield and the engine itself, which protects you from head-on gunfire." The armor plate was designed into the aircraft when its primary function was bomber escort. Therefore, the armor was quite effective in protecting pilots from attacks by other fighter aircraft from the rear or head-on. There was no armor protection for pilots against flak or ground fire that hit the aircraft from the side or from below.

ARS or **ARSvc**

Air Rescue Squadron/Service

Arty

Artillery

ASI

Airspeed Indicator

AT

Air Tactics

ATA

Actual Time of Arrival

ATAR

Anti-Tank Aircraft Rocket. See **HVAR**.

ATIS

Allied Translator & Interpreter Section

ATC

Air Training Command

AUDACIOUS [2]

Korean War (12 April 1951) Eighth Army plan for an orderly withdrawal.

Augur in

Pilot slang for crash. "Heard that two of my classmates augured in..."

AW

Automatic Weapons

AWS

Air Weather Service

Ayer, Capt. Elliot Dean

On 9 July 1952, a four-ship flight of the 67th Squadron "returning from a close support mission landed at K-46 airbase. The fourth airplane of the flight completed the 45,000th effective combat sortie of the 18th Fighter Bomber Group, six days short of two years of combat flying in the Korean conflict. This number of sorties was the greatest among completed by any combat fighter bomber wing in Korea." Captain Elliot Ayer, How Flight Leader, was credited with the 45,000th combat sortie. (USAFHRA. *Monthly Historical Report, 18th Fighter Bomber Group,* July 1952. p. 14.) Ayer was KIA 25 July 1952.

B-26

Douglas "Invader": twin-engine light bomber (USA)

B-29

Boeing "Superfortress": four-engine bomber (USA)

BA-64

North Korean armored car, a four-wheeled vehicle weighing 4,800 pounds combat loaded. It was powered by a four-cycle, 50 hp engine giving it a top road speed of 55 mph. It was armored with 3/8-inch rolled, steeply sloped plate to afford maximum protection against small arms fire. Armament consisted of one small caliber machine gun. The tires were made of solid sponge rubber. See **T-34** and **SU-76**.

Bailey Bridge

Army bridge that could be swiftly assembled and used for river crossings, etc.

Bailout Bottle

A small green oxygen bottle attached to a parachute to be used in the event of a high altitude bailout so the pilot would not lose consciousness on the way down. The 18th flew some escort missions for B-29s at altitudes at or above 25,000 feet. On such missions, the bottles were issued.

Bailout

The process of exiting the aircraft while it is airborne. Pilots were advised to "slow the airplane to the lowest speed that is reasonably safe—150 mph. The lower the speed at which you bail out, the less risk there is. But don't slow the airplane dangerously near the stalling point, particularly if you have no power. Lower the seat, duck your head, and jettison the canopy. Disconnect your headset and oxygen hose, and release the safety belt and shoulder harness. Pull yourself up onto the seat so that you're in a crouching position with your feet in the seat. Dive with head down toward the trailing edge of the right wing, unless a fire or some other condition makes it advisable to go out the left side." If the pilot had to exit the plane at high altitude, he was advised to "make a delayed free fall" before opening his chute. In this way "you not only escape the danger of cold, of lack of oxygen, and–if in a combat zone—the danger of gunfire, but you also eliminate the possibility of personal injury from the snap-out in the rarified air." At high altitudes the G-forces exerted on the pilot by the pull of the harness in during the opening snap are from two to four times as great as at lower altitudes.

BAR

Browning Automatic Rifle.

Barcus, Lt. Gen. Glenn O.

On 30 May 1952, Lt. Gen. Barcus replaced General Everest as Commander, Fifth Air Force. On 16 May 1953, General Barcus presented the Distinguished Unit Citation to the 18th Fighter-Bomber Group "in recognition of the Group's outstanding contributions to the cause of the United Nations during the period 22 April 1951 through 8 July 1951." During the opening months of World War II, Barcus was in command of the 22nd Fighter Squadron at Puerto Rico, followed by command of the 36th Group, and a period of duty in Trinidad to help form the Interceptor Command. In April 1942, he went to Washington as deputy director, Air Defense at Army Air Force Headquarters. In December 1942, Colonel Barcus assumed command of the Philadelphia Air Defense Wing. He remained there until April 1943, when he became commander of the First Fighter Command at Mitchell Field, N.Y. General Barcus went overseas in April 1944, proceeding to Naples, Italy, where he commanded the 64th Fighter Wing. In February 1945, he became commanding general of the 12th Tactical Air Command, with headquarters near Nancy, France. He remained in command of the 12th Tactical Air Command until ordered back to the United States in August 1946. In September he became chief of staff of the Tactical Air Command at Langley Field, and in March, 1947, was put in command of the 12th Air Force at March Field, Calif., remaining in command when it moved to Brooks Air Force Base, Texas. General Barcus assumed command of the First Air Force at Fort Slocum, N.Y., in September 1949, and a month later moved with it to Mitchell Air Force Base, N.Y. He became commanding general of the Tactical Air Command at Langley Air Force Base, Va., in July 1950. In June 1952, General Barcus was transferred to Korea where he assumed command of the Fifth Air Force. He remained there until the end of May 1953, when he returned to the United States to become vice commander, Air Training Command. On 31 May 1953, Lt. Gen. Samuel E. Anderson, USAF, assumed command of Fifth Air Force, replacing General Barcus.

Barrier cover

UN interceptor jet patrols 20-50 miles north of an attacking bomber stream.

Base leg

See **Final**.

Battalion

A battalion normally consisted of two or more companies or batteries under the command of a lieutenant colonel—a basic military organizational element. The three infantry battalions in the standard Army and Marine Corps regiments of the day all followed the same system for letter designating their companies. Companies A, B, and C in First Battalion were rifle companies; D was a weapons company. In Second Battalion, E, F, and G were rifle companies; H was a weapons company. Likewise in Third Battalion, I, K, and L were rifle companies (there was no J Company) and M was a weapons Company.

Battery

In the U.S. military, battery is the designation for a company-sized unit of artillery. Commanded by a captain, it is composed of approximately 100 officers and men and equipped with guns, howitzers, rocket launchers, searchlights, appropriate to its mission.

Battle Damage

"Any damage to the aircraft brought about by enemy action. Battle damage may be accomplished by direct means such as air-to-air or ground-to-air fire, or by indirect means such as cable traps." (Memorandum No. 40, Operations Analysis Office, Hq. Fifth Air Force, 31 March 1951)

Battle Fatigue

Called "Shell Shock" in the First World War, Battle Fatigue was the term used in World War II and Korea. Pilots also had nicknames for battle fatigue, at the least the early symptoms, including: clanky, flak happy,

Battle Formation

See Formations.

Battle Loss

"Any aircraft that is lost while on a combat mission due to direct enemy action." (Memorandum No. 40, Operations Analysis Office, Hq. Fifth Air Force, 31 March 1951)

BC

N.K. Border Constabulary (called *Bo An Dae*)

BCP

Break Cloud Procedure

BDA

Battle Damage Assessment

Bedcheck Charley

Enemy aircraft, nicknamed "Bedcheck Charlies," used to harass Allied positions. Two types of antique aircraft were most often used, including: Soviet-built Yakovlev YAK-18 training planes; and Polikarpov PO-2 wood and fabric biplanes, both with a cruising speed of about 100 knots. Even ground personnel were not immune to the perceived threat of enemy air attack, particularly at K-16 where "Bed Check Charlie," a small, two-place, enemy biplane made regular appearances. Hedgehopping down the valleys and hilly countryside to avoid air search radar, "Charlie" would arrive in the early morning hours, "dropping hand grenades, mortar shells, and strafing the area with a hand held sub-machine gun. No damage was inflicted by this 'bogie' other than a few barked shins, skinned elbows, caused when personnel stumbled over tent ropes en route to their fox holes," the 39th FIS reported. Bedcheck Charlie hit K-23/Pyongyang in November 1950," noted Col. Bill Myers.

Belly landing

A forced landing with wheels up. "Forced landings with wheels down should be made only when you're absolutely certain that such a procedures will be safe." See **Ditching**.

BG

Bombardment Group

BIG STICK

Korean War plan to destroy the Communist supply complex based on Sibyon-ni, to advance the Eighth Army left flank to the Yesong River, and to regain Kaesong.

BIG SWITCH

Name for the main POW exchange that followed the signing of the Korean Armistice agreement July 27, 1953. Operation Big Switch was conducted from August 5 through December 23, 1953. It was the final exchange of prisoners of war by both sides. [3]

Billets

Slang for living and sleeping quarters areas. "Up in the billets, a young pilot stirs and shakes off the four MIGs that have been chasing him all night, curls himself into a tighter ball under his blankets, and with a happy smile grins to himself: 'Hell, I'm glad I'm not on 'Strip' this morning!'" [4]

Bingo

A UN radio code word meaning to "withdraw," time to go home as the fuel turn-around state has been reached. By monitoring UN radio broadcasts, Communist air controllers would wait to hear the "Bingo" signal, then vector patrolling MIG flights across the Yalu River to attack the Sabres that were then getting low on fuel. By coordinating the attacks on the Sabres by southward pursing MIGs with those of MIGs heading north from Chongchon, the Red air force was able to "box in" the Sabres, some of whom would exhaust their fuel and have to bail out near Cho-do (see). UN patrols soon learned that the MIGs would not pursue them out to sea and began to return "home" over the Yellow Sea whenever possible.

Bird baths

Airman slang for taking a "bath" from one's helmet. "Bathed out of our helmets--bird baths."

Bird Dog

Search And Rescue. Also referred to light observation type aircraft. See **L-19**.

Blinking Squadron

Also, "**blinker noses**." Colloquial name for the 39th FIS based on the visual effect of its F-51 nose spinners (hubs over the propeller), one side of which were painted blue and the other white, producing a "blinking" effect when the engines were running. Ground troops called them "**winking spinners**." Until the assignment of the 39th FIS to the 18th Wing in Spring 1951, the 67th Squadron painted the spinners on its aircraft half red and half white.

Blockage and Escort Force (Task Force 95)

Organized Sept. 12, 1950, the U.N. Blockade and Escort Force was a major subordinate command of U.S. Naval Forces, Far East (NAVFE).

Blooding

Exposing new "peon" pilots to combat for the first time. "The 'blooding' of newly assigned pilot personnel was successfully accomplished. Mission level experience of such pilots is rapidly increasing."

BLT

Battalion Landing Team

BLUEHEARTS

Code name for the original plan for an amphibious landing behind enemy lines, abandoned by 10 July 1950. Succeeded by **CHROMITE.**

Bn

Battalion

BNR

Body not recovered.

Boffins

British and Australian slang meaning someone who is considered to know a lot about science and technology, but is not thought to be interested in other things. Probably synonymous with "geek." "…this was devised by the boffins to confuse the enemy as well as the pilot himself."

Bogeys

Unidentified aircraft or attacking aircraft, e.g. "Bogeys at six o'clock level."

Bomb

Bombardment

Bomb line

"The position forward of the front lines beyond which operations can be undertaken without direction from the close support control." The designated line, beyond which was considered enemy territory. Below the bomb line combat

operations were conducted only under the positive control of a Mosquito or FAC. "Accordingly the bomb (battle) line was withdrawn from the boundary (Manchurian-Korean) perimeter and the "chop line" as a line of "no combat" demarcation was abandoned." [5]

Bomber Command

A major subordinate command of Far East Air Force (FEAF), Bomber Command (Provisional) was established July 8, 1950, with headquarters at Yokota AB, Japan.

Bombs

Removable bomb racks on the F-51D were designed to hold 100-, 250-, or 500-pound bombs. 1000-pound bombs could be carried "to accomplish particular missions, but the extra weight is undesirable and restricts the airplane to straight and level flight." If bombs were not installed, "chemical smoke tanks" (napalm) or droppable fuel tanks could be carried.

BomCom

Bomber Command.

Bout-One

A composite unit of American and South Korean airmen organized by the 8th Fighter-Bomber Wing on June 27, 1950. Led by Major Dean E. Hess, the Korean and American pilots of "Bout-One" arrived in Taegu, South Korean on the evening of June 30th and reported to the local KMAG headquarters. Following the death of an inexperienced South Korean pilot, American pilots began to fly all the combat missions in the antiquated F-51s initially flown by the Bout-One pilots. See **51st Fighter Squadron (Provisional)**.

BOXER Boys

F-51 pilots who sailed with the **USS BOXER** (see) bringing many former Air National Guard (ANG) aircraft to Korea where they were hastily put into combat. "To the best of my knowledge," explained Col. Jim Peek, "all of the pilots on the BOXER were Active Duty Air Force Pilots recruited from Fighter Groups or Wings all over the U. S. In our case it was just a day or two after June 25th 1950 when our Group Commander then, Colonel Ashly B. Packard (later killed in a T-33 at Itazuke) called a meeting in the base theater of all pilots assigned or attached to the 27th. He had been an Air Attache in Korea during 1948-1949 and knew first hand about the country and its people. He gave us a good briefing about the invasion by the North Koreans and answered a lot of questions about the place. One question someone asked was, 'Where in the hell is Korea?' Air Force Headquarters requested all fighter bases to check their personnel records for pilots with a lot of P-51 experience. This is where the pilots on the BOXER came from, active duty personnel. Guard pilots were not called to duty until after the Chinese joined the fray and replacements were needed to fill the ranks of those KIA and those rotated to the ZI after 100 missions."

Box-in tactics

See **Bingo**.

Bradley, General of the Army Omar Nelson

Assumed duties as Army Chief of Staff Feb. 7, 1948, and the first Chairman, Joint Chiefs of Staff, Jan. 16, 1949. Promoted to General of the Army (five stars) in September 1950, he served as JCS chairman throughout the Korean War.

BRG

Bearing

Brigade (also Brig)

The organizational structure used throughout the Korean War by British, Canadian and Turkish forces. Consisting of a headquarters and two or more battalions, it was roughly analogous to an American regiment.

Brinson, Col. Sheldon S.

Succeeded Major Frank L. Orth as CO of the 18th FB Group on June 18, 1952. Orth "for a short period, was Commanding Officer of the Group." Prior to Orth's short tenure, Colonel Seymour Levensen commanded the Group. [Other records cite the turnover as taking place on 17 May 1952, probably to avoid noting the "bridging" period provided by Major Orth.]

British Commonwealth Division

British Commonwealth Forces—Britain, Canada, Australia, and New Zealand—that played a major part in the Korean War.

Bronze Star Medal

First authorized in World War II, the Bronze Star Medal was awarded in the name of the President of the United States for heroic or meritorious achievement or service in connection with military operations against an armed enemy not involving participation in aerial flight. Awards, denoted by a metallic V device worn on the medal ribbon, were made for heroism performed under circumstances of a lesser degree than those required for award of the Silver Star.

Brousseau, S/Sgt Norman

Crew Chief S/Sgt Norman Brousseau, A/2C

Harold Hudren and A/3C Freeman Finley worked for two months on refining and improving the process followed to change the engine on an F-51. The usual time for the complex job was approximately 125 hours. Finley and his team "whizzed through the job in the breath taking time of 40 hours and 30 minutes." The men were honored by the Group and lauded by Capt. William Wakeham, maintenance supervisor. "I defy any other three men to perform the same job in a comparable length of time." The *Truckbuster* noted, "The teamwork exhibited by these men, each of whom was from a different Squadron, reflects the attainment of cooperation that is possible at Dogpatch. The Squadrons represented were the Foxy Few, Blinker Nose and the Red Scarfers."

Browning Automatic Rifle (BAR)

The Browning Automatic Rifle M-1918A2 or "BAR" was the standard squad automatic weapon for both U.S. Army and Marine Corps Infantry units during World War II and the Korean War.

BS

Bombardment Squadron

Btry

Battery

BUCKSHOT 16

Korean War operation by the Republic of Korea 11th Division, Republic of Korea I Corps, to take North Korean prisoners.

Bug Out

Evacuate quickly. "So on the evening of August 5th we at Taegu air base were racing to complete our evacuation preparations before dark--planning to move out—to Bug Out—on 6 August 1950."

Bul

Bulletin

Burp Gun

The most distinctive small arm of the Korean War—the Soviet Pistolet-Pulemyot Shpagina obr 1941G (PPSh41) submachine-gun and its Chinese-manufactured counterpart.

Buy the farm/bought the farm

Pilot slang for killed or died.

BW

Bombardment Wing

C

Combat

C/

Chief

C/P

Co-pilot

C-46

The C-46 "Commando" was first delivered to the AAF in July 1942 for the Air Transport Command and Troop Carrier Command. During WW II, the AAF used over 3,100 C-46s to haul cargo and personnel and for towing gliders. The C-46 became famous during WW II while transporting war materials over the "Hump" from India to China after the Japanese had closed the Burma Road. The Commando had a greater cargo load capacity than the famous C-47 and it provided better performance at higher altitudes. However, the C-46 required extensive maintenance and had a relatively high loss rate. The C-46 had a wing span of 108 feet and a length of 76 ft. 4 inches. Two Pratt & Whitney R-2800s developed 2,000 hp each. It cost about $230,000.

C-47/R4D

Douglas "Skytrain": twin-engine transport plane. Also known affectionately as a "Goony bird." The Skytrain was adapted from the DC-3 commercial airliner that was introduced into service in 1936. First ordered in 1940, by the end of WW II, 9,348 had been purchased for AAF use. Skytrains carried personnel and cargo. During combat operations, they towed troop-carrying gliders and dropped paratroops into enemy territory. During the Korean War, Skytrains hauled supplies, dropped paratroops, evacuated wounded and dropped flares for night bombing attacks. The Skytrain had a wing span of 95 feet and a length of 64 feet 5 inches. It cost about $138,000.

C-54/R5D

The "Skymaster," was also known in civilian aviation as the DC-4. The Skymaster began service with the USAAC in 1942, and carried up to 26 passengers. Later versions carried up to 49 passengers. The U.S. Navy also used the Skymaster, which was designated the R5D. One Skymaster named the "Sacred Cow" was converted into service for President Franklin D. Roosevelt. The Skymaster had a speed of 273 mph, a ceiling of 22,507 feet and a range of 3,877 miles.

Cable Trap

A cable strung across the valleys as a hazard for low flying aircraft. (Memorandum No. 40, Operations Analysis Office, Hq. Fifth Air Force, 31 March 1951)

CAM

Camera

Campaigns

The Korean War consisted of 10 campaigns,

including: UN Defensive—June 27-Sept. 15, 1950; UN Offensive—Sept. 16-Nov. 2, 1950; CCF Intervention—Nov. 3, 1950-Jan. 24, 1951; First UN counteroffensive—Jan. 25-April 21, 1951; CCF Spring Offensive—April 22-July 8, 1951; UN Summer-Fall Offensive—July 9-Nov. 27, 1951; Second Korean Winter—Nov. 28, 1951-April 30, 1952; Korea Summer-Fall 1952—May 1-Nov. 30, 1952; Third Korean Winter—Dec. 1, 1952-April 30, 1953; Korea Summer-Fall—May 1-July 27, 1953.

CAP

Combat Air Patrol, or "CAP," is an aircraft patrol stationed over an objective area, a force to be protected, or in an air defense area whose mission is to intercept and destroy hostile aircraft before they can reach their targets. Often used as a verb, as in "we capped the crash site."

Capped

Provided combat air patrol for, e.g. "The procedures of capping a downed pilot were also changed in hopes that the change will cut down the losses suffered on capping missions."

CAS

Calibrated airspeed — indicated airspeed corrected for air density and **compressibility**. See **Close Air Support**.

Casualties

A broad term encompassing those killed or wounded in action, those who later died of their wounds, those missing in action and those taken as prisoners of war.

CAVU

Ceiling and visibility unlimited, i.e. cloudless (or scattered cloud) conditions with visibility in excess of ten kilometers.

CCAF

Chinese Communist Air Force

CCF

Chinese Communist Forces

CCRAK

Covert, Clandestine, and Related Activities in Korea.

CCS

Combined Chiefs of Staff

CCT

Combat Crew Training

CCTF

Combat Crew Training Flight, a provisional unit of the 18th Fighter-Bomber Wing established in early 1953 as the 18th Group converted from F-51s to F-86 fighters. See **MTD**.

CCTS

Combat Crew Training School. The 18th Group found it was necessary in November 1951 to establish a new training program at K-46 that covered "all phases of combat flying in F-51 type aircraft. Although the majority of replacement pilots required little training prior to being assigned to flights, it was found that some pilots had not graduated from CCTS before coming overseas. A brief course, approximately that of CCTS training given at Luke AFB, was initiated at K-46. A survey of new pilots revealed that very few had experience with napalm, rocket firing or high angle strafing." [6]

CDR

Commander

CE

Circular Error

Ceiling

Height above ground or water lowest layer of clouds below 20,000 feet that covers more than half of the sky. An aircraft's **service ceiling** is the density altitude at which its maximum rate of climb is no greater than 100 feet per minute. Its **absolute ceiling** is the highest altitude at which the aircraft can maintain level flight.

CEP

Circular Error Probable

CG

Commanding General; also Center of Gravity

CH

Compass Heading

Chairman, Joint Chiefs of Staff

Senior officer of the U.S. armed services. A statutory adviser to the National Security Council, he presides over the Joint Chiefs of Staff consisting of the chiefs of staff from the Army and Air Force and the Chief of Naval Operations. Unlike during the Korean War, today the Joint Chiefs of Staff also includes the Marine Corps Commandant.

Chandelle

A climbing turn beginning from approximately straight-and-level flight, and ending after the aircraft has completed 180 degrees of turn in a wings-level, nose-high attitude at the minimum controllable airspeed.

Cherokee strike

Term used by Vice Admiral Joseph J. "Jocko" Clark, the last commander of the Navy's 7th Fleet during the Korean War and a Cherokee descendent, for air strikes that concentrated his fleet's efforts on destroying enemy weapons and supplies behind enemy lines. The Cherokee Strikes served as a much-needed morale boost for American frontline troops.

China Lobby

Label given to those in and out of government who supported the Nationalist government of Chiang-Kai-Shek and opposed the Communist government of Mao Tse-tung.

Chinese Communist Forces (CCF)

Elements of the Chinese People's Liberation Army moved into Korea Oct. 4, 1950.

Chipyong-ni, Battle of

Northwest of Wonju in central Korea, the village ("ni" in Korean) of Chipyong was the site of a major battle Feb. 13-15, 1951.

Chmn

Chairman

Chodo

Island about one third up the West coast of North Korea controlled by U.N. forces. Air surveillance and air rescue personnel based there saved many lives. Facilities included a tactical air-direction center with limited capabilities, but helpful in providing local air-control and warning services in that area of Korea. When fighter-bombers or Sabres ventured into Northwest Korea, an SA-16 would be deployed from Seoul to orbit north of Cho-do. If a fighter pilot ran into trouble he "Maydayed" and tried to reach a pre-determined orbit-rescue point off the west coast. His own flight would provide RESCAP until the Albatross arrived. See **Bingo**. By December 1951 a detachment of H-5 helicopters were stationed at Cho-do for rescue alert. In February 1952, more capable H-19 helicopters were stationed on Cho-do.

CHOKE

A main supply route interdiction plan used by FAF during which last-light (flying at twilight) fighter-bombers attacked selected road bridges. Then, shortly after dark, fighter-bombers--usually B-26's--would attack vehicles stalled behind the blown-out bridges.

Chopline

The **FEAF CHOPLINE** or line of "no combat" demarcation was instituted on 15 October 1950, which limited the air operations to actions 20 miles south of the Manchurian border from longitude 12 degrees to the west coast. This was equally divided into three areas, Recce Areas I, II, and III. See **Bombline**.

CHOPSTICK 6

Korean War plan for the envelopment of the high ground south of P'yong-gang by a reinforced Republic of Korea division.

CHOPSTICK 16

Korean War plan for a two-division attack to drive the Communists from the area east and south of the Nam River.

Chosin Reservoir

The Chosin Reservoir (Changjin Reservoir in Korean) was part of North Korea's Japanese-built hydroelectric system located in northeastern Korea. The Reservoir was the site of one of the best-known battles of the Korean War from Nov. 27-Dec. 11, 1950.

CHROMITE

Korean War (September 13, 1950) landing at Inch'on. Planning for **Operation Chromite**, the code name for the Inchon invasion, began August 12, 1950, and was completed the following month. It replaced a similar plan that had been called **Operation Bluehearts**. The objectives of Operation CHROMITE were to: neutralize the fortifications on Wolmi Island that controlled the access to Inchon Harbor; successfully complete an amphibious landing and capture Inchon and seize Kimpo Airfield (K-14), just south of Seoul; and, to capture the city of Seoul. The plan included preparations for the Eighth U.S. Army (EUSA) to breakout of the Pusan Perimeter at the same time as the Inchon landing, pushing the North Korean Army northward, and thus trapping it between the two forces.

CIA

Central Intelligence Agency

CINCAFPAC

Commander-in-Chief Army Forces Pacific

CINCFE

Commander-in-Chief, Far East

CINCPAC

Commander in Chief, Pacific

CINCPACFLT

Commander-in-Chief, Pacific Fleet

CINCUNC

Commander-in-Chief, United Nations Command

Clamped

See **Socked-in**.

CLAM-UP

Korean War operation to delude the Communists by imposing silence along the front lines 10-15 February 1952. Outposts were temporarily abandoned in the hope that Communist ground troops would increase patrolling and that the enemy patrols would fall into ambuscades. **Clam-Up** ended on Feb. 16th without success.

Clanky

Air Force fighter pilot slang for combat fatigue. Also "**flak happy**."

Clark, Gen. Mark Wayne

On 12 May 1952, replaced General Matthew B. Ridgway as commander in chief, Far East Command and commander in chief, United Na-

tions Command.

Clearance

Authorization from air traffic control to proceed as requested or instructed. Used for ground and air maneuvering, e.g. "cleared for take-off."

Close Air Support

One of the three "classic" missions of tactical airpower, including **air superiority** and **interdiction**. CAS was the most complex of these three missions "since it involved an intimate cooperation of ground and air forces and an intricate system of communications." [7] Close air support involves the use of fighter, fighter-bomber and, in exceptional cases, bomber aircraft to strike enemy targets just in front of the battle lines. "Upon reaching the target designated by the TACP, the flight leader should observe the terrain and other conditions in order to establish the best axis and method of attack," 18th Fighter-Bomber Group Standardized Procedures for Combat Operations explained. "The objective is to deliver maximum firepower to enemy positions while absorbing a minimum of return fire from them. To accomplish this, the method of deploying aircraft to attack at different angles and altitudes has been proven highly successful. These aircraft, evenly spaced will provide almost continuous fire on enemy positions, while in the target area. After completing a bomb, rocket, or firing run, evasive action should be taken by a series of sharp turns, or a change in direction, or by hitting the deck. Aircraft making rocket-firing and gunnery runs at a high angle present a more difficult target for ground gun crews and at the same time provide a more effective concentration of fire against ground personnel and equipment. This type of attack is best utilized under good weather conditions, however, it is difficult to adapt to low ceiling conditions. [8]

CLR

Clear

CM-IN

Classified message-In

CO

Commanding Officer

Co(s)

Company(ies)

Cocktail Courier

On February 14, 1953 the R&R service was "enhanced by a direct flight from K-55 to Tachikawa Air Base, Japan, on a weekly basis—a C-124, known as the 'Cocktail Courier.'

CofS

Chief of Staff

Colson, Maj. Carl C.

In June 1951 Colson, of Cocoa, Florida, relieved Lt. Col. Henry W. "Hank" Lawrence as Commander of the 67th Squadron. In August, 1951, Major Colson created a fifth flight, Easy Flight, "to permit more effective operations, and to permit one flight to return aircraft to K-10 where better maintenance facilities are available, and to take care of additional duties for a period of one or two days before being returned to the advance base." During that period the operations section was led by Major Michael E. Adams, Operations Officer, with 1st Lt. Harold K. Wimberly serving as Assistance Operations Officer. Flight Commanders included: 1st Lt. Walter H. Burke (A-Flight); 1st Lt. George N. Leitner (B-Flight); 1st Lt. James W. Lee (C-Flight); Capt. Robert P. Pasqualicchio (D-Flight); and, 1st Lt. George L. Coyle, Jr. (E-Flight).

Combat Crew Training School

See **CCTS**.

ComCarCom

Combat Cargo Command

Comd

Command

Comdr

Commander

COMFAIRJAP

Commander, Fleet Air Wing Japan

COMINT

Communications intelligence (now known as SIGINT, i.e., signals intelligence)

Comm (also Comms)

Communication

COMNAVFE

Commander, Naval Forces Far East, Vice Adm. C. Turner Joy.

Company

In the U.S. Army and Marine Corps a company is the basic organizational unit.

Compressibility

Compression waves or shock waves that develop over the wings and other control surfaces of an aircraft as it approaches the speed of sound. Instead of following the contour of the airfoil, the air is disrupted by the shock waves and the "lift characteristics" of the airplane are largely destroyed—intense drag develops and "the stability, control and trim characteristics of the airplane are all affected. The buffets, the controls stiffen as the airplane begins to develop uncontrollable pitching and porpoising, or uncontrollable rolling and yawing. For F-51 pilots, the first effects of compressibility was a "nibbling" at the stick—a vibration, that soon developing a definite "walking" stick, the pilot would not be able to use the joy stick because it was moving of its own volition. A porpoising—pitching up and down—would then follow unless the pilot reduced speed. For example, if a pilot failed to cut his throttle during a steep angle dive, trying to regain control of the aircraft when it experienced compressibility could cause the plane to loose so much altitude that it would not have enough to recover before it crashed.

COMSEVENTHFLT

Commander, Seventh Fleet

COMUNBLOCKANDCORTFOR

Commander, United Nations Blockading and Escort Force

Con

Control

CONUS

Continental United States. See **ZI**.

Coolant

The Mustang's Merlin engine and four-blade prop both needed to be cooled. The engine cooling system is a high-pressure system (30 psi) with a coolant capacity of 16 ½ gallons. The coolant used was a mixture of ethylene glycol and water. The after cooling system cooled the supercharger fuel-air mixture.

Corps

Refers to a group of men and women who share similar functions such as the Medical Corps or the Signal Corps. It also designates an organizational unit subordinate to a field army composed of two or more divisions.

Cosmoline

A substance essentially the same as Vaseline, but of a stiffer consistency, that is obtained from the residues of the distillation of petroleum. Used as a coating on machinery (including aircraft) to reduce saltwater corrosion during sea transportation.

COUNTER

Korean War plan (June 6, 1952) for the 45th Infantry Division (I Corps) to capture strategic outpost sites. The 45th Infantry Division launched a two-phased series of attacks to establish 11 patrol bases in the Old Baldy area.

COURAGEOUS

Korean War operation for the March 23, 1951 advance to the Imjin River as a follow-on to **RIPPER.** Intelligence analysts concluded that the three divisions of the enemy I Corps are vulnerable. Once they are attacked and forced

to withdraw, their only route is across the Imjin River at the town of Munsan-ni. General Ridgway approved Operation Courageous, an enlargement of Ripper, to take advantage of that vulnerability. Paratroops jumped into the area around Munsan-ni before dawn on March 23. The air assault phase was code named **Operation Tomahawk**.

Cox, Lt. Col. Homer M.

Assumed command of the 18th Fighter-Bomber Group from Colonel Ira F. Wintermute on 20 February 1951.

CP

Command post

Crabtree, Lt. William

Second Lieutenant Billie R. Crabtree "was the first casualty of the unit [51st Provisional Squadron] … when be dove his F-51 too close to his target," on 25 July 1950, Colton recorded. "We had been fortunate, at first. We didn't suffer our first fatality for almost ten days after beginning our daily routine of intense ground attack combat operations against the North Korean enemy," recalled Lt. Col. Duane "Bud" Biteman, a friend and fellow fighter pilot, "when Second Lieutenant Billie Crabtree was unable to avoid his bomb blast, hitting the crest of a hill near Kwangju, near the west coast of South Korea. *(USAFHRA. "The Story of the 18th Fighter-Bomber Group in the Korean United Nations Police Action." 6002nd Tactical Support Wing, Public Information Office. S/Sgt Sandy Colton.)*

Crosswind leg

See **Final**.

Crow, Lt. Col. Julian

Commanding Officer, 67th Fighter-Bomber Squadron. The Executive Officer of the 12th Squadron, Major Julian F. Crow was reassigned in November 1951 as Commanding Officer of the 67th Squadron, succeeding Major Carl C. Colson.

CRS

Course, the intended direction of flight in the horizontal plane expressed in degrees of the compass.

CRS

Course

CS

Constant-speed (propeller). A variable-pitch propeller that maintains constant rpm by automatically changing blade angle.

CSGPO

Chief of Staff, G-3, Plans & Operations Div.

CSUSA

Chief of Staff, U.S. Army

CTF

Commander Task Force (Navy)

CTG

Commander Task Group (Navy)

CTU

Commander Task Unit (Navy)

CUDGEL

Korean War plan for an advance from the **WYOMING** line in the I and IX Corps sectors. See **Wrangler.**

CW

Continuous wave

D/

Director

D/F

Direction-finding. A new D/F station "was installed atop a hill near the base at K-10 and all flight leaders were requested to request a steer when returning to base. The D/F operators improved with practice and gave accurate steers toward the end of the month." [9]

DA

Department of the Army

DAF

Department of the Air Force

Dallas Squadron

See **51st Fighter Squadron (Provisional).**

DAUNTLESS

Korean War (April 11, 1951) plan for a limited advance by I and IX Corps against the Iron Triangle.

Davis, Maj. Murrit H.

Relieved Lt. Col. Thomas D. "Robby" Robertson as Commander, 39th FIS on 10 June 1951. Davis came to the 39th from the 41st Fighter-Interceptor Squadron in Japan, and was considered a capable commander and fighter pilot. "All personnel were saddened to lose Colonel Robertson, but the men soon recognized Major Davis' abilities and the unit retained its high level of esprit de corps under the new Squadron Commander." Davis was KIA on 14 August 1951 during a strike on Pyongyang, North Korea.

Deadstick

Descent and landing with engine(s) shut down and propeller(s) stopped. Also called "wind milling."

Death Valley

The rail route between Samdong-ni and Kowon that was so well protected by Red ground fire that Navy airmen called it "Death Valley."

Demilitarized Zone (DMZ)

Created by the 1953 Korean Armistice agreement, the DMZ consists of a buffer zone two kilometers on either side of a military demarcation line that follows the general location of the front lines at the close of the war.

Dep
Depot

DES
Descent

DEST
Destination

Det
Detachment

DF
Radio Direction Finding. "DF homing facilities on VHF are available to fighters at every major USAF base and at some USN bases. These could consist of temporary or permanent installations which guard various channels and which operate continuously during certain specified hours and on call, and during certain specified hours only. All homing stations guard DOG channel (121.50 mgs) for emergency use, and all homing stations at fighter bases guard the fighter "D" channel installed in fighter group aircraft." When requesting a DF steer, pilots were reminded that VHF/DF homing facilities were more or less limited in range to line of sight distances. "If a DF homer cannot be reached for a steer, sometimes additional altitude will bring a response. Steers have been given by DF homers to aircraft 275 miles out at 20,000 feet." *(18th Fighter-Bomber Wing Combat Operating Procedures)*

Dinghy
Inflatable, one-man rescue raft. "...Then up onto the wing, where the erk awaits you with your dinghy. This thing must save your life when you fall into cold water with sharks, and also serves as a cushion to sit on, since all parachutes are of the back type. This 'Cushion' is about a soft as sack full of broken bricks. A brief skirmish between you and the erk and the dinghy, and then you can climb into the cockpit." [10]

Dir
Director

DIR
Direct. Also **Depot Inspection Repair**.

DIS
Daily Intelligence Summary

DIST
Distance

Distinguished Flying Cross
Awarded in the name of the President of the United States for heroism or extraordinary achievement while participating in aerial flight.

Distinguished Service Cross
America's second highest award for bravery.

Ditching
A forced landing (see **belly landing**) in water. "Never attempt to ditch the F-51 except as a last resort. Fighter planes are not designed to float on water, and the F-51 has an even greater tendency to dive because of the airscoop underneath. It will go down in 1 ½ to 2 seconds."

Div
Division

Dive and Zoom
See **Yo-Yo** pattern.

Dive Bombing
"Dive bomb runs must originate from an altitude so that the aircraft can be aligned with the target long enough to make an accurate release of bombs and still recover from the dive and break away without entering the area of bomb blast. This entry altitude is usually above five thousands feet and varies with the steepness of the dive. The aircraft should be trimmed for the dive as soon as possible after entering bomb run in order to make a more effective alignment on the target. The point of release depends on the steepness of the dive. The greater the angle of dive, the less correction will be necessary for the bombs' trajectory. The high angle dive bomb run is the most effective means of pinpointing a target. In breaking away from the target after the bomb release, it is recommended that the break be made down and away from the target to the deck, taking evasive action." [11] See **Skip Bombing** and **Glide Bombing**.

Division
Basic combined arms organization for waging war. Normally commanded by a major general. During the Korean War it typically consisted of three regiments of infantry; a four-battalion division artillery (three battalions with 105-mm howitzers, one with 155-mm howitzers); an antiaircraft artillery battalion; a tank battalion; a reconnaissance company; an engineer battalion; a medical battalion; and supporting medical, ordnance, quartermaster and signal companies.

DoD
Department of Defense

Dog Patch Century Flight
Pilots assigned to the 18th Fighter-Bomber Wing who successfully completed 100 combat missions.

Doorstop
A comprehensive dispersal plan for Sabre squadrons prepared in January 1953 as a result of concerns regarding the danger of Communist air attack.

DOW
Died of wounds

Downwind
See **Final(s)**

DPRK
Democratic People's Republic of Korea

DR
Dead (deduced) reckoning. Plotting position by calculating the effects of speed, course, time and wind against last known position (fix).

Draft
Congress, which under the Constitution of the United States has the sole authority to raise armies, first legislated involuntary conscription—the draft—to fill the ranks of the military during the Civil War. It was again used in World War I and World War II. Although the draft laws were due to expire July 9, 1950, Congress quickly passed a two-year extension. By September 1950, 50,000 men were being drafted each month, and by 1952, 20,000 to 30,000 conscripts were sent to Korea each month.

Drop-tank
Gasoline tank, externally hung.

D.S.
Detached service, usually more than thirty days. Temporary Duty (**TDY**) was usually less than 30 days.

DTG
Distance To Go; Date Time Group (message address component)

DULUTH
Korean War line of defense to be established by Operation **SUNDIAL.**

DZ
Drop Zone

Dzus fasteners
Quick release fasteners on some external access panels.

EA
Engineer Aviation; Executive Assistant

EAD
Extended Active Duty

EAS
Equivalent Air Speed

Echelon formation
See **Formations.**

ECM
Electronic countermeasures

Eighth U.S. Army
The major U.S. Army headquarters in Japan when the Korean War began.

Eisenhower, General of the Army Dwight David
Although he retired from active duty in February 1948, he returned to active duty in 1951 to assume duties as supreme commander of the North Atlantic Treaty Organization (NATO). A year later, he resigned that post to run for President and in November 1952, he was elected the 34th President of the United States. During the period 2-5 December 1952, President-elect Eisenhower toured the front in Korea and met with South Korean President Syngman Rhee, during which visit his aircraft was escorted by 18th Group aircraft.

Elastic bridge
On August 19, 1950, nine Superfortresses of the 19th BG dropped fifty-four tons of one thousand-pound bombs on the west railway bridge at Seoul, called the "elastic bridge" because repeated air attacks had failed to bring it down. Thirty-seven USN dive-bombers from two aircraft carriers followed up the USAF attack. Aerial reconnaissance the next day revealed that two spans had collapsed.

Element
A "two ship" unit of a "four ship" aircraft **flight** (see).

Elsewhere
Early radio call sign for the 67th Fighter-Bomber Squadron. Major General Earle E. Partridge fired off a Letter of Commendation to the 67th Fighter-Bomber Squadron on November 9, 1950 that singled out the "Elsewhere Squadron" for a special commendation. "Within the Joint Operations Center, the code name 'Elsewhere,' is fast becoming a legend. It appears regularly in conjunction with reports of downed enemy aircraft," Partridge wrote. "I wish to commend the officers and airmen of the 67th Fighter Squadron of the 18th Fighter-Bomber Group for their fine display of courage, aggressiveness, and determination to seek out and destroy the enemy in the air. The exploits of this unit reflect a spirit of cooperation that is exemplary of the best traditions of the United States Air Force. We are now encountering an enemy who possesses aircraft of performance equal or superior to our own and who is daily growing bolder. We must depend upon the superior quality of our fighter pilots and the aggressive spirit exhibited by the "Elsewhere" squadron to maintain supremacy in the air over our Forces in North Korea."

Emergency Radio Set
See **AN/URC-4**.

Encl
Enclosure

ENG
Engine

Engr
Engineer

Erk
South African pilot slang for ground crew personnel. "Every man to his plane now. The erks are scraping the ice off the windscreens and cockpit canopies while you make a hurried inspection to see that all the essential parts; aircrews, engines, control surface, etc., are all there..." [12]

ESB
Engineer Special Brigade (Army)

Escape and Evasion Drop Tank
An externally carried F-51 drop tank "properly modified was prepared for swift transport to a downed pilot" in January 1951.

EST
Eastern Standard Time

Est
Estimate

EUSA
Eighth U.S. Army

EUSAK
Eighth United States Army in Korea, title created on July 13th at Taegu City, SK by Lt. Gen. Walton H. Walker upon assuming command of all American ground forces in Korea. The new command absorbed the Army personnel of USAFIK, ADCOM and KMAG, all of which were discontinued.

Everest, Lt. Gen. Frank Fort
Assumed command of Fifth Air Force on 1 June 1951, replacing General Timberlake. General Everest became commanding general of the Fifth Air Force, Far East Air Forces, in Korea in May 1951. Through his efforts, the Fifth Air Force became a powerful fighting machine that was able to attain, and maintain, air superiority over the enemy, the Air Force biography noted. A native of Council Bluffs, Iowa, where he was born in 1904, he graduated from the U.S. Military Academy June 9, 1928 and was commissioned a second lieutenant of Field Artillery. During WWII then Colonel Everest was assigned to Headquarters, U.S. Army Forces in the South Pacific Area, where he served successively as liaison officer to the commander, aircraft, South Pacific; commanding officer of the 11th Heavy Bomb Group at

New Hebrides Islands and Guadalcanal; and Army air officer on the staff of the commander of the South Pacific Theater. Following duty at Air Corps Headquarters as Air Force director of the Joint War Plans Committee in the Office of the Assistant Chief of Air Staff for Plans in January 1944, he was promoted to brigadier general in June. Following WWII he commanded the Yukon Sector, Alaskan Air Command, and was named assistant deputy chief of staff for operations at Air Force Headquarters in Washington. He became a major general in April 1948. In March 1950 he assumed the additional duty of senior Air Force member on the Military Liaison Committee to the Atomic Energy Commission. Following his tenure as Commander, Fifth Air Force, in mid-1952 he was appointed deputy commander of the Tactical Air Command at Langley Air Force Base, Va. He was named director of the Joint Staff in the Office of the Joint Chiefs of Staff, Washington, in April 1953. One year later he was designated deputy chief of staff for operations at Air Force Headquarters, a post he held until July 1, 1957, when he was appointed commander-in-chief of the U.S. Air Forces in Europe and promoted to a full general.

EVERREADY
Korean War plan covering eventualities of Republic of Korea domestic disturbances and disengaging United Nations Command forces

Ex
Executive Officer. The comparable term in the U.S. Navy is "XO."

EXEC
Execute

F/S
Fire Support

F2H
McDonnell "Banshee"--twin-engine jet fighter (USA)

F3D
Douglas "Skyknight"--twin-engine jet fighter (USA)

F4U
Vought "Corsair"--single-engine fighter (USA)

F-51D
North American "Mustang": single-engine fighter (USA). The Mustang was built by North American Aviation and was a single-place, low-wing monoplane powered by a Packard-built Rolls Royce engine. Originally designed primarily as a fighter airplane, it was later equipped to carry bombs, rockets and chemical tanks (napalm). The aircraft was equipped

with six .50-caliber machine guns as standard equipment. The Mustang's characteristics include: wing span (37 feet), length (32 feet 2 inches), gross weight (9,000 pounds with no external load/12,300 with maximum external load), engine (12-cylinder, liquid-cooled "Merlin" engine of 1490 horsepower driving a four-bladed constant-speed propeller and equipped with an injection-type carburetor).

F-51's with teeth
See **Tiger Squadron** (12th FBS).

F-80
Lockheed "Shooting Star": single-engine jet fighter (USA)

F-86
North American "Sabre": single-engine jet fighter (USA)

F9F
Grumman "Panther": single-engine jet fighter (USA)

FA
Field Artillery; Final Approach

FAC
Forward Air Controller

FAF or Fifth AF
Fifth Air Force

FAFIK
Fifth Air Force in Korea

Far East Air Forces (FEAF)
Activated at Brisbane, Australia, June 15, 1944, the Far East Air Force fought its way across the Pacific during World War II. When the Korean War began, it was part of the postwar occupation of Japan, with headquarters in Tokyo.

Far East Command
Shortly after the Korean War began, Far East Command was given operational command of the Republic of Korea (ROK) armed forces by ROK President Syngman Rhee. Soon after, the FECOM was designated as the U.N. Command (UNC), which gave it authority over Allied personnel as well.

FAWS
Fighter All Weather Squadron

FBG
Fighter Bomber Group

FBS
Fighter Bomber Squadron

FBW
Fighter Bomber Wing

FDC
Fire Direction Center

FEAF
Far East Air Forces (U.S.)

FEALogFor

Far East Air Logistics Force

FEAMCOM
Far East Materiel Command

FEC
Far East Command

FES
Far Eastern Squadron

FIG
Fighter-Interceptor Group

Fighting 39th
Nickname for the 39th Fighter-Interceptor Squadron. Also, "Cobra in the Clouds" Squadron. "Each section is taking pride in its own individual accomplishments as well as those of the Squadron as a whole. Although it is hard for us to compete with other outfits of the 'Jet Area' for the lime light, a decided amount of pride goes along with every combat sortie the Fighting 39th completes. Each man in the Squadron knows that he is doing his utmost in his contributions towards world peace."

Final(s)
Final approach. The part of a landing sequence or airport circuit procedure in which the aircraft has made its final turn and is inbound to the active runway. **Downwind** is the segment of the circuit paralleling the runway and flown on a reciprocal heading. **Base leg** is the crosswind segment bringing the aircraft from the downwind leg to **final approach**. The leg before downwind is called the **Crosswind leg**.

Finger formation
See **Formations.**

FIS
Fighter Interceptor Squadron

FIW
Fighter Interceptor Wing

Flak Happy
Air Force pilot slang for combat fatigue. Also "**clanky.**"

FLAK
Flieger Abwehr Kanonen, German anti-aircraft guns. Term carried over into subsequent wars and referred to ground fire coming from anti-aircraft guns as opposed to "pot shots" or ground fire from small arms. Flak was encountered "in increased intensity in the P'yongyang and Kangdong areas. This included 20-mm and 40-mm automatic weapons fire, "as well as small arms fire." One pilot, Captain Elzeard Deschamps, is presumed "missing in action" due to enemy anti-aircraft fire encountered over Kangdong airdrome." [13]

Flak traps
Ambush areas devised by Communist gunners

to lure UN pilots into traps—heavy concentrations of anti-aircraft guns. Traps include open parachutes hanging on trees, dummy troops made of straw, cables strung across valleys, and strings of lights at measured intervals along mountainsides that looked like a convoy. By July 1951 the Reds had 275 antiaircraft artillery guns and 600 automatic weapons emplaced in Korea. "Pyongyang was defended by 48 guns and more than 100 automatic weapons, making it one of the worst 'flak traps' in Korea." [14]

Flameout
Combustion failure in a jet turbine engine resulting in power loss.

Flight
A group of aircraft operating together. A "four-ship flight" consisted of four aircraft organized in two "elements." Two-, four-, and eight-aircraft Mustang flights were used during combat situations throughout the war. The majority of all flights consisted of four-aircraft flights where "two aircraft [an 'element'] were designated to furnish top (aerial) cover during armed reconnaissance flights or during strafing passes against enemy personnel, materiel and rolling stock."

Flims
See **Flimsy.**

Flimsy
Slang for "flimsies," the extremely thin paper used as 2nd, 3rd or 4th carbon copies. See **JOC Alert Missions**.

FLT
Flight

Fluid four
A flight formation of four aircraft spaced generally in fingertip formation. The two element leaders applying the firepower, while the wingmen covered the rear.

Fly away kits
Basically a system of plans and physical components (e.g. packing crates, boxes) designed to enable a unit to shift its operating location quickly and without much loss in mission performance.

Flying Boxcar
C-119, twin engine, transport aircraft

Flying Cheetahs
Nickname for the 2 Squadron, South African Air Force operationally attached to the 18th Fighter-Bomber Wing for most of the Korean War period.

Flying kit
SAAF slang for the collection of equipment worn

by Mustang pilots, including: gun belt, radio vest, Escape and Evasion vest (with its multitude of pockets filled with vital items necessary to sustain life behind enemy lines), Mae West, helmet and oxygen mask.

Flying Tigers of Korea

Term first used by South Korean President Syngman Rhee in reference to the 51st Provisional Squadron formed from Bout One and Dallas volunteers in the early days of the Korean Conflict. Later, the 51st Provisional became the 12th Fighter-Bomber Squadron that retained the sharks "grin" nose art.

FM

Frequency Modulation

FO

Field Order

Fonecon

Telephone conversation

Ford, Col. Ernest G.

Commander, 18th Fighter-Bomber Wing, 2 February 1952-7 March 1952, succeeding BG Turner C. Rogers.

Formations

    Element: two aircraft.

    Flight: two elements.

    Section: two flights.

    Squadron: two or more sections.

    Group: two or more squadrons.

    Trail formation: aircraft following single file approximately two ship lengths distance and "stacked down" approximately 15 feet below the one ahead.

    Close trail formation: each aircraft "stacked down" about 15' below 2/3s behind the one ahead and above. Propeller will be midway between scoop and tail section.

    Echelon formation: aircraft flying staggered "line abreast" approximately 3' apart and below and with the wing of each succeeding aircraft about 2/3's behind the nose of adjacent aircraft.

    Finger formation: visually approximating the positions of the right four fingers held closely together. "Middle finger" in front, the other "fingers" to the left (one aircraft) and right (two aircraft) flying 3' apart and below each other. "Wings overlapping approximately 3 feet laterally, stack down one ship height, and echelon depth that is necessary to keep #2 wing directly opposite star insignia on lead aircraft."

    Battle or tactical formation: a "finger formation"—wingtip of #2 aircraft will be directly opposite star insignia of lead aircraft— space laterally will be that necessary for wingman to accomplish a 180 degree turn into element lead and pull out 180 degrees to the line of flight of element leader. The horizontal separation of the battle or tactical formation is extended to one "turning diameter" between each aircraft.

Foster, 1st Lt. William G.

In October 1950, a four-aircraft flight led by 1st Lt. William G. Foster, napalm bombed, rocketed and strafed an enemy pocket of resistance in the vicinity of Chong-san, east of Taejon…with such effectiveness that an entire enemy regiment surrendered to UN Forces in that area. The other three pilots in that flight included: Capt. Charles H. Spencer, of Penn Yan, N.Y., who was flying his first Korean mission as wingman for Foster; 1st Lt. George N. Olsen, Pennyville, Ill., with 64 missions was flying the number three position as leader of the second element; and Capt. Edward J. Mason. While en route home the pilots were called by an area controller who asked, "Did you guys hear about the regimental surrender?" "Hear about?" answered Mason, "Hell, we did it."

FPM

Feet Per Minute

Frag Order

The daily Wing operations orders generally directed the Fighter-Bomber Group to perform missions as directed by daily Fifth Air Force Operations orders. The Fighter Group published as a daily operations order the "fragment" which concerned the Squadrons. Thus, the Group orders were known as "frag orders."

Freund, Lt. Col. Albert J.

Succeeded Major Frank Orth as Commanding Officer of the 12th Squadron on 5 August 1952. "Col. Freund came to the unit from the Pilot Training Center at Luke AFB, while Major Orth went the way of all happy warriors to his Valhalla in the states," the 12th noted in its report. Freund relieved Col. Sheldon S. Brinson as 18th FBG Commander on 25 November 1952 and was himself relieved on 24 January 1953, when he was assigned to Headquarters, Fifth AF. A major change occurred in the 12th when Colonel Freund "was elevated to Group Commanding Officer and Major [Vernon] Harwood assumed leadership of the Foxey Few." Harwood had been the 18th Group Training Officer and had been attached to the 67th Squadron.

Frozen Chosin

Korean in the winter.

FSCC

Fire Support Coordination Centers.

Ftr

Fighter

Ftr-Bmr

Fighter-Bomber

Ftr-Escort

Fighter-Escort

Ftr-Intcp

Fighter-Interceptor

Fwd

Forward

g

The force (acceleration) of gravity, normally 1g on earth. Zero g (0g) is weightlessness, as experienced by orbiting astronauts. **G** can be expressed in positive (+) and negative (-) values. During a normal loop a pilot experiences positive g, tending to force him down in his seat. In an outside loop, with the pilot's head on the outside of the vertical circle, negative **g** forces him up against his straps.

G.I.

Government Issue, "but in a broad sense meaning service personnel."

G/A

Go Around

G/S

Groundspeed. The speed an aircraft makes over the ground, a product of its airspeed and wind speed. Also, **Glide Slope**.

G-2

Intelligence section of divisional or higher staff.

G-3

Operations and training section of divisional or higher staff.

Gaggle

Pilot slang for a "loose formation of attacking aircraft." Also, referred to a 16-ship formation—four flights, one from each 18th squadron—a "gaggle" or "wing gaggle."

Gang

River in the Korean language.

Gardiner-Atkinson, Lt. Alan "Shadow"

2nd Squadron pilot SAAF, who on 2 May 1952, flew the 8,000th combat sortie for the "Flying Cheetahs." Lieutenant Gardiner-Atkinson, 27, of Melville, Johannesburg, "smiled as he climbed down from his cockpit to learn that he had had the honor of bringing the Squadron's total to 8,000 strikes. He had just led a flight of four Mustangs through a barrage of heavy flak in a raid on vital Communist rail supply lines near MIG Alley, deep behind enemy lines." (USAFHRA. *Truckbuster. Biweekly newspaper of the 18th Fighter-Bomber Wing.* May 16, 1952.)

GCA

Ground-controlled approach. A landing approach in which a ground controller provides verbal guidance to a pilot using precision navigation aids that monitor the aircraft's approach path. See **Shooting GCS's.**

GCI

Ground Controlled Intercept

GED

General Educational Development

GEN

General

GHQ

General Headquarters

Glide Bombing

See **Skip Bombing**.

GLO

Ground Liaison Officer

Globemaster

C-124; four engine strategic transport aircraft introduced into USAF service during the Korean War. Also known as an "aluminum overcast."

GMT

Greenwich Mean Time

GO

General Orders

Golf balls

Pilot slang for "flak" or anti-aircraft fire. "There was a hell of a fire-fight going on down there," Capt. Jack Hawley, of Bridgeport, Mich., said, "and they weren't all firing at each other. Some of them were firing at us. Golf balls were going by us from all angles. I think that's when rigor mortis of my trigger finger set in."

Goony bird

See **C-47/R4D.**

Great Debate

Also known as the "MacArthur Hearings," the so-called Great Debate on the Korean War began in May 1951 with Congressional hearings before the 26-man joint Senate Foreign Relations and Armed Services committees.

Ground pounders

Pilot slang for non-rated (not aviators), staff officers.

Group

In the Air Force, two-four squadron combat organization, normally commanded by a colonel, in the U.S. Army a group is a command structure controlling several battalion sized elements and is subordinate to a brigade.

Group

See **Formations.**

GS

General Staff

GS

Glideslope—the vertical guidance component of an instrument landing system that establishes a safe glide path (usually three degrees) to a runway. Also **Ground Speed.**

Gun camera

The F-51D could be equipped with a gun camera mounted in the leading edge of the left wing. The camera was loaded and adjusted from the left wheel well. A small door covered the camera when the landing gear was down. A three-position switch on the front switch panel controlled guns and camera. With the switch flicked up to GUNS, CAMERA & SIGHT, the guns fired and the camera operated with the pilot pressed the trigger on the stick. If the switch were pushed down to CAMERA & SIGHT, the pilots could take photographs without firing the guns. Both guns and camera were heated electrically to enable their operation even at high altitude.

Gunnery

The common error in air-to-ground gunnery "is allowing the burst of fire to travel from the first point of fire, through the target and beyond. The most destructive fire is that which is held on the desired target for the length of the time actual firing is accomplished. There are occasions when a dispersed fire is desired, however, most targets are stationary and by "walking" your rounds through your target only a small percentage of them are effective. Here again a steep angle of attack is desired, with the subsequent break-away for evasive action. Depending on the nature of the target, the number of passes will be made to be most effective, that is if it is a heavily defended area a second pass should not be made whereas close support attacks can be pressed." [15]

GW

Gross Weight

H/A (S)

High Angle Strafe

H-19

Helicopter

H-5

Helicopter

HAB

High Angle Bomb

Hagerstrom, Maj. James P.

Major Hagerstrom assumed command of the 67th Squadron on 3 February 1953, succeeding Major Max J. King, and "started the transition program to train pilots to fly the F-86 Sa-

bre jets. "The transition in a combat zone was very difficult and with only a few experienced jet pilots, was accomplished very efficiently," the 67th reported. "The Squadron received very few of the new F-86 aircraft and time was critical. Most of the pilots had never flown a jet aircraft and this made the job seem almost impossible." On 25 February 1953, the 67th flew its first combat mission in the F-86F type aircraft was flown by 18th FBW pilots during a four plane flight on a Yalu sweep. Major Hagerstrom, Commander of the 67th Squadron and flight leader, "shot down one MIG-15 type aircraft," the Group reported. Maj. Hagerstrom, destroyed his fifth MiG on 27 March 1953, to become the twenty-eighth Korean War jet air ace—the first 18th Fighter -omber Group jet ace. Completed combat tour with 8.5 MIG's destroyed and two damaged.

Hammer mission

Name given by 18th Fighter-Bomber Group to missions in which group Mustangs were teamed with 67th Tactical Reconnaissance Wing aircraft to attack "specific enemy artillery positions, supply and troop areas" following the completion of the primary mission in late 1951—rail interdiction.

Hangar flying

Pilot slang for anecdotal experience passed along pilot-to-pilot. "The combination of pilots new to jet aircraft but with a great deal of combat experience and pilots with jet training but no combat experience proved very good," the 67th reported. "By exchanging knowledge and much 'hangar flying', a very effective team developed as the squadron combat record proves," the 67th reported in March 1953.

Hangul

The Korean phonetic writing system, developed by scholars in the court of King Sejong in the fifteenth century, which is used either by itself or in conjunction with Chinese characters. The Korean language is one of the oldest in the world and belongs to the Ural-Altaic family, which includes Finnish and Hungarian. It does not belong to the tonal family of languages such as Mandarin Chinese and Vietnamese, in which meanings change depending on tonal inflection. Korean was written in Chinese ideographs (i.e., characters that represents ideas instead of sounds) until the 15th century. In 1443 Emperor Sejong devised a simple phonetic alphabet called Hangul and consisting of 24 easily learned characters—roughly equivalent to the 26-character Western ABCs.

Harwood, Major Vernon

Commanding Officer, 12th Squadron. A major change occurred in the 12th on 21 November 1952, when Colonel [Albert J.] Freund "was elevated to Group Commanding Officer and Major [Vernon] Harwood assumed leadership of the Foxey Few." Harwood had been the 18th Group Training Officer and had been attached to the 67th Squadron. On 3 February 1953, Major Evans assumed command of the 12th Fighter-Bomber Squadron from Major Harwood, who was reassigned to the Wing Staff as Inspector General.

Hawley, Major Jack

Flew the last combat mission with the F-51 Mustang on January 23, 1953. Awarded the Silver Star. Departed for the Z.I. on 1 May 1953. Major Jack Hawley, Executive Officer of the 67th Squadron, "won the distinction of completing the last combat sortie." Hawley "was given the honor of leading the last F-51 mission because he had been a member of the Squadron longer than anyone else. This ended the era of the famed Mustang. The Mustang was gone but would never be forgotten," the 67th accurately predicted.

HC

High capacity

Hdg

Heading. The direction in which an aircraft's nose points in flight in the horizontal plane, expressed in compass degrees.

HDG

Heading

HE

High explosive

Heara, S/Sgt Howard T.

Two airmen of the 39th FIS armament section "were hurt quite seriously on 24 June 1951 at K-16 when one of the [Korean] laborers dropped a box of napalm igniters. S/Sgt Howard T. Heara and S/Sgt Niel D. Irving attempted to pull the exploding box of phosphorus igniters from the hangar to save the aircraft and other ammunition stored in the general area and received severe burns about their face, neck and arms. Both were immediately evacuated to a nearby hospital and are now in the Tokyo Army Hospital where they are reported to be doing very well. Both airmen are being recommended for the Soldier's Medal."

Heartbreak Ridge

Named by news correspondents covering the action, "Heartbreak Ridge" was an extension of Bloody Ridge three miles to the south and was located in the eastern sector of the Eighth U.S. Army defensive line in the Punchbowl area.

HEAT

High explosive, antitank

Hess, Maj. Dean E.

At the beginning of WWII, Hess was an ordained minister of the Christian Church, living in Cleveland, Ohio. Deciding that he could not expect his parishioners to bear arms for the U.S. if he was not willing to do so, he enlisted in the Aviation Cadet Program and became a pilot. Eventually, he was sent to France in 1944, where he flew P-47's on 63 combat missions. After the war he briefly returned to the pulpit, but was recalled to active duty in 1948 and stationed in Japan. In June 1950, when South Korea was invaded by North Korea, he was immediately assigned as commanding officer of a detachment of USAF personnel training South Korean pilots to fly F-51 type fighters. As Commander of Detachment "1" of 36th Fighter Bomber Squadron (8th Grp) designated "Bout-One" organized at Itazuke, his assigned mission was to train South Korean pilots in F-51s. "Bout One" arrived at Taegu in the evening of 30 June 1950, when Hess reported for duty to KMAG headquarters. Despite numerous obstacles, Hess was able to expand this training into operational flights, which he often led. By June 1951 when he left Korea, he had flown 250 combat missions. During this period, Hess launched an unofficial program that provided food and shelter to the real victims of the war, children who had lost their parents and their homes. So many children were given shelter that Hess' airfield could no longer accommodate them and they were taken to a central orphanage in Seoul. When the Communists began to overrun the city, Hess persuaded the Air Force to lend assistance and, in the midst of last ditch defensive holding actions by U.N. troops, 15 C-54s were flown to Seoul under "Operation Kiddy Car" to evacuate hundreds of children to Cheju Island off the southern coast of Korea where Hess had established an orphanage. With contributions from U.N. soldiers, the orphanage was gradually able to accept more and more children. By the time Hess was transferred from Korea, his orphanage had taken in more than 1,054 Korean children who most likely would otherwise have died. In 1957, Hess published his story in a book entitled "Battle Hymn" which was made into a motion picture which starred Rock Hudson as Dean Hess. Hess' royalties from both the book and the movie were used to construct a new orphanage near Seoul, Korea. Colonel Hess retired from the USAF in 1969.

HF

High Frequency

High timers

Aircraft with above average hours of flight time i.e. required inordinate maintenance to keep them serviceable for the missions they had to perform.

HIGHBOY

Korean War I Corps artillery operation to bring direct fire on enemy positions and bunkers not accessible to other artillery and mortar fire.

HIGHTIDE

During an air refueling test on June 7, 1952, code named Operation HIGHTIDE, thirty-five F-84 ThunderJets took off from Japan, refueled from KB-29M aircraft over Korea, and attacked targets in the north.

Hist

History, Historical

Hit and run

Due to the "vastly increased amount of flak utilized by the enemy," it was becoming "common practice" to use the tactic of "hit-and-run"—"striking those targets closely protected by the enemy no more than twice per mission. It is believed this effects a valuable saving in equipment and personnel while still accomplishing the assigned mission." [16]

Hit the deck

Slang term meaning to either fall onto the ground, or if flying an airplane, to fly as close to the ground as possible (without touching).

Holy Land

Site of peace negotiations at Panmunjom. "In fact, the whole Kaesong area—whose "Holy Land" status protected it from air attacks, even though the truce negotiations had not met there very long—was probably a Communist military concentration point." [17]

HOME COMING

Korean War plan for limited operation offered as a substitute for **BIG STICK**

Honcho pilots

Term used by FEAF pilots for Communist pilots who were highly trained, capable and confident—probably instructor pilots—from "honcho" meaning "boss" in Japanese.

HP

Holding Pattern; horsepower

Hq

Headquarters

Hungnam, Evacuation of

A seaport on North Korea's eastern coast, Hungnam was the port from which the five divisions of the U.S. X Corps were evacuated following the massive Chinese Communist Forces intervention in November 1950 and the subsequent retreat from the Chosin Reservoir. During the first week of November, U.S. forces began to encounter elements of Chinese military units. By 15 November, elements of the U.S. 7th Infantry Division reached Hyesanjin on the Manchurian border. On 27 November eight full corps of CCF troops struck simultaneously at the U.S. 8th Army in the west and at the 5th and 7th Marine Regiments near the Chosen Reservoir. Hopelessly outnumbered and in the dead of a brutal winter, U.S. forces began a fighting withdrawal to force their way out of the massive trap. Aided by close air support from Fifth Air Force and Navy TF 77, U.S. forces linked up at Chinhung-ni on 9 December, the same day that General MacArthur ordered the evacuation of the 10th Corps from Hungnam. The evacuation of U.S. forces from Hungnam and Wonsan was a logistical achievement comparable to the evacuation of the British Army from Dunkirk in 1940. Over 105,000 soldiers, 91,000 civilians, and 17,500 vehicles were taken from Hungnam.

Hunter Groups

Volunteer members of Communist gunnery groups that were promised "hero" decorations and furloughs for destroying three UN aircraft during any 90-day period.

Hunter-Killer Plan

A roadblock plan developed in September 1952 during which the "hunter" crew reconnoitered an assigned roadblock area and determined the best location to establish a roadblock with bombs or other ordnance. After making the roadblock, a "killer" would arrive later to attack backed up vehicles. The locate-block-wait-attack process could be repeated as long as results were obtained.

Hv

Heavy

HVAR

High Velocity Aircraft Rocket. USAF fighter-bombers used the HVAR to knock out Communist tanks, trains, and bunkers. Originally developed by the U.S. Navy in World War II, the HVAR's warhead carried a deadly load of TNT to the target at 1,360 feet per second. Two types of aircraft rockets were employed in Korea, the 5.0" HVAR and the 6.5" ATAR (anti-tank aircraft rocket). The 5.0" HVAR was the

standard USAF and USN aircraft rocket and was used with a MK-148 nose fuse and a MK-149 tail fuse installed in the warhead. The warhead was a blast type with approximately eight pounds of HE (high explosive) filler. In July, 1950, when an urgent need was identified for a shaped charged anti-tank aircraft rocket, the 6.5" ATAR development was accelerated and rushed to the theater. The first 200 ATARs reached the FAF early in August 1950. The ATAR used the standard 5.0" HVAR and had a shaped charge warhead, with a filler weight of approximately 19 pounds. It was detonated by an electrical fuse using a M-36 special detonator.

I&E

Information and Education

I&R

Intelligence & Reconnaissance

IAS

Indicated Air Speed. The airspeed as seen by the pilot on his airspeed indicator. The IAS will differ from True Air Speed (see) at air densities other than a reference density.

ID

Infantry Division

IDENT

Identification

IF

Intermediate Frequency; Infrared

IFF

Identification Friend or Foe, electronic identification system.

IFR

Instrument flight rules prescribed for the operation of aircraft in instrument meteorological conditions, i.e. "bad weather." Also, **In-Flight Refueling**.

IG

Inspector General

In. hg

Inches of mercury

INBD

Inbound

Inchon Invasion

The X Corps amphibious invasion at Inchon on Korea's western coast Sept. 15, 1950, ranks as one of the boldest military maneuvers in history.

Inf

Infantry

Infiltration

Enemy soldiers posing as refugees (wearing traditional Korean white robes over their uniforms) easily blended in with the millions of

South Koreans who had fled their homes to avoid the war. Once behind friendly lines, these infiltrators regrouped and attacked Allied positions from the rear.

Info

Information

INST

Instrument

Instr

Instruction

INTC

Intercept

Intel

Intelligence

Intelligence Section

The 18th Fighter-Bomber Group Intelligence Section had the mission of keeping the Group Commander "informed of any change in enemy air order of battle, capabilities or intentions of the enemy, and all other items of an intelligence nature; also to disseminate to, and collect from, all combat pilots, intelligence information that was received pertinent to their mission. To train non-combat ready pilots in map reading, aircraft recognition, and escape and evasion as applied to this theater of operations; to provide continuation training for combat pilots in aircraft recognition, escape and evasion and current information necessary to accomplished the combat mission of this organization." [18]

Interdiction

Generic term used by the Air Force meaning any air action that prevents, or delays, or destroys enemy movements of men, equipment and supplies to the zone of a ground battle.

Interrog

Interrogation

Interv

Interview

INTSUM

Intelligence Summary

Inverted Flying

Upside down flying in the Mustang was limited to no more than ten seconds because "the oil pressure falls off."

IP

Instructor Pilot; Interception Point.

IR

Instrument rating.

Iron Triangle

The so-called "Iron Triangle" of the Korean War--Chorwon-Kumhwa-Pyonggang--was a triangularly shaped area of relatively flat terrain about 30 miles north of the 38th Parallel in the

642

mountains of east-central North Korea.

JADF

Japan Air Defense Force

JAG

Judge Advocate General

JALCO

Joint Airlift Control Organization

JAMESTOWN

Korean War defensive line to be established by **Operation COMMANDO.**

JATO

Jet-Assisted Take Off

JCS

Joint Chiefs of Staff

Jet Stream

A combat tactic used by Sabre jets in which flights were planned to arrive in patrol areas at five-minute intervals, provided a minimum of four separate high-speed forces within easy supporting distance of each other. See **Train formation**.

JLC

Japan Logistical Command

Jnl

Journal

JOC Alert Missions

When on JOC alert, the "pilots stood by in Squadron Operations awaiting word from Combat Operations that they were to scramble. Fifteen minutes was allowed to obtain the 'flims' [19] (which gave controllers, coordinates, time on target and mission number) and the authentication sheets, to brief, and to get airborne. As soon as the four or eight aircraft committed were landed from a mission, the same number was expected to be ready to go again. There was normally at least an hour or so between each 'scramble.' However, because the missions were rotated among the three Squadrons, forty minutes was allowed normally between receipt of the mission information at combat operations and the time on target, since the front was 18 minutes away at the closest point and 25 at the furthest," the 12th reported. [20]

JOC

Joint Operations Center. "The physical make-up of the center included an Air Force combat operations section and an Army air-ground operations section." [21] The Tactical Air Control Center (TACC), was designed to operate in close association with the JOC and serve as the focal point for aircraft control and warning activities of the tactical air force.

Joto

Slang meaning "OK." "This afternoon the mo-

bile UHF repair team came and fixed up our radios for us. They took until after dark, but everything is joto now," noted Lt. Ken Barber near the Yalu River on 14 November 1950.

Josephine

Radio code word meaning "low on," as in "Josephine ammo" or "Josephine fuel."

JP-1

Jet fuel (refined kerosene). Produced in various "grades," e.g. JP-3 (Navy) or JP-4 (F-86F).

JSPOG

Joint Strategic Plans and Operations Group

K

K-site, Korean Airbase

K-1

Pusan West

K-2

Taegu

K-3

Pohang

K-5

Taejon

K-6

Pyongtaek

K-8

Kunsan

K-9

Pusan East

K-10

Chinhae, approximately 3 miles southeast of Chinhae, Korea. K-10 served as the headquarters and main base of operations for the 18th Fighter-Bomber Group from January 1951 until June 1952.

K-13

Suwon

K-14

Kimpo

K-16

Seoul

K-40

Cheju-do Island

K-46

Approximately 7 mi. NNE of Wonju—127 degrees 57 minutes 30 seconds longitude west, 38 degrees 26 minutes 30 seconds North--approximately five miles southeast of Hoensong, Korea. The 18th Group used the K-46 air strip as a forward combat operations base until June 1952, when the Wing, Group and squadrons made it their headquarters, as well.

K-47

Chunchon

K-55

Osan-ni, approximately 12 miles southeast of

Suwon, Korea. Became the headquarters and operating base for the 18th Fighter-Bomber Wing in January 1953.

Kaesong

A city in western Korea just south of the 38th Parallel, Kaesong was the ancient capital of Korea. It was the first city to fall to the North Koreans June 25, 1950.

KANSAS-WYOMING

Korean War defensive lines in the vicinity of the 38th Parallel

KATUSA

Korean Augmentation to the U.S. Army.

KComZ

Korean Communications Zone

KG

Kilogram

KHz

Kilohertz, the frequency of a radio carrier wave measured in thousands of cycles per second. 1 kHz = 1,000 Hertz.

KIA

Killed in Action

(Operation) KILLER

Launched Feb. 21, 1951, Operation Killer (and its extensions, Operations Ripper, Courageous, Rugged and Dauntless) marked the beginning of the Allied counteroffensive to drive the Chinese Communist Forces and the North Korean People's Army out of South Korea. "The Eighth Army launched Operation KILLER to destroy large numbers of enemy troops while moving the UN line northward to the Han River." [22]

King, Lt. Col. Max J.

18th FBW Operations Officer, Feb. 18, 1953. DFC and BS in Spring 1953. On 23 January 1953, King as CO of the 67th Squadron led George and How flights on the last F-51 mission. Turned over command of the 67th to Major James P. Hagerstrom on 3 February 1953.

Km

Kilometer

KMAG

Korean Military Advisory Group (Army). See **EUSAK.**

KMC

Korean Marine Corps

KMC

Korean Marine Corps

Knot (kt)

One nautical mile per hour (never one knot per hour), the standard unit of aviation speed measurement. One knot equals 1.1515 mph; one nautical mile equals 6,080 feet.

Koje-do

Location of major prisoner of war camps. In May 1952 major riots took place at Koje-do.

Korean Communications Zone

(KCOMZ) Op Plan 14-54   See **Operation GLORY.**

KPA

Korean People's Army

KT

Knots

Kunu-ri, Battle of

The site of one of the major battles of the Korean War, Kunu-ri is located in northwestern Korea about 20 miles upstream from the mouth of the Chongchon River and some 75 air miles Southeast of the Manchurian border.

L-19

In the late 1940's the United States Army issued a requirement for a light two seat observation and liaison monoplane aircraft. Cessna Aircraft. Combat roles for the L-17 included artillery spotting, scouting and reconnaissance. "For the first time, the U.S. Army began using its own aircraft, the L-19 Bird Dog, for forward air control, artillery spotting, and other front-line duties, relieving Fifth Air Force of demands for these types of missions." [23]

LAB

Low Angle Bomb (Napalm)

LAS

Low Angle Strafe

LAT

Latitude

Lawrence, Lt. Col. Henry W. "Hank"

On 31 March 1951, Lt. Col. Lawrence relieved Lt. Col. William E. May as Commanding Officer of the 67th Squadron. Lawrence was relieved by Major Carl C. Colson in June 1951.

LCVP

Landing craft, vehicle, personnel

Ldr

Leader

Levenson, Col. Seymour

Commander, 18th Fighter-Bomber Group. On 30 November 1951, Colonel Seymour M. Levenson, assumed command of the 18th Fighter-Bomber Group from Colonel Ralph H. "Salty" Saltsman, "the ever popular and efficient Group Commander," who departed for the States. Lt. Col. Henry W. Lawrence was assigned as Group Executive Officer.

LITTLE SWITCH

Operation Little Switch, April 20–May 3, 1953, was the initial exchange of sick and wounded prisoners of the Korean War that was agreed to during the truce talks at Panmunjom on April 11, 1953. The Communist side repatriated 684 U.N. sick and wounded troops, while the UNC turned over 1,030 Chinese and 5,194 Koreans. The exchange was marked by demonstrations by the prisoners designed to embarrass UN forces by throwing away food and clothing that had been issued to them.

Log

Logistical

LON

Longitude

Long, Lt. Col. Stanley A.

Commanding Officer, 67th Fighter-Bomber Squadron from April 1952, succeeding Lt. Col. Julian Crow. Born in August 1918, during WWII he flew with the 11th AF in the Aleutian Theater as CO of the 54th Fighter Squadron flying the P-38 Lightning aircraft. During 100 missions in the Lightning, he scored three kills on Japanese aircraft. Between WWII and the Korean War, he was the owner and operator of "Long's Air Activities" and taught flying courses to civilian pilots.

Loran

Low-frequency radio long-range navigation system; measures time difference between reception of synchronized signals transmitted from ground transmitters.

Low, Col. Curtis R.

Commander, 18th Fighter-Bomber Wing, 1 December 1950-1 February 1951. On 5 July 1951, Col. Low received the Korean Presidential Unit Citation on behalf of the Wing" presented by Maj. Gen. Kim Chung Yul, chief of staff of the Republic of Korea Air Force.

Ltr

Letter

Lufberry

A tight circling turn, usually horizontal. A common practice when attacked from the rear was to make a tight turn, the 'Lufberry Circle', causing the less maneuverable jets to fly past. "It is important that one man control the rescue. It will be his responsibility to establish high and low cover and to neutralize the ground fire in the vicinity of the downed pilot prior to the arrival of the rescue aircraft. When the rescue aircraft reaches the location of the downed pilot, a luftberry [tight turning circle] should be established around the rescue aircraft so as to discourage ground fire and keep the rescue operation under constant observation." [18th Fighter-Bomber Wing Combat Operating Procedures] Additional insights were provided by Lt. Col. Duane "Bud" Biteman. The Lufberry, in the described case, is a slight misuse of the term. The original Lufberry maneuver was developed by a French-American Raoul Luftberry, who moved to Connecticut in 1904 and became a U.S. citizen. In WWI he joined the Lafayette Escadrille, was eventually credited with 17 "kills" and was killed in combat on 19 May 1918. A Lufberry is nothing more than a *very tight turn*, usually almost horizontal, to prevent the trailing attacker, who is also in a *very tight turn*, from sighting far enough ahead of your aircraft to "lead it" and for his bullets to possibly strike your aircraft. It's an effective defensive maneuver, but sooner or later one or the other aircraft is going to have to break out of the circle—and that is the moment of greatest danger because the enemy can follow and fire straight on. The use of the term Lufberry in the unit history report is therefore erroneous, and instead should have been described simply as a "tight circle" around the downed pilot, rather than a Lufberry. It takes at least "Two to Tango" in order to fly a Lufberry Circle.

LW

Light Weight

M

Mach number; Manual

M&S

Maintenance and Supply

MacArthur, General of the Army Douglas

General of the Army (five star rank) MacArthur was designated commander in chief of the United Nations Command by President Harry S Truman July 8, 1950, and given command of the Republic of Korea Armed Forces by ROK President Syngman Rhee July 14, 1950. In mid-April, 195, President Truman shocked the world by replacing General MacArthur, who had publicly criticized the administration's Korean War policies, with Lt. Gen. Matthew B. Ridgway, USA.

Mach number

Ratio of true airspeed to the speed of sound. Mach 1 is the speed of sound at sea level, ISA, approximately 1,100 feet per second or 760 mph.

Mae West

Air crew life vest for use in a ditching or over water bailout. (Note the correct spelling - it was named for the movie actress) "...Then over all that goes the 'Mae West,' which, when inflated, makes the origin of the name quite obvious. The item was designed to save the

wearer from drowning, but not from freezing."
Truckbuster, September 30, 1952.

MAG
Magnetic

MAINT
Maintenance

MAN
Manual

MAP'
Missed Approach

MARDIV
Marine Division

Martin, Col. Maurice L.
Colonel Maurice L. Martin assumed command of the 18th Fighter-Bomber Group on 24 January 1953, relieving Lt. Col. Albert J. Freund, who was reassigned to Headquarters, Fifth AF. On 13 March 1953, Colonel Martin, 18th Group Commander, engaged two MIGs while leading a two Squadron SAAF flight and shot down one. Martin assumed command of the 18th Fighter-Bomber Wing, 5 July 5, 1953, succeeding Col. John C. Edward.

MASH
Mobile Army Surgical Hospital

MATS
Military Air Transport Service

MAW
Marine Aircraft Wing

Maximum Effort
A strike by a large number of planes on a single target. When intelligence analysts and tactical planners determined that a particular target was important enough to justify a major strike, a squadron or more likely a group, would be tasked to hit a target with all its available resources—"maximum effort"—Col. Joe Peterburs explained. "The Group would put together a force from all four squadrons and we would get from 30-50 birds in the air all hitting the same target at the same time."

May, Lt. Col. William
Commanding Officer, 67th Fighter-Bomber Squadron, succeeded Major Arnold Mullins on 14 November 1950. On 1 March 1951, Lt. Col. May "abandoned his aircraft successfully after being struck by intense enemy ground fire behind enemy lines. He was rescued by a helicopter from the heavy cruiser St. Paul." May was hospitalized for burns. "Lt. Col. May was also shot down," Lt. Ken Barber recorded. "He was hit bad and flames were licking at his feet. He jettisoned his canopy and the flames really sucked up into his face, burning it, and he had to bail out—right over the enemy front lines."

All four of the ships covering him were hit with small arms fire. The helicopter came in—then backed off. Capt. Croner told him to get the hell back in and pick up that man. This time the copter did, dropping a rope ladder up which Col. May scrambled! The 'copter' had plenty of holes in it. Col. May is on a hospital ship—only burned around the face. Sure is lucky." On 31 March 1951, Lt. Col. Henry W. Lawrence relieved Lt. Col. May as Commanding Officer of the 67th Squadron.

Mayday
International radio distress call (from the French, *m'aidez* or "help me."). It signifies imminent danger to life requiring immediate assistance. Pilots were advised to "transmit 'Mayday' three times, followed by the call sign of your plane three times," followed by detailed information regarding estimated position, time, course, speed, altitude, intentions, etc.

McBride, Col. William P.
Commander, 18th Fighter-Bomber Group, in May 1951, succeeding Lt. Col. Homer M. Cox, who was transferred to Japan. On 5 June 1951, while leading a flight of four F-51s of the 67th Squadron, Col. McBride "who took command of the Group during the month of June, was struck in the face by automatic weapons fire and had to belly land at K-16. He has been in the Tokyo General Hospital since that date and has had to undergo several operations." Lt. Col. Ralph H. Saltsman, Jr. assumed command of the 18th F-B Group on 5 June 1951 and Lt. Col. Henry W. Lawrence "was brought up from the 67th Squadron to serve as Group Executive. Major Carl C. Colson moved from Group Operations to replace Colonel Lawrence as commander of the 67th." (USAFHRA. *Monthly Historical Report, 18th Fighter Bomber Group*, June 1951, p. 2.)

McGee, Major Charles E.
Led a 67th Squadron flight of four F-51's on 28 December 1950 in a close support mission of UN ground forces in the H'wachon Reservoir area where enemy forces "occupied positions approximately 50 yards north of friendly troops." Following the attack, approximately 125 CCF troops surrendered. McGee flew the 7,000th combat sortie for the 18th Wing on 28 January 1951.

Med
Medical Staff

Medal of Honor
The highest American military award for battlefield bravery.

MedTk
Medium Tank

Mellow Control
On July 20, 1950 control of tactical support aircraft was assumed at Taegu by the FAF-Eighth Army JOC. Its radio control station at Taegu was given the call sign of "Mellow." Fighter aircraft were directed to the front by **Mellow Control** (Tactical Air Control Center) and **Mosquito Mellow**. When they arrived in the operating area, airborne Mosquitoes FACs directed them to specific targets.

Meteor
British twin jet fighter aircraft used by the RAAF during the Korean War, primarily for air-to-ground interdiction and close air support missions.

MFA
Military Flying Area

MHz
Megahertz, the frequency of radio carrier waves measured in millions of cycles per second.

MIA
Missing in Action

MIG Alley
The area between the Chongchon and Yalu Rivers in northwestern Korea—roughly bordered by Sinuiju/Antung, Changju , Huichon and Sinanju—where Communist air forces were numerically superior.

MIG-15
Mikoyan "Fagot": single-engine jet fighter (Soviet)

MIG-21
Mikoyan "Fishbed": single-engine jet fighter (Soviet)

Mil
Military

Milk run
Easy mission or assignment.

Million dollar wound
A wound serious enough to get you sent home, but from which one would recover with no permanent disabilities. "One man was shot through the fat of his leg--the million dollar wound, another broke his leg, one had his helmet creased by a bullet." (Lt. Ken Barber's Korean War diary)

MILSPEC
Military Specifications

MIS
Military Intelligence Service

Mission assignment
"Normally, all mission assignments will be extracted form the Fifth Air Force Operations Or-

der for the day by A-3 [Operations Officer] of the 18th Fighter-Bomber Wing, who will coordinate the assignment with S-3 section of the Group. Breakdown of commitments will be accomplished by Group Operations and distributed to each squadron in sufficient time to accomplish the assigned mission. Flight Scheduling for each mission will be at the discretion of the individual Squadron Commanders, however, care should be exercised to insure equitable distribution of missions to pilots in his organization." [24]

MLR

Main Line of Resistance or the location of the main battle lines or front lines.

MN

Magnetic North

Monologue

Early radio call sign for the 12th Fighter-Bomber Squadron.

Moolah

An offer in May 1953 to Red pilots of $50,000 and political asylum if they would deliver their MIG-15 to the UN forces. The objective was to obtain a flyable MIG-15 for testing and evaluation. Even if the ploy did not produce an airplane prior to the Armistice, General Clark hoped to make Red air commanders suspicious of regarding the loyalty of their pilots.

Mort

Mortar

Mortars

High-angle fire weapons, making them particularly suitable for Korea's mountainous terrain.

Mosquito Mellow

Air borne forward air control aircraft, whose crew included U.S. Army personnel, relayed information to aircraft and could divert air strikes for greater efficiency. See **Mellow Control**.

Mosquito

A Fifth Air Force (FAF) **fragmentary operations order** issued on July 15, 1950 assigned airborne controllers radio call signs as "Mosquito Able," Mosquito Baker," and "Mosquito How." The catchy call signs soon became the unofficial nickname for the "Mosquito squadron." Soon, pilots were calling airborne controllers and their planes "Mosquitoes." By August 1, 1950, the 614th Tactical Control Squadron (Airborne) was created and assigned to the FAF at Taegu. Almost immediately, the Eighth Army began to assign officers and NCOs to the "mosquito" squadron as observers to ride in the back seat of the T-6s patrolling the lines and controlling air strikes. Because the T-6s often flew far below the "radio horizon," the 614th kept another plane orbiting at a much greater altitude—"Mosquito Mellow"—that relayed messages of the airborne controllers into the **TACC**. Mosquitos were seldom permitted to penetrate more than several miles into or over enemy territory.

MPC

Military Payment Certificate

MS

Manuscript

Msg

Message

MSgt

Master Sergeant

MSL

Mean Sea Level

MSR

Main Supply Route

MSTS

Military Sea Transportation Service

MTBF

Mean Time Between Failures

MTD

Mobile Training Detachment. "Pilots were scheduled to attend a 10 day MTD course consisting of 40 hours of instruction and a short ground school course conducted by the **CCTF** unit (see). Concurrently, they started flying in the T-33 for jet familiarization and progressed into the F-86 early in February," the 12th reported.

Mustang

(Air Force) Name of the F-51 Mustang fighter plane, a single engine, propeller driven aircraft, primarily used for fighter-bomber missions during the Korean War. (Navy) Officer promoted from the enlisted ranks.

N

North

N/A

Not Applicable

Naktong Perimeter, Battle of

Also known as the "Pusan Perimeter," the Naktong Perimeter battle was the name given to Eighth U.S. Army's initial defense of the Republic of Korea.

Napalm

An acronym derived from naphthenic and palmitic acids whose salts are used in its manufacture. NAPALM is a jellied gasoline used in flame throwers, fougasses and aerial bombs. Napalm was used in two forms, the 110-gallon drop tank with one or two igniters and the AN/M-76 gasoline jelly bomb using an AN/M-103 nose fuse and an AN/M-101-A2 tail fuse. Normal loading for napalm was two tanks or bombs per fighter-bomber aircraft. "Napalm destroyed or neutralized more T-34 tanks than all other airborne weapons combined," according to FAF operational analyses. "Approximately 10 times as many tanks were claimed to have been destroyed (or 14 times as many hit) by rockets as by napalm...it can only be concluded that whereas relatively large effort has been expended in shooting rockets at enemy tanks, and apparently resulting in hits, actually only a small fraction were hits. Had actual hits been obtained, a much larger number of tanks would have been found due to rockets." [25] Because napalm is generally used against relatively small targets, and because it must spread to a large area when dropped, it is released at a low altitude where the bomb will have a skipping effect on impact, the Combat Operations Manual for the 18th Fighter-Bomber Wing explained. "The bomb run should not be a shallow one as you present much too fine a target for the enemy. A high angle dive with a level out before release at 50'-100' followed by a sharp break in either direction will prove to be the most effective while subjecting yourself to a minimum possibility of being hit. Be prepared for instability resulting from a 'hung-up' bomb when at release altitude, as aircraft have been known to execute a roll if not properly checked." Eighteenth Wing pilots dropped over 22,000 napalm bombs during the Korean War.

Narr

Narrative

Natl

National

NAV

Navigation

NAVAID

Navigational Aid

NAVFE

U.S. Naval Forces, Far East

NCO

Non-commissioned officer

Night hecklers

See **Bed Check Charley**.

NKA

North Korean Army

NKAF

North Korean Air Force

NKPA

North Korean People's Army

NM

Nautical Mile

Norman, Col. Henry H.

Commander, 18th Fighter-Bomber Group until 16 June 1950 when he was succeeded by Lt. Col. Ira L. "Ike" Wintermute.

Nose ups

A sudden stop or runway surface problem could cause a taxiing aircraft, particularly the F-51 to pitch forward onto its nose doing significant damage to the prop and engine in the process. "Whenever the ground is softened by rains, the parking and taxiing problems are also a menace. The utmost caution is necessary to avoid mud-holes which could cause nose-ups or gear damage." [26]

NOTAM

Notices to Airmen, issued by aviation authorities to inform pilots of new or changed aeronautical facilities, services, procedures or hazards, temporary or permanent.

Nr

Number

o/r

On Request.

o/t

Other Times.

Oak Leaf Cluster

A metallic oak leaf cluster is worn on the ribbon of a medal to denote subsequent awards of the same decoration in the Army and Air Force.

OAT

Outside Air Temperature. OAT affects the measurement of indicated airspeed and its value is needed to calculate true airspeed.

OB

Order of Battle

OCMH

Office of the Chief of Military History

Ofc

Office

Off

Officer, Officers

OJT

On-the-Job-Training. "All airmen received [in December 1951 by the 18th Group] were either recruits who possessed only technical school training or airmen of the top three pay grades who had been on recruiting duty or away from normal operations for a period of several years. Intensive on-the-job training materially assisted in improving the qualifications of airmen but at the cost of decreased efficiency" for the squadrons," noted Group Commander, Col. Seymour Levenson.

OP

Operational

OPAREA

Operating Area

Operation Glory

The Armistice Agreement signed in Panmunjom in June 1953 included a provision agreeing to the exchange of military war dead on both sides. On July 20, 1954, it was agreed that the exchange of deceased personnel should formally commence on 1 September 1954 and end no later than 30 October, if possible. Implementation of Korean Communications Zone (KCOMZ) Op Plan 14-54 – better known as "Operation GLORY" – was put into effect on 22 July 1954. On August 30, 1954, the disinterment of all enemy deceased military personnel was completed, and all remains delivered and stored at "Glory Railhead," near Munsan-Ni, Korea. The exchange of deceased military personnel between the United Nations in South Korea, and the Communists in North Korea, continued daily, except Sundays, until September 21, 1954. A final tally indicated that 4,023 UN deceased personnel had been received from the North Koreans, and that 13,528 had been delivered to them. [27]

Operational Damage

"Any damage to the aircraft not due to enemy action. Operational damage includes engine failure, canopy failure, fragments or debris from the aircraft's own armament, or damage sustained in scraping trees or terrain." (Memorandum No. 40, Operations Analysis Office, Hq. Fifth Air Force, 31 March 1951)

Operational Loss

"Any aircraft that is lost on a combat mission due to aircraft malfunction or pilot error." (Memorandum No. 40, Operations Analysis Office, Hq. Fifth Air Force, 31 March 1951)

OPLR

Outpost Line of Resistance, a series of strong points in advance of the MLR (main line of resistance).

Opns

Operations

OPPLAN

Operational/operations Plan

OPT

Optimum

Ord

Order

ORT

Operational Readiness Test

Orth, Maj. Frank L.

Succeeded Lt. Col. Joseph T. Crane, Jr. as CO of the 12th Squadron on June 18, 1952. Orth had "considerable World War II fighter experience to recommend him for the job," the 12th reported. For a short period, Orth was Commander of the 18th Group, before turning it over to Col. Sheldon S. Brinson on June 18, 1952.

OSAF

Office of the Secretary of the Air Force

OSI

Office of Special Investigation

OTC

Officer in Tactical Command

Out of Commission for Parts

See **AOCP**.

OVERWHELMING

Korean War (1951) plan for an offensive by Eighth Army to the P'yonggang-Wonsan line (cancelled).

Paengnyong-do

A small island on Korea's west coast south of Cho-do (See) on which a lightweight air search and control radar was operated.

Papasan

Slang term used to designate the male head of a Korean family. To be a "real" Papasan the titleholder had to wear a very high black stovepipe hat.

Paradrops

Slang for "parachute drops." "The F-51s provided a fighter escort for the parachute drops—paradrops—at Sukchon and Sunchon, where the 187th Regimental Combat Team was being landed to cut off retreating North Korean troops."

Partridge, Gen. Earle Everard

General Partridge was named commander of Fifth Air Force in Nagoya, Japan, in October 1948. When the Korean War began, Partridge took the Fifth Air Force to Korea where he commanded it until June 1951. When the 24th Infantry Division fought the North Koreans at Taejon in early July, Partridge sent the Fifth Air Force to furnish close support and throughout the critical days in July the Fifth Air Force and the Eighth Army set a brilliant example of air and ground cooperation at its best. On 4 March 1951, General Partridge visited K-10 to present decorations to members of the 18th Fighter Bomber Wing and to present the Wing with a scroll honoring it upon completion of 10,000 effective combat sorties as of 24 February. "This record was compiled by pilots assigned to the 18th Fighter-Bomber Group and 2 Squadron, South African Air Force. The ceremonies were very impressive in that, for the first time, an honor guard of officers and airmen were on hand." On May 20th, General Stratemeyer, FEAF Commander, suffered a severe heart attack. He was succeeded by General Partridge, and MGen Edward J. Timberlake, Jr., USAF, took his place as Fifth Air Force Commander. Earle Everard Partridge was born in Wichendon, Mass., enlisted in the Army in July 1918 at Fort Slocum, N.Y., and went to France in August 1918 to join the 79th Division, participating in the St. Mihiel and Argonne operations prior to the Armistice. When the division returned in June 1919 he was honorably discharged. He reenlisted in 1920, attended West Point and took his Commission in the Air Service. In mid-July 1936 Partridge became a test pilot at Wright Field, flying many of the planes which were later used in World War II. During WWII his experience included Air War Planning and Joint Strategy. In 1943, he was sent overseas to Africa and eventually served as chief of staff of both the 12th Bomber Command and the Fifteenth Air Force, deputy commander of the Eighth Air Force and commanding general of the 3rd Bomb Division. Following an assignment at Headquarters Army Air Forces in January 1946 as assistant chief of staff for operations, he was ordered to Japan in October 1948 as commanding general of the Fifth Air Force, serving through the first year of the Korean War. Partridge was promoted to lieutenant general in April 1951. On his return to the United States in June Partridge commanded the newly formed Air Research and Development Command at Baltimore, Md., until June 1953 when he went to Headquarters U.S. Air Force as Deputy Chief of Operations for Operations. Going to Japan in April 1954 as a four-star general he became commander of the Far East Air Forces at Tokyo. Partridge returned home in July 1955 and was named commander in chief of the North American Air Defense Command and its Air Force Component, the Air Defense Command, at Ent Air Force Base, Colorado Springs. He retired from active duty July 31, 1959.

Pathfinder technique

A "pathfinder" flight involved a flight of two experienced pilots leaving a tactical airfield about ten minutes ahead of the main fighter-bomber strike, reconnoitering the assigned target area, and then marking the objective for the fighter-bombers by making the first attack.

Patton, 1st Lt. George Vernon

67th Squadron pilot KIA on 13 June 1952. "I was in Japan awaiting transportation home," 1st Lt. Wilfred "Budd" Stapley recalled, "when I got word that George had been shot down on his last scheduled mission. It was during a mission to Ping Pong [Pyongyang, NK] and his wingman said a 90-mm shell hit his aircraft in the cockpit. The aircraft fell in pieces." Patton, the namesake and nephew of General George Patton, was also an Army brat. His father, Stapley recalled, was a career army officer. The young Patton had flown a combat tour during WWII as a tail gunner on a B-17. While they were roommates at Craig AFB, Alabama during Advanced Single Engine flight training, Stapley recalled Patton "as the most dedicated person to doing the best job possible that I ever saw. The Air Force lost a future General when it lost George Patton." On 27 January 1952, Patton had been hit by ground fire while over his target and forced to bail out. He was picked up and returned to K-46 with minor injuries, the unit history reported dryly. "George had beaten the odds once before in Korea," Stapley remembered. George Patton was on a close air support mission when he was hit. Wrestling the badly damaged Mustang for control and trying to gain enough altitude to bail out, Patton also tried to get "disconnected" enough to bail out—but he was "hung up" on his equipment, straps, cables and harness. As he's fighting to keep the plane in the air and to get himself clear enough to bail out, the plane is heading south—closer to the no-man's land between the UN and Communist forces. Finally, when he was clear, he bailed out—and landed literally between the lines—in a mine field. Friendly troops were trying to tell him he was in a mine field, but he didn't hear or understand the warnings. "Stay down. Stay down," they yelled, "we'll come out and get you." Caught in the middle of a combat zone, Patton was in no frame of mind to sit there and wait to be rescued. After all, he was so close to friendly forces that he could see and hear them—almost. All he had to do to be rescued was get over to them…as fast as he could run. And run, he did, right through a mine field that he was later told was designed to ensure no person on foot could get through—alive. "You are the luckiest guy…alive," they told him when he reached friendly troops south of the "bomb line." To calm his nerves, they offered him a drink…and then another. By the time he had been picked up by a helicopter and

returned to K-46, his "nerves" were much better. "George said after he found that out, it took about a pint of Kentucky's finest to settle his nerves," Stapley remembered.

PB4Y

Consolidated "Privateer": four-engine patrol plane (USA)

PBM

Martin "Mariner": twin-engine flying boat (USA)

PDC

Pre-Departure Clearance

Perego, Col. Frank S.

Commander, 18th Fighter-Bomber Wing, 1 January 1953-15 June 1953, succeeding Col. William H. Clark. Morale that had taken a steep dive in late August 1952, "shot up considerably when the unpopular uniform regulations imposed upon the squadron were abrogated when Col. Perego assumed command of the Wing. The pilots and other members of the squadron immediately donned their weird assortment of headgear which are so important to their individuality," the 12th reported.

PERF

Performance

Pers

Personnel

Pickle

To push the bomb release--"pickle button"--on the B-8 grip in the F-86 aircraft.

PIF

See **Pilot Information Files.**

Piggy-back F-51

A "big morale booster," the 39th FIS reported in June 1951, "in the maintenance section was the squadron's 'piggy-back' F-51 [a Mustang with the 85-gallon fuselage tank removed to allow a second passenger behind the pilot]. Many of the airmen had the opportunity to ride in this "T-51" and received the thrill of their lives when the pilot put the plane through a few aerobatics." [28] One Journalist, S/Sgt William J. "Sandy" Colson was in the Pig during a combat mission when the aircraft was being flown by Lt. Col. Ira Wintermute, 18th Group Commander at the time. Also, simply "the Pig."

PILEDRIVER

Korean War (1951) counterattack operation

Pilot Information Files

Pilot Information Files were set up in every squadron ready room. To augment these files and to disseminate information to all pilots, 18th FB Group Operations established a writing of "PIF" Memos which call items of flying safety, pilot techniques, and operational conditions to the pilot's attention in brief and concise form." [29]

Pincer and envelopment technique

Coordinated "trains" of 60-80 MIG's that crossed the Yalu at altitudes above 35,000 feet. A "west coast train" and the "central train" dropped off flights or small sections that engaged UN Sabre patrols. However, the main bodies continued south to converge over Pyongyang where they would begin a return trip to the Yalu. While en route, a portion of the formation would drop down to 15,000 feet to attack UN fighter-bombers, homeward bound Sabres, or other straggler aircraft.

Ping pong

Pilot slang for Pyongyang, capitol of North Korea.

PINK

Korean War (December 1950) emergency shipment of logistical support from the Continental United States to build up the Far East Command.

PIR

Periodic Intelligence Report

Piss Call Charlie

A lone North Korean bomber "who would fly over the base [K-9, K-16 or K-46] at about the same time each night, just before midnight, and drop a bomb somewhere on or near the airfield."

PLA

People's Liberation Army

Plat

Platoon

PLM

Production Line Maintenance System.

PLR

Periodic Logistics Report

PMB

Provisional Marine Brigade

PO-2

Polikarpov: light night bomber biplane (Soviet).

POE

Port of Embarkation

POL

Petroleum, oil, and lubricants

POLECHARGE

Korean War plan for the capture of hill objectives on the **JAMESTOWN** line during **Operation COMMANDO.**

Police Action

President Harry S Truman used this phrase to describe the U.S. intervention in Korea.

POR

Periodic Operations Report

Pork Chop Hill, Battle of

Site of one of the last U.S. battles of the Korean War July 6-10, 1953.

Porpoising

Pitching up and down. See **Compressibility**.

POS

Position

Post-holing

Technique of cratering airfields or roads to reduce their usefulness or require extensive repairs. When the technique was used on airfields, reported Col. Bill Myers, the bombs were fused with various time delays. When "postholing roads with 500-lb GP bombs it was found that a dive angle of 30 degrees with an air speed of 300 mph and release points of 800 feet produced the best results. For destruction of tunnels, **skip bomb** tactics were used." [30]

POW

Prisoner of War

Powdered eggs

"Powdered eggs and powdered milk were simply that," remembered Lt. Col. William Cothern, USAF (Ret). "Easy to ship and store they were reconstituted to (scrambled eggs) and whole milk, although they were not considered 'gourmet food' by the troops."

Powdered Milk

See **Powdered eggs**.

Prang

Pilot slang for crash or badly damaged. "I had three other guys let the torque get the best of them and prang on take off," Colonel Joe Peterburs, former training officer for the 18th Fighter-Bomber Wing and the 12th Squadron in 1952. In September 1951, the *Truckbuster* ran a photograph of Capt. Alonzo Wagner, 39th FIS, standing behind a "practically non-existent elevator...ribs and little else." Wagner said he thought the fighter "acted a little funny" when he came in for a landing. "It's a good thing I didn't realize how badly pranged that elevator was or I'd probably have bailed out."

Pre-briefed Targets

"Targets that are of such a nature as to warrant assignment of a specific mission before take off are pre-briefed targets and generally include bridges, rail and road cuts, flak batteries, marshalling yards, etc. As the primary mission is the destruction of a particular target, the most direct route to that area should be taken, circumnavigating flak areas, which

could cause disruption of the mission. The armament load will be determined by the particular type of mission, which in turn will have a direct bearing on the type of tactics employed. Upon completion of the assigned mission, the flight will return to base, providing all armament has been expended. If the flight has not expended all armament and has sufficient fuel, they will perform an armed reconnaissance of the area en route to the base." [31]

PRESSURE PUMP

On July 11, 1952, in the first raid of Operation PRESSURE PUMP, nearly every operational air unit in the Far East attacked thirty targets in Pyongyang, in the largest single strike of the war to that date.

PROC

Procedure

PROF

Profile

Project Rebirth

Established at **FEAMCOM** in January 1951 to provide Depot Inspection and Repair of "war-weary F-51 aircraft," began functioning effectively in February 1951.

Project Spartan

A personnel-cutting purge instituted by FEAF in early 1953. Units already undermanned for the mission, reported severe consequences as a result of the cuts. "Our Personnel Services Section was confronted by every imaginable obstacle," the 18th Wing reported in early 1953, "the most serious of which was the skimpy personnel authorization, especially after we were 'Spartanized.' We were able to develop a full, well-rounded program only because of the tenacity and caliber of the personnel we were fortunate enough to have assigned. These men, all of them, worked a 12- to 14-hour day, not once in a while, but every single day of the period covered by this history [six month]. They gave unstintingly of their time, their efforts, and their talents. All of us who reaped the fruits of their labors are, indeed, indebted to these few men." [32]

Project Spotlight

As a part of Project SPOTLIGHT, an RB-26 located five locomotives in one marshaling yard, and two B-26 light bombers destroyed four and damaged the fifth on 26 December 1952... Light bomber attacks against locomotives traveling at night continued in Operation SPOTLIGHT, which maintained locomotive kills at the same high level as in January.

PSP

Pierced Steel Plank, used to create temporary runways.

Psychological Warfare

Operations at tactical, operational and strategic levels. On the battlefield, tanks were painted to resemble tigers in an attempt to spread panic among the enemy troops. On the other side, CCF troops used bugles, whistles and loudspeakers to scare the Allied defenders. At the operational level, both sides made extensive use of pamphlets to undermine their opponent's morale and encourage them to desert.

Pub

Publication

Punchbowl, Battles of

A peculiar terrain feature in eastern Korea along what would become the demarcation line when the Armistice was signed. The Punchbowl was an ancient volcanic crater some four to five miles in diameter rimmed by hills ranging from 1,000 to 2,000 feet.

Pusan

Located in southeastern Korea near the delta of the Naktong River, Pusan was and is South Korea's second largest city.

PW

Prisoner of War

Pyongyang

Capital of North Korea.

QTY

Quantity

QUAD

Quadrant

R&R

Rest and Recuperation or "rape and rampage" as it was sometimes known. Selected by their units, participants were flown to Japan on Air Force transports for five days temporary duty in Japan. On arrival they were paid, issued uniforms, fed and provided with a billet in a Special Services hotel or on one of the many military bases in Japan. Then they were left alone to "rest and recuperate."

R&R

Rearming and Refueling ramp. An R&R Operation meant "a situation whereby a sufficient number of personnel and equipment are sent to a forward strip to refuel and to rearm the tactical planes and to brief and debrief the pilots. The aircraft operate from the strip during the day but return to home base over night," an 18th Fighter-Bomber Wing directive explained. An R&R operation required four officers and 28 Airmen from the fighter group,

plus 5 airmen for napalm mixing, 3 Airmen for refueling operations, 4 mechanics, 4 cooks and 2 medical corpsmen.

R/C

Rate of Climb

RAAF

Royal Australian Air Force

Rad

Radio

RAD

Radial; Radio

RAF

Royal Air Force

RAN

Royal Australian Navy

Rashin

A port city 17 miles from the Soviet frontier on Korea's eastern coast, the town of Rashin is connected to the Soviet port of Vladivostok, which is less than 110 miles away by both rail and road.

Rat Killer

On November 12, 1951, General Ridgway ordered the U.S. Eighth Army to cease offensive operations and begin "Operation Ratkiller," an active defense of the Main Line of Resistance. In January 1952, the Army announced the results of Operation Ratkiller," its campaign to eliminate guerrillas and bandits in the Chirisan mountains.

Rated Officer

Air Force officer having earned his wings as a pilot.

Razon

A 1,000-pound, radio-guided bomb

RB-26

Douglas "Invader": twin-engine reconnaissance plane (USA)

RCC

Rescue Control Center

RCS

Reports Control Symbol

RCT

Regimental Combat Team

RDF

Radio Direction Finding--name first used for what became Radar

Rec

Recoilless

Recce areas

Reconnaissance areas or sectors.

Recd

Received

Recce

See **Armed reconnaissance**. The 67th re-

ported, "due to difficulties encountered in seeking camouflaged targets while carrying external tanks on low altitude reconnaissance missions, Squadron Operations gained the prerogative to **recce** without tanks on routes within 260 miles of the base." [33]

Recoilless Rifles

Developed in the closing days of World War II by the U.S. military as infantry antitank weapons, three 57-mm recoilless rifles were authorized in the weapons platoon of each rifle company, and a 75-mm recoilless rifle platoon was authorized in the weapons company of the infantry battalion.

Recon

Reconnaissance

Reconnaissance

Process of seeking out of information about enemy positions and dispositions.

RED COW

Operation Red Cow was conducted from 8-25 October 1952 during which Mosquito controllers directed the efforts of fighter-bomber sorties against 24 troop and artillery targets close to the MLR and the neutral zone.

REF

Reference

Regt

Regiment

REM

Remote

REMCO

Rear Echelon Maintenance Combined Operations

Rep

Representative

Res

Research

RESCAP

Rescue Combat Air Patrol. An aircraft patrol stationed over a combat search and rescue objective area whose mission is to intercept and destroy hostile aircraft. Its primary mission is to protect the search and rescue task forces during recovery operations.

Rev

Review

RF

Radio Frequency

Ridgway, Gen. Matthew Bunker

Named to command the Eighth U.S. Army in December 1950, General Ridgway was chosen to replace General of the Army Douglas MacArthur in May 1951.

RIPPER

Korean War (March 7 - April 4, 1951) offensive designed around the strategy of continuing to destroy enemy soldiers and equipment while minimizing United Nation losses. Taking and holding new ground was not one of Ripper's goals. Ripper's objective was to establish the **Idaho Line** beginning on the Han River eight miles east of Seoul and being anchored at Hapyong-dong on the east coast. **Operation Ripper** drove CCF back to the 38th Parallel and retook Seoul. Fifth Air Force flew close air support missions to support the operation.

RMK

Remarks

RN

Royal Navy

RNZN

Royal New Zealand Navy

Robertson, Lt. Col. Thomas D. "Robby"

Robertson commanded the 39th Fighter-Interceptor Squadron from 30 November 1950 until 10 June 1951, was reassigned to Headquarters FAF as the ALO for the 10th Corps. On 30 June 1951, Capt. Charles D. Sumner, a 39th FIS pilot who was serving as B Flight Commander, received heavy damage to his Mustang while over the enemy lines, starting a fire in his right wing and wheel well. He nursed the crippled plane back to K-16 and made a beautiful wheels-up landing--then found he could not get the canopy off to leave the burning ship. With the assistance of the K-16 crash crew, Lt. Col. Robertson, and several of the squadron's airmen, Sumner's canopy was pulled to one side sufficient to jerk him from the burning ship. Other than first and second-degree burns and a sprained back, Captain Sumner survived the close call very well. Robertson, T/Sgt Coleman and S/Sgt Dick of the squadron are being recommended for the Soldier's Medal for their heroic actions in saving Captain Sumner from a seemingly inevitable death." (USAFHRA. Monthly Historical Report, 39th Fighter-Interceptor Squadron, June 1951, p. 7.)

Rockets

The F-51D could carry six 5-inch rockets, five under each wing. A safety-wired latch keep the rocket from slipping forward and falling off. When the rocket was ignited, its forward thrust shears the safety wire, allowing it to shoot forward from the launchers. Rocket control switches were located on the front switch panel. Pressing the button on top of the control stick fired the rockets. Rockets could be fired one at a time or "in train," a salvo of all ten rockets released within about one second. Rockets could not be jettisoned, nor released in a "safe" condition. When an "emergency situation" (e.g. belly landing) made it "desirable for you to get rid of the rockets," pilots were advised to "use good judgment in doing so. Fire them into terrain where the resultant explosions will not endanger human lives." The 5" rocket is most effectively fired from an F-51 in a high angle of attack, 18th Fighter-Bomber Group Standardized Procedures for Combat Operations explained. "Quite obviously there are two types of error in firing: vertical and horizontal. Vertical error is minimized by using a high angle of attack and the correct mil depression. The horizontal error is minimized by firing the rockets when the line of flight of the aircraft coincides with the longitudinal axis of the aircraft. Regardless of what direction the rocket is pointed at the instant of release, its vertical line of trajectory will parallel the line of flight of the aircraft. The optimum release point for the 5" HVAR rocket is at a slant range of about 2,500 feet. (When using the 5" rocket equipped with the VT fuse, a minimum slant range of 3,200 feet will be observed as a release point). If a dive angle of 60 degrees is used a sight depression of 10 mils will cause your rockets to hit at the aiming point you had at the instant of release."

Rogers, BGen Turner Clifton

Commander, 18th Fighter-Bomber Wing, 1 February 1951-2 February 1952, succeeding Col. Curtis R. Low. Rogers was born in Taylorsville, N.C. and graduated from the U.S. Military Academy at West Point, N.Y. on June 12, 1936. The following fall, Lieutenant Rogers began flying training and graduated from primary and advanced flying schools at Randolph and Kelly fields in Texas. In March 1942 Lieutenant Colonel Rogers was named chief of the personnel section in the Directorate of Air Defense at Army Air Forces headquarters, and a year later became chief of the fighter and reconnaissance section. In March 1944 he was appointed chief of the Fighter Division at Headquarters Fourth Air Force. He was promoted to colonel on May 12, 1944. Following WWII he served as captain of the Fighter Evaluation Team, Air Evaluation Board, in the Southwest Pacific and as a staff planning officer in the War Plans Division at Air Force headquarters. He graduated from the Air War College at Maxwell Air Force Base, Ala. June 1950. Colonel Rogers was then transferred to Korea as assistant deputy for operations of the Fifth Air Force. "January 1941 was the date of my first command, a newly activated pursuit squadron of no other officers, forty airmen, and no aircraft. When both officers and machines arrived, I was transferred to staff work in Washington, D.C. Ten years of pushing papers preceded a fighter-wing command in Japan — an assignment that was foiled by the commencement of the Korean War. I was almost resigned to my fate when General 'Pat' Partridge came to my rescue and broke the jinx by giving me the 18th Fighter-Bomber Wing in Korea, which coincidentally had been my first organizational assignment out of flying school. This was a highlight of my career." In February 1951 "TeeCee" Rogers assumed command of the 18th Fighter-Bomber Wing and flew 50 combat missions in F-51 Mustangs. He became brigadier general on Oct. 9, 1951. He was awarded the Legion of Merit and one oak leaf cluster plus the Distinguished Flying Cross while in Korea. Returning to the United States in February 1952, his assignments included command of the Air Training Command's Crew Training Air Force Jet Fighter-Bomber training at Luke Air Force Base, Ariz., command of the nation's Air Force ROTC program, and command of the Military Assistance Advisory Group, Japan. General Rogers provided this account of his first combat mission in Korea in 1951 after he had assumed command of the 18th Fighter-Bomber Wing. He had not flown an F-51 (Mustang) since 1943, and after a hurried checkout was scheduled for two-ship armed reconnaissance of central North Korea. "The engine was rough on take-off, but pride would not let the 'new wing commander' abort his first mission. All Korea was covered by overcast, but we found a hole and deposited our napalm and rockets on enemy targets. Then my engine coughed, and I sought altitude for a bailout. I left my leader, climbed into the overcast and chugged to fifteen thousand feet to get on top where I suddenly lost direction. I called for a steer, and hours seemed to pass before I received a clear response. Finally, I sighted familiar territory, and my confidence returned. Why land at K-6, the location of the direction station, when I had a forward detachment at K-13? I headed for K-13 only to fly into a blinding snowstorm, but I still knew I could find K-13. Next I recognized the enemy-held Han River below. I did a quick one-eighty, and now with my last tank reading zero, I prepared for the third time to leave the ship. Suddenly I caught a glimpse of a runway on my left—never has a piece of concrete looked so beautiful. The engine sputtered to a stop from fuel starvation just as I turned off the end of the runway."

ROK

Republic of Korea

ROKAF

Republic of Korea Air Force

ROKN

Republic of Korea Navy

RON

Remain Over Night

ROPE

Code name for aircraft decoy system

ROUNDUP

Korean War (January 1951) X Corps advance on Hongch'on-P'yonch'ang. Roundup followed Operation **THUNDERBOLT**. "As part of Operation ROUNDUP, designed to disrupt enemy preparations for a new offensive, the U.S. X Corps advanced with strong air support near Hoengsong, northeast of Wonju in central Korea." [34]

Rpt

Report

RT

Radio telephony or voice communications, as opposed to **WT**, wireless telegraphy. Also styled **RIF**.

RTE

Route

RTO

Rail Transportation Office

RUGGED

Korean War (April 1951) advance to the Imjin River

Runaway Prop

Failure of the propeller governor, the blades go to full low pitch, resulting in high engine speeds.

RW

Runway

S. Comm.

Senate Committee

S-1

Adjutant

S-2

Intelligence Officer

S-3

Operations and Training Officer

S-4

Supply Officer

SAAF

South African Air Force

Sabre or **Sabrejet**

F-86; jet powered fighter interceptor aircraft

SAC

Strategic Air Command

Saltsman, Col. Ralph H. "Salty"

Commander, 18th Fighter-Bomber Group, 5 June 1951-30 November 1951. Promoted to full Colonel in August 1951. The 67th reported, a major highlight of the month was the promotion of Lt. Col. Saltsman to Colonel. "Everybody was glad to see the Colonel have to dig into his purse for that kind of party and a big box of cigars. All agreed that the promotion was well deserved."

SAR

Special Action Report; Search and Rescue

Sariwon

A city in central North Korea that was one of the apexes of the "Iron Triangle," known for its heavy and accurate flak batteries. Many American jet and prop planes were shot down in this area.

SATURATE

On Feb. 25, 1952, FAF director of intelligence strongly recommended the implementation of "Operation Saturate," an around-the-clock concentration of available railway-interdiction effort against short segments of railway track, including Kunu-ri to Huichon, Sunchon to Samdong-ni, Sinanju to Namsi-dong and Pyongyang to Namchonjom. Operation Saturate was put into effect on March 3rd. Attacks were sustained throughout April and May. Soon after the operation began, flak batteries had been put into place along nearly all rail lines. Losses of tactical aircraft were high.

SCAB

Ship Control of Aircraft Bombing

SCAP

Supreme Commander for the Allied Powers, i.e. General MacArthur. Mustangs from the 18th Fighter-Bomber Group were called on to provide air cover for MacArthur's plane when he visited "the front."

SCARWAF

Special Category Army (Personnel) With Air Force, an acronym used during the transition period in the late 1940s when the U.S. Air Force was still detaching itself from its mother service the U.S. Army.

SCATTER

Korean War screening plan for the repatriation of prisoners of war.

Scosh

Slang for "little bit," as in "It got a scosh cold last night. It must have been 20 degrees below zero because it's been 5 degrees below all day today." (Lt. Kenneth Barber's diary of 14 November 1950 written about 50 miles south of the Yalu River in North Korea.)

SCR

Signal Corps Radio

SCR-300

A low power portable radio receiver and transmitter designed for two-way communication over short distances (three miles plus), primarily for infantry units. Also called "walkie-talkie."

SCR-536

A lighter version of the SCR-300, and designed for similar use. The models weighed about 5 pounds, as opposed to 32 to 38 pounds for the SCR-300. Also called "handie talkie."

Scramble

Immediate take-off order to pilots standing by for prompt take-off and combat operations. "…We alternated on strip alert with the 67th Fighter-Bomber Squadron between the morning and evening alert…we were not 'scrambled.'" See **JOC Alert Missions** and **Strip Alert**.

Scroung/scrounger

Slang term used to describe an individual with the ability to obtain supplies, parts or materiel outside of normal supply channels that were often unable to deliver the critical items. "Captain Becraft, supply officer, has been tied down to various other additional duties throughout the month but has given generously of his off-duty time to help this section in many ways. He has made several trips to Pusan Army Depots in an effort to obtain needed items, which are not available through out normal supply sources. He has proved himself a 'Scrounger Extraordinary,' a title usually reserved for men with less scruples," the 39th FIS reported.

Scud layer

Low clouds. "I kept a nervous eye on my fuel gauges as I used first one set of tanks, then another, and wasn't very encouraged when we noticed a widespread 'scud' layer—low clouds—extending out a hundred miles or so west from the little island of Okinawa." (Lt. Col. Duane E. 'Bud' Biteman, USAF (Ret.)

Seabees

Officially "amphibious construction battalions," the Navy's Seabees were part of Task Force 90.

SEATO

Southeast Asia Treaty Organization

Sebille, Maj. Louis

The 67ᵗʰ Fighter-Bomber Squadron lost both its Squadron Commanding Officer, Major Lou Sebille, and its Operations Officer, Captain Bob Howell, to enemy ground fire within hours of each other on August 5, 1950, near H'amchang. Maj. Sebille was later awarded the Medal of Honor for his final mission, the first of but two awarded to Air Force personnel during the entire Korean War. On August 5, 1951, Major Sebille, then Commander of the 67ᵗʰ, led a flight of three F-51 Mustangs in a close air support mission for United Nations troops in the vicinity of Hamchong, Republic of Korea. On Saturday morning, 5 August, Lt. Kenneth Barber was assigned to fly wingman for Major Sebille. Over the channel, Barber's coolant started acting up and the temperature jumped to 150 degrees. His oil pressure was OK, but the radio was also "poor." He contacted Sebille to report his situation. Sebille sent Barber back to Ashiya and continued the mission. "Captain Johnson was his element leader, and they went on," Barber noted in his diary. Three hours later, Captain Johnson returned with his wingman. "Major Sebille had gone in. Apparently, his coolant was hit by ground fire (which leaves the plane only from 3-10 minutes flying time before it overheats and freezes). Captain Johnson said, "Head SE and you'll make it to friendly territory." Sebille answered, "I'm hit bad. I can't make it. I'm going to get that bastard." Sebille "then turned and went back in the valley and crashed his plane into an enemy truck and the whole business went sky high. Damn!" Barber noted. It was the 26ᵗʰ mission for the squadron and his fifth. Major Sebille was credited with inflicting considerable damage to the enemy during the mission while sacrificing his own life in the effort.

Sec

Section

Section

See **Formations**.

Secy

Secretary

Seoul City Sue

The North Korean Axis Sally or Tokyo Rose.

Sep

Separate

Service ceiling

See **Ceiling**.

SFC

Sergeant First Class

SFCP

Spotting Fire Command Post

SFL

Simulated Forced Landing

Shackle Code

Encryption system used to authenticate highly sensitive radio transmissions.

Shirley Control

Allied fliers checked in with "Shirley Control" when leaving friendly territory and when reentering. "Shirley Control could also redirect your mission when you were up North," explained Budd Stapley.

Shooting G.C.A.s

Pilot slang for making a series of practice landings that were directed largely by personnel operating a Ground Controlled Approach (GCA) radar system. See **GCA**.

SHORAN

Short-range navigation system employing an airborne transmission device and two ground beacon stations for precision positioning and bombing. On February 17-18, 1951 "B-26s flew the first night bombing mission using shoran, a short range navigation system employing an airborne radar device and two ground beacon stations for precision bombing." [35]

SHOWDOWN

Korean War plan designed to improve IX Corps defensive line positions north of Kumhwa. On 13-14 October, 1952, the U.S. IX Corps sent two battalions forward to capture Communist positions on Triangle Hill and Sniper Ridge. The objectives were secured, but the fighting became a bloody seesaw contest.

Sig

Signal

Sitrep

Situation Report

Sitting duck mission

"It was a sitting duck mission—that is, we go up there and take whatever targets are given us. And that's just what those boats turned out to be: sitting ducks." Captain Richard D. Kimball, *Truckbuster*, September 30, 1952. "In sitting duck missions, aircraft were assigned to the Naval Forces near Chodo Island to attack shore defenses around the Chinnamipo Estuary," the 12ᵗʰ Squadron reported in 1953. The Group was also called on in January 1953 to fly sorties for "sitting duck" missions. "On these missions, a flight of four aircraft was dispatched to Chodo Island where they contacted the Naval forces stationed there.

They were then directed, usually by the Fire Control Section of one of the destroyers, into attacks on observed shore batteries or activities across the straits from Chodo Island."

Ski jump

The 3,200-foot runway at K-16 had a "hump" at the 2,200-foot point. Unless a Mustang pilot was very careful, it would tend to propel the heavily laden aircraft into the air before it had sufficient air speed. The premature leap into the air, followed by sudden, high-speed stall back onto the runway was catastrophic for many 18ᵗʰ Group pilots, including Lt. Mickey Rorkc, who was prematurely 'tossed into the air in a stalled condition' by the notorious 'ski jump' at the 2200' point of the short 3200 foot runway. Lt. Col. Duane "Bud" Biteman remembered "that particular bump at Seoul's K-16 airport very well." It taught him "personally, quickly and regularly, the benefits of sudden rudder-exercise stall recoveries until adequate take-off speed could be accumulated in overloaded, war-weary F-51 Mustangs."

Skip bombing

Skip bombing and **glide bombing** are "adaptations of dive-bombing and require more technique that does dive-bombing, the 18ᵗʰ Fighter-Bomber Group Standardized Procedures for Combat Operations explained. "The bomb in both instances is released from a lower altitude and should incorporate a delayed fuse. In glide bomb runs, allowance must be made for a bigger arc in bomb trajectory than was true of dive-bombing. Skip bomb runs are made from low altitudes with the aiming point in front of the target. A hit can be scored by either skipping the bomb into the target or by driving the bomb directly into the target. The most common error in skip bombing is aiming short of the target and skipping over it. In the case the aiming point should be moved back. As was the case in other bomb runs, accomplish evasive maneuvers at all times except while on the alignment run prior to bomb release." See **Post-holing**.

Skynight

F3D; USN and USMC jet fighter designed with powerful radar systems to search, find, and target enemy aircraft in darkness.

Slot

Number Four position in the Diamond formation was known as "the slot."

SMACK

Korean War plan January 25, 1953, for a combined air-tank-infantry-artillery assault on Spud

Hill by elements of the 31st Infantry Regiment (7th Infantry Division).

Snap out

See **Bailout**.

Snowball

During Operation SNOWBALL, October 1-3, 1951, 315th AD C-119s dropped experimental fifty-five-gallon drums filled with napalm behind enemy lines.

SO

Special Order

SOB

Souls on board, the number of persons on board an aircraft. Also **POB**.

Socked-in

Colloquialism referring to an airport closed to air traffic by bad weather; also, similarly "clamped," a term inherited from the British, recalled Col. Robert "Pancho" Pasqualicchio.

SOP

Standard operating procedure.

Sortie

One trip by one plane. From June 27, 1950 to July 27, 1953, U.N. aircraft flew more than 1,040,708 close support, counter-air, interdiction, cargo and miscellaneous sorties in support of the U.N. military operations in Korea.

SP

Self-propelled

Spam

A spicy canned ham product packaged in a 12-ounce can produced by the Hormel Company since 1937. A overnight success, Spam, as it was called following a naming contest, grabbed 18 percent of its market. Over five billion cans have been sold.

Spam-can

Pilot's term for the F-51 Mustang. "Ten pilots of this organization climbed into the old familiar 'Spam-can' and the mission was completed successfully."

Spinner

The "hub" for the propeller. Spinners were often painted in various colors and designs to create unique visual effects, e.g. "blinker noses."

Split Operation

A situation whereby the tactical effort in whole or in part is made at a forward base, while the administration, base supply and field maintenance is conducted at a rear installation.

Spot Promotions

Temporary promotions to the next highest rank. Used as a morale boosting policy, especially for junior officers/pilots.

Spotlight

See **Project Spotlight**.

Spring Thaw

An intensive aerial interdiction attack planned by FEAF in March 1953 that was expected to disrupt enemy supply lines, destroy transportation, and force him to consume supplies that were stored in forward areas.

Squadron

See **Formations**.

STAB

Stabilizer

Staging Operation

"A situation similar to refueling and rearming (see) except that aircraft are staged at the forward strip but rotated to their home base for inspection and heavy maintenance."

Stanton, Lt. Col. Carroll L.

Succeeded Major James P. Hagerstrom as CO of the 67th Squadron in May 1953.

Stars and Stripes

Stars and Stripes was the official military newspaper of the Far East.

Stf

Staff

Stooge

Pilot slang for "loiter" or linger unnecessarily long in a specific area. "Do not 'Stooge' at low air speed, straight and level, or in one small area. "Make a few turns then move down on a road a few miles farther over this area, then move to another road."

STRANGLE

Korean War (1951-1952) air operations plan to disrupt North Korean logistics through interdiction bombing. The FEAF Rail Interdiction Program—"Operation Strangle"—was conducted in Korea from the summer of 1951 to early 1952. Its official objective was to interfere with and disrupt the enemy's lines of communications to such an extent that he will be unable to contain a determined offensive by friendly forces or be unable to mount a sustained major offensive himself." [36] The name "Strangle" was "devised to glamorize the task for the benefit of ground officers who had never been charmed by "interdiction." [37] FAF set out to exploit all means of interdiction, including: bridge attacks, tunnel attacks, cratered roadbeds, delayed action bombs. Initially, Operation Strangle was successful in slowing and catching retreating Communist troops. Eventually, the flexibility of the Communist logistic system enabled the damage to be repaired or circumvented to a great extent.

Strategy

In its simplest sense, it is the use of means to accomplish ends. In its broadest sense, it has to do with the use of power—political, economic, and psychological as well as military—to achieve the political goals, aims, and objectives of a nation.

Stratemeyer, Gen. George Edward

Became the commanding general, Far East Air Force in April 1949 and was in command there when the Korean War began. He suffered a severe heart attack on 20 May 1951 and relinquished his command to Gen. Otto P. Weyland in June 1951. He retired from active duty Jan. 31, 1952. He was succeeded by General Partridge, and MGEN Edward J. Timberlake, Jr., USAF, took his place as Fifth Air Force Commander.

Strip alert

"The squadron was also called on to perform 'strip alert'—four or eight aircraft parked at the end of the take off runway in readiness for immediate take-off."

SU-76

A self-propelled gun mounted on a lengthened T-7 light tank chassis and armed with a 76-mm gun. Those used in Korea had open topped, lightly armored (1/2 inch plate) fighting compartments. See **T-34** and **BA-64**.

Summ

Summary

SUMMIT

During **Operation SUMMIT** on September 21, 1951, a U.S. Marine Corps Company of 228 Marines was lifted by 12 Sikorsky S-55s—the first helicopter deployment of a combat unit.

SUNDIAL

Korean War plan (postponed November 11, 1951) to establish the **DULUTH** defensive line. When **Operation Sundial** was postponed by UN commander Gen. Matthew B. Ridgway, offensive action was limited to small-unit attacks and patrolling the front lines. Developed by Ridgway's predecessor, Gen. James Van Fleet, **SUNDIAL** had called for an offensive move to a line named **Duluth**, south of Pyongyang.

Supp

Supplement

Surg

Surgical

Switch, Operation

Personnel rotation plan begun by the 18th Fighter-Bomber Wing in February 1951 "wherein airmen and officers (non-combat) who had served six months in Korea would be returned to 13th Air Force jurisdiction if detailed to the theatre."

T/C

Top of Climb

T/D

Top of Descent

T/O

Tables of Organization

T/O (TO)

Takeoff

T/O&E

Table of Organization and Equipment, i.e. the mix of equipment and supplies that had been determined was required for a unit/squadron to perform its missions.

T-34

The T-34/85 was a 29-ton, Christie-type, well armored, diesel powered, medium tank mounting an 85-mm gun and used extensively by North Korean and Chinese Communist Forces in Korea. Its bogie wheels were individually sprung and fitted with rubber tires. The rear sprockets drove the tank treads. See **Su-76** and **BA-64**.

TAC

Tactical Air Command

TACAN

Tactical Air Navigation system. An ultra-high frequency electronic navigation aid system that provides suitably equipped aircraft with a continuous indication of bearing and distance to the selected Tacan station. Used by military aircraft.

TACC

Tactical Air Control Center. On July 14, 1950, General Partridge created the 6132nd Tactical Air Control Group (Provisional). By July 23rd the 6132nd was able to establish a Tactical Air Control Center adjacent to the Joint Operations Center at Taegu and took over the operation of control station "Mellow." See **Mellow Control**.

TACP

Tactical Air Control Parties, provided ground control of close air support in concert with airborne T-6 aircraft "Mosquitos." Each TACP consisted of an experienced pilot officer, who served as a forward air controller (FAC), and the airmen needed to operate and maintain the party's vehicular-mounted communications equipment. Troops on the ground could communicate directly with airborne forward air controllers via the SCR-300 "walkie-talkie" if necessary. Combat squadrons were required to supply pilots for temporary duty with the

TACPs. "TACP still necessitates the absence of three officers per each 21-day period on a TDY basis with ground force elements. Their duties in the main are concerned with the coordination of air strikes by fighter type aircraft in close support of such ground units."

Tactical formation

See **Formations.**

TADC

Tactical Air Direction Center

Tadpoles

Tactical Air-Direction Posts.

Taejon

Located 100 miles south of Seoul and 130 miles northwest of Pusan, Taejon was the sixth largest city in South Korea.

TAF

Terminal Area Forecast.

TAGO

The Adjutant General's Office

TALONS

Korean War outline plan (Aug-Sept 1951) for a ground offensive to bolster the Eighth Army's eastern front. As the fight for Bloody Ridge continues, Gen. James Van Fleet, Eighth Army commander, developed a new operation called **Talons**. Its overall objective is to straighten the Kansas defense line running to the northeast. It called for advances of from one to 15 miles. On Sept. 5, when General Van Fleet is advised of the losses in taking Bloody Ridge, he immediately cancels Talons because it will require similar fighting. He is unwilling to pay the cost in casualties that will be required to make the advances.

TAMERLANE

A radio call sign for the 12th Squadron.

TAPE

Tactical Air Power Evaluation

TAPE

Tactical Air Power Evaluation Office. Organized and coordinated **WEE Teams** (see) for the Fifth Air Force. The TAPE Office was "organized to collect, tabulate, and present a wide variety of data pertaining to Fifth Air Force operations.

TARCAP

Tactical Air Reconnaissance Combat Air Patrol

Tarzon mission

The tarzon bomb was a six-ton version of the half-ton razon bomb (remotely controlled, radio-guided bomb). B-29 bombardiers managed to destroy 15 bridges in Korea with Razon bombs by the end of 1950, when the much larger 12,000-lb. Tarzon bomb was put into operational use. On January 13, 1951 a B-29

knocked two spans out of the important railway bridge at Kang-gye using the new 12,000-pound radio-controlled Tarzon bomb dropped from 15,000 feet. Overall, the tarzon bomb did not live up to expectations. However, these bombs were the precursors of today's precision-guided weapons.

TAS

True airspeed. IAS corrected for altitude and outside air temperature, as opposed to **IAS**, or indicated air speed. The speed at which the airplane is actually moving through the air.

Task Force Smith

The first U.S. ground unit to fight in the Korean War.

Task Force

A term widely used during the Korean War. It was used by the Army to identify an ad hoc organization composed of a variety of units temporarily assembled under a single designated commander to accomplish a specific mission. For the Navy, "task force," and "task group" were subdivisions of the fleet.

Taylor, Gen. Maxwell Davenport

General Taylor replaced Gen. James A. Van Fleet as commander of the Eighth U.S. Army in Korea, Feb. 11, 1953.

TBD

To Be Determined

TBO

Time Between Overhauls

TBS

To Be Specified

TC

Troop Carrier

TCG

Troop Carrier Group

TCVE

Military Sea Transportation Service aircraft ferry

TDY

Temporary Duty assignment, usually less than 30 days. DS or Detached Service was often more than 30 days.

Telecon

Teletypewriter conference

TEMP

Temperature

TF

Task Force (Navy)

TG

Task Group (Navy)

TGT

Target

THDG

True Heading

The Pass

A quarter-mile long defile near Kunu-ri topped on either side by embankments of dirt and loose rock. Heavily defended by anti-aircraft gun positions.

Three-in-one mission

Pilot slang meaning three missions during one sortie. The F-51s provided a fighter escort for the parachute drops—paradrops—at Sukchon and Sunchon, where the 187th Regimental Combat Team was being landed to cut off retreating North Korean troops. They then provided an escort home for General MacArthur's C-54, from which he had been observing the operation. They left the C-54 over the MLR, and then dove down to provide close air support for ROK forces near Wonsan, and finished up the day, after rearming and refueling, by providing a fighter escort for B-26s of the 3rd Bomb Wing.

THUNDERBOLT

The first UN offensive of 1951—a reconnaissance-in-force by the American I and IX Corps. The objectives included clearing the area south of the Han River and recapturing the port of Inchon and the airfield at Suwon. Thunderbolt was followed by Operation **ROUNDUP**. The Eighth U.S. Army launched **Operation ROUNDUP** to drive CCF troops north.

Thunderjet

F-84; jet powered fighter and fighter-bomber aircraft.

Tornado

RB-45, the first jet reconnaissance aircraft in the USAF.

TIAS

True Indicated Air Speed

TIG

The Inspector General

Tiger Squadron

Colloquial name for 12th FBS because it sported the familiar shark's teeth nose art.

Timberlake, MGen Edward J.

Assumed command as Fifth Air Force Commander on 20 May 1951, succeeding Lt. Gen. Earle E. Partridge, who relieved General Stratemeyer.

Tip Tanks

External aircraft fuel tanks mounted near the tips of the wings used to significantly extend combat range and "loiter time."

Tk

Tank

TMC

Transport Movement Control

TN

True North

to (do)

Province, used in combined form, as Kangwoon-do for Kangwon Province, or Chungch'ong-pukto for North Ch'ungch'ong Province. There are eight mainland provinces and one island province in the Republic of Korea. *Do*, or *to* also means island, as in Cheju-do.

TOD

Top of Descent

Todd, Maj. James M.

Commanding Officer, 39th FIS in March 1952. "The main disturbing morale factor," Major James M. Todd, new CO of the 39th FIS reported, "concerns pilots only and has to do with the limited number of aircraft in the squadron and prevalent feeling that the future won't be any better on that score and will likely become worse." Major Stanley Long took over as XO of the 12th after Major James M. Todd moved up to Commanding Officer.

TOMAHAWK

Korean War (March 23, 1951) airborne operation by the 187th Regimental Combat Team at Munsan-ni as part of **Operation COURAGEOUS.** One hundred twenty C-119s and C-46s dropped nearly 3,500 paratroopers of the 187th Regimental Combat Team near Munsan-ni in the second largest airborne operation of the war.

Top cover

Pilot slang for one or more aircraft positioned above attacking aircraft to deal with any attacks by enemy aircraft and to help pinpoint anti-aircraft positions on the ground. The "standard two-ship reconnaissance flights were continued with excellent results. This system calls for one aircraft to fly at 100 to 350 foot altitudes, depending on terrains, while the second aircraft remained at 500 to 1,000 foot altitudes to provide top cover." [38]

Tornado

RB-45, the first jet reconnaissance aircraft in the USAF.

TOUCHDOWN

Korean War operation (October 1951) to gain control of Heartbreak Ridge.

Track

Actual flight path of an aircraft over the ground.

Trail formation

See **Formations.**

Train formation

As a means of providing improved mutual cover, Sabre wings adopted a "train" type of squadron formation consisting of six flights, each of four aircraft. A refinement of the jet stream, the flights flew the usual 'fluid-four' formation, but remained in a loose trail formation, each flight following another within an easy supporting distance of about one mile. [39]

Trans

Transport, Transportation

Transl

Translation

TRS

Tactical Reconnaissance Squadron

Truckbusters

Nickname for the 18th Fighter-Bomber Wing. Also, *Truckbuster* was the name for the bimonthly newspaper published by the 18th Fighter-Bomber Wing during the Korean War.

Tumen River

The 324-mile Tumen River flows easterly from the mountains of central Korea and empties into the Sea of Japan.

TWR

Control tower.

UFN

Until further notice.

UHF

Ultra-high frequency; 300-3,000 MHz band.

UN

United Nations. When the Korean War broke out in June 1950, the U.N. was a relatively new organization.

UNC

United Nations Command

Uncle Joe's Boys

Euphemism for Communist forces, particularly pilots. "As we move into the month of June we anticipate another bad month for Uncle Joe's Boys," noted Major John Rees, CO of the 12th Squadron in May 1951.

UNCOK

United Nations Commission on Korea

UNCURK

United Nations Commission for the Unification and Rehabilitation of Korea

Unguibus Et Rostro

With talons and beak—was approved as the motto for the 18th Group on 21 Feb 1931 and for the 18th Wing on 17 Apr 1953 just prior to Korean Armistice.

Unknown Loss

"Any aircraft that is lost on a combat mission due to an undetermined cause." (Memorandum No. 40, Operations Analysis Office, Hq.

Fifth Air Force, 31 March 1951)

UNRC

United Nations Reception Center

Unsan, Battle of

Around dusk, Nov. 1, 1950, near the village of Unsan, a crossroads in west-central North Korea about 50 air miles southeast of the Yalu River, two 10,000-man CCF infantry divisions of the CCF's 39th Army, XIII Army Group, launched an attack on two battalions of the Eighth U.S. Army's Eighth Cavalry Regiment, First U.S. Cavalry Division and the 15th Regiment of the First Republic of Korea Division. This attack marked the beginning of recognized CCF intervention in the Korean War.

URC-4

Emergency radio "used by airmen forced down behind the enemy lines."

USA

U.S. Army; United States of America

USAF

U.S. Air Force

USAFI

United States Armed Forces Institute

USAFIK

U.S. Army Forces in Korea

USMC

U.S. Marine Corps

USO

United Service Organization

USS BOXER

On Sunday, July 23, 1950, the U.S. Navy aircraft carrier USS BOXERr (CV 21), arrived in Yokosuka, Japan following a record eight-day transit from Alameda, California. Her service with the 7th Fleet in the Far East during the first half of 1950 included conducting joint operations with Air Force units in the Philippines. She returned to San Diego, arriving 25 June 1950. With the outbreak of the Korean conflict she was pressed into service to carry desperately needed Air Force planes to Korea. On 23 July 1950 she completed a record crossing of the Pacific from Alameda, Calif., to Yokosuka, Japan, in just 8½ days, carrying 145 P-51 *Mustang* and six L-5 aircraft for the Air Force, 19 Navy planes, 1,012 troops and 2,000 tons of supplies. On her return trip—27 July-4 August—she cut the record to 7 days, 10 hours, and 36 minutes. She departed for the Far East on August 24ᵗʰ to join TF 77 in providing air support to the troops. Her planes covered the landing at Inchon September 15ᵗʰ and other ground action until November, when she departed for the west coast and a much-needed

overhaul.

USSR

Union of Soviet Socialist Republics

V

Velocity

V/

Vice

Van Fleet, Gen. James Andrew

When the Korean War began, General Van Fleet was commanding the Second U.S. Army at Fort George G. Meade, Md. He replaced Gen. Matthew Ridgway as commander of the Eighth U.S. Army in Korea who in turn replaced Gen. Douglas MacArthur in Tokyo.

Vandenberg, Gen. Hoyt Sanford

Air Force Chief of Staff at the beginning of the Korean War, he presided over the Air Force buildup for the war, participated in the decision to launch amphibious operations at Inchon in September 1950, and concurred in the decision to remove Gen. Douglas MacArthur from command in the spring of 1951. Vandenberg was succeeded by Gen. Nathan F. Twining as CSAF on June 30, 1953.

VFR

Visual Flight Rules, outline procedures for operating aircraft in visual meteorological conditions (VMC), generally defined as five miles visibility or more and 1,000 feet vertical and one nautical mile horizontal clearance from cloud.

VHF

Very high frequency; 30-300 MHz band, used for most civil air-to-ground communication. The F-51 was equipped with a VHF transmitter and receiver. The VHF antenna mast extended vertically above the fuselage aft of the cockpit. The VHF radio included a control box with five push buttons—an OFF switch and A, B, C, and D switches by which four different crystal-controlled frequencies could be selected. Pilots could transmit and receive on only one channel at a time.

Vis

Visibility.

VLF

Very low frequency; in the 3-30 kHz band.

VMF

Marine Fighter Squadron

VMF(N)

Marine night fighter squadron

VMO

Marine Observation Squadron

VP

Navy Patrol Squadron

VT

Variable Time (radar-controlled) proximity fuse.

Walker, General Walton Harris

When the war began, General Walker directed the commitment of EUSA to combat and its subsequent withdrawal into the Naktong Perimeter and is famous for his "stand or die" speech. Walker was killed on 24 December 1950 in a vehicle accident.

Walking stick

A dangerous condition during which external air forces could take effective control of the aircraft away from the pilot. See **Compressibility**.

WD

War Diary

WEE Teams

Weapons Effectiveness Evaluation Teams. Operational analysis teams fielded by Fifth Air Force Office of **Tactical Air Power Evaluation** (see) to determine the most effective weapons to use on designated targets, e.g. tanks, guns, positions. Each WEE Team was "a self-sustaining field unit and consisted of a team captain, an intelligence specialist, photographer, driver and Korean interpreter."

WESPAC

Western Pacific

Weyland, Lt. Gen. Otto Paul

Named commanding general of the Tactical Air Command in July 1950, he replaced General Stratemeyer as commanding general, Far East Air Force on 10 June 1951 and remaining in that position for the remainder of the war. Lt. Gen. Weyland assumed command on 10 June 1951 in Tokyo of Far East Air Forces, replacing General Partridge.

WIA

Wounded in Action.

Wigwam

Pilot slang for Waegwan, South Korea.

Wilkerson, Maj. Sam

In March 1951, the 12ᵗʰ Squadron was commanded by Wilkerson, who led the 43 officers and 139 airmen of the squadron. The 12ᵗʰ set a new record in March by destroying over 600 vehicles and damaging many others, the unit reported.

WINDR

Wind Direction

Windmill

Slang for helicopter, e.g. "…shortly thereafter the 'windmill' (helicopter) arrived and the downed pilot was safely removed to Kimpo,

AB."

Windmilling

See **Deadstick.**

Windscreen

SAAF slang term for "wind shield."

Wing gaggle

See **Gaggle.**

Wing

A major organizational element of the Air Force, Navy and Marine Corps.

Winking spinners

See **Blinking Squadron** (39th FIS).

Wintermute, Lt. Col. Ira L. "Ike"

Commander, 18th Fighter-Bomber Group from 16 June 1950-20 February 1951, when he was relieved by Lt. Col. Homer M. Cox. Wintermute was then assigned to the Thirteenth Air Force.

WIP

Work in progress.

Wkly

Weekly

WOJG

Warrant Officer Junior Grade

WOLFHOUND

During August 1950, whenever the NKPA punched a hold in the Pusan Perimeter, the 27th Wolfhound Regiment was dispatched to plug the hole, recalled Col. Bill Myers. "It was the only effective fighting unit at the time," he noted. Korean War (January 15-17, 1951) attack by the 25th Infantry Division in the Suwon-Osan area. When Chinese troops attempted to flank U.N forces in Korea they stretched their line so thin that the Eighth U.S. Army initiated **Operation Wolfhound** to exploit the gaps. The reconnaissance-in-force resulted in 1,800 Chinese casualties in the Osan-Suwon area with the loss of only three American lives. **Operation Wolfhound** was seen as the first sign of the aggressive attitude that General Ridgway had brought to Eighth Army.

Wonsan

A port city and rail center on Korea's eastern coast about 110 air miles north of the 38th Parallel at Korea's narrow waist.

WP

Waypoint.

WRANGLER

Korean War plan to follow up **CUDGEL** with an amphibious operation on the east coast of Korea

Wt

Weight

WT

Wireless telegraphy. See **RT.**

Wx

Weather.

X-3

Test Flight

X-C

Cross Country

XMIT

Transmit

Yak-18

Yakovlev: single-engine trainer (Soviet)

Yak-9

Yakovlev "Frank": single-engine fighter (Soviet)

Yalu River

The 491-mile long Yalu River flows from Mount Paektu in central North Korea westward to the Yellow Sea.

Yechon, Battle of

On July 20, 1950, at the town of Yechon, the first successful counterattack of the Korean War was launched.

Yellow Sea

The Yellow Sea lies between mainland China and the Korean Peninsula and forms the west border of Korea.

Yo-yo maneuvers

Developed shortly after Mustangs were introduced into the Korean conflict. "Instead of two or more ships going in to search or attack a target simultaneously, we'd keep one ship high—above 2000 feet, just high enough to stay out of much small arms (rifle and machine gun) range—while the other went down onto the deck. Then, if the enemy fired on the attacking plane, the top-cover could usually spot the muzzle blasts and be able to dive in to attack, while the first attacker would pull up to fly "shotgun," continuing the one up, one down coverage for as long as there were targets in the area." (Lt. Col. Duane Biteman).

Yo-Yo

All attacks pressed by enemy jet type fighters "were made from altitude and a "yo-yo" pattern (i.e. Dive and Zoom) would be established. With the conventional type aircraft an enemy peculiarity was revealed. Whether pressing an attack and/or fleeing from an attack, these fighters (Yak-9 type) would turn with great maneuverability and/or snap-roll, sometimes 3 or 4 snap-rolls, followed by a split "S". [40] Maneuver reintroduced in June 1951 by Communist MIG pilots in which 20 or more of them would establish orbits over UN air formations, then "preferably from up-sun and usually in ele-

ments of two, the MIG's dived downward and attacked United Nations aircraft from high astern,; and, finally, the elements zoomed back up into the pool of orbiting MIG's overhead." [41] "On another day, while in a mock dogfight with another pilot, I found myself turning the P-51 as tight as I could, and not improving my position. He was gaining slightly, or we were staying equal to each other in the turn. No matter how tight I turned, he was able to stay even. Without having any other ideas, I started diving the plane within the turn and pulling up towards my opponent's airplane and pulling up above the turning plane and diving at him. In this manner I was able to slowly gain and finally ended up on his tail. Years later the fighter school at Nellis AFB started calling this maneuver the Yo-Yo. I'd been doing it for years and didn't know what it was!" explained Col. Howard "Scrappy" Johnson.

Z

Zulu (Greenwich Mean Time)

Zone of the Interior (ZI)

During the Korean War, the military term Zone of the Interior or ZI was used in official documents to designate the continental United States.

Endnotes

[1] USAFHRA. Monthly Historical Report, 18th Fighter-Bomber Wing, January 1951, p. 4.

[2] Many operational code names of the Korean War-era were compiled by the U.S. Army Center for Military History at: http://www.army.mil/cmh-pg/reference/code.htm

[3] U. S. Army. January, 2002. http://korea50.army.mil/history/factsheets/opswitch.html

[4] USAFHRA. *The Truckbuster*. "Strip Alert." November 17, 1952, p. 3.

[5] USAFHRA. Monthly Historical Report, 67th Fighter-Bomber Squadron, November 1950.

[6] USAFHRA. Monthly Historical Report, 18th Fighter-Bomber Group, November 1951, p. 4.

[7] Futrell, Robert F. U.S. Air Force in Korea. (Washington, D.C. : USAF Office of Air Force History, 1983), p. 704.

[8] 18th Fighter-Bomber Group. Standardized Procedures for Combat Operations. 1952. p. 8.

[9] USAFHRA. Monthly Historical Report, 12th Fighter-Bomber Squadron, January 1950, p. 4.

[10] USAFHRA. The Truckbuster. "Strip Alert." November 17, 1952, p. 3.

[11] 18th Fighter-Bomber Group. Standardized Procedures for Combat Operations. 1952. p. 9.

[12] USAFHRA. The Truckbuster. "Strip Alert." November 17, 1952, p. 3.

[13] USAFHRA. Monthly Historical Report, 67th Fighter-Bomber Squadron, February 1951, p. 4.

[14] Futrell. , p. 517.

[15] 18th Fighter-Bomber Group. Standardized Procedures for Combat Operations. 1952. p. 10.

[16] USAFHRA. Monthly Historical Report, 12th Fighter-Bomber Squadron, June 1951, p. 4.

[17] Futrell. p. 623.

[18] USAFHRA. Monthly Historical Report, 18th Fighter-Bomber Group. August 1952, p. 9.

[20] USAFHRA. Monthly Historical Report, 12th Fighter-Bomber Squadron, January-June 1953, p. 17.

[21] Futrell. p. 79.

[22] USAFHRA. January 2002. The U.S. Air Force's First War: Korea 1950-1953 Significant Events. February 1951.

[23] USAFHRA. January 2002. The U.S. Air Force's First War: Korea 1950-1953 Significant Events. February 1951.

[24] 18th Fighter-Bomber Group Standardized Procedures for Combat Operations. 1951. p. 2.

[25] NARA. Fifth Air Force Operations Analysis Office Memorandum No. 35, March 1, 1951. CONFIDENTIAL Declassified.

[26] USAFHRA. Monthly Historical Report, 18th Fighter-Bomber Group, June 1951, p. 3.

[27] U.S. Army Quartermaster Corps, Graves Registration Division, Ft. Lee, Virginia. January, 2002. http://www.qmmuseum.lee.army.mil/korea/op_glory.htm

[28] USAFHRA. Monthly Historical Report, 39th Fighter-Interceptor Squadron, June 1951, p. 9.

[29] USAFHRA. Monthly Historical Report, 12th Fighter-Bomber Squadron, June 1952, p. 7.

[30] USAFHRA. Monthly Historical Report, 18th Fighter-Bomber Group, May 1951, p. 3.

[31] 18th Fighter-Bomber Group. Standardized Procedures for Combat Operations. 1952. p. 9.

[32] USAFHRA. Monthly Historical Report, 18th Fighter-Bomber Group, January-June 1953, p. 20.

[33] USAFHRA. Monthly Historical Report, 67th Fighter-Bomber Squadron, January 1951, p. 4.

[34] Adapted from USAFHRA. January 2002. The U.S. Air Force's First War: Korea 1950-1953 Significant Events. February 1951.

[35] Adapted from USAFHRA. January 2002. The U.S. Air Force's First War: Korea 1950-1953 Significant Events. February 1951.

[36] Futrell . p. 25.

[37] Futrell. p. 324.

[38] USAFHRA. Monthly Historical Report, 18th Fighter-Bomber Group , February 1951.

[39] Futrell. p. 610.

[40] USAFHRA. History of the 67th Fighter-Bomber Squadron, November 1950.

[41] Futrell. p. 311.

Suggested Readings

Blair, Clay. *The Forgotten War.* New York: Times Books, 1987.

Cleveland, W. M. *Mosquitos in Korea.* Portsmouth, N.H.: Peter E. Randall Publisher, 1991.

Cline, Maj. Tim. "Forward Air Control in the Korean War." *American Aviation Historical Society Journal,* Winter 1976.

Dorr, Robert F. and Warren Thompson. *The Korean Air War.* Osceola, Wisc.: Motorbooks International, 1994.

Futrell, Robert Frank. *The United States Air Force in Korea, 1950—1953.* Washington, D.C.: Center for Air Force History, 1981. (Revised edition)

Grant, William Newby. *P-51 Mustang.* London : Arms and Armour Press, 1980.

Hallion, Richard P. *The Naval Air War in Korea.* Baltimore, Md.: Nautical and Aviation Publishing Co. of America, 1986.

Jackson, Robert. Air war in Korea, 1950-1953. Osceola, WI : Motorbooks International, 1998.

Lewis, Michael, Maj., USAF. *Lt. Gen. Ned Almond, USA: A Ground Comman-der's Conflicting View with Airmen over CAS Doctrine and Employment.* Maxwell AFB, Ala.: Air University, 1997. (A School of Advanced Air-power Studies thesis.)

Marion, Forrest L. That Others May Live: USAF Air Rescue in Korea. Montgomery, AL: USAF Historical Research Agency, 2004.

—. "'The Dumbo's will get us in no time': Air Force SA-16 Combat Operations in the Korean War Theater, 1950-1953." *Air Power History* (Summer 1999), 16-29.

McLaren, David R. *Lockheed P—80/F—80 Shooting Star: A Photo Chronicle.* Atglen, Pa.: Schiffer Publishing Ltd., 1996.

—. *Mustangs over Korea The North American F—51 at War, 1950—1953.* Atglen, Pa.: Schiffer Publishing Ltd., 1999.

—. *Republic F—84, Thunderjet, Thunderstreak, and Thunderflash: A Pho-to Chronicle.* Atglen, Pa.: Schiffer Publishing Ltd., 1998.

Millett, Allan R. "Korea, 1950—1953." In *Case Studies in the Development of Close Air Support,* edited by Benjamin Franklin Cooling. Washington, D.C.: Office of Air Force History, 1990.

Momyer, William W. *Airpower in three wars.* Montgomery, AL: Air University Press, 2003.

Moore, Dermot Michael. *South Africa's Flying Cheetahs in Korea* Johannesburg : Ashanti Pub., 1991.

Wilson, David. *Lion over Korea: 77 Fighter Squadron RAAF, 1950—1953.* Canberra: Banner Books, 1994

Warnock, A. Timothy, ed. *USAF in Korea: A Chronology, 1950-1953.* Washington, D.C.: Air Force History and Museums Program/Air University Press: 2000.

Y'Blood, William T., ed. *The Three Wars of Lt. Gen. George E. Stratemeyer: His Korean War Diary.* Washington, D.C.: Air Force History and Muse-ums Program, 1999.

—. "The U.S. Air Force in Korea, 1950-1953." *Air Power History* (Summer 2000), 38-39, 42-43.

18ᴛʜ Fighter-Bomber Wing
Roll of Honor
Korean War Service

This list of 18th Wing veterans of the Korean War was compiled from many sources and with the help of many others. Special thanks is given to the following individuals and organizations without whose help even this incomplete listing would have been impossible:

Lt. Col. Duane "Bud" Biteman, founder of the 18th Fighter Wing Association and the first to begin gathering the names of Truckbuster Veterans. Also, Barry Agovino, Lt. Col. Kenneth H. Barber, Ross Bedford, Lt. Col. Grover C. Crocker, Lt. Col. Julian F. Crow, Mary (Frese) DeFranco, David Denfield, Charles R. "Bob" Grissom, George L. Jamison, Col. Edward Mason, Lt. Col. John McCann (Dallas Squadron member), Doris McKelvey, Col. Harry Moreland, Lt. Col. Richard H. Schiebel, Col. Fred L. Thomas, Major Joe Williams, and William J. "Bill" Wirges.

Aanes, Edward A.
Abercrombie, Aaron R.
Abernathy, Richard
Abram, J.C.
Abulencia, Don
Adams, Carroll P.,
Adams, Michael E.
Adams, Milton B.
Adams, Nathan J.
Adams, Virgil H.
Adelman, Fred J.
Adkisson, Houston T.
Agan, Herbert W.
Agovino, Barry L.
Aguire, Lionel A.
Ainslie, Robert E.
Albarado, Leon J., Jr.
Albright, Ralph W.
Albritton, Raz
Alden, Ike,
Aldrich, George D.
Alexander, Carl E.
Alfarone, Eduardo M.
Alfier, Alexander A.
Alldredge, Gordon D.
Allard, Joseph P.
Allard, Orin T.

Allen, Albert E.
Allen, James E.
Allen, James R.
Allender, E.W.
Alley, Billy B.
Allgood, Vernon L.
Allison, "Red"
Allmon, Dwight
Allston, James Hartford
Almeida, Fred
Alton, D.
Altvater, Ralph P.
Alvarez, E.S.
Alves, Abel R.
Ambrecht, Louis P.
Ames, Roger J.
Anderson, Charles T.
Anderson, Curtis A.
Anderson, Don
Anderson, Gene A.
Anderson, George B.
Anderson, Hany S.
Anderson, Leonard W.
Anderson, Lynn M.
Anderson, Orin M.
Anderson, R. H.
Anderson, Richard D.

Anderson, R.L.
Anderson, Wayne D.
Anderson, Wayne L.
Andes, Lloyd
Andres, Joseph E.
Andrews, Jay W., Jr.
Andrews, Richard T.
Andrews, William C., Jr.
Andridge, Herbert W., Jr.
Andriesse, Arnold N.
Andujar, Manual V.
Ankrum, Leo R.
Annandale, J. J. K.
Annett, B. J.
Anwyl, Ray
Armbrecht, Louis P.
Armfield, Albert V.
Armstrong, Bernie H.
Armstrong, Clyde O.
Armstrong, Jacob B.
Armstrong, Ray F.
Arnold, Henry R.
Arnold, Howard B., Jr.
Arnold, J.K.
Arredondo, William
Arthur, Albert L.
Ash, Curtis

Ashworth, Russell
Askounis, Gust
Aspgren, Clarence
Atkinson, Leland R.
Atwood, Howard R.
Aubuchon, Edward W., Jr.
Auebler, T.A.
Augustine, J.H.
Augustine, Richard
Auld, David H., Jr.
Ausman, Harold J.
Ayer, Elliot Dean
Ayers, Fay E.
Baade, J.L.
Baader, Ted J.
Baardseth, Albert R.
Babasa, Joseph Mathews, Jr.
Babcock, Robert
Babcock, Warren E.
Bach, George A.
Backman, Dale F.
Bacola, Simon
Bade, Jack
Badenhorst, W.J.J.
Badger, Thomas
Bails, Richard L.

Bailey, Gayle M.
Bailey, Kenneth F.
Baird, Floyd C.
Baird, James K.
Baker, Buford O.
Baker, David
Baker, Donald
Baker, Robert H.
Baldauf, Eugene J.
Baldwin, Ernest A.
Baldwin, Rexford
Bales, George C.
Ball, Harlan E.
Ball, Jackson W.
Ballard, Dewey E.
Ballhousen, G.W.
Banasky, George E.
Banfield, Kenneth C.
Bannon, Gerald P.
Baransky, Gus J.
Barbee, Joe. D.
Barber, B.J.
Barber, H. S. J.
Barber, James L.
Barber, Kenneth H.
Barber, William R.
Bardwell, Rex E.

Barhaugh, John H.
Barker, W.
Barmore, Jan W.
Barnard, Bruce
Barnes, Jack D.
Barnes, J.R.
Barnes, Lee
Barnes, Rufus R., Jr.
Barnes, Sam
Barnhill, Robert W.
Barr, Edgar E.
Barrett, James J.
Barringer, John E.
Barrow, C.D.
Barrow, Leonard J. Jr.
Barry, Lavern
Bartell, Ray R.
Bartholoma, John H.
Bartlett, Jack R.
Bartley, Joseph R.
Bartolich, Eugene
Bartow, Michael H.
Basham, Bill
Basista, John J.
Baskin, Homer R.
Bassing, Joseph E.
Batchelder, John H.
Bates, Allen S.
Batsel, Lee H.
Baughn, Richard
Bauman, Vince A.
Baumann, Ervin M.
Baxter, Walter H., III
Baxter, Thurston Richard
Beachler, Rob
Beadle, Glenn J.
Beals, William R.
Beamer, Harry R.
Beamer, James I.
Beamish, A. R.
Beauregard, Clarence
Beauregtard, Victor
Beaver, Charles R.
Bechtel, Paul S.
Beck, Howard G.
Becraft, Myron A.
Bedford, Donald R.
Bedford, Ross J.
Beeler, Clifford H.
Beggs, Cecil R.
Begley, W.R.
Beinkemper, Elmer H.
Bekker, F. N.
Belanger, Donald H.
Bell, Frank G.
Bell, John
Bell, J.P.
Bell, Roy E.
Bellows, James Mayo, Jr.
Benavidez, A.C.

Beneke, Walter C. "Tex"
Benner, Jack
Bennett, Chauncey A.
Benoit, Ben R.
Benson, Richard V.
Benson, Robert D.
Bentley, Ellis
Berkes, Thomas D.
Berkow, Joe
Berna, Peter P.
Bernard, John A.
Bernier, Howard
Berry, C. L.
Bertrand, Richard E.
Bethke, Floyd E.
Bettis, Allan Shields
Betz, John C.
Bever, William C.
Bickel, David W.
Biden, N. "Flash"
Bidgood, P. E.
Biederstadt, Roger
Bielefeldt, Vilas L.
Bierbaum, Henry
Biggs, Ernest E.
Bilgnaut, H. P.
Bingham, Victoria
Biondo, Michael
Birch, George
Birch, George A., Jr.
Birk, Leroy, A.
Bishop, Charles J.
Bishop, Ken
Bissett, R. G.
Bist, Stan J.
Biteman, Duane E. "Bud"
Bitzer, Medon Armin
Bjorklund, Frans W.
Blaauw, J. P. D.
Black, Elbert D.
Black, Fred E.
Black, Winston S.
Blackley, Peter
Blackwell, F.B.
Blackwell, Walter S.
Blair, James Birney
Blake, Louis B.
Blakeney, Lewis
Bland, J.D.
Blandford-Newton, J. A.
Blank, H.P.
Blank, Robert R.
Blankenship, Jack B.
Blatt, John M.
Bledsoe, Clayton C.
Blesse, Frederick C. "Boots"
Blood, Ralph
Bloodworth, William
Blose, James W.
Blum, Caroll A.

Bocquin, Victor E.
Bodak, John
Bodiford, Hugh
Bodine, Francis S.
Boehm, John L.
Boerner, Charles E., Jr.
Boeye, John F.
Boggan, Johnie J.
Boggs, Thomas, Jr.
Bohrer, John W.
Boisen, Martin H.
Boland, Lawrence J.
Boles, C.L.
Bolin, David L.
Bolitho, John C.
Bollinger, Robert M.
Bolt, Donald D.
Bolton, H. N.
Bolton, James C.
Bonanno, Frederick Ramon
Bond, Roy S.
Bonham, Earl I.
Bonk, Eugene
Bonner, Frederick M.
Boone, Robert
Borders, Andrew J.
Bordley, Arthur B.
Borges, Peter
Boriss, Frank H.
Borman, Frank
Borman, Fred A.
Borsare, Edward F.
Bortner, Jon J.
Bos, Earl B.
Bosak, Edward M.
Bosch, A. C. J.
Bosman, J. J.
Botha, J. C.
Botha, M. C.
Botha, W. P. B.
Bothwell, James W.
Bott, M.S.
Boucek, James A.
Boucher, Gerald V.
Boudreaux, Adam J.
Bough, Stan G.
Bourne, Sam L.
Bowers, Charles J.
Bowers, Richard W.
Bowman, Byran
Bowthorpe, Ben
Boyd, Percy K.
Boynton, Maynard A.
Bozeman, Wallace H.
Bracey, H.N., Jr.
Bracke, George P.
Bradford, Lee W.
Bradfute, Roland G.
Bradley, Charles H.
Bradley, John L.

Bragg, Ceibert O.
Braley, Alfred R.
Branch, Alva G.
Brannon, Gerald
Brashears, Virgil Jr.
Brass, Ernest H., Jr.
Bratcher, Thomas
Brazelton, Leonard G.
Brazill, William R.
Bresko, Joseph T.
Brett, Devol "Rock"
Bretting, Martin M.
Brewer, Edwin H.
Brewer, Owen T., Jr.
Brewster, Gordon F.
Bridges, Dewey R.
Bridges, William D. Jr.
Brinkmeyer, Vernon
Bristow, Henry C.
Britten, Morton D.
Britton, Louis E.
Britzke, John
Brizzi, Vincent H.
Broberg, Melvin E.
Brock, Foster D.
Brooks, Bruce J.
Brooks, David H.
Brooks, H. J.
Brooks, James W.
Brothers, Thomas J.
Broughton, Arthur
Brown, Cliff
Brown, D. M.
Brown, Donald S.
Brown, Elwood E.
Brown, Harvey L.
Brown, Jack F.
Brown, James D.
Brown, Jeff "Jiffy"
Brown, John
Brown, Norwood J.
Brown, Richard G.
Brown, Robert C.
Brown, W.C., Jr.
Brown, Warren G.
Brown, Willis Ray
Bruce, Jim
Bruce, Leonard K.
Bruce, Lloyd
Brumskin, J.A.
Brunner, Loren
Brunke, Charles R.
Bruno, Romano
Brunson, J. T.
Bruska, Ed
Bruton, Earl D.
Bryan, Frank T.
Bryan, William E., Jr.
Bryan, William F.
Bryant, Lynwood C.

Bryant, Wylie L.
Bublinec, Frank
Buchanan, Riley
Buchanan, Riley
Buck, A. J.
Buckley, Donald I.
Bughman, Niles J.
Buie, Archie
Buie, Archie P., Jr.
Bullard, Exum F.
Bullock, A.W.
Bunderson, Mack V.
Bunn, Russell A.
Bunting, Dr. John J.
Burge, Homer O.
Burger, C. E. R.
Burger, H.J.P.
Burger, W. J. W.
Burgess, Benjamin F.
Burke, Clarence L.
Burke, Joseph
Burke, Vernon W.
Burke, Walter H.
Burnell, Everett O.
Burkett, Marvin V.
Burkett, William M.
Burnett, Clifford H.
Burnette, Dewey W.
Burnette, Walter N.
Burnley, Robert S.
Burns, Allen A.
Burnsed, M/Sgt
Burpee, Chas. D., Jr.
Busby, Ernest C.
Busher, C. J.
Bushlow, Anthony J.
Bussio, L. F.
Bustamante, Benito
Butcher, James L.
Butler, James J.
Butler, Jerome F.
Butler, Merwin
Butler, T. C.
Buttry, Paul D.
Buttyan, Eugene C.
Buzze, Frank C.
Byers, James L.
Byers, Rex A.
Bynum, Richard E., Jr.
Byrd, Crawford
Byrd, Kenneth E.
Byrne, Ronald E., Jr.
Byrnes, Robert
Byrom, Richard
Cadwell, Harold J.
Cage, Dewitt E.
Cain, Louis J.
Cain, Louis J.
Cadwell, Harold L., Jr.
Caldwell, John W.

Caldwell, Perrin L.
Callaway, James E.
Calvello, Nicholas
Cameron, Burton G.
Cameron, J.P.
Cameron, Scott
Camp, James E.
Campbell, A.W.
Campbell, Charles N.
Campbell, Cornealius
Campbell, Donald J.
Campbell, James H.
Campbell, James Ray
Campbell, Robert E.
Campbell, Rodger J.
Canady, Craig R.
Canady, Robert M.
Cann, Robert A.
Cantwell, B. J.
Caple, Joe A.
Capolongo, Henry J., Jr.
Carbone, Richard J.
Cardenas, Jose V.
Cardiff, George
Cardile, Rosario,
Carleton, John E.
Carleton, John S.
Carleton, Myron L.
Carlos, Lloyd P.
Carlson, Don C.
Carlson, Ken
Carlson, Raymond J.
Carlson, Robert L.
Carlson, Tom
Carlson, Victor R.
Carmichael, John C.
Carnell, Frank W.
Carnes, Russell
Carothers, Earl T.
Carpenter, John W., III
Carr, Jack
Carr, John L.
Carr, Samuel L.
Carreiro, Joseph V.
Carriker, Clyde H.
Carrier, Pleasant Fez, Jr.
Carter, Conrad F.
Carter, F.W.
Carter, James F.
Carter, James H.
Carter, Michael J.
Carter, Ray I.
Carusi, Sandi
Case, David T.
Casey, John
Casillo, Robert M.
Cassady, Richard H.
Cassatt, Robert K., II
Cassel, C. E.
Casserly, Thomas F., III

Castleberry, Marvin H.
Catalano, Charles
Cato, Joe R.
Cattin, J. E.
Cayer, Marcel A.
Cayot, Leonard L.
Centolella, Raymond
Chadwell, John B.
Chadwick, E. W.
Champagne, Alide J.
Chandler, Bob
Chandler, Riley
Chaney, O. D.
Chapman, Percy A.
Chapman, Thomas, Jr.
Chappas, Charles H.
Charnabay, J.D.
Chatfield, James D. L.
Chatfield, Stanley F.
Chattick, Lawrence E.
Cherbonneaux, James W.
Cherry, Robert W.
Childers, Joe
Childers, John H.
Chilson, Robert E.
Chisholm, Rich K.
Chong, Arthur L.
Chouteau, Henry E.
Christensen, Donald I.
Christensen, Hans
Christensen, Grant S.
Christgau, Roger A.
Christian, Ervin M., Jr.
Christian, Robert W.
Christian, Thomas J.
Christy, Darvin P., Jr.
Church, William J.
Churchill, Robert W.
Cilliers, P. S.
Clapper, John W.
Clark, Bruce R.
Clark, Clement B.
Clark, Dennis J.
Clark, Everson O.
Clark, Frank H., III
Clark, G.H.
Clark, L. P.
Clark, Owen L.
Clark, Ralph P.
Clark, William H.
Clause, Robert X.
Clausen, C. R.
Clausen, Clayton
Clausen, Robert
Clawges, Owen B.
Clawson, Charles P.
Clawson, Richard
Clay, James E.
Cleek, John H.
Clees, Robert J.

Clees, Robert J.
Clement, Juston
Clement, Robert W.
Clements, Phil L.
Clements, W.H.
Cleveland, Grady L.
Clift, Bert G.
Clifton, Richard
Cloete, M. D. V.
Clulow, Patrick
Coalter, Jesse L.
Coats, Chester
Cobb, Vernon O.
Cochran, Drexel B.
Cochrane, D. T.
Cockroft, Beachem
Coetzee, J. H.
Coffman, Millard F.
Cogan, Eugene J.
Coghlan, Jack V.
Coghlin, Jack
Cohen, Joseph
Cohn, John A.
Cole, William W.
Coleman, David W.
Coleman, John Joseph
Coleman, John S.
Coleman, Oran O.
Coleman, Patrick E.
Colgan, Robert G.
Coll, R. P.
Colladay, Harold A.
Collier, Victor W.
Collins, Donald M.
Collins, John B., II
Collins, John C.
Collins, M. E.
Collins, Orval B.
Collins, R.C
Collins, R. J.
Colones, Thomas
Colson, Carl C.
Colson, James
Colton, William J.
Comer, Thomas
Commons, Howard O.
Compton, Henry M., Jr.
Condes, Pete M.
Conley, J. A.
Connally, Eugene F.
Connick, Andrew J.
Connolly, Robert
Connors, Archibald
Haddock, Jr. "Archie"
Conserva, Phillip J.
Contival, Corbert R.
Cook, Everett E.
Cook, Jack
Cook, James R.
Cooke, Ainsley M.

Cookman, Lawrence W.
Cooley, David M.
Cooley, Kenton
Coomer, Wynn A.
Coon, Robert E.
Cooney, A. J.
Cooper, George W.
Cooper, H. W.
Cooper, Hezekiah W.
Cooper, Nolan V.
Cooper, Winfield
Coorpender, Raymond F.
Copenhaver, Ulysses G.
Copps, Richard D.
Corbett, Robert S.,
Corkill, Dean
Corley, John G., II
Corley, Melvin V., Jr.
Corn, James T. "Charley"
Cornell, Melvin E.
Cornell, Tod O.
Cornwall, Roland S.
Cory, Phillip R.
Cosgrove, Lear J.
Cosper, James H.
Costenbader, Ralph K.
Cothern, Billie R.
Cotnoir, Leland E.
Cottrell, Charles R., Jr.
Coulombe, William J.
Counts, Roger L.
Coupe, Stephen G.
Courter, Robert F.
Coury, Robert A.
Covel, Ray L.
Covell, Arthur E.
Covington, Frank
Cowart, Octavio J.
Cowe, Alistair H.
Cox, A. W.
Cox, Hannibal M.
Cox, Homer M.
Cox, John P.
Coxon, N.
Coyle, George L., Jr.
Crabb, Jarred V.
Crabtree, Billie R.
Craig, Arthur D.
Crain, Franklin
Cram, Bruce H.
Cramer, Harold J.
Crampton, William C.
Crandall, Grover
Crane, Joseph T., Jr.
Cranston, Robert
Cravens, Richard C.
Crawford, Ben R.
Crawford, Charles
Crawford, Jack H.
Crawford, Richard W.

Crawford, Thomas M., Jr.
Cree, Danny D.
Cree, Ronald Ross
Creech, William B.
Creed, Lewis F., Jr.
Crider, Luther L.
Crist, Kempus W.
Croach, Arthur B.
Crocker, Grover C.
Crocker, John C.
Crockett, Stuart H.
Cronan, Robert A.
Croner, Charles R.
Crook, Heber J. Jr.
Crosby, William J., II
Cross, Adelbert D.
Cross, Frank, Jr.
Cross, Marvin
Crotzer, Malcolm C.
Crouch, Arthur B.
Crow, Jack W.
Crow, Julian F.
Crow, R. J., Jr.
Crowell, William I.
Crownrich, Roscoe L.
Crull, Thomas L.

Cudal, Dionicio

Cudworth, Richard W.
Culbertson, Francis R.
Cullen, Robert I.
Cummings, Charles E.
Cummings, Will E.
Cunningham, Relbin C.
Cunningham, R.J.
Cuny, Arthur E.
Currie, Alexander D.
Currier, George R.
Curris, Alexander D.
Curry, William D.
Curtis, Charles R.
Curtis, K. A.
Curtis, Neil
Curtis, Norvel W.
Cusick, Robert A., Jr.
Cuthill, Fred J.
Cutia, Christopher Robert
Cutshall, Donald R.
Cvitanovich, Tony
Cybulski, John R.
Dade, Maurice
Daggett, William E.
Dailey, Benjamin J.
Daisa, John W.
Dakin, John B. Jr.
Dale, Harold D., Jr.
Daleo, Lorenzo, Jr.
Daley, Robert F.
Dallas, Will E.
Dallavalle, Richard C.

Damewood, L. Dag
Damiano, Bert
Daniels, William F.
Dannenberg, James E.
Danner, Bobby L.
Daries, Duncan P.
Darnell, Weldon H.
Dascombe, Charles B.
Davenport, Bernell L.
Davey, Cal
David, Mike S.
Davidson, Hubert
Davies, C. W.
Davies, Duncan P.
Davies, Harold H.
Davis, Asa E.
Davis, C. H.
Davis, George H.
Davis, Jack A.
Davis, James T.
Davis, Jessie R., Jr.
Davis, John D.
Davis, Larry R.
Davis, Maurice G.
Davis, Murrit Herman
Davis, Owen C., Jr.
Davis, Ramon Roderick
Davis, Roy E.
Davis, Willie
Davison, Robert W.
Dawson, John W.
Dean, Fred F.
Dean, Julian A., Jr.
Dean, Zack W.
Deans, D. D.
Deardorff, Walt
DeBeer, J. A. B.
DeBoer, Jacob L.
DeBoor, Otto S.
DeBruler, Jasper D.
Decker, Richard G.
DeConstant, Jean W.
Degner, Hans W.
Dehnert, Robert E.
Deihl, Richard H.
deJong, C. L.
DeLaFontaine, M. S.
DeLaHarpe, S. G.
Demezas, Theodore H.
Denardo, Dan R.
Denault, R.L.
Denfield, David T., Jr.
Denman, John A.
Dennehy, Daniel J.
Denson, Gerald W.
DePol, Edward R.
Dermont, Stanley J.
Derrick, Ken S.
De Santis, Joseph
Deschamps, Elzeard. J.

DeTolt, A. C.
Dettre, Rexford H.
Deuschle, Raymond D.
Dewar, Harry B.
deWet, Jean
Dews, Edwin Lamar
Dexter, Robert C.
Diamond, C. P.
Diamond, Charles
Dibble, John H.
Dice, Carl J.
Dick, Lester H.
Dick, Lester W.
Dickens, Allen
Dickenson, E.
Dickey, Floyd D.
Dickinson, Ted
Dickman, Siegel M.
Diefendorf, Allen J.
Diehl, Conrad H., Jr.
Dille, John Adams, Jr.
Dillon, Barclay H.
Dillon, Daniel L.
Dillon, Edward
Dillon, James F.
Dillon, Louis H.
Dillon, William M.
Dilzell, William T.
Di Nino, Larry G.
Dinn, Wallace
Dinkey, Francis J.
Dishlong, Joe N.
Dishongh, Joe B.
DiSilvestro, Mario
Ditch, J.D.
Ditimer, Karl D.
Dittmer, F. S.
Dixon, Lionel A.
Dixon, Willie Joe
Dobson, George
Doherty, G. C.
Dolezal, Albert
Dominick, Lyle F.
Donovan, George V.
Donovan, Michael D.
Doody, Joseph, Jr.
Dorie, Arthur F.
Dormehl, W. J.
Dorris, Theodore E.
Doveton, G. D.
Dougherty, Philip J.
Douglas, Lucius
Douscet, M.J.
Dow, Robert
Dowd, Lawrence T.
Doyle, Robert M.
Drage, Donald D.
Drake, David C.
Draper, Parry D.
Dreckman, Harold Gene

Drezen, Richard Stanley
Driscoll, William F.
Drury, W. R.
Dube, Weldon M.
Duberger, Chas. R.
DuBois, Delois E.
Dubose, Jack M.
Duckworth, Frank
Dudock, Edward P.
Duff, Elmer H.
Duffie, Ben C.
Duffy, Donald T.
Duffy, Robert L.
Dugan, Harry E., Jr.
DuJat, Robert E.
Duke, Charles B.
Duley, Robert
Dulfer, John E.
Dumas, John R.
Duncan, John D.
Duncan, Sherwood M.
Dunham, Howard M.
Dunham, John
Dunlap, Elmer N. "Pappy"
Dunn, Russell
Dunnagan, Clifford L.
Dunnavant, Robert
Dupee, Reginiald D.
duPlooy, R. M.
DuPont, Charles J.
DuPrez, J. J.
Durant, William D., Jr.
Durgin, Allen C.
Dursteler, William S.
Dusenbury, James A.
Dutton, Albert H.
Dutton, J. R.
Duval, James
Dye, Rufus, Jr.
Dyer, Norman D.
Dykstra, John A.
Eagan, John D.
Eaker, Britten W.
Earp, Denis. J.
Earp-Jones, Rex C.
Easley, W.C.
Easley, David S.
Eastis, David W.
Eaton, Joseph
Eaton, Lyle C.
Ebbert, Clarence A.
Eberhardt, Donald E.
Ebersole, Howard R.
Eby, Otto J.
Eckhart, Paul D.
Eckstein, John E.
Ector, H. Haley
Edelman, Karl
Edens, Malcolm Brody
Edmonds, Frank

Edwards, Harold P.
Edwards, John C.
Edwards, Richard W.
Edwards, Ward R.
Ehlers, C. C.
Eichelberger, George B., Jr.
Eick, Harold D.
Elander, Bill J.
Eliott, Jack
Ellenwood, Robt L.
Ellet, Lloyd D.
Ellington, Bill E.
Ellinwood, Bruce
Elliott, Arlie R.
Elliot, Daniel S.
Elliott, Ernest E.
Elliott, Leighton
Elliott, Robert A.
Elliott, Roy K.
Ellis, Jewel H.
Ellis, Robert S.
Ellison, Joe D.
Elmor, Bill
Elson, William
Embery, Robert L.
Emerson, R. J.
Empey, Roland W.
Emrick, Robert W.
Encinias, Miguel
Englert, Charles R.
Entz, Donald C.
Epperly, H.R.
Erickson, Phillip R.
Erickson, Robert E.
Ernst, Raymond L.
Eschardies, Paul L.
Escott, Francis William
Estes, Robert R.
Ettinger, Frank G.
Eurbin, Edward J.
Evans, Douglas E.
Evans, Harry K.
Evans, Shelby A.
Everly, Fred C.
Evola, Joseph P.
Ewing, Veryl M.
Exel, Raymond D.
Fagan, Harley L.
Fagan, James B.
Fager, George
Fair, Robert L.
Fairburn, Craig
Falconer, E. W.
Falo, Tony
Faris, Ben H.
Farmer, Owen P. Jr.
Farnstrom, D. D.
Farnum, Ellery H.
Farr, Daniel E., II

Farr, James T.
Farro, Cyril E.
Farron, Leonard R.
Farver, Robert W.
Fassman, L. J.
Faulk, Melvin W.
Faulkinbury, James F.
Fay, F. W.
Fay, John J.
Feagin, Forest
Fears, Walter H.
Featherstone, D. W.
Feezel, Tommy L.
Feibelman, Max M.
Feller, Frederick J.
Fenstermacher, Gene L.
Ferguson, Arthur
Ferguson, Robert A.
Ferguson, Robert
Ferraro, R. E.
Ferris, George B., Jr.
Fetch, Robert M.
Fiedler, William
Field, Burton M.
Field, Charles H.
Fielder, James M.
Fields, Jack C.
Fields, Jerome G.
Fields, Robert L.
Fillmann, William F. "Bud"
Fincher, Deltis Herman
Finkbiner, Billy W.
Finke, Wendell H.
Finley, Bernard O.
Finnegan, Charles E.
Fischer, Kenneth E.
Fischer, Robert C.
Fish, Richard H.
Fishel, Martin D.
Fisher, Ellis L.
Fitzgerald, John H.
Fjelstad, Kenneth S.
Fladmark, Oscar R.
Flagg, Earle V.
Flake, Alma Ross
Fleenor, Kenneth R.
Fleming, Alec F.
Fleming, Dale
Fleming, John F.
Flentke, Donald L.
Fletcher, Westwood H.
Flores, E. C.
Florey, Henry J.
Flower, Jack
Flowers, Arthur L.
Fluhr, Robert S.
Foisy, Arthur R.
Fonck, Fred R.
Foore, Acie F.
Forbert, Sam, Jr.

Forbes, Don R.
Ford, Clyde W.
Ford, Ernest G.
Ford, James G.
Forrest, Henry N.
Forsman, Richard
Forsstrom, Don R.
Forster, Harold S.
Forsyth, Homer
Forte, Robert A.
Fortney, Roger D.
Fosnick, Frank
Foster, A. H.
Foster, Andrew W., Jr.
Foster, D. Brock
Foster, T.M.
Foster, William G.
Fouche, G. E.
Fountain, Zed D.
Fouquet, Raymond M.
Fourie, L. W. G.
Fowkes, William
Fowler, John H.
Fox, Robert E.
Foye, Robert
Francis, Magnus
Frank, Richard
Frankart, Ned Charles
Franklin, Everett
Frantz, Dolph G.
Fray, Douglas W.
Fred, Harry
Fredenberg, Gilbert H.
Freelove, Dale
Freeman, Archie H. Jr.
Freeman, Lloyd O.
French, David J.
French, William C.
Frese, Lawrence R.
Frese, Raymond J.
Freund, Albert J., Jr.
Freytag, Richard A.
Frick, Vance R.
Frisby, A. G.
Fritsch, James E.
Fritz, George R.
Frost, M.H.E.
Frownfelter, Clarence E.
Frye, Charles L.
Frye, Richard W.
Fryer, T. R.
Frylinck, C. D.
Fuhs, Quinton
Fulford, A. C.
Funakoshi, Walter Y.
Funk, Lloyd S.
Gabreski, Francis S.
Gabriel, Charles A.
Gaddie, Eugene
Gaines, Edwin F.

Galicia, Herman M.
Galindo, Braulio M.
Gallagher, Marvin G.
Gallespie, G.W.
Gallman, Lewis Joe
Galvin, Lester D. Jr.
Galyon, Hershel E.
Gandy, Pierce M.
Gannon, T.W.
Garces, John R. Jr.
Garcia, Homer
Garcia, Joe C.
Gardner, Edgar K.
Gardner, Gayle B.
Garet, James A.
Garlough, Graydon K.
Garnett, Jack
Garnett, Robert M.
Garst, James
Gasson, Reg. E.
Gates, P. T.
Gaunt, Frank L.
Gaura, Isadore M.
Gaudreau, E.R.
Gautreaux, John
Gavura, John D.
Gaworski, Edward
Gazaway, Mark M.
Gearheart, Wallace L.
Gearing, H. T.
Geary, George K.
Gedye, M. D.
Geer, D.B.
Geering, W. J.
Gehr, Richard
Geis, R. A.
Gelveles, C. J.
Gelveles, Charles J.
Gemeny, John G.
George, Billy Joe
George, Robert O.
Gerhardt, Steven N.
German, James S.
German, Stanley R.
Gerrielts, John "Tod"
Gertz, Henry E.
Gerwig, John W.
Geyer, James A.
Gibbs, George, Jr.
Gibbs, Richard
Giblin, Richard T.
Gibson, Paul
Gibson, William J.
Giddens, Ecchol
Giddens, George C.
Giesigo, Robert
Gifford, John E.
Gilchrist, John D.
Gilchrist, William D.
Gildenhuys, B. P. A.

Gilger, Edward K.
Gill, Gerald B.
Gill, James
Gillespie, C.W.
Gillespie, F. H.
Gilliam, Vinson E.
Gilliland, Gilbert L.
Gilliland, Thomas
Gilmer, Donald G.
Giordano, Howard P.
Giosige, Robert R.
Gipson, Edgar N.
Givan, Dean
Given, Robert B.
Gladen, Cyrus R.
Glagovich, Paul L.
Glaser, John R.
Glass, Robert P.
Glass, Thomas R.
Glazier, Lynwood N.
Glenn, W.C.
Glenny, James R.
Gleoggler, James K.
Glessner, James L.
Glinister, J. D.
Gloeckler, Harold C. Jr.
Gloesner, Milton F., Jr.
Glommen, Martell J.
Glotzbach, Marvin W.
Goans, Daniel E.
Gobler, W. J.
Godsmark, John
Goerke, Delton
Goetze, A. R.
Golden, Newman Camay
Golden, Robert
Goldfogle, Richard A.
Goldsmith, Rich L.
Gomes, Vernon L.
Gomez, Carl
Gongalski, Lloyd
Gonzaba, M. B.
Good, Glen
Good, Robert E.
Good, William O.
Goodridge, Robert L.
Goodwin, Harold
Gordon, Andrew F.
Gordon, Joseph T.
Gordon, R.T.
Gordon, Stuart
Goslin, John C.
Gossen, Edward J.
Gossett, C. J.
Gotchey, Robert
Gould, William R.
Gowan, Clarence
Graaff, R. J.
Grace, D. D.
Graham, Robert D.

Graham, Richard H.
Grant, Herbert W.
Grant, R.L.
Grant, Richard M.
Grasis, Harry E.
Graves, Theron J.
Gray, Arthur M.
Gray, David L.
Gray, Donald
Gray, George Elbert
Gray, Richard, Jr.
Grazier, Raymond C.
Greaney, Maurice
Greeff, H. M. C.
Green, George W.
Green, H.
Green, J. W.
Green, Richard W.
Green, W. B.
Green, William F.
Greene, William James
Greenwood, David W.
Greenwood, George R.
Greget, Tony M.
Gregg, Bernard
Gregg, James A.
Gregor, John R.
Gregory, J.A.
Gregory, Stewart M.
Grenier, Arthur E., Jr.
Gretchko, Stephen J., Jr.
Greyell, Robert S.
Gries, William C.
Grieson, John A.,
Griffin, Donald E.
Griffin, Monroe H., Jr.
Griffin, Tom H.
Griffith, Bill
Griffith, Edward O., Jr.
Griffith, Hugh A., Jr.
Griffiths, T.H.
Griggs, Archie L.
Griggs, L.A.
Griggs, Richard S.
Grimmer, Carl
Grischkowsky, Edgar R.
*Grisham, David Howard
"Snowflake"*
Grissom, Charles R.
Groenwald, J. G.
Grog, James
Gronmeyer, William
Gross, Morton A. A.
Grossman, John Frank
Grott, Francis Mike
Grubb, William H.
Gruber, Richard T.
Grumbles, Wilbur J.
Grunder, M. O.
Guarino, Larry N.

Guerin, Roland L.
Gunning, Basil W.
Gurnett, Tom J.
Gustavison, D. F.
Guthrie, C. V.
Guttersen, Laird
Guyton, Mike
Gwin, Roy F.
Haarwood, Vernon R.
Haedtler, Martin C.
Haen, R.C.
Hafkemeyer, Uwe G. L.
Hafliger, Ross
Hafter, Joseph A.
Hagelthorne, Al
Hager, John Robert
Hagerstrom, James P.
Haggarty, John
Hagood, Donald M.
Haimes, Donald F.
Haines, George E.
Haines, Marland P.
Haines, Richard W.
Haizlip, Bobby B.
Hale, Robert L.
Hall, Arthur I.
Hall, B.B.
Hall, Fred D.
Hall, Glen R.
Hall, James H.
Hall, James K.
Hall, R., Jr.
Halley, Mike
Hallion, Vincent
Hallowell, Donald J.
Halstrom, Arvid V.
Halton, William T.
Halverson, Richard
Ham, William A.
Hambrick, James M.
Hamby, Albert C.
Hames, Landel
Hamilton, Alfred
Hamilton, D. E.
Hamilton, Howard D.
Hamilton, Isaac M.
Hamilton, Richard H.
Hammer, Robert H.
Hamowitz, A.
Hampton, Duane E.
Handschy, Glen G.
Haner, Robert H.
Haney, Max
Hanna, E. W.
Hanna, Theodore M.
Hansard, John
Hansen, David A.
Hansen, Donald J.
Hanson, Austin L.
Hanson, Edward R.

Hanson, Maurice L.
Hanz, Vernon H.
Harbin, Carl A.
Harburn, R. A.
Hard, Robert E.
Harden, James M.
Hardiman, Pete J.
Harding, Charles C.
Hardman, Paul
Hargin, Robert S.
Harjung, Larry D.
Harkness, Grant D.
Harlow, Wilburn B.
Harper, Flamm D.
Harper, Henry, Jr.
Harper, Lee A.
Harper, R.M.
Harrington, Joseph W.
Harrington, Virginia "Joe"
Harris, Bill
Harris, Brooklyn
Harris, Charles A.
Harris, Garland E.
Harris, James P., Jr.
Harrison, James B.
Harrison, William J.
Hart, Charlie E.
Hart, Dallas W.
Hart, Richard L.
Hart, Thomas A.
Hart, Willard P.
Harter, Vic
Hartley, Harold G.
Hartnett, John V.
Hartwig, George W.
Harvan, Frank J.
Harvey, Frank E.
Harwood, Vernon R.
Hasel, Marvin P.
Haskett, William T., Jr.
Haskins, G. W. "Bill"
Hatcher, Charles G.
Hatcher, Max
Hatzenbuehler, Jim
Hausen, Jacob E.
Hausner, Sigmund
Hauver, Charles D.
Havner, Simeon P.
Hawk, John C.
Hawley, Jack
Hawn, Dave A.
Haydon, Billy
Hayes, Donald R,
Hayes, Robert G.
Haymaker, Ralph W.
Hayward, Douglas B.
Hayward, Robert
Head, Cotesworth B.
Head, Earl E.
Heagney, Gerald J.

Healy, Richard L.
Heara, Howard T.
Heard, Randolph C.
Heard, William E.
Hearn, Howard T.
Hearn, James
Hearne, P. J.
Heath, James Darrell
Heath, Robert H.
Hecht, Morris
Heckler, Earl R.
Heckmaster, Freddie D.
Hederstrom, Jack Holly
Heeter, James D.
Hefelfinger, Charles A.
Hefer, D. L.
Heffernan, Robert M.
Heidema, H. W.
Heilands, Richard
Heilman, Richard W.
Heinbuch, James
Heiner, Howard R.
Heins, William J.
Henciak, Jerome E.
Henderson, C. W.
Henderson, Clarence
Henderson, Jesse J.
Hendrix, Phil
Henley, Edwin R. "Bones"
Henman, Floyd J.
Henn De K., A.
Henna, Theodore
Henry, Ivan R.
Henry, James G.
Henthorn, Robert E.
Herda, George
Herendeen, Bob D.
Herman, Donald S.
Herman, Robert L.
Hernandez, Eladio L.
Herring, B.M.
Herzer, Ronald C.
Hesford, E. N.
Hess, Dean E.
Hester, Robert M.
Hettema, Joe C.
Hewitt, Lester R.
Heyne, L.
Hickenlooper, Selden B.
Hicks, Harold V.
Hicks, Layden P.
Higa, Ronald J.
Higgins, John J.
Hightower, Calvin D.
Hightower, D. C.
Hilburn, Ray M. "Pappy"
Hill, George R.
Hill, John E.
Hill, Roger W.
Hill, W.F.

Hilton, Arnold
Hinck, Robert B.
Hines, Beryle E.
Hinman, J.F.
Hintermeir, Richard H.
Hinton, Charles
Hinton, Edward
Hirose, Edwin M.
Hirshberg, Sid S.
Hisken, Perry C.
Hitchcock, Samuel L.
Hixson, Jack L.
Hoagland, Edward C., Jr.
Hoard, Moray T.
Hobart, Edward
Hobart, Edwin
Hobbs, Ralph
Hobson, Reese K., Jr.
Hockett, Steven W.
Hodge, Bob
Hodge, Felix
Hodges, Arnold
Hodges, Charles E.
Hodges, Edward F.
Hodges, Kenneth Sherrill
Hoeffer, Bobby J.
Hoffman, Donald Edward
Hoffman, Sam B.
Hogue, Jerry F.
Hohatch, F.T.
Hoke, John David
Holcomb, Francis A.
Holden, Robert G.
Holder, Wallace "Glenn"
Holis, Horace D.
Hollenbeck, Erwin L.
Holly, Gerald
Holman, Robt N.
Holman, Boyne L.
Holman, Robert
Holmes, Vern D.
Holmes, Kenneth E.
Holmes, R. D.
Holmgren, Henry G.
Holowell, Donald
Holtzhausen, J. O.
Holshausen, Ivan A.
Holsomback, Robert L.
Holt, Aubrey J.
Holt, Charles M.
Holton, Hayden H.
Holzhauzen, J. O.
Holzschuh, John A.
Homka, Peter
Honaker, Elmer D.
Honacker, William
Honaker, William F.
Hood, L. W.
Hook, Robert D.

Hope, Jon W.
Hopkins, Carroll J.
Hopkins, T.D.
Hopkins, Ted L.
Horan, Thomas F.
Horn, John Lucas
Hornaday, Warren
Hornbaker, David
Hornsby, Jack C.
Horscroft, H. B.
Horsley, James C., Jr.
Horton, Phillips R. "Hoot"
Horton, Ralph J., Jr.
Hosaki, Joe
Hoster, Bob M.
Hough, B.R.
Houghton, Robert M.
House, Dallas N.
House, Walt D.
Houseworth, William
Houston, John B.
Hoversten, Francis J.
Howard, Claude F.
Howard, Forrest E.
Howard, Jake L.
Howe, John F. G.
Howell, Phil V.
Howell, Robert N.
Hower, Merle F.
Howie, Charles L.
Hubbard, Thomas H.
Hudson, B. L.
Hudson, Charles R.
Hudson, Charles T.
Hudson, Fred Gray, III
Hudson, V.L.
Hueske, Dale H.
Huff, Richard A.
Huffman, David I.
Huggins, James V.
Hughes, Henry A.
Hughes, Patrick V.
Huhn, Arthur E.
Humer, Ross T.
Humphrey, Winston E.
Hundley, Everett L.
Hunt, Daniel R.
Hunter, L. S.
Hunter, W. Dean
Hupp, George G.
Hurd, John
Hurlburt, Prosper E.
Hurley, Joseph R.
Hutchinson, Arthur Earl
Hutchinson, Raymond
Hutchison, John A.
Hutton, Harry C.
Hyde, Leland S.
Hyde, Sam
Hyden, Oran P.

Hydorn, William E.
Hynson, Arthur B., Jr.
Iglehart, Richard A.
Illner, J. E.
Imberg, Ralph M.
Immelman, D. G.
In, Timothy J.
Inferrera, John A.
Inglesby, S. J. W.
Ingvalson, Roger
Irish, Howard
Irving, Niel D.
Irwin, Frederick G.
Isenhour, Benjamin H.
Ivey, Thomas E.
Ivins, Loraine Reid
Jackman, William Edwin
Jackson, C. E.
Jackson, Edgar A.
Jackson, Jack
Jackson, Johnnie H., Jr.
Jackson, Wayne T.
Jacobs, Charles D.
Jacobs, Mike
Jacobs, Ralph E.
Jacques, Paul D.
James, Daniel, Jr. "Chappie"
James, G.S.
James, Gregory E.
James, Richard D.
Jamison, George L.
Janca, R. D.
Janca, Robert D.
Jane, Edwin G., Jr.
Janes, J.L.
Jansen, John A.
Jansen, Reed C.
Jarman, James T.
Jarvis, Rowan M.
Jeangerard, Jack J.
Jeffers, Buck W.
Jefferson, William H.
Jennings, Wallace R.
Jensen, J. Harvey
Jensen, Orland
Jensen, Ralph A.
Jent, Robt E. "Bob"
Jergensen, Kenneth H.
Jernigan, Lewis L.
Jessie, Richard A.
Jimenez, F.M.
John, Donald D.
Johanson, John
Johnson, Albert J.
Johnson, Curtiss F.
Johnson, Harry L.
Johnson, Howard C.
Johnson, Lonzo
Johnson, Lorne A.
Johnson, Martin H.

Johnson, Robert E.
Johnson, Russ
Johnson, W.L.
Johnston, Karl E.
Johnston, William D., Jr.
Jonas, Dick
Jones, B.L.
Jones, Buford J.
Jones, Charles C.
Jones, E. J.
Jones, E. N.
Jones, George D.
Jones, Harry A.
Jones, James
Jones, John A.
Jones, Harvey A., Jr.
Jones, Milton D.
Jones, Oliver Eugene
Jones, Paul E.
Jones, Robert A.
Jones, Robert G.
Jones, Robert J.
Jones, Robert L.
Jones, Robert T.
Jones, William C.
Joppru, Richard
Jordan, Harry
Jordan, Robert M.
Jorgensen, Daniel B.
Joslin, Richard E.
Joubert, Joe A.
Joy, Louis J.
Joyce, H. T. R.
Joyce, J.
Joynt, C. S.
Juhrs, William A.
Juszczyk, Walter E.
Juzwik, Mathew A.
Kaiser, Bob
Kaiser, Miles
Kalich, Edward R.
Kanaga, Robert
Kane, Warren H.
Karll, Theodore
Karr, F.K.
Kasunic, Thomas W.
Katz, Jack
Kaufman, Robert
Kauslick, Albert A.
Kauttu, Paul A.
Kautz, Kenneth
Kavanagh, Francis M.
Kawamoto, Calvin K.
Kearns, Michael W.
Keddy, R.
Kee, T.W.
Keeler, Curtis H.
Keen, William H.
Keenan, Robert H.
Keever, J.A.

Keevy, Eric R.
Keith, James H., Jr.
Keller, Ben E.
Kelly, J.R.
Kelly, Victor C.
Kelley, Frederick S.
Kelso, Wilber R., III
Kelton, Stanley T.
Kemp, S. L.
Kempland, Donald E.
Kempthorn, Richard J.
Kennedy, James T.
Kennedy, Thomas M.
Kenney, Richard F.
Kenny, B. R.
Kent, Richard D.
Kephart, Thomas
Kepley, Fred
Kerins, James B.
Kerpan, Louis M.
Kerschitz, Frank J.
Ketola, Bruno
Key, Harrison E.
Keys, Ronald
Keys, Vernon R.
Keyser, Robert E.
Kibort, Bernard R.
Kiedinger, James W.
Kief, Jerry
Kiehart, John E.
Kilbride, Wade R.
Kilburn, V. T.
Kilpatrick, C.C.
Kilray, Ed J.
Kinder, Lawrence
Kinder, Lawrence D.
King, James W.
King, Maurice J.
King, Max J.
Kinkennan, H.
Kinney, Dennis F.
Kinsman, Renn S.
Kiozyinski, Edward
Kirby, H. E.
Kirchner, Duane W.
Kirsch, George A.
Kiser, James R.
Kitchen, Richard F.
Kline, Benjamin J.
Klinger, Daniel L.
Klinglesmith, Jerry D.
Kloss, Charles J.
Kniffen, Charles E.
Knight, Harold C.
Knight, James E.
Kniss, Paul R.
Knoesen, J. F.
Knowlton, William M.
Knutsen, David E.
Kobort, B.R.

Kobriger, James C.
Kochar, Robert P.
Kochy, Stephen B.
Koekemoer, J. J.
Koening, Richard
Kohlschreiber, Edward W.
Koken, Eugene H.
Kolb, Clifford C.
Koon, Kenneth F.
Korbol, Harold O.
Kothman, Kenneth K.
Kottal, John L.
Kotze, H. A.
Kotzenberg, R. P. G.
Krakovsky, Joseph L.
Kramer, John D.
Krause, Kenneth E.
Krause, Lyle R.
Krebs, H.S.
Krehbeil, Burman C.
Kretschmer, Conrad R.
Kriel, P. A.
Kriesl, Richard
Kriz, William J.
Krogman, Harry
Krohn, G. H.
Krueger, Arlon G.
Kruger, J. H.
Kruger, V. R.
Kruggel, Ewald G.
Kruzel, Joe J.
Kuhn, Phillip G.
Kulpa, Alexander M.
Kunts, Scott A.
Kuntz, Gerry
Kuntz, James G.
Kuntz, Scott A.
Kurtze, Warren
La Shomb, Eugene R.
Laakman, Henry E.
LaBonte, Richard
LaClare, Edward F.
Ladue, Mark L.
Lacy, Garvin H.
Lacy, Thomas E.
Lafferty, David K.
Lafferty, Thomas C.
Lamar, James L.
Lamb, M. J.
Lambert, A. G.
Lambert, John W.
LaMontagne, Armond J.
Lamphier, Thomas G.
Lampkin, Jerry E.
Landry, Barney M.
Landry, John F.
Lane, Joe V.
Lane, Thomas H.
Lang, Rick
Langford, R. M. R.

Langveld, R. E.
Lanning, Adam B., III
Lansdale, James F.
Lantz, Virgil P.
LaPointe, Percy J.
Larkin, Timothy J.
Larrick, Herschell G.
Larrick, Herschell G., Jr.
Larsen, George E.
Larsen, Marion D.
Larsen, Paul A.
Lauritzen, James R.
Lavin, John T.
Law, John F.
Lawson, B.O.
Lawrence, Henry W.
Lawrence, Louis J.
Laws, Louis W.
Lawson, Bobbie
Lawson, Jarvis J.
Lawyer, Richard
Layton, John D.,
Leach, Lawrence J.
Leah, D. R.
Leake, Daniel D.
Leamon, T. J.
Leathers, D. R.
Ledford, Otto C.
Lee, Dwight Earl
Lee, James W.
Lee, W. B.
Leedy, Robert
LeFebre, Frederick H.
LeFleur, Robert
LeGrange, J. P.
Leighton, Amos B .
Leisy, Robert E.
Leitner, George N.
Lellyet, J. N.
Lemmon, James J.
Lenhart, Warren T.
Leonard, R. L.
Lent, John W.
LeRoux, J. N.
Lesicka, Joseph
Lessig, Cecil P.
Letherbarrow, B. D.
Letley, P.
Lette, Leroy L.
Levandoski, Stephen A.
Leve, Kenneth
Levenson, Seymour M.
Levitt, Louie E.
Levy, Mark
Lewer, Richard C.
Lewis, Billy S.
Lewis, Charles H.
Lewis, Francis E., II
Lewis, James R. D.
Lewis, John E.

Lewis, Roy W.
Libby, Edward E.
Libby, Francis N.
Liebenberg, Terry
Lighter, W.W.
Lightfoot, Marion F.
Lightner, Jack A.
Lighty, William O.
Lincoln, C.R.
Lindquist, C.W.
Lindsay, Charles E.
Lines, Robert J.
Linkous, Billy S.
Linn, Howard A.
Linnell, Terry
Lionberger, Lyle J.
Litchfield, Henry L.
Little, Ian R.
Little, John E.
Littlefield, Laurence D.
Livermore, Ross E.
Livingston, Henry H.
Lock, D. A. S.
Locke, William
Lockhart, Tom G.
Locks, William
Loeding, Keith, V.
Loeffler, John L.
Loftus, John L.
Loftus, Martin J.
Logan, Joe A.
Lomas, Norman B.
Lomax, Jack
Lombard, Chris
Lombard, P. H.
Lombardo, J.F., Jr.
Long, James W.
Long, Stanley A.
Longshore, Lamar B.
Lothridge, Robert L.
Lottinger, Roy F.
Lovelace, Albert P.
Lovell, Carl E.
Lovett, James D.
Lovitt, Louis E.
Low, Curtis R.
Lowe, Charles R., Jr.
Lowery, Arthur A.
Lubner, Marvin
Lucas, Robert J.
Luck, Ronald E.
Ludwig, Thomas W.
Lufi, Eldon D.
Lukakis, George M.
Lull, Warren W.
Lull, Warren W., Jr.
Lund, Ralph G.
Lundin, Fred A.
Lundquist, Richard T.
Lundskow, Henry P.

Lundskow, Henry P., Jr.
Lunsford, Henry C.
Luow, J. J. E.
Lutrey, Theodore
Lynch, Donald H.
Lynd, Donald O.
Lyster, David K., Jr.
Maach, Jayson
MacArevey, James J.
MacArthurDavid W.
MacCallum, Carl
MacDonald, Lawrence J.
MacDougal, Donald A.
MacGillicuddy, H. C.
MacGregor, Wallace F.
MacGuarrie, Ernie L.
Mack, Fred E.
Maclachlan, Neil M.
MacLaughlin, D. W.
MacMillan, David W.
MacNair, Donald B.
MacPherson, T.F.
Macrina, J.A.
Maikoski, Arthur J.
Mailloux, Norman R.
Maistrelli, Alfred F.
Major, Thomas E.
Mallick, George W.
Malone, Harry K.
Malone, Robert
Maloney, Richard M.
Mammen, David B.
Manak, John J.
Mancini, Nicholas
Manjak, Thomas G.
Mann, Howard P.
Manning, Robert J.
Manning, William H.
Mannino, Cosmo R.
Mansfield, Ernest G.
Manthey, Norris K.
Manthos, Atlee G.
Maples, Richard G.
Marcellus, Jack K.
March, Theodore P.
Marchand, D. L.
Marcum, William A.
Marcozzi, Ralph E.
Marford, Donald P.
Markowitz, Robert S.
Markowski, Ignatious R.
Marksbury, Robert L.
Marley, C. F.
Marley, C. L.
Marmetschke, Adolph
Marquis, Robert L.
Marsden, Lee R.
Marshall, Gerald R.
Martin, B. E.
Martin, Billy R.

Martin, David E.
Martin, Maurice L.
Martin, W. L.
Martine, Ned J.
Marx, Jacob
Maskell, B. A. T.
Mason, Edward J.
Mason, Max A., Jr.
Mason, Richard P.
Mason, Tom
Massengale, Ken M.
Masterson, Robert A.
Matasick, Robt A.
Mathee, R. W. N.
Mathews, James L.
Mathis, James J.
Mathis, Peyton S.
Matson, Henry E.
Mau, Jerome R. "Jerry"
Maxwell, Allison
May, Britt
May, William S. "Bill"
Maynard, Charles
Mayo, Frank,
Mays, Pete
Maytubby, David A.
Mazurak, Eugene Z.
McAlpine, John Matheson
McBride, William P.
McCabe, James J.
McCafferty, George O.
McCain, Clifton S.
McCall, Craig C.
McCamish, Carl B.
McCann, John P.
McCarty, David L.
McCarty, James P.
McCaskill, Rod E.
McCauley, Clayburn L.
McClain, Keith E.
McClendon, Frank C.
McClendon, Wallace
McCloud, J.M.
McClure, James R.
McClure, Willie D.
McCune, Robert
McDade, Charles L.
McDannold, John C.
McDavid, G.G.
McDermott, L.G.
McDermott, Thomas L.
McDonald, Billy J.
McDonald, Calvin C.
McDonald, K. B.
McDonald, Marion R.
McDonald, Reginald
McDougall, Marlin
McDowell, Wayne S.
McDuff, L.R., Jr.
McElroy, William J., III

McEntee, J.J.
McEwen, D. E.
McEwen, Delbert E.
McGee, Charles E.
McGee, Joseph V.
McGonigal, "Mike" B.
McGowan, Clarence A.
McGrail, H.J.
McGrath, J.H.
McGuff, Paul H.
McIntyre, Marshall G.
McKaig, Malcolm C.
McKaig, Terri
McKay, Gordon H.
McKellar, D. W.
McKelvey, Raymond D.
McKenna, Edmond P.
McKenny, James L.
McKeown, Arthur J.
McKinney, C. G.
McKinney, Clell H., Jr.
McKnight, David T.
McKnight, James T.
McKnight, Thomas
McKown, James S., Jr.
McKulla, Lawrence
McLanahan, James D.
McLaren, William A.
McLean, Harvey B.
McLees, George C., Jr.
McLoughlin, John F.
McMahon, Richard
McMillan, Orville S.
McMillan, Max
McMillion, Fred
McMurray, K.A.
McMurray, Robert B.
McNamara, Donald A.
McNaull, Cloyd S.
McNeil, Thomas C.
McNichol, D.H.
McNichol, William J.
McPhail, Charles R.
McRae, Charles C.
McShane, William E.
McVay, Richard B.
McWhite, Gene P.
McZinney, Clell H., Jr.
Meadville, Gordon E.
Meaker, Jack,
Meakin, James
Mederstrom, Jack A.
Meiring, J. A.
Meisenheimer, William
Meister, Robert J.
Menke, Hans
Mentz, M.
Mercer, Raymond D.
Merrigan, T.L.
Merrill, Clinton D.

Merrill, David K.
Merritt, Jack
Mervyn, William J.
Messett, T. Mike
Mettlen, John L.
Meyer, Andy L.
Meyer, Bobby J.
Meyer, Carl F.
Mezeske, Carl P.
Michael, Ralph L.
Michelson, Edward D.
Middleton, Harry Richard
Miesbach, Delaine C.
Mignanelli, H.
Mikula, Walter S.
Millen, Reginald M.
Miller, Arden L.
Miller, Burnett W.
Miller, Cyril C.
Miller, Daniel J.
Miller, Donald L.
Miller, Donald R.
Miller, Donald W.
Miller, Elden R.
Miller, Frederick L.
Miller, Harold E.
Miller, Jack W.
Miller, Melford W.
Miller, Robert L., III
Miller, Robert T.
Miller, Roy S.
Miller, Wendell D.
Miller, Wilbur S.
Miller, William C.
Miller, William S.
Milliman, W.J.
Mills, Jewell I.
Mills, Robert J.
Mills, Warren N.
Mills, Warren W.
Miraldi, Leonard P.
Miska, Robert
Mitchel, Erbert W.
Mitchell, Donald R.
Mitchell, Hershel L.
Mitchell, John W.
Mitchell, Owen S.
Mitchell, Robt H.
Mitchell, W. E.
Moats, Donald M.
Moershfelder, Herbert L.
Mogus, Michael H.
Moir, John
Moll, Toby
Molland, Leland P.
Mommer, Frank C.
Monroe, Shelton Wilson
Montanari, Frank A.
Montgomery, J. S.

Montgomery, Joseph S.
Montgomery, K.R.
Moody, Hal P.
Moolman, C. J.
Moore, Bruce L.
Moore, Cecil L.
Moore, Forman W.
Moore, Harold W.
Moore, Harry Cecil
Moore, Herbert C.
Moore, James D.
Moore, Joseph F.
Moore, Lyle Earl, Jr.
Moore, Maury K.
Moore, Rufus
Moore, T. C.
Moore, V.T.
Moore, Walter W.
Moore, Willie J.
Moorhead, Robert B.
Mooser, Paul J.
Moran, Bryce
Moran, John D.
Morehouse, Charles R.
Morehouse, Donald C.
Moreland, Harry H.
Morford, Donald P.
Morgan, Barry E.
Morley, Berley F.
Morley, Edward C.
Morley, James A.
Moriarity, Joseph A.
Morphis, Edward O.
Morris, Alfred R.
Morris, Bennie L.
Morris, Cola R.
Morris, William C.
Morris, William O.
Morrison, John A.
Morrissey, Raymond A.
Morrow, Elton G.
Morton, James K.
Morton, Walter P., Jr.
Motley, James L.
Mowry, William
Moynash, Russel C.
Mucheck, Robert L.
Mueller, John S.
Muffley, Max M.
Mulanax, Robert L.
Muldoon, John L.
Mullen, Jack R.
Muller, A. M.
Mullins, Arnold "Moon"
Muncy, W.H.
Munnik, D. J.
Munson, James
Munson, John M.
Murden, H.C.
Muroz, Gilberto

Murphy, Bob
Murphy, Edward G.
Murphy, George P.
Murphy, John J.
Murphy, John R.
Murray, Andrew E.
Murray, Joseph M.
Murray, Norman D.
Myers, Bill E.
Myers, D.K.
Myers, James F.
Myers, Robert W.
Myrick, Arthur W.
Nabers, Charles
Naftanel, John C.
Nantel, Robert A.
Nardo, Patrick
Navarro, Michael
Nay, Howard N.
Naylor, Robert L.
Neal, Charles C., Jr.
Neale, James M.
Nebinger, Ed M.
Nebinger, Edward M.
Neillands, Richard G.
Nell, L. D.
Nelsen, Marion W.
Nelson, John A.
Nelson, Nels A.
Nelson, William
Neptune, Wayne K.
Nessbaum, V. L.
Netherton, Robert C.
Neveling, A. C.
Newell, Harry D.
Newell, Richard G.
Newenhof, G. E.
Newlander, Carl E. Jr.
Newler, Leon
Newlon, John W.
Newman, Robert D.
Newstrom, Carroll
Newton, J. G.
Nibert, John J.
Nebinger, Edward M.
Nibley, Owen S.
Nichols, David F.
Nickerson, Joseph H.
Niemela, John R.
Niklaus, Robert C.
Nissen, Robert E.
Nix, Glenn
Njus, Kasper M.
Noble, Glen K.
Noble, Peter
Nolan, Robert A.
Nolin, Louis G., Jr.
Nolli, John J.
Nooger, Abraham
Nordin, Glenn L.

Nordmeyer, Jim
Nordquist, Roger W.
Norman, Henry H.
Norman-Smith, P. I.
Norris, William C.
North, Ken
Northcott, Clyde A.
Nortje, J. F.
Noyd, Werner S.
Noyes, Ralph L.
Nugent, John R.
Nugent, Robert L.
Nunnery, Charles C.
Nygard, Albert V.
Nygard, Paul R.
O'Brian, Michael
O'Briant, Eric Franklin
O'Brien, Desmond
O'Brien, Edmund D.
O'Brien, James F.
O'Brien, Michael W.
O'Brien, Mike W.
O'Brien, P. J.
O'Connell, Charles J.
O'Connell, P. A.
O'Connell, Patrick J.
O'Dell, William R.
Odin, C. Vick
O'Donovan, Edward D.
O'Grady, Gillon
O'Neal, Floyd B.
O'Neal, Ray C.
Oakley, J. T.
Oates, Everett G.
Ochoa, Alex M.
Odegaard, Douglas M.
Odendaal, H. O. M.
Odiorne, John M.
Ohnstad, Alden O.
Olcott, Richard L.
Oliver, Harold D.
Olliviere, Lionel A.
Olsen, George N.
Olson, Floyd
Olson, J.
Olson, Leonard S.
Olson, Ralph M.
Oja, Floyd G.
Ondracek, Laddie
Oppelt, Robert J.
Oresky, Jerry L.
Orsutt, S. J.
Ortega, Joseph H.
Orth, Robert C.
Osborne, Robert C.
Osborne, Sherrod, Jr.
Osteen, Joe B.
Oswell, B. O.
Overton, Norris W.
Owens, Harley

Paden, William L.
Padilla, Alexander Beck
Padula, Arnold F.
Page, A. R.
Page, Garnet D.
Page, Lewis A., Jr.
Pagitt, Leo
Paige, Frank H.
Painter, Charles F.
Palinkas, Albert
Palmer, David E.
Palmer, Duncan
Palmer, James M.
Palmer, K.L.
Palmer, Millwood J.
Palmer, Richard W.
Palmer, Roy L.
Palmer, Roy L.
Palmer, Stanley A.
Palmisano, William P.
Palombo, Anthony
Panko, Johnnie
Pappas, Critton J.
Park, Wallace L.
Parker, Armand J.
Parker, Donald
Parker, Frank P.
Parker, Gary E.
Parker, Jean E.
Parker, Joe L.
Parker, John E.
Parker, Maurice E.
Parker, Raymond
Parker, Samuel W.
Parks, Al
Parks, Wallace L.
Parrish, Lonnie W.
Parsons, Carroll T.
Parsons, Douglas R.
Parsonson, L. W.
"Jimmy"
Pascoe, Donald L.
Pasqualicchio, Robert P.
Paterson, Guy G.
Patnoe, Royal A.
Patrick, Doyle L.
Patterson, Arnold M.
Patterson, Ben L.
Patterson, Charles
Patterson, Warren S.
Patterson, William L.
Patton, George Vernon
Patzkowsky, R.E.
Paul, Edward A.
Paulk, John R.
Pavey, Charles
Payne, Douglas H.
Payne, Dwight E.
Payner, Warner K.
Peacock, George

Peacock, Robert D.
Pearce, L. B. "Bunny"
Pearcy, J. L.
Pearson, Bernard Lee
Pedersen, Arthur M.
Pederson, Thomas C.
Pedings, James W.
Peek, James C.
Peel, William B.
Pelchat, George
Peltekis, James
Pelz, Francis M.
Pendergraft, William J.
Pennington, Harold E.
Penrose, Richard
Pensyl, Jon P.
Perciasepe, Joseph A.
Percy, Bernard D.
Perego, Frank S.
Perez, Fernando
Perkins, Richard V.
Perrault, Joe F.
Perri, Leo A.
Perrin, Wayne
Perry, Joel V.
Peterburs, Joseph A.
Peters, Jack T.
Peterson, Albert O.
Peterson, Herbert A.
Peterson, Lowell J.
Petit, Robert L.
Petrarca, Eliseo A.
Petrash, Paul M.
Pettit, Robert T.
Petzen, John A.
Pfeiler, Louis F.
Pfuhl, John,
Philipp, Joseph W.
Phillips, Ben S.
Phillips, Billy E.
Phillips, George W.
Phillips, R.W.
Pickard, Harold W.
Pickel, Creel C.
Pickering, Earl W., Jr.
Pidsley, A. R.
Pidsley, D. W.
Piekielniak, Mathew W.
Pielan, Robert D.
Pienaar, B. J.
Pienaar, E. A. C.
Pieper, William H.
Pierce, Maynard O.
Pieterse, L. M.
Piriczky, Richard E.
Pitchford, Donald L.
Pitt, Robert W.
Pittman, Paul D.
Pittman, Walter Everett
Plass, Frederick J.

Plevyak, Raymond
Thaddeus
Plotkin, Melvin
Pochari, Tom R.
Poleynard, Sidney L.
Polk, Charles W.
Pollard, Bill S.
Pollock, John C.
Polnisch, Arthur B.
Ponder, Charles E.
Poole, H.L.
Pope, Ernest L.
Porter, Fred H.
Porter, Harry H., Jr.
Post, Harry
Potgieter, Frederick E.
Pottebaum, Cletus J.
Potter, Charles W.
Potter, Clair W.
Potter, Forrest V.
Potter, Gerald O.
Powell, Calvin H.
Powell, Edgar N.
Powell, J. E. G.
Powell, Scott
Powers, Harold M.
Powers, Joe E., Jr.
Powers, William E.
Pratt, Leland
Prevosti, Mario V.
Price, Charles H.
Price, Gene
Price, Howard I.
Price, Maylon D.
Price, Samuel D.
Price, Walter L.
Prickett, Vernon C.
Prince, Darrell P.
Prince, Thomas
Pruczinski, Frederick R.
Prugh, R. L.
Pruitt, Arthur H.
Pryor, James A.
Pryor, Sterling D.
Purnell, Fred V.
Putty, John K.
Pylant, Roy, Jr.
Pyut, Wallace
Quessenberry, E.W.
Quinn, Dorian
Quinones, Fred
Quy, Harvey D.
Rabun, William H. Jr.
Race, William O.
Rackham, Edwin J.
Radatz, E.
Radeck, Arnold V.
Radzuikina, Frank J.
Rae, A. S.
Ragsdale, Darrel L.

Ragsdale, Herbert L.
Ralston, Gilbert R.
Ramp, Leland
Ramsdell, Earl W.
Ramsel, Douglas A.
Ramsey, Robert Douglas
Ranch, Leonard A.
Randall, Jim E. P.
Randalls, Jim
Randazza, Thomas
Rankin, George J.
Ransford, Albert
Rapson, George A.
Rasberry, William D.
Rasmusson, James R.
Raszka, Ted
Rathbun, Edward L.
Ratledge, Jim B.
Ratliff, Delon
Ray, Carl L.
Ray, J.E.
Raybon, Lavonne
Raymond, William D.
Reding, Donald G.
Redmon, W.
Redmond, Frederick V.
Reed, Cheston M.
Reed, Franklin D.
Reed, Walter D.
Reeder, Damon B.
Reedy, J.R.
Rees, John W.
Reese, Douglas
Reeves, J.K.
Regan, Frank M.
Region, Marion A.
Reich, Doug A.
Reid, James F.
Reid, Kenneth E.
Reid, Levi
Reinhardt, Lewis K.
Reints, James A.
Remias, Paul M.
Renken, Randall R.
Rensburg, Zulu Jan
Resnick, Hugh
Revelle, L.D.
Revisky, Robt J.
Reynes, Joseph
Reynold, Charles
Reynolds, Henry L.
Reynolds, Leslie R.
Reynolds, Willard R.
Rhinehart, Walter F.
Rhoads, Merle A.
Rice, Fleming A.
Rice, George
Rich, A. P.
Richard, Robert E.
Richards, Charles L.

Richards, Don
Richards, Ellis
Richards, Joseph
Richards, Paul A.
Richards, R.
Richardson, Peter W.
Richie, Carl S.
Richter, F. B.
Rickle, Lawrence
Rieman, John G.
Riggens, H.B.
Riggs, Charles E., Jr.
Riggs, Charles R.
Riha, Amos F.
Riley, H.G.
Riley, Ray M.
Riley, Robert A.
Rinkowski, Joseph
Ristow, Herald R.
Ritchie, Andrew J.
Ritter, William H.
Ritter, William R.
Rivers, Richard T.
Rives, Joel Orlander
Robb, Robert J.
Roberts, Donald R.
Roberson, Arval J.
Roberson, Herman G.
Robertson, Raymond D., Jr.
Robertson, Thomas D.
    "Robbie"
Robinson, Elbert T.
Robinson, Jim
Robinson, Joseph W.
Robison, Clark A.
Roche, Robert F.
Rock, Edward T.
Rock, Henry C.
Roche, Joseph M.
Rockmaker, Frederick
Roe, James E.
Roe, R. Thomas
Roehm, John
Rogers, Harold E.
Rogers, Jack R.
Rogers, Lee A.
Rogers, R. H.
Rogers, Turner Clifton
Rogers, William C.
Rogers, William T., Jr.
Rogge, Gene F.
Rogotta, W. G. A.
Rolfe, G. H.
Rollag, Stanley A.
Roller, Lenton D.
Roller, Oscar C., Jr.
Romano, Bruno
Root, Aavin L.
Rorke, Michael H.
Rosel, Robert L.

Rose, Thomas G.
Rose, W.E.
Rosen, Arnold
Rosenburg, Dale N.
Rosencrans, Sheldon D.
Rosengrant, Robert H.
Rosenhan, A.L.
Ross, A.R.
Ross, S. L.
Rothe, Charles J.
Roth, Harlon C.
Rothenbuecher, Stanley
Rouncivell, K. H.
Routhier, Arthur
Royko, Michael, Jr.
Row, Enoch
Rudd, Calvin P.
Rudolph, Allan Keith
Rueger, Walter E.
Ruiter, D. A.
Rumbaugh, Marvin G.
Rund, Elmer L.
Rundle, Michael F.
Runkle, Del
Runyan, Stanley
Rushing, Harry Eugene
Rushing, O. E. "Oscar"
Russell, Daniel J.
Russell, Robert L.
Rutan, Fred S.
Ruth, Neil B.
Ruth, Robert
Rutter, B.
Ryan, Eddie D.
Ryder, Edward J.
Ryder, Thomas H.
Rydowski, John J.
Rykken, Dick
Sackett, Charles T.
Sadvary, Peter
Said, Howard K.
Salade, William A.
Salinger, Richard B.
Salmen, Robert E.
Saltsman, Ralph H., Jr.
    "Salty"
Sampson, Jack R.
Sanborn, Chester G.
Sanders, Bobby R.
Sanders, William E.
Sanderson, William W., Jr.
Sandlin, Robert E.
Sandmann, Joseph A., Jr.
Sandoval, Arthur M.
Sanfilippo, Thomas F.
***Sankey, William Charles,
Jr.***
Sanny, Max J.
Santasiero, Ralph A.
Santomassino, Sisto

Santos, Ray
Sapp, Bill M.
Sapp, Marion
Sargen, Charles M.
Sarosi, Ralph G.
Sarwinski, George M.
Satenstein, Marvin
Sauber, L. L.
Saunders, Jesse L.
Sawyer, Donald
Sawyer, Harold A.
Sawyer, Jerome R.
Sayles, Harry S.
Scahill, John J.
Scarano, Peter A.
Schaefer, Clifford A.
Scharick, Joseph V.
Schartiger, Charles
Schatz, James
Schell, Wyrian T.
Scherer, Donald O.
Schiebel, Richard H.
Schierhoff, Kenneth R.
Schiffel, Frank
Schindler, Andrew R.
Schindler, Wilber J.
Schmidt, Norman
Schmidt, Reynold D. B.
Schmitt, John G.
Schmitz, Paul E.
Schmitz, Walter H.
Schnaitman, Ray G.
Schneider, Donald B.
Schneider, James J.
Schoeman, P. A.
Schoenfeldt, D. A.
Schoettel, Theodore
Schofield, Thomas D.
Schooley, Lester A.
Schoombee, F. J.
Schreffler, Charles E.
Schroeder, Frank A.
Schuler, Joseph L.
Schultz, James T.
Schurr, Lowell
Schuster, Harold
Schwab, Donald H.
Schwab, John D.,
Schwarz,Walter J.
Schwertfeger, Ronald
Scoggins, George F.
Scott, Cassius C.
Scott, Trevor C.
Scott, William L.
Scott, Winfield W., Jr.
Scott-Shaw, C.
Searles, DeWitt R.
***Sebille, Louis
    Joseph"Lou"***
Sechrengost, William H.

Seeberg, George B.
Seelander, John H.
Seele, Steven T., Sr.
Seery, D.
Sefca, Milan
Sefcovic, Anthony
Sefton, Jack W.
Seguin, Richard James
Seher, Roy
Seibel, Harold J.
Seidman, Herbert
Self, Douglas S.
Sejan, George
Self, Melvin L.
Selkregg, James
Selover, L. E.
Selva, Tony
Semans, T. D., III
Semrau, Roy J.
Sennewald, C.A.
Sepulveda, Manual F.
Sequin, Richard James
Severeid, D. R.
Severn, David V.
Seymoe, Joseph P.
Seymone, Joseph P.
Shallenberger, Charles F.
Sharman, Thomas E.
Sharpsteen, Bill
Shattuck, James W.
Shaughnessy, Ed J., Sr.
Shaw, William S.
Sheedy, P.W.
Shelander, John H.
Shelton, David K.
Shelton, William E.
Shepard, Allan
Shepard, Jack E.
Shepard, Thomas J.
Shepard, Willie C.
Sherline, Bernard L.
Sherrill, Alvan C.
Sherry, Thomas H.
Shields, Billy J.
Shimp, Robert O.
Shingledecker, R.S.
Shinn, David A.
Shipley, Robert C.
Shipp, Maxwell J.
Shirley, Donald G.
Shive, Steward S., Jr.
Shively, Earl E.
Shiver, Clifton W.
Shivers, Charence L.
Shockley, Thomas L.
Shoemaker, Kenneth
Shoults, Charles T.
Shriver, F.C.
Shuler, Lucien B.
Shultz, William B.

Shumway, Philip R.
Shurlow, Melvin
Shurtleff, John O.
Shusky, D.R.
Sicklesteel, Milton E.
Sieg, Prentis R.
Siegler, Richard M.
Siemiaszko, Lawrence J.
Sigur, Lawrence R.
Sillery, Augustine C.
Silverman, A.
Silvernail, Russell S., Jr.
Silvestro, Bruno S.
Simmons, Charles E.
Simmons, S.E.
Simon, Julius A.
Simone, P. S.
Simpson, Charles B.
Simpson, Deverne C.
Simpson, George M.
Simpson, Glen D.
Simpson, Orville L.
Simpson, Tipp
Sims, Randall F.
Singleton, B. W.
Singleton, Dean O.
Sisemore, Monard L.
Sivertsen, T.M. Howard
Sizemore, Robert
Skaar, Charles A.
Skala, James H.
Skinner, Eugene E.
Sklenicka, Vigilee
Skoff, Eugene S.
Skousen, Alma W.
Skow, Richard C.
Skowron, Edward R.
Slater, William S.
Slewinski, Edward J.
Slezak, William F.
Sloan, Owen
Slower, Jack E.
Slowinaki, Edward J.
Slown, Ed J.
Smallwood, J. T.
Smelley, Reginald T.
Smisek, William J.
Smith Don E.
Smith, Ben H.
Smith, C. Hunter
Smith, Chadwick B.
Smith, Charles J.
Smith, Clarence E.
Smith, D. T.
Smith, Donald R.
Smith, Donald W.
Smith, Eugene E., Jr.
Smith, Eugene G.
Smith, Eugene L.
Smith, G. v. E.

Smith, Graham
Smith, Grant
Smith, Homer A.
Smith, Howard E.
Smith, Jack D.
Smith, Jack H.
Smith, Jack S.
Smith, James A.
Smith, Jennings H.
Smith, Ken C.
Smith, L. B. B.
Smith, Martin L.
Smith, Owen B.
Smith, Robert E.
Smith, Robert G.
Smith, Robert Leslie
Smith, Ron B.
Smith, Roy C.
Smith, Terry R.
Smith, Truett B.
Smith, Vernon R.
Smith, William
Smith, Zed S.
Smithson, Joseph P.
Smits, J. F.
Smotherman, Mario
Smotherman, Marion K.
Sneed, William O.
Snell, George W.
Snell, Will H.
Snow, Clayton
Snow, Frank N.
Snow, Harold S.
Snowden, Herman L.
Snyder, Jack A.
Snyders, J. D. S.
Solem, Herman S.
Soloby, Andrew
Soltis, William J.
Somers, Davis M.
Sonderman, Clarence H.
  "Gus"
Sooter, Ralph J.
Sosa, Alfonso
Soule, Irving D., Jr.
Southard, Ramon D.
Southern, Elmon L.
Southwell, Richard
Souza, Melvin
Spangler, Warren E.
Spann, William D.
Sparkman, Jimmy R.
Sparkman, Paul J.
Sparks, Alan B.
Sparks, Gary E.
Specht, Donald
Spelsberg, Walter T.
Spence, Theodore H., Jr.
Spencer, Barthelomew
Spencer, Billy J.

Spencer, Charles H.
Spencer, John H.
Spencer, Ted E.
Spencer, Thomas E.
Sperry, Robert E.
Spillers, Robert
Spina, Ben
Spinnenweber, Joseph H.
Spraggins, Sherman E.
Sprague, Roger L.
Spraul, Rocke F.
Springer, Charles W.
Springett, Alfred A.
Spry, Donald J.
Staats, Robert L.
Stacklie, Robert L.
Stalder, Charles
Stallings, Guy H.
Stallings, Robert, Jr.
Stamm, A. P.
Stamper, William
Stanbro, Herbert
Stanfield, Don N.
Stanfield, F. Wheeler
Stange, Vernon G.
Stankard, Stephen M.
Stanley, James R.
Stanton, Carroll M.
Stanton, Eugene S.
Stapley, Wilfred C. "Budd"
Star, E.E.
Starck, John Shirley
Staring, John H.,
Starkley, William G.,
Staron, Edward W.
Starwalt, Wallace L.
Staudte, Raymond W.,
Steckel, Richard Edmund
Steel, Kenneth I.
Steele, Elmer R.
Steele, J. C.
Steffensen, Harry R.
Stegenga, Stuart
Steiner, James W.
Steinsick, D.M., Jr.
Stell, Glenn A.
Stenberg, Clayton C.
Stephens, James A.
Stephens, J.E.
Stephens, Leon B., Jr.
Stepp, Lloyd
Sterbonic, Peter
Stern, Howard L.
Sternard, Robert E.
Stetler, Robert L.
Steuwer, Donald J.
Stevenin, Eugene W., Jr.
Stevens, Paul W., Jr.
Stevenson, Charles A.
Steward, Vernon G.

Stewart, Bernard J.
Stewart, Clifford L.
Stewart, Don J.
Stewart, Everett
Stewart, Glenn E.
Stewart, Kenneth M.
Stewart, Raymond A. Jr.
Stichnot, Alfred J.
Stike, Lyndell
Stine, Morris R.
Stobnicke, Paul P.
Stocker, Robert C.
Stoik, Theodore M.
Stolfi, Vincent G.
Stoll, Robert H.
Stone, John W., Jr.
Stone, Richard L.
Stone, Roy T.
Stone, Theodore
Stoner, Charles W.
Storino, Henry E.
Stossell, Fred M.
Stotts, John H.
Strader, Charles R.
Straight, George E.
Strait, Virgil K.
Strand, William H.
Strange, Forrest L.
Stratton, Eldon
Strauss, Thomas A., Jr.
Streach, Richard A.
Street, James F.
Streit, John P.
Strickland, Edwin C.
Strom, Wallace D.
Strough, Robert
Struth, Thomas C.
Strydom, P. J.
Stuart, Marx H.
Stubbs, Leonard
Stull, Ned R.
Sturdevant, Archie B.
Sturgis, James E.
Stutz, W. L.
Suber, John A.
Sullivan, Allan R.
Sullivan, Arthur D.
Sullivan, David S.
Sullivan, Edward
Sullivan, Edward H.
Sullivan, James G., Jr.
Sullivan, Whitney B.
Summerlin, Bill
Sumner, Charles D., Jr.
Sumner, Ralph E.
Surra, John W.
Sutherland, Mont E.
Swanepoel, B.
Swanson, Archie B.
Swanson, John A.

Swartz, Francis A.
Swauger, James S.
Sweeney, J. M.
Sweet, Leon W., Jr.
Swemmer, F. A.
Sykes, G. T. D.
Sylvester, John L.
Szeeley, Walter
Tabor, Charles L.
Tacon, Avelin P.
Takas, Joe "Tuffy"
Talbott, David B.
Talley, Albert E.
Talley, Thomas W.
Tandy, Orval H.
Tappe, Charles J., Jr.
Tarcari, Louis
Tarr, Milton F.
Tarr, Ralph K., Jr.
Tassinari, Robert
Tatum, William A.
Taylor, Claude R. "Spud"
Taylor, David L.
Taylor, E.
Taylor, Eddie A.
Taylor, Henry
Taylor, John E., Jr.
Taylor, Milton B.
Taylor, Paul N.
Taylor, Richard E.
Taylor, Robert L
Taylor, William B.
Tedder, John Q.
Tellefsen, George M., Jr.
Tennant, Homer J.
Terrell, Frederick R.
Terry, David E.
Terry, Oscar E.
Terry, Robert I.
Thacker, John M.
Thierfelder, Kurt
Thom, George H.
Thomas, Alfred J.
Thomas, Frank M.
Thomas, Fred L.
Thomas, Jim C.
Thomas, Joe
Thomas, Kent E.
Thomas, Mike D.
Thomas, Norman L.
Thomas, Phillip H.
Thomas R. Humphrey
Thomas, Robert J.
Thomason, Donald
Thomasson, Jerry K.
Thompson, Charles O.
Thompson, Gordon M.
Thompson, Howard R.
Thompson, John F.
Thompson, John H.

Thompson, John S.
Thompson, Joseph M.
Thompson, Leon
Thompson, R. N.
Thompson, Raymond F.
Thompson, Thomas E.
Thompson, W. A.
Thompson, Warren E.
Thomson, Gordon M.
Thornton, Daniel C.
Thornton, Eric, Jr.
Thorsten, Stan
Thrackwray, A. L.
Thrasher, Joel
Thresher, Robert D.
Tichacek, Charles
Tichenor, Don E.
Tidwell, Robert L.
Tiedemann, Charles F.
Tift, Ralph E.
Tilden, Thomas V.
Tillman, Beacher M.
Tillman, Herman G.
Timlin, Thomas B.
Timmons, Paul D., Jr.
Tims, George E.
Timson, Carl A.
Tindall, J.
Tinius, John O.
Tinsman, Clarence
Tipton, Carl W.
Titchener, L. A.
Titus, Robert F.
Todd, James M.
Toedt, Dell
Tolbert, Dalphy E.
Tolda, C.
Toliver, Raymond F.
Tomajan, Don K.
Tomich, Max
Tompkins, Robert
Tompkins, Stuart E. Jr.
Tooey, William A.
Tores, Ismael
Toscano, John J.
Toumbacaris, George B.
Towell, Joseph P.
Towner, William R.
Trabanino, Rudolph
Trautman, Charles
Trautman, Donald D.
Trayer, George T.
Traynor, William C.
Treece, James A.
Treffeisen, Jay D.
Tripp, Harry B.
Trollope, Henry H.
Trotter, J. R.
Troutfetter, Bernard F.
Troutman, Charles R.

Troy, Donald W.
Trumbo, Charles E. "Slide"
Trumbull, Lawrence L.
Truter, C. J. D.
Tubbs, Shirley B.
Tucker, Charles H., Jr.
Tucker, Roy L.
Tulk, Robert E.
Tunks, Joy V.
Turcotte, Raymond R.
Turley, Hansel W.
Turner, James B.
Turner, R.
Tuthill, Frank
Twitchell, Wally
Tygret, T. L.
Tyler, Harry Melville
Tyler, Kermit A.
Tyndale, Harry J.
Ulitt, Carl E.
Unander, Paul E.
Unatin, Jerry
Underwood, Arthur D.
Upshaw, Don C.
Urban, Theodore J.
Urquhart, William Timmons
    "Tim"
Valencic, Joe A.
Valentine, Edward J.
Valentine, Richard M.
Valenzano, Peter J.
Valenzuela, Al Y.
Van Andel, Noel J.
Van Cleeve, J.W.
Van den Bos, Willem H.
Van der Merwe, E. P.
Van der Westhuizen, B.
Van derSpuy, Alex "Topper"
Van Heerdeen, W.
Van Hellen, Russell C.
Van Hoepen, Egbert L.
Van Matre, Everett S.
Van Rensberg, A. Janse
Van Sice, Robert B.
Van Vuureen, D. J. J.
Van Vuuren, C. H.
Vanover, Gilbert
Varble, T.A.
Varble, Thomas A.
Vargas, Marshall J.
Varley, N. F.
Varnum, John W.
Vaughan, M.R.
Vaughn, Ansel B.
Vaught, Robert H.
Velander, David A.
Venaman, Ralph L.
Venter, B. C.
Venter, J. H.
Verster, Jessie P.

Vest, Daurice C.
Vestal, John E.
Vezaldenos, James J.
Viccellio, Henry, Sr.
Vice, M.C.
Vikan, Dean F.
Vilano, Nicholas
Vincent, Thomas E.
Vinson, Alan E.
Visocan, William
Visser, P. J.
Vittitoe, Robert C.
Vivier, L.
Vogel, John S.
Vogt, Michael
Voit, Donovan P.
Volckmar, A. F.
Vollmer, Al
Volts, Edmund E.
Volts, Edmund E.
Voss, John D.
Vreeland, Al
Waggoner, Horace Q.
Wagner, Alphonzo T., Jr.
Wagnon, John A.
Waid, Frederick J.
Wakefield, King E.
Wakeham, William H.
Wakehouse, Ernest P.
Walek, G.
Walker, Douglas P.
Walker, Durrant G.
Walker, James C.
Walker, Raymond
Wall, William
Wall, Willie J., Jr.
Wallace, Charles E.
Wallace, Muncie
Wallace, William W.
Wallick, William P.
Walls, Bobby E.
Walter, Earl C.
Walters, William J.
Walton, James H.
Walton, Robert T.
Wanninger, John T.
Ward, Alfred S.
Ward, Clinton E.
Ward, D.P.
Ward, Harold L,
Ward, Lee M.
Ward, Lowell E.
Ward, Ralph R.
Ward, Richard H.
Ward, William L.
Warm, Melvin
Warner, Fred P.
Warren, Henry L.
Warren, J.M.
Warren, James W.

Warwick, Harry T.
Wasson, John C.
Waterman, Ralph E., Jr.
Waters, Elwood I.
Watson, Robert H.
Watterman, Ralph
Wayburn, Randall C.
Wayne, Lloyd G.
Weart, George S.
Weathersbee, Stanley M.
Weaver, Lyman F.
Webb, L. C.
Weber, Nelson T.
Weber, Robert W.
Webster, Frederick L., Jr.
Webster, Harold, Jr.
Webster, Neil A.
Weeks, Leonard M. "Tom'"
Weeks, Nolan
Weiger, William F.
Weilenmann, Walter H.
Weimerts, Stanley
Weir, Charles O.
Weirers, John T.
Weisinger, Robert L.
Weiss, Richard L.
Weiss, William A.
Weitzman, Martin J.
Welch, Fred S.
Welgoss, Theodore P.
Wells, Joe
Wells, M.C.
Wells, Perry P.
Wells, Travis D.
Welninski, Daniel W.
Welsh, Francis L.
Welthagen, D. H.
Welz, Henry D.
Wendt, Raymond
Wenner, G.M.
Wenner, William S.
Wennes, Gilbert J.
Wentworth, Harold F.
Wentzel, P. C.
Werkowski, Robt B.
Wertz, Roger
Wessels, M. H.
West, Fred G.
West, George
West, William
Westbrook, Charles C.
Westbrook, Robert B.
Westcott, Richard D.
Westhoff, Fr. Donald F.
Wheadon, Elmer M.
Wheatley, Joseph R.
Wheeler, George E.
Wheeler, Richard A.
Wheeler, James A.
Wheeling, Nicholas

Whicker, Donal
Whipple, Warren E.,
Whitaker, Gordon
White, Alexander J.
White, Bert L.
White, Clayton C.
White, Floyd
White, Hamilton R.
White, Hugh B.
White, Robert, Jr.
White, Taylor C., Jr.
White, Wilbur O.,
Whitehead, Ken R.
Whiteman, George
Whitfield, D. C. R.
Whitham, Clifford J.
Whitley, Robert A.
Whitney, Joh E.
Wickersham, Donald L.
Widmyer, Charles R.
Weinberg, Sydney
Wierck, Norbert J.
Wiggett, Barry A. A.
Wiggins, Willard C., Jr
Wilbanks, Borden D.
Wilcox, Floyd J.
Wild, A. W.
Wildasin, Henry M.
Wilder, John W.
Wiles, Earl E.
Wilkerson, Sam C., Jr.
Wilkinson, John D., Jr.
Will, Thomas H.
Willard, Jack L.
Wille, Thomas
Willers, J.
William, Eugene
Williams, Billy T.
Williams Paul R.
Williams, Claude P.
Williams, E.D.
Williams, Edward B., Jr.
Williams, Edward J.
Williams, Emmett T.
Williams, Frank M.
Williams, Herbert L.
Williams, Howard F.
Williams, Hugh L.
Williams, Joseph B.
Williams, Neal L.
Williams, Ray C.
Williams, R.G.
Williams, Waldo
Williamson, Jack D.
Williamson, Sam B.
Williamson, William B.
Wilmens, L. L.
Wilson, C.L.
Wilson, Clyde S.
Wilson, Eugene E.

Wilson, Vern R.
Wilson, Victor
Wilson, W. E. St E.
Wilson, Weldon S.
Wilson, William M.
Wimberley, Harold Kirk
Windham, Tom M.
Winford, Earl R.
Winfrey, Clifford G.
Wing, Virgil C.
Winstanley, Miles
Wintermute, Ira F.
Wirges, William J.
Witherspoon, James H.
Withey, Lewis H.
Wittbrodt, Glen H.
Wittig, James T.
Wittington, W.
Wohlter, F. L.
Wohosky, Robert
Wojcik, Frank J.
Wold, Glen A.
Wolf, Robert
Wolfe, George L.
Wolfe, Lawrence Ervin, Jr.
Wolfe, Leland Harry
Wolfe, Roland L.
Woliung, John G.
Wolterding, Daniel R.
Wolz, Henry D.
Wood, Carl J.
Wood, Franklin H.
Wood, George R.
Wood, John P.
Wood, Robert L.
Wood, Virgil T.
Woodard, Vance E.
Woodson, J.
Woodward, J.
Woodworth, Raymond H.
Worley, C.M.
Wormack, Thelbert B.
Worman, Kenneth E.
Worrell, A. Hunter
Worth, Nathan H.
Wright, Arlo E.
Wright, Albert E.
Wright, Gary J.
Wright, Jack McConnell
Wright, John O.
Wright, Tandy A.
Wroblewski, Leon
Wurffel, Karl
Wurst, Rodney C.
Wyatt, Billy B.
Wyatt, Elvin O.
Wyatt, Harold A.
Wyatt, Richard
Wyche, Wilton E.

Wysk, Mike, Jr.
Wythes, Keith W.
Yablonski, Henry S.
Yahne, Verne M.
Yankauer, Charles D.
Yarber, Irven
Yarnell, Robert E.
Yates, Eugene A., Jr.
Yeakley, R. J.
Yeingst, Sherwin M.
Yingling, John W.
Yorke, Harvey F.
Yost, John C.
Young, Arch
Young, Frank W.
Young, James A.
Young, Joe O.
Young, Lee R.
Yousko, J.R.
Zappe, John A.
Zaricir, Dewint H.
Zeliadt, Raymond R.
Zellinger, Marvin
Zenker, Paul
Zesiger, William J.
Zimmerman, William F.
Zink, John
Zych, Ray J.

Index

 # Notes & Recollections

Notes & Recollections

 # Notes & Recollections

 # Notes & Recollections

 # Notes & Recollections